The Browns Bible

The BROWNS BIBLE

THE COMPLETE GAME-BY-GAME HISTORY OF THE CLEVELAND BROWNS

Jonathan Knight

Black Squirrel Books™

An imprint of The Kent State University Press

Kent, Ohio 44242 www.KentStateUniversityPress.com

Black Squirrel Books™
Frisky, industrious black squirrels are a familiar sight on the Kent State University campus and the inspiration for Black Squirrel Books™, a trade imprint of The Kent State University Press.
www.KentStateUniversityPress.com

Library of Congress Catalog Card Number 2012043684
ISBN 978-1-60635-170-3
Manufactured in the United States of America

Library of Congress Cataloging-in-Publication Data
Knight, Jonathan, 1976–
The Browns bible : the complete game-by-game history of the Cleveland Browns / Jonathan Knight.
pages cm
ISBN 978-1-60635-170-3 (hardcover)∞
1. Cleveland Browns (Football team : 1946–1995)—History.
2. Cleveland Browns (Football team : 1999–)—History. I. Title.
GV956.C6K63 2013
796.332′640977132—dc23
2012043684

17 16 15 14 13 5 4 3 2 1

Contents

Preface

I've always been a sucker for complete collections. Even if I have absolutely no interest in it, I'm drawn to anything with the word "complete" slapped across it.

To me it's incredibly satisfying to hold something in your hands and know that within your grasp is absolutely everything ever created that made up that particular universe, whether it be the writings of Edgar Allan Poe or every episode of *I Love Lucy.*

And that's what you've got this very moment. In your hands you hold the complete history of the Cleveland Browns—every season they fought through, every game they ever played, every touchdown they ever scored.

Feels good, doesn't it? Even if you have no interest in the Browns, I would hope it's an intriguing concept, if for no other reason than because never before has a book like this been written for any NFL team.

Spread across these pages are summaries of each and every regular-season and postseason game the Browns have ever played. Along with the summaries, you'll find box scores listing how every point of every game was scored, plus the individual offensive statistics for each contest.

What began on a Friday night in September 1946 against the comically overmatched Miami Seahawks right up to today—it's all here. Altogether, it's just under 1,000 games played over the course of nearly 70 years.

To be sure, not every story is a happy one, nor is every game worth remembering. Included here among the championships and the winning streaks are the blowout losses and the miserable seasons that make the former all the more precious.

As satisfying as holding the final product may be, the long process of putting it together was equally rewarding. Game by game, statistic by statistic, *The Browns Bible* emerged out of the ether like a massive jigsaw puzzle, requiring a seemingly endless scavenger hunt to find some of the pieces. And then finding out that some of the pieces had pieces.

Most of the research was compiled from primary sources: back issues of the *Plain Dealer, Cleveland Press, Browns News/Illustrated, New York Times,* and the *Sporting News.* Profootballreference.com was an absolutely vital online resource, as was the Gridiron Uniform Database at nfluniforms.blogspot.com and the Bolding Sports Research site at mmbolding.com/BSR for its impressive array of details about the College All-Star Game, Playoff Bowl, and Shamrock Bowl. (Indeed, while the Browns are one of just a few teams that have never played in a Super Bowl, they're the only team ever to have played in the Shamrock Bowl.)

In addition to past editions of the Browns' media guides and a cavalcade of highlight film, a handful of books proved valuable:

- *PB: The Paul Brown Story,* by Paul Brown with Jack Clary (Atheneum, 1980)
- *The Best Show in Football,* by Andy Piascik (Taylor Trade Publishing, 2007)
- *Sam, Sipe & Company: The Story of the Cleveland Browns,* by Bill Levy (J. T. Zubal & P. D. Dole, Publishers, 1981)
- *Paul Brown,* by Andrew O'Toole (Clerisy Press, 2008)
- *Cleveland Browns: The Official Illustrated History,* Writer/Editorial Director Ron Smith (Sporting News, 1999)

Not surprisingly, the further back I went, the more challenging it became to fill in some of the missing pieces, and I had to dig even deeper than what was available via printed/online material. Special thanks to Tony Dick, the Browns' alumni relations manager, who opened up the vault of team history and allowed me to peruse the team's ample archives and access indispensable information. I also must thank Dave Finoli, a fantastic writer and researcher (even though he's from Pittsburgh), who dug into his personal archives, and Terence Jon Troup (aka "Coach T. J."), a statistical wizard who's forgotten more about football than I will ever know. With their help, I was ultimately able to compile complete box scores for each NFL game the Browns have played.

During the team's early years in the All-America Football Conference in the late 1940s, when pro football was still a novelty and the AAFC operated like a traveling circus, statistical record keeping was, at best, an afterthought (an amazing contrast to the fantasy football-driven obsession with individual statistics we know today). As a result, the box scores from those four seasons—while as complete as possible—are regrettably incomplete simply because many of those individual statistics have been lost to history.

Conversely, I hope that some of the information provided here will open up new insights into the Browns' storied canon. In addition to the game capsules, Browns historians should enjoy the sidebars sprinkled throughout the book and an appendix honeycombed with intriguing details that examine everything from the Browns' all-time record by jersey color, starting quarterbacks, month, and day of the week to how they've fared against former coaches and in classic ballparks.

Put it all together and, in my humble opinion, you've got the best Browns reference guide ever created, perfect for reliving memories and settling barroom bets. Want to relive the Browns' amazing 29-game unbeaten streak in the late 1940s? Interested in how Jim Brown performed week by week in his incredible 1,863-yard season of 1963? And when exactly was that Monday-night game in which Bernie Kosar threw for 400 yards against Miami? They're all in here.

Perhaps more importantly, this book can also bring your own memories of past Browns' games into sharper focus and connect the present with the past.

For this is not merely a book about the Cleveland Browns; this book *is* the Cleveland Browns.

All in your hands.

1946

THE ACTUAL FIRST-EVER BROWNS' GAME

While the two official "first games" in Browns history—the openers of the 1946 and 1950 seasons against the Miami Seahawks and Philadelphia Eagles, respectively—have received historical distinction, technically they don't mark the first time the Browns ever took the field in competition.

The first time they cracked helmets against an opposing team was on August 30, 1946, when they played an exhibition game against the AAFC's Brooklyn Dodgers at the Rubber Bowl in Akron, an event that drew a sell-out crowd of 35,964 to see the Browns quickly fall behind 13–0, then rally back for a 35–20 win. The Browns' first touchdown was a dazzling, one-handed, 6-yard reception by RB Fred Evans from QB Cliff Lewis.

But the first time the Browns actually took the field for a game was 10 days earlier—August 20, 1946—when they held an intrasquad scrimmage on a Tuesday night before 8,500 fans at Toledo Waite High School.

The team was split into a White Squad and a Brown Squad, with the Whites grinding out a 10–0 victory on the strength of an 89-yard touchdown run by RB Edgar Jones and a 32-yard Lou Groza field goal.

Friday, September 6
Browns 44, Miami Seahawks 0
Cleveland Stadium (60,135)
Brown jerseys/white pants

Taking the field for an official game for the first time, the Browns throttled the overmatched Seahawks before the largest crowd ever to watch a professional football game to that point. Five different players crossed the goal line, including WR Mac Speedie, who scored the first touchdown in team history on a 19-yard pass from starting QB Cliff Lewis on the eighth play of the game. Lewis was eventually replaced by Otto Graham, and Graham threw his first career touchdown pass early in the second quarter on a long strike to WR Dante Lavelli. RB Tom Colella—a stalwart with the Cleveland Rams the previous two seasons—extended the lead to 24–0 on the first rushing touchdown in Browns' history: a 50-yard scamper in the second quarter. The Cleveland offense was powerful, rolling up 345 total yards, but the defense was dominant, holding the Seahawks to 27 total yards, including minus one on the ground, and didn't allow Miami to penetrate the Cleveland 39. The Browns also forced four turnovers, two of which resulted in touchdowns by DBs: a three-yard fumble return by Don Greenwood and a 76-yard interception return by Ray Terrell as time expired.

Record: 1–0

	1	2	3	4		
Seahawks	0	0	0	0	=	0
Browns	10	17	0	17	=	44

CLE-Speedie 19-yd. pass from Lewis (Groza kick)
CLE-Groza 22-yd. FG
CLE-Lavelli 39-yd. pass from Graham (Groza kick)
CLE-Colella 50-yd. run (Groza kick)
CLE-Groza 27-yd. FG
CLE-Greenwood 3-yd. fumble return (Groza kick)
CLE-Groza 21-yd. FG
CLE-Terrell 76-yd. interception return (Groza kick)

Passing
MIA: Pugh 3–7–10 0 TD 0 INT, Tarrant 1–3–9 0 TD 0 INT, Johnston 1–1–9 0 TD 0 INT, Gafford 0–2–0 0 TD 1 INT, Price 0–2–0 0 TD 0 INT, McDonald 0–1–0 0 TD 1 INT
CLE: Graham 5–13–109 1 TD 0 INT, Lewis 2–3–31 1 TD 0 INT, Greenwood 1–1–27 0 TD 0 INT, Saban 0–3–0 0 TD 1 INT

Rushing
MIA: Reynolds 6–31, Johnston 5–11, Gloden 3–5, Nelson 3–5, Jones 2–2, Gafford 3-(-3), Tarrant 2-(-23), Pugh 2-(-29)
CLE: Smith 7–54, Colella 1–50, E. Jones 3–45, Evans 5–22, Motley 5–19, Greenwood 10–13, Fekete 2–3, Lund 1-(-1), Graham 2-(-5), Saban 2-(-6), Lewis 2-(-16)

Receiving
MIA: Pool 2–18, Scott 1–12, Mitchell 1–3, Nelson 1-(-5)
CLE: Lavelli 3–79, Motley 1–35, Coppage 1–27, Speedie 1–16, Terrell 1–11, Smith 1-(-1)

Friday, September 13
Browns 20, Chicago Rockets 6
Soldier Field (51,962)
Brown jerseys/white pants

On Friday the thirteenth, the Browns powered to their second victory behind a muscular running game that rolled to 225 yards and overwhelmed the celebrated Rockets in their inaugural game. The Browns, 10-point underdogs, took a 7–0 lead four minutes into the game on a 20-yard touchdown run by RB Marion Motley, who made quite an impact in his first start, picking up 122 yards on just 12 carries. They then blew the game open in the third quarter, soaring to a 20–0 lead after a long touchdown run around left end by Don Greenwood. The Cleveland defense, while not as dominant as the week before, was resilient, holding Chicago scoreless until the final quarter and persevering to keep the Rockets off the board on three separate trips inside the Cleveland 15. The Browns also spoiled the debut of heralded rookie RB and eventual Hall of Famer Elroy Hirsch, holding him to just 13 yards on nine carries.
Record: 2–0

	1	2	3	4		
Browns	7	0	13	0	=	20
Rockets	0	0	0	6	=	6

CLE-Motley 20-yd. run (Groza kick)
CLE-Groza 21-yd. FG
CLE-Groza 37-yd. FG
CLE-Greenwood 41-yd. run (Groza kick)
CHI-Hillenbrand 35-yd. run (kick failed)

Rushing
CLE-Motley 12–122
CHI-Hirsch 9–13

Sunday, September 22
Browns 28, Buffalo Bisons 0
Civic Stadium (30,302)
White jerseys/white pants

Playing their first Sunday game and wearing white jerseys for the first time on a balmy afternoon in Buffalo, the Browns sprinted to a three-touchdown lead in the first quarter and coasted to another easy victory and their second shutout in three weeks. After opening the scoring with a long Otto Graham touchdown pass two minutes into the contest, the Browns were in command throughout, tacking on a fourth touchdown when DE Chet Adams scooped up a fumble and sprinted 25 yards into the end zone. The Cleveland defense forced five turnovers and held the Bisons, playing without injured star RB Steve Juzwik, to just 164 total yards. Yet the Browns demonstrated some sloppy play as well, coughing up the football three times themselves while getting penalized 11 times for 95 yards.
Record: 3–0

	1	2	3	4		
Browns	21	0	0	7	=	28
Bisons	0	0	0	0	=	0

CLE-Yonakor 52-yd. pass from Graham (Groza kick)
CLE-Motley 33-yd. pass from Graham (Groza kick)
CLE-Smith 12-yd. run (Groza kick)
CLE-Adams 25-yd. fumble return (Groza kick)

Sunday, September 29
Browns 24, New York Yankees 7
Cleveland Stadium (57,084)
White jerseys/white pants

Setting the tone for a surprisingly one-sided rivalry, the Browns took an early lead and then held off a strong Yankees squad for their fourth straight win on a rainy afternoon. A pair of interceptions set up two Cleveland touchdowns in the first nine minutes, then an Otto Graham fumble led to New York's only touchdown in the final minute of a wild first quarter. With the teams combining for 10 turnovers, the score remained 14–7 until a Lou Groza field goal extended the Cleveland lead to 10 points in the fourth quarter. RB Edgar Jones then sealed the victory with a 43-yard touchdown run with less than three minutes to play. Now the only unbeaten, untied team in the AAFC, the Browns were once again led by their defense, which held their opponent under 200 total yards for the third time in four games. Cleveland also contained versatile New York RB Orban "Spec" Sanders, who managed only four yards on three carries and completed just two of six passes—though Sanders was playing on an injured knee. It was the first of three Cleveland victories over New York in 1946 as the Browns quickly became the bane of the Yankees.
Record: 4–0

	1	2	3	4		
Yankees	7	0	0	0	=	7
Browns	14	0	0	10	=	24

CLE-Lavelli 7-yd. pass from Graham (Groza kick)
CLE-Greenwood 2-yd. run (Groza kick)
NYY-Russell 14-yd. pass from Sanders (Johnson kick)
CLE-Groza 22-yd. FG
CLE-E. Jones 43-yd. run (Groza kick)

Passing
NYY: Perina 5–10–52 0 TD 0 INT, Kennedy 1–5–40 0 TD 3 INT, Sanders 2–6–20 1 TD 1 INT, Prokop 0–1–0 0 TD 0 INT
CLE: Graham 8–14–128 1 TD 1 INT

Rushing
NYY: Perina 5–15, Kennedy 4–8, Wagner 1–8, Proctor 3–6, Sanders 3–4, Cheatham 1–0, Johnson 3-(-1), Prokop 8-(-5)
CLE: E. Jones 11–81, Motley 13–47, Greenwood 9–44, Lewis 3–9, Smith 2–7, Colella 1–2, Steuber 2-(-1), Graham 3-(-34)

Sunday, October 6
Browns 26, Brooklyn Dodgers 7
Cleveland Stadium (43,713)
White jerseys/white pants

On a warm, sun-splashed afternoon in Cleveland, the Browns once again coasted to victory on the strength of a marvelous defensive performance. The Dodgers were held to just 49 rushing yards and only 177 total as the Browns collected six turnovers, bringing their season total to 24 in five games. Appropriately, the defense scored points of its own when DE Alton Coppage smothered Brooklyn QB Glenn Dobbs in the end zone for a 5–0 lead midway through the first quarter. Don Greenwood added a pair of one-yard touchdown runs before the half to extend the margin to 19–0, and the Browns never looked back.
Record: 5–0

	1	2	3	4		
Dodgers	0	0	7	0	=	7
Browns	12	7	0	7	=	26

CLE-Groza 15-yd. FG
CLE-Safety: Coppage tackled Dobbs in end zone
CLE-Greenwood 1-yd. run (Groza kick)
CLE-Greenwood 1-yd. run (Groza kick)
BRK-Mayne 4-yd. run (Martinovich kick)
CLE-Colella 4-yd. run (Groza kick)

Passing
BRK: Dobbs 11–23–106 0 TD 2 INT, Mayne 4–7–32 0 TD 2 INT
CLE: Graham 5–7–76 0 TD 0 INT, Lewis 2–2–18 0 TD 0 INT, E. Jones 1–1–14 0 TD 0 INT

Rushing
BRK: Mayne 9–21, Principe 5–15, Colmer 4–15, Armstrong 2–14, Daley 4–0, Dobbs 10-(-16)
CLE: Motley 5–43, E. Jones 9–28, Greenwood 9–26, Steuber 1–17, Lewis 3–8, Colella 2–8, Smith 2–8, Terrell 2–6, Graham 1-(-2)

Saturday, October 12
Browns 7, New York Yankees 0
Yankee Stadium (34,252)
White jerseys/white pants

Playing through a heavy downpour on a Saturday afternoon, the Browns managed to topple the Yankees for the second time in three weeks despite being completely outplayed from start to finish. Struggling to move the ball for the first time all season, the Browns managed a woeful 67 total yards of offense, including just 24 on the ground as the New York defense controlled the game. The Yankee offense, meanwhile, enjoyed success against the Browns, topping 230 total yards, but continually saw promising drives thwarted as they turned the ball over five times. The most costly was a fumble on a punt return following the first possession of the second half, which was recovered by the Browns' Ed Ulinski at the New York 33. From there, Otto Graham connected on a touchdown pass to Dante Lavelli for the game's only score—and half of the team's yardage for the day. The floundering Yankees reached the Cleveland 16 in the final seconds, but the Browns' defense rose up to halt the drive and secure their sixth consecutive victory. It was the third Cleveland shutout, as the Browns had permitted a total of just 20 points in their first six games.
Record: 6–0

	1	2	3	4		
Browns	0	0	7	0	=	7
Yankees	0	0	0	0	=	0

CLE-Lavelli 33-yd. pass from Graham (Groza kick)

Sunday, October 20
Browns 31, Los Angeles Dons 14
Cleveland Stadium (71,134)
Brown jerseys/white pants

For the first time, the Browns came from behind to secure a rousing victory over Los Angeles before a colossal crowd at the Stadium. In the first half the Browns remained in the doldrums that had set in the previous weekend in New York and the Dons nursed a 7–3 advantage late in the third quarter before a short Otto Graham touchdown run gave the Browns their first lead. It was the beginning of an electrifying 14-minute stretch in which the Browns scored 28 points to blow the game open. A long Graham-to-Mac Speedie scoring strike made the lead 10 points, and they then pulled away thanks to two long touchdown runs by Marion Motley, who finished with 145 yards on just eight carries—an average of better than 17 yards per rush. Still undefeated with the season now half-completed, the Browns looked unbeatable—but that would change in the next two weeks.
Record: 7–0

	1	2	3	4		
Dons	7	0	0	7	=	14
Browns	0	3	7	21	=	31

LA-Nowaskey 18-yd. pass from O'Rourke (Aguirre kick)
CLE-Groza 48-yd. FG
CLE-Graham 2-yd. run (Groza kick)
CLE-Speedie 47-yd. pass from Graham (Groza kick)
CLE-Motley 49-yd. run (Groza kick)
LA-O'Rourke 6-yd. run (Aguirre kick)
CLE-Motley 68-yd. run (Groza kick)

Passing
LA: Bertelli 5–7–81 0 TD 0 INT, O'Rourke 5–13–40 0 TD 1 INT, Aguirre 0–1–0 0 TD 0 INT
CLE: Graham 4–10–129 1 TD 0 INT

Rushing
LA: Elsey 8–65, O'Rourke 6–59, Kimbrough 10–51, Clarke 13–45, Vinnola 4–20, Polanski 4–15, Fenenbock 3–7, Bertelli 2-(-1)
CLE: Motley 8–145, E. Jones 10–52, Greenwood 9–27, Smith 3–21, Akins 1-(-6), Lewis 2-(-8), Graham 2-(-10)

Sunday, October 27
San Francisco 49ers 34, Browns 20
Cleveland Stadium (70,385)
Brown jerseys/white pants

Hindered by six costly turnovers, the Browns lost for the first time to a strong San Francisco team that would prove to be their fiercest rival in the AAFC. The potent 49er offense controlled the football for much of the first half as the visitors silenced another immense Cleveland crowd of 70,000-plus and took a 20–6 halftime lead that swelled to three touchdowns in the third quarter after a Marion Motley fumble led to another 49er touchdown. The Browns narrowed the margin to 27–13 early in the fourth quarter and had a chance to get back into the game when they got the ball back, but Otto Graham threw a momentum-killing interception at midfield that led to San Francisco QB Frankie Albert's third touchdown toss of the day, and the 49ers never looked back. While Motley, the league's leading rusher, was held to a harmless 22 yards, Dante Lavelli shined on an otherwise frustrating day for the Browns, catching eight passes for a whopping 183 yards.
Record: 7–1

	1	2	3	4		
49ers	3	17	7	7	=	34
Browns	0	6	0	14	=	20

SF-Vetrano 22-yd. FG
SF-Beals 16-yd. pass from Albert (Vetrano kick)
SF-Eshmont 6-yd. run (Vetrano kick)
CLE-Greenwood 3-yd. run (kick failed)
SF-Vetrano 19-yd. FG
SF-Durdan 9-yd. pass from Albert (Vetrano kick)
CLE-Lavelli 21-yd. pass from Graham (Rokisky kick)
SF-Beals 15-yd. pass from Albert (Vetrano kick)
CLE-Smith 3-yd. run (Speedie pass from Graham)

Passing
SF: Albert 14–21–176 3 TD 1 INT
CLE: Graham 14–19–284 1 TD 1 INT

Rushing
SF: Strzykalski 5–78, Standlee 9–49, Eshmont 11–33, Albert 6–9, Durdan 4–8, Casanega 2–8, Parsons 1–4, Vetrano 1–2, Hall 1-(-2), Franceschi 2-(-15)
CLE: Greenwood 11–38, Smith 6–31, Motley 4–22, Steuber 1–1, E. Jones 1-(-2), Lewis 3-(-15), Graham 6-(-20)

Receiving
SF: Beals 6–96, Eshmont 3–33, Franceschi 1–17, Fisk 2–15, Durdan 1–8, Strzykalski 1–7
CLE: Lavelli 8–183, Speedie 3–59, Smith 2–36, Young 1–6

Sunday, November 3
Los Angeles Dons 17, Browns 16
Los Angeles Memorial Coliseum (24,800)
White jerseys/white pants

After making their first cross-country flight, the Browns lost for the second straight week, this time squandering a nine-point lead in the last eight minutes to lose on a last-minute field goal. The Dons rocked the Browns on their heels with a touchdown on the first play of the game, a 75-yard scoring scamper off-tackle by RB Chuck Fenenbock. But the Browns persevered and took control over the next three quarters, aided by a 79-yard touchdown reception by Mac Speedie, to make it 16–7 two minutes before the half. But the Browns failed to convert the extra point—a miscue that would haunt them by day's end. They were still poised to win before a botched punt gave the Dons a first down at the Cleveland 23, and they cut the margin to 16–14 with seven minutes to play. The Browns then blew another chance to clinch victory a minute later when RB Ray Terrell fumbled at the Los Angeles 35. The Dons drove to the Cleveland 3, where Joe Aguirre kicked an 11-yard field goal with 18 seconds left. The consecutive losses allowed the 49ers to pull within a game of the first-place Browns in the Western Division going into their highly anticipated matchup the following week in San Francisco.
Record: 7–2

	1	2	3	4		
Browns	3	13	0	0	=	16
Dons	7	0	0	10	=	17

LA-Fenenbock 75-yd. run (Aguirre kick)
CLE-Groza 25-yd. FG
CLE-Lund 5-yd. run (Groza kick)
CLE-Speedie 79-yd. pass from Graham (kick failed)
LA-Gentry 8-yd. run (Aguirre kick)
LA-Aguirre 11-yd. FG

Passing
CLE: Graham 12–19–241 1 TD 1 INT
LA: Bertelli 5–9 0 TD, O'Rourke 3–6 0 TD

Rushing
CLE: Greenwood 9–17, Jones 5–13, Colella 4–12, Motley 6–11, Smith 2–10, Terrell 2–9, Lund 2–6, Steuber 1-(-1), Graham 4-(-34)
LA: Fenenbock 3–76, Kimbrough 14–40, Seymour 5–30, Clarke 9–22, Marefos 4–15, Nygren 4–9, Elsey 3–8, Polanski 3–7, Nowaskey 1–5, O'Rourke 2–3, Aguirre 1-(-5)

Receiving
CLE: Speedie 4–134

Sunday, November 10
Browns 14, San Francisco 49ers 7
Kezar Stadium (41,061)
White jerseys/white pants

Bouncing back from two straight disheartening defeats, the Browns pushed their division lead back to two games and avenged their first loss with a gritty win by the Bay. Former Case Western Reserve star Bill Lund made his first start at RB and sparked the Browns' opening drive, which resulted in a short Otto Graham-to-Dante Lavelli touchdown pass. A quarter later, Marion Motley turned a short pass into a 64-yard gain to set up another score and make it 14–0. Though Lund and Motley both would leave the game with injuries, the Browns endured, even after San Francisco QB Frankie Albert scooped up a loose ball and tumbled into the end zone from the Cleveland 1 on the second play of the fourth quarter. With five minutes to play, the 49ers drove to the Cleveland 19, but the Browns' defense held to keep their lead in the game and the division.
Record: 8–2

	1	2	3	4		
Browns	7	7	0	0	=	14
49ers	0	0	0	7	=	7

CLE-Lavelli 3-yd. pass from Graham (Groza kick)
CLE-Smith 3-yd. run (Groza kick)
SF-Albert 1-yd. fumble return (Vetrano kick)

Rushing
CLE: Lund 5–37, Motley 6–31, Jones 4–16, Smith 8–12, Terrell 7–11, Fekete 1–5, Colella 4–1, Greenwood 1-(-2), Graham 3-(-5)
SF: Standlee 12–89, Parsons 12–31, Strzykalski 6–24, Eshmont 6–11, Vetrano 1–3, Casanega 2–2, Mathews 1–1, Albert 7-(-1), Freitas 1-(-17)

Sunday, November 17
Browns 51, Chicago Rockets 14
Cleveland Stadium (60,457)
Brown jerseys/white pants

Exploding for 34 points in the second half, the Cleveland offense returned to form in a blowout victory over Chicago that saw seven different Browns score touchdowns.

Edgar Jones set the tone early with a 26-yard scoring sweep, the opening salvo in a performance that saw him rush for 100 yards on only five carries. After the Rockets cut a two-touchdown lead to 14–7, Lou Groza extended it back to double digits with a career-best 51-yard field goal. The home team then pulled away in the second half on the strength of three touchdowns on five plays in the fourth quarter. Otto Graham threw four touchdown passes—two each to Dante Lavelli and Mac Speedie, and LB Frank Gatski put the icing on the cake with a 36-yard interception return for a touchdown to cap the scoring. Amid the offensive fireworks, the Cleveland defense was dominant, limiting the Rockets to just 156 yards and forcing a season-high eight turnovers.

Record: 9–2

	1	2	3	4		
Rockets	0	7	7	0	=	14
Browns	7	10	14	20	=	51

CLE-E. Jones 26-yd. run (Groza kick)
CLE-Lavelli 8-yd. pass from Graham (Groza kick)
CHI-Hirsch 17-yd. pass from Hoernschemeyer (Nemeth kick)
CLE-Groza 51-yd. FG
CLE-Lavelli 34-yd. pass from Graham (Groza kick)
CLE-Speedie 39-yd. pass from Graham (Groza kick)
CHI-Lamana 20-yd. punt return (Nemeth kick)
CLE-Speedie 7-yd. pass from Graham (Groza kick)
CLE-Lund 21-yd. pass from Schwenk (Groza kick)
CLE-Gatski 36-yd. interception return (kick failed)

Passing
CHI: Hoernschemeyer 10–19–102 1 TD 3 INT, Hirsch 1–4–13 0 TD 1 INT, Hillenbrand 0–1–0 0 TD 1 INT
CLE: Graham 7–10–131 4 TD 0 INT, Schwenk 1–4–21 1 TD 0 INT

Rushing
CHI: Hoernschemeyer 7–29, Lewis 4–11, Hirsch 7–10, Hillenbrand 3–3, Kellagher 2–3, Clay 2-(-2), Schroeder 1-(-7), Williams 1-(-11)
CLE: E. Jones 5–100, Terrell 12–49, Greenwood 2–33, Fekete 4–13, Smith 3–10, Lund 3–7, Motley 1–3, Colella 3–0, Akins 1-(-3), Schwenk 3-(-8)

Receiving
CHI: Motley 2–28, Quillen 2–28, Hillenbrand 3–21, Heywood 2–18, Hirsch 1–17, Williams 1–3
CLE: Lavelli 4–84, Speedie 2–47, Lund 1–21, E. Jones 1–1

Sunday, November 24
Browns 42, Buffalo Bisons 17
Cleveland Stadium (37,054)
White jerseys/white pants

The Cleveland offense erupted for the second straight week, this time rallying from an early deficit to score five consecutive touchdowns and clinch the AAFC Western Division title in front of the smallest home crowd of the season. Matching the Browns' physical style of play, the Bisons overcame a Cleveland touchdown three minutes into the contest to take a 10–7 lead into the second quarter. The Browns were clinging to a 14–10 lead midway through the third as Buffalo drove deep into Cleveland territory, but Tom Colella then made a key interception to turn the game around. It was immediately followed by a pair of Cleveland touchdowns, the second of which was a 76-yard touchdown run by Marion Motley that blew the game open. RB Al Akins then burst through for his only career touchdown with the Browns on a 50-yard carry early in the fourth quarter as the Browns finished with a season-high 455 yards of offense, including a whopping 281 on the ground, another best for 1946.

Record: 10–2

	1	2	3	4		
Bisons	10	0	0	7	=	17
Browns	7	7	14	14	=	42

CLE-E. Jones 46-yd. run (Groza kick)
BUF-Kulbitski 1-yd. run (Zontini kick)
BUF-Zontini 40-yd. FG
CLE-E. Jones 37-yd. pass from Graham (Groza kick)
CLE-Speedie 4-yd. pass from Graham (Groza kick)
CLE-Motley 76-yd. run (Groza kick)
CLE-Akins 50-yd. run (Groza kick)
CLE-Schwenk 1-yd. run (Groza kick)
BUF-King 12-yd. pass from Terlep (Zontini kick)

Passing
BUF: Terlep 9–19–84 1 TD 1 INT, Dekdebrun 2–7–20 0 TD 1 INT
CLE: Graham 9–18–156 2 TD 0 INT, Schwenk 1–1–7 0 TD 0 INT, E. Jones 0–1–0 0 TD 0 INT

Rushing
BUF: Kulbitski 17–70, Mutryn 8–40, Johnston 5–20, Terlep 4–10, Dudish 5–5, Juzwik 4–4, Sandig 1–3, Dekdebrun 4-(-5), Zontini 1-(-10)

CLE: E. Jones 8–105, Motley 2–83, Akins 2–47, Terrell 5–14, Lavelli 1–14, Fekete 2–10, Evans 2–9, Graham 2–4, Lund 2–3, Schwenk 1–1, Colella 3-(-9)

Tuesday, December 3
Browns 34, Miami Seahawks 0
Orange Bowl (9,083)
White jerseys/white pants

Picking up where they left off in their domination of the Seahawks in the opener, the Browns once again coasted to an easy victory over Miami, led by a suffocating defense. After heavy rain postponed the contest to a Tuesday night, Cleveland forced a whopping nine turnovers and limited the Seahawks to 46 total yards, just eight rushing. Appropriately, the Browns' defense put the first points on the board on an interception return for a touchdown by Otto Graham—the only defensive score of his career—as the Browns soared to a 17–0 halftime lead. Lou Groza provided the other highlight as he set a pro football record for most field goals and extra points in a season, increasing his 1946 totals to 12 and 41, respectively. The victory was even more impressive considering the Browns decided not to play Marion Motley and Bill Willis after racist threats were made, and Miami officials threatened to enforce city laws barring black players from playing with whites. With the financially struggling Seahawks shifted to Baltimore after the season, this would be the last time the Browns would play in Miami's Orange Bowl for 14 years, when they returned for the first Playoff Bowl, and the last regular-season game they'd play in south Florida until 1970.
Record: 11–2

	1	2	3	4		
Browns	7	10	7	10	=	34
Seahawks	0	0	0	0	=	0

CLE-Graham 37-yd. interception return (Groza kick)
CLE-E. Jones 1-yd. run (Groza kick)
CLE-Groza 50-yd. FG
CLE-Smith 2-yd. run (Groza kick)
CLE-Groza 11-yd. FG
CLE-Fekete 16-yd. run (Groza kick)

Sunday, December 8
Browns 66, Brooklyn Dodgers 14
Ebbets Field (14,600)
White jerseys/white pants

The Browns closed out a magnificent regular season with their most dynamic offensive display, rolling up 451 yards with nine different players scoring touchdowns in a record-setting romp over the Dodgers. After the Browns sprinted to a 21–0 lead early in the second quarter, Brooklyn got on the board on a fumble return for a score. Then the Browns struck right back on the ensuing kickoff as Edgar Jones fumbled, picked up the ball, and then streaked down the middle of the field for a 96-yard touchdown. With many of the regulars resting in the second half, backup QB Bud Schwenk directed the Cleveland scoring express, throwing three touchdown passes on the day. Wanting to break the league scoring mark of 62 points set by Los Angeles the previous Sunday, Paul Brown called for an onside kick following the eighth touchdown that made it 59–14. He then re-inserted Otto Graham—who'd sat out the entire second half—back into the game to lead the Browns to their ninth touchdown and the new scoring record. The only down moment was when Lou Groza injured his ankle in the third quarter and was carried from the field. In his stead, Chet Adams kicked the final five extra points—the first after he returned an interception for a touchdown. The victory was a tune-up for the AAFC title game two weeks later in Cleveland against the New York Yankees.
Record: 12–2

	1	2	3	4		
Browns	14	14	17	21	=	66
Dodgers	0	7	0	7	=	14

CLE-Lund 22-yd. pass from Schwenk (Groza kick)
CLE-Motley 7-yd. run (Groza kick)
CLE-Speedie 11-yd. pass from Graham (Groza kick)
BRK-Judd 12-yd. fumble return (Martinovich kick)
CLE-E. Jones 96-yd. kickoff return (Groza kick)
CLE-Groza 31-yd. FG
CLE-Adams 4-yd. interception return (Adams kick)
CLE-Smith 2-yd. run (Adams kick)
CLE-Yonakor 18-yd. pass from Schwenk (Adams kick)
BRK-Judd 52-yd. pass from Armstrong (Martinovich kick)
CLE-Lavelli 37-yd. pass from Schwenk (Adams kick)
CLE-Colella 12-yd. pass from Graham (Adams kick)

1946 AAFC Championship
Sunday, December 22
Browns 14, New York Yankees 9
Cleveland Stadium (40,469)
White jerseys/white pants

As the Browns prepared for their first championship game, a nearly perfect season finally hit some turbulence.

The weekend before the game, the Browns faced their first off-field crisis when Jim Daniell, Mac Speedie, and Lou Rymkus were arrested after an altercation with police. Paul Brown determined that Daniell had been the instigator and released him. In retrospect, many felt Brown punished Daniell rather than Speedie and Rymkus because they were actually more valuable to the team, but Brown felt he had to make a point—he wouldn't tolerate such behavior, and he had complete authority.

Just like the teams' previous meeting in New York two months earlier, the inaugural AAFC title game was a defensive struggle. After the Browns limited the Yankees to a field goal after New York had first-and-goal at the Cleveland 7 in the first quarter, the Yankees did one better, keeping the Browns off the board after reaching the New York 3. The Browns' offense finally got rolling just before the half, propelled by seven consecutive completions by Otto Graham, and took a 7–3 lead on a short Marion Motley touchdown run.

New York surged back into the lead in the third quarter after an 80-yard drive capped by a Spec Sanders touchdown, but Rymkus—lucky to still be on the team—broke through and blocked the extra point. Though the Browns moved the ball throughout the second half, they were unable to put points on the board through the third quarter due primarily to Lou Groza's injury, which hindered him on three missed kicks on the day.

While the Cleveland defense continually stymied the Yankees, New York clung to the lead. Running out of chances, the Browns took over at their own 25 midway through the fourth quarter. Edgar Jones made a key third-down catch off his shoe-tops to keep the drive going and push the Browns into New York territory. Moments later Otto Graham connected with Dante Lavelli for a 16-yard touchdown pass with 4:31 left—the same pass pattern that had resulted in the winning touchdown when the teams met in the mud in October.

A nice kickoff return put the Yankees into Cleveland territory, but Graham came up with a clinching interception at the Cleveland 30 to help the Browns melt away the final minutes.

As jubilant fans rushed the field to tear down the goalposts, a triumphant Paul Brown was carried off the field as the city of Cleveland had captured a football championship for the second straight year—albeit with a completely different team in a completely different league. The game also marked the first in an incredible string of 10 straight championships the Browns would play for over the next decade.

	1	2	3	4		
Yankees	3	0	6	0	=	9
Browns	0	7	0	7	=	14

NYY-Johnson 21-yd. FG
CLE-Motley 2-yd. run (Groza kick)
NYY-Sanders 2-yd. run (kick failed)
CLE-Lavelli 16-yd. pass from Graham (Groza kick)

Passing
NYY: Parker 8–18–81 0 TD 1 INT, Sanders 0–2–0 0 TD 0 INT
CLE: Graham 16–27–213 1 TD 1 INT

Rushing
NYY: Sanders 14–55, Parker 9–5, Prokop 5–5, Wagner 1–0
CLE: Motley 13–98, E. Jones 10–16, Greenwood 5–14, Colella 4–14, Terrell 1-(-4), Lavelli 1-(-7), Graham 3-(-19)

Receiving
NYY: Russell 5–58, Schwartz 1–12, Masterson 1–7, Prokop 1–4
CLE: Lavelli 6–87, Speedie 6–71, E. Jones 3–45, Yonakor 1–8

1947

Rushing
BUF: Mutryn 12–114, Tomasetti 14–36, Rykovich 5–19, Koch 6–16, Evans 4–15, Juzwik 3–15, Ratterman 2-(-7)
CLE: Cowan 8–67, E. Jones 4–66, Lund 2–24, Motley 6–13, Graham 1–9, Adamle 2–5, Colella 2–4, Greenwood 1–4

Receiving
BUF: Juzwik 1–17, Tomasetti 1–4, Coppage 1–3
CLE: Lavelli 6–81, Speedie 5–39, Cowan 1–1

Friday, September 5
Browns 30, Buffalo Bills 14
Cleveland Stadium (63,263)
White jerseys/white pants

In defense of their All-America Football Conference title, the Browns roared out of the starting gate with four touchdowns in the first 30 minutes in the opener with Buffalo on a Friday night and persevered through a sloppy second half to win comfortably. RB Marion Motley highlighted the scoring display in the early going, notching a touchdown on a three-yard run in the first quarter, then crossing the goal line again minutes later following a 48-yard interception return. Following a long touchdown pass from QB Otto Graham to WR Dante Lavelli to make it 27–0, Paul Brown started a handful of younger, less experienced players in the third quarter, and Buffalo took advantage with two quick touchdowns to cut the margin to 13 points. A Lou Groza field goal in the fourth capped the scoring and put the game out of reach.
Record: 1–0

	1	2	3	4		
Bills	0	0	14	0	=	14
Browns	13	14	0	3	=	30

CLE-E. Jones 11-yd. run (kick failed)
CLE-Motley 3-yd. run (Groza kick)
CLE-Motley 48-yd. interception return (Groza kick)
CLE-Lavelli 51-yd. pass from Graham (Groza kick)
BUF-Tomasetti 3-yd. run (Juzwik kick)
BUF-Coppage 3-yd. pass from Ratterman (Juzwik kick)
CLE-Groza 17-yd. FG

Passing
BUF: Ratterman 3–16–24 1 TD 4 INT
CLE: Graham 12–23–129 1 TD 0 INT, Lewis 0–1–0 0 TD 1 INT

Friday, September 12
Browns 55, Brooklyn Dodgers 7
Ebbets Field (18,876)
White jerseys/white pants

Before a hostile Friday-night crowd at Ebbets Field gathered primarily to jeer the struggling gridiron Dodgers, the Browns scored three early touchdowns in a five-minute period to set the tone and turned the contest into a massacre with five more touchdowns in the second half. After a Marion Motley scoring run got the Browns on the board, lightning struck when RB Tom Colella returned the ensuing Brooklyn punt 82 yards for another touchdown, followed shortly by a 53-yard scoring toss from Otto Graham to Dante Lavelli to make it 20–0. Motley, who picked up 111 yards on just five carries, opened the second half with a 51-yard touchdown run, followed by a second scoring toss from Graham, who completed nine of 11 passes on the day. Backup RB Bill Boedeker scored twice in the fourth as Paul Brown cleared the bench, even getting both reserve quarterbacks—Ermal Allen and Cliff Lewis—into the game. The only sour note on the night was an elbow injury to RB Edgar "Special Delivery" Jones, who would be sidelined for the next five weeks.
Record: 2–0

	1	2	3	4		
Browns	20	0	21	14	=	55
Dodgers	0	7	0	0	=	7

CLE-Motley 13-yd. run (Groza kick)
CLE-Colella 82-yd. punt return (kick failed)
CLE-Lavelli 53-yd. pass from Graham (Groza kick)
BRK-Hoernschemeyer 6-yd. run (Martinovich kick)
CLE-Motley 51-yd. run (Groza kick)
CLE-Speedie 19-yd. pass from Graham (Groza kick)
CLE-Lund 28-yd. interception return (Groza kick)
CLE-Boedeker 2-yd. run (Groza kick)
CLE-Boedeker 8-yd. run (Groza kick)

Rushing
CLE: Motley 5–111

Sunday, September 21
Browns 28, Baltimore Colts 0
Cleveland Stadium (44,257)
White jerseys/white pants

For the third straight week, the Browns soared to a huge early lead and then kept the opponent at bay in the second half to cruise to an easy victory on a hot, sunny afternoon on the lakefront. This time, Cleveland took a 21–0 lead in the game's first 12 plays, scoring first on a short touchdown run by Marion Motley, then on an interception return by Tom Colella. It was 28–0 at the half, and neither team scored in the final two periods, thanks in part to Cleveland punter Horace Gillom, who blasted seven punts for an average of 55.7 yards per kick, including a 74-yarder. With the victory, the Browns became the only undefeated team left in the AAFC and assumed sole possession of first place in the Western Division.

Record: 3–0

	1	2	3	4		
Colts	0	0	0	0	=	0
Browns	21	7	0	0	=	28

CLE-Motley 2-yd. run (Groza kick)
CLE-Colella 23-yd. interception return (Groza kick)
CLE-Boedeker 6-yd. run (Groza kick)
CLE-Cowan 1-yd. run (Groza kick)

Passing
BAL: Schwenk 10–28–159 0 TD, Nemeth 0–2–0 0 TD
CLE: Graham 4–6–77 0 TD 0 INT, Lewis 2–4–25 0 TD 0 INT, Allen 2–3–20 0 TD 0 INT

Rushing
BAL: Hillenbrand 5–41, Black 4–34, Mobley 6–29, Castiglia 4–16, Wright 4–11, Dudish 3–5, Mertes 2–3, Vardian 2–3, Terrell 1–4
CLE: Motley 10–68, Dellerba 11–48, Lewis 4–35, Boedeker 4–8, Cowan 3–5, Allen 1–3, Mayne 1–2, Greenwood 1–4, Colella 1–0, Humble 1–0

Receiving
BAL: Hillenbrand 3–73, Sigurdson 2–25, Dudish 1–20, Bechtol 1–17, Jones 1–9, Davis 1–8, Vardian 1–7
CLE: Speedie 1–33, Greenwood 2–32, Shurnas 1–17, Gillom 1–10, Boedeker 1–9, Davis 1–8, Lavelli 1–6

Friday, September 26
Browns 41, Chicago Rockets 21
Soldier Field (18,450)
White jerseys/white pants

The Browns once again followed their established script of riding a huge first-half lead to a comfortable victory, this time over the winless Rockets on a Friday night in the Windy City. Thanks to a pair of Otto Graham scoring tosses, including a 70-yard bomb to Mac Speedie, it was 27–0 at halftime, and the Browns endured the second half without RB Marion Motley, who was knocked out of the game early in the second period with a head injury. Graham, who had been pulled in the third quarter, was reinserted after Chicago scored two quick touchdowns and sparked Cleveland's fourth touchdown that put the game away in the fourth quarter. Graham, who saw his string of consecutive passes without an interception end at 91, was then knocked out of the game himself with an injury.

Record: 4–0

	1	2	3	4		
Browns	10	17	0	14	=	41
Rockets	0	0	14	7	=	21

CLE-Groza 32-yd. FG
CLE-Speedie 70-yd. pass from Graham (Groza kick)
CLE-Yonakor 8-yd. pass from Graham (Groza kick)
CLE-Cowan 3-yd. run (Groza kick)
CLE-Groza 20-yd. FG
CHI-Quillen 23-yd. pass from Vacanti (Rokisky kick)
CHI-Dove 14-yd. pass from Vacanti (Rokisky kick)
CLE-Boedeker 14-yd. run (Groza kick)
CLE-Dellerba 10-yd. fumble return (Groza kick)
CHI-Bass pass from Vacanti (Rokisky kick)

Sunday, October 5
Browns 26, New York Yankees 17
Cleveland Stadium (80,067)
White jerseys/white pants

Before a capacity crowd at Cleveland Stadium, the 1946 AAFC title flag was hoisted above the bleachers and set the tone for a magnificent afternoon of football between the league's two top teams. After the Yankees took a 3–0 lead into the second period—marking the first time the Browns had trailed all season—the home team rebounded with 17 points to take a two-touchdown lead to the half. A blowout appeared imminent, but New York responded with two touchdowns in the first five minutes of the third quarter—

the second on an interception return—to tie the contest. Then it was the Browns' turn as they took the football 73 yards on the ensuing possession and went back on top on an Otto Graham-to-Mac Speedie scoring toss with five minutes left in the period. With nine minutes remaining in the game, the Yankees drove to the Cleveland 25 after blocking a Lou Groza field-goal attempt but were stymied by the Browns' defense. The Cleveland offense, which rolled up 217 yards on the ground, then took six minutes off the clock and put the game away with a 43-yard Groza field goal with three minutes to play. The victory, the Browns' eleventh straight, moved them to 5–0 on the season.

Record: 5–0

	1	2	3	4		
Yankees	3	0	14	0	=	17
Browns	0	17	6	3	=	26

NYY-Johnson 47-yd. FG
CLE-Cowan 42-yd. pass from Graham (Groza kick)
CLE-Colella 29-yd. run (Groza kick)
CLE-Groza 25-yd. FG
NYY-Cheatham 7-yd. pass from Sanders (Johnson kick)
NYY-Sweiger 20-yd. interception return (Johnson kick)
CLE-Speedie 10-yd. pass from Graham (kick failed)
CLE-Groza 43-yd. FG

Rushing
NYY: Sanders 11–56, Young 7–41, Sweiger 2–9, Prokop 2–4, Kennedy 1–1
CLE: Colella 5–63, Motley 12–59, Graham 3–31, Adamle 1–22, Cowan 4–19, Greenwood 2–17, Boedeker 1–4, Allen 1–1, Lewis 1–1

Receiving
NYY: Sweiger 4–36, Kurrasch 1–21, Russell 1–19, Alford 1–18, Cheatham 1–7, Young 3–0
CLE: Speedie 6–58, Lavelli 3–47, Cowan 1–42, Gillom 1–14

Sunday, October 12
Los Angeles Dons 13, Browns 10
Cleveland Stadium (63,124)
White jerseys/white pants

The euphoria of the previous Sunday evaporated in a frustrating 2–3 loss to the Dons as Cleveland fumbles led to all three Los Angeles scores. The Browns sprinted to a 10–0 lead in the first quarter and appeared on the cusp of overwhelming the visitors, but the tide turned when the Dons' Chuck Fenenbock returned a fumble 28 yards for LA's lone touchdown, then Ben Agajanian's 46-yard field goal tied the game in the third period. The teams appeared headed for a stalemate when Agajanian missed a 22-yard field goal with three minutes to play, but the Browns were penalized for having 12 men on the field, and Agajanian made the second attempt from 17 yards out to give the Dons the lead. The Browns drove into Los Angeles territory in the final minute, but Groza missed a 50-yard field goal. The loss spoiled wonderful efforts by both the Cleveland defense and offense, which rolled up nearly 400 total yards, paced by 233 through the air by Graham, who hit Mac Speedie eight times for 110 yards.

Record: 5–1

	1	2	3	4		
Dons	0	7	3	3	=	13
Browns	10	0	0	0	=	10

CLE-Groza 28-yd. FG
CLE-Motley 14-yd. run (Groza kick)
LA-Fenenbock 28-yd. fumble return (Agajanian kick)
LA-Agajanian 46-yd. FG
LA-Agajanian 17-yd. FG

Passing
LA: O'Rourke 5–19–59 0 TD 0 INT, Dobbs 1–3-(-3) 0 TD 0 INT
CLE: Graham 19–29–233 0 TD 1 INT

Rushing
LA: Kelly 6–27, Kimbrough 4–23, Piggott 3–18, Clarke 6–15, O'Rourke 5–15, Reinhard 2–6, Fenenbock 1–2, Dobbs 1-(-1)
CLE: Motley 13–87, Boedeker 7–33, Greenwood 6–41, Cowan 3–4, Graham 2–1, Lund 3-(-1), Mayne 3-(-3)

Receiving
LA: Fenenbock 2–26, Nowaskey 1–20, Gentry 1–15, Clarke 1-(-2), Kelly 1-(-3)
CLE: Speedie 8–110, Lavelli 5–83, Cowan 3–17, Greenwood 1–12, Colella 1–9, Boedeker 1–2

Sunday, October 19
Browns 31, Chicago Rockets 28
Cleveland Stadium (32,256)
Brown jerseys/white pants

Bouncing back from a disheartening loss the week before, the Browns built a 17-point fourth-quarter lead and then hung on as the Rockets—playing far better than their 0–7 record—scored twice in the final four minutes. The teams combined for 821 total yards, the Browns tallying 456 paced by Otto Graham's 239 through the air. Mac Speedie notched his second straight 100-yard game, tallying 166 yards on just five receptions. Chicago snuck to an early 7–3 lead, but trailed 17–7 going into the fourth quarter. A pair of touchdown runs by the Browns' Edgar Jones, back from injury, made it 31–14, giving the home team enough margin to withstand a pair of touchdown receptions by Chicago's Ray Ramsey in the waning moments.

Record: 6–1

	1	2	3	4		
Rockets	0	7	0	21	=	28
Browns	3	7	7	14	=	31

CLE-Groza 21-yd. FG
CHI-Hirsch 37-yd. pass from Vacanti (Rokisky kick)
CLE-Motley 22-yd. run (Groza kick)
CLE-Speedie 49-yd. pass from Graham (Groza kick)
CLE-E. Jones 2-yd. run (Groza kick)
CHI-Ramsey 11-yd. run (Rokisky kick)
CLE-E. Jones 3-yd. run (Groza kick)
CHI-Ramsey 7-yd. pass from Vacanti (Rokisky kick)
CHI-Ramsey 20-yd. pass from Vacanti (Rokisky kick)

Passing
CHI: Vacanti 10–20–179 3 TD 0 INT, Dekdebrun 7–10–81 0 TD 0 INT, Evans 0–1–0 0 TD 0 INT, Hirsch 0–1–0 0 TD 0 INT
CLE: Graham 10–17–239 1 TD

Rushing
CHI: Kellagher 6–46, Daley 8–30, Ramsey 6–26, Dekdebrun 2–6, Evans 1–2, Hirsch 5-(-2), Bass 1-(-3)
CLE: E. Jones 8–76, Motley 10–56, Cowan 7–21, Graham 2–8, Adamle 3–5, Mayne 1–3, Allen 1–2, Greenwood 1–2, Boedeker 2–0, Blandin 1-(-6)

Receiving
CHI: Hirsch 3–74, Ramsey 4–73, Daley 2–37, Morris 2–23, Kellagher 1–18, Mulready 1–9, Ebli 2–23, Lahey 2–4
CLE: Speedie 5–166, Boedeker 2–86, Yonakor 3–37, Lund 1–8

Sunday, October 26
Browns 14, San Francisco 49ers 7
Kezar Stadium (54,483)
Brown jerseys/white pants

With first place in the Western Division at stake and a heavy fog rolling in off the Bay, the Browns bounded to a 14–0 halftime lead and held off the 49ers with sterling performances on both sides of the ball. Otto Graham put forth one of the best showings of his career, throwing for 278 yards and tossing a pair of touchdown passes to Dante Lavelli and Mac Speedie to open up a lead the Browns wouldn't relinquish. Speedie set an AAFC record with 10 receptions for 141 yards to continually silence an enthusiastic San Francisco crowd that created a college atmosphere. But with the Browns fumbling away two other scoring chances, the 49ers stayed in the game. The home team scored on its first possession of the second half to cut the margin to seven but was thwarted by the Cleveland defense for the rest of the afternoon. Horace Gillom clinched the victory by intercepting a San Francisco pass in the final minutes, pushing the Browns to 7–1 on the season, now two victories ahead of the 49ers in the division race.

Record: 7–1

	1	2	3	4		
Browns	7	7	0	0	=	14
49ers	0	0	7	0	=	7

CLE-Lavelli 22-yd. pass from Graham (Groza kick)
CLE-Speedie 42-yd. pass from Graham (Groza kick)
SF-Standlee 1-yd. run (Vetrano kick)

Rushing
CLE: Motley 19–60, Jones 7–57, Boedeker 4–38, Mayne 5–11, Graham 4-(-14), Greenwood 1-(-16)
SF: Standlee 11–72, Strzykalski 12–68, Mathews 3–23, Eshmont 4–12, Albers 8-(-9)

Receiving
CLE: Speedie 10–141

Sunday, November 2
Browns 28, Buffalo Bills 7
Civic Stadium (43,167)
White jerseys/white pants

Before a record crowd at Buffalo's Civic Stadium, the Browns picked up where they'd left off the week before, rolling up 392 yards of total offense and scoring a touch-

down in each period to defeat an improving Buffalo team that hadn't lost in five weeks. The highlight of the game came midway through the second period after the Cleveland defense halted the Bills at the Browns' 1. On the next play, Otto Graham looped a screen pass to Mac Speedie that caught the Buffalo defense off-guard, and Speedie followed a handful of key blocks downfield for a 99-yard touchdown. It was one of 13 completions in 16 attempts for Graham, who totaled 246 yards through the air and three scores.
Record: 8–1

	1	2	3	4		
Browns	7	7	7	7	=	28
Bills	0	0	0	7	=	7

CLE-E. Jones 12-yd. run (Groza kick)
CLE-Speedie 99-yd. pass from Graham (Groza kick)
CLE-Lavelli 11-yd. pass from Graham (Groza kick)
CLE-Yonakor 39-yd. pass from Graham (Groza kick)
BUF-Baldwin 11-yd. pass from Ratterman (Armstrong kick)

Receiving
CLE: Speedie 2–107

Passing
CLE: Graham 13–16–246 3 TD

Sunday, November 9
Browns 13, Brooklyn Dodgers 12
Cleveland Stadium (30,279)
White jerseys/white pants

Before the smallest home crowd in their two years of existence, the Browns cashed in on some good fortune to knock off the lowly Dodgers by a single point. Brooklyn, playing with something to prove after its 48-point loss to the Browns two months earlier, took the opening possession 80 yards for a touchdown. But setting the tone for a miserable day for Dodger kicker Phil Martinovich, the extra-point conversion was blocked, breaking a string of 30 consecutive successful point-after attempts for Martinovich, for whom things would get even worse. He would go on to miss four field goals on the afternoon, all of them short, spoiling a strong performance by the Brooklyn offense, which tallied 251 yards on the ground. Martinovich's struggles provided enough cushion for the Browns, who scored on their first two possessions but never threatened again, tallying a season-low 261 total yards. In fact, after Otto Graham's second touchdown pass early in the second quarter, he didn't complete another, and things looked grim for the Browns when Brooklyn RB Monk Gafford broke free for a 79-yard touchdown with just under eight minutes to play in the game. But Martinovich missed the extra point that would have tied the game, and the Bills never threatened again. The Browns had dodged a huge bullet, and with the 49ers losing in New York, they were on the brink of clinching their second consecutive division title.
Record: 9–1

	1	2	3	4		
Dodgers	6	0	0	6	=	12
Browns	7	6	0	0	=	13

BRK-Colmer 4-yd. run (kick failed)
CLE-Lavelli 72-yd. pass from Graham (Groza kick)
CLE-Mayne 15-yd. pass from Graham (kick failed)
BRK-Gafford 79-yd. run (kick failed)

Passing
BRK: Hoernschemeyer 3–12–22 0 TD 0 INT
CLE: Graham 4–14–95 2 TD 2 INT

Rushing
BRK: Gafford 8–110, Colmer 16–76, Hoernschemeyer 14–48, Jones 4–10, Akins 2–6, Thompson 1–4, Perina 1-(-3)
CLE: Motley 19–76, E. Jones 15–69, Mayne 6–9, Colella 1–9, Adamle 1–4, Graham 3-(-1)

Receiving
BRK: Colmer 2–26, Perina 1-(-4)
CLE: Lavelli 2–80, Mayne 1–15, Motley 1–0

Sunday, November 16
Browns 37, San Francisco 49ers 14
Cleveland Stadium (76,504)
White jerseys/white pants

In their home finale, the Browns clinched the Western Division title in resounding fashion, routing the 49ers to secure their fifth straight win and tenth in 11 contests. Dante Lavelli led the way, snagging seven receptions—three for touchdowns—that covered 127 yards, as Otto Graham tossed for 222 through the air. The turning point of the contest came on the fourth play of the second half. With the 49ers driving and trailing only 16–7, Tom Colella intercepted a pass at midfield and returned it to the San Francisco 3, setting up a Graham touchdown plunge to open the floodgates. The Browns also demonstrated their depth after Lou Groza pulled a muscle in his leg during warm-ups as Chet Adams and Lou Saban combined to provide the kicking duties.
Record: 10–1

	1	2	3	4		
49ers	0	7	0	7	=	14
Browns	9	7	14	7	=	37

CLE-Adams 44-yd. FG
CLE-Lavelli 23-yd. pass from Graham (kick failed)
SF-Eshmont 8-yd. pass from Albert (Vetrano kick)
CLE-Lavelli 15-yd. pass from Graham (Adams kick)
CLE-Graham 1-yd. run (Saban kick)
CLE-Lavelli 64-yd. pass from Graham (Saban kick)
SF-Strzykalski 5-yd. run (Vetrano kick)
CLE-Adamle 1-yd. run (Saban kick)

Passing
SF: Albert 9–16–109 1 TD, Freitas 3–6–50 0 TD
CLE: Graham 15–24–222 3 TD 0 INT, Allen 1–1–62 0 TD 0 INT

Rushing
SF: Strzykalski 9–51, Standlee 10–40, Eshmont 11–39, Mathews 1–15, Beals 2–12, Albert 2–7, Yonamine 1–6, Vetrano 1–0
CLE: E. Jones 7–52, Motley 10–49, Dewar 4–18, Mayne 3–12, Greenwood 2–10, Adamle 3–8, Lund 2–5, Boedeker 1–1, Graham 1–1

Receiving
SF: Strzykalski 2–49, Carr 2–40, Susoeff 3–32, Beals 2–24, Eshmont 2–17, Parsons 1-(-3)
CLE: Lavelli 7–127, Lund 1–62, Speedie 5–49, Greenwood 1–21, E. Jones 1–13, Boedeker 1–12

Sunday, November 23
Browns 28, New York Yankees 28
Yankee Stadium (70,060)
White jerseys/white pants

Though they didn't record a victory, the Browns provided one of the great stories of franchise history by rallying from a 28–0 deficit to force a tie with the high-flying Yankees, setting the stage for a memorable title-game rematch three weeks later. The largest crowd ever to attend a football game at Yankee Stadium thrilled as the home team dominated the Browns in the first half. Parlaying an unstoppable running game sparked by Orban "Spec" Sanders, who rushed for 117 yards and three touchdowns in the first 30 minutes, and aided by three Cleveland turnovers, the Yankees scored four touchdowns before the Browns got on the board just before the intermission. New York then picked up where it left off in the third quarter, driving to the Browns' 1 on its first possession. But the Cleveland defense stiffened and kept the Yankees out of the end zone, giving the ball back to the Browns' offense. From that point on, the game belonged to the Browns. Otto Graham immediately hit Mac Speedie with an 82-yard pass to set up Cleveland's second touchdown, then the Browns cut the lead to seven going into the fourth period. With the Browns' defense stuffing Sanders, who only collected 30 yards in the second half, a short scoring run by Jim Dewar tied the game with five minutes to play, capping a 90-yard drive. New York drove to the Browns' 36 in the final seconds but failed to call time out to set up a potential game-winning field goal, and time expired. Graham, now with 20 touchdown passes on the season, set a league record with 325 passing yards. Interestingly, while this game was one of three professional football games played in New York City that day, it dramatically outdrew the other two. Only 11,866 witnessed the Brooklyn-Los Angeles AAFC game at Ebbets Field, while a modest 27,939 filed into the Polo Grounds to see the NFL contest between the Giants and Green Bay Packers.
Record: 10–1–1

	1	2	3	4		
Browns	0	7	14	7	=	28
Yankees	14	14	0	0	=	28

NY-Sanders 1-yd. run (Johnson kick)
NY-Sanders 3-yd. run (Johnson kick)
NY-Sanders 27-yd. run (Johnson kick)
NY-Young 5-yd. run (Johnson kick)
CLE-Boedeker 34-yd. pass from Graham (Saban kick)
CLE-Motley 12-yd. pass from Graham (Saban kick)
CLE-Motley 10-yd. run (Saban kick)
CLE-Dewar 5-yd. run (Saban kick)

Passing
CLE: Graham 15–28–325 2 TD 3 INT

Rushing
NY: Sanders 32–147

Thursday, November 27
Browns 27, Los Angeles Dons 17
Los Angeles Memorial Coliseum (45,009)
Brown jerseys/white pants

Despite getting only three days off following an emotionally draining game and having to travel the length of the continent, the Browns still pulled out a gritty Thanksgiving Day victory, while also avenging their only loss of the season. Trailing 10–0 early after Los Angeles scored on a short interception return for a touchdown, the Browns scored the next 20 points to take control of the contest. After the Dons sliced the lead back to three, they regained possession deep in their own territory with four minutes to play, but Mac Speedie picked off a lateral and returned it for a touchdown to clinch the victory. It was the fifth turnover forced by the Cleveland defense, atoning for a season-high 462 yards allowed.

Record: 11–1–1

	1	2	3	4		
Browns	7	7	6	7	=	27
Dons	10	0	0	7	=	17

LA-Agajanian 43-yd. FG
LA-Clarke 8-yd. interception return (Agajanian kick)
CLE-Motley 43-yd. run (Saban kick)
CLE-Colella 18-yd. pass from Graham (Saban kick)
CLE-Mayne 69-yd. pass from Graham (kick failed)
LA-Fenenbock 35-yd. pass from Dobbs (Agajanian kick)
CLE-Speedie 8-yd. fumble return (Saban kick)

Sunday, December 7
Browns 42, Baltimore Colts 0
Memorial Stadium (20,574)
White jerseys/white pants

In the regular-season finale, the Browns put on an incredible offensive performance amid rainy and gloomy conditions in Baltimore. Rolling up 559 yards of offense, the Browns cruised to six touchdowns and a shutout victory that served as a perfect primer for the following week's league championship game. While Otto Graham tossed three more touchdown passes to bring his season total to 25, the Cleveland ground game was unstoppable, accumulating 334 yards. The Browns' defense was equally dominant, limiting the Colts to just 186 yards and forcing four turnovers.

Record: 12–1–1

	1	2	3	4		
Browns	14	7	14	7	=	42
Colts	0	0	0	0	=	0

CLE-E. Jones 11-yd. pass from Graham (Groza kick)
CLE-Lavelli 8-yd. pass from Graham (Groza kick)
CLE-Jones 1-yd. run (Groza kick)
CLE-Mayne 36-yd. pass from Graham (Groza kick)
CLE-Lund 18-yd. pass from Lewis (Groza kick)
CLE-Lund 63-yd. run (Groza kick)

1947 AAFC Championship
Sunday, December 14
Browns 14, New York Yankees 3
Yankee Stadium (61,879)
White jerseys/white pants

Many figured the Yankees were due. After all, they'd come progressively closer each of the four times they'd faced the Browns over the previous two years, culminated by their jumping to a 28–0 lead in their most recent meeting three weeks earlier. The law of averages suggested that the Yankees were simply too talented to continue to lose to the Browns.

Instead, the Browns denied these expectations and once again overpowered the Yankees to capture their second straight All-America Football Conference crown.

Marion Motley set up the game's first score late in the first quarter when he exploded around the end for a 51-yard gain to the New York 13. Moments later, Otto Graham powered over from the 1 to make it 7–0. Though the temperature hovered in the low 40s and there was no rain, the field was still half-frozen from the early onset of winter, and the defenses took center stage for much of the remainder of the game.

After falling behind, the Yankees marched to the Cleveland 5, but the Browns held and forced them to settle for a field goal and their only points of the day. It seemed only fitting that the Cleveland defense set up the backbreaking touchdown. Tom Colella, a spark plug on both sides of the ball all season, made a shoestring interception midway through the third period and returned it into Yankee territory, where another powerful Motley run paved the way for a short scoring blast by Edgar Jones to make it 14–3 and essentially extinguish any Yankee hopes of stealing the title.

New York threatened to make a game of it early in the fourth when the Yankees reached the Cleveland 19, but RB Buddy Young fumbled and Lou Saban recovered for the Browns. It was the third turnover of the day for the New York offense, which was limited to 212 total yards. Spec Sanders, who'd run roughshod over Cleveland three weeks before, was held in check to the tune of 40 yards on 12 carries. Conversely, Motley picked up 109 on 13 carries, and Graham, limited to primarily short passes, completed 14 of 21 attempts.

With their second straight championship, the Browns had visions of becoming a dynasty. But the success of their first two seasons would pale to what would come next.

	1	2	3	4		
Browns	7	0	7	0	=	14
Yankees	0	3	0	0	=	3

CLE-Graham 1-yd. run (Groza kick)
NY-Johnson 12-yd. FG
CLE-E. Jones 4-yd. run (Saban kick)

Passing
CLE: Graham 14–21–112 0 TD 0 INT
NY: Sanders 7–17–89 0 TD 1 INT, Prokop 0–1–0 0 TD 0 INT

Rushing
CLE: Motley 13–109, Jones 10–27, Graham 4–21, Lewis 1–9, Colella 1–6, Mayne 4–0
NY: Young 16–69, Sanders 12–40, Prokop 5–14

Receiving
CLE: Lavelli 3–37, Jones 3–31, Speedie 4–25, Mayne 1–8, Colella 2–7, Lewis 1–4
NY: Young 2–25, Kurrasch 1–20, Davis 1–18, Russell 1–14, Sweiger 2–12

1948

Friday, September 3
Browns 19, Los Angeles Dons 14
Cleveland Stadium (60,193)
White jerseys/white pants

The Browns kept things close to the vest in the season opener, gradually building a 19–0 lead before a big Friday-night crowd, then endured a flurry of Los Angeles points in the final seconds. With WR Dante Lavelli out with a broken ankle and QB Otto Graham playing with an injured hand that affected the accuracy of his throws, the Cleveland offense lacked the explosiveness that had defined it over the previous two seasons, managing only 263 total yards in what would be the Browns' lowest tally of the season. RB Marion Motley was also nursing an injured back and left the game twice with different injuries. Still, taking advantage of four Los Angeles turnovers (which wiped out three of their own) the Browns were too much for the Dons, opening the scoring with a 51-yard Lou Groza field goal and then tacking on a Graham touchdown pass to rookie RB (and Akron native) Ara Parseghian, followed by a safety when LA QB Glenn Dobbs stepped out of his own end zone on a pass attempt. Browns RB Bill Boedeker capped the Cleveland scoring with a short touchdown run in the third quarter. The Dons didn't get on the board until 30 seconds remained, then recovered the football on the ensuing kickoff and added another touchdown with five seconds to play.

Record: 1–0

	1	2	3	4		
Dons	0	0	0	14	=	14
Browns	3	7	9	0	=	19

CLE-Groza 51-yd. FG
CLE-Parseghian 17-yd. pass from Graham (Groza kick)
CLE-Safety: Dobbs stepped out of end zone
CLE-Boedeker 6-yd. run (Groza kick)
LA-Kimbrough 2-yd. run (Agajanian kick)
LA-Aguirre 9-yd. pass from Dobbs (Agajanian kick)

Passing
LA: Dobbs 15–24–134 1 TD 1 INT, Wedemeyer 1–4–11 0 TD 1 INT
CLE: Graham 9–17–122 1 TD 1 INT

Rushing
LA: Kimbrough 7–28, Dobbs 4–15, Wedemeyer 4–15, Clarke 2–5, Clay 2–5, Kelly 1–1, Mitchell 1–0
CLE: Motley 11–57, Boedeker 6–30, E. Jones 7–22, Cline 3–9, Cowan 1–8, Graham 2–6, Sensanbaugher 2–6, Adamle 3–4, Parseghian 2-(-9)

Receiving
LA: Baldwin 3–44, Kimbrough 2–37, Wedemeyer 3–17, Gentry 2–17, Clarke 2–15, Mitchell 1–11, Aguirre 1–9, Durkota 2-(-5)
CLE: Cowan 2–37, Motley 1–36, Gillom 2–22, Parseghian 1–17, Speedie 3–10

Sunday, September 12
Browns 42, Buffalo Bills 13
Civic Stadium (35,340)
White jerseys/white pants

The Cleveland offense returned to form in the first of what would be three blowout victories over the Bills in 1948, rolling up more than 500 yards and six touchdowns. After a wild first half that saw the teams combine for five touchdowns in an 18-minute span, the Browns took over in the second half on the strength of three rushing scores and a dominating defense that allowed the Bills to cross midfield only once in the final two periods. Otto Graham threw two touchdowns and ran for another, with his primary target being speedie WR Mac, who tied an AAFC record with 10 receptions for 151 yards. Marion Motley was efficient on the ground, rushing for 140 yards on 16 carries and an 18-yard score that gave the Browns a 14–0 lead going into the second quarter.

Record: 2–0

	1	2	3	4		
Browns	14	7	7	14	=	42
Bills	0	13	0	0	=	13

CLE-Cowan 11-yd. pass from Graham (Groza kick)
CLE-Motley 18-yd. run (Groza kick)
BUF-Rykovich 25-yd. run (kick failed)
CLE-Speedie 10-yd. pass from Graham (Groza kick)
BUF-Mutryn 12-yd. run (Armstrong kick)

CLE-Graham 1-yd. run (Groza kick)
CLE-Colella 23-yd. run (Groza kick)
CLE-Sensanbaugher 3-yd. run (Groza kick)

Passing
CLE: Graham 11–21–189 2 TD 0 INT, Lewis 3–5–47 0 TD 0 INT
BUF: Ratterman 3–9–20 0 TD, Still 0–3–0 0 TD 0 INT

Rushing
CLE: Motley 16–140, Boedeker 6–40, E. Jones 4–26, Colella 1–23, Adamle 3–15, Cline 1–8, James 1–8, Parseghian 1–5, D. Jones 2–4, Sensanbaugher 1–3, Graham 1–1, Cowan 2-(-1)
BUF: Rykovich 13–101, Mutryn 18–76, Kulbitski 10–39, Gompers 2–13, Schneider 1–4, Tomasetti 1–1, Ratterman 1-(-4), Still 1-(-10)

Receiving
CLE: Speedie 10–151, Boedeker 1–51, Cowan 2–32, Gillom 2–24
BUF: O'Connor 2–18, Mutryn 1–7

Friday, September 17
Browns 28, Chicago Rockets 7
Soldier Field (30,874)
White jerseys/white pants

For the second straight week, the Browns turned a tight contest into a rout in the second half, cruising to a Friday-night win in Chicago. The game turned on the first series of the second half when, with Cleveland leading 14–7, Browns' DB Cliff Lewis intercepted a Chicago pass to set up a touchdown. Otto Graham tossed three scoring passes, including two to Bob Cowan in the third quarter, and opened the scoring with a 12-yard touchdown run in the first quarter. The game became sloppier as the night went on, with the teams combining for nine turnovers, six by the Rockets. The loss began an 11-game losing streak for Chicago, which would not win again until 1949.
Record: 3–0

	1	2	3	4		
Browns	7	7	14	0	=	28
Rockets	0	7	0	0	=	7

CLE-Graham 12-yd. run (Groza kick)
CLE-Boedeker 4-yd. pass from Graham (Groza kick)
CHI-Hirsch 13-yd. pass from Bertelli (Juzwik kick)
CLE-Cowan 39-yd. pass from Graham (Groza kick)
CLE-Cowan 40-yd. pass from Graham (Groza kick)

Sunday, September 26
Browns 21, Chicago Rockets 10
Cleveland Stadium (37,190)
White jerseys/white pants

Facing the Rockets for the second time in nine days, the Browns rallied from a 10–0 halftime deficit to defeat Chicago once again and improve to 4–0. The Rockets drew first blood on their first offensive play with a 74-yard touchdown pass from QB Jesse Freitas to Cleveland native Eddie Prokop, then, with the Cleveland offense sputtering, extended the lead to 10 points with a second-quarter field goal. It marked just the second time in their history the Browns had been held scoreless in the first half. But Cleveland righted the ship with a pair of third-quarter touchdowns—both long Otto Graham passes—to take the lead, and the Browns' defense didn't allow another point. Things got chippy between the two teams, and Mac Speedie was forced to leave the game after a Chicago defender scooped up a handful of dirt from the baseball infield portion of the field and threw it in his face. Speedie had proved to be a thorn in Chicago's side, catching five passes for 103 yards.
Record: 4–0

	1	2	3	4		
Rockets	7	3	0	0	=	10
Browns	0	0	14	7	=	21

CHI-Prokop 74-yd. pass from Freitas (McCarthy kick)
CHI-McCarthy 18-yd. FG
CLE-Boedeker 37-yd. pass from Graham (Groza kick)
CLE-D. Jones 43-yd. pass from Graham (Groza kick)
CLE-Boedeker 2-yd. run (Groza kick)

Passing
CHI: Freitas 9–17–161 1 TD 2 INT, Prokop 0–1–0 0 TD 0 INT, Vacanti 0–1–0 0 TD 0 INT
CLE: Graham 11–22–216 2 TD 1 INT, Motley 0–1–0 0 TD 0 INT

Rushing
CHI: Clarke 4–17, Prokop 6–14, Proctor 4–9, Hirsch 2–5, Livingstone 4–4, Freitas 1–1, Simmons 1–1, Fenenbock 1-(-6)
CLE: Motley 13–51, Boedeker 17–35, D. Jones 5–17, Parseghian 2–12, Adamle 1–7, Cline 2–4

Receiving
CHI: Prokop 2–82, Hirsch 2–29, Livingstone 1–15, McCarthy 1–15, Jensen 1–11, King 1–10, Simmons 1-(-1)
CLE: Speedie 5–103, Boedeker 2–45, D. Jones 1–43, Motley 2–24, Yonakor 1–1

Tuesday, October 5
Browns 14, Baltimore Colts 10
Memorial Stadium (22,359)
White jerseys/white pants

The day after the Indians defeated the Boston Red Sox in the first-ever American League playoff and earned a trip to the World Series, the Browns continued the city's winning ways by sloshing to a victory over the Colts in the second and final Tuesday game in franchise history. Played out in the midst of a heavy downpour that resulted in ankle-deep patches of mud, the teams moved the ball primarily on the ground, though the Colts scored via the air on a 78-yard screen pass from QB Y. A. Tittle to RB Billy Hillenbrand on the fourth play of the game. The Browns came back to tie on a short Edgar Jones touchdown run, then after the Colts took a 10–7 lead into the third quarter, another Jones score gave the Browns the lead for good. With Marion Motley picking up 130 yards in the mud, the Browns tallied 228 rushing yards while holding the Colts to just 112 total after their early touchdown.
Record: 5–0

	1	2	3	4		
Browns	7	0	7	0	=	14
Colts	7	3	0	0	=	10

BAL-Hillenbrand 78-yd. pass from Tittle (Grossman kick)
CLE-E. Jones 2-yd. run (Groza kick)
BAL-Grossman 40-yd. FG
CLE-E. Jones 12-yd. pass from Graham (Groza kick)

Sunday, October 10
Browns 30, Brooklyn Dodgers 17
Cleveland Stadium (31,187)
White jerseys/white pants

Just hours after the Indians dropped Game Five of the World Series to the Boston Braves, Cleveland Stadium was cleared, and the field was prepped for a night game between the undefeated Browns and winless Brooklyn Dodgers. Though there were 55,000 fewer fans in the park for the Browns game, those there for the nightcap got to see a victory as the home team scored two fourth-quarter touchdowns to break a 17–17 tie. The Browns surged to a 10–0 lead in the first quarter after a league-record 53-yard field goal by Lou Groza, but the Dodgers rebounded to knot the score. Brooklyn did it again in the third quarter after a Bill Boedeker touchdown run put the Browns up 17–10 when lineman Hank Foldberg returned a blocked Groza field goal 51 yards for a touchdown. The Browns returned the favor early in the fourth when DE George Young scooped up a fumble and returned it nine yards for what proved to be the winning points. Marion Motley then put the icing on the cake with a short touchdown run that capped a 17-play, 73-yard drive. Though the Browns' offense played well, Otto Graham did not throw a touchdown pass—breaking a string of 13 consecutive games in which he'd fired a scoring toss.
Record: 6–0

	1	2	3	4		
Dodgers	0	10	7	0	=	17
Browns	10	0	7	13	=	30

CLE-E. Jones 8-yd. run (Groza kick)
CLE-Groza 53-yd. FG
BRK-Colmer 2-yd. run (Tevis kick)
BRK-Tevis 36-yd. FG
CLE-Boedeker 10-yd. run (Groza kick)
BRK-Foldberg 51-yd. blocked field goal return (Brown kick)
CLE-Young 9-yd. fumble return (kick failed)
CLE-Motley 3-yd. run (Groza kick)

Sunday, October 17
Browns 31, Buffalo Bills 14
Cleveland Stadium (28,054)
White jerseys/white pants

In a game played in a driving rainstorm, the Browns took control early and kept the Bills at bay all afternoon to move to 7–0 on the season. Cleveland surged ahead on the third play of the game when Otto Graham connected with Edgar Jones for a 44-yard score. After a Marion Motley fumble set up the game-tying touchdown, the Browns added 10 more points before the first quarter expired. They put the game away with a pair of touchdown receptions in the second half by Mac Speedie, who caught seven passes for 142 yards. The defeat dropped Buffalo to 2–5 on the season, but the Bills would turn things around, winning six of their next eight games to capture the Eastern Division crown and set up a third meeting with the Browns in the league championship two months later.
Record: 7–0

	1	2	3	4		
Bills	7	0	0	7	=	14
Browns	17	0	7	7	=	31

CLE-E. Jones 44-yd. pass from Graham (Groza kick)
BUF-Baldwin 22-yd. pass from Still (Steuber kick)
CLE-Groza 45-yd. FG
CLE-Motley 3-yd. run (Groza kick)
CLE-Speedie 15-yd. pass from Graham (Groza kick)
BUF-Tomasetti 9-yd. pass from Ratterman (Steuber kick)
CLE-Speedie 30-yd. pass from Lewis (Groza kick)

Passing
BUF: Ratterman 13–24–174 1 TD 0 INT, Still 4–9–84 1 TD 2 INT, Mutryn 1–1–6 0 TD 0 INT, Steuber 1–1-(-4) 0 TD 0 INT
CLE: Graham 11–27–189 2 TD 0 INT, Lewis 1–1–30 1 TD 0 INT

Rushing
BUF: Tomasetti 6–31, Gompers 5–22, Steuber 3–17, Mutryn 7–13, Kulbitski 1–4, Still 2-(-1), Ratterman 1-(-1), Bumgardner 2-(-3)
CLE: Motley 13–99, E. Jones 6–26, Parseghian 3–22, Boedeker 6–21, Cline 1–14, Cowan 4–13, Graham 2–8, Lewis 1–7, Sensanbaugher 2-(-1)

Receiving
BUF: Mutryn 4–128, Baldwin 4–73, Tomasetti 3–18, O'Connor 6–48, Comer 1-(-3), Kulbitski 1-(-4)
CLE: Speedie 7–142, E. Jones 2–62, Boedeker 1–8, Gillom 1–8, Motley 1–1

Sunday, October 24
Browns 35, New York Yankees 7
Cleveland Stadium (46,912)
White jerseys/white pants

The Browns started the second half of the season with a nearly flawless offensive performance sparked by one of the best games of Otto Graham's career. Graham threw for 310 yards and four touchdown passes—three in the first half—and ran for another as the Browns roared to a 35–0 lead. Two of Graham's scoring passes went to Dante Lavelli, who made his first appearance of the season after recovering from a broken ankle in the preseason. Lavelli's first touchdown reception capped a 99-yard drive and gave the Browns a 7–0 lead—the opening salvo in what would be a 486-yard performance for the offense, which excelled despite coughing up four turnovers. It was the sixth loss in eight games for the surprisingly struggling Yankees, a far cry from their 11–2–1 campaign, which landed them in the AAFC title game the year before.

Record: 8–0

	1	2	3	4		
Yankees	0	0	0	7	=	7
Browns	7	14	7	7	=	35

CLE-Lavelli 29-yd. pass from Graham (Groza kick)
CLE-Cowan 63-yd. pass from Graham (Groza kick)
CLE-Speedie 9-yd. pass from Graham (Groza kick)
CLE-Lavelli 18-yd. pass from Graham (Groza kick)
CLE-Graham 22-yd. run (Groza kick)
NYY-Young 34-yd. pass from Layden (Johnson kick)

Passing
NYY: Layden 7–13–99 1 TD, Sanders 4–12–19 0 TD 1 INT, Schwenk 2–3–10 0 TD 1 INT, Kennedy 0–1–0 0 TD 0 INT
CLE: Graham 21–30–310 4 TD 2 INT, Terlep 1–2–27 0 TD 1 INT

Rushing
NYY: Layden 9–42, Sanders 10–41, Young 5–17, Tew 3–7, Daley 1–0
CLE: Lewis 1–39, Motley 5–31, Graham 2–28, E. Jones 3–14, Cowan 2–10, Cline 3–9, Lavelli 1–9, Sensanbaugher 2–5, Colella 3–3, Parseghian 1–1

Receiving
NYY: Young 3–41, Russell 2–37, Cleary 2–18, Schnellbacher 1–9, Iverson 2–7, Alford 1–7, Cheatham 1–6, Sweiger 1–3
CLE: Lavelli 5–89, Speedie 8–84, Cowan 2–77, Gillom 3–48, D. Jones 1–12, Boedeker 1–11, Young 1–9, Colella 1–7

Sunday, November 7
Browns 28, Baltimore Colts 7
Cleveland Stadium (32,314)
White jerseys/white pants

For the third straight game, the Browns took command early and cruised to an easy victory, handing the Colts their fifth loss in six weeks. With a balanced offensive attack, the Browns once again topped 400 yards and scored a touchdown in each quarter—rushing scores by Edgar Jones, Marion Motley, and Ara Parseghian, and a short Otto Graham-to-Jones touchdown strike in the third quarter.

Mac Speedie was the standout on offense, catching eight passes for 140 yards, while the Cleveland defense held Baltimore scoreless until a long Y. A. Tittle touchdown pass in the fourth quarter. Following this game, the Colts would rally to win three of their last four to force a playoff with Buffalo for the Eastern Division title. The Browns' victory moved the Browns to 9–0 and set up the first of two colossal matchups with the 10–0 49ers the following Sunday in Cleveland.

Record: 9–0

	1	2	3	4		
Colts	0	0	0	7	=	7
Browns	7	7	7	7	=	28

CLE-E. Jones 4-yd. run (Groza kick)
CLE-Motley 22-yd. run (Groza kick)
CLE-E. Jones 4-yd. pass from Graham (Groza kick)
CLE-Parseghian 15-yd. run (Groza kick)
BAL-Hillenbrand 69-yd. pass from Tittle (Grossman kick)

Passing
BAL: Tittle 14–29–169 1 TD 0 INT, O'Rourke 2–5–14 0 TD 0 INT
CLE: Graham 15–27–224 1 TD 2 INT

Rushing
BAL: Pfohl 9–35, Tittle 3–14, Hillenbrand 5–13, Mertes 8–12, O'Rourke 2–12, Leicht 3–4, Gambino 4-(-1)
CLE: Motley 12–79, D. Jones 7–43, Parseghian 3–25, E. Jones 8–16, Colella 3–13, Sensanbaugher 1–9, Cline 1–6, Boedeker 2-(-1)

Receiving
BAL: Hillenbrand 2–64, Williams 6–61, Leicht 3–17, Pohl 2–16, Gambino 2–14, Davies 1–11
CLE: Speedie 8–140, Lavelli 3–50, Motley 1–16, E. Jones 2–11, D. Jones 1–7

Sunday, November 14
Browns 14, San Francisco 49ers 7
Cleveland Stadium (82,769)
White jerseys/white pants

In perhaps the most anticipated game in the brief history of the AAFC, the league's best two teams put their undefeated records on the line in a battle for first place in the Western Division before the largest crowd ever to attend a Browns game in their AAFC era. Though both teams were known for their offense, surprisingly it was the defenses that took center stage, as neither team topped 300 total yards, with the Browns holding the 49ers to just 177 (after topping 400 yards in eight of their 10 games) and six turnovers. After the 49ers fumbled the opening kickoff, the teams traded punches with two first-quarter touchdowns, then the Browns took the lead for good on an Edgar Jones scoring run in the third quarter. While the Browns emerged victorious, they came out of the fierce battle dinged up, with a handful of key players, including Mac Speedie, Bill Willis, Tommy James, and Otto Graham all suffering serious injuries. While the game had been evenly played, the 49ers felt they'd given it away and vowed to enact revenge when they met the Browns in San Francisco two weeks later.

Record: 10–0

	1	2	3	4		
49ers	7	0	0	0	=	7
Browns	7	0	7	0	=	14

CLE-Graham 14-yd. run (Groza kick)
SF-Perry 1-yd. run (Vetrano kick)
CLE-E. Jones 4-yd. run (Groza kick)

Passing
SF: Albert 6–15–32 0 TD 3 INT
CLE: Graham 12–26–147 0 TD 1 INT

Rushing
SF: Strzykalski 13–65, Albert 4–20, Hall 7–17, Standlee 5–16, Perry 5–10, Lillywhite 2–10, Cason 1–9
CLE: E. Jones 16–84, Graham 3–32, Motley 8–24, Boedeker 6–22, Parseghian 7–18, Adamle 1–2, D. Jones 1–2, Cowan 1-(-1), Colella 1-(-4)

Receiving
SF: Susoeff 2–17, Strzykalski 2–14, Shoener 1–1, Beals 1-(-3)
CLE: Cowan 2–41, Speedie 2–41, D. Jones 4–36, Lavelli 3–15, Parseghian 1–14

Sunday, November 21
Browns 34, New York Yankees 21
Yankee Stadium (52,518)
Brown jerseys/white pants

On a cool, bright, autumn afternoon, before the largest crowd to witness a football game in New York City in 1948, the Browns scored two touchdowns in the first eight minutes to set the tone, then blew open the game after the

Yankees came back to tie in the second quarter. Marion Motley opened the scoring in the early going, taking a screen pass 78 yards for a touchdown. An Ara Parseghian interception returned to the New York 3 moments later set up the Browns' second score, but New York knotted the game at 14 after an interception return for a touchdown midway through the second quarter. The Browns then took control, scoring 20 straight points to take a 34–14 lead into the fourth period. Once again, victory was costly as Dante Lavelli, Edgar Jones, and lineman Chubby Grigg were all forced out of the game. And the mounting injuries would play an even greater role in the coming days as the Browns boarded a plane just after the win in New York to fly across the country to Los Angeles, continuing a stretch of three games in eight days.

Record: 11–0

	1	2	3	4		
Browns	14	13	7	0	=	34
Yankees	0	14	0	7	=	21

CLE-Motley 78-yd. pass from Graham (Groza kick)
CLE-E. Jones 1-yd. run (Groza kick)
NY-Alford 29-yd. pass from Layden (Johnson kick)
NY-Schnellbacher 40-yd. interception return (Johnson kick)
CLE-Groza 34-yd. FG
CLE-Cowan 9-yd. run (Groza kick)
CLE-Groza 18-yd. FG
CLE-Motley 12-yd. run (Groza kick)
NY-Kennedy 1-yd. run (Johnson kick)

Thursday, November 25
Browns 31, Los Angeles Dons 14
Los Angeles Memorial Coliseum (60,031)
Brown jerseys/white pants

Before a big crowd on Thanksgiving Day (for a game that began at 11:15 A.M. local time), the banged-up Browns endured an upset bid with 17 unanswered points in the second half to pull away from the Dons and notch their fifteenth consecutive victory. Despite a handful of key injuries and playing after only three days' rest and a cross-country flight, the Browns showed no ill effects, picking up nearly 400 yards of offense and surviving a difficult first half that saw the Dons twice take a touchdown lead. The Browns tied the contest at 14 in the final minute of the first half with an Otto Graham touchdown pass, then Graham gave the Browns a lead they wouldn't relinquish with a one-yard scoring plunge to open a 17-point third quarter. Once again, however, the Browns' victory was tainted by injury as Graham twisted his knee in the fourth quarter. It looked highly unlikely he would be able to play three days later in San Francisco, where the rested and vengeful 49ers awaited.

Record: 12–0

	1	2	3	4		
Browns	0	14	17	0	=	31
Dons	7	7	0	0	=	14

LA-Clay 1-yd. run (Agajanian kick)
CLE-Lavelli 49-yd. pass from Graham (Groza kick)
LA-Clay 1-yd. run (Agajanian kick)
CLE-Cowan 17-yd. pass from Graham (Groza kick)
CLE-Graham 1-yd. run (Groza kick)
CLE-Groza 36-yd. FG
CLE-Adamle 19-yd. run (Groza kick)

Passing
CLE: Graham 16–32–239 2 TD 0 INT
LA: Dobbs 11–22–137 0 TD 1 INT

Rushing
CLE: E. Jones 7–37, Adamle 3–37, D. Jones 6–32, Sensanbaugher 6–19, Parseghian 2–11, Motley 5–10, Boedeker 2–4, Cowan 1–3, Cline 2–2, Graham 1–1
LA: Dobbs 12–69, Wedemeyer 9–27, Clay 6–5, Reinhard 1–5, Graham 1–3, Durkota 1–2

Sunday, November 28
Browns 31, San Francisco 49ers 28
Kezar Stadium (59,785)
White jerseys/white pants

Capping the most trying week in franchise history with their third game in eight days, the Browns picked up one of their most impressive victories, rallying from an 11-point second-half deficit to defeat the 11–1 49ers and clinch their third straight Western Division title. Otto Graham, still nursing a knee sprained badly in Los Angeles three days earlier, wasn't expected to play, but surprised even his own teammates by entering the game and immediately throwing a 41-yard touchdown pass to Dante Lavelli to give the Browns an early lead. Despite Graham's heroics, the 49ers rebounded to take a 21–10 advantage early in the third quarter, and it appeared that the Browns' magic—and their 15-game winning streak—were destined to come to an end. But Graham wouldn't allow it, putting together arguably the most impressive performance of his career, throwing three more touchdown passes in the next eight minutes to put the Browns back up by 10. Along with his four scoring tosses, the gimpy Graham finished with 234 passing yards. After San Francisco cut the margin to 31–28 with seven minutes to play, the Browns' explosive offense switched gears to a ball-control mind-set and milked six minutes off the clock before surrendering the football. Somewhat lost in Graham's legendary performance, the Cleveland defense once again frustrated the powerful 49ers, forcing four turnovers, bringing their total in the teams' two games to 10, and holding an opponent under 300 total yards for the sixth straight game. In addition to earning another trip to the AAFC title game, the triumphant but weary Browns received an even more appealing reward: seven days off.

Record: 13–0

	1	2	3	4		
Browns	10	0	21	0	=	31
49ers	0	14	7	7	=	28

CLE-Lavelli 41-yd. pass from Graham (Groza kick)
CLE-Groza 24-yd. FG
SF-Perry 2-yd. run (Vetrano kick)
SF-Beals 4-yd. pass from Albert (Vetrano kick)
SF-Beals 29-yd. pass from Albert (Vetrano kick)
CLE-Motley 6-yd. pass from Graham (Groza kick)
CLE-D. Jones 20-yd. pass from Graham (Groza kick)
CLE-E. Jones 33-yd. pass from Graham (Groza kick)
SF-Perry 6-yd. pass from Albert (Vetrano kick)

Passing
CLE: Graham 11–23–234 4 TD 1 INT

Rushing
CLE: E. Jones 13–45, Motley 10–26, Adams 5–19, Colella 4–18, Cowan 5–14, D. Jones 2–8, Boedeker 2-(-2)
SF: Strzykalski 15–104, Perry 6–38, Crowe 1–9, Albert 7–6, Hall 3–5, Lillywhite 1–5, Eshmont 1–3, Cason 1–1, Standlee 1–1

Sunday, December 5
Browns 31, Brooklyn Dodgers 21
Ebbets Field (9,821)
Brown jerseys/white pants

With little to play for, the Browns still soared to a 31–0 lead and hung on for a victory over the Dodgers that completed a perfect regular season—the first in professional football since the 1942 Chicago Bears—and extended their winning streak to 17 games. Behind a powerful ground game that tallied more than 240 yards, the Browns were in command by halftime, leading 21–0. While the Dodgers' running game was completely halted by the Browns, limited to only 27 yards, Brooklyn QB Bob Chappuis heated up in the second half, tallying 318 passing yards. The 2–11 Dodgers made things more respectable in the final minutes, but in the end, they'd dug far too deep a hole. With Baltimore and Buffalo set to play a one-game playoff for the Eastern Division crown the following Sunday, the undefeated Browns would receive an extra week to rest and prepare for the AAFC championship game.

Record: 14–0

	1	2	3	4		
Browns	7	14	10	0	=	31
Dodgers	0	0	7	14	=	21

CLE-D. Jones 1-yd. run (Groza kick)
CLE-Lavelli 54-yd. pass from Graham (Groza kick)
CLE-Graham 1-yd. run (Groza kick)
CLE-Groza 37-yd. FG
CLE-Gillom 25-yd. pass from Graham (Groza kick)
BRK-Hoernschemeyer 38-yd. pass from Chappuis (Brown kick)
BRK-Hoernschemeyer 3-yd. run (Brown kick)
BRK-Gafford 60-yd. pass from Chappuis (Brown kick)

Passing
BRK: Chappuis 14–29–318 3 TD 3 INT

1948 AAFC Championship
Sunday, December 19
Browns 49, Buffalo Bills 7
Cleveland Stadium (22,981)
White jerseys/white pants

There was little reason to expect the third Browns–Bills matchup of 1948 to play out much differently than the previous two. Not only had the Browns had no trouble dispatching Buffalo by a combined total of 46 points, but they had two weeks to prepare for the conference title game while the Bills had to go to Baltimore and defeat the Colts to win their division crown, 28–17. So what happened the following Sunday came as no surprise.

On a cold afternoon, with fresh snow piled up along the sidelines, the Browns dominated the Bills on both sides of the ball—doubling them in total yardage—and coasted to a third straight title with their highest point total of 1948. The scoring opened in the final minute of the first quarter when Edgar Jones scored the first of two touchdowns, this one set up by a Tommy James interception—one of five Cleveland would collect. Minutes later, the lead was stretched to 14 points when DE George Young scooped up a fumble and rumbled 18 yards for a touchdown.

THE ALL-AMERICAN TEAM

The Browns dominated the short-lived All-America Football Conference, cruising to the championship in all four of its seasons and outscoring their opponents by an average of more than 16 points per game.

While their dominance helped them land a spot in the NFL when the leagues merged following the 1949 season, it also played a huge factor in the downfall of the league, smothering interest in most of the other teams.

The Browns' superiority is demonstrated in the AAFC's overall standings:

	W	L	T	PCT	POSTSEASON APP.	REC VS. BROWNS
Cleveland Browns	52	4	3	.907	4	—
San Francisco 49ers	39	15	2	.714	1	2–7
New York Yankees	35	20	2	.632	3	0–9–1
Los Angeles Dons	25	27	2	.482	0	2–6
Buffalo Bisons/Bills	24	28	5	.465	2	0–8–2
Baltimore Colts	10	30	1	.256	1	0–6
Chicago Rockets/Hornets	11	40	3	.232	0	0–8
Brooklyn Dodgers	8	32	2	.214	0	0–6
Miami Seahawks	3	11	0	.214	0	0–2

(includes postseason games)

With the Cleveland defense continually thwarting the overwhelmed Buffalo offense, the 14–0 lead appeared insurmountable. But the floodgates opened after the intermission. On the second play of the second half, James picked up his second interception, this one leading to an Edgar Jones's touchdown reception, and the rout was on. Marion Motley, who would roll to 133 yards on 14 carries, scored three touchdowns in the second half, and the Cleveland defense held Buffalo to a harmless 167 total yards—including just 63 rushing yards on 33 carries—while collecting eight turnovers. Buffalo's only touchdown, late in the third quarter, came after the Browns extended a drive with a roughing-the-punter penalty.

DB Lou Saban put the cherry atop the sundae in the fourth quarter, returning an interception 39 yards for a touchdown. For the third straight year, the Browns were AAFC champions, now having won 18 straight games and extending their unbeaten streak to 24 games.

The only worrisome aspect of the Browns' triumph was the small crowd (22,981) that witnessed it on a relatively mild winter day—nearly 40,000 smaller than the throng that watched the Browns defeat the Yankees in the title game the year before. Clearly, the Browns' dominance was beginning to sink the league, and the AAFC's days were numbered.

	1	2	3	4		
Bills	0	0	7	0	=	7
Browns	7	7	14	21	=	49

CLE-E. Jones 3-yd. run (Groza kick)
CLE-Young 18-yd. fumble return (Groza kick)
CLE-E. Jones 9-yd. pass from Graham (Groza kick)
CLE-Motley 29-yd. run (Groza kick)
BUF-Baldwin 10-yd. pass from Still (Armstrong kick)
CLE-Motley 31-yd. run (Groza kick)
CLE-Motley 5-yd. run (Groza kick)
CLE-Saban 39-yd. interception return (Groza kick)

Passing
BUF: Still 6–18–80 1 TD 2 INT, Ratterman 5–18–24 0 TD 3 INT
CLE: Graham 11–24–118 1 TD 1 INT, E. Jones 0–2–0 0 TD 0 INT

Rushing
BUF: Bumgardner 11–34, Tomasetti 11–20, Mutryn 8–8, Kulbitski 2–1, O'Connor 1–0
CLE: Motley 14–133, E. Jones 8–29, D. Jones 5–22, Cline 1–20, Parseghian 4–14, Sensanbaugher 2–2, Colella 1–1, Graham 1–0, Adamle 2-(-1), Terlep 2-(-5)

Receiving
BUF: O'Connor 3–41, Bumgardner 1–25, Kulbitski 1–14, Baldwin 1–10, Gibson 1–7, Mutryn 2–5, Schneider 1–4, Tomasetti 1-(-2)
CLE: E. Jones 3–39, Speedie 2–22, Lavelli 2–16, Gillom 1–15, D. Jones 2–13, Motley 1–13

1949

Monday, September 5
Browns 28, Buffalo Bills 28
Civic Stadium (31,839)
White jerseys/white pants

Kicking off the season on Labor Day evening, the Browns dug themselves a huge hole, then fought their way out of it with a stirring fourth-quarter rally. Facing Buffalo for the first of what would be a trio of hard-fought battles over the course of the season, the Browns watched a 7–7 halftime score turn into a 28–7 deficit in the third quarter as the Bills cashed in on a pair of Cleveland fumbles to build what appeared would be an insurmountable lead over the three-time defending league champs. But then the Browns' offense—stagnant since its first drive of the game—kicked into high gear. QB Otto Graham followed up his first-quarter touchdown strike to RB Edgar Jones with two more to cut the margin to seven points. After regaining possession at the Buffalo 48 with just over two minutes to play, Horace Gillom made the play of the day, fighting off three Buffalo defenders to catch a Graham pass at the Bills' 2. On the next snap, Graham hit WR Mac Speedie on his knees right beneath the goalposts for a touchdown, and Lou Saban—filling in for Lou Groza, sidelined with a pulled muscle—booted the game-tying extra point. Graham finished the day with 27 completions in 40 attempts for 330 yards and four scores, connecting on 14 of 16 passes in the crucial fourth quarter. Statistically the Browns were dominant, tallying 507 yards of total offense while holding Buffalo to 175. Though it wasn't a Cleveland victory, the Buffalo faithful left the ballpark stunned and in awe of a Browns team that now hadn't lost in 25 consecutive games.
Record: 0–0–1

	1	2	3	4		
Browns	7	0	0	21	=	28
Bills	0	7	21	0	=	28

CLE-E. Jones 12-yd. pass from Graham (Saban kick)
BUF-Cline 6-yd. run (Adams kick)
BUF-Ratterman 2-yd. run (Adams kick)
BUF-Ratterman 1-yd. run (Adams kick)
BUF-Mutryn 2-yd. run (Adams kick)
CLE-E. Jones 7-yd. pass from Graham (Saban kick)
CLE-E. Jones 38-yd. pass from Graham (Saban kick)
CLE-Speedie 2-yd. pass from Graham (Saban kick)

Passing
CLE: Graham 27–40–330 4 TD 1 INT

Sunday, September 11
Browns 21, Baltimore Colts 0
Cleveland Stadium (21,621)
White jerseys/white pants

Though the day would be clouded by the loss of a handful of key players to injury, the Browns had no trouble with Baltimore and posted the seventh shutout in their four years' of existence. The Browns took an early lead on the first of two rushing touchdowns by Edgar Jones—set up by a Warren Lahr interception—then blew the game open in the third quarter with two more scores, including a second touchdown by Jones. The Browns were dominant on both sides of the ball, collecting more than 400 yards of offense while holding the Colts to just 156—an achievement made even more impressive considering DE George Young was knocked out of the game with a broken cheekbone, and Marion Motley was forced to the sideline in the opening minutes.
Record: 1–0–1

	1	2	3	4		
Colts	0	0	0	0	=	0
Browns	7	0	14	0	=	21

CLE-E. Jones 3-yd. run (Saban kick)
CLE-Lavelli 24-yd. pass from Graham (Saban kick)
CLE-E. Jones 7-yd. run (Saban kick)

Passing
BAL: Tittle 8–21–156 0 TD 2 INT
CLE: Graham 14–20–234 1 TD 1 INT

Rushing
BAL: Pfohl 8–31, Tittle 6–24, Adamle 3–18, Wedemeyer 4–12, Stone 3–11, Gambino 4–3, Jagade 1–0
CLE: Boedeker 7–62, E. Jones 10–33, Sustersic 9–30, Parseghian 10–21, Lahr 1–7, Motley 2–3, Graham 1–0, James 2-(-2)

Receiving
BAL: Williams 4–48, Stone 1–21, Davis 1–15, Pfohl 2-(-9)
CLE: Lavelli 5–77, Speedie 3–29, E. Jones 2–27, Gillom 1–14, Parseghian 1–2

Sunday, September 18
Browns 14, New York Yankees 3
Cleveland Stadium (26,312)
White jerseys/white pants

The Browns' sorcery over their New York rivals continued on a rainy afternoon in Cleveland as the Yankees more than doubled the Browns' total yardage and didn't allow the Cleveland offense to score a single point—yet still fell in defeat. With the Browns' offense struggling, managing just 125 total yards in what would be their worst performance of the season, the Cleveland defense picked up the slack dramatically, scoring two touchdowns and continually thwarting New York scoring threats. Six times the Yankees drove inside the Cleveland 20, with three trips inside the 10, and yet New York was unable to cross the goal line and managed only a single field goal on the afternoon. The tide turned late in the first quarter when, after the Yankees were threatening to extend their early lead to 10–0, RB Buddy Young fumbled and Browns' Les Horvath scooped it up and sprinted 84 yards for the go-ahead touchdown. The rest of the game became a muddy stalemate as neither offense could get untracked. The Browns exacerbated the Yankees' frustration in the final moments when Tommy James returned an interception 27 yards for a touchdown with two seconds to play.

Record: 2–0–1

	1	2	3	4		
Yankees	3	0	0	0	=	3
Browns	7	0	0	7	=	14

NYY-Johnson 25-yd. FG
CLE-Horvath 84-yd. fumble return (Saban kick)
CLE-James 27-yd. interception return (Saban kick)

Passing
NYY: Panciera 5–17–112 0 TD 1 INT, Johnson 1–7–15 0 TD 0 INT
CLE: Graham 4–10–36 0 TD 2 INT, E. Jones 0–1–0 0 TD 0 INT

Rushing
NYY: Kennedy 12–88, Young 6–25, Howard 10–22, Landry 2–11, Layden 2–8, Johnson 1–8, Rowe 1–7, Colmer 2–2, Panciera 1–1
CLE: E. Jones 11–30, Sustersic 6–30, Adamle 3–15, D. Jones 8–10, Graham 1–4

Receiving
NYY: Alford 1–52, Young 1–20, Kennedy 1–16, Landry 1–15, Russell 1–14, Poole 1–10
CLE: Speedie 1–15, Lavelli 2–13, E. Jones 1–8

Sunday, September 25
Browns 28, Baltimore Colts 20
Memorial Stadium (36,387)
White jerseys/white pants

Two weeks after dominating the Colts in Cleveland, the Browns had to rally from a 13-point second-half deficit with three fourth-quarter touchdowns to pull out a victory in the rematch in Baltimore. With the Cleveland offense once again struggling for much of the day, the Colts held a 13–0 lead until late in the third quarter, when Edgar Jones scored on a 17-yard run, then Otto Graham gave the Browns their first lead four minutes into the fourth with a six-yard scoring romp. Less than a minute later, Browns' lineman Bill Willis intercepted Baltimore QB Y. A. Tittle at the Colts' 7 and rumbled to the 2, where Marion Motley made it a 21–13 lead. Showing uncharacteristic pluck, the 0–4 Colts cut the lead back to a point with a long Tittle touchdown pass with six minutes remaining, but the Browns put the game away with Jones's second touchdown of the day and his seventh of the young season.

Record: 3–0–1

	1	2	3	4		
Browns	0	0	7	21	=	28
Colts	0	13	0	7	=	20

BAL-Williams 7-yd. pass from Tittle (Grossman kick)
BAL-Grossman 33-yd. FG
BAL-Grossman 38-yd. FG
CLE-E. Jones 17-yd. run (Groza kick)
CLE-Graham 6-yd. run (Groza kick)
CLE-Motley 2-yd. run (Groza kick)
BAL-Stone 47-yd. pass from Tittle (Grossman kick)
CLE-E. Jones 2-yd. run (Groza kick)

Passing
CLE: Graham 9–24–104 0 TD 1 INT
BAL: Tittle 7–18–95 2 TD 1 INT, Vacanti 6–14–86 0 TD 0 INT, O'Rourke 0–1–0 0 TD 0 INT

Rushing
CLE: E. Jones 8–27, Motley 7–26, D. Jones 7–22, Adamle 4–13, Sustersic 1–9, Graham 1–6, Boedeker 3–4, James 1–0
BAL: Gambino 11–73, Wedemeyer 7–30, Pfohl 10–19, Stone 2–10, Tittle 2–10, Leicht 2–1, Vacanti 1-(-4)

Receiving
CLE: Lavelli 4–31, Motley 1–25, D. Jones 2–24, Horvath 1–17, Speedie 1–7

BAL: Stone 3–75, Davis 3–29, Wedemeyer 2–26, North 1–18, Williams 2–15, Leicht 1–12, Gambino 1–6

Sunday, October 2
Browns 42, Los Angeles Dons 7
Cleveland Stadium (30,465)
White jerseys/white pants

The Browns extended their amazing string to 29 consecutive games without a loss with a blowout victory over the last team to beat them nearly two full years before. With 550 total yards, Cleveland's offense was unstoppable, paced by Marion Motley's 139 yards on the ground and Otto Graham's 279 through the air. Graham opened the scoring early in the second quarter with a 74-yard toss to RB Bill Boedeker, then Motley, who averaged eight yards per carry for the day, scored the first of his two touchdowns. The Browns' defense got into the act as well, with Lou Saban returning an interception 20 yards for a score to stretch the lead to 21–0 in the third quarter and blow the game wide open.

Record: 4–0–1

	1	2	3	4		
Dons	0	0	0	7	=	7
Browns	0	14	14	14	=	42

CLE-Boedeker 74-yd. pass from Graham (Groza kick)
CLE-Motley 2-yd. run (Groza kick)
CLE-Saban 20-yd. interception return (Groza kick)
CLE-Motley 33-yd. run (Groza kick)
CLE-Speedie 3-yd. pass from Graham (Groza kick)
LAD-Brown recovered fumble in end zone (Nelson kick)
CLE-Sustersic 39-yd. run (Groza kick)

Passing
LAD: Dobbs 7–24–93 0 TD, Taliaferro 3–11–33 0 TD 1 INT
CLE: Graham 17–28–279 2 TD, Lewis 2–3–29 0 TD

Rushing
LAD: Grimes 9–66, Dobbs 4–38, Rodgers 6–32, Taliaferro 7–30, Howell 4–27
CLE: Motley 17–139, Sustersic 2–43, Boedeker 5–30, D. Jones 6–20, Graham 2–16, E. Jones 4–8, Lewis 4-(-15)

Receiving
LAD: Wilkins 4–72, Ford 1–37, Grimes 1–13, Rodgers 1–6, Howell 2–1, Reinhard 1–1
CLE: Speedie 9–135, Boedeker 2–86, Lavelli 4–36, Lahr 1–20, D. Jones 1–15, Gillom 1–7, Motley 1–7

Sunday, October 9
San Francisco 49ers 56, Browns 28
Kezar Stadium (59,720)
White jerseys/white pants

The Browns' unbeaten streak came to a screeching halt against the rival 49ers, who dominated the Cleveland defense with an astonishing performance that saw them score three touchdowns in the first quarter and tally 35 points by halftime. Burdened by an Otto Graham interception on the third play of the game—the first of six Cleveland turnovers—the Browns fell behind 21–0 in the opening minutes, but then quickly cut the lead down to 21–14. The 49ers answered with another barrage of points, pushing the lead back to 21 points in the third quarter, then to 28 after the Browns cut it to 42–28 early in the fourth. San Francisco romped to 507 total yards as QB Frankie Albert threw for 249 yards and five touchdowns, and Joe Perry added 156 rushing yards on just 16 carries. The victory put San Francisco ahead of the Browns by a half-game atop the league standings.

Record: 4–1–1

	1	2	3	4		
Browns	7	14	0	7	=	28
49ers	21	14	7	14	=	56

SF-Strzykalski 16-yd. pass from Albert (Vetrano kick)
SF-Strzykalski 1-yd. run (Vetrano kick)
SF-Perry 27-yd. pass from Albert (Vetrano kick)
CLE-Speedie 39-yd. pass from Graham (Groza kick)
CLE-Lavelli 25-yd. pass from Graham (Groza kick)
SF-Beals 15-yd. pass from Albert (Vetrano kick)
CLE-Speedie 13-yd. pass from Graham (Groza kick)
SF-Susoeff 8-yd. pass from Albert (Vetrano kick)
SF-Carr 24-yd. pass from Albert (Vetrano kick)
CLE-Motley 12-yd. run (Groza kick)
SF-Perry 49-yd. run (Vetrano kick)
SF-Carr 5-yd. run (Vetrano kick)

Passing
CLE: Graham 13–26–281 2 TD 4 INT
SF: Albert 16–24–249 5 TD 3 INT

Rushing
CLE: Motley 13–80, E. Jones 5–6, Graham 5–2, D. Jones 2–2, Adamle 2-(-4)
SF: Perry 16–155, Strzykalski 12–39, Lillywhite 5–27, Cason 3–8, Carr 2–8, Garlin 1–6, Albert 1–5, Cathcart 1–4, Standlee 1–2, Eshmont 2–1, Beals 1–1

Friday, October 14
Browns 61, Los Angeles Dons 14
Los Angeles Memorial Coliseum (27,427)
Brown jerseys/white pants

The Browns bounced back from their frustrating defeat in San Francisco with a Friday-night massacre of the Dons that saw Cleveland rack up more than 600 yards of offense and nine touchdowns. Otto Graham, who would throw for 362 yards and six touchdowns on the night in less than three quarters of action, tallied 214 yards in the game's first 17 minutes and connected with WR Dante Lavelli for four scores in the first half as Cleveland soared to a 34–7 advantage at the intermission. Lavelli finished the game with 209 yards on just seven receptions, and Mac Speedie added two more touchdowns in the third quarter. The only sour moment for the Browns occurred when Edgar Jones was forced out with a broken collarbone and was lost for the remainder of the regular season.
Record: 5–1–1

	1	2	3	4		
Browns	14	20	14	13	=	61
Dons	7	0	0	7	=	14

CLE-Lavelli 46-yd. pass from Graham (Groza kick)
LAD-Rodgers 2-yd. run (Nelson kick)
CLE-D. Jones 42-yd. pass from Graham (Groza kick)
CLE-Lavelli 31-yd. pass from Graham (Groza kick)
CLE-Lavelli 67-yd. pass from Graham (Groza kick)
CLE-Lavelli 2-yd. pass from Graham (kick failed)
CLE-Speedie 12-yd. pass from Graham (Groza kick)
CLE-Speedie 27-yd. pass from Lewis (Groza kick)
LAD-Taliaferro 9-yd. run (Nelson kick)
CLE-Lahr 2-yd. run (kick failed)
CLE-Lewis 2-yd. run (Groza kick)

Passing
CLE: Graham 15–24–362 6 TD 0 INT

Receiving
CLE: Lavelli 7–209

Sunday, October 30
Browns 30, San Francisco 49ers 28
Cleveland Stadium (72,189)
White jerseys/white pants

Before the largest crowd to see them all year, the Browns avenged their blowout loss in San Francisco three weeks earlier with a thrilling victory over the 49ers on a crisp October afternoon on the lake. Following a scoreless first quarter, the teams exploded for four touchdowns in an eight-minute period in the second and went to the locker rooms tied at 14. The Browns took their first lead early in the third quarter when Otto Graham broke free up the middle for a 20-yard scoring run, but the 49ers rallied to tie the contest again in the opening moments of the fourth period, and the massive crowd braced for an exciting finish. The Browns crept into the lead again on a Lou Groza field goal with 9:45 remaining, then the Cleveland defense came up with a huge stop to turn the momentum in favor of the home team. And the offense responded with a clutch drive capped by a fourth-down touchdown pass from Graham to Mac Speedie with five minutes left. The 49ers added one final score with 15 seconds to play, but it was too little, too late, as the Browns surged back into first place. Demonstrating how they'd revolutionized the game in just four years of existence, the teams had combined for nearly 900 yards of offense—more than 500 of which came through the air—and no turnovers.
Record: 6–1–1

	1	2	3	4		
49ers	0	14	0	14	=	28
Browns	0	14	7	9	=	30

SF-Eshmont 48-yd. pass from Albert (Vetrano kick)
CLE-Lavelli 9-yd. pass from Graham (Groza kick)
SF-Lillywhite 8-yd. run (Vetrano kick)
CLE-D. Jones 6-yd. run (Groza kick)
CLE-Graham 20-yd. run (Groza kick)
SF-Beals 22-yd. pass from Albert (Vetrano kick)
CLE-Groza 38-yd. FG
CLE-Speedie 12-yd. pass from Graham (kick failed)
SF-Albert 1-yd. run (Vetrano kick)

Passing
SF: Albert 14–27–253 2 TD 0 INT
CLE: Graham 14–25–271 2 TD 0 INT

Rushing
SF: Cathcart 11–116, Albert 5–57, Perry 10–27, Lillywhite 7–20, Standlee 2–2, Beals 1–2
CLE: Graham 8–43, Motley 9–34, D. Jones 13–33, Boedeker 4–16, Adamle 1–3, James 1–0

Receiving
SF: Cathcart 5–88, Beals 4–78, Eshmont 1–48, Shoener 1–24, Salata 1–14, Lillywhite 1–1
CLE: Speedie 6–99, Lavelli 3–73, Motley 3–55, Gillom 1–29, Boedeker 1–15

Sunday, November 6
Browns 35, Chicago Hornets 2
Cleveland Stadium (16,506)
White jerseys/white pants

The momentum from the previous Sunday's huge win over San Francisco carried over as the Browns throttled Chicago and coasted to an easy victory before the smallest crowd ever to attend a Browns' regular-season home game. The Cleveland offense was once again unstoppable, collecting 542 total yards, including 256 on the ground as Marion Motley rushed for 118 and a pair of touchdowns, including a 49-yard scamper that made it 21–0 in the third quarter. Former Ohio State RB Les Horvath, who'd played primarily on defense up until the previous week, scored the only two touchdowns of his career, the second on a 54-yard pass from backup QB Cliff Lewis to round out the scoring. The Cleveland defense limited Chicago to only 46 rushing yards, allowed no points, and forced six turnovers, with the only Hornet score coming on a blocked punt that resulted in a safety.

Record: 7–1–1

	1	2	3	4		
Hornets	0	0	0	2	=	2
Browns	7	7	7	14	=	35

CLE-D. Jones 4-yd. run (Groza kick)
CLE-Horvath 2-yd. run (Groza kick)
CLE-Motley 49-yd. run (Groza kick)
CHI-Safety: Gillom punt blocked out of end zone
CLE-Motley 3-yd. run (Saban kick)
CLE-Horvath 54-yd. pass from Lewis (Saban kick)

Passing
CHI: Hoernschemeyer 12–26–184 0 TD, Chappius 0–3–0 0 TD
CLE: Graham 14–19–242 0 TD, Lewis 1–3–54

Rushing
CHI: Hoernschemeyer 10–39, Sweiger 1–12, Collins 2–4, Buksar 1–1, Clement 1–1, Ramsey 3-(-11)
CLE: Motley 14–118, D. Jones 8–66, Boedeker 8–49, Adamle 1–13, Graham 2–3, Jones 1–3, Horvath 1–2, Lahr 1–2, Sustersic 2–0

Receiving
CHI: Patterson 5–51, Ramsey 1–48, Edwards 3–44, McCarthy 2–34, Foldberg 1–7
CLE: Gillom 6–93, Speedie 3–59, Horvath 1–54, D. Jones 2–41, Motley 1–36, Adamle 1–13

Sunday, November 13
Browns 7, Buffalo Bills 7
Cleveland Stadium (22,511)
White jerseys/white pants

Amid pouring rain on a dark afternoon, the Browns and Bills once again played four full quarters without determining a winner. A Browns' romp appeared possible when George Adamle intercepted Buffalo QB George Ratterman on the game's first play, followed by a one-yard touchdown run by Otto Graham two minutes in. But the Bills rebounded to tie the game on the fourth snap of the second quarter after recovering a fumbled punt return at the Cleveland 44. Most of the remainder of the contest was played in the mud-soaked midfield, though the Browns squandered a golden opportunity midway through the second quarter when Dub Jones fumbled at the Buffalo 4. Then, midway through the fourth, Cleveland pushed to the Buffalo 13, but a penalty and a sack ruined another opportunity to take the lead. The Browns had one final chance with 15 seconds left, but Lou Groza's 51-yard field-goal attempt fell short, and they had to settle for their second stalemate of 1949.

Record: 7–1–2

	1	2	3	4		
Bills	0	7	0	0	=	7
Browns	7	0	0	0	=	7

CLE-Graham 1-yd. run (Groza kick)
BUF-Mutryn 4-yd. run (Adams kick)

Passing
BUF: Ratterman 6–20–82 0 TD 2 INT
CLE: Graham 11–26–176 0 TD 0 INT

Rushing
BUF: Mutryn 16–83, Bumgardner 12–40, Tomasetti 6–19, Cline 11–6
CLE: Motley 15–50, Boedeker 4–28, Horvath 5–15, D. Jones 5–14, Graham 2–7

Receiving
BUF: Baldwin 5–65, Mutryn 1–17
CLE: Gillom 6–65, Boedeker 1–61, Speedie 3–45, D. Jones 1–5

Sunday, November 20
Browns 31, New York Yankees 0
Yankee Stadium (50,711)
Brown jerseys/white pants

Before the largest Yankee home crowd of the season, the Browns crushed their New York rivals, sprinting to a 31–0 halftime lead before taking their foot off the gas in the second half and coasting to victory. The tone was set in the opening minutes as the Browns drove 76 yards on the opening kickoff and scored on a Bill Boedeker touchdown catch, then quickly recovered a New York fumble and made it 14–0 on the first of Dub Jones's two touchdowns. Averaging 20 yards per completion, Otto Graham threw for 382 yards, primarily to Mac Speedie, who caught 11 of his 19 completions for 228 yards, which remains a franchise record. Collecting a season-high eight turnovers, the Cleveland defense continually thwarted the Yankees, highlighted by three instances in the second half when New York drove to the Cleveland 1 but came away with no points. With the Cleveland blowout victory, the one-sided rivalry drew to a close in appropriate fashion—the teams had met 10 times in four seasons and the Yankees, generally considered the second-best team in the AAFC, failed to win a single game.

Record: 8–1–2

	1	2	3	4		
Browns	17	14	0	0	=	31
Yankees	0	0	0	0	=	0

CLE-Boedeker 23-yd. pass from Graham (Groza kick)
CLE-D. Jones 1-yd. run (Groza kick)
CLE-Groza 30-yd. FG
CLE-D. Jones 1-yd. run (Groza kick)
CLE-Motley 1-yd. run (Groza kick)

Passing
CLE: Graham 19–34–382 1 TD 1 INT
NYY: Johnson 6–16–93 0 TD 4 INT, Panciera 4–10–44 0 TD 1 INT

Rushing
CLE: Motley 13–49, D. Jones 9–18, Graham 2–11, Boedeker 5–5, Horvath 1–4, D. Jones 1–3, Sustersic 1-(-4)
NYY: Young 6–66, Kennedy 6–42, Colmer 2–14, Layden 2–13, Howard 11–12, Landry 5–12, Panciera 1–2, Prokop 1–0, Kusserow 1-(-2)

Receiving
CLE: Speedie 11–228, Gillom 2–48, Boedeker 2–40, D. Jones 2–28, Motley 2–19
NYY: Garza 3–67, Young 2–22, Landry 1–16, Alford 2–12, Russell 1–11, Kennedy 1–9

Thursday, November 24
Browns 14, Chicago Hornets 6
Soldier Field (5,031)
Brown jerseys/white pants

After an early morning squall in Chicago had buried Soldier Field in snow, the players suited up and helped the Hornets' players clear snow off the tarp and remove it (the team couldn't afford a grounds crew). Yet with the field still soaked and slippery and just over 5,000 in attendance (in what would be the smallest crowd ever to attend a Browns game), this Thanksgiving Day clash turned out to be as sloppy as the field, with the teams combining for nine turnovers and just 19 combined first downs. The Browns jumped to a lead in the first minute after they recovered a Chicago fumble on the first play, then drove 63 yards for a second touchdown eight minutes later. A Browns' fumble set up the Hornets' only touchdown early in the second period, but a missed extra point would loom large and keep Chicago at arm's length for the remainder of the defensive struggle. The Hornets threatened in the fourth after recovering another Cleveland fumble and driving to the Browns' 3, but the Cleveland defense turned them away to secure the ninth victory of the season.

Record: 9–1–2

	1	2	3	4		
Browns	14	0	0	0	=	14
Hornets	0	6	0	0	=	6

CLE-Boedeker 6-yd. run (Groza kick)
CLE-Motley 6-yd. run (Groza kick)
CHI-Clement 1-yd. run (kick failed)

Passing
CLE: Graham 6–9–88 0 TD 0 INT
CHI: Hoernschemeyer 3–12–39 0 TD 2 INT, Clement 5–7–48 0 TD 1 INT

Rushing
CLE: D. Jones 10–46, Boedeker 5–33, E. Jones 3–23, Horvath 3–14, Lahr 2–11, Motley 5–11, Adamle 3–6, Lewis 2–3
CHI: Hoernschemeyer 23–91, Clement 7–19, Brown 1–2, Ramsey 2-(-1)

Receiving
CLE: Speedie 4–81, Motley 1–4, Gillom 1–3
CHI: Edwards 4–60, Sweiger 2–12, Foldberg 1–10, Patterson 1–5

AAFC Playoff
Sunday, December 4
Browns 31, Buffalo Bills 21
Cleveland Stadium (17,270)
White jerseys/white pants

After two titanic ties earlier in the season, the Browns and Bills saved the best for last.

With a trip to the AAFC title game on the line, the teams picked up where they'd left off, matching one another score for score on a frosty afternoon in Cleveland before a modest gathering of 17,270—the Browns' second-smallest crowd of the season despite the high stakes.

The Browns jumped to a 10–0 lead, drawing first blood on a 51-yard aerial strike from Otto Graham to Dante Lavelli. But the Bills bounced back with a pair of George Ratterman touchdown passes, the second with just 32 seconds remaining in the second quarter, to go up 14–10 at the intermission. The bundled-up Cleveland fans were nervous as the second half began, wondering if the odds might finally break in favor of the Bills after seven Cleveland victories over their Lake Erie neighbors.

But a Lou Saban interception and return to the Buffalo 2 in the opening minutes of the third quarter calmed the jittery nerves, as the Browns took the lead on an Edgar Jones touchdown. Buffalo then countered the pendulum of momentum with an 80-yard drive aided by a roughing-the-kicker penalty on the Browns and capped by Ratterman's third scoring pass of the day to take the lead right back at 21–17. Three plays later, the Browns struck back with a 49-yard touchdown pass from Graham to Dub Jones to surge ahead by three once more.

The defenses settled, and the score remained 24–21 deep into the fourth quarter when the Bills began a determined drive from their own 20. Reaching midfield with five minutes to play, the Bills once again appeared poised to snap their nine-game winless streak to the Browns and secure a spot in the league championship. But Browns DB Warren Lahr stepped in front of a Ratterman pass at the Cleveland 48 to intercept it and sprinted through the falling darkness to the end zone for the clinching touchdown. It was the fourth Buffalo turnover of the day, and the most crucial.

Despite the wintry conditions and both running games being thwarted, the teams combined for nearly 800 total yards and attempted a league-record 85 total passes, with Graham throwing for 326 yards and Ratterman tallying 293. Aiding the Browns' cause was the return of Edgar Jones, who'd been out of action for two months after breaking his collarbone in October. In addition to scoring the go-ahead touchdown in the third quarter, Jones added 69 yards on six receptions, while Dante Lavelli also returned from injury to add a touchdown, and Mac Speedie turned in another fine game with seven catches for 113 yards.

The stage was now set for the final game in AAFC history—appropriately pitting the ill-fated league's two most successful franchises against one another.

	1	2	3	4		
Bills	0	14	7	0	=	21
Browns	10	0	14	7	=	31

CLE-Lavelli 51-yd. pass from Graham (Groza kick)
CLE-Groza 31-yd. FG
BUF-Tomasetti 4-yd. pass from Ratterman (Adams kick)
BUF-Mutryn 8-yd. pass from Ratterman (Adams kick)
CLE-E. Jones 2-yd. run (Groza kick)
BUF-Mutryn 30-yd. pass from Ratterman (Adams kick)
CLE-D. Jones 49-yd. pass from Graham (Groza kick)
CLE-Lahr 52-yd. interception return (Groza kick)

Passing
BUF: Ratterman 21–39–293 3 TD 2 INT, Still 0–3–0 0 TD 0 INT
CLE: Graham 22–43–326 2 TD 2 INT

Rushing
BUF: Bumgardner 10–37, Mutryn 8–24, Cline 3–10, Tomasetti 4–9
CLE: Motley 8–38, D. Jones 5–21, E. Jones 6–10, Graham 1–3

Receiving
BUF: Mutryn 6–81, Bumgardner 4–80, Baldwin 2–54, Tomasetti 3–37, Lukens 4–32, Cline 2–9
CLE: Speedie 7–113, Lavelli 5–96, E. Jones 6–69, D. Jones 1–49, Motley 3-(-1)

1949 AAFC Championship
Sunday, December 11
Browns 21, San Francisco 49ers 7
Cleveland Stadium (22,550)
White jerseys/white pants

No one quite knew what to expect when the Browns and 49ers took the field for the 1949 AAFC Championship.

Their previous two meetings that fall had been both exciting and memorable. In the first, the 49ers had romped to

THE SHAMROCK BOWL

The Shamrock Bowl was a one-time event in 1949 structured after the NFL's highly successful College All-Star Game, founded by Texas oil tycoon Glen McCarthy to raise money for charity—and potentially introduce the city of Houston as a potential candidate to receive an NFL team. (Houston had been promised an All-America Conference team, but with the league folding, the city would have to wait.) The name of the game mirrored one of McCarthy's business ventures, the swanky Shamrock Hotel, which opened in Houston earlier that year.

On December 17, 1949, a week after the Browns had defeated the San Francisco 49ers in the All-America Conference title game (and nine days after it was announced that the league would disband, with three of its teams joining the NFL), the Browns faced a collection of AAFC All-Stars at Rice Stadium in Houston.

Amid heavy rain and strong thunderstorms on a Saturday afternoon, less than ten thousand fans watched a sloppy game that looked nothing like a showcase for the league's best players. The All-Stars took an early 6–0 advantage, but the Browns surged into the lead in the second quarter on a 39-yard touchdown pass from Otto Graham to Dub Jones on what would prove to be their only score of the day. The All-Stars responded with a 91-yard scoring drive to put them up 12–7.

The teams sloshed through the mud in an ugly second half that saw both units squander their few opportunities to score. After driving to the Cleveland 15, the All-Stars fumbled and the Browns' Lou Saban, playing in his final game, recovered to end the threat. A Cleveland march to the All-Stars' 13 ended in an interception, and another possession ended at the 16 with six minutes remaining when the Browns were stopped on downs.

Minutes later the Shamrock Bowl was essentially lost to history, serving as a disappointing curtain call for the AAFC.

a four-touchdown triumph, snapping the Browns' record unbeaten streak, and in the second, the Browns had pulled out a narrow victory in another offensive shootout.

San Francisco had been one of only two teams to defeat Cleveland in the previous four seasons, while the Browns were unbeaten in three title-game appearances.

But in what would be the finale for the All-America Football Conference, the Browns proved once and for all that they were indeed the league's finest, just as they were at its outset. In a surprisingly dull game, the Browns put forth a businesslike performance and dominated their West Coast rivals on a slippery field, controlling the contest from the outset and avoiding the drama that had permeated through several of the teams' previous meetings.

The Browns drew first blood on their second possession when Edgar Jones scored his second touchdown of the postseason, marking the beginning of another crucial performance for the now-healthy running back. The 7–0 advantage carried through until halftime as the Cleveland defense, eager to erase the memories of the 984 yards the 49ers had rung up in their previous two meetings, rose to the occasion, holding San Francisco to a modest 230 yards of offense. In the third quarter, Marion Motley blasted through the line for a 63-yard touchdown run to make it 14–0, and though the 49ers responded with a touchdown on their next possession to cut the lead back to seven, the Browns never relinquished their dominion on the contest.

The icing on the cake came with six minutes left when Dub Jones scored from four yards out, the third rushing touchdown for a ground attack that chewed up 217 yards for the day. In a last-ditch effort, the 49ers drove to the Cleveland 31 on the next series, but fittingly, the Browns stopped them on downs and then ran out the clock with 11 straight bruising runs into the line.

For the fourth straight year, the Browns were AAFC champions, having defeated a different team in each title clash.

Without a doubt, they were ready for the National Football League, which had absorbed the Browns, 49ers, and Colts from the AAFC three days earlier.

	1	2	3	4		
49ers	0	0	0	7	=	7
Browns	7	0	7	7	=	21

CLE-E. Jones 2-yd. run (Groza kick)
CLE-Motley 68-yd. run (Groza kick)
SF-Salata 23-yd. pass from Albert (Vetrano kick)
CLE-D. Jones 4-yd. run (Groza kick)

Passing
SF: Albert 9–24–108 1 TD 0 INT, Lillywhite 0–1–0 0 TD 0 INT
CLE: Graham 7–17–128 0 TD 0 INT

Rushing
SF: Albert 5–41, Perry 6–36, Standlee 10–21, Garlin 3–13, Cathcart 9–11
CLE: Motley 8–75, E. Jones 16–63, Graham 9–62, James 2–7, Lahr 1–7, D. Jones 4–2, Lewis 1–1

Receiving
SF: Salata 3–37, Beals 3–26, Shoener 2–25, Garlin 1–10
CLE: Lavelli 4–56, Speedie 1–37, D. Jones 1–25, E. Jones 1–10

1950

Saturday, September 16
Browns 35, Philadelphia Eagles 10
Municipal Stadium (71,237)
Brown jerseys/white pants

The Browns exploded into the NFL with an astonishing performance that resulted in a blowout victory over the two-time defending champion Philadelphia Eagles on their own home field on what would prove to be a historic Saturday night. Though a punt return for a touchdown by the Browns' Don Phelps a minute into the game was called back on a penalty (and cost the Browns the services of kicker Lou Groza, who was injured on the play), the upstarts from the All-America Football Conference quickly proved they were a match for the champs, soaring to a 14–3 halftime lead on a pair of Otto Graham touchdown passes. The first—the Browns' initial score in the NFL—was a 59-yard strike down the middle to wide-open RB Dub Jones to give Cleveland a lead it would not relinquish. Graham, having a marvelous night, added a third touchdown pass to cap the first series of the third quarter and then ran for another in the fourth as the Browns turned the "World Series of football" into a blowout. They totaled 448 yards for the game as Graham threw for 346, including seven completions to WR Mac Speedie for 109 yards. The Eagles, playing without injured star RB Steve Van Buren, turned the ball over five times, yet the Browns had their share of mistakes, coughing up the ball four times themselves while committing 12 penalties for 98 yards.
Record: 1–0

	1	2	3	4		
Browns	7	7	7	14	=	35
Eagles	3	0	0	7	=	10

PHI-Patton 15-yd. FG
CLE-D. Jones 59-yd. pass from Graham (Grigg kick)
CLE-Lavelli 26-yd. pass from Graham (Grigg kick)
CLE-Speedie 13-yd. pass from Graham (Grigg kick)
CLE-Graham 1-yd. run (Grigg kick)
PHI-Pihos 17-yd. pass from Mackrides (Patton kick)
CLE-Bumgardner 2-yd. run (Grigg kick)

Passing
CLE: Graham 21–38–346 3 TD 2 INT
PHI: Thompson 8–24–73 0 TD 2 INT, Mackrides 3–8–45 1 TD 1 INT

Rushing
CLE: D. Jones 6–72, Motley 11–48, Bumgardner 4–18, Graham 3–3
PHI: Ziegler 17–57, Scott 13–46, Craft 4–28, Myers 5–12, Mackrides 2–2, Parmer 2–2, Thompson 1–1

Receiving
CLE: Speedie 7–109, D. Jones 5–98, Lavelli 4–76, Bumgardner 3–37, Motley 2–26
PHI: Pihos 4–51, Myers 2–29, Ferrante 3–24, Ziegler 2–14

Sunday, September 24
Browns 31, Baltimore Colts 0
Memorial Stadium (15,201)
White jerseys/white pants

For the second straight week, the Browns rolled to an easy victory, this time over fellow AAFC transfer Baltimore. Cleveland scored on its first three possessions—including an Otto Graham-to-Dante Lavelli touchdown pass on the second play of the game—to sprint to a 17–0 lead, then capped the scoring in the second half with 60- and 61-yard touchdown runs by Dub Jones and Ken Carpenter. The Browns' running game was unstoppable, rolling to 295 yards, atoning for a sour day for Graham, who threw four interceptions. Carpenter's long run allowed him to hit the 100-yard rushing mark though he carried the football only three times, and Lavelli was equally dominant as a receiver, catching five passes for 115 yards.
Record: 2–0

	1	2	3	4		
Browns	17	0	7	7	=	31
Colts	0	0	0	0	=	0

CLE-Lavelli 38-yd. pass from Graham (Grigg kick)
CLE-Grigg 19-yd. FG
CLE-D. Jones 11-yd. run (Grigg kick)
CLE-D. Jones 60-yd. run (Grigg kick)
CLE-K. Carpenter 61-yd. run (Grigg kick)

Passing
CLE: Graham 11–23–177 1 TD 4 INT
BAL: Burk 8–16–81 0 TD 2 INT, Tittle 5–12–75 0 TD 2 INT

Rushing
CLE: K. Carpenter 3–100, D. Jones 5–77, Phelps 4–44, Bumgardner 4–40, Motley 3–19, Graham 2–8, Moselle 1–4, Cole 4–3
BAL: Mutryn 14–46, Mazzanti 4–9, Burk 1–9, Collins 8–0, Tittle 1–2, Buksar 1–0, Stone 1–0, Spavital 5-(-3)

Receiving
CLE: Lavelli 5–115, Speedie 2–24, Motley 2–17, Gillom 1–16, D. Jones 2–8
BAL: Owens 4–69, Oristaglio 5–55, Mutryn 3–21, Mazzanti 1–11

Sunday, October 1
New York Giants 6, Browns 0
Cleveland Stadium (37,647)
White jerseys/white pants

Beginning what would become a fierce rivalry, the Giants unveiled a newly designed defense constructed specifically for the high-flying Cleveland attack and outmuscled the Browns in a physical defensive struggle, handing the Browns their first shutout in team history (and the last for another eight years). The Giants scored all the points they'd need on a short Eddie Price touchdown run midway through the first quarter, then spent the rest of the day frustrating the Browns' offense. Cleveland didn't complete a pass or cross midfield in the first half of the home opener, then threatened to score twice in the final seven minutes of the game. From the New York 10, Otto Graham and Marion Motley collided on a handoff, and the ensuing fumble was recovered by the Giants to quell the threat. Then with three minutes to play, the Browns reached New York territory before a fourth-down pass to the end zone glanced off the hands of Mac Speedie to seal the Cleveland defeat.
Record: 2–1

	1	2	3	4		
Giants	6	0	0	0	=	6
Browns	0	0	0	0	=	0

NYG-Price 2-yd. run (kick failed)

Passing
NYG: Conerly 4–13–61 0 TD 0 INT
CLE: Graham 12–30–127 0 TD 3 INT, K. Carpenter 0–1–0 0 TD 1 INT

Rushing
NYG: Roberts 12–77, Clay 11–35, Scott 4–10, Price 5–8, Jackson 2–4, Conerly 2–2
CLE: Motley 17–53, D. Jones 10–27, Graham 4–26, K. Carpenter 6–7, Bumgardner 1–6, Phelps 1–4

Receiving
NYG: Scott 2–55, Clay 1–3, Roberts 1–3
CLE: Lavelli 4–67, Speedie 4–34, D. Jones 2–15, K. Carpenter 2–11

Saturday, October 7
Browns 30, Pittsburgh Steelers 17
Forbes Field (35,590)
White jerseys/white pants

The Browns bounced back from the tough loss to New York and opened what would prove to be another huge rivalry with a Saturday-night victory over the Steelers. Mirroring their previous trip to Pennsylvania three weeks earlier, the Browns took command early, leading 21–3 at the half on the strength of a pair of one-yard touchdown runs by Otto Graham, both of which were set up by Pittsburgh fumbles. The Steelers would give up six turnovers on the night, wiping out an otherwise brilliant offensive performance that saw them roll to 214 rushing yards and 345 total. As the Cleveland running game amassed 191 yards, Dub Jones scored a pair of touchdowns, including the clincher on a 48-yard run with nine minutes to play.
Record: 3–1

	1	2	3	4		
Browns	7	14	2	7	=	30
Steelers	3	0	7	7	=	17

PIT-Geri 30-yd. FG
CLE-Graham 1-yd. run (Groza kick)
CLE-Graham 1-yd. run (Groza kick)
CLE-D. Jones 7-yd. run (Groza kick)
CLE-Safety: Kissell tackled Chandnois in end zone
PIT-Seabright 13-yd. pass from Geri (Geri kick)
CLE-D. Jones 48-yd. run (Groza kick)
PIT-Shipkey 1-yd. run (Geri kick)

Passing
CLE: Graham 10–17–75 0 TD 0 INT
PIT: Geri 9–18–122 1 TD 1 INT, McWilliams 1–2–9 0 TD 0 INT

Rushing
CLE: D. Jones 10–76, Motley 12–64, K. Carpenter 12–47, Graham 4–5, James 1-(-1)

PIT: Geri 23–145, Chandnois 6–33, McWilliams 2–13, Nuzum 3–10, Rogel 3–7, Shipkey 5–6

Receiving
CLE: Speedie 5–38, K. Carpenter 2–24, Lavelli 1–13, D. Jones 1–2, Motley 1-(-2)
PIT: Rogel 4–42, Nickel 1–41, Jasante 3–23, Seabright 1–13, Chandnois 1–12

Sunday, October 15
Browns 34, Chicago Cardinals 24
Cleveland Stadium (33,774)
White jerseys/white pants

Trailing by two touchdowns late in the third quarter, the Browns put together a stirring rally to score 24 unanswered points to capture their fourth victory in five games. A 54-yard pass-and-lateral from Otto Graham to Dante Lavelli to Marion Motley set up a Lavelli touchdown reception a play later to cut Chicago's lead to 24–17, and another Cleveland touchdown on the ensuing series tied the game. With the outcome hanging in the balance, the Cleveland defense rose to the occasion in the fourth quarter, intercepting a pass to set up the go-ahead field goal and then stymying the Cardinals for the remainder of the game as Motley tacked on an insurance score in the final minutes. While the Cleveland running attack floundered, managing only 43 yards on 31 carries, the passing game exploded for 369 yards, with both Lavelli (131) and Mac Speedie (106) topping the century mark. The Browns turned out to be their own worst enemy, getting flagged 15 times for a whopping 159 yards, while Graham threw three interceptions to counter his otherwise sterling day.
Record: 4–1

	1	2	3	4		
Cardinals	10	7	7	0	=	24
Browns	7	3	7	17	=	34

CHI-Polsfoot 3-yd. pass from Hardy (Harder kick)
CHI-Harder 47-yd. FG
CLE-Graham 7-yd. run (Groza kick)
CLE-Groza 33-yd. FG
CHI-Harder 1-yd. run (Harder kick)
CHI-Shaw 36-yd. pass from Hardy (Harder kick)
CLE-Lavelli 29-yd. pass from Graham (Groza kick)
CLE-Lavelli 26-yd. pass from Graham (Groza kick)
CLE-Groza 19-yd. FG
CLE-Motley 2-yd. run (Groza kick)

Passing
CHI: Hardy 8–26–126 2 TD 2 INT, Tripucka 0–2–0 0 TD 0 INT
CLE: Graham 22–35–369 2 TD 3 INT

Rushing
CHI: Angsman 10–56, Harder 6–28, Paul 1–18, Tripucka 1–18, Trippi 9–17
CLE: Motley 9–28, Graham 7–24, D. Jones 9–11, Phelps 1-(-1), K. Carpenter 3-(-3), Bumgardner 1-(-6), Humble 1-(-10)

Receiving
CHI: Shaw 3–92, Trippi 2–28, Harder 1–3, Polsfoot 1–3, Angsman 1–0
CLE: Lavelli 6–131, Speedie 6–106, Motley 4–69, D. Jones 6–63

Sunday, October 22
New York Giants 17, Browns 13
Polo Grounds (41,734)
White jerseys/white pants

For the second time in four weeks, the Giants' defense dominated the Browns and this time rallied from a 10-point halftime deficit to surge into first place in the American Conference. After taking a 6–3 lead on Lou Groza's second field goal with 25 seconds left in the half, Cleveland caught a huge break when New York RB Jim Ostendarp let the football roll to a stop on the ensuing kickoff and the Browns recovered the live ball at the Giants' 1. Otto Graham then took it across the goal line to increase the Cleveland lead to 13–3, but that would be all the offense the Browns would muster, crossing midfield only once in the second half and managing just 130 total yards on the afternoon. Meanwhile, with Browns DE Len Ford out with an injury, the Giants' running game got rolling, picking up 211 yards on the day. After cutting the margin to three points on the first series of the second half, the Giants recovered a Rex Bumgardner fumble at the Cleveland 19 with eight minutes remaining in the game—one of seven Cleveland turnovers—to set up the winning touchdown by RB Joe Scott, who finished with 121 yards on just 16 carries. The defeat dropped the Browns into third place in the division, a half-game behind both the Giants and Eagles.
Record: 4–2

	1	2	3	4		
Browns	0	13	0	0	=	13
Giants	3	0	7	7	=	17

NYG-Poole 22-yd. FG
CLE-Groza 18-yd. FG
CLE-Groza 17-yd. FG
CLE-Graham 1-yd. run (Groza kick)
NYG-Griffith 4-yd. run (Poole kick)
NYG-Scott 2-yd. run (Poole kick)

Passing
CLE: Graham 10–18–118 0 TD 3 INT
NYG: Tidwell 2–9–17 0 TD 1 INT, Conerly 0–3–0 0 TD 0 INT

Rushing
CLE: D. Jones 9–28, Motley 5–21, Bumgardner 8–20, Graham 10–14
NYG: Scott 16–121, Price 13–68, Griffith 11–15, Clay 8–9, Roberts 3–0, Tidwell 1–1, Conerly 4-(-3)

Receiving
CLE: Speedie 5–65, Lavelli 2–32, Bumgardner 2–13, Motley 1–8
NYG: Swiacki 1–10, McChesney 1–7

Sunday, October 29
Browns 45, Pittsburgh Steelers 7
Cleveland Stadium (40,714)
White jerseys/white pants

The Browns' offense took out its frustrations from the week before on the Steelers, rolling up 533 total yards, while the defense forced eight turnovers in a blowout victory. Cruising to a 17–0 halftime lead that swelled to 31–0 going into the fourth quarter, the Browns tallied 338 rushing yards, led by an astonishing performance by Marion Motley, who scored a pair of touchdowns and picked up 188 yards on just 11 carries—an average of better than 17 yards per rush. Similarly, the Browns completed only six passes on the day but still managed 195 yards through the air, an average of 32 yards per completion. The highlight was an 80-yard touchdown pass from Otto Graham to Dub Jones in the fourth quarter. Though crippled by penalties (12 for 128 yards), the Browns' dominant offense and opportunistic defense never gave the Steelers a chance, completing their first season sweep of their turnpike rivals.
Record: 5–2

	1	2	3	4		
Steelers	0	0	0	7	=	7
Browns	7	10	14	14	=	45

CLE-Graham 1-yd. run (Groza kick)
CLE-Groza 13-yd. FG
CLE-Motley 33-yd. pass from Graham (Groza kick)
CLE-Motley 69-yd. run (Groza kick)
CLE-Phelps 14-yd. run (Groza kick)
PIT-Gage 29-yd. pass from Gasparella (Geri kick)
CLE-D. Jones 80-yd. pass from Graham (Groza kick)
CLE-Gillom 38-yd. pass from Lewis (Groza kick)

Passing
CLE: Graham 5–9–157 2 TD 0 INT, Lewis 1–1–38 1 TD 0 INT
PIT: Gasparella 7–15–118 1 TD 0 INT, Gage 5–13–67 0 TD 3 INT, Geri 1–6–35 0 TD 2 INT, Chandnois 0–2–0 0 TD 1 INT

Rushing
CLE: Motley 11–188, Phelps 13–87, K. Carpenter 7–28, Moselle 3–20, Cole 5–6, Graham 3–5, D. Jones 2–4
PIT: Rogel 6–55, Geri 19–35, Chandnois 7–25, Gage 7–12, Hollingsworth 1–2

Receiving
CLE: D. Jones 1–80, Gillom 1–38, Speedie 2–37, Motley 1–33, Lavelli 1–7
PIT: Chandnois 3–98, Jansante 4–47, Gage 2–43, Nickel 1–20, Rogel 2–9, Hartley 1–3

Sunday, November 5
Browns 10, Chicago Cardinals 7
Comiskey Park (38,456)
White jerseys/white pants

The Browns got all the points they'd need in the opening minutes, relying on another stout defensive performance to capture their sixth victory. Setting the tone with a 33-yard touchdown run by Dub Jones on their first offensive play after recovering a fumbled punt snap, the Browns tacked on a field goal on their next possession, then spent the rest of the afternoon stuffing Chicago's offense, which crossed midfield only twice and turned the ball over five times. The Browns' Horace Gillom also played a key role, averaging 52.3 yards on six punts to continually pin the Cardinals back. Despite losing Marion Motley to injury in the first half, the Cleveland ground game steamrolled to 237 yards. With Philadelphia's loss to Pittsburgh, the Browns assumed sole possession of first place in the conference, taking a half-game lead over both the Eagles and Giants.
Record: 6–2

	1	2	3	4		
Browns	10	0	0	0	=	10
Cardinals	0	7	0	0	=	7

CLE-D. Jones 33-yd. run (Groza kick)
CLE-Groza 17-yd. FG
CHI-Tripucka 1-yd. run (Yablonski kick)

Passing
CLE: Graham 10–21–114 0 TD 2 INT
CHI: Tripucka 8–17–139 0 TD 3 INT, Hardy 5–8–55 0 TD 1 INT

Rushing
CLE: D. Jones 12–69, Cole 10–57, Motley 8–33, Bumgardner 11–32, Graham 4–32, Adamle 3–8, Phelps 4–4, Lewis 1–2
CHI: Angsman 6–30, Hardy 1–19, Dimancheff 5–14, Yablonski 6–7, Trippi 3–1, Harder 2–1, Tripucka 1–1

Receiving
CLE: Speedie 4–45, Lavelli 3–30, Phelps 1–28, K. Carpenter 1–10, D. Jones 1–1
CHI: Shaw 5–111, Dimancheff 3–32, Trippi 2–27, Harder 1–10, Schwall 1–7, Yablonski 1–7

Sunday, November 12
Browns 34, San Francisco 49ers 14
Cleveland Stadium (28,786)
White jerseys/white pants

Mirroring their win over the Cardinals a month earlier, the Browns scored the game's final 20 points—17 of which came in the final four minutes—to turn a tight game with the struggling 49ers into a rout. Clinging to a 17–14 lead, Lou Groza booted a short field goal to extend the lead to six, then back-to-back San Francisco turnovers led to Browns touchdowns, including Dub Jones's second of the day. The mistake-prone 49ers turned the ball over nine times—including six fumbles, setting a record for Browns' opponents that still stands—wiping out a promising start that saw them go to halftime tied at 14 and allowing the Browns to put up 34 points despite gathering only 229 yards of offense. Though the Cleveland passing game failed to ignite, the ground game was effective once again, paced by Marion Motley, who tallied 114 yards on 21 carries.
Record: 7–2

	1	2	3	4		
49ers	7	7	0	0	=	14
Browns	7	7	3	17	=	34

SF-Albert 1-yd. run (Soltau kick)
CLE-D. Jones 7-yd. pass from Graham (Groza kick)
CLE-Motley 22-yd. run (Groza kick)
SF-Beals 28-yd. pass from Albert (Soltau kick)
CLE-Groza 22-yd. FG
CLE-Groza 10-yd. FG
CLE-D. Jones 3-yd. run (Groza kick)
CLE-Bumgardner 12-yd. run (Groza kick)

Passing
SF: Albert 11–22–168 1 TD 3 INT
CLE: Graham 7–17–74 1 TD 0 INT, Lewis 0–3–0 0 TD 0 INT

Rushing
CLE: Motley 21–114, Bumgardner 12–32, Graham 5–16, Phelps 2–3, D. Jones 5-(-5), K. Carpenter 1-(-5)
SF: Strzykalski 14–69, Perry 9–25, Sitko 3–17, Cathcart 9–9, Albert 2–3

Receiving
CLE: D. Jones 3–30, Speedie 2–29, Lavelli 2–15
SF: Loyd 5–102, Beals 1–28, Nix 2–24, Cathcart 1–9, Strzykalski 2–5

Sunday, November 19
Browns 20, Washington Redskins 14
Cleveland Stadium (21,908)
White jerseys/white pants

On the brink of a stunning loss to the 1–7 Redskins, the Browns rallied for an 80-yard scoring drive in the final minutes to maintain a tie for first place in the conference. The Browns assumed control early, taking a 10–0 lead in the second quarter, but allowed the Redskins to creep back into the game with an interception return for a touchdown. Washington then took a 14–13 lead in the final minute of the third quarter and were poised to pull off the upset until the Browns' gritty final drive. A 16-yard pass to Mac Speedie dug the Browns out of a third-down hole and helped set up Don Phelps's nine-yard touchdown run around left end with just over four minutes remaining. But the Redskins wouldn't go quietly, returning the ensuing kickoff 70 yards into Cleveland territory before the Browns halted Washington on downs to clinch a hard-earned victory. Cleveland rushed for 258 yards, paced by another strong showing by Marion Motley, who picked up 178 on 27 carries.
Record: 8–2

	1	2	3	4		
Redskins	0	7	7	0	=	14
Browns	0	13	0	7	=	20

CLE-Groza 30-yd. FG
CLE-Lavelli 4-yd. pass from Graham (Groza kick)
WAS-Haynes 40-yd. interception return (Dudley kick)
CLE-Groza 13-yd. FG
WAS-Goode 2-yd. run (Dudley kick)
CLE-Phelps 8-yd. run (Groza kick)

Passing
WAS: Gilmer 19–30–156 0 TD 2 INT, Justice 1–1–15 0 TD 0 INT
CLE: Graham 6–13–65 1 TD 2 INT

Rushing
WAS: Justice 12–56, Goode 12–20, Saenz 2–13, Gilmer 3–6, Dudley 1-(-2)
CLE: Motley 27–178, Bumgardner 12–45, Phelps 4–22, Graham 6–9, D. Jones 4–4

Receiving
WAS: Taylor 3–49, Saenz 4–45, Justice 5–32, Goode 5–24, Tereshinski 1–9, Dudley 1–8, DeMao 1–4
CLE: Lavelli 4–27, Bumgardner 1–21, Speedie 1–17

Sunday, December 3
Browns 13, Philadelphia Eagles 7
Cleveland Stadium (37,490)
White jerseys/white pants

In a driving rainstorm on a sloppy field, Paul Brown made a point to the Eagles in a gritty victory made possible entirely by the Cleveland defense. After many Eagles players stated the only reason the Browns won in their first meeting was because all they did was pass the ball, in the second meeting the Browns didn't attempt a pass, instead relying on their defense to lead the way. And it worked as DB Warren Lahr intercepted a pass and returned it 30 yards for a touchdown just over a minute into the game. Philadelphia turned the ball over three more times, including a fumble that set up a Lou Groza field goal just before the half to give the Browns a 10–0 lead. They stretched it to 13–0 in the third quarter when aided by an Eagle penalty on the second-half kickoff. The Eagles finally managed to put points on the board with just over a minute to play. Horace Gillom set a team record by punting 12 times as the Cleveland offense could manage only 69 total yards and just one first down in one of the most bizarre victories the Browns would ever capture. The triumph helped them keep pace with the Giants, who also moved to 9–2 with a blowout victory over the crosstown rival Yanks.
Record: 9–2

	1	2	3	4		
Eagles	0	0	0	7	=	7
Browns	7	3	3	0	=	13

CLE-Lahr 30-yd. interception return (Groza kick)
CLE-Groza 35-yd. FG
CLE-Groza 43-yd. FG
PHI-Parmer 2-yd. run (Patton kick)

Passing
PHI: Thompson 8–21–81 0 TD 2 INT, Mackrides 0–2–0 0 TD 0 INT

Rushing
PHI: Ziegler 10–50, Myers 5–14, Parmer 6–11, Ledbetter 3–8, Mackrides 2–5, Van Buren 10-(-2)
CLE: Phelps 7–28, Bumgardner 8–20, Motley 12–16, D. Jones 7–9, K. Carpenter 2–1, Graham 5-(-5)

Receiving
PHI: Ferrante 4–46, Myers 1–13, Armstrong 1–8, Ziegler 1–8, Pihos 1–6

Sunday, December 10
Browns 45, Washington Redskins 21
Griffith Stadium (21,908)
White jerseys/white pants

In a driving snow, the Browns scored 31 unanswered points to close out a fantastic inaugural season in the NFL with a convincing victory over the Redskins. Otto Graham, who had struggled since mid-season, put it all together in the finale, throwing for 321 yards and four touchdowns as the Browns' offense soared to 477 total yards to overcome three turnovers and 109 yards in Cleveland penalties. The Browns' hopes dimmed early when Marion Motley was ejected for fighting, and the Redskins soared to a 21–14 lead. But Graham's third touchdown pass tied the game at 21, then Warren Lahr pushed the Browns into the lead moments later when he intercepted a tipped pass flat on his back at the Washington 18, then got up and sprinted into the end zone to break the game open. The Browns added the icing on the cake in the fourth quarter with a punt return for a score by Don Phelps and what would prove to be the only touchdown of Lou Groza's career on a 23-yard reception on a tackle-eligible play. Dub Jones was Graham's primary target, catching 10 passes for 161 yards and a pair of scores. Meanwhile, the Giants held off the Eagles in a defensive struggle in Philadelphia, leaving New York and the Browns tied for first in the American Conference and setting up a playoff the following Sunday in Cleveland.

Record: 10–2

	1	2	3	4		
Browns	0	14	14	17	=	45
Redskins	7	7	7	0	=	21

WAS-Justice 5-yd. pass from Baugh (Dudley kick)
CLE-D. Jones 20-yd. pass from Graham (Groza kick)
WAS-Taylor 51-yd. pass from Gilmer (Dudley kick)
CLE-D. Jones 29-yd. pass from Graham (Groza kick)
WAS-Dudley 22-yd. run (Dudley kick)
CLE-Bumgardner 25-yd. pass from Graham (Groza kick)
CLE-Lahr 18-yd. interception return (Groza kick)
CLE-Groza 11-yd. FG
CLE-Groza 23-yd. pass from Graham (Groza kick)
CLE-Phelps 54-yd. punt return (Groza kick)

Passing
CLE: Graham 23–32–321 4 TD 1 INT
WAS: Baugh 7–17–87 1 TD 2 INT, Gilmer 1–5–51 1 TD 1 INT

Rushing
CLE: Motley 4–48, Cole 7–39, Bumgardner 6–24, Moselle 1–15, D. Jones 4–12, Graham 2–8, Phelps 3–7, K. Carpenter 1–6, Lewis 1-(-3)
WAS: Goode 18–81, Dudley 4–41, Justice 10–22, Gilmer 2–10, Baugh 2–4, Drazenovich 1–1, Saenz 1–1

Receiving
CLE: D. Jones 10–161, Lavelli 5–52, Speedie 4–44, Bumgardner 3–41, Groza 1–23
WAS: Taylor 3–89, Goodnight 2–25, Tereshinski 1–15, Justice 1–6, Thomas 1–3

American Conference Playoff
Sunday, December 17
Browns 8, New York Giants 3
Cleveland Stadium (33,054)
White jerseys/white pants

Though they'd lost to the Giants twice in the regular season, by virtue of a coin flip, the Browns would host New York in their playoff with a trip to the NFL Championship on the line. And on a bitterly cold day along Lake Erie, they battled the Giants in what remains one of the most memorable games in Cleveland history.

Following the script established in their first two meetings, the game was a fierce defensive struggle on a slippery, frozen field. With both teams wearing rubber-soled shoes for better footing, the Browns got rolling on their opening possession and drove deep into New York territory, capping the march with a short Lou Groza field goal. And with the Cleveland defense controlling the Giants, the score remained 3–0 into the fourth quarter.

With 10 minutes left, New York appeared to move into the driver's seat when RB Gene Roberts broke free on a sweep from the Cleveland 36. Browns' DL Bill Willis, having a magnificent day, caught Roberts at the Browns' 4 to prevent the touchdown, and then, through a flurry of penalties, the Cleveland defense prevented the Giants from crossing the goal line on seven consecutive plays. New York settled for a game-tying field goal with 6:10 remaining.

The Browns regained possession at their own 35, and Otto Graham began marching them downfield, rushing for 36 yards on the icy turf to push them into New York territory. Lou Groza booted a 28-yard field goal with 58 seconds left to put the Browns ahead 6–3, then the Cleveland defense rounded out the scoring by tackling New York QB Charlie Conerly in the end zone for a safety with eight seconds left.

It had truly been a defensive war, with neither team topping 200 yards of offense and combining for only six complete passes in 23 attempts. While the Giants contained Marion Motley, who ran only for 12 yards on seven carries, Graham scampered for 70 on eight rushes, primarily on the final drive.

Later that afternoon in Los Angeles, the Rams sprinted past the Bears in the National Conference playoff, setting up a Christmas Eve showdown between the Browns and Cleveland's former team for the NFL title.

	1	2	3	4		
Giants	0	0	0	3	=	3
Browns	3	0	0	5	=	8

CLE-Groza 11-yd. FG
NYG-Clay 20-yd. FG
CLE-Groza 28-yd. FG
CLE-Safety: Willis tackled Conerly in end zone

Passing
NYG: Conerly 3–12–48 0 TD 2 INT, Tidwell 0–3–0 0 TD 0 INT
CLE: Graham 3–8–43 0 TD 1 INT

Rushing
NYG: Roberts 12–76, Price 21–65, Conerly 1–2, Scott 3-(-2)
CLE: Graham 8–70, Bumgardner 13–39, D. Jones 12–32, Motley 7–12

Receiving
NYG: McChesney 1–19, Roberts 1–17, Sulaitis 1–12
CLE: Lavelli 2–35, Bumgardner 1–8

1950 NFL Championship
Sunday, December 24
Browns 30, Los Angeles Rams 28
Cleveland Stadium (29,751)
White jerseys/white pants

In a dramatic encounter, Cleveland's new team battled its old one on Christmas Eve for the NFL championship in a game that featured 11 future Hall of Famers and would forever be remembered as one of the best ever played.

Led by an electrifying offense, the Rams took the lead on their first play from scrimmage on an 82-yard touchdown pass from QB Bob Waterfield, who had led the team to the NFL title five years earlier in Cleveland. The Browns responded with a touchdown of their own on their opening drive, and the tone was set for an offensive shoot-out on the lake. Cleveland surged to a 20–14 lead midway through the third quarter on a pair of scoring receptions by Dante Lavelli, but the Rams regained control by scoring two touchdowns in 25 seconds, the second on a fumble return. Los Angeles took its 28–20 lead into the fourth quarter and appeared to be on its way to the title.

But Warren Lahr intercepted Waterfield early in the final stanza to set up Otto Graham's fourth touchdown pass of the day to cut the lead to a single point. The Browns then drove to the Los Angeles 24 with three minutes left, but Graham fumbled and the Rams recovered, apparently sealing the home team's fate. The Cleveland defense stuffed Los Angeles, and the Browns got the ball back at their own 32 with 1:50 left.

Graham atoned for his fumble with a 14-yard run and then three straight pass completions to march the Browns to the Rams' 11 in the final minute. Lou Groza booted a 16-yard field goal through the uprights to put the Browns ahead 30–28 with 28 seconds left, and after Lahr intercepted a desperate pass in the waning moments, the Browns had captured their first NFL championship in perhaps the most memorable game in team history. The fans rushed the field and tore down the goalposts in celebration of the first of the Browns' four NFL titles.

Though they'd turned the ball over a total of nine times, the teams had combined for nearly 800 total yards, 44 first downs, and eight touchdowns, as Waterfield threw for 312 yards and Graham for 298 to go along with a game-high 99 rushing yards. LA wideout Tom Fears (nine catches, 136 yards) and Lavelli (a still-current team playoff record 11 catches, 128 yards) also stood out in what became an unforgettable aerial display capping a historic title game and marvelous season for the Browns in their first year in the NFL.

	1	2	3	4		
Rams	14	0	14	0	=	28
Browns	7	6	7	10	=	30

LA-Davis 82-yd. pass from Waterfield (Waterfield kick)
CLE-D. Jones 27-yd. pass from Graham (Groza kick)
LA-Hoerner 3-yd. run (Waterfield kick)
CLE-Lavelli 37-yd. pass from Graham (kick failed)

THE START OF AN EPIC RIVALRY . . . ON THE BASKETBALL COURT

One of the great rivalries in pro football began on October 7, 1950, when the Cleveland Browns, playing their fourth NFL game, defeated the Pittsburgh Steelers at Forbes Field, 30–17. The teams would play more than 100 times over the next eight decades, with their fan bases developing a bitter, adversarial relationship.

Yet despite the blue-collar, rust-belt flavor of the series, it actually began in tank tops and satin shorts.

The first time the Browns met the Steelers was on February 2, 1947, in an exhibition basketball game played on a Sunday night at Cleveland Arena as part of a doubleheader with the Cleveland Rebels of the Basketball Association of America (renamed the National Basketball Association two years later), who would play the league-leading Washington Capitols later that evening.

The Rebels got walloped, 107–81, but the night wasn't a total loss for the hometown fans. With Dante Lavelli and Marion Motley each scoring 10 points, the Browns beat the Steelers, 37–29, setting the tone for the series on the football field as Cleveland went on to win the first eight meetings, 12 of the first 13, and 16 of the first 18.

CLE-Lavelli 39-yd. pass from Graham (Groza kick)
LA-Hoerner 1-yd. run (Waterfield kick)
LA-Brink 6-yd. fumble return (Waterfield kick)
CLE-Bumgardner 14-yd. pass from Graham (Groza kick)
CLE-Groza 16-yd. FG

Passing
LA: Waterfield 18–31–312 1 TD 4 INT, Van Brocklin 0–1–0 0 TD 1 INT
CLE: Graham 22–33–298 4 TD 1 INT

Rushing
LA: Hoerner 24–86, Smith 4–11, Davis 6–6, Waterfield 1–2, Pasquariello 1–1
CLE: Graham 12–99, Motley 6–9, D. Jones 2–4, Bumgardner 5–2

Receiving
LA: Fears 9–136, Davis 2–88, Smith 3–46, Hirsch 4–42
CLE: Lavelli 11–128, D. Jones 4–80, Bumgardner 4–46, Gillom 1–29, Speedie 1–17, Motley 1-(-2)

1951

Sunday, September 30
San Francisco 49ers 24, Browns 10
Kezar Stadium (52,219)
White jerseys/white pants

The Browns started fast, then faded as rain began to fall in the second half while renewing their AAFC rivalry with the 49ers. Cleveland jumped to a 7–0 lead on the fifth play of the game when Otto Graham connected with Dub Jones for an eight-yard touchdown pass, but the Browns managed little offense after that as San Francisco scored 17 straight points and then put the game away with a third touchdown in the fourth quarter. 49ers RB Verl Lillywhite torched the Browns for 145 yards on 17 carries, while the Browns struggled to just 55 rushing yards as a team. Jones's early touchdown paved the way for a big performance, as he tallied 143 receiving yards. The defeat marked the first time the Browns had ever lost a season opener.
Record: 0–1

	1	2	3	4		
Browns	7	0	3	0	=	10
49ers	7	3	7	7	=	24

CLE-D. Jones 81-yd. pass from Graham (Groza kick)
SF-Wilson 25-yd. pass from Albert (Soltau kick)
SF-Soltau 42-yd. FG
SF-Perry 6-yd. run (Soltau kick)
CLE-Groza 40-yd. FG
SF-Perry 6-yd. run (Soltau kick)

Passing
CLE: Graham 18–30–222 1 TD 2 INT
SF: Albert 7–14–78 1 TD 1 INT, Tittle 3–3–59 0 TD 0 INT

Rushing
CLE: Cole 4–20, Graham 5–13, Motley 2–12, K. Carpenter 2–7, D. Jones 6–3
SF: Lillywhite 17–145, Schabarum 14–60, Albert 4–17, White 2–11, Perry 10–4, Arenas 1–0

Receiving
CLE: D. Jones 5–143, Speedie 5–36, Lavelli 5–23, K. Carpenter 2–18, Motley 1–2
SF: Soltau 1–37, Perry 4–36, Wilson 2–34, Beals 2–24, Schabarum 1–6

Sunday, October 7
Browns 38, Los Angeles Rams 23
Los Angeles Memorial Coliseum (67,186)
White jerseys/white pants

The Browns wrapped up their West Coast trip with a convincing victory over the Rams in a rematch of the previous year's NFL title game. Under blazing conditions that saw the temperature soar to 114°F on the field, the Browns trailed by 10 points early, but exploded for three touchdowns in the third quarter to seize control—the third on an interception return by DB Warren Lahr. RB Ken Carpenter had a brilliant game, scoring three touchdowns, while Dub Jones and Marion Motley both topped 100 yards rushing. As a team, the Browns tallied 450 total yards, compiling nearly 300 on the ground to help atone for seven allowed sacks and a whopping 145 yards lost in penalties.
Record: 1–1

	1	2	3	4		
Browns	7	0	21	10	=	38
Rams	10	0	7	6	=	23

LA-Hirsch 34-yd. pass from Van Brocklin (Waterfield kick)
LA-Waterfield 47-yd. FG
CLE-K. Carpenter 45-yd. pass from Graham (Groza kick)
CLE-K. Carpenter 2-yd. run (Groza kick)
CLE-K. Carpenter 7-yd. run (Groza kick)
CLE-Lahr 23-yd. interception return (Groza kick)
LA-Davis 1-yd. run (Waterfield kick)
CLE-Groza 44-yd. FG
LA-Davis 14-yd. pass from Van Brocklin (kick failed)
CLE-D. Jones 1-yd. run (Groza kick)

Passing
CLE: Graham 10–19–219 1 TD 2 INT
LA: Van Brocklin 6–17–129 2 TD 2 INT, Waterfield 6–16–106 0 TD 1 INT

Rushing
CLE: D. Jones 15–110, Motley 13–106, K. Carpenter 8–39, Phelps 3–20, Bumgardner 6–16, Graham 3–2, Cole 1–0
LA: Towler 8–33, Davis 8–27, Smith 5–12, Kalmanir 3–9, Hoerner 1–6, Van Brocklin 1–4, Williams 2-(-3)

THE BROWNS AND THE COLLEGE ALL-STAR GAME

Once a long-standing football tradition, the annual College All-Star Game lasted more than four decades and drew huge crowds to Chicago's Soldier Field each August to see the defending NFL champion take on the best players from the college game.

From 1934 to 1976, 42 games were played, with the defending NFL champion winning 33, many by lopsided scores. The Browns played in the game four times, after each of their four NFL titles.

August 17, 1951
Browns 33, College All-Stars 0
92,180

The Browns completely dominated the All-Stars in a shutout victory before a massive crowd, rolling up 425 yards of offense while allowing only 106 and five first downs as the All-Stars crossed midfield once. Otto Graham threw two touchdowns while Dub Jones ran for two more and rushed for 105 yards in what proved to be the third-most lopsided All-Star Game.

August 12, 1955
College All-Stars 30, Browns 27
75,000

Beginning what they thought would be the post-Otto Graham era, the Browns watched the All-Stars control the contest in the second half and cruise to their first victory over the NFL champion in five years. With Notre Dame QB Ralph Guglielmi running an effective offense, the All-Stars chewed up the Cleveland defense for 200 rushing yards, scoring more points than any All-Star team in 21 years and setting a record with 20 first downs. The Browns crept to a 20–17 halftime lead, but the All-Stars roared back with 13 points to take a 30–20 lead after a scoring run by Toledo's Mel Triplett and the third field goal of the day by Ohio State kicker Tad Weed. The Browns marched 80 yards to cut the margin to three points, but never saw the ball again. Watching from the stands, Graham would soon be wooed back for one final season by head coach Paul Brown.

August 10, 1956
Browns 26, College All-Stars 0
75,000

Shutting out the All-Stars for the second time, the Browns began the actual post-Otto Graham era on a good note. The offense set the tone with an 80-yard drive for a touchdown in the first quarter, while the defense contained Ohio State RB Howard "Hopalong" Cassady and limited the All-Stars (who were hindered by an early head injury to Michigan State QB Earl Morrall) to just a pair of pass completions for 12 yards and only five first downs. Lou Groza set an All-Star Game record with four field goals.

August 6, 1965
Browns 24, College All-Stars 16
68,000

On a humid night interrupted by heavy rain and thunderstorms, a nice performance by the Browns was overshadowed by a first-quarter shoulder injury suffered by Paul Warfield, who would be sidelined for the next 10 weeks. After soaring to a 17–3 halftime lead, the Browns put the game away early in the third when Cleveland RB Jamie Caleb blocked a punt and LB Stan Sczurek recovered the football for a touchdown. Notre Dame QB John Huarte led the All-Stars to a pair of scores after that in relief of Navy's Roger Staubach, who joined Warfield at the hospital after injuring his own shoulder.

Receiving
CLE: D. Jones 3–57, K. Carpenter 1–45, Speedie 1–41, Lavelli 3–39, Gillom 1–20, Cole 1–17
LA: Hirsch 4–69, Smith 1–61, Towler 1–46, Fears 5–45, Davis 1–14

Sunday, October 14
Browns 45, Washington Redskins 0
Cleveland Stadium (33,968)
White jerseys/white pants

The Browns set the tone two minutes into the game when DE George Young grabbed a Washington fumble and roared 47 yards for a touchdown, the opening salvo in a Cleveland onslaught. After taking a 14–0 lead to the half, the Browns put up 31 points in the final two periods to hand the Redskins their worst defeat since their 73–0 blowout at the hands of the Chicago Bears in the 1940 NFL title game. While the defense forced seven turnovers, the Cleveland offense racked up 192 yards on the ground and all four of the Browns' touchdowns came via the running game. It marked the Browns' first home shutout since joining the NFL the year before.

Record: 2–1

	1	2	3	4		
Redskins	0	0	0	0	=	0
Browns	7	7	17	14	=	45

CLE-Young 47-yd. fumble return (Groza kick)
CLE-K. Carpenter 1-yd. run (Groza kick)

CLE-Groza 27-yd. FG
CLE-Graham 1-yd. run (Groza kick)
CLE-Cole 9-yd. run (Groza kick)
CLE-Phelps 13-yd. run (Groza kick)
CLE-Oristaglio 20-yd. pass from Lewis (Groza kick)

Passing
WAS: Gilmer 8–14–116 0 TD 1 INT, Baugh 4–8–56 0 TD 2 INT
CLE: Graham 8–15–135 0 TD 0 INT, Lewis 3–4–49 1 TD 0 INT

Rushing
WAS: Gilmer 4–28, Drazenovich 11–17, Goode 6–17, Papit 7–15, Heath 6–13, Dudley 3–8, Dowda 2–7, Thomas 2–1, Baugh 1-(-1)
CLE: Cole 9–54, Phelps 9–44, D. Jones 7–40, Bumgardner 5–40, K. Carpenter 7–15, Graham 2-(-1)

Receiving
WAS: Taylor 6–87, Papit 1–24, Tereshinski 1–21, Brito 1–14, Goode 1–13, Dudley 1–9, Thomas 1–4
CLE: Speedie 3–48, Lavelli 1–44, Gillom 2–29, Oristaglio 1–20, K. Carpenter 1–16, D. Jones 1–11, Bumgardner 1–10, Cole 1–6

Sunday, October 21
Browns 17, Pittsburgh Steelers 0
Cleveland Stadium (32,409)
White jerseys/white pants

For the second straight week, the Browns held their opponent scoreless, a rare achievement that would be accomplished only one other time in team history. Fittingly, in what became a low-scoring struggle, the defense and special teams scored the Browns' only touchdowns. Horace Gillom scooped up a loose ball after a wayward Pittsburgh punt bounced off a Steeler lineman and ran 38 yards for a touchdown. Warren Lahr then capped the victory with a 27-yard interception return for a touchdown in the third quarter. The Browns' defense collected four turnovers and halted five Pittsburgh drives inside Cleveland territory. The offense, meanwhile, put together its third straight dominating running performance, rolling up 197 yards on the ground, paced by sparingly used Emerson Cole's 126.
Record: 3–1

	1	2	3	4		
Steelers	0	0	0	0	=	0
Browns	0	10	7	0	=	17

CLE-Gillom 38-yd. fumble return (Groza kick)
CLE-Groza 25-yd. FG
CLE-Lahr 27-yd. interception return (Groza kick)

Passing
PIT: Mathews 8–21–111 0 TD 0 INT, Chandnois 3–6–21 0 TD 1 INT, Geri 0–4–0 0 TD 1 INT, Gasparella 0–1–0 0 TD 0 INT
CLE: Graham 9–15–67 0 TD 1 INT

Rushing
PIT: Chandnois 9–42, Geri 8–29, Rogel 6–23, Mathews 6–7, Nuzum 7–4
CLE: Cole 17–126, D. Jones 11–52, K. Carpenter 6–30, Bumgardner 4–5, Phelps 4–1, Graham 4-(-17)

Receiving
PIT: Nuzum 1–39, Jansante 4–36, Nickel 2–17, Chandnois 1–16, Minarik 2–13, Rogel 1–11
CLE: Lavelli 3–27, Speedie 3–27, Bumgardner 1–7, D. Jones 2–6

Sunday, October 28
Browns 14, New York Giants 13
Cleveland Stadium (56,947)
White jerseys/white pants

What began as a scoring showcase quickly became a bitter defensive battle as the Browns prevailed over the Giants to win their fourth straight and take over first place in the American Conference. Cleveland took the lead in the first minute of the game when Otto Graham connected with Dub Jones for a 64-yard touchdown, but another Graham toss minutes later was intercepted by Giants' DB—and future Dallas head coach—Tom Landry and returned 20 yards for the tying touchdown. WR Dante Lavelli reeled in another scoring toss from Graham to give the Browns back the lead late in the first quarter, but five minutes into the second period New York countered with another touchdown. The Giants' missed extra point proved to be the difference as neither team was able to score again. New York was held to less than 200 total yards, but had a chance to take the lead with a minute to play before another missed kick by Giants' kicker Ray Poole, this time on a 41-yard field-goal attempt, gave the football back to the Browns. In what became a sloppy game, the home team prevailed despite coughing up three turnovers, allowing four sacks, and accumulating 115 yards in penalties.
Record: 4–1

	1	2	3	4		
Giants	7	6	0	0	=	13
Browns	14	0	0	0	=	14

CLE-D. Jones 64-yd. pass from Graham (Groza kick)
NYG-Landry 20-yd. interception return (Poole kick)
CLE-Lavelli 26-yd. pass from Graham (Groza kick)
NYG-McChesney 29-yd. pass from Conerly (kick failed)

Passing
NYG: Conerly 9–13–117 1 TD 1 INT, Tidwell 0–1–0 0 TD 1 INT
CLE: Graham 16–24–216 2 TD 3 INT

Rushing
NYG: Price 24–61, Scott 12–52, Conerly 1-(-1), Tidwell 1-(-2)
CLE: Graham 8–26, Cole 5–12, Bumgardner 13–7, Motley 1–4, D. Jones 6–2

Receiving
NYG: Scott 3–48, McChesney 1–29, Stribling 3–34, Price 1–4, Sulaitis 1–2
CLE: D. Jones 7–116, Lavelli 6–68, Gillom 2–25, Bumgardner 1–7

Sunday, November 4
Browns 34, Chicago Cardinals 17
Comiskey Park (19,742)
White jerseys/white pants

Forcing five turnovers, the Browns scored a pair of early touchdowns to take control and coasted to an easy win in Chicago. After Dub Jones opened the scoring with a 24-yard touchdown run, the Cardinals fumbled the ensuing kickoff and the Browns recovered, leading to an Otto Graham score and a 14–0 lead. Browns' LB Alex Agase came up with a pair of turnovers bookending the intermission to put the Browns in the clear. He recovered a fumble that led to a Dante Lavelli touchdown, then intercepted a pass on Chicago's first possession of the third quarter, and the Browns cashed in with Graham's second touchdown run. Rolling up more than 400 yards of offense, once again, the Browns were able to overcome their own miscues as they were flagged for 125 yards in penalties.
Record: 5–1

	1	2	3	4		
Browns	14	10	7	3	=	34
Cardinals	7	3	0	7	=	17

CLE-D. Jones 24-yd. run (Groza kick)
CLE-Graham 1-yd. run (Groza kick)
CHI-Polsfoot 20-yd. pass from Hardy (Patton kick)
CLE-Groza 32-yd. FG
CHI-Patton 10-yd. FG
CLE-Lavelli 27-yd. pass from Graham (Groza kick)
CLE-Graham 1-yd. run (Groza kick)
CLE-Groza 21-yd. FG
CHI-Pasquariello 1-yd. run (Patton kick)

Passing
CLE: Graham 15–21–210 1 TD 0 INT
CHI: Hardy 12–20–164 1 TD 1 INT, Trippi 5–9–94 0 TD 0 INT

Rushing
CLE: K. Carpenter 18–118, D. Jones 12–78, Motley 7–28, Graham 4–11, Taseff 1–3, Jagade 2–0
CHI: Angsman 12–54, Cross 7–41, Paquariello 4–10, Hardy 2–4, Trippi 1-(-2), Sitko 2-(-16)

Receiving
CLE: Gillom 5–80, Lavelli 5–67, K. Carpenter 3–49, D. Jones 1–12, Motley 1–2
CHI: Polsfoot 8–129, Stonesifer 5–69, Cross 2–38, Angsman 1–13, Sitko 1–9

Sunday, November 11
Browns 20, Philadelphia Eagles 17
Cleveland Stadium (36,571)
White jerseys/white pants

The Browns rallied from a 10-point halftime deficit to pull out their sixth straight win and eleventh straight at home as Paul Brown collected his two-hundredth career coaching victory (combining high school, college, and pro games). Held to just 30 yards in the first half, the Browns got rolling in the third quarter to tie the score but gave the lead right back after fumbling a punt that led to an Eagle touchdown. The Browns fought back again and took the lead five minutes into the fourth after a Warren Lahr interception set up a short Lou Groza field goal. The Eagles then had two opportunities to score in the final 10 minutes, but the Browns recovered a fumble at their own 26, then Philadelphia missed a potentially game-tying 44-yard field goal with a minute to play. The sterling Cleveland running game was completely neutralized as Philadelphia held the Browns to just 18 rushing yards on 22 carries.
Record: 6–1

	1	2	3	4		
Eagles	3	7	7	0	=	17
Browns	0	0	10	10	=	20

PHI-Walston 30-yd. FG
PHI-Van Buren 2-yd. run (Walston kick)
CLE-Groza 37-yd. FG
CLE-K. Carpenter 24-yd. pass from Graham (Groza kick)
PHI-Burk 1-yd. run (Walston kick)
CLE-Lavelli 17-yd. pass from Graham (Groza kick)
CLE-Groza 13-yd. FG

Passing
PHI: Burk 8–26–85 0 TD 2 INT
CLE: Graham 14–30–192 2 TD 1 INT

Rushing
PHI: S. Van Buren 17–95, Ziegler 6–59, Parmer 14–55, Sandifer 6–20, E. Van Buren 3–10, Scott 1–7, Pollard 1–2, Burk 4–0
CLE: Motley 7–12, K. Carpenter 7–10, D. Jones 4–3, Bumgardner 1–2, Graham 3-(-9)

Receiving
PHI: Pihos 2–26, Scott 1–24, Walston 2–18, Ziegler 2–11, Sandifer 1–6
CLE: Lavelli 4–85, Speedie 3–60, K. Carpenter 1–24, D. Jones 2–17, Gillom 1–10, Motley 3-(-4)

Sunday, November 18
Browns 10, New York Giants 0
Polo Grounds (52,215)
White jerseys/white pants

In another defensive struggle on a crisp autumn afternoon, the Browns grabbed an early lead and then hung on for their third shutout of the season and seventh straight win. The Browns scored all of the game's points in the first eight minutes, taking a 3–0 lead on a Lou Groza field goal and then stretching it to 10–0 when Dub Jones turned a screen pass into a 68-yard touchdown. From that point on, it was all defense as neither team topped 200 total yards and combined for only 17 first downs. The Browns forced three key turnovers, including an early interception by Cliff Lewis that set up their field goal, and came up with a goal-line stand in the final minute to preserve the shutout.
Record: 7–1

	1	2	3	4		
Browns	10	0	0	0	=	10
Giants	0	0	0	0	=	0

CLE-Groza 34-yd. FG
CLE-D. Jones 68-yd. pass from Graham (Groza kick)

Passing
CLE: Graham 8–18–162 1 TD 3 INT
NYG: Conerly 13–23–140 0 TD 1 INT

Rushing
CLE: K. Carpenter 9–24, D. Jones 12–23, Motley 6–10, Graham 2-(-1)
NYG: Price 19–61, Griffith 8–32, Scott 9–7, Pritchard 2–0, Conerly 2-(-2)

Receiving
CLE: D. Jones 3–94, Lavelli 3–54, Speedie 1–9, Motley 1–7
NYG: Hudson 1–50, Scott 6–45, Wilkinson 2–19, McChesney 1–14, Mote 1–8, Sulaitis 1–6, Price 1-(-2)

Sunday, November 25
Browns 42, Chicago Bears 21
Cleveland Stadium (40,969)
White jerseys/white pants

Behind one of the greatest individual performances in NFL history, the Browns steamrolled over the 6–2 Bears. Dub Jones set a team mark and tied Ernie Nevers's 22-year-old league record with six touchdowns—four rushing, two receiving—as the Browns built a 42–7 fourth-quarter lead and rolled up 516 yards of offense. Jones, who compiled 116 rushing yards and 80 receiving, scored the last five times he touched the ball, including runs of 27 and 43 yards and a reception for 43 in the second half. Mac Speedie also turned in a dazzling performance with 144 yards on six receptions but was overshadowed by Jones. Also somewhat lost was a strong showing by Otto Graham, who completed 12 of 19 passes for 277 yards. Perhaps the most amazing part of the Browns' display was that they also overcame another dubious team record, committing 21 penalties for 209 yards. With the Bears also getting flagged 16 times, the teams combined for another single-game team record for penalties (37) and penalty yardage (374) that still stands.
Record: 8–1

	1	2	3	4		
Bears	0	0	7	14	=	21
Browns	0	14	14	14	=	42

CLE-D. Jones 2-yd. run (Groza kick)
CLE-D. Jones 34-yd. pass from Graham (Groza kick)

CLE-D. Jones 12-yd. run (Groza kick)
CHI-Gulyanics 3-yd. run (Blanda kick)
CLE-D. Jones 27-yd. run (Groza kick)
CLE-D. Jones 43-yd. run (Groza kick)
CLE-D. Jones 43-yd. pass from Graham (Groza kick)
CHI-Sprinkle 55-yd. fumble return (Blanda kick)
CHI-Hunsinger 19-yd. pass from Williams (White kick)

Passing
CHI: Romanik 10–29–119 0 TD 1 INT, Williams 3–6–34 1 TD 0 INT, Lujack 2–6–29 0 TD 1 INT
CLE: Graham 12–19–277 2 TD 1 INT

Rushing
CHI: Hunsinger 4–41, Dottley 6–23, Lujack 2–10, Gulyanics 7–9, Kindt 1–2, Romanik 1–2, Stone 2–0, Boone 1-(-1), Williams 1-(-4), Rykovich 5-(-8)
CLE: D. Jones 9–116, K. Carpenter 7–75, Motley 6–38, Bumgardner 6–27, Cole 2–8, Taseff 1–5, Graham 3–4

Receiving
CHI: Schroeder 3–60, Dottley 3–42, Hoffman 3–32, Hunsinger 1–19, Gulyanics 2–16, Stone 1–7, Rykovich 2–6
CLE: Speedie 6–144, D. Jones 3–80, Lavelli 2–33, K. Carpenter 1–20

Sunday, December 2
Browns 49, Chicago Cardinals 28
Cleveland Stadium (30,550)
White jerseys/white pants

Aided by eight turnovers, the Browns once again lit up the scoreboard with a season-high 49 points as they sprinted to a six-touchdown lead and then withstood a flurry of Cardinal scores in the final minutes. Otto Graham threw for four touchdowns in the first half and returned a Cleveland fumble for another in the final minutes. Three scoring strikes went to Mac Speedie, whose first score came 90 seconds into the game, and by the four-minute mark, Dante Lavelli added another to set the Browns off to the races. Dub Jones scored his eighth touchdown in three games to open the second half. Leading 42–0, Paul Brown pulled Graham and other first-stringers, but after a pair of Cleveland fumbles—two of five Browns' turnovers—led to two Chicago touchdowns, the Cardinals cut the margin to 42–28 in the fourth quarter and Brown was forced to return his starters to the game. The 49 points scored was the Browns' highest single-game total since joining the NFL and delivered their ninth straight victory.
Record: 9–1

	1	2	3	4		
Cardinals	0	0	14	14	=	28
Browns	14	14	14	7	=	49

CLE-Speedie 22-yd. pass from Graham (Groza kick)
CLE-Lavelli 21-yd. pass from Graham (Groza kick)
CLE-Speedie 39-yd. pass from Graham (Groza kick)
CLE-Speedie 6-yd. pass from Graham (Groza kick)
CLE-D. Jones 3-yd. run (Groza kick)
CLE-Bumgardner 1-yd. run (Groza kick)
CHI-Paul 35-yd. pass from Trippi (Patton kick)
CHI-Stonesifer 9-yd. pass from Trippi (Patton kick)
CHI-Angsman 1-yd. run (Patton kick)
CHI-Stonesifer 4-yd. pass from Trippi (Patton kick)
CLE-Graham 2-yd. fumble return (Groza kick)

Passing
CHI: Trippi 11–28–147 3 TD 1 INT, Hardy 8–17–97 0 TD 2 INT
CLE: Graham 14–29–217 4 TD 3 INT

Rushing
CHI: Trippi 4–50, Pasquariello 8–48, Cross 4–43, Hardy 3–35, Angsman 8-(-2), Sitko 2-(-18)
CLE: D. Jones 8–31, K. Carpenter 4–22, Cole 3–19, Motley 4–13, Taseff 2–3, Bumgardner 6–2, Lewis 2-(-11)

Receiving
CHI: Paul 2–68, Polsfoot 4–49, Ramsey 3–42, Stonesifer 4–40, Cross 2–33, Sitko 2–13, Angsman 1–3, Pasquariello 1-(-4)
CLE: Lavelli 5–78, Speedie 4–73, Motley 3–39, D. Jones 2–27

Sunday, December 9
Browns 28, Pittsburgh Steelers 0
Forbes Field (24,229)
White jerseys/white pants

The Browns goose-egged the Steelers for the second time on the season and collected their fourth shutout of 1951 to notch their 10th straight win and clinch the American Conference crown. After a night of rain, a slippery field didn't slow the Browns in a three-touchdown second quarter. Meanwhile, the Cleveland defense held the Steelers to just over 200 yards of offense and forced five turnovers, giving them 13 in their past two games. They put the icing on the cake in the fourth quarter when Parma native and John Carroll grad Carl Taseff scored his first professional touchdown on a three-yard run.
Record: 10–1

	1	2	3	4		
Browns	0	21	0	7	=	28
Steelers	0	0	0	0	=	0

CLE-K. Carpenter 24-yd. run (Groza kick)
CLE-Motley 8-yd. run (Groza kick)
CLE-Lavelli 7-yd. pass from Graham (Groza kick)
CLE-Taseff 3-yd. run (Groza kick)

Passing
CLE: Graham 12–18–128 1 TD 0 INT
PIT: Ortmann 13–27–136 0 TD 2 INT, Chandnois 3–5–44 0 TD 0 INT

Rushing
CLE: K. Carpenter 12–56, Motley 8–37, D. Jones 10–31, Bumgardner 2–17, Cole 5–13, Taseff 2–6
PIT: Ortmann 11–66, Rogel 9–24, Chandnois 4–3, Nuzum 3-(-2)

Receiving
CLE: Speedie 4–78, Lavelli 4–46, Cole 2–7, D. Jones 1–7, K. Carpenter 1-(-10)
PIT: Nickel 6–80, Minarik 7–77, Smith 1–16, Chandnois 2–7

Sunday, December 16
Browns 24, Philadelphia Eagles 9
Shibe Park (16,263)
Brown jerseys/white pants

Wrapping up a nearly perfect regular season, the Browns skated to their eleventh straight victory on a frozen field in bitter-cold conditions. The Cleveland defense was magnificent, collecting 10 sacks while holding the Eagles to just 73 total yards and nine first downs. With essentially nothing to play for, the offense looked unprepared and sloppy, but Otto Graham threw a pair of scores, and Carl Taseff scored his second (and last) Browns touchdown to build a 17–0 lead in the third quarter. After the game, the Browns returned to the warmth of their hotel and listened to a pair of late games on the radio that determined their opponent in the NFL title game the following week. With a Rams' victory over Green Bay and San Francisco's rally past Detroit, the Browns would travel to Los Angeles for a rematch with the Rams seven days later.
Record: 11–1

	1	2	3	4		
Browns	7	3	7	7	=	24
Eagles	0	0	2	7	=	9

CLE-Lavelli 12-yd. pass from Graham (Groza kick)
CLE-Groza 21-yd. FG
CLE-Taseff 1-yd. run (Groza kick)
PHI-Safety: Stickel tackled Graham in end zone
CLE-Bumgardner 18-yd. pass from Graham (Groza kick)
PHI-Walston 11-yd. pass from Burk (Walston kick)

Passing
CLE: Graham 11–27–160 2 TD 0 INT, Lewis 1–2–19 0 TD 1 INT
PHI: Burk 8–22–88 1 TD 0 INT, Rauch 1–2–8 0 TD 0 INT

Rushing
CLE: Taseff 7–32, Jagade 5–30, Motley 7–13, Bumgardner 2–10, K. Carpenter 5–6, D. Jones 4–3, Graham 1–1, Lewis 1–1
PHI: Parmer 7–28, Ziegler 14–24, Pollard 3–19, S. Van Buren 2–6, Scott 3-(-2), Burk 1-(-10)

Receiving
CLE: Speedie 4–73, Bumgardner 2–37, Lavelli 2–24, K. Carpenter 2–21, Taseff 1–18, Motley 1–6
PHI: Walston 6–67, Armstrong 1–13, Parmer 1–8, Pollard 1–8

1951 NFL Championship
Sunday, December 23
Los Angeles Rams 24, Browns 17
Los Angeles Memorial Coliseum (57,540)
White jerseys/white pants

For the first time in seven years, the city of Cleveland didn't celebrate a pro football championship as the Browns couldn't hang on to a narrow halftime lead and lost the NFL title game on a long touchdown in the fourth quarter on a bright, sunny day in southern California.

Favored by six-and-a-half points after knocking off the Rams in the 1950 title game and then again decisively in Week Two, the Browns may have been affected by a shortened week of practice brought on by an East Coast blizzard that hindered their travel plans. The team's equipment, flown separately, was delayed, and the team was unable to practice for several days.

Perhaps as a result, the Browns played below the level they'd established during their 11-game winning streak, struggling to establish their powerful running game while coughing up four turnovers to give Los Angeles control of the game in the second half. On the strength of a Dub Jones touchdown and an NFL postseason record 52-yard field goal by Lou Groza, the Browns took a 10–7 lead into the third quarter, but, aided by an Otto Graham fumble, the Rams bounced back to take a touchdown lead early in the fourth.

After a long Mac Speedie touchdown catch was wiped out on a holding penalty, the Cleveland defense kept the Rams out of the end zone on two separate series at the Browns' 1, and LA settled for a field goal on the second trip. A short Ken Carpenter scoring run tied the game at 17 midway through the final period, but the Rams answered moments later when WR Tom Fears got behind Browns' DB Tommy James to catch a long third-down pass from Norm Van Brocklin at midfield, then raced into the end zone for the go-ahead touchdown with eight minutes remaining.

Otto Graham, who would toss for 280 yards on the day, threw his third interception on the Browns' next offensive play, but Cleveland stayed alive when Bill Willis blocked a Los Angeles field goal with five minutes showing. Two minutes later, the Browns faced fourth-and-two at the Rams' 43, but Jones was caught for a two-yard loss and the Rams regained possession. They held the ball until just 10 seconds remained, and a pair of desperate Cleveland passes went for naught, giving the city of Los Angeles its first NFL title. It also marked the first time the Browns had ever ended their season with a defeat.

	1	2	3	4		
Browns	0	10	0	7	=	17
Rams	0	7	7	10	=	24

LA-Hoerner 1-yd. run (Waterfield kick)
CLE-Groza 52-yd. FG
CLE-D. Jones 17-yd. pass from Graham (Groza kick)
LA-Towler 1-yd. run (Waterfield kick)
LA-Waterfield 17-yd. FG
CLE-K. Carpenter 2-yd. run (Groza kick)
LA-Fears 73-yd. pass from Van Brocklin (Waterfield kick)

Passing
CLE: Graham 19–40–280 1 TD 3 INT, K. Carpenter 0–1–0 0 TD 0 INT
LA: Van Brocklin 4–6–128 1 TD 0 INT, Waterfield 9–24–125 0 TD 2 INT

Rushing
CLE: Graham 5–43, Motley 5–23, K. Carpenter 4–14, D. Jones 9–12
LA: Towler 16–36, Younger 4–20, Smith 9–15, Waterfield 2–8, Hoerner 5–5, Van Brocklin 1–3, Davis 6-(-6)

Receiving
CLE: Speedie 7–81, Lavelli 4–65, D. Jones 4–62, K. Carpenter 3–49, Motley 1–23
LA: Fears 4–146, Hirsch 4–66, Smith 1–18, Hoerner 1–13, Davis 3–10

1952

Sunday, September 28
Browns 37, Los Angeles Rams 7
Cleveland Stadium (57,832)
White jerseys/white pants

Providing instant payback following their tough loss in the title game the previous year, the Browns kicked off the season by throttling the defending NFL champions in a much-anticipated rematch in sun-splashed Cleveland. The Rams looked shell-shocked from the outset as the Browns took a 7–0 lead on a 41-yard pass from QB Otto Graham—now wearing No. 14 instead of No. 60—to RB Ken Carpenter three minutes into the game and led 23–0 at the half, earning a standing ovation from their fans as they returned to the locker room. Carpenter nearly outgained the Los Angeles offense by himself, rolling up 145 yards on 16 carries, while the Rams were limited to just 158 yards of total offense—less than half the Browns' total of 419. The high-flying quarterback combo of Bob Waterfield and Norm Van Brocklin was held to six completions in 27 pass attempts with three interceptions. The loss was so devastating for the Rams they replaced head coach Joe Stydahar two days later.

Record: 1–0

	1	2	3	4		
Rams	0	0	0	7	=	7
Browns	10	13	7	7	=	37

CLE-K. Carpenter 41-yd. pass from Graham (Groza kick)
CLE-Groza 27-yd. FG
CLE-D. Jones 3-yd. run (Groza kick)
CLE-Groza 14-yd. FG
CLE-Groza 14-yd. FG
CLE-Howard 13-yd. pass from Graham (Groza kick)
LA-Towler 15-yd. run (Waterfield kick)
CLE-Motley 16-yd. run (Groza kick)

Passing
LA: Van Brocklin 3–17–40 0 TD 2 INT, Waterfield 3–10–26 0 TD 1 INT
CLE: Graham 10–16–138 2 TD 1 INT

Rushing
LA: Towler 11–64, Smith 4–21, Quinlan 3–9, Myers 2–8, Younger 2-(-2)
CLE: K. Carpenter 16–145, Motley 10–69, D. Jones 7–53, Graham 4–10, Howard 5–8, Renfro 3–4, Ratterman 1–2

Receiving
LA: Fears 2–42, Towler 2–23, Myers 1–3, Younger 1-(-2)
CLE: K. Carpenter 3–54, D. Jones 1–38, Speedie 4–32, Howard 1–13, Motley 1–1

Saturday, October 4
Browns 21, Pittsburgh Steelers 20
Forbes Field (27,923)
Brown jerseys/white pants

The Browns overcame a handful of early mistakes and rallied from 13 points down in the third quarter to upend the opportunistic Steelers in a Saturday-night showdown. The difference in the game actually occurred in the first quarter when the Steelers' point-after attempt following their first touchdown was blocked, a mistake that haunted them in the final minutes. Pittsburgh took advantage of a handful of Cleveland mistakes, including the Browns' inability to score after having a first-and-goal at the Steeler 2 in the second quarter and a trio of interceptions thrown by Otto Graham from deep in his own territory that led to all three Pittsburgh touchdowns. But Graham, who would throw for 401 yards on the night, was effective down the stretch, hitting RB Dub Jones for a 17-yard scoring strike, then Sherman Howard for a 57-yard touchdown on the next series to give the Browns the winning points. The Browns then controlled the ball for much of the final period, with the defense twice stopping the Steelers near midfield in the final minutes.

Record: 2–0

	1	2	3	4		
Browns	7	0	14	0	=	21
Steelers	6	7	7	0	=	20

PIT-Nickel 10-yd. pass from Finks (kick failed)
CLE-Motley 68-yd. pass from Graham (Groza kick)
PIT-Nickel 30-yd. pass from Finks (Kerkorian kick)
PIT-Finks 1-yd. run (Kerkorian kick)
CLE-D. Jones 17-yd. pass from Graham (Groza kick)
CLE-Howard 57-yd. pass from Graham (Groza kick)

Passing
CLE: Graham 21–49–401 0 TD 4 INT
PIT: Finks 11–32–203 2 TD 0 INT, Kerkorian 1–2–7 0 TD 0 INT

Rushing
CLE: Motley 11–49, Howard 8–10, D. Jones 5–3, Graham 3–2
PIT: Rogel 11–46, Modzelewski 17–33, Calvin 1–8, Finks 2–4

Receiving
CLE: Speedie 5–99, D. Jones 4–98, Motley 5–93, Howard 5–86, Gillom 2–25
PIT: Mathews 4–92, Nickel 4–65, Hensley 2–23, Modzelewski 1–23, Rogel 1–7

Sunday, October 12
New York Giants 17, Browns 9
Cleveland Stadium (51,858)
White jerseys/white pants

For the third time in their six meetings, the Giants held the Browns without a touchdown and forced enough mistakes to pull out a key victory that pushed New York into sole possession of first place in the American Conference. With Dub Jones ineffective after pulling a muscle during warm-ups, the Browns' running game was impotent, held to 21 yards on 23 carries. Consequently, Cleveland was held to what would be a season-low 211 total yards. Still, the Browns hung close and, after a stunning 70-yard Charlie Conerly touchdown pass, gave the Giants the lead with less than a minute to play in the half, three Lou Groza field goals—including a 52-yarder into the wind—gave Cleveland a 9–7 lead midway through the third quarter. Otto Graham tallied 236 yards through the air—161 of which went to WR Mac Speedie on eight catches—but completed only 14 of 35 attempts as his receivers dropped a handful of passes, including a pair of would-be touchdowns. After the Giants crept to a 10–9 advantage early in the fourth quarter, Graham tossed the game-clinching interception to Giants' DB Tom Landry, who returned it 30 yards for a touchdown.
Record: 2–1

	1	2	3	4		
Giants	0	7	0	10	=	17
Browns	0	3	6	0	=	9

CLE-Groza 30-yd. FG
NY-Wilkinson 70-yd. pass from Conerly (Poole kick)
CLE-Groza 52-yd. FG
CLE-Groza 21-yd. FG
NY-Poole 25-yd. FG
NY-Landry 30-yd. interception return (Poole kick)

Passing
NYG: Conerly 4–9–101 1 TD 2 INT
CLE: Graham 14–34–236 0 TD 1 INT, Motley 0–1–0 0 TD 0 INT

Rushing
NYG: Price 19–67, Rote 9–62, Conerly 5–48, Gifford 8–27, Wilkinson 6–1, Scott 1-(-4)
CLE: Howard 5–7, D. Jones 7–6, Graham 1–5, Motley 10–3

Receiving
NYG: Wilkinson 1–70, Stribling 1–21, Coulter 1–9, Price 1–1
CLE: Speedie 8–161, Motley 1–42, Howard 1–13, D. Jones 3–11, Gillom 1–9

Sunday, October 19
Browns 49, Philadelphia Eagles 7
Shibe Park (27,874)
Brown jerseys/white pants

The Browns rebounded from a disappointing performance the previous week to crush the Eagles on the strength of an unstoppable offensive attack. Rolling up more than 500 yards of offense, including 290 through the air from Otto Graham along with four touchdown passes, the Browns romped to a 21–0 halftime lead, then put the nail in the coffin with three more touchdowns in the third quarter. With Dub Jones back, the Browns' running attack returned to form with 234 yards on the ground. The tone was set midway through the first quarter when DE Len Ford recovered an Eagle fumble in the end zone, and the Cleveland defense would limit an opponent to less than 200 yards for the third time in four games. Adding to the celebration in the Cleveland locker room was the news that the Giants had been upset at home by the Chicago Cardinals, pulling the Browns into a first-place tie atop the conference.
Record: 3–1

	1	2	3	4		
Browns	14	7	21	7	=	49
Eagles	0	0	0	7	=	7

CLE-Ford recovered fumble in end zone (Groza kick)
CLE-Brewster 47-yd. pass from Graham (Groza kick)
CLE-Howard 35-yd. pass from Graham (Groza kick)
CLE-D. Jones 63-yd. pass from Graham (Groza kick)
CLE-Speedie 8-yd. pass from Graham (Groza kick)
CLE-D. Jones 16-yd. run (Groza kick)
CLE-Gillom 11-yd. pass from Ratterman (Groza kick)
PHI-Goldston 4-yd. run (Walston kick)

Passing
CLE: Graham 18–30–290 4 TD 2 INT, Ratterman 1–1–11 1 TD 0 INT
PHI: Thomason 8–18–124 0 TD 0 INT, Enke 4–17–36 0 TD, 1 INT Burk 1–6–9 0 TD 1 INT

Rushing
CLE: Jagade 11–98, Howard 11–46, Motley 14–43, D. Jones 4–37, Bumgardner 4–12, Graham 2-(-2)
PHI: Stevens 1–36, Goldston 5–28, Brewer 4–5, Burk 1–1, Ziegler 1-(-5), Huzvar 4-(-9), Pollard 5-(-11)

Receiving
CLE: D. Jones 6–121, Brewster 3–80, Speedie 5–48, Howard 2–38, Gillom 1–11, Motley 2–3
PHI: Grant 6–82, Walston 3–44, Ziegler 1–37, Van Buren 1–9, Brewer 1-(-1), Huzvar 1-(-2)

Sunday, October 26
Browns 19, Washington Redskins 15
Cleveland Stadium (32,496)
White jerseys/white pants

On a warm, crisp October Sunday on the lake, the Browns avoided a crushing upset with a second-half rally against a determined Redskins squad. A pair of short touchdown runs by Chuck Drazenovich gave Washington a 13–6 lead at the half as the Browns' offense, fresh off a dominating performance in Philadelphia the week before, now struggled to move the football. Lou Groza's third and fourth field goals of the game narrowed the lead to one point in the fourth quarter, then a key 57-yard pass from Otto Graham to RB Sherman Howard put the Browns at the Redskins' 2, where Graham snuck over the goal line to put the Browns ahead with four minutes left. But Washington threatened to take the lead back on its next possession, driving deep into Cleveland territory before Ray Renfro recovered a fumble at the 18 with two minutes left. Rather than punt from their end zone against a Washington rush that had been ferocious all afternoon, the Browns took an intentional safety to round out the scoring in the final moments. And with the Giants falling to the Eagles, the Browns took over sole possession of first in the conference.

Record: 4–1

	1	2	3	4		
Redskins	0	13	0	2	=	15
Browns	3	3	3	10	=	19

CLE-Groza 24-yd. FG
WAS-Drazenovich 2-yd. run (kick failed)
CLE-Groza 29-yd. FG
WAS-Drazenovich 2-yd. run (LeBaron kick)
CLE-Groza 27-yd. FG
CLE-Groza 35-yd. FG
CLE-Graham 1-yd. run (Groza kick)
WAS-Safety: Berrang tackled Graham in end zone

Passing
WAS: LeBaron 7–17–123 0 TD 0 INT, Gilmer 3–4–41 0 TD 0 INT
CLE: Graham 11–29–190 0 TD 1 INT, D. Jones 0–1–0 0 TD 0 INT

Rushing
WAS: Gilmer 11–76, Heath 11–43, Papit 6–38, Rykovich 5–27, Justice 4–23, LeBaron 6–6, Cox 2–5, Drazenovich 3–2
CLE: Motley 8–44, Howard 5–24, D. Jones 7–13, Bumgardner 2–4, Graham 3-(-1)

Receiving
WAS: Rykovich 2–56, Brito 3–48, Heath 2–33, Justice 1–15, Cox 1–6, Gilmer 1–6
CLE: Speedie 4–80, Howard 2–69, D. Jones 3–32, Motley 2–9

Sunday, November 2
Detroit Lions 17, Browns 6
Briggs Stadium (56,029)
White jerseys/white pants

Meeting for the first time ever and establishing a fierce rivalry that would define professional football over the remainder of the decade, the Browns and Lions fought bitterly through a defensive slugfest. For the third time in four weeks, the Cleveland offense struggled to ignite and failed to tally points despite a handful of opportunities. With Otto Graham and Detroit QB Bobby Layne combining to throw six interceptions, the defenses controlled the tempo, particularly Detroit's, which held the Browns to just 214 yards. Still, the Browns trailed just 10–6 and had driven into Detroit territory with five minutes to play before a Graham pass down the middle was picked off. The Lions took over near midfield and, after a backbreaking 41-yard run by RB Bob Hoernschemeyer, put the game away on a short Layne scoring toss. The loss, combined with a New York win over the Cardinals, dropped the Browns back into a first-place tie with the Giants.

Record: 4–2

	1	2	3	4		
Browns	3	0	3	0	=	6
Lions	0	10	0	7	=	17

CLE-Groza 12-yd. FG
DET-Hart 7-yd. pass from Layne (Harder kick)
DET-Harder 43-yd. FG
CLE-Groza 41-yd. FG
DET-Hart 10-yd. pass from Layne (Harder kick)

Passing
CLE: Graham 13–32–165 0 TD 3 INT
DET: Layne 15–32–193 2 TD 3 INT, Girard 0–2–0 0 TD 0 INT

Rushing
CLE: Motley 9–44, K. Carpenter 5–39, Renfro 2–12, Graham 3–7, Jagade 1–3, D. Jones 6–2
DET: Hoernschemeyer 11–80, Layne 12–26, Girard 9–20, Harden 4–11, Cline 1–6, Hart 1-(-1)

Receiving
CLE: D. Jones 3–67, Speedie 5–40, Jagade 2–36, K. Carpenter 3–22
DET: Hart 8–99, Girard 5–62, Box 1–40, Hoernschemeyer 1-(-8)

Sunday, November 9
Browns 28, Chicago Cardinals 13
Cleveland Stadium (34,097)
White jerseys/white pants

The Browns returned to form with another lopsided victory over an outmatched opponent as Cleveland racked up more than twice as much yardage as Chicago despite an impressive Cardinals' running game. In the early going it appeared the offensive struggles of recent weeks would continue when the Browns were stopped just short of a first down on a fourth-down play from the Chicago 3, and the Cardinals parlayed their newfound momentum into a 6–0 lead. But the Browns' air attack was too much to handle. RB Marion Motley turned a screen pass into a 52-yard score to give the Browns a lead they would not relinquish. With the Cardinals hanging around, trailing by just one point at the half, Graham caught fire in the third quarter, completing eight straight passes, including a 43-yard scoring toss to Mac Speedie, who snagged 11 receptions on the day for 157 yards.

Record: 5–2

	1	2	3	4		
Cardinals	6	7	0	0	=	13
Browns	7	7	14	0	=	28

CHI-Trippi 2-yd. run (kick failed)
CLE-Motley 52-yd. pass from Graham (Groza kick)
CLE-K. Carpenter 4-yd. run (Groza kick)
CHI-Matson 17-yd. run (Geri kick)
CLE-Speedie 43-yd. pass from Graham (Groza kick)
CLE-K. Carpenter 1-yd. run (Groza kick)

Passing
CHI: Trippi 5–12–47 0 TD 0 INT, Panciera 0–8–0 0 TD 1 INT
CLE: Graham 18–24–249 2 TD 0 INT, Ratterman 1–4–9 0 TD 1 INT

Rushing
CHI: Matson 10–63, Fischer 1–59, Trippi 7–38, Cross 7–28, Angsman 5–27, Sitko 6–22, Pasquariello 2–2
CLE: Motley 13–94, K. Carpenter 13–37, Bumgardner 1–24, D. Jones 4–21, Jagade 3–14, Renfro 1-(-1), Graham 3-(-5)

Receiving
CHI: Stonesifer 4–36, Cross 1–11
CLE: Speedie 11–157, Motley 1–52, K. Carpenter 3–22, D. Jones 3–18, Lavelli 1–9

Sunday, November 16
Browns 29, Pittsburgh Steelers 28
Cleveland Stadium (34,973)
White jerseys/white pants

Just as they did six weeks before in Pittsburgh, the Browns held off the Steelers and hung on for a hard-fought one-point victory. Though they'd had to rally from a double-digit deficit to win in Pittsburgh, the second time around they surged to a 22–0 lead early in the third quarter, then survived a scoring onslaught by the Steelers as QB Jim

Finks tossed four touchdown passes. Also as in the first meeting, the difference came early, this time in the form of a Browns' safety when DEs George Young and Len Ford pinned Finks in the Pittsburgh end zone for the two points that would put the Browns over the top by the end of the afternoon. The Browns were dominant in the first half, not allowing a Steeler first down until the final two minutes of the second period, while a pair of 22-yard touchdown catches by Dante Lavelli—returning to action after missing four games to injury—provided the cushion. After the Steelers cut the margin to eight points late in the third, Cleveland's Rex Bumgardner intercepted Finks to set up the Browns' final touchdown, a two-yard Graham rush. After another quick Steeler touchdown, DB Warren Lahr ended Pittsburgh's comeback attempt with an interception at midfield with three minutes left. The Steelers added their final touchdown with 20 seconds remaining. The victory proved even more fruitful as the Giants fell to Green Bay, propelling the Browns once again into sole possession of first place in the American Conference.

Record: 6–2

	1	2	3	4		
Steelers	0	0	14	14	=	28
Browns	9	6	7	7	=	29

CLE-Lavelli 22-yd. pass from Graham (Groza kick)
CLE-Safety: Young tackled Finks in end zone
CLE-Groza 11-yd. FG
CLE-Groza 34-yd. FG
CLE-Lavelli 22-yd. pass from Graham (Groza kick)
PIT-Mathews 33-yd. pass from Finks (Kerkorian kick)
PIT-Butler 7-yd. pass from Finks (Kerkorian kick)
CLE-Graham 2-yd. run (Groza kick)
PIT-Mathews 38-yd. pass from Finks (Kerkorian kick)
PIT-Nickel 9-yd. pass from Finks (Kerkorian kick)

Passing
PIT: Finks 19–44–306 4 TD 2 INT, Mathews 2–4–74 0 TD 0 INT
CLE: Graham 21–40–239 2 TD 2 INT, Motley 0–1–0 0 TD 0 INT

Rushing
PIT: Chandnois 3–32, Mathews 5–9, Finks 2–5, Rogel 6–4
CLE: Motley 16–72, D. Jones 9–66, K. Carpenter 13–34, Graham 3–31, Renfro 2-(-2)

Receiving
PIT: Mathews 5–126, Nickel 9–120, Sulima 3–79, Chandnois 2–25, Spinks 1–23, Butler 1–7
CLE: Lavelli 6–107, D. Jones 7–62, Speedie 4–43, K. Carpenter 3–14, Motley 1–13

Sunday, November 23
Philadelphia Eagles 28, Browns 20
Cleveland Stadium (28,948)
White jerseys/white pants

Just when the Browns appeared ready to a coast to a third straight title-game appearance, they were tripped up by a rapidly improving Eagles team that won for the fourth time in five weeks after losing to the Browns by six touchdowns in Philadelphia in mid-October. The Eagles set the tone early, taking a 14–0 lead in the first eight minutes, but the Browns gradually chipped away and took a six-point advantage into the fourth quarter. But the Eagles, who did not commit a penalty in the game, pulled away in the final stanza with a pair of short touchdown runs by RB Ralph Goldston, championing a potent running attack that tallied 176 yards against the previously stalwart Cleveland defense. Mac Speedie paced the Browns' offense with 156 receiving yards. Following the Eagles' first-ever victory over Cleveland, Philadelphia, the Giants, and the Browns were now all tied atop the conference. And with the Browns set to close the season with three consecutive road games, including the finale in New York, their chances for the conference crown looked bleak.

Record: 6–3

	1	2	3	4		
Eagles	14	0	0	14	=	28
Browns	7	3	10	0	=	20

PHI-Ziegler 3-yd. run (Watson kick)
PHI-Walston 3-yd. pass from Thomason (Walston kick)
CLE-Speedie 28-yd. pass from Graham (Groza kick)
CLE-Groza 18-yd. FG
CLE-Speedie 48-yd. pass from Graham (Groza kick)
CLE-Groza 19-yd. FG
PHI-Goldston 2-yd. run (Walston kick)
PHI-Goldston 2-yd. run (Walston kick)

Passing
PHI: Thomason 7–18–109 1 TD 2 INT, Enke 2–5–80 0 TD 1 INT
CLE: Graham 14–36–227 2 TD 2 INT

Rushing
PHI: Goldston 13–55, Ziegler 15–47, Huzvar 7–23, Pollard 9–22, Stevens 4–10, Brewer 3–10, Enke 2–10,

Thomason 3–6, Burk 1-(-7)
CLE: K. Carpenter 9–78, Motley 7–8, D. Jones 1-(-1), Graham 1-(-3)

Receiving
PHI: Walston 4–121, Grant 3–54, Pollard 2–14
CLE: Speedie 7–156, D. Jones 3–53, Lavelli 2–17, K. Carpenter 2–1

Sunday, November 30
Browns 48, Washington Redskins 24
Griffith Stadium (22,679)
White jerseys/white pants

After a wobbly start reminiscent of the teams' first meeting in Cleveland, the Browns dominated the Redskins over the final three quarters and surged back into sole possession of first as the Eagles were defeated by the Cardinals, and the Giants were annihilated in Pittsburgh. It looked as though the Browns' fate would sway the same direction in the first five minutes as Washington sprinted to a 14–0 lead, then led 17–7 early in the second. But sparked by RB Chick Jagade, who scored Cleveland's first touchdown and rushed for 147 yards on just 16 carries, the Browns racked up 255 yards on the ground and took a lead into halftime. They then pulled away in the third quarter, highlighted by a 54-yard punt return for a touchdown by Ken Carpenter, who enjoyed a marvelous day returning kicks. Though the Browns continued to be mistake-prone, committing six turnovers and 12 penalties, they cruised to a much-needed victory.
Record: 7–3

	1	2	3	4		
Browns	7	14	13	14	=	48
Redskins	14	3	0	7	=	24

WAS-Taylor 30-yd. pass from LeBaron (Buksar kick)
WAS-Gilmer 7-yd. pass from LeBaron (Buksar kick)
CLE-Jagade 17-yd. run (Groza kick)
WAS-Buksar 17-yd. FG
CLE-Speedie 23-yd. pass from Graham (Groza kick)
CLE-Graham 1-yd. run (Groza kick)
CLE-D. Jones 39-yd. pass from Graham (Groza kick)
CLE-K. Carpenter 54-yd. punt return (run failed)
WAS-Heath 19-yd. pass from LeBaron (Buksar kick)
CLE-Lavelli 3-yd. pass from D. Jones (Groza kick)
CLE-Graham 2-yd. run (Groza kick)

Passing
CLE: Graham 9–20–195 2 TD 3 INT, D. Jones 1–1–3 1 TD 0 INT, Ratterman 0–1–0 0 TD 1 INT
WAS: LeBaron 11–16–116 3 TD 1 INT, Gilmer 4–17–48 0 TD 1 INT

Rushing
CLE: Jagade 16–147, Graham 9–61, K. Carpenter 7–23, Motley 3–21, D. Jones 2–5, Bumgardner 2-(-2)
WAS: Gilmer 13–27, Rykovich 6–12, Heath 5–12, LeBaron 3–10, Papit 2–7, Cloud 2–7

Receiving
CLE: Lavelli 5–106, D. Jones 3–59, Speedie 2–33
WAS: Heath 4–47, Taylor 2–41, Drazenovich 1–18, Justice 2–17, Williams 1–13, Cox 1–13, Gilmer 2–9, Brito 1–6, Rykovich 1–0

Sunday, December 7
Browns 10, Chicago Cardinals 0
Comiskey Park (24,541)
White jerseys/white pants

Two weeks after being considered a long shot for the conference title, the Browns secured at least a tie for the crown on a sunny and unseasonably warm Sunday afternoon in Comiskey Park with a shutout win over the Cardinals. Leading the way was the Cleveland defense, which limited Chicago to just 150 yards of total offense and forced five turnovers to offset a half-dozen by the Browns themselves on a muddy, sloppy field. Cleveland took command early when Otto Graham hit Dub Jones on a 56-yard touchdown pass on the fourth play of the game, which turned out to be the only score of the first half. A Walt Michaels interception midway through the third period set up a short Lou Groza field goal to cushion the lead. With the Giants losing to Washington and the Eagles defeating the Dallas Texans, the race now came down to the Browns and Eagles. The Browns would have two chances to win the conference outright: by beating the Giants in New York in the regular-season finale or by the Redskins pulling off a second straight upset over the Eagles.
Record: 8–3

	1	2	3	4		
Browns	7	0	3	0	=	10
Cardinals	0	0	0	0	=	0

CLE-D. Jones 56-yd. pass from Graham (Groza kick)
CLE-Groza 12-yd. FG

Passing
CLE: Graham 14–22–207 1 TD 2 INT
CHI: Trippi 9–16–49 0 TD 2 INT, Panciera 5–15–71 0 TD 2 INT

Rushing
CLE: Jagade 13–59, D. Jones 11–43, K. Carpenter 5–32, Graham 3–26, Motley 3-(-3)
CHI: Cross 3–15, Sitko 3–14, Pasquariello 4–10, Geri 3–6, Angsman 2–5, Matson 4–2, Karras 8–1, Trippi 1–1, Panciera 1-(-2)

Receiving
CLE: D. Jones 6–82, Jagade 3–64, Lavelli 4–54, Speedie 1–7
CHI: Stonesifer 7–56, Karras 2–31, Matson 1–19, Cross 4–14

Sunday, December 14
New York Giants 37, Browns 34
Polo Grounds (41,610)
White jerseys/white pants

It was an exciting, impressive battle between two of football's titans that turned out to mean essentially nothing. Once again prone to mistakes, the Browns saw a fourth-quarter rally fall short along with their effort to clinch the American Conference crown on their own, but thanks to the Washington Redskins' stunning fourth-quarter comeback win over the Philadelphia Eagles, the Browns took the title anyway. With both offenses firing on all cylinders, the Browns and Giants were tied at 20 midway through the third quarter, but then the Browns' mistakes began to catch up with them. Three Otto Graham interceptions led to 17 New York points and a blocked Cleveland punt gift-wrapped another Giant touchdown early in the third quarter. The Giants took a 34–20 advantage into the fourth quarter, and after the Browns sliced it to seven with 11 minutes to play on a long scoring pass from Graham to Chick Jagade (who took a lateral from Mac Speedie after Speedie caught an eight-yard pass), Browns' nemesis Tom Landry picked off a Graham pass to set up what proved to be the winning points on a short field goal to make it 37–27, and the Browns ran out of time. While the Browns' offense was hot, its inability to hold onto the football put pressure on the defense, which allowed the Giants to score more points than any team had against the Browns in their three seasons in the NFL.
Record: 8–4

	1	2	3	4		
Browns	7	6	7	14	=	34
Giants	7	6	21	3	=	37

CLE-Jagade 11-yd. run (Groza kick)
NY-Stribling 17-yd. pass from Conerly (Poole kick)
CLE-Groza 42-yd. FG
CLE-Groza 35-yd. FG
NY-Scott 1-yd. run (kick failed)
NY-Rote 16-yd. pass from Conerly (Poole kick)
CLE-Lavelli 15-yd. pass from Graham (Gain kick)
NY-Scott 31-yd. pass from Conerly (Poole kick)
NY-Wilkinson 22-yd. pass from Conerly (Poole kick)
CLE-Jagade 47-yd. lateral from Speedie, 8-yd. pass from Graham (Gain kick)
NY-Poole 15-yd. FG
CLE-K. Carpenter 5-yd. run (Gain kick)

Passing
CLE: Graham 18–32–279 1 TD 3 INT
NYG: Conerly 16–26–154 4 TD 0 INT, Rote 1–1–41 0 TD 0 INT

Rushing
CLE: Jagade 13–52, D. Jones 2–28, K. Carpenter 4–20, Renfro 2–13, Graham 7-(-1)
NYG: Scott 11–32, Rote 13–31, Amberg 1–3, Conerly 5–9, Wilkinson 2-(-2), Thomas 1-(-3)

Receiving
CLE: Jagade 4–103, Speedie 6–55, Lavelli 3–43, Brewster 1–37, K. Carpenter 2–23, D. Jones 1–10, Renfro 1–8
NYG: Rote 7–73, Scott 3–47, McChesney 1–41, Amberg 2–26, Wilkinson 1–22, Stribling 2–21, Hudson 1-(-5)

1952 NFL Championship
Sunday, December 28
Detroit Lions 17, Browns 7
Cleveland Stadium (50,934)
White jerseys/white pants

It had been a wild, unpredictable season that seemed to demand a wild, unpredictable finish. The Browns had swayed between dominant and disappointing all year, losing four games in 1952 after losing only three in 1950 and 1951 combined. And while their 8–4 record wouldn't have been good enough to secure even a second-place finish in the conference in either of the two previous years, it was enough to win it outright in 1952, thanks to the equally surprising bouts of schizophrenia by the powerful Giants and upstart Eagles.

Appropriately, after such a confusing season, things were not settled by the conclusion of play on the final Sunday. In the National Conference, the Detroit Lions and Los Angeles Rams were tied for first with identical 9–3 records and, by rule, had to square off in a one-game playoff for the conference crown even though the Lions had defeated the Rams both times they'd met in the regular season. On the Sunday before Christmas, the Lions made it a clean sweep, beating the Rams 31–21 to earn their first trip to the NFL Championship since 1935.

Eager to redeem themselves for their disappointing loss in the previous year's title game, as well as their lethargic performance in a loss to Detroit in October, the Browns had plenty of motivation and this time would have the home-field advantage as 50,934 filed into Cleveland Stadium on December 28. Yet for all this, the Browns instead packed the erratic nature of the entire season into their final 60 minutes of football.

Even without Dub Jones, sidelined with the ankle injury that knocked him out of the regular-season finale, they had no trouble moving the ball on offense but struggled to score points. They committed two costly turnovers and a handful of critical penalties. The tone was set on the Browns' opening drive when they marched to the Detroit 18, but came away with nothing when Lou Groza missed a short field goal.

After a scoreless first quarter, the Lions took possession at midfield following a meager 22-yard punt by the Browns' Horace Gillom and drew first blood on a two-yard scoring run by Bobby Layne. Mirroring the defensive flavor of their October clash, the score remained 7–0 until halftime. Midway through the third period, Detroit RB Doak Walker broke free on a run off right tackle and scored after a 67-yard scamper to give the Lions a 14–0 advantage.

With the contest beginning to slip away, the Browns suddenly began to dominate the game on both sides of the ball. Over the next 15 minutes of play, Cleveland held possession of the football for all but five plays. And yet when the stretch was over, the home team still trailed.

They answered Detroit's second score with an 11-play, 67-yard drive capped by a seven-yard touchdown run by Chick Jagade, who would tally 104 rushing yards on the day. The Cleveland defense quickly forced a Detroit punt, and the offense picked up where it left off, driving from its own 17 to the Detroit 5 following a 42-yard run by Marion Motley. With just under 10 minutes to play, the Browns were poised to tie the contest. Instead, they stumbled backward to the Detroit 22, and when an Otto Graham pass on fourth down fell incomplete, they still trailed 14–7.

Still, they had one final chance. The defense forced another Detroit punt, but Ken Carpenter fumbled the return, and the Lions recovered at the Browns' 23. Pat Harder kicked a 36-yard field goal moments later to put the game out of reach. Symbolically, a final harried Browns drive ended just short of the Detroit goal line as time expired.

Though they'd accumulated nearly 130 more yards of offense and twice as many first downs while running twice as many plays, the Browns had been beaten by the Lions for the second time in 1952, and they'd now squandered a chance to capture an NFL title for the second straight year.

Little did the Browns know that their frustrations with their Lake Erie neighbors were just beginning.

	1	2	3	4		
Lions	0	7	7	3	=	17
Browns	0	0	7	0	=	7

DET-Layne 2-yd. run (Harder kick)
DET-Walker 67-yd. run (Harder kick)
CLE-Jagade 7-yd. run (Groza kick)
DET-Harder 36-yd. FG

Rushing
DET: Walker 10–97, Layne 9–47, Harder 8–28, Hoernschemeyer 7–27
CLE: Jagade 15–104, Motley 6–74, Graham 7–23, Renfro 3–13, K. Carpenter 3–13

Passing
DET: Layne 7–9–68 0 TD 0 INT, Walker 0–1–0 0 TD 0 INT
CLE: Graham 20–35–191 0 TD 1 INT, Motley 0–1–0 0 TD 0 INT

Receiving
DET: Harder 2–18, Walker 2–11 Hart 1–15, Swiacki 1–14, Box 1–10
CLE: Brewster 2–53, Bumgardner 4–43, Lavelli 4–33, Renfro 4–26, Motley 3–21, K. Carpenter 2–7, Gillom 1–8

1953

Sunday, September 27

Browns 27, Green Bay Packers 0
Milwaukee County Stadium (22,604)
White jerseys/white pants

Setting the tone for a magnificent regular season, the Browns opened the campaign with a dominating victory over the Packers, posting their first opening-day shutout since their inaugural game seven years before. QB Otto Graham played brilliantly, completing 18 of 24 passes for 292 yards while rushing for two touchdowns in the first half as the Browns built a 17–0 lead at the intermission. Using a two-platoon halfback system, the Browns alternated between Dub Jones, Ken Carpenter, Billy Reynolds, and Ray Renfro in the backfield, and the quartet combined to catch 12 passes for 222 yards. A 41-yard screen pass to Jones set up Graham's first touchdown four minutes into the contest, then a 55-yard completion to Reynolds led to the first of Lou Groza's two field goals. After holding the Packers to just 148 total yards for the game, the Cleveland defense saved the shutout in the final minutes when LB Tommy Thompson reeled in an interception after Green Bay drove to the Cleveland 11.

Record: 1–0

	1	2	3	4		
Browns	7	10	10	0	=	27
Packers	0	0	0	0	=	0

CLE-Graham 1-yd. run (Groza kick)
CLE-Graham 15-yd. FG
CLE-Graham 1-yd. run (Groza kick)
CLE-Groza 29-yd. FG
CLE-K. Carpenter 5-yd. run (Groza kick)

Passing
CLE: Graham 18–24–292 0 TD 1 INT, Ratterman 2–2–12 0 TD 0 INT
GB: Rote 4–15–55 0 TD 2 INT, Parilli 4–12–11 0 TD 1 INT

Rushing
CLE: Motley 7–34, Renfro 6–27, K. Carpenter 6–22, Jagade 5–11, Graham 3–4, Reynolds 3–3, D. Jones 2–5
GB: Cone 6–35, Ferguson 8–20, Carmichael 3–15, Parilli 6–11, Rote 3–11, Coutre 1–4, Reid 2–8, Boone 2–11

Receiving
CLE: Renfro 6–97, D. Jones 2–61, Reynolds 1–55, Lavelli 4–45, Brewster 2–25, Gillom 1–11, K. Carpenter 3–9, Motley 1–1
GB: Reid 2–26, Mann 2–22, Ferguson 2–6, Elliott 1–7, Boone 1–5

Sunday, October 4

Browns 27, Chicago Cardinals 7
Comiskey Park (24,734)
White jerseys/white pants

For the second straight week, a potent air attack and a sterling defensive effort led to an easy Browns' victory. Cleveland took control early when WR Dante Lavelli made a diving catch of a long Otto Graham pass at the Chicago 15, then got up and ran into the end zone to complete a 55-yard touchdown two minutes into the contest. After another Browns' score, Chicago cut the margin to 14–7 before Graham threw two more touchdowns to open up a 20-point lead. The Cardinals had one final chance to get back into the game early in the third quarter, but were stuffed on fourth-and-goal at the Cleveland 2. While the Browns' defense forced five turnovers and recorded four sacks, Graham threw for 310 yards on just 15 completions, four of which went to Lavelli for 137 yards and two scores.

Record: 2–0

	1	2	3	4		
Browns	14	6	0	7	=	27
Cardinals	7	0	0	0	=	7

CLE-Lavelli 55-yd. pass from Graham (Groza kick)
CLE-Jagade 3-yd. run (Groza kick)
CHI-Trippi 11-yd. pass from Root (Summerall kick)
CLE-Renfro 48-yd. pass from Graham (kick failed)
CLE-Lavelli 34-yd. pass from Graham (Groza kick)

Passing
CLE: Graham 15–22–310 3 TD 0 INT
CHI: Root 11–25–113 1 TD 2 INT, Nagel 5–16–44 0 TD 2 INT, Trippi 0–1–0 0 TD 0 INT

Rushing
CLE: Jagade 15–30, Motley 1–14, K. Carpenter 2–12, Reynolds 1–12, Howard 4–5, Graham 1–5, Graham 1–5, Renfro 3-(2), D. Jones 4-(-5)
CHI: Olszewski 15–74, Trippi 4–22, Paul 3–9, Nagel 1–6

Receiving
CLE: Lavelli 4–137, Renfro 3–71, Jagade 2–40, D. Jones 3–35, Brewster 2–27
CHI: Stonesifer 7–71, Nagler 5–66, Paul 2–16, Ramsey 1–4, Olszewski 1–0

Saturday, October 10
Browns 37, Philadelphia Eagles 13
Cleveland Stadium (45,802)
Orange jerseys/white pants

In their home opener on a Saturday night, the Browns—wearing orange jerseys for the first time—rolled up and down the Cleveland Stadium turf, scoring the game's final 17 points to run away with a third straight easy victory. Compiling 416 total yards, the Browns were led by Otto Graham, who turned in another sterling performance with 328 passing yards, including six receptions by WR Pete Brewster for 122 yards. After the Eagles scored to knot the game at six late in the first quarter, the Browns roared back with a pair of touchdowns, including a dazzling one-handed catch for a score by Dante Lavelli. After the Eagles cut the margin to 20–13, RB Chick Jagade scored his second touchdown of the day and Lou Groza tacked on his third field goal. Cleveland then rounded out the scoring in the fourth quarter when 290-pound DT Jerry Helluin returned a fumble 42 yards for a touchdown. While the Browns allowed the Eagles to compile more than 400 yards themselves, they forced five turnovers and racked up seven sacks.
Record: 3–0

	1	2	3	4		
Eagles	6	0	7	0	=	13
Browns	6	14	7	10	=	37

CLE-Groza 20-yd. FG
CLE-Groza 16-yd. FG
PHI-Ziegler 1-yd. run (kick failed)
CLE-Jagade 14-yd. run (Groza kick)
CLE-Lavelli 25-yd. pass from Graham (Groza kick)
PHI-Burk 32-yd. run (Walston kick)
CLE-Jagade 13-yd. run (Groza kick)
CLE-Groza 27-yd. FG
CLE-Helluin 42-yd. fumble return (Groza kick)

Passing
PHI: Burk 14–34–269 0 TD 2 INT, Thomason 1–2–22 0 TD 1 INT, Ziegler 0–1–0 0 TD 0 INT
CLE: Graham 20–30–328 1 TD 0 INT, Ratterman 1–1–15 0 TD 0 INT

Rushing
PHI: Ziegler 9–49, Johnson 12–46, Williams 1–40, Burk 1–32, Brewer 6–11, Pollard 3–9
CLE: Jagade 8–61, K. Carpenter 3–36, D. Jones 1–10, Graham 2–8, Motley 4–5, Renfro 3–5

Receiving
PHI: Walston 4–110, Pihos 4–64, Williams 2–63, Brewer 3–27, Ziegler 2–27
CLE: Brewster 6–122, Lavelli 4–99, Gillom 2–39, Renfro 4–37, D. Jones 2–25, Motley 1–15, Reynolds 1–7, Jagade 1–1

Sunday, October 18
Browns 30, Washington Redskins 14
Griffith Stadium (33,963)
White jerseys/white pants

Trailing early in the fourth quarter, the Browns exploded for 17 points in the final minutes to cruise to another double-digit victory. After the Redskins went ahead 14–13 on an interception return for a touchdown, the Browns responded with a 25-yard scoring reception by Dante Lavelli on their next possession, then turned two Washington fumbles into scores to put the game away. The red-hot Cleveland offense once again topped 400 total yards, with Ray Renfro going over 100 yards on the ground on just seven carries.
Record: 4–0

	1	2	3	4		
Browns	3	10	0	17	=	30
Redskins	0	7	0	7	=	14

CLE-Groza 9-yd. FG
WAS-Taylor 61-yd. pass from Scarbath (Dudley kick)
CLE-Groza 29-yd. FG
CLE-Graham 1-yd. run (Groza kick)
WAS-Cloud 28-yd. interception return (Dudley kick)
CLE-Lavelli 25-yd. pass from Graham (Groza kick)
CLE-Reynolds 9-yd. run (Groza kick)
CLE-Groza 23-yd. FG

Passing
CLE: Graham 16–32–235 1 TD 1 INT, D. Jones 0–1–0 0 TD 0 INT
WAS: Scarbath 5–18–105 1 TD 0 INT, LeBaron 0–3–0 0 TD 1 INT

Rushing
CLE: Renfro 7–101, Graham 5–34, Reynolds 5–31, Jagade 8–21, K. Carpenter 3–6, D. Jones 4–4
WAS: Justice 13–79, Heath 8–32, Barry 3–22, Drazenovich 6–18, Dowda 1–3, Scarbath 1–3, LeBaron 2–2

Receiving
CLE: Lavelli 4–97, Jagade 5–52, Renfro 3–44, Brewster 2–31, D. Jones 1–10, Reynolds 1–1
WAS: Taylor 2–78, Heath 2–18, Dekker 1–9

Sunday, October 25
Browns 7, New York Giants 0
Polo Grounds (30,773)
White jerseys/white pants

Playing through a heavy rain and ankle-deep mud, the Browns endured in a defensive struggle to pick up their second shutout of the season. The defining moment came in the second quarter when the Browns lined up for a field goal and drew the Giants offside to pick up a first down, then moments later scored the game's lone touchdown on a four-yard scamper by Otto Graham. The Cleveland defense took it from there, not allowing the Giants to cross midfield until the fourth quarter. When they finally did, twice marching to the Cleveland 30, the Browns halted them with an interception by DB Ken Gorgal and then a fumble recovery by DE Len Ford. The Browns' defense held the Giants to just 133 total yards and eight first downs, while the offense struggled to just 178, with Graham completing only two passes on the day.
Record: 5–0

	1	2	3	4		
Browns	0	7	0	0	=	7
Giants	0	0	0	0	=	0

CLE-Graham 4-yd. run (Groza kick)

Passing
CLE: Graham 2–5–25 0 TD 1 INT
NYG: Conerly 9–19–95 0 TD 3 INT

NO SCORES AND LOW SCORES

In four memorable games in Browns' history, the Browns and their opponent combined for only one score:

October 12, 1946	vs. Brooklyn Dodgers	W 7–0
October 1, 1950	vs. NY Giants	L 0–6
October 25, 1953	at NY Giants	W 7–0
December 1, 1974	vs. San Francisco 49ers	W 7–0

On 15 occasions, the Browns have been involved in a game in which no touchdowns were scored:

December 17, 1950	vs. NY Giants	W 8–3*
November 21, 1954	vs. Philadelphia Eagles	W 6–0
September 29, 1957	vs. NY Giants	W 6–3
December 12, 1970	vs. Dallas Cowboys	L 2–6
September 13, 1981	vs. Houston Oilers	L 3–9
October 21, 1984	at Cincinnati Bengals	L 9–12
September 4, 1988	at Kansas City Chiefs	W 6–3
September 27, 1992	vs. Denver Broncos	L 0–12
October 1, 2000	vs. Baltimore Ravens	L 0–12
September 9, 2001	vs. Seattle Seahawks	L 6–9
September 7, 2003	vs. Indianapolis Colts	L 6–9
October 26, 2003	at New England Patriots	L 3–9
December 16, 2007	vs. Buffalo Bills	W 8–0
October 11, 2009	at Buffalo Bills	W 6–3
October 23, 2011	vs. Seattle Seahawks	W 6–3

*American Conference Playoff

Rushing
CLE: Reynolds 18–74, K. Carpenter 14–55, Graham 10–41, Jagade 3–5, Motley 3-(-6)
NYG: Grandelius 11–36, Conerly 1–24, Price 6–7, Clay 2–1, Rote 1-(-1)

Receiving
CLE: Lavelli 2–25
NYG: Rote 3–38, Pelfrey 2–37, Stribling 1–19, Avinger 1–4, Clay 1-(-1), Grandelius 1-(-2)

Sunday, November 1
Browns 27, Washington Redskins 3
Cleveland Stadium (47,845)
White jerseys/white pants

On the strength of a trio of second-half touchdowns, the Browns blew open a close game to win their sixth straight and take a three-game lead in the Eastern Conference. After taking a 6–3 lead at the half, Otto Graham rushed for a pair of short touchdowns, the second set up by a punt blocked by lineman Don Steinbrunner. Billy Reynolds then added another score in the waning minutes, capping a marvelous performance by the Browns' running game, which tallied 190 yards. DB Tommy James sparked the defense with three interceptions, all deep in Cleveland territory, as the Browns held an opponent without a touchdown for the third time in six games.

Record: 6–0

	1	2	3	4		
Redskins	0	3	0	0	=	3
Browns	3	3	7	14	=	27

CLE-Groza 42-yd. FG
WAS-Dudley 17-yd. FG
CLE-Groza 15-yd. FG
CLE-Graham 1-yd. run (Groza kick)
CLE-Graham 2-yd. run (Groza kick)
CLE-Reynolds 14-yd. run (Groza kick)

Passing
WAS: LeBaron 14–35–233 0 TD 4 INT
CLE: Graham 13–19–194 0 TD 1 INT, Ratterman 1–2–0 0 TD 0 INT, Renfro 0–1–0 0 TD 0 INT

Rushing
WAS: Barry 3–27, Justice 10–26, LeBaron 2–26, Rykovich 6–12, Heath 4–1, Baker 2–1
CLE: Reynolds 12–68, Howard 3–37, Motley 3–36, Renfro 8–29, Jagade 5–17, K. Carpenter 3–6, Graham 3–4, D. Jones 2–0, Gibron 1-(-7)

Receiving
WAS: Taylor 4–87, Justice 3–63, Rykovich 2–42, Dekker 3–30, Barry 2–11
CLE: D. Jones 3–84, Lavelli 3–48, Renfro 2–26, Brewster 1–20, K. Carpenter 1–11, Jagade 1–4, Reynolds 2–1, Gillom 1–0

Sunday, November 8
Browns 34, Pittsburgh Steelers 16
Cleveland Stadium (35,592)
White jerseys/white pants

After fumbling the opening kickoff and spotting the Steelers a 9–0 lead, the Browns erupted for 24 points in the second quarter to surge ahead, then pocketed their seventh straight victory with 10 more points in the fourth on the strength of another dazzling offensive performance. The key moment came in the final seconds of the half when the Steelers lined up for a go-ahead field goal. The Browns' Ray Renfro blocked the kick and returned it 79 yards for a touchdown to put Cleveland up 24–16 and break Pittsburgh's momentum. It was Renfro's second score of the day, coming after he'd broken around left end for a 44-yard score minutes earlier. The Cleveland defense held the Steelers scoreless in the second half while the offense rolled up 422 total yards, including more than 200 on the ground.

Record: 7–0

	1	2	3	4		
Steelers	9	7	0	0	=	16
Browns	0	24	0	10	=	34

PIT-Bolkovac 27-yd. FG
PIT-Mathews 2-yd. run (kick failed)
CLE-K. Carpenter 7-yd. run (Groza kick)
CLE-Groza 20-yd. FG
CLE-Renfro 44-yd. run (Groza kick)
PIT-Mathews 77-yd. pass from Finks (Bolkovac kick)
CLE-Renfro 79-yd. blocked field-goal return (Groza kick)
CLE-Lavelli 17-yd. pass from Graham (Groza kick)
CLE-Groza 14-yd. FG

Passing
PIT: Finks 17–45–219 1 TD 2 INT, Rogel 0–1–0 0 TD 0 INT
CLE: Graham 12–18–218 1 TD 2 INT

Rushing
PIT: Chandnois 11–73, Rogel 16–48, Mathews 8–29, Brandt 13–11, Finks 1-(-14)
CLE: Renfro 9–67, Jagade 7–53, Motley 3–39, K. Carpenter 4–17, Reynolds 5–15, D. Jones 2–9, Graham 3–4

Receiving
PIT: Mathews 4–113, Nickel 6–68, Chandnois 7–38
CLE: Jagade 2–51, D. Jones 2–38, Renfro 3–35, Lavelli 3–32, K. Carpenter 1–32, Brewster 1–30

Sunday, November 15
Browns 23, San Francisco 49ers 21
Cleveland Stadium (80,698)
White jerseys/white pants

In an entertaining, back-and-forth game reminiscent of their memorable AAFC battles, the Browns and 49ers renewed their rivalry and thrilled a colossal crowd on the lakefront. The most memorable moment of the game came in the second quarter, when San Francisco lineman Art Michalik landed an elbow in the face of Otto Graham, which forced the quarterback out of the game to receive 15 stitches in his mouth. But Graham returned in the second half "wearing a plastic protective apparatus on his helmet," as the *Plain Dealer* described what became the league's first facemask. The patched-up Graham completed nine of 10 passes in the second half and helped the Browns take a 20–7 lead. But after the 49ers cut the margin back to six points with six minutes to play, the Browns fumbled the ensuing kickoff, and San Francisco recovered at the Cleveland 25. The Browns' defense stiffened, and Len Ford sacked QB Y. A. Tittle on fourth-and-five to give the ball back to the Browns, who put the game away with a Lou Groza field goal with under four minutes to play. Michalik's hit created a testy atmosphere as the Browns were penalized 15 times for 124 yards, somewhat softening their 457-yard offensive outburst. Dante Lavelli once again led the way, catching six passes for 137 yards.

Record: 8–0

	1	2	3	4		
49ers	0	7	0	14	=	21
Browns	7	3	3	10	=	23

CLE-Reynolds 5-yd. run (Groza kick)
CLE-Groza 26-yd. FG
SF-McElhenny 6-yd. run (Soltau kick)
CLE-Groza 11-yd. FG
CLE-Renfro 34-yd. pass from Graham (Groza kick)
SF-McElhenny 31-yd. pass from Tittle (Soltau kick)
CLE-Groza 28-yd. FG
SF-Tittle 7-yd. run (Soltau kick)

Passing
SF: Tittle 17–27–214 1 TD 0 INT
CLE: Graham 17–24–286 1 TD 0 INT, Ratterman 0–3–0 0 TD 0 INT

Rushing
SF: McElhenny 10–83, Perry 13–38, Tittle 1–7, Arenas 3–6
CLE: Reynolds 11–66, Jagade 11–45, Graham 3–30, D. Jones 3–16, Renfro 8–9, K. Carpenter 3–4, Motley 3–4, Ratterman 1–3

Receiving
SF: Wilson 5–62, Soltau 3–48, McElhenny 2–37, Schabarum 2–34, Perry 4–33, Arenas 1–0
CLE: Lavelli 6–137, Renfro 4–91, Reynolds 2–42, D. Jones 2–11, Jagade 1–5, Brewster 1–0, Motley 1–0

Sunday, November 22
Browns 20, Pittsburgh Steelers 16
Forbes Field (32,904)
White jerseys/white pants

With the Cleveland offense muddling through a rare sub-par performance, the defense carried the Browns to their ninth straight win, coming from behind and then holding off the Steelers in the fourth quarter. After Pittsburgh took a 9–7 lead when Browns' DB Warren Lahr was driven into the end zone and tackled after making an interception, the Browns bounced back with 13 straight points to take a 20–9 advantage into the fourth. Pittsburgh cut the margin to four points, then drove to the Cleveland 43 on its next possession but failed to convert on a key fourth-down pass and gave the ball back to the Browns. Cleveland drove to the Pittsburgh 1, and though the Browns were stopped on fourth down, the Steelers were unable to dig out of the hole, and the Browns escaped with a tough victory. Though the Steelers rushed for 216 yards, they were limited to nine completions in 24 pass attempts and coughed up three turnovers.

Record: 9–0

	1	2	3	4		
Browns	7	10	3	0	=	20
Steelers	9	0	0	7	=	16

CLE-Renfro 54-yd. pass from Graham (Groza kick)
PIT-Finks 1-yd. run (Bolkovac kick)
PIT-Safety: Lahr tackled in end zone by Mathews
CLE-Groza 50-yd. FG
CLE-Brewster 31-yd. pass from Graham (Groza kick)
CLE-Groza 41-yd. FG
PIT-Mathews 1-yd. run (Bolkovac kick)

Passing
CLE: Graham 16–28–200 2 TD 1 INT, Renfro 0–1–0 0 TD 0 INT
PIT: Finks 9–20–72 0 TD 2 INT, Mackrides 0–3–0 0 TD 0 INT, Chandnois 0–1–0 0 TD 0 INT

Rushing
CLE: Reynolds 5–25, Jagade 3–17, K. Carpenter 2–11, Renfro 3–7, Graham 4–6, D. Jones 6-(-6)
PIT: Mathews 11–79, Rogel 14–73, Chandnois 17–60, Finks 2–3, Mackrides 1–1

Receiving
CLE: Renfro 5–65, Lavelli 5–49, Brewster 2–45, D. Jones 2–35, Jagade 2–6
PIT: Nickel 3–46, Butler 1–10, Chandnois 3–9, Mathews 2–7

Sunday, November 29
Browns 27, Chicago Cardinals 16
Cleveland Stadium (24,499)
White jerseys/white pants

Scoring 17 points in the final 11 minutes, the Browns overcame a surprisingly impressive performance by the winless Cardinals to move to 10–0 and clinch their eighth straight championship-game appearance. Trailing 14–10 early in the fourth quarter, the Browns turned things around after a missed Chicago field goal with a 70-yard pass from Otto Graham to Ray Renfro that set up a Lou Groza field goal. Moments later, Renfro broke free for an 18-yard scoring run to give the Browns the lead. After taking an intentional safety with a minute remaining, the Browns capped the scoring when DB Tommy James returned a fumble 37 yards for a touchdown in the final seconds.

Record: 10–0

	1	2	3	4		
Cardinals	0	0	14	2	=	16
Browns	0	10	0	17	=	27

CLE-Jagade 16-yd. run (Groza kick)
CLE-Groza 37-yd. FG
CHI-Nagler 5-yd. pass from Root (Summerall kick)
CHI-Root 1-yd. run (Summerall kick)
CLE-Groza 30-yd. FG
CLE-Renfro 18-yd. run (Groza kick)
CHI-Safety: Schmidt tackled Graham in end zone
CLE-James 37-yd. fumble return (Groza kick)

Passing
CHI: Root 13–31–227 1 TD 0 INT, Trippi 2–5–21 0 TD 0 INT
CLE: Graham 19–28–276 0 TD 0 INT

Rushing
CHI: Cross 2–81, Trippi 13–39, Olszewski 8–19, Paul 2–5, Root 5-(-11)
CLE: Jagade 12–57, Reynolds 5–20, K. Carpenter 2–19, Renfro 4–9, Graham 6–7, D. Jones 1–3

Receiving
CHI: Olszewski 1–77, Cross 3–56, Nagler 4–46, Stonesifer 4–39, Trippi 2–26, Paul 1–4
CLE: Renfro 4–105, Jagade 6–36, Brewster 3–47, D. Jones 2–40, Lavelli 3–36, K. Carpenter 1–12

Sunday, December 6
Browns 62, New York Giants 14
Cleveland Stadium (40,235)
White jerseys/white pants

In their home finale, the Browns put on an offensive display against the rival Giants, setting a team record for scoring that has never been topped in their years in the NFL. Rolling to nearly 500 total yards, the Browns scored 31 points in each half, with their delighted fans chanting for more. Making the performance even more amazing, Otto Graham didn't start and played only part of the third quarter. Backup George Ratterman had an amazing game, throwing for three touchdowns. Two of them went to Pete Brewster, who was equally impressive, collecting 182 yards on seven catches and a third score on a halfback-option pass by Ray Renfro. The defense also got into the act, forcing four turnovers, including a 34-yard interception return for a score by LB Walt Michaels. Additionally, with his twentieth and twenty-first field goals of the season, Lou Groza set a new NFL single-season record. With their eleventh straight victory, the Browns tied their own team record for victories in a season in their NFL era set two years before.

Record: 11–0

	1	2	3	4		
Giants	0	7	7	0	=	14
Browns	10	21	24	7	=	62

CLE-Groza 30-yd. FG
CLE-Brewster 22-yd. pass from Ratterman (Groza kick)
NYG-Long 22-yd. pass from Conerly (Clay kick)
CLE-Renfro 58-yd. run (Groza kick)
CLE-Brewster 23-yd. pass from Ratterman (Groza kick)
CLE-Brewster 36-yd. pass from Renfro (Groza kick)
NYG-Gifford 13-yd. pass from Conerly (Clay kick)
CLE-K. Carpenter 2-yd. run (Groza kick)
CLE-Renfro 60-yd. pass from Graham (Groza kick)
CLE-Groza 18-yd. FG
CLE-Michaels 34-yd. interception return (Groza kick)
CLE-K. Carpenter 22-yd. pass from Ratterman (Groza kick)

Passing
NYG: Conerly 15–39–213 2 TD 3 INT, Gifford 1–1–16 0 TD 0 INT
CLE: Ratterman 15–27–237 3 TD 0 INT, Graham 4–4–116 1 TD 0 INT, Renfro 1–1–36 1 TD 0 INT

Rushing
NYG: Price 9–25, Grandelius 3–17, Long 8–16, Gifford 5–14, Conerly 1–2
CLE: Renfro 4–66, Motley 6–25, Jagade 2–6, K. Carpenter 3–3, Ratterman 1–3, D. Jones 5–2, Graham 1–2, Reynolds 7-(-1)

Receiving
NYG: Long 5–118, Gifford 3–32, Anderson 2–30, Grandelius 3–26, Stribling 2–21, Pelfrey 1–2
CLE: Brewster 7–182, Renfro 2–71, Gillom 3–52, Lavelli 2–25, K. Carpenter 1–22, D. Jones 2–18, Motley 2–10, Reynolds 1–9

Sunday, December 13
Philadelphia Eagles 42, Browns 27
Connie Mack Stadium (38,654)
White jerseys/white pants

Allowing more points than they had in a single game in five years, the Browns saw their hopes for a perfect regular season go up in smoke in Philadelphia. The Eagles' offense, shut out in Washington the week before, was dominant, picking up 459 total yards and 31 first downs, taking command after the Browns took a 10–0 lead into the second quarter. The turning point came midway through the third quarter when, with the Browns trailing 21–20, the Eagles recovered an Otto Graham fumble and cashed it in for the second of four touchdowns on consecutive possessions. The Browns closed the regular season with an 11–1 record, tying their franchise-best mark in their NFL era two years before.
Record: 11–1

	1	2	3	4		
Browns	10	3	7	7	=	27
Eagles	0	14	14	14	=	42

CLE-Renfro 11-yd. run (Groza kick)
CLE-Groza 19-yd. FG
PHI-Pihos 15-yd. pass from Thomason (Walston kick)
PHI-Thomason 1-yd. run (Walston kick)
CLE-Groza 24-yd. FG
CLE-K. Carpenter 8-yd. pass from Graham (Groza kick)
PHI-Ledbetter 14-yd. pass from Thomason (Walston kick)
PHI-Johnson 2-yd. run (Walston kick)
PHI-Ledbetter 3-yd. run (Walston kick)
PHI-Walston 17-yd. pass from Thomason (Walston kick)
CLE-Lavelli 17-yd. pass from Ratterman (Groza kick)

Passing
CLE: Graham 15–24–241 1 TD 2 INT, Ratterman 4–6–61 1 TD 0 INT
PHI: Thomason 23–35–331 3 TD 0 INT

Rushing
CLE: Renfro 5–34, Jagade 7–21, Motley 2–10, K. Carpenter 1–4, D. Jones 1–0, Graham 2-(-2)
PHI: Johnson 18–81, Williams 5–28, Ledbetter 5–14, Thomason 5–9, Ziegler 1–6, Giancanelli 3–4, Parmer 1–2, Pollard 1–2

Receiving
CLE: Brewster 5–103, Renfro 3–80, Lavelli 5–52, K. Carpenter 2–23, Motley 1–23, D. Jones 2–16, Reynolds 1–5
PHI: Pihos 5–80, Johnson 4–75, Giancanelli 3–45, Williams 3–34, Parmer 3–29, Pollard 2–27, Walston 2–27, Ledbetter 1–14

1953 NFL Championship
Sunday, December 27
Detroit Lions 17, Browns 16
Briggs Stadium (54,577)
White jerseys/white pants

In one of the most frustrating defeats in team history, the Browns saved their worst performance of the season for their biggest game as they managed just 191 yards of offense and coughed up four turnovers as they lost the NFL title game for the third straight season.

On a bright winter afternoon, the tone was set four minutes into the contest when Otto Graham lost a fumble that led to Detroit's first touchdown, beginning a miserable performance for the star quarterback. Graham would complete just two of 15 passes on the day while throwing a pair of interceptions and at one point was replaced by backup George Ratterman.

Despite Graham's struggles—and a dropped touchdown pass by Dante Lavelli as he slipped on the muddy turf beneath the goalposts late in the first quarter—the Browns endured. Len Ford recovered a fumble at the Detroit 6 to set up a Lou Groza field goal early in the second quarter. Then, paced by the hard running of RB Chick Jagade—who rushed for 102 yards—the Browns scored their lone touchdown on a Jagade run following a Ken Gorgal interception on the third play of the second half. It began a string of 13 straight Cleveland points that gave the Browns a 16–10 advantage with 4:10 remaining. But with the title on the line, the Lions responded with an 80-yard drive, capped by a 33-yard scoring pass from QB Bobby

Layne to Jim Doran with 2:08 left. Ironically, it was the only score of the year for Doran, usually a defensive player filling in as a wideout only because of a series of Detroit injuries.

Graham's woeful day was capped on the Browns' next offensive play as he threw his second interception, helping the Lions run out the clock and secure their second straight NFL title.

	1	2	3	4		
Browns	0	3	7	6	=	16
Lions	7	3	0	7	=	17

DET-Walker 1-yd. run (Walker kick)
CLE-Groza 13-yd. FG
DET-Walker 23-yd. FG
CLE-Jagade 9-yd. run (Groza kick)
CLE-Groza 15-yd. FG
CLE-Groza 43-yd. FG
DET-Doran 33-yd. pass from Layne (Walker kick)

Passing
CLE: Graham 2–15–20 0 TD 2 INT, Ratterman 1–1–18 0 TD 0 INT
DET: Layne 12–25–179 1 TD 2 INT

Rushing
CLE: Jagade 15–102, D. Jones 3–28, Reynolds 6–17, K. Carpenter 3–15, Renfro 4–11, Graham 5–9
DET: Hoernschemeyer 17–51, Layne 9–44, Gedman 8–29, Walker 3–5

Receiving
CLE: Jagade 1–18, Lavelli 1–13, Reynolds 1–7
DET: Doran 4–95, Box 4–54, Dibble 1–22, Walker 1–10, Hoernschemeyer 2-(-2)

1954

Sunday, September 26
Philadelphia Eagles 28, Browns 10
Connie Mack Stadium (26,546)
White jerseys/white pants

Losing a season opener for just the second time in their history, the Browns were dominated by Philadelphia in a performance that suggested their championship-caliber run may have come to an end. After the Eagles dominated the first half, holding the Browns to just one first down, Cleveland clawed to within four points on a touchdown catch by WR Dante Lavelli and a field goal set up by a fumble recovered by DE Len Ford. But the Eagles were simply too much, outgaining the Browns in total yardage 397 to 142 while collecting four sacks and four turnovers.
Record: 0–1

	1	2	3	4		
Browns	0	0	10	0	=	10
Eagles	0	14	7	7	=	28

PHI-Walston 10-yd. pass from Thomason (Walston kick)
PHI-Williams 18-yd. pass from Thomason (Walston kick)
CLE-Lavelli 16-yd. pass from Graham (Groza kick)
CLE-Groza 11-yd. FG
PHI-Giancanelli 16-yd. pass from Burk (Walston kick)
PHI-Pihos 9-yd. pass from Burk (Walston kick)

Passing
CLE: Graham 9–23–130 1 TD 1 INT
PHI: Thomason 7–12–130 2 TD1 INT, Burk 12–18–93 2 TD 0 INT

Rushing
CLE: Bassett 3–22, Graham 3–9, Reynolds 3–7, Morrison 4–5, Renfro 4–5, D. Jones 2-(-1)
PHI: Parmer 17–80, Williams 8–53, Thomason 5–25, Ledbetter 5–20, Burk 4–6, Giancanelli 5–5, Moselle 2–4, Johnson 1-(-11)

Receiving
CLE: Brewster 2–44, Lavelli 2–36, Morrison 2–21, Renfro 1–18, D. Jones 1–11, Bassett 1–0
PHI: Pihos 6–86, Williams 5–83, Moselle 2–29, Giancanelli 1–16, Walston 2–14, Parmer 3-(-5)

Sunday, October 10
Browns 31, Chicago Cardinals 7
Cleveland Stadium (24,101)
White jerseys/white pants

After a Week Two matchup with the defending NFL champion Detroit Lions was rescheduled to the end of the season due to the Indians needing Cleveland Stadium for the World Series (though they were swept and the conflicting Game Five was never played), the Browns notched their first victory on a rainy afternoon in a blowout over the Cardinals. QB Otto Graham connected on his first nine passes, totaling 208 yards, and threw for three touchdowns as the Browns—20-point favorites—scored touchdowns on their first four possessions. They soared to a 31–0 halftime lead and never looked back, defeating the Cardinals for the ninth straight time. The Cleveland offense rolled to 431 total yards, including 346 passing by Graham and Ratterman combined, while the teams combined for more than 200 yards in penalties.
Record: 1–1

	1	2	3	4		
Cardinals	0	0	0	7	=	7
Browns	14	17	0	0	=	31

CLE-Brewster 23-yd. pass from Graham (Groza kick)
CLE-Brewster 10-yd. pass from Graham (Groza kick)
CLE-Renfro 64-yd. pass from Graham (Groza kick)
CLE-Bassett 14-yd. run (Groza kick)
CLE-Groza 41-yd. FG
CHI-Goble 8-yd. run (Summerall kick)

Passing
CHI: McHan 13–27–183 0 TD 2 INT, Romanik 0–3–0 0 TD 0 INT
CLE: Graham 14–18–266 3 TD 0 INT, Ratterman 5–9–80 0 TD 1 INT

Rushing
CHI: King 8–38, Olszewski 6–19, Goble 2–12, McHan 4–10, Trippi 3–4, Matson 3-(-5)
CLE: Morrison 7–53, Bassett 8–34, Hanulak 3–11, Renfro 2–11, Ratterman 2–9, Graham 1–6, Reynolds 7–4

THE TOP 10 GAMES OF OTTO GRAHAM'S NFL CAREER

(Based on Highest Passer Rating Minimum 15 Attempts)

10. November 27, 1955 at NY Giants (Browns tie, 35–35)
17 of 31 for 319 yards, 3 TD 1 INT
109.5 rating

9. October 10, 1953 vs. Philadelphia (Browns win, 37–13)
20 of 30 for 328 yards, 1 TD 0 INT
114.3 rating

8. November 4, 1951 at Chicago Cardinals (Browns win, 34–17)
15 of 21 for 210 yards, 1 TD 0 INT
119.2 rating

7. November 25, 1951 vs. Chicago Bears (Browns win, 42–21)
12 of 19 for 277 yards, 2 TD 1 INT
120 rating

6. December 24, 1950 vs. LA Rams (Browns win, 30–28)**
22 of 33 for 298 yards, 4 TD 1 INT
122.2 rating

5. December 10, 1950 at Washington (Browns win, 45–21)
23 of 32 for 321 yards, 4 TD 1 INT
130.34 rating

4. November 9, 1952 vs. Chicago Cardinals (Browns win, 28–13)
18 of 24 for 249 yards, 2 TD 0 INT
135.6 rating

3. October 9, 1955 vs. Philadelphia (Browns win, 21–17)
16 of 21 for 223 yards, 2 TD 0 INT
141.6 rating

2. October 4, 1953 at Chicago Cardinals (Browns win, 27–7)
15 of 22 for 310 yards 3 TD 0 INT
150.6 rating

1. October 10, 1954 vs. Chicago (Browns win, 31–7)
14 of 18 for 266 yards, 3 TD 0 INT
158.3* rating

*Perfect rating
**NFL Championship Game

Receiving
CHI: Matson 3–83, Stonesifer 4–43, Olszewski 2–21, Crittendon 1–15, King 1–12, Trippi 1–5, Ladd 1–4
CLE: Lavelli 6–88, Renfro 2–73, Brewster 4–59, D. Jones 2–49, Bassett 2–41, Gillom 2–18, Reynolds 1–18

Sunday, October 17
Pittsburgh Steelers 55, Browns 27
Forbes Field (33,262)
White jerseys/white pants

Thanks to a disastrous second quarter that saw Pittsburgh score four touchdowns, the Browns were crushed for the second time in three games, losing to the Steelers for the first time in their history. Cleveland held a 14–7 lead at the end of the first quarter, but Pittsburgh caught fire in the second period with 27 points to take a commanding halftime lead. The Steelers forced eight turnovers, including a pair of interceptions returned for touchdowns as Otto Graham was picked off five times. Steeler WR Ray Mathews had a career day with four touchdowns and 152 receiving yards as the Steelers rolled to 441 total yards, the most the Browns would allow all season. The Cleveland offense nearly matched Pittsburgh with 436 yards, but the giveaways proved too much for the Browns to overcome as they fell below the .500 mark once again.

Record: 1–2

	1	2	3	4		
Browns	14	6	0	7	=	27
Steelers	7	27	14	7	=	55

CLE-Reynolds 5-yd. run (Groza kick)
PIT-Mathews 7-yd. pass from Finks (Held kick)
CLE-D. Jones 37-yd. pass from Graham (Groza kick)
PIT-Rogel 14-yd. pass from Finks (kick failed)
PIT-Butler 41-yd. interception return (Held kick)
PIT-Lattner 12-yd. run (Held kick)
CLE-Lavelli 29-yd. pass from Graham (kick failed)
PIT-Mathews 78-yd. pass from Finks (Held kick)
PIT-Mathews 8-yd. pass from Finks (Held kick)
PIT-Mathews 3-yd. run (Held kick)
CLE-Lavelli 24-yd. pass from Graham (Groza kick)
PIT-Craft 81-yd. interception return (Held kick)

Passing
CLE: Graham 22–28–298 3 TD 5 INT, Renfro 0–1–0 0 TD 1 INT

PIT: Finks 11–15–239 4 TD 1 INT, Chandnois 1–1–13 0 TD 0 INT, Held 1–1–5 0 TD 0 INT

Rushing
CLE: Bassett 10–78, Renfro 8–53, Reynolds 5–24, Graham 2–11, Morrison 2–1
PIT: Mathews 11–83, Rogel 12–45, Lattner 7–19, Chandnois 5–14, Finks 4–10, Brandt 2–10, Elter 1–3

Receiving
CLE: Lavelli 7–134, D. Jones 4–61, Renfro 3–54, Brewster 2–21, Morrison 2–14, Bassett 3–11, Reynolds 1–3
PIT: Mathews 5–152, Nickel 2–47, Sulima 3–41, Rogel 1–13, Chandnois 2–4

Sunday, October 24
Browns 35, Chicago Cardinals 3
Comiskey Park (25,823)
White jerseys/white pants

For the second time in three weeks, the winless Cardinals provided the perfect elixir for the Browns after a blowout loss as Cleveland steamrolled to its second victory. After an Otto Graham interception on the game's third play set up a Chicago field goal, the Browns exploded for 35 unanswered points. The Cleveland defense rebounded from its shoddy performance against the Steelers to limit Chicago to 160 total yards and just eight first downs while forcing four turnovers. On offense, the Browns pulled away thanks to a pair of touchdowns by rookie RB Maurice Bassett—who would be married two days later. Otto Graham added two more short scoring runs as the Browns notched their 10th straight victory over the Cardinals.
Record: 2–2

	1	2	3	4		
Browns	7	14	14	0	=	35
Cardinals	3	0	0	0	=	3

CHI-Summerall 41-yd. FG
CLE-Graham 1-yd. run (Groza kick)
CLE-Bassett 8-yd. run (Groza kick)
CLE-Lavelli 26-yd. pass from Graham (Groza kick)
CLE-Graham 1-yd. run (Groza kick)
CLE-Bassett 7-yd. run (Groza kick)

Passing
CLE: Graham 16–24–182 1 TD 1 INT, Ratterman 7–11–74 0 TD 0 INT
CHI: McHan 6–17–126 0 TD 1 INT, Romanik 0–4–0 0 TD 1 INT

Rushing
CLE: Bassett 12–49, Renfro 4–16, Hanulak 4–11, Morrison 5–8, Reynolds 5–5, D. Jones 2–5, Graham 3–4, James 1-(-6)
CHI: McHan 5–28, King 6–16, Olszewski 9–10, Matson 3–6, Barry 1–3, Goble 1-(-3)

Receiving
CLE: Lavelli 8–98, Bassett 4–45, Hanulak 2–39, Brewster 3–31, D. Jones 2–22, Renfro 2–12, Reynolds 1–6, Morrison 1–3
CHI: Matson 2–78, Stonesifer 2–29, Olszewski 2–19

Sunday, October 31
Browns 24, New York Giants 14
Cleveland Stadium (30,448)
White jerseys/white pants

On an unseasonably cold Halloween afternoon that saw a mix of rain and snow showers, the Browns cruised to an impressive victory over the first-place Giants. Otto Graham rushed for a pair of touchdowns, the second set up early in the third quarter by a fumble recovery by DB Tommy James at the New York 25. Graham also tossed a 16-yard scoring pass to Dante Lavelli to break a 7–7 tie in the first half but tossed three interceptions. The Cleveland running game controlled the line of scrimmage, rolling up 169 yards on the ground while the defense limited the Giants to 10 first downs. The victory pulled the Browns within a half-game of New York and one back of Philadelphia and Pittsburgh.
Record: 3–2

	1	2	3	4		
Giants	0	7	0	7	=	14
Browns	7	7	7	3	=	24

CLE-Graham 1-yd. run (Groza kick)
NYG-Conerly 1-yd. run (Agajanian kick)
CLE-Lavelli 16-yd. pass from Graham (Groza kick)
CLE-Graham 1-yd. run (Groza kick)
CLE-Groza 17-yd. FG
NYG-Price 83-yd. pass from Gifford (Agajanian kick)

Passing
NYG: Gifford 1–1–83 1 TD 0 INT, Conerly 5–15–64 0 TD 2 INT, Rote 0–1–0 0 TD 0 INT
CLE: Graham 14–26–160 1 TD 3 INT

Rushing
NYG: Price 9–65, Long 8–29, Gifford 6–9, Conerly 7–8, Rote 4–5
CLE: Bassett 19–89, D. Jones 3–27, Reynolds 9–26, Graham 10–20, Renfro 3–6, Hanulak 2–1

Receiving
NYG: Price 3–99, Schnelker 1–29, MacAfee 1–16, Long 1–3
CLE: Renfro 5–71, Lavelli 2–50, Brewster 3–41, Reynolds 3–9, Bassett 1–11

Sunday, November 7
Browns 62, Washington Redskins 3
Cleveland Stadium (25,158)
White jerseys/white pants

In what is still the most lopsided victory in club history, the Browns annihilated the 1–5 Redskins on a sunshiny autumn afternoon on the lakefront. Interestingly, the Browns didn't start to pull away until backup QB George Ratterman replaced Otto Graham after Graham was ineffective following a shoulder injury early in the second quarter, though Cleveland still led 13–3. In less than two quarters of action, Ratterman completed 10 of 11 passes for 208 yards and three touchdowns and left with the Browns up 41–3. Behind Ratterman's spark and a well-balanced performance by RB Dub Jones, who rushed for 84 yards and caught passes for 93, Cleveland rolled up 515 total yards and 33 first downs. WR Pete Brewster added 114 yards on seven catches. Meanwhile, the Cleveland defense was equally dominant, holding Washington to just 64 yards and four first downs. The Browns' defense also added the Browns' eighth and final touchdown on an interception return by DB Ken Gorgal with 20 seconds left.
Record: 4–2

	1	2	3	4		
Redskins	0	3	0	0	=	3
Browns	13	14	21	14	=	62

CLE-Groza 11-yd. FG
CLE-Groza 43-yd. FG
CLE-Graham 5-yd. run (Groza kick)
WAS-Janowicz 37-yd. FG
CLE-Bassett 9-yd. run (Groza kick)
CLE-D. Jones 48-yd. pass from Ratterman (Groza kick)
CLE-Brewster 16-yd. pass from Ratterman (Groza kick)
CLE-Lavelli 28-yd. pass from Ratterman (Groza kick)
CLE-Morrison 1-yd. run (Konz kick)
CLE-Brewster 9-yd. pass from Graham (Konz kick)
CLE-Gorgal 53-yd. interception return (Konz kick)

Passing
WAS: Dorow 3–14–33 0 TD 3 INT, Scarbath 2–4–3 0 TD 0 INT, Janowicz 0–1–0 0 TD 0 INT, Gilmer 0–1–0 0 TD 0 INT
CLE: Ratterman 10–11–208 3 TD 0 INT, Graham 8–17–102 1 TD 1 INT

Rushing
WAS: Wells 10–25, Atkeson 7–11, Justice 2–7, Goode 3–4, Scudero 1-(-3), Dorow 1-(-5), Gilmer 1-(-6)
CLE: D. Jones 8–84, Renfro 3–31, Morrison 7–30, Graham 7–27, Hanulak 7–21, Lahr 3–18, Bassett 9–13, Ratterman 3–2

Receiving
WAS: Carson 2–20, Wells 2–10, Atkeson 1–6
CLE: Brewster 7–114, D. Jones 3–93, Lavelli 4–59, Bassett 2–34, Morrison 1–8, Hanulak 1–2

Sunday, November 14
Browns 39, Chicago Bears 10
Wrigley Field (48,773)
White jerseys/white pants

The Browns caught fire in the second half to blow open a close game with 33 points in the final two periods on a bright, chilly afternoon at Wrigley Field. After both teams failed to score a touchdown in the first half, the game turned early in the third period on a bad Chicago punt that gave the Browns a first down at the Bears' 28. Six plays later, Otto Graham scored on a one-yard run, and two plays after that, DB Warren Lahr returned an interception 27 yards for a touchdown to make it 23–3. Early in the fourth quarter, Len Ford trapped Chicago QB Zeke Bratkowski in the end zone for a safety, then the Browns added two more scores to wrap up another convincing victory. The Browns compiled 222 rushing yards, including 90 by RB Chet Hanulak in the second half alone. Conversely, the Cleveland defense limited the Bears to just 37 rushing yards on 22 carries. The game marked the Browns' twenty-fifth without a loss against Chicago teams (Rockets, Bears, and Cardinals) in both the AAFC and NFL.
Record: 5–2

	1	2	3	4		
Browns	3	3	17	16	=	39
Bears	0	3	0	7	=	10

CLE-Groza 33-yd. FG
CLE-Groza 33-yd. FG
CHI-Blanda 23-yd. FG
CLE-Graham 1-yd. run (Groza kick)
CLE-Lahr 27-yd. interception return (Groza kick)
CLE-Groza 37-yd. FG
CLE-Safety: Ford tackled Bratkowski in end zone
CLE-Lavelli 8-yd. pass from Graham (Groza kick)
CLE-Hanulak 7-yd. run (Groza kick)
CHI-Hill 65-yd. pass from Bratkowski (Perini kick)

Passing
CLE: Graham 11–23–120 1 TD 1 INT
CHI: Blanda 5–18–112 0 TD 0 INT, Bratkowski 6–14–104 1 TD 3 INT

Rushing
CLE: Hanulak 11–90, Bassett 15–58, D. Jones 8–35, Morrison 3–20, Graham 9–11, Reynolds 4–8
CHI: Stone 6–26, Hoffman 6–14, Bratkowski 3–13, Blanda 2–0, Kindt 4-(-6), Brown 1-(-10)

Receiving
CLE: Lavelli 6–75, Hanulak 1–20, Brewster 1–10, Morrison 2–9, Bassett 1–6
CHI: Hill 3–117, Stone 4–68, McColl 2–20, Kindt 1–7, Hoffman 1–4

Sunday, November 21
Browns 6, Philadelphia Eagles 0
Cleveland Stadium (41,537)
White jerseys/white pants

On the strength of another magnificent defensive performance, the Browns moved into first place with a physical victory over the Eagles on a dark, cold afternoon. Two Lou Groza field goals represented all the game's scoring as Cleveland limited Philadelphia to just 110 total yards while forcing four turnovers, including a pair of fumble recoveries inside the Cleveland 20. But the game was still in doubt when the Eagles reached the Cleveland 1 with three minutes left. After stuffing the Eagles on first and second down and a delay-of-game penalty on Philly, the Browns forced two straight incomplete passes, including a fourth-down toss knocked down by lineman Mike McCormack. An interception of a last-gasp Eagle pass by LB Walt Michaels clinched a hard-earned victory that propelled the Browns to the top of the Eastern Conference.
Record: 6–2

	1	2	3	4		
Eagles	0	0	0	0	=	0
Browns	3	0	3	0	=	6

CLE-Groza 11-yd. FG
CLE-Groza 31-yd. FG

Passing
PHI: Thomason 10–23–74 0 TD 2 INT
CLE: Graham 11–21–192 0 TD 2 INT

Rushing
PHI: Worden 16–35, Ledbetter 16–22
CLE: Bassett 18–95, Reynolds 8–22, Graham 11–10, Morrison 1–5, D. Jones 5–4, Hanulak 1–3

Receiving
PHI: Walston 3–44, Pihos 2–18, Williams 2–17, Worden 1-(-1), Ledbetter 2-(-4)
CLE: Brewster 2–69, Bassett 3–60, D. Jones 3–29, Lavelli 1–14, Morrison 1–14, Reynolds 1–6

Sunday, November 28
Browns 16, New York Giants 7
Polo Grounds (45,936)
Brown jerseys/white pants

Picking up their sixth straight victory, the Browns' defense was again dominant in a battle for first place in New York. The injury-riddled Giants could manage only 68 total yards and eight first downs for the game and, incredibly, were held to just four yards rushing on 21 carries. New York's only points came on a punt return for a touchdown in the third quarter. The Browns built a 13–0 halftime lead and then held off the Giants in the second half despite coughing up five turnovers for the game. Pete Brewster caught eight passes for 126 yards, but the highlight of the day was a booming 80-yard punt by Horace Gillom, a club record that still stands. The victory put the Browns a game and a half ahead of the Giants and Eagles with three to play.
Record: 7–2

	1	2	3	4		
Browns	10	3	3	0	=	16
Giants	0	0	7	0	=	7

CLE-Groza 18-yd. FG
CLE-Graham 1-yd. run (Groza kick)
CLE-Groza 10-yd. FG
NYG-Johnson 48-yd. punt return (Agajanian kick)
CLE-Groza 38-yd. FG

Passing
CLE: Graham 16–27–238 0 TD 2 INT
NYG: Clatterbuck 10–25–96 0 TD 0 INT, Conerly 1–1–7 0 TD 0 INT, Rote 0–1–0 0 TD 1 INT

Rushing
CLE: D. Jones 12–44, Reynolds 10–34, Bassett 5–22, Morrison 6–15, Hanulak 2–4, Graham 4-(-3)
NYG: Price 10–17, Epps 2–10, Johnson 2–0, Rote 4-(-3), Clatterbuck 3-(-20)

Receiving
CLE: Brewster 8–126, Lavelli 4–50, D. Jones 2–50, Reynolds 2–12
NYG: Price 4–32, Schnelker 2–19, Topp 2–19, Johnson 1–19, Rote 2–14

Sunday, December 5
Browns 34, Washington Redskins 14
Griffith Stadium (21,761)
White jerseys/white pants

On a gloomy afternoon in the nation's capital, the Browns clinched at least a tie for the conference title with an easy victory over the Redskins. After Washington scored on its first possession, the Browns scored the game's next 34 points, starting with the first of two touchdown runs by Maurice Bassett and then a 25-yard interception return for a score by DB Ken Konz. The Cleveland offense cruised to 445 total yards despite losing four turnovers and the Browns accumulating over 100 yards in penalties. Dante Lavelli paced an air attack that compiled over 300 yards with 128 on five receptions.
Record: 8–2

	1	2	3	4		
Browns	7	10	10	7	=	34
Redskins	7	0	0	7	=	14

WAS-Taylor 18-yd. pass from Dorow (Felton kick)
CLE-Bassett 5-yd. run (Groza kick)
CLE-Konz 25-yd. interception return (Groza kick)
CLE-Groza 9-yd. FG
CLE-Bassett 1-yd. run (Groza kick)
CLE-Groza 30-yd. FG
CLE-Ratterman 1-yd. run (Groza kick)
WAS-Justice 80-yd. pass from Dorow (Felton kick)

Passing
CLE: Graham 13–18–252 0 TD 1 INT, Ratterman 5–10–49 0 TD 1 INT
WAS: Dorow 5–7–120 2 TD 1 INT, Scarbath 2–12–23 0 TD 1 INT

Rushing
CLE: Graham 6–41, Morrison 6–34, Hanulak 5–34, Renfro 5–29, Bassett 11–20, Reynolds 2–6, D. Jones 2-(-3), Ratterman 2-(-1)
WAS: Goode 9–47, Wells 9–40, Justice 9–15, Dorow 6–7, Scarbath 1–4

Receiving
CLE: Lavelli 5–128, Brewster 6–98, D. Jones 2–32, Reynolds 1–22, Morrison 2–9, Bassett 1–8, Hanulak 1–4
WAS: Justice 2–85, Taylor 2–32, Carson 1–14, Wells 1–12

Sunday, December 12
Browns 42, Pittsburgh Steelers 7
Cleveland Stadium (28,064)
White jerseys/white pants

Behind three touchdowns by unheralded rookie RB Chet Hanulak on a damp, dark afternoon, the Browns avenged their earlier loss to Pittsburgh with a blowout victory that clinched their eighth straight victory and ninth straight division/conference title. Ken Konz returned an interception for a touchdown for the second straight week on the first play of the second quarter, then the Browns recovered a Pittsburgh fumble on the ensuing kickoff to set up Hanulak's second score and blow the game open. Two plays after the following kickoff, Len Ford recovered another Steeler fumble, leading to Hanulak's third touchdown. Playing for an injured Ray Renfro, Hanulak tallied 94 yards on just 12 carries as the Cleveland offense gathered 464 total yards, 292 on the ground. Meanwhile, the Browns' defense limited the Steelers to just 171 and forced six turnovers.
Record: 9–2

	1	2	3	4		
Steelers	0	0	7	0	=	7
Browns	7	21	0	14	=	42

CLE-Hanulak 13-yd. run (Groza kick)
CLE-Konz 54-yd. interception return (Groza kick)
CLE-Hanulak 3-yd. run (Groza kick)
CLE-Hanulak 8-yd. run (Groza kick)
PIT-Mathews 47-yd. pass from Finks (Bolkovac kick)
CLE-Morrison 2-yd. run (Groza kick)
CLE-Reynolds 3-yd. run (Groza kick)

Passing
PIT: Finks 7–20–93 1 TD 3 INT, Held 0–6–0 0 TD 0 INT, Mathews 0–1–0 0 TD 0 INT
CLE: Graham 7–9–137 0 TD 0 INT, Ratterman 5–12–54 0 TD 1 INT, Lahr 0–1–0 0 TD 1 INT

Rushing
PIT: Chandnois 11–34, Brandt 6–23, Mathews 6–22, Rogel 6–15, Held 1–2, Calvin 1–0
CLE: Hanulak 12–94, Morrison 9–56, Bassett 13–53, Reynolds 6–45, D. Jones 5–37, Ratterman 1–5, Graham 4–2

Receiving
PIT: Mathews 5–80, Sulima 1–7, Rogel 1–6
CLE: Lavelli 2–70, Brewster 4–63, Gillom 3–44, Bassett 2–11, Morrison 1–3

Sunday, December 19
Detroit Lions 14, Browns 10
Cleveland Stadium (34,168)
White jerseys/white pants

In a game that proved to be meaningless since both teams had already clinched their respective conferences, the Browns and Lions provided a preview of the following week's NFL title game in a game originally scheduled for the second week of the season but postponed due to the Indians' appearance in the World Series. Through snowy conditions, the Browns led for much of the game despite completing only one pass on the afternoon and managing a season-low 113 total yards. They appeared to have victory in their grasp in the closing minutes when they stopped the Lions on fourth down at their own 37, but Dub Jones then lost a fumble to give the Lions new life. After an exchange of punts, the Lions put together a sustained drive that ended with the game-winning touchdown on a Bobby Layne scoring pass with 50 seconds to play. It snapped the Browns' eight-game winning streak and marked their fourth straight loss to Detroit while setting an ominous tone for the next Sunday's championship.
Record: 9–3

	1	2	3	4		
Lions	0	0	7	7	=	14
Browns	7	0	3	0	=	10

CLE-Graham 1-yd. run (Groza kick)
DET-Dibble 26-yd. pass from Layne (Walker kick)
CLE-Groza 44-yd. FG
DET-Girard 11-yd. pass from Layne (Walker kick)

Passing
DET: Layne 18–36–183 2 TD, Hoernschemeyer 0–1–0 0 TD
CLE: Graham 1–6–15 0 TD 0 INT

Rushing
DET: Layne 6–24, Bowman 9–23, Walker 2–19, L. Carpenter 9–14, Hoernschemeyer 7–11, Girard 1–1
CLE: Bassett 21–55, Hanulak 12–29, Graham 3–12, D. Jones 4–7, Morrison 4–7, Reynolds 5–5

Receiving
DET: Girard 4–56, Hart 2–45, Dibble 2–38, Bowman 3–15, Walker 2–13, L. Carpenter 3–9, Hoernschemeyer 2–7
CLE: Hanulak 1–15

1954 NFL Championship
Sunday, December 26
Browns 56, Detroit Lions 10
Cleveland Stadium (43,827)
White jerseys/white pants

Meeting for the NFL title for the third straight season, the Browns finally solved the puzzle of the Detroit Lions with an emphatic blowout victory that secured Cleveland's second NFL championship.

On an unseasonably warm, sunny day after Christmas, the Lions, two-and-half-point favorites, appeared to continue their inexplicable spell over the Browns on the game's first play—a 50-yard run by FB Bill Bowman. The Browns caught a break when the Lions lost a fumble on the next play, but gave the gift right back with an interception that set up a Detroit field goal. From that point on, it was all Cleveland. The Browns scored five touchdowns in the first half to steamroll to a 35–10 lead, two by Ray Renfro, who returned to the lineup after missing six weeks with a knee injury.

The Cleveland defense stole the show, intercepting six Bobby Layne passes and forcing a total of nine turnovers, with Len Ford and Ken Konz each picking off two passes by Layne, who completed only 18 of 42 attempts.

But the game's individual standout was Otto Graham, who had played the worst game of his career against Detroit in the previous year's championship. Playing what he thought would be his final game, Graham ran for three touchdowns and threw for three more in one of the greatest performances in championship-game history.

The 46-point victory represented the second-largest margin in title-game history, behind only the 73–0 blowout by the Chicago Bears over the Washington Redskins in 1940. Making the performance even more amazing, the Browns' 56 points were more than they'd scored in their previous four games with Detroit combined.

Jubilant Cleveland fans rushed the field at game's end to tear down the goalposts as the Browns snapped their three-game championship losing streak and defeated the Lions for the first time in their history.

	1	2	3	4		
Lions	3	7	0	0	=	10
Browns	14	21	14	7	=	56

DET-Walker 36-yd. FG
CLE-Renfro 35-yd. pass from Graham (Groza kick)
CLE-Brewster 8-yd. pass from Graham (Groza kick)
CLE-Graham 1-yd. run (Groza kick)
DET-Bowman 5-yd. run (Walker kick)
CLE-Graham 5-yd. run (Groza kick)
CLE-Renfro 31-yd. pass from Graham (Groza kick)
CLE-Graham 1-yd. run (Groza kick)
CLE-Morrison 12-yd. run (Groza kick)
CLE-Hanulak 10-yd. run (Groza kick)

Passing
DET: Layne 18–42–177 0 TD 6 INT, Dublinski 1–2–18 0 TD 0 INT
CLE: Graham 9–12–163 3 TD 2 INT

Rushing
DET: L. Carpenter 8–64, Bowman 7–61, Walker 3–13, Layne 7–7, Hoernschemeyer 2–2, Dublinski 2-(-11)
CLE: Hanulak 5–44, Graham 9–27, Bassett 8–27, Morrison 10–19, Reynolds 6–16, D. Jones 3–3, Renfro 3–2, Ratterman 1–2

Receiving
DET: Dibble 4–63, Girard 5–57, Walker 2–39, Hart 1–19, L. Carpenter 6–17, Bowman 1–0
CLE: Renfro 5–94, Brewster 2–53, Bassett 1–10, Lavelli 1–6

1955

CLE: Morrison 15–117, Renfro 11–60, Bassett 7–30, Graham 8–8, Ratterman 3–4, Modzelewski 2–2

Receiving
WAS: Elter 1–70, Carson 4–66, Zagers 2–26, Cox 1–14
CLE: Bassett 5–52, Lavelli 2–39, Brewster 2–38, Morrison 3–30, Renfro 3–30

Sunday, September 25
Washington Redskins 27, Browns 17
Cleveland Stadium (30,041)
White jerseys/white pants

With QB Otto Graham still working his way back into playing shape after coming out of retirement just three weeks earlier, the Cleveland offense struggled in the first half as the Browns lost their second straight opener. Graham started, but after the Browns fell behind 13–3 at the half, he was replaced by George Ratterman, who led the Browns to two third-quarter touchdowns that pulled them within three points of the Redskins. But the game turned in the fourth quarter when Ratterman fumbled, and Washington recovered at the Cleveland 25. Four plays later the Redskins added an insurance touchdown run by QB Eddie LeBaron. Washington managed only a modest 260 total yards for the day, while Ratterman's second-half spark propelled the Browns to nearly 400 total yards, including 221 on the ground, paced by RB Fred Morrison's 117.
Record: 0–1

	1	2	3	4		
Redskins	6	7	7	7	=	27
Browns	0	3	14	0	=	17

WAS-Janowicz 4-yd. run (kick failed)
WAS-Carson 24-yd. pass from LeBaron (Janowicz kick)
CLE-Groza 44-yd. FG
CLE-Brewster 21-yd. pass from Ratterman (Groza kick)
WAS-Carson 17-yd. pass from LeBaron (Janowicz kick)
CLE-Renfro 8-yd. pass from Ratterman (Groza kick)
WAS-LeBaron 13-yd. run (Janowicz kick)

Passing
WAS: LeBaron 8–16–176 2 TD 1 INT
CLE: Ratterman 12–18–159 2 TD 0 INT, Graham 3–9–30 0 TD 2 INT, Renfro 0–1–0 0 TD 0 INT

Rushing
WAS: Atkeson 12–45, LeBaron 3–21, Elter 6–11, Zagers 3–10, Janowicz 3–8

Sunday, October 2
Browns 38, San Francisco 49ers 3
Kezar Stadium (46,150)
White jerseys/white pants

Otto Graham returned to form and led the Browns to a romp, handing the 49ers the worst home loss in their history. The tone was set early when San Francisco QB Y. A. Tittle's first pass was intercepted by Cleveland DB Tommy James. Moments later Graham scored the first of the Browns' five touchdowns on a one-yard plunge. The Browns then blew the game open with 17 points in the second quarter—including the first of two touchdowns by RB Ed Modzelewski—to take a 24–3 halftime lead, then left it to their fierce defense to contain the 49ers. San Francisco was held to just 139 yards and eight first downs, while the Browns tallied 357, topping 200 on the ground for the second straight week.
Record: 1–1

	1	2	3	4		
Browns	7	17	7	7	=	38
49ers	0	3	0	0	=	3

CLE-Graham 1-yd. run (Groza kick)
SF-Soltau 17-yd. FG
CLE-Modzelewski 1-yd. run (Groza kick)
CLE-Groza 32-yd. FG
CLE-Morrison 1-yd. run (Groza kick)
CLE-Modzelewski 1-yd. run (Groza kick)
CLE-Bassett 5-yd. run (Groza kick)

Passing
CLE: Graham 7–11–140 0 TD 0 INT, Ratterman 1–1–32 0 TD 0 INT
SF: Tittle 5–15–57 0 TD 2 INT, Duncan 1–3–27 0 TD 0 INT

Rushing
CLE: Morrison 20–80, Modzelewski 14–56, Graham 7–28, D. Jones 3–13, Renfro 8–10, Petitbon 3–10, Bassett 2–10, James 1–2, Ford 2–1

SF: Perry 10–23, Laughlin 5–18, Tittle 4–17, Hardy 1–14, Johnson 4–3, Arenas 1–0, McElhenny 1-(-3), Duncan 1-(-5)

Receiving
CLE: Brewster 2–59, D. Jones 1–43, Lavelli 2–37, Morrison 2–31, Renfro 1–11
SF: Wilson 2–28, Laughlin 1–27, Soltau 1–19, Arenas 1–7, McElhenny 1–3

Sunday, October 9
Browns 21, Philadelphia Eagles 17
Cleveland Stadium (43,974)
White jerseys/white pants

Trailing by three points with three minutes to play and backed up at their own 13, the Browns drove 87 yards in 11 plays to score the winning touchdown in the final minute. An Otto Graham fumble earlier in the fourth period set up the Eagles' go-ahead touchdown and put Philadelphia in a position to hand the Browns a second straight home defeat. But with the setting sun glistening right in Graham's eyes on the final drive, he pulled off three critical plays to keep the Browns' hopes alive: an 18-yard run on third-and-three, a 14-yard pass to WR Dante Lavelli on fourth and six with 1:30 left, and then a 36-yard run to the Philadelphia 8. Moments later, Graham hit Lavelli again—his sixth reception of the day—this time for a five-yard touchdown to give the Browns a dramatic victory. Once again, the Cleveland defense was superb, limiting an opponent to less than 200 yards for the second straight week. The Eagles stayed in the game thanks to three Cleveland fumbles, two of which set up Philly's touchdowns.
Record: 2–1

	1	2	3	4		
Eagles	7	3	0	7	=	17
Browns	0	14	0	7	=	21

PHI-Giancanelli 3-yd. run (Bielski kick)
CLE-Graham 3-yd. run (Groza kick)
PHI-Bielski 50-yd. FG
CLE-Modzelewski 28-yd. pass from Graham (Groza kick)
PHI-Pihos 4-yd. pass from Burk (Bielski kick)
CLE-Lavelli 5-yd. pass from Graham (Groza kick)

Passing
PHI: Burk 8–12–75 1 TD 0 INT, Thomason 5–18–61 0 TD 0 INT
CLE: Graham 16–21–223 2 TD 0 INT

Rushing
PHI: Giancanelli 13–40, Bielski 4–7, Ledbetter 1–3, Norton 7–2, Thomason 2-(-3), Burk 2-(-6)
CLE: Morrison 12–64, Modzelewski 15–43, Graham 8–40, Renfro 4–9, Bassett 3–9

Receiving
PHI: Walston 3–39, Norton 2–33, Pihos 3–26, Giancanelli 3–18, Stribling 1–14, Bawel 1–6
CLE: Lavelli 6–108, Brewster 2–38, Morrison 1–34, Modzelewski 5–32, Renfro 1–9, Bassett 1–2

Sunday, October 16
Browns 24, Washington Redskins 14
Griffith Stadium (29,168)
White jerseys/white pants

The Browns avenged their opening-day defeat on a crisp autumn afternoon in the nation's capital, blowing open a close game in the third quarter and coasting to victory. Clinging to a 10–7 halftime lead, Ed Modzelewski scored his second touchdown of the day on a short pass from Otto Graham at the outset of the third quarter, and moments later LB Walt Michaels put the Browns over the top with a 25-yard interception return for a touchdown, the second and final of his career. Though the Cleveland offense struggled and the team was penalized 11 times, for the third straight week, the Browns held their opponent under 200 total yards, this time collecting five turnovers. WR Pete Brewster was the standout on offense, catching six passes for 109 yards.
Record: 3–1

	1	2	3	4		
Browns	7	3	14	0	=	24
Redskins	7	0	0	7	=	14

CLE-Modzelewski 6-yd. run (Groza kick)
WAS-Atkeson 15-yd. run (Janowicz kick)
CLE-Groza 41-yd. FG
CLE-Modzelewski 5-yd. pass from Graham (Groza kick)
CLE-Michaels 25-yd. interception return (Groza kick)
WAS-Hecker 5-yd. pass from LeBaron (Janowicz kick)

Passing
CLE: Graham 9–16–138 1 TD 1 INT
WAS: LeBaron 5–15–40 1 TD 0 INT, Guglielmi 2–10–17 0 TD 2 INT

Rushing
CLE: Modzelewski 13–58, Morrison 6–12, Bassett 2–12, Smith 5–7, Graham 1–3, D. Jones 1–3, Renfro 5-(-3)
WAS: Janowicz 12–56, Zagers 8–26, Atkeson 5–26, Goode 6–20, LeBaron 1–3, Guglielmi 1–1, Dorow 1-(-1)

Receiving
CLE: Brewster 6–109, Lavelli 2–24, Modzelewski 1–5
WAS: Hecker 2–22, Janowicz 3–18, Jones 1–10, Cox 1–7

Sunday, October 23
Browns 41, Green Bay Packers 10
Cleveland Stadium (51,482)
White jerseys/white pants

Coasting to their fourth straight win, the Browns blew open a close game in the second half to crush the 3–1 Packers. After Green Bay took a 10–7 lead on a kickoff return for a touchdown early in the second quarter, the Browns bounced back with a 97-yard scoring drive, capped by a short Fred Morrison touchdown run, to surge back into the lead. Holding Green Bay scoreless from that point on, the Browns then sealed the victory with 20 fourth-quarter points, including two touchdown passes by backup QB George Ratterman. The Cleveland offense rolled up a season-best 454 yards of offense, while the defense was dominant for the fourth straight week, holding the Packers to only 161 yards and forcing three turnovers.
Record: 4–1

	1	2	3	4		
Packers	3	7	0	0	=	10
Browns	0	14	7	20	=	41

GB-Cone 27-yd. FG
CLE-Graham 1-yd. run (Groza kick)
GB-Carmichael 100-yd. kickoff return (Cone kick)
CLE-Morrison 4-yd. run (Groza kick)
CLE-Bassett 30-yd. run (Groza kick)
CLE-Groza 35-yd. FG
CLE-Groza 36-yd. FG
CLE-D. Jones 25-yd. pass from Ratterman (Groza kick)
CLE-Brewster 22-yd. pass from Ratterman (Groza kick)

Passing
GB: Rote 6–20–42 0 TD 2 INT, Brackins 0–2–0 0 TD 0 INT
CLE: Graham 7–12–187 0 TD 0 INT, Ratterman 3–3–84 2 TD 0 INT

Rushing
GB: Switzer 1–38, Ferguson 8–36, Reid 9–31, Rote 12–20, Johnson 2–14
CLE: Morrison 17–87, Bassett 9–58, Modzelewski 9–47, Smith 7–19, Graham 7-(-7)

Receiving
GB: Howton 2–19, Carmichael 2–14, Switzer 2–9
CLE: Renfro 3–91, Brewster 4–88, Morrison 1–49, D. Jones 1–26, Lavelli 1–17

Sunday, October 30
Browns 26, Chicago Cardinals 20
Comiskey Park (29,471)
White jerseys/white pants

On a gloomy, rainy afternoon on Chicago's south side, the Browns rolled to a big first-half lead and then held off Chicago to secure their fifth straight triumph and their eleventh straight over the Cardinals. Aided by a 60-yard punt return for a score by Don Paul and a safety after LB Chuck Noll blocked a punt that rolled out of the end zone, the Browns held a 23–6 advantage early in the third quarter. Chicago then cashed in on two Cleveland fumbles for a pair of touchdowns to narrow the margin to six in the fourth quarter. But the Browns' defense endured and clinched victory when Noll intercepted a pass in the final seconds—Chicago's fifth turnover of the day. Returning after injuring his shoulder in the previous game, Ed Modzelewski paced the Browns' offense by plowing for 121 yards and a touchdown through the mud. The Cleveland victory, combined with a Pittsburgh loss to Philadelphia, propelled the Browns into sole possession of first place in the Eastern Conference.
Record: 5–1

	1	2	3	4		
Browns	7	14	5	0	=	26
Cardinals	3	3	7	7	=	20

CLE-Modzelewski 5-yd. run (Groza kick)
CHI-Summerall 20-yd. FG
CLE-Paul 60-yd. punt return (Groza kick)
CLE-Renfro 4-yd. pass from Graham (Groza kick)
CHI-Summerall 14-yd. FG
CLE-Safety: Noll blocked punt out of end zone
CHI-McHan 1-yd. run (Summerall kick)
CHI-Groza 44-yd. FG
CHI-Stonesifer 18-yd. pass from Mann (Summerall kick)

Passing
CLE: Graham 4–12–62 1 TD 0 INT
CHI: McHan 7–26–102 0 TD 2 INT, Mann 2–3–36 1 TD 0 INT, Compton 1–5–26 0 TD 0 INT

Rushing
CLE: Modzelewski 28–121, Morrison 15–70, Bassett 2–11, Graham 2-(-6)
CHI: Matson 9–66, Olszewski 15–32, McHan 6–26, Mann 7–6, Carr 1–3, Goble 1–1

Receiving
CLE: Brewster 2–47, Morrison 1–11, Renfro 1–4
CHI: Stonesifer 3–55, Matson 3–44, Carr 2–33, Brubaker 1–31, Mann 1–1

Sunday, November 6
Browns 24, New York Giants 14
Cleveland Stadium (46,524)
White jerseys/white pants

Things looked bleak for the Browns at halftime, as they trailed the rival Giants 14–3, and Otto Graham was out for the day after being knocked unconscious on a hit in the second quarter. But led by a smothering defense, the Browns rallied behind George Ratterman for three second-half touchdowns to pick up their sixth straight victory. After moving up and down the field at will through the first half, the Giants could manage only 14 total yards in the second while Ratterman threw a pair of touchdown passes to put the Browns in front early in the fourth quarter. The Giants were poised to tie the game with less than 10 minutes to play, but Ben Agajanian missed a 23-yard field goal and the Browns drove 80 yards for the game-clinching touchdown—a short fourth-down scoring run by Ratterman in the waning seconds.
Record: 6–1

	1	2	3	4		
Giants	0	14	0	0	=	14
Browns	3	0	7	14	=	24

CLE-Groza 14-yd. FG
NYG-Gifford 6-yd. pass from Conerly (Agajanian kick)
NYG-Rote 71-yd. pass from Gifford (Agajanian kick)
CLE-Renfro 30-yd. pass from Ratterman (Groza kick)
CLE-Brewster 14-yd. pass from Ratterman (Groza kick)
CLE-Ratterman 4-yd. run (Groza kick)

Passing
NYG: Conerly 12–30–151 1 TD 3 INT, Gifford 1–1–71 1 TD 0 INT
CLE: Graham 5–10–57 0 TD 1 INT, Ratterman 10–15–163 2 TD 2 INT

Rushing
NYG: Epps 13–80, Gifford 6–17, Rote 3–10, Webster 3–5, Conerly 1-(-2)
CLE: Morrison 16–44, Modzelewski 18–36, Smith 5–15, Graham 1–14, D. Jones 1–9, Ratterman 3–4

Receiving
NYG: Rote 3–98, Schnelker 4–48, Gifford 4–46, MacAfee 2–30
CLE: Renfro 5–85, Modzelewski 3–63, Lavelli 4–37, Brewster 2–25, Smith 1–10

Sunday, November 13
Philadelphia Eagles 33, Browns 17
Connie Mack Stadium (39,303)
Brown jerseys/white pants

The Browns got off to a dazzling start, scoring on their first three possessions and soaring to a 17–0 lead in the first 12 minutes. But everything fell apart after that as the Eagles rallied to victory before a standing-room-only crowd at Connie Mack Stadium, the largest ever to watch a football game at the ballpark. With the Cleveland secondary riddled with injury, Philadelphia's offense caught fire, led by WR Bill Stribling's 123 receiving yards, and narrowed the lead to one point going into the fourth quarter. A minute into the final period, the Eagles blocked a punt to set up the go-ahead touchdown, then recovered a critical fumble after RB Dub Jones caught a long pass at the Eagle 37 to thwart the Browns' final scoring opportunity. Philadelphia put the game away when DB Bibbles Bawel returned an interception 40 yards for a score—one of seven Cleveland turnovers. The defeat allowed Washington to pull within a game of the Browns in the conference race.
Record: 6–2

	1	2	3	4		
Browns	17	0	0	0	=	17
Eagles	0	10	6	17	=	33

CLE-Groza 17-yd. FG
CLE-Renfro 61-yd. pass from Graham (Groza kick)
CLE-Graham 1-yd. run (Groza kick)
PHI-Stribling 2-yd. pass from Burk (Bielski kick)

PHI-Bielski 23-yd. FG
PHI-Stribling 21-yd. pass from Burk (kick failed)
PHI-Burk 1-yd. run (Bielski kick)
PHI-Bawel 40-yd. interception return (Bielski kick)
PHI-Bielski 40-yd. FG

Passing
CLE: Graham 7–17–150 1 TD 2 INT, Ratterman 1–3–5 0 TD 1 INT
PHI: Burk 12–28–198 2 TD 2 INT

Rushing
CLE: Modzelewski 19–83, Morrison 8–34, Graham 3–18, D. Jones 3–6, Bassett 2–0
PHI: Goode 8–60, Burk 6–34, Giancanelli 4–26, Parmer 7–18, Goldston 5–14, Bielski 1–1, Wegert 3-(-5)

Receiving
CLE: Renfro 1–61, D. Jones 1–46, Brewster 4–38, Bassett 1–5, Lavelli 1–5
PHI: Stribling 6–123, Pihos 3–46, Giancanelli 2–15, Walston 1–14

Sunday, November 20
Browns 41, Pittsburgh Steelers 14
Cleveland Stadium (53,509)
White jerseys/white pants

On a perfect afternoon for football, the Browns pulled away from a 14–14 second-quarter tie with the Steelers with 27 unanswered points to bounce back from a disappointing loss the week before. Dante Lavelli caught his second touchdown pass of the day—a 42-yard strike from Otto Graham—just before the half to break the tie, then the Browns tacked on two more touchdowns in the third quarter as the Cleveland defense thwarted Pittsburgh in the final two periods, limiting the Steelers to a mere 70 yards in the second half and collecting six sacks and five turnovers on the afternoon. DB Ken Konz, who'd scored on an interception return for a touchdown in the first quarter, capped a good day with a 42-yard punt return to set up another. Offensively, Fred Morrison rushed for 140 yards on 17 carries. The Redskins kept pace in Chicago, staying within a game of the Browns with three to play.
Record: 7–2

	1	2	3	4		
Steelers	7	7	0	0	=	14
Browns	7	14	13	7	=	41

PIT-Nickel 16-yd. pass from Finks (Weed kick)
CLE-Konz 15-yd. interception return (Groza kick)
CLE-Lavelli 6-yd. pass from Graham (Groza kick)
PIT-Nickel 30-yd. pass from Marchibroda (Weed kick)
CLE-Lavelli 42-yd. pass from Graham (Groza kick)
CLE-Modzelewski 3-yd. run (kick failed)
CLE-Graham 4-yd. run (Groza kick)
CLE-Bassett 5-yd. run (Groza kick)

Passing
PIT: Finks 9–19–113 1 TD 3 INT, Marchibroda 5–13–71 1 TD 1 INT
CLE: Graham 6–9–79 2 TD 0 INT, Ratterman 2–2–41 0 TD 0 INT

Rushing
PIT: Mathews 3–24, Rogel 9–16, Watson 7–16, Marchibroda 2–10, Campbell 2–1
CLE: Morrison 17–140, Modzelewski 16–44, Bassett 2–9, Smith 4–6, Graham 10–0

Receiving
PIT: Nickel 4–76, Campbell 1–36, Watson 5–27, O'Brien 2–20, McClairen 1–13, Mathews 1–12
CLE: Lavelli 3–64, Renfro 2–26, Bassett 1–25, Modzelewski 2–5

Sunday, November 27
Browns 35, New York Giants 35
Polo Grounds (45,699)
Brown jerseys/white pants

In the most exciting game of the season and the final NFL game ever played in the Polo Grounds, the Browns and Giants matched one another blow for blow in a shootout that saw the teams combine for three touchdowns in a frantic final eight minutes. The Browns rallied from an early 14–0 deficit with three touchdowns to take a lead in the third quarter, but the Giants came right back with two more scores to go up 28–21 in the fourth. After a short Ed Modzelewski touchdown run tied the game again, on the Giants' next play from scrimmage, Chuck Noll intercepted New York QB Charlie Conerly and returned it 14 yards for the go-ahead touchdown. The Giants then drove the length of the field to tie it again with less than three minutes to play, but the Browns were poised to escape with a victory as they drove inside the New York 20 in the final seconds. But Lou Groza's 21-yard field-goal attempt was blocked—his second blocked kick of the day—to preserve the tie. Otto Graham directed a precision passing attack as he threw for 319 yards, with two of his targets—Ray Renfro and Pete Brewster—both going over the 100-yard mark. The stalemate enabled Washington, winners in Pittsburgh, to pull within a half-game of the Browns in the Eastern Conference.

Record: 7–2–1

	1	2	3	4		
Browns	0	7	14	14	=	35
Giants	7	7	7	14	=	35

NYG-Webster 1-yd. run (Agajanian kick)
NYG-Epps 14-yd. run (Agajanian kick)
CLE-Brewster 16-yd. pass from Graham (Groza kick)
CLE-Renfro 42-yd. pass from Graham (Groza kick)
CLE-Brewster 41-yd. pass from Graham (Groza kick)
NYG-Schnelker recovered fumble in end zone (Agajanian kick)
NYG-Rote 16-yd. pass from Conerly (Agajanian kick)
CLE-Modzelewski 2-yd. run (Groza kick)
CLE-Noll 14-yd. interception return (Groza kick)
NYG-Gifford 23-yd. pass from Conerly (Agajanian kick)

Passing
CLE: Graham 17–31–319 3 TD 1 INT
NYG: Conerly 15–27–187 2 TD, Heinrich 3–7–41 0 TD 0 INT

Rushing
CLE: Morrison 7–47, Graham 9–37, Modzelewski 19–33, Smith 1–4, D. Jones 1–0, Gillom 1-(-15)
NYG: Gifford 8 59, Rote 4–34, Epps 9–29, Price 4–22, Conerly 1–3, Webster 2–0

Receiving
CLE: Renfro 5–130, Brewster 5–107, Lavelli 5–74, Modzelewski 2–8
NYG: Schnelker 7–81, Rote 6–69, Gifford 3–54, MacAfee 2–24

Sunday, December 4
Browns 30, Pittsburgh Steelers 7
Forbes Field (31,101)
White jerseys/white pants

On a sunny afternoon, the Browns dominated the Steelers on a sloppy field to secure their eighth win and, with the Giants' upset victory over the Redskins, clinch their 10th consecutive division/conference title. As had been the case so many times previously in 1955, the Cleveland defense led the way, holding Pittsburgh to 123 total yards and forcing five turnovers, with the Steelers' only score coming on a fumble return for a touchdown. On offense, the Browns chewed up yards on the ground, finishing with 273, with Fred Morrison leading the way with 104 on 13 carries. Otto Graham completed only four passes on the afternoon, but two were for touchdowns as the Browns built a 30–0 lead in the third quarter and cruised to another win and a sixth straight berth in the NFL Championship.

Record: 8–2–1

	1	2	3	4		
Browns	10	10	10	0	=	30
Steelers	0	0	0	7	=	7

CLE-Graham 4-yd. run (Groza kick)
CLE-Groza 16-yd. FG
CLE-Renfro 46-yd. pass from Graham (Groza kick)
CLE-Groza 22-yd. FG
CLE-Brewster 17-yd. pass from Graham (Groza kick)
CLE-Groza 46-yd. FG
PIT-O'Malley recovered blocked punt in end zone (Weed kick)

Passing
CLE: Graham 4–12–95 2 TD 0 INT, Ratterman 3–4–20 0 TD 0 INT
PIT: Finks 5–20–96 0 TD 3 INT, Marchibroda 2–4–23 0 TD 1 INT, Eaton 0–2–0 0 TD 0 INT

Rushing
CLE: Morrison 13–104, Smith 13–58, Modzelewski 17–51, Bassett 9–35, D. Jones 1–13, Graham 6–12
PIT: Rogel 6–17, Mathews 2–11, Watson 5–2, Finks 1–0, Marchibroda 2-(-4)

Receiving
CLE: Brewster 3–46, Renfro 1–46, Lavelli 1–22, Smith 1–2, Bassett 1-(-1)
PIT: Bernet 2–64, Watson 3–46, Mathews 1–15, Campbell 1-(-6)

Sunday, December 11
Browns 35, Chicago Cardinals 24
Cleveland Stadium (25,914)
White jerseys/white pants

On a snowy afternoon in Cleveland, the Browns closed the book on a superb regular season by rallying from a 10-point fourth-quarter deficit with three touchdowns in the final five minutes to stun the Cardinals and extend their unbeaten streak to four games going into the NFL title game. In his final home game, Otto Graham threw for three touchdown passes, including the go-ahead strike to Ray Renfro from 41 yards out in the waning minutes of the game. The Browns watched a 14–6 lead turn into a 24–14 deficit and appeared destined for their third defeat before Chuck Noll came up with a game-changing interception with seven minutes left that sparked the comeback. A Fred Morrison touchdown run moments later cut the Chicago lead to three, then after the Cleveland defense forced the Cardinals to punt after three plays, Renfro reeled in a tipped pass from Graham for the go-ahead touchdown. Rookie RB Bob Smith added some insurance in the final minutes when he broke loose for a 31-yard touchdown run, which would be the only score of his brief career. The rousing comeback served as a perfect tune-up for the league championship in two weeks against the Rams, who clinched the Western Conference crown with a win over the Packers.

Record: 9–2–1

	1	2	3	4		
Cardinals	6	6	12	0	=	24
Browns	14	0	0	21	=	35

CHI-Mann 30-yd. run (kick failed)
CLE-Renfro 19-yd. pass from Graham (Groza kick)
CLE-Lavelli 35-yd. pass from Graham (Groza kick)
CHI-Boydston 67-yd. pass from McHan (kick failed)
CHI-Matson 78-yd. punt return (kick failed)
CLE-Morrison 10-yd. run (Groza kick)
CLE-Renfro 41-yd. pass from Graham (Groza kick)
CLE-Smith 31-yd. run (Groza kick)

Passing
CHI: McHan 12–25–165 2 TD 2 INT, Compton 0–2–0 0 TD 0 INT
CLE: Graham 13–25–241 3 TD 1 INT

Rushing
CHI: Olszewski 1–30, Carr 9–23, Hill 7–23, Compton 1–13, Hammack 3–10, Bernardi 7–8, Trippi 6–8, Matson 2–5
CLE: Modzelewski 15–45, Smith 2–33, Graham 6–26, Morrison 10–25, Renfro 1–14

Receiving
CHI: Stonesifer 8–80, Boydston 1–67, Bernardi 1–23, Matson 2–5
CLE: Renfro 6–110, Lavelli 4–65, Brewster 2–36, Morrison 1–30

1955 NFL Championship
Monday, December 26
Browns 38, Los Angeles Rams 14
Los Angeles Memorial Coliseum (87,695)
White jerseys/white pants

Playing for an NFL title for the third time in six seasons, the 1955 encounter between the Browns and Rams was the least memorable of the series but would still be remembered as the curtain call for one of the greatest players in NFL history.

Before a record crowd that shattered the previous attendance mark for the NFL title game by nearly 30,000, the Browns followed the script they'd perfected during the regular season: blowing open a close game in the second half thanks to a marvelous defensive performance. This time, the tone was set early in the sunshiny first quarter as Ken Konz intercepted Los Angeles QB Norm Van Brocklin at the Cleveland 12 in what would be the first of seven Cleveland interceptions on the afternoon. Don Paul returned another 65 yards for a touchdown to make it 10–0 early in the second quarter, then a long touchdown reception by Dante Lavelli put the Browns up 17–7 at the intermission.

Cleveland pulled away in the third on a pair of rushing touchdowns by Graham, playing in his final NFL game. He then added a second aerial score in the fourth to close out a magnificent career that saw him play in 10 consecutive championship games. With a light fog rolling onto the field in the final minutes, Graham came off the field to the loudest ovation of the day from the otherwise disappointed Los Angeles fans.

It was the Browns' third NFL title in six seasons and seventh championship in 10, but would mark the final crown for Paul Brown. With Graham and several other stalwarts of the 1940s and 1950s coming to the ends of their careers, the Browns were about to enter a new era of their history.

	1	2	3	4		
Browns	3	14	14	7	=	38
Rams	0	7	0	7	=	14

CLE-Groza 26-yd. FG
CLE-Paul 65-yd. interception return (Groza kick)
LA-Quinlan 67-yd. pass from Van Brocklin (Richter kick)
CLE-Lavelli 50-yd. pass from Graham (Groza kick)
CLE-Graham 15-yd. run (Groza kick)
CLE-Graham 1-yd. run (Groza kick)
CLE-Renfro 35-yd. pass from Graham (Groza kick)
LA-Waller 4-yd. run (Richter kick)

Passing

CLE: Graham 14–25–209 2 TD 3 INT
LA: Van Brocklin 11–25–166 1 TD 6 INT, Wade 0–3–0 0 TD 1 INT

Rushing

CLE: Modzelewski 13–61, Bassett 11–49, Morrison 11–33, Graham 9–21, D. Jones 1–3, Smith 3–2
LA: Towler 14–64, Waller 11–48, Wade 1–4

Receiving

CLE: Lavelli 3–95, Renfro 2–49, Modzelewski 5–34, D. Jones 1–11, Brewster 1–9, Morrison 1–7, Bassett 1–4
LA: Quinlan 5–116, Waller 3–18, Fears 1–16, Hirsch 1–9, Towler 1–7

1956

Sunday, September 30
Chicago Cardinals 9, Browns 7
Comiskey Park (20,966)
White jerseys/white pants

On a sunny afternoon in Chicago, the Browns began the post-Otto Graham era by losing on opening day for the third consecutive year as the Cardinals used some late heroics to secure their first-ever win over the Browns after 12 straight losses. Though the Cleveland offense struggled, accumulating just over 200 yards and only eight first downs on the day, the Browns took a one-point lead into the fourth quarter thanks to a 46-yard scoring pass from new starting QB George Ratterman to WR Ray Renfro on their first possession. The Browns' offense managed little else the remainder of the game, seeing their only other scoring opportunity go awry when Lou Groza had a 42-yard field goal blocked in the third quarter. The Cardinals controlled the ball for much of the game but still trailed until beginning their final march midway through the final period. After driving inside the Cleveland 5, Pat Summerall kicked the game-winner with 29 seconds left, atoning for missing an 18-yard kick in the second quarter. Despite allowing 276 rushing yards, the Cleveland defense endured, holding Chicago without a touchdown. The cause was aided by DB Don Paul, who picked off two passes against his former team.

Record: 0–1

	1	2	3	4		
Browns	7	0	0	0	=	7
Cardinals	3	3	0	3	=	9

CHI-Summerall 12-yd. FG
CLE-Renfro 46-yd. pass from Ratterman (Groza kick)
CHI-Summerall 16-yd. FG
CHI-Summerall 9-yd. FG

Passing
CLE: Ratterman 6–12–89 1 TD 2 INT, Parilli 1–1–34 0 TD 0 INT
CHI: Root 4–8–35 0 TD 2 INT, McHan 3–7–33 0 TD 1 INT, Matson 0–1–0 0 TD

Rushing
CLE: Morrison 14–67, Bassett 4–26, Modzelewski 7–15, Ratterman 2–0
CHI: Matson 20–144, Olszewski 17–63, McHan 8–34, Mann 5–28, Bernardi 2–6, Childress 1–1

Receiving
CLE: Renfro 3–72, P. Carpenter 1–34, Brewster 1–16, Bassett 2–1
CHI: Stonesifer 3–35, Nagler 1–17, Olszewski 1–13, Matson 1–4, Mann 1-(-1)

Saturday, October 6
Browns 14, Pittsburgh Steelers 10
Forbes Field (35,398)
White jerseys/white pants

With points at a premium for the second straight week, the Browns rallied for a fourth-quarter touchdown and then made a key defensive play in the waning moments to secure their first victory of the season in a Saturday-night clash with the Steelers. Trailing 10–7 midway through the final period, RB Ed Modzelewski exploded for a 13-yard touchdown run on a trap play to give the Browns the lead, but Pittsburgh drove to the Cleveland 2 with just over a minute to play. After a two-yard loss on third down, a fourth-down pass was knocked away by Cleveland DB Warren Lahr, and the Browns regained possession and ran out the clock. George Ratterman played well, completing 14 of 17 passes—including 11 straight at one point, but it was the Cleveland running game that led the way, rolling to 214 yards.

Record: 1–1

	1	2	3	4		
Browns	0	7	0	7	=	14
Steelers	0	10	0	0	=	10

CLE-Ratterman 1-yd. run (Groza kick)
PIT-Glick 30-yd. FG
PIT-Chandnois 1-yd. run (Glick kick)
CLE-Modzelewski 13-yd. run (Groza kick)

Passing
CLE: Ratterman 14–17–122 0 TD 0 INT
PIT: Marchibroda 13–25–153 0 TD 0 INT

Rushing
CLE: Morrison 12–69, P. Carpenter 8–62, Modzelewski 13–56, Smith 2–10, Renfro 2–9, Ratterman 4–8
PIT: Marchibroda 6–40, Chandnois 11–21, Watson 6–21, Rogel 9–12, Varrichione 1–2

Receiving
CLE: Lavelli 3–54, Renfro 2–24, Brewster 2–17, P. Carpenter 3–13, Morrison 2–8, Modzelewski 2–6
PIT: Perry 4–68, Mathews 5–61, Chandnois 1–11, Rogel 1–7, Nickel 1–6, Watson 1–0

Sunday, October 14
New York Giants 21, Browns 9
Cleveland Stadium (60,042)
White jerseys/white pants

In their home opener, the Browns were completely dominated by the eventual NFL champion Giants and were forced to abandon Paul Brown's innovative use of electronic communications via QB George Ratterman's helmet due to technical problems in the early going. Though New York controlled both lines of scrimmage from the outset, the game went to halftime tied at seven after the Browns blocked a field goal, and LB Galen Fiss returned the ball 55 yards to set up a short Ed Modzelewski touchdown leap. The second half was all Giants as RB Alex Webster scored two of his three touchdowns, the second of which put the game away with nine minutes remaining and was followed by a deliberate safety by the Giants with two minutes left. The Browns could manage only 134 total yards, including a mere 40 on the ground on 25 carries, while the Giants cruised to 256 rushing yards and 330 total, while collecting seven sacks. After the helmet communicator raised lively debate among reporters and coaches, NFL commissioner Bert Bell banned the invention the following week.
Record: 1–2

	1	2	3	4		
Giants	0	7	7	7	=	21
Browns	0	7	0	2	=	9

NYG-Webster 2-yd. pass from Heinrich (Gifford kick)
CLE-Modzelewski 1-yd. run (Groza kick)
NYG-Webster 1-yd. run (Chandler kick)
NYG-Webster 34-yd. run (Chandler kick)
CLE-Safety: Wren tackled Conerly in end zone

Passing
NYG: Heinrich 6–8–44 1 TD 2 INT, Conerly 3–5–30 0 TD 0 INT
CLE: Ratterman 17–25–156 0 TD 1 INT

Rushing
NYG: Webster 16–94, Triplett 19–91, Gifford 11–73, Heinrich 1–1, Conerly 5-(-3)
CLE: Modzelewski 14–28, Ratterman 3–10, Morrison 8–2

Receiving
NYG: Gifford 4–42, Schnelker 2–20, MacAfee 1–12, Webster 2–0
CLE: Lavelli 5–74, Brewster 3–38, P. Carpenter 3–31, Modzelewski 5–9, Morrison 1–4

Sunday, October 21
Washington Redskins 20, Browns 9
Griffith Stadium (23,332)
White jerseys/white pants

For the second straight week, the Browns' offense was held scoreless in the second half as they were unable to hold onto a third-quarter lead and dropped to 1–3 for the first time in team history. The Browns got off to a good start, driving to the Washington 26 on their first possession before George Ratterman suffered what proved to be a career-ending knee injury and was replaced by backup QB Babe Parilli. Behind a trio of Lou Groza field goals, the Browns crept to a 9–7 halftime lead, but the winless Redskins scored 13 points in the second half to win going away. While the Cleveland defense once again did an admirable job, the offense managed just 216 total yards and turned the ball over four times.
Record: 1–3

	1	2	3	4		
Browns	3	6	0	0	=	9
Redskins	0	7	7	6	=	20

CLE-Groza 30-yd. FG
WAS-Elter 5-yd. run (Baker kick)
CLE-Groza 47-yd. FG
CLE-Groza 12-yd. FG
WAS-James 9-yd. pass from LeBaron (Baker kick)
WAS-Baker 16-yd. FG
WAS-Baker 32-yd. FG

Passing
CLE: Parilli 8–17–93 0 TD 2 INT, Ratterman 2–3–31 0 TD 0 INT
WAS: LeBaron 4–9–38 1 TD 2 INT, Dorow 0–1–0 0 TD 0 INT

Rushing
CLE: Modzelewski 13–47, P. Carpenter 9–33, Parilli 6–19, Morrison 1–8, Quinlan 1–3, Ratterman 1–1
WAS: Elter 16–91, Atkeson 9–34, Runnels 6–27, James 6–26, Baker 4–17, LeBaron 2–5

Receiving
CLE: Lavelli 5–68, Brewster 3–38, Renfro 1–18, P. Carpenter 1–0
WAS: Baker 1–17, Meilinger 2–12, James 1–9

Sunday, October 28
Pittsburgh Steelers 24, Browns 16
Cleveland Stadium (50,358)
White jerseys/white pants

After sprinting to a 13–0 lead in the first three minutes, the Browns fell apart and were dominated by the Steelers in their fourth dispiriting loss. Babe Parilli made his first pro start at QB and hit WR Dante Lavelli for a 68-yard touchdown pass on the game's fourth play, and three plays later DB Don Paul returned an interception 35 yards for another score. Parilli would struggle the remainder of the afternoon, throwing three interceptions as Pittsburgh bounced back with a trio of touchdowns in the second quarter to take control of the contest. After having a field goal blocked in the second quarter, Lou Groza cut the Pittsburgh lead to 21–16 early in the fourth, but the Steelers sealed the victory with a field goal of their own in the final minutes, dropping the Browns to their fourth loss in five games.
Record: 1–4

	1	2	3	4		
Steelers	0	21	0	3	=	24
Browns	13	0	0	3	=	16

CLE-Lavelli 68-yd. pass from Parilli (kick failed)
CLE-Paul 35-yd. interception return (Groza kick)
PIT-Nickel 10-yd. pass from Marchibroda (Glick kick)
PIT-Chandnois 1-yd. run (Glick kick)
PIT-Perry 75-yd. pass from Marchibroda (Glick kick)
CLE-Groza 28-yd. FG
PIT-Glick 11-yd. FG

Passing
PIT: Marchibroda 12–19–227 2 TD 3 INT, Chandnois 0–1–0 0 TD 0 INT
CLE: Parilli 7–16–126 1 TD 3 INT

Rushing
PIT: Rogel 10–62, Chandnois 13–37, Perry 1–14, Shepard 2–13, Watson 3–6, Marchibroda 3–4, Baldacci 1–3
CLE: P. Carpenter 21–82, Modzelewski 14–63, Parilli 3–29, Morrison 1–2

Receiving
PIT: Perry 2–112, Nickel 4–55, Rogel 3–24, Chandnois 2–20, Mathews 1–16
CLE: Lavelli 1–68, Brewster 4–50, Renfro 1–8, Modzelewski 1–0

Sunday, November 4
Browns 24, Green Bay Packers 7
Milwaukee County Stadium (28,590)
White jerseys/white pants

On a chilly, damp day in Milwaukee, the Browns took control early and picked up a much-needed victory. In the opening minutes, LB Chuck Noll scooped up a Green Bay fumble and returned it 39 yards for a touchdown. A Ray Renfro scoring reception and a Lou Groza field goal set up by another Green Bay fumble stretched the advantage to 17–0 before the Packers got on the board in the fourth quarter. Led by RB Preston Carpenter (21 carries, 91 yards) and Ed Modzelewski (22 carries, 90 yards), the Browns rolled up 222 rushing yards, attempting only four passes all afternoon.
Record: 2–4

	1	2	3	4		
Browns	7	7	0	10	=	24
Packers	0	0	0	7	=	7

CLE-Noll 39-yd. fumble return (Groza kick)
CLE-Renfro 26-yd. pass from Parilli (Groza kick)
CLE-Groza 13-yd. FG
GB-Howton 10-yd. pass from Rote (Cone kick)
CLE-Morrison 1-yd. run (Groza kick)

Passing
CLE: Parilli 2–3–57 1 TD 1 INT, O'Connell 0–1–0 0 TD 0 INT
GB: Rote 12–26–159 1 TD 0 INT, Starr 2–3–9 0 TD 0 INT

Rushing
CLE: P. Carpenter 21–91, Modzelewski 22–90, Morrison 2–24, Parilli 6–14, O'Connell 2–3, Bassett 1–0
GB: Carmichael 6–66, Rote 7–28, Johnson 6–22, Ferguson 1–7, Reid 1–3, Cone 5–1

Receiving
CLE: Quinlan 1–31, Renfro 1–26
GB: Cone 4–71, Howton 3–56, Johnson 3–19, Knafelc 1–19, Carmichael 2–3, Losch 1–0

Sunday, November 11
Baltimore Colts 21, Browns 7
Cleveland Stadium (42,404)
White jerseys/white pants

Behind a dominating ground attack, the Colts broke open a 7–7 game with two fourth-quarter touchdowns to drop the Browns to their fifth defeat. Cleveland took the lead on a Ray Renfro touchdown catch on its first possession, but the offense was stymied for the remainder of the afternoon, turning the ball over four times. A fumbled punt return set up the Colts' first touchdown, and a goal-line stand by Baltimore in the second quarter preserved the 7–7 tie. After Babe Parilli fumbled in Baltimore territory in the fourth quarter, Colts' RB Lenny Moore broke free for a 70-yard touchdown run to give the Colts the lead and they added an insurance touchdown in the final minutes. With both Moore and RB Alan Ameche topping the century mark, Baltimore rolled to 305 rushing yards, picking up only five net yards passing on the afternoon. Making matters worse for the Browns, Parilli was injured and lost for the rest of the season.
Record: 2–5

	1	2	3	4		
Colts	7	0	0	14	=	21
Browns	7	0	0	0	=	7

CLE-Renfro 27-yd. pass from Parilli (Groza kick)
BAL-Ameche 1-yd. run (Feamster kick)
BAL-Moore 70-yd. run (Feamster kick)
BAL-Dupre 12-yd. run (Feamster kick)

Passing
BAL: Unitas 5–14–21 0 TD 0 INT
CLE: Parilli 6–12–99 1 TD 1 INT, O'Connell 5–12–57 0 TD 0 INT

Rushing
BAL: Moore 11–120, Ameche 18–108, Unitas 4–40, Dupre 7–34, Vessels 2–2, Womble 1–1
CLE: Modzelewski 14–91, P. Carpenter 16–38, Parilli 3–3, O'Connell 2–3, Morrison 1–0

Receiving
BAL: Dupre 2–11, Mutscheller 2–7, Ameche 1–3
CLE: Renfro 5–100, Quinlan 3–32, Brewster 1–19, Modzelewski 1–6, P. Carpenter 1-(-1)

Sunday, November 18
Browns 16, Philadelphia Eagles 0
Connie Mack Stadium (25,894)
White jerseys/white pants

Behind a brilliant defensive performance, the Browns cruised to an easy victory in Philadelphia, posting their first shutout in two years. The Browns held the Eagles to just 71 total yards, picking up four sacks and three turnovers as Philadelphia didn't cross midfield the entire game. With Tommy O'Connell—signed after George Ratterman went down a month earlier—making his first NFL start at QB, the Browns extended a 3–0 lead to 10 points on the first possession of the second half when O'Connell hit RB Maurice Bassett for a 31-yard score. The Cleveland ground game was effective, totaling 233 yards, and was paced by Preston Carpenter's 133 on 24 carries. But the Browns' back luck in 1956 continued when Ed Modzelewski was lost for the remainder of the season with a broken leg and dislocated ankle.
Record: 3–5

	1	2	3	4		
Browns	0	3	7	6	=	16
Eagles	0	0	0	0	=	0

CLE-Groza 22-yd. FG
CLE-Bassett 31-yd. pass from O'Connell (Groza kick)
CLE-Groza 41-yd. FG
CLE-Groza 15-yd. FG

Passing
CLE: O'Connell 4–11–63 1 TD 0 INT
PHI: Thomason 4–12–39 0 TD 2 INT

Rushing
CLE: P. Carpenter 24–133, Modzelewski 10–41, Morrison 12–30, Bassett 7–24, Renfro 1–5
PHI: Schaefer 6–21, Giancanelli 7–20, Bielski 5–16, Keller 8–8, Thomason 3–3

Receiving
CLE: Bassett 1–31, Brewster 1–13, Lavelli 1–13, Modzelewski 1–6
PHI: Burnine 1–13, Walston 1–11, Schaefer 1–9, Bielski 1–6

Sunday, November 25
Washington Redskins 20, Browns 17
Cleveland Stadium (22,878)
White jerseys/white pants

On the brink of salvaging a season split with the Redskins, the Browns couldn't close out the victory and instead lost a defensive battle in the waning moments to a red-hot Washington team. After the 'Skins got on the scoreboard on a fumble return for a touchdown, the Browns tied the game on a 65-yard punt return for a score by Ken Konz, then surged ahead after Cleveland lineman Bob Gain recovered a fumble to set up a short touchdown run by Maurice Bassett. Clinging to a 17–13 lead with time running out, the Browns gave the Redskins new life with a roughing-the-punter penalty that resulted in a first down and kept Washington's drive alive. Moments later, QB Eddie LeBaron hit WR John Carson for a 26-yard touchdown with 1:30 to play to give the Redskins their fifth straight victory.
Record: 3–6

	1	2	3	4		
Redskins	7	0	6	7	=	20
Browns	7	7	0	3	=	17

WAS-Hecker 17-yd. fumble return (Baker kick)
CLE-Konz 65-yd. punt return (Groza kick)
CLE-Bassett 1-yd. run (Groza kick)
WAS-Baker 31-yd. FG
WAS-Baker 19-yd. FG
CLE-Groza 42-yd. FG
WAS-Carson 26-yd. pass from LeBaron (Baker kick)

Passing
WAS: LeBaron 8–16–108 1 TD 1 INT, Dorow 2–4–32 0 TD 0 INT
CLE: O'Connell 6–12–48 0 TD 1 INT

Rushing
WAS: Elter 11–40, Runnels 9–23, Wells 6–12, LeBaron 5–10, Baker 4–8, Dorow 1–4
CLE: P. Carpenter 29–89, Bassett 15–43, O'Connell 1–3, Quinlan 1–1

Receiving
WAS: Carson 4–73, Meilinger 3–42, Elter 2–26, Wells 1–1
CLE: Brewster 3–40, Lavelli 1–7, P. Carpenter 2–1

Sunday, December 2
Browns 17, Philadelphia Eagles 14
Cleveland Stadium (20,654)
White jerseys/white pants

Despite five turnovers and two penalties called on the Cleveland fans, the Browns endured for a last-minute victory over the Eagles, their first home triumph of the season. With a cold rain falling and snow piled up in the stands, fans expressed their disapproval over the officials not penalizing the Eagles for knocking down the intended Cleveland receiver on a play that resulted in an interception by pelting snowballs at the officials. They in turn penalized the Browns five yards for unsportsmanlike conduct for the fans' behavior. Later, when the Eagles were pinned back near the bleachers, fans flung snowballs at them, resulting in a 15-yard penalty. With the sloppy game tied at 14 with time running out, the Eagles had to punt from their own end zone, and the ensuing return and a personal foul on Philadelphia gave the Browns a first down at the Eagles' 28 to set up Lou Groza's winning field goal with 29 seconds left. Preston Carpenter paced the Browns' offense with 116 rushing yards on 23 carries, while Tommy O'Connell tossed a pair of touchdown passes, the first a fourth-down connection with wideout Pete Brewster.
Record: 4–6

	1	2	3	4		
Eagles	7	0	7	0	=	14
Browns	7	7	0	3	=	17

PHI-Thomason 1-yd. run (Walston kick)
CLE-Brewster 3-yd. pass from O'Connell (Groza kick)
CLE-Renfro 46-yd. pass from O'Connell (Groza kick)
PHI-Keller 20-yd. run (Walston kick)
CLE-Groza 37-yd. FG

Passing
PHI: Burk 9–18–91 0 TD 2 INT, Thomason 4–10–39 0 TD 1 INT
CLE: O'Connell 9–18–115 2 TD 2 INT

Rushing
PHI: Bielski 11–51, Keller 9–43, Berzinski 6–34, Schaefer 2–16, Burk 4–3, Thomason 1–1
CLE: P. Carpenter 23–116, Bassett 14–36, Morrison 5–21, Renfro 1–10, O'Connell 4-(-6)

Receiving
PHI: Walston 5–49, Burnine 1–22, Retzlaff 1–20, Berzinski 2–18, Wegert 3–17, Bielski 1–4
CLE: Renfro 1–46, Brewster 3–28, Lavelli 2–26, P. Carpenter 2–18, Bassett 1–3

Sunday, December 9
Browns 24, New York Giants 7
Yankee Stadium (27,707)
Brown jerseys/white pants

The 11-point underdog Browns put together their most impressive performance of the season, overwhelming the eventual league-champion Giants on their own home field. On a dark afternoon that saw a mixture of rain and snow, the Browns took control early on a muddy field after recovering a fumbled punt return by New York. They then drove to the one-yard line, where Tommy O'Connell plunged over the goal line to make it 7–0. After the Giants tied the game, the Browns surged ahead again with 10 second-quarter points, then stretched it to 24–7 on another O'Connell score early in the third quarter, capping an 82-yard drive. The Cleveland defense kept the Giants in check from there, holding star RB Frank Gifford to just 16 yards on six carries. Meanwhile, the Browns rolled up 193 yards on the ground, paced by Fred Morrison's 112 on 19 rushes. The Giants, booed off the field by their fans at the game's conclusion, wound up clinching the Eastern Conference title later that afternoon anyway when the Chicago Cardinals were defeated by the Chicago Bears.
Record: 5–6

	1	2	3	4		
Browns	7	10	7	0	=	24
Giants	0	7	0	0	=	7

CLE-O'Connell 1 yd. run (Groza kick)
NYG-Gifford 6-yd. pass from Conerly (Agajanian kick)
CLE-Groza 41-yd. FG
CLE-Morrison 6-yd. pass from O'Connell (Groza kick)
CLE-O'Connell 1-yd. run (Groza kick)

Passing
CLE: O'Connell 7–11–106 1 TD 1 INT
NYG: Conerly 10–24–103 1 TD 1 INT, Clatterbuck 2–3–17 0 TD 0 INT, Heinrich 2–4–6 0 TD 0 INT

Rushing
CLE: Morrison 19–112, P. Carpenter 23–70, O'Connell 7–11
NYG: Webster 11–46, Triplett 6–41, Gifford 6–16

Receiving
CLE: Brewster 3–64, P. Carpenter 2–28, Morrison 2–14
NYG: Gifford 6–56, Rote 1–21, Filipski 2–16, MacAfee 1–15, Webster 2–12, Chandler 1–5, Triplett 1–1

Sunday, December 16
Chicago Cardinals 24, Browns 7
Cleveland Stadium (25,312)
White jerseys/white pants

On a gloomy afternoon, the Browns ended the season the same way they began it—scoring an early touchdown and then mustering no other offense as they were defeated by the Cardinals. After drawing first blood when rookie holder Billy Kinard ran for a 27-yard touchdown on a fake field goal, it was downhill for the Cleveland offense as Tommy O'Connell threw four interceptions. The Cardinals took the lead with a pair of second-quarter touchdowns and controlled the line of scrimmage throughout the game, rushing for 221 yards while completing only two passes. The game was the final ever played by eventual Hall of Fame WR Dante Lavelli, who concluded his magnificent 11-year career. The Browns' seventh defeat marked the first losing season in team history and the first time Paul Brown had suffered a losing campaign since 1943, when he was the head coach of the war-riddled Ohio State Buckeyes.
Record: 5–7

	1	2	3	4		
Cardinals	0	14	3	7	=	24
Browns	7	0	0	0	=	7

CLE-Kinard 27-yd. run (Groza kick)
CHI-McHan 1-yd. run (Summerall kick)
CHI-Matson 1-yd. run (Summerall kick)
CHI-Summerall 15-yd. FG
CHI-McHan 3-yd. run (Summerall kick)

Passing
CHI: McHan 2–7–31 0 TD 1 INT, Matson 0–1–0 0 TD 0 INT
CLE: O'Connell 11–31–162 0 TD 4 INT

Rushing
CHI: Olszewski 18–90, Matson 22–80, Childress 6–22, McHan 8–15, Mann 4–13, Root 1–1
CLE: P. Carpenter 14–42, Kinard 1–27, O'Connell 8–26, Morrison 8–5

Receiving
CHI: Stonesifer 1–25, Olszewski 1–6
CLE: Brewster 4–94, Lavelli 2–34, Renfro 3–31, Morrison 1–3, P. Carpenter 1–0

1957

Sunday, September 29
Browns 6, New York Giants 3
Cleveland Stadium (58,095)
Brown jerseys/white pants

Setting the tone for a comeback season, the Browns stunned the defending world champions with a dramatic opening-day victory in the final seconds—the Browns' first Week One triumph in four years. In a titanic defensive struggle, neither the Browns nor the Giants could cross the goal line or accumulate 200 yards of offense, but the home team came up with a gutsy drive when it was needed most. New York was poised to take the lead midway through the fourth quarter, but kicker Ben Agajanian missed a chip-shot 16-yard field goal, and the score remained 3–3. With five minutes left, the Browns regained possession at their own 20 and gradually began marching upfield. The key play was a 15-yard run on third-and-11 by rookie RB Jim Brown, playing in his first NFL game, who blasted over left tackle to the New York 44. Brown, who picked up 31 yards on the winning drive, finished his first game with 89 on 21 carries. The rookie's heroics pushed the Browns into field-goal range, and Lou Groza booted a 47-yard attempt through a stiff lake breeze and between the uprights with 21 seconds remaining to put the Browns ahead 6–3. A last-gasp drive by the Giants reached midfield, where a desperation 54-yard kick by Agajanian fell well short as time expired. The Cleveland defense started off the season in brilliant fashion, limiting the Giants to just three pass completions in 16 attempts and picking off a pair of passes. This also marked the first time the Browns wore brown jerseys for a home game in 10 years and also the first game the Browns played with each player's numerals on his helmet, a change that would last through the 1960 season.

Record: 1–0

	1	2	3	4		
Giants	0	3	0	0	=	3
Browns	0	3	0	3	=	6

NYG-Agajanian 32-yd. FG
CLE-Groza 29-yd. FG
CLE-Groza 47-yd. FG

Passing
NYG: Conerly 2–11–35 0 TD 2 INT, Heinrich 1–5–4 0 TD 0 INT
CLE: O'Connell 4–8–46 0 TD 0 INT, Borton 0–1–0 0 TD 0 INT, Hanulak 0–1–0 0 TD 0 INT

Rushing
NYG: Webster 13–69, Triplett 11–51, Gifford 11–39, Epps 3–4, Conerly 1-(-8)
CLE: Brown 21–89, Hanulak 17–16, Campbell 1–14, Renfro 1–6, O'Connell 1-(-3)

Receiving
NYG: Rote 1–24, Epps 1–11, Webster 1–4
CLE: Brewster 1–25, Renfro 2–15, Brown 1–6

Saturday, October 5
Browns 23, Pittsburgh Steelers 12
Forbes Field (35,570)
White jerseys/white pants

The day after Sputnik was launched by the Soviet Union, the Browns were clinging to a one-point lead in the second half in a Saturday-night affair at Forbes Field when a little-used rookie RB named Milt Campbell helped propel the Browns to a victory over an improved Steelers team. After the Browns took a 13–6 lead in the third quarter on a halfback-option touchdown pass from Chet Hanulak to WR Ray Renfro and a trio of Lou Groza field goals, the Steelers were poised to tie the game following QB Earl Morrall's second touchdown pass later in the period. But Campbell broke through the Pittsburgh line to block the extra point and keep the Browns ahead. Then, after DB Junior Wren intercepted a pass to set up another Groza field goal in the fourth, Campbell put the game away when he reeled in a 25-yard touchdown pass from QB Tommy O'Connell. It would be the only touchdown—and only reception—of Campbell's one-year NFL career, but it turned out to be memorable. For the second straight week, the Cleveland defense was strong, holding the Steelers to just 63 rushing yards while forcing four turnovers and collecting nine sacks behind a ferocious pass rush. Pittsburgh was equally impressive in holding Jim Brown to 39 yards on 15 carries.

Record: 2–0

	1	2	3	4		
Browns	0	10	3	10	=	23
Steelers	0	6	6	0	=	12

CLE-Renfro 32-yd. pass from Hanulak (Groza kick)
PIT-Girard 21-yd. pass from Morrall (kick failed)
CLE-Groza 29-yd. FG
CLE-Groza 45-yd. FG
PIT-Girard 32-yd. pass from Morrall (kick failed)
CLE-Groza 14-yd. FG
CLE-Campbell 25-yd. pass from O'Connell (Groza kick)

Passing
CLE: O'Connell 10–17–122 1 TD 0 INT, Hanulak 1–1–32 1 TD 0 INT, Campbell 0–1–0 0 TD 0 INT
PIT: Morrall 17–25–255 2 TD 1 INT

Rushing
CLE: Hanulak 11–40, Brown 15–39, Campbell 4–11, Modzelewski 2–6, O'Connell 3–5, Reynolds 1–5
PIT: Bowman 10–31, Derby 8–26, Rogel 1–4, Morrall 1–1, Young 1–1

Receiving
CLE: P. Carpenter 4–65, Campbell 1–25, Renfro 1–32, Brewster 1–18, Clarke 1–10, Brown 3–4
PIT: Derby 4–79, Bowman 6–57, McClairen 3–53, Girard 2–53, Mathews 1–17, Rogel 1-(-4)

Sunday, October 13
Browns 24, Philadelphia Eagles 7
Cleveland Stadium (53,493)
Brown jerseys/white pants

In a game marred by on-field fisticuffs that resulted in seven players being ejected, the Browns rolled over the winless Eagles on a perfect October afternoon thanks to another dominant performance by their defense. Holding Philadelphia to a mere 107 total yards, the Browns soared a 17–0 halftime lead and took a 24–0 advantage into the fourth quarter. After a 56-yard pass from Tommy O'Connell to WR Pete Brewster on the game's first play, Jim Brown scored his first NFL touchdown on a short pass from O'Connell to put the Browns up 7–0. Brown's score was followed minutes later by a 64-yard scoring jaunt by RB Chet Hanulak. The Eagles' only points came in the waning minutes on an interception return for a touchdown by DB Jimmy Harris. Once again looking like a title contender, the Browns moved to 3–0 for only the second time since joining the NFL.
Record: 3–0

	1	2	3	4		
Eagles	0	0	0	7	=	7
Browns	14	3	7	0	=	24

CLE-Brown 5-yd. pass from O'Connell (Groza kick)
CLE-Hanulak 64-yd. run (Groza kick)
CLE-Groza 22-yd. FG
CLE-Reynolds 5-yd. run (Groza kick)
PHI-Harris 65-yd. interception return (Walston kick)

Passing
PHI: Dorow 6–12–56 0 TD 1 INT, Jurgensen 4–10–17 0 TD 1 INT, Thomason 0–1–0 0 TD 1 INT
CLE: O'Connell 5–7–120 1 TD 0 INT, Borton 0–2–0 0 TD 1 INT, Plum 0–2–0 0 TD 0 INT

Rushing
PHI: Peaks 10–22, Worden 5–19, McDonald 2–17, Keller 5–13, Thomason 1–5, Youngelman 1–3, Dorow 3–1, Barnes 1–1, Jurgensen 2-(-18)
CLE: Hanulak 8–89, Reynolds 18–42, Brown 10–28, Modzelewski 2–2, Plum 2–2, O'Connell 1–2

Receiving
PHI: Retzlaff 4–52, Burnine 1–16, Stribling 2–13, Walston 1–6, Bielski 1-(-5), Gaona 1-(-9)
CLE: Brewster 4–105, Brown 1–5

Sunday, October 20
Philadelphia Eagles 17, Browns 7
Connie Mack Stadium (22,443)
White jerseys/white pants

Seven days after dominating the Eagles in Cleveland, the tables were turned on the Browns in the rematch in Philadelphia as the Eagles cashed in on six turnovers and 10 penalties to upset the Browns and drop them into a tie with the Giants for first place in the Eastern Conference. The Browns struggled from the outset, not picking up a first down until the second quarter, and spent much of the day pinned deep in their own territory. Tommy O'Connell was knocked out of the game and replaced as quarterback by rookie Milt Plum, but neither could get the Cleveland offense rolling and combined to throw four interceptions, two to Eagles' LB Chuck Benardik. The Browns' lone touchdown was a one-yard plunge by Jim Brown with just over six minutes to play and marked the rookie's first rushing touchdown. The surprising loss snapped an eight-game losing streak for Philadelphia that dated back to 1956 and signified the last time the Browns would play in legendary Connie Mack Stadium (a.k.a. Shibe Park). It also marked the only time in Browns' UFL history they played the same team in back-to-back weeks in the regular season (on three occasions they would play the same team two weeks in a row in the season finale followed by a postseason game—the Lions in 1954, the Giants in 1958, and the Houston Oilers in 1988).

Record: 3–1

	1	2	3	4		
Browns	0	0	0	7	=	7
Eagles	3	7	0	7	=	17

PHI-Walston 12-yd. FG
PHI-Ryan 46-yd. pass from Jurgensen (Walston kick)
PHI-Jurgensen 1-yd. run (Walston kick)
CLE-Brown 1-yd. run (Groza kick)

Passing
CLE: O'Connell 6–12–116 0 TD 3 INT, Plum 7–13–78 0 TD 1 INT
PHI: Jurgensen 6–9–84 1 TD 0 INT, Barnes 0–1–0 0 TD 0 INT

Rushing
CLE: Brown 12–53, L. Carpenter 9–30, Renfro 1–16, Reynolds 3–6, Plum 1–5, McCormack 1–4, Hanulak 3–3, O'Connell 2-(-14)
PHI: Barnes 22–87, Peaks 18–72, Worden 3–21, Jurgensen 2–6

Receiving
CLE: Clarke 2–55, L. Carpenter 3–40, Renfro 2–30, Brewster 2–29, P. Carpenter 1–16, Brown 2–12, Reynolds 1–12
PHI: Ryan 2–66, Barnes 4–18

Sunday, October 27
Browns 17, Chicago Cardinals 7
Comiskey Park (26,341)
White jerseys/white pants

Though the offense struggled for the second straight week, the Cleveland defense came to the rescue on a bright but chilly afternoon to propel the Browns to their fourth victory and—with a Giants' loss to Washington—back into sole possession of first place in the Eastern Conference. Trailing 7–3 late in the third quarter, the Browns' defense turned the game around when DE Len Ford recovered a fumble at the Philadelphia 10. Moments later Jim Brown scored on a fourth-down play to give the Browns the lead. Cleveland then salted the game away with less than five minutes remaining on another fourth-down touchdown when Tommy O'Connell, who'd replaced Milt Plum in the second half, hit Preston Carpenter to make it 17–7. In another defensive battle, the Cardinals were limited to just seven first downs and 157 total yards. After scoring their only touchdown three minutes into the game, the Cards were kept off the board for the remainder of the contest and didn't cross midfield in the second half.

Record: 4–1

	1	2	3	4		
Browns	3	0	7	7	=	17
Cardinals	7	0	0	0	=	7

CHI-Matson 19-yd. run (Summerall kick)
CLE-Groza 30-yd. FG
CLE-Brown 1-yd. run (Groza kick)
CLE-P. Carpenter 14-yd. pass from O'Connell (Groza kick)

Passing
CLE: O'Connell 2–3–31 1 TD 0 INT, Plum 3–9–11 0 TD 1 INT
CHI: McHan 4–10–64 0 TD 0 INT, Marchibroda 0–2–0 0 TD 1 INT, Matson 0–1–0 0 TD 0 INT

Rushing
CLE: Hanulak 21–74, Brown 22–70, Reynolds 5–9, Plum 2–9
CHI: Matson 16–63, Olszewski 10–31, McHan 3–9

Receiving
CLE: Brewster 1–17, P. Carpenter 1–14, Brown 2–7, Renfro 1–4
CHI: Lewis 2–49, Nagler 1–9, Matson 1–6

Sunday, November 3
Browns 21, Washington Redskins 17
Cleveland Stadium (52,936)
Brown jerseys/white pants

Once again sparked by a marvelous defensive performance, the Browns scored a pair of third-quarter touchdowns to take control of a tight contest, then held off the Redskins in the final minutes to capture their fifth win in six games. Leading the way for the Cleveland offense was Jim Brown, who topped the century mark for the first time, finishing with 109 rushing yards and a pair of touchdowns, including the go-ahead score in the third quarter. After a one-yard plunge by Tommy O'Connell, who came off the bench to spark the offense in the second half, made it 21–10 late in the third quarter, the Redskins found new life when Bert Zagers returned a punt 56 yards for a touchdown with 5:46 remaining to cut the lead back to four points. Cleveland marched from its own 29 to the Washington 29, then faced fourth-and-eight. Paul Brown rolled the dice and went for it, and Preston Carpenter came through with a 12-yard run around left end to move the chains and allow the Browns to run out the rest of the clock. For the fourth time in the first six games, the Browns held their opponent to less than 200 yards of total offense, while Brown's heroics sparked a 231-yard rushing performance by the Browns' resurgent offense.

Record: 5–1

	1	2	3	4		
Redskins	7	3	0	7	=	17
Browns	7	0	14	0	=	21

CLE-Brown 1-yd. run (Groza kick)
WAS-Sutton 8-yd. run (Baker kick)
WAS-Baker 10-yd. FG
CLE-Brown 9-yd. run (Groza kick)
CLE-O'Connell 1-yd. run (Groza kick)
WAS-Zagers 56-yd. punt return (Baker kick)

Passing
WAS: LeBaron 3–7–17 0 TD 1 INT, Bukich 2–5–47 0 TD 0 INT
CLE: O'Connell 8–12–122 0 TD 1 INT

Rushing
WAS: Bosseler 15–58, Podoley 5–33, Sutton 10–17, Elter 2–3, Bukich 1-(-5)
CLE: Brown 21–109, Hanulak 20–50, P. Carpenter 1–39, L. Carpenter 12–35, O'Connell 2–3, Reynolds 2-(-5)

Receiving
WAS: Podoley 2–35, Carson 1–13, Walton 1–12, Bosseler 1–4
CLE: Brewster 5–103, P. Carpenter 2–19, Brown 1–0

Sunday, November 10
Browns 24, Pittsburgh Steelers 0
Cleveland Stadium (53,709)
Brown jerseys/white pants

With the temperature hovering around the freezing mark on an unseasonably frigid November afternoon, the Browns surpassed their win total from 1956 with a businesslike romp over the Steelers. Though both teams would turn the ball over four times, the Browns overcame their mistakes with a pair of Tommy O'Connell touchdown passes, first a 49-yard strike to Ray Renfro, then a 13-yard toss to Preston Carpenter on a rollout to make it 17–0 in the third quarter. When Pittsburgh threatened to make a game of it in the fourth quarter, driving inside the Cleveland 10 with eight minutes to play, DB Don Paul scooped up a Steeler fumble and sprinted 89 yards for the game-clinching touchdown—and a team record—to secure the Browns' eleventh shutout since joining the NFL.

Record: 6–1

	1	2	3	4		
Steelers	0	0	0	0	=	0
Browns	3	7	7	7	=	24

CLE-Groza 34-yd. FG
CLE-Renfro 49-yd. pass from O'Connell (Groza kick)
CLE-P. Carpenter 13-yd. pass from O'Connell (Groza kick)
CLE-Paul 89-yd. fumble return (Groza kick)

Passing
PIT: Morrall 15–33–193 0 TD 1 INT, Kemp 2–4–18 0 TD 1 INT
CLE: O'Connell 7–11–156 2 TD 1 INT, Plum 1–1–12 0 TD 0 INT

Rushing
PIT: Wells 14–86, Young 10–27, Watson 1–3, Kemp 1–0, Mathews 1-(-9), Morrall 3-(-17)
CLE: Brown 14–76, Hanulak 16–38, O'Connell 1–7, Plum 2–4, Modzelewski 1–2, L. Carpenter 2-(-4)

Receiving
PIT: McClairen 7–82, Girard 2–52, Mathews 2–25, Watson 2–20, Young 2–17, Wells 2–15
CLE: Renfro 2–85, P. Carpenter 4–48, Brewster 1–23, Clarke 1–12

Sunday, November 17
Browns 30, Washington Redskins 30
Griffith Stadium (27,722)
White jerseys/white pants

Trailing by 10 with five minutes remaining, the Browns rallied for a late touchdown, and then Lou Groza drilled a 23-yard field goal with 15 seconds to play to force a tie and keep the Browns a half-game ahead of the Giants in the Eastern Conference. After the Browns took a 13–9 lead with six minutes to play in the third quarter, the Cleveland defense, which had been stellar all season, suffered its first real lapse, surrendering 21 points in the next 16 minutes of play and allowing the Redskins to take control of the contest. It took the Browns just over a minute to cut the margin to 30–27 as they drove 63 yards in three plays—a drive capped by a great catch-and-lateral by Preston Carpenter to Pete Brewster—then the defense came up big when it had to, forcing a three-and-out, and the Browns got the football back at their own 34. Facing fourth-and-two at the Washington 44 in the final minute, Tommy O'Connell—who threw for more than 300 yards on the day—connected with Ray Renfro for 27 yards to set up Groza's game-tying kick with 15 seconds left. The Cleveland offense rolled up a season-high 425 total yards as three different receivers topped the century mark: Brewster (6–124), Renfro (4–113), and Carpenter (6–112).

Record: 6–1–1

	1	2	3	4		
Browns	3	7	3	17	=	30
Redskins	6	3	14	7	=	30

CLE-Groza 19-yd. FG
WAS-Elter 4-yd. run (kick failed)
WAS-Baker 25-yd. FG
CLE-Hanulak 3-yd. run (Groza kick)
CLE-Groza 35-yd. FG
WAS-Elter 18-yd. run (Baker kick)
WAS-Bosseler 2-yd. run (Baker kick)
CLE-Brewster 10-yd. pass from O'Connell (Groza kick)
WAS-Meilinger 34-yd. pass from LeBaron (Baker kick)
CLE-Brewster 23-yd. lateral from P. Carpenter, 17-yd. pass from O'Connell (Groza kick)
CLE-Groza 23-yd. FG

Passing
CLE: O'Connell 16–24–324 1 TD 1 INT
WAS: LeBaron 7–10–177 1 TD 0 INT

Rushing
CLE: Brown 15–68, Hanulak 14–26, O'Connell 3-(-12)
WAS: Elter 9–57, Bosseler 17–48, Podoley 11–41, LeBaron 2–7, Sutton 3–0

Receiving
CLE: Brewster 6–124, Renfro 4–113, P. Carpenter 6–112
WAS: Carson 2–51, Meilinger 2–46, Braatz 1–37, Podoley 1–36, Bosseler 1–7

Sunday, November 24
Browns 45, Los Angeles Rams 31
Cleveland Stadium (65,407)
Brown jerseys/white pants

The Browns' largest home crowd in four years witnessed not only a stirring Cleveland come-from-behind victory, but the arrival of a legend. In just his ninth game, rookie Jim Brown set an NFL record with 237 rushing yards on 31 carries and added four touchdowns, three in the second half, as he sparked a Cleveland rally from an 11-point third-quarter deficit. After the Rams returned a Brown fumble for a touchdown early in the second half to stretch their lead to 28–17, things looked bleak for the home team, particularly after Tommy O'Connell was forced out of the game with an injury in the first quarter. Then Brown scored three consecutive touchdowns to put the Browns up by 10. After they first cut the margin to 28–24, DT Don Colo stripped Rams' QB Norm Van Brocklin of the football and then recovered at the Los Angeles 7 to set up the go-ahead score. With the Rams driving at midfield, another Los Angeles fumble was recovered by Cleveland DT Bob Gain, and 10 plays later, Brown crossed the goal line for the fourth time. After the Rams cut the margin back to seven with a field goal, RB Lew Carpenter put it away with a one-yard touchdown in the final minutes, his second of the day. Behind Brown's amazing performance, Cleveland rolled up a whopping 330 rushing yards and averaged nearly six yards per carry as a team. Interestingly, the man whose record Brown broke was Rams' RB Tommy Wilson, who'd rushed for 223 in the season finale in 1956, and got to witness his name being erased from the record book from the opposing sideline. Though he tied it four years later, Brown's dazzling day against the Rams would remain a team record for 52 years.

Record: 7–1–1

	1	2	3	4		
Rams	0	21	7	3	=	31
Browns	7	10	14	14	=	45

CLE-L. Carpenter 23-yd. run (Groza kick)
LA-Hirsch 14-yd. pass from Van Brocklin (Cothren kick)
CLE-Brown 69-yd. run (Groza kick)
LA-Wilson 1-yd. run (Cothren kick)
LA-Hirsch 20-yd. pass from Van Brocklin (Cothren kick)
CLE-Groza 48-yd. FG
LA-Hauser 29-yd. fumble return (Cothren kick)
CLE-Brown 1-yd. run (Groza kick)
CLE-Brown 1-yd. run (Groza kick)

CLE-Brown 3-yd. run (Groza kick)
LA-Cothren 42-yd. FG
CLE-L. Carpenter 1-yd. run (Groza kick)

Passing
LA: Van Brocklin 7–17–123 2 TD 3 INT
CLE: Plum 6–9–62 0 TD 0 INT, O'Connell 0–4–0 0 TD 2 INT

Rushing
LA: Arnett 11–52, Marconi 8–48, Younger 6–39, Wilson 8–34, Waller 2–1
CLE: Brown 31–237, L. Carpenter 15–70, Plum 6–18, Modzelewski 2–5, Hanulak 4–0

Receiving
LA: Boyd 4–86, Hirsch 2–34, Arnett 1–3
CLE: Brown 3–21, Hanulak 1–19, Renfro 1–13, Brewster 1–9

Sunday, December 1
Browns 31, Chicago Cardinals 0
Cleveland Stadium (40,525)
Brown jerseys/white pants

With their second shutout of the season, the Browns secured their sixth straight home victory and, with a San Francisco triumph over New York, put themselves in a position to clinch the Eastern Conference title with a win the following week. The struggling Cardinals were no match for the soaring Browns, who took a 21–0 halftime lead and then continued to stymie Chicago in the second half, holding the Cards to 166 total yards for the day while forcing four turnovers. After throwing two touchdown passes to Ray Renfro in the second quarter despite being doubtful to start with a nagging shoulder injury, Tommy O'Connell saw his injury-plagued season continue as he was carried off the field in the third quarter after hurting his ankle. At the conclusion of the game, enthralled home fans, celebrating a perfect home schedule and the Browns' return to elite status, stormed the field and tore down both goalposts.
Record: 8–1–1

	1	2	3	4		
Cardinals	0	0	0	0	=	0
Browns	7	14	3	7	=	31

CLE-L. Carpenter 10-yd. run (Groza kick)
CLE-Renfro 65-yd. pass from O'Connell (Groza kick)
CLE-Renfro 23-yd. pass from O'Connell (Groza kick)
CLE-Groza 25-yd. FG
CLE-Hanulak 5-yd. run (Groza kick)

Passing
CHI: Marchibroda 2–5–18 0 TD 1 INT, McHan 1–12–9 0 TD 1 INT, Larson 2–3–2 0 TD 1 INT, Sears 0–1–0 0 TD 0 INT
CLE: O'Connell 5–12–177 2 TD 0 INT, Plum 1–5–8 0 TD 1 INT

Rushing
CHI: Matson 16–65, Childress 12–62, Mann 7–26, McHan 1–4, Larson 2-(-7)
CLE: L. Carpenter 15–67, Brown 10–57, Hanulak 6–21, P. Carpenter 1–12, O'Connell 1–7, Modzelewski 3–6, Plum 1-(-1), Campbell 2-(-2)

Receiving
CHI: Nagler 2–19, Childress 2–18, Sears 1-(-8)
CLE: Renfro 3–109, Brewster 2–68, Hanulak 1–8

Sunday, December 8
Detroit Lions 20, Browns 7
Briggs Stadium (55,814)
White jerseys/white pants

With the Giants losing in Pittsburgh on Saturday, the Browns unexpectedly clinched the Eastern Conference title a day early and thus came out flat in their showdown with the Lions, who were fighting for their lives in a three-way race in the Western Conference. While the Cleveland defense was at its usual high level, the offense was sluggish and managed only 69 yards on the ground on 34 carries, with Jim Brown held to 38. Still, Cleveland had a chance to take the lead early in the fourth quarter, driving to the Detroit 4 with the Lions leading 10–7. But with the conference title clinched, Paul Brown opted to play for the win rather than the tie, and the Browns were stopped on fourth down—one of a trio of fourth-down stops for the Lions on the day. Detroit, who'd lost QB Bobby Layne to a season-ending ankle injury in the second quarter, went on to add 10 points in the final minutes with backup Tobin Rote at the controls to win going away. Similarly, the Browns were without their own No. 1 QB as Tommy O'Connell was unable to play due to the shoulder and ankle injuries he'd suffered in previous weeks, and rookie Milt Plum played admirably in his absence despite suffering from intestinal flu, tossing a 58-yard touchdown pass to Ray Renfro in the third quarter for the Browns' only score.
Record: 8–2–1

	1	2	3	4		
Browns	0	0	7	0	=	7
Lions	3	0	7	10	=	20

DET-Martin 27-yd. FG
DET-Middleton 10-yd. pass from Rote (Martin kick)
CLE-Renfro 58-yd. pass from Plum (Groza kick)
DET-Martin 27-yd. FG
DET-Johnson 4-yd. run (Martin kick)

Passing
CLE: Plum 12–21–190 1 TD 1 INT, Borton 3–3–22 0 TD 0 INT
DET: Rote 5–16–89 1 TD 0 INT, Layne 2–6–15 0 TD 0 INT, Gedman 0–1–0 0 TD 0 INT

Rushing
CLE: Brown 16–38, Hanulak 5–18, Plum 5–13, L. Carpenter 8–0
DET: Gedman 3–67, Johnson 13–49, Rote 4–30, Hart 1–4, Cassady 6–1

Receiving
CLE: Brewster 4–63, Renfro 1–58, P. Carpenter 6–48, L. Carpenter 1–21, Brown 2–11, Hanulak 1–11
DET: Middleton 3–63, Junker 1–17, Cassady 1–13, Johnson 2–11

Sunday, December 15
Browns 34, New York Giants 28
Yankee Stadium (54,294)
White jerseys/white pants

After fans had pointed to the season finale in New York all season anticipating a battle for the Eastern Conference title, the Browns-Giants matchup in Week 12 turned out to be something of an anticlimax since the Browns had already clinched the crown the week before. Still, with the game serving as nothing more than a tune-up for the NFL title game for the Browns and a farewell appearance for the Giants before their home fans, the teams put on a remarkable show, combining for more than 40 first downs and 800 yards in a seesaw offensive shootout that saw neither team lead by more than seven points. Milt Plum was efficient once again, completing 11 of 16 passes for 229 yards and rushing for 68 more, while Preston Carpenter paced a ground attack that racked up 298 total yards with 117 of his own and the go-ahead touchdown run on an end-around early in the third quarter to put the Browns ahead 24–21. The Giants took the lead back on an Alex Webster one-yard score early in the fourth quarter, but the Browns responded with a 68-yard scoring drive, paced by a 28-yard Plum run to set up Lew Carpenter's two-yard touchdown. The Giants had one final chance to win, driving to the Cleveland 13 with less than two minutes remaining, but Browns' DB Ken Konz intercepted Giants' QB Charlie Conerly at the two-yard line to secure Cleveland's ninth victory and complete a season sweep of the defending NFL champs.

Record: 9–2–1

	1	2	3	4		
Browns	7	10	7	10	=	34
Giants	14	7	0	7	=	28

CLE-Renfro 38-yd. pass from Plum (Groza kick)
NYG-Gifford 9-yd. run (Agajanian kick)
NYG-Gifford 21-yd. pass from Heinrich (Agajanian kick)
CLE-Brown 20-yd. run (Groza kick)
NYG-Heinrich 7-yd. run (Agajanian kick)
CLE-Groza 15-yd. FG
CLE-P. Carpenter 35-yd. run (Groza kick)
CLE-Groza 15-yd. FG
NYG-Webster 1-yd. run (Agajanian kick)
CLE-L. Carpenter 2-yd. run (Groza kick)

Passing
CLE: Plum 11–16–229 1 TD 1 INT
NYG: Heinrich 7–15–175 1 TD 1 INT, Conerly 10–17–113 0 TD 2 INT

Rushing
CLE: L. Carpenter 22–117, Brown 15–78, Plum 7–68, P. Carpenter 1–35
NYG: Webster 15–42, Gifford 2–36, Heinrich 2–9, Conerly 1–9, Epps 4–6, Triplett 2–6

Receiving
CLE: Renfro 4–130, P. Carpenter 3–76, Brewster 2–30, L. Carpenter 1–4, Brown 1-(-11)
NYG: Schnelker 3–83, Webster 5–71, Rote 3–53, MacAfee 4–47, Gifford 1–21, Triplett 1–13

1957 NFL Championship
Sunday, December 29
Detroit Lions 59, Browns 14
Briggs Stadium (55,263)
White jerseys/white pants

For the fourth time in six seasons, the Browns and Lions squared off for the NFL title, and after Detroit had won two of the three previous meetings, it appeared the Browns were in prime position to even the series and capture their fourth NFL championship in eight years. With the

Lions playing without star QB Bobby Layne and having expended immeasurable energy and emotion in a Western Conference playoff the week before in which they'd rallied from a 27–7 third-quarter deficit to defeat the 49ers on the road, the rested Browns were favored by three points. Thus, what actually happened on a sunny, cold afternoon at Briggs Stadium was almost inexplicable.

The Lions, supposedly weary and battered, came out on fire, while it was the Browns who played as if their tanks were empty. Aided by a handful of Cleveland mistakes, Detroit surged to a 17–0 lead in the first quarter and led 31–7 at halftime. In the first 30 minutes, the Browns had turned the ball over six times, with the most damaging an interception by Lions' DB Terry Barr in the waning minutes of the half that he returned 19 yards for a touchdown to put Detroit up by 24 and essentially extinguish any hopes of a Cleveland comeback.

While they managed to hang onto the ball in the second half, the Cleveland defense, which had been superb all season, continued to be overwhelmed by Detroit's backup QB Tobin Rote, who had the finest game of his career, throwing for 280 yards and four touchdowns while rushing for another. The Lions finished the day with 438 total yards, while the Browns, alternating between hurting QBs Tommy O'Connell and Milt Plum, did most of their damage on the ground, collecting 218 rushing yards.

When the final gun sounded, Detroit had tallied eight touchdowns and had handed the Browns the worst loss in their history, avenging their 56–10 defeat in the teams' previous title-game meeting three years earlier. It would be Paul Brown's final appearance in an NFL championship game, and the Browns would not return for another seven years. For the Lions, who had been so dominant throughout the 1950s, the 1957 title game would mark not only their fourth and final NFL crown but the franchise's last appearance in a championship game.

	1	2	3	4		
Browns	0	7	7	0	=	14
Lions	17	14	14	14	=	59

DET-Martin 31-yd. FG
DET-Rote 1-yd. run (Martin kick)
DET-Gedman 1-yd. run (Martin kick)
CLE-Brown 29-yd. run (Groza kick)
DET-Junker 26-yd. pass from Rote (Martin kick)
DET-Barr 19-yd. interception return (Martin kick)
CLE-L. Carpenter 5-yd. run (Groza kick)
DET-Doran 78-yd. pass from Rote (Martin kick)
DET-Junker 23-yd. pass from Rote (Martin kick)
DET-Middleton 32-yd. pass from Rote (Martin kick)
DET-Cassady 16-yd. pass from Reichow (Martin kick)

Passing
CLE: O'Connell 4–8–61 0 TD 2 INT, Plum 5–12–51 0 TD 2 INT, Hanulak 0–1–0 0 TD 1 INT
DET: Rote 12–19–280 4 TD 0 INT, Reichow 1–2–16 1 TD 0 INT

Rushing
CLE: L. Carpenter 14–82, Brown 20–69, Plum 3–46, Renfro 1–21
DET: Cassady 8–48, Johnson 7–34, Gedman 12–28, Rote 7–27, Reichow 1–0

Receiving
CLE: Brewster 3–52, P. Carpenter 4–43, Renfro 1–9, L. Carpenter 1–8
DET: Junker 5–109, Doran 3–101, Middleton 1–32, Cassady 2–22, Johnson 1–16, Tracy 1–16

1958

Sunday, September 28
Browns 30, Los Angeles Rams 27
Los Angeles Memorial Coliseum (69,993)
White jerseys/white pants

By scoring 16 points in the fourth quarter, the Browns rallied for a stunning victory over the Rams on a sun-drenched afternoon in southern California. Tallying 470 total yards, the Rams built a 10-point halftime lead that they stretched to 27–14 going into the fourth quarter. But the Browns weren't to be denied. A touchdown pass from Milt Plum (now the Browns' starting QB after Tommy O'Connell retired to become an assistant coach at Illinois, his alma mater) to WR Ray Renfro cut the margin to seven with 12 minutes to play. Then Browns' DB Junior Wren recovered a fumble at the Rams' 41 and returned it to the 7. Moments later, RB Jim Brown tied the game with his second touchdown in what became a colossal afternoon, as he finished with 171 yards on 24 carries. The Browns' defense rose to the occasion, forcing the red-hot LA offense to punt, and the Browns drove deep into Rams' territory, then took their first lead on a short Lou Groza field goal off the baseball infield portion of the field (being used by the Los Angeles Dodgers for the first time that year) with 23 seconds left. But the Rams weren't done, completing a long toss to the Cleveland 41 in the waning moments, but a 48-yard field goal sailed wide, clinching a thrilling Browns' win.

Record: 1–0

	1	2	3	4		
Browns	0	7	7	16	=	30
Rams	3	14	10	0	=	27

LA-Cothren 40-yd. FG
LA-Lundy 20-yd. pass from Wade (Cothren kick)
CLE-Mitchell 4-yd. pass from Plum (Groza kick)
LA-Shofner 55-yd. pass from Wade (Cothren kick)
CLE-Brown 38-yd. run (Groza kick)
LA-Wilson 13-yd. run (Cothren kick)
LA-Cothren 11-yd. FG
CLE-Renfro 21-yd. pass from Plum (kick failed)
CLE-Brown 5-yd. run (Groza kick)
CLE-Groza 9-yd. FG

Passing
CLE: Plum 13–25–141 2 TD 2 INT
LA: Wade 17–22–289 2 TD

Rushing
CLE: Brown 24–171, Mitchell 10–50, Bolden 2–21, Plum 2–15
LA: Wilson 13–108, Arnett 13–68, Wade 3–23, Marconi 1–4, Waller 1-(-1)

Receiving
CLE: Brewster 3–49, P. Carpenter 4–45, Mitchell 5–26, Renfro 1–21
LA: Shofner 6–149, Lundy 3–59, Arnett 3–26, Wilson 2–25, Clarke 2–15, Marconi 1–15

Sunday, October 5
Browns 45, Pittsburgh Steelers 12
Pitt Stadium (31,130)
White jerseys/white pants

Led by another sterling offensive performance, the Browns won their second straight, routing the Steelers in their home opener. Milt Plum started the game with stunning accuracy, completing his first eight passes for 132 yards, and finished the game 13 of 14 for 197 and a pair of touchdowns. RB Preston Carpenter was his primary target, catching seven passes for 131 yards. Jim Brown was once again a force, tallying 129 yards on just 17 carries with three touchdowns—including a 59-yard scoring run—as the Browns rolled up more than 400 total yards and took command early by sprinting to a 21–0 lead early in the third quarter. The Cleveland defense kept the Steelers at bay by forcing a whopping nine turnovers, including five fumbles.

Record: 2–0

	1	2	3	4		
Browns	7	17	14	7	=	45
Steelers	0	10	0	2	=	12

CLE-Brown 23-yd. run (Groza kick)
CLE-Mitchell 21-yd. pass from Plum (Groza kick)
CLE-Brewster 8-yd. pass from Plum (Groza kick)
PIT-Tracy 1-yd. run (Miller kick)
PIT-Miner 31-yd. FG

CLE-Groza 32-yd. FG
CLE-Brown 59-yd. run (Groza kick)
CLE-Brown 3-yd. run (Groza kick)
CLE-P. Carpenter 4-yd. pass from Ninowski (Groza kick)
PIT-Safety: Ninowski tackled by Stautner in end zone

Passing
CLE: Plum 13–14–197 2 TD 0 INT, Ninowski 3–7-45 1 TD 2 INT
PIT: Morrall 7–22–158 0 TD 4 INT, Dawson 1–2-11 0 TD 0 INT, Tracy 0–1-0 0 TD 0 INT

Rushing
CLE: Brown 17–129, Mitchell 8–65, Modzelewski 2–6, Bolden 4–1, L. Carpenter 4-(-1), Plum 1-(-8)
PIT: Tracy 11–54, Younger 8–28, Christy 3–16, Krutko 1–5, Dawson 1–1, Morrall 2-(-4)

Receiving
CLE: P. Carpenter 7–131, Renfro 2–40, Mitchell 2–36, Brown 3–17, Modzelewski 1–10, Brewster 1–8
PIT: Orr 1–66, Tracy 3–34, McClairen 1–20, Lucas 1–17, Younger 1–17, Mathews 1–15

Sunday, October 12
Browns 35, Chicago Cardinals 28
Cleveland Stadium (65,403)
Brown jerseys/white pants

Before the largest crowd for a home opener in team history, the Browns put on a clinic in running the football, dominating the line of scrimmage as both Jim Brown and rookie RB Bobby Mitchell were unstoppable, each rushing for more than 140 yards. As a team, the Browns tallied a team-record 332 rushing yards and five touchdowns, averaging more than six yards per carry. Brown (182 yards on 34 carries) set the tone with two first-quarter touchdowns, followed by a third score early in the fourth quarter, while Mitchell (147 yards on 11 carries) opened the floodgates with a 63-yard touchdown run. After the Cardinals cut the margin to 21–14 in the third quarter, the Browns stretched the advantage to 35–14 early in the fourth, then endured as Chicago scored two late touchdowns to pull within a single score before time expired. The Browns' defense struggled, but forced four turnovers to help the Browns stay in control and move to 3–0 for the second straight year.
Record: 3–0

	1	2	3	4		
Cardinals	0	7	7	14	=	28
Browns	14	7	7	7	=	35

CLE-Brown 3-yd. run (Groza kick)
CLE-Brown 1-yd. run (Groza kick)
CHI-Matson 14-yd. run (Conrad kick)
CLE-Mitchell 63-yd. run (Groza kick)
CHI-Nagler 24-yd. pass from Reynolds (Conrad kick)
CLE-Plum 1-yd. run (Groza kick)
CLE-Brown 7-yd. run (Groza kick)
CHI-Crow 91-yd. pass from Reynolds (Conrad kick)
CHI-Crow 27-yd. pass from Reynolds (Conrad kick)

Passing
CHI: Reynolds 11–18–239 3 TD 2 INT, Hill 1–1-18 0 TD 0 INT, McHan 0–9-0 0 TD 0 INT
CLE: Plum 7–15–122 0 TD 1 INT

Rushing
CHI: Matson 10–62, Reynolds 4–46, Crow 6–38, Sears 1–2, McHan 1–0
CLE: Brown 34–182, Mitchell 11–147, P. Carpenter 2–12, Renfro 1–12, L. Carpenter 2–1, Plum 4-(-22)

Receiving
CHI: Crow 4–152, Lewis 5–62, Nagler 1–24, Matson 2–19
CLE: Clarke 2–57, Renfro 2–32, P. Carpenter 2–25, Brown 1–8

Sunday, October 19
Browns 27, Pittsburgh Steelers 10
Cleveland Stadium (66,852)
Brown jerseys/white pants

On a perfect autumn afternoon, the Browns built a two-game lead in the Eastern Conference by overwhelming the Steelers for the second time in three weeks. After Pittsburgh grabbed an early 7–0 lead on a long halfback-option touchdown pass, the Browns exploded for 27 consecutive points to collect their fourth straight win over Pittsburgh. Jim Brown was once again dominant, running for 153 yards and bringing his season total to 635 in just four games. For the second straight week, Bobby Mitchell also went over the century mark with 108 yards on 13 carries as the Browns picked up 264 yards on the ground and more than 400 total. One of the lone pieces of bad news to come out of the game was the loss of offensive lineman

Mike McCormack with a knee injury that would keep him sidelined for three weeks. The game also saw Milt Plum's debut as a kicker as he filled in for Lou Groza—out with a head injury—and connected on a pair of extra points.
Record: 4–0

	1	2	3	4		
Steelers	7	0	0	3	=	10
Browns	7	14	0	6	=	27

PIT-Mathews 64-yd. pass from Tracy (Miner kick)
CLE-Brown 27-yd. pass from Plum (Groza kick)
CLE-Brown 48-yd. run (Plum kick)
CLE-Renfro 36-yd. pass from Plum (Plum kick)
CLE-Mitchell 7-yd. pass from Plum (kick failed)
PIT-Miner 47-yd. FG

Passing
PIT: Layne 14–26–133 0 TD 1 INT, Tracy 1–1-64 1 TD 0 INT, Dawson 0–1-0 0 TD 0 INT
CLE: Plum 8–18–138 3 TD 2 INT, Ninowski 1–2-34 0 TD 0 INT

Rushing
PIT: Tracy 14–78, Younger 13–14, Christy 2–6, Krutko 1-(-5), Layne 2-(-6)
CLE: Brown 19–153, Mitchell 13–108, Bolden 1–3, Ninowski 2–1, Plum 1-(-1)

Receiving
PIT: Mathews 2–72, Younger 6–39, Tracy 2–39, Orr 3–32, Lucas 1–11, McClairen 1–4
CLE: Mitchell 3–38, Renfro 1–36, Clarke 1–34, Brown 1–27, Brewster 1–24, P. Carpenter 2–13

Sunday, October 26
Browns 38, Chicago Cardinals 24
Comiskey Park (30,933)
White jerseys/white pants

Behind yet another epic performance by Jim Brown, the Browns surmounted a second-half deficit on a gray afternoon on Chicago's south side to win comfortably and improve to 5–0 for the first time in five years. Brown scored four of Cleveland's five touchdowns—bringing his season total to 14—and rushed for 180 yards, averaging more than seven yards per carry for the day. With the Browns trailing 24–17 early in the third quarter, Brown ripped off back-to-back scoring runs of 41 and 62 yards to give the Browns the lead, then put the game away with a two-yard touchdown run in the fourth. Cleveland's other touchdown came in the second quarter when rookie RB Leroy Bolden returned a kickoff 102 yards for a touchdown—the longest in the Browns' history to this point and the only score of Bolden's brief career—to give the Browns a 17–14 lead. The Cleveland special teams also got into the act, recovering a fumbled punt return to set up the game's first touchdown, then later blocking a field goal (though the Cardinals recovered the ball and ran for a first down, ultimately scoring a touchdown on the drive). While the passing game took a back seat to the dominant running attack, Ray Renfro managed to catch five passes for 108 yards as Milt Plum completed 10 of his 14 passes.
Record: 5–0

	1	2	3	4		
Browns	10	7	14	7	=	38
Cardinals	7	14	3	0	=	24

CLE-Brown 7-yd. run (Groza kick)
CHI-McHan 1-yd. run (Conrad kick)
CLE-Groza 12-yd. FG
CHI-Nagler 7-yd. pass from McHan (Conrad kick)
CLE-Bolden 102-yd. kickoff return (Groza kick)
CHI-Childress 23-yd. run on lateral (Conrad kick)
CHI-Conrad 32-yd. FG
CLE-Brown 41-yd. run (Groza kick)
CLE-Brown 62-yd. run (Groza kick)
CLE-Brown 2-yd. run (Groza kick)

Passing
CLE: Plum 10–14–126 0 TD 0 INT
CHI: McHan 8–19–113 1 TD 1 INT, Reynolds 2–3-28 0 TD 0 INT

Rushing
CLE: Brown 24–180, Mitchell 11–44, Bolden 3–34, Plum 3–6, Modzelewski 1–2, Renfro 1–0
CHI: Childress 12–55, Matson 14–50, Reynolds 2–20, Crow 3–10, Sears 2–5, McHan 4-(-4)

Receiving
CLE: Renfro 5–108, Brewster 1–16, P. Carpenter 1–9, Mitchell 1–3, Brown 2-(-10)
CHI: Nagler 4–70, Sears 2–28, Childress 1–23, Boydston 1–11, Matson 2–9

Sunday, November 2
New York Giants 21, Browns 17
Cleveland Stadium (78,404)
Brown jerseys/white pants

Before the fourth-largest crowd in team history, the Browns squandered a chance to build a three-game cushion between themselves and the rival Giants by blowing a 10-point halftime lead to lose for the first time in 1958. The Browns built a 17–7 advantage in the second quarter on the strength of a 58-yard touchdown run by Jim Brown and a 46-yard interception return for a score by DB Ken Konz. But the second half was an entirely different story as the Giants took control, taking the lead three minutes into the fourth quarter on the second of two Charlie Conerly touchdown passes to RB Alex Webster. After cruising through the first half, the Cleveland offense was thwarted in the final two quarters, picking up only 27 total yards and not crossing midfield. Jim Brown again topped 100 yards, but other than his touchdown run, was well contained by the New York defense. The loss—what would prove to be the first of six straight by the Browns to the Giants—pulled New York to within one game of the Browns in the conference and set up added emphasis on the teams' rematch in the regular-season finale at Yankee Stadium in December.
Record: 5–1

	1	2	3	4		
Giants	0	7	7	7	=	21
Browns	3	14	0	0	=	17

CLE-Groza 41-yd. FG
NYG-Schnelker 39-yd. pass from Conerly (Summerall kick)
CLE-Brown 58-yd. run (Groza kick)
CLE-Konz 46-yd. interception return (Groza kick)
NYG-Webster 15-yd. pass from Conerly (Summerall kick)
NYG-Webster 10-yd. pass from Conerly (Summerall kick)

Passing
NYG: Conerly 12–23–194 3 TD 3 INT
CLE: Plum 4–14–26 0 TD 2 INT

Rushing
NYG: Triplett 20–116, King 8–32, Webster 12–30, Maynard 2-(-5), Conerly 3-(-12)
CLE: Brown 13–113, Mitchell 13–65, Plum 3–12, Freeman 1–9, Bolden 1-(-5), P. Carpenter 1-(-10)

Receiving
NYG: Schnelker 3–87, Webster 7–81, Maynard 2–29
CLE: P. Carpenter 3–25, Mitchell 1–1

Sunday, November 9
Detroit Lions 30, Browns 10
Cleveland Stadium (75,563)
Brown jerseys/white pants

Hoping to jump-start an offense that struggled mightily in the second half the week before, Paul Brown tapped backup QB Jim Ninowski to start in place of Milt Plum before another colossal crowd at the Stadium—the largest in five years—in a rematch of the previous year's NFL title game. But this one went much the same way as the teams' last meeting as the Lions—1-4-1 going in—soared to a 20–3 halftime lead and stretched it to 30–3 before the Browns finally reached the end zone behind Plum, who was inserted in the second half. Detroit QB Tobin Rote, who'd carved up the Browns in the '57 title game, was impressive once again, throwing for 246 yards and three touchdowns. The loss was doubly painful as the Giants toppled the undefeated Colts to move into a first-place tie with the Browns atop the conference. One of the few bright spots for the Browns on this dark day was Jim Brown surpassing the 1,000-yard rushing mark after just seven games.
Record: 5–2

	1	2	3	4		
Lions	3	17	7	3	=	30
Browns	0	3	0	7	=	10

DET-Martin 43-yd. FG
CLE-Groza 11-yd. FG
DET-Martin 37-yd. FG
DET-Gibbons 4-yd. pass from Rote (Martin kick)
DET-Cassady 34-yd. pass from Rote (Martin kick)
DET-Gedman 13-yd. pass from Rote (Martin kick)
DET-Martin 48-yd. FG
CLE-Renfro 12-yd. pass from Plum (Groza kick)

Passing
DET: Rote 17–30–246 3 TD 0 INT
CLE: Plum 6–9-63 1 TD 0 INT, Ninowski 4–8-60 0 TD 1 INT

Rushing
DET: Johnson 8–53, Gedman 12–21, Rote 4–10, Cassady 2–10, Lewis 1-(-3)
CLE: Brown 21–83, Mitchell 9–39, Renfro 1–5, Bolden 4–1, Plum 2–1

Receiving
DET: Doran 5–70, Middleton 2–66, Cassady 4–63, Gibbons 3–35, Gedman 3–12
CLE: P. Carpenter 3–45, Renfro 2–36, Brewster 1–28, Brown 2–7, Mitchell 2–7

Sunday, November 16
Browns 20, Washington Redskins 10
Griffith Stadium (32,372)
White jerseys/white pants

The Browns rebounded from back-to-back tough losses to muscle out a victory over the Redskins in the fourth quarter, which—combined with the Giants' surprising loss to Pittsburgh—once again gave the Browns sole possession of first place. Knotted in a 10–10 tie throughout the second half, the Browns persevered thanks to their defense, which limited Washington to just over 200 total yards and forced five turnovers. With 2:10 to play, Cleveland broke the stalemate when Lou Groza connected on a 26-yard field goal, capping a seven-minute drive. DB Don Paul then intercepted a pass to set up the icing on the cake in the final seconds—Jim Brown's second touchdown of the day. With 152 more yards, Brown set a new single-season league rushing record, still with four games to play.
Record: 6–2

	1	2	3	4		
Browns	7	3	0	10	=	20
Redskins	7	3	0	0	=	10

CLE-Brown 1-yd. run (Groza kick)
WAS-Podoley 64-yd. pass from Guglielmi (Baker kick)
WAS-Baker 35-yd. FG
CLE-Groza 10-yd. FG
CLE-Groza 26-yd. FG
CLE-Brown 5-yd. run (Groza kick)

Passing
CLE: Plum 12–27–193 0 TD 3 INT
WAS: Guglielmi 5–12–126 1 TD 2 INT, LeBaron 4–8-38 0 TD 0 INT, Sutton 0–1-0 0 TD 0 INT

Rushing
CLE: Brown 27–152, L. Carpenter 13–61, Plum 5–24
WAS: Olszewski 10–41, Guglielmi 6–13, Podoley 4–12, Sutton 3–12, Watson 2-(-1), LeBaron 1-(-12)

Receiving
CLE: P. Carpenter 4–115, Renfro 2–29, Brewster 2–27, L. Carpenter 2–23, Brown 2-(-1)
WAS: Podoley 2–76, Olszewski 4–43, Anderson 2–32, Walton 1–13

Sunday, November 23
Browns 28, Philadelphia Eagles 14
Cleveland Stadium (51,319)
Brown jerseys/white pants

Setting the tone on the opening kickoff, Bobby Mitchell raced 98 yards for a touchdown to pave the way for a Browns' victory over the struggling Eagles. Mitchell then added a 68-yard punt return for a score later in the first quarter to make it 14–0 and became the only player in Browns' history to return a kickoff and punt for a touchdown in the same game. After the Eagles cut the Cleveland lead to 21–14, the Browns responded with a touchdown pass from Milt Plum to Ray Renfro to salt the game away with 10 minutes left. Mitchell's returns helped push the Browns over the hump despite Jim Brown being held to just 66 yards on 20 carries. The Giants kept pace with a blowout win over the Redskins, staying one game back of the Browns with three to play.
Record: 7–2

	1	2	3	4		
Eagles	0	7	7	0	=	14
Browns	14	7	0	7	=	28

CLE-Mitchell 98-yd. kickoff return (Groza kick)
CLE-Mitchell 68-yd. punt return (Groza kick)
PHI-Barnes 2-yd. run (Walston kick)
CLE-L. Carpenter 1-yd. run (Groza kick)
PHI-McDonald 31-yd. pass from Van Brocklin (Walston kick)
CLE-Renfro 34-yd. pass from Plum (Groza kick)

Passing
PHI: Van Brocklin 18–29–210 1 TD 0 INT, Barnes 0–1-0 0 TD 0 INT
CLE: Plum 8–11–143 1 TD 0 INT

Rushing
PHI: Barnes 19–66, Peaks 12–44, Kowalczyk 3–6, Van Brocklin 1-(-1)
CLE: Brown 20–66, L. Carpenter 12–43, Plum 3–27, Mitchell 4-(-1)

Receiving
PHI: McDonald 3–60, Retzlaff 5–47, Peaks 3–46, Barnes 4–43, Bielski 3–14
CLE: Renfro 2–46, Brown 2–43, Brewster 2–34, Mitchell 2–20

Sunday, November 30
Browns 21, Washington Redskins 14
Cleveland Stadium (33,240)
Brown jerseys/white pants

On a frigid Sunday on the lake that saw the temperature plummet to 15°F, the Browns rallied from behind in the fourth quarter for a critical victory that kept them ahead of the fast-charging Giants. Trailing 14–7 after three periods, the Browns capped a 91-yard drive to tie the contest with a three-yard scoring run by RB Lew Carpenter, who rushed for 95 yards on 13 carries. Just as with Bobby Mitchell's two scores the week before, Carpenter's heroics were timely as Jim Brown was once again stymied, this time held to just 12 rushing yards on 11 carries. With time running out, Milt Plum—who'd donned basketball shoes for better traction on the glassy turf going into the fourth quarter—led the Browns on another drive, then ended it with a one-yard touchdown plunge with less than two minutes to play. Junior Wren clinched the victory with an interception in the final seconds, the only turnover by either team on the day. Throwing for 219 yards despite completing only 10 passes, Plum also came up big on the Browns' first touchdown, hitting Ray Renfro on a rollout pass on fourth-and-11 from the Washington 29.

Record: 8–2

	1	2	3	4		
Redskins	7	0	7	0	=	14
Browns	7	0	0	14	=	21

CLE-Renfro 29-yd. pass from Plum (Groza kick)
WAS-Bosseler 4-yd. run (Baker kick)
WAS-Watson 7-yd. pass from LeBaron (Baker kick)
CLE-L. Carpenter 3-yd. run (Groza kick)
CLE-Plum 1-yd. run (Groza kick)

Passing
WAS: LeBaron 13–18–189 1 TD 1 INT
CLE: Plum 10–19–219 1 TD 0 INT

Rushing
WAS: Bosseler 14–71, Scudero 16–63, Sutton 8–18, Podoley 1–8, LeBaron 1-(-10)
CLE: L. Carpenter 13–95, Plum 5–23, Brown 11–12

Receiving
WAS: Anderson 3–42, Watson 4–40, Sutton 4–19, Walton 1–18, Bosseler 1–10
CLE: Renfro 3–100, Brewster 3–72, Brown 1–21, L. Carpenter 2–15, P. Carpenter 1–11

Sunday, December 7
Browns 21, Philadelphia Eagles 14
Franklin Field (36,773)
White jerseys/white pants

On a bright, chilly day in Philadelphia, the Browns clinched a tie for the conference title by following an almost identical script that had resulted in victory each of the previous two weeks. Jim Brown returned to form, rushing for 128 yards on 21 carries, while Lew Carpenter added another 100 on 21 carries of his own as the Browns tallied 240 yards on the ground. Yet the hero of the day was Milt Plum, who ran for the first two Cleveland touchdowns, then connected with Ray Renfro from 48 yards for the game-winning score on the last play of the third quarter. The Renfro touchdown was Plum's fifth and final completion of the day, though he still tossed for 111 yards. The day was almost perfect for the Browns as the Giants trailed Detroit in the fourth quarter and were on the brink of elimination from the race but rallied for a narrow victory to stay one game back of the Browns heading into their showdown at Yankee Stadium the following Sunday in the regular-season finale.

Record: 9–2

	1	2	3	4		
Browns	14	0	7	0	=	21
Eagles	7	7	0	0	=	14

CLE-Plum 10-yd. run (Groza kick)
PHI-McDonald 26-yd. pass from Van Brocklin (Walston kick)
CLE-Plum 1-yd. run (Groza kick)
PHI-McDonald 4-yd. pass from Barnes (Walston kick)
CLE-Renfro 48-yd. pass from Plum (Groza kick)

Passing
CLE: Plum 5–11–111 1 TD 1 INT
PHI: Van Brocklin 15–27–154 1 TD 2 INT, Barnes 1–1–4 1 TD 0 INT

Rushing
CLE: Brown 21–128, L. Carpenter 21–100, Plum 6–29, Mitchell 1-(-17)
PHI: Barnes 12–74, Peaks 13–50, McDonald 1–5

Receiving
CLE: Renfro 2–61, Brown 2–26, Brewster 1–24
PHI: McDonald 5–58, Retzlaff 4–47, Barnes 2–29, Peaks 4–17, Bielski 1–7

Sunday, December 14
New York Giants 13, Browns 10
Yankee Stadium (63,192)
White jerseys/white pants

Seconds away from a trip to the NFL title game, the Browns saw their fate suddenly change direction in an epic battle with the rival Giants at snow-swept Yankee Stadium. Surging ahead on the first play of the game when Jim Brown exploded through the line for a 65-yard touchdown, the Browns seemed in control for much of the afternoon, particularly since they needed only a tie to clinch the conference title. Thus, after the Giants knotted the game at 10 five minutes into the fourth quarter, the Browns were still in the driver's seat. They appeared to have things wrapped up as the Giants desperately drove down the field in the final minutes when Frank Gifford appeared to fumble at the Cleveland 30 after catching a pass and the Browns recovered. But the pass was ruled incomplete and the Giants maintained possession. They reached the Cleveland 41 and faced fourth down, then decided to send out Pat Summerall—who'd missed from 33 yards earlier in the period—to attempt a 49-yard field goal off the snowy turf. Incredibly, Summerall's kick was good, giving the Giants their first lead with 2:07 to play. When a desperation 55-yard field-goal attempt by Lou Groza fell short in the final seconds, New York had won the game, catching the Browns in the process and forcing a playoff for the Eastern Conference title the following week.
Record: 9–3

	1	2	3	4		
Browns	7	3	0	0	=	10
Giants	0	3	0	10	=	13

CLE-Brown 65-yd. run (Groza kick)
NYG-Summerall 46-yd. FG
CLE-Groza 22-yd. FG
NYG-Schnelker 8-yd. pass from Gifford (Summerall kick)
NYG-Summerall 49-yd. FG

Passing
CLE: Plum 6–12–140 0 TD 0 INT
NYG: Conerly 10–29–102 0 TD 0 INT, Gifford 2–3-46 0 TD 0 INT, Heinrich 3–5-22 0 TD 0 INT

Rushing
CLE: Brown 26–148, L. Carpenter 8–9, Plum 2–1, Freeman 1-(-8)
NYG: Webster 8–40, King 3–11, Triplett 5–8, Gifford 6–5

Receiving
CLE: Renfro 2–64, P. Carpenter 2–55, Brewster 1–12, L. Carpenter 1–9
NYG: Webster 5–58, Rote 2–48, Gifford 4–35, Schnelker 2–20, King 2–9

Eastern Conference Playoff
Sunday, December 21
New York Giants 10, Browns 0
Yankee Stadium (61,174)
White jerseys/white pants

The Browns' unscheduled and unwanted return trip to New York was even more frustrating than the one the week before as the Giants' defense completely dominated Cleveland and coasted to victory and a trip to the NFL Championship.

The Browns, who had gone 113 consecutive games without being shut out, were held to a pitiful 86 total yards of offense. Jim Brown was harnessed, held to a harmless eight yards rushing on seven carries, as the run-oriented Browns managed just 24 yards on the ground. The Cleveland passing game wasn't much better, held to 10 completions in 27 attempts with three interceptions. The New York offense, meanwhile, nearly quadrupled the Browns in total yardage and built a 10–0 halftime lead that proved to be enough.

Still, Cleveland was still alive until it squandered two golden opportunities after recovering a pair of Giant fumbles. After the second, the Browns reached the New York 4, but a sack and a fourth-down interception kept them off the board. By the fourth quarter, the beleaguered Browns were beaten, and ran only eight offensive plays for the period. In becoming the first team to ever defeat the Browns three times in one season, the Giants earned a trip to the league title game the following week to face the upstart Baltimore Colts, and the two teams put on one of the most memorable shows in the history of football, with Baltimore winning in overtime, 23–17.

	1	2	3	4		
Browns	0	0	0	0	=	0
Giants	7	3	0	0	=	10

NYG-Conerly 10-yd. run (Summerall kick)
NYG-Summerall 26-yd. FG

Passing
CLE: Plum 7–12–83 0 TD 2 INT, Ninowski 3–15–31 0 TD 1 INT

NYG: Conerly 7–11–75 0 TD 0 INT, Heinrich 1–7-31 0 TD 2 INT

Rushing
CLE: Plum 3–13, Brown 7–8, L. Carpenter 3–3
NYG: Gifford 23–95, Webster 15–62, King 10–26, Triplett 5–18

Receiving
CLE: Brewster 3–56, Brown 2–18, P. Carpenter 2–18, Renfro 1–17, L. Carpenter 2–5
NYG: Schnelker 2–46, Webster 3–44, Rote 1–11, King 1–6, Gifford 1-(-1)

1959

Saturday, September 26

Pittsburgh Steelers 17, Browns 7

Forbes Field (33,844)

White jerseys/white pants

On a Saturday night in the Steel City, the Browns immediately dug themselves a hole in the Eastern Conference race, allowing the Steelers to score 17 second-half points and pull off the upset. Old Cleveland nemesis Bobby Layne was the catalyst, throwing for 209 yards and a pair of touchdowns, rushing for 49 more, and kicking both extra points and a field goal. The Browns' lone score was set up by an interception by DB Ken Konz, but the offense mustered little after that, only threatening to score one other time and coming away empty when Lou Groza missed a 28-yard field goal in the third quarter. Adding insult to injury, Pittsburgh's clinching touchdown was scored by WR Pete Brewster, who'd played for the Browns for seven years before being traded to the Steelers a month before the season began.

Record: 0–1

	1	2	3	4		
Browns	0	7	0	0	=	7
Steelers	0	0	10	7	=	17

CLE-Plum 1-yd. run (Groza kick)
PIT-Layne 26-yd. FG
PIT-Orr 20-yd. pass from Layne (Layne kick)
PIT-Brewster 19-yd. pass from Layne (Layne kick)

Passing
CLE: Plum 13–23–146 0 TD 1 INT
PIT: Layne 13–20–209 2 TD 2 INT

Rushing
CLE: Brown 19–81, Mitchell 9–46, Plum 4–12
PIT: Tracy 17–51, Layne 5–49, Krutko 8–15, Elter 2–6

Receiving
CLE: Howton 4–57, P. Carpenter 4–47, Brown 2–34, Mitchell 3–8
PIT: Orr 6–89, Brewster 3–72, Mathews 2–44, Elter 1–3, Tracy 1–1

Sunday, October 4

Browns 34, Chicago Cardinals 7

Soldier Field (19,935)

White jerseys/white pants

On a rainy afternoon in Chicago, the Browns rebounded from their disappointing start to the season to rout the Cardinals behind the power running of Jim Brown, who rushed for 147 yards on 37 carries, the most attempts in a single game in his career. QB Milt Plum was equally effective despite the elements, completing 11 of 14 passes for 154 yards and a pair of scores, while the Cardinals struggled to hold onto the slippery football, fumbling five times. Cleveland DB Junior Wren returned one 44 yards for a touchdown in the third quarter to make it 28–0 and thwart any hopes of a Chicago comeback.

Record: 1–1

	1	2	3	4		
Browns	7	14	7	6	=	34
Cardinals	0	0	7	0	=	7

CLE-Brown 2-yd. run (Groza kick)
CLE-Brown 1-yd. run (Groza kick)
CLE-Renfro 5-yd. pass from Plum (Groza kick)
CLE-Wren 44-yd. fumble return (Groza kick)
CHI-Hill 1-yd. run (Conrad kick)
CLE-Howton 36-yd. pass from Plum (kick failed)

Passing
CLE: Plum 11–14–154 2 TD 0 INT
CHI: Hill 11–25–147 0 TD 0 INT, Reynolds 6–13–50 0 TD 1 INT

Rushing
CLE: Brown 37–147, Mitchell 7–12, Plum 1–1
CHI: Crow 7–60, Hammack 5–26, Conrad 4–8, Hickman 1–5, Childress 1–3, Hill 1–2, Reynolds 1-(-3)

Receiving
CLE: Renfro 5–54, Howton 2–46, Mitchell 1–24, Brown 2–22, P. Carpenter 1–11
CHI: Lewis 8–106, Tracey 3–31, Randle 3–22, Crow 2–22, Hickman 1–11, Hammack 1–5

Sunday, October 11
New York Giants 10, Browns 6
Cleveland Stadium (65,534)
Brown jerseys/white pants

On a bright, blustery afternoon, the Browns were stymied by the defending conference champions before the largest crowd for a home opener in team history—breaking the mark set the previous season. The Browns had no trouble moving the ball for much of the day, rolling up 343 total yards, but squandered several scoring opportunities, starting late in the second quarter when Milt Plum was intercepted in the end zone after the Browns had recovered a New York fumble on the Giants' 9. Sparked by the turnaround, the Giants drove 80 yards in just over a minute and scored their lone touchdown. After the New York defense kept the Browns at bay for much of the second half, the Giants extended their lead to 10–0 on a Pat Summerall field goal with six minutes left. The Browns rallied to get on the board with 2:40 left on a Milt Plum scoring toss to RB Bobby Mitchell, but it was too little, too late, and the Browns had lost a critical game that would haunt them for the rest of the season.

Record: 1–2

	1	2	3	4		
Giants	0	7	0	3	=	10
Browns	0	0	0	6	=	6

NY-Conerly 1-yd. run (Summerall kick)
NY-Summerall 31-yd. FG
CLE-Mitchell 33-yd. pass from Plum (kick failed)

Passing
NYG: Conerly 9–17–106 0 TD 0 INT
CLE: Plum 18–37–211 1 TD 1 INT

Rushing
NYG: Triplett 14–58, Gifford 10–52, Conerly 4–26, Webster 4–12, Morrison 2–8
CLE: Brown 22–86, Mitchell 12–49, Plum 2–4

Receiving
NYG: Schnelker 3–48, Gifford 3–40, Rote 1–13, Morrison 2–5
CLE: Howton 7–82, Renfro 5–51, Mitchell 2–36, P. Carpenter 2–27, Brown 2–15

Sunday, October 18
Browns 17, Chicago Cardinals 7
Cleveland Stadium (46,422)
Brown jerseys/white pants

For the second time in three weeks, the Browns jumped out to an early lead over the Cardinals and hung on, this time for a much more narrow victory that kept their conference-title hopes alive. After Bobby Mitchell capped an 82-yard drive with a 15-yard scoring pass from Milt Plum to open the scoring, moments later DB Bernie Parrish returned an interception 37 yards for a score to make it 14–0. After collecting 135 of their 169 rushing yards in the first half, the Browns failed to capitalize on a handful of other scoring opportunities in the second half. But the Cleveland defense was magnificent, permitting the Cardinals to cross midfield only once aside from their lone touchdown, a 62-yard pass by QB John Roach, who filled in after Chicago's top two quarterbacks left the game with injuries on successive plays in the second quarter. Though Roach performed admirably, he threw a key interception to LB Walt Michaels midway through the fourth quarter that halted the Cardinals' newfound momentum.

Record: 2–2

	1	2	3	4		
Cardinals	0	0	7	0	=	7
Browns	14	0	3	0	=	17

CLE-Mitchell 15-yd. pass from Plum (Groza kick)
CLE-Parrish 37-yd. interception return (Groza kick)
CLE-Groza 18-yd. FG
CHI-Lewis 62-yd. pass from Roach (Conrad kick)

Passing
CHI: Hill 1–3–9 0 TD 1 INT, Roach 6–16–113 1 TD 1 INT, Reynolds 0–1–0 0 TD 0 INT
CLE: Plum 12–22–126 1 TD 0 INT

Rushing
CHI: Crow 18–71, Childress 6–13, Conrad 5–9, Roach 1–5
CLE: Brown 27–123, Mitchell 16–45, Plum 1–1

Receiving
CHI: Lewis 2–78, Conrad 2–21, Tracey 2–14, Crow 1–9
CLE: P. Carpenter 3–37, Mitchell 4–35, Brown 3–22, Plum 1–20, Renfro 1–12

Sunday, October 25
Browns 34, Washington Redskins 7
Cleveland Stadium (42,732)
Brown jerseys/white pants

Once again, the Cleveland defense came through with a strong performance to spark another victory on a rainy, gloomy afternoon on the lake. Spearheaded by five turnovers, including a pair of interceptions by DB Jim Shofner (the first on the second play of the game)—and later a key goal-line stand that kept the Browns' lead 13–0 at the half, the Browns pulled away with three touchdowns in the final two periods. They opened the scoring when Bobby Mitchell took a flare pass 76 yards for a touchdown in the first quarter, the first of four touchdown tosses on the day for Milt Plum, who threw for 253 yards. Jim Brown added 122 yards on the ground and Cleveland's second touchdown.
Record: 3–2

	1	2	3	4		
Redskins	0	0	7	0	=	7
Browns	6	7	7	14	=	34

CLE-Mitchell 76-yd. pass from Plum (kick failed)
CLE-Brown 30-yd. run (Groza kick)
CLE-Mitchell 15-yd. pass from Plum (Groza kick)
WAS-Anderson 28-yd. pass from Guglielmi (Baker kick)
CLE-P. Carpenter 12-yd. pass from Plum (Groza kick)
CLE-Modzelewski 10-yd. pass from Plum (Groza kick)

Passing
WAS: Guglielmi 5–15–76 1 TD, Day 3–4–40 0 TD
CLE: Plum 13–18–253 4 TD 0 INT, Ninowski 3–5–41 0 TD 0 INT

Rushing
WAS: James 13–79, Bosseler 15–60, Olszewski 3–18, Guglielmi 4-(-4)
CLE: Brown 17–122, Mitchell 7–23, Ninowski 1–11, Ptacek 2–7, Bolden 2–6, P. Carpenter 1–4, Plum 1-(-1)

Receiving
WAS: Anderson 4–85, Carson 2–24, Bosseler 1–7, Podoley 1–0
CLE: Mitchell 3–107, Renfro 3–65, Clarke 2–35, Howton 3–27, P. Carpenter 2–27, Brown 2–23, Modzelewski 1–10

Sunday, November 1
Browns 38, Baltimore Colts 31
Memorial Stadium (57,557)
White jerseys/white pants

In one of the most thrilling games in team history, the Browns stunned the defending world champions on their own home field behind a legendary individual performance. Jim Brown carried the football 32 times for 178 yards and five touchdowns, leading a furious offensive charge that saw the Browns roll up 397 total yards. Brown set the tone early in the second quarter when he took a pitchout on third-and-10 from the Cleveland 30 and blasted 70 yards for the Browns' first touchdown. Fittingly, he then clinched victory with his fifth score from a yard out with 1:32 remaining, capping a clutch 74-yard drive after the Colts had cut the margin to 31–24 with six minutes left. Brown's performance overshadowed a masterful showing by Baltimore QB Johnny Unitas, who threw for 397 yards and four scores, but all for naught. Milt Plum added 200 yards through the air as the teams combined for more than 800 yards and just one punt. While the Cleveland defense was on its heels most of the day, Junior Wren picked off two Unitas passes in the second half that proved to be huge. The first came early in the third quarter and set up Cleveland's third touchdown, and the second came in the fourth in the end zone, halting a potential scoring drive. Bernie Parrish did the same late in the second quarter, reeling in a Unitas pass at the Cleveland 4 to preserve the Browns' lead into halftime.
Record: 4–2

	1	2	3	4		
Browns	3	14	14	7	=	38
Colts	3	7	7	14	=	31

CLE-Groza 16-yd. FG
BAL-Myhra 23-yd. FG
CLE-Brown 70-yd. run (Groza kick)
BAL-Moore 3-yd. pass from Unitas (Myhra kick)
CLE-Brown 17-yd. run (Groza kick)
CLE-Brown 3-yd. run (Groza kick)
BAL-Richardson 8-yd. pass from Unitas (Myhra kick)
CLE-Brown 1-yd. run (Groza kick)
BAL-Berry 10-yd. pass from Unitas (Myhra kick)
CLE-Brown 1-yd. run (Groza kick)
BAL-Mutscheller 5-yd. pass from Unitas (Myhra kick)

Passing
CLE: Plum 14–23–200 0 TD 2 INT
BAL: Unitas 23–41–397 4 TD 3 INT

Rushing
CLE: Brown 32–178, Mitchell 8–23, Plum 2-(-4)
BAL: Ameche 9–18, Unitas 2–11, Moore 5–9, Sommer 2–6, Pricer 1–1

Receiving
CLE: Mitchell 5–66, P. Carpenter 3–56, Howton 3–48, Renfro 2–30, Brown 1–0
BAL: Berry 11–156, Moore 5–115, Mutscheller 4–84, Sommer 1–25, Richardson 2–17

Sunday, November 8
Browns 28, Philadelphia Eagles 7
Cleveland Stadium (58,275)
Brown jerseys/white pants

On a crisp, sun-splashed afternoon, the Browns vaulted to a 21–0 first-half lead and cruised to an easy victory over Philadelphia, their fourth straight. Jim Brown was the catalyst once again, picking up 125 yards and a pair of touchdowns, the first capping an 87-yard drive late in the first quarter. On the next play, Walt Michaels recovered a Philadelphia fumble, and moments later, Brown made it 14–0. The Browns then pushed the advantage to 21–0 on their next possession on a Milt Plum scoring toss to WR Ray Renfro. Defensively, Junior Wren halted a potential scoring drive with an end-zone interception, and two other opportunities were halted when the Browns stuffed the Eagles on fourth down in Cleveland territory. After the Eagles cut the margin to 14, Bobby Mitchell capped the scoring with a 65-yard touchdown run in the fourth quarter.
Record: 5–2

	1	2	3	4		
Eagles	0	0	0	7	=	7
Browns	7	14	0	7	=	28

CLE-Brown 20-yd. run (Groza kick)
CLE-Brown 1-yd. run (Groza kick)
CLE-Renfro 4-yd. pass from Plum (Groza kick)
PHI-Barnes 4-yd. pass from Van Brocklin (Walston kick)
CLE-Mitchell 65-yd. run (Groza kick)

Passing
PHI: Van Brocklin 23–40–260 1 TD 1 INT, Barnes 0–1–0 0 TD 1 INT
CLE: Plum 12–20–146 1 TD 0 INT

Rushing
PHI: Barnes 13–35, Peaks 9–32, Kowalczyk 1–0
CLE: Brown 29–125, Mitchell 5–63, Plum 2-(-5)

Receiving
PHI: Retzlaff 6–94, McDonald 4–65, Peaks 4–38, Barnes 6–33, Walston 2–17, Sapp 1–13
CLE: Howton 4–62, Renfro 2–32, Mitchell 3–18, P. Carpenter 2–17, Brown 1–17

Sunday, November 15
Browns 31, Washington Redskins 17
Griffith Stadium (32,266)
White jerseys/white pants

Behind a career performance by Bobby Mitchell, the Browns broke open a tight game in the second half and captured their fifth straight victory. On 14 carries, Mitchell accumulated 232 yards and scored three touchdowns, including a 90-yard scoring scamper on a pitchout on the second play of the game—still the longest run from scrimmage in Browns' history. After the game was delayed for 12 minutes in the early going after the Redskins protested about the type of cleats the Browns were using, and the officials forced them to change shoes, Cleveland bounced to a quick 14–0 lead. Behind 177 first-half rushing yards by Johnny Olszewski, the Redskins rallied to tie the contest at the half. After Lou Groza put Cleveland ahead again, an interception by LB Galen Fiss set up Mitchell's second touchdown to make it 24–14. Washington again cut the margin to seven before Mitchell put the game away with his third score. Mitchell, who didn't carry the football again, fell five yards short of the team record of 237 set by Jim Brown two years earlier. The Browns, who rolled up 442 total yards, got more good news when they learned that Pittsburgh had upset the Giants, pulling Cleveland into a tie for first place in the Eastern Conference with four games to play.
Record: 6–2

	1	2	3	4		
Browns	14	0	10	7	=	31
Redskins	7	7	3	0	=	17

CLE-Mitchell 90-yd. run (Groza kick)
CLE-Renfro 39-yd. pass from Plum (Groza kick)
WAS-James 4-yd. run (Baker kick)
WAS-Olszewski 19-yd. run (Baker kick)
CLE-Groza 35-yd. FG
CLE-Mitchell 5-yd. run (Groza kick)
WAS-Baker 14-yd. FG
CLE-Mitchell 23-yd. run

Passing
CLE: Plum 17–25–170 1 TD 0 INT
WAS: LeBaron 3–10–51 0 TD 2 INT, Guglielmi 4–7–47 0 TD 0 INT

Rushing
CLE: Mitchell 14–232, Brown 16–40, Ptacek 1–6, Plum 1-(-2)
WAS: Olszewski 18–190, James 8–30, Sutton 7–26, Guglielmi 1–11, LeBaron 1-(-2)

Receiving
CLE: Renfro 5–96, P. Carpenter 3–52, Howton 3–20, Brown 3–13, Modzelewski 1-(-5), Mitchell 2-(-6)
WAS: Walton 4–52, Anderson 1–35, James 1–11, Olszewski 1–0

Sunday, November 22
Pittsburgh Steelers 21, Browns 20
Cleveland Stadium (68,563)
Brown jerseys/white pants

With the Browns on a roll, they suffered a stunning last-minute home loss to the struggling Steelers that tumbled them out of first place. After a fourth-down touchdown plunge by RB Tom Tracy, Pittsburgh jumped to a 14–0 lead in the second quarter, but the Browns fought back on the strength of a marvelous performance by Ray Renfro, who caught three touchdown passes along with 161 receiving yards. His third score, a 70-yard bomb, gave Cleveland its first lead at 20–14 with just over six minutes to play in the game. But because Lou Groza missed the point after following the Browns' first score, the home team's lead remained six points instead of seven. The Steelers responded with a gritty 83-yard drive that ended when Bobby Layne found WR Gern Nagler between the goal-posts with 40 seconds left. The Browns frantically drove to the Pittsburgh 42 in the waning moments, and Groza attempted a potential game-winning field goal from the 49. But it missed—Groza's third missed field goal of the afternoon—and the Steelers escaped with the upset. It marked the Steelers' first-ever season sweep of the Browns, something that wouldn't happen again for 15 years. And with the Giants defeating the Cardinals, New York once again took over sole possession of first place in the conference.
Record: 6–3

	1	2	3	4		
Steelers	0	14	0	7	=	21
Browns	0	6	0	14	=	20

PIT-Tracy 4-yd. run (Layne kick)
PIT-Tracy 1-yd. run (Layne kick)
CLE-Renfro 30-yd. pass from Plum (kick failed)
CLE-Renfro 27-yd. pass from Plum (Groza kick)
CLE-Renfro 70-yd. pass from Plum (Groza kick)
PIT-Nagler 17-yd. pass from Layne (Layne kick)

Passing
PIT: Layne 12–20–126 1 TD 0 INT, Mathews 1–1–38 0 TD 0 INT
CLE: Plum 17–29–269 3 TD 0 INT

Rushing
PIT: Tracy 24–99, Barnett 17–50, Layne 4–19, Luna 1–10, Mathews 1–4
CLE: Brown 15–111, Mitchell 7–15

Receiving
PIT: Orr 4–86, Nagler 4–63, Barnett 4–20, Mathews 1-(-5)
CLE: Renfro 5–161, Howton 5–77, P. Carpenter 1–13, Brown 4–10, Mitchell 2–8

Sunday, November 29
San Francisco 49ers 21, Browns 20
Cleveland Stadium (56,854)
Brown jerseys/white pants

A half-frozen, subdued crowd watched the Browns' title hopes go up in smoke during a disastrous second quarter in which the 49ers lit up the scoreboard with three touchdowns, two as a result of Cleveland turnovers. The Browns caught an early break when Galen Fiss recovered a San Francisco fumble on the 49ers' 8 and returned it to the 1, setting up a Jim Brown score to give the Browns a 7–0 lead going into the second period. But cashing in on Cleveland's mistakes, the 49ers vaulted to a 14-point lead and then hung on after the Browns cut the margin to 21–20 two minutes into the fourth quarter on Brown's second touchdown. The home team had one final chance to surge back ahead minutes later after driving to the San Francisco 42, but Milt Plum tossed his second interception to halt the drive. Thus, despite a tremendous effort by the Cleveland defense, which held the 49ers to just 200 total yards, the Browns dropped their second straight one-point loss at home, permitting the Giants to clinch at least a tie for the conference title with a blowout win over the Redskins. The contest also marked the first time in team history that the Browns did not commit a penalty in a game.
Record: 6–4

	1	2	3	4		
49ers	0	21	0	0	=	21
Browns	7	3	3	7	=	20

CLE-Brown 1-yd. run (Groza kick)
SF-Wilson 2-yd. pass from Brodie (Davis kick)
SF-Smith 21-yd. pass from Brodie (Davis kick)
SF-McElhenny 12-yd. run (Davis kick)
CLE-Groza 32-yd. FG
CLE-Groza 48-yd. FG
CLE-Brown 2-yd. run (Groza kick)

Passing
SF: Brodie 10–22–141 2 TD 0 INT
CLE: Plum 11–26–116 0 TD 2 INT

Rushing
SF: Smith 15–28, Perry 9–23, McElhenny 3–9, Brodie 2-(-1)
CLE: Brown 28–114, Mitchell 12–76, Plum 3-(-8)

Receiving
SF: Smith 4–60, Wilson 2–27, Owens 1–23, McElhenny 1–18, Dugan 1–12, Perry 1–1
CLE: P. Carpenter 2–42, Howton 2–26, Mitchell 4–20, Renfro 1–17, Brown 2–11

Sunday, December 6
New York Giants 48, Browns 7
Yankee Stadium (68,436)
White jerseys/white pants

The dim hopes the Browns still held for climbing back into the Eastern Conference race were extinguished in a humiliating loss to the Giants, who, by beating the Browns for the fifth straight time, clinched the conference crown outright and secured a spot in the NFL Championship for the second straight year. It would be the second-worst defeat in Cleveland history, and things started badly when Jim Brown was forced out of a game for the first time in his career in the first quarter when he was kicked in the head at the bottom of a pileup. With their catalyst out, the Cleveland offense was helpless, committing five turnovers and accumulating a meager 136 total yards—just 26 through the air. The Giants, meanwhile, couldn't be stopped, racking up more than 500 total yards—including 401 passing as they soared to a 48–0 lead in the fourth quarter. The Browns' lone score came on a nifty 78-yard punt return by Bobby Mitchell early in the final period. When New York fans preemptively stormed the field and tore down the goal posts with 1:53 remaining, a frustrated Paul Brown took his players off the field and refused to send them back out for 20 minutes until order was restored.

Record: 6–5

	1	2	3	4		
Browns	0	0	0	7	=	7
Giants	7	17	24	0	=	48

NY-Schnelker 3-yd. pass from Conerly (Summerall kick)
NY-Summerall 40-yd. FG
NY-Gifford 2-yd. run (Summerall kick)
NY-Crow 30-yd. interception return (Summerall kick)
NY-Gifford 31-yd. pass from Conerly (Summerall kick)
NY-Summerall 22-yd. FG
NY-Rote 19-yd. pass from Conerly (Chandler kick)
NY-Webster 6-yd. pass from Heinrich (Chandler kick)
CLE-Mitchell 78-yd. punt return (Groza kick)

Passing
CLE: Plum 6–15–36 0 TD 2 INT, Ninowski 0–5–0 0 TD 1 INT
NYG: Conerly 14–21–271 3 TD 0 INT, Heinrich 8–16–92 1 TD 1 INT, Gifford 1–2–38 0 TD 0 INT, Morrison 0–1–0 0 TD 0 INT

Rushing
CLE: Brown 15–50, Mitchell 10–32, Modzelewski 6–18, Bolden 2–5, Plum 2–5
NYG: Gifford 9–46, Triplett 5–29, Webster 8–25, Conerly 3–14, King 4–11, Morrison 2–0

Receiving
CLE: Modzelewski 1–13, Clarke 1–9, Mitchell 3–7, Howton 1–7
NYG: Gifford 7–129, Schnelker 6–102, Rote 3–79, King 1–35, Morrison 2–34, Webster 3–17, Biscaha 1–5

Sunday, December 13
Browns 28, Philadelphia Eagles 21
Franklin Field (45,952)
White jerseys/white pants

Playing for nothing more than pride and a share of second place, the Browns rallied from behind with a pair of fourth-quarter touchdowns to clinch the 13th winning record in their 14 seasons. After taking an early lead on a long touchdown pass from Milt Plum to RB Preston Carpenter, for the third straight week, the Browns were victimized by a disastrous second quarter that saw Philadelphia score three touchdowns—two in the final three minutes—to take a halftime lead. Controlling the action through much of the third quarter, the Eagles threatened to break the game open late in the period when they marched to the Cleveland 1 and had a first-and-goal. But the Cleveland defense kept the Eagles out of the end zone on four successive plays, providing a dramatic momentum swing. The Browns' offense responded with a 13-play, 99-yard drive that ended with a Jim Brown touchdown to tie the game five minutes into the fourth period. The Browns, capping a marvelous offensive performance that tallied 450 total yards, then scored the winning points on another short Brown scoring run with three minutes left. Bernie Parrish then secured the triumph by intercepting Norm Van Brocklin at midfield. The Browns' star running back finished with 152 yards on 33 carries and captured his third straight rushing title with 1,329 yards on the season. Bobby Mitchell added another 127 yards on 24 carries as the Browns rolled up 296 on the ground.

Record: 7–5

	1	2	3	4		
Browns	7	7	0	14	=	28
Eagles	0	21	0	0	=	21

CLE-P. Carpenter 43-yd. pass from Plum (Groza kick)
PHI-Barnes 27-yd. run (Walston kick)
CLE-Mitchell 5-yd. run (Groza kick)
PHI-Owens 3-yd. fumble return (Walston kick)
PHI-Walston 18-yd. pass from Van Brocklin (Walston kick)
CLE-Brown 1-yd. run (Groza kick)
CLE-Brown 4-yd. run (Groza kick)

Passing
CLE: Plum 12–14–165 1 TD 0 INT
PHI: Van Brocklin 15–22–246 1 TD 1 INT

Rushing
CLE: Brown 33–152, Mitchell 24–127, Plum 2–17
PHI: Barnes 13–50, Kowalczyk 6–12, Van Brocklin 1–0, Peaks 5-(-2)

Receiving
CLE: Howton 5–61, P. Carpenter 1–43, Mitchell 3–28, Brown 2–23, Renfro 1–10
PHI: Retzlaff 4–81, McDonald 4–60, Barnes 3–48, Walston 3–44, Bielski 1–13

1960

Sunday, September 25
Browns 41, Philadelphia Eagles 24
Franklin Field (56,303)
White jerseys/white pants

Behind an unstoppable running attack and an opportunistic defense, the Browns overwhelmed the host Eagles, who would lose only one other game all season as they went on to win the NFL title. The tone was set on the third play of the game when DB Bernie Parrish intercepted Philadelphia QB Norm Van Brocklin, then on Cleveland's first offensive play, RB Bobby Mitchell swept around end for a 31-yard touchdown—his first of three on the day. Another interception—the first of two by Browns' DB Don Fleming—set up a second Cleveland touchdown, and the Browns never looked back. Cleveland finished with 329 rushing yards, led by Mitchell's 156 and Jim Brown's 153. Mitchell later added a 30-yard scoring run and caught an 11-yard touchdown pass from QB Milt Plum with two minutes left in the fourth. The game also marked the debut of new Browns' kicker Sam Baker, who replaced Lou Groza after he retired following the 1959 season—only to return in 1961 and play seven more seasons.

Record: 1–0

	1	2	3	4		
Browns	14	10	7	10	=	41
Eagles	3	7	0	14	=	24

CLE-Mitchell 31-yd. run (Baker kick)
CLE-Brown 1-yd. run (Baker kick)
PHI-Walston 21-yd. FG
CLE-Baker 36-yd. FG
PHI-McDonald 24-yd. pass from Van Brocklin (Walston kick)
CLE-Plum 1-yd. run (Baker kick)
CLE-Mitchell 30-yd. run (Baker kick)
CLE-Baker 15-yd. FG
PHI-Walston 10-yd. pass from Van Brocklin (Walston kick)
CLE-Mitchell 11-yd. pass from Plum (Baker kick)
PHI-Retzlaff 6-yd. pass from Jurgensen (Walston kick)

Passing
CLE: Plum 9–11–67 1 TD 0 INT
PHI: Van Brocklin 16–30–251 2 TD 3 INT, Jurgensen 5–6–57 1 TD 0 INT

Rushing
CLE: Mitchell 14–156, Brown 24–153, Plum 4–10, Gautt 2–10
PHI: Barnes 10–56, Dean 11–30, Peaks 11–20, Van Brocklin 1–0

Receiving
CLE: Mitchell 5–34, Renfro 1–27, Kreitling 1–18, Brown 2-(-12)
PHI: Retzlaff 5–80, Walston 4–75, McDonald 5–67, Peaks 4–35, Dean 1–31, Barnes 2–20

Sunday, October 2
Browns 28, Pittsburgh Steelers 20
Cleveland Stadium (67,692)
Brown jerseys/white pants

In their home opener, the Browns used a series of big plays to build a 21–0 halftime lead and then held off the Steelers in the second half to move to 2–0. Mirroring the start of the previous week's game, the Browns recovered a Pittsburgh fumble on the first play and cashed in on a touchdown plunge by Milt Plum. After Bobby Mitchell extended the lead to 14–0 with a short scoring run in the second quarter, WR Rich Kreitling reeled in a 60-yard touchdown pass from Plum, the highlight of a great day for Kreitling that saw him accumulate 157 receiving yards on just three catches, setting a team record by averaging better than 52 yards per catch. After Pittsburgh cut the margin to 21–13 early in the fourth quarter, the Browns caught a break when Bobby Mitchell was ruled down at the Pittsburgh 2 before fumbling, and Jim Brown scored on the next play. The Browns then secured the win with a goal-line stand on Pittsburgh's next possession. Both teams topped 400 total yards, with Plum throwing for 308 on a mere 10 completions to just three receivers.

Record: 2–0

	1	2	3	4		
Steelers	0	0	7	13	=	20
Browns	7	14	0	7	=	28

CLE-Plum 1-yd. run (Baker kick)
CLE-Mitchell 5-yd. run (Baker kick)
CLE-Kreitling 60-yd. pass from Plum (Baker kick)

THE PLACEKICKING PLACEHOLDERS

The one position at which the Browns have been amazingly consistent over the years is placekicker, at which five players have served in the role over the majority of the past 60-plus years: Lou Groza (1946–59, 1961–67), Don Cockroft (1968–80), Matt Bahr (1981–89), Matt Stover (1991–95), and Phil Dawson (1999–2012).

Starting in 1960, when Lou Groza retired for a season, only to return the following year (and remain the Browns' kicker for the next seven years), only three times in their history have the Browns entered a season with someone other than one of these five as their kicker.

1960
Sam Baker
12 of 20 field-goal attempts, 44 of 46 extra points = 80 points

1981
Dave Jacobs
4 of 12 field-goal attempts, 9 of 10 extra points = 21 points
(After five games, the Browns traded for Matt Bahr, who replaced Jacobs.)

1990
Jerry Kauric
14 of 20 field-goal attempts, 24 of 27 extra points = 66 points

During the reign of the Browns' five kickers, a handful of substitutes have filled in, primarily when the regular kicker was injured or a stronger leg was required for a long attempt.

Chet Adams
1946: 5 of 5 extra points = 5 points
1947: 1 of 1 field-goal attempts, 1 of 2 extra points = 4 points

Lou Saban
1947: 10 of 11 extra points = 10 points
1949: 0 of 2 field-goal attempts, 11 of 11 extra points = 11 points

Mac Speedie
1946: 1 of 1 extra points = 1 point

John Rokisky
1946: 1 of 1 extra points = 1 point

Chubby Grigg
1950: 1 of 2 field-goal attempts, 9 of 9 extra points = 12 points

Bob Gain
1952: 3 of 3 extra points = 3 points

Ken Konz
1954: 3 of 3 extra points = 3 points

Milt Plum
1958: 2 of 2 extra points = 2 points

Jim Houston
1966: 1 of 1 extra points = 1 point

Steve Cox
1981: 0 of 1 field-goal attempts = 0 points
1982: 0 of 1 field-goal attempts = 0 points
1983: 1 of 1 field-goal attempts = 3 points
1984: 1 of 3 field-goal attempts = 3 points

Mark Moseley
1986: 6 of 7 field-goal attempts, 13 of 14 extra points = 31 points

Jeff Jaeger*
1987: 14 of 22 field-goal attempts, 33 of 33 extra points = 75 points

Brian Franco**
1987: 3 of 4 field-goal attempts, 2 of 2 extra points = 11 points

Brett Conway
2003: 5 of 7 field-goal attempts, 3 of 3 extra points = 18 points

Billy Cundiff
2009: 6 of 6 field-goal attempts, 4 of 4 extra points = 22 points

**Served as kicker for most of the season as Matt Bahr recovered from a knee injury; Bahr returned for the final three games of the regular season*

***Kicker for strike-replacement games*

PIT-Tracy 40-yd. pass from Layne (Layne kick)
PIT-Tracy 1-yd. run (kick failed)
CLE-Brown 2-yd. run (Baker kick)
PIT-Dial 3-yd. pass from Layne (Rechichar kick)

Passing
PIT: Layne 14–21–296 2 TD 1 INT, P. Carpenter 1–1–2 0 TD 0 INT, Tracy 1-1-(-2) 0 TD 0 INT
CLE: Plum 10–14–308 1 TD 0 INT

Rushing
PIT: Tracy 15–51, Scales 7–22, P. Carpenter 2–19, Layne 3–9, Krutko 4–8, Johnson 1–1, Barnett 1–0
CLE: Brown 19–87, Mitchell 16–52, Plum 5-(-7)

Receiving
PIT: P. Carpenter 3–100, Dial 6–98, Orr 4–51, Tracy 2–49, Scales 1-(-2)
CLE: Kreitling 3–157, Nagler 4–79, Mitchell 3–72

Sunday, October 16
Browns 48, Dallas Cowboys 7
Cotton Bowl (28,500)
White jerseys/white pants

In their first game ever against the expansion Cowboys, the Browns rolled to a 28–0 halftime lead and cruised to an easy victory. With the Texas State Fair ongoing outside the Cotton Bowl, Bobby Mitchell added an exclamation point to another fantastic performance by returning the second-half kickoff 90 yards for a touchdown, his third of the day and seventh of the young season. Now the only undefeated team remaining in the NFL, Cleveland forced six Dallas turnovers, including a 34-yard interception return for a touchdown by DE Larry Stephens. The second half saw mostly backups get into the action, including reserve QB Len Dawson, who was acquired from Pittsburgh in the offseason and made his Cleveland debut and only appearance of the season. Dallas also inserted rookie QB Don Meredith, who saw his first NFL action.

Record: 3–0

	1	2	3	4		
Browns	7	21	14	6	=	48
Cowboys	0	0	0	7	=	7

CLE-Mitchell 46-yd. pass from Plum (Baker kick)
CLE-Brown 5-yd. run (Baker kick)
CLE-Mitchell 30-yd. run (Baker kick)
CLE-Stephens 34-yd. interception return (Baker kick)
CLE-Mitchell 90-yd. kickoff return (Baker kick)
CLE-Nagler 6-yd. pass from Plum (Baker kick)
CLE-Caleb 5-yd. run (kick failed)
DAL-Howton 12-yd. pass from Heinrich (Cone kick)

Passing
CLE: Plum 6–8–106 2 TD 0 INT, Dawson 8–13–23 0 TD 0 INT
DAL: Heinrich 6–15–88 1 TD 2 INT, LeBaron 2–6–6 0 TD 2 INT, Meredith 1–6–6 0 TD 0 INT

Rushing
CLE: Gautt 12–77, Caleb 5–52, Mitchell 9–46, Brown 7–25, Dawson 1–0
DAL: McIlhenny 12–43, Dupre 8–19, Babb 3–12, LeBaron 1–11, Heinrich 1–3

Receiving
CLE: Mitchell 1–46, Murphy 2–36, Brown 1–24, Nagler 2–22, Renfro 1–12, Williams 1–5, Clarke 1–2, Caleb 5-(-18)
DAL: Howton 2–53, Dugan 2–21, Doran 1–14, Babb 1–6, McIlhenny 2–4, Dupre 1–2

Sunday, October 23
Philadelphia Eagles 31, Browns 29
Cleveland Stadium (64,850)
Brown jerseys/white pants

A critical pass-interference penalty on the Browns in the final seconds gave the Eagles the opportunity to kick the game-winning field goal to cap an impressive comeback in an exciting back-and-forth contest on a blustery afternoon on the lake. The Eagles set the tone for the day with a 49-yard touchdown pass on their first play, but the Browns rebounded to take control. Following an 86-yard touchdown reception by backup WR Leon Clarke and a 71-yard scoring gallop by Jim Brown early in the third quarter, the Browns built a 22–7 lead. It then evaporated as the Eagles scored three straight touchdowns. Now trailing by six, Cleveland drove 88 yards in 11 plays to take the lead back on a short Milt Plum-to-Bobby Mitchell touchdown pass. The Eagles were pinned back at their own 10 with 1:50 remaining but quickly drove into Cleveland territory. DB Bobby Franklin appeared to clinch a Browns' victory with an interception with time running out, but Browns' LB Vince Costello was penalized for pass interference, giving Philadelphia a first down. Moments later, Bobby Walston kicked a 38-yard field goal with 10 seconds on the clock to give the Eagles a narrow victory. The last-minute heroics spoiled a spectacular performance by the Cleveland offense, which tallied 451 yards, including 167 on the ground from Brown. But 114 yards in penalties, capped by the damaging pass-interference call, proved too much for the Browns to overcome as they lost for the first time in 1960.

Record: 3–1

	1	2	3	4		
Eagles	7	0	14	10	=	31
Browns	3	12	7	7	=	29

PHI-Walston 49-yd. pass from Van Brocklin (Walston kick)
CLE-Baker 12-yd. FG
CLE-Baker 23-yd. FG
CLE-Clarke 86-yd. pass from Plum (kick failed)
CLE-Baker 44-yd. FG
CLE-Brown 71-yd. run (Baker kick)
PHI-Barnes 2-yd. run (Walston kick)
PHI-McDonald 57-yd. pass from Van Brocklin (Walston kick)
PHI-Barnes 8-yd. pass from Van Brocklin (Walston kick)
CLE-Mitchell 3-yd. pass from Plum (Baker kick)
PHI-Walston 38-yd. FG

Passing
PHI: Van Brocklin 17–26–292 3 TD 1 INT
CLE: Plum 16–22–289 2 TD 0 INT

Rushing
PHI: Peaks 13–102, Barnes 9–25, Dean 1–8, Van Brocklin 1–1
CLE: Brown 22–167, Mitchell 14–35

Receiving
PHI: Walston 4–94, Retzlaff 3–80, McDonald 2–66, Barnes 7–48, Peaks 1–4
CLE: Clarke 1–86, Mitchell 7–70, Brown 4–57, Kreitling 2–39, Nagler 2–37

Sunday, October 30
Browns 31, Washington Redskins 10
Griffith Stadium (32,086)
White jerseys/white pants

With a touchdown just before and another just after the half, the Browns pulled away from the Redskins in a blowout victory that propelled them into a tie with Philadelphia for first place in the East. Leading 7–3 in the final moments of the second quarter, the Browns surprised Washington with a halfback-option touchdown pass from Bobby Mitchell—the first pass attempt of his career—then opened the floodgates on the third play of the second half when Milt Plum connected with WR Gern Nagler for a 53-yard score to give the Browns an 18-point lead. Mitchell ran for another touchdown later in the period, and a Don Fleming interception set up a Cleveland field goal. Meanwhile, the Browns' defense forced four Redskin turnovers to keep the home team at bay and stymied Washington's running game, holding the 'Skins to less than three yards per carry as a team.
Record: 4–1

	1	2	3	4		
Browns	0	14	17	0	=	31
Redskins	0	3	0	7	=	10

CLE-Brown 25-yd. run (Baker kick)
WAS-Khayat 12-yd. FG
CLE-Renfro 23-yd. pass from Mitchell (Baker kick)
CLE-Nagler 53-yd. pass from Plum (Baker kick)
CLE-Baker 21-yd. FG
CLE-Mitchell 3-yd. run (Baker kick)
WAS-Bosseler 1-yd. run (Khayat kick)

Passing
CLE: Plum 14–19–204 1 TD 0 INT, Mitchell 1–1–23 1 TD 0 INT
WAS: Guglielmi 15–28–175 0 TD 3 INT

Rushing
CLE: Brown 12–60, Mitchell 6–38, Gautt 3–27, Plum 1–6, Caleb 2–4
WAS: Bosseler 11–34, Guglielmi 10–29, Podoley 6–19, Olszewski 6–14, Vereb 5–9

Receiving
CLE: Nagler 3–81, Renfro 3–43, Mitchell 3–41, Brown 2–26, Kreitling 3–25, Clarke 1–11
WAS: Podoley 3–54, Walton 3–39, Anderson 2–33, Vereb 4–29, Bosseler 2–15, Olszewski 1–5

Sunday, November 6
New York Giants 17, Browns 13
Cleveland Stadium (82,842)
Brown jerseys/white pants

On a chilly afternoon before the largest crowd in the team's 14-year history, the Browns' title hopes took a serious hit as they were utterly dominated by the Giants, who collected their sixth straight victory over Cleveland. The Browns were held to just 95 total yards, a team-record-low six rushing on 24 carries, while New York steamrolled to better than 300 total, including 209 on the ground. Still, the Browns were in it right to the end, leading 13–10 midway through the third quarter after DB Jim Shofner recovered a Giant fumble at the New York 13 to set up a fourth-down touchdown pass from Milt Plum to WR Ray Renfro. But the Giants answered with a 14-play, 80-yard drive to take the lead back in the final minutes of the period, then staved off Cleveland's last threat midway through the fourth when Plum fumbled after the Browns reached the New York 19. The Browns were unable to cross midfield again and now found themselves a game behind Philadelphia and a half-game back of the Giants at the season's midpoint.
Record: 4–2

	1	2	3	4		
Giants	0	10	7	0	=	17
Browns	0	6	7	0	=	13

CLE-Baker 21-yd. FG
CLE-Baker 22-yd. FG
NYG-Summerall 15-yd. FG

NYG-Triplett 1-yd. run (Summerall kick)
CLE-Renfro 6-yd. pass from Plum (Baker kick)
NYG-Gifford 6-yd. run (Summerall kick)

Passing
NYG: Conerly 6–17–105 0 TD 0 INT, Summerall 0–1–0 0 TD 0 INT
CLE: Plum 13–25–101 1 TD 0 INT

Rushing
NYG: Triplett 25–137, Gifford 13–71, Morrison 5–5, Webster 2–4, Conerly 1-(-8)
CLE: Brown 11–29, Mitchell 9–14, Kreitling 1-(-2), Plum 3-(-35)

Receiving
NYG: Gifford 2–44, Morrison 1–35, Schnelker 1–11, Triplett 1–8, Rote 1–7
CLE: Mitchell 7–57, Nagler 2–23, Kreitling 1–17, Renfro 2–10, Brown 1-(-6)

Sunday, November 13
Browns 28, St. Louis Cardinals 27
Cleveland Stadium (49,192)
Brown jerseys/white pants

After scoring on their first possession and taking command of the game in the first half, the Browns allowed the Cardinals to creep back into the contest by coughing up three fumbles and permitting 20 second-half points before escaping with a one-point win. A two-touchdown halftime lead was trimmed to 21–20 before Jim Brown provided what proved to be the winning points with a three-yard scoring run early in the fourth quarter. It capped an impressive day that saw him rush for 173 yards and surge into the league lead in rushing. St. Louis scored again in the final minute on a long touchdown pass to pull back within a single point, but the Browns recovered the ensuing onside kick to secure their fifth victory and keep pace with the Giants and Eagles, who both won as well. With Brown leading the way, the Cleveland ground game picked up 234 yards, while Milt Plum connected on 11 of 15 passes as the Browns' offense bounced back from their sub-par performance against New York to top 400 total yards for the third time on the season.
Record: 5–2

	1	2	3	4		
Cardinals	0	7	10	10	=	27
Browns	7	14	0	7	=	28

CLE-Brown 1-yd. run (Baker kick)
CLE-Renfro 66-yd. pass from Plum (Baker kick)
STL-Childress 52-yd. pass from Crow (Conrad kick)
CLE-Clarke 5-yd. pass from Plum (Baker kick)
STL-Perry 40-yd. FG
STL-Mestnik 5-yd. run (Conrad kick)
STL-Perry 28-yd. FG
CLE-Brown 3-yd. run (Baker kick)
STL-Randle 43-yd. pass from Roach (Conrad kick)

Passing
STL: Roach 12–20–186 1 TD 2 INT, Crow 1–1–52 1 TD 0 INT
CLE: Plum 11–15–194 2 TD 0 INT

Rushing
STL: Mestnik 16–76, Childress 4–46, Crow 8–42, Conrad 4–7, Roach 1-(-1)
CLE: Brown 28–173, Mitchell 11–61, Plum 1–0

Receiving
STL: Randle 7–104, Childress 2–81, Crow 3–32, McInnis 1–21
CLE: Nagler 4–85, Renfro 2–77, Kreitling 1–18, Brown 3–9, Clarke 1–5

Sunday, November 20
Pittsburgh Steelers 14, Browns 10
Forbes Field (35,215)
White jerseys/white pants

Despite another brilliant offensive showing that saw them roll up more than 400 yards for the second straight week, the Browns could cash in for only 10 points and squandered a late lead in a demoralizing loss to the struggling Steelers, who hadn't won in a month. With points at a premium on a cold day, the Browns took a 10–7 lead with just under seven minutes to play on a short scoring reception by Rich Kreitling from Milt Plum, who threw for a season-high 328 yards. But the Cleveland defense was unable to maintain the advantage, permitting the Steelers to drive 75 yards and take the lead on a fourth-down touchdown run by Tom Tracy with 2:41 left. The Browns weren't done, driving from their own 24 to the Steeler 10, converting a fourth-and-24 with a 27-yard Plum pass to Gern Nagler, who caught 10 passes for 177 yards on the day. But on the game's final play, diving WR Leon Clarke couldn't hang on to a Plum pass in the end zone, and the Browns lost for the third time on the season.
Record: 5–3

	1	2	3	4		
Browns	0	0	3	7	=	10
Steelers	7	0	0	7	=	14

PIT-Johnson 3-yd. run (Layne kick)
CLE-Baker 19-yd. FG
CLE-Kreitling 6-yd. pass from Plum (Baker kick)
PIT-Tracy 4-yd. run (Layne kick)

Passing
CLE: Plum 23–37–328 1 TD 0 INT
PIT: Layne 10–23–174 0 TD 2 INT, P. Carpenter 0–1–0 0 TD 0 INT

Rushing
CLE: Brown 17–86, Mitchell 10–50, Kreitling 1-(-15)
PIT: Tracy 19–78, Johnson 16–73, P. Carpenter 1–3, Layne 1-(-5)

Receiving
CLE: Nagler 10–177, Renfro 5–57, Mitchell 3–45, Clarke 4–43, Kreitling 1–6
PIT: Dial 3–62, P. Carpenter 3–45, Orr 2–37, Brewster 1–18, Johnson 1–12

Sunday, November 27
Browns 17, St. Louis Cardinals 17
Busch Stadium (26,146)
White jerseys/white pants

In their first-ever trip to St. Louis, the Browns forced six turnovers but were unable to hold onto a 10-point second-half lead and had to settle for a stalemate with the Cardinals. Two Milt Plum touchdown passes sparked the Browns to a 17–7 halftime lead, but St. Louis came back to tie the contest in the fourth quarter as the Browns were held scoreless in the second half. Cleveland had a golden opportunity to squeak out the victory when Don Fleming intercepted a pass to set up a 23-yard field-goal attempt by Sam Baker with 3:37 left. But Baker missed, and the Cardinals threatened to take victory before Bobby Franklin made his second interception of the day—the team's fifth—at the Cleveland 13 in the final minute. Jim Brown paced the Browns' offense, rushing for 132 yards on 24 carries, but the Cardinals outgained the Browns on the ground and overall. Meanwhile, the Eagles knocked off the Giants in a first-place battle in Philadelphia to increase their lead over the Browns to two-and-a-half games with three to play.
Record: 5–3–1

	1	2	3	4		
Browns	0	17	0	0	=	17
Cardinals	0	7	3	7	=	17

CLE-Nagler 20-yd. pass from Plum (Baker kick)
STL-Crow 2-yd. run (Conrad kick)
CLE-Clarke 2-yd. pass from Plum (Baker kick)
CLE-Baker 42-yd. FG
STL-Perry 23-yd. FG
STL-Randle 12-yd. pass from Roach (Conrad kick)

Passing
CLE: Plum 13–19–108 2 TD 0 INT
STL: Roach 9–19–119 1 TD 5 INT, Crow 1–1–8 0 TD 0 INT

Rushing
CLE: Brown 24–132, Gautt 5–35, Mitchell 7–30, Baker 1-(-11)
STL: Hammack 17–80, Crow 12–71, Childress 7–47, Roach 2–3, Conrad 2-(-6)

Receiving
CLE: Nagler 4–35, Mitchell 3–34, Renfro 3–30, Kreitling 1–16, Clarke 1–2, Brown 1-(-9)
STL: Randle 6–75, Crow 1–30, McInnis 2–18, Conrad 1–4

Sunday, December 4
Browns 27, Washington Redskins 16
Cleveland Stadium (35,211)
Brown jerseys/white pants

Two touchdowns in the final five minutes of the first half allowed the Browns to take control of the game and cruise to victory on an overcast afternoon. Down 13–10, Milt Plum connected with Rich Kreitling for a touchdown to put the Browns ahead, then an interception by Jim Shofner set up another Plum scoring toss, this one to Bobby Mitchell, with just 27 seconds left to put the Browns up by 11. With the defense collecting eight sacks—four by DE Paul Wiggin in a six-play period in the fourth quarter—the Browns held Washington to just 178 yards of offense and picked up their sixth win. Unfortunately, it was for naught as the Eagles clinched the Eastern Conference title with their ninth straight victory. Jim Brown had another spectacular day, rushing for 135 yards on just 15 carries to go over the 1,000-yard mark for the season and surpass Marion Motley's franchise record of 4,713 career rushing yards. Another streak came to an end when Milt Plum threw his first interception of the season after a string of 195 straight passes without getting picked off.
Record: 6–3–1

	1	2	3	4		
Redskins	10	3	3	0	=	16
Browns	7	17	0	3	=	27

WAS-James 27-yd. run (Khayat kick)
CLE-Brown 30-yd. pass from Plum (Baker kick)
WAS-Khayat 37-yd. FG
WAS-Khayat 31-yd. FG
CLE-Baker 16-yd. FG
CLE-Kreitling 12-yd. pass from Plum (Baker kick)
CLE-Mitchell 29-yd. pass from Plum (Baker kick)
WAS-Khayat 35-yd. FG
CLE-Baker 15-yd. FG

Passing
WAS: Guglielmi 17–26–125 0 TD 1 INT
CLE: Plum 10–28–212 3 TD 1 INT

Rushing
WAS: Olszewski 13–43, James 5–41, Bosseler 9–27, Guglielmi 10–8, Horner 1–2
CLE: Brown 15–135, Mitchell 4–3, Plum 1–1

Receiving
WAS: Anderson 6–45, Osborne 6–38, Horner 2–16, Olszewski 2–15, Haley 1–11
CLE: Mitchell 4–80, Brown 2–64, Nagler 2–42, Renfro 1–14, Kreitling 1–12

Sunday, December 11
Browns 42, Chicago Bears 0
Cleveland Stadium (38,155)
Brown jerseys/white pants

Aided by eight Chicago turnovers, including three interception returns for touchdowns, the Browns handed the Bears the worst defeat in their history. Browns' DB Bernie Parrish started the fireworks when he intercepted a pass at the Cleveland 8 and returned it for a touchdown to extend the Browns' advantage to 14–0. Two plays later, Bobby Franklin picked off another Chicago pass and returned it 31 yards for a touchdown, the beginning of a career day. Franklin would intercept two more passes, returning one 37 yards for another touchdown in the fourth quarter, just as a massive snowstorm began to sweep into Cleveland off the lake. With seven total interceptions, four in the second quarter alone, the Browns wound up setting an NFL record with 213 yards in interception-return yardage. With little required, the Browns' offense didn't do much, though Jim Brown quietly rushed for 100 yards yet again.
Record: 7–3–1

	1	2	3	4		
Bears	0	0	0	0	=	0
Browns	7	21	0	14	=	42

CLE-Clarke 27-yd. pass from Plum (Baker kick)
CLE-Parrish 92-yd. interception return (Baker kick)
CLE-Franklin 31-yd. interception return (Baker kick)
CLE-Brown 4-yd. run (Baker kick)
CLE-Franklin 37-yd. interception return (Baker kick)
CLE-Gautt 3-yd. run (Baker kick)

Passing
CHI: Brown 6–16–95 0 TD 2 INT, Bratkowski 5–16–27 0 TD 5 INT
CLE: Plum 7–12–84 1 TD 0 INT

Rushing
CHI: Douglas 5–44, Casares 8–23, Galimore 6–17, Morris 4–13, Adams 1–4, Brown 1–4, Bratkowski 1-(-2)
CLE: Brown 22–100, Mitchell 9–14, Gautt 6–10, Caleb 1–4, Plum 1–3

Receiving
CHI: Dooley 7–101, Cola 1–14, Dewveall 1–13, Morris 2-(-6)
CLE: Clarke 2–35, Renfro 2–32, Gautt 1–10, Kreitling 1–4, Brown 1–3

Sunday, December 18
Browns 48, New York Giants 34
Yankee Stadium (56,517)
White jerseys/white pants

On a frozen, slippery field, the Browns closed out the regular season with a flourish, exploding for 27 points in a seven-minute period in the fourth quarter to overcome a 13-point deficit and snap a six-game losing streak to the Giants. After falling behind 14–0 in the game's first four minutes, the Browns rallied to take a lead late in the second quarter. They then fell behind again 34–21 on the fourth play of the second half on a 70-yard touchdown reception by WR Bob Schnelker, who finished the day with 180 receiving yards. After cutting the margin to six, the Browns took the lead when Paul Wiggin intercepted a pass and returned it 20 yards for the go-ahead touchdown with nine minutes left. After a key defensive stop, the Browns added another score on a Jim Brown touchdown run four plays later. DE Bob Gain put the icing on the cake with the first touchdown of his career off another interception—the Browns' fifth defensive touchdown in two weeks. In what became a wild game, both teams topped 400 yards, as Milt Plum threw four touchdown passes and was also picked

off four times—after throwing only one interception over the previous 11 games. Jim Brown topped 100 yards to give him a league-leading 1,257 for the season, while Bobby Mitchell caught nine passes—two for touchdowns—for 133 yards. The victory clinched second place for the Browns and secured a trip to the first-ever Playoff Bowl in Miami three weeks later.
Record: 8–3–1

	1	2	3	4		
Browns	7	14	0	27	=	48
Giants	14	13	7	0	=	34

NYG-Lynch 16-yd. interception return (Summerall kick)
NYG-Rote 23-yd. pass from Conerly (Summerall kick)
CLE-Renfro 31-yd. pass from Plum (Baker kick)
NYG-Summerall 11-yd. FG
CLE-Mitchell 69-yd. pass from Plum (Baker kick)
NYG-Summerall 31-yd. FG
CLE-Mitchell 7-yd. pass from Plum (Baker kick)
NYG-Rote 18-yd. pass from Conerly (Summerall kick)
NYG-Schnelker 70-yd. pass from Conerly (Summerall kick)
CLE-Brown 37-yd. pass from Plum (Baker kick)
CLE-Wiggin 20-yd. interception return (Baker kick)
CLE-Brown 11-yd. run (Baker kick)
CLE-Gain 22-yd. interception return (run failed)

Passing
CLE: Plum 19–40–296 4 TD 4 INT
NYG: Conerly 16–29–282 3 TD 1 INT, Grosscup 2–6–26 0 TD 1 INT, Shaw 0–3–0 0 TD 0 INT

Rushing
CLE: Brown 14–110, Mitchell 2–7, Plum 1-(-2)
NYG: Triplett 7–72, King 9–39, Morrison 6–20, Webster 4–17, Sutton 3–12, Conerly 1–2, Chandler 1-(-5), Grosscup 1-(-6)

Receiving
CLE: Mitchell 9–133, Renfro 4–76, Brown 2–48, Nagler 3–35, Kreitling 1–4
NYG: Schnelker 8–180, Rote 4–80, Morrison 2–28, Webster 2–18, King 2–2

1960 Playoff Bowl
Sunday, January 7
Detroit Lions 17, Browns 16
Orange Bowl (34,981)
White jerseys/white pants

To extend its season by a week and offer another showcase of postseason football to differentiate itself from the first-year American Football League, the NFL organized the inaugural Bert Bell Benefit Bowl—nicknamed the "Playoff Bowl"—following the 1960 season. Played a week after the NFL Championship, it would pit the second-place teams from each division against one another in Miami's Orange Bowl.

Ironically, the first Playoff Bowl (or "Runner-Up Bowl" as it would come to be known) pitted the Browns against the Detroit Lions, two teams that had cracked helmets for the NFL title three times in the previous eight seasons. On a sun-splashed afternoon and before a disappointing crowd of less than 35,000, the Browns scored the only points of the first half on a Milt Plum touchdown pass to Rich Kreitling, who separated his shoulder on the play and had to leave the game.

The Lions clawed back to take a 10–7 lead into the fourth quarter, then after the Browns tied it with a field goal, they squandered a golden opportunity to take the lead back after recovering a Detroit fumble on the ensuing kickoff. Plum—who struggled all day—threw an interception three plays later, and the Lions drove 58 yards to surge ahead with five minutes remaining.

One play later, it appeared the Browns would tie the game once again when Plum hit Bobby Mitchell on a short pass over the middle, and Mitchell turned it into an 89-yard touchdown. But center John Morrow's snap on the extra point was low, and the kick was blocked by Detroit DB Dick "Night Train" Layne, keeping the Lions in the lead. The Browns had one last chance, regaining possession at their own 12 with 1:35 remaining, but Plum promptly threw his fourth interception of the game—the third by Detroit DB Gary Lowe—and the Lions secured their eighth victory in nine games against Cleveland, though the NFL recognized the Playoff Bowl only as an exhibition.

Thus, Jim Brown's 132 rushing yards didn't count, but neither did Plum's four interceptions, sparing him the indignity of throwing eight in the final two games of the season after throwing just one in the first 11.

The Browns would return to the Playoff Bowl three years later, becoming one of six teams to make multiple trips to the often-forgotten postseason exhibition contest.

	1	2	3	4		
Lions	0	0	10	7	=	17
Browns	0	7	0	9	=	16

CLE-Kreitling 9-yd. pass from Plum (Baker kick)
DET-Pietrosante 5-yd. run (Martin kick)
DET-Martin 12-yd. FG
CLE-Baker 27-yd. FG
DET-Webb 1-yd. run (Martin kick)
CLE-Mitchell 89-yd. pass from Plum (kick failed)

1961

Sunday, September 17
Philadelphia Eagles 27, Browns 20
Franklin Field (60,671)
White jerseys/white pants

A myriad of untimely mistakes cost the Browns a chance to knock off the defending world champions on their own home field as the Eagles cashed in on four Cleveland turnovers to thwart an otherwise sterling effort. Philadelphia set the tone for the afternoon on the opening kickoff when Timmy Brown returned it for a touchdown from five yards deep in his end zone. But the Browns endured to take a 10–7 lead midway through a wild first quarter on a 60-yard scoring pass from Milt Plum to rookie WR Charley Ferguson. After the Eagles took a 17–10 lead at the half—dodging a bullet when Cleveland WR Ray Renfro fumbled at the Philadelphia 2 after a 54-yard reception in the final seconds—the Browns cut the margin to four in the third period and were poised to take control of the game, forcing a Philadelphia punt. But RB Bobby Mitchell fumbled the return—his second cough-up of the day—and the Eagles recovered. Moments later, it was 24–13, and the Browns' uphill struggle was too steep. Mitchell atoned for his earlier miscues with a touchdown reception to cut the margin to 27–20 with eight minutes to play, and the Browns got one last chance when the Eagles missed a 12-yard field-goal attempt with two minutes remaining. Plum quickly guided Cleveland to the Eagles' 40 but then was intercepted to secure Philadelphia's triumph. Thus, a 432-yard effort by the Cleveland offense, sparked by 329 passing yards by Plum and 99 rushing yards by RB Jim Brown, went for naught.

Record: 0–1

	1	2	3	4		
Browns	10	0	3	7	=	20
Eagles	10	7	7	3	=	27

PHI-Brown 105-yd. kickoff return (Walston kick)
CLE-Groza 20-yd. FG
CLE-Ferguson 60-yd. pass from Plum (Groza kick)
PHI-Walston 22-yd. FG
PHI-Walston 18-yd. pass from Jurgensen (Walston kick)
CLE-Groza 21-yd. FG
PHI-McDonald 6-yd. pass from Jurgensen (Walston kick)
PHI-Walston 18-yd. FG
CLE-Mitchell 12-yd. pass from Plum (Groza kick)

Passing
CLE: Plum 18–30–329 2 TD 1 INT
PHI: Jurgensen 11–17–183 2 TD 1 INT

Rushing
CLE: Brown 19–99, Mitchell 10–4, Plum 1–0
PHI: Barnes 13–83, Peaks 13–47, Dean 4–12, Sapp 2–4, Jurgensen 1–1

Receiving
CLE: Renfro 4–104, Ferguson 2–68, Mitchell 6–59, Brown 3–41, Clarke 2–36, Nagler 1–21
PHI: Retzlaff 3–71, McDonald 4–53, Dean 1–35, Walston 1–18, Peaks 1–8, Sapp 1-(-2)

Sunday, September 24
Browns 20, St. Louis Cardinals 17
Cleveland Stadium (50,443)
Brown jerseys/white pants

Fighting through a ferocious defensive battle, the Browns rallied from a two-touchdown deficit and emerged victorious on a hot afternoon on the lake thanks to the last-minute heroics of Lou Groza and a remarkable defensive play in the final seconds. After St. Louis jumped to a 14–0 advantage early in the second quarter, a Cardinal field goal with 10 minutes left in the game gave them a 17–10 lead. But it took the Browns just four plays to drive 76 yards and equalize matters on a 41-yard touchdown pass from Milt Plum to RB Tom Watkins, who was replacing Bobby Mitchell, sidelined with a concussion in the second quarter. The Cleveland defense, strong all day as it held St. Louis to 185 total yards and picked up a trio of turnovers, forced the Cardinals to punt on their next possession and gave the offense the opportunity to drive deep into St. Louis territory with time running out and give the Browns their first lead on a 19-yard Groza field goal with 40 seconds left. But St. Louis wasn't done yet, driving to the Cleveland 24 in the frenzied final moments, where QB Charley Johnson lofted a pass to the end zone for WR Sonny Randle, who'd already scored twice on the day. Browns' DB Jim Shofner out-leapt Randle to reel in the game-clinching interception, and the Browns were in the win column for the first time in 1961.

Record: 1–1

	1	2	3	4		
Cardinals	7	7	0	3	=	17
Browns	0	10	0	10	=	20

STL-Randle 5-yd. pass from Etcheverry (Perry kick)
STL-Randle 7-yd. pass from Etcheverry (Perry kick)
CLE-Watkins 16-yd. pass from Plum (Groza kick)
CLE-Groza 12-yd. FG
STL-Perry 10-yd. FG
CLE-Clarke 41-yd. pass from Plum (Groza kick)
CLE-Groza 19-yd. FG

Passing
STL: Etcheverry 9–19–94 2 TD 1 INT, Johnson 4–11–43 0 TD 1 INT
CLE: Plum 16–32–134 2 TD 3 INT

Rushing
STL: Gautt 16–62, Anderson 2–19, McInnis 2–10, Conrad 5–7, Etcheverry 1-(-3)
CLE: Brown 22–94, Watkins 5–27, Mitchell 1–6, Plum 2-(-16)

Receiving
STL: Conrad 5–57, Randle 4–44, Stacy 4–36
CLE: Renfro 4–46, Clarke 1–41, Watkins 2–21, Brown 7–17, Kreitling 1–9, Mitchell 1–0

Sunday, October 1
Browns 25, Dallas Cowboys 7
Cleveland Stadium (43,638)
Brown jerseys/white pants

On a damp, rainy day in Cleveland, the Browns and Cowboys had trouble holding onto the slippery football, combining for seven turnovers. But the Cleveland defense and a powerful running attack led the Browns to a win over the second-year Cowboys, off to a 2–0 start after going winless the year before. Starting for Bobby Mitchell, still suffering the after-effects of a concussion the week before, RB Tom Watkins rung up 92 yards on 14 carries and was a nice complement to Jim Brown, who tallied 98. Down 15–0 late in the second quarter, the Cowboys had a chance to get back into the game with a first-and-goal situation at the Cleveland 6, but the Browns' defense stopped the Cowboys on downs and controlled the game from that point on.
Record: 2–1

	1	2	3	4		
Cowboys	0	0	0	7	=	7
Browns	9	6	3	7	=	25

CLE-Brown 7-yd. run (kick failed)
CLE-Groza 28-yd. FG
CLE-Kreitling 16-yd. pass from Plum (kick failed)
CLE-Groza 27-yd. FG
CLE-Kreitling 8-yd. pass from Plum (Groza kick)
DAL-Perkins 7-yd. pass from Meredith (Green kick)

Passing
DAL: Meredith 11–23–128 1 TD 2 INT, LeBaron 1–2–1 0 TD 0 INT
CLE: Plum 8–17–100 2 TD 1 INT

Rushing
DAL: Perkins 16–36, Marsh 8–11, Meredith 1–3, Dupre 1–2
CLE: Brown 22–98, Watkins 14–92, Plum 4–21, Powell 1–5

Receiving
DAL: Marsh 6–53, Perkins 2–27, Bielski 1–23, Clarke 2–12, Howton 1–4
CLE: Renfro 3–36, Kreitling 3–29, Brown 1–28, Nagler 1–7

Sunday, October 8
Browns 31, Washington Redskins 7
Cleveland Stadium (46,186)
Brown jerseys/white pants

Bobby Mitchell returned to the lineup with a vengeance, scoring three touchdowns—on a reception, a run, and a punt return—and propelling the Browns to a second straight blowout victory while handing the Redskins their twelfth straight defeat. Mitchell finished the day with 184 total yards (41 rushing, 60 receiving, 83 on punt returns), twice breaking free for long touchdowns in the second quarter. The first came on a 52-yard pass from Milt Plum, the second on a 64-yard punt return. Then, after a touchdown reception by future University of Nebraska head coach Tom Osborne cut the Browns' lead to 10 before the half, Mitchell broke the game open again with a 31-yard scoring scamper in the fourth quarter. Mitchell's explosiveness was timely, as Jim Brown was held to just 24 yards on 17 carries. Another highlight came in the fourth quarter when backup QB (and eventual Hall of Famer) Len Dawson threw what would be his only touchdown pass for the Browns: a 17-yard strike to Ray Renfro to round out the scoring.
Record: 3–1

	1	2	3	4		
Redskins	0	7	0	0	=	7
Browns	3	14	0	14	=	31

CLE-Groza 34-yd. FG
CLE-Mitchell 52-yd. pass from Plum (Groza kick)
CLE-Mitchell 64-yd. punt return (Groza kick)
WAS-Osborne 6-yd. pass from Snead (Aveni kick)
CLE-Mitchell 31-yd. run (Groza kick)
CLE-Renfro 17-yd. pass from Dawson (Groza kick)

Passing
WAS: Snead 13–27–200 1 TD 2 INT, Izo 2–2–31 0 TD 0 INT
CLE: Plum 16–26–184 1 TD 0 INT, Dawson 1–1–17 1 TD 0 INT

Rushing
WAS: Bosseler 6–16, Cunningham 7–15, Horner 7–12, James 1–1
CLE: Mitchell 4–41, Watkins 6–26, Brown 17–24

Receiving
WAS: Dugan 7–120, Anderson 2–59, Osborne 3–36, James 1–12, Cunningham 2–4
CLE: Mitchell 3–60, Renfro 3–50, Brown 7–41, Kreitling 3–35, Nagler 1–15

Sunday, October 15
Green Bay Packers 49, Browns 17
Cleveland Stadium (75,042)
Brown jerseys/white pants

With more than 75,000 fans packed into Cleveland Stadium on a drizzly afternoon for what they hoped would be a preview of the NFL title game, the Packers rolled up nearly 500 yards of offense and obliterated the Browns in the first-ever matchup between coaching legends Vince Lombardi and Paul Brown. Packers' RB Jim Taylor, leading the league in rushing, set the tone early with two quick touchdowns in the first period, then went for the jugular in the third period with a 45-yard scoring romp to make it 28–3. He then added a fourth early in the final period. Taylor finished the day with 158 yards on the ground as Green Bay tallied 216 rushing yards, complementing 272 through the air as QB Bart Starr was nearly perfect, completing 15 of 17 passes. Conversely, Milt Plum threw a pair of touchdown passes—the second to Ray Renfro, who tallied 100 yards on seven catches—but the Cleveland offense just couldn't keep up with the mighty Packers, who would roll to their first NFL title in what would be a golden decade.

Record: 3–2

	1	2	3	4		
Packers	14	7	7	21	=	49
Browns	0	3	7	7	=	17

GB-Taylor 26-yd. run (Hornung kick)
GB-Taylor 1-yd. run (Hornung kick)
CLE-Groza 27-yd. FG
GB-Hornung 3-yd. run (Hornung kick)
GB-Taylor 45-yd. run (Hornung kick)
CLE-Nagler 21-yd. pass from Plum (Groza kick)
GB-Taylor 4-yd. run (Hornung kick)
CLE-Renfro 13-yd. pass from Plum (Groza kick)
GB-McGee 45-yd. pass from Starr (Hornung kick)
GB-Roach 1-yd. run (Hornung kick)

Passing
GB: Starr 15–17–272 1 TD 0 INT
CLE: Plum 17–26–187 2 TD 1 INT

Rushing
GB: Taylor 21–158, Hornung 7–37, Pitts 3–22, Moore 2–4, Roach 2-(-5)
CLE: Brown 16–72, Mitchell 9–39, Watkins 5–10, Plum 3–0

Receiving
GB: McGee 5–120, Kramer 5–74, Dowler 2–56, Taylor 3–22
CLE: Renfro 7–100, Nagler 2–32, Kreitling 2–26, Mitchell 4–18, Brown 2–11

Sunday, October 22
Browns 30, Pittsburgh Steelers 28
Forbes Field (29,266)
White jerseys/white pants

Rallying from behind in the fourth quarter, the Browns stayed within a game of the front-running Eagles and Giants in the Eastern Conference with a thrilling victory over the Steelers on a bright, crisp autumn afternoon in Pittsburgh. With Milt Plum still nursing a dislocated thumb on his throwing hand suffered against Green Bay, Len Dawson started at QB and directed the Browns to a 10–0 halftime lead. But the game turned when a Dawson screen pass was intercepted, leading to Pittsburgh's first score. After the

Steelers took the lead moments later, Paul Brown yanked Dawson and sent Plum into the fray. The sore-thumbed signal-caller completed six of eight passes for 88 yards and led the Browns to 20 points in less than a half as the game became a seesaw battle. An interception by Cleveland DB Bobby Franklin set up a Bobby Mitchell touchdown run to give the Browns back the lead early in the fourth, but then Mitchell gave it right back with a fumble that set up a Pittsburgh score to make it 21–20. But Mitchell responded on the next possession with an 18-yard scoring sweep around right end, his third touchdown of the game. Then on the next play following the kickoff, DE Paul Wiggin recovered a fumble at the Steeler 10 to set up a Lou Groza field goal to give the Browns breathing room at 30–21. But fitting with the tone of the wild contest, the Steelers came right back with an 88-yard touchdown reception by WR Buddy Dial—who would tally an incredible 235 receiving yards for the day—with two minutes left and then forced a Cleveland punt with 36 seconds remaining. But two incomplete passes and a fumble later, the Browns had finally clinched a hard-earned victory that saw both Jim Brown and Bobby Mitchell rush for over 100 yards and the Cleveland defense collect six sacks.

Record: 4–2

	1	2	3	4		
Browns	3	7	3	17	=	30
Steelers	0	0	14	14	=	28

CLE-Groza 24-yd. FG
CLE-Mitchell 6-yd. run (Groza kick)
PIT-Dial 12-yd. pass from Bukich (Michaels kick)
PIT-Tracy 1-yd. run (Michaels kick)
CLE-Groza 36-yd. FG
CLE-Mitchell 9-yd. run (Groza kick)
PIT-Tracy 1-yd. run (Michaels kick)
CLE-Mitchell 18-yd. run (Groza kick)
CLE-Groza 12-yd. FG
PIT-Dial 88-yd. pass from Bukich (Michaels kick)

Passing
CLE: Plum 6–8–88 0 TD 0 INT, Dawson 6–12–68 0 TD 2 INT
PIT: Bukich 15–24–275 2 TD 1 INT

Rushing
CLE: Mitchell 14–119, Brown 29–114, Watkins 2–6, Plum 1–0, Dawson 1-(-10)
PIT: Johnson 8–35, Tracy 12–34, Scales 4–10, Hoak 2–8

Receiving
CLE: Mitchell 4–47, Kreitling 3–42, Clarke 2–30, Nagler 2–25, Renfro 1–12
PIT: Dial 9–235, P. Carpenter 1–21, Coronado 1–14, Scales 3–7, Johnson 1-(-2)

Sunday, October 29
Browns 21, St. Louis Cardinals 10
Busch Stadium (26,696)
White jerseys/white pants

The Browns took care of the Cardinals in a businesslike fashion on a warm, bright afternoon in St. Louis, jumping to a 14–0 lead in the first quarter and controlling the game from that point on. Cleveland drew first blood with some trickery, sending holder Bobby Franklin around left end for a touchdown on a fake field goal. Then, after recovering a St. Louis fumble, the Browns extended the lead on a Ray Renfro scoring reception, one of just five passes Cleveland completed on the day. The air attack was unnecessary since both Jim Brown and Bobby Mitchell surpassed 100 rushing yards in what was expected to be Mitchell's final game of the season, as he'd been called to active duty in the Army and would report to Fort Meade in Maryland the following week. The Browns' defense was also strong, limiting the Cardinals to less than 200 yards of offense while collecting four sacks and forcing three turnovers.

Record: 5–2

	1	2	3	4		
Browns	14	7	0	0	=	21
Cardinals	0	3	7	0	=	10

CLE-Franklin 12-yd. run (Groza kick)
CLE-Renfro 12-yd. pass from Plum (Groza kick)
STL-Perry 31-yd. FG
CLE-Mitchell 56-yd. run (Groza kick)
STL-Guglielmi 3-yd. run (Perry kick)

Passing
CLE: Plum 5–9–117 1 TD 0 INT
STL: Guglielmi 9–20–140 0 TD 0 INT, Etcheverry 1–4–12 0 TD 1 INT

Rushing
CLE: Brown 28–109, Mitchell 19–104, Franklin 1–12, Watkins 1–2, Plum 2-(-3)
STL: Crow 8–40, Mestnik 8–25, Gautt 6–9, Guglielmi 1–3, Anderson 1–0

Receiving
CLE: Renfro 4–68, Crespino 1–49
STL: Conrad 3–62, Anderson 4–46, Randle 2–36, Gautt 1–8

Sunday, November 5
Pittsburgh Steelers 17, Browns 13
Cleveland Stadium (62,723)
Brown jerseys/white pants

With a stunning loss to the visiting Steelers, who entered the contest with a 2–5 record, the Browns dropped into third place in the Eastern Conference and fell two games behind the Eagles. Cleveland seemed on its way to its sixth victory in seven games, taking a 10–0 lead midway through the third quarter, but Pittsburgh rebounded to tie the game going into the final period. Again, the Browns seemed on the brink of triumph when Lou Groza connected on a 37-yard field goal with 3:51 remaining to go ahead, 13–10. But then the Cleveland special team suffered its third crucial meltdown of the afternoon, allowing Bob Schnelker to return the ensuing kickoff 50 yards to the Cleveland 38. Moments later, Schnelker reeled in the winning touchdown pass. The Browns were forced to punt on their next possession and only got the ball back as time expired. Both of Pittsburgh's other scores were set up by long returns—one on a kickoff and another on a punt. Jim Brown, who bulled to 95 rushing yards in the first half, was stymied in the second, collecting only 15. Worse still, Tom Watkins, tapped to replace Bobby Mitchell, was lost for a month with a shoulder injury suffered in the fourth quarter.

Record: 5–3

	1	2	3	4		
Steelers	0	0	10	7	=	17
Browns	7	0	3	3	=	13

CLE-Brown 3-yd. run (Groza kick)
CLE-Groza 27-yd. FG
PIT-Bukich 1-yd. run (Michaels kick)
PIT-Michaels 10-yd. FG
CLE-Groza 37-yd. FG
PIT-Schnelker 26-yd. pass from Bukich (Michaels kick)

Passing
PIT: Bukich 12–18–203 1 TD 2 INT
CLE: Plum 10–19–140 0 TD 1 INT

Rushing
PIT: Johnson 22–105, Tracy 17–54, Hoak 1–1, Bukich 2–0
CLE: Brown 18–110, Watkins 10–46, Mitchell 4-(-8)

Receiving
PIT: Schnelker 7–160, Dial 1–16, Johnson 1–13, Tracy 2–11, P. Carpenter 1–3
CLE: Watkins 2–45, Brown 4–38, Kreitling 2–27, Renfro 1–19, Nagler 1–11

Sunday, November 12
Browns 17, Washington Redskins 6
D.C. Stadium (28,975)
White jerseys/white pants

In their first game in brand-new D.C. Stadium, the Browns bounced back from their disheartening loss to Pittsburgh to handle the winless Redskins on a gray, nippy day in the nation's capital and claw back within a game of first place. Jim Brown did a little bit of everything, rushing for 133 yards, catching five passes for 35 more, while also throwing for a touchdown on a halfback option on the first pass attempt of his career. The Browns also received a bonus when Bobby Mitchell was granted a weekend pass from his Army duties to play in the game, and he added 38 rushing yards. While Washington hung close for much of the game, three missed field goals and an extra point doomed the woeful Redskins, who saw their final chance to stay in the game fade early in the fourth when the Browns' Jim Shofner intercepted a fourth-down Redskin pass at the Cleveland 3. With the Giants blowing out the Eagles in their much-anticipated showdown in New York, the Browns were now within one game of the conference's two front-runners.

Record: 6–3

	1	2	3	4		
Browns	3	7	7	0	=	17
Redskins	0	0	6	0	=	6

CLE-Groza 48-yd. FG
CLE-Renfro 37-yd. pass from Brown (Groza kick)
WAS-Bosseler 1-yd. run (kick failed)
CLE-Kreitling 9-yd. pass from Plum (Groza kick)

Passing
CLE: Plum 12–15–92 1 TD 0 INT, Brown 1–1–37 1 TD 0 INT
WAS: Snead 17–29–173 0 TD 1 INT

Rushing
CLE: Brown 20–133, Mitchell 8–38, Plum 1–8
WAS: Horner 13–72, Bosseler 8–21, Cunningham 3–5, Snead 1-(-2)

Receiving
CLE: Renfro 3–61, Brown 5–35, Nagler 4–24, Kreitling 1–9
WAS: Anderson 5–65, Dugan 5–65, Bosseler 3–18, Horner 2–10, Osborne 1–10, Cunningham 1–5

Sunday, November 19
Browns 45, Philadelphia Eagles 24
Cleveland Stadium (68,399)
Brown jerseys/white pants

Behind another amazing performance by Jim Brown on a chilly day on the lakefront, the Browns romped over the defending world champions, stayed in the thick of the conference race, and picked up one of the most satisfying victories in team history. With 237 yards on 34 carries, Brown tied the NFL record he'd set four years before, while adding a quartet of touchdowns and 52 more yards receiving. Somewhat lost amid Brown's achievement was an outstanding performance by Milt Plum, who threw for 246 yards, and Bobby Mitchell—free on another weekend pass—who scored twice and tallied 198 total yards. As a team, the Browns rolled up more than 500 yards of offense, catching fire in the second half to score 31 points and rip open a game they'd led just 14–10 at the half. The victory pulled the Browns into a second-place tie with Philadelphia, with both a game back of the Giants, who romped over Pittsburgh and would come to Cleveland the following Sunday for a battle for first place in one of the most anticipated games in Browns' history.
Record: 7–3

	1	2	3	4		
Eagles	3	7	0	14	=	24
Browns	0	14	10	21	=	45

PHI-Walston 34-yd. FG
CLE-Brown 34-yd. run (Groza kick)
PHI-Dean 2-yd. run (Walston kick)
CLE-Brown 3-yd. run (Groza kick)
CLE-Mitchell 18-yd. pass from Plum (Groza kick)
CLE-Groza 17-yd. FG
CLE-Brown 1-yd. run (Groza kick)
CLE-Brown 8-yd. run (Groza kick)
PHI-McDonald 6-yd. pass from Jurgensen (Walston kick)
CLE-Mitchell 91-yd. kickoff return (Groza kick)
PHI-Brown 39-yd. pass from Jurgensen (Walston kick)

Passing
PHI: Jurgensen 18–32–230 2 TD 1 INT
CLE: Plum 16–21–246 1 TD 0 INT, Brown 0–1–0 0 TD 0 INT

Rushing
PHI: Brown 2–49, Dean 9–31, Peaks 8–17
CLE: Brown 34–237, Mitchell 8–43, Plum 2-(-21)

Receiving
PHI: Brown 2–58, Dean 6–51, Walston 4–43, Peaks 3–43, McDonald 2–25, Retzlaff 1–10
CLE: Renfro 4–73, Mitchell 4–54, Brown 3–52, Kreitling 2–26, Clarke 2–25, Nagler 1–16

Sunday, November 26
New York Giants 37, Browns 21
Cleveland Stadium (80,455)
Brown jerseys/white pants

Before their largest home crowd of the season on a surprisingly warm November afternoon, the Browns put on a good show in the first half of their battle for first place with the rival Giants, but the game got away from them in an eight-minute stretch of the second half. In a blink, a 14–14 game turned into a 20-point New York lead, the barrage capped by a 35-yard interception return for a touchdown by Giants' DB Erich Barnes. The teams were evenly matched, but the Giants took advantage of scoring opportunities and the Browns did not. The New York defense held the Browns to just 66 rushing yards, as both teams' air attacks led the way. Milt Plum threw for 284 yards, connecting with Ray Renfro seven times for 166 and a pair of scores, the first of which gave the Browns a short-lived 7–0 lead in the first quarter. But the Giants were simply too much, dropping the Browns to two games off the pace in the Eastern Conference with three to play.
Record: 7–4

	1	2	3	4		
Giants	0	14	6	17	=	37
Browns	7	7	0	7	=	21

CLE-Renfro 43-yd. pass from Plum (Groza kick)
NYG-Tittle 5-yd. run (Summerall kick)
NYG-Gaiters 1-yd. run (Summerall kick)
CLE-Brown 1-yd. run (Groza kick)
NYG-Summerall 34-yd. FG
NYG-Summerall 17-yd. FG
NYG-Gaiters 11-yd. run (Summerall kick)
NYG-Barnes 35-yd. interception return (Summerall kick)
CLE-Renfro 15-yd. from Plum (Groza kick)
NYG-Summerall 11-yd. FG

Passing
NYG: Tittle 17–26–233 0 TD 1 INT, Gaiters 1–1–27 0 TD 0 INT
CLE: Plum 19–33–284 2 TD 1 INT, Dawson 0–2–0 0 TD 1 INT

Rushing
NYG: Gaiters 15–63, Webster 15–49, Tittle 4–4
CLE: Brown 20–68, Mitchell 2–2, Plum 1-(-4)

Receiving
NYG: Shofner 6–97, Webster 4–65, Rote 5–58, Walton 3–40
CLE: Renfro 7–166, Mitchell 5–54, Brown 5–46, Clarke 1–11, Nagler 1–7

Sunday, December 3
Browns 38, Dallas Cowboys 17
Cotton Bowl (23,500)
White jerseys/white pants

Taking control of the game with two fumble returns for touchdowns in the first quarter, the Browns coasted to a much-needed victory that, combined with a Giants' loss to Green Bay, pulled them back to within a game of first place in the conference. DB Bernie Parrish, who would enjoy the best game of his career, opened the scoring on a mild, sunny afternoon in Dallas by returning a fumble 34 yards for a touchdown. LB Vince Costello scooped up another minutes later and rumbled 30 yards to make it 14–0. After the first of Jim Brown's two touchdowns on the day, Cleveland had a 21–0 lead less than 10 minutes into the contest and matched each Dallas score with one of its own from that point on. In addition to the touchdown on the fumble return, Parrish added three interceptions as the defense racked up six turnovers. Offensively, Bobby Mitchell—free on another weekend pass—exploded for 140 yards on 12 carries as the Browns totaled 230 on the ground.
Record: 8–4

	1	2	3	4		
Browns	21	3	0	14	=	38
Cowboys	0	10	0	7	=	17

CLE-Parrish 34-yd. fumble return (Groza kick)
CLE-Costello 30-yd. fumble return (Groza kick)
CLE-Brown 1-yd. run (Groza kick)
DAL-Doran 16-yd. pass from LeBaron (Bielski kick)
CLE-Groza 20-yd. FG
DAL-Bielski 36-yd. FG
CLE-Brown 21-yd. pass from Plum (Groza kick)
DAL-Doran 5-yd. pass from LeBaron (Green kick)
CLE-Plum 1-yd. run (Groza kick)

Passing
CLE: Plum 10–13–143 1 TD 0 INT
DAL: LeBaron 14–27–202 2 TD 3 INT

Rushing
CLE: Mitchell 12–140, Brown 18–86, Plum 5–4
DAL: Perkins 20–123, Marsh 6–25, Lockett 3–19, LeBaron 3–7

Receiving
CLE: Brown 4–51, Nagler 2–41, Renfro 2–31, Mitchell 2–20
DAL: Clarke 2–76, Howton 5–63, Doran 3–50, Perkins 2–15, Bielski 1–2, Marsh 1-(-4)

Sunday, December 10
Chicago Bears 17, Browns 14
Wrigley Field (38,717)
White jerseys/white pants

A season of ups and downs took its final dip in frosty Wrigley Field as the Browns were eliminated from the conference race when they squandered a 14–0 fourth-quarter lead and lost to the Bears for the first time ever. The Browns got off to a quick start, hitting the scoreboard when Jim Brown took a flare pass and sprinted 77 yards for a touchdown six minutes into the game. After the Bears fumbled on the ensuing kickoff and the Browns recovered, three minutes later, TE Bobby Crespino reeled in a touchdown pass from Milt Plum right under the goalposts, and it appeared the Browns would coast to their ninth victory. The score remained 14–0 until the fourth quarter, when the Bears cut it to seven, then quickly forced the Browns to punt. Three plays later, Chicago knotted the score on a long touchdown pass. Clinging to their final hopes of a conference title, the Browns made a crucial mistake when Milt Plum fumbled at the Cleveland 20 and the Bears recovered, setting up the go-ahead field goal with three-and-a-half minutes to play. After a frenzied flurry of action in the final minutes, the Browns had one last chance with time running out when Bobby Mitchell caught a 35-yard pass over the middle, weaving his way toward the sideline. Just after he stepped out of bounds, the final gun sounded, and the officials declared the game complete over the protests of Paul Brown, who argued that there was time left for one more play. The loss proved even more frustrating with news coming in from Philadelphia that the Giants had defeated the Eagles. Had the Browns hung on to defeat Chicago, they would have had a chance to tie for the conference lead by defeating the Giants in the season finale the following week. Lost in the disappointment was Lou Groza becoming the NFL's all-time leading scorer, finishing the game with 826 total points.

Record: 8–5

	1	2	3	4		
Browns	14	0	0	0	=	14
Bears	0	0	0	17	=	17

CLE-Brown 77-yd. pass from Plum (Groza kick)
CLE-Crespino 13-yd. pass from Plum (Groza kick)
CHI-Galimore 3-yd. run (LeClerc kick)
CHI-Coia 64-yd. pass from Brown (LeClerc kick)
CHI-LeClerc 9-yd. FG

Passing
CLE: Plum 17–28–281 2 TD 1 INT, Brown 0–1–0 0 TD 0 INT
CHI: Brown 16–31–222 1 TD 2 INT

Rushing
CLE: Brown 18–62, Mitchell 7–15, Plum 2-(-2)
CHI: Galimore 13–67, Casares 14–43, Brown 1-(-2)

Receiving
CLE: Brown 5–99, Renfro 4–57, Mitchell 2–52, Nagler 3–42, Kreitling 2–18, Crespino 1–13
CHI: Dooley 6–90, Coia 3–85, Ditka 4–35, Galimore 3–12

Sunday, December 17
Browns 7, New York Giants 7
Yankee Stadium (61,084)
White jerseys/white pants

Playing for nothing but pride, the Browns put forth an admirable effort in the season finale, matching the Giants blow-for-blow in a titanic defensive battle on a cold, misty afternoon at Yankee Stadium. The Cleveland defense capped a wonderful season, collecting four sacks and three turnovers, but the New York defense was even better, continually thwarting the Browns' scoring opportunities. After the Browns tied the game in the third quarter on one of just seven of Milt Plum's completions on the day, they failed to capitalize on back-to-back scoring chances in the fourth quarter. First, Ray Renfro dropped a long third-down pass inside the Giants 10, then on the following snap, Lou Groza was short on a 48-yard field goal. Another field-goal attempt went awry midway through the third quarter after the Browns recovered a Giant fumble deep in New York territory. The snap was muffed, and the kick was blocked. But the Giants also failed to cash in, allowing a field goal to be blocked on the last play of the half, then Pat Summerall missed a chip-shot 13-yard boot midway through the fourth. But the tie was as good as a victory for the Giants, since it clinched the Eastern Conference title outright and secured a spot in the NFL title game against Green Bay. Jim Brown provided two-thirds of the Browns' offense, topping the 100-yard mark for the sixth time on the season and finishing with 1,408 yards to top the Packers' Jim Taylor by 101 for his fifth rushing title.

Record: 8–5–1

	1	2	3	4		
Browns	0	0	7	0	=	7
Giants	7	0	0	0	=	7

NYG-Wells 7-yd. pass from Tittle (Summerall kick)
CLE-Clarke 35-yd. pass from Plum (Groza kick)

Passing
CLE: Plum 7–25–91 1 TD 1 INT
NYG: Tittle 10–19–116 1 TD 0 INT, Conerly 4–9–46 0 TD 1 INT

Rushing
CLE: Brown 24–102, Mitchell 3–5
NYG: Webster 21–91, Wells 16–52, Conerly 2-(-1), Tittle 1-(-6)

Receiving
CLE: Clarke 3–68, Renfro 1–11, Kreitling 2–8, Mitchell 1–4
NYG: Shofner 6–92, Webster 3–36, Rote 3–25, Wells 2–9

1962

Sunday, September 16
Browns 17, New York Giants 7
Cleveland Stadium (81,115)
Brown jerseys/white pants

Before the largest crowd for a home opener in team history, the Browns picked up what turned out to be their most impressive victory of the year, handing the eventual conference champions one of just two losses for 1962. The Browns took the lead late in the first quarter after converting on a third-and-24 situation when QB Jim Ninowski, returning to the Browns after two seasons in Detroit, shoveled a desperation toss to RB Jim Brown, who turned the makeshift play into a 27-yard gain. Five plays later, Brown—who finished with 134 rushing yards on the day—exploded off left tackle for a nine-yard touchdown run to give the Browns the lead. After the Giants tied the game on the first series of the second half, the Browns surged ahead again on a Ninowski touchdown pass to WR Rich Kreitling. Then a 64-yard pass to Kreitling on a flea-flicker play set up an insurance field goal in the fourth quarter. The Cleveland defense also played well, coming up with four New York turnovers, including a diving interception by DB Ross Fichtner in the end zone to halt the Giants' first possession, and later a fumble recovery by DB Jim Shofner.
Record: 1–0

	1	2	3	4		
Giants	0	0	7	0	=	7
Browns	7	0	7	3	=	17

CLE-Brown 9-yd. run (Groza kick)
NYG-Webster 1-yd. run (Chandler kick)
CLE-Kreitling 17-yd. pass from Ninowski (Groza kick)
CLE-Groza 29-yd. FG

Passing
NYG: Tittle 16–27–198 0 TD 3 INT, Guglielmi 1–2–9 0 TD 0 INT, Gaiters 0–2–0 0 TD 0 INT
CLE: Ninowski 8–19–147 1 TD 1 INT

Rushing
NYG: Webster 12–37, Gaiters 7–35, Counts 6–23, Tittle 1–7, Guglielmi 1-(-15)
CLE: Brown 17–134, Wilson 18–76, Ninowski 3–5, Green 1–1, Scales 1–0

Receiving
NYG: Shofner 5–76, Webster 5–50, Gaiters 3–34, Walton 2–23, Counts 1–12, Gifford 1–12
CLE: Kreitling 4–92, Brown 2–32, Wilson 2–23

THE PERFECT PRESEASONS

While fans tend to put too much emphasis on how the Browns fare in the preseason, there's not always a direct correlation between how the team does in its exhibition games and how it fares once the contests count.

Seven times in their history, the Browns have gone through their preseason schedule unbeaten; in six of those seasons they wound up reaching the postseason:

1946: 1–0
Regular season: 12–2, AAFC champions
1947: 1–0
Regular season: 12–1–1, AAFC champions
1949: 2–0–1
Regular season: 9–1–2, AAFC champions
1950: 5–0
Regular season: 10–2, NFL champions
1962: 5–0
Regular season: 7–6–1, third in Eastern Conference
1982: 4–0
Regular season: 4–5, playoff qualifier
1986: 4–0
Regular season: 12–4, AFC Central champions

At the opposite end of the spectrum, the Browns have also gone winless in the preseason twice, forecasting mixed results:

1972: 0–6
Regular season: 10–4, second in AFC Central, wild-card berth
2008: 0–4
Regular season: 4–12, fourth in AFC North

Sunday, September 23
Washington Redskins 17, Browns 16
Cleveland Stadium (57,491)
Brown jerseys/white pants

The Browns were on the brink of a second straight victory only to see it ripped away by a former teammate and back-to-back special teams breakdowns in the final moments. Squandering ample opportunities to turn the game into a rout, the Browns crept to a 16–10 lead in the fourth quarter and had the ball at the Washington 33, but Jim Brown fumbled, and the Redskins recovered with 3:40 remaining. The Redskins then reached midfield when QB Norm Snead fired a short pass to former Cleveland RB Bobby Mitchell—traded to the Redskins the previous offseason—and Mitchell scampered for a 50-yard touchdown with 1:34 remaining. The Browns quickly scurried into Washington territory, but Lou Groza's 28-yard field-goal attempt was blocked. Since the Browns recovered the ball after the block and it wasn't fourth down, they got the opportunity to kick again, but Groza's 50-yard attempt was also blocked, sealing their fate. It was a fitting conclusion to a frustrating day for the Browns, who gave the Redskins their first touchdown on an interception return and then had another drive halted on fourth down from the Washington 2.

Record: 1–1

	1	2	3	4		
Redskins	7	0	3	7	=	17
Browns	3	10	0	3	=	16

WAS-Steffen 39-yd. interception return (Khayat kick)
CLE-Groza 32-yd. FG
CLE-Wilson 1-yd. run (Groza kick)
CLE-Groza 12-yd. FG
WAS-Khayat 33-yd. FG
CLE-Groza 37-yd. FG
WAS-Mitchell 50-yd. pass from Snead (Khayat kick)

Passing
WAS: Snead 8–18–147 1 TD 3 INT
CLE: Ninowski 19–34–224 0 TD 1 INT

Rushing
WAS: Bosseler 12–59, Cunningham 7–38, Jackson 4–8, Snead 1-(-10)
CLE: Brown 20–88, Wilson 12–28, Ninowski 2–15

Receiving
WAS: Mitchell 3–94, Anderson 1–21, Dugan 2–19, Cunningham 1–11, Bosseler 1–2
CLE: Kreitling 8–72, Brewer 4–58, Renfro 3–44, Brown 3–42, Wilson 1–8

Sunday, September 30
Philadelphia Eagles 35, Browns 7
Franklin Field (60,671)
White jerseys/white pants

After both teams scored touchdowns on their opening possessions, the Eagles dominated the rest of the game and cruised to a blowout victory. The Browns turned the ball over six times, including three interceptions by Jim Ninowski, who completed just nine of 27 passes and was replaced by recently acquired backup Frank Ryan in the fourth quarter. Jim Brown scored Cleveland's only touchdown, but was limited to 38 yards on 12 carries. The Cleveland defense collected four turnovers, including two interceptions by Ross Fichtner, but it wasn't enough to overcome the offensive mistakes.

Record: 1–2

	1	2	3	4		
Browns	7	0	0	0	=	7
Eagles	7	7	7	14	=	35

PHI-McDonald 31-yd. pass from Jurgensen (Walston kick)
CLE-Brown 5-yd. run (Groza kick)
PHI-Jurgensen 1-yd. run (Walston kick)
PHI-Peaks 1-yd. run (Walston kick)
PHI-Lucas 15-yd. pass from Jurgensen (Walston kick)
PHI-Sapp 1-yd. run (Walston kick)

Passing
CLE: Ninowski 9–27–60 0 TD 3 INT, Ryan 4–5–58 0 TD 0 INT, Brown 1–1–28 0 TD 0 INT
PHI: Jurgensen 18–24–265 2 TD 2 INT, Hill 1–3–23 0 TD 1 INT

Rushing
CLE: Brown 12–38, Wilson 9–33, Green 2–18, Ryan 2–16, Ninowski 1-(-1)
PHI: Brown 15–72, Peaks 12–30, Sapp 6–5, Douglas 1–2, Jurgensen 1–1

Receiving
CLE: Renfro 5–74, Brewer 2–28, Kreitling 2–17, Clarke 1–13, Green 2–10, Brown 2–4
PHI: McDonald 6–140, Lucas 4–76, Brown 6–42, Peaks 3–30

Sunday, October 7
Browns 19, Dallas Cowboys 10
Cleveland Stadium (44,040)
Brown jerseys/white pants

Thanks to a new play just added to the playbook the previous week, the Browns evened their record with a gritty win over the Cowboys. With the score tied 10–10 in the final minute of the third quarter, Jim Ninowski rolled out on a newly designed play from midfield and fired a pass downfield to Jim Brown, who caught it and carried two defenders into the end zone for a 50-yard touchdown to give the Browns a 16–10 lead. The extra point failed due to a bad snap, but Lou Groza booted the clinching field goal in the final seconds, his second of the game after being honored at halftime for his 17 years of service to the team. His second field goal once again made him the NFL's all-time leading scorer. Neither team could manage much offense, with both tallying less than 240 total yards, and the Browns could manage only 62 on the ground.

Record: 2–2

	1	2	3	4		
Cowboys	0	3	7	0	=	10
Browns	7	0	9	3	=	19

CLE-Brown 2-yd. run (Groza kick)
DAL-Baker 15-yd. FG
CLE-Groza 35-yd. FG
DAL-Clarke 36-yd. pass from Meredith (Baker kick)
CLE-Brown 50-yd. pass from Ninowski (kick failed)
CLE-Groza 42-yd. FG

Passing
DAL: Meredith 6–13–104 1 TD 0 INT, LeBaron 5–8–40 0 TD 0 INT
CLE: Ninowski 15–25–169 1 TD 1 INT

Rushing
DAL: Perkins 18–74, Marsh 6–16, Meredith 3–12, LeBaron 1-(-1)
CLE: Brown 18–71, Green 6–1, Ninowski 3-(-4), Wilson 1-(-6)

Receiving
DAL: Clarke 3–70, Norman 1–29, Marsh 4–26, Folkins 2–12, Howton 1–7
CLE: Kreitling 3–62, Brown 4–55, Clarke 2–29, Renfro 2–17, Brewer 2–11, Green 2-(-5)

Sunday, October 14
Baltimore Colts 36, Browns 14
Cleveland Stadium (80,132)
Brown jerseys/white pants

After a disastrous first half, the Browns threatened to make it interesting with back-to-back touchdowns, but the Colts pulled away in the final five minutes to drop Cleveland under .500 on a warm afternoon on the lake. Baltimore surged to a 23–0 lead at the intermission, then the Browns pulled within nine points on a pair of Jim Ninowski touchdown passes. They got the ball back early in the fourth quarter before an interception halted their momentum. Johnny Unitas's third scoring toss of the day was followed by a fumble return for a touchdown to deliver a convincing victory for the Colts. Though Jim Brown snagged a 53-yard scoring pass to put the Browns on the board in the third quarter, he had a miserable day running the football, as he was held to just 11 yards on 14 carries and lost the fumble that resulted in Baltimore's final touchdown—one of five Cleveland turnovers on the day.

Record: 2–3

	1	2	3	4		
Colts	13	10	0	13	=	36
Browns	0	0	7	7	=	14

BAL-Owens 24-yd. pass from Unitas (Bielski kick)
BAL-Matte 18-yd. pass from Unitas (kick failed)
BAL-Bielski 4-yd. pass from Matte (Harris kick)
BAL-Harris 17-yd. FG
CLE-Brown 53-yd. pass from Ninowski (Groza kick)
CLE-Kreitling 18-yd. pass from Ninowski (Groza kick)
BAL-Owens 9-yd. pass from Unitas (kick failed)
BAL-Braase 10-yd. fumble return (Bielski kick)

Passing
BAL: Unitas 18–31–225 3 TD 1 INT, Matte 1–3–4 1 TD 0 INT
CLE: Ninowski 16–32–223 2 TD 2 INT

Rushing
BAL: Perry 8–57, Matte 12–44, Smolinski 9–30, Hawkins 2–15, Orr 1–14, Unitas 3–11
CLE: Brown 14–11, Wilson 4–9

Receiving
BAL: Owens 6–81, Matte 3–45, Mackey 2–33, Perry 4–29, Orr 1–18, Smolinski 1–12, Berry 1–7, Bielski 1–4
CLE: Brown 3–85, Kreitling 5–65, Wilson 4–37, Clarke 3–27, Renfro 1–9

Sunday, October 21
Browns 34, St. Louis Cardinals 7
Busch Stadium (23,256)
White jerseys/white pants

With the United States embroiled in the Cuban Missile Crisis, the Browns dominated the Cardinals on a bright afternoon in St. Louis with their finest offensive display of the season. While the Cleveland defense held St. Louis to a mere nine total yards in the first half, the Browns soared to

a 20–0 lead and never looked back. The Browns tallied 487 total yards and 26 first downs as Jim Ninowski threw for 339 yards and three touchdown passes. His primary target was WR Ray Renfro, who caught six passes for 152 yards, while rookie WR Gary Collins caught the first of what would be 331 career receptions with the Browns. Meanwhile, the Cleveland defense forced three turnovers, including a pair of interceptions by Ross Fichtner, and the Browns overcame 110 yards in penalties to climb back to the .500 mark.
Record: 3–3

	1	2	3	4		
Browns	6	14	0	14	=	34
Cardinals	0	0	7	0	=	7

CLE-Groza 12-yd. FG
CLE-Groza 27-yd. FG
CLE-Scales 5-yd. run (Groza kick)
CLE-Brewer 37-yd. pass from Ninowski (Groza kick)
STL-Crow 5-yd. pass from Johnson (Perry kick)
CLE-Brown 4-yd. pass from Ninowski (Groza kick)
CLE-Renfro 38-yd. pass from Ninowski (Groza kick)

Passing
CLE: Ninowski 19–29–339 3 TD 0 INT, Ryan 1–2–42 0 TD 0 INT
STL: Johnson 12–34–107 1 TD 3 INT, Crow 1–1–7 0 TD 0 INT

Rushing
CLE: Brown 17–57, Scales 12–55, Ryan 1–23, Green 1–1
STL: Gautt 6–48, Crow 9–28, Johnson 4–14

Receiving
CLE: Renfro 6–152, Brewer 4–73, Kreitling 3–51, Wilson 1–42, Brown 4–35, Scales 1–22, Collins 1–6
STL: Randle 4–35, Conrad 3–35, Gautt 2–28, Crow 3–15, Childress 1–1

Sunday, October 28
Browns 41, Pittsburgh Steelers 14
Pitt Stadium (35,417)
White jerseys/white pants

The Browns put together their second straight dominating offensive performance and exploded for 34 second-half points to roll to a blowout win on a dark, rainy day in Pittsburgh. After the Browns took an early lead on a fumble return for a touchdown by LB Vince Costello, in the second quarter Jim Ninowski was knocked out of the game and lost for the season with a broken collarbone. After throwing a costly interception that set up Pittsburgh's first score, newly aquired backup Frank Ryan filled in nicely, throwing a pair of touchdown passes in the second half as the Browns pulled away. While the offense lit up the scoreboard, the defense was equally powerful, collecting 10 sacks and forcing four turnovers while holding the Steelers to just 205 total yards.
Record: 4–3

	1	2	3	4		
Browns	7	0	17	17	=	41
Steelers	0	0	7	7	=	14

CLE-Costello 21-yd. fumble return (Groza kick)
CLE-Groza 37-yd. FG
CLE-Scales 12-yd. run (Groza kick)
PIT-Hoak 1-yd. run (Michaels kick)
CLE-Brown 15-yd. pass from Ryan (Groza kick)
CLE-Groza 51-yd. FG
CLE-Brown 1-yd. run (Groza kick)
PIT-Dial 6-yd. pass from Brown (Michaels kick)
CLE-Green 8-yd. pass from Ryan (Groza kick)

Passing
CLE: Ryan 11–18–144 2 TD 2 INT, Ninowski 1–7–16 0 TD 0 INT
PIT: Brown 6–7–88 1 TD 0 INT, Layne 3–9–44 0 TD 1 INT

Rushing
CLE: Brown 21–93, Scales 11–55, Green 3–42, Ryan 3–9, Wilson 2–1
PIT: Johnson 16–94, Womack 15–55, Ferguson 3–23, Hoak 2–1, Mack 1-(-9)

Receiving
CLE: Renfro 2–53, Brown 4–36, Collins 1–22, Scales 2–16, Kreitling 1–16, Crespino 1–9, Green 1–8
PIT: Dial 5–66, Hill 2–31, Mack 1–29, Ferguson 1–6

Sunday, November 4
Browns 14, Philadelphia Eagles 14
Cleveland Stadium (63,848)
Brown jerseys/white pants

Frank Ryan made his first start for the Browns, and while he ran for 80 yards and a touchdown, he had a tough day throwing the ball as the Cleveland offense struggled to put points on the board and had to settle for a stalemate against the struggling Eagles. The day started sourly when Jim Brown lost a fumble on the Browns' first play that set up a Philadelphia touchdown—the first of a combined eight turnovers in what became a sloppy game. The Browns saw a handful of other scoring opportunities go awry, including two missed field goals—with another blocked—and a fumble return for a touchdown wiped out by a penalty. Still, after Ryan's touchdown tied the game with five minutes left, the Browns appeared poised to take the lead when Vince Costello intercepted a pass and returned it into Philadelphia territory. But Lou Groza missed a 45-yard attempt, and then the Eagles missed a kick of their own in the final minutes to preserve the tie.

Record: 4–3–1

	1	2	3	4		
Eagles	7	0	7	0	=	14
Browns	0	7	0	7	=	14

PHI-Peaks 22-yd. run (Walston kick)
CLE-Scales 5-yd. run (Groza kick)
PHI-Brown 5-yd. pass from Jurgensen (Walston kick)
CLE-Ryan 9-yd. run (Groza kick)

Passing
PHI: Jurgensen 15–27–142 1 TD 3 INT
CLE: Ryan 10–23–119 0 TD 2 INT, Scales 0–1–0 0 TD 1 INT

Rushing
PHI: Peaks 14–33, Brown 11–30, Jurgensen 1–2
CLE: Ryan 9–80, Brown 20–69, Scales 10–33

Receiving
PHI: Peaks 4–50, Brown 5–44, Cassady 3–26, Lucas 1–17, McDonald 2–5
CLE: Renfro 2–54, Brown 4–31, Kreitling 2–24, Scales 2–10

Sunday, November 11
Washington Redskins 17, Browns 9
D.C. Stadium (48,169)
White jerseys/white pants

On another tough day for the offense, the Browns accumulated almost as many penalty yards as total yards and a handful of mistakes paved the way for an easy Washington victory. With Jim Brown held to just 27 yards on nine carries, the Browns managed only 191 yards of offense, but racked up 141 yards on 11 penalties as the Redskins rolled to a 17–0 lead early in the third quarter and then withstood a pair of late Cleveland scores to close out the win. A 65-yard touchdown pass from Frank Ryan to Ray Renfro put the Browns on the board, but a miss on the point after kept the Browns two scores down after a field goal later in the period. A Rich Kreitling touchdown reception that would have cut the Redskins' lead to a point early in the fourth was wiped out by a penalty and the Browns failed to draw any closer.

Record: 4–4–1

	1	2	3	4		
Browns	0	0	9	0	=	9
Redskins	0	10	7	0	=	17

WAS-Bosseler 1-yd. run (Khayat kick)
WAS-Khayat 28-yd. FG
WAS-Bosseler 1-yd. run (Khayat kick)
CLE-Renfro 65-yd. pass from Ryan (kick failed)
CLE-Groza 25-yd. FG

Passing
CLE: Ryan 11–18–118 1 TD 2 INT
WAS: Snead 14–23–112 0 TD 2 INT

Rushing
CLE: Ryan 6–48, Brown 9–27, Scales 6–14
WAS: Barnes 20–67, Cunningham 5–39, Bosseler 12–33, Snead 1–3

Receiving
CLE: Renfro 1–65, Clarke 2–24, Kreitling 2–24, Scales 2–12, Brown 4-(-7)
WAS: Bosseler 5–37, Dugan 3–30, Junker 1–18, Mitchell 2–14, James 1–14, Anderson 1–8, Cunningham 1-(-9)

Sunday, November 18
Browns 38, St. Louis Cardinals 14
Cleveland Stadium (41,815)
Brown jerseys/white pants

Sparked by four touchdowns by Jim Brown and the suddenly potent aerial combination of newcomers Frank Ryan and Gary Collins, the Browns rolled to a blowout victory over St. Louis on a chilly afternoon in Cleveland. Collins, filling in for an injured Ray Renfro, had a breakout game with six receptions for 88 yards and his first pro touchdown, while Ryan tossed for 241 yards on just 13 completions. On defense, LB Galen Fiss picked off two passes that led to scores as the Browns blew open a 7–0 game with a 17-point third quarter. For just the second (and final) time in franchise history, the Browns did not commit a penalty in a game.

Record: 5–4–1

	1	2	3	4		
Cardinals	0	0	0	14	=	14
Browns	0	7	17	14	=	38

CLE-Collins 12-yd. pass from Ryan (Groza kick)
CLE-Brown 3-yd. run (Groza kick)
CLE-Brown 4-yd. run (Groza kick)
CLE-Groza 24-yd. FG
STL-Gautt 1-yd. run (Perry kick)
CLE-Brown 16-yd. run (Groza kick)
STL-Hammack 23-yd. run (Perry kick)
CLE-Brown 7-yd. run (Groza kick)

Passing
STL: Johnson 9–21–91 0 TD 0 INT, Etcheverry 6–11–58 0 TD 2 INT
CLE: Ryan 13–21–241 1 TD 0 INT

Rushing
STL: Gautt 15–69, Crow 14–65, Hammack 2–34, Johnson 2–29, Childress 1–12, Etcheverry 1–1
CLE: Brown 19–79, Scales 5–44, Green 4–13, Ryan 10–0

Receiving
STL: Conrad 3–39, Gautt 3–29, Randle 3–26, Anderson 1–16, Childress 2–15, Crow 2–14, McInnis 1–10
CLE: Collins 6–88, Green 2–75, Kreitling 2–41, Brown 2–27, Clarke 1–10

Sunday, November 25
Browns 35, Pittsburgh Steelers 14
Cleveland Stadium (53,601)
Brown jerseys/white pants

With a dazzling offensive performance on a bright November afternoon, the Browns blew open a tight game with three fourth-quarter touchdowns to move into second place in the Eastern Conference. Cleveland rolled to 418 total yards, paced by Frank Ryan throwing for 284 and three touchdowns. Jim Brown rushed for 110 yards—topping the century mark for the first time in nine games, the longest drought of his career—and catching passes for 56 more while scoring three touchdowns. Gary Collins came up big for the second straight week, snagging a touchdown catch in the final minute of the first half. While one-sided, the game was relatively crisp, with just one penalty called.
Record: 6–4–1

	1	2	3	4		
Steelers	0	0	7	7	=	14
Browns	0	14	0	21	=	35

CLE-Brown 34-yd. pass from Ryan (Groza kick)
CLE-Collins 12-yd. pass from Ryan (Groza kick)
PIT-Womack 15-yd. run (Michaels kick)
CLE-Renfro 31-yd. pass from Ryan (Groza kick)
PIT-Johnson 6-yd. run (Michaels kick)
CLE-Brown 1-yd. run (Groza kick)
CLE-Brown 1-yd. run (Groza kick)

Passing
PIT: Layne 13–23–155 0 TD 1 INT
CLE: Ryan 21–33–284 3 TD 0 INT

Rushing
PIT: Johnson 15–68, Womack 9–51, Hoak 12–22, Burrell 2–3
CLE: Brown 19–110, Green 8–45, Ryan 3–0

Receiving
PIT: Burrell 2–74, Johnson 7–29, Carpenter 2–27, Hoak 1–19, Womack 1–6
CLE: Renfro 3–78, Kreitling 5–70, Brown 5–56, Collins 3–37, Brewer 3–30, Green 1–9, Crespino 1–4

Sunday, December 2
Dallas Cowboys 45, Browns 21
Cotton Bowl (24,226)
White jerseys/white pants

The Browns were unable to keep up with the suddenly fiery Cowboys, who exploded for four touchdowns in the second half to coast to their first-ever victory over Cleveland, setting single-game team records for points scored and first downs. The Browns kept pace through two quarters, trailing just 17–14 at the half, as Frank Ryan had another sterling day, throwing for 268 yards and three touchdowns. Rich Kreitling was the primary target, catching seven passes for 125 yards and a score. But due to their struggling rushing attack, which managed just 61 yards as Jim Brown was held to 29 on eight carries, they were unable to keep the ball away from the red-hot Dallas attack. The Cowboys rolled to 217 rushing yards and nearly 400 total along with 28 first downs behind the hot hand of QB Don Meredith, who completed 10 of 12 passes and a pair of touchdowns.
Record: 6–5–1

	1	2	3	4		
Browns	7	7	0	7	=	21
Cowboys	3	14	14	14	=	45

DAL-Baker 15-yd. FG
CLE-Brewer 15-yd. pass from Ryan (Groza kick)
DAL-Clarke 2-yd. pass from Meredith (Baker kick)
DAL-Folkins 5-yd. pass from Meredith (Baker kick)
CLE-Kreitling 28-yd. pass from Ryan (Groza kick)
DAL-Perkins 1-yd. run (Baker kick)
DAL-Perkins 1-yd. run (Baker kick)
DAL-Lockett 1-yd. run (Baker kick)
DAL-Howton 12-yd. pass from LeBaron (Baker kick)
CLE-Renfro 11-yd. pass from Ryan

Passing
CLE: Ryan 19–31–268 3 TD 1 INT, Brown 0–1–0 0 TD 0 INT
DAL: Meredith 10–12–147 2 TD 0 INT, LeBaron 6–8–53 1 TD 1 INT

Rushing
CLE: Brown 8–29, Green 4–16, Ryan 1–16
DAL: Marsh 17–117, Perkins 22–92, Lockett 2–8

Receiving
CLE: Kreitling 7–125, Brewer 4–60, Renfro 4–60, Brown 4–23
DAL: Howton 4–77, Marsh 4–52, Folkins 4–36, Clarke 3–20, Perkins 1–15

Sunday, December 9
New York Giants 17, Browns 13
Yankee Stadium (62,794)
White jerseys/white pants

In a crisply played game that saw just one penalty, the Browns threw a scare into the red-hot Giants, but New York endured to pull out its eighth straight win and drop the Browns out of second place. After backup QB Ralph Guglielmi led the Giants to a pair of touchdowns, the Browns cut the lead to 14–13 going into the fourth quarter on a Jim Brown touchdown run. But the New York defense hunkered down in the fourth quarter, and the Giants tacked on an insurance field goal to secure the victory. While the Cleveland run game failed to ignite, rookie RB Ernie Green had a breakout game, catching nine passes for 97 yards.
Record: 6–6–1

	1	2	3	4		
Browns	0	3	10	0	=	13
Giants	0	7	7	3	=	17

NYG-Walton 7-yd. pass from Guglielmi (Chandler kick)
CLE-Groza 16-yd. FG
CLE-Groza 39-yd. FG
NYG-Morrison 1-yd. run (Chandler kick)
CLE-Brown 4-yd. run (Groza kick)
NYG-Chandler 17-yd. FG

Passing
CLE: Ryan 17–33–185 0 TD 0 INT
NYG: Guglielmi 5–10–82 1 TD 0 INT, Tittle 1–2–12 0 TD 0 INT, Gifford 1–1–12 0 TD 0 INT

Rushing
CLE: Brown 14–55, Ryan 5–22, Scales 2–10, Green 2–2
NYG: King 21–92, Guglielmi 8–50, Webster 6–31, Morrison 9–28, Tittle 1–10

Receiving
CLE: Green 9–97, Brown 3–42, Brewer 2–20, Renfro 1–16, Scales 1–7, Clarke 1–3
NYG: Gifford 3–60, King 2–24, Shofner 1–15, Walton 1–7

Saturday, December 15
Browns 13, San Francisco 49ers 10
Kezar Stadium (35,274)
White jerseys/white pants

On a rainy, foggy Saturday afternoon in San Francisco, the Browns used a strong running game and defensive performance to secure a winning record for the season. Jim Brown sloshed through the mud for 135 yards and a pair of touchdowns as the Browns took a 13–10 halftime lead, then neither team scored in the second half. After slipping in the mud for a four-yard loss on the second-to-last play of the game, Brown was stopped short of his fifth straight 1,000-yard season after already being denied the NFL rushing title for the first time. Meanwhile, the Cleveland defense collected six sacks and, after San Francisco scored a touchdown on its first possession, the 49ers were almost completely shut down for the remainder of the game. The triumph turned out to be the final game Paul Brown would coach for the Browns, as he was fired four weeks later and replaced by assistant Blanton Collier.
Record: 7–6–1

	1	2	3	4		
Browns	6	7	0	0	=	13
49ers	7	3	0	0	=	10

SF-Brodie 1-yd. run (Davis kick)
CLE-Brown 5-yd. run (pass failed)
CLE-Brown 12-yd. run (Groza kick)
SF-Davis 14-yd. FG

Passing
CLE: Ryan 5–10–82 0 TD 0 INT
SF: Brodie 13–20–152 0 TD 1 INT

Rushing
CLE: Brown 22–135, Scales 9–28, Ryan 2–28
SF: Smith 27–90, Brodie 5–31, Vollenweider 5–23, Winston 1-(-15)

Receiving
CLE: Brown 3–56, Renfro 1–16, Brewer 1–10
SF: Stickles 3–73, Conner 3–34, Smith 3–33, McFarland 1–8, Vollenweider 2–2, Winston 1–2

1963

Sunday, September 15
Browns 37, Washington Redskins 14
Cleveland Stadium (57,618)
Brown jerseys/white pants

In Blanton Collier's first game as head coach, the Browns' offense erupted to spark a romp over Washington on a crisp afternoon in Cleveland. The Browns tallied a whopping 543 total yards, led by RB Jim Brown, who rushed for 162 on just 15 carries and caught three passes for 100 more. Frank Ryan—now the Browns' full-time starting QB—also led the charge, throwing for 334 yards and a pair of touchdowns. Ryan's first score came on the Browns' fourth play—a four-yard toss to WR Bobby Crespino—after the Redskins fumbled the opening kickoff. An 83-yard touchdown pass to Brown followed in the second quarter. Fittingly, Brown capped Cleveland's touchdown barrage with an 80-yard romp in the fourth quarter after the 'Skins had cut the margin to 27–14 following a 99-yard touchdown reception by former Browns' RB Bobby Mitchell. With Collier at the helm, a new era had begun with the kind of impressive offensive display that would define the remainder of the decade.

Record: 1–0

	1	2	3	4		
Redskins	0	7	7	0	=	14
Browns	10	14	3	10	=	37

CLE-Crespino 4-yd. pass from Ryan (Groza kick)
CLE-Groza 42-yd. FG
WAS-Richter 7-yd. pass from Snead (Khayat kick)
CLE-Brown 83-yd. pass from Ryan (Groza kick)
CLE-Brown 10-yd. run (Groza kick)
CLE-Groza 24-yd. FG
WAS-Mitchell 99-yd. pass from Izo (Khayat kick)
CLE-Brown 80-yd. run (Groza kick)
CLE-Groza 39-yd. FG

Passing
WAS: Izo 8–17–153 1 TD 1 INT, Snead 5–15–75 1 TD 1 INT
CLE: Ryan 21–31–334 2 TD 2 INT, Brown 0–1–0 0 TD 0 INT

Rushing
WAS: James 14–40, Bosseler 6–25, Snead 1–4, Izo 1–2
CLE: Brown 15–162, Webb 6–37, Green 4–10, Ryan 4–8

Receiving
WAS: Mitchell 4–122, Dugan 3–53, Richter 3–27, Bosseler 1–15, Cunningham 2–11
CLE: Brown 3–100, Brewer 4–81, Collins 4–52, Kreitling 3–48, Green 4–35, Hutchinson 1–17, Crespino 1–4, Webb 1-(-3)

Sunday, September 22
Browns 41, Dallas Cowboys 24
Cotton Bowl (28,710)
White jerseys/white pants

Amid intense heat in the Cotton Bowl, the Cleveland offense once again was unstoppable as the Browns blew open a close game in the fourth quarter to win comfortably over the Cowboys. Jim Brown came within five yards of matching his own single-game record, tallying 232 on just 20 carries, including touchdown runs of 71 and 62 yards. WR Gary Collins snagged a pair of touchdown receptions—his first big game in what would be a breakout season—as the Browns topped 450 total yards and sprinted to a 24–7 lead in the second quarter. After Dallas narrowed the margin to 27–24 going into the fourth, the Browns converted on a key third-and-17 situation to keep alive a drive that would result in Collins' second touchdown and give them some breathing room before Brown opened the floodgates with his second score.

Record: 2–0

	1	2	3	4		
Browns	14	10	3	14	=	41
Cowboys	7	10	7	0	=	24

CLE-Collins 17-yd. pass from Ryan (Groza kick)
DAL-Perkins 19-yd. run (Baker kick)
CLE-Ryan 7-yd. run (Groza kick)
CLE-Groza 32-yd. FG
CLE-Brown 71-yd. run (Groza kick)
DAL-Clarke 23-yd. pass from LeBaron (Baker kick)
DAL-Baker 13-yd. FG
CLE-Groza 15-yd. FG
DAL-Perkins 1-yd. run (Baker kick)
CLE-Collins 4-yd. pass from Ryan (Groza kick)
CLE-Brown 62-yd. run (Groza kick)

Passing
CLE: Ryan 11–18–188 2 TD 2 INT, Brown 0–1–0 0 TD 0 INT
DAL: LeBaron 9–13–132 1 TD 1 INT, Meredith 6–13–77 0 TD 1 INT

Rushing
CLE: Brown 20–232, Ryan 3–17, Webb 3–10, Green 5–6
DAL: Perkins 22–95, Meredith 4–32, Marsh 5-(-9)

Receiving
CLE: Collins 5–85, Green 3–57, Hutchinson 1–17, Renfro 1–16, Brewer 1–13
DAL: Norman 1–49, Clarke 2–43, Folkins 2–32, Marsh 4–29, Barnes 2–25, Howton 2–21, Perkins 2–10

Sunday, September 29
Browns 20, Los Angeles Rams 6
Cleveland Stadium (54,713)
Brown jerseys/white pants

Though the offense wasn't as dominant as the previous two weeks and hindered its own cause with four turnovers, the Cleveland defense rose to the occasion, keeping the Rams out of the end zone and driving the Browns to a 3–0 record on a rainy afternoon. The turning point came early in the third quarter when the Rams recovered a fumble deep in Cleveland territory and shortly after had first-and-goal at the Browns' 5. The Cleveland defense thwarted the Rams on four straight plays to keep the lead and switch the momentum back to the home team. A Frank Ryan-to-WR Rich Kreitling touchdown pass pushed the lead to 10, then Ryan's second scoring pass, a 39-yarder to WR Ray Renfro, put the contest away with 10 minutes remaining.
Record: 3–0

	1	2	3	4		
Rams	3	0	0	3	=	6
Browns	0	7	6	7	=	20

LA-Villanueva 13-yd. FG
CLE-Brown 17-yd. run (Groza kick)
CLE-Kreitling 14-yd. pass from Ryan (kick failed)
LA-Villanueva 45-yd. FG
CLE-Renfro 39-yd. pass from Ryan (Groza kick)

Passing
LA: Bratkowski 8–14–85 0 TD 1 INT, Gabriel 6–10–65 0 TD 1 INT
CLE: Ryan 9–15–152 2 TD 0 INT, Groza 0–1–0 0 TD 1 INT

Rushing
LA: Arnett 18–39, Bass 12–38, Gabriel 1–8
CLE: Brown 22–95, Green 8–70, Franklin 1-(-10), Ryan 5-(-24)

Receiving
LA: Phillips 2–47, Atkins 2–32, Adams 3–26, Arnett 2–26, Bass 5–19
CLE: Brewer 3–62, Renfro 1–39, Green 2–26, Kreitling 1–14, Collins 1–11, Brown 1–0

Saturday, October 5
Browns 35, Pittsburgh Steelers 23
Cleveland Stadium (84,684)
Brown jerseys/white pants

On an electric Saturday night before the largest crowd in team history, the Browns rallied from behind in the fourth quarter to knock off the unbeaten Steelers and maintain sole possession of first place in the Eastern Conference. Trailing 23–21 after three periods, the Browns took the lead with 12 minutes remaining on Gary Collins's second touchdown catch of the evening, set up by a 52-yard punt return by Jim Shofner. After Pittsburgh missed a field goal, the home team put the plucky Steelers away with just over four minutes left. After a 73-yard punt by Collins pinned the Steelers deep in their own territory, Browns' LB Galen Fiss intercepted a pass, and moments later Frank Ryan connected on his third touchdown pass of the night, a 19-yard strike to Rich Kreitling. Jim Brown was once again the spark plug on offense, tallying 175 yards on 21 carries to bring his season total to 664 yards in just four games.
Record: 4–0

	1	2	3	4		
Steelers	3	17	3	0	=	23
Browns	7	7	7	14	=	35

PIT-Michaels 18-yd. FG
CLE-Brown 8-yd. run (Groza kick)
PIT-Michaels 8-yd. FG
PIT-Dial 24-yd. pass from Brown (Michaels kick)
CLE-Collins 15-yd. pass from Ryan (Groza kick)
PIT-Dial 41-yd. pass from Brown (Michaels kick)
CLE-Ryan 13-yd. run (Groza kick)
PIT-Michaels 8-yd. FG
CLE-Collins 20-yd. pass from Ryan (Groza kick)
CLE-Kreitling 19-yd. pass from Ryan (Groza kick)

SATURDAY NIGHT WITH THE STEELERS

From their first-ever meeting in their rich rivalry, the Browns and Steelers established a tradition of playing on Saturday nights, adding some spice to the rivalry long before the era of prime-time games in the NFL.

Starting with five games at Forbes Field between 1950 and 1959, the tradition really caught fire when it moved to Cleveland Stadium for eight games starting in 1963, each of which drew more than eighty thousand fans. With the dawn of *Monday Night Football* in 1970 and football's gradual introduction to prime-time television, the Saturday-night clashes eventually faded away.

Interestingly, the Browns won 11 of the 13 games, seven of the eight played in Cleveland.

October 7, 1950
(Forbes Field—35,590)
Browns 30, Steelers 17

October 4, 1952
(Forbes Field—27,923)
Browns 21, Steelers 20

October 6, 1956
(Forbes Field—35,398)
Browns 14, Steelers 10

October 5, 1957
(Forbes Field—35,570)
Browns 23, Steelers 12

September 26, 1959
(Forbes Field—33,844)
Steelers 17, Browns 7

October 5, 1963
(Cleveland Stadium—84,684)
Browns 35, Steelers 23

October 10, 1964
(Cleveland Stadium—80,530)
Steelers 23, Browns 7

October 9, 1965
(Cleveland Stadium—80,187)
Browns 24, Steelers 19

October 8, 1966
(Cleveland Stadium—82,687)
Browns 41, Steelers 10

October 7, 1967
(Cleveland Stadium—82,949)
Browns 21, Steelers 10

October 5, 1968
(Cleveland Stadium—81,865)
Browns 31, Steelers 24

October 18, 1969
(Cleveland Stadium—84,078)
Browns 42, Steelers 31

October 3, 1970
(Cleveland Stadium—84,439)
Browns 15, Steelers 7

Passing
PIT: Brown 18–35–289 2 TD 1 INT, Nofsinger 1–1–27 0 TD 0 INT
CLE: Ryan 9–21–148 3 TD 0 INT

Rushing
PIT: Hoak 19–54, Ferguson 12–37, Brown 1–7, Mack 1–0, Tracy 2-(-1)
CLE: Brown 21–175, Ryan 8–54, Green 4-(-10)

Receiving
PIT: Dial 7–144, Mack 6–130, Hoak 2–18, P. Carpenter 1–17, Ferguson 3–7
CLE: Collins 5–95, Kreitling 1–19, Brown 1–15, Green 1–13, Brewer 1–6

Sunday, October 13
Browns 35, New York Giants 24
Yankee Stadium (62,956)
White jerseys/white pants

In a highly anticipated matchup with the rival Giants before a big crowd at Yankee Stadium, the Browns rallied from a 10-point deficit with three second-half touchdowns to score a huge victory that opened up a two-game conference lead. Down 17–7 in the second quarter, the Browns caught fire behind three touchdown passes by Frank Ryan and the second and third of Jim Brown's three touchdowns. The Browns took their first lead when Brown broke free on a screen pass, turning it into a 72-yard touchdown, then expanded the margin when he swept around left end for a 32-yard scoring run. Brown wound up with 209 total yards (123 rushing, 86 receiving). After the Giants cut the margin to 28–24 with 11 minutes to play, the Browns answered with a 12-play, 80-yard drive capped by a diving touchdown catch by Rich Kreitling with less than four minutes left. Though the Cleveland defense was dinged up, it held the Giants to just over 200 total yards, including just 72 on the ground.

Record: 5–0

	1	2	3	4		
Browns	7	7	14	7	=	35
Giants	14	3	0	7	=	24

NYG-Lynch 47-yd. interception return (Chandler kick)
CLE-Brown 1-yd. run (Groza kick)
NYG-Webster 1-yd. run (Chandler kick)
NYG-Chandler 25-yd. FG
CLE-Kreitling 10-yd. pass from Ryan (Groza kick)
CLE-Brown 72-yd. pass from Ryan (Groza kick)
CLE-Brown 32-yd. run (Groza kick)
NYG-King 14-yd. pass from Tittle (Chandler kick)
CLE-Kreitling 11-yd. pass from Ryan (Groza kick)

Passing
CLE: Ryan 12–16–169 3 TD 1 INT
NYG: Tittle 17–31–178 1 TD 0 INT

Rushing
CLE: Brown 23–123, Green 12–69, Ryan 4–18
NYG: Morrison 9–38, Gifford 1–12, King 6–11, Tittle 1–7, Webster 4–2, McElhenny 1–2, Chandler 1–0

Receiving
CLE: Brown 4–86, Kreitling 3–36, Brewer 3–35, Green 1–7, Collins 1–5
NYG: Shofner 5–54, Gifford 4–49, Walton 2–31, Morrison 4–20, King 1–14, Webster 1–10

Sunday, October 20
Browns 37, Philadelphia Eagles 7
Cleveland Stadium (75,174)
Brown jerseys/white pants

The Browns moved to 6–0 for the first time in 10 years, crushing the Eagles with another dominant performance by the offense, now ranked No. 1 in the league. Rolling up 500 total yards while holding the Eagles to 161, the Browns took a 20–7 halftime lead and then blew the game open in the fourth quarter, starting with Frank Ryan's fourth touchdown pass, the third to Gary Collins. Jim Brown was impressive as usual, tallying 144 yards on 25 carries and giving him 8,390 for his career, breaking the NFL record held by San Francisco's Joe Perry. Ryan wound up throwing for 203 yards in spearheading an offense that collected 29 first downs, while LB Vince Costello picked off a pair of passes, the first of which set up the Browns' first touchdown.
Record: 6–0

	1	2	3	4		
Eagles	0	7	0	0	=	7
Browns	6	14	0	17	=	37

CLE-Collins 35-yd. pass from Ryan (kick failed)
CLE-Brown 10-yd. pass from Ryan (Groza kick)
PHI-Goodwin 4-yd. pass from Jurgensen (Clark kick)
CLE-Collins 17-yd. pass from Ryan (Groza kick)
CLE-Collins 14-yd. pass from Ryan (Groza kick)
CLE-Groza 43-yd. FG
CLE-Scales 2-yd. run (Groza kick)

Passing
PHI: Jurgensen 7–13–76 1 TD 1 INT, Hill 2–8–17 0 TD 2 INT
CLE: Ryan 15–23–203 4 TD 1 INT, Ninowski 4–5–86 0 TD 0 INT

Rushing
PHI: Brown 10–38, Dean 6–34, Peaks 2–9
CLE: Brown 25–144, Green 9–57, Ryan 7–20, Scales 2-(-3)

Receiving
PHI: Brown 2–42, Dean 2–29, Goodwin 2–11, Retzlaff 2–7, McDonald 1–4
CLE: Brewer 5–98, Collins 5–82, Kreitling 1–45, Brown 3–21, Crespino 1–18, Green 2–13, Hutchinson 1–7, Webb 1–5

Sunday, October 27
New York Giants 33, Browns 6
Cleveland Stadium (84,213)
Brown jerseys/white pants

With a chance to essentially eliminate their archrivals from the conference race before a colossal home crowd, the high-flying Browns hit a brick wall and were obliterated by the Giants in one of the most disappointing performances in team history. The New York offensive and defensive lines completely dominated the contest, for which the tone was set on the Browns' first play when Jim Brown fumbled, followed by a Frank Ryan interception on their second offensive play. Taking advantage of the early mistakes, the Giants jumped out early, leading 17–0 after the first quarter and 23–0 at the half. The Browns' offense, which entered the game ranked number 1 in the league, was held to a meager 142 total yards and only six first downs for the entire game as the Giants ran 40 more plays. Ryan completed just one of nine passes for minus-six yards before being yanked for Jim Ninowski, while Brown was held to a modest 40 yards on nine carries. The Browns' lone touchdown—a short toss from Ninowski to Rich Kreitling—came with less than six minutes to play and was one of just five completed Cleveland passes on the day in 20 attempts. For as dispiriting as the defeat was, the Browns still held a one-game lead on the Giants at the season's midpoint.
Record: 6–1

	1	2	3	4		
Giants	17	6	10	0	=	33
Browns	0	0	0	6	=	6

NYG-Chandler 29-yd. FG
NYG-Shofner 23-yd. pass from Tittle (Chandler kick)
NYG-McElhenny 6-yd. pass from Tittle (Chandler kick)
NYG-Chandler 34-yd. FG

NYG-Chandler 33-yd. FG
NYG-Chandler 42-yd. FG
NYG-Webster 2-yd. run (Chandler kick)
CLE-Kreitling 10-yd. pass from Ninowski (kick failed)

Passing
NYG: Tittle 21–31–214 2 TD 1 INT, Griffing 1–2–6 0 TD 0 INT
CLE: Ninowski 4–11–120 1 TD 1 INT, Ryan 1–9-(-6) 0 TD 1 INT

Rushing
NYG: Webster 16–53, McElhenny 13–53, King 10–49, Morrison 5–27
CLE: Brown 9–40, Ryan 4–19, Webb 1–4

Receiving
NYG: Shofner 7–108, Thomas 3–32, Walton 4–26, King 3–25, Webster 3–17, McElhenny 1–6, Morrison 1–6
CLE: Hutchinson 2–97, Scales 1–13, Kreitling 1–10, Green 1-(-6)

Sunday, November 3
Browns 23, Philadelphia Eagles 17
Franklin Field (60,671)
White jerseys/white pants

Though the overall performance was erratic, the Browns bounced back from the New York blowout to edge the Eagles on the road on a bright, windy day at Franklin Field. While the passing game was once again nonexistent, Jim Brown and the Cleveland running attack were back at full strength, rolling up 274 yards, 223 by Brown, who opened the scoring with a 62-yard jaunt on the fourth play of the game. After the Eagles took a 10–7 lead early in the second period, the Browns crept to a six-point intermission advantage on three straight Lou Groza field goals. An interception by DB Ross Fichtner set up the Browns' second touchdown, a Frank Ryan-to-RB Ernie Green scoring pass that made it 23–10 and proved too much for the Eagles to overcome. Philadelphia cut the margin to six points with just over a minute left, then recovered an onside kick and quickly scurried to the Cleveland 36. With the Browns' lead in jeopardy, DB Larry Benz picked off Eagles' QB King Hill to secure the victory, though Brown fumbled on the final play of the game and Philadelphia recovered as the final gun sounded. Brown topped the 1,000-yard mark for the season, pushing his total to 1,194 as the Browns matched their victory total from 1962 with six games still to play. Meanwhile, in St. Louis, the Giants kept pace with a win over the Cardinals to keep the Browns' lead at just one game.

Record: 7–1

	1	2	3	4		
Browns	7	9	7	0	=	23
Eagles	3	7	0	7	=	17

CLE-Brown 62-yd. run (Groza kick)
PHI-Clark 22-yd. FG
PHI-Peaks 2-yd. run (Clark kick)
CLE-Groza 9-yd. FG
CLE-Groza 22-yd. FG
CLE-Groza 34-yd. FG
CLE-Green 21-yd. pass from Ryan (Groza kick)
PHI-Goodwin 14-yd. pass from Hill (Clark kick)

Passing
CLE: Ryan 4–9–70 1 TD 1 INT
PHI: Hill 14–30–201 1 TD 2 INT

Rushing
CLE: Brown 28–223, Green 5–23, Ryan 5–21, Webb 2–7
PHI: Brown 17–87, Peaks 13–51, Dean 3–14

Receiving
CLE: Green 3–44, Collins 1–26
PHI: Retzlaff 3–66, Brown 3–49, Peaks 4–42, McDonald 1–22, Goodwin 1–14, Dean 2–8

Sunday, November 10
Pittsburgh Steelers 9, Browns 7
Pitt Stadium (54,497)
White jerseys/white pants

For the third straight game, the Browns' passing game failed to ignite and the offense struggled to put points on the board, resulting in a frustrating defeat to the improved Steelers in a rugged defensive battle. The Browns took a 7–0 lead into the third quarter, then the game turned when Pittsburgh LB Bob Schmitz pinned Jim Brown trying to sweep around left end in the end zone for a safety. The Steelers then took the lead early in the fourth quarter with an 82-yard scoring drive and continued to thwart the Browns' offense, which picked up only two first downs in the second half. Despite being outgained by more than 150 yards, the Browns stayed close thanks to the struggles of Pittsburgh kicker Lou Michaels, who missed five field-goal attempts. Cleveland's last scoring chance came late in the third quarter when Ernie Green broke free on a run to the Pittsburgh 20, but then fumbled and the Steelers recovered, sparking the game-winning drive. With the defeat, and a New York blowout triumph over Philadelphia, the Browns slipped into a tie for first place in the conference.

Record: 7–2

	1	2	3	4		
Browns	0	7	0	0	=	7
Steelers	0	0	2	7	=	9

CLE-Collins 4-yd. pass from Ryan (Groza kick)
PIT-Safety: Schmitz tackled Brown in end zone
PIT-Ballman 9-yd. pass from Brown (Michaels kick)

Passing
CLE: Ryan 11–25–93 1 TD 0 INT, Brown 0–1–0 0 TD 0 INT
PIT: Brown 13–27–215 1 TD 1 INT

Rushing
CLE: Brown 19–99, Green 4–30, Ryan 7–5
PIT: Johnson 27–131, Hoak 15–53, Sapp 3–6, Brown 4-(-3)

Receiving
CLE: Collins 3–25, Green 2–22, Kreitling 1–17, Renfro 1–16, Brown 4–14
PIT: Dial 5–114, Mack 2–37, Hoak 1–21, Ballman 2–20, P. Carpenter 1–19, Johnson 2–4

Sunday, November 17
St. Louis Cardinals 20, Browns 14
Cleveland Stadium (75,932)
Brown jerseys/white pants

Despite a change at quarterback and another triumphant performance by Jim Brown, the Browns' slump continued as they lost for the third time in four weeks. Things started out perfectly when Brown broke free on the second play of the game for a 59-yard touchdown run. But the Cardinals rebounded with 20 straight points, and the Browns could manage little offense until the final minutes of the game when a touchdown pass from Jim Ninowski—starting in place of struggling Frank Ryan—cut the St. Louis lead to 20–14 with 4:28 left. The Browns got the ball back in the final minute and scrambled to the St. Louis 30 before time expired. Brown was the lone silver lining, rushing for 154 yards, but Ninowski failed to spark the passing game, and four turnovers crippled the offensive effort. The defeat, combined with a Giants' blowout victory over San Francisco, dropped the Browns into a second-place tie with the Cardinals.
Record: 7–3

	1	2	3	4		
Cardinals	3	10	0	7	=	20
Browns	7	0	0	7	=	14

CLE-Brown 59-yd. run (Groza kick)
STL-Bakken 42-yd. FG
STL-Randle 41-yd. pass from Johnson (Bakken kick)
STL-Bakken 9-yd. FG
STL-Triplett 19-yd. pass from Johnson (Bakken kick)
CLE-Green 15-yd. pass from Ninowski (Groza kick)

Passing
STL: Johnson 25–34–285 2 TD 2 INT
CLE: Ninowski 15–28–167 1 TD 2 INT

Rushing
STL: Childress 11–48, Thornton 6–13, Triplett 6–9
CLE: Brown 22–154, Green 5–24, Ninowski 4-(-21)

Receiving
STL: Randle 4–90, Triplett 7–64, Conrad 5–59, Smith 3–39, Childress 4–16, Hammack 1–15, Thornton 1–2
CLE: Brewer 5–66, Green 5–46, Brown 2–21, Collins 2–20, Kreitling 1–14

Sunday, November 24
Browns 27, Dallas Cowboys 17
Cleveland Stadium (55,096)
Brown jerseys/white pants

Played before a subdued home crowd just 48 hours after the assassination of President John Kennedy, the Browns once again put forth a shaky performance but managed to hold off the struggling Cowboys. Nursing a 13–10 lead early in the fourth quarter, Ross Fichtner blew the game open when he returned an interception 36 yards for a touchdown. It was followed by an interception by DE Paul Wiggin moments later that set up Gary Collins's second scoring reception of the game. Frank Ryan returned to the lineup, but struggled, throwing three interceptions as the Browns turned the ball over five times, the final resulting in a fumble return for a touchdown for the Cowboys in the final seconds. But the Cleveland defense atoned for the miscues by intercepting Dallas QB Don Meredith four times. Though Jim Brown was contained, held to 51 yards on 17 carries, Ernie Green rose to the occasion with 97 yards on just seven rushes. With the Cardinals' upset of the Giants in Yankee Stadium, the three teams were now knotted in a three-way tie atop the conference with three games to play. A halftime ceremony honoring Ray Renfro, wrapping up his twelfth and final season with the Browns, was canceled in the aftermath of the assassination.
Record: 8–3

	1	2	3	4		
Cowboys	3	7	0	7	=	17
Browns	10	3	0	14	=	27

CLE-Collins 11-yd. pass from Ryan (Groza kick)
DAL-Baker 20-yd. FG
CLE-Groza 24-yd. FG
CLE-Groza 10-yd. FG
DAL-Marsh 20-yd. run (Baker kick)
CLE-Fichtner 36-yd. interception return (Groza kick)
CLE-Collins 16-yd. pass from Ryan (Groza kick)
DAL-Green 20-yd. fumble return (Baker kick)

Passing
DAL: Meredith 13–30–93 0 TD 4 INT, LeBaron 0–5–0 0 TD 0 INT
CLE: Ryan 13–26–162 2 TD 3 INT, Brown 0–1–0 0 TD 0 INT

Rushing
DAL: Perkins 17–77, Marsh 6–47, Meredith 1–1
CLE: Green 7–97, Brown 17–51, Ryan 4–27

Receiving
DAL: Clarke 2–27, Marsh 4–26, Perkins 3–25, Barnes 2–8, Norman 1–4, Howton 1–3
CLE: Brewer 4–52, Hutchinson 1–35, Collins 2–27, Kreitling 1–24, Brown 3–15, Renfro 1–11, Green 1-(-2)

Sunday, December 1
Browns 24, St. Louis Cardinals 10
Busch Stadium (32,531)
White jerseys/white pants

With their title hopes hanging in the balance, the Browns came through with a gritty performance on a bright, cold day in St. Louis, returning to their early-season form to avenge their loss to the Cardinals two weeks earlier. Rolling up 400 yards of offense for the game while holding St. Louis to less than 200, the Browns roared to a 21–3 halftime lead on the strength of two short touchdown runs by Jim Brown, who bounced back from a poor showing the week before to tally 179 yards on 29 carries. Pushing his season total to 1,677 yards, Brown broke his own five-year-old NFL single-season record of 1,527 yards. Frank Ryan also responded with his best showing in over a month, throwing for 210 yards on just 10 completions—four to Gary Collins for an even 100 yards. The win nearly catapulted the Browns back into sole possession of first place, but the Giants rallied for a come-from-behind victory in Dallas to keep the two rivals tied atop the conference standings.
Record: 9–3

	1	2	3	4		
Browns	7	14	0	3	=	24
Cardinals	0	3	7	0	=	10

CLE-Kreitling 23-yd. pass from Ryan (Groza kick)
STL-Bakken 33-yd. FG
CLE-Brown 1-yd. run (Groza kick)
CLE-Brown 3-yd. run (Groza kick)
STL-Childress 8-yd. run (Bakken kick)
CLE-Groza 19-yd. FG

Passing
CLE: Ryan 10–18–210 1 TD 1 INT
STL: Johnson 9–26–58 0 TD 0 INT

Rushing
CLE: Brown 29–179, Green 9–34, Ryan 6–27
STL: Triplett 16–102, Childress 10–45, Stovall 1–32, Conrad 1–0

Receiving
CLE: Collins 4–100, Hutchinson 2–63, Kreitling 4–47
STL: Randle 3–25, Conrad 2–20, Childress 4–13

Sunday, December 8
Detroit Lions 38, Browns 10
Tiger Stadium (51,382)
White jerseys/white pants

Detroit's inexplicable spell over the Browns continued as the Lions moved to 5–0 against Cleveland in the regular season and 9–1 overall with a blowout victory that, combined with the Giants' win over Washington, eliminated the Browns from the Eastern Conference title race. The Browns looked as listless as the cold, gray afternoon, turning the football over five times while permitting the Lions to roll up 447 total yards. Still, the Browns hung tough after falling behind 14–0, cutting the margin to four points at the half following a Frank Ryan touchdown bomb to Gary Collins. But the Browns' chances evaporated in the third quarter when Detroit scored on its first possession, then added another touchdown when Ryan was stripped of the football deep in his own territory and the Lions recovered in the end zone. Detroit QB Earl Morrall spearheaded a potent air attack, averaging more than 20 yards per completion, while Ryan struggled and was replaced by Jim Ninowski, who fared little better, throwing three interceptions.

Record: 9–4

	1	2	3	4		
Browns	0	10	0	0	=	10
Lions	7	7	17	7	=	38

DET-Barr 75-yd. pass from Morrall (Walker kick)
DET-Lewis 5-yd. run (Walker kick)
CLE-Groza 19-yd. FG
CLE-Collins 49-yd. pass from Ryan (Groza kick)
DET-Cogdill 29-yd. pass from Morrall (Walker kick)
DET-Walker 23-yd. FG
DET-McCord recovers fumble in end zone (Walker kick)
DET-Pietrosante 2-yd. run (Walker kick)

Passing
CLE: Ryan 5–15–87 1 TD 0 INT, Ninowski 6–17–50 0 TD 3 INT
DET: Morrall 13–25–271 2 TD 1 INT

Rushing
CLE: Green 7–90, Brown 13–61, Ryan 2–7, Ninowski 1–2
DET: Lewis 22–97, Pietrosante 15–55, Watkins 4–19, Ryder 3–5

Receiving
CLE: Collins 5–98, Kreitling 2–32, Brewer 2–9, Brown 2-(-2)
DET: Barr 4–118, Cogdill 4–93, Gibbons 3–44, Lewis 2–16

Sunday, December 15
Browns 27, Washington Redskins 20
D.C. Stadium (40,865)
White jerseys/white pants

With their conference-title hopes thwarted, the Browns closed a satisfying regular season by holding off the Redskins at frosty D.C. Stadium to clinch second place and earn their second trip to the Playoff Bowl. Jumping to a 13–0 lead in the second quarter, the Browns overcame three turnovers and a kickoff return for a touchdown by former teammate Bobby Mitchell thanks to a solid performance by Frank Ryan and Jim Brown's ninth 100-yard game of the season. Ryan tossed three touchdown passes, bringing his season total to 28, which tied the team record set by Otto Graham 15 years earlier. And with 125 yards in the finale, Brown pushed his 1963 tally to 1,863 rushing yards—an NFL single-season record that would stand for 10 years. Gary Collins also capped an impressive season with two more touchdown receptions, bringing his league-leading total to 13 for the year, in what would be the best of his career and the first of four double-digit touchdown seasons. Yet after coughing up two fumbles in the fourth quarter, the Browns still needed help in the form of a roughing-the-punter penalty on Washington with two minutes left that permitted them to run out the clock rather than give the Redskins one last chance to tie the game. Cleveland's 10 victories were the most they'd managed in a season in nine years, and the campaign would continue thanks to a Giants' win over Pittsburgh and a Dallas upset of St. Louis to give the Browns sole possession of second place in the Eastern Conference and punch their ticket to Miami to face the Green Bay Packers three weeks later.

Record: 10–4

	1	2	3	4		
Browns	10	10	0	7	=	27
Redskins	0	7	7	6	=	20

CLE-Groza 42-yd. FG
CLE-Collins 34-yd. pass from Ryan (Groza kick)
CLE-Groza 42-yd. FG
WAS-Mitchell 92-yd. kickoff return (Khayat kick)
CLE-Green 33-yd. pass from Ryan (Groza kick)
WAS-Barnes 1-yd. run (Khayat kick)
CLE-Collins 9-yd. pass from Ryan (Groza kick)
WAS-Barnes 23-yd. pass from Snead (kick failed)

Passing
CLE: Ryan 14–30–216 3 TD 1 INT
WAS: Snead 11–26–169 1 TD 0 INT, Barnes 1–1–32 0 TD 0 INT, Anderson 0–1–0 0 TD 0 INT

Rushing
CLE: Brown 28–125, Green 8–26, Ryan 3–25
WAS: Barnes 12–40, Snead 2–12, Cunningham 3–4, Mitchell 1–0

Receiving
CLE: Kreitling 3–80, Green 3–50, Collins 5–48, Brewer 1–32, Hutchinson 1–8, Brown 1-(-2)
WAS: Mitchell 4–99, Anderson 2–46, Barnes 4–40, Cunningham 2–16

1964 Playoff Bowl
Sunday, January 5
Green Bay Packers 40, Browns 23
Orange Bowl (54,921)
Brown jerseys/white pants

Two weeks after watching the Chicago Bears defeat the New York Giants for the league title, the Browns and Packers battled in the annual consolation match in Miami's Orange Bowl with a record 54,000-plus in the stands (three times the previous year's total) and another 40 million fans watching the last football game of the season on television. Though the game was technically an exhibition and the statistics didn't count, the teams put forth an impressive offensive performance, combining for more than 1,000 yards on a warm but overcast afternoon.

Though the teams were fairly even statistically, the Packers took command early and were never truly challenged. QB Bart Starr threw three touchdown passes in the first half as the Packers sprinted to a 21–3 lead, then expanded it to 38–10 early in the fourth quarter before the Browns managed to make it more respectable with two late touchdowns, the second set up by an interception by DB Bernie Parrish. Fittingly, Green Bay rounded out the scoring when lineman Jerry Kramer tackled Frank Ryan in the end zone for a safety in the closing seconds.

Starr, named the game's MVP, completed 15 of 18 passes for 259 yards, including a Playoff-Bowl-record 99-yard scoring toss down the sideline to RB Tom Moore in the first quarter after the Packers stopped the Browns on the Green Bay 1.

Frank Ryan set another Playoff Bowl record by throwing for 310 yards, but for all the offensive fireworks, Jim Brown was held to 56 yards on 11 carries and fellow 1,000-yard rusher Jim Taylor was limited to 48 yards on 13 carries for Green Bay.

Though it ended on a sour note, the Browns' 1963 season was a satisfying one and set the tone for an even more memorable one in 1964.

	1	2	3	4		
Browns	0	10	0	13	=	23
Packers	14	14	7	5	=	40

GB-R. Kramer 18-yd. pass from Starr (J. Kramer kick)
GB-Moore 99-yd. pass from Starr (J. Kramer kick)
CLE-Groza 35-yd. FG
GB-McGee 15-yd. pass from Starr (J. Kramer kick)
CLE-Green 5-yd. run (Groza kick)
GB-Taylor 1-yd. run (J. Kramer kick)
GB-Moore 1-yd. run (J. Kramer kick)
GB-J. Kramer 8-yd. FG
CLE-Kreitling 20-yd. pass from Ryan (Groza kick)
CLE-Crespino 25-yd. pass from Ryan (kick failed)
GB-Safety: J. Kramer tackled Ryan in end zone

1964

Sunday, September 13
Browns 27, Washington Redskins 17
D.C. Stadium (47,577)
Brown jerseys/white pants

Through a steady rain, the Browns committed two early turnovers and fell behind by 10 points, then took control and held off Washington for their third straight opening-day win. Recovering four Washington fumbles, the Browns were able to rally to victory despite a sub-par offensive performance. The game turned late in the second quarter when the Browns recovered a fumbled punt return, and a play later QB Frank Ryan hit WR Gary Collins for the first touchdown of the season. After a quick defensive stop, the Browns then drove 70 yards and took the lead on the first of two Jim Brown one-yard scores. Trailing 20–10 late in the third quarter, the Redskins were poised to cut the margin, but then fumbled at the Cleveland 5. RB Ernie Green added a fourth-quarter touchdown to put the game away.
Record: 1–0

	1	2	3	4		
Browns	0	13	7	7	=	27
Redskins	0	10	0	3	=	13

WAS-Martin 12-yd. FG
WAS-Taylor 17-yd. run (Martin kick)
CLE-Collins 23-yd. pass from Ryan (kick failed)
CLE-Brown 1-yd. run (Groza kick)
CLE-Brown 1-yd. run (Groza kick)
WAS-Martin 14-yd. FG
CLE-Green 1-yd. run (Groza kick)

Passing
CLE: Ryan 8–19–112 1 TD 3 INT
WAS: Jurgensen 17–30–235 0 TD 0 INT

Rushing
CLE: Brown 23–89, Green 11–37, Ryan 3–17
WAS: Taylor 14–62, Bosseler 3–14, Lockett 3–10, Jurgensen 2–10

Receiving
CLE: Green 2–51, Collins 2–34, Brewer 4–27
WAS: Mitchell 4–115, Taylor 8–88, Coia 2–13, Richter 1–11, Lockett 1–6, Bosseler 1–2

Sunday, September 20
Browns 33, St. Louis Cardinals 33
Cleveland Stadium (76,954)
White jerseys/white pants

Under a bright September sun in the home opener, the Browns battled to a stalemate in a wild game with St. Louis. In a seesaw offensive shoot-out, the Browns were on the brink of defeat, trailing 30–26 and facing fourth-and-19 at the St. Louis 45 with just over a minute remaining. But Gary Collins reeled in a clutch 43-yard reception to give the Browns a first down at the Cardinals' 2, and moments later Jim Brown swept around right end to give the Browns a 33–30 lead with 48 seconds left. It was just enough time for St. Louis to mount a final drive, marching 54 yards in just over 30 seconds, and kick the tying field goal just before time expired. Though the Cleveland passing game struggled to ignite, Collins led the charge with 105 receiving yards, while rookie WR Paul Warfield caught his first NFL touchdown on a 40-yard strike from Frank Ryan just before the half.
Record: 1–0–1

	1	2	3	4		
Cardinals	10	3	10	10	=	33
Browns	6	10	7	10	=	33

STL-Crow 22-yd. pass from Johnson (Bakken kick)
CLE-Groza 32-yd. FG
CLE-Groza 12-yd. FG
STL-Bakken 30-yd. FG
CLE-Groza 37-yd. FG
STL-Bakken 51-yd. FG
CLE-Warfield 40-yd. pass from Ryan (Groza kick)
STL-Randle 38-yd. pass from Johnson (Bakken kick)
STL-Bakken 44-yd. FG
CLE-Collins 7-yd. pass from Ryan (Groza kick)
STL-Randle 50-yd. pass from Johnson (Bakken kick)
CLE-Groza 25-yd. FG
CLE-Brown 1-yd. run (Groza kick)
STL-Bakken 28-yd. FG

Passing
STL: Johnson 14–27–241 3 TD 1 INT
CLE: Ryan 12–26–189 2 TD 2 INT

Rushing
STL: Crow 11–58, Childress 14–52, Gautt 1–4, Johnson 1–0
CLE: Brown 21–79, Green 5–19, Ryan 3–16, Kelly 1–1

Receiving
STL: Randle 4–121, Childress 3–50, Conrad 3–31, Crow 3–29, Anderson 1–10
CLE: Collins 6–105, Warfield 3–63, Brown 2–14, Hutchinson 1–7

Sunday, September 27
Browns 28, Philadelphia Eagles 20
Franklin Field (60,671)
White jerseys/white pants

On a bright, breezy day in Philadelphia, the Browns' offense got rolling in the second half to rally to a victory over the Eagles. After a shaky first half, Frank Ryan caught fire, throwing for 151 yards and three touchdowns in the final two quarters as the Browns rebounded from a six-point halftime deficit to take a 15-point advantage in the fourth quarter. Jim Brown turned in his first 100-yard rushing game of the season, while Paul Warfield had his first big game as a pro, reeling in six catches for 97 yards. An interception by DB Ross Fichtner set up the game-clinching touchdown five minutes into the fourth quarter on Gary Collins's third score in three weeks.
Record: 2–0–1

	1	2	3	4		
Browns	7	0	14	7	=	28
Eagles	7	6	0	7	=	20

CLE-Green 37-yd. run (Groza kick)
PHI-Matson 1-yd. run (Baker kick)
PHI-Baker 12-yd. FG
PHI-Baker 42-yd. FG
CLE-Warfield 24-yd. pass from Ryan (Groza kick)
CLE-Brown 40-yd. pass from Ryan (Groza kick)
CLE-Collins 12-yd. pass from Ryan (Groza kick)
PHI-Matson 7-yd. run (Baker kick)

Passing
CLE: Ryan 11–26–193 3 TD 1 INT
PHI: Snead 19–28–183 0 TD 2 INT

Rushing
CLE: Brown 25–104, Green 8–61, Ryan 1–4
PHI: Gros 15–61, Matson 9–58, Woodeshick 3–22, Snead 1–18, Brown 5–12

Receiving
CLE: Warfield 6–97, Brown 2–53, Collins 2–29, Green 1–14
PHI: Goodwin 3–64, Poage 4–41, Matson 3–26, Gros 4–23, Retzlaff 2–15, Woodeshick 3–14

Sunday, October 4
Browns 27, Dallas Cowboys 6
Cleveland Stadium (72,062)
White jerseys/white pants

Aided by two long Frank Ryan touchdown passes in the second half, the Browns pulled away from Dallas on a bright, breezy autumn afternoon to remain unbeaten after four games. Leading 13–6 at the half, Ryan connected with Paul Warfield for a 40-yard score, then with Gary Collins for a 38-yard touchdown strike to give Cleveland an insurmountable lead. Collins's touchdown made it six consecutive games he'd scored, setting a team record. Warfield tallied the first 100-yard day of his career with 123 on five catches as Ryan compiled 256 passing yards on just 15 completions. One of the only setbacks for the Browns on this day was the career-ending broken leg suffered by DE Bob Gain, a five-time Pro Bowler.
Record: 3–0–1

	1	2	3	4		
Cowboys	0	6	0	0	=	6
Browns	7	6	7	7	=	27

CLE-Green 7-yd. pass from Ryan (Groza kick)
CLE-Groza 19-yd. FG
DAL-Norman 5-yd. pass from Roach (kick failed)
CLE-Groza 21-yd. FG
CLE-Warfield 40-yd. pass from Ryan (Groza kick)
CLE-Collins 38-yd. pass from Ryan (Groza kick)

Passing
DAL: Roach 13–26–132 1 TD 0 INT
CLE: Ryan 15–26–256 3 TD 1 INT

Rushing
DAL: Perkins 18–80, Marsh 10–43, Clarke 2–9, Roach 3–0
CLE: Brown 23–89, Green 5–20, Ryan 2–7

Receiving
DAL: Norman 2–42, Clarke 5–37, McDonald 2–34, Folkins 1–8, Perkins 1–6, Marsh 2–5
CLE: Warfield 5–123, Collins 3–62, Green 5–47, Brown 2–24

Saturday, October 10
Pittsburgh Steelers 23, Browns 7
Cleveland Stadium (80,530)
White jerseys/white pants

On a chilly Saturday night, the high-flying Browns were ripped apart by the Steelers and suffered their first loss of the season. Thirteen-point underdogs, the Steelers roared to a 16–0 lead in the second quarter and dominated the Browns all night. The catalyst was RB John Henry Johnson, who rushed for 200 yards and three touchdowns as Pittsburgh dominated the line of scrimmage, running 76 plays to the Browns' 45 and rolling up 477 total yards. Cleveland's lone touchdown came on a reception by Gary Collins, who extended his scoring string to seven straight games. Despite the ugly defeat, the Browns remained tied for first when the Cardinals were blown out by Baltimore the following Monday night.

Record: 3–1–1

	1	2	3	4		
Steelers	10	6	7	0	=	23
Browns	0	7	0	0	=	7

PIT-Clark 21-yd. FG
PIT-Johnson 33-yd. run (Clark kick)
PIT-Johnson 45-yd. run (kick failed)
CLE-Collins 18-yd. pass from Ryan (Groza kick)
PIT-Johnson 5-yd. run (Clark kick)

Passing
PIT: Brown 9–11–128 0 TD 0 INT
CLE: Ryan 13–29–167 1 TD 0 INT

Rushing
PIT: Johnson 30–200, Peaks 21–96, Brown 5–27, Hoak 5–23, Sapp 2–9, Ballman 1-(-1)
CLE: Brown 8–59, Ryan 2–33, Green 2–4

Receiving
PIT: Powers 2–51, Ballman 4–48, Peaks 2–25, Johnson 1–4
CLE: Brown 5–77, Warfield 3–34, Collins 2–32, Green 3–24

Sunday, October 18
Browns 20, Dallas Cowboys 16
Cotton Bowl (37,456)
Brown jerseys/white pants

In another lethargic performance, the Browns were on the brink of losing to the struggling Cowboys midway through the fourth quarter on an overcast day in the Cotton Bowl. Trailing by three points with less than seven minutes remaining, DB Bernie Parrish picked off Dallas QB Don Meredith and raced 54 yards for the go-ahead touchdown, the Browns' fifth takeaway of the afternoon. The Browns then caught a break moments later when a Cowboy touchdown pass was called back because Meredith was over the line of scrimmage when he threw the ball. Cleveland stopped Dallas on downs with three minutes left, then recovered a Meredith fumble to halt the Cowboys' final drive and secure a much-needed victory. Though Jim Brown exploded for 188 rushing yards—including a 71-yard run on the game's first play to set up a touchdown—the offense struggled all day and managed just 95 passing yards from Frank Ryan while allowing four sacks. But the Cleveland defense rose to the occasion, forcing five turnovers while controlling the Dallas offense. The win allowed the Browns to keep pace with St. Louis, who defeated Washington.

Record: 4–1–1

	1	2	3	4		
Browns	7	6	0	7	=	20
Cowboys	0	6	10	0	=	16

CLE-Green 1-yd. run (Groza kick)
DAL-Van Raaphorst 34-yd. FG
CLE-Groza 34-yd. FG
CLE-Groza 30-yd. FG
DAL-Van Raaphorst 20-yd. FG
DAL-Van Raaphorst 37-yd. FG
DAL-Perkins 1-yd. run (Van Raaphorst kick)
CLE-Parrish 54-yd. interception return (Groza kick)

Passing
CLE: Ryan 9–20–95 1 TD 0 INT
DAL: Meredith 16–36–228 0 TD 1 INT, Roach 3–7–23 0 TD 1 INT

Rushing
CLE: Brown 26–188, Green 6–13, Ryan 5-(-6)
DAL: Perkins 21–96, Marsh 5–8, Meredith 1–3, Clarke 3-(-11)

Receiving
CLE: Collins 3–38, Warfield 2–36, Brewer 1–12, Brown 1–9, Hutchinson 1–5, Green 1-(-5)
DAL: Clarke 7–93, McDonald 4–85, Perkins 3–23, Folkins 2–19, Dial 1–17, Marsh 1–11, Norman 1–3

Sunday, October 25
Browns 42, New York Giants 20
Cleveland Stadium (81,050)
White jerseys/white pants

On a bright, warm October afternoon, the Browns exploded for a quartet of touchdowns in the fourth quarter to roll to a convincing victory over struggling New York. The Browns got on the board in the second quarter on a 68-yard punt return by rookie RB Leroy Kelly, his first pro touchdown, and were clinging to a one-point advantage going into the fourth quarter. Two fumble returns for touchdowns by DE Paul Wiggin and RB Charlie Scales on a New York kickoff return opened the floodgates as the Browns rolled to 42 points—28 in the final period—despite managing only 225 yards of offense. Conversely, the Cleveland defense allowed the Giants to pile up 426 yards, but forced six turnovers. The victory, combined with a stunning Cardinals' loss to Dallas, allowed the Browns to take over sole possession of first place in the Eastern Conference.
Record: 5–1–1

	1	2	3	4		
Giants	6	0	7	7	=	20
Browns	0	7	7	28	=	42

NYG-James 1-yd. run (kick failed)
CLE-Kelly 68-yd. punt return (Groza kick)
CLE-Warfield 11-yd. pass from Ryan (Groza kick)
NYG-Tittle 7-yd. run (Chandler kick)
CLE-Wiggin 2-yd. fumble return (Groza kick)
CLE-Collins 9-yd. pass from Ryan (Groza kick)
CLE-Scales 23-yd. fumble return (Groza kick)
NYG-Wheelwright 20-yd. pass from Wood (Chandler kick)
CLE-Brewer 11-yd. pass from Ninowski (Groza kick)

Passing
NYG: Tittle 19–31–177 0 TD 3 INT, Thurlow 2–2–47 0 TD 0 INT, Wood 3–3–44 1 TD 0 INT
CLE: Ryan 8–17–86 2 TD 3 INT, Ninowski 2–3–52 1 TD 0 INT

Rushing
NYG: Wheelwright 20–94, James 10–34, Tittle 2–14, Thurlow 3–11, Wood 1–8
CLE: Brown 12–56, Green 7–28, Ryan 3–21, Ninowski 1-(-8)

Receiving
NYG: Thomas 4–83, Wheelwright 5–68, Shofner 5–31, Crespino 2–27, Morrison 3–23, Thurlow 2–20, Owens 1–14, James 1–2, Webster 1–0
CLE: Brewer 4–80, Warfield 3–33, Collins 2–22, Green 1–3

Sunday, November 1
Browns 30, Pittsburgh Steelers 17
Pitt Stadium (49,568)
White jerseys/white pants

Three weeks after getting dominated by Pittsburgh in Cleveland, the Browns turned the tables on the Steelers on a balmy afternoon to pick up another key victory. After sprinting to a 10–0 lead after the first NFL score by rookie WR Clifton McNeil, filling in for injured Gary Collins, the Browns saw the Steelers rally back to tie with two scores in the final five minutes of the first half. Then the first of two interceptions by DB Larry Benz set up the first of two Ernie Green touchdown runs early in the third quarter as the Browns pulled away. After Pittsburgh narrowed the margin to six points midway through the fourth, Cleveland embarked on a 73-yard drive capped by Green's second score to clinch victory with a minute to play. The Browns rolled up 412 yards while holding Pittsburgh to 251, as the Cleveland defense collected five sacks and contained Pittsburgh RB John Henry Johnson, limiting him to 100 yards—half of his total from their first meeting. Meanwhile, Jim Brown rushed for 149, and Green added another 86 as the Browns tallied 250 yards on the ground. With the Cardinals once again getting upset, this time by the Giants, the Browns leapt to a two-game lead atop the conference.
Record: 6–1–1

	1	2	3	4		
Browns	0	10	10	10	=	30
Steelers	0	10	0	7	=	17

CLE-Groza 36-yd. FG
CLE-McNeil 25-yd. pass from Ryan (Groza kick)
PIT-Peaks 5-yd. run (Clark kick)
PIT-Clark 26-yd. FG
CLE-Green 7-yd. run (Groza kick)
CLE-Groza 22-yd. FG
CLE-Groza 16-yd. FG
PIT-Johnson 1-yd. run (Clark kick)
CLE-Green 13-yd. run (Groza kick)

Passing
CLE: Ryan 15–28–179 1 TD 0 INT
PIT: Brown 8–23–128 0 TD 2 INT

Rushing
CLE: Brown 23–149, Green 17–86, Ryan 3–15
PIT: Johnson 16–100, Peaks 16–59, Ballman 1–5, Brown 1–1, Hoak 1–0

Receiving
CLE: Brewer 4–67, Brown 5–37, McNeil 2–32, Warfield 2–24, Green 2–19
PIT: Powers 2–36, Ballman 2–31, Hoak 1–20, Burrell 1–19, Johnson 1–17, Peaks 1–5

Sunday, November 8
Browns 34, Washington Redskins 24
Cleveland Stadium (76,385)
White jerseys/white pants

On a perfect autumn afternoon, the Browns put together their finest offensive performance of the season thus far, rolling to nearly 400 total yards and an impressive win over Washington. Playing on an injured foot, Jim Brown tossed a 13-yard touchdown pass to Gary Collins in the third quarter to open up a 17-point lead, then capped the Browns' scoring with a two-yard run in the fourth quarter that marked the one-hundredth touchdown of his career. Paul Warfield added to his quickly growing collection of impressive touchdowns when he reeled in a 62-yard bomb from Frank Ryan later in the period. Former Brown Bobby Mitchell proved to be a thorn in Cleveland's side, compiling 113 rushing yards and two touchdowns. The victory kept the Browns two games up on St. Louis, who held off the Steelers.
Record: 7–1–1

	1	2	3	4		
Redskins	0	3	7	14	=	24
Browns	0	13	14	7	=	34

WAS-Martin 30-yd. FG
CLE-Green 21-yd. run (Groza kick)
CLE-Groza 11-yd. FG
CLE-Groza 38-yd. FG
CLE-Collins 13-yd. pass from Brown (Groza kick)
WAS-Mitchell 14-yd. pass from Jurgensen (Martin kick)
CLE-Warfield 62-yd. pass from Ryan (Groza kick)
WAS-Taylor 10-yd. pass from Ryan (Martin kick)
CLE-Brown 2-yd. run (Groza kick)
WAS-Mitchell 14-yd. pass from Jurgensen (Martin kick)

Passing
WAS: Jurgensen 21–36–261 3 TD 1 INT, Taylor 0–1–0 0 TD 0 INT
CLE: Ryan 11–19–162 1 TD 1 INT, Brown 1–1–13 1 TD 0 INT

Rushing
WAS: Taylor 17–67, Lockett 5–20, Jurgensen 2–14
CLE: Brown 18–121, Green 11–53, Ryan 5–36

Receiving
WAS: Mitchell 7–113, Taylor 7–77, Lockett 4–41, P. Carpenter 2–26, Coia 1–4
CLE: Warfield 3–82, Collins 3–42, Brown 3–28, Green 2–14, Brewer 1–9

Sunday, November 15
Browns 37, Detroit Lions 21
Cleveland Stadium (83,064)
White jerseys/white pants

Before a colossal crowd on a surprisingly warm November afternoon, the Browns' quest for a title cleared another obstacle as they overcame a shaky start to notch their first regular-season victory over longtime stumbling block Detroit. The Lions sprinted to an early lead on two touchdown passes by former Browns' QB Milt Plum, including a 92-yard strike. But the Browns bounced back to pull within one point at the intermission, then held Detroit scoreless in the second half and took control with 17 unanswered points, capped by a 65-yard interception return for a score by DB Walter Beach as time expired. The Cleveland offense was once again clicking, with Jim Brown rushing for 147 yards and a pair of scores and Paul Warfield adding 92 yards receiving. With St. Louis tying the Giants, the Browns' conference lead swelled to two-and-a-half games with four to play.
Record: 8–1–1

	1	2	3	4		
Lions	14	7	0	0	=	21
Browns	7	13	7	10	=	37

CLE-Brown 6-yd. run (Groza kick)
DET-Lewis 92-yd. pass from Plum (Walker kick)
DET-Gibbons 4-yd. pass from Plum (Walker kick)
CLE-Groza 38-yd. FG
CLE-Brown 2-yd. run (Groza kick)
DET-Barr 39-yd. pass from Plum (Walker kick)
CLE-Groza 47-yd. FG
CLE-Warfield 8-yd. pass from Ryan (Groza kick)
CLE-Groza 36-yd. FG
CLE-Beach 65-yd. interception return (Groza kick)

Passing
DET: Plum 15–27–236 3 TD 1 INT, Gibbs 1–2–3 0 TD 1 INT
CLE: Ryan 15–25–179 1 TD 2 INT

Rushing
DET: Pietrosante 14–70, Watkins 7–30, Lewis 7–6
CLE: Brown 24–147, Green 11–57, Ryan 2–14

Receiving
DET: Lewis 1–92, Cogdill 5–50, Barr 2–44, Gibbons 5–27, Pietrosante 2–21, Watkins 1–5
CLE: Warfield 5–92, Brown 5–47, Collins 2–24, Green 2–11, Brewer 1–5

Sunday, November 22
Green Bay Packers 28, Browns 21
Milwaukee County Stadium (48,065)
White jerseys/white pants

With a second-half surge, the Packers overcame a halftime deficit and snapped the Browns' five-game winning streak. With the Browns up 14–7 early in the third quarter, the tide turned when the Packers completed a 55-yard pass on fourth-and-one to set up the first of two short touchdown runs by RB Jim Taylor to tie the game. Two more Green Bay touchdowns followed after Cleveland turnovers as the Packers held Jim Brown to eight yards in the second half and built a 28–14 lead. The Browns pulled within seven on Paul Warfield's second touchdown catch with eight minutes left, but two more turnovers allowed the Packers to hold on for the upset. And with the Cardinals rolling to victory in Philadelphia, the Browns' conference lead was trimmed to a game-and-a-half.
Record: 8–2–1

	1	2	3	4		
Browns	14	0	0	7	=	21
Packers	7	0	14	7	=	28

CLE-Warfield 48-yd. pass from Ryan (Groza kick)
GB-Pitts 19-yd. run (Hornung kick)
CLE-Brown 1-yd. run (Groza kick)
GB-Taylor 1-yd. run (Hornung kick)
GB-Starr 4-yd. run (Hornung kick)
GB-Taylor 5-yd. run (Hornung kick)
CLE-Warfield 19-yd. pass from Ryan (Groza kick)

Passing
CLE: Ryan 17–28–197 2 TD 2 INT
GB: Starr 13–18–131 0 TD 0 INT

Rushing
CLE: Brown 20–74, Green 7–46, Ryan 1–18
GB: Taylor 22–63, Moore 10–46, Pitts 7–41, Starr 2–6

Receiving
CLE: Warfield 7–126, Collins 4–69, Green 1–2, Brown 5–0
GB: McGee 4–81, Kramer 2–36, Taylor 4–5, Dowler 1–4, Pitts 1–3, Moore 1–2

Sunday, November 29
Browns 38, Philadelphia Eagles 24
Cleveland Stadium (79,289)
White jerseys/white pants

Bouncing back from a tough loss, the Browns built a huge lead on big plays by the special teams and defense and then held off the Eagles in the second half to pick up their ninth victory. The tone was set on a crazy sequence on the opening kickoff in which the Eagles fumbled, and both teams had numerous chances to recover the football, which bounced and rolled nearly 20 yards into the Philadelphia end zone, where Browns' backup lineman Roger Shoals finally pounced on it for a touchdown. The Browns then pulled away as their special teams added another score when LB Sid Williams blocked a punt and then recovered it in the end zone. Moments later, Cleveland LB Jim Houston returned an interception 42 yards for another touchdown. The lead swelled to 24–3 early in the third quarter, then Frank Ryan tossed a pair of touchdown passes to Johnny Brewer, and the defense picked off two more passes in the fourth quarter to secure the win. Meanwhile, in Pittsburgh, the Cardinals rallied for a one-point win to keep the Browns from clinching at least a tie for the conference title with two games remaining.
Record: 9–2–1

	1	2	3	4		
Eagles	3	0	7	14	=	24
Browns	7	14	10	7	=	38

CLE-Shoals recovered fumble in end zone (Groza kick)
PHI-Baker 14-yd. FG
CLE-Williams recovered blocked punt in end zone (Groza kick)
CLE-Houston 42-yd. interception return (Groza kick)

CLE-Groza 37-yd. FG
PHI-Brown 20-yd. run (Baker kick)
CLE-Brewer 24-yd. pass from Ryan (Groza kick)
PHI-Goodwin 19-yd. pass from Snead (Baker kick)
CLE-Brewer 13-yd. pass from Ryan (Groza kick)
PHI-Retzlaff 32-yd. pass from Snead (Baker kick)

Passing
PHI: Snead 10–15–165 2 TD 1 INT, Hill 10–18–101 0 TD 1 INT, Brown 0–1–0 0 TD 1 INT
CLE: Ryan 13–25–145 2 TD 1 INT

Rushing
PHI: Brown 10–40, Woodeshick 4–36, Lang 3–28, Gros 7–27, Hill 1-(-2)
CLE: Brown 22–133, Green 8–24, Kelly 1–2, Ryan 1-(-2)

Receiving
PHI: Retzlaff 5–100, Goodwin 6–72, Lang 4–46, Gros 3–29, Poage 2–19
CLE: Brewer 5–61, Collins 3–39, Green 1–17, Warfield 2–16, Brown 2–12

Sunday, December 6
St. Louis Cardinals 28, Browns 19
Busch Stadium (31,585)
Brown jerseys/white pants

The Browns squandered an opportunity to eliminate the Cardinals and clinch the conference title, digging themselves a massive hole in the second quarter that they were unable to climb out of on a frigid day in. After sneaking to a 3–0 lead, the Browns allowed three straight touchdowns to fall behind by 18 points. Leading the charge for St. Louis was a stellar performance by QB Charley Johnson, who threw for two touchdowns and ran for two more, including the clincher in the third quarter after the Browns had narrowed the margin to 21–9. The victory pulled the Cardinals within a half-game of the Browns and gave them a chance to sneak past Cleveland for the conference title in the final week of the regular season with a Browns' loss in New York on Saturday and a St. Louis win over Philadelphia the following afternoon.
Record: 9–3–1

	1	2	3	4		
Browns	3	3	3	10	=	19
Cardinals	0	21	7	0	=	28

CLE-Groza 22-yd. FG
STL-Childress 46-yd. pass from Johnson (Bakken kick)
STL-Johnson 1-yd. run (Bakken kick)
STL-Conrad 8-yd. pass from Johnson (Bakken kick)
CLE-Groza 39-yd. FG
CLE-Groza 17-yd. FG
STL-Johnson 1-yd. run (Bakken kick)
CLE-Groza 36-yd. FG
CLE-Green 30-yd. pass from Ryan (Groza kick)

Passing
CLE: Ryan 15–33–242 1 TD 2 INT
STL: Johnson 15–22–167 2 TD 1 INT

Rushing
CLE: Brown 15–59, Ryan 4–30, Green 3–17
STL: Crow 21–72, Childress 9–44, Thornton 6–26, Gautt 6–6, Johnson 3–2

Receiving
CLE: Warfield 6–91, Brewer 4–60, Green 2–60, Brown 3–31
STL: Smith 5–50, Childress 1–46, Gambrell 3–25, Crow 2–20, Conrad 3–19, Gautt 1–7

Saturday, December 12
Browns 52, New York Giants 20
Yankee Stadium (63,007)
White jerseys/white pants

The Browns clinched their first title-game appearance in seven years with a dominating performance in Yankee Stadium that resulted in a romp over the rival Giants. On a gray, damp Saturday afternoon in the Bronx, the Browns fell behind 7–3 on the final touchdown pass of Y. A. Tittle's career, then took control of the contest with three touchdowns in the second quarter. The Browns then followed that with another trio of scores in the third as they put forth their highest point total in 11 years. Frank Ryan played the finest game of his career, completing 12 of 13 passes for 202 yards with five passing touchdowns and one rushing as the Cleveland attack racked up better than 400 yards. Paul Warfield went over the 100-yard receiving mark while Jim Brown added 99 on the ground to finish the season with a league-high 1,446 and tied the NFL record with his one hundred-fifth career touchdown.
Record: 10–3–1

	1	2	3	4		
Browns	3	21	21	7	=	52
Giants	0	7	0	13	=	20

CLE-Groza 39-yd. FG
NYG-James 7-yd. pass from Tittle (Chandler kick)
CLE-Ryan 13-yd. run (Groza kick)
CLE-Collins 11-yd. pass from Ryan (Groza kick)
CLE-Green 1-yd. pass from Ryan (Groza kick)
CLE-Green 25-yd. pass from Ryan (Groza kick)
CLE-Warfield 8-yd. pass from Ryan (Groza kick)
CLE-Brown 8-yd. pass from Ryan (Groza kick)
NYG-Thomas 10-yd. pass from Wood (Chandler kick)
CLE-Roberts 24-yd. pass from Ninowski (Groza kick)
NYG-Thomas 1-yd. pass from Wood (no kick)

Passing
CLE: Ryan 12–13–202 5 TD 0 INT, Ninowski 4–6–73 1 TD 0 INT
NYG: Wood 12–21–209 2 TD 0 INT, Tittle 10–15–93 1 TD 2 INT, Thurlow 0–1–0 0 TD 0 INT

Rushing
CLE: Brown 20–99, Green 8–26, Ryan 2–14, Kelly 4–9, Scales 2–5
NYG: Wheelwright 12–46, Thurlow 4–21, James 3–6, Tittle 1–3

Receiving
CLE: Warfield 5–103, Collins 3–48, McNeil 2–37, Green 2–26, Roberts 1–24, Brewer 1–17, Hutchinson 1–12, Brown 1–8
NYG: Morrison 8–147, Thomas 4–41, Jones 2–41, Wheelwright 3–26, Gifford 2–23, Thurlow 1–17, James 2–7

1964 NFL Championship
Sunday, December 27
Browns 27, Baltimore Colts 0
Cleveland Stadium (79,544)
White jerseys/white pants

On a windy and bitterly cold afternoon, the Browns put together perhaps the greatest performance in team history as they stunned the 12–2 Colts to win their fourth NFL title before the second-largest championship-game crowd in league history.

Baltimore, a seven-point favorite, had the only real opportunity to score in the first half, but bobbled a snap on a field-goal attempt, which kept the game scoreless at halftime. Then, with the wind—at times gusting up to 30 mph—at their backs in the third quarter, the Browns exploded for 17 points, including a pair of touchdown receptions by Gary Collins, who played the finest game of his career. Collins added a third touchdown in the fourth quarter, this one from 51 yards, to round out the scoring as the Cleveland offense rolled to 339 total yards.

But even more dominant on this day was the Cleveland defense, which held the league's top offense to just 181 total yards while forcing four turnovers. They intercepted Baltimore QB Johnny Unitas twice, limiting him to only 95 passing yards. Meanwhile, Jim Brown rushed for 114—highlighted by a 46-yard run that set up the Browns' first touchdown—and Collins caught five passes for 130 yards and a new title-game record with three touchdowns to earn MVP honors.

As the clock ticked down to zero, thousands of fans rushed the field and tore down the goalposts—still the last time Browns' fans were able to partake in such a celebration.

	1	2	3	4		
Colts	0	0	0	0	=	0
Browns	0	0	17	10	=	27

CLE-Groza 43-yd. FG
CLE-Collins 18-yd. pass from Ryan (Groza kick)
CLE-Collins 42-yd. pass from Ryan (Groza kick)
CLE-Groza 10-yd. FG
CLE-Collins 51-yd. pass from Ryan (Groza kick)

Passing
BAL: Unitas 12–20–95 0 TD 2 INT
CLE: Ryan 11–18–206 3 TD 1 INT

Rushing
BAL: Moore 9–40, Hill 9–31, Unitas 6–30, Boyd 1-(-9)
CLE: Brown 27–114, Green 10–29, Ryan 3–2, Warfield 1-(-3)

Receiving
BAL: Berry 3–38, Orr 2–31, Lorick 3–18, Moore 2–4, Hill 1–2, Mackey 1–2
CLE: Collins 5–130, Brown 3–37, Brewer 2–26, Warfield 1–13

1965

Receiving
CLE: Roberts 2–91, Collins 2–50, Brown 3–16, Green 1-(-5)
WAS: Mitchell 4–51, Taylor 2–41, P. Carpenter 2–30, Hughley 2–30, Coia 1–21, Smith 1–16, Lewis 1–13, Jencks 1–12, Casares 1–5

Sunday, September 19
Browns 17, Washington Redskins 7
D.C. Stadium (48,208)
White jerseys/white pants

The Browns opened up defense of their NFL title with a tough victory over the Redskins on a hot, humid afternoon in the nation's capital. After an early Lou Groza field goal, the Browns pulled off the play of the day in the second quarter when QB Frank Ryan connected with WR Walter "The Flea" Roberts for an 80-yard touchdown pass in what proved to be the Browns' longest play of the season. Ryan added another scoring pass to Gary Collins in the third quarter to open up a 17–0 lead, and the defense took it from there. Washington was held to just 24 rushing yards and completed less than half its pass attempts as the Browns picked up their fourth straight opening-day victory.
Record: 1–0

	1	2	3	4		
Browns	3	7	7	0	=	17
Redskins	0	0	0	7	=	7

CLE-Groza 20-yd. FG
CLE-Roberts 80-yd. pass from Ryan (Groza kick)
CLE-Collins 35-yd. pass from Ryan (Groza kick)
WAS-Coia 21-yd. pass from Shiner (Jencks kick)

Passing
CLE: Ryan 8–19–152 2 TD 1 INT
WAS: Jurgensen 9–21–124 0 TD 1 INT, Shiner 6–12–95 1 TD 0 INT

Rushing
CLE: Green 11–89, Brown 21–65, Kelly 6–19, Scales 1–4, Ryan 2–3
WAS: Taylor 8–21, Hughley 4–7, Casares 2–5, Atkins 1–1, Lewis 1–0, Shiner 2-(-10)

Sunday, September 26
St. Louis Cardinals 49, Browns 13
Cleveland Stadium (80,161)
White jerseys/white pants

On a sunshiny afternoon, the Browns opened their home schedule with a throttling at the hands of the Cardinals, who dominated from start to finish. St. Louis set the tone early with a 78-yard touchdown pass by QB Charley Johnson, the first of a career-best six he'd throw on the day, including three to WR Sonny Randle, who reeled in 198 receiving yards. After the Browns took a brief 10–7 lead early in the second quarter, a 65-yard kickoff return by St. Louis set up the first of four consecutive touchdowns in the second quarter, with the other three set up by Frank Ryan interceptions. The Cardinals rolled to 489 yards of offense while picking off six Cleveland passes, four thrown by Ryan, who sat out the second half with an injured foot. The Browns' self-destructive offense was paced by Jim Brown, who rushed for 110 yards on 17 carries, and Gary Collins, who caught six passes for 116, including Cleveland's only touchdown.
Record: 1–1

	1	2	3	4		
Cardinals	7	28	14	0	=	49
Browns	3	7	3	0	=	13

STL-Crenshaw 78-yd. pass from Johnson (Bakken kick)
CLE-Groza 34-yd. FG
CLE-Collins 13-yd. pass from Ryan (Groza kick)
STL-Randle 32-yd. pass from Johnson (Bakken kick)
STL-Triplett 4-yd. run (Bakken kick)
STL-Randle 7-yd. pass from Johnson (Bakken kick)
STL-Conrad 9-yd. pass from Johnson (Bakken kick)
CLE-Groza 47-yd. FG
STL-Randle 56-yd. pass from Johnson (Bakken kick)
STL-Gambrell 3-yd. pass from Johnson (Bakken kick)

Passing
STL: Johnson 11–19–310 6 TD 1 INT, Humphrey 2–5–19 0 TD 1 INT
CLE: Ninowski 8–17–148 0 TD 2 INT, Ryan 5–15–61 1 TD 4 INT

Rushing
STL: Gautt 14–64, Thornton 11–59, Crenshaw 10–25, Triplett 8–22, Johnson 1-(-1)
CLE: Brown 17–110, Green 3–7, Kelly 1–5

Receiving
STL: Randle 7–198, Crenshaw 1–78, Conrad 3–42, Gambrell 2–11
CLE: Collins 6–116, Brewer 4–56, Roberts 2–23, Brown 1–14

Sunday, October 3
Browns 35, Philadelphia Eagles 17
Franklin Field (60,759)
White jerseys/white pants

Trailing by three points in the fourth quarter on a breezy afternoon in Philadelphia, the Browns exploded for three touchdowns in the final 11 minutes to pull away for a convincing victory. The game turned on a fumbled punt return by Philadelphia RB Tim Brown that was recovered by Cleveland LB Sid Williams at the Eagles' 2. On the next play, Jim Brown leapt into the end zone to give the Browns a 21–17 lead. After the ensuing kickoff, Browns' DB Ross Fichtner intercepted a pass at the Philadelphia 32 and rushed into the end zone for another score. Another interception by DB Larry Benz set up Jim Brown's third score of the day to seal the victory. With QB Jim Ninowski starting in place of injured Frank Ryan, the Browns' passing game struggled, but the offense was sparked by 133 rushing yards from Brown. Meanwhile, the Cleveland defense aided the cause by forcing six turnovers.
Record: 2–1

	1	2	3	4		
Browns	0	7	7	21	=	35
Eagles	0	10	0	7	=	17

PHI-Retzlaff 2-yd. pass from Hill (Lloyd kick)
CLE-Brown 4-yd. run (Groza kick)
PHI-Lloyd 42-yd. FG
CLE-Collins 13-yd. pass from Ninowski (Groza kick)
PHI-Gros 2-yd. pass from Hill (Lloyd kick)
CLE-Brown 2-yd. run (Groza kick)
CLE-Fichtner 32-yd. interception return (Groza kick)
CLE-Brown 4-yd. run (Groza kick)

Passing
CLE: Ninowski 9–20–103 1 TD 0 INT
PHI: Hill 12–25–170 2 TD 4 INT, Concannon 2–5–53 0 TD 1 INT, Snead 0–1–0 0 TD 0 INT

Rushing
CLE: Brown 27–133, Green 9–44, Ninowski 2–34, Kelly 4–25, Scales 1–3
PHI: Gros 14–85, Brown 8–63, Concannon 1–12, Hill 1–3

Receiving
CLE: Collins 3–34, Green 2–31, Brown 2–25, Roberts 2–13
PHI: Retzlaff 6–76, Brown 3–72, Goodwin 2–40, Gros 3–35

Saturday, October 9
Browns 24, Pittsburgh Steelers 19
Cleveland Stadium (80,187)
White jerseys/white pants

Continuing their annual Saturday-night tradition with the rival Steelers, the Browns rallied for a last-minute touchdown to pick up an exciting victory in the rain and mud. Clinging to a five-point lead with five minutes left, the Browns allowed Pittsburgh's Roy Jefferson to return a punt 67 yards to the Cleveland 26. Four plays later, RB Dick Hoak scored to put the Steelers, 17-point underdogs, up 19–17. The Browns took over at their own 22 and, thanks to two key receptions by RB Leroy Kelly, marched downfield, then scored the winning touchdown on a Frank Ryan-to-Gary Collins 14-yard pass with 44 seconds left. The persistent Steelers hung tough throughout the night despite another dazzling performance by Jim Brown, who rushed for 168 yards and scored a pair of touchdowns.
Record: 3–1

	1	2	3	4		
Steelers	0	6	6	7	=	19
Browns	10	0	7	7	=	24

CLE-Groza 38-yd. FG
CLE-Brown 4-yd. pass from Ryan (Groza kick)
PIT-Nelsen 1-yd. run (kick failed)
PIT-Hoak 42-yd. run (kick failed)
CLE-Brown 1-yd. (Groza kick)
PIT-Hoak 15-yd. run (Clark kick)
CLE-Collins 14-yd. pass from Ryan (Groza kick)

Passing
PIT: Nelsen 9–20–92 0 TD 0 INT
CLE: Ryan 12–22–153 2 TD 0 INT, Brown 0–1–0 0 TD 0 INT

Rushing
PIT: Hoak 15–107, Lind 13–56, Butler 2–8, Nelsen 6–4
CLE: Brown 29–168, Kelly 13–67, Ryan 2–8, Franklin 1-(-11)

Receiving
PIT: Thomas 4–51, Hoak 4–33, Martha 1–8
CLE: Kelly 5–60, Collins 4–54, Roberts 1–25, Brewer 1–10, Brown 1–4

Sunday, October 17
Browns 23, Dallas Cowboys 17
Cleveland Stadium (80,432)
White jerseys/white pants

On a perfect autumn afternoon, the Browns roared to a 17–0 lead and then hung on to capture their fourth victory in five weeks. After taking control in the second quarter, the Browns allowed Dallas to creep back into the game when they fumbled the kickoff following a Cowboy field goal and Dallas recovered, resulting in a touchdown just before the half. The Browns further aided the Cowboys when two long touchdowns were called back on penalties, including a 67-yard punt return by RB Leroy Kelly. After extending their lead with a pair of Lou Groza field goals, the Browns squandered another opportunity when Groza missed a chip shot early in the fourth that would have put them up by 16. Dallas pulled within six points on a touchdown with just over a minute to play, but the Browns recovered the ensuing onside kick, and then Larry Benz intercepted a desperation Cowboy pass in the final moments to close the books.
Record: 4–1

	1	2	3	4		
Cowboys	0	10	0	7	=	17
Browns	10	7	6	0	=	23

CLE-Brown 10-yd. run (Groza kick)
CLE-Groza 48-yd. FG
CLE-Roberts 29-yd. pass from Ryan (Groza kick)
DAL-Villanueva 16-yd. FG
DAL-Norman 5-yd. pass from Meredith (Villanueva kick)
CLE-Groza 16-yd. FG
CLE-Groza 19-yd. FG
DAL-Gent 20-yd. pass from Meredith (Villanueva kick)

Passing
DAL: Meredith 14–31–185 2 TD 0 INT, Rhome 1–5–19 0 TD 0 INT, Morton 0–3–0 0 TD 1 INT
CLE: Ryan 14–27–242 1 TD 0 INT

Rushing
DAL: Perkins 11–27, Dunn 5–21, Meredith 2–19, Reeves 3–12
CLE: Brown 22–85, Green 10–15, Kelly 2–3, Ryan 1–2

Receiving
DAL: Clarke 4–81, Hayes 5–50, Gent 2–38, Perkins 2–22, Dunn 1–8, Norman 1–5
CLE: Roberts 2–73, Collins 4–55, Brown 5–53, Kelly 1–52, McNeil 1–6, Green 1–3

Sunday, October 24
Browns 38, New York Giants 14
Yankee Stadium (62,864)
White jerseys/white pants

On a beautiful autumn afternoon in the Bronx, the Cleveland offense put on an impressive display as the Browns rolled to an easy victory and took over sole possession of first place in the Eastern Conference. A balanced offensive attack piled up 526 total yards, including 177 rushing by Jim Brown, who also threw a touchdown pass to Gary Collins on a halfback-option play. Frank Ryan threw for three more scores, two to Walter Roberts in the second quarter, and Collins collected 121 receiving yards on just three catches. After New York took a 7–3 lead into the second quarter, the Browns responded with five straight touchdowns to take a commanding lead and coasted to their fourth straight victory. Combined with a St. Louis loss to the Redskins, the victory propelled the Browns atop the conference standings.
Record: 5–1

	1	2	3	4		
Browns	3	14	14	7	=	38
Giants	7	0	0	7	=	14

CLE-Groza 24-yd. FG
NYG-Frederickson 1-yd. run (Timberlake kick)
CLE-Roberts 21-yd. pass from Ryan (Groza kick)
CLE-Roberts 4-yd. pass from Ryan (Groza kick)
CLE-Collins 39-yd. pass from Brown (Groza kick)
CLE-Brown 5-yd. pass from Ryan (Groza kick)
CLE-Green 1-yd. run (Groza kick)
NYG-Mercein 2-yd. run (Timberlake kick)

Passing
CLE: Ryan 10–15–177 3 TD 0 INT, Ninowski 4–8–81 0 TD 0 INT, Brown 1–1–39 1 TD 0 INT
NYG: Morrall 10–21–145 0 TD 0 INT, Wood 3–6–47 0 TD 0 INT, Koy 0–1–0 0 TD 0 INT

Rushing
CLE: Brown 24–177, Green 15–35, Scales 3–26, Ryan 1–5
NYG: Frederickson 14–51, Thurlow 5–33, Wheelwright 4–23, Koy 1–6, Reed 1–6, Mercein 1–2, Morrall 1-(-1)

Receiving
CLE: Collins 3–121, Green 4–54, Roberts 3–51, McNeil 1–31, Hutchinson 1–22, Brown 3–18
NYG: Morrison 5–71, Shofner 2–49, Frederickson 3–29, Jones 1–17, Thomas 1–14, Wheelwright 1–12

Sunday, October 31
Minnesota Vikings 27, Browns 17
Cleveland Stadium (83,505)
White jerseys/white pants

The high-flying Browns hit a brick wall on a breezy Halloween afternoon on the lakefront as the Vikings dominated both lines of scrimmage and coasted to an upset victory in the teams' first-ever meeting. The Cleveland offense was held to just 167 total yards, including a mere 34 rushing on 28 attempts as Jim Brown was limited to 39 on 18 carries. Frank Ryan also struggled, managing just four completions in 15 pass attempts and was pulled for backup Jim Ninowski. Meanwhile, the Cleveland defense was torched for 196 yards on the ground and 408 total by the Vikings, who took a 24–10 lead early in the fourth quarter. A Brown touchdown cut the lead to seven, but Minnesota put the game away with a field goal with just over a minute left. The Browns remained alone in first place thanks to a New York victory over the Cardinals.
Record: 5–2

	1	2	3	4		
Vikings	7	14	0	6	=	27
Browns	3	7	0	7	=	17

CLE-Groza 20-yd. FG
MIN-Brown 1-yd. run (Cox kick)
CLE-Green 1-yd. run (Groza kick)
MIN-Mason 72-yd. pass from Tarkenton (Cox kick)
MIN-Brown 2-yd. pass from Tarkenton (Cox kick)
MIN-Cox 30-yd. FG
CLE-Brown 1-yd. run (Groza kick)
MIN-Cox 18-yd. FG

Passing
MIN: Tarkenton 17–27–234 2 TD 0 INT
CLE: Ryan 4–15–75 0 TD 0 INT, Ninowski 5–7–62 0 TD 0 INT, Groza 0–1–0 0 TD 0 INT

Rushing
MIN: Brown 26–138, Mason 12–66, King 1–1, Tarkenton 2-(-9)
CLE: Brown 18–39, Kelly 4–4, Ryan 2-(-4), Green 4-(-5)

Receiving
MIN: Mason 1–72, Flatley 6–65, Brown 5–46, Phillips 4–41, King 1–10
CLE: Collins 4–116, Brewer 1–15, Brown 2–9, Kelly 1–1, Green 1-(-4)

Sunday, November 7
Browns 38, Philadelphia Eagles 34
Cleveland Stadium (72,807)
White jerseys/white pants

With both offenses combining for nearly 1,000 yards, the Browns maintained their conference lead with a wild victory over Philadelphia. Lighting up the scoreboard as a sunny afternoon soon became caked by a soupy fog rolling in off the lake, the Browns and Eagles seesawed through three quarters before the Browns caught a break in the fourth that put them over the top. Clinging to a four-point lead, the Browns were punting back to Philadelphia when a roughing-the-punter penalty on the Eagles (aided by some dramatics by punter Gary Collins) gave the Browns a much-needed first down. Moments later, Collins caught his second touchdown of the day to put the Browns up 38–27 and provide the insurance to withstand one final Eagle score with less than two minutes remaining. The Eagles regained possession deep in their own territory with under a minute to play and frantically drove to the Cleveland 35 before time expired. Philly rolled to 582 total yards, the most the Browns would allow all year, as QB Norm Snead threw for 362 yards and a trio of scoring passes, and Timmy Brown rushed for a whopping 186 yards on just 16 carries. While impressive, the Cleveland offense was well off the pace with 369 yards, paced by 131 rushing by Jim Brown—who also added three touchdowns—and 128 receiving by Collins. The Cleveland special teams also helped contribute to the scoring onslaught when Walter

Roberts returned the kickoff following Philadelphia's first touchdown 88 yards to set up the Browns' first score.
Record: 6–2

	1	2	3	4		
Eagles	14	3	10	7	=	34
Browns	7	14	10	7	=	38

PHI-Brown 54-yd. run (Baker kick)
CLE-Collins 2-yd. pass from Ryan (Groza kick)
PHI-Retzlaff 6-yd. pass from Snead (Baker kick)
CLE-Brown 7-yd. run (Groza kick)
PHI-Baker 12-yd. FG
CLE-Brown 32-yd. pass from Ryan (Groza kick)
PHI-Retzlaff 39-yd. pass from Snead (Baker kick)
CLE-Groza 49-yd. FG
PHI-Baker 39-yd. FG
CLE-Brown 1-yd. run (Groza kick)
CLE-Collins 7-yd. pass from Ryan (Groza kick)
PHI-Retzlaff 22-yd. pass from Snead (Baker kick)

Passing
PHI: Snead 18–36–362 3 TD 2 INT
CLE: Ryan 16–24–220 3 TD 1 INT

Rushing
PHI: Brown 16–186, Gros 11–30, Snead 3–14
CLE: Brown 20–131, Green 7–29, Ryan 1–17, Roberts 1–10

Receiving
PHI: Retzlaff 7–151, Poage 3–84, Glass 4–51, Brown 2–38, Gill 1–27, Gros 1–11
CLE: Collins 8–128, Brown 5–60, Green 2–21, Roberts 1–11

Sunday, November 14
Browns 34, New York Giants 21
Cleveland Stadium (82,426)
White jerseys/white pants

On the strength of another explosive offensive performance, the Browns cruised to their fourth straight victory over the Giants on a crisp, chilly afternoon. Picking up 459 total yards of offense, the Browns carried a three-point lead into the fourth quarter, then sealed the victory with 10 points in the final stanza. Jim Brown led the way, scoring three touchdowns and rushing for 156 yards, putting him over the 1,000-yard mark for the season for the seventh time in his career. RB Ernie Green was just as potent a weapon, rushing for 62 yards and catching seven passes for 160 and the game's first touchdown. Combined with a St. Louis loss to the Bears, the Browns surged to a two-game lead in the Eastern Conference with five to play.
Record: 7–2

	1	2	3	4		
Giants	7	7	7	0	=	21
Browns	14	3	7	10	=	34

CLE-Green 26-yd. pass from Ryan (Groza kick)
NYG-Thomas 21-yd. pass from Morrall (Timberlake kick)
CLE-Brown 3-yd. run (Groza kick)
CLE-Groza 19-yd. FG
NYG-Jones 79-yd. pass from Morrall (Timberlake kick)
CLE-Brown 4-yd. run (Groza kick)
NYG-Crespino 2-yd. pass from Morrall (Timberlake kick)
CLE-Brown 17-yd. run (Groza kick)
CLE-Groza 37-yd. FG

Passing
NYG: Morrall 18–30–261 3 TD 2 INT
CLE: Ryan 13–24–236 1 TD 1 INT

Rushing
NYG: Thurlow 12–51, Frederickson 14–40, Reed 3–11, Morrison 1–7, Morrall 2-(-2)
CLE: Brown 20–156, Green 11–62, Roberts 1–14

Receiving
NYG: Jones 4–118, Thomas 4–60, Frederickson 5–41, Morrison 2–21, Reed 2–19, Crespino 1–2
CLE: Green 7–160, Brown 3–36, McNeil 1–32, Roberts 1–9, Kelly 1-(-1)

Sunday, November 21
Browns 24, Dallas Cowboys 17
Cotton Bowl (76,251)
Brown jerseys/white pants

Before a record crowd at the Cotton Bowl, the Browns built a two-touchdown lead and then hung on through an anxious final period to secure their seventh victory in eight weeks. Though the Cleveland offense struggled, managing just 200 total yards, the defense and special teams rose to the occasion to help the Browns take control. Leroy Kelly returned a punt 67 yards for a score just before the half to open up a 17–3 lead, while the defense collected four sacks and forced three turnovers. The momentum shifted in the fourth quarter when a Lou Groza field-goal attempt was

blocked and the Cowboys converted it into a touchdown to cut the margin to 24–17. Dallas was then poised to tie the game with four minutes remaining, but Cleveland LB Vince Costello intercepted a short Don Meredith pass in the end zone to preserve the lead. A Jim Brown fumble gave the ball back to Dallas at the Cleveland 40 two minutes later, and the Cowboys drove to the 23 and had one final chance to tie the game. Then Cleveland DB Ross Fichtner picked off another Meredith pass to end the threat and clinch a tough victory. With the Cardinals losing at home to New York, the Browns opened up a comfortable three-game conference lead with just four games to play.
Record: 8–2

	1	2	3	4		
Browns	0	17	7	0	=	24
Cowboys	0	3	7	7	=	17

DAL-Villanueva 10-yd. FG
CLE-Groza 46-yd. FG
CLE-Brown 3-yd. run (Groza kick)
CLE-Kelly 67-yd. punt return (Groza kick)
DAL-Norman 2-yd. pass from Meredith (Villanueva kick)
CLE-Collins 5-yd. pass from Ryan (Groza kick)
DAL-Hayes 45-yd. pass from Meredith (Villanueva kick)

Passing
CLE: Ryan 9–18–75 1 TD 0 INT
DAL: Meredith 17–29–201 2 TD 3 INT

Rushing
CLE: Brown 19–99, Green 8–28, Ryan 2–14, Kelly 1-(-6)
DAL: Perkins 22–86, Meredith 2–14, Dunn 3–10, Hayes 1–8, Clarke 1–6

Receiving
CLE: Green 2–23, Collins 2–18, Brown 3–17, Kelly 1–10, Roberts 1–7
DAL: Hayes 6–84, Clarke 4–62, Dunn 3–25, Gent 2–16, Dial 1–12, Norman 1–2

Sunday, November 28
Browns 42, Pittsburgh Steelers 21
Pitt Stadium (42,757)
White jerseys/white pants

On a windy, cold Sunday after Thanksgiving, the Browns clinched a conference title earlier than ever before, coasting to an easy victory over the struggling Steelers. The Cleveland defense led the way in the first half, holding Pittsburgh scoreless as the Browns took a 7–0 lead on a 56-yard punt return by Leroy Kelly early in the second quarter. A wild, eight-touchdown second half began on the first play after the kickoff when Jim Brown broke loose for a 68-yard run to set up the first of his four scores. Brown finished with 146 yards on just 20 carries, posting his seventh 100-yard rushing day of the season. With the Cleveland passing game thwarted by the high winds, the Browns rolled to 241 rushing yards and answered each Pittsburgh touchdown with one of their own as they picked up their fourth straight victory. Though the Steelers outgained the Browns in total yardage, the Cleveland defense collected seven sacks. A St. Louis loss to Philadelphia nailed down the Browns' second straight title-game appearance.
Record: 9–2

	1	2	3	4		
Browns	0	7	14	21	=	42
Steelers	0	0	7	14	=	21

CLE-Kelly 56-yd. punt return (Groza kick)
CLE-Brown 2-yd. run (Groza kick)
CLE-Brown 2-yd. run (Groza kick)
PIT-Ballman 87-yd. pass from Nelsen (Clark kick)
CLE-Brown 15-yd. run (Groza kick)
PIT-Butler 43-yd. pass from Nelsen (Clark kick)
CLE-Brewer 25-yd. pass from Ninowski (Groza kick)
PIT-Thomas 80-yd. pass from Nelsen (Clark kick)
CLE-Brown 27-yd. pass from Ninowski (Groza kick)

Passing
CLE: Ninowski 3–4–72 2 TD 0 INT, Ryan 3–9–61 0 TD 0 INT
PIT: Nelsen 9–22–285 3 TD 0 INT

Rushing
CLE: Brown 20–146, Green 13–57, Ninowski 1–14, Scales 2–12, Kelly 3–6, Ryan 3–6
PIT: Peaks 14–87, Hoak 9–37, Nelsen 1–14, Butler 2-(-1)

Receiving
CLE: Collins 3–74, Brown 2–34, Brewer 1–25
PIT: Ballman 3–118, Thomas 1–80, Butler 1–43, Folkins 2–25, Hoak 1–22, Lind 1-(-3)

Sunday, December 5
Browns 24, Washington Redskins 16
Cleveland Stadium (77,765)
White jerseys/white pants

Despite four turnovers in the home finale, the Browns overcame a nine-point halftime deficit and scored the game's final 17 points to pick up their fifth straight victory.

Cleveland took a 17–16 lead early in the fourth quarter on TE Tom Hutchinson's first career touchdown reception, then after DE Bill Glass stripped the football from Washington QB Sonny Jurgensen on a sack and Browns' LB Jim Houston recovered, Jim Brown's NFL-record twentieth touchdown of the season put the game away with less than two minutes to play. Brown finished with 141 yards on the ground, his fifty-eighth and final 100-yard rushing game. At the conclusion of a home schedule that saw the Browns draw a record 557,283, the fans charged the field and tore down the goalposts to celebrate another magnificent season.

Record: 10–2

	1	2	3	4		
Redskins	6	10	0	0	=	16
Browns	0	7	3	14	=	24

WAS-Taylor 2-yd. run (kick failed)
CLE-Collins 7-yd. pass from Ryan (Groza kick)
WAS-Richter 6-yd. pass from Jurgensen (Jencks kick)
WAS-Jencks 20-yd. FG
CLE-Groza 42-yd. FG
CLE-Hutchinson 14-yd. pass from Ryan (Groza kick)
CLE-Brown 5-yd. run (Groza kick)

Passing
WAS: Jurgensen 18–35–155 1 TD 2 INT
CLE: Ryan 9–22–124 2 TD 3 INT

Rushing
WAS: Taylor 16–70, Hughley 4–5, Lewis 2–5, Jurgensen 1-(-17)
CLE: Brown 27–141, Green 8–43, Collins 1–16, Ryan 2–0

Receiving
WAS: Mitchell 4–78, Coia 5–34, Taylor 3–25, Hughley 2–12, Richter 1–6, Smith 1–2, Lewis 2-(-2)
CLE: Collins 5–53, Brown 1–29, Brewer 1–17, Hutchinson 1–14, Roberts 1–11

Sunday, December 12
Los Angeles Rams 42, Browns 7
Los Angeles Memorial Coliseum (49,048)
Brown jerseys/white pants

In a driving rain, the Browns' winning streak came to a screeching halt as they were pulverized by the 3–9 Rams. Unable to adapt to a muddy field, the Browns were held to a season-low 119 total yards and a mere six first downs as Jim Ninowski, getting the start at QB, was unable to spark the offense. Jim Brown was also nullified, held to just 20 rushing yards on 13 carries. The bad news kept coming when WR Paul Warfield, making his first appearance of the season after fracturing a shoulder in the College All-Star Game, caught three passes but was then injured again and wouldn't return to action until the following season. Meanwhile, the Rams were unstoppable, rolling to 469 total yards behind a fabulous performance by QB Roman Gabriel, who threw for 323 yards and five touchdowns and ran for another. His primary target was WR Tommy McDonald, who caught three of the scoring passes and tallied 200 receiving yards on the afternoon. The defeat marked the first Browns' loss to Los Angeles in 14 years, snapping a five-game winning streak over the Rams.

Record: 10–3

	1	2	3	4		
Browns	0	7	0	0	=	7
Rams	7	14	7	14	=	42

LA-McKeever 5-yd. pass from Gabriel (Gossett kick)
LA-Brown 22-yd. pass from Gabriel (Gossett kick)
LA-McDonald 46-yd. pass from Gabriel (Gossett kick)
CLE-Green 3-yd. pass from Ninowski (Groza kick)
LA-Gabriel 9-yd. run (Gossett kick)
LA-McDonald 42-yd. pass from Gabriel (Gossett kick)
LA-McDonald 43-yd. pass from Gabriel (Gossett kick)

Passing
CLE: Ninowski 11–27–83 1 TD 1 INT
LA: Gabriel 15–31–323 5 TD 1 INT

Rushing
CLE: Brown 13–20, Kelly 3–16, Roberts 1–6, Green 1–0, Ninowski 1-(-2)
LA: Bass 12–64, Gabriel 3–34, Brown 7–29, Wilson 6–24, Josephson 3–10, Stiger 2–8

Receiving
CLE: Collins 2–31, Warfield 3–30, Brown 3–13, Green 3–9
LA: McDonald 6–200, Snow 3–47, Brown 2–45, McKeever 3–22, Bass 1–9

Sunday, December 19
Browns 27, St. Louis Cardinals 24
Busch Stadium (29,348)
Brown jerseys/white pants

In a wild regular-season finale on a sunny but frigid day in St. Louis, the Browns rallied from behind in the fourth quarter to capture their eleventh victory and send the once-contending Cardinals to their eighth defeat in nine games. In what proved to be his final regular-season game, Jim Brown was ejected in the second quarter after getting into a fight with St. Louis DE Joe Robb, spoiling a chance for another 100-yard game after he'd rushed for 74 yards on his first 12 carries. Behind Brown, Cleveland surged to a 17–0 lead, but after his ejection, the Cardinals roared back. A 96-yard interception return for a touchdown by DB Larry Wilson—one of three interceptions he'd collect on the day—turned the game around, and the Cardinals scored 24 straight points to take control. After narrowing the St. Louis lead to 24–20, an interception by Vince Costello in Cardinals' territory set up the game-winning points on the next play when Frank Ryan hit Tom Hutchinson for a 24-yard touchdown with four minutes remaining. The Cardinals had one final chance, driving to the Cleveland 23 in the waning moments, but eschewed a potential tying field goal and were stopped on fourth down. The Cleveland defense was magnificent, holding the Cardinals to just 160 yards—the lowest tally the Browns allowed all season—and forced four turnovers.

Record: 11–3

	1	2	3	4		
Browns	7	10	0	10	=	27
Cardinals	0	7	10	7	=	24

CLE-Collins 13-yd. pass from Ryan (Groza kick)
CLE-Brown 3-yd. run (Groza kick)
CLE-Groza 44-yd. FG
STL-Wilson 96-yd. interception return (Bakken kick)
STL-Nofsinger 1-yd. run (Bakken kick)
STL-Bakken 23-yd. FG
STL-Triplett 5-yd. pass from Nofsinger (Bakken kick)
CLE-Groza 45-yd. FG
CLE-Hutchinson 24-yd. pass from Ryan (Groza kick)

Passing
CLE: Ryan 16–33–175 2 TD 3 INT
STL: Nofsinger 8–20–47 1 TD 1 INT, Humphrey 5–14–26 0 TD 3 INT

Rushing
CLE: Brown 12–74, Green 11–32, Ryan 3–21, Scales 4–14
STL: Crenshaw 8–59, Triplett 16–50, Nofsinger 4–1

Receiving
CLE: Hutchinson 4–77, Brewer 5–51, Collins 4–34, Scales 1–7, Green 2–6
STL: Conrad 3–26, Crenshaw 4–17, Randle 2–13, Triplett 3–10, Smith 1–7

1965 NFL Championship
Sunday, January 2
Green Bay Packers 23, Browns 12
Lambeau Field (50,852)
White jerseys/white pants

Amid miserable conditions that saw a combination of snow, sleet, rain, and fog, the Browns were overwhelmed in the second half and lost the NFL title game for the fifth time in team history.

Arriving late to Lambeau Field due to snarled traffic in the nasty weather, the Browns made a game of it in the first half and trailed just 13–12 at the intermission after a Gary Collins touchdown reception and a pair of Lou Groza field goals. But the Packers parlayed the momentum they'd picked up in their exciting overtime playoff victory over Baltimore the previous week and dominated play in the final 30 minutes to capture their fourth world title in six years.

Unfazed by the muddy conditions, the Packers controlled the line of scrimmage, rushing for more than 200 yards as a team and running 69 offensive plays to Cleveland's 39. A touchdown by RB Paul Hornung on a sweep gave them an eight-point lead in the third quarter and the Packers never looked back. After Lou Groza had a field goal blocked in the third quarter, Cleveland had few opportunities in the second half and ran just four offensive plays in the fourth period.

In what turned out to be his final game, Jim Brown was limited to 50 yards on 12 carries as the Browns' offense managed just 161 yards and eight first downs for the day. Meanwhile, the Packers' powerful combination of Hornung and RB Jim Taylor—who rushed for 96 yards and was named the game's MVP—was simply too much for the Browns, who were unable to successfully defend their world title.

	1	2	3	4		
Browns	9	3	0	0	=	12
Packers	7	6	7	3	=	23

GB-Dale 47-yd. pass from Starr (Chandler kick)
CLE-Collins 17-yd. pass from Ryan (kick failed)
CLE-Groza 24-yd. FG
GB-Chandler 15-yd. FG
GB-Chandler 23-yd. FG
CLE-Groza 28-yd. FG
GB-Hornung 13-yd. run (Chandler kick)
GB-Chandler 29-yd. FG

Passing
CLE: Ryan 8–18–115 1 TD 2 INT
GB: Starr 10–18–147 1 TD 1 INT, Hornung 0–1–0 0 TD 0 INT

Rushing
CLE: Brown 12–50, Ryan 3–9, Green 3–5
GB: Hornung 18–105, Taylor 27–96, Moore 2–3

Receiving
CLE: Brown 3–44, Collins 3–41, Warfield 2–30
GB: Dale 2–60, Dowler 5–59, Taylor 2–20, Hornung 1–8

1966

Sunday, September 11
Browns 38, Washington Redskins 14
D.C. Stadium (48,643)
White jerseys/white pants

With the football world watching to see how the Browns would fare following Jim Brown's sudden retirement, things looked grim early as the Redskins took advantage of a fumble by Cleveland RB Ernie Green and soared to a 14–0 lead. Outgained by more than 100 yards in the first half, the Browns trailed at the intermission but reverted back to their championship form in the final two periods. QB Frank Ryan threw three touchdown passes, and the Cleveland defense limited Washington to 97 total yards in the second half, picking off QB Sonny Jurgensen five times. After Browns' DB Walter Beach recovered a fumble on the second play of the third quarter, a 20-yard scoring pass from Ryan to WR Gary Collins tied the game, and the Browns took the lead with a Lou Groza field goal on their next possession. Then they piled on 21 points in the fourth quarter to win going away. Green and RB Leroy Kelly combined to rush for 142 yards as the Browns won their seventh straight over Washington, now coached by former Browns' QB Otto Graham.
Record: 1–0

	1	2	3	4		
Browns	7	0	10	21	=	38
Redskins	14	0	0	0	=	14

WAS-Taylor 5-yd. run (Gogolak kick)
WAS-Taylor 34-yd. pass from Jurgensen (Gogolak kick)
CLE-Kelly 29-yd. run (Groza kick)
CLE-Collins 20-yd. pass from Ryan (Groza kick)
CLE-Groza 35-yd. FG
CLE-Warfield 16-yd. pass from Ryan (Groza kick)
CLE-Green 1-yd. run (Groza kick)
CLE-Collins 5-yd. pass from Ryan (Groza kick)

Passing
CLE: Ryan 13–25–159 3 TD 0 INT
WAS: Jurgensen 17–35–240 1 TD 5 INT

Rushing
CLE: Green 11–88, Kelly 16–54, Ryan 4–11, Harraway 2–6, Ninowski 1-(-11)
WAS: Taylor 9–62, Whitfield 10–31, Rector 5–8, Kantor 1–2

Receiving
CLE: Warfield 4–59, Morin 3–51, Collins 3–44, Green 3–5
WAS: Taylor 5–94, Mitchell 2–56, P. Carpenter 3–31, Whitfield 3–29, Mazurek 1–15, Rector 2–9, Smith 1–6

Sunday, September 18
Green Bay Packers 21, Browns 20
Cleveland Stadium (83,943)
White jerseys/white pants

A massive crowd gathered for the home opener, hoping to see the Browns enact revenge for their loss to Vince Lombardi's Packers in the NFL Championship eight months before. For much of the sunny afternoon, it appeared they'd go home happy. Frank Ryan connected with Gary Collins for a pair of touchdown passes to put the Browns up 14–0 in the second quarter. After the Packers narrowed the lead on a gutsy fourth-down scoring pass from QB Bart Starr to RB Paul Hornung from the Cleveland 44, a Lou Groza field goal that hit the crossbar yet still bounced over put the Browns up by 10 at the half. Trailing 20–14 midway through the fourth quarter, Green Bay marched 76 yards to the Cleveland 9, where on fourth-and-eight, RB Jim Taylor took a swing pass from Starr and maneuvered through three defenders on his way to the end zone for the go-ahead touchdown with 2:34 left. The Browns quickly drove into Packer territory in the final minute, but Green Bay recovered a Ryan fumble to clinch the victory.
Record: 1–1

	1	2	3	4		
Packers	0	7	7	7	=	21
Browns	7	10	0	3	=	20

CLE-Collins 11-yd. pass from Ryan (Groza kick)
CLE-Collins 24-yd. pass from Ryan (Groza kick)
GB-Hornung 44-yd. pass from Starr (Chandler kick)
CLE-Groza 42-yd. FG
GB-Taylor 1-yd. run (Chandler kick)
CLE-Groza 46-yd. FG
GB-Taylor 9-yd. pass from Starr (Chandler kick)

Passing
GB: Starr 20–30–238 2 TD 0 INT
CLE: Ryan 15–24–184 2 TD 0 INT

Rushing
GB: Hornung 14–51, Taylor 17–42, Starr 4–17, Pitts 3–8
CLE: Green 9–52, Kelly 11–51, Ryan 2–7

Receiving
GB: Hornung 3–69, Taylor 8–64, Dowler 4–61, Dale 2–23, Fleming 2–15, Anderson 1–6
CLE: Collins 4–70, Warfield 3–54, Green 5–33, Kelly 3–27

Sunday, September 25
St. Louis Cardinals 34, Browns 28
Cleveland Stadium (74,814)
White jerseys/white pants

Amid constant rain showers on a gloomy day on the lake, the Browns once again squandered a double-digit lead in the second half to lose at home to a title contender. The Browns recovered three Cardinal fumbles in the first two periods, but could parlay them into only seven points. Still, on the strength of the first 100-yard game of Leroy Kelly's young career and 279 passing yards from Frank Ryan, the Browns surged to a 28–14 advantage early in the third quarter. A pair of touchdown passes by St. Louis QB Charley Johnson tied it going into the fourth, and a 23-yard scoring scamper by RB Prentice Gautt put the Cardinals ahead for good. Just like the week before, the Browns had one final chance to win in the final moments, but after driving to the St. Louis 11, they were stopped on fourth down. The Browns were now under .500 for the first time in Blanton Collier's tenure as head coach.
Record: 1–2

	1	2	3	4		
Cardinals	7	7	14	6	=	34
Browns	14	7	7	0	=	28

CLE-Green 23-yd. pass from Ryan (Groza kick)
STL-Shivers 94-yd. kickoff return (Bakken kick)
CLE-Kelly 1-yd. run (Groza kick)
STL-Randle 33-yd. pass from Johnson (Bakken kick)
CLE-Kelly 6-yd. run (Groza kick)
CLE-Kelly 57-yd. run (Groza kick)
STL-Smith 58-yd. pass from Johnson (Bakken kick)
STL-Gambrell 9-yd. pass from Johnson (Bakken kick)
STL-Gautt 23-yd. run (kick failed)

Passing
STL: Johnson 11–20–218 3 TD 2 INT
CLE: Ryan 21–41–279 1 TD 1 INT

Rushing
STL: Gautt 6–50, Crenshaw 9–31, Roland 10–24, Johnson 3–2
CLE: Kelly 19–109, Green 10–22, Ryan 3–12

Receiving
STL: Smith 3–83, Conrad 4–65, Randle 1–33, Roland 1–16, Gautt 1–12, Gambrell 1–9
CLE: Morin 6–97, Warfield 3–79, Green 5–59, Kelly 6–36, Collins 1–8

Sunday, October 2
Browns 28, New York Giants 7
Yankee Stadium (62,916)
White jerseys/white pants

After back-to-back heartbreaks, the Browns rebounded to dominate the Giants and pull back into the Eastern Conference race. Leading just 14–7 going into the fourth quarter, they slammed the door with a scoring run by Ernie Green and Frank Ryan's second touchdown pass. The real star of the game was Leroy Kelly, who had a breakthrough game, picking up 138 yards on 20 carries, sparking an offensive attack that rolled up 418 yards. Ernie Green added 73 more rushing yards, while Gary Collins tacked on 88 yards receiving on just four receptions. The Cleveland defense also played well, holding the Giants to 50 yards rushing and forcing six turnovers.
Record: 2–2

	1	2	3	4		
Browns	7	7	0	14	=	28
Giants	0	7	0	0	=	7

CLE-Morin 20-yd. pass from Ryan (Groza kick)
CLE-Kelly 3-yd. run (Groza kick)
NYG-Jones 17-yd. pass from Wood (Gogolak kick)
CLE-Green 14-yd. run (Groza kick)
CLE-Warfield 9-yd. pass from Ryan (Groza kick)

Passing
CLE: Ryan 14–24–171 2 TD 1 INT
NYG: Morrall 10–23–177 0 TD 3 INT, Wood 3–6–75 1 TD 1 INT

Rushing
CLE: Kelly 20–138, Green 18–73, Ryan 8–47
NYG: Lewis 9–24, Mercein 7–21, Koy 1–7, Wood 1-(-2)

Receiving
CLE: Collins 4–88, Morin 4–48, Green 4–18, Warfield 2–17
NYG: Jones 4–88, Thomas 3–88, Mercein 4–35, Lewis 1–22, Morrison 1–19

Saturday, October 8
Browns 41, Pittsburgh Steelers 10
Cleveland Stadium (82,687)
White jerseys/white pants

In their annual Saturday-night showdown with Pittsburgh, the Browns overwhelmed the Steelers in the first half, outgaining them 289 yards to 20, picking up 19 first downs to Pittsburgh's one, and jumping to a 21–0 lead. The Steelers hung tough, cutting the margin to 11 points going into the fourth quarter, but the Browns made sure the big crowd went home happy with an exclamatory 20-point final period, highlighted by WR Paul Warfield scooping up a fumble by teammate Milt Morin and taking it three yards for a touchdown. For the night, the Browns collected a whopping 467 yards of offense as both Leroy Kelly and Ernie Green topped 100 yards on the ground, while the Cleveland defense picked off five Pittsburgh passes and held the Steelers to just 22 rushing yards.
Record: 3–2

	1	2	3	4		
Steelers	0	0	10	0	=	10
Browns	14	7	0	20	=	41

CLE-Collins 23-yd. pass from Ryan (Groza kick)
CLE-Collins 14-yd. pass from Ryan (Groza kick)
CLE-Kelly 2-yd. run (Groza kick)
PIT-Jefferson 23-yd. pass from Izo (Clark kick)
PIT-Clark 16-yd. FG
CLE-Kelly 10-yd. run (kick failed)
CLE-Warfield 3-yd. fumble return (Groza kick)
CLE-Smith 24-yd. pass from Ninowski (Groza kick)

Passing
PIT: Izo 17–31–177 1 TD 3 INT, Smith 1–7–19 0 TD 2 INT
CLE: Ryan 14–21–179 2 TD 0 INT, Ninowski 4–6–67 1 TD 0 INT, Groza 1-1-(-7)

Rushing
PIT: Hoak 7–36, Lind 3–4, Asbury 4–0, Izo 2-(-18)
CLE: Kelly 19–113, Green 16–103, Pietrosante 3–12, Ryan 2–11, Harraway 1–3, Schultz 1–3, Ninowski 1-(-4)

Receiving
PIT: Hilton 5–58, Jefferson 2–42, Hoak 7–40, Ballman 1–26, Asbury 2–19, Wilburn 1–11
CLE: Collins 6–68, Morin 4–52, Warfield 2–41, Kelly 3–34, Green 2–27, Smith 1–24, Costello 1-(-7)

Sunday, October 23
Browns 30, Dallas Cowboys 21
Cleveland Stadium (84,721)
White jerseys/white pants

Before the largest crowd in team history, the Browns rocketed back into the Eastern Conference race by blasting the undefeated Cowboys on a perfect autumn afternoon. The Browns intercepted Dallas QB Don Meredith four times—including three by DB Ross Fichtner—giving them 13 in their last three contests and collected five sacks behind a voracious defensive attack. After stuffing Dallas on fourth-and-one at the Cleveland 35 early in the third quarter, the home team blew open a 13–7 game with 17 third-quarter points—capped by a 21-yard scoring reception by Paul Warfield—to put the game out of reach. With St. Louis suffering its first loss, the Browns pulled within a game-and-a-half of first place and a half-game of the second-place Cowboys.
Record: 4–2

	1	2	3	4		
Cowboys	7	0	0	14	=	21
Browns	10	3	17	0	=	30

CLE-Groza 39-yd. FG
DAL-Meredith 3-yd. run (Villanueva kick)
CLE-Morin 15-yd. pass from Ryan (Groza kick)
CLE-Groza 30-yd. FG
CLE-Groza 47-yd. FG
CLE-Kelly 2-yd. run (Groza kick)
CLE-Warfield 21-yd. pass from Ryan (Groza kick)
DAL-Perkins 1-yd. run (Villanueva kick)
DAL-Clarke 1-yd. pass from Meredith (Villanueva kick)

Passing
DAL: Meredith 26–45–288 1 TD 4 INT
CLE: Ryan 9–24–159 2 TD 0 INT

Rushing
DAL: Reeves 10–49, Perkins 15–44, Meredith 3–32, Renfro 3–31
CLE: Green 11–56, Kelly 12–25, Ryan 8–24

Receiving
DAL: Hayes 7–108, Reeves 4–42, Clarke 3–40, Gent 3–39, Renfro 3–23, Perkins 4–18, Norman 2–18
CLE: Collins 3–75, Warfield 3–39, Green 2–30, Morin 1–15

Sunday, October 30
Browns 49, Atlanta Falcons 17
Atlanta Stadium (57,235)
White jerseys/white pants

Things unfolded exactly as expected for the red-hot Browns against the expansion and winless Falcons. Steamrolling Atlanta for more than 500 yards of offense and seven touchdowns, Cleveland won its fourth straight and kept pace with the victorious Cardinals and Cowboys. The tone was set in the opening moments when Leroy Kelly exploded through the line for a 70-yard scoring run, what would be the longest play of his Hall of Fame career. Frank Ryan threw for four touchdowns, and backup Jim Ninowski relieved him to toss two more in the fourth quarter.
Record: 5–2

	1	2	3	4		
Browns	14	7	7	21	=	49
Falcons	0	10	0	7	=	17

CLE-Kelly 70-yd. run (Groza kick)
CLE-Warfield 36-yd. pass from Ryan (Groza kick)
ATL-Wheelwright 1-yd. run (Kirouac kick)
CLE-Collins 17-yd. pass from Ryan (Houston pass from Ninowski)
ATL-Kirouac 23-yd. FG
CLE-Green 6-yd. pass from Ryan (Groza kick)
ATL-Hawkins 22-yd. pass from Johnson (Kirouac kick)
CLE-McNeil 44-yd. pass from Ninowski (Groza kick)
CLE-Smith 15-yd. pass from Ninowski (Groza kick)

Passing
CLE: Ryan 13–21–223 4 TD 1 INT, Ninowski 3–4–72 2 TD 0 INT
ATL: Johnson 14–25–158 1 TD 1 INT

Rushing
CLE: Kelly 14–98, Green 10–74, Ryan 1–16, Schultz 3–14, Harraway 2–10, Pietrosante 1–1
ATL: Coffey 17–117, Johnson 4–40, Wheelwright 11–32, Dunn 3–10, Scales 1–5

Receiving
CLE: Warfield 3–78, Green 3–49, Collins 4–48, McNeil 1–44, Kelly 1–30, Smith 2–28, Morin 2–18
ATL: Hawkins 4–64, Burke 5–60, Barnes 1–16, Dunn 2–13, Coffey 1–4, Scales 1–1

Sunday, November 6
Pittsburgh Steelers 16, Browns 6
Pitt Stadium (39,690)
Brown jerseys/white pants

Four weeks after dominating the Steelers in Cleveland, the Browns saw their title hopes dimmed after a sloppy, lethargic performance in Pittsburgh. Despite committing six turnovers—including five interceptions by Frank Ryan—the Browns, 16-point favorites, led 6–3 at the half and still had a chance to pull out a tie until the Steelers kicked a game-clinching field goal with less than a minute to play. Losers of five straight games coming in, the Steelers took the lead with a touchdown in the opening moments of the fourth quarter, then picked off Ryan after the Browns drove to the Pittsburgh 19 on the following possession. They never threatened to score again. With the Cardinals winning in New York, the Browns were now two full games off the pace and had already lost to St. Louis in the teams' first meeting.
Record: 5–3

	1	2	3	4		
Browns	0	6	0	0	=	6
Steelers	0	3	3	10	=	16

CLE-Collins 24-yd. pass from Ryan (kick failed)
PIT-Clark 28-yd. FG
PIT-Clark 25-yd. FG
PIT-Ballman 8-yd. pass from Smith (Clark kick)
PIT-Clark 42-yd. FG

Passing
CLE: Ryan 19–37–228 1 TD 5 INT
PIT: Smith 11–19–151 1 TD 0 INT

Rushing
CLE: Kelly 19–82, Green 10–49
PIT: Asbury 17–94, Hoak 6–18, Smith 6–15, Butler 3–8

Receiving
CLE: Collins 7–93, Green 3–37, Kelly 4–35, Smith 2–26, Morin 1–16, Warfield 1–12, Roberts 1–9
PIT: Ballman 6–77, Hilton 4–59, Jefferson 1–15

Sunday, November 13
Browns 27, Philadelphia Eagles 7
Cleveland Stadium (77,968)
White jerseys/white pants

On a sunny but cold afternoon, the Browns once again started slow, but got rolling in the second half to capture their seventh consecutive win over the Eagles and rebound from the disaster in Pittsburgh. Frank Ryan, booed loudly at the outset, threw two touchdown passes in the second half to put the game away after the Browns' lead was just 7–0 at halftime. Gary Collins helped turn the tide by averaging 41 yards per punt and twice running for first downs out of the punt formation. But the best news of the day came from Pittsburgh, where the Steelers shocked the first-place Cardinals, allowing both the Browns and Cowboys to claw to within one game of St. Louis.
Record: 6–3

	1	2	3	4		
Eagles	0	0	0	7	=	7
Browns	0	7	7	13	=	27

CLE-Green 27-yd. run (Groza kick)
CLE-Morin 16-yd. pass from Ryan (Groza kick)
CLE-Groza 22-yd. FG
CLE-Warfield 28 yd. pass from Ryan (Groza kick)
CLE-Groza 29-yd. FG
PHI-Gros 1-yd. run (Baker kick)

Passing
PHI: K. Hill 8–16–105 0 TD 1 INT, Snead 10–15–87 0 TD 1 INT
CLE: Ryan 12–26–168 2 TD 0 INT, Ninowski 3–5–26 0 TD 0 INT, Kelly 0–1–0 0 TD 0 INT

Rushing
PHI: Gros 15–72, Brown 11–43
CLE: Green 13–73, Kelly 13–60, Collins 2–38, Pietrosante 1–2, Ryan 1-(-4)

Receiving
PHI: Retzlaff 4–61, F. Hill 5–59, Gros 5–32, Goodwin 2–22, Brown 2–18
CLE: Collins 5–69, Warfield 3–64, Kelly 2–19, Morin 1–16, Green 2–12, Roberts 1–10, Smith 1–4

Sunday, November 20
Browns 14, Washington Redskins 3
Cleveland Stadium (78,466)
White jerseys/white pants

Once again nursing a narrow lead at the half, the Browns pulled away in the third quarter to pick up a key home win. Ernie Green set up the game's first touchdown with a 35-yard draw, then scored on a five-yard pass from Frank Ryan. Aided by two missed field goals by the Redskins, the Browns took control when Leroy Kelly broke loose for a 56-yard touchdown run midway through the third quarter to make it 14–0. Kelly finished the day with an even 100 yards rushing on just 14 carries. With the Cardinals idle, a Dallas win in Pittsburgh pulled the Cowboys into a tie for first, while the Browns closed to within a half-game.
Record: 7–3

	1	2	3	4		
Redskins	0	0	3	0	=	3
Browns	7	0	7	0	=	14

CLE-Green 5-yd. pass from Ryan (Groza kick)
CLE-Kelly 56-yd. run (Groza kick)
WAS-Gogolak 20-yd. FG

Passing
WAS: Jurgensen 27–38–178 0 TD 2 INT
CLE: Ryan 9–17–112 1 TD 0 INT

Rushing
WAS: Whitfield 16–98, Thurlow 10–36, Looney 2–21, Barrington 3–11, Taylor 2–6, Jurgensen 2-(-4)
CLE: Kelly 14–100, Green 9–50, Ryan 1–9

Receiving
WAS: Taylor 9–60, Smith 6–56, Mitchell 3–23, Thurlow 3–15, Whitfield 3–12, Barrington 1–11, Johnson 1–1, Looney 1–0
CLE: Warfield 2–36, Kelly 2–33, Green 3–27, Collins 1–8, Smith 1–8

Thursday, November 24
Dallas Cowboys 26, Browns 14
Cotton Bowl (75,504)
Brown jerseys/white pants

In the biggest game of the season for the Browns—labeled "High Dusk" because of its 6 P.M. kickoff—the Cowboys avenged their October loss in Cleveland with a huge win in a Thanksgiving Day showdown that took on the flavor of a championship game. Cleveland's kicking game struggled on this breezy Texas evening as Lou Groza came up short on a pair of field goals and had another blocked. On the Cowboys' ensuing possession, they drove down the field and scored the game-clinching touchdown. Trailing by one after a seesaw first half, the Cowboys' Danny Villaneuva kicked his third and fourth field goals of the night in the third quarter to put Dallas ahead for good. Leroy Kelly rushed for 115 yards as the Browns' offense consistently moved the ball but couldn't translate yards into points. After a St. Louis win three days later, the Browns' title hopes were once again slim.

Record: 7–4

	1	2	3	4		
Browns	0	14	0	0	=	14
Cowboys	6	7	6	7	=	26

DAL-Villanueva 11-yd. FG
DAL-Villanueva 31-yd. FG
CLE-Kelly 1-yd. run (Groza kick)
DAL-Reeves 6-yd. pass from Meredith (Villanueva kick)
CLE-Green 16-yd. pass from Ryan (Groza kick)
DAL-Villanueva 12-yd. FG
DAL-Villanueva 13-yd. FG
DAL-Perkins 9-yd. run (Villanueva kick)

Passing
CLE: Ryan 12–26–190 1 TD 0 INT
DAL: Meredith 16–24–131 1 TD 0 INT

Rushing
CLE: Kelly 15–115, Green 8–24, Ryan 3–18
DAL: Perkins 23–111, Reeves 14–49, Meredith 3–20, Garrison 1–2, Clarke 1-(-9)

Receiving
CLE: Collins 5–92, Kelly 2–25, Warfield 1–23, Smith 2–22, Green 1–16, Pietrosante 1–12
DAL: Hayes 6–54, Reeves 4–32, Clarke 4–21, Gent 1–12, Perkins 1–12

Sunday, December 4
Browns 49, New York Giants 40
Cleveland Stadium (61,651)
White jerseys/white pants

Down 20 points in the third quarter on a bitterly cold day at the Stadium, the Browns pulled off what remains the greatest comeback in team history to avoid a humiliating loss. Deemed 26-point underdogs going in, the 1–9–1 Giants had their way with the Browns in the first half on the glassy, frozen turf, returning the opening kickoff for a touchdown and soaring to a 31–14 halftime lead, then adding to it early in the third quarter. The Browns rallied with two of Leroy Kelly's three touchdown runs on the day but still trailed 40–28 with just over five minutes remaining in the game. It took less than two minutes for Frank Ryan to motor the Browns down the field and cut the margin to five with a scoring strike to TE Ralph Smith. Then the Cleveland defense stopped New York cold on a crucial third-and-three to get the ball back to the offense. Ryan, who would throw for 326 yards, picked up where he left off, directing the Browns to the New York 31, then tossed a screen pass to Ernie Green, who wove his way through a myriad of Giants' defenders to reach the end zone and give the Browns their first lead with 1:20 remaining. DE Bill Glass put the icing on the cake when he scooped up a New York fumble on the next series and rumbled 13 yards for the game-clinching touchdown. After scoring 35 points in the second half and rolling up 447 yards of offense for the game, the Browns thrilled their frosty home crowd with one of the most exciting victories in their history and kept their hopes for a Playoff Bowl berth alive.

Record: 8–4

	1	2	3	4		
Giants	14	17	6	3	=	40
Browns	7	7	14	21	=	49

NYG-Childs 90-yd. kickoff return (Gogolak kick)
NYG-Wood 5-yd. run (Gogolak kick)
CLE-Kelly 1-yd. run (Groza kick)
NYG-Wood 16-yd. run (Gogolak kick)
CLE-Collins 3-yd. pass from Ryan (Groza kick)
NYG-Morrison 33-yd. pass from Wood (Gogolak kick)
NYG-Gogolak 26-yd. FG
NYG-Gogolak 13-yd. FG
CLE-Kelly 3-yd. run (Groza kick)
NYG-Gogolak 38-yd. FG
CLE-Kelly 2-yd. run (Groza kick)
NYG-Gogolak 16-yd. FG
CLE-Smith 19-yd. pass from Ryan (Groza kick)
CLE-Green 31-yd. pass from Ryan (Groza kick)
CLE-Glass 13-yd. fumble return (Groza kick)

Passing
NYG: Wood 9–18–120 1 TD 0 INT, Kennedy 1–2–13 0 TD 0 INT
CLE: Ryan 16–27–326 3 TD 3 INT

Rushing
NYG: Jacobs 26–94, Wood 6–72, Morrison 17–58, Kennedy 1-(-12)
CLE: Kelly 13–126, Green 4–5, Ryan 1-(-1)

Receiving
NYG: Morrison 5–75, Jacobs 2–21, Thomas 1–20, Jones 1–13, Crespino 1–4
CLE: Collins 5–120, Kelly 4–71, Green 4–68, Smith 3–67

Sunday, December 11
Philadelphia Eagles 33, Browns 21
Franklin Field (58,074)
White jerseys/white pants

For the second straight week, the Browns played a miserable first half and trailed by 20 in the third quarter, but this time there was no miraculous comeback. After taking a lead early in the second quarter on a fake field-goal pass from Jim Ninowski to LB Jim Houston on the only reception of his career, the Browns were dominated for the remainder of the half. Symbolizing the day (and the differing rules of the era), when a long Lou Groza field-goal attempt at the end of the first half fell short, Philadelphia's Al Nelson caught it at the goal line and returned it 100 yards for a touchdown to make it 27–7. An interception return for a touchdown for Ross Fichtner (who'd appeared on the cover of *Sports Illustrated* two weeks before) and a Frank Ryan scoring toss to Gary Collins cut the margin to six early in the fourth quarter. But a pair of Philadelphia field goals put the game out of reach. Making the loss more painful, both the Cardinals and Cowboys were defeated as well, and the Browns missed a golden opportunity to get back into the conference race.
Record: 8–5

	1	2	3	4		
Browns	0	7	7	7	=	21
Eagles	6	21	0	6	=	33

PHI-Baker 37-yd. FG
PHI-Baker 38-yd. FG
CLE-Houston 10-yd. pass from Ninowski (Groza kick)
PHI-Concannon 9-yd. run (Baker kick)
PHI-Woodeshick 44-yd. pass from Concannon (Baker kick)
PHI-Nelson 100-yd. FG return (Baker kick)
CLE-Fichtner 39-yd. interception return (Groza kick)
CLE-Collins 10-yd. pass from Ryan (Groza kick)
PHI-Baker 42-yd. FG
PHI-Baker 30-yd. FG

Passing
CLE: Ryan 16–39–229 1 TD 3 INT, Ninowski 1–1–10 1 TD 0 INT
PHI: Concannon 7–23–120 1 TD 4 INT

Rushing
CLE: Green 10–61, Kelly 12–51, Ryan 2–6
PHI: Woodeshick 14–82, Concannon 7–40, Brown 9–30, Lang 6–30, Matson 5–21, Gros 3–0

Receiving
CLE: Warfield 3–78, Kelly 5–56, Green 4–54, Collins 3–37, Houston 1–10, Smith 1–4
PHI: Woodeshick 1–44, Goodwin 2–25, Brown 2–21, Retzlaff 1–20, Gros 1–10

Saturday, December 17
Browns 38, St. Louis Cardinals 10
Busch Stadium (47,721)
White jerseys/white pants

Playing for nothing more than pride and a chance to go to the Playoff Bowl, the Browns crushed the suddenly slumping Cardinals, who lost four of their last five games to finish fourth after standing alone atop the Eastern Conference in early November. After falling behind by 10 in the second quarter, the Browns abandoned their floundering running game and turned to the air. The result was a 38-point explosion over the final three periods, highlighted by four touchdown passes by Frank Ryan, giving him a team-record 29 for the season. Throwing for 367 yards on this gloomy Saturday afternoon in St. Louis, Ryan's primary targets were Paul Warfield, who reeled in six receptions for 161 yards, and Gary Collins, who added five catches, two for touchdowns, for 126 more. While the aerial assault was entertaining, the Browns' inability to move the ball on the ground cost Leroy Kelly (12 carries, 19 yards) the league rushing title, as he was passed by Chicago's Gale Sayers after a 197-yard performance in his finale. Still, Kelly finished 1966 with 1,141 yards and proved he was a viable replacement for Jim Brown. The Browns' hopes of earning a trip to Miami were also thwarted the following afternoon when the Eagles defeated the Redskins. Though the Browns and Eagles had finished with identical records and had split their two decisions, Philadelphia would represent the Eastern Conference in the Playoff Bowl because the Browns had been there more recently (1963) than the Eagles (1961).
Record: 9–5

	1	2	3	4		
Browns	0	10	14	14	=	38
Cardinals	0	10	0	0	=	10

STL-Bakken 10-yd. FG
STL-Nofsinger 1-yd. run (Bakken kick)
CLE-Collins 42-yd. pass from Ryan (Groza kick)
CLE-Groza 37-yd. FG
CLE-Collins 44-yd. pass from Ryan (Groza kick)
CLE-Kelly 1-yd. run (Groza kick)
CLE-Green 19-yd. pass from Ryan (Groza kick)
CLE-McNeil 50-yd. pass from Ryan (Groza kick)

Passing
CLE: Ryan 17–30–367 4 TD 0 INT, Ninowski 0–2–0 0 TD 1 INT
STL: Nofsinger 9–17–126 0 TD 1 INT, Hart 4–11–29 0 TD 0 INT, Roland 0–1–0 0 TD 0 INT

Rushing
CLE: Harraway 2–21, Green 5–20, Kelly 12–19, Schultz 3–15, Pietrosante 2–5, Ninowski 1–4
STL: Roland 10–30, Gautt 8–30, Crenshaw 6–26, Gambrell 1–24, Smith 1–8, Shivers 1–5, Bryant 1–4, Nofsinger 1–1

Receiving
CLE: Warfield 6–161, Collins 5–126, McNeil 1–50, Morin 1–20, Green 4–10
STL: Gambrell 5–111, Conrad 4–35, Roland 1–10, Crenshaw 3-(1)

1967

Sunday, September 17
Dallas Cowboys 21, Browns 14
Cleveland Stadium (81,039)
White jerseys/white pants

Despite an admirable defensive performance, the Browns were unable to cash in on several scoring opportunities and lost their opening game for the first time in six years. After Dallas took a 14–7 halftime lead on a pair of scoring passes by QB Don Meredith, the Cowboys scored what proved to be the winning points on an interception return of a tipped Frank Ryan pass on the first play of the third quarter. The Browns went on to recover three Dallas fumbles in the final two periods but were unable to translate any of the takeaways into points as Lou Groza missed two short field goals, and a botched snap spoiled another. After a touchdown catch by WR Gary Collins cut the Cowboys' lead to seven, the Browns' final chance came after recovering a fumble at the Cleveland 37 with two minutes left. They were stopped on fourth down moments later. Dallas held the Browns to just 11 yards rushing and forced six turnovers of their own in the first of what would be two disappointing Cleveland performances against Dallas in 1967.

Record: 0–1

	1	2	3	4		
Cowboys	7	7	7	0	=	21
Browns	7	0	7	0	=	14

CLE-Kelly 5-yd. run (Groza kick)
DAL-Hayes 22-yd. pass from Meredith (Deters kick)
DAL-Reeves 7-yd. pass from Meredith (Deters kick)
DAL-Howley 28-yd. interception return (Deters kick)
CLE-Collins 12-yd. pass from Ryan (Groza kick)

Passing
DAL: Meredith 14–23–205 2 TD 1 INT
CLE: Ryan 17–37–239 1 TD 3 INT

Rushing
DAL: Reeves 18–114, Perkins 13–57, Shy 6–16, Meredith 4–6, Baynham 1–3, Villanueva 1-(-15)
CLE: Kelly 8–11, Green 8–4, Shiner 1-(-4)

Receiving
DAL: Hayes 5–125, Reeves 2–33, Rentzel 3–30, Perkins 2–13, Norman 1–9, Baynham 1-(-5)
CLE: Green 7–85, Collins 5–77, Warfield 3–46, Kelly 1–17, Smith 1–14

Sunday, September 24
Detroit Lions 31, Browns 14
Tiger Stadium (57,383)
White jerseys/white pants

For the first time in their history, the Browns lost the first two games of a season as they were dominated by the Lions in Detroit. Aided by a 51-yard punt return by rookie DB Ben Davis, Cleveland sprinted to a 14–3 lead early in the second quarter. But the Lions controlled the contest from there, scoring four unanswered touchdowns with an offensive attack led by former Browns' QB Milt Plum. After the Lions cut the margin to four at the half, they put together three long scoring drives in the final two periods and tallied 461 total yards for the afternoon. While the Cleveland passing game struggled, RB Leroy Kelly paced the offense with 141 yards on the ground, including 102 in the first half.

Record: 0–2

	1	2	3	4		
Browns	7	7	0	0	=	14
Lions	3	7	7	14	=	31

CLE-Kelly 4-yd. run (Groza kick)
DET-Yepremian 33-yd. FG
CLE-Warfield 42-yd. pass from Ryan (Groza kick)
DET-Watkins 4-yd. run (Yepremian kick)
DET-Farr 5-yd. pass from Plum (Yepremian kick)
DET-Watkins 4-yd. run (Yepremian kick)
DET-Nowatzke 3-yd. run (Yepremian kick)

Passing
CLE: Ryan 9–19–87 1 TD 2 INT
DET: Plum 16–27–229 1 TD 0 INT

Rushing
CLE: Kelly 16–141, Green 8–50, Ryan 1–0

DET: Watkins 24–115, Farr 15–75, Nowatzke 9–36, Marsh 1–7, Felts 1–4, Plum 1–1

Receiving
CLE: Warfield 2–48, Smith 2–26, Kelly 2–14, Barney 1–3, Green 1–1, Pietrosante 1-(-5)
DET: Malinchak 5–88, Farr 7–82, Studstill 2–36, Watkins 1–14, Nowatzke 1–9

Sunday, October 1
Browns 42, New Orleans Saints 7
Tulane Stadium (77,045)
Brown jerseys/white pants

The Browns broke into the win column with a resounding victory over the expansion New Orleans Saints, who were loudly booed by their massive crowd and pelted by beer cans and whiskey bottles. After creeping to a 14–7 halftime lead, the Browns exploded for four second-half touchdowns, including a second scoring reception by WR Paul Warfield, who collected 107 receiving yards on the day. Leroy Kelly also topped 100 yards rushing, while RB Ernie Green scored a pair of touchdowns. Frank Ryan threw three touchdown passes despite leaving the game for a cortisone shot after injuring his shoulder in the second period. While Cleveland rolled up more than 400 yards of offense, the defense forced five turnovers, highlighted by an 88-yard return by DB Ross Fichtner on a lateral after an interception by DB Erich Barnes at the Cleveland 5. The long return set up a Kelly touchdown and put the Browns up 21–7, permanently shifting the momentum.
Record: 1–2

	1	2	3	4		
Browns	7	7	14	14	=	42
Saints	0	7	0	0	=	7

CLE-Warfield 18-yd. pass from Ryan (Groza kick)
NO-Taylor 2-yd. run (Durkee kick)
CLE-Green 41-yd. pass from Ryan (Groza kick)
CLE-Kelly 1-yd. run (Groza kick)
CLE-Green 2-yd. run (Groza kick)
CLE-Warfield 49-yd. pass from Ryan (Groza kick)
CLE-Smith recovered fumble in end zone (Groza kick)

Passing
CLE: Ryan 11–21–205 3 TD 2 INT, Lane 2–4–43 0 TD 0 INT, Shiner 0–1–0 0 TD 1 INT
NO: Kilmer 11–25–135 0 TD 3 INT, Cuozzo 7–12–87 0 TD 1 INT, Wood 1–3–9 0 TD 0 INT

Rushing
CLE: Kelly 20–110, Green 17–46, Pietrosante 2–35, Conjar 6–7
NO: Taylor 10–34, Gilliam 1–19, McCall 6–10, Cuozzo 2–6, Barrington 1–2, Kilmer 1-(-3)

Receiving
CLE: Warfield 4–107, Green 4–66, Smith 4–62, Kelly 1–13
NO: Gilliam 8–77, Poage 4–73, McCall 1–26, Taylor 3–21, Abramowicz 1–15, Roberts 1–12, Kramer 1–7

Saturday, October 7
Browns 21, Pittsburgh Steelers 10
Cleveland Stadium (82,949)
White jerseys/white pants

In their annual Saturday-night showdown with the Steelers, the Browns stuffed the Pittsburgh running game and coasted to a victory to claw to the .500 mark. The Steelers gained just 70 rushing yards, averaging less than three yards per carry on the night, while the Browns' offense was led by the one-two punch of Ernie Green (108 yards on 11 carries) and Leroy Kelly (80 on 25). Leading 7–3 at the half, the Browns broke the game open on the first series of the third quarter when TE Ralph Smith reeled in a 49-yard touchdown pass. Green then capped the scoring with a 15-yard scoring reception later in the period, Ryan's third touchdown pass on the evening.
Record: 2–2

	1	2	3	4		
Steelers	3	0	7	0	=	10
Browns	0	7	14	0	=	21

PIT-Clark 43-yd. FG
CLE-Warfield 17-yd. pass from Ryan (Groza kick)
CLE-Smith 49-yd. pass from Ryan (Groza kick)
PIT-Hoak 8-yd. pass from Nix (Clark kick)
CLE-Green 15-yd. pass from Ryan (Groza kick)

Passing
PIT: Nix 23–34–218 1 TD 3 INT, Hoak 0–1–0 0 TD 0 INT
CLE: Ryan 11–25–190 3 TD 3 INT

Rushing
PIT: Hoak 10–29, Asbury 11–16, Hilton 1–15, Nix 2–8, Gros 1–2
CLE: Green 11–108, Kelly 25–80, Ryan 1-(-2), Warfield 1-(-8)

Receiving
PIT: Compton 10–108, Wilburn 5–49, Gros 3–25, Hoak 3–20, Hilton 2–16
CLE: Smith 2–60, Warfield 3–45, Collins 3–40, Green 2–25, Kelly 1–20

Sunday, October 15
Browns 20, St. Louis Cardinals 16
Cleveland Stadium (77,813)
White jerseys/white pants

The Browns sprinted to a quick lead and then held off the Cardinals in the second half to clinch their first home win over St. Louis in five years. Two scores within a 90-second period in the first quarter put Cleveland up 10–0, then the lead swelled to 17–6 at the half. Both Browns' touchdowns were set up by turnovers: an interception by Erich Barnes and a fumble recovery by DE Bill Glass. The Cardinals cut the margin to a single point early in the fourth quarter, but the Cleveland defense rose to the occasion, picking off two passes and forcing punts on the final three St. Louis possessions. Lou Groza's second field goal provided insurance with 58 seconds left. The victory moved the Browns into a three-way tie for first atop the new Century Division with the Giants and Cardinals.
Record: 3–2

	1	2	3	4		
Cardinals	0	6	7	3	=	16
Browns	10	7	0	3	=	20

CLE-Groza 40-yd. FG
CLE-Kelly 20-yd. pass from Ryan (Groza kick)
STL-Bakken 42-yd. FG
CLE-Collins 32-yd. pass from Ryan (Groza kick)
STL-Bakken 26-yd. FG
STL-Hart 1-yd. run (Bakken kick)
STL-Bakken 14-yd. FG
CLE-Groza 34-yd. FG

Passing
STL: Hart 15–35–228 0 TD 3 INT
CLE: Ryan 7–18–133 2 TD 1 INT

Rushing
STL: Roland 23–66, Crenshaw 7–23, Gautt 6–21, Smith 1–18, Hart 2–4
CLE: Kelly 15–63, Green 12–38, Ryan 4–8

Receiving
STL: Smith 3–90, Gautt 2–58, Williams 6–57, Roland 1–9, Crenshaw 2–7, Conrad 1–7
CLE: Collins 2–42, Green 2–33, Kelly 2–30, Warfield 1–28

Sunday, October 22
Browns 24, Chicago Bears 0
Cleveland Stadium (83,183)
White jerseys/white pants

On a sun-splashed autumn afternoon, the Browns dominated George Halas's Bears to remain tied for first in the division with St. Louis. The Cleveland defense held the Bears—playing without star RB Gale Sayers—to just 136 total yards and collected five sacks as the Browns posted their first shutout since their NFL title-game victory over Baltimore three years before. Leroy Kelly, the NFL's leading rusher, ran for 111 yards, and Ernie Green added 86 more. Gary Collins caught seven passes for 106 yards and two scores as the Browns broke open a scoreless game at halftime and pulled away with a 17-point fourth quarter.
Record: 4–2

	1	2	3	4		
Bears	0	0	0	0	=	0
Browns	0	0	7	17	=	24

CLE-Collins 9-yd. pass from Ryan (Groza kick)
CLE-Kelly 22-yd. run (Groza kick)
CLE-Groza 24-yd. FG
CLE-Collins 6-yd. pass from Ryan (Groza kick)

Passing
CHI: Concannon 12–19–141 0 TD 1 INT, Bukich 3–8–14 0 TD 0 INT
CLE: Ryan 12–27–181 2 TD 0 INT, Shiner 2–2–18 0 TD 0 INT

Rushing
CHI: Piccolo 4–11, Bull 4–10, Concannon 7–3, Livingston 5–3, Jones 1–2, Bukich 1-(-9)
CLE: Kelly 18–111, Green 18–86, Ryan 1-(-8)

Receiving
CHI: Gordon 4–50, Piccolo 3–32, Morris 4–29, Jones 1–28, Bull 3–16
CLE: Collins 7–106, Green 5–39, Warfield 1–33, Kelly 1–21

Sunday, October 29
New York Giants 38, Browns 34
Yankee Stadium (62,903)
Brown jerseys/white pants

In a wild game on a perfect afternoon for football in New York City, the Browns nearly rallied all the way back from an 18-point deficit in the second half but fell just short to fall into a three-way tie for first in the Century Division. After taking a 10–0 lead with two quick scores in the opening minutes, the Browns were overwhelmed by the Giants over the next two periods as New York soared to a 35–17 lead after three touchdown passes and one rushing by QB Fran Tarkenton, who threw for 285 yards. But the Browns fought back, and after back-to-back scoring receptions by Paul Warfield, the New York lead was down to a single point. The Browns' last scoring threat stalled at the Giant 34 with a fourth-down sack, and the Giants added an insurance field goal in the final minutes. Frank Ryan nearly matched Tarkenton's display, throwing for 279 yards and three touchdowns, with Warfield snagging five receptions for 126 yards.

Record: 4–3

	1	2	3	4		
Browns	10	7	10	7	=	34
Giants	0	21	14	3	=	38

CLE-Collins 14-yd. pass from Ryan (Groza kick)
CLE-Groza 11-yd. FG
NYG-Tarkenton 15-yd. run (Gogolak kick)
NYG-Frederickson 3-yd. run (Gogolak kick)
CLE-Kelly 8-yd. run (Groza kick)
NYG-Thomas 32-yd. pass from Tarkenton (Gogolak kick)
NYG-Morrison 30-yd. pass from Tarkenton (Gogolak kick)
NYG-Morrison 12-yd. pass from Tarkenton (Gogolak kick)
CLE-Groza 37-yd. FG
CLE-Warfield 33-yd. pass from Ryan (Groza kick)
CLE-Warfield 32-yd. pass from Ryan (Groza kick)
NYG-Gogolak 47-yd. FG

Passing
CLE: Ryan 13–25–279 3 TD 1 INT
NYG: Tarkenton 18–30–285 3 TD 1 INT

Rushing
CLE: Kelly 11–68, Conjar 1–16, Green 9–13, Ryan 4–13
NYG: Frederickson 13–56, Koy 13–54, Tarkenton 7–29, Jones 1-(-2)

Receiving
CLE: Warfield 5–126, Collins 3–59, Kelly 3–58, Green 2–36
NYG: Thomas 5–110, Morrison 3–57, Jones 3–54, Koy 5–42, Frederickson 2–22

Sunday, November 5
Browns 34, Pittsburgh Steelers 14
Pitt Stadium (47,131)
Brown jerseys/white pants

For the second time in four weeks, the Browns knocked off the Steelers, though this encounter in Pittsburgh on a bright, chilly afternoon was much more lopsided. The Browns scored three early touchdowns and soared to a 31–7 third-quarter lead behind a dominating running attack that rolled up 181 yards behind Ernie Green's 83 and Leroy Kelly's 82. Rookie Ben Davis returned a punt 52 yards for a touchdown to open the floodgates in the second quarter, while once again the Cleveland defense stuffed Pittsburgh's ground game, holding the Steelers to less than three yards per rush.

Record: 5–3

	1	2	3	4		
Browns	14	10	7	3	=	34
Steelers	0	7	0	7	=	14

CLE-Collins 3-yd. pass from Ryan (Groza kick)
CLE-Kelly 41-yd. pass from Ryan (Groza kick)
CLE-Davis 52-yd. punt return (Groza kick)
PIT-Jefferson 18-yd. pass from Nelsen (Clark kick)
CLE-Groza 37-yd. FG
CLE-Green 27-yd. run (Groza kick)
CLE-Groza 35-yd. FG
PIT-Wilburn 13-yd. pass from Nelsen (Clark kick)

Passing
CLE: Ryan 13–21–161 2 TD 0 INT, Shiner 1–5–16 0 TD 0 INT
PIT: Nelsen 10–22–214 2 TD 1 INT, Nix 4–7–40 0 TD 1 INT, Hoak 0–1–0 0 TD 0 INT

Rushing
CLE: Green 12–83, Kelly 15–82, Conjar 4–20, Pietrosante 2–10, Ryan 3-(-2), Harraway 4-(-12)
PIT: Shy 9–31, Gros 7–27, Hoak 7–27, Asbury 1–7, Nix 2-(-6), Nelsen 2-(-14)

Receiving
CLE: Warfield 3–61, Kelly 3–49, Collins 3–36, Green 4–25
PIT: Hilton 6–88, Shy 1–55, Wilburn 2–42, Hoak 2–33, Jefferson 2–31, Gros 1–5

Sunday, November 12
Green Bay Packers 55, Browns 7
Milwaukee County Stadium (50,074)
White jerseys/white pants

In their worst defeat ever, the Browns were annihilated by the defending world champions and suffered their fifth straight loss to the Packers before a record crowd at County Stadium. Green Bay quickly set the tone by returning the opening kickoff for a touchdown, then intercepted Frank Ryan's first pass to set up another score. Green Bay's lead swelled to 28–0 before the Browns got on the board with a 59-yard touchdown run by Ernie Green. But the Packers' Travis Williams again returned the ensuing kickoff for another touchdown, capping Green Bay's 35-point first quarter. RB Donny Anderson scored four of the Packers' seven touchdowns as Green Bay rolled to 456 total yards and snagged seven Cleveland turnovers. The humiliating loss dropped the Browns a half-game behind St. Louis in the division race.
Record: 5–4

	1	2	3	4		
Browns	7	0	0	0	=	7
Packers	35	10	3	7	=	55

GB-Williams 87-yd. kickoff return (Chandler kick)
GB-Fleming 14-yd. pass from Starr (Chandler kick)
GB-Anderson 2-yd. run (Chandler kick)
GB-Anderson 27-yd. pass from Starr (Chandler kick)
CLE-Green 59-yd. run (Groza kick)
GB-Williams 85-yd. kickoff return (Chandler kick)
GB-Chandler 24-yd. FG
GB-Chandler 30-yd. FG
GB-Anderson 3-yd. run (Chandler kick)

Passing
CLE: Ryan 7–21–97 0 TD 4 INT, Shiner 0–1–0 0 TD 0 INT
GB: Starr 14–21–249 2 TD 1 INT, Horn 1–3–17 0 TD 0 INT

Rushing
CLE: Kelly 14–82, Green 4–74, Pietrosante 1–9, Ryan 1–0, Shiner 1-(-3)
GB: Wilson 16–100, Anderson 17–56, Williams 4–43, Mercein 6–24, Starr 2–12

Receiving
CLE: Conjar 3–40, Warfield 2–24, Smith 1–18, Morin 1–15
GB: Anderson 5–103, Dale 5–94, Dowler 2–26, Brown 1–17, Fleming 1–14, Wilson 1–12

Sunday, November 19
Browns 14, Minnesota Vikings 10
Cleveland Stadium (68,431)
White jerseys/white pants

The Browns bounced back from their blowout loss to pull out a gritty victory over the Vikings on an overcast, windy afternoon on the lake to take over sole possession of first place in the Century Division. After Minnesota took a 10–0 lead in what became a defensive battle, a Leroy Kelly touchdown cut the margin to three before the half. But the Vikings were poised to win, still leading with just over three minutes to play and had the ball at midfield. But DT Jim Kanicki caused a fumble, and Browns' DE Walter Johnson recovered to give Cleveland new life. Nine plays later, sparked by a 30-yard Kelly run, the Browns' star tailback slammed into the end zone again from the Minnesota 1 to provide the winning points with 28 seconds remaining. It capped a brilliant day for the Cleveland running game, which tallied 210 yards, led by Kelly's 123. It atoned for an off-day for the Browns' passing game, which contributed only 93 yards by Frank Ryan and allowed eight sacks. The Cleveland defense limited the Vikings to just over 200 yards of offense and held them scoreless in the second half to keep the Browns in the game.
Record: 6–4

	1	2	3	4		
Vikings	7	3	0	0	=	10
Browns	0	7	0	7	=	14

MIN-Osborn 4-yd. run (Cox kick)
MIN-Cox 20-yd. FG
CLE-Kelly 1-yd. run (Groza kick)
CLE-Kelly 1-yd. run (Groza kick)

Passing
MIN: Vander Kelen 4–12–70 0 TD 1 INT, Kapp 7–13–40 0 TD 0 INT
CLE: Ryan 11–21–93 0 TD 0 INT

Rushing
MIN: Osborn 17–59, Brown 11–33, Kapp 3–6, Vander Kelen 1–1
CLE: Kelly 26–123, Green 13–78, Ryan 2–9

Receiving
MIN: Phillips 3–59, Washington 2–18, Brown 1–11, Flatley 1–11, Lindsey 1–7, McKeever 1–4, Osborn 2–0
CLE: Collins 3–37, Warfield 2–28, Green 4–25, Smith 1–3, Kelly 1–0

Sunday, November 26
Browns 42, Washington Redskins 37
Cleveland Stadium (72,798)
White jerseys/white pants

In an offensive showcase that saw the teams combine for more than 900 yards of total offense and 50 first downs, the Browns built a commanding lead and then held off the Redskins in the fourth quarter to stay a game ahead of the Giants in the division race. After Washington cut an 18-point Cleveland lead to five, the Redskins regained possession at their own 23 with 1:33 to play and quickly drove into Cleveland territory. Facing fourth down with 20 seconds to go, Washington QB Sonny Jurgensen was sacked by Bill Glass—the Browns' fifth of the day—to wrap up a thrilling victory. Leroy Kelly once again led the way on offense, rushing for 163 yards and a pair of touchdowns as he went over the 1,000-yard mark for the second straight season. The Browns also added a pair of dazzling touchdowns on big plays—first when LB Johnny Brewer picked off a pass tipped by LB Jim Houston and raced 70 yards for a touchdown, then when Carl Ward set a team record that still stands with a 104-yard kickoff return for a score. The Cleveland defense struggled to stop Jurgensen, who threw for 418 yards, as three Washington receivers topped the 100-yard mark. The Browns also overcame a whopping 148 yards in penalties.
Record: 7–4

	1	2	3	4		
Redskins	0	17	7	13	=	37
Browns	14	14	7	7	=	42

CLE-Kelly 42-yd. run (Groza kick)
CLE-Brewer 70-yd. interception return (Groza kick)
WAS-Taylor 23-yd. pass from Jurgensen (Mingo kick)
WAS-Mingo 27-yd. FG
CLE-Ward 104-yd. kickoff return (Groza kick)
CLE-Warfield 48-yd. pass from Ryan (Groza kick)
WAS-Taylor 15-yd. pass from Jurgensen (Mingo kick)
CLE-Green 1-yd. run (Groza kick)
WAS-Allen 1-yd. run (Mingo kick)
CLE-Kelly 21-yd. run (Groza kick)
WAS-Mitchell 48-yd. pass from Jurgensen (Mingo kick)
WAS-Allen 1-yd. run (kick failed)

Passing
WAS: Jurgensen 32–50–418 3 TD 1 INT
CLE: Ryan 11–17–233 1 TD 0 INT

Rushing
WAS: Allen 14–59, Whitfield 14–28, Jurgensen 1–21
CLE: Kelly 20–163, Green 13–41, Ryan 1-(-1)

Receiving
WAS: Taylor 11–123, Mitchell 6–106, Whitfield 8–102, Smith 4–63, Allen 3–24
CLE: Warfield 3–96, Collins 3–58, Kelly 2–44, Green 2–24, Smith 1–11

Sunday, December 3
Browns 24, New York Giants 14
Cleveland Stadium (78,594)
White jerseys/white pants

The Browns eliminated the Giants from the division race and maintained a one-and-a-half-game lead over St. Louis with a businesslike victory on a chilly December afternoon. After the Browns built a 17–0 halftime lead, the Giants cut the margin to 10 points and were poised to draw closer after driving to the Cleveland 24 in the fourth quarter. But for the second straight week, the Browns came up with a huge interception return for a touchdown, this time by Jim Houston, to put the game out of reach. It capped a good day for Houston, who also blocked a New York field-goal attempt in the first quarter. The Cleveland running game again rode to the rescue of an ineffective air attack, compiling 183 yards as the Browns averaged more than six yards per carry.
Record: 8–4

	1	2	3	4		
Giants	0	0	7	7	=	14
Browns	10	7	0	7	=	24

CLE-Groza 15-yd. FG
CLE-Kelly 1-yd. run (Groza kick)
CLE-Collins 24-yd. pass from Ryan (Groza kick)
NYG-Morrison 9-yd. run (Gogolak kick)
CLE-Houston 79-yd. interception return (Groza kick)
NYG-Thomas 7-yd. pass from Tarkenton (Gogolak kick)

Passing
NYG: Tarkenton 26–43–218 1 TD 2 INT
CLE: Ryan 6–13–61 1 TD 1 INT, Kelly 0–1–0 0 TD 0 INT

Rushing
NYG: Morrison 15–86, Koy 13–60, Tarkenton 1–15
CLE: Kelly 17–94, Green 8–41, Ryan 2–21, Warfield 1–18, Collins 1–6, Pietrosante 1–3

Receiving
NYG: Thomas 9–79, Jones 5–76, Morrison 9–43, Koy 2–15, Crespino 1–5
CLE: Collins 3–45, Kelly 2–9, Green 1–7

THE TEAM OF THE CENTURY

As the NFL expanded in the 1960s—and prepared for the merger with the American Football League in 1970—the league was split into four divisions for the first time in 1967: the Capital, Century, Coastal, and Central. This alignment would last through 1969 and serve as the template for the new structure once the AFL was enveloped.

In those three seasons, the Browns dominated the Century Division, rolling to titles each year. The St. Louis Cardinals and Pittsburgh Steelers remained rivals all three seasons, while the New York Giants were replaced by the New Orleans Saints for 1968 before switching back from the Capital Division for 1969.

In the short-lived era of the Century Division, the Browns were the only team to post an overall winning record:

Cleveland Browns	**29–12–1 (.702)**
St. Louis Cardinals	**19–20–3 (.488)**
New York Giants	**13–15 (.464)**
New Orleans Saints	**4–9–1 (.321)**
Pittsburgh Steelers	**7–33–2 (.190)**

The Browns also notched a 14–4 record against Century Division opponents.

Sunday, December 10
Browns 20, St. Louis Cardinals 16
Busch Stadium (47,782)
White jerseys/white pants

Through a layer of fog in St. Louis, the Browns completed a season sweep of the Cardinals and clinched the first Century Division title. Winning by the identical score as their first meeting, the Browns took an early lead on a leaping touchdown catch by wideout Paul Warfield over two defenders. The Cardinals fought back to take a 9–7 halftime lead, but the Browns rallied to go up by 11 following an interception return for a touchdown by Jim Houston for the second straight game. St. Louis pulled back within four points midway through the fourth period, but the Browns ate up the next seven minutes and halted the Cardinals on their final harried drive. Cleveland's offense compiled its worst performance of the season, managing just 131 total yards and eight first downs as Leroy Kelly was negated, held to 15 yards on 15 carries.
Record: 9–4

	1	2	3	4		
Browns	0	7	6	7	=	20
Cardinals	0	9	0	7	=	16

STL-Bakken 12-yd. FG
CLE-Warfield 38-yd. pass from Ryan (Groza kick)
STL-Bakken 42-yd. FG
STL-Bakken 26-yd. FG
CLE-Groza 33-yd. FG
CLE-Groza 23-yd. FG
CLE-Houston 18-yd. interception return (Groza kick)
STL-Smith 15-yd. pass from Hart (Bakken kick)

Passing
CLE: Ryan 8–15–66 1 TD 0 INT
STL: Hart 18–36–182 1 TD 1 INT, Smith 0–1–0 0 TD 1 INT

Rushing
CLE: Green 12–48, Ryan 2–19, Kelly 15–15
STL: Gautt 16–63, Roland 12–27, Crenshaw 5–19, Williams 1–7, Hart 1–6, Thornton 1–3, Latourette 1-(-4)

Receiving
CLE: Warfield 2–57, Kelly 1–6, Green 5–3
STL: Smith 6–91, Conrad 5–46, Gambrell 3–21, Gautt 2–15, Williams 2–9

Sunday, December 17
Philadelphia Eagles 28, Browns 24
Franklin Field (60,658)
White jerseys/white pants

Resting most of their starters in preparation for the playoffs, the Browns dug a deep hole against the mediocre Eagles, and then saw a fourth-quarter rally fall short. After Philadelphia grabbed a 28–10 lead midway through the final period, two touchdown passes from Cleveland's Gary Lane—who went the distance at quarterback—to WR Clifton McNeil pulled the Browns within four, but they could draw no closer. With 62 rushing yards, Leroy Kelly finished the season with 1,205 to lead the NFL, once again averaging more than five yards per carry. While essentially meaningless, the defeat would set a tone that would carry over into the Browns' final two frustrating games.

Record: 9–5

	1	2	3	4		
Browns	7	3	0	14	=	24
Eagles	0	7	7	14	=	28

CLE-Kelly 2-yd. run (Groza kick)
PHI-Lang 1-yd. pass from Snead (Baker kick)
CLE-Groza 32-yd. FG
PHI-Lang 8-yd. run (Baker kick)
PHI-Woodeshick 43-yd. pass from Snead (Baker kick)
PHI-Hawkins 60-yd. pass from Snead (Baker kick)
CLE-McNeil 5-yd. pass from Lane (Groza kick)
CLE-McNeil 5-yd. pass from Lane (Groza kick)

Passing
CLE: Lane 19–39–211 2 TD 1 INT
PHI: Snead 14–28–234 3 TD 0 INT

Rushing
CLE: Kelly 15–62, Conjar 9–35, Lane 2–21, Pietrosante 4–16, Harraway 1-(-2)
PHI: Woodeshick 15–70, Lang 8–48, Snead 1–7

Receiving
CLE: Morin 6–75, Pietrosante 5–61, McNeil 3–33, Conjar 3–28, Smith 1–11, Warfield 1–3
PHI: Hawkins 3–98, Woodeshick 4–75, Ballman 4–58, Ditka 1–5, Lang 2-(-2)

Eastern Conference Playoff
Sunday, December 24
Dallas Cowboys 52, Browns 14
Cotton Bowl (70,786)
Brown jerseys/white pants

With a trip to the NFL title game on the line on a sunny Christmas Eve in Texas, the Browns gave up a smorgasbord of big plays to the Cowboys, who cruised to a lopsided victory in the first of three straight playoff matchups between the teams.

The catalyst for Dallas was WR Bob Hayes, who compiled 285 total yards, including an 86-yard touchdown reception and punt returns of 64 and 58 yards that set up scores. The Cowboys sprinted to 24 points before the Browns got on the board with a Milt Morin touchdown catch late in the second quarter. Dallas then tacked on four more touchdowns in the second half—including a 60-yard interception return—to top the 50-point mark.

The Browns' lone highlight came in the final minutes when Paul Warfield caught a 75-yard touchdown pass to close out the scoring. While Warfield compiled 99 receiving yards for the game, Leroy Kelly also put forth a nice effort, rushing for 96 yards on 15 carries, while Lou Groza booted two extra points in what would be his final NFL game. But the Dallas offense, which rolled up more than 400 total yards, was simply unstoppable, and the Cowboys earned a trip to Green Bay to face the Packers the following Sunday in what would become known as the "Ice Bowl."

	1	2	3	4		
Browns	0	7	0	7	=	14
Cowboys	14	10	21	7	=	52

DAL-Baynham 3-yd. pass from Meredith (Villanueva kick)
DAL-Perkins 4-yd. run (Villanueva kick)
DAL-Hayes 86-yd. pass from Meredith (Villanueva kick)
DAL-Villanueva 10-yd. FG
CLE-Morin 13-yd. pass from Ryan (Groza kick)
DAL-Baynham 1-yd. run (Villanueva kick)
DAL-Perkins 1-yd. run (Villanueva kick)
DAL-Green 60-yd. interception return (Villanueva kick)
DAL-Baynham 1-yd. run (Villanueva kick)
CLE-Warfield 75-yd. pass from Ryan (Groza kick)

Passing
CLE: Ryan 14–30–194 2 TD 1 INT
DAL: Meredith 11–13–212 2 TD 0 INT, Morton 1–3–13 0 TD 1 INT

Rushing
CLE: Kelly 15–96, Green 10–49, Ryan 2–14
DAL: Perkins 18–74, Baynham 13–50, Garrison 9–33, Clarke 1–8, Reeves 3–7, Meredith 2–6

Receiving
CLE: Warfield 3–99, Kelly 4–39, Morin 3–35, Green 3–18, Collins 1–3
DAL: Hayes 5–144, Rentzel 3–65, Reeves 1–9, Perkins 1–4, Baynham 2–3

1968 Playoff Bowl
Sunday, January 7
Los Angeles Rams 30, Browns 6
Orange Bowl (37,102)
White jerseys/white pants

In their third trip to the Playoff Bowl, the Browns once again were defeated, this time in a blowout to the powerful 11–1–2 Los Angeles Rams, champions of the Coastal Division, who'd been overwhelmed by the Packers in their divisional playoff.

On a hot and humid afternoon in Miami before a largely apathetic crowd, the Rams soared to a 17–0 halftime lead and never looked back, dominating the struggling Cleveland offense. The Browns' lone points came in the fourth quarter when Leroy Kelly—held to just 59 yards rushing on the day—scored on a two-yard touchdown run on a drive orchestrated by backup QB Gary Lane. Fittingly, the extra point was blocked by Rams' lineman Deacon Jones.

Los Angeles QB Roman Gabriel was named MVP as the Western Conference won for the seventh time in eight Playoff Bowls. The exhibition would be abandoned two years later following the AFL/NFL merger with the Browns matching the Detroit Lions and Dallas Cowboys for most appearances with three.

	1	2	3	4		
Rams	10	7	3	10	=	30
Browns	0	0	0	6	=	6

LA-Casey 21-yd. pass from Gabriel (Gossett kick)
LA-Gossett 41-yd. FG
LA-Truax 2-yd. pass from Gabriel (Gossett kick)
LA-Gossett 46-yd. FG
CLE-Kelly 2-yd. run (kick failed)
LA-Ellison 9-yd. run (Gossett kick)
LA-Gossett 19-yd. FG

1968

Sunday, September 15
Browns 24, New Orleans Saints 10
Tulane Stadium (74,215)
Brown jerseys/white pants

Two touchdowns in the final two minutes propelled the Browns to an opening-day victory in New Orleans against the second-year Saints. After both teams scored 10 points in the second quarter, heavy rain swept through the stadium, and the game remained tied late into the fourth. Then an interception by Browns' DB Ernie Kellermann returned to the New Orleans 46 sparked the winning drive. RB Leroy Kelly put the Browns ahead for good moments later when he swept around right end for an eight-yard touchdown with less than two minutes remaining. Cleveland put the icing on the cake when DE Bill Glass intercepted a pass and returned it 17 yards for another score to make the final 24–10. It capped a nice day for the Browns' defense, which collected three turnovers and three sacks while limiting New Orleans to just over 200 total yards. Kelly paced the Cleveland offensive attack with 107 yards on 20 carries while scoring a pair of touchdowns, and rookie kicker Don Cockroft had an impressive debut, booting a field goal and connecting on three extra points.

Record: 1–0

	1	2	3	4		
Browns	0	10	0	14	=	24
Saints	0	10	0	0	=	10

NO-Kilmer 1-yd. run (Durkee kick)
CLE-Kelly 30-yd. pass from Ryan (Cockroft kick)
CLE-Cockroft 22-yd. FG
NO-Durkee 40-yd. FG
CLE-Kelly 8-yd. run (Cockroft kick)
CLE-Glass 17-yd. interception return (Cockroft kick)

Passing
CLE: Ryan 10–20–201 1 TD 1 INT
NO: Kilmer 15–31–152 0 TD 3 INT

Rushing
CLE: Kelly 20–107, Harraway 13–29, Ryan 2–17
NO: Schultz 15–55, Barrington 7–27, Baker 4–2, Kilmer 2–1

Receiving
CLE: Collins 4–94, Warfield 3–65, Kelly 1–30, Harraway 2–12
NO: Abramowicz 2–67, Hester 1–22, Parks 3–20, Gilliam 2–16, Schultz 3–12, Barrington 3–11, Stickles 1–4

Sunday, September 22
Dallas Cowboys 28, Browns 7
Cotton Bowl (68,733)
Brown jerseys/white pants

On a hot, humid afternoon in the Cotton Bowl, the Cowboys pulled away in the second half and coasted to an easy victory over the Browns—their fourth straight over Cleveland. Dallas built a 14–0 lead after a fumble return for a touchdown, but the Browns cut the margin to seven points at the half following a long touchdown pass from QB Frank Ryan to WR Paul Warfield. A pair of touchdowns by Dallas RB Dan Reeves in the second half put the Cowboys in the clear as the Browns' offense was unable to pose any serious threats in the final two quarters. Cleveland allowed five sacks on the day and failed to cash in on a pair of Don Cockroft field-goal attempts—a miss from 48 yards and a block from 36. Newly acquired QB Bill Nelsen made his Cleveland debut in the final minutes, completing his first two passes.

Record: 1–1

	1	2	3	4		
Browns	0	7	0	0	=	7
Cowboys	0	14	7	7	=	28

DAL-Baynham 2-yd. run (Clark kick)
DAL-Townes 20-yd. fumble return (Clark kick)
CLE-Warfield 55-yd. pass from Ryan (Cockroft kick)
DAL-Reeves 4-yd. run (Clark kick)
DAL-Reeves 1-yd. run (Clark kick)

Passing
CLE: Ryan 10–17–194 1 TD 0 INT, Nelsen 2–2–3 0 TD 0 INT
DAL: Meredith 10–17–156 0 TD 0 INT

Rushing
CLE: Kelly 13–58, Harraway 10–18, Ryan 3–11
DAL: Reeves 17–98, Perkins 18–70, Meredith 3–20, Baynham 3–13, Garrison 3–2

Receiving
CLE: Warfield 3–85, Kelly 2–39, Harraway 2–38, Collins 1–17, Morin 2–15, Smith 1–4, Leigh 1-(-1)
DAL: Rentzel 4–68, Garrison 1–27, Hayes 2–22, Perkins 1–15, Reeves 1–15, Norman 1–9

Sunday, September 29
Los Angeles Rams 24, Browns 6
Cleveland Stadium (82,514)
Brown jerseys/white pants

Wearing brown jerseys at home for the first time in five years (and last time for seven years), the Browns were completely humiliated by the undefeated Rams before a massive crowd stunned into silence in the home opener. Despite an ineffective offense, the Browns made a game of it in the first half, cashing in on a long Frank Ryan-to-Paul Warfield scoring pass for the second straight week to pull within 10–6 at the intermission. But Cleveland was unable to cross midfield for the rest of the game as the Rams forced three turnovers, collected four sacks, and held the Browns to a harmless 129 total yards and just six first downs. In what proved to be the final start of his NFL career, Frank Ryan was miserable, completing only three of 13 passes while throwing a pair of interceptions. Meanwhile, the Browns' defense hung tough for as long as it could, but the Rams' first 10 points were set up by turnovers, and Los Angeles wound up running nearly twice as many offensive plays. With the rout, the Rams picked up their first win in Cleveland since moving to Los Angeles 23 years before. The embarrassing defeat seemed to suggest 1968 was going to signify a down year for a young Browns team.

Record: 1–2

	1	2	3	4		
Rams	10	0	0	14	=	24
Browns	0	6	0	0	=	6

LA-Gossett 22-yd. FG
LA-Mason 6-yd. run (Gossett kick)
CLE-Warfield 57-yd. pass from Ryan (kick failed)
LA-Casey 26-yd. pass from Gabriel (Gossett kick)
LA-Mason 4-yd. run (Gossett kick)

Passing
LA: Gabriel 17–34–176 1 TD 1 INT
CLE: Ryan 3–13–103 1 TD 2 INT, Kelly 0–1–0 0 TD 0 INT, Nelsen 1–2-(-6) 0 TD 0 INT

Rushing
LA: Bass 23–134, Mason 17–54, Dyer 1–0, Gabriel 1–0
CLE: Kelly 11–49, Ryan 4–21, Leigh 1–5, Harraway 4-(-9)

Receiving
LA: Casey 4–55, Truax 5–52, Snow 3–44, Bass 3–17, Mason 2–8
CLE: Warfield 1–57, Collins 2–46, Kelly 1-(-6)

Saturday, October 5
Browns 31, Pittsburgh Steelers 24
Cleveland Stadium (81,865)
White jerseys/white pants

The Browns got back on the right track in their annual Saturday-night affair with the Steelers, breaking open a tie game in the third quarter to pick up a desperately needed victory. Former Steeler Bill Nelsen made his first Cleveland start against his former team, replacing the ineffective Frank Ryan and provided the spark the Browns were looking for. Cleveland rolled to nearly 400 total yards as Nelsen completed 16 of 25 passes, and the running game rolled up 176 yards, with 128 coming from Leroy Kelly. After Pittsburgh fought back from a 14–3 deficit to tie the game at 17 in the third quarter, the Browns responded with a pair of touchdowns. The first came on a short Kelly run after the Steelers fumbled a punt return. They scored the second when, after a 25-yard gain, Kelly lateraled the ball to WR Eppie Barney, who took it the final eight yards for what proved to be the winning touchdown. Pittsburgh pulled back within seven on a fumble return for a score in the final minutes but could draw no closer.

Record: 2–2

	1	2	3	4		
Steelers	3	7	7	7	=	24
Browns	7	10	7	7	=	31

PIT-Lusteg 25-yd. FG
CLE-Leigh 20-yd. run (Cockroft kick)
CLE-Warfield 28-yd. pass from Nelsen (Cockroft kick)
PIT-Jefferson 13-yd. pass from Shiner (Lusteg kick)
CLE-Cockroft 27-yd. FG
PIT-Jefferson 23-yd. pass from Shiner (Lusteg kick)
CLE-Kelly 2-yd. run (Cockroft kick)
CLE-Barney 8-yd. lateral from Kelly (Cockroft kick)
PIT-Martha 60-yd. fumble return (Lusteg kick)

Passing
PIT: Shiner 11–24–141 2 TD 1 INT, Hoak 2–3–24 0 TD 0 INT
CLE: Nelsen 16–25–190 1 TD 1 INT

Rushing
PIT: Gros 15–58, Hoak 12–58
CLE: Kelly 25–128, Leigh 8–53, Harraway 3-(-2), Nelsen 2-(-3)

Receiving
PIT: Jefferson 5–78, Wilburn 5–66, Gros 3–21
CLE: Collins 2–73, Warfield 5–70, Morin 3–46, Barney 3–16, Leigh 1-(-7), Kelly 2-(-8)

Sunday, October 13
St. Louis Cardinals 27, Browns 21
Cleveland Stadium (79,349)
White jerseys/white pants

The Browns were unable to build on the previous week's victory as a comeback attempt fell short on a warm October afternoon on the lakefront. Though the Cardinals had been struggling, losing three of their first four games, they jumped to a 20–0 lead in the second quarter before the Browns clawed back into the contest. Bill Nelsen, making his second start, threw for a pair of touchdowns—including a 65-yard strike to Paul Warfield—to cut the margin to six points early in the third quarter. After St. Louis pushed the lead back to 13, Nelsen scored on a one-yard plunge early in the fourth quarter to make it 27–21. They then appeared poised to take the lead after regaining possession near midfield, but Nelsen was hit on a pass attempt and intercepted to halt the Browns' momentum. Cleveland later drove to the St. Louis 48 with three minutes left but was forced to punt and didn't regain possession until less than a minute remained. Nelsen created several big plays, throwing for 324 yards, including 151 to TE Milt Morin in what proved to be the finest game of his career. But the Browns' running game was nonexistent, collecting just 22 yards as Leroy Kelly was held to just five on 11 carries.
Record: 2–3

	1	2	3	4		
Cardinals	3	17	7	0	=	27
Browns	0	7	7	7	=	21

STL-Bakken 43-yd. FG
STL-Hart 1-yd. run (Bakken kick)
STL-Bakken 21-yd. FG
STL-Shivers 2-yd. run (Bakken kick)
CLE-Morin 22-yd. pass from Nelsen (Cockroft kick)
CLE-Warfield 65-yd. pass from Nelsen (Cockroft kick)
STL-Williams 33-yd. pass from Hart (Bakken kick)
CLE-Nelsen 1-yd. run (Cockroft kick)

Passing
STL: Hart 9–24–140 1 TD 2 INT
CLE: Nelsen 17–39–324 2 TD 2 INT, Kelly 0–1–0 0 TD 0 INT

Rushing
STL: Crenshaw 19–94, Roland 12–30, Edwards 3–12, Shivers 2–8, Hart 2–3, Williams 1–0
CLE: Harraway 5–16, Kelly 11–5, Nelsen 1–1

Receiving
STL: Williams 4–84, Smith 2–31, Crenshaw 1–18, Roland 2–7
CLE: Morin 8–151, Warfield 3–93, Kelly 2–46, Barney 2–31, Harraway 2–3

Sunday, October 20
Browns 30, Baltimore Colts 20
Memorial Stadium (60,238)
White jerseys/white pants

The Browns turned their season around on a gorgeous autumn afternoon in Baltimore with a stunning upset of the 5–0 Colts. Entering the game as 15-point underdogs, the Browns set the tone early with the first of three Bill Nelsen touchdown passes against a defense that had allowed only 58 points in its five games. A fourth-down strike to Eppie Barney early in the third quarter put the Browns up 21–7, then after a pair of Baltimore field goals, Cleveland put the game away on a short Leroy Kelly touchdown run in the fourth quarter. Kelly turned in one of the finest performances of his career, rushing for 130 yards against the mighty Baltimore defense along with a pair of touchdowns. Another key factor was the season debut of RB Ernie Green, who'd missed the first five games with a knee injury. Conversely, the Browns' defense forced five turnovers, including three interceptions of veteran QB Johnny Unitas, who replaced starter Earl Morrall in the second half, but completed only one of 11 passes. The victory marked the beginning of what would become an eight-game winning streak for the Browns and represented the only loss in what would be a magnificent Colts' campaign.
Record: 3–3

THE BEST TEAMS THE BROWNS HAVE BEATEN

Almost every year, the Browns will tally at least one victory over a team in the midst of a stellar season. But over their history they've notched a handful of memorable victories over some truly remarkable teams enjoying dominant seasons. Below is a list of the greatest teams the Browns have defeated.

t11. **1981 San Francisco 49ers (13–3 .813)**
Browns defeated, 15–12
1995 Kansas City Chiefs (13–3 .813)
Browns defeated, 35–17

t9. **1951 New York Giants (9–2–1 .818)**
Browns defeated, 14–13 and 10–0
1954 Detroit Lions (9–2–1 .818)
*Browns defeated, 56–10***

t7. **1950 New York Giants (10–2 .833)**
*Browns defeated, 8–3**
1960 Philadelphia Eagles (10–2 .833)
Browns defeated, 41–24

6. **1969 Dallas Cowboys (11–2–1 .846)**
Browns defeated, 42–10 and 38–14†

t3. **1962 New York Giants (12–2 .857)**
Browns defeated, 17–7
1964 Baltimore Colts (12–2 .857)
*Browns defeated, 27–0***
1968 Dallas Cowboys (12–2 .857)
Browns defeated, 31–20†

2. **2010 New England Patriots (14–2 .875)**
Browns defeated, 34–14

1. **1968 Baltimore Colts (13–1 .929)**
Browns defeated, 30–20

**American Division playoff*
***NFL Championship Game*
†Eastern Conference playoff

	1	2	3	4		
Browns	7	7	7	9	=	30
Colts	0	7	6	7	=	20

CLE-Kelly 2-yd. pass from Nelsen (Cockroft kick)
BAL-Matte 23-yd. run (Michaels kick)
CLE-Warfield 6-yd. pass from Nelsen (Cockroft kick)
CLE-Barney 2-yd. pass from Nelsen (Cockroft kick)
BAL-Michaels 17-yd. FG
BAL-Michaels 33-yd. FG
CLE-Kelly 4-yd. run (kick failed)
CLE-Cockroft 11-yd. FG
BAL-Richardson 8-yd. pass from Morrall (Michaels kick)

Passing
CLE: Nelsen 15–23–137 3 TD 0 INT
BAL: Morrall 10–18–130 1 TD 1 INT, Unitas 1–11–12 0 TD 3 INT

Rushing
CLE: Kelly 30–130, Nelsen 4–32, Green 5–12, Leigh 4–5
BAL: Matte 13–64, Hill 9–23, Morrall 1–0, Unitas 1-(-6)

Receiving
CLE: Warfield 5–46, Morin 3–41, Kelly 2–18, Barney 2–17, Green 2–11, Leigh 1–4
BAL: Mackey 3–41, Orr 3–38, Matte 2–37, Hill 2–18, Richardson 1–8

Sunday, October 27
Browns 30, Atlanta Falcons 7
Cleveland Stadium (67,723)
White jerseys/white pants

Picking up where they left off the week before, the Browns cruised to an easy victory over the struggling Falcons behind an explosive offensive performance. They set the tone with an 80-yard march on their first possession as Bill Nelsen completed his first six pass attempts, and the Browns took a 20–0 lead at the half. It swelled to 30–0 in the fourth quarter following another touchdown reception by Paul Warfield, who extended his scoring streak to six games. The Cleveland offense rolled to 444 total yards—112 rushing by Leroy Kelly—while the defense racked up eight sacks and held the Falcons scoreless until the final minute of the game. With the win, the Browns moved over the .500 mark for good and remained tied with St. Louis for first place in the Century Division.
Record: 4–3

	1	2	3	4		
Falcons	0	0	0	7	=	7
Browns	7	13	3	7	=	30

CLE-Kelly 5-yd. run (Cockroft kick)
CLE-Kelly 1-yd. run (Cockroft kick)
CLE-Cockroft 25-yd. FG
CLE-Cockroft 42-yd. FG
CLE-Cockroft 34-yd. FG
CLE-Warfield 22-yd. pass from Nelsen (Cockroft kick)
ATL-Donohoe 7-yd. pass from Berry (Etter kick)

Passing
ATL: Berry 8–10–107 1 TD 1 INT, Johnson 6–15–70 0 TD 1 INT, Wages 1–1–21 0 TD 0 INT
CLE: Nelsen 18–27–248 1 TD 0 INT

Rushing
ATL: Butler 13–73, McCarthy 5–27, Johnson 1–26, Berry 1–13, Dunn 3–4, Lee 3–4
CLE: Kelly 19–112, Green 9–45, Leigh 4–41, Morrison 1-(-2)

Receiving
ATL: Long 4–73, Flatley 3–45, Butler 3–36, McCarthy 2–27, Donohoe 1–7, Wages 1–7
CLE: Morin 5–98, Warfield 4–80, Barney 3–34, Kelly 3–29, Smith 1–7, Green 2–0

Sunday, November 3
Browns 33, San Francisco 49ers 21
Kezar Stadium (31,359)
White jerseys/white pants

Behind what proved to be the finest game of Leroy Kelly's Hall of Fame career, the Browns rallied from an early deficit to pick up a key win in San Francisco. Kelly rolled up 174 yards on 27 carries and provided the winning points on a short touchdown run in the third quarter that put the Browns ahead 23–14 after they'd trailed 14–3 early in the second quarter. Don Cockroft kicked four field goals, and Bill Nelsen threw a pair of touchdowns to Milt Morin while the Cleveland defense forced five turnovers and limited San Francisco to less than three yards per carry on the ground. With a St. Louis victory in Philadelphia, the Browns and Cardinals remained tied for first place in the division.
Record: 5–3

	1	2	3	4		
Browns	3	13	10	7	=	33
49ers	7	7	0	7	=	21

CLE-Cockroft 18-yd. FG
SF-Crow 4-yd. pass from Brodie (Patera kick)
SF-McNeil 9-yd. pass from Brodie (Patera kick)
CLE-Morin 32-yd. pass from Nelsen (Cockroft kick)
CLE-Cockroft 46-yd. FG
CLE-Cockroft 14-yd. FG
CLE-Kelly 2-yd. run (Cockroft kick)
CLE-Cockroft 16-yd. FG
CLE-Morin 15-yd. pass from Nelsen (Cockroft kick)
SF-Windsor 5-yd. pass from Brodie (Patera kick)

Passing
CLE: Nelsen 11–33–148 2 TD 2 INT
SF: Brodie 23–37–241 3 TD 2 INT

Rushing
CLE: Kelly 27–174, Harraway 9–37, Leigh 2–13
SF: Willard 13–39, Lewis 8–23, Tucker 1–16, Daniels 1–2, Brodie 1-(-10)

Receiving
CLE: Morin 6–71, Warfield 4–63, Barney 1–14
SF: McNeil 5–92, Witcher 4–54, Willard 4–26, Cunningham 2–25, Crow 3–23, Windsor 2–18, Tucker 3–3

Sunday, November 10
Browns 35, New Orleans Saints 17
Cleveland Stadium (71,025)
White jerseys/white pants

Sparked by another marvelous performance by Leroy Kelly and the Cleveland offense, the Browns rolled to their fourth straight victory. Kelly rushed for 127 yards and added 104 yards receiving while scoring three touchdowns as the offense rolled up a season-high 467 total yards. Bill Nelsen threw four touchdown passes but also three interceptions as the Browns turned the ball over six times. Cleveland's giveaways helped the Saints pull within 14–10 in the third quarter, but the Browns responded with a 68-yard touchdown on a screen pass to Kelly to open up the floodgates. With the win, and a Cardinals' tie against Pittsburgh, the Browns took over sole possession of first place in the division.
Record: 6–3

	1	2	3	4		
Saints	3	0	7	7	=	17
Browns	0	14	14	7	=	35

NO-Durkee 42-yd. FG
CLE-Kelly 5-yd. pass from Nelsen (Cockroft kick)
CLE-Warfield 12-yd. pass from Nelsen (Cockroft kick)
NO-Abramowicz 8-yd. pass from Sweetan (Durkee kick)
CLE-Kelly 68-yd. pass from Nelsen (Cockroft kick)
CLE-Kelly 1-yd. run (Cockroft kick)
CLE-Morin 9-yd. pass from Nelsen (Cockroft kick)
NO-Hester 7-yd. pass from South (Durkee kick)

Passing
NO: Sweetan 10–27–103 1 TD 2 INT, South 5–15–50 1 TD 1 INT, Parks 0–1–0 0 TD 0 INT
CLE: Nelsen 10–24–262 4 TD 3 INT

Rushing
NO: McCall 9–41, Barrington 6–41, Lorick 7–23, Poage 1–22, Schultz 4–19, Wheelwright 2–14, Sweetan 1–1
CLE: Kelly 17–127, Harraway 9–79, Green 4–10, Morrison 2–4, Leigh 2–2, Nelsen 1–0

Receiving
NO: Abramowicz 6–69, Lorick 3–45, McCall 2–15, Poage 1–11, Hester 1–7, Parks 1–6, Barrington 1–0
CLE: Warfield 5–107, Kelly 3–104, McDonald 1–42, Morin 1–9

Sunday, November 17
Browns 45, Pittsburgh Steelers 24
Pitt Stadium (41,572)
Brown jerseys/white pants

With the Cleveland offense once again on a roll, the Browns' defense also got into the act in a blowout victory over Pittsburgh. Though Leroy Kelly was held to just 19 yards rushing, Bill Nelsen and the passing game rode to the rescue, collecting 352 yards through the air and five touchdown passes. After Nelsen threw for 258 yards and three scores against his former team, he left the game with an injury in the fourth quarter and was replaced by Frank Ryan, who promptly added two more scoring passes (and two quick interceptions) as the Browns scored 21 points in the final period to win going away. While the offense stole the show with nearly 400 yards, the defense forced seven turnovers, including six interceptions. Combined with a St. Louis loss to Baltimore, the victory enabled the Browns to open up a game-and-a-half lead in the Century Division.
Record: 7–3

	1	2	3	4		
Browns	14	10	0	21	=	45
Steelers	7	3	0	14	=	24

CLE-Kelly 7-yd. run (Cockroft kick)
PIT-Wilburn 10-yd. pass from Shiner (Lusteg kick)
CLE-Green 62-yd. pass from Nelsen (Cockroft kick)
PIT-Lusteg 13-yd. FG
CLE-Green 11-yd. pass from Nelsen (Cockroft kick)
CLE-Cockroft 27-yd. FG
CLE-Morin 2-yd. pass from Nelsen (Cockroft kick)
PIT-May 27-yd. interception return (Lusteg kick)
CLE-Warfield 36-yd. pass from Ryan (Cockroft kick)
PIT-Wilburn 19-yd. pass from Shiner (Lusteg kick)
CLE-Harraway 33-yd. pass from Ryan (Cockroft kick)

Passing
CLE: Nelsen 18–27–258 3 TD 1 INT, Ryan 4–7–94 2 TD 2 INT, Kelly 0–1–0 0 TD 0 INT
PIT: Shiner 17–35–188 2 TD 5 INT, Hoak 0–1–0 0 TD 1 INT

Rushing
CLE: Kelly 11–19, Green 9–16, Harraway 5–13, Morrison 1–1, Nelsen 1-(-2)
PIT: Gros 13–109, Hoak 11–34, Jefferson 1–22

Receiving
CLE: Morin 5–103, Green 5–84, Warfield 4–68, Barney 4–43, Harraway 1–33, McDonald 1–13, Kelly 2–8
PIT: Wilburn 7–79, Hoak 4–45, Jefferson 3–39, Gros 2–17, Shy 1–8

Sunday, November 24
Browns 47, Philadelphia Eagles 13
Cleveland Stadium (62,338)
White jerseys/white pants

The winning streak hit six as the Browns dominated the winless Eagles on the strength of another sterling offensive performance. After Philly pulled to within 10–6 midway through the second quarter, the Browns erupted for 30 straight points to turn the contest into a rout. Cleveland collected 438 total yards, including better than 200 on the ground as Leroy Kelly—who hadn't practiced all week with a bruised shin—rushed for 108 yards and two scores and threw a touchdown pass to Paul Warfield on a halfback-option play. With another big day, Kelly went over the 1,000-yard rushing mark for the season. Milt Morin notched his second straight 100-yard receiving day, while the defense forced six turnovers.
Record: 8–3

	1	2	3	4		
Eagles	0	6	0	7	=	13
Browns	10	10	14	13	=	47

CLE-Warfield 12-yd. pass from Nelsen (Cockroft kick)
CLE-Cockroft 28-yd. FG
PHI-Baker 18-yd. FG
PHI-Baker 25-yd. FG
CLE-Warfield 34-yd. pass from Kelly (Cockroft kick)
CLE-Cockroft 26-yd. FG
CLE-Kelly 36-yd. run (Cockroft kick)
CLE-Kelly 1-yd. run (Cockroft kick)
CLE-Morrison 1-yd. run (kick failed)
CLE-Morrison 29-yd. pass from Ryan (Cockroft kick)
PHI-Hill 7-yd. pass from Snead (Baker kick)

Passing
PHI: Snead 27–48–286 1 TD 3 INT
CLE: Nelsen 10–21–177 1 TD 0 INT, Ryan 3–5–35 1 TD 0 INT, Kelly 1–1–34 1 TD 0 INT

Rushing
PHI: Woodeshick 14–46, Pinder 4–9, Snead 2–2
CLE: Kelly 20–108, Harraway 4–30, Green 5–25, Ryan 2–15, Smith 1–13, Morin 1–8, Morrison 3–2, Nelsen 1–0

Receiving
PHI: Ballman 9–86, Woodeshick 6–86, Hill 7–71, Hawkins 2–29, Pinder 3–14
CLE: Morin 2–108, Warfield 3–54, Morrison 1–29, Green 3–24, Barney 2–24, McDonald 1–11, Harraway 2-(-4)

Sunday, December 1
Browns 45, New York Giants 10
Cleveland Stadium (83,193)
White jerseys/white pants

Before a massive crowd on a rainy afternoon at the Stadium, the Browns extended their winning streak to seven by dominating the 7–4 Giants in the mud. Leroy Kelly ran for four touchdowns—bringing his season total to 18—including three in the third quarter as the Browns quickly wiped out an early 3–0 New York lead. Paul Warfield was unaffected by the foul conditions, catching six passes for a season-high 137 yards and a score, while the Browns' defense forced five turnovers and limited the Giants to just 182 total yards. The Cardinals kept pace with a win in Pittsburgh, but remained a game-and-a-half behind Cleveland with two to play.
Record: 9–3

	1	2	3	4		
Giants	3	0	0	7	=	10
Browns	0	17	21	7	=	45

NYG-Gogolak 46-yd. FG
CLE-Warfield 29-yd. pass from Nelsen (Cockroft kick)
CLE-Kelly 9-yd. run (Cockroft kick)
CLE-Cockroft 37-yd. FG
CLE-Kelly 8-yd. run (Cockroft kick)
CLE-Kelly 7-yd. run (Cockroft kick)
CLE-Kelly 5-yd. run (Cockroft kick)
NYG-Koy 1-yd. run (Gogolak kick)
CLE-McDonald 12-yd. pass from Ryan (Cockroft kick)

Passing
NYG: Tarkenton 8–20–59 0 TD 1 INT, Wood 2–4–23 0 TD 1 INT, Duhon 1–1–5 0 TD 0 INT
CLE: Nelsen 13–25–204 1 TD 0 INT, Ryan 1–4–12 1 TD 1INT

Rushing
NYG: Koy 10–32, Duhon 5–20, Tarkenton 2–16, Frederickson 5–15, Blye 3–15, Wood 1–2
CLE: Kelly 16–56, Harraway 8–37, Green 6–34, Leigh 2–25, Morrison 3–20

Receiving
NYG: Duhon 3–29, Blye 2–18, Thomas 2–15, Frederickson 1–9, Koy 1–6, Morrison 1–6, Jones 1–4
CLE: Warfield 6–137, Kelly 3–35, Morin 1–14, McDonald 1–12, Barney 1–10, Green 2–8

Sunday, December 8
Browns 24, Washington Redskins 21
D.C. Stadium (50,661)
White jerseys/white pants

The winning streak reached eight as the Browns clinched their second straight Century Division title with a come-from-behind victory in the nation's capital. While the offense struggled in the first half, the Browns stayed close thanks to a 40-yard interception return for a touchdown by DB Erich Barnes and trailed 14–7 going into the third quarter. A short Leroy Kelly scoring run tied the game, then the Browns scored 10 points in the fourth quarter to surge ahead. The Redskins made it interesting in the final moments when former Browns' QB Jim Ninowski—in for an injured Sonny Jurgensen—threw a touchdown pass with a minute to play to pull Washington within three, then the Redskins recovered an onside kick. But the Browns' defense stopped them on downs to secure their tenth victory of the season. Kelly rushed for 99 yards before leaving with an injury, while Milt Morin had another strong performance, catching six passes for 133 yards.
Record: 10–3

	1	2	3	4		
Browns	0	7	7	10	=	24
Redskins	7	7	0	7	=	21

WAS-Smith 5-yd. pass from Jurgensen (Gogolak kick)
CLE-Barnes 40-yd. interception return (Cockroft kick)
WAS-Larson 2-yd. pass from Jurgensen (Gogolak kick)
CLE-Kelly 1-yd. run (Cockroft kick)

CLE-Cockroft 20-yd. FG
CLE-Warfield 38-yd. pass from Nelsen (Cockroft kick)
WAS-Taylor 31-yd. pass from Ninowski (Gogolak kick)

Passing
CLE: Nelsen 12–22–205 1 TD 1 INT
WAS: Jurgensen 12–23–127 2 TD 3 INT, Ninowski 9–16–115 1 TD 0 INT, Beban 0–1–0 0 TD 0 INT

Rushing
CLE: Kelly 18–99, Harraway 10–31, Green 3–10, Morrison 4–8, Nelsen 1–1
WAS: Brunet 13–59, Larson 10–43, Jurgensen 1–7, Smith 3–5

Receiving
CLE: Morin 6–133, Warfield 1–38, Green 2–15, Morrison 1–11, McDonald 1–6, Kelly 1–2
WAS: Smith 7–103, Taylor 2–44, Larson 4–36, Richter 2–19, Smith 1–15, Brunet 4–13, Mitchell 1–12

Saturday, December 14
St. Louis Cardinals 27, Browns 16
Busch Stadium (39,746)
White jerseys/white pants

On a bright but very cold Saturday afternoon, the Browns' winning streak came to an end as they closed out the regular season with a defeat in an essentially meaningless contest with the Cardinals. Despite a lethargic performance, the Browns hung around, tying the contest in the third quarter on a 45-yard touchdown run by Leroy Kelly, then pulled within four after a St. Louis touchdown gave the Cardinals the lead once again. St. Louis scored the clinching touchdown with just under seven minutes to play as the Cards completed a season sweep of the Browns but still finished a half-game behind them in the Century Division. Leroy Kelly rushed for 67 yards and a touchdown to finish the season with 1,239 to lead the NFL, while Paul Warfield topped the 100-yard mark for the third time in six weeks and finished his campaign with 1,067 receiving yards—a franchise record.
Record: 10–4

	1	2	3	4		
Browns	3	3	7	3	=	16
Cardinals	7	6	7	7	=	27

STL-Conrad 28-yd. pass from Hart (Bakken kick)
CLE-Cockroft 50-yd. FG
STL-Bakken 33-yd. FG
CLE-Cockroft 16-yd. FG
STL-Bakken 37-yd. FG
CLE-Kelly 45-yd. run (Cockroft kick)
STL-Conrad 20-yd. pass from Hart (Bakken kick)
CLE-Cockroft 15-yd. FG
STL-Smith 36-yd. run (Bakken kick)

Passing
CLE: Nelsen 9–23–216 0 TD 0 INT
STL: Hart 9–21–121 2 TD 0 INT, Johnson 0–1–0 0 TD 0 INT

Rushing
CLE: Kelly 10–67, Harraway 11–55, Morrison 4–6, Nelsen 2–1
STL: Crenshaw 20–69, Roland 8–51, Smith 2–36, Lane 6–25, Edwards 3–25, Hart 1–2, Shivers 1-(-5)

Receiving
CLE: Warfield 3–104, Harraway 3–80, McDonald 2–29, Morin 1–3
STL: Conrad 4–71, Smith 3–43, Daanen 1–10, Crenshaw 1-(-3)

Eastern Conference Playoff
Saturday, December 21
Browns 31, Dallas Cowboys 20
Cleveland Stadium (81,497)
White jerseys/white pants

Before a colossal crowd, the Browns notched one of the most impressive victories in franchise history, stunning a powerful Cowboys team to earn a trip to the NFL title game for the first time in four years.

The Capital Division–champion Cowboys, who finished a dominating regular season with a 12–2 record, were expected to roll over the Browns much as they had in the teams' first meeting in September. But the Browns' defense set the tone for a big day early with an interception by DB Mike Howell that set up a Cleveland field goal. Aided by a fumble return for a touchdown, Dallas surged to a 10–3 lead, and it appeared they would carry the advantage to the intermission before Bill Nelsen connected with Leroy Kelly for a 45-yard touchdown pass in the final minute of the half to tie the game.

Then everything changed in the first three minutes of the third quarter. On the first play of the second half, Cleveland LB Dale Lindsey batted a Don Meredith pass into the air and intercepted it, then returned it 27 yards for the go-ahead touchdown to the delight of the sellout crowd. Three plays later, DB Ben Davis intercepted another Meredith pass, and a snap after that, Kelly broke loose for his second touchdown of the day to put the Browns ahead 24–10. They'd scored three touchdowns in just over three minutes of play to take control of the contest.

After a Dallas field goal, the Cowboys were poised to draw within a touchdown early in the fourth quarter, but Erich Barnes came up with a key interception to halt their momentum. A long Nelsen pass to Paul Warfield set up a backbreaking touchdown run by Ernie Green to make it 31–13 with just over five minutes to play, and the Browns were in the clear. After Dallas scored a meaningless touchdown in the waning moments, fans swarmed the field in celebration of a marvelous Cleveland victory.

The defense led the way, intercepting four Dallas passes and holding the explosive Cowboy offense to just 86 rushing yards and 12 pass completions in 32 attempts, forcing starting QB Don Meredith to the bench. Offensively, Nelsen threw for 203 yards and Kelly ran for 87, while Paul Warfield caught four passes for 86 yards.

The following afternoon, Baltimore defeated Minnesota to earn a trip to Cleveland for an NFL title game few predicted.

	1	2	3	4		
Cowboys	7	3	3	7	=	20
Browns	3	7	14	7	=	31

CLE-Cockroft 38-yd. FG
DAL-Howley 44-yd. fumble return (Clark kick)
DAL-Clark 16-yd. FG
CLE-Kelly 45-yd. pass from Nelsen (Cockroft kick)
CLE-Lindsey 27-yd. interception return (Cockroft kick)
CLE-Kelly 35-yd. run (Cockroft kick)
DAL-Clark 47-yd. FG
CLE-Green 2-yd. run (Cockroft kick)
DAL-Garrison 2-yd. pass from Morton (Clark kick)

Passing
DAL: Morton 9–23–163 1 TD 1 INT, Meredith 3–9–42 0 TD 3 INT
CLE: Nelsen 13–25–203 1 TD 1 INT

Rushing
DAL: Perkins 14–51, Morton 2–14, Baynham 10–7, Garrison 1–6, Meredith 1–5, Shy 2–3
CLE: Kelly 20–87, Harraway 5–12, Green 3–5, Nelsen 2-(-2)

Receiving
DAL: Hayes 5–83, Rentzel 3–75, Baynham 1–34, Garrison 2–8, Norman 1–5
CLE: Warfield 4–86, Morin 4–47, Kelly 2–46, Collins 2–26, Harraway 1-(-2)

1968 NFL Championship
Sunday, December 29
Baltimore Colts 34, Browns 0
Cleveland Stadium (80,628)
White jerseys/white pants

Four years after the Browns' surprising rout of Baltimore in the NFL title game, the tables were turned as the visiting Colts crushed Cleveland on a cold, gray afternoon to advance to Super Bowl III. In so doing, Baltimore also avenged its only loss of the regular season, a 30–20 defeat at home to the Browns in October.

After squandering a few early scoring opportunities, the lifeless Browns lost control of the game in the second quarter as the Colts exploded for 17 points. It seemed the momentum would swing after Erich Barnes recovered a Baltimore fumble at the Cleveland 14 with the Colts ahead 10–0, but moments later, Bill Nelsen threw an interception that set up another Baltimore score. The Browns had one last chance to get back into the game when they drove into field-goal range on the first possession of the third quarter. But after Don Cockroft missed a 50-yard field goal, the Colts were penalized for jumping offside, then Cockroft missed the second attempt from 45 yards—a microcosm of the entire game.

With the sullen home crowd watching grimly, Cleveland native and Shaw High School alumnus Tom Matte rushed for three touchdowns as the Colts rolled to 353 total yards, 184 on the ground. Meanwhile, the Baltimore defense was dominant, limiting the Browns to just 173 total yards while forcing three turnovers and collecting four sacks as the Colts posted their fourth shutout of the season. Leroy Kelly, the NFL's leading rusher during the regular season, managed just 28 yards on 13 carries, while Nelsen and Frank Ryan combined to complete only 13 of 32 passes. It marked the only time the Browns were ever shut out in their postseason history.

The Colts, heavy favorites going into the Super Bowl, were then the victims of one of the greatest upsets in NFL history as they were toppled by Joe Namath and the Jets.

	1	2	3	4		
Colts	0	17	7	10	=	34
Browns	0	0	0	0	=	0

BAL-Michaels 28-yd. FG
BAL-Matte 1-yd. run (Michaels kick)
BAL-Matte 12-yd. run (Michaels kick)
BAL-Matte 2-yd. run (Michaels kick)
BAL-Michaels 10-yd. FG
BAL-Brown 4-yd. run (Michaels kick)

Passing
BAL: Morrall 11–25–169 0 TD 1 INT
CLE: Nelsen 11–26–132 0 TD 2 INT, Ryan 2–6–19 0 TD 0 INT

Rushing
BAL: Matte 17–88, Hill 11–60, Brown 5–18, Cole 3–14, Mackey 2–4, Morrall 1–0
CLE: Kelly 13–28, Harraway 6–26, Green 1–2, Ryan 2–0

Receiving
BAL: Richardson 3–78, Mackey 2–34, Orr 2–33, Matte 2–15, Mitchell 1–7, Cole 1–2
CLE: Morin 3–41, Harraway 4–40, Warfield 2–30, Kelly 3–27, Collins 1–13

1969

Sunday, September 21
Browns 27, Philadelphia Eagles 20
Franklin Field (60,698)
White jerseys/white pants

Despite losing RB Leroy Kelly to a pulled hamstring in the opening minutes, the Browns overwhelmed the Eagles on opening day with superior depth and a strong defense. Three plays after Kelly was sidelined, QB Bill Nelsen hit WR Gary Collins for a 35-yard touchdown pass that gave the visitors a lead they would not relinquish. Rookie RB Ron Johnson, playing in his first NFL game, filled in marvelously for Kelly, picking up 118 yards on 17 carries and scoring a pair of touchdowns, including a 48-yard scamper in the third quarter to put the Browns up 27–7. Though Johnson would go on to much success with the New York Giants in the 1970s, this would be the only 100-yard game of his one-year Cleveland career. All three of the Eagles' touchdowns were freakish—one set up after Cleveland DB Erich Barnes deflected a field-goal attempt at the crossbar, and the Eagles recovered to give them a first down at the Cleveland 2, another on an interception return, and the third in the final minute after Philadelphia recovered an onside kick. The Eagles recovered another onside kick moments later and had a final opportunity to tie, but Browns' DB Mike Howell intercepted Philly QB Norm Snead to secure the Cleveland win.

Record: 1–0

	1	2	3	4		
Browns	7	6	14	0	=	27
Eagles	0	7	0	13	=	20

CLE-Collins 35-yd. pass from Nelsen (Cockroft kick)
CLE-Cockroft 22-yd. FG
PHI-Woodeshick 1-yd. run (Baker kick)
CLE-Cockroft 37-yd. FG
CLE-R. Johnson 1-yd. run (Cockroft kick)
CLE-R. Johnson 48-yd. run (Cockroft kick)
PHI-Scarpati 34-yd. interception return (kick failed)
PHI-Hawkins 41-yd. pass from Snead (Baker kick)

Passing
CLE: Nelsen 11–26–177 1 TD 2 INT, Morrison 1–1–16 0 TD 0 INT, Rhome 1–1–3 0 TD 0 INT
PHI: Snead 11–24–148 1 TD 2 INT, Mira 1–7–20 0 TD 0 INT

Rushing
CLE: R. Johnson 17–118, Morrison 16–48, Kelly 3–9, Nelsen 1-(-2)
PHI: Woodeshick 14–63, Keyes 3–10, Mira 2–10, Wilson 3–5, Snead 2–0

Receiving
CLE: Collins 3–58, Morin 2–38, Morrison 2–32, Hooker 2–21, R. Johnson 2–21, Glass 1–17, Warfield 1–9
PHI: Hawkins 4–92, Ballman 3–45, Jackson 2–17, Keyes 1–11, Wilson 1–6, Woodeshick 1-(-3)

Sunday, September 28
Browns 27, Washington Redskins 23
Cleveland Stadium (82,581)
White jerseys/white pants

With injured Leroy Kelly on one sideline and Vince Lombardi on the other, the Browns rallied from behind in the fourth quarter to capture a thrilling victory over the Redskins and snap a frustrating six-game losing streak against Lombardi in the last game he'd ever coach against the Browns. As the afternoon alternated between bright sunshine and dark rain showers, the Browns and Redskins played a fitting seesaw affair that saw the home team surge to a 20–10 lead with 10 minutes left. Then after Washington cut the margin to three points, the 'Skins recovered a Bill Nelsen fumble, and a play later, scored again to go up 23–20 with just over four minutes remaining. Taking over at their own 26, the Browns quickly marched to the Washington 15, where Nelsen found Gary Collins in the corner of the end zone for the winning points with 1:09 left. Washington threatened in the final seconds as QB Sonny Jurgensen broke loose for a 33-yard gain, but time expired on the play. Propelling the Browns' eleventh straight win over Washington was RB Reece Morrison, who exploded for 131 yards on 24 carries.

Record: 2–0

	1	2	3	4		
Redskins	7	0	3	13	=	23
Browns	0	10	7	10	=	27

WAS-Smith 6-yd. pass from Jurgensen (Knight kick)
CLE-R. Johnson 1-yd. run (Cockroft kick)
CLE-Cockroft 41-yd. FG
WAS-Knight 32-yd. FG
CLE-R. Johnson 17-yd. run (Cockroft kick)
CLE-Cockroft 23-yd. FG
WAS-Harraway 1-yd. run (kick failed)
WAS-Long 13-yd. pass from Jurgensen (Knight kick)
CLE-Collins 15-yd. pass from Nelsen (Cockroft kick)

Passing
WAS: Jurgensen 14–18–121 2 TD 0 INT
CLE: Nelsen 12–21–152 1 TD 1 INT

Rushing
WAS: Brown 14–95, Harraway 10–44, Jurgensen 1–33, Dyer 1–5
CLE: Morrison 24–131, R. Johnson 20–73, Nelsen 1-(-5)

Receiving
WAS: Long 4–59, Smith 3–21, Taylor 2–19, Dyer 1–17, Allen 1–5, Brown 3–0
CLE: Warfield 4–69, Morrison 4–39, Morin 2–22, Collins 1–15, R. Johnson 1–7

Sunday, October 5
Detroit Lions 28, Browns 21
Cleveland Stadium (82,933)
White jerseys/white pants

With a 3–0 record in their grasp, the Browns imploded in the second half, squandering a 14-point lead and losing for the first time in 1969. Leading 21–7 after three first-half touchdown passes by Bill Nelsen, the Browns were poised to stretch their lead to 17 points midway through the third quarter, but the snap on a short Don Cockroft field-goal attempt was high, and the Lions recovered the football at midfield. The miscue turned the game completely around as Detroit would score the game's final 21 points to win. The tying touchdown, early in the fourth, came after Bill Nelsen fumbled the snap from center, and the Lions recovered at the Cleveland 31. It was one of six turnovers on the day for the Browns, who were stymied offensively. Leroy Kelly returned to action but was far from full strength, held to just 16 yards on 10 carries. Paul Warfield was the lone bright spot, snagging seven receptions for 106 yards and the game's first touchdown.
Record: 2–1

	1	2	3	4		
Lions	0	7	7	14	=	28
Browns	7	14	0	0	=	21

CLE-Warfield 21-yd. pass from Nelsen (Cockroft kick)
DET-McCullouch 13-yd. pass from Munson (Mann kick)
CLE-Collins 23-yd. pass from Nelsen (Cockroft kick)
CLE-Collins 23-yd. pass from Nelsen (Cockroft kick)
DET-Wright 26-yd. pass from Munson (Mann kick)
DET-Eddy 1-yd. run (Mann kick)
DET-Farr 2-yd. run (Mann kick)

Passing
DET: Munson 11–20–169 2 TD 1 INT, Landry 2–3–25 0 TD 1 INT
CLE: Nelsen 13–29–196 3 TD 3 INT

Rushing
DET: Farr 19–64, Eddy 11–55, Munson 2–13, Watkins 4–12
CLE: R. Johnson 12–59, Kelly 10–16, Morrison 2–5, Nelsen 1-(-1)

Receiving
DET: Wright 3–51, Sanders 4–47, Watkins 3–43, McCullouch 2–37, Farr 1–16
CLE: Warfield 7–106, Collins 3–67, Morin 2–22, Kelly 1–1

Sunday, October 12
Browns 27, New Orleans Saints 17
Tulane Stadium (71,274)
White jerseys/white pants

On a hot, muggy afternoon in Louisiana, the Browns jumped to a double-digit lead over the winless Saints and hung on for a crucial win. Forcing four New Orleans turnovers, the Browns took control in a wild second quarter that saw 30 points scored. After the Browns crept to a 10–7 lead, DT Marv Upshaw knocked the ball from Saints' QB Billy Kilmer, and fellow DT Walter Johnson recovered at the New Orleans 12 and rumbled into the end zone for a touchdown to put Cleveland up by 10. Seconds later, Kilmer fumbled again, and DE Jack Gregory recovered for the Browns at the New Orleans 28, setting up a short Don Cockroft field goal. With 57 rushing yards, 52 receiving yards, and a pair of touchdowns, Leroy Kelly returned to form, and Bill Nelsen tossed for 214 yards as the Browns didn't turn the football over after committing 13 turnovers in their first three games.
Record: 3–1

	1	2	3	4		
Browns	0	20	0	7	=	27
Saints	0	10	7	0	=	17

CLE-Kelly 4-yd. pass from Nelsen (Cockroft kick)
NO-Livingston 1-yd. run (Dempsey kick)
CLE-Cockroft 28-yd. FG
CLE-W. Johnson 12-yd. fumble return (Cockroft kick)
CLE-Cockroft 30-yd. FG
NO-Dempsey 22-yd. FG
NO-Baker 1-yd. run (Dempsey kick)
CLE-Kelly 1-yd. run (Cockroft kick)

Passing
CLE: Nelsen 15–25–214 1 TD 0 INT, Kelly 0–1–0 0 TD 0 INT
NO: Kilmer 13–19–163 0 TD 1 INT

Rushing
CLE: Kelly 17–57, R. Johnson 7–17, B. Scott 11–13, Morrison 2–5
NO: Baker 13–74, Livingston 14–54, Barrington 1–17, Wheelwright 3–16

Receiving
CLE: Warfield 5–93, Kelly 3–52, Glass 1–40, Collins 2–28, R. Johnson 2–10
NO: Abramowicz 3–43, Dodd 1–34, Poage 2–26, Parks 2–24, Livingston 2–14, Barrington 1–12, Wheelwright 1–10, Baker 1–0

Saturday, October 18
Browns 42, Pittsburgh Steelers 31
Cleveland Stadium (84,078)
White jerseys/white pants

On a chilly October Saturday night, the Browns picked off four Steeler passes in the second half—returning two for touchdowns—to blow open a tight game and defeat first-year head coach Chuck Noll in their first meeting. Trailing 14–10 in the third quarter, the Steelers drove to the Cleveland 23, only to squander the opportunity to take the lead by fumbling—one of eight Pittsburgh turnovers on the night. Erich Barnes returned an interception 55 yards for a score, followed by a 40-yard return for six points early in the fourth by DB Walt Sumner. Gary Collins was the catalyst on offense, catching seven of Bill Nelsen's 12 completions on the night for 103 yards and a pair of touchdowns, the second of which made it 35–10 in a wild fourth period that saw each team score three touchdowns.
Record: 4–1

	1	2	3	4		
Steelers	0	10	0	21	=	31
Browns	7	7	7	21	=	42

CLE-Collins 4-yd. pass from Nelsen (Cockroft kick)
PIT-Hoak 4-yd. run (Mingo kick)
CLE-Kelly 1-yd. run (Cockroft kick)
PIT-Mingo 38-yd. FG
CLE-Barnes 55-yd. interception return (Cockroft kick)
CLE-Sumner 40-yd. interception return (Cockroft kick)
CLE-Collins 48-yd. pass from Nelsen (Cockroft kick)
PIT-Gros 15-yd. pass from Hanratty (Mingo kick)
PIT-Jefferson 10-yd. pass from Nix (Mingo kick)
CLE-Morrison 1-yd. run (Cockroft kick)
PIT-Jefferson 15-yd. pass from Hanratty (Mingo kick)

Passing
PIT: Hanratty 6–11–132 2 TD 3 INT, Nix 7–13–57 1 TD 1 INT, Shiner 3–9–27 0 TD 0 INT
CLE: Nelsen 12–25–171 2 TD 3 INT, Rhome 0–2–0 0 TD 0 INT, R. Johnson 0–1–0 0 TD 0 INT

Rushing
PIT: Hoak 11–51, Hanratty 1–31, Nix 3–21, Bankston 3–15, Gros 5–14, Campbell 1–5, Shiner 1–1, McCall 2-(-1)
CLE: Morrison 3–60, Kelly 18–51, R. Johnson 13–33

Receiving
PIT: Jefferson 7–110, Campbell 1–32, Gros 3–25, Cropper 2–24, Adams 1–19, Hoak 1–4, Bankston 1–2
CLE: Collins 7–103, Kelly 1–36, R. Johnson 3–20, Morin 1–12

Sunday, October 26
Browns 21, St. Louis Cardinals 21
Cleveland Stadium (81,186)
White jerseys/white pants

On the brink of securing a third straight victory, the Browns were instead forced to settle for a tie when the Cardinals rallied for a touchdown with eight seconds remaining. With two minutes left the Browns had pulled ahead in a hard-fought contest when Gary Collins made a dazzling third-down catch for a 12-yard touchdown to make it 21–14 just moments after Collins left the game with an ankle injury. Appropriately, it was Cardinals' WR John Gilliam who caught the tying touchdown pass, his third of the day, to give him a whopping 192 yards on just four receptions. Cardinals' QB Charley Johnson tossed for 306 yards as St. Louis rolled up 445 total. Leroy Kelly paced the Browns by rushing for 71 yards and a touchdown and threw for another on a halfback-option toss to Paul Warfield to open the scoring in the first quarter.

Record: 4–1–1

	1	2	3	4		
Cardinals	7	0	7	7	=	21
Browns	7	0	7	7	=	21

CLE-Warfield 36-yd. pass from Kelly (Cockroft kick)
STL-Gilliam 84-yd. pass from Johnson (Bakken kick)
STL-Gilliam 75-yd. pass from Johnson (Bakken kick)
CLE-Kelly 2-yd. run (Cockroft kick)
CLE-Collins 12-yd. pass from Nelsen (Cockroft kick)
STL-Gilliam 15-yd. pass from Johnson (Bakken kick)

Passing
STL: Johnson 15–30–306 3 TD 1 INT
CLE: Nelsen 19–28–198 1 TD 1 INT, Kelly 1–2–36 1 TD 0 INT

Rushing
STL: Roland 16–56, Edwards 12–52, Johnson 3–31
CLE: Kelly 16–71, R. Johnson 13–35

Receiving
STL: Gilliam 4–192, Williams 3–41, Smith 3–33, Roland 3–27, Edwards 2–13
CLE: Collins 9–95, Warfield 4–88, R. Johnson 4–27, Morin 2–24, Kelly 1–0

Sunday, November 2
Browns 42, Dallas Cowboys 10
Cleveland Stadium (84,850)
White jerseys/white pants

In one of the most stunning performances in team history, the Browns obliterated the undefeated Cowboys with a nearly flawless effort on a damp, chilly afternoon before the third-largest crowd ever to see a football game in Cleveland. The Cowboys, 6–0 going in, were looking to avenge their playoff loss to the Browns on the same field 10 months earlier, and were seven-point favorites. But the Browns set the tone by scoring on their first offensive play—a 48-yard strike from Bill Nelsen to Paul Warfield—and were dominant from that point on, soaring to a 28–3 advantage at the half and never looked back. Nelsen played one of the finest games of his career, throwing for 255 yards and a team-record five touchdowns—two each to Warfield and Gary Collins—against a Dallas defense that had permitted only seven touchdowns in its first six games. On the other side of the ball, the Cleveland defense racked up six sacks and forced six turnovers, including three interceptions of Cowboys' QB Craig Morton, who yielded to rookie Roger Staubach in the fourth quarter. What's more, Dallas rookie RB Calvin Hill, the league's leading rusher, was held to just 52 yards. The victory snapped Dallas's 11-game regular-season winning streak and marked their first road defeat in nearly two years. Now with a two-and-a-half-game lead on the Giants at the season's midpoint, the Browns were in the driver's seat in the Century Division.

Record: 5–1–1

	1	2	3	4		
Cowboys	0	3	0	7	=	10
Browns	14	14	0	14	=	42

CLE-Warfield 48-yd. pass from Nelsen (Cockroft kick)
CLE-Collins 10-yd. pass from Nelsen (Cockroft kick)
CLE-R. Johnson 1-yd. run (Cockroft kick)
DAL-Clark 14-yd. FG
CLE-Warfield 21-yd. pass from Nelsen (Cockroft kick)
CLE-Collins 7-yd. pass from Nelsen (Cockroft kick)
DAL-Hill 1-yd. run (Clark kick)
CLE-Glass 10-yd. pass from Nelsen (Cockroft kick)

Passing
DAL: Morton 11–22–147 0 TD 3 INT, Staubach 6–11–74 0 TD 0 INT
CLE: Nelsen 18–25–255 5 TD 1 INT, Kelly 0–1–0 0 TD 0 INT

Rushing
DAL: Garrison 14–70, Hill 12–52, Staubach 1–7, Reeves 1–6, Shy 1–5
CLE: Kelly 19–65, Warfield 1–16, R. Johnson 10–13, B. Scott 3–1

Receiving
DAL: Homan 4–53, Rentzel 2–40, Hayes 2–40, Ditka 3–34, Hill 2–21, Garrison 2–14, Conrad 1–12, Norman 1–7
CLE: Morin 7–101, Warfield 3–84, Collins 5–47, Glass 1–10, R. Johnson 1–7, Kelly 1–6

Sunday, November 9
Minnesota Vikings 51, Browns 3
Metropolitan Stadium (47,700)
White jerseys/white pants

For as perfectly as things had gone the week before against Dallas, everything fell apart seven days later against a powerful Minnesota team that simply obliterated the Browns. Aided by four Cleveland turnovers, the Vikings scored on their first nine possessions, outgained the Browns 454 total yards to 151, and picked up 31 first downs to Cleveland's eight. Minnesota WR Gene Washington caught seven passes for 119 yards and three touchdowns, almost outperforming the entire Browns' roster. It matched the most lopsided loss in Browns' history, mirroring a 48-point defeat to Green Bay two years earlier, and 10 years would pass before Cleveland permitted more than 50 points in a game again. More importantly, it set a bad tone for the rematch in the NFL Championship two months later.
Record: 5–2–1

	1	2	3	4		
Browns	0	3	0	0	=	3
Vikings	10	17	7	17	=	51

MIN-Washington 16-yd. pass from Kapp (Cox)
MIN-Cox 32-yd. FG
MIN-Washington 10-yd. pass from Kapp (Cox kick)
CLE-Cockroft 28-yd. FG
MIN-Cox 28-yd. FG
MIN-Washington 1-yd. pass from Kapp (Cox kick)
MIN-Osborn 5-yd. run (Cox kick)
MIN-Jones 1-yd. run (Cox kick)
MIN-Cox 32-yd. FG
MIN-Lindsey 2-yd. run (Cox kick)

Passing
CLE: Nelsen 7–16–95 0 TD 3 INT, Rhome 5–11–30 0 TD 1 INT
MIN: Kapp 16–24–223 3 TD 0 INT, Cuozzo 4–8–51 0 TD 0 INT, Lee 0–1–0 0 TD 0 INT

Rushing
CLE: Kelly 6–24, Morrison 1–15, B. Scott 1–2, R. Johnson 2–1
MIN: Reed 9–51, Osborn 10–48, Brown 7–46, Jones 8–34, Lee 1–5, Lindsey 1–2, Harris 2–1, Kapp 1–1

Receiving
CLE: Jones 2–33, Kelly 2–28, Warfield 1–27, Collins 2–23, R. Johnson 2–17, Morin 1–6, Leigh 2-(-9)
MIN: Washington 7–119, Beasley 4–57, Grim 3–43, Henderson 3–39, Osborn 2–11, Brown 1–5

Sunday, November 16
Browns 24, Pittsburgh Steelers 3
Pitt Stadium (47,670)
Brown jerseys/white pants

Rebounding nicely after utter disaster in Minnesota the week before, the Browns dominated the Steelers on a bright, chilly day in Pittsburgh to all but clinch the Century Division title. Bill Nelsen threw for 290 yards and a pair of scores as he defeated his former team for the fourth straight time since joining the Browns. Paul Warfield was Nelsen's primary target, snagging five receptions for 132 yards, while Leroy Kelly rushed for 97 yards. The turning point of the game came in the second quarter with the Browns leading 7–3, when Pittsburgh blew a chance to take the lead by fumbling at the Cleveland 4. The Browns stretched the lead to seven points at the half, then put it away with a pair of touchdowns in the fourth quarter. Meanwhile, with a St. Louis defeat to Detroit, the Browns' divisional lead stretched to three games with five to play.
Record: 6–2–1

	1	2	3	4		
Browns	7	3	0	14	=	24
Steelers	3	0	0	0	=	3

CLE-Collins 26-yd. pass from Nelsen (Cockroft kick)
PIT-Mingo 31-yd. FG
CLE-Cockroft 28-yd. FG
CLE-Warfield 12-yd. pass from Nelsen (Cockroft kick)
CLE-Kelly 1-yd. run (Cockroft kick)

Passing
CLE: Nelsen 18–32–290 2 TD 2 INT
PIT: Hanratty 11–22–149 0 TD 1 INT

Rushing
CLE: Kelly 24–97, R. Johnson 8–23, Morin 1–8, B. Scott 1-(-1)
PIT: Bankston 15–96, Hanratty 5–54, Hoak 7–21

Receiving
CLE: Warfield 5–132, Collins 6–91, Morin 3–37, R. Johnson 3–29, Kelly 1–1
PIT: Wilburn 4–71, Jefferson 4–58, Hoak 1–16, Henderson 1–8, Bankston 1-(-4)

Sunday, November 23
Browns 28, New York Giants 17
Cleveland Stadium (80,595)
White jerseys/white pants

On a damp, cold day, the Browns forced six turnovers and held off the Giants to clinch a tie for the division title. Putting together his finest performance of the season thus far, Leroy Kelly rushed for 124 yards—the nineteenth 100-yard game of his career—and scored three touchdowns to give the Browns a 21–0 lead in the second quarter. Behind QB Fran Tarkenton, who threw for 279 yards, New York then rallied to score the next 17 points to cut the margin to four. The Browns responded with a Bill Nelsen-to-Gary Collins scoring toss early in the fourth quarter, but the Giants then drove to the Cleveland 2 and were poised to pull within one score again. Tarkenton was hit as he threw a pass into the end zone, and the ball was intercepted by Browns' LB John Garlington with 10:27 remaining. With New York's momentum halted for good, the Browns then melted five minutes off the clock with their ensuing drive and coasted to victory.

Record: 7–2–1

	1	2	3	4		
Giants	0	10	7	0	=	17
Browns	14	7	0	7	=	28

CLE-Kelly 23-yd. run (Cockroft kick)
CLE-Kelly 30-yd. run (Cockroft kick)
CLE-Kelly 1-yd. run (Cockroft kick)
NYG-Gogolak 27-yd. FG
NYG-Thomas 23-yd. pass from Tarkenton (Gogolak kick)
NYG-Coffey 2-yd. pass from Tarkenton (Gogolak kick)
CLE-Collins 24-yd. pass from Nelsen (Cockroft kick)

Passing
NYG: Tarkenton 22–32–279 2 TD 3 INT
CLE: Nelsen 7–17–123 1 TD 1 INT, Kelly 0–1–0 0 TD 0 INT

Rushing
NYG: Coffey 18–83, Morrison 9–24, Tarkenton 1–10
CLE: Kelly 18–124, R. Johnson 10–29

Receiving
NYG: Herrmann 3–85, White 7–79, Morrison 5–68, Thomas 3–41, Jones 2–9, Coffey 2-(-3)
CLE: Collins 2–40, Warfield 1–30, Kelly 1–25, B. Scott 1–14, Morin 1–12, R. Johnson 1–2

Sunday, November 30
Browns 28, Chicago Bears 24
Wrigley Field (45,050)
White jerseys/white pants

After falling behind by two touchdowns to the 1–9 Bears, the Browns came back to win their eighth game of the season and clinch their third consecutive Century Division title. Chicago got out to a strong start in the first half behind the power running of RB Gayle Sayers, who picked up 89 yards in the first 30 minutes and scored a touchdown to give the Bears a 14–0 lead early in the second quarter. The Browns cut the lead to seven at the half, then tied it in the third before falling behind again after a fumble set up a Chicago field goal with eight minutes to play. But the Browns responded with an eight-play, 90-yard drive and scored the winning touchdown on a seven-yard Ron Johnson run. The Bears drove into Cleveland territory in the final minute but were stymied by the Cleveland defense, which rose to the occasion in the second half, holding Sayers to 37 yards and not allowing another touchdown. Offensively, Bill Nelsen had another sterling day, tossing for 290 yards and a pair of scores, while Gary Collins caught six passes for 126. Interestingly, this would be the last game the Browns would play in Chicago for 17 years, as well as the last the Browns would play at historic Wrigley Field.

Record: 8–2–1

	1	2	3	4		
Browns	0	14	7	7	=	28
Bears	7	14	0	3	=	24

CHI-Wallace 21-yd. pass from Douglass (Percival kick)
CHI-Sayers 1-yd. run (Percival kick)
CLE-Warfield 10-yd. pass from Nelsen (Cockroft kick)
CHI-Hull 4-yd. run (Percival kick)
CLE-R. Johnson 1-yd. run (Percival kick)
CLE-Glass 24-yd. pass from Nelsen (Cockroft kick)
CHI-Percival 10-yd. FG
CLE-R. Johnson 7-yd. run (Cockroft kick)

Passing
CLE: Nelsen 16–30–290 2 TD 0 INT
CHI: Douglass 10–27–145 1 TD 0 INT

Rushing
CLE: Kelly 15–41, R. Johnson 11–29, B. Scott 4–4, Nelsen 1-(-6)
CHI: Sayers 20–126, Hull 11–50, Douglass 4–49, Gordon 1–6, Montgomery 1–6, Wallace 1–0

Receiving
CLE: Collins 6–126, Morin 4–64, Kelly 3–53, Glass 1–24, R. Johnson 1–13, Warfield 1–10
CHI: Wallace 3–75, Gordon 3–21, Sayers 1–21, Hull 2–16, Simmons 1–12

Sunday, December 7
Browns 20, Green Bay Packers 7
Cleveland Stadium (82,137)
White jerseys/white pants

Just as they'd snapped their losing streak against Vince Lombardi earlier in the season, the Browns finally managed to beat the Packers, ending an eight-game skid that stretched over the previous 13 years. In the wind, rain, and mud of Cleveland Stadium, Leroy Kelly sloshed to 151 yards to pace the offense, but it was the Browns' defense that led the way, limiting the Packers to 218 total yards and not allowing any points until the final two minutes of the contest. The Browns took control by scoring 10 points in the final three minutes of the first half, including a leaping 30-yard touchdown catch by Paul Warfield. DB Ernie Kellermann then broke the game open in the third when he returned an interception 40 yards for a touchdown to make it 20–0. Despite the foul weather conditions, more than 82,000 filed into the ballpark for the home finale, marking the first time in NFL history a team had drawn 80,000 fans for each of its home games in a season.
Record: 9–2–1

	1	2	3	4		
Packers	0	0	0	7	=	7
Browns	0	13	7	0	=	20

CLE-Cockroft 20-yd. FG
CLE-Warfield 30-yd. pass from Nelsen (Cockroft kick)
CLE-Cockroft 45-yd. FG
CLE-Kellermann 40-yd. interception return
GB-Hampton 29-yd. pass from Horn (Lusteg kick)

Passing
GB: Horn 10–23–122 1 TD 1 INT
CLE: Nelsen 10–24–137 1 TD 0 INT

Rushing
GB: T. Williams 14–47, Hampton 8–33, Anderson 4–12, P. Williams 2–5, Grabowski 1–2
CLE: Kelly 22–151, R. Johnson 7–21, Morrison 2–7, Warfield 1–7, Nelsen 1–3

Receiving
GB: Hampton 3–38, Dowler 1–22, P. Williams 1–18, Dale 1–17, Spilis 1–14, Anderson 1–10, T. Williams 2–3
CLE: Morin 5–63, Warfield 2–44, Collins 1–24, B. Scott 1–6, R. Johnson 1–0

BARNSTORMING IN CLASSIC BALLPARKS

Back in the days when baseball and football teams used to share homes, the Browns played a handful of games at some of the most hallowed ballparks in the history of sports:

Yankee Stadium
Browns' record: 11–6–2
Browns' first game: 1946 Browns' last game: 1969

Comiskey Park
Browns' record: 8–1
Browns' first game: 1950 Browns' last game: 1958

Griffith Stadium
Browns' record: 8–1–1
Browns' first game: 1950 Browns' last game: 1960

Forbes Field
Browns' record: 8–3
Browns' first game: 1950 Browns' last game: 1961

Ebbets Field
Browns' record: 3–0
Browns' first game: 1946 Browns' last game: 1948

Polo Grounds
Browns' record: 3–2–1
Browns' first game: 1950 Browns' last game: 1955

Shibe Park/Connie Mack Stadium
Browns' record: 3–4
Browns' first game: 1951 Browns' last game: 1957

Wrigley Field
Browns' record: 2–1
Browns' first game: 1954 Browns' last game: 1969

Briggs Stadium/Tiger Stadium
Browns' record: 0–6
Browns' first game: 1952 Browns' last game: 1967

Sunday, December 14
Browns 27, St. Louis Cardinals 21
Busch Stadium (44,924)
White jerseys/white pants

The Browns took a 20-point lead into the fourth quarter, then hung on and took advantage of a bizarre penalty to hold off the Cardinals to capture their fifth straight victory. After falling behind 7–0 early, the Browns scored the next 27 points, including a pair of touchdown receptions by Paul Warfield. His second touchdown, an 82-yarder, made it 27–7 with four minutes left in the third period. As the Browns gradually replaced starters with backups, the Cardinals crept back into the game, and with a minute to go, trailed only 27–21, and Browns' punter Don Cockroft was kicking from inside his own 10. The kick was blocked but hit the foot of a Cardinal defender in the ensuing scramble, resulting in a 15-yard penalty and a Cleveland first down, allowing the Browns to run out the clock.
Record: 10–2–1

	1	2	3	4		
Browns	7	6	14	0	=	27
Cardinals	7	0	0	14	=	21

STL-Roland 3-yd. run (Bakken kick)
CLE Warfield 4-yd. pass from Nelsen (Cockroft kick)
CLE-Cockroft 25-yd. FG
CLE-Cockroft 33-yd. FG
CLE-Kelly 5-yd. run (Cockroft kick)
CLE-Warfield 82-yd. pass from Nelsen (Cockroft kick)
STL-Lane 2-yd. run (Bakken kick)
STL-Johnson 1-yd. run (Bakken kick)

Passing
CLE: Nelsen 15–26–235 2 TD 1 INT, Rhome 1–5–2 0 TD 0 INT
STL: Johnson 9–18–102 0 TD 1 INT, Hart 6–19–70 0 TD 0 INT

Rushing
CLE: Kelly 14–52, B. Scott 10–32, R. Johnson 4–11, Morrison 5–9, Rhome 1–0
STL: Roland 7–32, Edwards 9–22, Lane 3–10, Johnson 1–1, Gilliam 1-(-4)

Receiving
CLE: Warfield 4–119, Morin 4–66, Collins 3–27, Kelly 3–23, R. Johnson 1–2, B. Scott 1–0
STL: Edwards 3–62, Lane 5–47, Gilliam 3–45, Williams 2–16, Smith 2–2

Sunday, December 21
New York Giants 27, Browns 14
Yankee Stadium (62,966)
White jerseys/white pants

With little to play for, the Browns got caught looking ahead to the Eastern Conference playoff the following weekend in Dallas and allowed two fourth-quarter touchdowns to fall to the Giants on a damp, frosty afternoon in the Bronx. New York thrust a heavy blitz at Bill Nelsen, sacking him five times while forcing three Cleveland turnovers. The most critical came in the fourth quarter after the Giants took a 20–14 lead. The Browns were on the march, and a pass to Milt Morin would have put them inside the New York 30, but Morin fumbled and the Giants recovered, ending the threat. One of the lone highlights for the Browns was the play of rookie RB Bo Scott, who, in his second start, rushed for 85 yards on just nine carries.
Record: 10–3–1

	1	2	3	4		
Browns	7	0	7	0	=	14
Giants	0	13	0	14	=	27

CLE-Warfield 40-yd. pass from Nelsen (Cockroft kick)
NYG-Gogolak 25-yd. FG
NYG-Gogolak 45-yd. FG
NYG-Koy 1-yd. run (Gogolak kick)
CLE-Kelly 2-yd. run (Cockroft kick)
NYG-Morrison 1-yd. pass from Tarkenton (Gogolak kick)
NYG-Morrison 1-yd. run (Gogolak kick)

Passing
CLE: Nelsen 17–28–210 1 TD 1 INT
NYG: Tarkenton 14–26–257 1 TD 0 INT

Rushing
CLE: B. Scott 9–85, Kelly 14–59, Morin 1–22, Morrison 5–21, R. Johnson 3–9
NYG: Koy 20–95, Morrison 9–25, Houston 1–11, Tarkenton 1–0

Receiving
CLE: Warfield 4–75, Collins 4–42, Kelly 3–42, Morin 3–28, B. Scott 1–14, R. Johnson 2–9
NYG: Morrison 6–134, Houston 2–69, Wilson 3–35, Jones 1–11, Koy 2–8

Eastern Conference Playoff
Sunday, December 28
Browns 38, Dallas Cowboys 14
Cotton Bowl (69,321)
Brown jerseys/white pants

The Cowboys entered their third game with the Browns in the past 365 days figuring enough was enough. True, Cleveland was talented, but the Cowboys had been dominant in both 1968 and 1969. For them to be defeated a third consecutive time by the Browns—after being dominated in their previous two contests—would be both stunning and go against all laws of probability. Plus, this time, with the game in the Cotton Bowl, it seemed natural to expect the Cowboys to come out on top.

Instead, the Browns put forth perhaps the most impressive pressure performance in team history, dominating the mighty Cowboys from the opening snap and rolling to a blowout victory on a rainy, gloomy afternoon in Dallas. Bill Nelsen repeatedly frustrated what was considered one of the best defenses in NFL history, throwing for 219 yards—184 in the first half—and leading the Browns to 344 total yards. Paul Warfield sliced up the Dallas secondary for eight receptions for 99 yards, while Bo Scott rushed for a pair of touchdowns in his first postseason appearance. When Leroy Kelly added another early in the fourth, the Cowboys had allowed as many rushing touchdowns on the day as they had in the entire 1969 season.

After the Browns scored 10 points in the last two minutes of the half to go up 17–0, the fans began booing the home team, which hadn't crossed midfield in the first half. Things only got worse when Cleveland LB Jim Houston intercepted Cowboys' QB Craig Morton on Dallas's first possession of the second half and returned it to the Cowboys' 19, setting up another Browns' touchdown. It was one of three turnovers forced by the Cleveland defense, labeled "rubber-band" by Dallas coach Tom Landry for its ability to stretch but not break. It was a comment that roused the unit, which limited the Cowboys' offense to just 217 total yards. It frustrated Morton, who completed only eight of his 24 passes, and completely contained star RB Calvin Hill, holding him to just 17 yards.

Appropriately, the defense provided the exclamation point midway through the fourth when DB Walt Sumner picked off another Morton pass at the Cleveland 12 and sprinted untouched down the sideline for an 88-yard touchdown to make it 38–7. Succumbing to the Cotton Bowl chants of "We Want Roger!," Landry inserted rookie Roger Staubach into his first playoff game, and he rounded out the scoring with a short touchdown pass in the waning moments.

With their third straight thunderous victory over the Cowboys, the Browns would play for the NFL championship for the eleventh time in 20 seasons.

	1	2	3	4		
Browns	7	10	7	14	=	38
Cowboys	0	0	7	7	=	14

CLE-B. Scott 2-yd. run (Cockroft kick)
CLE-Morin 6-yd. pass from Nelsen (Cockroft kick)
CLE-Cockroft 29-yd. FG
CLE-B. Scott 2-yd. run
DAL-Morton 2-yd. run (Clark kick)
CLE-Kelly 1-yd. run (Cockroft kick)
CLE-Sumner 88-yd. interception return (Cockroft kick)
DAL-Rentzel 5-yd. pass from Staubach (Clark kick)

Passing
CLE: Nelsen 18–27–219 1 TD 0 INT, Rhome 2–2–35 0 TD 0 INT
DAL: Morton 8–24–92 0 TD 2 INT, Staubach 4–5–44 1 TD 0 INT

Rushing
CLE: Kelly 19–66, B. Scott 11–33, Morrison 2–3, Cockroft 1–0, R. Johnson 2-(-5)
DAL: Garrison 9–49, Staubach 3–22, Hill 8–17, Morton 4–12, Shy 1–0

Receiving
CLE: Warfield 8–99, Morin 4–52, B. Scott 2–39, Collins 2–19, Morrison 1–18, Jones 1–17, Kelly 2–10
DAL: Hayes 4–44, Rentzel 3–41, Norman 1–26, Garrison 2–15, Hill 1–7, Reeves 1–3

1969 NFL Championship
Sunday, January 4
Minnesota Vikings 27, Browns 7
Metropolitan Stadium (47,900)
White jerseys/white pants

Just as the Browns' playoff encounter with Dallas eerily mirrored the teams' regular-season meeting two months earlier, so too did their rematch with the Minnesota Vikings for the 1969 NFL Championship—the last game played under that title. Once again, the Vikings were simply too much for the Browns and steamrolled their way to their first NFL title and a spot in Super Bowl IV.

On a sunny but brutally cold afternoon in Bloomington, with the temperature hovering in single digits and the wind chill below zero, the Browns looked nervous and hesitant in the early going. Between their cautious play and the tenuous footing on an icy field, the Browns quickly fell behind. The Vikings scored two touchdowns in the first eight minutes of play, the second coming on a 75-yard pass from QB Joe Kapp to WR Gene Washington, who broke free when Browns' DB Erich Barnes slipped and fell at midfield.

Things got no better in the second quarter. Bill Nelsen took a sharp hit and his arm went numb, remaining so for the rest of the game. The Minnesota lead stretched to 24–0 at the half and was 27–0 going into the fourth before the Browns finally got on the board with a short touchdown pass from Nelsen to Gary Collins.

Parlaying a perfect game plan in the frigid conditions, the Minnesota offense rolled up 222 yards on the ground, paced by RB Dave Osborn's 108 on 18 carries. Kapp completed only seven passes, but three went to Washington for 120 yards. On the other side of the ball, the Cleveland offense was further hindered by three turnovers. Adding insult to the Browns' second stomping at the hands of the Vikings came the following week, when Minnesota was thwarted by the upstart Kansas City Chiefs of the American Football League in the Super Bowl.

Frustrating as it was, it proved to be the final game in a golden era of Browns' history. With the AFL/NFL merger about to occur, the Browns' string of postseason dominance came to end on this frosty day in Minnesota. Seventeen years would pass before the Browns won another postseason game and found themselves one game away from the Super Bowl.

	1	2	3	4		
Browns	0	0	0	7	=	7
Vikings	14	10	3	0	=	27

MIN-Kapp 7-yd. run (Cox kick)
MIN-Washington 75-yd. pass from Kapp (Cox kick)
MIN-Cox 30-yd. FG
MIN-Osborn 20-yd. FG
MIN-Cox 32-yd. FG
CLE-Collins 3-yd. pass from Nelsen (Cockroft kick)

Passing
CLE: Nelsen 17–33–181 1 TD 2 INT
MIN: Kapp 7–13–169 1 TD 0 INT

Rushing
CLE: Kelly 15–80, B. Scott 6–17
MIN: Osborn 18–108, Kapp 8–57, Brown 12–43, Reed 5–7, Jones 2–7

Receiving
CLE: B. Scott 5–56, Warfield 4–47, Collins 5–43, Morin 1–18, Kelly 2–17
MIN: Washington 3–120, Brown 1–20, Henderson 2–17, Beasley 1–12

1970

Monday, September 21
Browns 31, New York Jets 21
Cleveland Stadium (85,703)
White jerseys/white pants

On a historic evening, the Browns played their first game as a member of the American Football Conference and hosted the initial broadcast of ABC's *Monday Night Football,* holding off the Jets for an exciting victory before the largest home crowd in team history. The Browns jumped to a quick 14–0 lead with touchdowns on their first two possessions. They then added a third score when WR Homer Jones—acquired in the offseason to replace Paul Warfield, who was traded so the Browns could draft QB Mike Phipps—returned the second-half kickoff 94 yards for a touchdown to make it 21–7. With QB Joe Namath picking apart the Cleveland defense, including hitting WR George Sauer 10 times for a whopping 172 yards, the Jets battled back to pull within three points at 24–21 and regained possession with just over a minute left. Cleveland LB Billy Andrews then made a diving interception and scampered 25 yards for the game-clinching touchdown. It was the fourth New York turnover, as the Jets' mistakes wiped out a convincing 454–221 advantage in total yardage. New York also rolled up 161 yards in penalties (the Browns added 101) and committed two of their turnovers inside the Cleveland 20, allowing the Browns to escape with a victory on a memorable evening.
Record: 1–0

	1	2	3	4		
Jets	0	7	7	7	=	21
Browns	14	0	10	7	=	31

CLE-Collins 8-yd. pass from Nelsen (Cockroft kick)
CLE-B. Scott 2-yd. run (Cockroft kick)
NYJ-Boozer 5-yd. run (Turner kick)
CLE-Jones 94-yd. kickoff return (Cockroft kick)
NYJ-Boozer 10-yd. run (Turner kick)
CLE-Cockroft 27-yd. FG
NYJ-Sauer 33-yd. pass from Namath (Turner kick)
CLE-Andrews 25-yd. interception return (Cockroft kick)

Passing
NYJ: Namath 18–31–298 1 TD 3 INT, Woodall 1–2–7 0 TD 0 INT
CLE: Nelsen 12–27–145 1 TD 0 INT

Rushing
NYJ: Snell 16–108, Boozer 15–58, Nock 1–3, White 1–0, Namath 1-(-1)
CLE: Kelly 20–62, B. Scott 9–12, Nelsen 1–2

Receiving
NYJ: Sauer 10–172, Maynard 4–69, Boozer 3–38, Caster 1–19, Stewart 1–7
CLE: Morin 5–90, B. Scott 4–21, Collins 2–21, Hooker 1–13

Sunday, September 27
San Francisco 49ers 34, Browns 31
Kezar Stadium (37,502)
White jerseys/white pants

In a wild offensive shootout, the Browns rallied from an 11-point deficit but were unable to hang onto a fourth-quarter lead and suffered their first loss in 1970. After San Francisco surged to a 21–10 advantage in the second quarter, the Browns roared back with three touchdowns to take a 31–27 advantage on Leroy Kelly's second score early in the fourth quarter. But on that drive, QB Bill Nelsen injured his knee and left the game, and backup Don Gault threw an interception on Cleveland's next series that led to the go-ahead 49ers' touchdown on a long pass. The Browns were unable to move the ball on their final possession, and San Francisco escaped with an exciting victory. Both teams compiled more than 400 yards of offense, with Nelsen throwing for 308 yards and connecting with WR Fair Hooker for 157.
Record: 1–1

	1	2	3	4		
Browns	7	10	7	7	=	31
49ers	14	7	0	13	=	34

SF-Willard 5-yd. pass from Brodie (Gossett kick)
CLE-B. Scott 3-yd. run (Cockroft kick)
SF-Phillips 35-yd. interception return (Gossett kick)
CLE-Cockroft 20-yd. FG
SF-Thomas 15-yd. pass from Brodie (Gossett kick)

CLE-Hooker 8-yd. pass from Nelsen (Cockroft kick)
CLE-Kelly 33-yd. run (Cockroft kick)
SF-Willard 9-yd. run (kick failed)
CLE-Kelly 8-yd. run (Cockroft kick)
SF-Thomas 61-yd. pass from Brodie (Gossett kick)

Passing
CLE: Nelsen 14–25–308 1 TD 1 INT, Gault 1–3–23 0 TD 1 INT
SF: Brodie 20–31–277 3 TD 0 INT

Rushing
CLE: Kelly 16–74, B. Scott 15–48
SF: Willard 22–105, Tucker 4–23, Cunningham 7–15, Thomas 3–8, Brodie 2–7

Receiving
CLE: Hooker 4–157, Collins 4–68, Kelly 2–54, Morin 2–42, B. Scott 3–10
SF: Thomas 4–78, Witcher 2–41, Washington 5–40, Cunningham 2–36, Windsor 3–35, Riley 1–21, Isenbarger 1–15, Kwalick 1–6, Willard 1–5

Saturday, October 3
Browns 15, Pittsburgh Steelers 7
Cleveland Stadium (84,349)
White jerseys/white pants

Closing out their Saturday-night tradition, the Browns and Steelers fought through a defensive war that saw the Browns score two third-quarter touchdowns to take control and then hold off Pittsburgh on a damp, chilly evening. The Cleveland defense opened the scoring when DE Ron Snidow tackled rookie Steelers' QB Terry Bradshaw in the end zone for a safety, but Bradshaw returned the favor with a 22-yard touchdown run that put Pittsburgh up 7–2 at the half. With the Cleveland offense sputtering, Blanton Collier replaced Don Gault—who'd completed just one of 16 passes—with rookie Mike Phipps in the third quarter. On his first possession, Phipps drove the Browns 90 yards and connected with RB Reece Morrison for a 53-yard touchdown to give them the lead. Fittingly, the Cleveland defense added the final score when DB Erich Barnes returned an interception 38 yards for a touchdown to make it 15–7. The Steelers threatened to score twice in the fourth quarter, but a 47-yard field-goal attempt hit the crossbar, then Browns' DB Walt Sumner halted another drive with an interception after Pittsburgh marched to the Cleveland 12. Thanks to a smothering defense that racked up seven sacks, the Browns emerged victorious despite accumulating less than 200 yards of offense.
Record: 2–1

	1	2	3	4		
Steelers	0	7	0	0	=	7
Browns	2	0	13	0	=	15

CLE-Safety: Snidow tackled Bradshaw in end zone
PIT-Bradshaw 22-yd. run (Mingo kick)
CLE-Morrison 53-yd. pass from Phipps (kick failed)
CLE-Barnes 38-yd. interception return (Cockroft kick)

Passing
PIT: Bradshaw 13–29–207 0 TD 3 INT
CLE: Phipps 3–5–86 1 TD 0 INT, Gault 1–16–44 0 TD 2 INT

Rushing
PIT: Pearson 13–56, Bradshaw 4–44, Fuqua 7–26, Hoak 2–8
CLE: Morrison 21–29, Minniear 7–23, Phipps 1–9, Kelly 5–8

Receiving
PIT: Shanklin 2–80, Bryant 3–35, Smith 3–30, Fuqua 2–20, Staggers 1–20, Hughes 1–18, Hoak 1–4
CLE: Glass 2–63, Morrison 1–53, Hooker 1–14

Sunday, October 11
Browns 30, Cincinnati Bengals 27
Cleveland Stadium (83,520)
White jerseys/white pants

In another historic game, Paul Brown returned to Cleveland, this time as the coach of the Cincinnati Bengals as the two Ohio teams met for the first time on an overcast, mild afternoon by the lake. The Bengals jumped to a quick 10–0 lead, but the Browns fought back to take command in a hard-hitting contest. Browns' DE Walter Johnson pinned Bengals' QB Virgil Carter in the end zone for a safety to open their scoring, then RB Leroy Kelly's second touchdown gave the Browns their first lead early in the fourth quarter. Erich Barnes intercepted a pass and returned it to the Cincinnati 6, and moments later RB Bo Scott scored to put Cleveland up by 10. The Bengals responded with a touchdown of their own to slice the margin back to a field goal, but the Browns converted on a pair of critical third downs in the final minutes to melt the clock and preserve a hard-earned victory. As Paul Brown jogged off the field without shaking Blanton Collier's hand (as was Brown's usual preference), the crowd booed him mercilessly, bringing to a close the first act in what would become a long, bitter rivalry.
Record: 3–1

	1	2	3	4		
Bengals	10	7	3	7	=	27
Browns	2	14	0	14	=	30

CIN-Muhlmann 50-yd. FG
CIN-Phillips 2-yd. run (Muhlmann kick)
CLE-Safety: Johnson tackled Carter in end zone
CLE-Kelly 3-yd. pass from Nelsen (Cockroft kick)
CIN-Berry 58-yd. fumble return (Muhlmann kick)
CLE-Morin 4-yd. pass from Nelsen (Cockroft kick)
CIN-Muhlmann 23-yd. FG
CLE-Kelly 1-yd. run (Cockroft kick)
CLE-B. Scott 1-yd. run (Cockroft kick)
CIN-Thomas 16-yd. pass from Carter (Muhlmann kick)

Passing
CIN: Carter 20–28–218 1 TD 1 INT
CLE: Nelsen 17–29–226 2 TD 1 INT

Rushing
CIN: Phillips 13–33, Robinson 6–17, Johnson 1–4
CLE: Kelly 29–84, B. Scott 10–44, Morin 1–2, Nelsen 1–0

Receiving
CIN: Thomas 7–82, Crabtree 3–55, Coslet 3–48, Robinson 3–21, Phillips 4–12
CLE: Kelly 5–79, Collins 5–65, Morin 4–40, B. Scott 2–29, Hooker 1–13

Sunday, October 18
Detroit Lions 41, Browns 24
Cleveland Stadium (83,577)
White jerseys/white pants

In contrast to the perfect autumn afternoon, the Browns were downright horrible, coughing up six turnovers and giving up 38 points in the first half in a blowout loss to Detroit. After squandering an early lead, the Browns pulled within 17–14 midway through the second quarter before the Lions scored three touchdowns in the next three minutes to build an insurmountable advantage. Bill Nelsen threw three interceptions—two of which were returned for touchdowns—and added a fumble as the Browns continually made self-inflicted errors. The only bright spot was a 100-yard rushing performance by Leroy Kelly, who was in Army reserve training until noon on Sunday, then took a private plane from Port Clinton, Ohio, to Cleveland to arrive shortly before kickoff.
Record: 3–2

	1	2	3	4		
Lions	14	24	3	0	=	41
Browns	7	7	0	10	=	24

CLE-Collins 14-yd. pass from Nelsen (Cockroft kick)
DET-Hand 62-yd. interception return (Mann kick)
DET-Taylor 2-yd. pass from Munson (Mann kick)
DET-Mann 51-yd. FG
CLE-Hooker 16-yd. pass from Nelsen (Cockroft kick)
DET-Walton 28-yd. pass from Munson (Mann kick)
DET-Weger 29-yd. interception return (Mann kick)
DET-Walton 34-yd. pass from Munson (Mann kick)
DET-Mann 34-yd. FG
CLE-Cockroft 47-yd. FG
CLE-B. Scott 3-yd. run (Cockroft kick)

Passing
DET: Munson 10–20–187 3 TD 1 INT, Landry 1–1–13 0 TD 0 INT
CLE: Phipps 6–13–141 0 TD 2 INT, Nelsen 6–16–65 2 TD 3 INT

Rushing
DET: Taylor 13–51, Farr 6–27, Triplett 6–15, Eddy 3–11, Munson 1–11
CLE: Kelly 24–106, B. Scott 7–24, Phipps 2–17

Receiving
DET: Walton 4–158, McCullouch 2–24, Farr 2–11, Triplett 1–13, Taylor 1–2, Freitas 1-(-8)
CLE: Glass 2–74, Hooker 4–52, Morin 3–36, B. Scott 2–30, Collins 1–14

Sunday, October 25
Browns 28, Miami Dolphins 0
Orange Bowl (75,313)
White jerseys/white pants

Playing a regular-season game in Miami for the first time in 24 years, the Browns put together a nearly flawless performance to dominate the 4–1 Dolphins and post their first shutout in three seasons. The Cleveland defense was brilliant, holding Miami to just 165 total yards and only one first down in the second half while adding a touchdown on an interception return by Dale Lindsey. They also collected four sacks and limited former teammate Paul Warfield to just 69 yards receiving. On offense, Bill Nelsen turned in a fine performance, completing 20 of 26 passes for 229 yards as nine different Browns caught passes. The impressive victory gave the Browns a two-game lead in the AFC Central.
Record: 4–2

	1	2	3	4		
Browns	0	14	7	7	=	28
Dolphins	0	0	0	0	=	0

CLE-B. Scott 13-yd. pass from Nelsen (Cockroft kick)
CLE-Lindsey 56-yd. interception return (Cockroft kick)
CLE-Collins 21-yd. pass from Nelsen (Cockroft kick)
CLE-Minniear 1-yd. run (Cockroft kick)

Passing
CLE: Nelsen 20–26–229 2 TD 1 INT, Phipps 3–3–23 0 TD 0 INT
MIA: Griese 5–12–67 0 TD 3 INT, Stofa 2–8–11 0 TD 0 INT

Rushing
CLE: B. Scott 13–41, Morrison 12–22, Kelly 6–16, Minniear 3–8
MIA: Kiick 8–40, Csonka 10–33, Morris 4–30, Seiple 1–24, Griese 1–1, Noonan 1-(-9)

Receiving
CLE: Hooker 5–80, Morin 4–40, B. Scott 4–30, Glass 2–28, Collins 2–25, Jones 2–22, Kelly 2–16, Morrison 1–12, Minniear 1-(-1)
MIA: Warfield 3–69, Morris 1–19, Fleming 2-(-2), Csonka 1-(-8)

Sunday, November 1
San Diego Chargers 27, Browns 10
Cleveland Stadium (80,047)
White jerseys/white pants

Turning the ball over four times, the Browns' momentum came to a screeching halt with a mistake-riddled home defeat to the struggling Chargers. A pair of untimely fumbles changed the complexion of the game—the first by Bo Scott at the San Diego 8 to cost the Browns a chance to build on a 3–0 lead, and the second by Walt Sumner on a punt return that the Chargers ran back for their second touchdown. Cleveland pulled within four points at the half, but San Diego cruised in the second, tacking on 13 points to win just their second game of the season. The loss allowed Pittsburgh—a winner in Cincinnati the following evening—to narrow the Browns' lead in the new AFC Central Division to one game at the midpoint of the season. The game marked the seventeenth straight home game in which the Browns drew more than 80,000 fans.
Record: 4–3

	1	2	3	4		
Chargers	0	14	7	6	=	27
Browns	3	7	0	0	=	10

CLE-Cockroft 11-yd. FG
SD-Alworth 44-yd. pass from Hadl (Mercer kick)
SD-Detwiler 20-yd. fumble return (Mercer kick)
CLE-B. Scott 9-yd. pass from Nelsen (Cockroft kick)
SD-Hubbert 1-yd. run (Mercer kick)
SD-Mercer 37-yd. FG
SD-Mercer 12-yd. FG

Passing
SD: Hadl 13–21–206 1 TD 0 INT
CLE: Nelsen 11–23–144 1 TD 1 INT, Phipps 1–1–20 0 TD 0 INT

Rushing
SD: Hubbert 16–61, Post 11–44, Hadl 2–19, Smith 1–4, Queen 1–3
CLE: B. Scott 13–82, Morrison 21–76

Receiving
SD: Frazier 5–83, Alworth 4–76, Post 3–41, Hubbert 1–6
CLE: Morin 3–51, Glass 3–45, Collins 2–37, Hooker 1–13, B. Scott 2–9, Morrison 1–9

Sunday, November 8
Oakland Raiders 23, Browns 20
Oakland–Alameda County Coliseum (54,463)
White jerseys/white pants

Despite a rousing comeback, the Browns dropped back to .500 with a heartbreaking last-minute loss in Oakland. The Raiders built a 13–0 second-quarter lead, but the Browns roared back with 20 straight points to take a 20–13 advantage with just over four minutes remaining. Then 43-year-old Oakland backup QB George Blanda, who entered the game early in the final period after Daryle Lamonica was knocked out, led the Raiders on a quick scoring drive to tie the game with just over a minute to play. Rather than settling for the tie, the Browns went for the win, and Bill Nelsen threw an interception at midfield with 34 seconds left. It opened the door for Blanda to kick a 52-yard field goal with three seconds showing to give the Raiders their sixteenth straight home victory and hand the Browns a stunning defeat. While Nelsen struggled, completing only nine of 28 passes with three interceptions, Bo Scott topped 100 rushing yards for the first time in his career, most of which came when he exploded for a dazzling 63-yard touchdown run in the third quarter.
Record: 4–4

	1	2	3	4		
Browns	0	10	7	3	=	20
Raiders	3	10	0	10	=	23

OAK-Blanda 43-yd. FG
OAK-Smith 27-yd. pass from Lamonica (Blanda kick)
OAK-Blanda 9-yd. FG
CLE-Kelly 10-yd. pass from Nelsen (Cockroft kick)
CLE-Cockroft 42-yd. FG
CLE-B. Scott 63-yd. run (Cockroft kick)
CLE-Cockroft 32-yd. FG
OAK-Wells 14-yd. pass from Blanda (Blanda kick)
OAK-Blanda 52-yd. FG

Passing
CLE: Nelsen 9–28–110 1 TD 3 INT
OAK: Blanda 7–12–102 1 TD 1 INT, Lamonica 7–20–68 1 TD 0 INT

Rushing
CLE: B. Scott 14–101, Kelly 18–31, Nelsen 1-(-2)
OAK: Smith 16–73, Dixon 14–47, Hubbard 6–21, Todd 4–15, Blanda 1–4

Receiving
CLE: Kelly 5–65, Morin 2–25, B. Scott 2–20
OAK: Wells 2–45, Smith 4–43, Sherman 4–35, Biletnikoff 1–17, Chester 1–13, Dixon 1–9, Todd 1–8

Sunday, November 15
Cincinnati Bengals 14, Browns 10
Riverfront Stadium (60,007)
Brown jerseys/white pants

Before the largest crowd ever to witness a sporting event in Cincinnati, the Browns saw a 10-point lead evaporate and lost an important division game on a chilly afternoon at brand-new Riverfront Stadium. With Bill Nelsen hobbling, Mike Phipps made his first NFL start and drove the Browns to a touchdown on their first possession. They extended the lead to 10–0 early in the second, but the Bengals bounced back with a pair of scores to take the lead following an 85-yard drive late in the third quarter. The Cleveland offense struggled throughout the second half, but had one final chance after the Bengals fumbled a punt return in their own territory in the fourth quarter. The Browns moved to the Cincinnati 30, but a Phipps fourth-down pass was knocked away, and the Bengals were able to run out the clock to pull within a game of the Browns and Steelers in the AFC Central.
Record: 4–5

	1	2	3	4		
Browns	7	3	0	0	=	10
Bengals	0	7	7	0	=	14

CLE-Kelly 9-yd. run (Cockroft kick)
CLE-Cockroft 15-yd. FG
CIN-Phillips 13-yd. pass from Carter (Muhlmann kick)
CIN-Robinson 1-yd. run (Muhlmann kick)

Passing
CLE: Phipps 11–25–170 0 TD 1 INT
CIN: Carter 10–17–123 1 TD 0 INT

Rushing
CLE: Kelly 21–60, Phipps 4–57, B. Scott 9–35, Morrison 1–1
CIN: Carter 9–110, Robinson 14–63, Phillips 9–34, Crabtree 1–3

Receiving
CLE: Morin 3–78, Collins 2–30, Glass 2–28, B. Scott 2–16, Kelly 1–10, Hooker 1–8
CIN: Myers 3–67, Phillips 2–17, Trumpy 2–16, Robinson 2–13, Thomas 1–10

Sunday, November 22
Browns 28, Houston Oilers 14
Cleveland Stadium (74,723)
White jerseys/white pants

Initiating another intra-division rivalry, the Browns snapped a three-game losing streak to regain sole possession of first place with a convincing win over Houston on a blustery day. Forcing four Oiler turnovers, the Browns surged to a 28–7 lead as TE Chip Glass scored a pair of third-quarter touchdowns, including a 78-yard strike from Bill Nelsen. The Browns' quarterback played well in his return, tossing three scoring passes while averaging better than 22 yards per completion. The victory pushed the Browns back to the .500 mark and gave them a one-game cushion over Pittsburgh and fast-charging Cincinnati.
Record: 5–5

	1	2	3	4		
Oilers	0	7	0	7	=	14
Browns	7	7	14	0	=	28

CLE-B. Scott 14-yd. pass from Nelsen (Cockroft kick)
HOU-Dawkins 40-yd. run (Gerela kick)
CLE-Kelly 2-yd. run (Cockroft kick)

CLE-Glass 7-yd. pass from Nelsen (Cockroft kick)
CLE-Glass 78-yd. pass from Nelsen (Cockroft kick)
HOU-Dawkins 8-yd. run (Gerela kick)

Passing
HOU: Johnson 20–37–168 0 TD 3 INT
CLE: Nelsen 10–22–229 3 TD 0 INT

Rushing
HOU: Dawkins 22–143, Richardson 9–28, Hopkins 3–7, Smiley 1–0
CLE: B. Scott 15–63, Kelly 17–46, Morrison 3–9, Minniear 2–8

Receiving
HOU: Reed 8–65, LeVias 5–44, Dawkins 3–17, Joiner 1–17, Richardson 1–13, Haik 1–7, Hopkins 1–5
CLE: Glass 3–102, Morin 2–49, B. Scott 2–33, Hooker 1–20, Collins 1–16, Jones 1–9

Sunday, November 29
Pittsburgh Steelers 28, Browns 9
Three Rivers Stadium (50,214)
White jerseys/white pants

Beginning a miserable run in their first game at new Three Rivers Stadium, the Browns were dominated by the Steelers on a wet, dark afternoon in Pittsburgh and tumbled into a three-way tie for first place in the division. Outgaining the Browns 425 yards to 171 for the game, the Steelers led just 14–9 in the third quarter before Terry Bradshaw tossed a pair of long touchdown passes to put Pittsburgh in the clear. It would be the Browns' worst offensive performance of the season, as they averaged less than two yards per rush as a team, and Leroy Kelly failed to gain a yard on 10 carries. It was the first in what would become a string of 16 consecutive Browns' losses at Three Rivers.
Record: 5–6

	1	2	3	4		
Browns	3	3	3	0	=	9
Steelers	7	7	7	7	=	28

PIT-Shanklin 8-yd. pass from Hanratty (Watson kick)
CLE-Cockroft 16-yd. FG
CLE-Cockroft 38-yd. FG
PIT-Beatty 30-yd. interception return (Watson kick)
CLE-Cockroft 46-yd. FG
PIT-Shanklin 81-yd. pass from Bradshaw (Watson kick)
PIT-Fuqua 57-yd. pass from Bradshaw (Watson kick)

Passing
CLE: Nelsen 11–29–85 0 TD 1 INT, Phipps 4–10–72 0 TD 0 INT
PIT: Bradshaw 4–9–197 2 TD 0 INT, Hanratty 6–8–69 1 TD 0 INT

Rushing
CLE: B. Scott 10–34, Phipps 2–8, Kelly 10–0, Nelsen 1–0
PIT: Pearson 14–61, Bradshaw 5–49, Fuqua 12–33, Hoak 4–14, Smith 1–6, Wilburn 2–5

Receiving
CLE: Hooker 4–50, Morin 2–39, B. Scott 5–32, Jones 1–20, Kelly 3–16
PIT: Shanklin 3–121, Fuqua 4–116, Wilburn 2–29, Smith 1–0

Monday, December 7
Browns 21, Houston Oilers 10
Houston Astrodome (50,582)
White jerseys/white pants

In their first game in the Astrodome, the Browns dominated the second half to defeat the Oilers on *Monday Night Football* and remained tied for first with Cincinnati in the AFC Central. The game turned late in the second quarter when the Browns stopped Houston on fourth-and-goal at the Cleveland 1, then embarked on a quick 99-yard drive to take a 7–3 lead on a Gary Collins touchdown with eight seconds left in the half. From that point on, it was all Cleveland as the Browns scored on the first possession of the third quarter and built a 21–3 fourth-quarter lead.

THE BROWNS' RUST-BELT RIVALRY: HOME AND AWAY

BROWNS VS. STEELERS IN PITTSBURGH
(By Stadium)
Forbes Field (1950–61): 8–3
Pitt Stadium (1958–69): 7–2
Three Rivers Stadium (1970–2000): 5–24
Heinz Field (2001–12): 1–12
ALL-TIME: 21–41

BROWNS VS. STEELERS IN CLEVELAND
(By Stadium)
Cleveland Stadium (1950–95): 33–13
Cleveland Browns Stadium (1999–2012): 3–10
ALL-TIME: 36–23

Leroy Kelly bounced back from a tough day in Pittsburgh to tally 108 rushing yards—the twenty-second 100-yard game of his career—as the Browns rolled to 194 on the ground. It was also the first game following Blanton Collier's announcement that he would retire as head coach after the season.

Record: 6–6

	1	2	3	4		
Browns	0	7	7	7	=	21
Oilers	3	0	0	7	=	10

HOU-Gerela 43-yd. FG
CLE-Collins 1-yd. pass from Nelsen (Cockroft kick)
CLE-B. Scott 2-yd. run (Cockroft kick)
CLE-Kelly 1-yd. run (Cockroft kick)
HOU-Beirne 9-yd. pass from Rhome (Gerela kick)

Passing
CLE: Nelsen 15–27–161 1 TD 2 INT
HOU: Rhome 6–10–73 1 TD 1 INT, Johnson 5–18–49 0 TD 0 INT

Rushing
CLE: Kelly 20–108, B. Scott 11–61, Morrison 10–37, Nelsen 3-(-4), Brown 1-(-8)
HOU: Dawkins 15–81, Richardson 8–29

Receiving
CLE: Jones 3–30, Morin 1–29, Hooker 2–28, Collins 3–23, Morrison 2–21, B. Scott 3–18, Glass 1–12
HOU: Reed 4–44, Beirne 2–34, Richardson 1–25, Joiner 2–12, Dawkins 2–7

Saturday, December 12
Dallas Cowboys 6, Browns 2
Cleveland Stadium (75,458)
White jerseys/white pants

In a steady rain and on a slippery, muddy field, the Browns' hopes for the division title took a severe blow as they fell to the eventual NFC champions by the most unusual final score in team history. Playing for the second time in six days, Cleveland's only points came in the first quarter when Dallas WR Bob Hayes received a Cleveland punt inside his own 10-yard line and, trying to evade tacklers after recovering his own fumble, scampered backward into the end zone, where he was caught by the Browns' Chuck Reynolds for a safety. The 2–0 lead lasted until the third quarter, when Dallas blocked a Browns' punt to set up the go-ahead field goal. The Cowboys added another three points in the fourth quarter, but the Browns squandered a pair of opportunities to score. The first came when Gary Collins fumbled after catching a pass inside the Dallas 10. The second came with less than two minutes remaining when intended receiver Bo Scott slipped, and a Bill Nelsen pass was intercepted after the Browns drove to the Cowboy 17. Aided by the elements, the Browns' defense limited the Cowboys to just 174 total yards, and while the Cleveland offense was much more effective, it coughed up four turnovers. The following afternoon, the Bengals defeated Houston, and the Browns fell out of first place for the first time all season.

Record: 6–7

	1	2	3	4		
Cowboys	0	0	3	3	=	6
Browns	2	0	0	0	=	2

CLE-Safety: Reynolds tackled Hayes in end zone
DAL-Clark 39-yd. FG
DAL-Clark 31-yd. FG

Passing
DAL: Morton 8–17–72 0 TD 0 INT
CLE: Nelsen 23–39–239 0 TD 3 INT

Rushing
DAL: Thomas 19–70, Garrison 19–55, Hill 1–0, Morton 2-(-3)
CLE: B. Scott 12–45, Kelly 7–18

Receiving
DAL: Hayes 3–43, Garrison 2–11, Ditka 1–8, Thomas 1–6, Rucker 1–4
CLE: Morin 5–62, Kelly 5–52, Collins 4–52, B. Scott 6–51, Jones 2–17, Glass 1–5

Sunday, December 20
Browns 27, Denver Broncos 13
Mile High Stadium (51,001)
White jerseys/white pants

In Blanton Collier's final game as head coach, the inspired Browns overwhelmed the Broncos on a bright, chilly day in Denver. Despite knowing their final chance for the AFC Central crown evaporated when the Bengals crushed the Boston Patriots earlier that afternoon, the Browns were sharp, sprinting to a 27–6 lead thanks to a pair of Bill Nelsen touchdown passes in the third quarter.

Mike Phipps tossed two interceptions and coughed up a fumble in relief of Nelsen in the fourth quarter to allow the Broncos to pull within two touchdowns, but the Browns hung on to finish the season at .500. An interception by Cleveland DB Ben Davis—who'd missed nearly all of the previous two seasons with a knee injury—clinched the win. The players hoisted Collier up for a victory ride off the field to close out his marvelous eight-year tenure.

Record: 7–7

	1	2	3	4		
Browns	0	10	17	0	=	27
Broncos	3	3	0	7	=	13

DEN-Howfield 48-yd. FG
CLE-Cockroft 32-yd. FG
CLE-B. Scott 2-yd. run (Cockroft kick)
DEN-Howfield 30-yd. FG
CLE-Cockroft 34-yd. FG
CLE-Jones 43-yd. pass from Nelsen (Cockroft kick)
CLE-B. Scott 23-yd. pass from Nelsen (Cockroft kick)
DEN-Crenshaw 1-yd. run (Howfield kick)

Passing
CLE: Nelsen 11–22–215 2 TD 0 INT, Phipps 1–3–17 0 TD 2 INT
DEN: Pastrana 10–26–116 0 TD 3 INT

Rushing
CLE: Kelly 13–43, B. Scott 13–35, Phipps 2–3, Morrison 5–1
DEN: Little 13–44, Pastrana 7–42, Crenshaw 9–35, Turner 4–34, Anderson 4–24

Receiving
CLE: B. Scott 3–52, Glass 3–46, Jones 1–43, Hooker 3–42, Morin 1–30, Kelly 1–19
DEN: Denson 4–48, Masters 4–41, Van Heusen 1–17, Little 1–10

1971

Sunday, September 19
Browns 31, Houston Oilers 0
Cleveland Stadium (73,387)
White jerseys/white pants

On a damp, dark day, the Browns cruised to victory in the season opener as Nick Skorich won his first game as Cleveland head coach. Allaying fans' fears after a 1–5 preseason, the Browns took control in the second quarter behind the precision passing of QB Bill Nelsen, who completed five straight third-down passes at one point, and RB Leroy Kelly, who scored a pair of one-yard touchdowns. The Cleveland defense rose to the occasion, holding Houston to just 35 yards rushing and forcing six turnovers, including five interceptions: two each by DBs Walt Sumner and rookie Clarence Scott in his first game. Leading 24–0 in the fourth quarter, Skorich inserted backup QB Mike Phipps, who threw a touchdown pass to WR Frank Pitts, acquired from Kansas City 10 days earlier.

Record: 1–0

	1	2	3	4		
Oilers	0	0	0	0	=	0
Browns	7	10	7	7	=	31

CLE-Kelly 1-yd. run (Cockroft kick)
CLE-Kelly 1-yd. run (Cockroft kick)
CLE-Cockroft 24-yd. FG
CLE-Collins 8-yd. pass from Nelsen (Cockroft kick)
CLE-Pitts 18-yd. pass from Phipps (Cockroft kick)

Passing
HOU: Dickey 8–20–144 0 TD 3 INT, Johnson 9–19–101 0 TD 2 INT
CLE: Nelsen 17–31–254 1 TD 1 INT, Phipps 2–7–26 1 TD 0 INT, Kelly 0–1–0 0 TD 0 INT

Rushing
HOU: Campbell 11–22, Dawkins 3–13, Hopkins 1–0
CLE: Kelly 17–60, B. Scott 11–53, Cockroft 1–12, Cornell 1-(-4), Nelsen 1-(-5), Brown 3-(-8)

Receiving
HOU: Joiner 4–92, Burrough 4–82, Beirne 3–47, Campbell 3–15, Dawkins 2–5, Reed 1–4
CLE: Morin 4–74, Hooker 5–69, Collins 4–69, Kelly 4–42, Pitts 2–26

Sunday, September 26
Browns 14, Baltimore Colts 13
Memorial Stadium (56,837)
White jerseys/white pants

In the mud and rain at Memorial Stadium, the Browns stunned the defending world champions on the strength of a suffocating defense that limited the Colts to just 178 total yards and forced a whopping eight turnovers. Cleveland took command of the low-scoring affair when Leroy Kelly scored his second touchdown of the game with 11:29 left to put the visitors ahead 14–6. But the Colts crept back into the game when they blocked a Don Cockroft punt that was returned for a touchdown by Kent State alumnus Don Nottingham and cut the Cleveland lead to one point with just over four minutes remaining. The Colts, who completed only three passes on the day, would get two chances to win the game in the final minutes, and inserted legendary QB Johnny Unitas in the hopes of sparking a comeback. But both drives were halted by Browns' interceptions, one by Clarence Scott, and the second in the final seconds by Walt Sumner, his second of the game and fourth in two weeks. Now 7–0 all-time in the city of Baltimore, the Browns moved into sole possession of first place in the AFC Central.

Record: 2–0

	1	2	3	4		
Browns	0	7	0	7	=	14
Colts	0	3	3	7	=	13

BAL-O'Brien 27-yd. FG
CLE-Kelly 3-yd. run (Cockroft kick)
BAL-O'Brien 32-yd. FG
CLE-Kelly 1-yd. run (Cockroft kick)
BAL-Nottingham 20-yd. blocked punt return (O'Brien kick)

Passing
CLE: Nelsen 13–26–161 0 TD 2 INT, Kelly 0–1–0 0 TD 0 INT
BAL: Morrall 3–13–49 0 TD 3 INT, Unitas 0–5–0 0 TD 2 INT

Rushing
CLE: B. Scott 19–68, Kelly 19–56, Nelsen 1-(-1), Morrison 1-(-5)
BAL: Bulaich 11–63, Matte 11–41, Nottingham 8–40, Morrall 1-(-7)

Receiving
CLE: Hooker 6–78, Collins 3–58, B. Scott 3–17, Morin 1–8
BAL: Matte 1–22, Mackey 1–16, Perkins 1–11

Monday, October 4
Oakland Raiders 34, Browns 20
Cleveland Stadium (84,285)
White jerseys/white pants

Before a massive crowd and a national television audience on *Monday Night Football,* the Browns squandered a 10-point fourth-quarter lead by allowing the Raiders to score 24 points in the final period and soar to a comfortable victory. The Browns built a 14–0 advantage in the second quarter on a 22-yard scoring strike from Bill Nelsen to Leroy Kelly, who had a terrific night with 82 yards rushing and 84 more receiving. But the Raiders rallied for 10 points in the final five minutes of the half to stay close and prevent the Browns from pulling away. After a pair of Don Cockroft field goals extended the Cleveland lead to 20–10 early in the fourth period, Oakland caught fire, scoring a pair of touchdowns within five minutes to take their first lead with nine minutes remaining. The Raiders then pulled away with 10 more points to hand the Browns their first-ever Monday-night loss and their initial defeat of 1971.
Record: 2–1

	1	2	3	4		
Raiders	0	10	0	24	=	34
Browns	0	14	3	3	=	20

CLE-B. Scott 3-yd. run (Cockroft kick)
CLE-Kelly 22-yd. pass from Nelsen (Cockroft kick)
OAK-Chester 20-yd. pass from Lamonica (Blanda kick)
OAK-Blanda 20-yd. FG
CLE-Cockroft 27-yd. FG
CLE-Cockroft 14-yd. FG
OAK-Chester 13-yd. pass from Lamonica (Blanda kick)
OAK-Davis 5-yd. run (Blanda kick)
OAK-Blanda 26-yd. FG
OAK-Banaszak 1-yd. run (Blanda kick)

Passing
OAK: Lamonica 11–21–184 2 TD 1 INT
CLE: Nelsen 15–25–195 1 TD 2 INT

Rushing
OAK: Hubbard 15–103, Banaszak 8–57, Davis 3–11, Lamonica 1-(-3)
CLE: Kelly 22–82, B. Scott 17–75, Morin 1–1, Nelsen 3-(-2)

Receiving
OAK: Biletnikoff 2–60, Hubbard 2–44, Chester 3–43, Davis 2–15, Sherman 1–11, Highsmith 1–11
CLE: Kelly 6–84, Morin 4–65, B. Scott 3–24, Collins 2–22

Sunday, October 10
Browns 27, Pittsburgh Steelers 17
Cleveland Stadium (83,391)
White jerseys/white pants

Midway through the fourth quarter, the game seemed to be following the identical script as the one six days before in which the Browns watched a comfortable first-half lead evaporate in a disheartening defeat. But this time, facing the division-rival Steelers, the Browns found the killer instinct to put together a 16-play, 85-yard drive to score the game-clinching touchdown after Pittsburgh had cut a 17-point lead to three early in the fourth quarter. Bill Nelsen sparked the Cleveland offense, throwing for 236 yards and a touchdown pass to TE Milt Morin, who had one of the finest days of his career with eight receptions for 126 yards. His touchdown made it 10–0 in the first quarter, followed by an 18-yard scoring romp by RB Bo Scott to put the Browns in command. But, buoyed by a pair of Terry Bradshaw touchdown passes, the Steelers pulled within 20–17 and were poised to tie the game with 8:40 left. But kicker Roy Gerela missed a chip-shot field goal and the momentum swung back to the Browns, who responded with their clutch drive, which catapulted them back into first place all alone in the AFC Central.
Record: 3–1

	1	2	3	4		
Steelers	0	7	3	7	=	17
Browns	10	10	0	7	=	27

CLE-Cockroft 25-yd. FG
CLE-Morin 19-yd. pass from Nelsen (Cockroft kick)
CLE-B. Scott 18-yd. run (Cockroft kick)
PIT-Smith 22-yd. pass from Bradshaw (Gerela kick)
CLE-Cockroft 20-yd. FG
PIT-Gerela 33-yd. FG
PIT-Shanklin 11-yd. pass from Bradshaw (Gerela kick)
CLE-Kelly 7-yd. run (Cockroft kick)

Passing
PIT: Bradshaw 12–27–126 2 TD 1 INT, Walden 1–1–10 0 TD 0 INT
CLE: Nelsen 18–27–236 1 TD 1 INT

Rushing
PIT: Pearson 7–73, Fuqua 10–22, Bradshaw 3–15
CLE: B. Scott 22–73, Kelly 17–63, Nelsen 1-(-5)

Receiving
PIT: Smith 3–36, Fuqua 3–32, Adams 4–31, Lewis 1–22, Shanklin 2–15
CLE: Morin 8–126, B. Scott 4–54, Hooker 1–30, Kelly 5–26

Sunday, October 17
Browns 27, Cincinnati Bengals 24
Riverfront Stadium (60,824)
Brown jerseys/white pants

After trailing by 11 points with nine minutes to play, Bo Scott scored two of his three touchdowns in the waning moments to stun the Bengals and deliver the Browns' first-ever win in Cincinnati. A record crowd at year-old Riverfront Stadium watched the home team roll to 232 rushing yards and lead throughout the game. But the momentum shifted when Cleveland DE Jack Gregory recovered a fumble by rookie QB Ken Anderson at the Cincinnati 10 midway through the fourth quarter. Moments later, Scott caught a seven-yard scoring pass from Bill Nelsen to cut the deficit to four points. The Browns regained possession at their own 48 with just over a minute left and quickly drove downfield to take the lead when Scott bulled his way into the end zone past five tacklers from four yards out with 39 seconds left. The Bengals had one final chance, but the Browns' defense stiffened at the Cincinnati 42, forcing three straight Anderson incompletions and then sacking him to end the game.
Record: 4–1

	1	2	3	4		
Browns	0	6	7	14	=	27
Bengals	7	3	7	7	=	24

CIN-Robinson 10-yd. run (Muhlmann kick)
CLE-Cockroft 35-yd. FG
CIN-Muhlmann 12-yd. FG
CLE-Cockroft 22-yd. FG
CIN-Johnson 3-yd. run (Muhlmann kick)
CLE-B. Scott 3-yd. run (Cockroft kick)
CIN-Johnson 49-yd. run (Muhlmann kick)
CLE-B. Scott 7-yd. pass from Nelsen (Cockroft kick)
CLE-B. Scott 4-yd. run (Cockroft kick)

Passing
CLE: Nelsen 18–34–213 1 TD 2 INT, Kelly 0–1–0 0 TD 0 INT
CIN: Anderson 10–21–122 0 TD 1 INT, Willis 0–1–0 0 TD 0 INT

Rushing
CLE: B. Scott 14–42, Kelly 11–24, Cornell 1-(-2)
CIN: Johnson 15–98, Phillips 13–87, Robinson 4–34, Anderson 4–9, Willis 3–2, Lewis 1–2

Receiving
CLE: Morin 8–97, Hooker 3–73, Collins 2–24, Kelly 2–18, B. Scott 3–1
CIN: Myers 3–43, Trumpy 3–43, Phillips 3–31, Johnson 1–5

Sunday, October 24
Denver Broncos 27, Browns 0
Cleveland Stadium (75,674)
White jerseys/white pants

Having won four of their first five, the high-flying Browns hit a brick wall on a damp, gloomy day against the 1–3–1 Broncos, getting dominated in one of the worst performances in team history. The Browns were held to a harmless 60 total yards and turned the ball over four times, while the Broncos rolled up 365 yards, a whopping 280 on the ground. Denver set the tone by driving 92 yards for a touchdown on the game's first possession, the opening salvo in a first-half assault that saw the Broncos build a 24–0 lead. Held to just 24 rushing yards on the day, the Browns did little better through the air, completing only seven of 27 passes with three interceptions. With a Steelers' win over Houston, the Browns' division lead was trimmed to one game.
Record: 4–2

	1	2	3	4		
Broncos	7	17	3	0	=	27
Browns	0	0	0	0	=	0

DEN-Masters 7-yd. pass from Horn (Turner kick)
DEN-Anderson 6-yd. run (Turner kick)
DEN-Forsberg 40-yd. interception return (Turner kick)
DEN-Turner 10-yd. FG
DEN-Turner 36-yd. FG

Passing
DEN: Horn 8–16–85 1 TD 0 INT
CLE: Nelsen 6–19–69 0 TD 1 INT, Phipps 1–8–12 0 TD 2 INT

Rushing
DEN: Little 25–113, Anderson 16–71, Lynch 10–53, Masters 1–37, Simmons 1–7, Turner 2–3, Gehrke 1–2, Mosier 1-(-6)
CLE: Kelly 10–19, Cornell 1–6, B. Scott 4-(-1)

Receiving
DEN: Masters 3–39, Little 2–23, Simmons 1–13, Anderson 1–8, Lynch 1–2
CLE: Morin 1–31, Hooker 3–24, Kelly 1–13, Pitts 1–11, B. Scott 1–2

Sunday, October 31
Atlanta Falcons 31, Browns 14
Cleveland Stadium (76,825)
White jerseys/white pants

On Halloween afternoon, the Browns put forth another horrific showing and were throttled at home by a sub-.500 team for the second straight week. The Falcons took control in the opening seconds, scoring a touchdown on the game's third play, then returning an interception for a touchdown on the Browns' third play to take a quick 14–0 lead. Thwarted by four Bill Nelsen interceptions, the Browns' offense could never get untracked and managed only 153 total yards for the day. Atlanta's lead swelled to 28–0 in the third quarter before the Browns got on the board when a blocked punt by rookie lineman Doug Dieken set up a Bo Scott touchdown run. Fortunately for the Browns, Pittsburgh lost again to Baltimore, thus Cleveland kept its one-game division lead.
Record: 4–3

	1	2	3	4		
Falcons	14	7	7	3	=	31
Browns	0	0	7	7	=	14

ATL-Burrow 39-yd. pass from Shiner (Bell kick)
ATL-Hansen 40-yd. interception return (Bell kick)
ATL-Mitchell 23-yd. pass from Shiner (Bell kick)
ATL-Butler 1-yd. run (Bell kick)
CLE-B. Scott 12-yd. run (Cockroft kick)
ATL-Bell 27-yd. FG
CLE-Collins 24-yd. pass from Nelsen (Cockroft kick)

Passing
ATL: Shiner 6–9–115 2 TD 0 INT, Lothridge 1–1–27 0 TD 0 INT
CLE: Nelsen 9–19–108 1 TD 4 INT

Rushing
ATL: Butler 21–63, Malone 13–56, Wages 9–25, Belton 6–22, Campbell 4–13, Chesson 1-(-4)
CLE: B. Scott 11–46, Kelly 9–19

Receiving
ATL: Burrow 2–71, Mitchell 3–35, Mallory 1–27, Chesson 1–9
CLE: Collins 2–36, Morin 3–30, Hooker 3–30, B. Scott 1–12

Sunday, November 7
Pittsburgh Steelers 26, Browns 9
Three Rivers Stadium (50,202)
White jerseys/white pants

The Browns' slide continued as they were dominated at Three Rivers Stadium for the second straight year, allowing the Steelers to pull into a first-place tie. Trailing 16–0 at the half, the Browns clawed within a touchdown early in the fourth period, but a blocked punt set up a Steelers' field goal to extend the margin back to 10 points. The home team then put the game away when QB Terry Hanratty, who replaced injured Terry Bradshaw in the second quarter, threw a long touchdown pass. The blocked punt capped a lousy day for the Cleveland special teams, which saw Don Cockroft miss a 42-yard field goal and have a 44-yard attempt blocked. The unit did score the Browns' first points when LB Doug Dicken tackled Pittsburgh punter Bobby Walden in the end zone after Walden fumbled the football receiving the snap. While the Cleveland offense again struggled, Leroy Kelly broke out of a month-long slump to rush for 102 yards.
Record: 4–4

	1	2	3	4		
Browns	0	0	2	7	=	9
Steelers	10	6	0	10	=	26

PIT-Gerela 45-yd. FG
PIT-Bradshaw 1-yd. run (Gerela kick)
PIT-Gerela 23-yd. FG
PIT-Gerela 17-yd. FG
CLE-Safety: Dicken tackled Walden in end zone
CLE-B. Scott 1-yd. run (Cockroft kick)
PIT-Gerela 13-yd. FG
PIT-Smith 40-yd. pass from Hanratty (Gerela kick)

Passing
CLE: Nelsen 10–19–114 0 TD 2 INT, Phipps 0–3–0 0 TD 0 INT
PIT: Hanratty 3–10–93 1 TD 0 INT, Bradshaw 4–11–70 0 TD 1 INT

Rushing
CLE: Kelly 22–102, B. Scott 9–27, Nelsen 1-(-7)
PIT: Fuqua 30–131, Bradshaw 4–37, Pearson 9–36, Bankston 5–26, Walden 1-(-7)

Receiving
CLE: Hooker 4–77, B. Scott 5–20, Morin 1–17
PIT: Smith 3–82, Pearson 1–29, Shanklin 1–24, Bankston 1–14, Fuqua 1–14

Sunday, November 14
Kansas City Chiefs 13, Browns 7
Kansas City Municipal Stadium (50,388)
White jerseys/white pants

The Browns' losing streak reached four—at that point the longest in team history—but there were signs of hope in defeat to a powerful Kansas City team on its way to the AFC West title. Hoping to spark a stagnant offense, Nick Skorich started Mike Phipps at quarterback for the second time in his brief career, but the move backfired as Phipps struggled, completing only nine of 22 passes with a pair of interceptions, and Cleveland was held scoreless until the final minutes. Bill Nelsen was sharp after replacing Phipps, and his late touchdown pass kept the Browns in the game, making a missed field goal by Don Cockroft with 10 minutes left all the more critical. Sparked by Frank Pitts, who scorched his old team for 129 receiving yards on five catches, the Browns' offense awoke, tallying nearly 300 total yards, mostly through the air. Meanwhile, the Cleveland defense hung tough, holding the Chiefs scoreless in the second half while collecting three sacks and a pair of turnovers. And in Miami, the Steelers failed to capitalize on the opportunity, falling to the Dolphins, and Pittsburgh and Cleveland remained tied for first in the division with 4–5 records.
Record: 4–5

	1	2	3	4		
Browns	0	0	0	7	=	7
Chiefs	3	10	0	0	=	13

KC-Stenerud 14-yd. FG
KC-Stenerud 27-yd. FG
KC-Hayes 26-yd. pass from Dawson (Stenerud kick)
CLE-Morin 18-yd. pass from Nelsen (Cockroft kick)

Passing
CLE: Nelsen 7–11–130 1 TD 0 INT, Phipps 9–22–117 0 TD 2 INT
KC: Dawson 15–24–234 1 TD 0 INT

Rushing
CLE: Kelly 9–30, B. Scott 10–15
KC: Podolak 20–69, Hayes 9–52, Otis 11–44, McVea 1–12, Dawson 1–8, Frazier 1-(-2)

Receiving
CLE: Pitts 5–129, Hooker 4–46, B. Scott 3–22, Cornell 1–18, Morin 1–18, Kelly 2–14
KC: Taylor 3–66, Stroud 3–55, Podolak 4–50, Hayes 2–35, Wright 3–28

Sunday, November 21
Browns 27, New England Patriots 7
Cleveland Stadium (65,238)
White jerseys/white pants

Finally returning to form, the Browns picked up their first victory in a month, pulling away from the Patriots in the second half to climb back to .500 on a windy, chilly afternoon. After the Browns set the tone by driving 72 yards in 17 plays on their first possession, the Cleveland defense led the way, intercepting four passes thrown by rookie QB Jim Plunkett, including two by LB Billy Andrews. Andrews's second interception set up Leroy Kelly's second touchdown of the day that put the Browns in the clear, making it 24–7 in the fourth quarter. Kelly topped 100 yards as the Browns tallied 175 rushing, while Frank Pitts had a second straight big day through the air, capped by a 35-yard scoring reception that extended the Browns' lead to 10 points in the third quarter. The Steelers kept pace with a win over the New York Giants and the teams remained knotted for first with four games to play.
Record: 5–5

	1	2	3	4		
Patriots	0	7	0	0	=	7
Browns	10	0	7	10	=	27

CLE-Kelly 7-yd. pass from Nelsen (Cockroft kick)
CLE-Cockroft 34-yd. FG
NE-Beer 18-yd. pass from Plunkett (Gogolak kick)
CLE-Pitts 35-yd. pass from Nelsen (Cockroft kick)
CLE-Kelly 1-yd. run (Cockroft kick)
CLE-Cockroft 31-yd. FG

Passing
NE: Plunkett 13–32–169 1 TD 4 INT
CLE: Nelsen 12–23–158 2 TD 0 INT, Phipps 0–3–0 0 TD 0 INT

Rushing
NE: Nance 14–62, Garrett 12–56, Plunkett 1–5
CLE: Kelly 23–113, B. Scott 14–43, Phipps 1–15, Morrison 4–3, Nelsen 1–1

Receiving
NE: Vataha 4–65, Sellers 2–26, Rucker 2–24, Garrett 2–24, Beer 1–18, Nance 2–12
CLE: Pitts 4–75, Hooker 2–27, Kelly 2–21, Morin 2–16, B. Scott 1–14, Collins 1–5

Sunday, November 28
Browns 37, Houston Oilers 24
Houston Astrodome (37,921)
White jerseys/white pants

After struggling through a miserable first half, the Browns caught fire in the second, exploding for 24 points to overcome the Oilers and—with a Steelers' loss to Denver—take over sole possession of first in the AFC Central. The Browns gift-wrapped all of Houston's points in the first half, with one coming on a return of a Leroy Kelly fumble for a touchdown and the other 10 points set up by interceptions. The Browns turned the tables early in the third quarter when DB Ben Davis recovered a Houston fumble—one of five Oiler turnovers on the day—to set up the go-ahead touchdown, and they never looked back. After Houston narrowed the margin to 34–24, the Oilers recovered another Kelly fumble with eight minutes to play and appeared poised to make a game of it. But the Cleveland defense stopped Houston on downs and Don Cockroft tacked on an insurance field goal in the closing minutes to give the Browns a much-needed division victory. Despite the two fumbles, Kelly finished with 107 yards on the day, moving him into sixth place on the NFL's all-time rushing list.

Record: 6–5

	1	2	3	4		
Browns	3	10	14	10	=	37
Oilers	0	17	0	7	=	24

CLE-Cockroft 40-yd. FG
HOU-Moseley 27-yd. FG
HOU-Boyette 19-yd. fumble return (Moseley kick)
CLE-Cockroft 35-yd. FG
CLE-Kelly 1-yd. run (Cockroft kick)
HOU-Joiner 20-yd. pass from Campbell (Moseley kick)
CLE-B. Scott 1-yd. run (Cockroft kick)
CLE-Pitts 18-yd. pass from Nelsen (Cockroft kick)
CLE-B. Scott 4-yd. run (Cockroft kick)
HOU-Pastorini 1-yd. run (Moseley kick)
CLE-Cockroft 39-yd. FG

Passing
CLE: Nelsen 11–22–162 1 TD 2 INT, Phipps 0–2–0 0 TD 0 INT
HOU: Pastorini 4–8–90 0 TD 1 INT, Johnson 9–19–83 0 TD 2 INT, Campbell 1–1–20 1 TD 0 INT

Rushing
CLE: Kelly 23–107, B. Scott 13–39, Cornell 5–14
HOU: Holmes 9–23, Pastorini 3–12, Campbell 5–7, Post 1–3, Walsh 2–1

Receiving
CLE: Jones 4–66, Pitts 3–63, Hooker 3–29, Kelly 1–4
HOU: Joiner 2–73, Reed 3–43, Campbell 2–36, Burrough 3–15, Beirne 1–14, Post 2–13, Walsh 1-(-1)

Sunday, December 5
Browns 31, Cincinnati Bengals 27
Cleveland Stadium (82,705)
White jerseys/white pants

In a thrilling back-and-forth contest, the Browns overcame a 13-point deficit to defeat the Bengals in the final minutes and, with a surprising Pittsburgh loss in Houston, clinch their first-ever AFC Central Division title. Before a massive home crowd, the Browns caught a break on the opening kickoff, recovering a Cincinnati fumble that resulted in a short Leroy Kelly touchdown run and a 7–0 lead. The remainder of the first half belonged to the Bengals, who scored 20 straight points to take control of the contest. But everything changed just before the half when Bill Nelsen hit Fair Hooker deep down the middle for a 39-yard touchdown pass with five seconds left in the second quarter to cut the Cincinnati lead to 20–14. The Browns then took the lead on a dazzling 53-yard scoring reception by Frank Pitts but lost it when Bengals' RB Essex Johnson broke free for an 86-yard touchdown run on the first play of the fourth quarter. After a short Don Cockroft field goal cut the lead to 27–24, the Browns got the ball back at their own 20 with eight minutes left. Nelsen completed two key third-down passes, and Leroy

Kelly capped the final dazzling performance of his legendary career by sweeping around left end and stretching across the goal line for a four-yard touchdown run with 1:48 remaining. Cleveland DB Ernie Kellermann secured the victory a play later with an interception, and, with the news of Pittsburgh's defeat filtering into the stadium, fans swarmed the field at the game's conclusion to celebrate the Browns' division championship.

Record: 7–5

	1	2	3	4		
Bengals	10	10	0	7	=	27
Browns	7	7	7	10	=	31

CLE-Kelly 1-yd. run (Cockroft kick)
CIN-Muhlmann 46-yd. FG
CIN-Dressler 4-yd. run (Muhlmann kick)
CIN-Willis 9-yd. run (Muhlmann kick)
CIN-Muhlmann 24-yd. FG
CLE-Hooker 39-yd. pass from Nelsen (Cockroft kick)
CLE-Pitts 53-yd. pass from Nelsen (Cockroft kick)
CIN-Johnson 86-yd. run (Muhlmann kick)
CLE-Cockroft 12-yd. FG
CLE-Kelly 4-yd. run (Cockroft kick)

Passing
CIN: Carter 13–28–118 0 TD 1 INT
CLE: Nelsen 14–28–224 2 TD 2 INT

Rushing
CIN: Johnson 4–109, Willis 17–79, Dressler 12–39, Carter 1–5
CLE: Kelly 23–127, B. Scott 12–61, Nelsen 3-(-6)

Receiving
CIN: Trumpy 3–43, Dressler 6–26, Myers 3–26, Johnson 1–23
CLE: Pitts 5–103, Hooker 5–80, Morin 3–35, B. Scott 1–6

Sunday, December 12
Browns 21, New Orleans Saints 17
Tulane Stadium (72,794)
Brown jerseys/white pants

Despite seven turnovers, the Browns managed to hold off the Saints and pick up their eighth victory on a warm, humid afternoon in New Orleans. The Browns lost five fumbles, and Leroy Kelly was held to just 13 yards on 11 carries, but thanks to a ferocious Cleveland pass rush, the Saints saw their 10–7 halftime lead evaporate in the second half. Starting Saints' QB Edd Hargett completed only one of 12 passes (and would never play another game in the NFL) and was replaced by rookie Archie Manning. After a Kelly touchdown run gave the Browns the lead for good in the third quarter, Cleveland DT Walter Johnson recovered a Manning fumble in the end zone to provide what proved to be the winning points. Clinging to a four-point lead and with the division already clinched, Nick Skorich inserted Mike Phipps late in the fourth quarter, and Phipps helped the Browns run out the clock and extend their winning streak to four games.

Record: 8–5

	1	2	3	4		
Browns	7	0	7	7	=	21
Saints	0	10	0	7	=	17

CLE-B. Scott 2-yd. run (Cockroft kick)
NO-Durkee 28-yd. FG
NO-Robinson 4-yd. run (Durkee kick)
CLE-Kelly 1-yd. run (Cockroft kick)
CLE-Johnson recovered fumble in end zone (Cockroft kick)
NO-Strong 7-yd. run (Durkee kick)

Passing
CLE: Nelsen 9–18–130 0 TD 2 INT, Phipps 1–2–24 0 TD 0 INT, Kelly 1–1–23 0 TD 0 INT
NO: Manning 6–11–91 0 TD 0 INT, Hargett 1–12–10 0 TD 0 INT

Rushing
CLE: Brown 8–55, B. Scott 14–46, Phipps 5–20, Kelly 11–13, Nelsen 1–0, Cornell 3-(-2)
NO: Strong 14–88, Gresham 16–60, Hargett 1–11, Robinson 1–4, Manning 1-(-4)

Receiving
CLE: Hooker 3–52, B. Scott 3–51, Pitts 4–50, Morin 1–24
NO: Newland 2–63, Parks 2–29, Abramowicz 1–11, Gresham 1–5, Manning 1-(-7)

Sunday, December 19
Browns 20, Washington Redskins 13
RFK Stadium (53,041)
White jerseys/white pants

With both teams already having clinched postseason berths, the Browns closed out the regular season on a high note, coming from behind to beat the Redskins and go into the playoffs riding a five-game winning streak. The final recep-

tion of WR Gary Collins's 10-year career resulted in his seventieth touchdown and gave the Browns a 10–3 lead in the second quarter, but the Redskins scored 10 points before the half to surge ahead. A Don Cockroft field goal tied it in the third, then an interception by Browns' DB Mike Howell and a 68-yard return to the Washington 6 set up a short Bill Nelsen-to-Chip Glass touchdown pass to provide the winning points in the fourth quarter. Browns' DT Jerry Sherk intercepted a pass to halt another Washington drive, and LB John Garlington knocked away a fourth-down Billy Kilmer pass from the Cleveland 8 with time running out to clinch Cleveland's twelfth straight victory over the Redskins.
Record: 9–5

	1	2	3	4		
Browns	3	7	3	7	=	20
Redskins	0	13	0	0	=	13

CLE-Cockroft 30-yd. FG
WAS-Knight 18-yd. FG
CLE-Collins 17-yd. pass from Nelsen (Cockroft kick)
WAS-Brown 29-yd. pass from Kilmer (Knight kick)
WAS-Knight 35-yd. FG
CLE-Cockroft 32-yd. FG
CLE-Glass 4-yd. pass from Nelsen (Cockroft kick)

Passing
CLE: Nelsen 15–23–165 2 TD 2 INT
WAS: Kilmer 18–33–229 1 TD 2 INT

Rushing
CLE: Kelly 18–50, B. Scott 9–19, Nelsen 1–0
WAS: Brown 26–81, Harraway 9–36

Receiving
CLE: Morin 3–40, Hooker 3–34, Pitts 3–30, Kelly 2–30, Collins 1–17, B. Scott 2–10, Glass 1–4
WAS: Brown 4–69, McNeil 3–55, Jefferson 4–46, Harraway 4–32, Smith 3–27

AFC Divisional Playoff
Sunday, December 26
Baltimore Colts 20, Browns 3
Cleveland Stadium (74,082)
White jerseys/white pants

On a gray, rainy day after Christmas, the Browns saw their streaky season come to an end as they were overwhelmed by the defending Super Bowl champions, who avenged their early-season defeat to the Browns in Baltimore with a dominating performance that propelled the Colts to the AFC Championship.

Baltimore set the tone early, as 38-year-old QB Johnny Unitas completed eight of his first nine passes, and the Colts fended off two Cleveland scoring threats in the first quarter. A 39-yard pass to Browns' WR Fair Hooker on the fourth play of the game went for naught when he was hit from behind by former Ohio State QB Rex Kern, now a DB for the Colts, and lost the football at the Baltimore 12. Then a 48-yard punt return by Leroy Kelly proved fruitless as a Don Cockroft field-goal attempt was blocked by Baltimore lineman Bubba Smith. The Colts followed with a 92-yard touchdown drive and never looked back.

The missed opportunities were too much for the Browns to overcome as Baltimore RB Don Nottingham scored a pair of second-quarter touchdowns—the second set up by an interception—to put the visitors in control. The Colts' defense throttled the Browns for the remainder of the day, collecting five sacks and five turnovers while holding the Browns—whose offensive line was riddled with injury and illness—to just 165 yards. Bubba Smith also added another blocked field goal.

As an eerie fog rolled in off the lake, Baltimore tacked on a pair of second-half field goals and punched their ticket for a trip to Miami for the AFC title game the following week.

	1	2	3	4		
Colts	0	14	3	3	=	20
Browns	0	0	3	0	=	3

BAL-Nottingham 1-yd. run (O'Brien kick)
BAL-Nottingham 7-yd. run (O'Brien kick)
CLE-Cockroft 14-yd. FG
BAL-O'Brien 42-yd. FG
BAL-O'Brien 15-yd. FG

Passing
BAL: Unitas 13–21–143 0 TD 1 INT
CLE: Nelsen 9–21–104 0 TD 3 INT, Phipps 3–6–27 0 TD 0 INT

Rushing
BAL: Nottingham 23–92, Matte 16–26, McCauley 3–9, Nowatzke 1–1
CLE: Kelly 14–49, B. Scott 8–25, Nelsen 2-(-5)

Receiving
BAL: Mitchell 5–73, Hinton 2–30, Matte 3–22, Perkins 1–10, Nottingham 1–5, Havrilak 1–3
CLE: B. Scott 5–41, Hooker 1–39, Kelly 4–24, Morin 1–16, Glass 1–11

1972

Sunday, September 17
Green Bay Packers 26, Browns 10
Cleveland Stadium (75,771)
White jerseys/white pants

The preseason funk that saw the Browns lose all six of their exhibition contests carried over into the opener as they were overwhelmed on their home field by the Packers. The Cleveland offense was miserable, coughing up four turnovers and managing just 188 total yards as the team's only touchdown came on a 55-yard return of a blocked field goal by DB Clarence Scott in the second quarter, which gave the Browns a brief 10–7 lead. From that point on, it was all Green Bay as the Packers scored the game's final 19 points. Browns' QB Bill Nelsen made what proved to be the final start of his career, then was relieved by Mike Phipps in the third quarter, though together they completed just 14 of 33 passes and tossed a trio of interceptions. The Browns' running game was even worse, averaging less than three yards per carry, and starting center Jim Copeland was lost for the season with a dislocated hip.

Record: 0–1

	1	2	3	4		
Packers	7	10	3	6	=	26
Browns	3	7	0	0	=	10

GB-McGeorge 23-yd. pass from Hunter (Marcol kick)
CLE-Cockroft 21-yd. FG
CLE-C. Scott 55-yd. blocked field goal return (Cockroft kick)
GB-Marcol 41-yd. FG
GB-McGeorge 2-yd. pass from Hunter (Marcol kick)
GB-Marcol 19-yd. FG
GB-Marcol 19-yd. FG
GB-Marcol 17-yd. FG

Passing
GB: Hunter 7–17–150 2 TD 0 INT
CLE: Nelsen 9–19–84 0 TD 2 INT, Phipps 5–14–49 0 TD 1 INT

Rushing
GB: Brockington 23–83, Lane 16–45, Hudson 6–11, Williams 3–6
CLE: B. Scott 9–33, Kelly 13–26, Phipps 1–3

Receiving
GB: Lane 2–63, Glass 1–31, McGeorge 2–25, Brockington 1–20, Davis 1–11
CLE: Morin 3–48, Kelly 3–30, Hooker 3–28, B. Scott 3–12, Pitts 1–8, Richardson 1–7

Sunday, September 24
Browns 27, Philadelphia Eagles 17
Veterans Stadium (65,720)
White jerseys/white pants

The Browns bounced back from their miserable performance in the opener to take a 24-point second-half lead over Philadelphia and then held off the Eagles to pick up their first victory of the season. Mike Phipps made his first start of the season and threw for a touchdown and ran for another while the Cleveland running game rebounded to collect 155 yards. The Browns' defense, meanwhile, forced three turnovers and tallied five sacks as Nick Skorich picked up his first victory over the team he coached a decade earlier.

Record: 1–1

	1	2	3	4		
Browns	3	17	7	0	=	27
Eagles	0	3	7	7	=	17

CLE-Cockroft 10-yd. FG
PHI-Dempsey 18-yd. FG
CLE-Cockroft 44-yd. FG
CLE-B. Scott 1-yd. run (Cockroft kick)
CLE-Pitts 22-yd. pass from Phipps (Cockroft kick)
CLE-Phipps 4-yd. run (Cockroft kick)
PHI-Jackson 20-yd. pass from Reaves (Dempsey kick)
PHI-Reaves 1-yd. run (Dempsey kick)

Passing
CLE: Phipps 9–20–152 1 TD 1 INT
PHI: Liske 14–25–186 0 TD 2 INT, Reaves 8–14–108 1 TD 0 INT

Rushing
CLE: B. Scott 10–74, Kelly 17–66, Phipps 5–12, Brown 4–3
PHI: Reaves 6–23, Baker 9–22, James 4–15, Watkins 4–12, Sullivan 1-(-6)

Receiving
CLE: Pitts 3–58, Kelly 2–50, Morin 2–42, Hooker 1–7, B. Scott 1-(-5)
PHI: Jackson 7–131, Baker 7–62, Ballman 3–46, Hawkins 3–45, Sullivan 1–7, James 1–3

Sunday, October 1
Browns 27, Cincinnati Bengals 6
Cleveland Stadium (81,564)
White jerseys/white pants

Pulling away with a pair of touchdowns in the fourth quarter, the Browns overwhelmed the undefeated Bengals to pull off the upset and surge into contention in the AFC Central. With the defense forcing four turnovers and not allowing a touchdown, the Browns took a 13–3 lead after three quarters and then sealed the victory with a pair of late scores. The first was a long touchdown reception by WR Frank Pitts, and the second came when DE Wes Grant hit Cincinnati QB Ken Anderson and stripped the ball, then fellow DE Bob Briggs returned it for a score. RB Leroy Kelly paced the Cleveland running game with 83 yards and moved into fifth place on the NFL's all-time rushing list. The Browns' victory was clouded somewhat with the loss of another starter as DE Ron Snidow suffered a broken leg and would miss the remainder of the season.
Record: 2–1

	1	2	3	4		
Bengals	0	3	0	3	=	6
Browns	10	0	3	14	=	27

CLE-Kelly 2-yd. run (Cockroft kick)
CLE-Cockroft 31-yd. FG
CIN-Muhlmann 26-yd. FG
CLE-Cockroft 30-yd. FG
CIN-Muhlmann 14-yd. FG
CLE-Pitts 68-yd. pass from Phipps (Cockroft kick)
CLE-Briggs 11-yd. fumble return (Cockroft kick)

Passing
CIN: Anderson 21–43–221 0 TD 2 INT
CLE: Phipps 12–24–198 1 TD 0 INT

Rushing
CIN: Johnson 15–71, Phillips 6–25, Anderson 2–18, Willis 5–11, Dressler 2–3
CLE: Kelly 22–83, Brown 11–28, Phipps 1-(-2)

Receiving
CIN: Johnson 2–51, Myers 4–50, Thomas 3–43, Phillips 5–30, Trumpy 4–28, Willis 1–9, Buie 1–5, Dressler 1–5
CLE: Pitts 4–105, Hooker 4–47, Morin 2–34, Brown 1–15, Kelly 1-(-3)

Sunday, October 8
Kansas City Chiefs 31, Browns 7
Cleveland Stadium (83,819)
White jerseys/white pants

Before the largest crowd to attend a Cleveland game all season—which included Sen. Ted Kennedy—the Browns gave away a team-record eight turnovers and were blown out on their home field by the Chiefs on a bright, breezy October afternoon. The tone was set on the opening kickoff when Browns' RB Ken Brown fumbled, the first of three he'd cough up in the game. Mike Phipps added four interceptions as the Cleveland offense barely topped 200 total yards. Despite the miserable performance, the Browns pulled within a touchdown midway through the second quarter before Kansas City scored 17 unanswered points to pull away and move to 3–1 on the season.
Record: 2–2

	1	2	3	4		
Chiefs	7	14	7	3	=	31
Browns	0	7	0	0	=	7

KC-Frazier 3-yd. pass from Livingston (Stenerud kick)
KC-Stroud 8-yd. pass from Livingston (Stenerud kick)
CLE-Hooker 16-yd. pass from Phipps (Cockroft kick)
KC-Taylor 34-yd. pass from Livingston (Stenerud kick)
KC-Adamle 1-yd. run (Stenerud kick)
KC-Stenerud 34-yd. FG

Passing
KC: Livingston 8–18–81 3 TD 1 INT
CLE: Phipps 12–27–121 1 TD 4 INT, Kelly 0–1–0 0 TD 0 INT

Rushing
KC: Adamle 20–88, Hayes 13–86, Livingston 5–39, Kinney 9–12, Taylor 1-(-4)
CLE: Brown 7–48, Kelly 10–29, Phipps 3–24, Cornell 3-(-4)

Receiving
KC: Taylor 2–38, Homan 1–22, Adamle 3–10, Stroud 1–8, Frazier 1–3
CLE: Hooker 3–36, Morin 2–31, Pitts 4–30, Brown 1–17, Cornell 2–7

Sunday, October 15
Chicago Bears 17, Browns 0
Cleveland Stadium (72,339)
White jerseys/white pants

For the second straight week, the Browns were humiliated on their home field, this time against a struggling Chicago team that was winless over its previous nine games. On a bright, chilly afternoon, the Browns' offense was once again invisible, managing just 163 total yards and nine first downs while allowing five sacks. Meanwhile, while the Browns' defense held the Bears to just two completed passes, it allowed 256 rushing yards, more than six times Cleveland's ground total. Though he completed only two of nine passes, Chicago QB Bobby Douglass continually burned the Browns, rushing for 117 yards on just 11 carries, including a 57-yard touchdown run in the fourth quarter. The defeat dropped the Browns two games behind first-place Cincinnati with the season on the brink of disaster.
Record: 2–3

	1	2	3	4		
Bears	7	0	3	7	=	17
Browns	0	0	0	0	=	0

CHI-Thomas 41-yd. pass from Douglass (Percival kick)
CHI-Percival 8-yd. FG
CHI-Douglass 57-yd. run (Percival kick)

Passing
CHI: Douglass 2–9–62 1 TD 1 INT
CLE: Phipps 9–19–126 0 TD 0 INT, Nelsen 4–10–43 0 TD 0 INT

Rushing
CHI: Douglass 11–117, Harrison 14–51, Shy 9–41, Pinder 10–36, Thomas 1–8, Lawson 1–7, Farmer 1-(-2), Huarte 1-(-2)
CLE: Phipps 6–26, Kelly 10–14, B. Scott 7-(-3)

Receiving
CHI: Thomas 2–62
CLE: Morin 5–86, Hooker 3–43, B. Scott 2–30, Kelly 2–7, Pitts 1–3

Sunday, October 22
Browns 23, Houston Oilers 17
Houston Astrodome (38,113)
White jerseys/white pants

Following a tumultuous week in which Nick Skorich benched starting center Fred Hoaglin for recently acquired Bob DeMarco and released safety Mike Howell so rookie Thom Darden could take his place in the lineup, the Browns rallied for a much-needed victory in Houston. In a seesaw game, the Browns trailed by a point in the fourth quarter when they put together an 80-yard drive capped by a one-yard Mike Phipps scoring plunge that gave them the lead. The key play on the march was a long third-down completion to Fair Hooker that pushed the Browns into Houston territory. The Cleveland defense held off the Oilers from there, and the Browns evened their record and pulled within a game of first place in the AFC Central.
Record: 3–3

	1	2	3	4		
Browns	0	13	3	7	=	23
Oilers	7	0	7	3	=	17

HOU-Joiner 51-yd. pass from Pastorini (Butler kick)
CLE-Cockroft 33-yd. FG
CLE-Cockroft 33-yd. FG
CLE-Pitts 27-yd. pass from Phipps (Cockroft kick)
HOU-Burrough 80-yd. pass from Pastorini (Butler kick)
CLE-Cockroft 26-yd. FG
HOU-Butler 46-yd. FG
CLE-Phipps 1-yd. run (Cockroft kick)

Passing
CLE: Phipps 9–19–127 1 TD 0 INT
HOU: Pastorini 17–27–239 2 TD 0 INT

Rushing
CLE: Kelly 22–69, B. Scott 11–37, Phipps 5–28, Brown 1–1
HOU: Granger 8–37, Pastorini 4–33, Rodgers 8–31, Holmes 13–23, Walsh 2–16, Joiner 1–3

Receiving
CLE: Hooker 3–56, Pitts 2–33, B. Scott 1–21, Morin 1–16, Kelly 2–1
HOU: Burrough 1–80, Joiner 4–75, Reed 4–35, Holmes 2–22, Granger 4–18, Rodgers 1–9, Walsh 1–0

Sunday, October 29
Browns 27, Denver Broncos 20
Mile High Stadium (51,656)
White jerseys/white pants

On a chilly, windy afternoon in the Rocky Mountains, the Browns put together an impressive performance to rally to victory over the Broncos. Down 17–10 in the third quarter, the Browns pulled within four points on a career-best 57-yard field goal by Don Cockroft, then the second-longest in NFL history. The Browns surged ahead on the only touchdown reception in WR Paul Staroba's career, then after Denver tied the score at 20, Mike Phipps led the Browns on a 74-yard drive, and for the second straight week, provided the winning points with a one-yard touchdown run, this time with just 2:50 to play. Denver quickly drove to the Cleveland 17, but Thom Darden then clinched the victory with his first career interception. The Browns' offense rolled to 343 total yards, including 172 on the ground in what proved to be their last victory in Denver for 18 years.
Record: 4–3

	1	2	3	4		
Browns	3	7	3	14	=	27
Broncos	10	0	7	3	=	20

CLE-Cockroft 27-yd. FG
DEN-Anderson 28-yd. pass from Johnson (Turner kick)
DEN-Turner 32-yd. FG
CLE-Morin 2-yd. pass from Phipps (Cockroft kick)
DEN-Little 19-yd. pass from Johnson (Turner kick)
CLE-Cockroft 57-yd. FG
CLE-Staroba 19-yd. pass from Phipps (Cockroft kick)
DEN-Turner 43-yd. FG
CLE-Phipps 1-yd. run (Cockroft kick)

Passing
CLE: Phipps 15–33–178 2 TD 1 INT
DEN: Johnson 14–24–140 2 TD 1 INT

Rushing
CLE: B. Scott 14–66, Kelly 14–60, Phipps 8–28, Pitts 2–16, Brown 1–2
DEN: Little 14–79, Anderson 8–67

Receiving
CLE: Morin 4–51, Hooker 3–51, Pitts 3–33, Kelly 2–20, Staroba 1–19, Glass 1–8, B. Scott 1-(-4)
DEN: Anderson 7–86, Sherman 4–40, Little 3–14

Sunday, November 5
Browns 20, Houston Oilers 0
Cleveland Stadium (61,985)
White jerseys/white pants

On an overcast afternoon, the Browns blew open a narrow game with a pair of fourth-quarter touchdowns to win their third straight and pull into a second-place tie with Cincinnati. The key sequence of the game took place in the first quarter, when the Browns kept Houston out of the end zone on four straight plays inside the Cleveland 7, including a fourth-down attempt from the 1. A pair of Don Cockroft field goals were the game's only points until Leroy Kelly broke through for scoring runs of one and 14 yards in the final stanza. The Cleveland defense, posting its second straight home shutout of Houston, limited the Oilers to just over 200 total yards and collected four sacks. The Browns remained a game back of front-running Pittsburgh, which blew out the Bengals in a battle for first place.
Record: 5–3

	1	2	3	4		
Oilers	0	0	0	0	=	0
Browns	3	0	3	14	=	20

CLE-Cockroft 19-yd. FG
CLE-Cockroft 32-yd. FG
CLE-Kelly 1-yd. run (Cockroft kick)
CLE-Kelly 14-yd. run (Cockroft kick)

Passing
HOU: Pastorini 7–14–68 0 TD INT, Nix 8–10–47 0 TD 0 INT
CLE: Phipps 9–20–152 0 TD 0 INT

Rushing
HOU: Robinson 15–77, Willis 10–33, Pastorini 1–17, Rodgers 3-(-8)
CLE: Kelly 19–72, B. Scott 12–60, Phipps 6–16, Lefear 1–4

Receiving
HOU: Willis 7–64, Burrough 3–27, Smith 2–11, Robinson 1–6, Reed 1–4, Rodgers 1–3
CLE: Morin 3–70, Hooker 2–39, B. Scott 2–31, Kelly 2–12

Monday, November 13
Browns 21, San Diego Chargers 17
San Diego Stadium (54,205)
White jerseys/white pants

On the brink of defeat, the Browns pulled out a miraculous win with a last-minute touchdown on *Monday Night Football* to extend their winning streak to four games. After RB Ken Brown scored with 10 minutes remaining, the Browns were clinging to a 14–10 lead when San Diego regained possession with just over four minutes to play and drove to the go-ahead score. The Browns took over at their own 36 with 1:01 remaining, and after two quick completions across midfield, Mike Phipps lofted a long pass down the right sideline that Frank Pitts reeled in for a 38-yard touchdown with 41 seconds left. The victory enabled the Browns to stay within a game of first-place Pittsburgh heading into their much-anticipated matchup the following Sunday.

Record: 6–3

	1	2	3	4		
Browns	0	7	0	14	=	21
Chargers	0	3	7	7	=	17

SD-Partee 26-yd. FG
CLE-Phipps 1-yd. run (Cockroft kick)
SD-Edwards 4-yd. pass from Hadl (Partee kick)
CLE-Brown 2-yd. run (Cockroft kick)
SD-Garrett 3-yd. run (Partee kick)
CLE-Pitts 38-yd. pass from Phipps (Cockroft kick)

Passing
CLE: Phipps 13–21–186 1 TD 1 INT
SD: Hadl 12–21–140 1 TD 1 INT

Rushing
CLE: Kelly 17–67, B. Scott 6–21, Phipps 4–17, Pitts 1–13, Brown 2–6
SD: Edwards 17–91, Garrett 24–89, Hadl 3–11

Receiving
CLE: Pitts 5–96, Kelly 1–27, Brown 2–26, Morin 1–18, Glass 1–13, Hooker 1–5, B. Scott 2–1
SD: Norman 3–47, Edwards 3–34, Garrison 2–30, Garrett 4–29

Sunday, November 19
Browns 26, Pittsburgh Steelers 24
Cleveland Stadium (83,009)
White jerseys/white pants

In one of the most dramatic finishes in team history, the Browns pulled out another last-minute victory before a colossal crowd in the most anticipated meeting in their rivalry with the Steelers. Sloshing through the mud on a dark, rainy afternoon, the Browns build a 20–3 second-quarter lead only to see it evaporate into a 24–23 deficit following a 75-yard touchdown run by Pittsburgh rookie RB Franco Harris midway through the fourth quarter. The Browns responded by driving to the Steeler 19, but Don Cockroft missed a short field goal wide right, apparently sealing the Browns' defeat. But the Cleveland defense responded by stopping Pittsburgh on third and short with a minute left, and the Browns regained possession at their own 42 following the Steeler punt. Mike Phipps completed back-to-back passes to propel the Browns into field-goal range, and Cockroft returned to essentially the same spot on the field where he'd missed moments earlier. This time, he connected from 26 yards with 13 seconds remaining and was mobbed by his teammates, then again moments later when the crowd rushed the field after the final gun. The Cleveland offense rolled up a season-high 389 yards, including 217 rushing, paced by Leroy Kelly's 107 in what would be the final 100-yard game of his 10-year Hall of Fame career. The victory moved the Browns into a tie for first with the Steelers with four games to play.

Record: 7–3

	1	2	3	4		
Steelers	3	7	7	7	=	24
Browns	10	10	3	3	=	26

PIT-Gerela 39-yd. FG
CLE-Cockroft 26-yd. FG
CLE-Phipps 1-yd. run (Cockroft kick)
CLE-Cockroft 38-yd. FG
CLE-Pitts 17-yd. pass from Phipps (Cockroft kick)
PIT-Mullins 3-yd. pass from Bradshaw (Gerela kick)
CLE-Cockroft 12-yd. FG
PIT-Fuqua 1-yd. run (Gerela kick)
PIT-Harris 75-yd. run (Gerela kick)
CLE-Cockroft 26-yd. FG

Passing
PIT: Bradshaw 10–21–136 1 TD 1 INT
CLE: Phipps 14–25–194 1 TD 2 INT

Rushing
PIT: Harris 12–136, Fuqua 13–46, Bradshaw 3–17, Lewis 1–12
CLE: Kelly 21–107, B. Scott 14–84, Phipps 3–26

Receiving
PIT: Shanklin 5–108, Lewis 3–24, Mullins 1–3, Harris 1–1
CLE: Morin 4–77, Pitts 3–43, Hooker 2–25, Glass 2–24, B. Scott 2–15, Kelly 1–10

Sunday, November 26
Browns 27, Buffalo Bills 10
Cleveland Stadium (70,104)
White jerseys/white pants

After spotting Buffalo a 10–0 lead in the teams' first-ever meeting, the Browns bounced back with 27 unanswered points to cruise to their sixth straight victory in a snowy, sleety home finale. The Browns tied the game at the half and then dominated the final two quarters, highlighted by a 36-yard touchdown return of an interception by DE Nick Roman on a pass tipped by LB Dale Lindsey. While Buffalo RB O. J. Simpson rushed for 93 yards and went over the 1,000-yard mark for the season, the Browns' defense held the Bills to just 175 total yards and collected five sacks. The victory allowed the Browns to keep pace with the Steelers and stay tied atop the AFC Central.
Record: 8–3

	1	2	3	4		
Bills	10	0	0	0	=	10
Browns	0	10	7	10	=	27

BUF-Simpson 6-yd. run (Leypoldt kick)
BUF-Leypoldt 38-yd. FG
CLE-Cockroft 33-yd. FG
CLE-Kelly 13-yd. pass from Phipps (Cockroft kick)
CLE-Brown 1-yd. run (Cockroft kick)
CLE-Roman 36-yd. interception return (Cockroft kick)
CLE-Cockroft 49-yd. FG

Passing
BUF: Shaw 3–6–34 0 TD 0 INT, Hart 2–6–22 0 TD 1 INT
CLE: Phipps 11–22–145 1 TD 2 INT

Rushing
BUF: Simpson 27–93, Braxton 10–34, Shaw 3–17, Patrick 1–2, Hart 3–1
CLE: Kelly 18–58, B. Scott 8–40, Brown 5–25, Cornell 2–5, Lefear 1–3, Phipps 2–1

Receiving
BUF: Simpson 2–25, Chandler 1–13, Braxton 1–9, Koy 1–9
CLE: B. Scott 6–62, Pitts 2–36, Morin 1–18, Glass 1–16, Kelly 1–13

Sunday, December 3
Pittsburgh Steelers 30, Browns 0
Three Rivers Stadium (50,350)
White jerseys/white pants

Two weeks after their trip to Cleveland, the Steelers avenged their narrow defeat to the Browns with a blowout victory that snapped the Browns' six-game winning streak and put Pittsburgh in the driver's seat to the division title. After Don Cockroft missed a 37-yard field goal in the first quarter, the Browns never threatened to score again and were limited to a season-low 126 total yards as they coughed up three turnovers and allowed four sacks. Meanwhile, Pittsburgh scored 20 points in the second half and the Browns were shut out for the second time in the same season for the first time in team history.
Record: 8–4

	1	2	3	4		
Browns	0	0	0	0	=	0
Steelers	3	7	7	13	=	30

PIT-Gerela 36-yd. FG
PIT-Harris 1-yd. run (Gerela kick)
PIT-Harris 11-yd. run (Gerela kick)
PIT-McMakin 78-yd. pass from Bradshaw (Gerela kick)
PIT-Gerela 44-yd. FG
PIT-Gerela 37-yd. FG

Passing
CLE: Phipps 9–20–59 0 TD 1 INT
PIT: Bradshaw 9–17–162 1 TD 0 INT

Rushing
CLE: Kelly 11–40, B. Scott 10–31, Phipps 7–29, Lefear 1-(-1)
PIT: Harris 20–102, Fuqua 12–31, Bradshaw 5–27, Bleier 1–17, Pearson 3–7, Davis 2–0

Receiving
CLE: Morin 1–24, Hooker 3–22, Kelly 3–12, Brown 1–6, B. Scott 1-(-5)
PIT: McMakin 3–113, Harris 4–26, Shanklin 2–23

Saturday, December 9
Browns 27, Cincinnati Bengals 24
Riverfront Stadium (59,524)
White jerseys/white pants

In the only Saturday meeting in series history, the Browns eliminated the Bengals from the playoff race with an impressive road win, their fifth in six meetings with Cincinnati. Thanks to a long touchdown strike from Mike Phipps to Frank Pitts and a short Leroy Kelly scoring run, the Browns grabbed a 14–0 lead in the second quarter, but the Bengals rebounded with 17 straight points to go ahead early in the third. With the score tied at 24, the Browns scored the winning points on a 27-yard field goal by Don Cockroft with 4:03 remaining. Cincinnati then drove to the Cleveland 7, but LB Billy Andrews intercepted Bengals' QB Virgil Carter at the goal line to preserve the victory. Though the Browns' offense struggled—and Phipps was knocked out of the game after being knocked unconscious on the touchdown pass to Pitts, then returned (replaced briefly by Bill Nelsen in the final appearance of his battle-scarred career)—the defense rose to the occasion, collecting four sacks and four turnovers. The victory proved even more satisfying on Monday night when Oakland defeated the Jets, allowing the Browns to clinch the AFC wild-card spot and ensure a trip to the playoffs for the second straight year.
Record: 9–4

	1	2	3	4		
Browns	0	14	10	3	=	27
Bengals	0	10	14	0	=	24

CLE-Pitts 50-yd. pass from Phipps (Cockroft kick)
CLE-Kelly 5-yd. run (Cockroft kick)
CIN-Carter 8-yd. run (Muhlmann kick)
CIN-Muhlmann 31-yd. FG
CIN-Johnson 9-yd. run (Muhlmann kick)
CLE-Hooker 20-yd. pass from Phipps (Cockroft kick)
CLE-Cockroft 27-yd. FG
CIN-Dressler 1-yd. run (Muhlmann kick)
CLE-Cockroft 27-yd. FG

Passing
CLE: Phipps 10–24–151 2 TD 1 INT, Nelsen 1–2–14 0 TD 1 INT
CIN: Carter 7–16–95 0 TD 2 INT, Anderson 6–10–59 0 TD 0 INT

Rushing
CLE: B. Scott 12–59, Kelly 12–42, Phipps 4–10, Nelsen 1-(-2)
CIN: Dressler 14–75, Johnson 13–48, Phillips 5–23, Carter 4–22, Lewis 1–15, Anderson 1–11

Receiving
CLE: Pitts 4–77, Hooker 3–44, Kelly 3–25, B. Scott 1–19
CIN: Myers 8–116, Joiner 1–17, Dressler 2–11, Coslet 1–8, Johnson 1–2

Sunday, December 17
Browns 26, New York Jets 10
Shea Stadium (62,614)
White jerseys/white pants

On frozen turf that better resembled a skating rink, the Browns overcame the Jets and the high winds whipping through Flushing Meadows to pick up their tenth victory of the season and their eighth in nine weeks. Though the Jets were playing without injured QB Joe Namath, the game was tied at 10 early in the third quarter before the Browns pulled away. The big play was an 80-yard scoring pass from Mike Phipps to Frank Pitts, which gave the Browns the lead for good and opened the floodgates. Phipps and Pitts hooked up for another score in the fourth period, though Don Cockroft's string of 88 consecutive extra points came to an end afterward. Despite the conditions, the Browns tallied 342 total yards while holding New York to 206.
Record: 10–4

	1	2	3	4		
Browns	7	3	7	9	=	26
Jets	7	0	3	0	=	10

CLE-B. Scott 27-yd. run (Cockroft kick)
NYJ-Boozer 3-yd. run (Howfield kick)
CLE-Cockroft 8-yd. FG
NYJ-Howfield 19-yd. FG
CLE-Pitts 80-yd. pass from Phipps (Cockroft kick)
CLE-Pitts 7-yd. pass from Phipps (kick failed)
CLE-Cockroft 13-yd. FG

Passing
CLE: Phipps 7–17–156 2 TD 2 INT
NYJ: Davis 5–12–44 0 TD 1 INT

Rushing
CLE: Kelly 18–78, B. Scott 10–69, Phipps 5–38, Cornell 2–7, Brown 1–1
NYJ: Boozer 22–106, Bjorklund 7–28, McClain 5–24, Davis 3–24

Receiving
CLE: Pitts 4–98, Hooker 1–38, Morin 1–25, B. Scott 1-(-5)
NYJ: Bjorklund 3–19, Caster 1–19, Boozer 1–6

Holidays with the Browns

Labor Day (0–26–1)
1949:
Browns 28, Buffalo Bills 28

1981:
San Diego Chargers 44, Browns 14

1984:
Seattle Seahawks 33, Browns 0

Halloween (2–3)
1954:
Browns 24, New York Giants 14

1965:
Minnesota Vikings 27, Browns 17

1971:
Atlanta Falcons 31, Browns 14

1976:
Cincinnati Bengals 21, Browns 6

1999:
Browns 21, New Orleans Saints 16

Thanksgiving (3–3)
1947:
Browns 27, Los Angeles Dons 17

1948:
Browns 31, Los Angeles Dons 14

1949:
Browns 14, Chicago Hornets 6

1966:
Dallas Cowboys 26, Browns 14

1982:
Dallas Cowboys 31, Browns 14

1989:
Detroit Lions 13, Browns 10

Christmas Eve (2–7)
1950:
NFL Championship
Browns 30, Los Angeles Rams 28

1967:
Eastern Conference Playoff
Dallas Cowboys 52, Browns 14

1972:
AFC Divisional Playoff
Miami Dolphins 20, Browns 14

1988:
AFC Wild Card Game
Houston Oilers 24, Browns 23

1994:
Browns 35, Seattle Seahawks 9

1995:
Jacksonville Jaguars 24, Browns 21

2005:
Pittsburgh Steelers 41, Browns 0

2006:
Tampa Bay Buccaneers 22, Browns 7

2011:
Baltimore Ravens 20, Cleveland Browns 14

New Year's Eve (0–1)
2006:
Houston Texans 14, Browns 6

New Year's Day (1–1)
1995:
AFC First-Round Playoff
Browns 20, New England Patriots 13

2011:
Pittsburgh Steelers 13, Browns 9

Overall Record:
8–17–1

AFC Divisional Playoff
Sunday, December 24
Miami Dolphins 20, Browns 14
Orange Bowl (78,196)
Brown jerseys/white pants

On a sun-drenched Christmas Eve in Miami, the Browns came within minutes of an historic upset as they came closer to beating the undefeated Dolphins than any other team in 1972.

Things started poorly for the Browns, 13-point underdogs, as Mike Phipps's first pass was intercepted, then the Dolphins took the lead on a blocked punt return for a touchdown. Things got worse when Frank Pitts dropped a potential touchdown pass, and Phipps was picked off on the next play, leading to a Miami field goal and a 10–0 lead.

But gradually, the Browns crept back into the game. A Phipps scramble for a touchdown got the Browns on the board in the third quarter, then Miami DB Dick Anderson fumbled after intercepting Phipps, and Browns' WR Fair Hooker recovered to give the Browns new life. Two plays later, Hooker reeled in a 27-yard touchdown pass to give the Browns a 14–13 lead with 8:11 remaining.

But the Dolphins kept their perfect season alive with a clutch 80-yard drive—aided by two key receptions by former Browns' WR Paul Warfield—capped by an eight-yard touchdown run by RB Jim Kiick with four minutes left. After being forced to punt, the Browns had one final chance, driving to the Miami 34 before Phipps was picked off for the fifth time, allowing the Dolphins to run out the clock and secure their fifteenth straight victory on the season.

Though Miami had escaped, the Browns had outplayed them, tallying more yardage while holding the Dolphins' triumphant trio of running backs—Mercury Morris, Jim Kiick, and Larry Csonka—all under 75 yards. Unheralded Browns' RB Bo Scott wound up leading all rushers with 94 yards on 16 carries.

The following week the Dolphins defeated Pittsburgh in the AFC Championship, then held off Washington in Super Bowl VII to complete the only perfect season in modern NFL history. Conversely, the playoff appearance would be the Browns' last for eight years.

	1	2	3	4		
Browns	0	0	7	7	=	14
Dolphins	10	0	0	10	=	20

MIA-Babb 5-yd. blocked punt return (Yepremian kick)
MIA-Yepremian 40-yd. FG
CLE-Phipps 5-yd. run (Cockroft kick)
MIA-Yepremian 46-yd. FG
CLE-Hooker 27-yd. pass from Phipps (Cockroft kick)
MIA-Kiick 8-yd. run (Yepremian kick)

Passing
CLE: Phipps 9–23–131 1 TD 5 INT
MIA: Morrall 6–13–88 0 TD 0 INT

Rushing
CLE: B. Scott 16–94, Phipps 8–47, Brown 4–13, Kelly 4–11
MIA: Morris 15–72, Kiick 14–50, Warfield 2–41, Csonka 12–32, Morrall 4–3

Receiving
CLE: Hooker 3–53, B. Scott 4–30, Kelly 1–27, Morin 1–21
MIA: Twilly 3–33, Warfield 2–50, Kiick 1–5

1973

Sunday, September 16
Browns 24, Baltimore Colts 14
Cleveland Stadium (74,303)
White jerseys/white pants

A ferocious defensive effort overcame a handful of mistakes on offense and special teams and propelled the Browns to victory on opening day. Holding the Colts to just 129 total yards for the game and sacking rookie QB Bert Jones (son of former Browns' star RB Dub Jones) five times in his NFL debut, the Browns' soared to a 17–7 halftime lead after DB Clarence Scott returned the first interception of Jones's career 45 yards for a touchdown late in the second quarter. But thanks to three Cleveland fumbles, the Colts hung in the game, cutting the margin to three when LB Ted Hendricks blocked a Don Cockroft punt and returned the football for a touchdown. But the Browns, playing without offensive linemen John Demarie and Bob McKay, responded with a drive deep into Baltimore territory, capped when QB Mike Phipps hit WR Frank Pitts in the corner of the end zone on a third-down pass to push the lead back to 10 on their second scoring connection of the afternoon. The Cleveland defense took it from there, holding the Colts to just 11 yards of offense in the second half.

Record: 1–0

	1	2	3	4		
Colts	0	7	7	0	=	14
Browns	7	10	7	0	=	24

CLE-Pitts 26-yd. pass from Phipps (Cockroft kick)
BAL-Speyrer 33-yd. pass from Jones (Hunt kick)
CLE-Cockroft 14-yd. FG
CLE-C. Scott 45-yd. interception return (Cockroft kick)
BAL-Hendricks 2-yd. blocked punt return (Hunt kick)
CLE-Pitts 8-yd. pass from Phipps (Cockroft kick)

Passing
BAL: Jones 6–22–56 1 TD 1 INT
CLE: Phipps 12–26–150 2 TD 0 INT

Rushing
BAL: Nottingham 16–64, McCauley 16–53, Jones 3–24, Lee 1-(-16)
CLE: Phipps 7–55, Brown 8–40, McKinnis 11–27, Lefear 7–19, Kelly 9–6

Receiving
BAL: Speyrer 1–33, Chester 2–14, Mitchell 1–8, Nottingham 1–5, McCauley 1-(-4)
CLE: Hooker 5–62, Pitts 4–56, Morin 2–37, McKinnis 1-(-5)

Sunday, September 23
Pittsburgh Steelers 33, Browns 6
Three Rivers Stadium (49,396)
White jerseys/white pants

As was becoming their custom in Three Rivers Stadium since its opening three years before, the Browns were simply overwhelmed by the Steelers in a lopsided defeat. For the fourth straight year, Cleveland was unable to score a touchdown in Pittsburgh, as the Steelers rolled to a 16–3 halftime lead and then blew the game open in the third quarter. The Browns held their ground for much of the first quarter before the Steelers scored their first touchdown on the final play of the period to break a 3–3 tie. The turning point came early in the second quarter. Trailing by 10, the Browns attempted a fake field goal from the Pittsburgh 9, which was snuffed out by the Steelers. Aided by three Mike Phipps interceptions, the Steelers racked up 196 yards on the ground while smothering the Cleveland offense.

Record: 1–1

	1	2	3	4		
Browns	3	0	0	3	=	6
Steelers	10	6	10	7	=	33

PIT-Gerela 12-yd. FG
CLE-Cockroft 43-yd. FG
PIT-Fuqua 4-yd. run (Gerela kick)
PIT-Gerela 40-yd. FG
PIT-Gerela 26-yd. FG
PIT-Gerela 44-yd. FG
PIT-Lewis 8-yd. pass from Bradshaw (Gerela kick)
CLE-Cockroft 28-yd. FG
PIT-Lewis 53-yd. pass from Hanratty (Gerela kick)

Passing
CLE: Phipps 15–29–157 0 TD 3 INT, Horn 0–1–0 0 TD 0 INT
PIT: Bradshaw 5–14–140 1 TD 1 INT, Hanratty 1–1–53 1 TD 0 INT

Rushing
CLE: Kelly 13–39, Phipps 4–30, Lefear 5–13, McKinnis 6–9, Brown 6–0, Richardson 1-(-7)
PIT: Fuqua 16–80, Pearson 9–74, Bradshaw 2–16, Harris 4–14, Davis 4–12

Receiving
CLE: Richardson 4–49, Pitts 2–33, Morin 2–27, Kelly 4–25, Lefear 2–14, Hooker 1–9
PIT: Lewis 3–92, Shanklin 2–92, Harris 1–9

Sunday, September 30
Browns 12, New York Giants 10
Cleveland Stadium (76,065)
White jerseys/white pants

After a disastrous first half that saw the Browns throw two interceptions, miss two field goals, and manage only 79 yards, they turned everything around in the final 30 minutes, rallying from a 10-point deficit to knock off the Giants in the waning moments. The Cleveland defense, battered the week before in Pittsburgh, hunkered down to dominate New York in the second half, not allowing another point while limiting the Giants to only two first downs. For the contest, the Giants managed only 123 total yards, including just 49 on the ground, though their top RB—former Brown Ron Johnson—was out with an injury. The tide began to turn in the third quarter when DB Thom Darden returned an interception 36 yards to the Giants' 7 to set up one of Don Cockroft's four field goals on the afternoon. Mike Phipps struggled much of the day, throwing a pair of interceptions while being sacked six times, but put it together when it counted. Trailing 10–9 with just over seven minutes left, the Browns took possession at their own 18 and drove 79 yards in nine plays to the New York 3, where Cockroft kicked the game-winner from 10 yards out with 2:45 to play. Two plays later, DB Walt Sumner intercepted a Norm Snead pass, allowing the Browns to melt most of the final two minutes. When the Giants got the ball back for one final play, Sumner intercepted Snead again to clinch the victory. Somewhat lost in the second-half comeback was the NFL debut of the Browns' rookie RB from Oklahoma, Greg Pruitt, who carried the ball only twice for six yards, but added 30 more on a pair of receptions.
Record: 2–1

	1	2	3	4		
Giants	0	10	0	0	=	10
Browns	0	0	6	6	=	12

NYG-Gogolak 20-yd. FG
NYG-Tucker 20-yd. pass from Snead (Gogolak kick)
CLE-Cockroft 11-yd. FG
CLE-Cockroft 27-yd. FG
CLE-Cockroft 30-yd. FG
CLE-Cockroft 10-yd. FG

Passing
NYG: Snead 9–19–82 1 TD 3 INT
CLE: Phipps 9–20–134 0 TD 2 INT, Horn 1–2–12 0 TD 0 INT

Rushing
NYG: Orduna 15–36, Evans 10–13
CLE: Kelly 25–63, Brown 13–45, Phipps 6–27, G. Pruitt 2–6

Receiving
NYG: Grim 3–24, Tucker 1–20, Ballman 1–16, Herrmann 1–12, Evans 3–10
CLE: Richardson 3–70, G. Pruitt 2–30, Brown 3–21, McKinnis 1–4

Sunday, October 7
Browns 17, Cincinnati Bengals 10
Cleveland Stadium (70,805)
White jerseys/white pants

After struggling mightily over the first three weeks, the Cleveland offense rose to the occasion to lead the way to a key divisional victory over the Bengals—the Browns' fifth straight over their in-state rivals. The running game—paced by workmanlike performances by Ken Brown and Leroy Kelly—exploded for 216 yards and a pair of touchdowns and the Browns did not turn the football over while collecting three Cincinnati giveaways. After the Bengals snuck to an early 3–0 lead, Browns' DB Ben Davis recovered a fumble at the Cleveland 37 that halted Cincinnati's momentum and set up Cleveland's first score. Leroy Kelly gave the Browns a lead they would not relinquish with a three-yard touchdown run to snap a string of 10 consecutive quarters without a Browns' touchdown. Then in the third period, a second fumble recovery by Davis led to another Kelly touchdown to make it 14–3. After the Bengals cut the lead back to four points when WR Isaac Curtis made a remarkable one-handed catch on a 60-

yard touchdown, the Browns pushed the margin back to a touchdown minutes later and completed the scoring with a Don Cockroft field goal. The defense took it from there, and the Browns were victorious for the third time in four weeks.

Record: 3–1

	1	2	3	4		
Bengals	3	0	0	7	=	10
Browns	0	7	7	3	=	17

CIN-Muhlmann 38-yd. FG
CLE-Kelly 3-yd. run (Cockroft kick)
CLE-Kelly 7-yd. run (Cockroft kick)
CIN-Curtis 60-yd. pass from Anderson (Muhlmann kick)
CLE-Cockroft 24-yd. FG

Passing
CIN: Anderson 11–23–177 1 TD 1 INT
CLE: Phipps 9–18–77 0 TD 0 INT

Rushing
CIN: Johnson 12–52, Clark 12–44
CLE: Brown 26–93, Kelly 21–73, Phipps 4–52, G. Pruitt 1-(-2)

Receiving
CIN: Curtis 3–80, Johnson 3–38, Joiner 1–26, Coslet 1–18, Clark 2–10, Trumpy 1–5
CLE: Morin 4–32, Kelly 2–24, Brown 2–13, Hooker 1–8

Monday, October 15
Miami Dolphins 17, Browns 9
Cleveland Stadium (72,070)
White jerseys/white pants

Though it ended in defeat, the Browns put forth a marvelous effort before a national audience on *Monday Night Football*, giving the defending Super Bowl champions all they could handle in a titanic defensive struggle. The Dolphins, winners of 18 of their last 19 regular-season games, were nine-point favorites going into a rematch of the teams' fierce divisional playoff in the Orange Bowl 10 months earlier, but found themselves down 6–3 at the half. After Miami drew first blood in the second quarter, an interception by Ben Davis set up the game-tying field goal, followed by a 44-yard kick by Don Cockroft to give the Browns the lead. But the margin could have been larger had the Browns not squandered other opportunities, including a missed 34-yard field goal. In the second half, the Dolphins' bruising RB Larry Csonka took over, scoring a touchdown to put Miami up, followed by another Cockroft field goal to cut the Miami lead to 10–9 going into the fourth quarter. The Browns had two opportunities to take the lead in the final period, but Cockroft was short on a 52-yard field-goal attempt, then after Cleveland regained possession with eight minutes left, a third-down pass by Mike Phipps was intercepted at midfield. Csonka then bulled his way into the end zone after five straight carries to put the game away. Despite Miami's effective running game (114 yards by Csonka and 94 more by Mercury Morris), the defenses took center stage, with neither team topping 250 total yards. Miami QB Bob Griese was held to three pass completions for the game and was picked off twice, while Phipps was sacked five times.

Record: 3–2

	1	2	3	4		
Dolphins	0	3	7	7	=	17
Browns	0	6	3	0	=	9

MIA-Yepremian 36-yd. FG
CLE-Cockroft 30-yd. FG
CLE-Cockroft 44-yd. FG
MIA-Csonka 2-yd. run (Yepremian kick)
CLE-Cockroft 35-yd. FG
MIA-Csonka 2-yd. run (Yepremian kick)

Passing
MIA: Griese 3–11–51 0 TD 2 INT
CLE: Phipps 8–16–93 0 TD 1 INT

Rushing
MIA: Csonka 21–114, Morris 13–94, Kiick 2–8, Briscoe 1–2, Griese 3-(-6)
CLE: Kelly 14–65, Brown 17–55, Phipps 7–34

Receiving
MIA: Warfield 1–33, Briscoe 1–14, Kiick 1–4
CLE: Morin 2–42, Brown 3–30, Pitts 3–21

Sunday, October 21
Browns 42, Houston Oilers 13
Cleveland Stadium (61,146)
White jerseys/white pants

The Browns got back into the win column with a near-perfect performance against the hapless Oilers, who were throttled for their seventeenth straight defeat on a beautiful autumn afternoon in Cleveland. The smallest crowd for a Browns home game in 10 years watched its team almost effortlessly cruise to a huge halftime lead, scoring more points (28) than the Oilers accumulated in total yardage (24). Houston would manage only 106 total yards and four first downs for the game but made things more respectable with 13 third-quarter points, only to then surrender two more Cleveland touchdowns in the fourth period. The Browns rolled up what would be a season-high 366 total yards, sparked by the efficient play of Mike Phipps, who ran for two touchdowns and threw for two more. An inspired effort by Greg Pruitt, who averaged better than five yards per carry on 11 rushes, led a dominating running attack that collected 264 yards. The 42 points were the most the Browns had scored in a game in four years, and it would be another four years before they topped it.

Record: 4–2

	1	2	3	4		
Oilers	0	0	13	0	=	13
Browns	14	14	0	14	=	42

CLE-Kelly 8-yd. run (Cockroft kick)
CLE-Phipps 1-yd. run (Cockroft kick)
CLE-Hooker 21-yd. pass from Phipps (Cockroft kick)
CLE-Pitts 3-yd. pass from Phipps (Cockroft kick)
HOU-Hinton 34-yd. pass from Pastorini (Butler kick)
HOU-Butler 9-yd. FG
HOU-Butler 31-yd. FG
CLE-Phipps 13-yd. run (Cockroft kick)
CLE-B. Scott 2-yd. pass from Horn (Cockroft kick)

Passing
HOU: Pastorini 6–19–118 1 TD 1 INT, Dickey 2–3-(-2) 0 TD 0 INT
CLE: Phipps 11–19–146 2 TD 1 INT, Horn 1–2–2 1 TD 0 INT

Rushing
HOU: Pastorini 3–19, Jolley 2–5, Gresham 7–1, Willis 6-(-2)
CLE: Brown 14–61, G. Pruitt 11–56, B. Scott 13–46, Lefear 3–44, Kelly 6–38, Phipps 4–15, Richardson 1–4

Receiving
HOU: Willis 2–51, Gresham 3–35, Hinton 1–34, Jolley 1–0, Burrough 1-(-4)
CLE: Hooker 3–52, Morin 3–38, Kelly 1–33, Pitts 3–18, B. Scott 2–7

Sunday, October 28
Browns 16, San Diego Chargers 16
Cleveland Stadium (68,244)
White jerseys/white pants

Following a crisp performance the week before, the Browns fell flat against the struggling Chargers and were lucky to escape with a last-minute tie in the mud and rain. Behind strong play by rookie QB Dan Fouts, who'd replaced veteran Johnny Unitas behind center three weeks before, the Chargers—who'd won only once in their first six games—took a 10–3 halftime lead over the sluggish Browns. Though Mike Phipps was in the midst of another frustrating game, the Cleveland special teams sparked a comeback by blocking a San Diego field-goal attempt early in the fourth quarter that led to a field goal for the Browns to cut the Chargers' lead to four. Minutes later, DT Jerry Sherk stripped the ball from Chargers' RB Mike Garrett, and ballhawking Ben Davis recovered at the San Diego 32 and returned it to the 9. The Browns then took their first lead moments later when Greg Pruitt scored his first professional touchdown on a magnificent play in which he shook off a vicious facemask tackle and changed direction to scamper nine yards into the end zone. But with time running out, Fouts connected with WR Willie McGee for a 50-yard gain to the Cleveland 17. With 30 seconds showing, Ray Wersching booted a 16-yard field goal to knot the score for good. The Fouts-led Chargers rolled up 339 yards, nearly twice as much as the Browns, who were 12-point favorites.

Record: 4–2–1

	1	2	3	4		
Chargers	0	10	3	3	=	16
Browns	0	3	3	10	=	16

SD-Wersching 11-yd. FG
CLE-Cockroft 40-yd. FG
SD-Garrett 1-yd. pass from Fouts (Holliday run)
CLE-Cockroft 17-yd. FG
SD-Wersching 8-yd. FG
CLE-Cockroft 42-yd. FG
CLE-G. Pruitt 7-yd. run (Cockroft kick)
SD-Wersching 16-yd. FG

Passing
SD: Fouts 8–16–135 1 TD 1 INT
CLE: Phipps 10–21–92 0 TD 2 INT

Rushing
SD: Garrett 19–130, Edwards 15–44, Holmes 6–16, Fouts 1–16, Jones 3-(-2)

CLE: Lefear 7–47, Brown 12–39, G. Pruitt 5–24, B. Scott 5–11, Phipps 1–4, Richardson 1-(-7)

Receiving
SD: McGee 1–50, Garrett 5–47, Holliday 2–38
CLE: Lefear 2–24, Brown 2–21, B. Scott 2–13, Morin 1–19, Glass 1–13, Richardson 1–7, Pitts 1-(-5)

Sunday, November 4
Minnesota Vikings 26, Browns 3
Metropolitan Stadium (45,590)
White jerseys/white pants

Facing the undefeated Vikings and one of the greatest defenses in recent memory, the Browns were dominated on both sides of the ball and simply overwhelmed by a superior team. The Browns were held to a mere four first downs and only 145 total yards of offense, while Minnesota rolled up 23 and 353. Yet the Browns hung around in the first half. Catching a break by recovering a Vikings' fumble on the opening kickoff, the Browns jumped to a quick 3–0 lead and trailed by only six at the intermission despite handing the Vikings two turnovers in Cleveland territory. But Minnesota pulled away in the second half, wearing down a Browns' defense riddled by the flu to move to 8–0 on the season.
Record: 4–3–1

	1	2	3	4		
Browns	3	0	0	0	=	3
Vikings	3	6	7	10	=	26

CLE-Cockroft 27-yd. FG
MIN-Cox 16-yd. FG
MIN-Cox 23-yd. FG
MIN-Cox 33-yd. FG
MIN-Reed 3-yd. run (Cox kick)
MIN-Voigt 7-yd. pass from Tarkenton (Cox kick)
MIN-Cox 41-yd. FG

Passing
CLE: Phipps 10–20–82 0 TD 2 INT, Horn 2–3–8 0 TD 0 INT
MIN: Tarkenton 13–22–166 1 TD 0 INT, Berry 1–2–5 0 TD 0 INT

Rushing
CLE: Brown 7–25, Phipps 2–22, Kelly 4–19, Lefear 1–7, McKinnis 1–0, Cockroft 1-(-3)
MIN: Reed 22–79, Marinaro 15–48, Tarkenton 5–33, Osborn 5–28, Brown 2–10, McClanahan 1–3, Berry 1–0

Receiving
CLE: Pitts 4–36, Morin 1–29, Brown 4–26, Richardson 1–5, Lefear 1–0, Kelly 1-(-6)
MIN: Marinaro 6–65, Gilliam 2–50, Voigt 3–28, Dale 1–18, Osborn 1–5, Reed 1–5

Sunday, November 11
Browns 23, Houston Oilers 13
Houston Astrodome (37,230)
White jerseys/white pants

It wasn't quite the blowout of the teams' first meeting in Cleveland three weeks before, but the Browns followed a similar script: jump to a big first-half lead and then hold off the scuffling Oilers. Behind an impressive performance by Greg Pruitt, the Browns scored all the points they'd need in the first quarter, jumping to a 17–0 lead. With Pruitt leading the way, the Browns rolled up 180 yards on the ground. Late in the period, Pruitt swept around right end for a 53-yard touchdown run, the Browns' longest of the season. The teams swapped field goals in the second half before the Oilers pulled within 10 in the final minutes, but it wasn't enough to prevent their eighth straight loss to the Browns.
Record: 5–3–1

	1	2	3	4		
Browns	17	0	3	3	=	23
Oilers	0	3	3	7	=	13

CLE-Cockroft 30-yd. FG
CLE-Phipps 1-yd. run (Cockroft kick)
CLE-G. Pruitt 53-yd. run (Cockroft kick)
HOU-Butler 27-yd. FG
HOU-Butler 46-yd. FG
CLE-Cockroft 22-yd. FG
CLE-Cockroft 45-yd. FG
HOU-Alston 39-yd. pass from Dickey (Butler kick)

Passing
CLE: Phipps 8–17–132 0 TD 1 INT
HOU: Dickey 12–22–139 1 TD 0 INT, Pastorini 8–15–84 0 TD 1 INT, Willis 0–1–0 0 TD 0 INT

Rushing
CLE: G. Pruitt 5–66, Brown 17–59, McKinnis 6–33, Kelly 5–12, Phipps 2–8, Lefear 2–2
HOU: Thomas 7–42, Willis 14–38, Gresham 6–26

Receiving
CLE: Glass 1–47, Morin 3–46, Kelly 1–23, Pitts 1–10, Brown 1–4, G. Pruitt 1–2
HOU: Hinton 4–69, Parks 4–51, Alston 3–48, Burrough 3–34, Gresham 2–24, Willis 4-(-3)

Sunday, November 18
Browns 7, Oakland Raiders 3
Oakland–Alameda County Coliseum (47,398)
White jerseys/white pants

Thanks to a tremendous defensive effort on a blustery day by the Bay, the Browns completely thwarted a talented and heavily favored Oakland team and collected a victory that buoyed their hopes for a playoff berth. The Raiders, boasting the league's top offense going in, were limited to only 172 yards of offense as the Browns sacked QB Ken Stabler, the NFL's leading passer, five times. In a game that featured 21 punts, the Browns were little better offensively but broke through for the game's only touchdown when WR Fair Hooker beat veteran DB Willie Brown for a seven-yard touchdown reception in the second quarter. The visitors were also able to withstand three turnovers, including a Mike Phipps fumble at midfield in the fourth quarter that led to Oakland's only points—a short George Blanda field goal. Each team had the ball twice after that, with the Browns melting most of the final two minutes before punting back to the Raiders, who were unable to muster a threat before time expired. It would be 14 years before the Browns beat the silver and black again, as the Raiders would win the next eight meetings.
Record: 6–3–1

	1	2	3	4		
Browns	0	7	0	0	=	7
Raiders	0	0	0	3	=	3

CLE-Hooker 7-yd. pass from Phipps (Cockroft kick)
OAK-Blanda 23-yd. FG

Passing
CLE: Phipps 9–17–96 1 TD 0 INT
OAK: Stabler 17–33–122 0 TD 0 INT

Rushing
CLE: Brown 22–82, Phipps 6–28, G. Pruitt 4–27, Kelly 9–20, B. Scott 1–1
OAK: Hubbard 12–48, Davis 6–20, Smith 6–15, Stabler 1–13, Banaszak 1–1

Receiving
CLE: Pitts 4–62, Kelly 2–21, Hooker 1–7, Brown 2–6
OAK: Branch 4–43, Biletnikoff 3–27, Smith 2–21, Siani 2–17, Davis 1–6, Moore 1–6, Hubbard 4–2

Sunday, November 25
Browns 21, Pittsburgh Steelers 16
Cleveland Stadium (67,773)
White jerseys/white pants

For the second straight year, the Browns and Steelers fought to the bitter end on a gloomy November day in Cleveland, once again with the home team pulling out a thrilling victory in the final minute. A seesaw game reached its climax in the final period starting when Pittsburgh kicked a field goal to go ahead 16–14 with eight minutes to play. Following a Cleveland punt, the Steelers were driving, hoping to put the game away with time running out when DE Joe "Turkey" Jones stripped the football from Pittsburgh QB Joe Gilliam, in for an injured Terry Hanratty. Browns' LB John Garlington recovered at the Cleveland 39 and the Browns had new life. It looked as though it would be for naught two plays later when Mike Phipps was swarmed by Steelers on third-and-nine, but he ducked down twice to avoid the rush and floated a pass to Greg Pruitt in the flat, who wove his way through a broken field for a 42-yard gain to the Pittsburgh 18. Moments later Pruitt finished his heroics with a majestic 19-yard sweep around left end for a touchdown with just under a minute left. Yet the drama wasn't complete—the Steelers drove to the Cleveland 15 in the waning seconds before Gilliam threw four straight incomplete passes to end the final threat. It was the ninth straight loss in Cleveland for the Steelers, who, despite outgaining the Browns by 130 yards and forcing four turnovers, now led the Browns by only a half-game in the AFC Central. With back-to-back wins over teams that had made the playoffs the year before, the Browns were in good position to secure their third straight postseason berth themselves.
Record: 7–3–1

	1	2	3	4		
Steelers	7	3	3	3	=	16
Browns	7	7	0	7	=	21

PIT-Shanklin 9-yd. pass from Gilliam (Gerela kick)
CLE-Phipps 1-yd. run (Cockroft kick)
CLE-G. Pruitt 15-yd. pass from Phipps (Cockroft kick)
PIT-Gerela 24-yd. FG

PIT-Gerela 14-yd. FG
PIT-Gerela 20-yd. FG
CLE-G. Pruitt 19-yd. run (Cockroft kick)

Passing
PIT: Gilliam 12–29–197 1 TD 1 INT, Hanratty 1–1–27 0 TD 0 INT
CLE: Phipps 5–17–146 1 TD 3 INT

Rushing
PIT: Pearson 16–94, Harris 22–48, Gilliam 2–14, Fuqua 3–13, Bleier 1–1
CLE: G. Pruitt 5–31, Phipps 6–24, B. Scott 7–19, Brown 5–18, Kelly 11–12

Receiving
PIT: Shanklin 4–87, Lewis 7–65, Brown 1–45, McMakin 1–27
CLE: G. Pruitt 2–57, Brown 1–46, Kelly 1–36, Pitts 1–7

Sunday, December 2
Browns 20, Kansas City Chiefs 20
Arrowhead Stadium (70,296)
White jerseys/white pants

As the bright winter afternoon in Kansas City turned dark and the lights above brand-new Arrowhead Stadium illuminated the field below, the Browns put together a fierce fourth-quarter rally to turn a potential defeat into a tie and keep their playoff hopes alive. The Chiefs had victory in their grasp after they stretched a four-point lead to 20–6 in the fourth quarter. Now trailing by two touchdowns with just over six minutes to play and not having reached the end zone the entire game, the Browns cut the lead to seven when Greg Pruitt burst through the right side and made it into the clear down the sideline for a 65-yard touchdown run, which gave Pruitt the first 100-yard game of his career. Then the Browns' defense, which had struggled all afternoon, forced a critical three-and-out and the Cleveland offense regained possession at its own 24. With the sun settling into the Missouri horizon, and the blustery afternoon turning to evening, the Browns maneuvered to midfield, where Mike Phipps, who was sacked seven times on the day, hit TE Milt Morin for a 51-yard touchdown pass to tie the game. The stalemate—which marked the first time the Browns had tied two games in the same season since 1949—set up a three-way knot atop the AFC Central with the Browns, Bengals, and Steelers.
Record: 7–3–2

	1	2	3	4		
Browns	0	3	3	14	=	20
Chiefs	7	0	3	10	=	20

KC-Wright 11-yd. pass from Livingston (Stenerud kick)
CLE-Cockroft 44-yd. FG
KC-Stenerud 15-yd. FG
CLE-Cockroft 28-yd. FG
KC-Stenerud 13-yd. FG
KC-Podolak 2-yd. run (Stenerud kick)
CLE-G. Pruitt 65-yd. run (Cockroft kick)
CLE-Morin 51-yd. pass from Phipps (Cockroft kick)

Passing
CLE: Phipps 13–27–171 1 TD 1 INT, G. Pruitt 0–1–0 0 TD 0 INT
KC: Livingston 7–11–70 1 TD 0 INT, Beathard 4–11–67 0 TD 0 INT

Rushing
CLE: G. Pruitt 15–110, Phipps 4–19, Kelly 4–9, Brown 3–4, McKinnis 2–2, B. Scott 3–0
KC: Ellison 20–108, Podolak 26–84, Wright 1–9, Livingston 1–5, Beathard 3–1, Butler 1–1

Receiving
CLE: Morin 3–86, Pitts 4–35, Hooker 2–18, Brown 1–17, McKinnis 1–12, G. Pruitt 1–7, B. Scott 1-(-4)
KC: Wright 5–70, Taylor 2–41, Butler 1–14, Podolak 3–12

Sunday, December 9
Cincinnati Bengals 34, Browns 17
Riverfront Stadium (58,266)
White jerseys/white pants

The Browns' playoff hopes were crippled along the Ohio River as the red-hot Bengals dominated Cleveland on both sides of the ball to win their fifth straight and close in on their second AFC Central Division title. Cincinnati rookie WR Isaac Curtis burned the Browns for three touchdowns in the first half—including a 70-yarder—as the home team soared to a 21–3 halftime lead. But the Browns rebounded in the third quarter. After the Bengals made it 24–3 with a field goal, the Browns cut the margin to seven after a short touchdown reception by WR Gloster Richardson, followed by DB Van Green returning a Bengals' fumble 15 yards for a touchdown. But on the ensuing possession, Bengals' QB Ken Anderson scrambled for a first down on a key third-and-10 play and the drive ended in a momentum-killing touchdown. Cincinnati more than doubled the Browns in total yardage (374–148), forced three turnovers, and sacked Mike Phipps five times. A week after his breakthrough game in Kansas City, Greg Pruitt was held to 12 yards on six carries as Cleveland running backs combined for just 36 yards on the ground.

Record: 7–4–2

	1	2	3	4		
Browns	0	3	14	0	=	17
Bengals	7	14	10	3	=	34

CIN-Curtis 9-yd. pass from Anderson (Muhlmann kick)
CLE-Cockroft 40-yd. FG
CIN-Curtis 70-yd. pass from Anderson (Muhlmann kick)
CIN-Curtis 20-yd. pass from Anderson (Muhlmann kick)
CIN-Muhlmann 10-yd. FG
CLE-Richardson 6-yd. pass from Phipps (Cockroft kick)
CLE-Green 15-yd. fumble return (Cockroft kick)
CIN-Clark 1-yd. run (Muhlmann kick)
CIN-Muhlmann 45-yd. FG

Passing
CLE: Phipps 13–27–111 1 TD 2 INT
CIN: Anderson 11–19–201 3 TD 0 INT

Rushing
CLE: Phipps 4–42, G. Pruitt 6–12, Brown 4–12, Kelly 4–9, Lefear 1–3, B. Scott 4–0
CIN: Johnson 19–91, Clark 22–69, Anderson 4–10, Elliott 1–3

Receiving
CLE: Richardson 3–44, Morin 2–27, Hooker 3–26, G. Pruitt 2–11, Brown 3–3
CIN: Curtis 5–117, Joiner 5–70, Trumpy 1–14

Sunday, December 16
Los Angeles Rams 30, Browns 17
Los Angeles Memorial Coliseum (73,948)
White jerseys/white pants

With their playoff hopes essentially gone and Greg Pruitt seeing only limited action while suffering from food poisoning, the Browns didn't put up much of a fight against the NFC West-champion Rams. Cleveland lost three fumbles in the first quarter—and would turn the ball over five times on the day—as Los Angeles jumped to a quick 13–0 lead that ballooned to 27–10 at halftime. Eventual Hall-of-Famer Leroy Kelly played his final game, carrying seven times for 24 yards, while the season finale also marked the last game for longtime LB Dale Lindsey and Canton-bound offensive lineman Gene Hickerson. While Mike Phipps threw for a touchdown and ran for another, the Cleveland offensive attack once again failed to ignite. Conversely, the Rams rolled up 231 yards on the ground, led by RB Lawrence McCutcheon, whose son would play DB for the Browns a quarter-century later. The up-and-down season closed with the Browns scoring the second-least amount of points in team history.

Record: 7–5–2

	1	2	3	4		
Browns	7	3	0	7	=	17
Rams	13	14	3	0	=	30

LA-Ray 48-yd. FG
LA-Ray 27-yd. FG
LA-Klein 23-yd. pass from Hadl (Ray kick)
CLE-Phipps 25-yd. run (Cockroft kick)
LA-Jackson 8-yd. pass from Hadl (Ray kick)
CLE-Cockroft 22-yd. FG
LA-Baker 4-yd. run (Ray kick)
LA-Ray 15-yd. FG
CLE-Pitts 14-yd. pass from Phipps (Cockroft kick)

Passing
CLE: Phipps 16–25–132 1 TD 2 INT
LA: Hadl 6–14–92 2 TD 0 INT, Harris 1–4–4 0 TD 0 INT

Rushing
CLE: G. Pruitt 7–39, Phipps 3–35, Kelly 7–24, McKinnis 2–6, Brown 6–4, B. Scott 1–2
LA: McCutcheon 19–83, Bertelsen 11–66, Josephson 5–36, Scribner 3–15, Smith 3–13, Baker 3–9, Harris 1–9

Receiving
CLE: Pitts 4–44, Holden 3–27, Kelly 3–24, Hooker 2–14, Morin 2–13, B. Scott 1–7, G. Pruitt 1–3
LA: Jackson 3–48, Klein 1–23, Curran 1–13, Snow 1–8, McCutcheon 1–4

1974

Receiving
CLE: Morin 2–27, Brown 3–9, Dunbar 1–1, B. Scott 3–0
CIN: Curtis 5–117, Myers 2–28, Trumpy 1–25, Chandler 1–9, Clark 1–9

Sunday, September 15
Cincinnati Bengals 33, Browns 7
Riverfront Stadium (53,113)
White jerseys/white pants

With expectations for the new season already subdued, the Browns suffered their worst opening-day loss in franchise history and their worst loss ever to Paul Brown's Bengals. Things looked good early as the Browns hung tough with the defending AFC Central champs and took a 7–0 lead with just 23 seconds left in the first half. But thanks to a 49-yard reception by Cincy WR Isaac Curtis, the Bengals tied the game with a second left and then pulled away in the third quarter. While the Cleveland running game was powerful, rolling up 200 yards, the Browns were held to just three net yards passing as QB Mike Phipps was sacked five times.
Record: 0–1

	1	2	3	4		
Browns	0	7	0	0	=	7
Bengals	0	7	16	10	=	33

CLE-Morin 7-yd. pass from Phipps (Cockroft kick)
CIN-Clark 1-yd. run (Muhlmann kick)
CIN-Curtis 19-yd. pass from Anderson (Muhlmann kick)
CIN-Safety: Carpenter tackled Phipps in end zone
CIN-Trumpy 25-yd. pass from Anderson (Muhlmann kick)
CIN-Parrish 62-yd. punt return (Muhlmann kick)
CIN-Muhlmann 32-yd. FG

Passing
CLE: Phipps 9–22–37 1 TD 1 INT
CIN: Anderson 9–17–179 2 TD 0 INT, Clark 1–1–9 0 TD 0 INT

Rushing
CLE: Brown 12–78, G. Pruitt 12–64, B. Scott 8–36, Phipps 3–22
CIN: Clark 14–74, Dressler 7–31, Davis 6–23, Elliott 4–21, Williams 1–15, Anderson 1–2, Johnson 1–0

Sunday, September 22
Browns 20, Houston Oilers 7
Cleveland Stadium (58,988)
White jerseys/white pants

In front of the smallest crowd for a home opener in Cleveland in 11 years, the Browns took advantage of six turnovers and won an ugly game over division-rival Houston. A touchdown run by RB Greg Pruitt in the second quarter wiped out an early deficit, while the Cleveland defense held the Oilers to just 35 rushing yards and limited QB Lynn Dickey to two completions in 15 attempts in the second half. Yet the victory was dampened by the loss of two starters to knee injuries: WR Steve Holden, who wouldn't return until mid-season, and center Jim Copeland, who would miss the rest of the year. Copeland's injury led to the signing of Ohio State grad Tom DeLeone the following Thursday. Amid these gathering storm clouds, it would be more than a month before the Browns tasted victory again.
Record: 1–1

	1	2	3	4		
Oilers	7	0	0	0	=	7
Browns	3	7	10	0	=	20

CLE-Cockroft 27-yd. FG
HOU-Alston 9-yd. pass from Dickey (Butler kick)
CLE-G. Pruitt 9-yd. run (Cockroft kick)
CLE-Cockroft 41-yd. FG
CLE-Brown 5-yd. pass from Phipps (Cockroft kick)

Passing
HOU: Dickey 9–26–163 1 TD 3 INT, Coleman 0–1–0 0 TD 0 INT
CLE: Phipps 15–29–141 1 TD 0 INT

Rushing
HOU: Washington 8–24, Amundson 5–9, Coleman 10–2
CLE: G. Pruitt 14–89, Phipps 5–37, B. Scott 7–32, Brown 10–27, McKinnis 6–25, Holden 1–6

Receiving
HOU: Alston 2–42, Burrough 2–40, Parks 2–30, Amundson 1–29, Washington 1–15, Gresham 1–7
CLE: Holden 5–83, Brown 5–37, Dunbar 1–15, B. Scott 3–13, McKinnis 1-(-7)

Sunday, September 29
St. Louis Cardinals 29, Browns 7
Busch Stadium (43,472)
Brown jerseys/white pants

With many preoccupied St. Louis fans listening to portable radios to stay tuned to the exploits of the baseball Cardinals in the heat of a pennant race, the gridiron Cards turned a 7–0 game at the half into a blowout by battering the Browns in a wild third quarter. St. Louis RB Terry Metcalf, showing his six-year-old son Eric how it's done, returned the second-half kickoff 94 yards for a touchdown and also accumulated 68 yards on a trio of punt returns, giving the Cardinals good field position all afternoon. With their strong running attack stifled, the Browns' lone score was a 55-yard halfback option toss from Greg Pruitt to WR Gloster Richardson. Perhaps the most significant moment of the game came in garbage time late in the fourth quarter when backup QB Brian Sipe made his professional debut.
Record: 1–2

	1	2	3	4		
Browns	0	0	7	0	=	7
Cardinals	0	7	22	0	=	29

STL-Thompson 56-yd. interception return (Bakken kick)
STL-Metcalf 94-yd. kickoff return (Bakken kick)
CLE-Richardson 55-yd. pass from Pruitt (Cockroft kick)
STL-Gray 68-yd. pass from Hart (kick failed)
STL-Bakken 44-yd. FG
STL-Anderson 1-yd. run (kick failed)

Passing
CLE: Phipps 12–26–117 0 TD 1 INT, G. Pruitt 1–1–55 1 TD 0 INT, Sipe 1–2–6 0 TD 0 INT
STL: Hart 4–11–107 1 TD 0 INT

Rushing
CLE: Phipps 7–38, G. Pruitt 8–21, Brown 6–19, B. Scott 5–9, McKinnis 2–4, Lefear 1–2
STL: Anderson 14–60, Willard 10–44, Otis 8–19, Belton 3–19, Hart 1–16, Metcalf 6–13

Receiving
CLE: Richardson 2–71, Dunbar 3–37, Brown 4–27, Lefear 2–14, Morin 1–14, B. Scott 1–9, McKinnis 1–6
STL: Gray 1–68, Thomas 1–27, Metcalf 2–12

Sunday, October 6
Oakland Raiders 40, Browns 24
Cleveland Stadium (65,247)
White jerseys/white pants

The Browns surprised even themselves by surging to a 10–0 lead over John Madden's Raiders thanks to an interception return for a touchdown by LB Charlie Hall on the game's second play and a long punt return by Greg Pruitt that set up a field goal minutes later. After Pruitt caught a scoring pass from Mike Phipps, the Browns led 17–7 going into the second quarter, but the Raiders scored 30 points in the next 30 minutes of play to turn it into a blowout. The turning point came midway through the second quarter when Cleveland RB Ken Brown was pinned in the end zone for an Oakland safety following an interception by Browns' DB Thom Darden at the Cleveland 1. The Browns, who committed six turnovers and were outgained by more than 200 yards, had now dropped three of their first four games for the first time in 18 years.
Record: 1–3

	1	2	3	4		
Raiders	7	16	14	3	=	40
Browns	17	0	0	7	=	24

CLE-Hall 29-yd. interception return (Cockroft kick)
CLE-Cockroft 46-yd. FG
OAK-Biletnikoff 11-yd. pass from Stabler (Blanda kick)
CLE-G. Pruitt 34-yd. pass from Phipps (Cockroft kick)
OAK-Davis 45-yd. pass from Stabler (Blanda kick)
OAK-Safety: Sistrunk tackled Brown in end zone
OAK-Banaszak 3-yd. run (Blanda kick)
OAK-Branch 10-yd. pass from Stabler (Blanda kick)
OAK-Davis 1-yd. run (Blanda kick)
CLE-McKinnis 44-yd. run (Cockroft kick)
OAK-Blanda 30-yd. FG

Passing
OAK: Stabler 19–33–237 3 TD 2 INT, Lamonica 1–2–13 0 TD 1 INT, Guy 0–1–0 0 TD 1 INT, Lawrence 0–1–0 0 TD 0 INT
CLE: Phipps 8–15–127 1 TD 2 INT, Sipe 2–6–22 0 TD 3 INT

Rushing
OAK: Davis 18–116, Hubbard 14–46, Hart 3–30, Banaszak 8–23, Smith 3–9, van Eeghen 2–1, Lamonica 1-(-3)
CLE: McKinnis 2–50, Phipps 3–34, Brown 7–23, B. Scott 3–9, G. Pruitt 6–8, Lefear 1–0

Receiving
OAK: Davis 4–82, Branch 4–56, Biletnikoff 4–46, Hubbard 4–33, Moore 2–16, Banaszak 1–9, Siani 1–8
CLE: G. Pruitt 2–45, Richardson 2–41, Morin 1–24, Dunbar 1–21, McKinnis 1–10, Lefear 2–7, Brown 1–1

Sunday, October 13
Cincinnati Bengals 34, Browns 24
Cleveland Stadium (70,897)
White jerseys/white pants

With the Cleveland papers questioning Nick Skorich's job security, the Bengals ravaged the Browns' defense and captured their first-ever victory in Cleveland. The Browns rushed for a whopping 263 yards, with four players topping the 50-yard tally, but they also allowed more than 450 yards for a second straight week. Greg Pruitt continued to emerge as the heart of the Cleveland offense, rushing for 83 yards and throwing another long touchdown pass, but Mike Phipps was sacked five times and completed only 10 of 27 passes. With the defeat, the Browns dropped to 1–4 for the first time in their history.
Record: 1–4

	1	2	3	4		
Bengals	13	7	7	7	–	34
Browns	3	7	7	7	=	24

CIN-Clark 2-yd. run (kick failed)
CLE-Cockroft 27-yd. FG
CIN-Elliott 28-yd. pass from Anderson (Muhlmann kick)
CIN-Joiner 65-yd. pass from Anderson (Muhlmann kick)
CLE-Morin 9-yd. pass from Phipps (Cockroft kick)
CLE-Brown 20-yd. run (Cockroft kick)
CIN-Anderson 19-yd. run (Muhlmann kick)
CIN-Curtis 18-yd. pass from Anderson (Muhlmann kick)
CLE-Richardson 60-yd. pass from G. Pruitt (Cockroft kick)

Passing
CIN: Anderson 19–29–278 3 TD 1 INT
CLE: Phipps 10–27–83 1 TD 1 INT, G. Pruitt 1–1–60 1 TD 0 INT

Rushing
CIN: Elliott 10–83, Anderson 4–46, Davis 7–28, Clark 13–26, Joiner 1–4, Dressler 2–2
CLE: G. Pruitt 11–83, McKinnis 10–69, Brown 6–57, Phipps 6–54

Receiving
CIN: Joiner 4–88, Trumpy 2–55, Myers 4–45, Elliott 4–41, Clark 3–23, Curtis 1–18, Davis 1–8
CLE: Richardson 1–60, Morin 3–30, McKinnis 4–23, Sullivan 1–17, Brown 2–13

Sunday, October 20
Pittsburgh Steelers 20, Browns 16
Three Rivers Stadium (48,100)
White jerseys/white pants

Though 15-point underdogs, the Browns played well and had a chance to win in the final minutes on a dark afternoon in Pittsburgh spotted with October snow flurries. Nick Skorich's attempt to shake things up by making several changes to the starting lineup didn't pay off at first as the Steelers jumped to a 14–0 lead. But the Browns scored two touchdowns in less than two minutes to cut the margin to one point at the half. When Pittsburgh DE L. C. Greenwood blocked Don Cockroft's second point-after attempt, the complexion of the second half changed. Most notably, rather than attempting a game-tying field goal on fourth down at the Pittsburgh 17 when trailing by four points in the final minutes, the Browns were forced to go for it, and a desperation pass by Mike Phipps was intercepted.
Record: 1–5

	1	2	3	4		
Browns	0	13	0	3	=	16
Steelers	7	7	3	3	=	20

PIT-Pearson 6-yd. run (Gerela kick)
PIT-Harris 1-yd. run (Gerela kick)
CLE-Phipps 18-yd. run (Cockroft kick)
CLE-Morin 9-yd. pass from Phipps (kick failed)
PIT-Gerela 31-yd. FG
CLE-Cockroft 21-yd. FG
PIT-Gerela 26-yd. FG

Passing
CLE: Phipps 10–23–160 1 TD 1 INT
PIT: Gilliam 5–18–78 0 TD 0 INT

Rushing
CLE: McKinnis 13–46, Phipps 4–38, G. Pruitt 8–37, Brown 10–14
PIT: Harris 14–81, Bleier 9–48, Pearson 10–21, Fuqua 5–11, Davis 3–9, Gilliam 3–4, Stallworth 1-(-9)

Receiving
CLE: Richardson 2–62, Morin 3–46, McKinnis 4–38, Pruitt 1–14
PIT: Shanklin 2–42, Stallworth 1–14, Grossman 1–12, Lewis 1–10

Sunday, October 27
Browns 23, Denver Broncos 21
Cleveland Stadium (60,478)
White jerseys/white pants

Trailing 21–9 in the fourth quarter in the midst of another lethargic performance, the Browns were well on their way to their fifth straight loss in what was becoming a nightmarish season. But things turned around shortly after Nick Skorich replaced Mike Phipps with Brian Sipe early in the final period. Aided by a 27-yard gain by Don Cockroft on a fake punt from the Denver 43, Sipe converted a fourth-and-10 pass to Steve Holden three plays later and then scrambled into the end zone for the Browns' first touchdown with less than six minutes to play to cut the lead to five. After a key defensive stop, Greg Pruitt returned the ensuing punt 72 yards to the Denver 3. With 1:56 left, Sipe took a quarterback sneak from the 1, bounced off the line and circled into the end zone to give the Browns their first lead. The Broncos drove to the Cleveland 34 in the waning seconds, but a 51-yard field-goal attempt by Jim Turner fell short.
Record: 2–5

	1	2	3	4		
Broncos	7	7	7	0	=	21
Browns	0	3	6	14	=	23

DEN-Odoms 12-yd. pass from Johnson (Turner kick)
DEN-Simmons 13-yd. pass from Johnson (Turner kick)
CLE-Cockroft 27-yd. FG
CLE-Cockroft 30-yd. FG
CLE-Cockroft 25-yd. FG
DEN-Armstrong 33-yd. run (Turner kick)
CLE-Sipe 8-yd. run (Cockroft kick)
CLE-Sipe 1-yd. run (Cockroft kick)

Passing
DEN: Johnson 14–27–207 2 TD 0 INT
CLE: Phipps 8–25–170 0 TD 1 INT, Sipe 4–6–32 0 TD 0 INT, Cockroft 1–1–27 0 TD 0 INT

Rushing
DEN: Armstrong 17–142, Little 13–41, Keyworth 1–2, Ross 1–1
CLE: McKinnis 7–23, G. Pruitt 7–22, Brown 7–15, Sipe 5–12

Receiving
DEN: Odoms 4–59, Little 4–37, Van Heusen 1–37, Simmons 2–34, Armstrong 2–23, Moses 1–17
CLE: McKinnis 6–111, Thaxton 1–34, Richardson 2–32, Green 1–27, Holden 2–21, G. Pruitt 1–4

Sunday, November 3
San Diego Chargers 36, Browns 35
San Diego Stadium (36,631)
White jerseys/white pants

Returning to his hometown of San Diego, Brian Sipe made his first professional start and provided a portent of things to come as the Browns and Chargers put on one of the most exciting contests of the season. With Sipe sparking the offense, the Browns scored two early touchdowns and led 21–7 at the half. But Dan Fouts got hot in the second, tossing four touchdown passes to bring the Chargers back to take a one-point lead on a field goal with 55 seconds remaining. The Browns weren't done yet as Greg Pruitt returned the ensuing kickoff 61 yards. Sipe directed the Browns to the San Diego 10 and was running one more play to position the ball for a field-goal attempt when he fumbled the center snap and Chargers' LB Charles Anthony recovered with 18 seconds left, ending one of the most exciting—and heartbreaking—Browns' games of the decade.
Record: 2–6

	1	2	3	4		
Browns	14	7	0	14	=	35
Chargers	0	7	12	17	=	36

CLE-Holden 6-yd. pass from Sipe (Cockroft kick)
CLE-G. Pruitt 3-yd. run (Cockroft kick)
SD-Matthews 1-yd. run (Partee kick)
CLE-Sipe 1-yd. run (Cockroft kick)
SD-Woods 43-yd. pass from Fouts (kick failed)
SD-Bonner 1-yd. pass from Fouts (kick failed)
CLE-McKinnis 6-yd. run (Cockroft kick)
SD-Davis 70-yd. pass from Fouts (Partee kick)
CLE-Sipe 1-yd. run (Cockroft kick)
SD-Woods 75-yd. pass from Fouts (Partee kick)
SD-Wersching 40-yd. FG

Passing
CLE: Sipe 16–23–186 1 TD 1 INT
SD: Fouts 12–21–333 4 TD 1 INT

Rushing
CLE: McKinnis 11–48, G. Pruitt 17–47, Brown 9–21, Sipe 2–2, Thaxton 1-(10)
SD: Woods 18–51, Matthews 11–37, Fouts 7–24, Davis 1-(-9)

Receiving
CLE: Holden 6–85, G. Pruitt 3–38, Thaxton 3–37, Brown 2–16, McKinnis 2–10
SD: Davis 4–142, Woods 3–119, Garrison 3–68, Matthews 1–3, Bonner 1–1

Sunday, November 10
Browns 21, New England Patriots 14
Schaefer Stadium (61,279)
White jerseys/white pants

Rebounding from their crushing defeat the week before, the Browns pulled off a stunning upset over the 6–2 Patriots. Greg Pruitt set the tone by returning the opening kickoff 88 yards for a touchdown, and moments later Thom Darden recovered a Patriots' fumble and rumbled 29 yards for another score to give the Browns a 14–0 lead less than two minutes into the game. The Patriots came back to tie the score at the half, but the Cleveland defense harassed New England QB Jim Plunkett all day, picking off four passes (two by Darden) and keeping the game knotted until a 25-yard punt return by Pruitt set up Ken Brown's four-yard touchdown run to put the Browns ahead for a good four minutes into the fourth quarter.
Record: 3–6

	1	2	3	4		
Browns	14	0	0	7	=	21
Patriots	0	14	0	0	=	14

CLE-G. Pruitt 88-yd. kickoff return (Cockroft kick)
CLE-Darden 29-yd. fumble return (Cockroft kick)
NE-Cunningham 1-yd. run (Smith kick)
NE-Cunningham 1-yd. run (Smith kick)
CLE-Brown 4-yd. run (Cockroft kick)

Passing
CLE: Sipe 10–18–116 0 TD 0 INT
NE: Plunkett 9–21–134 0 TD 4 INT

Rushing
CLE: McKinnis 15–59, Brown 10–23, G. Pruitt 6–10, Sipe 3–8
NE: Cunningham 20–75, Herron 18–61, Plunkett 7–28

Receiving
CLE: G. Pruitt 4–46, Sullivan 2–26, Morin 1–19, McKinnis 2–16, Brown 1–9
NE: Herron 4–42, Vataha 2–40, Rucker 1–28, Adams 1–18, Cunningham 1–6

Sunday, November 17
Pittsburgh Steelers 26, Browns 16
Cleveland Stadium (77,739)
White jerseys/white pants

The largest home crowd of the season packed into Cleveland Stadium to watch a sloppy contest between the two rivals, who combined for 13 turnovers on a sunny but chilly November afternoon on the lake. The Browns rallied from a seven-point halftime deficit when DE Van Green picked off Pittsburgh QB Terry Hanratty early in the third quarter and returned it 36 yards for a touchdown to knot the score. The Browns then pulled ahead 16–13 on a short Don Cockroft field goal and carried the lead into the fourth. After Pittsburgh tied it up again, DT Joe Greene recovered a botched handoff between Brian Sipe and RB Billy Lefear, then lateraled it to DB J. T. Thomas, who rumbled 14 more yards for the go-ahead, backbreaking touchdown. After adding a late field goal as insurance, the Steelers had picked up their first win in Cleveland in 10 years and their first season sweep of the Browns since 1959.
Record: 3–7

	1	2	3	4		
Steelers	7	6	0	13	=	26
Browns	3	3	10	0	=	16

CLE-Cockroft 44-yd. FG
PIT-Shanklin 28-yd. pass from Hanratty (Gerela kick)
PIT-Gerela 32-yd. FG
CLE-Cockroft 35-yd. FG
PIT-Gerela 32-yd. FG
CLE-Green 36-yd. interception return (Cockroft kick)
CLE-Cockroft 18-yd. FG
PIT-Gerela 23-yd. FG
PIT-Thomas 14-yd. fumble return (Gerela kick)
PIT-Gerela 22-yd. FG

Passing
PIT: Hanratty 2–15–63 1 TD 3 INT, Gilliam 1–4–18 0 TD 0 INT
CLE: Sipe 15–30–162 0 TD 3 INT, Phipps 0–5–0 0 TD 0 INT

Rushing
PIT: Harris 23–156, Davis 9–52, Fuqua 8–31, Hanratty 1-(-6)
CLE: McKinnis 14–49, Sipe 2–17, Brown 5–16, Lefear 4–0, G. Pruitt 6-(-2)

Receiving
PIT: Shanklin 3–81
CLE: Morin 6–59, Sullivan 2–49, Holden 2–27, G. Pruitt 3–12, Brown 1–12, McKinnis 1–3

Sunday, November 24
Buffalo Bills 15, Browns 10
Cleveland Stadium (66,504)
White jerseys/white pants

In the rain and mud, Buffalo RB O. J. Simpson battled through the elements and the flu to rush for 115 yards and a touchdown, leading the Bills to their first-ever triumph over the Browns. After the Browns took a lead on a Don Cockroft field goal early in the second quarter, the Bills surged to a nine-point halftime advantage and controlled the game in the second half despite completing only one pass on the afternoon. Mike Phipps returned to action and threw three interceptions in relief of an ineffective Brian Sipe, though he led the Browns to their only touchdown with four seconds left in the game. The defeat clinched the Browns' first losing record in 18 years.
Record: 3–8

	1	2	3	4		
Bills	0	12	0	3	=	15
Browns	0	3	0	7	=	10

CLE-Cockroft 21-yd. FG
BUF-Simpson 41-yd. FG
BUF-Leypoldt 41-yd. FG
BUF-Safety: Kadish tackled Sipe in end zone
BUF-Leypoldt 42-yd. FG
CLE-Brown 3-yd. pass from Phipps (Cockroft kick)

Passing
BUF: Ferguson 1–7–9 0 TD 0 INT
CLE: Phipps 10–19–102 1 TD 3 INT, Sipe 6–10–37 0 TD 0 INT

Rushing
BUF: Simpson 22–115, Braxton 10–49, Watkins 6–24, Ferguson 2–0
CLE: Brown 15–73, McKinnis 16–49, Phipps 3–17, Sipe 2–4, G. Pruitt 1–4

Receiving
BUF: Rashad 1–9
CLE: Morin 4–46, Hooker 2–34, Holden 3–24, Brown 3–21, McKinnis 3–10, G. Pruitt 1–4

Sunday, December 1
Browns 7, San Francisco 49ers 0
Cleveland Stadium (24,559)
White jerseys/white pants

Amid miserable conditions before the smallest Cleveland crowd since 1956, the Browns and 49ers fought through a cocktail of snow showers and driving sleet upon a muddy field. Neither team scored through the first three quarters, and the game appeared destined for a scoreless tie before Cleveland rookie DB Eddie Brown, in for injured Walt Sumner, intercepted his third pass of the day (the Browns' fifth) and, with his eyes covered in mud, sloshed 24 yards to the San Francisco 24. Moments later, Ken Brown barreled across the goal line from the 49ers' 1 with 3:21 remaining for the game's only score. After the 49ers drove to the Cleveland 28 in the final seconds, Thom Darden sealed the victory when he intercepted a desperation San Francisco pass in the end zone on the final play.
Record: 4–8

	1	2	3	4		
49ers	0	0	0	0	=	0
Browns	0	0	0	7	=	7

CLE-Brown 1-yd. run (Cockroft kick)

Passing
SF: Owen 6–23–74 0 TD 5 INT
CLE: Sipe 5–13–42 0 TD 0 INT, Phipps 4–7–25 0 TD 1 INT

Rushing
SF: Jackson 19–91, Schreiber 18–55, Owen 2–11, Johnson 2–4, Williams 1-(-2)
CLE: G. Pruitt 10–55, McKinnis 12–50, Brown 10–50, Sipe 2–1, Phipps 1–1

Receiving
SF: Mitchell 1–24, Johnson 2–23, Abramowicz 1–18, Beasley 1–8, Jackson 1–1
CLE: Holden 4–36, Brown 3–23, G. Pruitt 1–5, McKinnis 1–3

Sunday, December 8
Dallas Cowboys 41, Browns 17
Texas Stadium (48,754)
Brown jerseys/white pants

Surrendering 469 total yards to the playoff-bound Cowboys, the Browns clinched the first last-place finish in their history with a lopsided defeat in Dallas. Cowboys' QB Roger Staubach threw a pair of scoring passes to WR Golden Richards in the first two minutes of the game, but the Browns hung tough and cut the lead to three on a Ken Brown touchdown run early in the third quarter. Dallas then pulled away with three touchdowns in the next five minutes. The Cowboys were aided by five Cleveland turnovers, including four interceptions by Mike Phipps, who made his first start in six weeks.
Record: 4–9

	1	2	3	4		
Browns	0	10	7	0	=	17
Cowboys	14	6	21	0	=	41

DAL-Richards 35-yd. pass from Staubach (Herrera kick)
DAL-Richards 41-yd. pass from Staubach (Herrera kick)
CLE-Holden 4-yd. pass from Phipps (Cockroft kick)
DAL-Herrera 39-yd. FG
CLE-Cockroft 28-yd. FG
DAL-Herrera 19-yd. FG
CLE-Brown 12-yd. run (Cockroft kick)
DAL-Garrison 3-yd. run (Herrera kick)
DAL-DuPree 42-yd. pass from Staubach (Herrera kick)
DAL-Garrison 1 yd. run (Herrera kick)

Passing
CLE: Phipps 15–29–195 1 TD 4 INT
DAL: Staubach 14–24–230 3 TD 1 INT, Longley 1–1–60 TD 0 INT

Rushing
CLE: McKinnis 10–32, Brown 8–28, Phipps 4–27, G. Pruitt 5–0
DAL: Newhouse 12–69, Hill 14–66, Young 6–46, Dennison 4–31, Staubach 3–22, Garrison 7–18

Receiving
CLE: Holden 5–87, G. Pruitt 2–36, McKinnis 3–32, Morin 2–25, Brown 2–10, Hooker 1–5
DAL: Richards 3–92, DuPree 3–74, Pearson 3–40, Garrison 2–9, Hill 1–8, Fugett 1–6, Newhouse 1–4, Young 1–3

Sunday, December 15
Houston Oilers 28, Browns 24
Houston Astrodome (37,910)
Brown jerseys/white pants

The Browns closed out the worst season in their history with a disheartening defeat in the Astrodome, their first-ever loss to the Oilers. Mistakes once again did in the Browns, who took a 17–14 lead midway through the third quarter only to fall behind 28–17 in the fourth thanks to numerous miscues, including four turnovers and 13 penalties for a whopping 134 yards. Greg Pruitt was one of the lone bright spots, topping 100 yards rushing for the only time all season, while adding 70 yards on three catches and scoring the game-tying touchdown on a short run in the third quarter. The game would be the last for Nick Skorich as Cleveland's head coach, as he was fired the following week and was replaced by offensive line coach Forrest Gregg a month later.
Record: 4–10

	1	2	3	4		
Browns	7	0	10	7	=	24
Oilers	0	7	14	7	=	28

CLE-Holden 41-yd. pass from Phipps (Cockroft kick)
HOU-Alston 7-yd. pass from Pastorini (Butler kick)
HOU-Johnson 6-yd. pass from Pastorini (Butler kick)
CLE-G. Pruitt 4-yd. run (Cockroft kick)
CLE-Cockroft 37-yd. FG
HOU-Willis 5-yd. run (Butler kick)
HOU-Rodgers 20-yd. run (Butler kick)
CLE-Hooker 9-yd. pass from Phipps (Cockroft kick)

Passing
CLE: Phipps 16–29–227 2 TD 2 INT
HOU: Pastorini 12–25–121 2 TD 2 INT

Rushing
CLE: G. Pruitt 15–102, McKinnis 6–15, Brown 10–14, Phipps 3–11
HOU: Willis 11–68, Washington 10–58, Rodgers 7–47, Amundson 10–14, Johnson 1–3, Pastorini 3-(-8)

Receiving
CLE: Holden 3–89, G. Pruitt 3–70, Morin 4–40, Brown 2–16, Hooker 1–9, McKinnis 3–3
HOU: Parks 2–40, Alston 2–38, Willis 5–23, Johnson 3–20

1975

Sunday, September 21
Cincinnati Bengals 24, Browns 17
Riverfront Stadium (52,874)
White jerseys/orange pants

In Forrest Gregg's first game as head coach (and wearing orange pants for the first time), the Browns fell behind 24–3 midway through the third quarter, then launched a furious comeback that nearly toppled the playoff-bound Bengals. A 77-yard drive was capped by a marvelous touchdown run by RB Greg Pruitt, who took a handoff running right from the Cincinnati 8, then reversed direction and angled into the end zone for the first touchdown in what would be a great individual campaign. Less than a minute later, LB Charlie Hall recovered a fumble by Bengals' QB Ken Anderson in the end zone for a touchdown that cut the margin to seven. Cincinnati also fumbled the ensuing kickoff, with the Browns recovering. They drove to the Bengals' 3, but were then turned away after two fumbled center exchanges and a fruitless fourth-down run. The Browns were again poised to tie the game when they drove to the Cincinnati 1 on their next series, but RB Hugh McKinnis was stopped on fourth down midway through the fourth quarter, and the Bengals ran out the remaining seven minutes to escape. Altogether, the Browns had run six plays inside the Cincinnati 2 and failed to score any points. While the effort was admirable, the defeat forecasted a frustrating season.
Record: 0–1

	1	2	3	4		
Browns	0	3	14	0	=	17
Bengals	14	3	7	0	=	24

CIN-Curtis 27-yd. pass from Anderson (Green kick)
CIN-Clark 14-yd. run (Green kick)
CLE-Cockroft 18-yd. FG
CIN-Green 44-yd. FG
CIN-Elliot 3-yd. run (Green kick)
CLE-G. Pruitt 8-yd. run (Cockroft kick)
CLE-Hall recovered fumble in end zone (Cockroft kick)

Passing
CLE: Phipps 14–22–156 0 TD 0 INT
CIN: Anderson 17–27–287 1 TD 0 INT

Rushing
CLE: G. Pruitt 17–66, McKinnis 8–19, Phipps 5–19, Pritchett 1–1, Holden 1–0
CIN: Elliott 13–72, Clark 18–51, Anderson 5–10, Johnson 2–3, Curtis 2-(-9)

Receiving
CLE: Roan 6–69, Rucker 4–57, Holden 1–15, McKinnis 1–11, G. Pruitt 2–4
CIN: Curtis 6–127, Johnson 3–47, Trumpy 3–38, Elliott 1–28, Myers 2–25, Joiner 1–14, Clark 1–8

Sunday, September 28
Minnesota Vikings 42, Browns 10
Cleveland Stadium (68,064)
Brown jerseys/orange pants

In their home opener, the Browns were crushed by the defending NFC champions, beginning what would become a horrid home stand. The Cleveland offense was overwhelmed, coughing up four turnovers and allowing five sacks, with the Browns' only touchdown coming on a batted wide receiver-option pass thrown by rookie Willie Miller and caught by recently acquired WR Reggie Rucker in the fourth quarter. Brian Sipe made his 1975 debut, replacing Mike Phipps in the second half with the Browns down 28–3, but Sipe promptly threw three interceptions. The only real individual standout for Cleveland was DB Clarence Scott, who picked off two Fran Tarkenton passes.
Record: 0–2

	1	2	3	4		
Vikings	7	14	7	14	=	42
Browns	0	3	0	7	=	10

MIN-Gilliam 29-yd. pass from Tarkenton (Cox kick)
MIN-Foreman 1-yd. run (Cox kick)
CLE-Cockroft 38-yd. FG
MIN-Foreman 13-yd. pass from Tarkenton (Cox kick)
MIN-Tarkenton 2-yd. run (Cox kick)
MIN-Miller 1-yd. run (Cox kick)
CLE-Rucker 26-yd. pass from W. Miller (Cockroft kick)
MIN-Lash 33-yd. pass from Lee (Cox kick)

Passing
MIN: Tarkenton 17–27–170 2 TD 2 INT, Lee 2–5–65 1 TD 0 INT

CLE: Phipps 7–17–84 0 TD 1 INT, Sipe 6–11–46 0 TD 3 INT, W. Miller 1–1–26 1 TD 0 INT

Rushing
MIN: McClanahan 12–61, Foreman 11–33, Marinaro 8–28, Osborn 3–8, Miller 3–5, Tarkenton 1–2
CLE: G. Pruitt 11–50, Pritchett 8–46, Sipe 2–24, Brown 2–10

Receiving
MIN: Foreman 7–61, Gilliam 4–60, Marinaro 4–32, Lash 1–33, Miller 1–32, Voigt 1–9, McClanahan 1–8
CLE: Rucker 3–66, Roan 4–56, Pritchett 4–26, W. Miller 1–6, G. Pruitt 2–2

Sunday, October 5
Pittsburgh Steelers 42, Browns 6
Cleveland Stadium (73,595)
Brown jerseys/orange pants

On a bright, warm autumn afternoon, things went from bad to worse for the hapless Browns as they were annihilated on their own home field by the defending Super Bowl champions and dropped to 0–3 for the first time in their history. The Cleveland defense was abysmal, surrendering more than 500 total yards as the Steelers averaged nearly eight yards per offensive play. Pittsburgh soared to a 28–0 halftime lead before the Browns got on the board on a touchdown run by RB Hugh McKinnis. Several fights broke out on the field throughout the game, including a scuffle between Browns' center Tom DeLeone and Steelers' DT Joe Greene after Greene kicked Cleveland lineman Bob McKay in the stomach and groin. Both DeLeone and Greene were ejected.
Record: 0–3

	1	2	3	4		
Steelers	7	21	0	14	=	42
Browns	0	0	0	6	=	6

PIT-Stallworth 3-yd. pass from Bradshaw (Gerela kick)
PIT-Harris 1-yd. run (Gerela kick)
PIT-Collier 1-yd. run (Gerela kick)
PIT-Swann 43-yd. pass from Gilliam (Gerela kick)
CLE-McKinnis 7-yd. run (kick failed)
PIT-Garrett 45-yd. pass from Gilliam (Gerela kick)
PIT-Harrison 3-yd. run (Gerela kick)

Passing
PIT: Gilliam 11–15–221 2 TD 0 INT, Bradshaw 7–8–151 1 TD 0 INT
CLE: Phipps 16–31–136 0 TD 2 INT

Rushing
PIT: Harris 17–57, Bleier 10–37, Fuqua 4–21, Harrison 4–14, Collier 3–10, Hanratty 1–0, Bradshaw 1-(-5)
CLE: G. Pruitt 14–54, McKinnis 9–46, Pritchett 5–10, Phipps 2–9, Brown 1–3

Receiving
PIT: Swann 5–126, Stallworth 4–109, Garrett 3–84, Grossman 3–30, Brown 1–20, Harris 1–9, Bleier 1-(-6)
CLE: Roan 1–31, G. Pruitt 6–30, McKinnis 3–17, Rucker 1–15, W. Miller 2–14, Lefear 1–14, Holden 1–9, Brown 1–6

Sunday, October 12
Houston Oilers 40, Browns 10
Cleveland Stadium (46,531)
Brown jerseys/orange pants

The Browns' miserable stretch continued as they committed five turnovers in another lopsided home loss, this one to division-rival Houston, who won in Cleveland for the first time. Things actually started well for the Browns, who took their first lead of the season in the first quarter and held a 10–3 advantage early in the second. But it was downhill from there as Mike Phipps threw four interceptions, and Houston WR Billy "White Shoes" Johnson returned the second-half kickoff for a touchdown to blow the game open. The Browns had now been out scored 124–26 over their last three games.
Record: 0–4

	1	2	3	4		
Oilers	3	17	13	7	=	40
Browns	3	7	0	0	=	10

CLE-Cockroft 39-yd. FG
HOU-Butler 46-yd. FG
CLE-McKinnis 1-yd. run (Cockroft kick)
HOU-Alston 6-yd. pass from Pastorini (Butler kick)
HOU-Alston 5-yd. pass from Pastorini (Butler kick)
HOU-Butler 33-yd. FG
HOU-Johnson 81-yd. kickoff return (Butler kick)
HOU-Butler 25-yd. FG
HOU-Butler 21-yd. FG
HOU-Alston 11-yd. pass from Pastorini (Butler kick)

Passing
HOU: Pastorini 12–20–124 3 TD 0 INT, Dickey 0–1–0 0 TD 0 INT
CLE: Phipps 9–15–89 0 TD 4 INT, Sipe 7–14–83 0 TD 0 INT, Cockroft 1–1–1 0 TD 0 INT

Rushing
HOU: Coleman 14–110, Willis 14–60, Hardeman 9–57, Holmes 4–15, Rodgers 4–12, Edwards 1-(-4)
CLE: G. Pruitt 12–51, McKinnis 8–42, Phipps 3–9, Pritchett 2–2, Hynoski 1–0, W. Miller 1-(-2)

Receiving
HOU: Johnson 3–37, Willis 3–31, Alston 3–22, Burrough 1–14, Coleman 1–12, Sawyer 1–8
CLE: Rucker 6–66, Holden 3–47, McKinnis 2–24, Roan 2–19, Hynoski 1–15, G. Pruitt 2–1, Craig 1–1

Sunday, October 19
Denver Broncos 16, Browns 15
Mile High Stadium (52,590)
White jerseys/orange pants

The string of humiliating losses came to an end, but the Browns still couldn't pull out a victory, suffering a heartbreaking loss on the final play of the game on a bright, beautiful afternoon outside the Rocky Mountains. Though they didn't score a touchdown, the Browns led for most of the game as Don Cockroft tied an NFL record with five field goals, allowing Cleveland to build a 15–6 lead early in the fourth quarter. The Broncos cut the lead to two points, but the Browns dodged a huge bullet and appeared to have victory in their grasp after LB Dick Ambrose—making his first career start—recovered a Denver fumble in the Cleveland end zone with 2:18 to play to prevent the go-ahead touchdown. The offense was unable to kill the clock and Denver regained possession at its own 32 with 1:43 remaining. The Broncos then converted on two clutch fourth downs, including a 10-yard run by QB Steve Ramsey to the Cleveland 36 with four seconds left, to set up a team-record 53-yard field goal by Jim Turner as time expired. It was a bitter pill to swallow for the Browns, who forced six turnovers in an inspired effort that went for naught.
Record: 0–5

	1	2	3	4		
Browns	3	6	3	3	=	15
Broncos	3	3	0	10	=	16

CLE-Cockroft 24-yd. FG
DEN-Turner 25-yd. FG
CLE-Cockroft 49-yd. FG
DEN-Turner 48-yd. FG
CLE-Cockroft 43-yd. FG
CLE-Cockroft 20-yd. FG
CLE-Cockroft 42-yd. FG
DEN-Keyworth 1-yd. run (Turner kick)
DEN-Turner 53-yd. FG

Passing
CLE: Sipe 12–25–111 0 TD 0 INT, Phipps 2–8–28 0 TD 1 INT
DEN: Johnson 9–22–110 0 TD 1 INT, Ramsey 10–12–94 0 TD 0 INT, Van Heusen 1–1–30 0 TD 0 INT

Rushing
CLE: G. Pruitt 19–64, Pritchett 12–38, McKinnis 5–15, Brown 7–14, Sipe 2–13
DEN: Keyworth 11–62, Ross 6–18, Johnson 1–13, Ramsey 1–10, Upchurch 1–7, Little 6-(-2)

Receiving
CLE: Roan 5–52, Rucker 3–37, W. Miller 2–23, G. Pruitt 3–20, McKinnis 1–7
DEN: Keyworth 6–45, Dolbin 2–36, Moses 2–35, Ross 2–34, Little 3–27, Odoms 2–24, Upchurch 2–21, Van Heusen 1–12

Sunday, October 26
Washington Redskins 23, Browns 7
Cleveland Stadium (56,702)
Brown jerseys/orange pants

On another bright, beautiful October afternoon, the Browns fought valiantly for three quarters, but the superior Redskins pulled away in the fourth, dropping Cleveland to its sixth straight loss of the season. The Browns appeared to have momentum after a touchdown pass from Brian Sipe to TE Oscar Roan pulled them within 9–7 midway through the third quarter, then they forced a Washington punt. But Pete Athas fumbled the return at midfield, and the Redskins cashed in for the backbreaking touchdown early in the fourth quarter and cruised to a 16-point victory. It was one of four turnovers on the day for the Browns, who continued to struggle even with Sipe making his first start of the season. The defeat snapped a 12-game Browns' winning streak over the Redskins.
Record: 0–6

	1	2	3	4		
Redskins	0	6	3	14	=	23
Browns	0	0	7	0	=	7

WAS-Thomas 3-yd. pass from Kilmer (kick failed)
WAS-Moseley 37-yd. FG
CLE-Roan 15-yd. pass from Sipe (Cockroft kick)
WAS-Brown 11-yd. pass from Kilmer (Moseley kick)
WAS-Thomas 1-yd. run (Moseley kick)

Passing
WAS: Kilmer 15–33–207 2 TD 0 INT
CLE: Sipe 11–20–117 1 TD 0 INT

Rushing
WAS: Thomas 27–124, Denson 4–22, Brown 6–21, Brunet 4–20, Nelson 2–3
CLE: G. Pruitt 14–48, Sipe 5–23, Pritchett 4–17, Poole 2–13, McKinnis 2-(-1)

Receiving
WAS: Grant 5–78, Taylor 3–49, Thomas 2–30, Smith 2–23, Brown 1–11, Nelson 1–10, Denson 1–6
CLE: Roan 5–71, Rucker 3–29, McKinnis 1–9, W. Miller 1–5, G. Pruitt 1–3

Sunday, November 2
Baltimore Colts 21, Browns 7
Memorial Stadium (35,235)
White jerseys/orange pants

For the first time in their history, the Browns lost a game in Baltimore as the eventual AFC East-champion Colts marched to a 21–0 halftime lead and never looked back, dropping the Browns to 0–7. The Browns, who had won seven straight games at Memorial Stadium, managed just 23 yards in the first half and didn't get on the scoreboard until midway through the fourth quarter. The Cleveland defense played well, limiting the Colts to just 228 yards while collecting five sacks, but the offense struggled again as Mike Phipps relieved starter Brian Sipe late in the second quarter. Phipps didn't do much better, completing just eight of 26 passes, and suffered a foot injury that would sideline him for the next two weeks.
Record: 0–7

	1	2	3	4		
Browns	0	0	0	7	=	7
Colts	7	14	0	0	=	21

BAL-McCauley 1-yd. run (Linhart kick)
BAL-Chester 2-yd. pass from Jones (Linhart kick)
BAL-Mitchell 35-yd. pass from Jones (Linhart kick)
CLE-McKinnis 1-yd. run (Cockroft kick)

Passing
CLE: Phipps 8–26–118 0 TD 2 INT, Sipe 9–18–70 0 TD 0 INT
BAL: Jones 16–26–153 2 TD 1 INT

Rushing
CLE: Poole 12–69, G. Pruitt 7–25, McKinnis 4–20, Phipps 2–15, Pritchett 3–0, Holden 1-(-4)
BAL: Jones 4–49, Olds 8–32, Mitchell 11–27, McCauley 7–11, Leaks 3-(-2)

Receiving
CLE: Rucker 4–65, McKinnis 2–30, G. Pruitt 3–28, Roan 3–25, Pritchett 3–21, Holden 1–14, Poole 1–5
BAL: Mitchell 4–69, Chester 5–47, Doughty 2–16, McCauley 2–15, Johnson 1–10, Olds 2-(-4)

Sunday, November 9
Detroit Lions 21, Browns 10
Pontiac Silverdome (75,283)
White jerseys/orange pants

The Browns' losing streak reached eight with an ugly loss in the brand-new Pontiac Silverdome. The Lions jumped to a quick 7–0 lead a minute into the game and extended it to 14–0 at the half before the Browns got on the board in the third quarter. They were poised to make a game of it when they drove to the Detroit 34 midway through the fourth, but former Browns' DB Ben Davis intercepted a pass that bounced off Greg Pruitt's hands and returned it 67 yards for the game-clinching touchdown. It capped a miserable day for Cleveland QB Will Cureton, who was making the only appearance of his brief career and completed only 10 of 32 passes. Making matters worse, Browns' RB Larry Poole was lost for the season with a broken arm in the second quarter.
Record: 0–8

	1	2	3	4		
Browns	0	0	3	7	=	10
Lions	7	7	0	7	=	21

DET-Taylor 1-yd. run (Mann kick)
DET-Jarvis 21-yd. pass from Reed (Mann kick)
CLE-Cockroft 32-yd. FG
DET-Davis 67-yd. interception return (Mann kick)
CLE-Roan 12-yd. pass from Cureton (Cockroft kick)

Passing
CLE: Cureton 10–32–95 1 TD 1 INT
DET: Reed 10–17–133 1 TD 1 INT, Concannon 1–2–30 0 TD 0 INT

Rushing
CLE: G. Pruitt 16–72, Poole 3–32, Pritchett 8–14, McKinnis 1–4, Brown 2–3, Cureton 1–1
DET: Taylor 19–81, Bussey 10–38, King 6–17, Reed 2–3, Thompson 3-(-2), Briscoe 1-(-9)

Receiving
CLE: Rucker 3–24, Holden 2–24, Roan 3–23, G. Pruitt 1–16, Pritchett 1–8
DET: Jarvis 3–78, Briscoe 4–51, McMakin 1–30, Thompson 2–10, King 1-(-6)

Sunday, November 16
Oakland Raiders 38, Browns 17
Oakland-Alameda County Coliseum (50,461)
White jerseys/orange pants

The Browns hung tough with the eventual AFC West champions, but the Raiders pulled away in the second half to deliver Cleveland's ninth straight loss in 1975 and eleventh straight overall. Oakland, 21-point favorites, found itself tied with the Browns midway through the third quarter, then closed out the game with three straight touchdowns to win comfortably. Raiders' QB Ken Stabler threw four touchdown passes as Oakland rolled up 427 total yards, nearly twice the Browns' total. Greg Pruitt paced the Cleveland offense with 103 yards on only 12 carries, and Mike Phipps started at quarterback for the first time in four weeks, but threw three interceptions.
Record: 0–9

	1	2	3	4		
Browns	7	3	7	0	=	17
Raiders	7	10	7	14	=	38

OAK-Branch 22-yd. pass from Stabler (Blanda kick)
CLE-G. Pruitt 10-yd. run (Cockroft kick)
OAK-Branch 21-yd. pass from Stabler (Blanda kick)
CLE-Cockroft 25-yd. FG
OAK-Blanda 28-yd. FG

THE BROWNS' BEST AND WORST STARTS

In general, the Browns have traditionally not been a team that either roars or stumbles out of the starting gate. But there have been a handful of memorable stretches to begin seasons.

Best Starts		**Worst Starts**	
3–0	6–0	0–3	0–7
1957	1963	1984	1999
1960		2006	
1978	7–0	2008	0–9
1993	1946	2010	1975
4–0	11–0	0–4	
1979	1953	2009	
5–0	14–0	0–5	
1947	1948*	2012	
1958			

**Perfect season*

CLE-C. Miller 1-yd. run (Cockroft kick)
OAK-Biletnikoff 15-yd. pass from Stabler (Blanda kick)
OAK-Davis 31-yd. pass from Stabler (Blanda kick)
OAK-Davis 26-yd. run (Blanda kick)

Passing
CLE: Phipps 14–30–116 0 TD 3 INT
OAK: Stabler 16–25–220 4 TD 1 INT

Rushing
CLE: G. Pruitt 12–103, McKinnis 9–25, C. Miller 5–5, Pritchett 4–2
OAK: Davis 17–120, Hubbard 12–44, Phillips 6–26, Banaszak 7–18, van Eeghen 3–5, Hart 1–4

Receiving
CLE: Roan 3–32, Holden 1–22, C. Miller 2–20, G. Pruitt 4–17, Rucker 2–16, McKinnis 1–5, Pritchett 1–4
OAK: Biletnikoff 6–73, Branch 5–70, Davis 1–31, Moore 1–21, Siani 1–18, Banaszak 1–5, Hart 1–2

Sunday, November 23
Browns 35, Cincinnati Bengals 23
Cleveland Stadium (56,427)
Brown jerseys/orange pants

With a dramatic 20-point fourth quarter on a sunshiny November afternoon, the Browns' 11-game losing streak finally came to an end with one of the greatest upsets in team history. The Browns' Billy Lefear returned the opening kickoff 92 yards to set up a short Greg Pruitt touchdown run, but LeFear broke his leg on the play and would never again play in the NFL. The 8–1 Bengals controlled the contest through the first half and led 23–12 early in the third before QB Ken Anderson left the game with a bruised chest, and the Browns gradually fought back. Early in the fourth quarter, TE Oscar Roan made a leaping catch in the end zone for a touchdown that pulled the Browns within a point. After forcing a Bengals' punt, the Browns drove back downfield and took the lead on a touchdown catch by Greg Pruitt, who darted through Cincinnati defenders just as he'd done all day, tallying 304 total yards. The Bengals had one final chance, but Cleveland DB Jim Hill picked off a pass near midfield and returned it 56 yards for the game-clinching touchdown to cap a spirited comeback that saw the Browns score the game's last 23 points, 20 in the fourth quarter. In their best performance of the year, the Browns tallied 439 total yards of offense as embattled Mike Phipps played the best game of his career, throwing for 298 yards. He was swarmed by fans who'd rushed the field after the final gun. Meanwhile, Pruitt rushed for 121 yards on 17 carries and caught seven passes for 106 more. The game also marked retiring Paul Brown's final trip to Cleveland as a coach.

Record: 1–9

	1	2	3	4		
Bengals	13	7	3	0	=	23
Browns	9	3	3	20	=	35

CLE-G. Pruitt 2-yd. run (kick failed)
CLE-Cockroft 27-yd. FG
CIN-Trumpy 35-yd. pass from Anderson (Green kick)
CIN-Fritts 4-yd. run (kick failed)
CIN-Curtis 30-yd. pass from Anderson (Green kick)
CLE-Cockroft 32-yd. FG
CIN-Green 21-yd. FG
CLE-Cockroft 43-yd. FG
CLE-Roan 5-yd. pass from Phipps (Cockroft kick)
CLE-G. Pruitt 13-yd. pass from Phipps (Cockroft kick)
CLE-Hill 56-yd. interception return (kick failed)

Passing
CIN: Anderson 13–20–292 2 TD 0 INT, Reaves 4–11–68 0 TD 1 INT
CLE: Phipps 23–36–298 2 TD 0 INT

Rushing
CIN: Elliott 13–35, Williams 4–18, Clark 6–15, Fritts 3–4, Anderson 1–1, Reaves 1–1
CLE: G. Pruitt 17–121, Pritchett 13–40, Phipps 2–7, C. Miller 1-(-2)

Receiving
CIN: Joiner 7–200, Curtis 2–77, Trumpy 2–44, Elliott 3–21, Williams 1–9, Clark 1–7, Coslet 1–2
CLE: G. Pruitt 7–106, Holden 5–93, Rucker 6–64, Roan 3–25, Pritchett 2–10

Sunday, November 30
Browns 17, New Orleans Saints 16
Cleveland Stadium (44,753)
Brown jerseys/orange pants

The Browns won back-to-back games for the first time in two years, putting together another fourth-quarter rally to top the Saints in the mud on a dark, rainy afternoon. New Orleans built a 16–3 lead in the third quarter, but the Saints failed to convert their second extra point, a mistake that would come back to haunt them. After New Orleans RB Mike Strachan injured his ankle and couldn't play in the second half after rushing for 99 yards in the first, the Browns cut the margin to six points with a touchdown catch over the middle by Reggie Rucker early in the fourth. They then regained possession at their own 3 with just under 11 minutes remaining and embarked on an impressive 15-play, 97-yard drive that ended with an eight-yard Greg Pruitt scoring run to give them the lead with 3:12 to play. The Cleveland defense then forced a New Orleans punt, and a last-gasp Saints' drive in the final minute ended at the Cleveland 43 when time expired.

Record: 2–9

	1	2	3	4		
Saints	3	7	6	0	=	16
Browns	0	0	3	14	=	17

NO-Szaro 28-yd. FG
NO-Maxson 1-yd. run (Szaro kick)
CLE-Cockroft 28-yd. FG
NO-Maxson 1-yd. run (run failed)
CLE-Rucker 22-yd. pass from Phipps (Cockroft kick)
CLE-G. Pruitt 8-yd. run (Cockroft kick)

Passing
NO: Manning 6–10–92 0 TD 0 INT
CLE: Phipps 17–29–162 1 TD 1 INT

Rushing
NO: Strachan 21–99, Maxson 16–45, Manning 4–17, Rogers 6–8, Jones 1–5, McNeill 3–3
CLE: G. Pruitt 19–77, Pritchett 8–18, McKinnis 2–4

Receiving
NO: Hamilton 2–70, Maxson 3–11, Seal 1–11
CLE: Rucker 7–83, McKinnis 2–19, G. Pruitt 4–18, Roan 1–16, Parris 1–12, Holden 1–11, Pritchett 1–3

Sunday, December 7
Pittsburgh Steelers 31, Browns 17
Three Rivers Stadium (47,962)
White jerseys/orange pants

The Browns' modest winning streak came to a halt despite another admirable performance against the 10–1 Steelers. Following a one-yard Greg Pruitt touchdown run that gave the Browns a 10–7 lead in the second quarter, Browns' WR Willie Miller scooped up a Pittsburgh fumble on the ensuing kickoff and returned it 17 yards for a touchdown to put Cleveland up by 10 less than two minutes before the half. The Pittsburgh defense didn't allow another score, and the Steelers scored the game's final 24 points, though the Browns held them to just 258 yards of offense and sacked Terry Bradshaw four times.
Record: 2–10

	1	2	3	4		
Browns	3	14	0	0	=	17
Steelers	7	3	14	7	=	31

CLE-Cockroft 26-yd. FG
PIT-Harris 3-yd. run (Gerela kick)
CLE-G. Pruitt 1-yd. run (Cockroft kick)
CLE-W. Miller 17-yd. fumble return (Cockroft kick)
PIT-Gerela 32-yd. FG
PIT-Swann 3-yd. pass from Bradshaw (Gerela kick)
PIT-Swann 18-yd. pass from Bradshaw (Gerela kick)
PIT-Harris 8-yd. run (Gerela kick)

Passing
CLE: Phipps 14–37–145 0 TD 3 INT
PIT: Bradshaw 11–25–135 2 TD 0 INT

Rushing
CLE: G. Pruitt 19–85, McKinnis 8–20, Phipps 3–11, Pritchett 2–6
PIT: Harris 25–103, Bradshaw 3–30, Bleier 9–24, Harrison 1–2, Collier 1–1

Receiving
CLE: Rucker 5–39, Holden 1–28, Morin 1–19, Pritchett 1–18, McKinnis 2–17, G. Pruitt 3–15, Hynoski 1–9
PIT: Swann 5–67, Bleier 2–24, Lewis 1–20, Harris 2–15, Grossman 1–9

Sunday, December 14
Browns 40, Kansas City Chiefs 14
Cleveland Stadium (44,368)
Brown jerseys/orange pants

The Browns took out a season's worth of frustration on Kansas City on an unseasonably warm December afternoon and picked up their third victory in four weeks. Posting their finest overall performance of 1975 on both sides of the ball, the Browns rolled to 481 total yards while allowing just 146 as they exploded for 30 second-half points. The spark was Greg Pruitt, who rushed for 214 yards and three touchdowns, passing the 1,000-yard mark for the season. It was the first time a Brown hit 1,000 rushing yards in seven years as Pruitt joined Jim Brown and Leroy Kelly as the only Cleveland running backs to hit the four-digit mark in rushing. Reggie Rucker also enjoyed his finest day of the season, catching six passes for 130 yards and caught a touchdown early in the fourth quarter that capped a five-minute period in which the Browns scored 23 points. While the offense lit up the scoreboard, the defense quietly put together its best showing of the season, collecting four turnovers and five sacks and holding the Chiefs to just over two yards per offensive play. Rookie DE Mack Mitchell collected four of the sacks himself, one of which resulted in a stripped football to create a Cleveland safety in the third quarter.
Record: 3–10

	1	2	3	4		
Chiefs	0	0	0	14	=	14
Browns	7	3	16	14	=	40

CLE-G. Pruitt 11-yd. run (Cockroft kick)
CLE-Cockroft 26-yd. FG
CLE-McKinnis 1-yd. run (Cockroft kick)
CLE-Safety: East tackled Getty in end zone
CLE-G. Pruitt 3-yd. run (Cockroft kick)
CLE-Rucker 40-yd. pass from Phipps (Cockroft kick)
KC-Green 1-yd. run (Stenerud kick)
CLE-G. Pruitt 14-yd. run (Cockroft kick)
KC-Masters 9-yd. pass from Adams (Stenerud kick)

Passing
KC: Adams 13–31–141 1 TD 1 INT
CLE: Phipps 14–20–204 1 TD 0 INT, Cockroft 1-1-(-1) 0 TD 0 INT

Rushing
KC: Kinney 10–29, Green 15–9, Dressler 2–5, Adams 2–4

CLE: G. Pruitt 26–214, McKinnis 14–65, Phipps 1–0, Brown 1–0, Hynoski 1–0, Pritchett 1-(-1)

Receiving
KC: Green 4–57, Pearson 3–32, Brunson 2–20, Podolak 1–13, Masters 1–9, Kinney 1–6, Dressler 1–4
CLE: Rucker 6–130, Holden 2–25, G. Pruitt 3–23, Pritchett 2–18, McKinnis 1–8, Green 1-(-1)

Sunday, December 21
Houston Oilers 21, Browns 10
Houston Astrodome (43,770)
White jerseys/orange pants

The Browns' worst season in their 30 years of existence closed out with a whimper as they were dominated by the Oilers in the finale, giving Houston its first-ever season sweep of Cleveland. The Browns fell behind 21–0 at the half before showing signs of life in the final two quarters, highlighted by Mike Phipps completing 10 straight passes at one point and throwing for more than 200 yards for the third time in the last five games. The defeat wrapped up Cleveland's year with a 3–11 record—a game behind its 1974 showing and the worst mark in team history. It would be 15 years before the team notched a worse campaign.
Record: 3–11

	1	2	3	4		
Browns	0	0	3	7	=	10
Oilers	14	7	0	0	=	21

HOU-Hardeman 2-yd. run (Butler kick)
HOU-Burrough 75-yd. pass from Pastorini (Butler kick)
HOU-Coleman 2-yd. run (Butler kick)
CLE-Cockroft 42-yd. FG
CLE-Brown 4-yd. run (Cockroft kick)

Passing
CLE: Phipps 24–42–213 0 TD 2 INT, Hynoski 0–1–0 0 TD 0 INT
HOU: Pastorini 11–23–166 1 TD 2 INT

Rushing
CLE: Hynoski 5–38, G. Pruitt 14–37, Brown 3–15, Pritchett 4–6, McKinnis 1–0
HOU: Coleman 12–54, Hardeman 9–45, Willis 18–42, Rodgers 5–25

Receiving
CLE: Rucker 7–79, Roan 5–44, Holden 3–32, Brown 1–17, G. Pruitt 3–16, W. Miller 1–9, McKinnis 1–8, Hynoski 2–7, Pritchett 1–1
HOU: Burrough 5–129, Coleman 2–22, Johnson 1–15, Alston 2–10, Willis 1-(-10)

1976

Sunday, September 12
Browns 38, New York Jets 17
Cleveland Stadium (67,496)
White jerseys/orange pants

On what proved to be a fateful afternoon, the Browns took control in the second quarter and helped the memories of their worst season fade with a convincing victory in a sun-splashed opener. After falling behind 10–0 in the first quarter, the Browns exploded for three touchdowns in the second behind red-hot QB Mike Phipps, who completed eight of nine passes in the period, including the go-ahead touchdown toss to veteran WR Paul Warfield, making his return in Cleveland after six seasons in Miami and the World Football League. But Phipps's career took a dramatic turn early in the third quarter when he separated his right shoulder and was replaced by backup Brian Sipe, who kept the offense rolling to close out the victory. While both quarterbacks played well, throwing for a total of five touchdown passes, WR Reggie Rucker stole the show with three scoring receptions, and RB Greg Pruitt rolled to 124 yards on the ground and another 51 receiving as the Browns compiled nearly 400 total yards, setting the tone for a turnaround season.

Record: 1–0

	1	2	3	4		
Jets	10	0	0	7	=	17
Browns	0	21	10	7	=	38

NYJ-Leahy 41-yd. FG
NYJ-Davis 20-yd. run (Leahy kick)
CLE-Rucker 13-yd. pass from Phipps (Cockroft kick)
CLE-Warfield 23-yd. pass from Phipps (Cockroft kick)
CLE-Rucker 4-yd. pass from Phipps (Cockroft kick)
CLE-Cockroft 32-yd. FG
CLE-Rucker 8-yd. pass from Sipe (Cockroft kick)
NYJ-Todd 8-yd. run (Leahy kick)
CLE-Holden 26-yd. pass from Sipe (Cockroft kick)

Passing
NYJ: Namath 15–31–137 0 TD 1 INT, Todd 4–5–25 0 TD 1 INT
CLE: Phipps 11–15–100 3 TD 0 INT, Sipe 7–10–83 2 TD 0 INT

Rushing
NYJ: Marinaro 11–36, Davis 8–36, Gaines 6–29, Todd 3–10
CLE: G. Pruitt 17–124, C. Miller 15–47, Phipps 3–26, M. Pruitt 5–7, Rucker 1–3, Sipe 1–0

Receiving
NYJ: Marinaro 3–40, Caster 5–39, Knight 2–36, Giammona 4–18, Gaines 2–16, Buckey 2–7, Davis 1–6
CLE: G. Pruitt 4–51, Rucker 5–37, Warfield 3–32, Holden 1–26, Roan 1–17, C. Miller 2–8, Duncan 1–7, M. Pruitt 1–5

Sunday, September 19
Pittsburgh Steelers 31, Browns 14
Three Rivers Stadium (49,169)
White jerseys/orange pants

A third-quarter blocked punt swung the game's momentum and launched a Pittsburgh comeback as the Browns watched a promising first half turn into a blowout loss. Brian Sipe threw a pair of second-quarter touchdowns as the Browns soared to a 14–0 halftime lead, but the Steelers blocked a Cleveland punt early in the second half, which led to their first touchdown and changed the complexion of the game. By the end of the quarter, the Steelers led by three, then tacked on two more touchdowns in the fourth period to win going away. The Browns aided Pittsburgh's cause with four lost fumbles—two by rookie RB Mike Pruitt, making his first NFL start—spoiling an otherwise impressive performance by the Browns' offense against the two-time defending Super Bowl champions.

Record: 1–1

	1	2	3	4		
Browns	0	14	0	0	=	14
Steelers	0	0	17	14	=	31

CLE-Rucker 14-yd. pass from Sipe (Cockroft kick)
CLE-Roan 17-yd. pass from Sipe (Cockroft kick)
PIT-Stallworth 14-yd. pass from Bradshaw (Gerela kick)
PIT-Gerela 47-yd. FG
PIT-Harris 2-yd. run (Gerela kick)
PIT-Stallworth 5-yd. pass from Bradshaw (Gerela kick)
PIT-Bradshaw 7-yd. run (Gerela kick)

Passing
CLE: Sipe 15–34–193 2 TD 0 INT
PIT: Bradshaw 7–23–77 2 TD 0 INT

Rushing
CLE: M. Pruitt 13–70, G. Pruitt 20–69, Duncan 1–3, Poole 1–3, Sipe 1–0
PIT: Harris 25–118, Bleier 12–62, Bradshaw 6–32, Deloplaine 1–5, Harrison 1–4

Receiving
CLE: G. Pruitt 6–83, Warfield 2–49, Roan 3–31, Rucker 2–31, M. Pruitt 2-(-1)
PIT: Grossman 2–38, Stallworth 2–19, Harris 2–10, Bleier 1–10

Sunday, September 26
Denver Broncos 44, Browns 13
Mile High Stadium (62,775)
White jerseys/orange pants

With an utterly miserable performance, the Browns dropped below the .500 mark as Denver cruised to an easy win on a damp afternoon in the Rockies. Following the first of two punt returns for touchdowns and a Cleveland fumble on the ensuing kickoff, the Broncos soared to a 14–0 lead four minutes into the game, then recovered another key cough-up by Mike Pruitt and returned it for a touchdown early in the third after the Browns had trimmed the lead to 10 points. The teams combined for seven turnovers and 21 penalties, with the Browns collecting 121 yards in infractions compared to just 227 total yards.
Record: 1–2

	1	2	3	4		
Browns	0	7	0	6	=	13
Broncos	17	0	20	7	=	44

DEN-Upchurch 73-yd. punt return (Turner kick)
DEN-Armstrong 1-yd. run (Turner kick)
DEN-Turner 47-yd. FG
CLE-Roan 5-yd. pass from Sipe (Cockroft kick)
DEN-Jones 43-yd. fumble return (Turner kick)
DEN-Upchurch 47-yd. punt return (kick failed)
DEN-Moses 36-yd. pass from Ramsey (Turner kick)
CLE-G. Pruitt 8-yd. run (kick failed)
DEN-Kiick 12-yd. pass from Ramsey (Turner kick)

Passing
CLE: Sipe 18–31–134 1 TD 2 INT, Mays 2–6–24 0 TD 0 INT
DEN: Ramsey 10–20–166 2 TD 2 INT, Weese 1–1–11 0 TD 0 INT

Rushing
CLE: G. Pruitt 16–56, M. Pruitt 14–21, Poole 1–4, Duncan 2–2
DEN: Armstrong 18–23, Perrin 7–11, Kiick 3–10, Dolbin 1–8, Franckowiak 2–3, Weese 1–0

Receiving
CLE: M. Pruitt 4–29, Holden 2–27, Parris 2–24, Roan 3–22, G. Pruitt 5–18, Rucker 1–16, Duncan 2–11, Warfield 1–11
DEN: Moses 2–52, Armstrong 2–40, Dolbin 3–37, Kiick 2–23, Upchurch 1–16, Keyworth 1–9

Sunday, October 3
Cincinnati Bengals 45, Browns 24
Cleveland Stadium (75,817)
White jerseys/orange pants

The Browns were blitzed for 40-plus points for the second straight week, spoiling another admirable performance by the offense with Brian Sipe at the helm. After the Browns tied the game at seven midway through a wild first quarter, Cincinnati returned the ensuing kickoff to take a lead it would not relinquish. The advantage swelled to 31–10 in the second quarter, then a pair of Sipe scoring tosses cut the margin to seven, and the Browns drove to the Cincinnati 13 on their next series. But Don Cockroft missed a short field goal, and the Bengals bounced back with two fourth-quarter touchdowns to close out the victory. Leading the Cleveland offense to more than 400 yards, Sipe set team records for completions in a game (26) and most attempts in a game without an interception (42), as he threw for 290 yards. His primary target was Reggie Rucker, who had another outstanding day, catching nine passes for 141 yards and a score.
Record: 1–3

	1	2	3	4		
Bengals	21	10	0	14	=	45
Browns	7	10	7	0	=	24

CIN-Elliott 19-yd. pass from Anderson (Bahr kick)
CLE-C. Miller 6-yd. run (Cockroft kick)
CIN-Shelby 97-yd. kickoff return (Bahr kick)
CIN-Curtis 44-yd. pass from Anderson (Bahr kick)
CIN-Bahr 40-yd. FG
CLE-Cockroft 33-yd. FG

CIN-Curtis 7-yd. pass from Anderson (Bahr kick)
CLE-Rucker 26-yd. pass from Sipe (Sipe run)
CLE-G. Pruitt 4-yd. pass from Sipe (Cockroft kick)
CIN-Elliott 29-yd. pass from Anderson (Bahr kick)
CIN-Clark 1-yd. run (Bahr kick)

Passing
CIN: Anderson 19–27–265 4 TD 2 INT
CLE: Sipe 26–42–290 2 TD 0 INT

Rushing
CIN: Griffin 16–75, Clark 13–53, Anderson 4–6, Elliott 3-(-1)
CLE: G. Pruitt 15–70, C. Miller 5–24, Poole 2–17, Duncan 2–14, M. Pruitt 2–2, Sipe 1–0

Receiving
CIN: Elliott 5–89, Curtis 5–87, Myers 3–38, Trumpy 1–21, Griffin 2–12, Clark 2–11, Brooks 1–7
CLE: Rucker 9–141, Holden 5–75, G. Pruitt 8–39, Roan 3–31, Poole 1–4

Sunday, October 10
Browns 18, Pittsburgh Steelers 16
Cleveland Stadium (76,411)
White jerseys/orange pants

With the season on the brink of mirroring the disasters of the previous two, the Browns rallied from behind in the second half to pick up an emblematic victory over their archrivals. The heavily favored Steelers took a 10–6 lead in the second quarter, and the chances for a Cleveland comeback looked bleak when Brian Sipe was knocked out of the game with a concussion. With Mike Phipps still out with a shoulder injury, the Browns' hopes rested on third-stringer Dave Mays, an offseason dentist and the first African American quarterback in team history. Browns' DB Clarence Scott blocked a Pittsburgh field-goal attempt early in the third quarter that swung the momentum, and Mays led the Browns to their only touchdown, a one-yard Cleo Miller plunge to give them the lead. The Cleveland defense then took over, holding Pittsburgh to 196 total yards for the day. Two more Don Cockroft field goals extended the margin to 18–10 with two minutes remaining, and a last-gasp Steelers touchdown wasn't enough to catch up. But the play of the game came with 11 minutes left when Browns' DE Joe "Turkey" Jones picked up Pittsburgh QB Terry Bradshaw and flung him to the ground on his head, knocking Bradshaw out of the game with a neck injury. The defeat dropped the two-time defending Super Bowl champs to 1–4 but would mark their final defeat of the regular season as they went on to win nine straight to capture another AFC Central title.

Record: 2–3

	1	2	3	4		
Steelers	7	3	0	6	=	16
Browns	3	3	9	3	=	18

CLE-Cockroft 43-yd. FG
PIT-Harris 1-yd. run (Gerela kick)
CLE-Cockroft 28-yd. FG
PIT-Gerela 30-yd. FG
CLE-C. Miller 1-yd. run (kick failed)
CLE-Cockroft 50-yd. FG
CLE-Cockroft 40-yd. FG
PIT-Kruczek 22-yd. run (kick failed)

Passing
PIT: Bradshaw 10–18–75 0 TD 1 INT, Kruczek 3–5–59 0 TD 0 INT
CLE: Sipe 4–14–80 0 TD 0 INT, Mays 5–9–70 0 TD 0 INT, G. Pruitt 1–1–29 0 TD 0 INT, Cockroft 0–1–0 0 TD 0 INT

Rushing
PIT: Harris 13–39, Kruczek 2–30, Bleier 8–25, Bradshaw 2–17
CLE: G. Pruitt 22–76, C. Miller 23–57, Mays 3–14

Receiving
PIT: Swann 3–74, Grossman 3–41, Harris 6–13, Lewis 1–6
CLE: Rucker 3–77, Warfield 3–65, G. Pruitt 3–29, C. Miller 1–8

Sunday, October 17
Browns 20, Atlanta Falcons 17
Fulton County Stadium (33,364)
White jerseys/orange pants

Behind an unstoppable running attack, the Browns took a two-touchdown lead, lost it, and then rallied for their first road victory in nearly two years, snapping an 11-game losing streak. Cleveland tallied 321 yards on the ground, paced by an incredible performance by Greg Pruitt, who rushed for 191 yards and a pair of touchdowns, including the game-winner early in the fourth quarter. Leading by three, the Browns embarked on a drive that ate up nearly 10 minutes of the final period, not giving up the ball until just over a minute remained. After the Falcons drove into

Cleveland territory in the final seconds, DB Thom Darden clinched the victory with his fifth interception of the year. With Pruitt leading the way, along with Cleo Miller, who added another 82 rushing yards and the Browns' other touchdown, the Cleveland offense picked up a season-high 432 yards.

Record: 3–3

	1	2	3	4		
Browns	14	0	6	0	=	20
Falcons	0	14	3	0	=	17

CLE-G. Pruitt 1-yd. run (Cockroft kick)
CLE-C. Miller 1-yd. run (Cockroft kick)
ATL-Bean 23-yd. run (Mike-Mayer kick)
ATL-Gilliam 18-yd. pass from McQuilken (Mike-Mayer kick)
ATL-Mike-Mayer 33-yd. FG
CLE-G. Pruitt 2-yd. run (run failed)

Passing
CLE: Sipe 12–18–134 0 TD 2 INT
ATL: McQuilken 15–28–180 1 TD 1 INT

Rushing
CLE: G. Pruitt 26–191, C. Miller 22–82, Sipe 5–25, Poole 3 23, Phipps 1–0
ATL: Bean 14–54, Thompson 8–23, McQuilken 2–9, Stanback 2–3

Receiving
CLE: Warfield 4–69, Rucker 3–31, G. Pruitt 3–21, Roan 1–11, C. Miller 1–2
ATL: Jenkins 6–74, Mitchell 2–47, Gilliam 3–38, Thompson 3–12, Bean 1–9

Sunday, October 24
Browns 21, San Diego Chargers 17
Cleveland Stadium (60,018)
White jerseys/orange pants

In a game eerily similar to the week before, the Browns scored two early touchdowns, then fell behind before scoring the winning points early in the fourth quarter to capture their third straight victory on a cold, rainy afternoon. Greg Pruitt got off to a great start, tallying 100 yards in total offense in a little over a quarter of action before leaving the game with a badly sprained ankle that would hamper him for the rest of the season. With Pruitt out, San Diego rallied for 17 straight points to take the lead before Brian Sipe led the Browns on an 82-yard drive capped by a 10-yard scoring pass to TE Oscar Roan in the first minute of the fourth quarter. The Cleveland defense held San Diego scoreless in the final period and limited the Chargers to just a field goal in the second half. Cleveland RB Larry Poole did a nice job filling in for Pruitt, rushing for a game-high 64 yards in relief, while Sipe hit on 23 of 28 passes—completing 12 straight at one point.

Record: 4–3

	1	2	3	4		
Chargers	0	14	3	0	=	17
Browns	14	0	0	7	=	21

CLE-Rucker 3-yd. pass from Sipe (Cockroft kick)
CLE-G. Pruitt 1-yd. run (Cockroft kick)
SD-Joiner 16-yd. pass from Fouts (Wersching kick)
SD-Scarber 11-yd. pass from Woods (Wersching kick)
SD-Wersching 22-yd. FG
CLE-Roan 10-yd. pass from Sipe (Cockroft kick)

Passing
SD: Fouts 23–35–235 1 TD 1 INT, Woods 1–1–11 1 TD 0 INT
CLE: Sipe 23–28–246 2 TD 2 INT

Rushing
SD: Young 14–48, Morris 4–13, Scarber 4–9, Woods 2–4, Matthews 1–4, Fouts 2–0
CLE: Poole 16–64, G. Pruitt 7–40, C. Miller 8–34, Sipe 3-(-1)

Receiving
SD: Joiner 5–94, Young 6–44, Morris 2–28, Scarber 3–21, Curran 3–20, Dorsey 1–16, Woods 2–13, Matthews 2–10
CLE: Warfield 5–76, G. Pruitt 6–60, Poole 7–55, Rucker 4–45, Roan 1–10

Sunday, October 31
Cincinnati Bengals 21, Browns 6
Riverfront Stadium (54,776)
White jerseys/orange pants

Despite an admirable effort by hobbling Greg Pruitt, the Browns couldn't cash in on a handful of scoring opportunities and were overwhelmed by the division-leading Bengals on Halloween. Playing on his badly injured ankle, Pruitt rushed for 124 yards, but four Cleveland trips inside the Cincinnati 10 resulted in just six points. The turning point came early in the third quarter when the Browns drove to the Cincinnati 7 trailing 14–6 but lost their momentum when Pruitt fumbled. Clarence Scott picked off a pair of Ken Anderson passes, but the Cleveland defense allowed the Bengals to roll to 385 total yards, including 203 on the ground.

Record: 4–4

	1	2	3	4		
Browns	3	3	0	0	=	6
Bengals	7	7	0	7	=	21

CIN-Clark 1-yd. run (Bahr kick)
CLE-Cockroft 18-yd. FG
CLE-Cockroft 26-yd. FG
CIN-Curtis 69-yd. pass from Anderson (Bahr kick)
CIN-Clark 1-yd. run (Bahr kick)

Passing
CLE: Sipe 12–27–171 0 TD 1 INT
CIN: Anderson 15–24–182 1 TD 2 INT

Rushing
CLE: G. Pruitt 18–124, C. Miller 11–57, Poole 2–1
CIN: Clark 21–100, Griffin 8–51, Elliott 8–35, Curtis 1–14, Davis 1–5, Fritts 2-(-2)

Receiving
CLE: C. Miller 2–46, Warfield 2–36, Rucker 2–32, Roan 2–29, G. Pruitt 4–28
CIN: Curtis 6–116, Clark 5–32, Brooks 2–17, Elliott 1–12, Myers 1–5

Sunday, November 7
Browns 21, Houston Oilers 7
Houston Astrodome (39,828)
White jerseys/orange pants

Behind a sterling defensive effort and a late spark provided by Brian Sipe, the Browns held off the Oilers to surge over the .500 mark again. The defense got the Browns on the board 90 seconds into the game by forcing a fumble deep in Houston territory that resulted in a Cleveland safety, then a pair of Don Cockroft field goals extended the lead to 8–0 at the half. Mike Phipps made his first start since opening day, but struggled and with the Browns clinging to a one-point lead in the fourth quarter, was pulled in favor of Brian Sipe. Sipe quickly led Cleveland to a touchdown on a halfback-option toss by Greg Pruitt. Then an interception by LB Bob Babich set up another score on Sipe's only pass of the day to seal the victory. The defense limited Houston to 188 total yards while collecting four sacks and three turnovers, while Sipe's late heroics marked a changing of the guard at quarterback. Mike Phipps would never start another game for the Browns and was traded away after the season as Sipe assumed the role of full-time starting quarterback.

Record: 5–4

	1	2	3	4		
Browns	5	3	0	13	=	21
Oilers	0	7	0	0	=	7

CLE-Safety: Mitchell tackled Drungo in end zone
CLE-Cockroft 30-yd. FG
CLE-Cockroft 40-yd. FG
HOU-Coleman 7-yd. pass from Hadl (Butler kick)
CLE-Duncan 10-yd. pass from G. Pruitt (kick failed)
CLE-Roan 23-yd. pass from Sipe (Cockroft kick)

Passing
CLE: Phipps 7–17–35 0 TD 0 INT, Sipe 1–1–23 1 TD 0 INT, G. Pruitt 1–1–10 1 TD 0 INT
HOU: Hadl 12–20–106 1 TD 1 INT, Pastorini 1–1-(-4) 0 TD 0 INT

Rushing
CLE: G. Pruitt 18–79, Poole 10–76, C. Miller 8–29, M. Pruitt 7–14, Duncan 1–2
HOU: Coleman 12–70, Hardeman 12–25, Burrough 1–12, Hadl 2–8, Johnson 1–5, Dawkins 2–3, Willis 1–2

Receiving
CLE: Roan 1–23, Warfield 1–20, Duncan 1–10, C. Miller 2–9, Rucker 2–9, G. Pruitt 2-(-3)
HOU: Burrough 3–24, Coleman 3–24, Alston 2–23, Sawyer 1–11, Hardeman 2–10, Thomas 2–10

Sunday, November 14
Browns 24, Philadelphia Eagles 3
Cleveland Stadium (62,120)
White jerseys/orange pants

With the defense again leading the way, the Browns coasted to an easy victory over Philadelphia. DT Jerry Sherk collected four sacks as the Browns held the Eagles to just 164 total yards and picked off four passes, including a return for a touchdown by DB Ron Bolton in the fourth quarter. The offense didn't lose stride despite the departure of hobbling Greg Pruitt after just five carries as Brian Sipe once again directed an effective attack, hitting Reggie Rucker six times for 99 yards and a score.

Record: 6–4

	1	2	3	4		
Eagles	0	0	3	0	=	3
Browns	0	10	0	14	=	24

CLE-Cockroft 32-yd. FG
CLE-Rucker 20-yd. pass from Sipe (Cockroft kick)
PHI-Muhlmann 33-yd. FG
CLE-Warfield 9-yd. pass from Sipe (Cockroft kick)
CLE-Bolton 37-yd. interception return (Cockroft kick)

Passing
PHI: Boryla 14–24–73 0 TD 4 INT
CLE: Sipe 15–21–198 2 TD 0 INT, Mays 2–4–7 0 TD 0 INT

Rushing
PHI: Hampton 16–94, Olds 5–28, Smith 1–12, Sullivan 2–9, Boryla 1–0, McAlister 1–0
CLE: Poole 12–60, C. Miller 11–51, M. Pruitt 6–20, G. Pruitt 5–0, Duncan 1–0, Mays 1–0, Sipe 1–0

Receiving
PHI: Young 2–31, Smith 2–17, Carmichael 2–15, McAlister 3–12, Lusk 1–9, Hampton 2–1, Olds 2-(-12)
CLE: Rucker 6–99, Warfield 5–47, Parris 2–34, C. Miller 1–19, Poole 2–13, M. Pruitt 1-(-7)

Sunday, November 21
Browns 24, Tampa Bay Buccaneers 7
Tampa Stadium (36,930)
Brown jerseys/orange pants

Tied with the winless, expansion Buccaneers midway through the third quarter, the Browns got rolling when Greg Pruitt entered the game, quickly scoring the go-ahead touchdown on a Brian Sipe-to-Paul Warfield strike, and they pulled away for their third straight victory. On the first play of the fourth quarter, a fierce Cleveland pass rush knocked the ball away from Tampa Bay QB Steve Spurrier, and Turkey Jones recovered the football in the end zone for a touchdown to put the Browns up 21–7 and put them in the clear. The defense limited the Bucs to just 66 total yards in the second half while Pruitt rushed for 44 yards in limited action.

Record: 7–4

	1	2	3	4		
Browns	7	0	7	10	=	24
Buccaneers	0	7	0	0	=	7

CLE-C. Miller 2-yd. run (Cockroft kick)
TB-Johnson 12-yd. pass from Spurrier (Green kick)
CLE-Warfield 15-yd. pass from Sipe (Cockroft kick)
CLE-Jones recovered fumble in end zone (Cockroft kick)
CLE-Cockroft 32-yd. FG

Passing
CLE: Sipe 10–18–131 1 TD 0 INT, Phipps 2–5–11 0 TD 0 INT
TB: Spurrier 15–28–135 1 TD 0 INT, Dickinson 2–3–29 0 TD 1 INT, Davis 1–1-(-7) 0 TD 0 INT

Rushing
CLE: C. Miller 14–49, G. Pruitt 10–44, Poole 13–38, Sipe 1–10, M. Pruitt 2–4, Duncan 1–4
TB: Williams 11–39, McNeill 4–37, Carter 12–25, Spurrier 1–1

Receiving
CLE: Warfield 4–79, Rucker 3–25, Logan 1–18, C. Miller 1–15, Duncan 1–4, Poole 1–4, G. Pruitt 1-(-3)
TB: Moore 5–56, Owens 4–50, Johnson 4–31, McKay 1–11, Williams 1–9, Carter 2–7, Novak 1-(-7)

Sunday, November 28
Browns 17, Miami Dolphins 13
Cleveland Stadium (74,715)
White jerseys/orange pants

On a snowy afternoon, the Browns overcame five turnovers by the offense and used a late defensive stand to clinch a narrow victory over the Dolphins. Aided by a struggling Miami kicking game that missed a pair of field goals and an extra point, the Browns took a four-point lead with a field goal with two minutes to play, but Miami quickly drove deep into Cleveland territory with just over a minute left. Out of time outs, the Dolphins reached the Cleveland 3 in the final seconds, but an ill-advised handoff to RB Norm Bulaich was stuffed by Turkey Jones and time expired, giving the Browns their fourth straight victory. Brian Sipe threw a pair of touchdown passes, including a dazzling, leaping catch by Paul Warfield on his thirty-fourth birthday to open the scoring in the second quarter. The victory ensured the Browns' highest win total in four years.

Record: 8–4

	1	2	3	4		
Dolphins	0	6	0	7	=	13
Browns	0	7	7	3	=	17

CLE-Warfield 12-yd. pass from Sipe (Cockroft kick)
MIA-Seiple 4-yd. pass from Griese (kick failed)
CLE-Rucker 18-yd. pass from Sipe (Cockroft kick)
MIA-Solomon 9-yd. pass from Griese (Yepremian kick)
CLE-Cockroft 19-yd. FG

Passing
MIA: Griese 22–33–209 2 TD 0 INT
CLE: Sipe 15–22–191 2 TD 3 INT, G. Pruitt 0–1–0 0 TD 0 INT

Rushing
MIA: Malone 12–67, Bulaich 15–53, Seiple 1–7, Griese 3–6, Solomon 2–1
CLE: Poole 17–69, C. Miller 11–57, G. Pruitt 2–7

Receiving
MIA: Bulaich 7–53, Harris 5–52, Malone 2–39, Solomon 3–33, Tillman 2–13, Seiple 2–12, Mandich 1–7
CLE: Rucker 4–77, Warfield 4–60, C. Miller 3–24, Parris 1–15, Logan 1–10, G. Pruitt 1–5, Poole 1–0

Sunday, December 5
Browns 13, Houston Oilers 10
Cleveland Stadium (56,025)
White jerseys/orange pants

In another defensive struggle on a bitterly cold day, the Browns endured to hold off the Oilers and pick up their fifth straight win, representing their longest streak in four years. The Cleveland defense held the Oilers to 175 yards of offense and only nine first downs while forcing four turnovers. The Browns, who committed five turnovers themselves, got on the scoreboard on the first play of the second quarter when Brian Sipe was flushed out of the pocket and lofted a long touchdown pass on the run to Paul Warfield. The Browns then added a pair of field goals to take a 13–3 lead in the fourth quarter. Houston cut the margin to three on a touchdown bomb with four minutes to play, but an interception by Cleveland LB Charlie Hall with 1:28 remaining sealed the victory. RB Cleo Miller had his best day as a pro, rushing for 99 yards on 17 carries, while rookie WR Ricky Feacher ripped off a key 49-yard punt return to set up the Browns' touchdown.
Record: 9–4

	1	2	3	4		
Oilers	0	0	3	7	=	10
Browns	0	7	3	3	=	13

CLE-Warfield 37-yd. pass from Sipe (Cockroft kick)
CLE-Cockroft 29-yd. FG
HOU-Butler 31-yd. FG
CLE-Cockroft 46-yd. FG
HOU-Burrough 54-yd. pass from Pastorini (Butler kick)

Passing
HOU: Pastorini 13–19–127 1 TD 1 INT, Hadl 4–10–25 0 TD 2 INT
CLE: Sipe 9–22–114 1 TD 2 INT

Rushing
HOU: Coleman 8–25, Dawkins 6–15, Pastorini 1–11, Hadl 1–6, Willis 7–1
CLE: C. Miller 17–99, G. Pruitt 24–74, Warfield 1–3, Sipe 2–0

Receiving
HOU: Burrough 3–69, Johnson 4–51, Sawyer 3–14, Willis 3–11, Taylor 1–7, Dawkins 1–3, Thomas 1–1, Coleman 1-(-4)
CLE: Warfield 2–50, Rucker 2–29, Logan 1–16, C. Miller 3–14, G. Pruitt 1–5

Sunday, December 12
Kansas City Chiefs 39, Browns 14
Arrowhead Stadium (34,340)
White jerseys/orange pants

Already having been eliminated from playoff contention, the Browns saw their winning streak and their hopes of a 10-win season go up in smoke with a miserable performance that saw them commit six turnovers and more than 100 yards in penalties. They took a lead early in the second quarter on a short Larry Poole touchdown run, but the Chiefs scored 22 straight points to take control of the contest behind an amazing performance by RB Ed Podolak, who rushed for 137 yards, added 71 more receiving, and scored three touchdowns. One of the lone bright spots for the Browns was Greg Pruitt, topping the 1,000-yard mark for the second straight year. Finishing with a 9–5 record, the Browns improved their 1975 tally by six games, the best one-season turnaround in franchise history.
Record: 9–5

	1	2	3	4		
Browns	0	7	7	0	=	14
Chiefs	0	15	17	7	=	39

BIGGEST TURNAROUNDS

There have been a handful of turnaround seasons in Browns history, reflecting both remarkable improvement and dramatic collapse compared to the previous year. Here are the Browns' most dramatic jumps in overall record from one season to the next.

Biggest Improvements

Plus 6 games

1976
(3–11 to 9–5)

2007
(4–12 to 10–6)

Plus 4½ games

1958
(5–7 to 9–2–1)

Plus 4 games

1986
(8–8 to 12–4)

1994
(7–9 to 11–5)

2001
(3–13 to 7–9)

Biggest Declines

Minus 6½ games

1990
(9–6–1 to 3–13)

Minus 6 games

1981
(11–5 to 5–11)

1995
(11–5 to 5–11)

2008
(10–6 to 4–12)

Minus 4½ games

1956
(9–2–1 to 5–7)

Minus 4 games

1974
(7–5–2 to 4–10)

1984
(9–7 to 5–11)

2003
(9–7 to 5–11)

CLE-Poole 1-yd. run (Cockroft kick)
KC-Podolak 22-yd. run (kick failed)
KC-Podolak 2-yd. run (kick failed)
KC-Stenerud 27-yd. FG
KC-Podolak 2-yd. run (Stenerud kick)
CLE-Warfield 13-yd. pass from Sipe (Cockroft kick)
KC-Lane 2-yd. run (Stenerud kick)
KC-Stenerud 42-yd. FG
KC-White 10-yd. pass from Adams (Stenerud kick)

Passing
CLE: Sipe 11–24–125 1 TD 2 INT, Mays 0–1–0 0 TD 0 INT
KC: Adams 15–29–201 1 TD 0 INT, Livingston 3–6–36 0 TD 1 INT

Rushing
CLE: G. Pruitt 9–46, Sipe 3–37, C. Miller 8–27, Rucker 1–27, Duncan 3–19, Poole 1–1, M. Pruitt 3–0, Mays 1–0
KC: Podolak 29–137, Lane 12–50, Adams 2–13, Harrison 1-(-2)

Receiving
CLE: Logan 2–60, Rucker 3–27, Warfield 2–19, Duncan 1–17, G. Pruitt 1–8, Poole 2-(-6)
KC: Podolak 4–71, Marshall 3–67, White 5–64, Lane 6–35

1977

Sunday, September 18
Browns 13, Cincinnati Bengals 3
Riverfront Stadium (52,847)
White jerseys/orange pants

In a stunning upset, the Browns outmuscled the heavily favored Bengals on their home field to secure their first win in Cincinnati in five years and hand the Bengals their first-ever opening-day defeat. The Bengals, 12-point favorites and picked by many to reach the Super Bowl, had won six of their last seven games over Cleveland but were completely thwarted by the Browns. On a hot, humid afternoon, the Browns sprinted to a 13–0 lead after Cleveland DT Earl Edwards recovered a fumble by Cincy RB Archie Griffin to set up in a short Don Cockroft field goal. RB Larry Poole then swept around right end for a 12-yard touchdown in the second quarter. The Cleveland defense, playing without injured DT Jerry Sherk, stymied the Bengals' offense all day, sacking QB Ken Anderson three times and forcing three turnovers. The Browns' offense also struggled, averaging just three yards per rush, while Brian Sipe—making his first opening-day start at quarterback—was sacked four times but completed 15 of 21 passes.

Record: 1–0

	1	2	3	4		
Browns	3	10	0	0	=	13
Bengals	0	0	3	0	=	3

CLE-Cockroft 41-yd. FG
CLE-Cockroft 25-yd. FG
CLE-Poole 12-yd. run (Cockroft kick)
CIN-Bahr 25-yd. FG

Passing
CLE: Sipe 15–21–198 0 TD 1 INT, G. Pruitt 0–1–0 0 TD 0 INT
CIN: Anderson 16–34–157 0 TD 1 INT

Rushing
CLE: C. Miller 11–47, G. Pruitt 13–27, M. Pruitt 7–23, Poole 4–21, Sipe 2-(-6)
CIN: Griffin 18–36, Anderson 4–34, Davis 5–19, Elliott 4–12, Johnson 2–3

Receiving
CLE: Logan 4–78, G. Pruitt 4–61, Rucker 1–22, Roan 2–16, Parris 1–16, Craig 1–5
CIN: Curtis 3–46, Elliott 4–23, Corbett 2–24, McDaniel 2–21, Brooks 1–15, Davis 2–13, McInally 1–9, Griffin 1–6

Monday, September 26
Browns 30, New England Patriots 27 (OT)
Cleveland Stadium (76,418)
White jerseys/orange pants

In one of the most exciting games in team history, the Browns rallied from a 10-point second-half deficit to defeat the powerful New England Patriots in the first overtime game in franchise history. Making their first appearance on *Monday Night Football* in four years, it appeared the Browns would pull out the victory in regulation when Don Cockroft kicked a 37-yard field goal with 50 seconds remaining, but the Patriots quickly drove down the field to tie the game in the waning moments to force overtime. The Browns quickly took care of business in sudden-death, winning the coin toss and driving 53 yards on their first possession—sparked by a pair of key third-down conversions and a 22-yard pass from Brian Sipe to WR Dave Logan. A play later, Don Cockroft split the uprights from 35 yards out to end the game and put the Browns at 2–0 for the first time in six years. Though he was limping on a sore ankle by the end of the night, Greg Pruitt sparked the Cleveland offense, rushing for 151 yards on 26 carries while adding 51 yards receiving and a touchdown pass to open the scoring. After a short Cockroft field goal was blocked early in the fourth quarter and the Patriots took a 24–17 lead, Pruitt tied the game again with an eight-yard scoring reception. It was only the second time a Monday-night game had gone to overtime and remains the only occasion in which the Browns went to sudden-death in a prime-time game.

Record: 2–0

	1	2	3	4	OT		
Patriots	0	17	0	10	0	=	27
Browns	7	0	10	10	3	=	30

CLE-Duncan 5-yd. pass from G. Pruitt (Cockroft kick)
NE-Cunningham 8-yd. pass from Grogan (Smith kick)

NE-Smith 35-yd. FG
NE-Calhoun 2-yd. run (Smith kick)
CLE-Parris 26-yd. pass from Sipe (Cockroft kick)
CLE-Cockroft 37-yd. FG
NE-Francis 6-yd. pass from Grogan (Smith kick)
CLE-G. Pruitt 8-yd. pass from Sipe (Cockroft kick)
CLE-Cockroft 37-yd. FG
NE-Smith 34-yd. FG
CLE-Cockroft 35-yd. FG

Passing
NE: Grogan 15–23–172 2 TD 1 INT
CLE: Sipe 18–25–199 2 TD 2 INT, G. Pruitt 1–2–5 1 TD 0 INT

Rushing
NE: Cunningham 18–70, Calhoun 13–49, Grogan 4–18, Forte 5–4
CLE: G. Pruitt 26–151, C. Miller 11–31, Poole 3–10, Sipe 2–6, Rucker 1–3, Coleman 1-(-3)

Receiving
NE: Cunningham 7–52, Francis 2–34, Forte 2–25, Burks 1–22, Calhoun 1–21, Morgan 1–9, Stingley 1–9
CLE: G. Pruitt 4–51, Parris 3–48, Logan 2–41, Rucker 3–22, C. Miller 4–19, Roan 2–18, Duncan 1–5

Sunday, October 2
Pittsburgh Steelers 28, Browns 14
Cleveland Stadium (80,588)
White jerseys/orange pants

Playing flat and uninspired football after back-to-back emotional wins, the Browns were overwhelmed by the powerful Steelers in a sloppy game that saw the teams combine for 21 penalties for 186 yards. Despite being dominated by the Pittsburgh defense, which held Cleveland to just 165 total yards for the game and forced five turnovers, the Browns took a 14–7 lead in the second quarter on a one-yard scoring run by RB Cleo Miller set up by an interception by LB Gerald Irons. The Steelers knotted the score before the half when a long Terry Bradshaw pass was tipped by Browns' DB Thom Darden into the arms of Pittsburgh WR Frank Lewis for a 65-yard score. The Steelers then pulled away with two more touchdowns in the second half. The Browns' comeback hopes were thwarted when Brian Sipe left the game with 10 minutes remaining after injuring his elbow and shoulder on a late hit by Pittsburgh DT Steve Furness. A week after a dazzling performance against New England, Greg Pruitt was held to 34 rushing yards on 17 carries and didn't catch a pass.
Record: 2–1

	1	2	3	4		
Steelers	7	7	7	7	=	28
Browns	7	7	0	0	=	14

PIT-Swann 5-yd. pass from Bradshaw (Gerela kick)
CLE-Logan 22-yd. pass from Sipe (Cockroft kick)
CLE-C. Miller 1-yd. run (Cockroft kick)
PIT-Lewis 65-yd. pass from Bradshaw (Gerela kick)
PIT-Swann 14-yd. pass from Bradshaw (Gerela kick)
PIT-Bradshaw 1-yd. run (Gerela kick)

Passing
PIT: Bradshaw 10–17–143 3 TD 2 INT
CLE: Sipe 9–20–81 1 TD 1 INT, Mays 1–3–4 0 TD 2 INT, Logan 0–1–0 0 TD 0 INT

Rushing
PIT: Harris 22–72, Bleier 15–67, Harrison 8–39, Smith 4–29, Bradshaw 6–9, Thornton 1–2
CLE: C. Miller 11–49, G. Pruitt 17–34, Poole 1-(-3)

Receiving
PIT: Swann 7–71, Lewis 1–65, Bleier 2–7
CLE: Roan 3–43, Logan 2–27, C. Miller 4–8, Rucker 1–7

Sunday, October 9
Oakland Raiders 26, Browns 10
Cleveland Stadium (80,236)
White jerseys/orange pants

The Browns hung with the defending Super Bowl champions for a half before things fell apart in the third quarter, and the Raiders coasted to their seventh straight victory. Oakland led just 9–3 at the half as the teams combined for four field goals, but after the Browns fumbled the second-half kickoff, Oakland scored 10 quick points and extended the lead to 26–3 in the fourth quarter. Oakland RB Mark van Eeghen was the catalyst in what became a defensive struggle, rushing for 114 yards and both of the Raiders' touchdowns. Committing five turnovers for the second straight week, the Browns were hindered by a hobbling Greg Pruitt, who injured his ankle early in the game, and an ineffective Brian Sipe, who hadn't recovered from the injuries suffered against Pittsburgh the week before. An impressive defensive performance that limited the Raiders to 259 total yards was led by LB Dick Ambrose, who collected a whopping 18 tackles.
Record: 2–2

	1	2	3	4		
Raiders	3	6	10	7	=	26
Browns	3	0	0	7	=	10

OAK-Mann 39-yd. FG
CLE-Cockroft 41-yd. FG
OAK-Mann 28-yd. FG
OAK-Mann 27-yd. FG
OAK-van Eeghen 3-yd. run (Mann kick)
OAK-Mann 39-yd. FG
OAK-van Eeghen 3-yd. run (Mann kick)
CLE-Rucker 20-yd. pass from Sipe (Cockroft kick)

Passing
OAK: Stabler 9–19–107 0 TD 1 INT, Rae 0–1–0 0 TD 1 INT
CLE: Sipe 12–27–141 1 TD 2 INT

Rushing
OAK: van Eeghen 25–114, Davis 12–41, Banaszak 7–19, Robiskie 1–5, Garrett 3-(-8)
CLE: M. Pruitt 5–36, G. Pruitt 6–35, C. Miller 5–19, Poole 7–12, Sipe 3–11

Receiving
OAK: Casper 3–45, Branch 3–37, Biletnikoff 1–12, van Eeghen 1–7, Banaszak 1–6
CLE: Rucker 4–52, C. Miller 2–35, Poole 2–25, Roan 1–10, Parris 1–9, M. Pruitt 1–6, G. Pruitt 1–4

Sunday, October 16
Browns 24, Houston Oilers 23
Houston Astrodome (47,888)
White jerseys/orange pants

After a tough start in a wild first half, the Browns roared to an 11-point lead, then had to rally from behind to win on a last-second field goal against the first-place Oilers. Down 10–0 early following a punt return for a touchdown by Houston WR Billy "White Shoes" Johnson, the Browns responded with three straight touchdowns, including a 49-yard interception return for a score by DB Clarence Scott, to take a 21–10 advantage early in the second quarter. The Oilers shaved the margin to one point at the half, then took the lead on a fourth-quarter field goal. Running out of chances, the Browns regained possession with 4:20 to play and marched 54 yards, sparked by injured Greg Pruitt coming off the bench to give the Browns the boost they needed. Inching into field-goal range, the Browns pulled a rabbit out of their hat when Pruitt fired a 13-yard halfback-option pass to Cleo Miller to push the Browns into high-percentage range for Don Cockroft. As time expired, Cockroft connected from 30 yards out to give the Browns their second last-play victory of the season. In another defensive battle, the Browns were held to 170 total yards and managed only 71 passing yards on the day. But the Browns' two longest plays—Pruitt's 13-yard pass and an 18-yard toss from Brian Sipe to TE Gary Parris—came on the game-winning drive.

Record: 3–2

	1	2	3	4		
Browns	14	7	0	3	=	24
Oilers	10	10	0	3	=	23

HOU-Johnson 87-yd. punt return (Fritsch kick)
HOU-Fritsch 25-yd. FG
CLE-C. Miller 6-yd. run (Cockroft kick)
CLE-C. Scott 49-yd. interception return (Cockroft kick)
CLE-Roan 8-yd. pass from Sipe (Cockroft kick)
HOU-Fritsch 37-yd. FG
HOU-Hadl 6-yd. run (Fritsch kick)
HOU-Fritsch 36-yd. FG
CLE-Cockroft 30-yd. FG

Passing
CLE: Sipe 8–19–58 1 TD 1 INT, G. Pruitt 1–1–13 0 TD 0 INT
HOU: Pastorini 8–15–89 0 TD 0 INT, Hadl 6–14–59 0 TD 2 INT

Rushing
CLE: Poole 14–52, C. Miller 12–42, G. Pruitt 4–13, Warfield 1–2
HOU: Wilson 23–56, Coleman 12–44, Hadl 1–6, Hardeman 1–3

Receiving
CLE: Parris 2–24, C. Miller 2–17, Roan 2–16, Poole 2–11, Warfield 1–3
HOU: Burrough 5–92, Wilson 5–31, Coleman 2–18, Giles 1–4, Hardeman 1–3

Sunday, October 23
Browns 27, Buffalo Bills 16
Rich Stadium (60,905)
White jerseys/orange pants

Trailing the woeful Bills late in the second quarter, the Browns parlayed a lucky bounce into a momentum-changing touchdown and cruised to victory. From the Cleveland 48, a Brian Sipe pass for Reggie Rucker was deflected directly to Paul Warfield at the Buffalo 20, and he sprinted into the end zone for a serendipitous touchdown and a 13–7 Cleveland lead. Another halfback-option pass by Greg Pruitt in the third quarter resulted in a touchdown to Cleo Miller and a 20–10 advantage. However, aided by the second punt return for a touchdown the Browns had allowed in two weeks, the Bills hung around until the visitors put the game away on a Sipe-to-Garry Parris touchdown pass with eight minutes remaining. The Bills, who'd snapped a 14-game losing streak the week before, crippled their own cause with 12 penalties for a whopping 139 yards and four turnovers—two interceptions by Thom Darden and a pair of fumble recoveries by DE Mack Mitchell. Meanwhile, Cleo Miller out-played Buffalo RB O. J. Simpson, picking up 117 yards on 21 carries, while Simpson managed just 99 despite picking up 71 in the first half. With the win, the Browns remained tied with the Steelers for first place in the AFC Central Division.

Record: 4–2

	1	2	3	4		
Browns	0	13	7	7	=	27
Bills	7	3	6	0	=	16

BUF-Gant 38-yd. pass from Ferguson (Long kick)
CLE-Cockroft 41-yd. FG
CLE-Cockroft 27-yd. FG
CLE-Warfield 52-yd. pass from Sipe (Cockroft kick)
BUF-Long 41-yd. FG
CLE-C. Miller 6-yd. pass from G. Pruitt (Cockroft kick)
BUF-Moody 91-yd. punt return (kick failed)
CLE-Parris 9-yd. pass from Sipe (Cockroft kick)

Passing
CLE: Sipe 14–22–143 2 TD 2 INT, G. Pruitt 1–2–6 1 TD 0 INT
BUF: Ferguson 11–29–199 1 TD 2 INT

Rushing
CLE: C. Miller 21–117, G. Pruitt 21–90, Poole 2–7, M. Pruitt 2–5, Sipe 2–0
BUF: Simpson 19–99, Ferguson 3–54, Braxton 3–9

Receiving
CLE: Warfield 1–52, Rucker 4–46, C. Miller 5–20, Parris 2–15, G. Pruitt 2–12, Poole 1–4
BUF: Gant 5–111, Piccone 3–52, Chandler 2–27, Braxton 1–9

Sunday, October 30
Browns 44, Kansas City Chiefs 7
Cleveland Stadium (60,381)
White jerseys/orange pants

On a beautiful, golden, autumn, afternoon, the Browns obliterated the struggling Chiefs to win their third straight and—with a Pittsburgh loss in Baltimore—assumed sole possession of first place in the AFC Central at the season's midpoint. Behind an unstoppable running game, the Browns rolled up 526 total yards, the most they'd compiled in a game in 12 years while putting up their highest point total in nine seasons. Breaking free for a 78-yard touchdown run in the third quarter, Greg Pruitt averaged nearly 10 yards per carry in rushing for 153 yards, and Mike Pruitt—in the first big performance of his career—added 96 more as the Browns tallied 322 yards on the ground. Buoyed by the season debut of previously injured DT Jerry Sherk, the defense also got into the action, forcing six turnovers and collecting four sacks. Thom Darden blew the game open in the second quarter when he scored on an interception return, and the Browns held the Chiefs scoreless until the final minute of the game. Things actually could have been much worse for the Chiefs had the Browns not been plagued with three turnovers themselves and 103 yards in penalties.

Record: 5–2

	1	2	3	4		
Chiefs	0	0	0	7	=	7
Browns	13	17	7	7	=	44

CLE-Parris 7-yd. pass from Sipe (Cockroft kick)
CLE-Cockroft 29-yd. FG
CLE-Cockroft 34-yd. FG
CLE-Cockroft 27-yd. FG
CLE-Darden 18-yd. interception return (Cockroft kick)
CLE-M. Pruitt 1-yd. run (Cockroft kick)
CLE-G. Pruitt 78-yd. run (Cockroft kick)
CLE-Parris 2-yd. pass from Mays (Cockroft kick)
KC-Brockington 22-yd. pass from Livingston (Stenerud kick)

Passing
KC: Livingston 12–22–121 1 TD 1 INT, Adams 2–10–31 0 TD 2 INT
CLE: Sipe 12–25–200 1 TD 2 INT, Mays 4–6–28 1 TD 0 INT

Rushing
KC: Podolak 9–87, Brockington 3–20, Reed 7–18, Bailey 5–7, Livingston 1–5, Adams 1–0
CLE: G. Pruitt 18–153, M. Pruitt 20–96, C. Miller 9–42, Duncan 3–21, Poole 2–7, Rucker 1–3

Receiving
KC: Brunson 4–54, White 5–44, Brockington 1–22, Marshall 1–15, Reed 1–12, Bailey 2–5
CLE: Rucker 4–94, G. Pruitt 2–46, Poole 2–38, C. Miller 2–21, Warfield 1–11, Logan 3–9, Parris 2–9

Sunday, November 6
Cincinnati Bengals 10, Browns 7
Cleveland Stadium (81,932)
White jerseys/orange pants

What promised to be a miserable second half of the season began with a drab, sloppy performance against the Bengals, who avenged their opening-day loss with a victory in another defensive struggle. The Browns were once again their own worst enemy, committing 12 penalties and turning the ball over four times, including a pair of fumbles by Cleo Miller. After the Browns tied the game at seven just before the half, the Bengals crept ahead in the third quarter and clung to the lead into the fourth, then came through on the key possession of the game. Pinned back at their own 5 with 4:11 left, Cincinnati melted almost four minutes off the clock to secure victory, aided by a crucial third-down pass-interference penalty on Browns' DB Ron Bolton. Still, with a Pittsburgh loss in Denver, the Browns remained alone in first place.
Record: 5–3

	1	2	3	4		
Bengals	7	0	3	0	=	10
Browns	0	7	0	0	=	7

CIN-Johnson 11-yd. run (Bahr kick)
CLE-Roan 4-yd. pass from Sipe (Cockroft kick)
CIN-Bahr 47-yd. FG

Passing
CIN: Anderson 14–19–153 0 TD 1 INT
CLE: Sipe 20–28–189 1 TD 2 INT

Rushing
CIN: Johnson 15–40, Elliott 5–21, Griffin 5–19, Anderson 3–4, Davis 1–0
CLE: C. Miller 11–70, G. Pruitt 15–54, M. Pruitt 5–7

Receiving
CIN: Curtis 5–70, Trumpy 2–36, Elliott 5–28, McInally 1–12, Johnson 1–7
CLE: Rucker 3–47, Miller 4–37, G. Pruitt 3–29, Roan 2–25, Parris 2–21, Warfield 3–19, M. Pruitt 2–6, Poole 1–5

Sunday, November 13
Pittsburgh Steelers 35, Browns 31
Three Rivers Stadium (47,055)
White jerseys/orange pants

The Browns tumbled back into a first-place tie with a disastrous loss in Pittsburgh that saw Brian Sipe suffer an injured shoulder that would sideline him for the remainder of the season. The 4–4 Steelers, losers of two straight, were dominant in the first half, soaring to a 28–3 lead, then hung on through a barrage of three fourth-quarter Cleveland touchdowns—all receptions by RB Larry Poole—amid snow flurries at Three Rivers. After the Browns narrowed the Pittsburgh lead to 35–31 with 59 seconds left, they quickly stopped the Steelers and got the ball back at their own 36 but managed only two incomplete passes before time expired. Browns' backup QB Dave Mays tossed for 269 yards in just over two quarters of play, but it wasn't enough to overcome Pittsburgh's early onslaught. The Steelers were led by Terry Bradshaw's 226 passing yards in the first half, while wideouts Lynn Swann and John Stallworth both finished the day with more than 125 yards receiving. In addition to Mays' heroics, the Browns were paced offensively by Reggie Rucker, who went over the 100-yard receiving mark, and Greg Pruitt, who rushed for 108 yards on 19 carries. The teams combined for more than 800 yards of offense and 48 first downs but also eight turnovers.
Record: 5–4

	1	2	3	4		
Browns	3	0	7	21	=	31
Steelers	7	21	0	7	=	35

CLE-Cockroft 44-yd. FG
PIT-Swann 39-yd. pass from Bradshaw (Gerela kick)
PIT-Bleier 2-yd. run (Gerela kick)
PIT-Stallworth 38-yd. pass from Bradshaw (Gerela kick)
PIT-Harris 16-yd. run (Gerela kick)
CLE-C. Miller 5-yd. run (Cockroft kick)
PIT-Stallworth 9-yd. pass from Bradshaw (Gerela kick)
CLE-Poole 5-yd. pass from Mays (Cockroft kick)
CLE-Poole 13-yd. pass from Mays (Cockroft kick)
CLE-Poole 3-yd. pass from Mays (Cockroft kick)

Passing
CLE: Mays 17–32–269 3 TD 2 INT, Sipe 4–8–24 0 TD 1 INT
PIT: Bradshaw 13–21–283 3 TD 0 INT, Graff 2–2-(-6)

Rushing
CLE: G. Pruitt 19–108, C. Miller 6–18, Poole 4–7, Sipe 1–3, Mays 1–2
PIT: Harris 28–99, Bleier 16–73, Graff 2-(-1)

Receiving
CLE: Rucker 4–104, Warfield 4–52, Poole 6–50, G. Pruitt 2–32, Parris 1–24, C. Miller 3–22, Logan 1–9
PIT: Swann 5–129, Stallworth 6–126, Cunningham 1–21, Harris 2–1, Bleier 1–0

Sunday, November 20
Browns 21, New York Giants 7
Giants Stadium (72,576)
White jerseys/orange pants

The Browns rebounded from back-to-back losses with a much-needed victory on a bright November Sunday in the Meadowlands that kept them tied for first with Pittsburgh with four games remaining. Behind Dave Mays, making his first NFL start, the Browns scored on their first possession, then took the lead for good when LB Gerald Irons returned an interception 53 yards for a score in the third quarter and put the game away on the final touchdown reception of Paul Warfield's Hall of Fame career. Continuing an unsettling trend, the Browns were once again plagued by self-inflicted mistakes to the tune of 15 penalties for 117 yards. The Cleveland defense helped atone for the miscues by collecting six sacks and forcing four turnovers, including a pair of interceptions by DB Oliver Davis. Though no one knew it at the time, the victory would mark not only the Browns' final win of 1977, but Forrest Gregg's final win as Cleveland's coach.
Record: 6–4

	1	2	3	4		
Browns	7	0	7	7	=	21
Giants	0	7	0	0	=	7

CLE-G. Pruitt 2-yd. run (Cockroft kick)
NYG-Moorehead 15-yd. pass from Golsteyn (Danelo kick)
CLE-Irons 53-yd. interception return (Cockroft kick)
CLE-Warfield 18-yd. pass from Mays (Cockroft kick)

Passing
CLE: Mays 13–24–138 1 TD 1 INT
NYG: Golsteyn 12–25–150 1 TD 3 INT, Pisarcik 0–1–0 0 TD 0 INT

Rushing
CLE: G. Pruitt 25–96, C. Miller 14–44
NYG: Hammond 10–53, Spencer 6–31, Kotar 6–24, Watkins 2–6, Csonka 4–4, Bell 2-(-2)

Receiving
CLE: G. Pruitt 5–71, C. Miller 3–33, Warfield 2–33, Poole 2–4, Rucker 1-(-3)
NYG: Perkins 3–61, Hammond 5–42, Moorehead 3–36, Shirk 1–11

Sunday, November 27
Los Angeles Rams 9, Browns 0
Cleveland Stadium (70,352)
White jerseys/orange pants

On a dark, frosty afternoon on the lake, the Browns put forth a miserable performance as they were shut out for the first time in five years and fell out of first place. Managing just 181 total yards while running just 51 plays to the Rams' 80, the Browns turned the ball over six times and saw Dave Mays twice leave the game with injury, leaving the quarterbacking duties to untested third-stringer Terry Luck. The lone bright spot for Cleveland was DB Ron Bolton tying a team record with three interceptions of Los Angeles QB Pat Haden, who'd gone 106 attempts without getting picked off. Amid snow flurries in the second half, neither team scored as the Rams controlled the line of scrimmage behind the power running of RB Lawrence McCutcheon, father of future Browns' DB Daylon McCutcheon, who rushed for 104 yards.
Record: 6–5

	1	2	3	4		
Rams	6	3	0	0	=	9
Browns	0	0	0	0	=	0

LA-Cappelletti 7-yd. run (kick failed)
LA-Septien 18-yd. FG

Passing
LA: Haden 21–29–172 0 TD 3 INT
CLE: Mays 10–18–96 0 TD 2 INT, Luck 3–8–23 0 TD 1 INT, G. Pruitt 0–1–0 0 TD 0 INT

Rushing
LA: McCutcheon 24–104, Capelletti 14–55, Haden 3–39, Bryant 2–7, Tyler 5–6, Nelson 1–5
CLE: C. Miller 9–50, G. Pruitt 11–39, Mays 2–1

Receiving
LA: Waddy 6–68, Jackson 5–44, Nelson 4–39, Cappelletti 5–15, McCutcheon 1–6
CLE: Warfield 3–46, G. Pruitt 3–25, Rucker 1–18, Parris 2–15, Roan 1–8, C. Miller 3–7

Sunday, December 4
San Diego Chargers 37, Browns 14
San Diego Stadium (37,312)
White jerseys/orange pants

On one of the uglier days in team history, the Browns not only were crushed on the field by the San Diego Chargers but also began coming apart internally afterward as Forrest Gregg accused the players of quitting, further straining a growing rift in the locker room. Overwhelmed from the start, the Browns trailed 27–0 at the half and extended their scoreless string to seven consecutive quarters before adding a pair of meaningless touchdowns in the final period. While the Cleveland offense struggled to put points on the board, the Browns' defense was equally toothless, permitting the Chargers to roll up 425 total yards and not forcing a punt all day.
Record: 6–6

	1	2	3	4		
Browns	0	0	0	14	=	14
Chargers	14	13	3	7	=	37

SD-Woods 29-yd. run (Benirschke kick)
SD-Bauer 15-yd. pass from Fouts (Benirschke kick)
SD-Benirschke 35-yd. FG
SD-Joiner 30-yd. pass from Fouts (Benirschke kick)
SD-Benirschke 36-yd. FG
SD-Benirschke 24-yd. FG
CLE-Rucker 16-yd. pass from Mays (Cockroft kick)
SD-Dorsey 67-yd. pass from Fouts (Benirschke kick)
CLE-Miller 6-yd. run (Cockroft kick)

Passing
CLE: Mays 19–30–228 1 TD 1 INT, Logan 0–1–0 0 TD 0 INT
SD: Fouts 14–20–237 3 TD 0 INT, Olander 2–3–25 0 TD 0 INT

Rushing
CLE: G. Pruitt 16–67, C. Miller 10–45, Mays 1-(-1)
SD: Woods 11–62, Matthews 11–59, Barnes 8–17, Fouts 1–11, Williams 3–9, Young 2–9, Bauer 1–0

Receiving
CLE: G. Pruitt 6–98, C. Miller 5–48, Rucker 2–32, Logan 2–21, Parris 3–18, Warfield 1–11
SD: Dorsey 4–108, Joiner 2–46, Woods 2–26, Rodgers 1–24, Young 3–23, Bauer 1–15, Barnes 1–10, Matthews 1–6, Curran 1–4

Sunday, December 11
Houston Oilers 19, Browns 15
Cleveland Stadium (30,898)
White jerseys/orange pants

The collapsing Browns hit rock-bottom on a frozen field in the home finale as they statistically dominated the Oilers but handed the game over with an incredible eight turnovers. The bumbling Browns fell behind 19–6 in the third quarter after Billy "White Shoes" Johnson returned a punt for a touchdown against Cleveland for the second time in 1977, and things should have been worse had Houston not botched two point-after attempts. The Browns stayed alive thanks to a safety recorded by Jerry Sherk when he pinned RB Rob Carpenter in the end zone. They were also buoyed by an admirable performance by Terry Luck, who entered the game at quarterback in the second quarter and wound up throwing for 188 yards and the only touchdown pass of his brief NFL career with 3:05 remaining, which cut the Houston lead to four points. The Browns regained possession with 1:29 left but were pinned back at their own 3 and could do no damage. Despite outgaining Houston in total yardage 400–167, the Browns fell for the third straight week. And in the days to follow, Forrest Gregg would resign as coach when he discovered Art Modell was about to fire him at season's end.
Record: 6–7

	1	2	3	4		
Oilers	7	6	6	0	=	19
Browns	0	6	2	7	=	15

HOU-Coleman 3-yd. run (Dempsey kick)
CLE-Cockroft 26-yd. FG
HOU-Coleman 2-yd. run (kick failed)
CLE-Cockroft 40-yd. FG

CHANGING HORSES IN MID-RACE

Three times in their history, the Browns have turned to an assistant coach to guide the team to the finish of a tumultuous season. None of these instances saw any discernible improvement in the team's fortunes.

1977
Dick Modzelewski replaces Forrest Gregg
Duration: One game
Record at time of replacement: 6–7
Record after replacement: 0–1
Before replacement: Browns outscored opponents, 250–247 (an average score of 19.2–19)
After replacement: Browns outscored, 20–19

1990
Jim Shofner replaces Bud Carson
Duration: Seven games
Record at time of replacement: 2–7
Record after replacement: 1–6
Before replacement: Browns outscored, 235–128 (an average score of 26–14)
After replacement: Browns outscored, 227–100 (an average score of 32–14)

2004
Terry Robiskie replaces Butch Davis
Duration: Five games
Record at time of replacement: 3–8
Record after replacement: 1–4
Before replacement: Browns outscored, 266–225 (an average score of 24–21)
After replacement: Browns outscored, 124–51 (an average score of 25–10)

Browns' all-time record under interim coaches: 2–11

Marty Schottenheimer's promotion to replace Sam Rutigliano midway through the 1984 season doesn't qualify because Schottenheimer was named full-time head coach upon his promotion, not interim coach. But perhaps because of this distinction, the results are quite a bit different than those of the Browns' interim coaches.

1984
Marty Schottenheimer replaces Sam Rutigliano
Record at time of replacement: 1–7
Record after replacement: 4–4
Before replacement: Browns outscored, 150–102 (an average score of 19–13)
After replacement: Browns outscored opponents, 148–147 (an average score of 19–18)

HOU-Johnson 72-yd. punt return (kick failed)
CLE-Safety: Sherk tackled Carpenter in end zone
CLE-Parris 3-yd. pass from Luck (Cockroft kick)

Passing
HOU: Pastorini 7–12–74 0 TD 1 INT
CLE: Luck 16–27–188 1 TD 2 INT, Mays 3–8–34 0 TD 2 INT

Rushing
HOU: Coleman 20–66, Carpenter 15–48, Pastorini 1-(-3)
CLE: G. Pruitt 23–92, C. Miller 15–84, Poole 1–5, Luck 2-(-3)

Receiving
HOU: Foster 1–56, Barber 1–11, Johnson 1–10, Coleman 3–1, Burrough 1-(-4)
CLE: Rucker 6–97, G. Pruitt 5–42, C. Miller 3–24, Warfield 2–24, Logan 1–21, Parris 2–14

Sunday, December 18
Seattle Seahawks 20, Browns 19
Seattle Kingdome (61,583)
White jerseys/orange pants

Under the direction of defensive coordinator Dick Modzelewski, promoted to interim head coach after Forrest Gregg's resignation the week before, the Browns squandered a nine-point halftime lead and lost their first meeting against the second-year Seahawks in the final minute. Once again plagued by self-inflicted errors—104 yards in penalties, five turnovers, and a missed extra point that proved to be the difference—the Browns still were on the brink of victory when Don Cockroft booted a 33-yard field goal with 1:51 remaining to extend their lead to 19–14. But Seattle marched 80 yards in less than a minute and scored the winning points when QB Jim Zorn hit WR Steve Largent in the corner of the end zone with 52 seconds to play. In his final NFL game, Terry Luck made his only start and threw four costly interceptions but also caught a touchdown pass on a halfback-option toss by Greg Pruitt in the first quarter. Pruitt also ran for a score as he racked up 127 yards on 22 carries and surpassed the 1,000-yard mark for the third straight season. He was backed up by Cleo Miller's 98 on 18 carries as the Browns rolled up 259 rushing yards. The schizophrenic season ended with the Browns losing six of their last seven to clinch their third losing record in four years.

Record: 6–8

	1	2	3	4		
Browns	6	10	0	3	=	19
Seahawks	0	7	0	13	=	20

CLE-Luck 4-yd. pass from G. Pruitt (kick failed)
CLE-G. Pruitt 5-yd. run (Cockroft kick)
SEA-Smith 20-yd. run (Leypoldt kick)
CLE-Cockroft 24-yd. FG
SEA-Sims 5-yd. run (Leypoldt kick)
CLE-Cockroft 33-yd. FG
SEA-Largent 15-yd. pass from Zorn (kick failed)

Passing
CLE: Luck 6–15–105 0 TD 4 INT, G. Pruitt 1–2–4 1 TD 0 INT
SEA: Zorn 10–24–132 1 TD 2 INT

Rushing
CLE: G. Pruitt 22–127, C. Miller 18–98, M. Pruitt 8–38, Luck 1–1, Duncan 2-(-5)
SEA: Testerman 16–79, Smith 10–54, Zorn 3–34, Hunter 2–19, Sims 1–5

Receiving
CLE: Logan 4–78, Rucker 2–27, Luck 1–4
SEA: Howard 3–40, McCullum 2–34, Smith 2–32, Largent 1–15, Testerman 2–11

1978

Sunday, September 3
Browns 24, San Francisco 49ers 7
Cleveland Stadium (68,973)
White jerseys/orange pants

In Sam Rutigliano's debut as Cleveland's head coach, the Browns scored 10 points in the final six minutes of the contest to clinch a victory over San Francisco. The Cleveland defense forced six turnovers, setting the tone when a fumble recovery led to a short touchdown by RB Greg Pruitt three minutes into the game. After the 49ers tied the contest in the second quarter, rookie TE Ozzie Newsome, making his NFL debut, scored on a 33-yard reverse in the final minute of the half. The lead remained seven points until WR Reggie Rucker caught a 69-yard touchdown pass from QB Brian Sipe with 6:03 remaining, set up by a recovery of a fumble by San Francisco RB O. J. Simpson. In his first game with the 49ers, Simpson was held to 78 yards on 22 carries, including 11 on six carries in the second half.

Record: 1–0

	1	2	3	4		
49ers	0	7	0	0	=	7
Browns	7	7	0	10	=	24

CLE-G. Pruitt 2-yd. run (Cockroft kick)
SF-MacAfee 7-yd. pass from DeBerg (Wersching kick)
CLE-Newsome 33-yd. run (Cockroft kick)
CLE-Rucker 69-yd. pass from Sipe (Cockroft kick)
CLE-Cockroft 23-yd. FG

Passing
SF: DeBerg 16–32–174 1 TD 3 INT
CLE: Sipe 12–25–190 1 TD 0 INT, G. Pruitt 0–1–0 0 TD 0 INT

Rushing
SF: Simpson 22–78, Boykin 15–52, Williams 1–1, DeBerg 2–0
CLE: G. Pruitt 22–106, Newsome 1–33, Sipe 4–32, C. Miller 10–31, M. Pruitt 2–6, Sullivan 2–5

Receiving
SF: LeCount 5–63, Solomon 3–54, MacAfee 3–22, Simpson 3–20, Boykin 2–15
CLE: Rucker 3–113, G. Pruitt 3–25, Logan 1–24, C. Miller 3–15, M. Pruitt 1–7, Newsome 1–6

Sunday, September 10
Browns 13, Cincinnati Bengals 10 (OT)
Cleveland Stadium (72,691)
White jerseys/orange pants

On a steamy afternoon, the Browns rallied from a 10-point second-half deficit to force overtime and then pulled out a hard-earned victory over the rival Bengals. Cincinnati held a 10–0 lead late in the third quarter until the Browns got on the board with a short Don Cockroft field goal, then tied it on a Reggie Rucker touchdown reception with 10 minutes remaining in the game. The Bengals had a chance to win the game in regulation, but kicker Chris Bahr was wide left on a 37-yard field goal as time expired. The Browns won the overtime coin flip and, after first dropping the football at the Cleveland 6, RB Larry Collins scooped it up and returned it 41 yards. An 18-yard reception by Ozzie Newsome and a facemask penalty on the Bengals pushed the Browns into field-goal range, and Cockroft drilled a 27-yard boot four minutes into sudden-death to move the Browns to 2–0. Greg Pruitt paced the Cleveland offense with 120 rushing yards on 22 carries but left the game with an injured calf that would sideline him for the next month.

Record: 2–0

	1	2	3	4	OT		
Bengals	7	3	0	0	0	=	10
Browns	0	0	3	7	3	=	13

CIN-Bass 51-yd. pass from Reaves (Bahr kick)
CIN-Bahr 37-yd. FG
CLE-Cockroft 32-yd. FG
CLE-Rucker 13-yd. pass from Sipe (Cockroft kick)
CLE-Cockroft 27-yd. FG

Passing
CIN: Reaves 15–26–169 1 TD 1 INT
CLE: Sipe 16–32–219 1 TD 1INT

Rushing
CIN: Johnson 21–81, Griffin 13–32, Davis 1–2, Turner 1–0
CLE: G. Pruitt 22–120, M. Pruitt 10–44, C. Miller 3–3, Sipe 2–2

Receiving
CIN: Bass 1–51, Griffin 6–36, Walker 2–32, Curtis 2–21, Corbett 1–14, McInally 1–11, Clark 1–2, Johnson 1–2
CLE: Rucker 4–77, Logan 3–61, Newsome 3–42, G. Pruitt 5–36, M. Pruitt 1–3

Sunday, September 17
Browns 24, Atlanta Falcons 16
Fulton County Stadium (56,648)
Brown jerseys/orange pants

On another steamy September afternoon, the Browns moved to 3–0 for the first time in 15 years with an impressive road victory over the playoff-bound Falcons, who would not lose another game on their home field all season. Playing without injured Greg Pruitt, the Cleveland offense didn't miss a beat as Brian Sipe threw a pair of touchdown passes, including the first scoring reception of Ozzie Newsome's Hall of Fame career. Sipe also ran for the clinching score with just over a minute remaining on a busted play in which he scooped up a fumbled snap and darted into the end zone from two yards out. Down 17–10 in the fourth quarter, the Falcons scored a touchdown and were poised to tie the score, but missed the extra point in what proved to be the turning point of the game. For good measure, Cleveland DB Thom Darden picked off an Atlanta pass in the end zone as time expired—the fourth turnover forced by a Cleveland defense that also collected six sacks. In what also became a sloppy game, the teams combined for 27 penalties for 246 yards.
Record: 3–0

	1	2	3	4		
Browns	0	17	0	7	=	24
Falcons	3	7	0	6	=	16

ATL-Steinfort 24-yd. FG
CLE-Cockroft 43-yd. FG
CLE-Newsome 2-yd. pass from Sipe (Cockroft kick)
ATL-Stanback 15-yd. run (Steinfort kick)
CLE-Rucker 27-yd. pass from Sipe (Cockroft kick)
ATL-Strong 2-yd. run (kick failed)
CLE-Sipe 2-yd. run (Cockroft kick)

Passing
CLE: Sipe 20–35–219 2 TD 0 INT
ATL: Bartkowski 7–15–126 0 TD 2 INT, Jones 4–13–62 0 TD 2 INT

Rushing
CLE: M. Pruitt 15–65, C. Miller 7–24, Rucker 1–9, Collins 5–7, Newsome 1–6, Sullivan 3–2, Sipe 2-(-3)
ATL: Stanback 7–31, Patton 7–23, Strong 5–19, Bean 10–14, Bartkowski 1–0

Receiving
CLE: Logan 5–63, Rucker 4–60, Feacher 3–57, Newsome 4–19, C. Miller 2–13, Parris 1–4, M. Pruitt 1–3
ATL: Francis 2–61, Ryckman 3–48, Mitchell 3–42, Pearson 1–17, Jackson 1–13, Patton 1–7

Sunday, September 24
Pittsburgh Steelers 15, Browns 9 (OT)
Three Rivers Stadium (49,573)
White jerseys/orange pants

Thanks to one of the most controversial plays in Browns' history, the Steelers escaped with an overtime victory that stretched Cleveland's Three Rivers Stadium losing streak to nine games. On the opening kickoff of sudden-death, Pittsburgh's Larry Anderson slipped on the turf, fell, then got back up and fumbled, and the loose ball was recovered by Cleveland WR Ricky Feacher at the Steelers' 22, within chip-shot field-goal range. But the officials incorrectly ruled Anderson was down before the fumble and Pittsburgh maintained possession. The Steelers then drove 79 yards and won the game on a 37-yard flea-flicker pass from QB Terry Bradshaw to TE Bennie Cunningham. In what was a battle for first place between two undefeated teams, the Browns took a 9–3 advantage into the fourth, but the Steelers tied the game with 2:35 remaining. Cleveland then drove to the Pittsburgh 36 in the final minute, but a key play by Pittsburgh LB Jack Lambert pushed the Browns out of field-goal range. The Cleveland offense struggled, managing just 199 total yards while permitting five sacks to a Pittsburgh team that would go 14–2 and win the Super Bowl.
Record: 3–1

	1	2	3	4	OT		
Browns	0	6	3	0	0	=	9
Steelers	3	0	0	6	6	=	15

PIT-Gerela 19-yd. FG
CLE-Cockroft 43-yd. FG
CLE-Cockroft 30-yd. FG
CLE-Cockroft 41-yd. FG
PIT-Gerela 33-yd. FG
PIT-Gerela 36-yd. FG
PIT-Cunningham 37-yd. pass from Bradshaw

Passing
CLE: Sipe 14–32–139 0 TD 2 INT
PIT: Bradshaw 14–32–208 1 TD 2 INT

Rushing
CLE: M. Pruitt 14–42, Newsome 2–24, C. Miller 6–17, Sipe 3–9, Rucker 1–5, Collins 6–0
PIT: Harris 26–84, Bleier 9–28, Bradshaw 2–27

Receiving
CLE: Logan 3–46, Rucker 2–37, Sullivan 1–20, Newsome 2–19, C. Miller 1–12, Collins 1–4, M. Pruitt 4–1
PIT: Swann 6–83, Cunningham 2–69, Stallworth 2–40, Harris 3–9, Bleier 1–7

Sunday, October 1
Houston Oilers 16, Browns 13
Cleveland Stadium (72,776)
White jerseys/orange pants

For the second straight week, the Browns felt they were robbed by the officials on the key play of the game as they lost another heartbreaker, this time on a field goal in the final seconds. Though the Cleveland offense struggled all afternoon, the Browns were in position to take the lead in a tie game with under two minutes to play, but RB Mike Pruitt fumbled at midfield and Houston recovered. Moments later, Oilers' QB Dan Pastorini lofted a long pass down the left sideline for WR Ken Burrough. Cleveland DB Ron Bolton leapt up and appeared to intercept the football before Burrough reached over him to grab the ball as they hit the ground at the Cleveland 4. The officials ruled simultaneous possession and, by rule, rewarded Burrough with a reception with a minute to play. Outraged fans in the bleachers pelted the field with bottles and debris, causing a 10-minute delay and prompting the officials to switch ends of the field. Houston kicked the game-winning field goal with 14 seconds remaining, and the Browns were handed a frustrating defeat for the second straight week. Cleveland led the AFC title game-bound Oilers 10–0 at the half, but managed only 182 total yards for the game and gave away four turnovers, including three interceptions by Brian Sipe, who completed only 12 of 32 passes. The game also marked the Cleveland debut of veteran RB Calvin Hill, who signed with the Browns the week before.
Record: 3–2

	1	2	3	4		
Oilers	0	0	6	10	=	16
Browns	3	7	0	3	=	13

CLE-Cockroft 41-yd. FG
CLE-Logan 7-yd. pass from Sipe (Cockroft kick)
HOU-Caster 41-yd. pass from Pastorini (kick failed)
HOU-Carpenter 7-yd. run (Fritsch kick)
CLE-Cockroft 40-yd. FG
HOU-Fritsch 19-yd. FG

Passing
HOU: Pastorini 14–29–215 1 TD 1 INT
CLE: Sipe 12–32–106 1 TD 3 INT

Rushing
HOU: Wilson 16–72, Coleman 19–63, Carpenter 9–29, Pastorini 2–0
CLE: M. Pruitt 11–41, C. Miller 5–18, Hill 6–16, Collins 1–3

Receiving
HOU: Burrough 3–68, Coleman 4–63, Caster 2–49, Renfro 2–26, Barber 2–11, Wilson 1-(-2)
CLE: Rucker 3–48, Logan 2–28, Newsome 2–11, Hill 2–10, M. Pruitt 1–5, C. Miller 2–4

Sunday, October 8
Browns 24, New Orleans Saints 16
Louisiana Superdome (50,158)
White jerseys/orange pants

Thanks to a balanced running attack, the Browns bounced back into the win column with a triumph in their first-ever game in the Louisiana Superdome. With Greg Pruitt still sidelined, Cleveland managed 179 rushing yards behind sterling performances by Cleo Miller and Calvin Hill and roared to a 24–9 lead following a leaping touchdown reception by Ozzie Newsome. The Browns then snuffed out New Orleans's last chance to get back into the game with a goal-line stand with three minutes left. While Saints' QB Archie Manning threw for 249 yards, the Browns' defense held the Saints to just 67 rushing yards, barely three yards per carry. The triumph propelled the Browns into sole possession of second place in the AFC Central.
Record: 4–2

	1	2	3	4		
Browns	7	7	7	3	=	24
Saints	0	9	0	7	=	16

CLE-C. Miller 1-yd. run (Cockroft kick)
CLE-Collins 3-yd. run (Cockroft kick)
NO-Mauti 16-yd. pass from Manning (kick failed)
NO-Szaro 20-yd. FG
CLE-Newsome 14-yd. pass from Sipe (Cockroft kick)
CLE-Cockroft 40-yd. FG
NO-Manning 1-yd. run (Szaro kick)

Passing
CLE: Sipe 11–17–103 1 TD 1 INT
NO: Manning 24–39–249 1 TD 1 INT

Rushing
CLE: C. Miller 21–93, Hill 13–53, M. Pruitt 4–10, Collins 3–9, M. Miller 1–8, Newsome 1–8, Sipe 1-(-2)
NO: Strachan 9–38, Manning 3–14, Galbreath 8–11, Holmes 2–4

Receiving
CLE: Hill 4–36, Newsome 4–35, Logan 1–16, Rucker 1–14, C. Miller 1–2
NO: Childs 7–86, Chandler 4–59, Harris 3–32, Mauti 2–31, Galbreath 6–23, Owens 1–16, Strachan 1–2

Sunday, October 15
Pittsburgh Steelers 34, Browns 14
Cleveland Stadium (81,302)
White jerseys/orange pants

Before their largest home crowd of the season, the Browns continually shot themselves in the foot with four turnovers and 10 penalties and were overwhelmed by the undefeated Steelers. Cleveland hung close in the first half and took a 7–6 lead just before the intermission on a touchdown reception by WR Dave Logan that capped a drive highlighted by the ejection of Pittsburgh LB Jack Lambert. But the Steelers took the lead right back with a 95-yard return for a touchdown on the ensuing kickoff by Larry Anderson (who'd lost the ball on the phantom fumble in overtime during the teams' first meeting three weeks before) and never looked back. The Cleveland offense showed signs of life with 360 yards against the strong Pittsburgh defense, but couldn't overcome its own mistakes as the Browns fell three games behind the Steelers in the division race and into a second-place tie with Houston.
Record: 4–3

	1	2	3	4		
Steelers	6	7	14	7	=	34
Browns	0	7	0	7	=	14

PIT-Gerela 23-yd. FG
PIT-Gerela 44-yd FG
CLE-Logan 17-yd. pass from Sipe (Cockroft kick)
PIT-Anderson 95-yd. kickoff return (Gerela kick)
PIT-Swann 28-yd. pass from Bradshaw (Gerela kick)
PIT-Bleier 1-yd. run (Gerela kick)
CLE-Rucker 18-yd pass from Sipe (Cockroft kick)
PIT-Stallworth 32-yd. pass from Bradshaw (Gerela kick)

Passing
PIT: Bradshaw 10–21–175 2 TD 0 INT
CLE: Sipe 17–30–213 2 TD 2 INT, M. Miller 2–5–39 0 TD 0 INT

Rushing
PIT: Bleier 13–57, Harris 15–41, Thornton 5–38, Deloplaine 3–34, Bradshaw 1–0, Kruczek 1-(-2)
CLE: Hill 10–42, M. Miller 3–33, C. Miller 11–24, Sipe 2–11, M. Pruitt 5–10, G. Pruitt 6–8, Newsome 1–4

Receiving
PIT: Swann 5–76, Stallworth 2–68, Grossman 2–25, Bell 1–6
CLE: Rucker 4–95, Newsome 3–47, Logan 2–38, Hill 3–34, M. Pruitt 3–19, C. Miller 3–11, G. Pruitt 1–8

Sunday, October 22
Kansas City Chiefs 17, Browns 3
Arrowhead Stadium (41,157)
White jerseys/orange pants

The Browns got off to a great start as WR Keith Wright returned the opening kickoff 86 yards to set up a Don Cockroft field goal, but it was downhill from there as they lost for the fourth time in five weeks. The Chiefs, who had lost their previous six games, went on to score 17 unanswered points. Despite the return of Greg Pruitt, the Browns' offense was held to a season-low 162 total yards, nearly topped by the team's 103 yards in penalties. An ineffective Brian Sipe was replaced by backup Mark Miller to start the second half with the Browns down 10–3, and Miller drove the offense across midfield in the fourth quarter before throwing an interception. Kansas City responded with an 80-yard drive for the game-clinching touchdown. Held without a catch for the first time in nearly four years, Reggie Rucker saw his 55-game receiving streak come to a close.
Record: 4–4

	1	2	3	4		
Browns	3	0	0	0	=	3
Chiefs	3	7	0	7	=	17

CLE-Cockroft 20-yd. FG
KC-Stenerud 21-yd. FG
KC-Morgado 8-yd. run (Stenerud kick)
KC-Morgado 2-yd. run (Stenerud kick)

Passing
CLE: Sipe 7–11–40 0 TD 1 INT, M. Miller 3–7–27 0 TD 1 INT
KC: Livingston 8–13–57 0 TD 0 INT

Rushing
CLE: M. Pruitt 10–57, G. Pruitt 16–46, Hill 2–6, C. Miller 2–4, Sipe 1–1, Newsome 1-(-3)
KC: Reed 14–97, Morgado 18–74, Bailey 7–14, Livingston 2–6, Belton 2–3, Lane 1-(-1), McKnight 3-(-3)

Receiving
CLE: G. Pruitt 6–34, Feacher 1–19, Newsome 1–12, M. Pruitt 1–5, Wright 1-(-3)
KC: Belton 1–22, Lane 3–13, Marshall 1–12, White 1–5, Bailey 1–3, Reed 1–2

Sunday, October 29
Browns 41, Buffalo Bills 20
Cleveland Stadium (51,409)
Brown jerseys/orange pants

Behind a dazzling offensive performance, the Browns snapped their losing skid and surged back over the .500 mark on a sunny autumn afternoon. A week after its worst showing of the season, the Cleveland offense put together its best, exploding for 532 total yards, including a whopping 309 on the ground as Mike Pruitt rushed for a career-high 173 on just 21 carries. Pruitt's day was capped by a picture-perfect 71-yard scoring scamper late in the third quarter, his second of the game. Calvin Hill scored his first two touchdowns in a Browns' uniform, while Reggie Rucker caught two of Brian Sipe's three touchdown passes as Sipe notched a perfect passer rating of 158.3, becoming the twenty-second quarterback in NFL history to accomplish the feat (ironically, New England's Steve Grogan would also do it the same afternoon). Sipe became the second Browns quarterback ever to reach a perfect score, matching Frank Ryan's performance in the 1964 regular-season finale. Overshadowed by the offensive fireworks, the Cleveland defense forced three turnovers, including a pair of interceptions by Thom Darden. The big plays on both sides of the ball helped overcome 12 Cleveland penalties for 135 yards. The victory, combined with a Houston loss to Cincinnati, pulled the Browns back into a tie for second place.
Record: 5–4

THE TOP 10 GAMES OF BRIAN SIPE'S CAREER

(Based on highest passer rating—minimum 15 attempts)

10. November 9, 1980 at Baltimore (Browns win, 28–27)
22 of 29 for 212 yards, 2 TD 0 INT
118.7 rating

9. September 28, 1980 at Tampa Bay (Browns win, 34–27)
22 of 32 for 318 yards, 3 TD 1 INT
119 rating

8. October 25, 1981 vs. Baltimore (Browns win, 42–28)
30 of 41 for 444 yards, 4 TD 2 INT
120.4 rating

7. November 27, 1983 vs. Baltimore (Browns win, 41–23)
20 of 33 for 313 yards, 3 TD 0 INT
122.4 rating

6. November 23, 1980 vs. Cincinnati (Browns win, 31–7)
27 of 36 for 310 yards, 4 TD 0 INT
125.9 rating

5. September 11, 1983 at Detroit (Browns win, 31–26)
18 of 29 for 234 yards, 4 TD 0 INT
127 rating

4. December 18, 1983 vs. Pittsburgh (Browns win, 30–17)
14 of 22 for 199 yards, 4 TD 0 INT
132.4 rating

3. November 14, 1976 vs. Philadelphia (Browns win, 24–3)
15 of 21 for 198 yards, 2 TD 0 INT
132.6 rating

2. November 19, 1978 at Baltimore (Browns win, 45–24)
15 of 22 for 309 yards, 4 TD 0 INT
150.6 rating

1. October 29, 1978 vs. Buffalo (Browns win, 41–20)
12 of 15 for 217 yards, 3 TD 0 INT
158.3 rating*

*Perfect rating

	1	2	3	4		
Bills	0	7	6	7	=	20
Browns	7	13	14	7	=	41

CLE-Rucker 16-yd. pass from Sipe (Cockroft kick)
CLE-Hill 15-yd. pass from Sipe (kick failed)
BUF-Miller 2-yd. run (Dempsey kick)
CLE-M. Pruitt 1-yd. run (Cockroft kick)
CLE-Rucker 44-yd. pass from Sipe (Cockroft kick)
CLE-M. Pruitt 71-yd. run (Cockroft kick)
BUF-Johnson 1-yd. run (kick failed)
CLE-Hill 3-yd. pass from M. Miller (Cockroft kick)
BUF-Piccone 5-yd. pass from Mays (Dempsey kick)

Passing
BUF: Ferguson 13–23–185 0 TD 2 INT, Mays 4–15–39 1 TD 0 INT
CLE: Sipe 12–15–217 3 TD 0 INT, M. Miller 2–2–17 1 TD 0 INT

Rushing
BUF: Brown 7–33, Miller 11–23, Hooks 3–20, Johnson 4–6
CLE: M. Pruitt 21–173, G. Pruitt 13–87, Hill 6–21, Collins 5–15, Sipe 1–11, Newsome 1–2

Receiving
BUF: Chandler 7–114, Gant 3–29, Brooks 2–29, Piccone 2–18, Lewis 1–15, Miller 1–10, Brown 1–9
CLE: Newsome 4–96, Rucker 4–89, Hill 2–18, Logan 1–15, M. Pruitt 1–14, G. Pruitt 2–2

Sunday, November 5
Houston Oilers 14, Browns 10
Houston Astrodome (45,827)
White jerseys/orange pants

For the second time in a month, the Browns stood tall against the powerful Oilers and held a lead in the fourth quarter, but Houston once again pulled out a narrow victory. The dominant offensive performance the week before didn't carry over as the Browns were held to under 200 total yards of offense and just 10 first downs, including a meager 28 yards rushing on 22 carries. Brian Sipe was sacked seven times though completed four passes to Ozzie Newsome for 124 yards, the first 100-yard game of Newsome's career. After a short Sipe touchdown run just before the half gave the Browns a 7–0 lead, Houston tied it early in the third quarter on a 72-yard touchdown catch by TE Mike Barber. The Browns surged ahead again with a field goal late in the third quarter, but Houston took the lead for good on a touchdown run by RB Rob Carpenter midway through the fourth period and held off the Browns for the rest of the game.
Record: 7–3

	1	2	3	4		
Browns	0	7	3	0	=	10
Oilers	0	0	7	7	=	14

CLE-Sipe 2-yd. run (Cockroft kick)
HOU-Barber 72-yd. pass from Pastorini (Fritsch kick)
CLE-Cockroft 40-yd. FG
HOU-Carpenter 2-yd. run (Fritsch kick)

Passing
CLE: Sipe 15–28–220 0 TD 1 INT, M. Miller 0–1–0 0 TD 0 INT
HOU: Pastorini 17–25–242 1 TD 2 INT

Rushing
CLE: G. Pruitt 13–16, M. Pruitt 6–8, Sipe 3–4
HOU: Campbell 19–71, Carpenter 12–54, Wilson 8–35, Pastorini 2-(-4)

Receiving
CLE: Newsome 4–124, G. Pruitt 6–46, Logan 2–28, Hill 1–10, M. Pruitt 1–8, Rucker 1–4
HOU: Barber 3–92, Burrough 5–64, Renfro 3–31, Caster 2–23, Carpenter 2–17, Campbell 2–15

Sunday, November 12
Denver Broncos 19, Browns 7
Cleveland Stadium (70,856)
Brown jerseys/orange pants

Despite another strong defensive performance, the Browns lost for the fourth time in five weeks and dipped below the .500 mark for the first time in 1978. After Don Cockroft missed a pair of short field goals in the first half, the Browns recovered a Denver fumble at the Broncos' 12 and pulled within three points midway through the third period. Down 13–7 with three minutes left in the game, it appeared the Browns would have one final chance to win, but WR Keith Wright dropped a Denver punt and the Broncos recovered, setting up the clinching touchdown with 1:39 remaining. It was the last of several missed opportunities for the Browns, who proved capable of playing with the defending AFC champions.
Record: 5–6

	1	2	3	4		
Broncos	0	7	6	6	=	19
Browns	0	0	7	0	=	7

DEN-Odoms 25-yd. pass from Morton (Turner kick)
DEN-Turner 44-yd. FG
CLE-M. Pruitt 1-yd. run (Cockroft kick)
DEN-Turner 20-yd. FG
DEN-Perrin 2-yd. run (kick failed)

Passing
DEN: Morton 18–28–230 1 TD 0 INT
CLE: Sipe 16–27–152 0 TD 2 INT

Rushing
DEN: Keyworth 14–52, Canada 5–17, Armstrong 5–15, Perrin 3–10, Lytle 4–7, Morton 3–7, Preston 2–1
CLE: M. Pruitt 15–50, Hill 12–50, Newsome 1–9, G. Pruitt 2–1

Receiving
DEN: Moses 5–115, Odoms 5–58, Keyworth 4–27, Preston 2–20, Dolbin 1–9, Armstrong 1–1
CLE: M. Pruitt 6–47, Hill 4–45, Logan 3–36, C. Miller 1–15, G. Pruitt 2–9

Sunday, November 19
Browns 45, Baltimore Colts 24
Memorial Stadium (45,341)
White jerseys/orange pants

Just when it appeared the bottom was about to drop out on the Browns' season, they rebounded with their highest point total in 10 years to notch a resounding come-from-behind victory to even their record. Despite playing without injured QB Bert Jones, the Colts dominated play in the early going, taking a 10–0 lead midway through the second quarter. But the Browns quickly caught fire, sprinting to 17 points before the intermission, then four more touchdowns in the second half. Brian Sipe had another fantastic game, throwing for a career-best 309 yards and four touchdowns—three to Calvin Hill, who tallied 113 receiving yards. Reggie Rucker accounted for another 123 yards and a touchdown, while DB Oliver Davis scored the Browns' only defensive touchdown of the season on a 39-yard interception return in the third quarter.
Record: 6–6

	1	2	3	4		
Browns	0	17	14	14	=	45
Colts	7	3	7	7	=	24

BAL-McCauley 2-yd. run (Linhart kick)
BAL-Linhart 23-yd. FG
CLE-Hill 53-yd. pass from Sipe (Cockroft kick)
CLE-M. Pruitt 1-yd. run (Cockroft kick)
CLE-Cockroft 45-yd. FG
CLE-Hill 37-yd. pass from Sipe (Cockroft kick)
CLE-Davis 29-yd. interception return (Cockroft kick)
BAL-Carr 24-yd. pass from Troup (Linhart kick)
CLE-Hill 23-yd. pass from Sipe (Cockroft kick)
BAL-Alston 2-yd. pass from Troup (Linhart kick)
CLE-Rucker 25-yd. pass from Sipe (Cockroft kick)

Passing
CLE: Sipe 15–22–309 4 TD 0 INT
BAL: Troup 24–38–296 2 TD 1 INT

Rushing
CLE: G. Pruitt 18–69, Hill 6–36, Sipe 1–19, M. Miller 1–17, M. Pruitt 11–15, Evans 1–12, C. Miller 2–3
BAL: Washington 9–34, Leaks 6–18, Lee 5–12, McCauley 3-(-2)

Receiving
CLE: Rucker 6–123, Hill 3–113, Newsome 2–38, C. Miller 1–23, Logan 2–13, G. Pruitt 1-(-1)
BAL: Carr 5–98, Washington 6–76, McCauley 6–49, Alston 4–45, McCall 1–19, Lee 2–9

Sunday, November 26
Browns 30, Los Angeles Rams 19
Cleveland Stadium (55,158)
Brown jerseys/orange pants

The Browns kept their slim playoff hopes alive with a decisive upset of the Rams, who entered the contest with a league-best 10–2 record. The Browns began to build a commanding lead late in the first half after an Ozzie Newsome end-around touchdown run and a blocked field goal led to a Mike Pruitt touchdown run. A Reggie Rucker touchdown catch in the third period made it 24–9, and the Browns sealed the victory early in the fourth quarter when Greg Pruitt took a pitch around left end for a dazzling 57-yard touchdown run. The Cleveland defense forced five turnovers, including four interceptions, while the teams combined for more than 200 yards in penalties.
Record: 7–6

	1	2	3	4		
Rams	3	6	0	10	=	19
Browns	10	7	7	6	=	30

LA-Corral 25-yd. FG
CLE-Cockroft 41-yd. FG
CLE-Newsome 9-yd. run (Cockroft kick)
LA-Corral 46-yd. FG
CLE-M. Pruitt 1-yd. run (Cockroft kick)
LA-Corral 27-yd. FG
CLE-Rucker 31-yd. pass from Sipe (Cockroft kick)
LA-Corral 48-yd. FG
CLE-G. Pruitt 57-yd. run (kick failed)
LA-Jessie 22-yd. pass from Haden (Corral kick)

Passing
LA: Haden 20–39–197 1 TD 3 INT, Ferragamo 2–6–26 0 TD 1 INT
CLE: Sipe 15–23–246 1 TD 0 INT, G. Pruitt 0–1–0 0 TD 1 INT

Rushing
LA: Bryant 9–44, Cappelletti 10–43, McCutcheon 5–32, Haden 2–26, Waddy 2–4, Latin 3-(-1)
CLE: G. Pruitt 9–74, Hill 11–36, C. Miller 2–9, M. Pruitt 3–6, Newsome 2–6, Sipe 5-(-1)

Receiving
LA: Young 7–81, Cappelletti 7–68, Jessie 2–27, Miller 3–24, Waddy 2–16, Bryant 1–7
CLE: Newsome 3–73, Rucker 3–71, Logan 3–70, Hill 3–25, G. Pruitt 2–11, C. Miller 1-(-4)

Sunday, December 3
Seattle Seahawks 47, Browns 24
Seattle Kingdome (62,262)
White jerseys/orange pants

A horrendous performance by the Cleveland defense resulted in a blowout defeat in Seattle that extinguished the Browns' playoff hopes. Rolling up more than 400 total yards, the Seahawks took control of the game early, and after a bad punt snap resulted in a safety, Seattle led, 23–0. The Browns' offense got rolling from that point on, scoring 24 points and compiling 452 yards but was crippled by six turnovers. Greg Pruitt enjoyed his finest day of the season, rushing for 113 yards on just 12 carries while catching a trio of passes for 46 more yards, while Brian Sipe threw for 250 yards and three touchdown passes.
Record: 7–7

	1	2	3	4		
Browns	0	10	7	7	=	24
Seahawks	14	9	7	17	=	47

SEA-Smith 1-yd. run (Herrera kick)
SEA-Sims 9-yd. run (Herrera kick)
SEA-Largent 27-yd. pass from Zorn (Herrera kick)
SEA-Safety: Raible tackled Evans in end zone
CLE-Logan 7-yd. pass from Sipe (Cockroft kick)
CLE-Cockroft 40-yd. FG
SEA-Sims 19-yd. run (Herrera kick)
CLE-G. Pruitt 26-yd. pass from Sipe (Cockroft kick)
SEA-Herrera 38-yd. FG
SEA-Sims 9-yd. run (Herrera kick)
CLE-Logan 5-yd. pass from Sipe (Cockroft kick)
SEA-Simpson 40-yd. interception return (Herrera kick)

Passing
CLE: Sipe 20–36–250 3 TD 1 INT, Evans 1–1–19 0 TD 0 INT, M. Miller 0–3–0 0 TD 1 INT, G. Pruitt 0–1–0 0 TD 1 INT
SEA: Zorn 15–24–219 1 TD 1 INT, Myer 2–3–16 0 TD 0 INT

Rushing
CLE: G. Pruitt 12–113, C. Miller 5–36, Collins 2–30, M. Pruitt 2–11, Hill 1–3, Evans 1–0, Sipe 1–0
SEA: Sims 23–91, Smith 15–87, Testerman 1–5, Hunter 2–0, Zorn 1–0

Receiving
CLE: Rucker 4–86, Wright 4–56, G. Pruitt 3–46, Logan 5–43, Newsome 3–19, C. Miller 2–19
SEA: Largent 8–108, McCullum 3–41, Sawyer 2–32, Smith 1–27, Raible 2–21, Sims 1–6

Sunday, December 10
Browns 37, New York Jets 34 (OT)
Cleveland Stadium (36,881)
Brown jerseys/orange pants

In the wildest game of the season, the Browns squandered a 17-point fourth-quarter lead, but then rallied to force overtime and pulled out a thrilling victory over the Jets. On a windy, bitterly cold afternoon, Cleveland controlled the contest for three quarters, but saw a 27–10 advantage evaporate as the Jets scored 24 straight points to take a 34–27 lead with 1:16 to play. Aided by a 26-yard reception by Greg Pruitt, the Browns drove 73 yards in 62 seconds and tied the game on an 18-yard Brian Sipe-to-Calvin Hill touchdown pass in the corner of the end zone with 14 seconds showing. The Browns won the toss in sudden-death and Greg Pruitt returned the kickoff 31 yards, then carried the football three straight times to reach the New York 5, where Don Cockroft kicked the game-winning field goal three minutes into the extra session. Pruitt finished the day with 138 yards on 21 carries, pacing an offense that topped the 500-yard mark for the second time on the year. Sipe threw for 283 yards, and the Browns' defense picked off four New York passes, including the tenth interception of the year by Thom Darden, setting a new team record and securing the league lead.

Record: 8–7

	1	2	3	4	OT		
Jets	0	10	0	24	0	=	34
Browns	7	10	10	7	3	=	37

CLE-Hill 2-yd. run (Cockroft kick)
CLE-G. Pruitt 22-yd. pass from Sipe (Cockroft kick)
NYJ-Leahy 45-yd. FG
CLE-Cockroft 26-yd. FG
NYJ-Harper 3-yd. pass from Robinson (Leahy kick)
CLE-Cockroft 22-yd. FG
CLE-Sipe 2-yd. run (Cockroft kick)
NYJ-Shuler 4-yd. pass from Robinson (Leahy kick)
NYJ-Harper 20-yd. pass from Robinson (Leahy kick)
NYJ-Leahy 39-yd. FG
NYJ-Long 1-yd. run (Leahy kick)
CLE-Hill 18-yd. pass from Sipe (Cockroft kick)
CLE-Cockroft 22-yd. FG

Passing
NYJ: Robinson 22–44–289 3 TD 4 INT
CLE: Sipe 20–32–283 2 TD 1 INT

Rushing
NYJ: Harper 4–49, Long 11–30, Dierking 6–24
CLE: G. Pruitt 21–138, C. Miller 11–62, Hill 8–18, M. Pruitt 3–11, Sipe 2–4, Newsome 1–3

Receiving
NYJ: Harper 4–81, Gaffney 4–68, Walker 4–66, Dierking 5–42, Long 2–15, Barkum 2–13, Shuler 1–4
CLE: Rucker 4–76, G. Pruitt 6–69, C. Miller 3–42, Newsome 1–29, Hill 2–26, Wright 3–23, Logan 1–18

Sunday, December 17
Cincinnati Bengals 48, Browns 16
Riverfront Stadium (46,985)
White jerseys/orange pants

The Browns' roller-coaster season ended on a down note as they were thumped by the 3–12 Bengals with a miserable performance in the finale. The struggling Bengals steamrolled to a season-best 494 total yards and cruised to a 24–6 lead early in the third quarter, sparked by a spectacular day by RB Pete Johnson, who picked up 160 yards on 27 rushes. After a 70-yard scoring run by Greg Pruitt, the Browns cut the margin to eight points going into the fourth, but the Bengals erupted for 24 unanswered points to turn the game into a rout. With Brian Sipe knocked out early with a concussion, Cleveland coughed up six turnovers as backup QB Mark Miller completed only six of 21 passes. Once again Greg Pruitt paced the offense, rushing for 182 yards on 22 carries for his fifth 100-yard game of the season. But after missing action due to injuries early in the year, he finished 40 yards short of his fourth straight 1,000-yard campaign. Despite the ugly loss, Sam Rutigliano was given a contract extension after the game through the 1983 season.

Record: 8–8

	1	2	3	4		
Browns	6	0	10	0	=	16
Bengals	0	17	7	24	=	48

CLE-M. Miller 5-yd. run (kick failed)
CIN-Bahr 23-yd. FG
CIN-Bass 40-yd. pass from Anderson (Bahr kick)
CIN-Griffin 6-yd. pass from Anderson (Bahr kick)
CIN-Walker 3-yd. pass from Griffin (Bahr kick)
CLE-G. Pruitt 70-yd. run (Cockroft kick)
CLE-Cockroft 19-yd. FG
CIN-Anderson 3-yd. run (Bahr kick)
CIN-Bahr 49-yd. FG
CIN-Johnson 12-yd. run (Bahr kick)
CIN-Perry 16-yd. interception return (Bahr kick)

Passing
CLE: M. Miller 6–21–129 0 TD 2 INT, Sipe 0–2–0 0 TD 0 INT
CIN: Anderson 14–22–256 2 TD 1 INT, Griffin 1–1–3 1 TD 0 INT

Rushing
CLE: G. Pruitt 22–182, C. Miller 4–12, M. Pruitt 3–11, Hill 5–8, M. Miller 2–5, Newsome 1–4
CIN: Johnson 27–160, Griffin 17–65, Anderson 3–18, Davis 1–2

Receiving
CLE: Logan 3–86, Newsome 1–19, Hill 1–17, G. Pruitt 1–7
CIN: Curtis 7–138, Bass 2–62, Johnson 2–25, Brooks 1–20, Griffin 2–8, Corbett 1–5, Walker 1–3

1979

Sunday, September 2
Browns 25, New York Jets 22 (OT)
Shea Stadium (48,472)
White jerseys/orange pants

The Browns set the tone for a remarkable season with a nail-biting, emotionally exhausting 75-minute battle at Shea Stadium. The drama began early in the fourth when the Browns, leading 19–13, decided to go for it on fourth-and-inches at the New York 14 rather than kick a field goal. They were stuffed, and the Jets responded with the game-tying touchdown but missed a chance to take the lead when the extra-point attempt went awry. Browns' WR Ricky Feacher fumbled the ensuing kickoff and the Jets recovered, cashing in for a 22–19 lead on a field goal with 1:58 to play. But the Browns weren't to be denied, driving from their own 14 to the Jets' 18 with time running out, and Don Cockroft sent the game to overtime with a 35-yard field goal with four seconds remaining. Momentum swung dramatically back and forth in sudden-death, with the Browns surviving a blocked punt with the aid of a ferocious pass rush that pinned New York QB Matt Robinson five times, including three by newly acquired DE Lyle Alzado. With 35 seconds left in overtime, Robinson launched a desperation pass from his own 38 that was intercepted by DB Oliver Davis, who weaved his way to the New York 31, giving the Browns one last chance. A key pass from QB Brian Sipe, who threw for 302 yards, to WR Dave Logan, who caught six passes for 115 yards, pushed them into field-goal range, and with 18 seconds left, Cockroft kicked his fourth field goal of the day into the falling dusk to give the Browns a memorable opening-day victory.
Record: 1–0

	1	2	3	4	OT		
Browns	7	3	9	3	3	=	25
Jets	3	7	3	9	0	=	22

NYJ-Leahy 34-yd. FG
CLE-G. Pruitt 12-yd. pass from Sipe (Cockroft kick)
NYJ-Robinson 1-yd. run (Leahy kick)
CLE-Cockroft 31-yd. FG
CLE-Newsome 17-yd. pass from Sipe (kick failed)
NYJ-Leahy 24-yd. FG
CLE-Cockroft 36-yd. FG
NYJ-Long 5-yd. run (kick failed)
NYJ-Leahy 21-yd. FG
CLE-Cockroft 35-yd. FG
CLE-Cockroft 27-yd. FG

Passing
CLE: Sipe 21–36–302 2 TD 3 INT
NYJ: Robinson 17–31–191 0 TD 2 INT

Rushing
CLE: G. Pruitt 20–81, M. Pruitt 16–49, Hill 2–1
NYJ: Dierking 14–94, Long 21–69, Harper 7–44, Gaines 6–18, Robinson 3–4

Receiving
CLE: Logan 6–115, Rucker 4–74, G. Pruitt 3–39, Newsome 3–31, M. Pruitt 3–18, Wright 1–13, Feacher 1–12
NYJ: Walker 5–65, Barkum 3–33, Gaffney 3–33, Long 1–27, Gaines 3–22, Dierking 1–8, Harper 1–3

Sunday, September 9
Browns 27, Kansas City Chiefs 24
Arrowhead Stadium (42,181)
White jerseys/orange pants

For the second straight week, the Browns went right down to the final gun, rallying from behind and scoring the winning points in the final minutes of play. For much of the afternoon, it appeared the Browns would coast to victory as they took a 20–0 lead early in the third quarter. But the Chiefs caught fire, scoring three touchdowns in 13 minutes behind the heroics of backup QB Steve Fuller. Trailing 24–20 with two minutes to play, the Browns mounted a clutch drive into Kansas City territory, marching 76 yards in eight plays. When Kansas City DB Tim Collier and Browns' RB Greg Pruitt were both ejected for fighting after an incomplete pass, Cleveland WR Reggie Rucker noticed that Collier's replacement was untested rookie M. L. Carter and told Brian Sipe he could beat Carter over the middle. On the next snap from the Kansas City 21, Sipe lofted a pass into the end zone, which Rucker caught behind Carter and just in front of the goalpost with 52 seconds remaining to give the Browns their second consecutive heart-stopping victory.
Record: 2–0

	1	2	3	4		
Browns	10	7	3	7	=	27
Chiefs	0	0	7	17	=	24

CLE-Cockroft 27-yd. FG
CLE-Rucker 17-yd. pass from Sipe (Cockroft kick)
CLE-Newsome 20-yd. pass from Sipe (Cockroft kick)
CLE-Cockroft 32-yd. FG
KC-Smith 17-yd. pass from Fuller (Stenerud kick)
KC-Reed 9-yd. run (Stenerud kick)
KC-McKnight 1-yd. run (Stenerud kick)
KC-Stenerud 30-yd. FG
CLE-Rucker 21-yd. pass from Sipe (Cockroft kick)

Passing
CLE: Sipe 19–35–243 3 TD 1 INT
KC: Fuller 14–25–148 1 TD 0 INT, Livingston 2–10–26 0 TD 1 INT

Rushing
CLE: M. Pruitt 14–77, G. Pruitt 14–69, C. Miller 3–11, Sipe 4–6, Hill 2–1
KC: McKnight 14–44, Reed 12–37, Belton 3–17, Morgado 1–2, Fuller 2–1

Receiving
CLE: Newsome 6–77, G. Pruitt 4–52, Rucker 3–48, Logan 2–30, C. Miller 2–28, M. Pruitt 2–8
KC: Smith 5–65, Gaunty 3–48, Marshall 2–29, Reed 3–17, McKnight 3–15

Sunday, September 16
Browns 13, Baltimore Colts 10
Cleveland Stadium (73,889)
White jerseys/orange pants

Once again firming their reputation as the "Kardiac Kids," the Browns rallied from behind for a narrow victory with a game-winning field goal in the last two minutes. After quickly falling behind 10–0 in the game's first 10 minutes, the Browns rebounded and tied the game in the third quarter of what became a defensive struggle. Pinned deep in their own territory late in the fourth quarter, the Browns pulled off the play of the day—a 74-yard pass from Brian Sipe to TE Ozzie Newsome that set up a 28-yard field goal by Don Cockroft with 1:51 remaining. The Colts had one final chance, driving to the Cleveland 11, but Toni Linhart missed a 28-yard field goal with six seconds left that would have forced overtime—his third miss of the afternoon, all within 32 yards. Despite a sub-par performance, the Browns had escaped and were now 3–0.
Record: 3–0

	1	2	3	4		
Colts	10	0	0	0	=	10
Browns	0	3	7	3	=	13

BAL-Braziel recovers fumble in end zone (Linhart kick)
BAL-Linhart 26-yd. FG
CLE-Cockroft 37-yd. FG
CLE-Logan 35-yd. pass from Sipe (Cockroft kick)
CLE-Cockroft 28-yd. FG

Passing
BAL: Landry 17–29–185 0 TD 0 INT
CLE: Sipe 14–32–218 1 TD 2 INT

Rushing
BAL: Washington 19–59, Hardeman 9–33, McCauley 5–6
CLE: G. Pruitt 17–64, M. Pruitt 14–63, Sipe 1-(-3)

Receiving
BAL: Carr 7–79, McCauley 4–70, Washington 5–33, Hardeman 1–3
CLE: Newsome 3–84, Logan 5–77, G. Pruitt 2–18, C. Miller 2–17, Rucker 1–15, Hill 1–7

Monday, September 24
Browns 26, Dallas Cowboys 7
Cleveland Stadium (80,123)
White jerseys/orange pants

In one of the most rousing victories in team history, the Browns crushed the undefeated defending NFC champions before a capacity crowd and a *Monday Night Football* television audience. Cleveland took command early and never looked back, scoring three touchdowns in the first seven minutes to roar to a 20–0 lead. Brian Sipe opened the scoring with a pair of dazzling touchdown tosses to Dave Logan and Ozzie Newsome, then DB Thom Darden electrified the crowd by intercepting legendary Dallas QB Roger Staubach at the Cowboys' 39—Staubach's first interception in 150 attempts—and returned it for a touchdown. Darden added another interception later as the Browns tightened the screws after a long Staubach touchdown pass later in the first quarter, keeping the explosive Dallas offense off the scoreboard in the final three periods. Cleveland LB Dick Ambrose recovered a fumble at the Cleveland 9 to thwart one second-quarter drive, while the Browns caught breaks when Dallas missed two field goals. DT Jerry Sherk led the charge, picking up three sacks as the Browns forced five turnovers. The only sour point of a magical evening came after the final gun when fans storming the field as the Browns departed by the home-team dugout caused Lyle Alzado to stumble down the steps, injuring his knee. Now 4–0 for the first time in 16 years and tied with Pittsburgh atop the AFC Central, the Browns and their fans believed anything was possible in 1979.

Record: 4–0

	1	2	3	4		
Cowboys	7	0	0	0	=	7
Browns	20	0	0	6	=	26

CLE-Logan 23-yd. pass from Sipe (kick failed)
CLE-Newsome 52-yd. pass from Sipe (Cockroft kick)
CLE-Darden 39-yd. interception return (Cockroft kick)
DAL-Hill 48-yd. pass from Staubach (Septien kick)
CLE-M. Pruitt 2-yd. run (kick failed)

Passing
DAL: Staubach 21–39–303 1 TD 2 INT
CLE: Sipe 15–28–239 2 TD 1 INT

Rushing
DAL: Dorsett 14–64, Laidlaw 13–49, Staubach 2–11, DuPree 1-(-1)
CLE: M. Pruitt 14–31, Hill 7–24, G. Pruitt 6–15, C. Miller 2–7, Moriarty 2–5, Sipe 1–1, Feacher 1-(-1)

Receiving
DAL: D. Pearson 5–109, Hill 3–70, P. Pearson 3–34, DuPree 3–29, Wilson 1–21, Saldi 1–15, Laidlaw 3–9, Dorsett 1–9, Cosbie 1–7
CLE: Rucker 5–57, C. Miller 3–55, Newsome 3–53, Logan 2–42, G. Pruitt 1–27, M. Pruitt 1–5

Sunday, September 30
Houston Oilers 31, Browns 10
Houston Astrodome (48,915)
White jerseys/orange pants

Coming off four straight emotional victories, playing without two key starters, and overdue for a letdown, the Browns were brought back to reality in Houston, as the Oilers parlayed four turnovers into a blowout victory. With both Greg Pruitt and Lyle Alzado sidelined with injuries, a Browns' fumble on a center snap on the second play of the game set the tone, followed by a short field-goal miss by Don Cockroft midway through the second quarter with the Browns down 10–3. Moments later, the Houston lead ballooned to 24–3, capped by an interception return for a touchdown by DB J. C. Wilson. Cleveland cut the margin back to 14 before the half, but Houston responded with a touchdown on the first series of the third quarter—RB Earl Campbell's third of the afternoon—to put the game out of reach. The loss prevented Cleveland from taking over sole possession of first place, since the Steelers lost a narrow decision at home to Philadelphia to create a three-way tie atop the Central with the Browns and Houston. Worse still, in the final minutes, Browns' WR Keith Wright, leading the league in kickoff returns, was lost for the season with a knee injury.

Record: 4–1

	1	2	3	4		
Browns	0	10	0	0	=	10
Oilers	10	14	7	0	=	31

HOU-Fritsch 28-yd. FG
HOU-Campbell 2-yd. run (Fritsch kick)
CLE-Cockroft 46-yd. FG
HOU-Campbell 2-yd. run (Fritsch kick)
HOU-Wilson 34-yd. interception return (Fritsch kick)
CLE-Sipe 1-yd. run (Cockroft kick)
HOU-Campbell 1-yd. run (Fritsch kick)

Passing
CLE: Sipe 18–35–222 0 TD 2 INT, M. Miller 2–8–31 0 TD 1 INT
HOU: Pastorini 8–13–102 0 TD 0 INT

Rushing
CLE: C. Miller 4–59, M. Pruitt 13–32, Hill 4–14, Sipe 3–3
HOU: Campbell 18–76, Carpenter 11–57, Wilson 5–46, King 3–9, Clark 3–3, Pastorini 2–3

Receiving
CLE: Hill 6–68, Logan 2–58, Rucker 2–36, Newsome 2–21, C. Miller 4–19, Moriarty 1–17, Weathers 1–14, Feacher 1–12, M. Pruitt 1–8
HOU: Barber 2–39, Coleman 2–21, Burrough 2–18, Wilson 1–17, Clark 1–7

Sunday, October 7
Pittsburgh Steelers 51, Browns 35
Cleveland Stadium (81,260)
White jerseys/orange pants

In one of the most highly anticipated games in recent memory, the Browns' defense was annihilated by the red-hot offense of the defending world champions in a battle for first place in the AFC Central Division before a capacity crowd and a national-television audience. Aided by a myriad of Browns' mistakes—including a missed field goal, two fumbles, and an interception thrown at the Pittsburgh 1—the Steelers scored touchdowns on each of their first four possessions and led 27–0 one minute into the second quarter before the Cleveland offense came alive. From that point on, the teams traded touchdowns in a dazzling offensive display, but the early hole was simply too much for the Browns to overcome. The teams combined for 980 total yards, 45 first downs, and 12 touchdowns with Pittsburgh rolling up an astonishing 361 yards on the ground—the most ever against a Cleveland defense. Conversely, the Browns did most of their damage through the air. Brian Sipe tossed for 351 yards and tied a team record with five touchdown passes, while Pittsburgh RB Franco Harris was almost untouchable, running for 153 yards on 19 carries and a pair of scores. Following a brilliant one-handed touchdown catch by Dave Logan (which would grace the cover of *Sports Illustrated* the following year), the Browns narrowed the lead to nine points with nine minutes to play and had Pittsburgh pinned back at its own 6, but the Steelers converted on three successive third-and-long situations on the ensuing possession to melt more than eight minutes off the clock and secure victory with their seventh touchdown of the afternoon. With the Oilers falling to St. Louis, the Steelers left town that October evening with sole possession of first in the division.

Record: 4–2

	1	2	3	4		
Steelers	21	9	7	14	=	51
Browns	0	14	7	14	=	35

PIT-Cunningham 7-yd. pass from Bradshaw (Bahr kick)
PIT-Thornton 10-yd. pass from Bradshaw (Bahr kick)
PIT-Harris 71-yd. run (Bahr kick)
PIT-Smith 14-yd. pass from Bradshaw (kick failed)
CLE-Rucker 32-yd. pass from Sipe (Cockroft kick)
CLE-Newsome 18-yd. pass from Sipe (Cockroft kick)
PIT-Bahr 42-yd. FG
PIT-Harris 25-yd. run (Bahr kick)
CLE-Hill 14-yd. pass from Sipe (Cockroft kick)
PIT-Bleier 70-yd. run (Bahr kick)
CLE-Logan 30-yd. pass from Sipe (Cockroft kick)
CLE-Logan 13-yd. pass from Sipe (Cockroft kick)
PIT-Thornton 1-yd. run (Bahr kick)

Passing
PIT: Bradshaw 12–21–161 3 TD 0 INT
CLE: Sipe 22–41–351 5 TD 3 INT, Evans 1–1–14 0 TD 0 INT

Rushing
PIT: Harris 19–153, Thornton 18–98, Bleier 4–81, Hawthorne 4–29
CLE: M. Pruitt 15–73, Hill 5–8, Hall 1–7, Sipe 2–4, C. Miller 1–1

Receiving
PIT: Stallworth 4–96, Cunningham 4–29, Smith 2–17, Thornton 1–10, Bleier 1–9
CLE: Newsome 6–97, Logan 5–91, Hill 4–68, Rucker 2–56, M. Pruitt 4–33, Feacher 1–14, Adams 1–6

Sunday, October 14
Washington Redskins 13, Browns 9
Cleveland Stadium (63,323)
White jerseys/orange pants

Though showing dramatic improvement over the week before, the Cleveland defense couldn't come up with a stop when it needed it, allowing the Redskins to drive 80 yards in eight plays in the final two minutes to score the winning touchdown with 27 seconds remaining and send the Browns to a third straight loss. Conversely, the Browns struggled to put points on the board, squandering an extra-point attempt and missing two field goals, the second of which would have put the Browns up by six with 1:55 to play. The key play of the Redskins' final drive was a short pass from QB Joe Theismann to WR Danny Buggs, which turned into a 34-yard gain into Cleveland territory after the Browns' Oliver Davis missed a tackle. Moments later, Theismann hit RB Clarence Harmon for the game-winning score from 14 yards out. The loss was made even more painful for the Browns with the news that the Steelers had been upset by the winless Bengals, and the Browns had missed another chance to climb back into first place.

Record: 4–3

	1	2	3	4		
Redskins	0	3	3	7	=	13
Browns	0	6	3	0	=	9

WAS-Moseley 35-yd. FG
CLE-Hill 1-yd. run (kick failed)
WAS-Moseley 17-yd. FG
CLE-Cockroft 37-yd. FG
WAS-Harmon 14-yd. pass from Theismann (Moseley kick)

Passing
WAS: Theismann 14–24–233 1 TD 1 INT
CLE: Sipe 13–25–160 0 TD 1 INT

Rushing
WAS: Riggins 14–31, Hardeman 8–28, Malone 7–15, Harmon 2–9, Theismann 1–6
CLE: M. Pruitt 22–85, Hill 4–35, Sipe 3–24, C. Miller 4–16, Moriarty 2–7

Receiving
WAS: McDaniel 2–77, Harmon 4–60, Buggs 3–54, Warren 4–32, Hardeman 1–10
CLE: Logan 5–97, Rucker 2–26, Hill 4–20, M. Pruitt 1–15, C. Miller 1–2

Sunday, October 21
Browns 28, Cincinnati Bengals 27
Cleveland Stadium (75,119)
Brown jerseys/orange pants

Trailing 20–7 in the third quarter, with the specter of a fourth straight loss looming before them, the Browns rallied for three quick touchdowns to take control of a hard-fought contest, then hung on for a one-point victory. The key play of the game turned out to be the point-after attempt following Cincinnati's third touchdown, which was blocked by Browns' LB Curtis Weathers and turned out to be the difference in the final score. Moments later, Ozzie Newsome made a dazzling one-handed catch to spark the Cleveland offense, and Brian Sipe threw touchdown passes to Ricky Feacher, Mike Pruitt, and Newsome—giving Sipe 17 scoring strikes for the season—to take a 28–20 lead six minutes into the fourth quarter. Not to be denied, the 1–6 Bengals cut the margin to 28–27 on a touchdown run by RB Pete Johnson with 6:26 to play, then forced a Cleveland punt. But the Bengals fumbled the return, and the Browns recovered at the Cincinnati 39. Still not able to put the game away, the Browns clung to a one-point lead when Don Cockroft missed a 43-yard field goal with 1:48 left. But the Cleveland defense, frustrated by Cincy QB Ken Anderson for most of the day, stopped the Bengals on downs to secure the win and snap the losing streak. Mike Pruitt rose to the occasion with 135 yards on 19 carries, marking the second 100-yard game of his four-year career.
Record: 5–3

	1	2	3	4		
Bengals	7	0	13	7	=	27
Browns	7	0	7	14	=	28

CIN-Bass 9-yd. pass from Anderson (Bahr kick)
CLE-Rucker 6-yd. pass from Sipe (Cockroft kick)
CIN-Johnson 1-yd. run (Bahr kick)
CIN-Curtis 8-yd. pass from Anderson (kick failed)
CLE-Feacher 2-yd. pass from Sipe (Cockroft kick)
CLE-M. Pruitt 50-yd. pass from Sipe (Cockroft kick)
CLE-Newsome 27-yd. pass from Sipe (Cockroft kick)
CIN-Johnson 32-yd. run (Bahr kick)

Passing
CIN: Anderson 20–32–318 2 TD 0 INT
CLE: Sipe 18–34–197 4 TD 3 INT

Rushing
CIN: Johnson 15–63, Griffin 6–15, Dinkel 1–9, Alexander 6–8, Turner 1–7
CLE: M. Pruitt 19–135, Hill 1–3, C. Miller 1–3, G. Pruitt 4–1, Adams 1–1, Sipe 6-(-19)

Receiving
CIN: Curtis 6–108, Bass 5–100, Ross 5–72, Griffin 3–28, Turner 1–10
CLE: Newsome 5–90, M. Pruitt 4–54, G. Pruitt 4–19, Hill 2–13, Logan 1–13, Rucker 1–6, Feacher 1–2

Sunday, October 28
Browns 38, St. Louis Cardinals 20
Busch Stadium (47,845)
White jerseys/orange pants

The good news was the Browns overwhelmed the struggling Cardinals with a dominating second-half performance to win easily and stay within a game of Pittsburgh in the AFC Central. The bad news was that Greg Pruitt was lost for the season with a knee injury. Even without Pruitt for much of the day, the Browns' running game was overpowering, rolling up 226 yards and four touchdowns, including a one-yard plunge by Cleveland native Pat Moriarty and the only rushing touchdown of five-foot-seven RB Dino Hall's career, a 52-yarder to put the game away in the fourth quarter. Trailing by three at the half, the Browns scored four straight touchdowns to take control of the game and beat the Cardinals for the first time since 1969.
Record: 6–3

	1	2	3	4		
Browns	10	0	7	21	=	38
Cardinals	6	7	0	7	=	20

STL-Neils 72-yd. fumble return (kick failed)
CLE-M. Pruitt 1-yd. run (Cockroft kick)
CLE-Cockroft 51-yd. FG
STL-Anderson 3-yd. run (Parris pass from Wehrli)
CLE-Moriarty 1-yd. run (Cockroft kick)
CLE-Logan 6-yd. pass from Sipe (Cockroft kick)

CLE-C. Miller 39-yd. run (Cockroft kick)
CLE-Hall 52-yd. run (Cockroft kick)
STL-Tilley 24-yd. pass from Pisarkiewicz (Little kick)

Passing
CLE: Sipe 20–28–208 1 TD 0 INT
STL: Hart 10–21–109 0 TD 2 INT, Pisarkiewicz 6–10–77 1 TD 0 INT

Rushing
CLE: C. Miller 11–80, Hall 2–61, Hill 9–43, M. Pruitt 8–41, Adams 1–3, G. Pruitt 1–3, Sipe 1–0, M. Miller 1-(-2), Moriarty 8-(-3)
STL: Anderson 17–68, Lott 3–22, Morris 5–19

Receiving
CLE: Hill 7–81, Rucker 4–76, Newsome 4–19, C. Miller 3–18, Logan 2–14
STL: Parris 3–60, Tilley 2–41, Brown 3–36, Morris 3–15, Anderson 2–14, Stief 1–13, Childs 1–4, Lott 1–3

Sunday, November 4
Browns 24, Philadelphia Eagles 19
Veterans Stadium (69,019)
White jerseys/orange pants

Trailing the playoff-bound Eagles 19–10 with less than four minutes to play, the Browns rallied for two touchdowns to take the lead, then held off Philadelphia on the last play of the game to escape with another thrilling victory. A short Brian Sipe-to-Ozzie Newsome scoring pass cut the lead to two points with 3:21 remaining, then after the Cleveland defense came up with a key stop, the Browns got the ball back. They quickly drove 71 yards in five plays and took the lead when Mike Pruitt broke through the line for a 24-yard touchdown run with 55 seconds left, putting him over the century mark for the day. But the Browns weren't out of the woods yet, as the Eagles drove to the Cleveland 10 and had one final chance with one second left. Browns' LB Charlie Hall intercepted QB Ron Jaworski at the goal line to clinch victory, Cleveland's fourth takeaway of the game. Reggie Rucker aided the Browns' attack with 106 receiving yards, while the Cleveland defense was continually frustrated by Eagles' RB Wilbert Montgomery, who skewered the Browns for 197 yards on 30 carries. The victory kept the Browns tied for second with the Oilers, both one game back of Pittsburgh but also cost them the services of DT Jerry Sherk for the remainder of the season as he suffered a leg injury that led to a dangerous staph infection.
Record: 7–3

	1	2	3	4		
Eagles	7	3	0	14	=	24
Browns	6	7	6	0	=	19

PHI-Carmichael 19-yd. pass from Jaworski (kick failed)
CLE-Rucker 21-yd. pass from Sipe (Cockroft kick)
CLE-Cockroft 39-yd. FG
PHI-Montgomery 52-yd. run (Franklin kick)
PHI-Franklin 42-yd. FG
PHI-Franklin 39-yd. FG
CLE-Newsome 5-yd. pass from Sipe (Cockroft kick)
CLE-M. Pruitt 24-yd. run (Cockroft kick)

Passing
CLE: Sipe 20–35–222 2 TD 3 INT
PHI: Jaworski 16–23–205 1 TD 2 INT

Rushing
CLE: M. Pruitt 17–104, Hall 4–35, Hill 7–18, Sipe 1-(-3)
PHI: Montgomery 30–197, Harris 7–23, Jaworski 3–16

Receiving
CLE: Rucker 5–106, C. Miller 4–38, Logan 3–35, Hill 3–23, Newsome 2–23, M. Pruitt 3-(-3)
PHI: Carmichael 5–95, Krepfle 3–41, Montgomery 3–40, Smith 1–22, Campfield 2–6, Harris 2–1

Sunday, November 11
Seattle Seahawks 29, Browns 24
Cleveland Stadium (72,440)
Brown jerseys/orange pants

The Browns' playoff drive hit some major turbulence as they couldn't overcome a myriad of mistakes against the sub-par Seahawks on a dark, cold day on the lake. Cashing in on two Cleveland turnovers, Seattle took a 16–0 lead in the second quarter, then persevered after the Browns scored the next 17 points to take a one-point lead into the fourth. After Seattle took the lead back at 22–17, Don Cockroft missed a 44-yard field goal early in the fourth quarter that would have pulled the Browns back within two points. On the next play, Seattle RB Al Hunter broke loose for a 67-yard run to the Cleveland 6, leading to another touchdown—Sherman Smith's third of the day—that proved to be too much for the Browns. After Cleveland cut the lead back to 29–24, the Seahawks ran out the final 7:29 to drop the Browns to their fourth loss. Aided by a 65-yard touchdown run on the second play of the third quarter, Mike Pruitt tallied 141 yards on just 15 carries to pace the Cleveland offense, while the passing

game uncharacteristically struggled. The loss dropped the Browns two games back of Pittsburgh and tumbled them into third place in the division behind 8–3 Houston.
Record: 7–4

	1	2	3	4		
Seahawks	7	9	0	13	=	29
Browns	0	3	14	7	=	24

SEA-Smith 5-yd. run (Herrera kick)
SEA-Smith 2-yd. run (kick failed)
SEA-Herrera 34-yd. FG
CLE-Cockroft 28-yd. FG
CLE-M. Pruitt 65-yd. run (Cockroft kick)
CLE-M. Pruitt 1-yd. run (Cockroft kick)
SEA-Hunter 5-yd. run (kick failed)
SEA-Smith 2-yd. run (Herrera kick)
CLE-Sipe 3-yd. run (Cockroft kick)

Passing
SEA: Zorn 15–27–249 0 TD 0 INT, Smith 1–1–11 0 TD 0 INT
CLE: Sipe 13–29–177 0 TD 2 INT

Rushing
SEA: Hunter 13–95, Smith 14–54, Moore 5–15, Zorn 5–14, Doornink 5–11
CLE: M. Pruitt 15–141, Sipe 7–34, Hill 5–30, Hall 4–10

Receiving
SEA: Largent 3–93, McCullum 3–45, Raible 1–41, Moore 3–36, Smith 2–14, Peets 1–11, Hunter 1–9, Doornink 1–7, Bell 1–4
CLE: Newsome 3–61, M. Pruitt 4–47, Logan 3–46, Rucker 1–18, Hill 2–5

Sunday, November 18
Browns 30, Miami Dolphins 24 (OT)
Cleveland Stadium (80,374)
Brown jerseys/orange pants

On a sun-splashed afternoon, the Browns continued their season-long trend of exciting come-from-behind victories to pick up a thrilling win over Miami and pull back within a game of first place in the AFC Central. After a nip-and-tuck battle all afternoon, the Dolphins surged ahead with 11 minutes to play and were poised to pull out victory before Brian Sipe hit Ozzie Newsome for a 34-yard touchdown pass with 1:21 remaining to send the game to overtime. Cleveland won the coin toss and on the first possession, carefully drove to the Miami 39. From there, Sipe lofted a long pass for Reggie Rucker, who caught it in the end zone and was smothered by his teammates in front of the bleachers. Despite fighting the flu, Sipe was brilliant, throwing for 358 yards and three touchdowns as the Cleveland offense surged for nearly 500 total yards. Rucker also came up big, catching nine passes for 177 yards. The victory, combined with a Pittsburgh loss to San Diego, gave the Browns new life in the division race, pulling them within a game of the Steelers heading into their showdown the following Sunday at Three Rivers Stadium.
Record: 8–4

	1	2	3	4	OT		
Dolphins	0	3	7	14	0	=	24
Browns	7	0	10	7	6	=	30

CLE-Moriarty 2-yd. run (Cockroft kick)
MIA-von Schamann 38-yd. FG
MIA-Williams 9-yd. run (von Schamann kick)
CLE-Newsome 14-yd. pass from Sipe (Cockroft kick)
CLE-Cockroft 43-yd. FG
MIA-Hardy 2-yd. pass from Strock (von Schamann kick)
MIA-Williams 4-yd. pass from Strock (von Schamann kick)
CLE-Newsome 34-yd. pass from Sipe (Cockroft kick)
CLE-Rucker 39-yd. pass from Sipe

Passing
MIA: Griese 10–21–115 0 TD 2 INT, Strock 6–10–89 2 TD 1 INT
CLE: Sipe 23–42–358 3 TD 0 INT

Rushing
MIA: Williams 10–65, Csonka 12–44, Davis 7–9, Griese 1–3
CLE: M. Pruitt 19–93, Sipe 5–30, Hall 3–15, Hill 2–6, C. Miller 1–2, Moriarty 1–2

Receiving
MIA: Harris 4–119, Moore 3–42, Hardy 3–39, Davis 4–8, Williams 1–4, Csonka 1-(-8)
CLE: Rucker 9–177, Newsome 4–76, Logan 5–63, Hill 3–21, M. Pruitt 2–21

Sunday, November 25
Pittsburgh Steelers 33, Browns 30 (OT)
Three Rivers Stadium (48,773)
White jerseys/orange pants

In perhaps the greatest game in the history of the rivalry, the Browns and Steelers put on a show on a gray November afternoon in Pittsburgh that would never be forgotten, battling for nearly 75 minutes of play before a victor could be decided. It seemed as though the Browns would finally pick up their first victory at Three Rivers in their tenth attempt, as they roared out of the locker room to take a 20–6 lead late in the first half and carried a two-touchdown advantage into what promised to be a wild fourth quarter. The Browns still led 30–20 before Pittsburgh RB Franco Harris cut the margin to three with 4:42 remaining. The Steelers' defense, which had been shredded by the Browns' passing attack all day, forced a Cleveland punt, and the Steelers tied the game on a short Matt Bahr field goal with 24 seconds left in regulation. For the second straight year in Pittsburgh, the two teams went to sudden-death overtime, where on the first play from scrimmage, Brian Sipe scrambled for 34 yards to the Pittsburgh 34. But after a sack—one of seven on the day for the Pittsburgh defense—a long third-down Sipe pass was picked off by Steelers' DB Mel Blount at the Pittsburgh 4. The roles reversed moments later after the Steelers drove to the Cleveland 33, where Terry Bradshaw was intercepted by Browns' DB Ron Bolton, thwarting the drive. After a Cleveland punt, the Steelers began driving again and aided by a 28-yard Bradshaw scramble to the Cleveland 38 on third-and-10, gradually crept into field-goal range. With nine seconds left, Bahr was called upon again and drilled a 37-yard field goal to give the Steelers a hard-earned victory and deal the Browns a crushing defeat. For the second time in 1979, the Cleveland defense was slaughtered by the Pittsburgh offense, which racked up a whopping 606 total yards (the most the Browns ever allowed) and 36 first downs. Bradshaw threw for 364 yards, and Harris led an unstoppable running attack with 151 rushing yards. Meanwhile, Sipe tossed for 333 yards and three touchdowns, with his primary target being Dave Logan, who caught seven passes for 135 yards. The defeat all but eliminated the Browns from the division race, dropping them two games back of both Pittsburgh and Houston with three to play.

Record: 8–5

	1	2	3	4	OT		
Browns	10	10	7	3	0	=	30
Steelers	3	10	0	17	3	=	33

CLE-Newsome 21-yd. pass from Sipe (Cockroft kick)
CLE-Cockroft 20-yd. FG
PIT-Bahr 45-yd. FG
CLE-Cockroft 32-yd. FG
PIT-Bahr 34-yd. FG
CLE-Logan 16-yd. pass from Sipe (Cockroft kick)
PIT-Harris 2-yd. pass from Bradshaw (Bahr kick)
CLE-Hill 3-yd. pass from Sipe (Cockroft kick)
PIT-Harris 1-yd. run (Bahr kick)
CLE-Cockroft 40-yd. FG
PIT-Harris 3-yd. run (Bahr kick)
PIT-Bahr 21-yd. FG
PIT-Bahr 37-yd. FG

Passing
CLE: Sipe 23–38–333 3 TD 1 INT
PIT: Bradshaw 30–44–364 1 TD 1 INT

Rushing
CLE: Sipe 3–30, M. Pruitt 14–27, Hill 5–10, C. Miller 1-(-2), Hall 1-(-3)
PIT: Harris 32–151, Bleier 10–61, Bradshaw 3–43

Receiving
CLE: Logan 7–135, Newsome 5–77, Hill 4–51, Rucker 2–36, M. Pruitt 3–21, Hall 1–8, C. Miller 1–5
PIT: Harris 9–81, Stallworth 6–75, Cunningham 4–68, Swann 3–48, Grossman 1–47, Bleier 7–45

Sunday, December 2
Browns 14, Houston Oilers 7
Cleveland Stadium (69,112)
Brown jerseys/orange pants

Amid thick snow showers, the Browns rebounded from their difficult loss in Pittsburgh to pick up their most satisfying victory of the year, knocking off the red-hot Oilers on the strength of a powerful running game and a resurgent defense. With the unit riddled with injury on the defensive line, the Browns switched to an improvised 3–4 defensive scheme that stymied the 10–3 Oilers all day. Houston's only score came after an ill-advised surprise onside kick by the Browns after they took a 7–0 lead on a short dump pass to Mike Pruitt that turned into a 42-yard score. With the defenses and the elements containing the offenses for much of the afternoon—and the Browns aiding Houston's cause by throwing an interception in the end zone and missing two field goals—the Browns retook the lead two minutes into the fourth quarter on a short touchdown run by Mike Pruitt, who rushed for 111 yards on the day and surpassed the 1,000-yard mark for the season for the first time in his career. With time running out, the Oilers drove from their own 20 into Cleveland territory and threatened to send the game to overtime, but Browns' DE Jack Gregory recovered an Earl Campbell fumble at the Cleveland 23 with 32 seconds left to clinch the victory. With the loss, the Oilers tumbled out of first place, and the Steelers reclaimed sole possession of the top spot in the division.

Record: 9–5

	1	2	3	4		
Oilers	7	0	0	0	=	7
Browns	7	0	0	7	=	14

CLE-M. Pruitt 42-yd. pass from Sipe (Cockroft kick)
HOU-Campbell 11-yd. run (Fritsch kick)
CLE-M. Pruitt 1-yd. run (Cockroft kick)

Passing
HOU: Pastorini 16–31–133 0 TD 1 INT
CLE: Sipe 13–26–172 1 TD 1 INT

Rushing
HOU: Campbell 22–108, Carpenter 1–9, Wilson 3–4
CLE: M. Pruitt 25–111, Sipe 5–42, C. Miller 7–32, Hall 1–7, Newsome 1–6, Moriarty 1–0

Receiving
HOU: Burrough 1–35, Campbell 6–34, Renfro 3–27, Caster 2–21, Barber 3–13, Coleman 1–3
CLE: M. Pruitt 4–67, Newsome 4–42, Logan 1–21, Feacher 1–16, Rucker 1–14, C. Miller 2–12

Sunday, December 9
Oakland Raiders 19, Browns 14
Oakland–Alameda County Coliseum (52,641)
White jerseys/orange pants

In a battle of two teams fighting for the last wild-card spot in the AFC, the Raiders jumped to a 13–0 halftime lead and held off the Browns in the second half. The Browns' offense was sluggish in the early going, as Brian Sipe was sacked five times in the first half, while the defense got off to a rough start, allowing a long touchdown pass three minutes into the game that set the tone. The Browns clawed back into the contest on the strength of two Mike Pruitt touchdown runs, the first a career-best 77-yard jaunt that burned an all-out Oakland blitz. The second cut the Oakland lead to 16–14 midway through the third quarter, but the Browns didn't threaten again. After the Raiders pushed the lead to five points with a field goal with 1:48 left in the game, the Browns got the ball back at their own 24, but Sipe threw four consecutive incomplete passes to give the ball back to the Raiders. Pruitt paced the struggling Cleveland offense, totaling 149 yards on 20 carries, but it wasn't enough, and the Browns would now need help in the final week of the season to secure a playoff spot.
Record: 9–6

	1	2	3	4		
Browns	0	0	7	7	=	14
Raiders	7	6	0	6	=	19

OAK-Branch 39-yd. Stabler (Breech kick)
OAK-Breech 25-yd. FG
OAK-Breech 38-yd. FG
CLE-M. Pruitt 77-yd. run (Cockroft kick)
OAK-Breech 23-yd. FG
CLE-M. Pruitt 2-yd. run (Cockroft kick)
OAK-Breech 45-yd. FG

Passing
CLE: Sipe 14–29–153 0 TD 2 INT
OAK: Stabler 23–34–196 1 TD 1 INT

Rushing
CLE: M. Pruitt 20–149, Sipe 2–21, C. Miller 2–1, Hall 2-(-2)
OAK: Whittington 22–74, van Eeghen 11–38, Russell 3–14, Jensen 1–4

Receiving
CLE: Logan 5–59, M. Pruitt 3–44, Hill 2–24, Newsome 2–14, C. Miller 1–8, Rucker 1–4
OAK: Branch 6–81, Casper 5–49, Ramsey 4–28, van Eeghen 4–21, Chester 1–10, Russell 1–5, Whittington 2–2

Sunday, December 16
Cincinnati Bengals 16, Browns 12
Riverfront Stadium (42,183)
White jerseys/orange pants

Needing to win and a series of other games to go their way to sneak into the playoffs, the Browns couldn't take care of business on a rainy day in Cincinnati against the 3–12 Bengals. Outgaining the Bengals by more than 150 yards, the Browns were their own worst enemy, coughing up four turnovers while missing a field goal and two extra points, allowing the Bengals to take a seven-point lead into the fourth quarter. The Browns could have tied on a Mike Pruitt touchdown run, but the botched point after kept the Bengals ahead by a point. The Browns forced a Cincinnati punt with just over two minutes to play, but Cleveland's Dino Hall fumbled the return—after fumbling earlier to set up Cincinnati's first touchdown—and the Bengals recovered at the Browns' 31. Cincinnati tacked on a field goal with 1:51 remaining, forcing the Browns to score a touchdown to win. They drove to the Bengals' 5 with five seconds left, but a Brian Sipe pass intended for Reggie Rucker in the end zone was tipped away by Cincinnati DB Dick Jauron, and the Browns' roller-coaster season had come to an end.

Record: 9–7

	1	2	3	4		
Browns	6	0	0	6	=	12
Bengals	0	6	7	3	=	16

CLE-Logan 33-yd. pass from Sipe (kick failed)
CIN-Johnson 1-yd. run (pass failed)
CIN-Thompson 5-yd. run (Bahr kick)
CLE-M. Pruitt 1-yd. run (run failed)
CIN-Bahr 43-yd. FG

Passing
CLE: Sipe 20–42–238 1 TD 1 INT
CIN: Anderson 9–10–47 0 TD 0 INT, Thompson 4–12–27 0 TD 0 INT

Rushing
CLE: M. Pruitt 19–83, Hall 4–22, Sipe 1–8, C. Miller 2–3
CIN: Johnson 19–67, Griffin 11–45, Anderson 1–21, Thompson 5–15, Kreider 1–0, Alexander 1-(-2)

Receiving
CLE: Logan 5–86, C. Miller 3–49, Feacher 2–47, M. Pruitt 6–34, Newsome 3–16, Hall 1–6
CIN: Ross 4–29, Johnson 3–17, Bass 3–12, Griffin 2–11, Curtis 1–5

1980

Sunday, September 7
New England Patriots 34, Browns 17
Schaefer Stadium (49,222)
Brown jerseys/orange pants

The modest expectations for the Browns going into the season were immediately dampened on a sun-drenched Sunday in Foxboro as they were dominated in the opener by the Patriots, who pulled away in the second half, turning a 13–3 advantage at the intermission into a 34–3 lead early in the fourth quarter. The game turned early in the third after the Browns recovered a fumble at the New England 38 and were poised to pull within one score. But RB Mike Pruitt returned the favor with a fumble of his own, and moments later the Patriots scored again on a long touchdown pass. The already-suspect Cleveland defense allowed a paltry 452 yards, including 186 rushing, while the struggling Browns' offense—the heart of the team the year before—struggled to just 263 and didn't reach the end zone until the outcome was already decided. It marked the first time the Browns had lost a season opener in five years and seemed to forecast a disappointing season.

Record: 0–1

	1	2	3	4		
Browns	0	3	0	14	=	17
Patriots	3	10	14	7	=	34

NE-Smith 37-yd. FG
NE-Smith 35-yd. FG
NE-Jackson 10-yd. pass from Grogan (Smith kick)
CLE-Cockroft 25-yd. FG
NE-Morgan 67-yd. pass from Grogan (Smith kick)
NE-Calhoun 2-yd. run (Smith kick)
NE-Hasselbeck 17-yd. pass from Grogan (Smith kick)
CLE-Logan 10-yd. pass from Sipe (Cockroft kick)
CLE-Wright 11-yd. pass from Sipe (Cockroft kick)

Passing
CLE: Sipe 22–35–233 2 TD 0 INT
NE: Grogan 17–26–277 3 TD 1 INT

Rushing
CLE: M. Pruitt 11–50, White 4–2, Sipe 2-(-4)
NE: Ferguson 19–64, Calhoun 14–51, Grogan 3–23, Morgan 1–14, Foreman 5–13, Tatupu 3–9, Jackson 1–8, Johnson 3–4

Receiving
CLE: Hill 3–67, M. Pruitt 5–49, Logan 4–44, Newsome 3–32, Adams 1–18, Rucker 2–12, Wright 1–11, White 3–0
NE: Morgan 3–102, Jackson 4–77, Hasselbeck 2–26, Johnson 2–22, Pennywell 1–16, Francis 1–14, Ferguson 1–11, Foreman 2–9, Calhoun 1–0

Monday, September 15
Houston Oilers 16, Browns 7
Cleveland Stadium (80,243)
White jerseys/orange pants

Before a colossal home crowd and a *Monday Night Football* television audience, the Browns were once again completely outplayed, this time by a division rival, to drop to 0–2. The Cleveland offense, so explosive in 1979, was completely thwarted for the second straight week, this time accumulating only 181 total yards, less than half of Houston's total, as the Oilers held the football for more than 42 minutes, including all but four minutes of the second half. The Browns actually led at halftime after a short Brian Sipe-to-RB Calvin Hill scoring pass but could do nothing with the few opportunities they had in the final two periods. The Browns ran just 42 plays on the night, just over half of Houston's 77, and looked like a team in no way ready to contend in football's toughest division.

Record: 0–2

	1	2	3	4		
Oilers	0	3	7	6	=	16
Browns	0	7	0	0	=	7

CLE-Hill 3-yd. pass from Sipe (Cockroft kick)
HOU-Fritsch 25-yd. FG
HOU-Wilson 2-yd. run (Fritsch kick)
HOU-Fritsch 29-yd. FG
HOU-Fritsch 17-yd. FG

Passing
HOU: Stabler 23–28–187 0 TD 0 INT
CLE: Sipe 12–25–106 1 TD 1 INT

Rushing
HOU: Campbell 18–106, Coleman 8–36, Wilson 9–27, Carpenter 13–23
CLE: M. Pruitt 12–59, White 4–16

Receiving
HOU: Barber 5–47, Carpenter 5–44, Johnson 5–40, Renfro 3–31, Wilson 3–12, Campbell 1–8, Caster 1–5
CLE: M. Pruitt 4–40, Logan 3–37, Hill 2–12, Newsome 2–12, Rucker 1–5

Sunday, September 21
Browns 20, Kansas City Chiefs 13
Cleveland Stadium (63,614)
White jerseys/orange pants

The Browns bounced back from their flat performance on Monday night to hold off the Chiefs and salvage their season with the first of several narrow victories. In a see-saw game, the Browns scored what turned out to be the winning points on a dazzling catch-and-run for a 31-yard touchdown by rookie RB Charles White with three minutes left in the third quarter. They then halted a potential Kansas City scoring drive by recovering a fumble at the Cleveland 12 with nine minutes remaining in the game. On the ensuing drive, the Browns melted the next eight minutes off the clock, and after three Kansas City desperation passes to the end zone from midfield fell incomplete, the Browns had broken into the win column. The Cleveland defense stepped up for the first time, collecting four sacks and halting the KC running game, while the offense racked up nearly 400 total yards. Seeing his first substantial action, White was the catalyst on offense, scoring the first two touchdowns of his career while tallying 159 total yards, including 100 on seven catches.
Record: 1–2

	1	2	3	4		
Chiefs	0	6	7	0	=	13
Browns	0	7	13	0	=	20

KC-Lowery 38-yd. FG
KC-Lowery 22-yd. FG
CLE-White 2-yd. run (Cockroft kick)
CLE-Wright 12-yd. pass from Sipe (kick failed)
KC-Samuels 16-yd. pass from Fuller (Lowery kick)
CLE-White 31-yd. pass from Sipe (Cockroft kick)

Passing
KC: Fuller 15–26–193 1 TD 0 INT
CLE: Sipe 23–36–295 2 TD 1 INT

Rushing
KC: McKnight 13–35, Fuller 5–26, Gant 5–14, Hadnot 5–13, Reed 6–6
CLE: White 15–59, M. Pruitt 15–34, Sipe 1–7, Newsome 1–4, Evans 1-(-1)

Receiving
KC: Samuels 4–79, Gant 1–33, McKnight 4–32, Smith 3–20, Marshall 1–18, Williams 1–6, Reed 1–5
CLE: White 7–100, Newsome 6–55, Logan 3–39, Adams 1–39, Rucker 3–35, M. Pruitt 2–15, Wright 1–12

Sunday, September 28
Browns 34, Tampa Bay Buccaneers 27
Tampa Stadium (65,540)
White jerseys/orange pants

With the heat index over 100°F at sultry Tampa Stadium, the Browns rallied from an early 10-point deficit to take command with four straight touchdowns, then held off a furious rally from the defending NFC Central champs to score a critical victory that turned their season around. After falling behind 13–3 in the second quarter, the Browns caught fire, paced by the red-hot Brian Sipe, who at one point completed 13 consecutive passes. The Browns' lead stretched to 31–13 with 10 minutes left in the game on a long scoring reception by Calvin Hill—his second of the day—but the Buccaneers narrowed the margin to seven in the final minute and then recovered an onside kick and were poised to tie the game and send it to overtime. Tampa reached the Browns' 20, but time expired and the Browns had escaped in true Kardiac Kids fashion. In what became an aerial shoot-out, each offense hit 400 total yards, while Sipe and Buccaneers' QB Doug Williams combined to throw for more than 650 yards and six touchdowns, though each team also accumulated more than 100 yards in penalties. With the exciting victory, the Browns had kept pace with the rest of the AFC Central and proved there would be some excitement in 1980 after all.
Record: 2–2

	1	2	3	4		
Browns	0	17	7	10	=	34
Buccaneers	6	7	0	14	=	27

TB-Yepremian 37-yd. FG
TB-Yepremian 35-yd. FG
CLE-Cockroft 35-yd. FG
TB-Jones 41-yd. pass from Williams (Yepremian kick)
CLE-White 8-yd. run (Cockroft kick)
CLE-Hill 3-yd. pass from Sipe (Cockroft kick)
CLE-Feacher 13-yd. pass from Sipe (Cockroft kick)

CLE-Hill 43-yd. pass from Sipe (Cockroft kick)
TB-Jones 3-yd. pass from Williams (Yepremian kick)
CLE-Cockroft 36-yd. FG
TB-Eckwood 7-yd. pass from Williams (Yepremian kick)

Passing
CLE: Sipe 22–32–318 3 TD 1 INT
TB: Williams 30–56–343 3 TD 2 INT

Rushing
CLE: M. Pruitt 15–48, White 11–27, G. Pruitt 3–19, C. Miller 1–0, Sipe 1(-2)
TB: Hagins 1–26, Eckwood 11–22, Bell 11–17, Williams 2–15

Receiving
CLE: Rucker 4–79, Logan 2–50, Adams 2–46, Hill 2–46, M. Pruitt 5–39, Feacher 3–25, Newsome 2–25, Oden 1–5, White 1–3
TB: Jones 7–106, Eckwood 10–101, Davis 4–45, Mucker 2–37, Giles 2–22, Bell 3–21, Obradovich 1–8, Davis 1–3

Sunday, October 5
Denver Broncos 19, Browns 16
Cleveland Stadium (81,065)
White jerseys/orange pants

The newfound momentum of the previous two weeks evaporated in a frustrating loss to Denver that turned on a bizarre play just before the half. Following an impressive over-the-shoulder catch by Reggie Rucker for a long touchdown midway through the second quarter, the Browns led 10–6 and were poised to take command as they drove to the Denver 1 in the final minute of the half. But a rollout pass by Brian Sipe was deflected into the arms of Broncos' LB Randy Gradishar, who returned it 93 yards for the go-ahead touchdown. The second half was a nip-and-tuck struggle that saw the Broncos take a 19–16 lead with under six minutes left, then survive when a 54-yard field-goal attempt by Don Cockroft fell short with two-and-a-half minutes remaining. Denver then ran out the clock, and the Browns dipped below .500 once again despite outgaining the Broncos by more than 100 yards and out-playing them for much of the day. In the end, the Gradishar touchdown and 97 yards in penalties proved too much for the Browns to overcome.
Record: 2–3

	1	2	3	4		
Broncos	3	10	3	3	=	19
Browns	3	10	3	0	=	16

DEN-Steinfort 18-yd. FG
CLE-Cockroft 24-yd. FG
DEN-Steinfort 47-yd. FG
CLE-Rucker 40-yd. pass from Sipe (Cockroft kick)
DEN-Gradishar 93-yd. interception return (Steinfort kick)
CLE-Cockroft 45-yd. FG
DEN-Steinfort 41-yd. FG
CLE-Cockroft 40-yd. FG
DEN-Steinfort 19-yd. FG

Passing
DEN: Morton 9–12–109 0 TD 0 INT, Robinson 5–14–57 0 TD 1 INT
CLE: Sipe 20–40–258 1 TD 1 INT

Rushing
DEN: Armstrong 12–36, Jensen 10–27, Lytle 5–7, Morton 4–5, Robinson 2–4, McCutcheon 1–3
CLE: M. Pruitt 9–60, White 11–32, Newsome 1–9, G. Pruitt 2–2

Receiving
DEN: Upchurch 5–53, Moses 2–53, Jensen 4–44, Larson 1–7, Egloff 1–5, Armstrong 1–4
CLE: Rucker 3–83, M. Pruitt 5–49, Newsome 4–37, G. Pruitt 4–34, Logan 3–32, Feacher 1–23

Sunday, October 12
Browns 27, Seattle Seahawks 3
Seattle Kingdome (61,366)
White jerseys/orange pants

Once again getting back on track after a tough loss, the Browns dominated Seattle to pick up their first win ever over the Seahawks. Cleveland blew open a tight contest just before the half when sparingly used WR Keith Wright found open space on a broken play and reeled in a 39-yard touchdown pass from a scrambling Brian Sipe to put the Browns ahead 13–3. The Cleveland defense rose to the occasion in the second half, continually stymieing the Seahawks, as the offense tacked on another pair of touchdowns to pull away. Topping the 100-yard mark for the first time on the season, Mike Pruitt led a ferocious running attack and scored two touchdowns while Sipe averaged nearly 20 yards per completion and wasn't sacked thanks to a marvelous performance by the Cleveland offensive line. Meanwhile, the Browns' defense racked up five sacks and held an opponent without a touchdown for the first time in three years. The victory also pulled the Browns within a game of first place as the Steelers were upset at home by the lowly Bengals.
Record: 3–3

	1	2	3	4		
Browns	7	6	7	7	=	27
Seahawks	0	3	0	0	=	3

CLE-M. Pruitt 2-yd. run (Cockroft kick)
SEA-Herrera 29-yd. FG
CLE-Wright 39-yd. pass from Sipe (kick failed)
CLE-White 3-yd. run (Cockroft kick)
CLE-M. Pruitt 22-yd. run (Cockroft kick)

Passing
CLE: Sipe 12–24–211 1 TD 0 INT
SEA: Zorn 23–29–222 0 TD 0 INT

Rushing
CLE: M. Pruitt 24–116, White 10–37, Sipe 1–11, Hall 1–7, C. Miller 1–5, G. Pruitt 1–0
SEA: Moore 6–37, Zorn 3–34, Doornink 7–23, Jodat 11–24

Receiving
CLE: Newsome 2–60, Wright 1–39, Logan 2–38, White 2–27, Feacher 1–26, M. Pruitt 3–13, Oden 1–8
SEA: McCullum 5–61, Moore 6–53, Doornink 4–39, Jodat 3–24, Green 1–19, Sawyer 2–17, Largent 2–9

Sunday, October 19
Browns 26, Green Bay Packers 21
Cleveland Stadium (75,548)
White jerseys/orange pants

In one of the most memorable finishes in franchise history, the Browns—in full Kardiac Kids mode—scored a dramatic touchdown in the final seconds to snatch victory from the jaws of defeat. After controlling the contest early and taking a 13–0 lead early in the third quarter, the Browns watched the Packers score three straight touchdowns to take an eight-point advantage midway through the fourth period. They quickly cut the lead to one, then regained possession at their own 13 with less than two minutes left. The Browns drove into Green Bay territory, but then were set back with a holding penalty and faced third-and-20 from the Packer 46 with 25 seconds left. Brian Sipe lofted a long pass for WR Dave Logan, who out-leaped his defender to catch it at the 19, then skipped into the end zone for the game-winning touchdown with 16 seconds to play as the Stadium crowd erupted. It capped a near-perfect day for Sipe, who, despite playing with several nagging injuries, threw for 391 yards as the Browns rolled up nearly 500 yards of offense. The last-minute magic helped overcome another mistake-riddled performance that saw the Browns amass more than 100 yards in penalties and squander a handful of scoring opportunities.

Record: 4–3

	1	2	3	4		
Packers	0	0	14	7	=	21
Browns	0	10	3	13	=	26

CLE-Cockroft 40-yd. FG
CLE-M. Pruitt 1-yd. run (Cockroft kick)
CLE-Cockroft 42-yd. FG
GB-Dickey 7-yd. run (Birney kick)
GB-Ellis 1-yd. run (Birney kick)
GB-Lofton 26-yd. pass from Dickey (Birney kick)
CLE-Newsome 19-yd. pass from Sipe (Cockroft kick)
CLE-Logan 46-yd. pass from Sipe (kick failed)

Passing
GB: Dickey 17–22–230 1 TD 3 INT
CLE: Sipe 24–39–391 2 TD 0 INT

Rushing
GB: Ellis 9–32, Middleton 13–25, Atkins 5–14, Ivery 7–11, Dickey 3–8
CLE: M. Pruitt 16–43, Sipe 2–33, White 7–13, G. Pruitt 1-(-2)

Receiving
GB: Lofton 8–136, Thompson 1–43, Ellis 2–22, Ivery 1–12, Middleton 4–11, Coffman 1–6
CLE: Hill 5–94, Rucker 5–81, M. Pruitt 6–61, Newsome 5–60, Logan 2–52, G. Pruitt 1–43

Sunday, October 26
Browns 27, Pittsburgh Steelers 26
Cleveland Stadium (79,095)
Brown jerseys/orange pants

Facing the injury-riddled defending world champions, the Browns put together a remarkable second-half comeback to notch a thrilling victory—their first over Pittsburgh in four years. Pittsburgh cashed in on a handful of Cleveland mistakes to take command of the game early and controlled the contest into the second half. Trailing 26–14 early in the fourth quarter, the Browns cut the margin to five on RB Greg Pruitt's second touchdown catch of the game with nine minutes left, then scored the winning points when Brian Sipe lobbed a third-down, 18-yard touchdown pass to TE Ozzie Newsome with 5:38 remaining. The Cleveland defense, on fire down the stretch, thwarted the Steelers' comeback attempts, most notably when DB Ron Bolton came up with a huge interception in Cleveland territory with less than two minutes remaining. When the clock finally hit zero, the Browns had secured one of the most dramatic wins and set the stage for a remarkable second half of the season. Sipe was magnificent once again, throwing for 349 yards and four touchdowns, with Dave Logan his primary target, catching eight passes for 131 yards.

Record: 5–3

	1	2	3	4		
Steelers	10	3	13	0	=	26
Browns	0	7	7	13	=	27

PIT-Hawthorne 1-yd. run (Bahr kick)
PIT-Bahr 27-yd. FG
CLE-Hill 5-yd. pass from Sipe (Cockroft kick)
PIT-Bahr 22-yd. FG
PIT-Hawthorne 2-yd. run (Bahr kick)
CLE-G. Pruitt 6-yd. pass from Sipe (Cockroft kick)
PIT-Thornton 2-yd. run (kick failed)
CLE-G. Pruitt 7-yd. pass from Sipe (kick failed)
CLE-Newsome 18-yd. pass from Sipe (Cockroft kick)

Passing
PIT: Stoudt 18–37–310 0 TD 1 INT
CLE: Sipe 28–46–349 4 TD 1 INT

Rushing
PIT: Stoudt 4–21, Davis 9–20, Bleier 5–19, Hawthorne 9–16, Thornton 7–11
CLE: M. Pruitt 17–82, G. Pruitt 5–8, White 1–1, Evans 1–0, McDonald 1–0

Receiving
PIT: Bell 4–125, Smith 4–75, Sweeney 2–49, Bleier 4–33, Grossman 1–13, Hawthorne 2–11, Cunningham 1–4
CLE: Logan 8–131, G. Pruitt 8–71, Newsome 4–55, Rucker 3–47, Hill 2–20, Adams 1–10, White 1–10, M. Pruitt 1–5

Monday, November 3
Browns 27, Chicago Bears 21

Cleveland Stadium (83,224)
Brown jerseys/orange pants

Before the largest crowd to attend a Browns' game in eight years, Mike Pruitt scored two fourth-quarter touchdowns to help the Browns hold off the Bears and clinch a victory on *Monday Night Football.* After holding a 13–0 lead late in the third quarter, the Browns saw the Bears narrow the margin to six points with less than five minutes left. On a critical third-and-one a minute later, Pruitt exploded through the line for a 56-yard touchdown run with 3:35 to play that turned out to be the game-winning score after the Bears tacked on another touchdown in the final seconds. With the offense firing on all cylinders, Pruitt finished with 129 yards on the ground, while Brian Sipe tossed for another 298, and in one night moved from third to first on the Browns' all-time passing yardage list, leapfrogging both Frank Ryan and Otto Graham. Meanwhile, the Cleveland defense did its part, holding RB Walter Payton—averaging nearly 100 yards per game—to just 30 on 11 carries. The victory, the Browns' fourth straight, kept them locked in a three-way tie with Houston and Pittsburgh atop the AFC Central.

Record: 6–3

	1	2	3	4		
Bears	0	0	7	14	=	21
Browns	3	7	3	14	=	27

CLE-Cockroft 23-yd. FG
CLE-Rucker 4-yd. pass from Sipe (Cockroft kick)
CLE-Cockroft 42-yd. FG
CHI-Evans 7-yd. run (Thomas kick)
CLE-M. Pruitt 1-yd. run (Cockroft kick)
CHI-Baschnagel 17-yd. pass from Evans (Thomas kick)
CLE-M. Pruitt 56-yd. run (Cockroft kick)
CHI-Earl 6-yd. pass from Evans (Thomas kick)

Passing
CHI: Evans 18–33–201 2 TD 1 INT
CLE: Sipe 23–39–298 1 TD 2 INT

Rushing
CHI: Evans 6–46, Payton 11–30, Harper 4–10
CLE: M. Pruitt 27–129, G. Pruitt 4–17, White 4–14, Sipe 2–7, C. Miller 1–3

Receiving
CHI: Earl 5–63, Baschnagel 3–37, Watts 2–36, Payton 5–31, Scott 1–16, Fisher 1–13, Williams 1–5
CLE: Newsome 5–97, Hill 4–63, G. Pruitt 4–45, Logan 3–41, Rucker 3–24, M. Pruitt 1–12, White 2–11, Oden 1–5

Sunday, November 9
Browns 28, Baltimore Colts 27
Memorial Stadium (45,369)
Brown jerseys/orange pants

For the second time in seven days, the Browns built a comfortable fourth-quarter lead, then hung on for dear life to escape with a narrow victory. On a rainy afternoon in Baltimore (the last time the Browns would play there against the Colts), the Browns' offense started the contest on fire and roared to a 21–6 lead, sparked by a pair of touchdown runs by Charles White, as the Browns picked up nearly 300 total yards in the first half. Leading 28–13 throughout the fourth quarter, the Browns allowed the Colts to score two touchdowns in the final 90 seconds, aided by an untimely Mike Pruitt fumble, to cut the lead to a single point. But the Browns recovered the ensuing onside kick with 19 seconds left to clinch victory, with the difference being a missed extra point by Baltimore kicker Steve Mike-Mayer in the second quarter. Cleveland topped 400 total yards for the fourth consecutive week, this time propelled by a running attack that topped 200 yards. The fifth straight victory, representing the Browns' longest winning streak in four years, kept them tied with Houston atop the AFC Central.
Record: 7–3

	1	2	3	4		
Browns	14	7	0	7	=	28
Colts	0	6	7	14	=	27

CLE-White 5-yd. run (Cockroft kick)
CLE-Logan 39-yd. pass from Sipe (Cockroft kick)
BAL-McCall 23-yd. pass from Jones (kick failed)
CLE-White 5-yd. run (Cockroft kick)
BAL-Dickey 5-yd. run (Mike-Mayer kick)
CLE-G. Pruitt 12-yd. pass from Sipe (Cockroft kick)
BAL-McCall 2-yd. pass from Jones (Mike-Mayer kick)
BAL-McCauley 5-yd. pass from Jones (Mike-Mayer kick)

Passing
CLE: Sipe 22–29–212 2 TD 0 INT
BAL: Jones 27–39–289 3 TD 1 INT

Rushing
CLE: M. Pruitt 18–103, White 15–77, C. Miller 3–29, G. Pruitt 2–4, McDonald 1-(-2)
BAL: Dickey 14–87, Franklin 4–19, Jones 1–6, Washington 2-(-2)

Receiving
CLE: Logan 5–85, G. Pruitt 5–47, Rucker 4–36, Feacher 1–16, M. Pruitt 4–13, Newsome 2–13, White 1–2
BAL: Washington 7–64, Butler 4–56, Siani 2–42, McCall 3–33, McCauley 4–27, Carr 2–20, Franklin 2–19, DeRoo 1–16, Dickey 1–12, Sims 1–0

Sunday, November 16
Pittsburgh Steelers 16, Browns 13
Three Rivers Stadium (54,563)
White jerseys/orange pants

For the eleventh straight year, the Browns were unable to pull out a victory at Three Rivers Stadium, losing in the final seconds just as they had the previous two seasons. Matching the Steelers' physical style of play in what became a fierce defensive struggle, the Browns intercepted Pittsburgh QB Terry Bradshaw four times and grabbed a 13–7 halftime lead thanks to a pair of Brian Sipe touchdown passes, the second an impressive juggling catch by Dave Logan. But a flubbed snap on the first extra-point attempt would prove costly later. Still clinging to a six-point lead with less than two minutes left, the Browns took an intentional safety rather than risk punting from the end zone, and the Steelers quickly drove to the Cleveland 3, where Bradshaw hit WR Lynn Swann for the game-winning touchdown with 11 seconds left. The defeat dropped the Browns into a tie with the Steelers for second place, both a game back of Houston.
Record: 7–4

	1	2	3	4		
Browns	0	13	0	0	=	13
Steelers	0	7	0	9	=	16

PIT-Smith 10-yd. pass from Bradshaw (Bahr kick)
CLE-Newsome 4-yd. pass from Bradshaw (Bahr kick)
CLE-Logan 15-yd. pass from Sipe (Cockroft kick)
PIT-Safety: Toews tackled Evans in end zone
PIT-Swann 3-yd. pass from Bradshaw (Bahr kick)

Passing
CLE: Sipe 15–34–178 2 TD 1 INT
PIT: Bradshaw 19–35–263 2 TD 4 INT

Rushing
CLE: M. Pruitt 15–55, G. Pruitt 5–23, Hall 1–19, White 2–3, Evans 1-(-5)
PIT: Harris 15–40, Bradshaw 3–21, Bleier 9–18

Receiving
CLE: M. Pruitt 5–49, Newsome 3–42, Rucker 2–42, G. Pruitt 4–30, Logan 1–15
PIT: Swann 9–138, Bell 2–46, Smith 2–33, Grossman 3–28, Harris 2–11, Bleier 1–7

Sunday, November 23
Browns 31, Cincinnati Bengals 7
Cleveland Stadium (79,253)
Brown jerseys/orange pants

The Browns rebounded from their tough loss in Pittsburgh by blowing open a tight game with Cincinnati in the second half and cruising to their eighth victory of the season. For the second time in 1980, Brian Sipe threw four touchdown passes in a game, this time to four different receivers. The fourth provided an exclamation point on a satisfying victory—a 55-yard bomb to Ricky Feacher, who outfought two defenders to catch the ball, then glided into the end zone after the pair of Bengals collided and fell to the ground. While the Cleveland running game struggled, managing only 31 yards on 16 carries, Sipe was magnificent once again, topping the 300-yard mark for the fourth time on the season. The victory also pulled the Browns into a tie for first place when the Oilers were upset by the New York Jets.
Record: 8–4

	1	2	3	4		
Bengals	7	0	0	0	=	7
Browns	0	14	14	3	=	31

CIN-Alexander 6-yd. run (Vitiello kick)
CLE-Rucker 16-yd. pass from Sipe (Cockroft kick)
CLE-Hill 5-yd. pass from Sipe (Cockroft kick)
CLE-G. Pruitt 2-yd. pass from Sipe (Cockroft kick)
CLE-Feacher 55-yd. pass from Sipe (Cockroft kick)
CLE-Cockroft 31-yd. FG

Passing
CIN: Anderson 18–25–187 0 TD 2 INT, Thompson 7–15–81 0 TD 0 INT
CLE: Sipe 27–36–310 4 TD 1 INT

Rushing
CIN: Turner 11–62, Alexander 13–52, Anderson 3–20, Griffin 2–8, Poole 1–7, Thompson 1–1
CLE: M. Pruitt 5–14, Hill 1–11, G. Pruitt 5–9, C. Miller 2–8, McDonald 1–0, White 1-(-3), Adams 1-(-8)

Receiving
CIN: Ross 4–74, McInally 6–62, Kreider 3–36, Alexander 4–30, Corbett 3–28, Turner 3–21, Curtis 1–14, Poole 1–3
CLE: Rucker 7–82, G. Pruitt 6–67, Feacher 1–55, Logan 6–50, M. Pruitt 3–24, Hill 3–18, Newsome 1–14

Sunday, November 30
Browns 17, Houston Oilers 14
Houston Astrodome (51,514)
White jerseys/orange pants

Scoring one of the hallmark victories of the season, the Browns outmuscled the talented Oilers to claim sole possession of first place. Silencing the home crowd by taking a 14–0 lead three minutes into the second quarter on a pair of touchdown runs by unheralded RB Cleo Miller, the Browns kept the Oilers at bay all afternoon, forcing five turnovers. After Houston cut the lead in half, early in the third quarter Miller exploded through the line for a 50-yard run—the longest of his career—to set up a field goal that provided the winning points. Houston quickly cut the margin back to three, then the defenses took center stage. Houston mounted one final threat, driving to the Cleveland 35 with 1:32 left, but Browns' DB Clarence Scott intercepted Ken Stabler to clinch victory. Though the Cleveland offense had been thwarted, held to less than 200 yards for just the second time all season (their first meeting with the Oilers was the other), the Browns managed to escape with a hard-earned victory thanks primarily to their opportunistic defense, which contained RB Earl Campbell and continually frustrated the Oilers' offense. Upon arriving back in Cleveland, the Browns were greeted by thousands of adoring fans who packed into Hopkins Airport to welcome them back after the huge victory.
Record: 9–4

	1	2	3	4		
Browns	7	7	3	0	=	17
Oilers	0	7	7	0	=	14

CLE-C. Miller 6-yd. run (Cockroft kick)
CLE-C. Miller 1-yd. run (Cockroft kick)
HOU-Campbell 1-yd. run (Fritsch kick)
CLE-Cockroft 25-yd. FG
CLE-Casper 30-yd. pass from Stabler (Fritsch kick)

Passing
CLE: Sipe 13–21–93 0 TD 1 INT
HOU: Stabler 17–26–219 1 TD 2 INT

Rushing
CLE: C. Miller 8–69, M. Pruitt 16–50, G. Pruitt 3–4, White 1–1, Sipe 3-(-3)
HOU: Campbell 27–109, Wilson 3–5, Stabler 1–0

Receiving
CLE: Rucker 3–31, Adams 2–26, M. Pruitt 2–17, G. Pruitt 3–8, Newsome 1–7, Hill 1–3, C. Miller 1–1
HOU: Casper 7–150, Renfro 2–23, Barber 2–19, Wilson 4–13, Caster 1–12, Campbell 1–2

Sunday, December 7
Browns 17, New York Jets 14
Cleveland Stadium (78,454)
Brown jerseys/orange pants

Following the same script that had worked all season, the Browns surged to an early lead, then used some fourth-quarter heroics to pull out a narrow victory on an unseasonably mild December afternoon. With both teams squandering scoring opportunities in the first half, the Browns led just 3–0 at the intermission, then stretched it to 10–0 midway through the third quarter. The Jets then crept into the lead two minutes into the fourth quarter following back-to-back touchdowns, but the Browns surged back ahead on the next possession when Brian Sipe hit Greg Pruitt on a short touchdown pass with 9:27 to play. After halting a Jets' drive into Cleveland territory on the next series, the Browns regained possession with just under six minutes remaining and held the football until the clock hit zero. Guiding the Browns to the 10-victory mark for the first time in eight years, Sipe was once again masterful, throwing for 340 yards, with Reggie Rucker collecting 108, Dave Logan 87, and Greg Pruitt snagging 10 receptions. Following a Houston victory over Pittsburgh the previous Thursday night, the Browns remained a game ahead of the Oilers with two more to play.
Record: 10–4

	1	2	3	4		
Jets	0	0	7	7	=	14
Browns	0	3	7	7	=	17

CLE-Cockroft 34-yd. FG
CLE-M. Pruitt 9-yd. run (Cockroft kick)
NYJ-Jones 39-yd. pass from Todd (Leahy kick)
NYJ-Shuler 5-yd. pass from Todd (Leahy kick)
CLE-G. Pruitt 5-yd. pass from Sipe (Cockroft kick)

Passing
NYJ: Todd 19–28–214 2 TD 2 INT
CLE: Sipe 30–41–340 1 TD 1 INT

Rushing
NYJ: Newton 9–55, Dierking 6–21, Long 2–9, Todd 1–7, Harper 1–1
CLE: M. Pruitt 16–52, Adams 1–15, G. Pruitt 3–11, C. Miller 2–1, Sipe 5–0

Receiving
NYJ: Newton 6–64, Harper 3–55, Jones 1–39, Dierking 6–19, Walker 1–17, Barkum 1–15, Shuler 1–5
CLE: Rucker 5–108, Logan 6–87, G. Pruitt 10–75, M. Pruitt 6–42, Newsome 3–28

Sunday, December 14
Minnesota Vikings 28, Browns 23
Metropolitan Stadium (42,202)
White jerseys/orange pants

In one of the most stunning defeats in team history, the Browns saw a 14-point lead evaporate in the final seven minutes and lost on the final play of the game. With a chance to clinch a playoff berth, the Browns were in control the entire game, building a 23–9 margin midway through the fourth quarter. Aided by an interception on an ill-advised Brian Sipe pass, the Vikings cut the lead to 23–22 with 1:35 to play, but a missed extra point earlier kept the Browns in the lead. Minnesota regained possession at its own 20 with 14 seconds left, and after a trick lateral play moved the Vikings to the Cleveland 46 with five seconds remaining, a Hail Mary pass by QB Tommy Kramer was batted by DBs Thom Darden and Ron Bolton at the goal line and into the arms of Minnesota WR Ahmad Rashad in the end zone for the game-winning touchdown. The Cleveland defense had fallen apart in the second half, allowing the Vikings to score 28 points in 30 minutes and finish with a total of 530 total yards, including 456 through the air, the most the Browns had ever allowed in a single game. The victory allowed Minnesota to clinch the NFC Central, while the heart-wrenching defeat dropped the Browns back into a tie for first with Houston. The entire season would boil down to the finale in Cincinnati.
Record: 10–5

	1	2	3	4		
Browns	7	6	3	7	=	23
Vikings	0	0	9	19	=	28

CLE-Hill 18-yd. pass from Sipe (Cockroft kick)
CLE-Sipe 2-yd. run (kick failed)
MIN-Senser 31-yd. pass from Kramer (kick failed)
CLE-Cockroft 32-yd. FG
MIN-Danmeier 24-yd. FG
CLE-C. Miller 1-yd. run (Cockroft kick)
MIN-Brown 7-yd. pass from Kramer (kick failed)
MIN-Rashad 12-yd. pass from Kramer (Danmeier kick)
MIN-Rashad 46-yd. pass from Kramer (kick failed)

Passing
CLE: Sipe 20–33–232 1 TD 1 INT
MIN: Kramer 38–49–456 4 TD 0 INT

Rushing
CLE: M. Pruitt 19–88, G. Pruitt 5–20, C. Miller 7–17, Sipe 2–9
MIN: Brown 10–49, Young 3–11, Kramer 2–11, White 1–4

Receiving
CLE: Logan 2–56, Hill 3–44, M. Pruitt 5–32, Feacher 1–30, Rucker 3–29, Newsome 3–27, G. Pruitt 3–14
MIN: Rashad 9–142, Senser 7–79, White 4–79, Young 9–72, Brown 7–58, LeCount 1–16, Tucker 1–10

Sunday, December 21
Browns 27, Cincinnati Bengals 24
Riverfront Stadium (50,058)
White jerseys/orange pants

In the epic finale of a storybook regular season, the Browns came from behind for another thrilling victory to clinch their first division title in eight years. After the Bengals controlled the game early and took a 10–0 lead, the Browns rallied to tie the game at the half, then endured through a seesaw second half that saw the teams exchange four touchdowns in a wild third quarter. After the defenses recovered to control the action through the fourth, the Browns took over near midfield with six minutes to play and drove deep into Cincinnati territory, where they took a 27–24 lead on a short field goal with 1:25 left. The Bengals quickly marched to the Cleveland 34 in the final seconds, but time expired after another completion into field-goal range, and the Browns had survived yet again. Brian Sipe had endured a ferocious Cincinnati pass rush that collected six sacks to throw for 308 yards and three touchdowns, two to sparingly used WR Ricky Feacher in the third quarter. The Cleveland defense struggled again, but managed to force four turnovers to keep the spirited Bengals from pulling the upset. When the Browns arrived back in Cleveland, 15,000 fans were waiting there to celebrate the thrilling climax of the Kardiac Kids' unforgettable season.
Record: 11–5

	1	2	3	4		
Browns	0	10	14	3	=	27
Bengals	3	7	14	0	=	24

CIN-Breech 42-yd. FG
CIN-Thompson 13-yd. run (Breech kick)
CLE-Rucker 42-yd. pass from Sipe (Cockroft kick)
CLE-Cockroft 26-yd. FG
CIN-R. Griffin 52-yd. interception return (Breech kick)
CLE-Feacher 35-yd. pass from Sipe (Cockroft kick)
CLE-Feacher 34-yd. pass from Sipe (Cockroft kick)
CIN-McInally 59-yd. pass from Thompson (Breech kick)
CLE-Cockroft 22-yd. FG

Passing
CLE: Sipe 24–44–308 3 TD 2 INT
CIN: Thompson 12–30–197 1 TD 2 INT, Anderson 4–6–54 0 TD 0 INT

Rushing
CLE: M. Pruitt 14–51, C. Miller 3–7, G. Pruitt 1–2, Sipe 1-(-3)
CIN: Alexander 8–50, Johnson 16–42, Thompson 4–30, A. Griffin 2–3, Harris 1–0

Receiving
CLE: Rucker 4–74, Feacher 2–69, Logan 1–65, Newsome 5–30, Adams 1–26, Hill 2–16, M. Pruitt 6–11, G. Pruitt 2–10, C. Miller 1–7
CIN: McInally 3–86, Ross 5–77, Kreider 3–54, Curtis 2–17, Harris 1–7, Alexander 1–5, A. Griffin 1–5

AFC Divisional Playoff
Sunday, January 4
Oakland Raiders 14, Browns 12
Cleveland Stadium (77,655)
Brown jerseys/orange pants

On a frozen, glassy field and with the windchill factor at –36°F, the Browns and Oakland Raiders played a game that wound up being as memorable as the weather conditions.

With the miserable surface and bitter cold neutralizing much of the athletic talent, the teams carefully managed what they could, primarily exchanging punts and trying to avoid mistakes. The Raiders made the first miscue when QB Jim Plunkett was intercepted by the Browns' Ron Bolton, who returned it 42 yards for a touchdown with six minutes left in the first half. But, as would be the case all day, the Browns' kicking team failed when called upon as Don Cockroft's point-after attempt barely fluttered over the line of scrimmage—one of four failed field-goal or extra-point attempts for the Browns on the day.

Oakland took a 7–6 lead at the half, but the Browns began adapting to the cold in the third quarter and converted on a pair of field goals to take a 12–7 lead. The Raiders skated downfield and took the lead back at 14–12 with nine minutes remaining. The Browns appeared poised for a game-winning drive with just over four minutes left, but a Brian Sipe fumble gave the ball back to the Raiders in Cleveland territory, and it appeared Oakland was headed to victory. A crucial stop on fourth-and-inches by the Browns' defense gave the ball back to Sipe and Co. at their own 15 with 2:22 left.

They quickly maneuvered downfield, sparked by a 29-yard pass to Ozzie Newsome and a 23-yard toss to Greg Pruitt. Mike Pruitt plowed for a 14-yard gain to the Oakland 14, and a play later, Sam Rutigliano opted to attempt one more pass before kicking a field goal. With 49 seconds left, the playcall was "Red Right 88," and Sipe tried to fire a pass toward Newsome crossing through the end zone. But Oakland DB Mike Davis stepped in front of Newsome to intercept the pass and end the Browns' fairy-tale season.

The Raiders advanced to the AFC Championship, and the following week they upset San Diego to advance to Super Bowl XV, then knocked off the favored Philadelphia Eagles to become the first wild-card team to win an NFL title.

The Browns, meanwhile, were left to ponder what might have been after the first of four heartbreaking postseason defeats in the 1980s.

	1	2	3	4		
Raiders	0	7	0	7	=	14
Browns	0	6	6	0	=	12

CLE-Bolton 42-yd. interception return (kick failed)
OAK-van Eeghen 1-yd. run (Bahr kick)
CLE-Cockroft 30-yd. FG
CLE-Cockroft 30-yd. FG
OAK-van Eeghen 1-yd. run (Bahr kick)

Passing
OAK: Plunkett 14–30–149 0 TD 2 INT
CLE: Sipe 13–40–183 0 TD 3 INT

Rushing
OAK: van Eeghen 20–45, King 12–23, Plunkett 4–8, Whittington 1–1, Jensen 1-(-1)
CLE: M. Pruitt 13–48, Hill 2–23, Sipe 6–13, G. Pruitt 4–11, C. Miller 1–1, McDonald 1-(-11)

Receiving
OAK: Chester 3–64, van Eeghen 3–23, Branch 2–23, Chandler 1–15, King 4–14, Whittington 1–10
CLE: G. Pruitt 3–54, Newsome 4–51, Rucker 2–38, Logan 2–36, Hill 2–4

1981

Monday, September 7
San Diego Chargers 44, Browns 14
Cleveland Stadium (78,904)
White jerseys/orange pants

With massive expectations surrounding the Browns in their first game following their magical 1980 season, they were annihilated on their home field before a sellout crowd and a *Monday Night Football* television audience. Setting the tone by scoring on their first possession, the Chargers' offense was unstoppable, rolling up 535 total yards and 28 first downs, coasting to a 27–7 lead early in the third quarter. After the Browns cut the margin to 13 and threatened to get back into the game, the Chargers scored the last 17 points of the contest to win going away. The Cleveland offense was potent, collecting 419 yards, and was paced by Brian Sipe's team-record 57 pass attempts, but the Browns could do little more than play catch-up all night to a San Diego offense that just had too many weapons firing on all cylinders: QB Dan Fouts threw for 330 yards and three second-half touchdowns, while RB Chuck Muncie rushed for 161 yards on 24 carries, and TE Charlie Joiner reeled in 191 receiving yards.

Record: 0–1

	1	2	3	4		
Chargers	10	10	14	10	=	44
Browns	0	7	7	0	=	14

SD-Brooks 4-yd. run (Benirschke kick)
SD-Benirschke 50-yd. FG
CLE-Feacher 18-yd. pass from Sipe (Jacobs kick)
SD-Muncie 9-yd. run (Benirschke kick)
SD-Benirschke 43-yd. FG
SD-Brooks 13-yd. pass from Fouts (Benirschke kick)
CLE-G. Pruitt 4-yd. pass from Sipe (Jacobs kick)
SD-Bauer 4-yd. pass from Fouts (Benirschke kick)
SD-Benirschke 32-yd. FG
SD-Smith 38-yd. pass from Fouts (Benirschke kick)

Passing
SD: Fouts 19–25–330 3 TD 0 INT
CLE: Sipe 31–57–375 2 TD 2 INT

Rushing
SD: Muncie 24–161, Brooks 8–28, Cappelletti 5–14, Fouts 2–9, Luther 2-(-7)
CLE: M. Pruitt 8–30, G. Pruitt 1–11, Sipe 4–10, Hill 1–2

Receiving
SD: Joiner 6–191, Smith 1–38, Muncie 4–23, Winslow 2–23, Brooks 1–21, Scales 1–16, Brooks 2–9, Sievers 1–5, Bauer 1–4
CLE: Newsome 6–87, G. Pruitt 7–86, Logan 4–71, Rucker 5–68, M. Pruitt 6–30, Feacher 1–18, Hill 2–15

Sunday September 13
Houston Oilers 9, Browns 3
Cleveland Stadium (79,483)
White jerseys/orange pants

The Browns' defense rebounded from a horrid performance in week one, holding the Oilers to 209 total yards without allowing a touchdown and limiting All-Pro RB Earl Campbell to just 42 yards on 17 carries. But it wasn't enough as the Browns repeatedly squandered scoring opportunities. New kicker David Jacobs, in his second game after replacing retired Don Cockroft, had two field-goal attempts blocked and missed another from 41 yards out, wasting several impressive drives by the Cleveland offense, which ran 31 more plays than the Oilers and held the football for eight minutes longer. Still, the Browns had a final chance to win when they drove to the Houston 39 with a minute to play, but the drive ended with four straight incomplete passes by Brian Sipe, who fired 53 attempts on the afternoon.

Record: 0–2

	1	2	3	4		
Oilers	3	0	3	3	=	9
Browns	0	3	0	0	=	3

HOU-Fritsch 42-yd. FG
CLE-Jacobs 29-yd. FG
HOU-Fritsch 27-yd. FG
HOU-Fritsch 36-yd. FG

Passing
HOU: Stabler 10–18–131 0 TD 1 INT
CLE: Sipe 25–53–234 0 TD 1 INT

Rushing
HOU: Campbell 17–42, Carpenter 7–40, Armstrong 4–10, Stabler 2-(-1)
CLE: White 9–40, M. Pruitt 5–30, C. Miller 6–16, G. Pruitt 4–13

Receiving
HOU: Burrough 3–57, Armstrong 1–48, Carpenter 5–13, Renfro 1–13
CLE: G. Pruitt 9–65, Newsome 6–57, Feacher 1–41, C. Miller 4–28, Adams 1–24, Logan 2–20, M. Pruitt 1–7, White 1-(-8)

Sunday, September 20
Browns 20, Cincinnati Bengals 17
Riverfront Stadium (52,170)
Brown jerseys/orange pants

After two frustrating games to open the season, the Browns put it all together in week three, dominating a Cincinnati team bound for the Super Bowl on its own home turf. Rolling up more than 400 yards of offense, including 185 on the ground, the Browns sprinted to a 13–0 halftime lead, then hung on after the Bengals twice cut the margin to three in the fourth quarter. With RB Cleo Miller rushing for 96 yards, and Mike Pruitt collecting 70, the Browns held a whopping 24-minute advantage in time of possession and responded with a clutch 77-yard drive—capped by a Pruitt scoring run—to push the lead back to 20–10 midway through the fourth quarter. The Bengals would go on to win 11 of their next 12 home games and not drop a game to a divisional opponent at Riverfront for more than two years.

Record: 1–2

	1	2	3	4		
Browns	3	10	0	7	=	20
Bengals	0	0	3	14	=	17

CLE-Jacobs 28-yd. FG
CLE-Jacobs 30-yd. FG
CLE-Newsome 4-yd. pass from Sipe (Jacobs kick)
CIN-Breech 21-yd. FG
CIN-Collinsworth 41-yd. pass from Anderson (Breech kick)
CLE-M. Pruitt 12-yd. run (Jacobs kick)
CIN-Johnson 1-yd. run (Breech kick)

Passing
CLE: Sipe 24–35–259 1 TD 0 INT
CIN: Anderson 16–25–238 1 TD 0 INT

Rushing
CLE: C. Miller 22–96, M. Pruitt 13–70, White 6–12, Sipe 2–5, G. Pruitt 2–2
CIN: Anderson 2–28, Johnson 8–21, Griffin 4-(-1)

Receiving
CLE: White 7–73, Rucker 2–63, Newsome 5–42, Feacher 2–30, C. Miller 3–24, M. Pruitt 3–20, G. Pruitt 2–7

CIN: Curtis 4–79, Collinsworth 3–66, Ross 3–35, Kreider 2–25, McInally 2–19, Griffin 1–17, Johnson 1-(-3)

Sunday, September 27
Browns 28, Atlanta Falcons 17
Cleveland Stadium (78,283)
White jerseys/orange pants

With a second straight sterling overall performance against an undefeated team, the Browns clawed back to the .500 mark. Once again dominating time of possession and collecting more than 100 total yards more than their opponent, the Browns rallied from an early 10–0 deficit and took control of the contest with a pair of touchdowns in the final 39 seconds of the half, the second following a fumble recovered by Cleveland LB Clay Matthews. The Browns then made their lead 28–10 by scoring on the first series of the second half and held off the Falcons from there. RBs Mike Pruitt (20 carries, 99 yards) and Charles White (17 carries, 72 yards) led a ferocious running attack, while the defense forced four turnovers that helped atone for five by the Browns' offense. Atlanta Pro Bowl QB Steve Bartowski was limited to 12 completions in 30 attempts and sacked three times as the Cleveland defense put forth its third consecutive strong showing.

Record: 2–2

	1	2	3	4		
Falcons	3	7	0	7	=	17
Browns	0	21	7	0	=	28

ATL-Luckhurst 35-yd. FG
ATL-Jenkins 18-yd. pass from Bartowski (Luckhurst kick)
CLE-M. Pruitt 13-yd. pass from Sipe (Jacobs kick)
CLE-Newsome 23-yd. pass from Sipe (Jacobs kick)
CLE-Sipe 1-yd. run (Jacobs kick)
CLE-M. Pruitt 1-yd. rush (Jacobs kick)
ATL-Jenkins 5-yd. pass from Bartowski (Luckhurst kick)

Passing
ATL: Bartowski 12–30–176 2 TD 2 INT
CLE: Sipe 21–34–215 2 TD 2 INT

Rushing
ATL: Andrews 16–97, Cain 6–13, Daykin 1–2
CLE: M. Pruitt 20–99, White 17–72, C. Miller 3–9, Sipe 4-(-2)

Receiving
ATL: Jenkins 6–136, Cain 3–20, C. Miller 1–11, Andrews 2–9
CLE: Newsome 6–78, M. Pruitt 4–33, White 4–32, Logan 2–32, G. Pruitt 3–26, Rucker 1–8, C. Miller 1–6

Sunday, October 4
Los Angeles Rams 27, Browns 16
Anaheim Stadium (63,924)
Brown jerseys/orange pants

The momentum of the previous two weeks evaporated in Anaheim as the Browns rolled up more penalty yards (88) than rushing yards (78) and were dominated by a sub-par Rams team. In addition to allowing Los Angeles to control the line of scrimmage with more than 200 yards on the ground and 400 total, the Browns had two touchdowns wiped out on penalties and missed an extra point after having a field goal blocked. Consequently, David Jacobs, who'd made only four of 12 field-goal attempts on the season, was released the following day. For all their struggles and with Brian Sipe suffering a concussion midway through the third quarter, the Browns trailed by only four going into the fourth before the Rams padded the lead.
Record: 2–3

	1	2	3	4		
Browns	3	0	7	6	=	16
Rams	7	7	0	13	=	27

CLE-Jacobs 35-yd. FG
LA-Tyler 2-yd. run (Corral kick)
LA-Tyler 1-yd. pass from Haden (Corral kick)
CLE-M. Pruitt 1-yd. run (Jacobs kick)
LA-Guman 4-yd. run (Corral kick)
LA-Corral 38-yd. FG
LA-Corral 41-yd. FG
CLE-Newsome 38-yd. pass from Sipe (kick failed)

Passing
CLE: Sipe 14–28–250 1 TD 1 INT
LA: Haden 21–31–205 1 TD 0 INT

Rushing
CLE: M. Pruitt 17–56, White 6–12, G. Pruitt 1–7, Hill 1–3, Sipe 1–0
LA: Bryant 19–93, Guman 13–54, Tyler 12–29, Dennard 1–21, Haden 1–16

Receiving
CLE: Feacher 2–71, Rucker 3–65, Newsome 2–56, M. Pruitt 5–40, G. Pruitt 1–9, Hill 1–9
LA: Dennard 7–90, Tyler 6–45, Waddy 2–33, Guman 2–15, Bryant 2–9, C. Miller 1–7, Childs 1–6

Sunday, October 11
Pittsburgh Steelers 13, Browns 7
Three Rivers Stadium (53,255)
White jerseys/orange pants

Squandering a chance to win in the final moments for the fourth consecutive year, the Browns dropped to 0–12 at Three Rivers Stadium when a valiant comeback effort by backup QB Paul McDonald fell just short. It was a frustrating game for both teams, symbolized by the Browns' 445 total yards resulting in only seven points. Brian Sipe was forced to leave the game late in the third quarter after a vicious hit by Pittsburgh LB Jack Lambert, and McDonald, facing the first pressure situation of his career, drove the Browns from their own 3 to the Steelers' 12 with six clutch completions in the waning minutes. With 1:53 left, McDonald's pass to TE Ozzie Newsome in the end zone was tipped and intercepted by Pittsburgh DB J. T. Thomas, and the Steelers had dodged a bullet. The Browns, who'd seen five drives inside the Pittsburgh 40 result in no points, were also saddled with 12 penalties for 97 yards, nearly matching the Steelers' eight for 95. Newsome caught five passes on the day, including Cleveland's only touchdown, for 120 yards. The game also marked the Browns' debut of kicker Matt Bahr, acquired from San Francisco earlier in the week, who kicked an extra point against his former team, the Steelers.
Record: 2–4

	1	2	3	4		
Browns	0	7	0	0	=	7
Steelers	7	3	0	3	=	13

PIT-Stallworth 9-yd. pass from Bradshaw (Trout kick)
PIT-Trout 19-yd. FG
CLE-Newsome 29-yd. pass from Sipe (Bahr kick)
PIT-Trout 23-yd. FG

Passing
CLE: Sipe 12–26–183 1 TD 1 INT, McDonald 8–16–106 0 TD 1 INT
PIT: Bradshaw 19–33–199 1 TD 1 INT

Rushing
CLE: White 12–65, M. Pruitt 14–50, Sipe 3–27, Newsome 1–14, G. Pruitt 2–10
PIT: Harris 13–80, Pollard 9–33, Davis 2–28, Bradshaw 3–20, Thornton 1–5

Receiving
CLE: Newsome 5–120, M. Pruitt 4–44, Rucker 2–40, White 5–37, Logan 1–20, Hill 2–17, Fulton 1–11
PIT: Swann 6–90, Cunningham 4–61, Stallworth 3–22, Harris 4–13, Pollard 2–13

Sunday, October 18
Browns 20, New Orleans Saints 17
Cleveland Stadium (76,059)
Brown jerseys/orange pants

The Browns rallied from a fourth-quarter deficit to avoid a disastrous defeat at home against the 1–5 Saints. Trailing throughout the second half, the Browns surged ahead when Mike Pruitt scored from a yard out with 4:18 remaining but weren't in the clear until New Orleans missed a 37-yard field goal with 1:11 left. While the Browns were hot offensively, paced by 270 passing yards by Brian Sipe and 113 receiving by RB Greg Pruitt, the Saints stayed in the game on the strength of a 79-yard scoring run by rookie RB George Rogers and another touchdown on a fake field goal. Browns' LB Curtis Weathers came up with one of the key plays of the game, blocking a Saints' field goal with 9:44 to play.
Record: 3–4

	1	2	3	4		
Saints	7	7	3	0	=	17
Browns	10	0	3	7	=	20

CLE-Bahr 34-yd. FG
NO-Rogers 79-yd. run (Ricardo kick)
CLE-M. Pruitt 8-yd. run (Bahr kick)
NO-Wilson 8-yd. pass from Myers (Ricardo kick)
NO-Ricardo 21-yd. FG
CLE-Bahr 19-yd. FG
CLE-M. Pruitt 1-yd. run (Bahr kick)

Passing
NO: Manning 16–28–199 0 TD 0 INT, Myers 1–1–8 1 TD 0 INT
CLE: Sipe 25–42–270 0 TD 0 INT

Rushing
NO: G. Rogers 18–122, J. Rogers 3–12, Holmes 2–8, Wilson 1–0
CLE: M. Pruitt 18–83, White 11–19, Sipe 3-(-8)

Receiving
NO: Wilson 3–75, G. Rogers 2–36, Hardy 2–32, Merkens 2–22, Groth 1–17, Tyler 3–11, Holmes 3–7, Martini 1–7
CLE: G. Pruitt 7–113, Newsome 7–65, Feacher 3–49, Rucker 1–15, White 2–13, Hill 2–10, M. Pruitt 3–5

Sunday, October 25
Browns 42, Baltimore Colts 28
Cleveland Stadium (78,986)
Brown jerseys/orange pants

The Browns once again pulled back to the .500 mark on the strength of the most impressive offensive performance in team history. The Cleveland offense riddled the Colts for a team-record 562 total yards, paced by 444 through the air by Brian Sipe, setting another franchise mark. Sipe, who twice completed 11 straight passes in the game, tossed four touchdown passes and had five different receivers all collect over 50 yards. Greg Pruitt led the pack with 104 on nine catches, marking his second 100-yard receiving game in three weeks. Yet for all the offensive dominance, the Colts managed to stay in the game thanks to six Cleveland turnovers and the good fortune of scoring a touchdown after the Browns had blocked a Baltimore field-goal attempt. Ahead 28–7 at the half, the Browns let Baltimore back in the game with turnovers on their first three possessions of the third quarter. After the 1–6 Colts pulled to within 35–28 early in the fourth, they were threatening to tie the game on their ensuing drive before Browns' DB Thom Darden came up with a critical interception at the Cleveland 11. Sipe and Co. then drove 89 yards and put the game away when Mike Pruitt scored from 16 yards out with 7:28 to play.
Record: 4–4

	1	2	3	4		
Colts	0	7	14	7	=	28
Browns	7	21	7	7	=	42

CLE-Newsome 1-yd. pass from Sipe (Bahr kick)
CLE-G. Pruitt 22-yd. pass from Sipe (Bahr kick)
CLE-Logan 40-yd. pass from Sipe (Bahr kick)
BAL-Dickey 3-yd. pass from Jones (Wood kick)
CLE-White 2-yd. run (Bahr kick)
BAL-Landry 11-yd. run on lateral (Wood kick)
BAL-Butler 36-yd. pass from Jones (Wood kick)
CLE-Feacher 28-yd. pass from Sipe (Bahr kick)
BAL-Butler 5-yd. pass from Jones (Wood kick)
CLE-M. Pruitt 16-yd. run (Bahr kick)

Passing
BAL: Jones 17–37–249 3 TD 2 INT
CLE: Sipe 30–41–444 4 TD 2 INT

Rushing
BAL: McMillan 14–57, Dickey 14–36, Jones 1–17, McCauley 1–6, Dixon 2–2
CLE: M. Pruitt 16–87, White 6–21, C. Miller 5–20, G. Pruitt 3–11, Feacher 1-(-1), Sipe 2-(-7)

Receiving
BAL: McCauley 4–73, Carr 3–58, Butler 3–56, Dickey 3–24, McMillan 1–17, Dixon 2–16, McCall 1–5
CLE: G. Pruitt 9–104, Newsome 5–85, Rucker 4–72, Logan 3–69, Feacher 5–55, M. Pruitt 3–38, White 1–21

Sunday, November 1
Buffalo Bills 22, Browns 13
Rich Stadium (78,266)
Brown jerseys/orange pants

The Browns' high-flying offense was shifted into reverse, and the defense was helpless to stop a red-hot Buffalo attack that roared for 469 yards. The Bills were led by RB Joe Cribbs, who by himself outgained the Browns, accumulating 248 total yards and three touchdowns. Despite being dramatically out-played and having two touchdowns called back on penalties, the Browns pulled to within two points midway through the fourth quarter on a Brian Sipe-to-Ozzie Newsome scoring pass. But two minutes later, Cribbs reeled in a 60-yard touchdown pass on third-and-10 to ice the game for the Bills. With center Tom DeLeone out for the remainder of the season after breaking an ankle the previous week, the Cleveland offensive line fell apart. Consequently, the Browns could pick up only 71 rushing yards, and Sipe's rough season continued as he threw three interceptions and was sacked six times.
Record: 4–5

	1	2	3	4		
Browns	0	3	3	7	=	13
Bills	6	7	2	7	=	22

BUF-Cribbs 58-yd. pass from Ferguson (run failed)
BUF-Cribbs 15-yd. pass from Ferguson (Mike-Mayer kick)
CLE-Bahr 36-yd. FG
CLE-Bahr 39-yd. FG
BUF-Safety: McDonald tackled in end zone
CLE-Newsome 12-yd. pass from Sipe (Bahr kick)
BUF-Cribbs 60-yd. pass from Ferguson (Mike-Mayer kick)

Passing
CLE: Sipe 14–37–199 1 TD 3 INT, McDonald 0–1–0 0 TD 0 INT
BUF: Ferguson 14–30–297 3 TD 1 INT

Rushing
CLE: M. Pruitt 13–39, G. Pruitt 3–22, Sipe 2–6, White 2–4
BUF: Cribbs 23–85, Brown 14–58, Leaks 3–15, Brammer 1–11, Hooks 2–4, Ferguson 1-(-1)

Receiving
CLE: Feacher 2–62, Newsome 3–52, M. Pruitt 4–20, G. Pruitt 2–19, Logan 1–19, C. Miller 1–16, Rucker 1–11
BUF: Cribbs 5–163, Lewis 5–97, Butler 3–29, Hooks 1–8

Sunday, November 8
Denver Broncos 23, Browns 20 (OT)
Mile High Stadium (74,859)
White jerseys/orange pants

Still in contention in the AFC playoff race going in, a heartbreaking loss to the Broncos in Denver all but eliminated the Browns, who once again were their own worst enemy. After rallying to tie the game with 29 seconds left in regulation with a short Matt Bahr field goal, the Browns were on the march on their first possession of overtime when Brian Sipe hit RB Calvin Hill with a long pass at midfield. But Hill fumbled the football along the sideline and the Broncos recovered at their own 48, setting up Fred Steinfort's 30-yard field goal to win the game four minutes into sudden-death. It was the Browns' fourth turnover of the game against the league's best defense, though the Cleveland defense stepped up with six sacks of Denver QB Craig Morton. With the defeat, the Browns tumbled into last place in the AFC Central.
Record: 4–6

	1	2	3	4	OT		
Browns	0	7	7	6	0	=	20
Broncos	3	7	3	7	3	=	23

DEN-Steinfort 45-yd. FG
CLE-C. Miller 1-yd. rush (Bahr kick)
DEN-Watson 5-yd. pass from Morton (Steinfort kick)
DEN-Steinfort 43-yd. FG
CLE-Logan 23-yd. pass from Sipe (Bahr kick)
DEN-Preston 4-yd. run (Steinfort kick)
CLE-Bahr 27-yd. FG
CLE-Bahr 32-yd. FG
DEN-Steinfort 30-yd. FG

Passing
CLE: Sipe 20–42–290 1 TD 2 INT
DEN: Morton 21–33–291 1 TD 0 INT

Rushing
CLE: M. Pruitt 12–57, Sipe 3–10, C. Miller 6–9, Newsome 1–6
DEN: Parros 13–66, Preston 11–29, Reed 8–14, Morton 1–5, Upchurch 1–2, Lytle 2–0

Receiving
CLE: Newsome 3–89, Logan 5–86, Hill 4–42, Rucker 1–33, M. Pruitt 5–30, C. Miller 2–10
DEN: Odoms 5–71, Preston 4–61, Watson 3–55, Upchurch 3–49, Parros 3–22, Reed 2–15, Egloff 1–18

Sunday, November 15
Browns 15, San Francisco 49ers 12
Candlestick Park (52,445)
White jerseys/orange pants

Despite a lethargic performance for much of the game, the Browns rallied from a fourth-quarter deficit to stun the 8–2 49ers on their own field with 10 points in the final seven minutes. A 21-yard touchdown pass from Brian Sipe to WR Reggie Rucker with 6:46 remaining tied the contest at 12, then after regaining possession, Sipe and Rucker hooked up again for a 38-yard gain to the San Francisco 22. It set up a 24-yard field goal with 43 seconds remaining by Matt Bahr, who'd begun the season with the 49ers before being traded to Cleveland. The Browns then iced the victory moments later when DB Judson Flint picked off Joe Montana. The key play of the game came earlier in the fourth after San Francisco recovered a fumble on a punt return deep in Cleveland territory while up seven. Poised to extend the margin to double digits, the 49ers' momentum was halted when rookie DB Hanford Dixon deflected a Montana pass into the arms of LB Dick Ambrose at the Cleveland 6, thwarting the drive. It would be the only home loss of the season for the 49ers, who would go on to finish 13–3 and win their first Super Bowl two months later. For as rousing as the victory was, it also marked the Browns' final win of the 1981 season.
Record: 5–6

	1	2	3	4		
Browns	2	3	0	10	=	15
49ers	0	6	6	0	=	12

CLE-Safety: Intentional grounding by Montana in end zone
SF-Wersching 28-yd. FG
CLE-Bahr 28-yd. FG
SF-Wersching 29-yd. FG
SF-Wersching 28-yd. FG
SF-Wersching 28-yd. FG
CLE-Rucker 21-yd. pass from Sipe (Bahr kick)
CLE-Bahr 24-yd. FG

Passing
CLE: Sipe 16–33–180 1 TD 1 INT
SF: Montana 24–42–213 0 TD 2 INT

Rushing
CLE: M. Pruitt 18–76, G. Pruitt 5–26, White 2–7, Sipe 1-(-3)
SF: Easley 16–59, Hofer 10–33, Patton 4–15, Davis 2–6, Montana 2–5, Solomon 1–0

Receiving
CLE: Rucker 3–77, Newsome 3–36, G. Pruitt 4–33, White 2–12, M. Pruitt 3–11, Feacher 1–11
SF: Hofer 7–64, Clark 6–52, Solomon 3–35, Cooper 3–21, Young 2–16, Patton 1–11, Shumann 1–8, Easley 1–6

Sunday, November 22
Pittsburgh Steelers 32, Browns 10
Cleveland Stadium (77,958)
Brown jerseys/orange pants

The Browns' last-minute magic of the week before evaporated in the snow and wind of Cleveland Stadium as the Steelers scored the last 20 points of the game to rout the mistake-prone home team, which committed 11 penalties for 94 yards and handed Pittsburgh seven turnovers. Emblematic of the sloppy conditions, Brian Sipe suffered through the worst game of his career, tossing a team-record six interceptions. Still, the Browns made a game of it for three quarters. After the Browns scored on their opening drive, they trailed only 12–10 at the half following a Sipe-to-WR Dave Logan scoring pass. The Steelers even kept Cleveland closer by missing

SUPER BOWL SWEEP

The 1981 Browns are one of just 15 teams in NFL history that defeated both teams that eventually reached the Super Bowl in the same season. They were also the first—and now one of only three—that defeated both Super Bowl teams on their own home fields.

1978 Los Angeles Rams
defeated Dallas Cowboys 27–14
defeated Pittsburgh Steelers 10–7
Steelers beat Cowboys in Super Bowl XIII

1979 San Diego Chargers
defeated Los Angeles Rams 40–16
defeated Pittsburgh Steelers 35–7
Steelers beat Rams in Super Bowl XIV

1980 Dallas Cowboys
defeated Oakland Raiders 19–13
defeated Philadelphia Eagles 35–27
Raiders beat Eagles in Super Bowl XV

1980 San Diego Chargers
defeated Oakland Raiders 30–24 (OT)
defeated Philadelphia Eagles 22–21
Raiders beat Eagles in Super Bowl XV

1981 Cleveland Browns*
defeated Cincinnati Bengals 20–17
defeated San Francisco 49ers 15–12
49ers beat Bengals in Super Bowl XVI

1985 Miami Dolphins
defeated Chicago Bears 38–24
defeated New England Patriots 30–27
Bears beat Patriots in Super Bowl XX

1986 Seattle Seahawks
defeated New York Giants 17–12
defeated Denver Broncos 41–16
Giants beat Broncos in Super Bowl XXI

1993 Miami Dolphins*
defeated Buffalo Bills 22–13
defeated Dallas Cowboys 16–14
Cowboys beat Bills in Super bowl XXVIII

1996 Dallas Cowboys
defeated Green Bay Packers 21–6
defeated New England Patriots 12–6
Packers beat Patriots in Super Bowl XXXI

2000 Washington Redskins
defeated New York Giants 16–6
defeated Baltimore Ravens 10–3
Ravens beat Giants in Super Bowl XXXV

2000 Tennessee Titans
defeated New York Giants 28–14
defeated Baltimore Ravens 14–6
Ravens beat Giants in Super Bowl XXXV

2004 Pittsburgh Steelers
defeated New England Patriots 34–20
defeated Philadelphia Eagles 27–3
Patriots beat Eagles in Super Bowl XXXIX

2005 Jacksonville Jaguars
defeated Seattle Seahawks 26–14
defeated Pittsburgh Steelers 23–17 OT
Steelers beat Seahawks in Super Bowl XL

2008 New York Giants*
defeated Pittsburgh Steelers 21–14
defeated Arizona Cardinals 37–29
Steelers beat Cardinals in Super Bowl XLIII

2010 New England Patriots
defeated Pittsburgh Steelers 39–26
defeated Green Bay Packers 31–27
Packers beat Steelers in Super Bowl XLV

**Won both games on the road*

the extra point after each of their first three touchdowns. But the Browns let the game get away in the second half despite snatching five takeaways themselves and rolling up 146 rushing yards on a muddy field.

Record: 5–7

	1	2	3	4		
Steelers	12	0	6	14	=	32
Browns	3	7	0	0	=	10

CLE-Bahr 33-yd. FG
PIT-Hawthorne 1-yd. run (kick failed)
PIT-Thornton 3-yd. run (kick failed)
CLE-Logan 13-yd. pass from Sipe (Bahr kick)
PIT-Harris 2-yd. run (kick failed)
PIT-Pinney 1-yd. pass from Bradshaw (Trout kick)
PIT-Moser 5-yd. pass from Bradshaw (Trout kick)

Passing
PIT: Bradshaw 17–32–223 2 TD 2 INT
CLE: Sipe 18–39–227 1 TD 6 INT

Rushing
PIT: Harris 20–75, Thornton 15–52, Malone 1–5, Bradshaw 2–4, Hawthorne 4–3, Davis 1–0
CLE: M. Pruitt 16–96, Sipe 4–27, G. Pruitt 7–17, White 1–6

Receiving
PIT: Smith 3–72, Stallworth 2–40, Harris 3–36, Thornton 4–31, Swann 1–19, Hawthorne 1–12, Grossman 1–7, Moser 1–5, Pinney 1–1
CLE: Feacher 4–79, Newsome 5–61, M. Pruitt 3–31, G. Pruitt 3–19, Rucker 1–18, Logan 1–13, Oden 1–6

Sunday, November 29
Cincinnati Bengals 41, Browns 21
Cleveland Stadium (75,186)
Brown jerseys/orange pants

For the first time in six years, the Browns dropped three games below .500 as the soaring Bengals captured their fifth straight victory, dominating the Browns from the outset and winning in Cleveland for the first time since 1977. Three Browns' fumbles led to three Bengals' touchdowns, including two in the first eight minutes of the game as Cincinnati took a 21–0 lead early in the second period and never looked back. Bengals' QB Ken Anderson tossed four touchdown passes in the first half—two to rookie WR Cris Collinsworth—and directed Cincinnati on a key scoring drive early in the fourth quarter after the Browns had cut the margin to 28–14. Paul McDonald threw his first career touchdown pass in mop-up time in the waning minutes. Total yardage and first downs were almost identical, but Cleveland's three early turnovers doomed any hopes of an upset as the Bengals moved one step closer to their first AFC Central title in eight years.
Record: 5–8

	1	2	3	4		
Bengals	14	14	0	13	=	41
Browns	0	7	0	14	=	21

CIN-Johnson 5-yd. pass from Anderson (Breech kick)
CIN-Collinsworth 39-yd. pass from Anderson (Breech kick)
CIN-Collinsworth 7-yd. pass from Anderson (Breech kick)
CLE-Feacher 30-yd. pass from Sipe (Bahr kick)
CIN-Harris 2-yd. pass from Anderson (Breech kick)
CLE-M. Pruitt 1-yd. run (Bahr kick)
CIN-Johnson 11-yd. run (kick failed)
CIN-Johnson 1-yd. run (Breech kick)
CLE-G. Pruitt 7-yd. pass from McDonald (Bahr kick)

Passing
CIN: Anderson 26–32–235 4 TD 0 INT, Thompson 1–2–19 0 TD 0 INT
CLE: Sipe 19–28–217 1 TD 0 INT, McDonald 3–6–60 1 TD 0 INT

Rushing
CIN: Johnson 21–105, Alexander 4–11, Bass 1–9, Anderson 2–7, Hargrove 1-(-2)
CLE: M. Pruitt 21–83, Sipe 4–43, G. Pruitt 1–1, C. Miller 1–0, White 2-(-2)

Receiving
CIN: Collinsworth 5–76, Ross 6–66, Curtis 3–39, Johnson 7–37, Harris 3–25, Alexander 2–8, Kreider 1–3
CLE: Feacher 3–98, Newsome 4–58, M. Pruitt 8–57, G. Pruitt 4–30, Rucker 1–21, Logan 2–13

Thursday, December 3
Houston Oilers 17, Browns 13
Houston Astrodome (44,502)
Brown jerseys/orange pants

In perhaps the most frustrating loss of the season, the Browns utterly dominated the Oilers from start to finish on a nationally televised Thursday-night game but still lost by blowing several scoring opportunities. Three times the Browns drove inside the Houston 5, but were unable to score a touchdown, including when they had first-and-goal at the Oiler 3 with 1:10 remaining and failed to cross the goal line for the game-winning touchdown on four successive plays. The Browns' statistical dominance was staggering—outgaining Houston by more than 200 total yards, collecting 28 first downs to Houston's seven, and holding the ball more than 20 minutes longer—yet all for naught. Aided by two Brian Sipe interceptions and a blocked punt, the Oilers surged to a 17–6 lead late in the third period. The Browns pulled back within four with a one-yard touchdown by Cleo Miller in the fourth quarter but were unable to score again. Offensively, the Browns rolled up 190 rushing yards, spearheaded by 155 from Mike Pruitt, while the Cleveland defense limited Earl Campbell to 31 yards on 15 carries. The defeat clinched Cleveland's first losing record in four years.
Record: 5–9

	1	2	3	4		
Browns	3	3	0	7	=	13
Oilers	3	0	14	0	=	17

CLE-Bahr 18-yd. FG
HOU-Fritsch 32-yd. FG
CLE-Bahr 19-yd. FG
HOU-Casper 30-yd. pass from Nielsen (Fritsch kick)
HOU-Campbell 1-yd. run (Fritsch kick)
CLE-C. Miller 1-yd. run (Bahr kick)

Passing
CLE: Sipe 21–31–206 0 TD 2 INT
HOU: Nielsen 7–11–86 1 TD 0 INT, Stabler 5–9–48 0 TD 1 INT

Rushing
CLE: M. Pruitt 32–155, C. Miller 8–17, Sipe 1–12, G. Pruitt 1–3, White 1–3
HOU: Campbell 15–31, Coleman 1–3, Wilson 2–2, Nielsen 2-(-2)

Receiving
CLE: M. Pruitt 7–58, Logan 4–38, G. Pruitt 4–37, Newsome 3–26, Rucker 1–24, C. Miller 2–23
HOU: Casper 2–39, Barber 1–35, Armstrong 1–19, Brooks 2–16, Coleman 1–10, Burrough 2–9, Campbell 2–3, Wilson 1–3

Saturday, December 12
New York Jets 14, Browns 13
Cleveland Stadium (56,866)
Brown jerseys/orange pants

For the second straight week, the Browns were denied victory by not taking advantage of opportunities, highlighted by a blocked field goal, a dropped interception, and a dropped touchdown pass, all of which led to a one-point loss to the playoff-bound Jets on a Saturday afternoon. Trailing 14–3 at halftime, the Browns got back into the game on a touchdown reception by RB Calvin Hill, playing his final game in Cleveland. While the defense held the Jets scoreless in the second half, a short Matt Bahr field goal cut the New York lead to a point midway through the fourth quarter. But the Browns went three and out on their next possession and never saw the ball again, finishing their home schedule with a disappointing 3–5 mark.
Record: 5–10

	1	2	3	4		
Jets	0	14	0	0	=	14
Browns	0	3	7	3	=	13

NYJ-J. Jones 28-yd. pass from Todd (Leahy kick)
CLE-Bahr 26-yd. FG
NYJ-Harper 7-yd. pass from Todd (Leahy kick)
CLE-Hill 8-yd. pass from Sipe (Bahr kick)
CLE-Bahr 20-yd. FG

Passing
NYJ: Todd 15–28–159 2 TD 2 INT
CLE: Sipe 20–35–280 1 TD 0 INT

Rushing
NYJ: Dierking 13–76, Long 5–27, McNeil 4–21, Newton 7–20, Harper 2–13, Todd 3–7
CLE: M. Pruitt 15–41, Sipe 3–19, White 4–15, G. Pruitt 1–1, C. Miller 1-(-2)

Receiving
NYJ: J. Jones 5–83, Harper 4–42, Gaffney 1–10, Barkum 2–9, B. Jones 1–9, Dierking 1–5, McNeil 1–1
CLE: Newsome 5–79, Feacher 2–75, G. Pruitt 5–44, C. Miller 3–32, Rucker 1–17, Logan 1–15, Hill 1–8, M. Pruitt 1–6, White 1–4

Sunday, December 20
Seattle Seahawks 42, Browns 21
Seattle Kingdome (51,435)
White jerseys/orange pants

A disappointing season closed with a thud as the Browns committed a whopping 10 turnovers—including one on each of their first five possessions—to hand the Seahawks a blowout victory. In addition to three interceptions, the Browns fumbled the ball nine times, losing seven, as Seattle scored touchdowns on an interception return and then a fumble return in the first half to explode to a 28–0 lead. Paul McDonald replaced an ineffective Brian Sipe in the second quarter and threw for 297 yards and three touchdowns, helping the Browns roll up 452 yards of offense, though the outcome of the contest was never in doubt. The Browns also allowed six sacks and committed 88 yards in penalties. One of the few highlights was Calvin Hill scoring a touchdown on a swing pass in the final quarter of his last game.
Record: 5–11

	1	2	3	4		
Browns	0	7	7	7	=	21
Seahawks	14	14	14	0	=	42

SEA-Easley 82-yd. interception return (Alvarez kick)
SEA-Brown 2-yd. run (Alvarez kick)
SEA-Largent 4-yd. pass from Krieg (Alvarez kick)
SEA-Johnson 31-yd. fumble return (Alvarez kick)
CLE-G. Pruitt 5-yd. pass from McDonald (Bahr kick)
SEA-Johns 10-yd. pass from Krieg (Alvarez kick)
SEA-Largent 14-yd. pass from Krieg (Alvarez kick)
CLE-Logan 16-yd. pass from McDonald (Bahr kick)
CLE-Hill 8-yd. pass from McDonald (Bahr kick)

Passing
CLE: McDonald 24–34–297 3 TD 1 INT, Sipe 3–6–47 0 TD 2 INT
SEA: Krieg 14–21–206 3 TD 1 INT, Largent 0–1–0 0 TD 0 INT

Rushing
CLE: White 18–68, M. Pruitt 9–51, Hill 2–18, Sipe 1–14, McDonald 2–0
SEA: Ivory 9–38, Brown 7–21, Hughes 8–18, Largent 1–8, Lane 3–6, Krieg 2–5, Smith 2-(-2)

Receiving
CLE: Logan 5–101, Feacher 3–65, Hill 5–49, G. Pruitt 5–44, White 4–35, Fulton 1–27, M. Pruitt 3–12, Newsome 1–11
SEA: Largent 6–80, Sawyer 2–40, Brown 1–35, Smith 1–15, Tice 1–14, Johns 1–10, Hughes 1–6, McCullum 1–6

1982

Sunday, September 12
Browns 21, Seattle Seahawks 7
Seattle Kingdome (55,907)
White jerseys/orange pants

Less than nine months after closing out the 1981 season with a horrific performance in the Kingdome, the Browns opened 1982 with a dominant victory over the Seahawks. Parlaying a ferocious running game that rolled up 200 yards and three touchdowns, the Browns roared to a 21–0 halftime lead and never looked back. RB Mike Pruitt rushed for 136 yards and two scores, while the Cleveland defense held Seattle to just 180 total yards and collected eight sacks, three by rookie LB Chip Banks in his first NFL game. The only bad news on this day was the loss of LB Clay Matthews with a broken ankle. He would be sidelined for the next four months, and his absence would haunt the defense for the remainder of the season.

Record: 1–0

	1	2	3	4		
Browns	7	14	0	0	=	21
Seahawks	0	0	7	0	=	7

CLE-M. Pruitt 3-yd. run (Bahr kick)
CLE-White 18-yd. run (Bahr kick)
CLE-M. Pruitt 2-yd. run (Bahr kick)
SEA-Ivory 2-yd. run (Johnson kick)

Passing
CLE: Sipe 11–23–138 0 TD 0 INT
SEA: Krieg 22–38–203 0 TD 1 INT, Smith 0–1–0 0 TD 0 INT

Rushing
CLE: M. Pruitt 30–136, White 14–73, Sipe 3-(-9)
SEA: Doornink 5–14, Ivory 4–10, Smith 4–10, Krieg 1–4, Hughes 1–2

Receiving
CLE: White 5–66, Logan 2–33, Newsome 2–22, M. Pruitt 2–17
SEA: Largent 6–71, Ivory 4–26, Doornink 1–22, Tice 4–15, Brown 1–15, Walker 1–14, Johns 2–12, Carr 1–12, Smith 1–11, Sawyer 1–5

Sunday, September 19
Philadelphia Eagles 24, Browns 21
Cleveland Stadium (78,830)
White jerseys/orange pants

When the dust settled at the end of a wild fourth quarter that saw the teams combine for five touchdowns, the Browns had suffered one of the most heartbreaking defeats in their history. After taking a 14–3 lead early in the final period, the Browns were unable to keep up the momentum as QB Ron Jaworski led the Eagles to two quick scores to give them a 17–14 lead with 4:09 to play. The Browns responded with an 80-yard drive and took the lead when TE Ozzie Newsome miraculously scored on a 34-yard pass he tipped and took out of the hands of Philadelphia DB Roynell Young at the goal line with 57 seconds left. But the staggering Browns' defense was unable to stop the Eagles from cruising 65 yards in four plays and scoring the winning touchdown with 22 seconds left.

Record: 1–1

	1	2	3	4		
Eagles	0	3	0	21	=	24
Browns	7	0	0	14	=	21

CLE-Newsome 19-yd. pass from Sipe (Bahr kick)
PHI-Franklin 47-yd. FG
CLE-White 3-yd. run (Bahr kick)
PHI-Smith 41-yd. pass from Jaworski (Franklin kick)
PHI-Campfield 11-yd. pass from Jaworski (Franklin kick)
CLE-Newsome 34-yd. pass from Sipe (Bahr kick)
PHI-Harris 2-yd. run (Franklin kick)

Passing
PHI: Jaworski 25–41–334 2 TD 1 INT
CLE: Sipe 20–41–239 2 TD 2 INT

Rushing
PHI: Harrington 11–52, Montgomery 12–38, Harris 1–2, Jaworski 1–1
CLE: White 10–45, C. Miller 7–40, M. Pruitt 11–32, Sipe 2–22

Receiving
PHI: Carmichael 6–100, Smith 4–83, Montgomery 4–48, Campfield 4–32, Quick 2–28, Spagnola 2–21, Kab 1–13, Harrington 2–9
CLE: Newsome 8–122, Feacher 4–37, Hall 1–31, White 3–15, C. Miller 2–15, M. Pruitt 1–12, Walker 1–7

Sunday, November 21
Browns 10, New England Patriots 7
Cleveland Stadium (51,281)
Brown jerseys/orange pants

A cold, steady rain and mud-slopped field fit the performance of the teams, both of whom looked rusty in their first game back after the 57-day players' strike. With disgruntled fans booing the sloppy play, neither team scored until the fourth quarter, when WR Ricky Feacher's defender slipped on the wet turf on an out pattern, enabling Feacher to turn it into a 40-yard touchdown. The Patriots tied it with 3:18 remaining, and the game appeared headed for overtime before Browns' DB Clinton Burrell caused and recovered a fumble at the New England 20 with 1:24 left. Matt Bahr ended it with a 24-yard field goal on the game's final play. With neither team topping 270 yards of total offense, the Browns limited New England to just three pass completions on the afternoon.

Record: 2–1

	1	2	3	4		
Patriots	0	0	0	7	=	7
Browns	0	0	0	10	=	10

CLE-Feacher 40-yd. pass from Sipe (Bahr kick)
NE-Brown 38-yd. pass from Cavanaugh (Robinson kick)
CLE-Bahr 24-yd. FG

Passing
NE: Cavanaugh 3–11–96 1 TD 0 INT
CLE: Sipe 13–32–138 1 TD 0 INT

Rushing
NE: Collins 18–80, van Eeghen 13–63, Tatupu 2–13, Cunningham 2–6, Toler 1–4, Cavanaugh 2–3
CLE: White 16–48, M. Pruitt 13–31, Sipe 4–18

Receiving
NE: Hasselbeck 1–41, Brown 1–38, Morgan 1–17
CLE: Feacher 4–78, White 3–18, Logan 2–16, M. Pruitt 2–12, Newsome 1–10, Hall 1–4

THE LOST GAMES OF '82

Had they played out the entire season, would the 1982 Browns still have been a playoff team? Here's a rundown of the games that were canceled, and how each team fared in the shortened season:

September 27 CINCINNATI (7–2)
The Bengals, fresh off their Super Bowl appearance in 1981, cruised through their nine games on the strength of a potent offense and handled the Browns fairly easily despite a lackluster performance in December. Though it would have been a home game on *Monday Night Football* in front of a big crowd, it's hard to see the Browns winning this one.

October 3 at Washington (8–1)
Many of the Redskins' key players, including QB Joe Theismann and RB John Riggins, were in the twilight of their careers, but Washington put it all together in 1982 to secure the best record in the NFC. It's highly unlikely the Browns could have defeated the eventual Super Bowl champions on their home field.

October 10 at LA Raiders (8–1)
In their first year in Los Angeles, the Raiders' silver-and-black, bad-boy reputation was embraced by their new city, and they delivered with a fantastic season. Combine the Browns' long history of struggling on the West Coast with the Raiders' meteoric rise to the NFL elite, and it's difficult to imagine the Browns coming out on top (as evidenced by their lopsided playoff loss to the Raiders in January).

October 17 BALTIMORE (0–8–1)
In their second-to-last year in Baltimore, the Colts were downright embarrassing, failing to win a single game while being outscored by 14 points every Sunday. Particularly with this game to have been played in Cleveland, this likely would have been an easy Browns' win.

October 31 HOUSTON (1–8)
When they met in Houston in late December, the Browns struggled and were lucky to pull out a come-from-behind victory in the final six minutes. But in addition to being overmatched, the Oilers were in a four-season stretch in which they lost 23 straight road games. This is another game that probably would have been a chip shot for the Browns.

November 7 NY GIANTS (4–5)
In their final season before the arrival of Bill Parcells as head coach, the '82 Giants had an erratic season very similar to the Browns', just missing a playoff berth. Though the Giants appear to have an edge on paper, boasting a slightly better offense and a much better defense, this one would have been a toss-up.

November 14 at Miami (7–2)
Once again, the Browns would have had to play a team that wound up in the Super Bowl on its own home field. Boasting the NFL's best defense, the Dolphins almost assuredly would have made things difficult for a Cleveland offense that struggled to put points on the board for much of the season.

Thursday, November 25
Dallas Cowboys 31, Browns 14
Texas Stadium (46,267)
Brown jerseys/orange pants

The Browns' doldrums from the previous Sunday carried over to Thanksgiving as they were annihilated in Texas Stadium. The Cowboys collected nearly 500 total yards, including a whopping 299 on the ground as they coasted to a 31–0 third-quarter lead aided by five Cleveland turnovers and four Dallas sacks. Paul McDonald relieved an ineffective Brian Sipe at quarterback in the second half and directed the Browns to a pair of meaningless touchdowns in the fourth quarter. After Sipe tossed three interceptions, McDonald threw for 151 yards in limited action, while Dallas RB Tony Dorsett rushed for 116 yards and a pair of touchdowns for the NFC Championship-bound Cowboys. It marked the Browns' first Thanksgiving Day appearance in 16 years and just their second since joining the NFL.
Record: 2–2

	1	2	3	4		
Browns	0	0	0	14	=	14
Cowboys	0	17	14	0	=	31

DAL-DuPree 4-yd. pass from White (Septien kick)
DAL-Dorsett 1-yd. run (Septien kick)
DAL-Septien 40-yd. FG
DAL-Springs 2-yd. pass from White (Septien kick)
DAL-Dorsett 5-yd. run (Septien kick)
CLE-Hall 18-yd. pass from McDonald (Bahr kick)
CLE-Pruitt 2-yd. run (Bahr kick)

Passing
CLE: McDonald 9–15–151 1 TD 1 INT, Sipe 11–23–85 0 TD 3 INT
DAL: White 13–22–215 2 TD 1 INT, Hogeboom 0–2–0 0 TD 1 INT

Rushing
CLE: M. Pruitt 14–65, White 4–11, Sipe 2–6
DAL: Dorsett 20–116, Springs 12–73, Newsome 5–47, Newhouse 4–25, Peoples 7–22, White 2–16, Hogeboom 2–0

Receiving
CLE: Feacher 4–47, Walker 1–46, White 8–45, Hall 3–43, Newsome 2–40, Logan 1–11, M. Pruitt 1–4
DAL: Pearson 3–87, Hill 4–76, Dorsett 2–26, Cosbie 1–12, Springs 2–10, DuPree 1–4

Sunday, December 5
San Diego Chargers 30, Browns 13
Cleveland Stadium (54,064)
Brown jerseys/orange pants

Once again amid cold, rainy conditions at Cleveland Stadium, the Browns' defense was overwhelmed by a far superior offense, and the team suffered a lopsided defeat. Though fans were jeering him before the game even began, Brian Sipe turned in a memorable individual performance, completing a team-record 33 passes out of 48 attempts for 338 yards—surpassing the 20,000-yard mark for his career—and set another franchise mark by connecting on 14 straight attempts. But two early interceptions led to a pair of San Diego touchdowns, and the Browns could score only six points in a string of five trips inside the Chargers' 30. Ozzie Newsome caught a then-career-best 10 passes for 140 yards and the Browns' only touchdown, which brought them within 14 points in the third quarter after trailing 27–3 at the half. Newsome also extended his streak of consecutive games with at least one reception to a team-record 45.
Record: 2–3

	1	2	3	4		
Chargers	14	13	0	3	=	30
Browns	3	0	10	0	=	13

SD-Muncie 1-yd. run (Benirschke kick)
SD-Muncie 1-yd. run (Benirschke kick)
CLE-Bahr 46-yd. FG
SD-Brooks 1-yd. run (Benirschke kick)
SD-Brooks 11-yd. run (kick failed)
CLE-Bahr 34-yd. FG
CLE-Newsome 4-yd. pass from Sipe (Bahr kick)
SD-Benirschke 24-yd. FG

Passing
SD: Fouts 18–23–252 0 TD 2 INT
CLE: Sipe 33–48–338 1 TD 2 INT

Rushing
SD: Brooks 22–96, Muncie 8–22, Fouts 3–5, Bell 1–4, Cappelletti 2–3
CLE: M. Pruitt 18–77, White 2–16, C. Miller 1-(-3)

Receiving
SD: Joiner 7–92, Chandler 5–84, Muncie 3–49, Winslow 2–18, Brooks 1–9
CLE: Newsome 10–140, Logan 5–71, Feacher 3–44, Pruitt 9–43, White 4–31, C. Miller 1–5, Oden 1–4

Sunday, December 12
Cincinnati Bengals 23, Browns 10
Riverfront Stadium (54,305)
White jerseys/orange pants

For the fourth straight week, the Cleveland offense failed to reach the end zone in the first half, and the Browns dug a hole they could not pull themselves out of, losing their third straight game. Moving to 5–1, the Bengals benefited from a myriad of Browns' mistakes, including four Cleveland turnovers and five Cincinnati first downs as a result of Browns' penalties. Still, the Browns' defense kept the team in the game, narrowing a 14–3 halftime deficit to four points when DB Clinton Burrell returned an interception 14 yards for the Browns' only touchdown four minutes into the third quarter. Down 17–10 in the fourth quarter, the Browns had two chances to tie the game but saw a pair of promising drives end with turnovers, including a Mike Pruitt fumble at the Bengals' 6. For the second straight game, Ozzie Newsome caught 10 passes, this time for 88 yards. The defense, which held the Bengals to a modest 256 total yards, was led by newly acquired lineman Bob Golic, who replaced injured Henry Bradley and collected seven tackles and the first two sacks of his NFL career.

Record: 2–4

	1	2	3	4		
Browns	0	3	7	0	=	10
Bengals	0	14	3	6	=	23

CIN-Johnson 3-yd. run (Breech kick)
CIN-Anderson 1-yd. run (Breech kick)
CLE-Bahr 29-yd. FG
CLE-Burrell 14-yd. interception return (Bahr kick)
CIN-Breech 44-yd. FG
CIN-Breech 21-yd. FG
CIN-Breech 36-yd. FG

Passing
CLE: Sipe 13–18–126 0 TD 1 INT, McDonald 5–13–54 0 TD 2 INT
CIN: Anderson 18–28–183 0 TD 1 INT

Rushing
CLE: M. Pruitt 13–40, Hall 2–14, Sipe 2–7, White 1–3, Cox 1–0
CIN: Johnson 19–54, Alexander 8–27, Anderson 7–24, Harris 1-(-8)

Receiving
CLE: Newsome 10–88, Logan 2–41, White 3–29, M. Pruitt 3–22
CIN: Collinsworth 6–64, Ross 4–49, Johnson 4–40, Curtis 2–17, Griffin 2–13

Sunday, December 19
Browns 10, Pittsburgh Steelers 9
Cleveland Stadium (67,139)
Brown jerseys/orange pants

On another rainy, muddy Sunday in Cleveland, the Browns' offense sputtered, but the defense responded with a dominant performance to lead the home team to a narrow victory and snap its losing streak. Looking to provide a spark for the offense, Sam Rutigliano gave Paul McDonald his first career start in place of Brian Sipe at quarterback, ending Sipe's string of 70 consecutive starts. Though sacked six times, McDonald was effective in adverse conditions, particularly in the absence of any type of running attack (just 38 yards on 27 carries). The game was won by the Cleveland defense, led by DB Hanford Dixon, who picked off three Terry Bradshaw passes—the first interceptions of Dixon's career—while adding two forced fumbles and a sack. The Browns surged ahead 10–7 on a one-yard plunge by RB Johnny Davis with a minute remaining in the third quarter following a 16-yard Pittsburgh punt from the end zone. The Browns then halted three of four Steelers' drives in the final quarter with interceptions and hung on for a win that kept their playoff hopes alive. The game marked the first time in 20 years a Browns-Steelers game in Cleveland didn't sell out.

Record: 3–4

	1	2	3	4		
Steelers	0	7	0	2	=	9
Browns	3	0	7	0	=	10

CLE-Bahr 44-yd. FG
PIT-Stallworth 6-yd. pass from Bradshaw (Anderson kick)
CLE-Davis 1-yd. run (Bahr kick)
PIT-Safety: Cox ran out of end zone

Passing
PIT: Bradshaw 12–39–144 1 TD 4 INT
CLE: McDonald 19–40–227 0 TD 1 INT

Rushing
PIT: Harris 14–65, Pollard 7–30, Davis 2–2, Hawthorne 2–1
CLE: C. Miller 7–20, M. Pruitt 6–17, White 7–16, Davis 2–1, McDonald 4-(-5), Cox 1-(-11)

Receiving
PIT: Smith 4–74, Cunningham 3–33, Harris 3–24, Pollard 1–7, Stallworth 1–6
CLE: Walker 4–57, Logan 4–52, Newsome 4–42, White 3–37, Feacher 2–25, Fulton 1–9, M. Pruitt 1–5

Sunday, December 26
Browns 20, Houston Oilers 14
Houston Astrodome (36,559)
Brown jerseys/orange pants

On the day after Christmas, the Oilers gift-wrapped a critical victory for the Browns as they fought for a spot in the expanded playoff tournament. Though just 1–6 going in, the Oilers had the better of play early and were poised to take a 14–3 lead midway through the second quarter before RB Earl Campbell fumbled at the Cleveland 1, and Clinton Burrell recovered for the Browns. The momentum of the game then turned when Cleveland drove 96 yards for the go-ahead touchdown on a 56-yard scoring pass from Paul McDonald to WR Dave Logan down the left sideline. The Oilers rebounded to take a 14–10 lead into the fourth quarter and were in position to milk the clock, leading by a point with just over six minutes to play. But Campbell couldn't handle a pitchout, and Burrell again recovered, this time at the Houston 1, where RB Charles White leapt into the end zone on the next play to put the Browns ahead for good with 5:36 remaining. The Browns secured victory when DB Judson Flint made an acrobatic interception at the Cleveland 37 with 1:26 left—Houston's sixth turnover of the afternoon.
Record: 4–4

	1	2	3	4		
Browns	0	10	0	10	=	20
Oilers	7	0	7	0	=	14

HOU-Renfro 8-yd. pass from Nielsen (Kempf kick)
CLE-Bahr 18-yd. FG
CLE-Logan 56-yd. pass from McDonald (Bahr kick)
HOU-Craft 3-yd. run (Kempf kick)
CLE-Bahr 24-yd. FG
CLE-White 1-yd. run (Bahr kick)

Passing
CLE: McDonald 18–34–248 1 TD 0 INT
HOU: Nielsen 18–33–266 1 TD 3 INT, Manning 1–4–5 0 TD 1 INT

Rushing
CLE: M. Pruitt 27–88, White 10–34, McDonald 2-(-11)
HOU: Campbell 17–43, Manning 2–19, Edwards 3–13, Craft 2–9, Allen 1–9, Armstrong 3–7, Nielsen 3–5

Receiving
CLE: Logan 4–83, Feacher 4–68, Newsome 3–46, White 4–36, M. Pruitt 2–12, Walker 1–3
HOU: Bailey 7–97, Casper 3–64, Campbell 1–46, Edwards 2–27, Craft 3–20, Armstrong 2–9, Renfro 1–8

Sunday, January 2
Pittsburgh Steelers 37, Browns 21
Three Rivers Stadium (52,312)
White jerseys/orange pants

Though they suffered their thirteenth consecutive disheartening defeat in Three Rivers Stadium, by sunset the Browns still managed to secure a playoff spot—an appropriate end to a bizarre regular season. Though they were completely out-played for much of the game and coughed up six turnovers, the Browns still had a chance to win with five minutes to play after they'd narrowed a 20-point fourth-quarter Pittsburgh lead to six on a pair of Paul McDonald touchdown passes. But with the game in the balance, Terry Bradshaw hit WR Lynn Swann with a 60-yard pass on third-and-11 to set up a short field goal with 2:39 to play to push the lead to nine point. A late interception thrown by McDonald, who posted his first career 300-yard game, led to a final Pittsburgh touchdown. Ozzie Newsome topped the 100-yard receiving mark for the third time in the brief season, as did Ricky Feacher for the first time in his career. In a dramatic contrast from their meeting two weeks earlier, the Steelers had their way with the Cleveland defense, rolling up 521 total yards. But the sting of the defeat was softened when word came in from Foxboro that the Patriots had defeated the Buffalo Bills, making the Browns (along with the Detroit Lions at the same time) the first team in NFL history to qualify for the playoffs with a losing record.
Record: 4–5

	1	2	3	4		
Browns	0	7	0	14	=	21
Steelers	7	6	7	17	=	37

PIT-Pinney 3-yd. pass from Bradshaw (Anderson kick)
CLE-Feacher 1-yd. pass from McDonald (Bahr kick)
PIT-Rodgers 18-yd. blocked punt return (run failed)

PIT-Harris 6-yd. run (Anderson kick)
PIT-Smith 38-yd. pass from Bradshaw (Anderson kick)
CLE-Logan 8-yd. pass from McDonald (Bahr kick)
CLE-Feacher 12-yd. pass from McDonald (Bahr kick)
PIT-Anderson 34-yd. FG
PIT-Abercrombie 1-yd. run (Anderson kick)

Passing
CLE: McDonald 22–47–313 3 TD 4 INT
PIT: Bradshaw 14–24–269 2 TD 2 INT

Rushing
CLE: M. Pruitt 11–30, White 5–13, C. Miller 1–4, Davis 2–2, McDonald 1–3
PIT: Harris 23–120, Abercrombie 10–73, Swann 1–25, Davis 7–22, Pollard 7–22, Bradshaw 1-(-1)

Receiving
CLE: Newsome 9–123, Feacher 7–109, Logan 3–39, Walker 1–23, M. Pruitt 1–13, White 1–6
PIT: Swann 5–114, Smith 2–76, Stallworth 3–44, Harris 3–32, Pinney 1–3

AFC First-Round Playoff
Saturday, January 8
Los Angeles Raiders 27, Browns 10

Los Angeles Memorial Coliseum (56,555)
White jerseys/orange pants

Going in, it promised to be the wildest weekend in NFL postseason history. In two days, 16 teams—including two of which failed to win more games than they lost during the abbreviated regular season—would play in eight playoff games.

Amid this loopy setup, the Browns jetted across the country to face the top-seeded Los Angeles Raiders and former teammates Greg Pruitt and Lyle Alzado. Yet an ominous tone was set on the flight west when Art Modell collapsed and lost consciousness for 30 seconds, sending a chill through the plane. Modell was treated and revived after what was later determined to be a reaction to blood-pressure medication he was taking.

After an up-and-down, somewhat unpredictable season, the Browns' first road postseason game in 10 years unfolded exactly the way almost everyone expected. The Raiders completed a 64-yard pass on their first play from scrimmage and controlled the game from that point forward, though the Browns hung around for nearly three quarters.

Two interceptions of Los Angeles QB Jim Plunkett thwarted early Raider drives, and Matt Bahr tied an NFL playoff record with a 52-yard field goal early in the second quarter. Then, Paul McDonald, making the only postseason appearance of his career, completed a 43-yard touchdown bomb to Ricky Feacher with two minutes left in the first half to tie the game at 10. Though they looked like the better team throughout the first half, the Raiders led just 13–10 at the intermission.

And the Browns threatened to surge ahead on the first possession of the third quarter when they drove to the Raiders' 14, but former ally Alzado stripped Charles White on a carry up the middle and the Raiders recovered. Twelve plays later, rookie RB Marcus Allen capped an 89-yard drive with a three-yard touchdown run to make it 20–10. After forcing a Cleveland punt, the Raiders, who would tally 510 total yards on the day, put the game out of reach with another touchdown with 12 minutes remaining.

Though several Browns put forth admirable individual efforts—including Ricky Feacher, who posted the finest day of his career with 124 receiving yards—they simply did not have the horses to keep up with the mighty Raiders, who would fall to the New York Jets in a stunning upset in the divisional playoff the following week.

	1	2	3	4		
Browns	0	10	0	0	=	10
Raiders	3	10	7	7	=	27

LA-Bahr 27-yd. FG
CLE-Bahr 52-yd. FG
LA-Allen 2-yd. run (Bahr kick)
CLE-Feacher 43-yd. pass from McDonald (Bahr kick)
LA-Bahr 37-yd. FG
LA-Allen 3-yd. run (Bahr kick)
LA-Hawkins 1-yd. run (Bahr kick)

Passing
CLE: McDonald 18–37–281 1 TD 0 INT
LA: Plunkett 24–37–386 0 TD 2 INT

Rushing
CLE: White 9–30, M. Pruitt 8–19, McDonald 1–7
LA: Allen 17–72, King 7–30, G. Pruitt 3–15, Hawkins 4–10, Plunkett 2–10, Willis 3–3

Receiving
CLE: Feacher 4–124, Newsome 4–51, Walker 4–47, Logan 1–27, M. Pruitt 3–17, White 2–15
LA: Branch 5–121, Christensen 6–93, Allen 6–75, Barnwell 2–38, Ramsey 1–25, G. Pruitt 2–14, King 1–11, Hawkins 1–9

1983

Sunday, September 4
Minnesota Vikings 27, Browns 21
Cleveland Stadium (70,087)
White jerseys/orange pants

An inspired fourth-quarter rally couldn't overcome a sluggish first-half performance as the Browns dropped their home opener for the fourth straight year. After permitting the Vikings to collect more than 250 yards of offense and dominate Cleveland in the first half, the struggling Browns fell behind by 10 at the intermission, then trailed 27–14 going into the fourth quarter. With 2:35 remaining, QB Brian Sipe hit WR Willis Adams for a 23-yard score—Sipe's third touchdown pass of the day—to cut the margin to six, then with just over a minute left, the Vikings decided to go for it on fourth-and-one at their own 41. The Browns' defense held and suddenly the home team was in a position to steal a victory. But two plays later, Sipe was intercepted—the Browns' fourth turnover—to end the comeback.

Record: 0–1

	1	2	3	4		
Vikings	7	10	10	0	=	27
Browns	0	7	7	7	=	21

MIN-Brown 1-yd. run (Ricardo kick)
MIN-Ricardo 23-yd. FG
CLE-Feacher 18-yd. pass from Sipe (Bahr kick)
MIN-Brown 5-yd. run (Ricardo kick)
CLE-M. Pruitt 6-yd. pass from Sipe (Bahr kick)
MIN-Brown 10-yd. pass from Kramer (Ricardo kick)
MIN-Ricardo 38-yd. FG
CLE-Adams 23-yd. pass from Sipe (Bahr kick)

Passing
MIN: Kramer 22–33–198 1 TD 1 INT
CLE: Sipe 20–33–223 3 TD 2 INT, McDonald 0–1–0 0 TD 1 INT

Rushing
MIN: Brown 19–74, Nelson 10–70, LeCount 1–40, Galbreath 2–7, Young 1–3, Kramer 6-(-5)
CLE: M. Pruitt 17–94, Davis 3–12, Sipe 3–7, Walker 1–3

Receiving
MIN: Brown 6–63, White 4–43, Bruer 3–19, Nelson 2–19, Young 2–16, LeCount 2–15, Lewis 1–12, Galbreath 1–7, Jones 1–4
CLE: Logan 4–83, Feacher 3–50, Newsome 5–35, Jones 3–25, Adams 1–23, M. Pruitt 3–8, Davis 1-(-1)

Sunday, September 11
Browns 31, Detroit Lions 26
Pontiac Silverdome (60,095)
White jerseys/orange pants

The Browns survived a wild fourth quarter to prevail in an offensive shootout in Detroit and pick up their first win over the Lions in 19 years and their only victory ever in the Motor City. Brian Sipe threw four touchdown passes—the last of which gave him 135 for his career and made him the Browns' all-time leader—to give the Browns a 28–17 lead midway through the final period. But Detroit cut the lead to two points minutes later following a touchdown and a safety when Sipe was pinned in the end zone. A critical interception by Browns' DB Mike Whitwell set up a Matt Bahr field goal to make it 31–26 with two minutes to play, but Detroit QB Gary Danielson, who'd replaced Eric Hipple in the fourth quarter, drove the Lions to the Cleveland 38 with a minute left. The Browns' defense, which had permitted the Lions to roll up 435 total yards, finally held, stopping Detroit on downs to secure the victory. RB Mike Pruitt propelled the Cleveland offense with 137 yards on 24 carries, though the Browns were crippled by 16 penalties totaling 140 yards. Five Detroit turnovers balanced the scales, leading to 17 Cleveland points.

Record: 1–1

	1	2	3	4		
Browns	7	7	7	10	=	31
Lions	7	7	3	9	=	26

DET-Thompson 80-yd. pass from Hipple (Murray kick)
CLE-Feacher 42-yd. pass from Sipe (Bahr kick)
CLE-M. Pruitt 6-yd. pass from Sipe (Bahr kick)
DET-Norris 5-yd. pass from Hipple (Murray kick)
DET-Murray 43-yd. FG
CLE-Newsome 15-yd. pass from Sipe (Bahr kick)
CLE-Logan 22-yd. pass from Sipe (Bahr kick)

DET-Norris 15-yd. pass from Danielson (Murray kick)
DET-Safety: English tackled Sipe in end zone
CLE-Bahr 25-yd. FG

Passing
CLE: Sipe 18–29–234 4 TD 0 INT
DET: Hipple 15–25–233 1 TD 2 INT, Danielson 10–17–126 1 TD 1 INT

Rushing
CLE: M. Pruitt 24–137, Davis 5–20, Sipe 5–3
DET: Sims 11–54, Jones 10–44, Thompson 1–5, Bussey 1–4, Hipple 1–0, Danielson 1-(-1)

Receiving
CLE: Feacher 3–66, Holt 3–59, Walker 5–35, Logan 2–35, Newsome 3–33, M. Pruitt 1–6, Adams 1–0
DET: Thompson 8–179, Norris 4–48, Nicholas 3–39, Chadwick 2–33, Sims 4–29, Jones 3–20, Scott 1–11

Thursday, September 15
Browns 17, Cincinnati Bengals 7
Cleveland Stadium (79,700)
Brown jerseys/orange pants

Behind a sterling defensive effort, the Browns treated a massive home crowd to a huge victory over the rival Bengals on a cool Thursday night before a national-television audience. The tone was set in the opening minutes when Cleveland LB Chip Banks intercepted a pass by Cincinnati QB Ken Anderson to thwart a Bengals' scoring threat, then TE Ozzie Newsome made an amazing diving catch for a 19-yard touchdown to cap the ensuing possession. With the Cleveland defense containing the Bengals through the second half, the Browns stretched a three-point halftime lead to 10 on a Mike Pruitt touchdown, then put the game away when DB Clarence Scott picked off Anderson in the end zone with 1:35 remaining.
Record: 2–1

	1	2	3	4		
Bengals	0	7	0	0	=	7
Browns	7	3	7	0	=	17

CLE-Newsome 19-yd. pass from Sipe (Bahr kick)
CLE-Bahr 19-yd. FG
CIN-Kinnebrew 1-yd. run (Breech kick)
CLE-M. Pruitt 1-yd. run (Bahr kick)

Passing
CIN: Anderson 26–40–207 0 TD 2 INT
CLE: Sipe 21–31–201 1 TD 2 INT, Walker 1–1–25 0 TD 0 INT

Rushing
CIN: Alexander 11–46, Anderson 4–21, Kinnebrew 4–19, Tate 2–16
CLE: M. Pruitt 25–83, Walker 1–2, Davis 1–1, Sipe 1-(-2)

Receiving
CIN: Collinsworth 6–83, Alexander 6–33, Kreider 3–33, Ross 3–18, Verser 1–18, Curtis 2–13, Tate 3–5, Kinnebrew 2–4
CLE: Newsome 5–50, Feacher 2–40, Holt 2–39, Jones 3–36, M. Pruitt 5–16, Adams 1–16, Walker 2–15, Logan 1–10, Davis 1–4

Sunday, September 25
Browns 30, San Diego Chargers 24 (OT)
Jack Murphy Stadium (49,482)
Brown jerseys/orange pants

In what would prove to be the most exciting game of the season, the Browns prevailed in an aerial battle that saw the teams combine for more than 800 yards of offense and 50 first downs. Both Brian Sipe (327) and Dan Fouts (351) topped 300 yards passing and threw for three touchdowns. Fouts's last two, both to WR Wes Chandler in a six-minute period of the third quarter, turned an 11-point deficit into a three-point San Diego lead that persevered into the final moments of the fourth quarter. With time running out, Sipe guided the Browns deep into Chargers' territory and Matt Bahr tied the contest at 24 with a 32-yard field goal with 18 seconds remaining. Then, on the first possession of overtime, the Browns reached midfield when Sipe hit TE Harry Holt over the middle at the San Diego 25, and Holt broke free to rumble into the end zone for the game-winning touchdown. In a game full of heroes, WR Dave Logan turned in the final 100-yard game of his career, snagging eight receptions for 121 yards. The win propelled the Browns into sole possession of first place in the AFC Central.
Record: 3–1

	1	2	3	4	OT		
Browns	7	7	7	3	6	=	30
Chargers	3	7	14	0	0	=	24

SD-Benirschke 37-yd. FG
CLE-M. Pruitt 1-yd. run (Bahr kick)
CLE-Newsome 11-yd. pass from Sipe (Bahr kick)
SD-Sievers 15-yd. pass from Fouts (Benirschke kick)
CLE-Jones 27-yd. pass from Sipe (Bahr kick)
SD-Chandler 25-yd. pass from Fouts (Benirschke kick)
SD-Chandler 34-yd. pass from Fouts (Benirschke kick)
CLE-Bahr 32-yd. FG
CLE-Holt 48-yd. pass from Sipe (no kick)

Passing
CLE: Sipe 27–44–327 3 TD 0 INT, Walker 0–1–0 0 TD 1 INT
SD: Fouts 24–38–351 3 TD 0 INT

Rushing
CLE: M. Pruitt 24–63, Walker 3–19, Jones 1–19, Hall 1–2
SD: Muncie 18–60, Brooks 7–12, Fouts 1-(-2)

Receiving
CLE: Logan 8–121, Newsome 7–65, Holt 2–53, Jones 2–39, M. Pruitt 5–21, Adams 1–17, Walker 2–11
SD: Chandler 6–134, Winslow 8–108, Joiner 3–45, Muncie 5–42, Sievers 1–15, Brooks 1–7

Sunday, October 2
Seattle Seahawks 24, Browns 9
Cleveland Stadium (75,446)
White jerseys/orange pants

Playing sloppy football all afternoon, the Browns gift-wrapped a victory for Seattle in a loss that would prove to haunt the team at season's end. Committing four turnovers and 10 penalties, the Browns rolled up more than 400 total yards and outgained Seattle by nearly 150 yet played from behind all day. Despite the mistakes, the Browns were still in position to win when RB Boyce Green scored his first NFL touchdown and pulled the Browns within one point with 12 minutes remaining. After Matt Bahr missed the extra point that would have tied the game (his first miss in 78 point-after attempts), Seattle made it 17–9 after recovering a Brian Sipe fumble at the Cleveland 15 with just over eight minutes play. The Browns' last chance ended in disaster when a fourth-down Sipe screen pass was picked off by Seattle DE Jacob Green and returned 73 yards for a touchdown with 1:50 left. Combined with a Sipe interception that set up Seattle's first touchdown in the opening minutes of the third quarter, the Seahawks tallied 21 of their 24 points off Cleveland turnovers.
Record: 3–2

	1	2	3	4		
Seahawks	3	0	7	14	=	24
Browns	0	3	0	6	=	9

SEA-Johnson 24-yd. FG
CLE-Bahr 40-yd. FG
SEA-Warner 1-yd. run (Johnson kick)
CLE-Green 5-yd. pass from Sipe (kick failed)
SEA-Warner 1-yd. run (Johnson kick)
SEA-Green 73-yd. interception return (Johnson kick)

Passing
SEA: Zorn 11–17–122 0 TD 1 INT
CLE: Sipe 25–40–310 1 TD 3 INT

Rushing
SEA: Warner 24–94, Hughes 5–28, Zorn 6–15
CLE: M. Pruitt 24–107, Sipe 2–13, Holt 2–5

Receiving
SEA: Walker 1–32, Largent 2–30, Warner 5–28, Young 1–18, Metzelaars 1–11, Hughes 1–3
CLE: Holt 6–77, Adams 4–73, Newsome 5–55, Logan 3–44, M. Pruitt 3–30, Jones 2–23, Green 1–5, Walker 1–3

Sunday, October 9
Browns 10, New York Jets 7
Cleveland Stadium (78,235)
White jerseys/orange pants

On a blustery day, the Cleveland offensive line contained the heralded "New York Sack Exchange," and a stalwart defense gave the Browns a chance to win in the final minute. While the Cleveland running game was held in check, including just six yards from Mike Pruitt, Brian Sipe threw for 294 yards to spark the Browns' offense. A 7–0 lead following a Sipe-to-WR Bobby Jones touchdown pass in the second quarter held up until the waning moments of the fourth quarter, when the Jets drove 83 yards and tied the game with 1:28 remaining. Taking over at their own 35, the Browns quickly zipped into New York territory with long Sipe completions to Harry Holt and Dave Logan to set up a game-winning 44-yard field goal by Matt Bahr as time expired. LB Tom Cousineau led a ferocious defensive charge, racking up 15 tackles, an interception, and a fumble recovery in the finest game of his career. Marring the victory somewhat was the loss of LB Dick Ambrose, who left the game with a broken ankle and, despite valiant comeback attempts each of the next two seasons, would never play again.
Record: 4–2

	1	2	3	4		
Jets	0	0	0	7	=	7
Browns	0	7	0	3	=	10

CLE-Jones 32-yd. pass from Sipe (Bahr kick)
NYJ-Harper 15-yd. pass from Todd (Leahy kick)
CLE-Bahr 44-yd. FG

Passing
NYJ: Todd 22–31–197 1 TD 1 INT
CLE: Sipe 21–34–294 1 TD 2 INT, McDonald 1–2–3 0 TD 0 INT

Rushing
NYJ: Crutchfield 15–81, Harper 6–32, Jones 1–6, Todd 3–4, Augustyniak 2–1
CLE: Green 16–48, Sipe 2–11, M. Pruitt 6–6, Davis 1–1

Receiving
NYJ: Harper 7–58, Jones 2–37, Walker 3–32, Shuler 2–17, Gaffney 2–15, Dierking 2–12, Barkum 1–11, Augustyniak 2–10, Crutchfield 1–5
CLE: Holt 4–75, Jones 5–68, Logan 3–66, Newsome 5–57, Adams 1–16, Green 3–8, Hall 1–7

Sunday, October 16
Pittsburgh Steelers 44, Browns 17
Three Rivers Stadium (59,263)
White jerseys/orange pants

The Three Rivers jinx, now reaching 14 years, plummeted to a new level of frustration as the Steelers sprinted to a 17–0 lead in the first six minutes of the game and pounded the Browns from start to finish in a battle for first place in the AFC Central. Brian Sipe threw for 310 yards and guided the Browns to a whopping 449 yards of offense but threw six interceptions to match a team record he'd set against the Steelers two years before, including one on each of Cleveland's first three possessions. Pittsburgh LB Mike Merriweather returned one interception 31 yards for a score, while Steelers' DB Greg Best later scooped up a fumble and rumbled 94 yards for an exclamation-point touchdown in the fourth quarter. The lone bright spot for the Browns was RB Boyce Green, who rushed for 137 yards on 28 carries with a pair of touchdowns in his first pro start, becoming the first Cleveland runner to top the century mark in Pittsburgh in six years. Ozzie Newsome added 103 yards on nine catches.
Record: 4–3

	1	2	3	4		
Browns	3	7	7	0	=	17
Steelers	20	14	0	10	=	44

PIT-Anderson 18-yd. FG
PIT-Abercrombie 1-yd. run (Anderson kick)
PIT-Merriweather 31-yd. interception return (Anderson kick)
CLE-Bahr 27-yd. FG
PIT-Anderson 29-yd. FG
CLE-Green 23-yd. run (Bahr kick)
PIT-Harris 1-yd. run (Anderson kick)
PIT-Sweeney 40-yd. pass from Stoudt (Anderson kick)
CLE-Green 1-yd. run (Bahr kick)
PIT-Anderson 26-yd. FG
PIT-Best 94-yd. fumble return (Anderson kick)

Passing
CLE: Sipe 27–49–310 0 TD 6 INT
PIT: Stoudt 14–18–194 1 TD 0 INT

Rushing
CLE: Green 28–137, Walker 3–22
PIT: Abercrombie 15–65, Harris 15–38, Stoudt 5–28, Pollard 4–15

Receiving
CLE: Newsome 9–103, Jones 6–88, Green 5–35, Logan 1–22, Walker 1–21, Hall 2–17, Davis 2–12, Stracka 1–12
PIT: Sweeney 4–69, Capers 1–36, Harris 3–28, Abercrombie 3–27, Cunningham 2–21, Garrity 1–13

Sunday, October 23
Cincinnati Bengals 28, Browns 21
Riverfront Stadium (50,047)
Brown jerseys/orange pants

Despite facing the floundering 1–6 Bengals without their starting quarterback, the Browns were unable to hold a fourth-quarter lead and lost a winnable game that dropped them two games back of the Steelers in the division race at the season's midpoint. After the Browns took a 14–7 halftime lead, the Bengals responded each time Cleveland was poised to build a comfortable advantage, tying the contest at 14 and then again at 21 with 12 minutes to play. The winning points were provided by the Cincinnati defense when veteran DB Ken Riley, playing in his final season, returned an interception 42 yards for a touchdown with 9:23 remaining—the third interception return for a touchdown the Browns had allowed in four weeks. The

Browns responded with a drive into Bengals' territory, but a fake field-goal attempt from the Cincy 24 was snuffed out, and the lead remained seven points. Cleveland was forced to punt on its final possession, and Bengals' backup QB Turk Schonert, in for injured Ken Anderson, ran out the clock to drop the Browns to .500.

Record: 4–4

	1	2	3	4		
Browns	0	14	7	0	=	21
Bengals	0	7	7	14	=	28

CIN-Johnson 1-yd. run (Breech kick)
CLE-Newsome 5-yd. pass from Sipe (Bahr kick)
CLE-Jones 8-yd. pass from Sipe (Bahr kick)
CIN-Schonert 1-yd. run (Breech kick)
CLE-Newsome 17-yd. pass from Sipe (Bahr kick)
CIN-Alexander 4-yd. run (Breech kick)
CIN-Riley 42-yd. interception return (Breech kick)

Passing
CLE: Sipe 19–35–225 3 TD 2 INT, McDonald 1–1-(-5) 0 TD 0 INT
CIN: Schonert 16–20–163 0 TD 0 INT

Rushing
CLE: Green 6–31, M. Pruitt 12–28, Walker 1–8, Sipe 1–7
CIN: Johnson 14–46, Schonert 10–36, Alexander 12–35, Tate 3–13, Wilson 3–4

Receiving
CLE: Newsome 7–69, Walker 4–57, Adams 1–38, Jones 3–37, Holt 2–14, Green 3–5
CIN: Curtis 3–60, Ross 1–20, Wilson 3–19, Holman 2–15, Collinsworth 2–14, Kreider 2–14, Harris 1–8, Tate 1–8, Alexander 1–5

Sunday, October 30
Browns 25, Houston Oilers 19 (OT)
Cleveland Stadium (66,955)
Brown jerseys/orange pants

Thanks to some special-teams trickery and late heroics, the Browns avoided a disastrous defeat to the 0–8 Oilers on a chilly afternoon in Cleveland. With Brian Sipe sidelined with a sore arm, Paul McDonald got his first start of the season, but the offense struggled throughout the first half. Trailing 10–3 in the final minute of the second quarter, the Browns pulled off a fake field goal and McDonald lofted a pass to LT Doug Dieken, an eligible receiver on the play, who caught it and rumbled into the end zone for the tying touchdown. Despite a fiery halftime speech from Sam Rutigliano, the Browns weren't much better in the second half, falling behind 19–13 late in the third period, though they'd caught a break when Houston missed the extra point after its second touchdown. Still trailing late in the game, the Browns tied it with 49 seconds remaining on Matt Bahr's fourth field goal of the game and sent the contest to overtime. On the Oilers' second possession, Browns' DB Mike Whitwell intercepted QB Gifford Nielsen at the Houston 35 and returned it to the 20. On the next play, Boyce Green burst through the line, broke two tackles, and carried two more defenders the final five yards into the end zone for the game-winning touchdown. Green finished with 107 yards on just 14 carries as the Oilers lost their fifteenth straight game.

Record: 5–4

	1	2	3	4	OT		
Oilers	7	3	9	0	0	=	19
Browns	3	7	3	6	6	=	25

CLE-Bahr 37-yd. FG
HOU-Renfro 19-yd. pass from Nielsen (Kempf kick)
HOU-Kempf 19-yd. FG
CLE-Dieken 14-yd. pass from McDonald (Bahr kick)
HOU-Renfro 38-yd. pass from Nielsen (kick failed)
CLE-Bahr 37-yd. FG
HOU-Kempf 24-yd. FG
CLE-Bahr 29-yd. FG
CLE-Bahr 30-yd. FG
CLE-Green 20-yd. run

Passing
HOU: Nielsen 11–27–155 2 TD 1 INT
CLE: McDonald 19–41–209 1 TD 2 INT

Rushing
HOU: Moriarty 15–61, Craft 12–38, Nielsen 5–15, Walls 1–7, Brown 2-(-1)
CLE: Green 14–107, M. Pruitt 18–66, Walker 2–8, McDonald 2–7

Receiving
HOU: Renfro 4–73, Smith 4–44, Dressel 2–31, McCloskey 1–7
CLE: Logan 3–56, Newsome 4–41, Green 4–40, Jones 2–31, Dieken 1–14, Walker 1–13, Holt 1–6, Davis 1–5, M. Pruitt 2–3

Sunday, November 6
Green Bay Packers 35, Browns 21
Milwaukee County Coliseum (54,089)
White jerseys/orange pants

Despite facing the NFL's worst defense and accumulating 456 yards, the Browns could manage only two offensive touchdowns as they failed to capitalize on three golden scoring opportunities and committed four turnovers in a frustrating defeat. Two of the Cleveland turnovers came inside the Green Bay 15, and another chance for points evaporated on a bad snap on a field-goal attempt. With the Browns consistently shooting themselves in the foot, the Packers took a 28–7 lead into the fourth quarter, then recovered the ensuing onside kick after the Browns cut the lead to seven points with just over a minute to play following a pair of touchdown passes by Brian Sipe, who returned to action to replace a struggling Paul McDonald. Green Bay then tacked on a final touchdown to make the final margin a comfortable 14 points. Cleveland's lone highlight of the first half came when NT Bob Golic corralled a tipped Lynn Dickey pass and rumbled into the end zone from the Packers' 7 for the only interception and only touchdown of his career. With the loss, the Browns dropped back to .500 and were now three games back of the Steelers in the division race.

Record: 5 5

	1	2	3	4		
Browns	7	0	0	14	=	21
Packers	7	14	7	7	=	35

GB-Jefferson 18-yd. pass from Dickey (Stenerud kick)
CLE-Golic 7-yd. interception return (Bahr kick)
GB-Coffman 4-yd. pass from Dickey (Stenerud kick)
GB-Lewis 10-yd. pass from Dickey (Stenerud kick)
GB-Ellis 2-yd. pass from Dickey (Stenerud kick)
CLE-Jones 20-yd. pass from Sipe (Bahr kick)
CLE-Walker 19-yd. pass from Sipe (Bahir kick)
GB-Ellis 25-yd. run (Stenerud kick)

Passing
CLE: Sipe 16–27–231 2 TD 1 INT, McDonald 11–23–134 0 TD 1 INT
GB: Dickey 20–33–228 4 TD 3 INT

Rushing
CLE: M. Pruitt 16–73, Walker 2–19, Green 4–14, McDonald 1–10, Sipe 2–3
GB: Ellis 17–86, Clark 12–50, Meade 5–18, Huckleby 3–3, Dickey 2–1, Lofton 1-(-4)

Receiving
CLE: Jones 4–93, Newsome 8–90, Logan 4–73, Walker 4–41, M. Pruitt 5–40, Adams 1–18, Green 1–10
GB: Jefferson 7–102, Lofton 2–64, Clark 3–20, Epps 1–12, Lewis 1–10, Coffman 2–9, Meade 1–6, Ellis 3–5

Sunday, November 13
Browns 20, Tampa Bay Buccaneers 0
Cleveland Stadium (56,091)
Brown jerseys/orange pants

Posting their first shutout in nine years, the Browns picked up a much-needed victory over the 1–9 Buccaneers before a lethargic crowd at the Stadium on a sunshiny, crisp November afternoon. The Browns grabbed an early 10–0 lead, then kept things close to the vest for the remainder of the contest as the Cleveland defense handled the NFL's worst offense. The Browns controlled Tampa Bay RB James Wilder, holding him to 62 yards on the ground a week after he rolled up 219 against Minnesota. Leading 13–0, the Browns milked more than seven minutes off the clock with a final fourth-quarter drive that ended with Mike Pruitt's second touchdown of the day.

Record: 6–5

	1	2	3	4		
Buccaneers	0	0	0	0	=	0
Browns	10	0	3	7	=	20

CLE-Bahr 27-yd. FG
CLE-M. Pruitt 1-yd. run (Bahr kick)
CLE-Bahr 42-yd. FG
CLE-M. Pruitt 1-yd. run (Bahr kick)

Passing
TB: Thompson 17–31–182 0 TD 0 INT
CLE: Sipe 14–26–174 0 TD 0 INT

Rushing
TB: Wilder 19–62, Thompson 1–4, Carter 1–0
CLE: M. Pruitt 23–60, Green 6–23, Sipe 4–12, Davis 2–5, Walker 2–4, Adams 1–2, Belk (1-(-5)

Receiving
TB: House 5–110, Bell 4–34, Carter 2–14, Wilder 4–10, Carver 1–10, Armstrong 1–4
CLE: Newsome 3–81, M. Pruitt 4–26, Walker 2–25, Adams 2–22, Green 1–8, Logan 1–7, Jones 1–5

Sunday, November 20
Browns 30, New England Patriots 0
Sullivan Stadium (40,987)
White jerseys/orange pants

The Browns collected their most impressive victory of the year on the strength of what Sam Rutigliano called the team's best performance in his tenure as head coach. A ferocious defensive effort notched a second straight shutout—the first back-to-back goose-eggs for the Browns in 32 years—over a Patriots team fighting with the Browns for a playoff spot. New England, leading the league in rushing at 178 yards per game, was held to 190 total yards of offense as the Browns forced five turnovers and collected five sacks in a nearly flawless performance. Chip Banks led the way with a pair of sacks and opened the floodgates in the second quarter when he returned an interception 65 yards for a touchdown. The Browns then gambled with an onside kick on the ensuing kickoff, recovered and stretched the lead to 17–0 on a short Brian Sipe touchdown pass to WR Rocky Belk, then never looked back. While the defense stole the show, and the passing game was unusually quiet, the Browns' running game was powerful, rolling up 176 yards, paced by Mike Pruitt's 136 on 24 carries. DB Hanford Dixon and LB Tom Cousineau each intercepted two passes as the Browns scored 20 points off Patriots' turnovers. The victory reignited the Browns' playoff drive and positioned them in the thick of the race with four games to play.
Record: 7–5

	1	2	3	4		
Browns	3	17	3	7	=	30
Patriots	0	0	0	0	=	0

CLE-Bahr 22-yd. FG
CLE-Banks 65-yd. interception return (Bahr kick)
CLE-Belk 2-yd. pass from Sipe (Bahr kick)
CLE-Bahr 20-yd. FG
CLE-Bahr 20-yd. FG
CLE-M. Pruitt 6-yd. run (Bahr kick)

Passing
CLE: Sipe 9–20–71 1 TD 1 INT
NE: Grogan 9–20–74 0 TD 3 INT, Eason 4–11–34 0 TD 2 INT

Rushing
CLE: M. Pruitt 24–136, Green 10–37, Davis 1–3, Sipe 2–2, Walker 1-(-2)
NE: Collins 10–48, Tatupu 5–23, van Eeghen 3–13, Eason 2–11, Grogan 1–11, Weathers 2–8

Receiving
CLE: Belk 2–41, Green 2–4, Adams 1–9, Feacher 1–5, Holt 1–4, Newsome 1–4, Walker 1–4
NE: Collins 4–35, van Eeghen 4–31, Jones 1–12, Ramsey 1–10, Dawson 1–10, Starring 1–6, Morgan 1–4

Sunday, November 27
Browns 41, Baltimore Colts 23
Cleveland Stadium (65,812)
Brown jerseys/orange pants

The Browns moved into the driver's seat in the AFC wild-card race and pulled within one game of the Steelers in the AFC Central with a comfortable win over the Colts. Brian Sipe, whose sore arm kept him from practicing all week, threw for 313 yards and three touchdowns—all in the first half—as the Browns took control with 28 points in the first two periods, then blew the game open in the third quarter. Rolling up 417 total yards, the offense was firing on all cylinders as Mike Pruitt rushed for 110 yards and a pair of touchdowns. Ozzie Newsome added 108 receiving yards—66 on a second-quarter touchdown—and became the Browns' all-time leader in receptions with 332, surpassing WR Gary Collins. Chip Banks added a sack and another interception as he continued to emerge as one of the defense's most dominating components. It would be the last time the Browns ever played the "Baltimore" Colts.
Record: 8–5

	1	2	3	4		
Colts	3	14	0	6	=	23
Browns	14	14	10	3	=	41

CLE-M. Pruitt 4-yd. run (Bahr kick)
BAL-Allegre 31-yd. FG
CLE-Adams 15-yd. pass from Sipe (Bahr kick)
BAL-McMillan 4-yd. pass from Pagel (Allegre kick)
CLE-Newsome 66-yd. pass from Sipe (Bahr kick)
BAL-McMillan 2-yd. run (Allegre kick)
CLE-Logan 9-yd. pass from Sipe (Bahr kick)
CLE-Bahr 26-yd. FG
CLE-M. Pruitt 2-yd. run (Bahr kick)
BAL-Butler 7-yd. pass from Pagel (kick failed)
CLE-Bahr 27-yd. FG

Passing
BAL: Pagel 15–26–164 2 TD 2 INT
CLE: Sipe 20–33–313 3 TD 0 INT

Rushing
BAL: McMillan 11–50, Dickey 14–38, Pagel 5–38, Williams 6–36, Moore 5–33
CLE: M. Pruitt 24–110, Green 2–0

Receiving
BAL: Porter 4–71, Williams 2–32, McMillan 3–22, Butler 2–14, Sherwin 2–11, Dickey 1–11, Moore 1–3
CLE: Newsome 8–108, Adams 3–86, Logan 3–64, Belk 1–23, Hall 1–9, Holt 1–8, Walker 1–8, M. Pruitt 2–7

Sunday, December 4
Denver Broncos 27, Browns 6
Mile High Stadium (70,912)
White jerseys/orange pants

Facing rookie QB John Elway for the first time, the Browns were flattened by the Broncos and lost a golden opportunity to climb into first place as the Steelers were upset at home by the Bengals. Elway, who'd struggled all season, enjoyed a breakthrough performance, throwing for 284 yards and a pair of touchdowns while leading Denver's twenty-sixth-ranked offense to 411 total yards. A 3–0 Cleveland lead vanished in a disastrous second quarter that saw the Broncos score three touchdowns. While Elway showed his potential, Brian Sipe struggled, throwing three interceptions that led to 17 Denver points, while the Cleveland rushing game was held to just 65 yards. The lone high point came just before the half when Steve Cox set a team record with a 58-yard field goal. The loss pulled the front-running Browns back into the fray of a five-team race for the AFC's two wild-card spots.
Record: 8–6

	1	2	3	4		
Browns	3	3	0	0	=	6
Broncos	0	21	3	3	=	27

CLE-Bahr 47-yd. FG
DEN-Winder 3-yd. run (Karlis kick)
DEN-Sampson 39-yd. pass from Elway (Karlis kick)
DEN-Sampson 49-yd. pass from Elway (Karlis kick)
CLE-Cox 58-yd. FG
DEN-Karlis 20-yd. FG
DEN-Karlis 50-yd. FG

Passing
CLE: Sipe 22–47–231 0 TD 3 INT
DEN: Elway 16–24–284 2 TD 1 INT

Rushing
CLE: Green 4–27, M. Pruitt 11–25, Walker 1–13
DEN: Winder 20–71, Elway 6–18, Willhite 8–15, Myles 3–15, Poole 4–8

Receiving
CLE: Newsome 8–78, Adams 3–56, Walker 4–33, Jones 2–28, Logan 2–14, Belk 1–13, Green 2–9
DEN: Sampson 3–101, Watson 3–47, Egloff 2–37, Myles 2–31, Sawyer 2–28, Poole 3–25, Willhite 1–15

Sunday, December 11
Houston Oilers 34, Browns 27
Houston Astrodome (29,746)
Brown jerseys/orange pants

With a playoff spot hanging in the balance, the Browns suffered a stunning and crushing defeat to the miserable Houston Oilers, who entered the contest with a 1–13 record. Played before the smallest crowd to watch the Browns in nine years, the game was defined by Mike Pruitt, who rolled up great numbers with 153 rushing yards and three touchdowns but lost three fumbles and had a pass bounce off him for an Oilers' interception. Two of Pruitt's fumbles led directly to Houston touchdowns as the Oilers soared to a 24–6 lead late in the second quarter. Yet the Browns bounced back with Pruitt's three touchdowns in an eight-minute stretch to take a 27–24 lead midway through the third quarter. The Oilers surged back into the lead on a long touchdown pass by Cleveland native Oliver Luck with six minutes to play, but the Browns were in Houston territory and poised to tie when Pruitt coughed up his third fumble with 4:37 left. The Browns wouldn't threaten again. With the Steelers clinching the division with a victory the day before, the Browns would need to win the finale over Pittsburgh the following week and get help to secure a playoff spot.
Record: 8–7

	1	2	3	4		
Browns	3	10	14	0	=	27
Oilers	10	14	3	7	=	34

CLE-Bahr 44-yd. FG
HOU-Kempf 40-yd. FG
HOU-Smith 24-yd. pass from Bryant (Kempf kick)
HOU-Campbell 2-yd. run (Kempf kick)
CLE-Bahr 45-yd. FG
HOU-Brown 93-yd. kickoff return (Kempf kick)
CLE-M. Pruitt 2-yd. run (Bahr kick)

CLE-M. Pruitt 1-yd. run (Bahr kick)
CLE-M. Pruitt 4-yd. run (Bahr kick)
HOU-Kempf 35-yd. FG
HOU-Smith 43-yd. pass from Luck (Kempf kick)

Passing
CLE: Sipe 18–26–223 0 TD 1 INT
DEN: Luck 13–24–178 1 TD 0 INT, Bryant 1–1–24 1 TD 0 INT

Rushing
CLE: M. Pruitt 30–153, Green 2–7, Sipe 2–2
HOU: Campbell 32–130, Luck 5–8, Crutchfield 3–7, Smith 1–7

Receiving
CLE: Holt 5–81, Newsome 7–71, Logan 2–32, Jones 1–18, Feacher 1–11, Green 2–10
HOU: Smith 7–150, Bryant 3–20, Campbell 1–9, Dressel 1–8, McCloskey 1–8, Arnold 1–7

Sunday, December 18
Browns 30, Pittsburgh Steelers 17
Cleveland Stadium (72,313)
Brown jerseys/orange pants

In an emotional game that represented the end of an era in team history, the Browns overwhelmed their rivals in a final desperate bid to make the playoffs. But the victory amid snow flurries wasn't enough as the Browns were eliminated when Seattle defeated New England, giving the Seahawks and Denver the two wild-card spots—both teams Cleveland had lost to. The contest also represented the final game of Brian Sipe's NFL career, and he went out in memorable fashion, throwing four touchdown passes and enduring a vicious cheap shot to the head from Steelers' LB Jack Lambert, which led to a brawl along the Cleveland sideline and Lambert's ejection. The Browns' defense closed the books on a breakthrough season, sacking Pittsburgh quarterbacks six times while holding longtime nemesis Franco Harris to 56 yards on 20 carries in his final game against Cleveland. Nine days later, concluding a season-long story line, Sipe signed a contract with the New Jersey Generals of the United States Football League—concluding his 10-year NFL career—and Paul McDonald would be handed the reins of the Cleveland quarterback job.
Record: 9–7

	1	2	3	4		
Steelers	3	7	0	7	=	17
Browns	9	14	7	0	=	30

PIT-Anderson 34-yd. FG
CLE-Belk 64-yd. pass from Sipe (kick failed)
CLE-Bahr 30-yd. FG
CLE-Holt 3-yd. pass from Sipe (Bahr kick)
PIT-Stoudt 3-yd. run (Anderson kick)
CLE-Feacher 4-yd. pass from Sipe (Bahr kick)
CLE-Holt 1-yd. pass from Sipe (Bahr kick)
PIT-Harris 2-yd. pass from Malone (Anderson kick)

Passing
PIT: Malone 7–12–108 1 TD 1 INT, Stoudt 7–21–94 0 TD 1 INT
CLE: Sipe 14–22–199 4 TD 0 INT

Rushing
PIT: Harris 20–56, Abercrombie 6–40, Stoudt 4–29, Pollard 2–4
CLE: Green 12–66, M. Pruitt 15–43, Walker 2–4, Holt 1–3, Sipe 2-(-2)

Receiving
PIT: Hawthorne 5–66, Garrity 2–57, Capers 1–21, Harris 3–18, Sweeney 1–18, Cunningham 1–13, Abercrombie 1–9
CLE: Belk 1–64, Feacher 3–45, Green 1–33, Newsome 4–30, Jones 2–16, Walker 1–7, Holt 2–4

1984

Monday, September 3
Seattle Seahawks 33, Browns 0
Seattle Kingdome (59,540)
White jerseys/white pants

In their worst opening-day performance, the Browns were obliterated by the Seahawks on Labor Day afternoon (rescheduled due to a Sunday conflict at the Kingdome with the baseball Mariners). In their first game with Paul McDonald as their full-time starting QB, the Browns' offense was completely thwarted, held to 120 total yards while allowing seven sacks and turning the ball over five times. McDonald, meanwhile, struggled through an inauspicious debut as he completed only eight of 27 passes. The Cleveland special teams were just as dreadful, permitting three long punt returns and a blocked punt. It was the worst shutout defeat in Cleveland history—the first time the Browns were shut out on opening day—and set the tone for a troubled season.

Record: 0–1

	1	2	3	4		
Browns	0	0	0	0	=	0
Seahawks	7	13	13	0	=	33

SEA-Tice 5-yd. pass from Krieg (Johnson kick)
SEA-Johnson 22-yd. FG
SEA-Johns 7-yd. pass from Krieg (Johnson kick)
SEA-Johnson 50-yd. FG
SEA-Johnson 41-yd. FG
SEA-Johnson 24-yd. FG
SEA-Turner 34-yd. pass from Krieg (Johnson kick)

Passing
CLE: McDonald 8–27–114 0 TD 2 INT, Flick 1–1–2 0 TD 0 INT
SEA: Krieg 14–28–179 3 TD 1 INT

Rushing
CLE: M. Pruitt 15–43, Green 3–9
SEA: Warner 10–40, Hughes 11–38, Dixon 15–36, Lane 1–15, Krieg 3–9, Bryant 2–4, Zorn 4–3

Receiving
CLE: Harris 2–45, Feacher 3–35, Newsome 2–22, Holt 1–12, Green 1–2
SEA: Johns 3–49, Metzelaars 3–46, Turner 1–34, Warner 1–19, Largent 2–17, Bryant 1–9, Tice 1–5, Doornink 1–0, Dixon 1–0

Sunday, September 9
Los Angeles Rams 20, Browns 17
Anaheim Stadium (43,043)
White jerseys/white pants

Rebounding nicely after their miserable opener six days before, the Browns were poised to pull off a victory over the Rams, taking a lead into the fourth quarter but permitted 10 points in the final 15 minutes and then saw a final comeback attempt thwarted in the final minute. Los Angeles drew first blood when a Paul McDonald pass was tipped, intercepted, and returned for an 81-yard touchdown in the first quarter. But the Browns hung tough to take a 17–10 lead with a minute left in the third quarter on a touchdown reception by TE Ozzie Newsome. After the Rams tied the score on the next possession (scored by speedy WR Ron Brown, whom the Browns had drafted two years earlier only to see him bypass the NFL to train for the Olympics), Cleveland missed a chance to take the lead back when Matt Bahr missed a 46-yard field goal with five minutes left. Led by RB Eric Dickerson—on his way to a record-breaking 2,105 rushing yards for the season—the Rams moved downfield and surged ahead by three on a field goal with 1:25 left. Out of time outs, the Browns drove from their own 17 to the Los Angeles 49 with 35 seconds remaining. After Browns' WR Duriel Harris was ruled out of bounds on a reception at the Rams' 20, he argued with an official and was penalized 15 yards for unsportsmanlike conduct, stalling the Browns' final chance. Thus, despite outgaining the Rams by more than 100 yards, holding them to just 226 total, the Browns lost the game to drop to 0–2. Rookie WR Brian Brennan was one of the few individual standouts for the Cleveland offense, catching the first five passes of his NFL career for 75 yards.

Record: 0–2

	1	2	3	4		
Browns	7	3	7	0	=	17
Rams	7	3	0	10	=	20

LA-Irvin 81-yd. interception return (Lansford kick)
CLE-M. Pruitt 6-yd. run (Bahr kick)
LA-Lansford 37-yd. FG
CLE-Bahr 25-yd. FG
CLE-Newsome 4-yd. pass from McDonald (Bahr kick)
LA-Brown 5-yd. pass from Ferragamo (Lansford kick)
LA-Lansford 27-yd. FG

Passing
CLE: McDonald 18–35–263 1 TD 1 INT
LA: Ferragamo 12–20–101 1 TD 2 INT

Rushing
CLE: M. Pruitt 27–78, Green 2–2, McDonald 1–2
LA: Dickerson 27–102, Crutchfield 5–30, Ellard 1–4

Receiving
CLE: Brennan 5–75, Newsome 8–65, Feacher 1–64, Harris 2–50, M. Pruitt 2–9
LA: Hill 2–23, Ellard 2–21, Brown 2–11, Guman 1–11, Hill 1–11, Dickerson 2–9, McDonald 1–8, Farmer 1–7

Sunday, September 16
Denver Broncos 24, Browns 14
Cleveland Stadium (61,980)
Brown jerseys/white pants

Playing on prime-time television on a Sunday night for the first time ever, the Browns leapt to a 14–0 lead, only to see second-year QB John Elway rally the Broncos to a halftime lead that held up. After a pair of short touchdown runs by RB Mike Pruitt, the Browns' offense struggled for the remainder of the game, with four turnovers and seven sacks allowed. After two Elway scoring passes tied the score, a Paul McDonald fumble in the last minute of the first half led to a Denver field goal that gave the Broncos a 17–14 lead. The margin held up into the final minutes after Matt Bahr missed a 36-yard field goal that could have tied the score late in the third quarter. The Browns had one last chance, starting at their own 22 with 1:53 remaining, and McDonald drove them to the Denver 46. But on the next play, he was intercepted by Denver DB Randy Robbins, who returned it 62 yards for the game-clinching touchdown with 37 seconds left. The loss dropped the Browns to 0–3 for the first time in nine years.
Record: 0–3

	1	2	3	4		
Broncos	0	17	0	7	=	24
Browns	7	7	0	0	=	14

CLE-M. Pruitt 1-yd. run (Bahr kick)
CLE-M. Pruitt 2-yd. run (Bahr kick)
DEN-Sampson 23-yd. pass from Elway (Karlis kick)
DEN-Johnson 18-yd. pass from Elway (Karlis kick)
DEN-Karlis 25-yd. FG
DEN-Robbins 62-yd. interception return (Karlis kick)

Passing
DEN: Elway 15–35–170 2 TD 1 INT
CLE: McDonald 22–42–282 0 TD 3 INT

Rushing
DEN: Winder 17–76, Elway 6–42, Willhite 2–8, Lang 1–6, Parros 1–1
CLE: M. Pruitt 24–67, Green 3–9, McDonald 2–3

Receiving
DEN: Johnson 4–64, Winder 7–56, Sampson 1–23, Watson 1–20, Kay 2–7
CLE: Harris 5–104, Brennan 7–84, Holt 5–59, Feacher 1–18, Newsome 2–12, Green 1–4, White 1–1

Sunday, September 23
Browns 20, Pittsburgh Steelers 10
Cleveland Stadium (77,312)
Brown jerseys/white pants

The misery of the previous three weeks evaporated on a warm, overcast afternoon in Cleveland as the Browns took control of a tight game with the eventual division-champion Steelers and cruised to an impressive victory. Surrendering a defensive touchdown for the third straight game, the Browns trailed 7–0 at the half but came alive in the third quarter. After driving for a field goal on their first possession, the Browns recovered a Steelers' fumble caused by Cleveland DB Don Rogers and parlayed it into the go-ahead touchdown when Paul McDonald read a Pittsburgh blitz and dumped a pass for wide-open RB Boyce Green for a 44-yard score. After the Steelers tied the game at 10, McDonald drove his team to the eventual winning score on his second touchdown pass of the game early in the fourth quarter. It would be the Browns' best offensive performance of the season, as they tallied 413 total yards, 293 coming through the air as McDonald atoned for three straight sub-par performances. But the rousing victory would be the Browns' last for nearly two months and wound up being the final triumph of Sam Rutigliano's NFL career.
Record: 1–3

	1	2	3	4		
Steelers	0	7	3	0	=	10
Browns	0	0	10	10	=	20

PIT-Washington 69-yd. interception return (Anderson kick)
CLE-Bahr 18-yd. FG
CLE-Green 44-yd. pass from McDonald (Bahr kick)
PIT-Anderson 46-yd. FG
CLE-Harris 3-yd. pass from McDonald (Bahr kick)
CLE-Bahr 48-yd. FG

Passing
PIT: Woodley 9–25–153 0 TD 1 INT
CLE: McDonald 15–28–293 2 TD 1 INT

Rushing
PIT: Veals 12–35, Erenberg 12–23, Gillespie 2–12, Woodley 2–1
CLE: M. Pruitt 26–83, Green 16–41, McDonald 3–4

Receiving
PIT: Stallworth 3–68, Lipps 3–43, Thompson 1–25, Gillespie 1–12, Erenberg 1–5
CLE: Newsome 6–99, Holt 3–89, Green 3–76, Brennan 1–19, M. Pruitt 1–7, Harris 1–3

Sunday, September 30
Kansas City Chiefs 10, Browns 6
Arrowhead Stadium (40,785)
White jerseys/white pants

Despite an abysmal offensive performance, the Browns still nearly pulled out a victory in Kansas City on the strength of its overburdened defense, taking a 6–3 lead into the fourth quarter. Accumulating only 186 total yards for the game, Cleveland allowed a club-record 11 sacks and was burdened by a handful of dropped passes and four interceptions by Paul McDonald. But the Browns' defense also forced four turnovers to keep the Chiefs from blowing the game open and made a fourth-down stand at the Cleveland 4 with 4:38 remaining, which gave the offense one last chance. The Browns reached the Kansas City 30 with a minute left before McDonald was picked off by Chiefs' DB Kevin Ross to end the threat and drop the Browns to 1–4.
Record: 1–4

	1	2	3	4		
Browns	0	3	3	0	=	6
Chiefs	0	3	0	7	=	10

CLE-Bahr 34-yd. FG
KC-Lowery 42-yd. FG
CLE-Bahr 23-yd. FG
KC-Jackson 9-yd. pass from Blackledge (Lowery kick)

Passing
CLE: McDonald 17–38–186 0 TD 4 INT
KC: Blackledge 15–33–155 1 TD 2 INT

Rushing
CLE: M. Pruitt 20–67, Holt 1–12, Green 5-(-1)
KC: Brown 13–35, Lacy 6–24, Jackson 4–22, Heard 4–11, Blackledge 4–3

Receiving
CLE: Newsome 7–74, Walker 4–44, Harris 2–26, Feacher 1–22, Adams 1–8, Holt 1–8, M. Pruitt 1–4
KC: Marshall 4–63, Brown 4–29, Jackson 4–29, Paige 1–15, Carson 1–13, Scott 1–6

Sunday, October 7
New England Patriots 17, Browns 16
Cleveland Stadium (53,036)
Brown jerseys/white pants

The Browns suffered another heart-wrenching loss, this one eerily reminiscent of their playoff defeat to Oakland four years earlier. Controlling the game for most of the afternoon, the Browns took a 16–3 lead in the third quarter but then saw it disappear with a pair of New England touchdowns. The Browns appeared to take the lead back with 3:12 remaining when Matt Bahr apparently made a 36-yard field goal, but the officials ruled it was no good. With time running out, Paul McDonald—enjoying the finest day of his career with 320 yards passing—drove the Browns from their own 30 to the Patriots' 21 before the Browns suffered a massive breakdown in communications. Unsure whether to kick a field goal or run another play, the Browns let nearly 30 seconds run off the clock before calling time out with 23 seconds left. McDonald wanted to kick the field goal, but Sam Rutigliano opted to run one more play. The playcall was botched in the huddle and Duriel Harris, who'd already caught eight passes for 136 yards and was the intended receiver on the play, ran the incorrect route. Then, after McDonald released the pass, Harris slipped, and Patriots' DB Raymond Clayborn intercepted it at the 5, then ran 87 yards to clinch the New England victory. As the frustrated fans left the ballpark, a chant of "Good-bye, Sam" began rising, foreshadowing what was to come in the following weeks.
Record: 1–5

	1	2	3	4		
Patriots	3	0	7	7	=	17
Browns	0	9	7	0	=	16

NE-Franklin 45-yd. FG
CLE-Bahr 24-yd. FG
CLE-Bahr 48-yd. FG
CLE-Bahr 27-yd. FG
CLE-Harris 16-yd. pass from McDonald (Bahr kick)
NE-Starring 42-yd. pass from Eason (Franklin kick)
NE-Collins 2-yd. run (Franklin kick)

Passing
NE: Eason 14–21–178 1 TD 0 INT
CLE: McDonald 23–37–320 1 TD 1 INT

Rushing
NE: Tatupu 20–83, Eason 3–20, Collins 2–6, Fryar 1–0
CLE: Green 19–33, Byner 5–11

Receiving
NE: Starring 3–77, Ramsey 6–65, Tatupu 2–14, Dawson 2–12, Fryar 1–10
CLE: Harris 8–136, Newsome 6–55, Feacher 3–45, Brennan 1–29, Walker 2–26, Stracka 1–15, Byner 2–14

Sunday, October 14
New York Jets 24, Browns 20
Cleveland Stadium (55,673)
Brown jerseys/white pants

For the fifth time in seven weeks, the Browns saw an opportunity to win a close game in the final two minutes go awry, this time spoiling the finest day of Ozzie Newsome's career. After the Browns rallied from a 10-point deficit to take a 20–17 lead two minutes into the fourth quarter, they failed to add to it when Matt Bahr missed a 31-yard field goal. The Jets cashed in and took the lead back following an 80-yard drive. But as was their custom, the Browns had one final chance, driving to the New York 28 with two minutes left. After the Cleveland offensive line handled the celebrated "New York Sack Exchange" all day, it allowed three straight sacks, two by DE Mark Gastineau, to secure the Jets' victory. Consequently, a second straight strong offensive performance went for naught, highlighted by 14 receptions for 191 yards by Newsome, both franchise records.
Record: 1–6

	1	2	3	4		
Jets	7	10	0	7	=	24
Browns	7	7	3	3	=	20

NYJ-McNeil 3-yd. run (Leahy kick)
CLE-M. Pruitt 1-yd. run (Bahr kick)
NYJ-Leahy 30-yd. FG
NYJ-McNeil 8-yd. run (Leahy kick)
CLE-M. Pruitt 1-yd. run (Bahr kick)
CLE-Bahr 49-yd. FG
CLE-Bahr 18-yd. FG
NYJ-Paige 1-yd. run (Leahy kick)

Passing
NYJ: Ryan 11–25–145 0 TD 2 INT
CLE: McDonald 25–37–299 0 TD 0 INT

Rushing
NYJ: Hector 10–97, McNeil 11–54, Barber 3–20, Ryan 7–13, Paige 2–8
CLE: M. Pruitt 20–79, White 11–30, McDonald 1–8

Receiving
NYJ: Hector 3–42, Shuler 2–41, Humphery 2–30, Gaffney 1–14, McNeil 2–10, Dennison 1–8
CLE: Newsome 14–191, Harris 2–26, Adams 1–24, Feacher 3–22, White 2–13, Brennan 1–9, M. Pruitt 1–9, McDonald 1-(-4)

Sunday, October 21
Cincinnati Bengals 12, Browns 9
Riverfront Stadium (50,667)
Brown jerseys/white pants

Once again, the Browns lost a winnable game, this time on the final play in a battle between two 1–6 teams at rainy Riverfront Stadium. Combining for six turnovers, neither team could reach the end zone, though the second of the Browns' three field goals was a memorable one—a 60-yard boot by Steve Cox, setting a new team record and marking the second-longest in NFL history. After regular kicker Matt Bahr connected on a 47-yard field goal with 2:02 remaining to tie the contest at nine, it appeared the Browns and Bengals were headed for overtime. But Cincinnati QB Turk Schonert—the third Bengal quarterback used—connected on a 42-yard pass to WR Mike Martin (his first catch of the year) through the heart of the Browns' defense, which had played well all day, to push them into field-goal range. Cincy kicker Jim Breech booted the game's seventh field goal, this one from 33 yards out as time expired, to drop the Browns to 1–7. The Cleveland offense again was its own worst enemy, allowing five sacks and coughing up four turnovers, thwarting another 300-yard passing performance by Paul McDonald. The next day, Art Modell announced the firing of Sam Rutigliano as Browns' head coach, replacing him with defensive coordinator Marty Schottenheimer.

Record: 1–7

	1	2	3	4		
Browns	3	3	0	3	=	9
Bengals	3	3	0	6	=	12

CIN-Breech 24-yd. FG
CLE-Bahr 50-yd. FG
CIN-Breech 23-yd. FG
CLE-Cox 60-yd. FG
CIN-Breech 25-yd. FG
CLE-Bahr 47-yd. FG
CIN-Breech 33-yd. FG

Passing
CLE: McDonald 27–47–300 0 TD 2 INT
CIN: Schonert 9–15–130 0 TD 0 INT, Anderson 8–12–68 0 TD 1 INT, Esiason 1–7–4 0 TD 0 INT

Rushing
CLE: White 12–28, Byner 3–17, M. Pruitt 4–11
CIN: Jennings 8–38, Alexander 12–29, Brooks 6–24, Anderson 2–17, Esiason 4–11, Kinnebrew 1–1

Receiving
CLE: Adams 8–94, Harris 5–71, Byner 3–36, Walker 3–34, Newsome 4–20, Bolden 1–19, White 2–15, Feacher 1–11
CIN: Martin 1–42, Holman 2–39, Jennings 4–26, Alexander 3–26, Collinsworth 3–24, Curtis 2–19, Verser 1–17, Brooks 1–5, Harris 1–4

Sunday, October 28
New Orleans Saints 16, Browns 14
Cleveland Stadium (52,489)
Brown jerseys/white pants

The Marty Schottenheimer era began exactly the same way the Sam Rutigliano era ended—with the Browns losing on a field goal on the last play of the game. On a dark, rainy afternoon in Cleveland, the Browns lost their fifth straight game by a combined total of 14 points, once again failing to capitalize on opportunities and being victimized by bad luck. Clinging to a 14–13 lead with less than two minutes to play, the Browns appeared to clinch victory when Brian Brennan made a diving third-down catch good for 40 yards to the New Orleans 5, but the Browns were penalized for holding and forced to punt. Out of time outs, the Saints took over at their own 23, and thanks to a 36-yard pass, moved into Cleveland territory in the final seconds. With no time remaining, New Orleans kicker Morten Andersen launched a 53-yard field goal through the rain and swirling wind to hand the Browns yet another heartbreaking defeat on the longest field goal in the history of Cleveland Stadium. While the Cleveland offense managed to hold onto the ball, committing no turnovers for the first time all year, the defense—ranked No. 1 in the AFC—had trouble stopping the mediocre Saints, as they tallied nearly 400 yards and notched their first victory ever over the Browns.

Record: 1–8

	1	2	3	4		
Saints	0	10	0	6	=	16
Browns	0	7	7	0	=	14

NO-Gajan 2-yd. pass from Todd (Andersen kick)
CLE-Newsome 5-yd. pass from McDonald (Bahr kick)
NO-Andersen 26-yd. FG
CLE-Newsome 5-yd. pass from McDonald (Bahr kick)
NO-Andersen 21-yd. FG
NO-Andersen 53-yd. FG

Passing
NO: Todd 21–27–294 1 TD 0 INT
CLE: McDonald 16–23–193 2 TD 0 INT

Rushing
NO: Gajan 7–52, Rogers 11–26, Wilson 3–19, Campbell 6–9, Todd 3–8, Duckett 1-(-3)
CLE: Green 23–74, M. Pruitt 5–11, Davis 1–6, McDonald 1–0, Walker 1-(-8)

Receiving
NO: Young 4–101, Wilson 4–47, Scott 1–36, Groth 3–33, Gajan 6–29, Brenner 1–27, Anthony 1–11, Miller 1–10
CLE: Adams 4–62, Newsome 4–42, Harris 3–31, Brennan 2–26, Byner 1–21, Davis 1–6, Green 1–5

Sunday, November 4
Browns 13, Buffalo Bills 10
Rich Stadium (33,343)
Brown jerseys/white pants

Finally, the football literally bounced the Browns' way. With the specter of an embarrassing defeat to the 0–9 Bills staring them in the face on a cold, rainy day in Buffalo, the

Browns finally received a small measure of justice for all the bad breaks they'd suffered earlier in the season on a third-down play midway through the fourth quarter. Trailing 10–6, Paul McDonald completed a pass to WR Willis Adams for 13 yards on third-and-20, but Adams fumbled as he was tackled. The ball bounced off the wet Astroturf and right into the arms of rookie RB Earnest Byner trailing the play. Byner cruised down the sideline for a 55-yard touchdown to give the Browns the lead—and Byner the first touchdown of his career. The Cleveland defense, which had dominated the woeful Bills all day, held on from there, and Marty Schottenheimer collected his first win as a head coach, appropriately against the first team he'd ever played for. Schottenheimer's grind-it-out style was showcased as the Browns focused on the running game, plowing for 211 yards on the ground, paced by Boyce Green with a career-high 156 on 29 carries—the highest total by a Cleveland RB in six years. The Browns' defense also rose to the occasion, permitting only 183 yards with the only Buffalo points coming on a fumble return for a touchdown and a field goal set up by a Green fumble.

Record: 2–8

	1	2	3	4		
Browns	3	3	0	7	=	13
Bills	0	7	3	0	=	10

CLE-Bahr 28-yd. FG
BUF-Keating 34-yd. fumble return (Nelson kick)
CLE-Bahr 36-yd. FG
BUF-Nelson 42-yd. FG
CLE-Byner 55-yd. fumble return (Bahr kick)

Passing
CLE: McDonald 7–18–86 0 TD 1 INT
BUF: Ferguson 16–24–110 0 TD 2 INT

Rushing
CLE: Green 29–156, Byner 9–58, McDonald 5-(-3)
BUF: Bell 20–82, Neal 5–17, Williams 2–8, Moore 1–1, Ferguson 1-(-2)

Receiving
CLE: Newsome 4–53, Harris 2–20, Adams 1–13
BUF: Dawkins 3–38, Bell 6–27, Hunter 3–14, Franklin 1–9, White 1–8, Moore 1–7, Riddick 1–7

Sunday, November 11
San Francisco 49ers 41, Browns 7
Cleveland Stadium (60,092)
Brown jerseys/white pants

On another dank, rainy afternoon, the Browns were simply overwhelmed by the eventual Super Bowl champions, demonstrating how far they had to go before being considered a title contender. The tone was set on the opening kickoff when Earnest Byner, the hero from the week before, fumbled, setting up the first of seven 49ers' scores. The strong Cleveland defense was ripped apart by a cruising San Francisco offense led by a nearly flawless performance by Joe Montana to the tune of 468 total yards. Meanwhile the Cleveland offense once again became its own worst enemy with six dropped passes and four turnovers. The Browns managed their only score on a remarkable play when WR Bruce Davis out-leaped two defenders to reel in a tipped ball for a touchdown. The 49ers moved to 10–1 on the year, winning their fourth straight in what would become a 12-game winning streak, culminating with a win in Super Bowl XIX.

Record: 2–9

	1	2	3	4		
49ers	6	7	14	14	=	41
Browns	0	0	0	7	=	7

SF-Wersching 47-yd. FG
SF-Wersching 26-yd. FG
SF-Craig 20-yd. run (Wersching kick)
SF-Craig 2-yd. run (Wersching kick)
SF-Solomon 60-yd. pass from Montana (Wersching kick)
SF-Solomon 2-yd. pass from Montana (Wersching kick)
SF-Ring 5-yd. run (Wersching kick)
CLE-Davis 18-yd. pass from McDonald (Bahr kick)

Passing
SF: Montana 24–30–263 2 TD 1 INT
CLE: McDonald 13–33–220 1 TD 1 INT

Rushing
SF: Tyler 17–87, Ring 6–48, Craig 9–45, Harmon 5–29, Montana 2–4,
CLE: Green 13–38, Byner 5–5, McDonald 2–0

Receiving
SF: Solomon 5–105, Craig 8–49, Cooper 2–35, Nehemiah 1–23, Frank 1–21, Clark 2–19, Tyler 4–12, Ring 1-(-1)
CLE: Davis 4–64, Newsome 2–56, Brennan 1–52, Adams 3–30, Green 2–11, Byner 1–7

Sunday, November 18
Browns 23, Atlanta Falcons 7
Fulton County Stadium (28,280)
White jerseys/white pants

Behind a dominating defensive performance, the Browns picked up their third win. Before the smallest crowd to attend a Browns' game in 10 years, the Cleveland defense collected 11 sacks of Atlanta quarterbacks, setting a new team record, and held the Falcons to just over 200 total yards while forcing four turnovers. The key play came early in the fourth quarter. With the Browns clinging to a 13–7 lead, Cleveland NT Dave Puzzuoli sacked Atlanta QB Steve Bartkowski and caused a fumble that was recovered by first-year DB Frank Minnifield at the Atlanta 16. On the next play, Paul McDonald connected with Ozzie Newsome for a touchdown that gave the Browns the breathing room they needed to secure victory. LB Clay Matthews led the charge on defense, notching three sacks, while an interception by DB Hanford Dixon set up the field goal that put the Browns ahead for good. The Cleveland defense also contained Atlanta's All-Pro RB Gerald Riggs, who would rush for more than 1,400 yards on the season, but was held to a season-low 71 on 21 carries. On offense, Boyce Green paced the attack, topping the 100-yard mark for the second time in three weeks and the fourth and final time in his career.
Record: 3–9

	1	2	3	4		
Browns	10	3	0	10	=	23
Falcons	7	0	0	0	=	7

ATL-Bailey 20-yd pass from Bartkowski (Luckhurst kick)
CLE-Davis 43-yd. pass from McDonald (Bahr kick)
CLE-Bahr 27-yd. FG
CLE-Bahr 46-yd. FG
CLE-Newsome 16-yd. pass from McDonald (Bahr kick)
CLE-Bahr 20-yd. FG

Passing
CLE: McDonald 13–23–205 2 TD 1 INT, Cox 1–1–16 0 TD 0 INT
ATL: Bartkowski 19–28–191 1 TD 1 INT, Moroski 4–10–43 0 TD 1 INT

Rushing
CLE: Green 30–121, Byner 2–0, McDonald 2-(-8)
ATL: Riggs 21–71, Bartkowski 1–0

Receiving
CLE: Newsome 5–97, Davis 2–49, Brennan 3–37, Feacher 1–16, Holt 2–13, Green 1–9
ATL: Bailey 4–55, Cox 4–44, Riggs 6–41, Jackson 3–38, Hodge 2–29, Benson 1–8, Tuttle 1–7, Cain 1–7, Landrum 1–5

Sunday, November 25
Browns 27, Houston Oilers 10
Cleveland Stadium (46,077)
Brown jerseys/white pants

For the first time all season, the Browns won back-to-back games, this time dominating the 2–10 Oilers in the brilliant November sunshine at Cleveland Stadium. The Browns' defense again led the way, limiting the Oilers to just 147 total yards, the lowest tally of the season for the improving Cleveland unit. Houston's only touchdown came on a fumble return that tied the game at seven in the first quarter—the fifth defensive touchdown scored against the Browns in 1984. But Cleveland rebounded to take a 20–7 halftime lead, following Matt Bahr's second field goal set up by an interception and 47-yard return by DB Al Gross. Rookie Brian Brennan scored the first two touchdowns of his career, while Paul McDonald tossed three scoring passes and connected with Ozzie Newsome 10 times for 102 yards as the Cleveland offense tallied a season-high 27 points. Incredibly, with the win, the 4–9 Browns remained mathematically alive for the AFC Central Division title, trailing division-leader Pittsburgh by only three games with three to play.
Record: 4–9

	1	2	3	4		
Oilers	7	0	0	3	=	10
Browns	7	13	0	7	=	27

CLE-Brennan 14-yd. pass from McDonald (Bahr kick)
HOU-Bostic 25-yd. fumble return (Cooper kick)
CLE-Bahr 18-yd. FG
CLE-Newsome 12-yd. pass from McDonald (Bahr kick)
CLE-Bahr 29-yd. FG
HOU-Cooper 29-yd. FG
CLE-Brennan 7-yd. pass from McDonald (Bahr kick)

Passing
HOU: Moon 9–20–84 0 TD 2 INT
CLE: McDonald 16–26–151 3 TD 1 INT

Rushing
HOU: Moriarty 16–81, Edwards 3–20, Joyner 3–4, Moon 3–4
CLE: Green 26–74, Byner 9–41, Davis 1–5, White 1–4, McDonald 1-(-4)

Receiving
HOU: Williams 2–22, Dressel 1–15, Bryant 1–14, Holston 1–11, McCloskey 1–11, Walls 1–9, Edwards 1–6, Moriarty 1-(-4)
CLE: Newsome 10–102, Brennan 4–34, Walker 1–9, Holt 1–6

Sunday, December 2
Cincinnati Bengals 20, Browns 17 (OT)
Cleveland Stadium (51,774)
Brown jerseys/white pants

Reverting back to the agonizing style of defeat that had plagued them throughout the first half of the season, the Browns dropped another heartbreaker, blowing a lead in the final seconds of regulation and losing in overtime to the resurgent Bengals. The Browns appeared on their way to a third straight win as they built a 17–7 second-half lead on the forty-seventh and final touchdown Mike Pruitt would score with the Browns. After the Bengals narrowed the margin to seven points, the Browns were poised to pin Cincy deep in its own territory with a punt with a minute to play. But a blown blocking scheme resulted in the Bengals blocking the punt and taking over at the Cleveland 27. Then a pass-interference penalty on Hanford Dixon in the end zone with 19 seconds to play gave the Bengals a first down at the Cleveland 1, and with seven seconds left, they tied it on a bizarre tackle-eligible play that saw QB Boomer Esiason hit All-Pro offensive lineman Anthony Munoz with the first touchdown of his career to send the game to overtime. The Browns won the toss in the extra session but were forced to punt and suffered another special-teams breakdown, allowing a 30-yard return to set up the winning field goal. It spoiled an otherwise crisp performance for the Browns, who committed no turnovers, allowed only one sack, and committed just one penalty aside from Dixon's interference call. The defeat extinguished the Browns' fledging chance in the division race and secured the fourth double-digit-loss season in team history.
Record: 4–10

	1	2	3	4	OT		
Bengals	7	0	0	10	3	=	20
Browns	0	10	0	7	0	=	17

CIN-Jennings 15-yd. pass from Schonert (Breech kick)
CLE-Bahr 24-yd. FG
CLE-Brennan 21-yd. pass from McDonald (Bahr kick)
CLE-M. Pruitt 1-yd. run (Bahr kick)
CIN-Breech 22-yd. FG
CIN-Munoz 1-yd. pass from Esiason (Breech kick)
CIN-Breech 35-yd. FG

Passing
CIN: Schonert 16–21–138 1 TD 1 INT, Esiason 12–20–108 1 TD 0 INT
CLE: McDonald 18–24–191 1 TD 0 INT

Rushing
CIN: Jennings 9–38, Alexander 13–37, Schonert 2–18, Brooks 3–16, Kinnebrew 5–7, Martin 1–3
CLE: M. Pruitt 17–58, Green 12–35, Byner 3–3

Receiving
CIN: Kreider 6–85, Harris 5–53, Jennings 5–29, Verser 1–22, Alexander 3–12, Martin 1–11, Kinnebrew 2–10, Holman 1–8, Collinsworth 1–7, Kern 1–5, Brooks 1–3, Munoz 1–1
CLE: Newsome 8–62, Brennan 5–55, Feacher 3–54, Adams 1–11, Byner 1–9

Sunday, December 9
Pittsburgh Steelers 23, Browns 20
Three Rivers Stadium (55,825)
White jerseys/white pants

Appropriately, the Browns' final loss of the 1984 season typified the entire year. Trailing 17–6 late in the first half, the Browns rebounded to tie the game at 20 in the fourth quarter, then stayed alive minutes later when Hanford Dixon intercepted a pass in the end zone to thwart a potential Steelers' scoring drive. But once again the Browns' mistakes—this time exemplified by four Paul McDonald interceptions—proved too much, and the Steelers pulled out the victory with a drive in the final minutes that resulted in the game-winning field goal with five seconds to play. It was the ninth time in 1984 the Browns lost a game in the final two minutes and marked their eighth defeat by seven points or less. Somewhat lost amid the disappointment of the Browns' fifteenth straight defeat at Three Rivers Stadium was a strong performance by rookie Earnest Byner, who notched the first 100-yard rushing game of his career, tallying 103 yards on just 15 carries.
Record: 4–11

	1	2	3	4		
Browns	3	10	0	7	=	20
Steelers	7	10	3	3	=	23

CLE-Bahr 29-yd. FG
PIT-Lipps 61-yd. pass from Malone (Anderson kick)
PIT-Anderson 40-yd. FG
CLE-Bahr 49-yd. FG
PIT-Pollard 1-yd. run (Anderson kick)
CLE-Feacher 16-yd. pass from McDonald (Bahr kick)
PIT-Anderson 22-yd. FG
CLE-McDonald 3-yd. run (Bahr kick)
PIT-Anderson 34-yd. FG

Passing
CLE: McDonald 19–33–211 1 TD 4 INT
PIT: Malone 11–22–203 1 TD 2 INT, Campbell 2–4–26 0 TD 0 INT

Rushing
CLE: Byner 15–103, Green 11–25, M. Pruitt 5–9, McDonald 1–3
PIT: Abercrombie 15–74, Pollard 9–37, Malone 4–8, Erenberg 1–6, Campbell 1–0

Receiving
CLE: Feacher 3–56, Young 1–47, Newsome 5–33, Holt 3–31, Adams 2–19, Brennan 3–16, Green 2–9
PIT: Lipps 3–97, Pollard 5–62, Stallworth 2–37, Erenberg 1–22, Abercrombie 2–11

Sunday, December 16
Browns 27, Houston Oilers 20
Houston Astrodome (33,676)
White jerseys/white pants

The Browns closed the season on a winning note, using a bruising running attack to secure their fourth victory in seven weeks and complete a season sweep of Houston for the first time in eight years. The catalyst was Earnest Byner—now seeing much more playing time under Marty Schottenheimer—who soared to 188 yards on 21 carries, including two touchdowns. Byner's longest run, a 54-yard scamper, set up a Matt Bahr field goal that extended the Cleveland lead to 27–20 with just over two minutes to play. The Cleveland defense then stopped the Oilers on downs to clinch the victory. First-year Houston QB Warren Moon threw for more than 300 yards—the first passer to accomplish the feat against the Browns all year—while the Browns hindered their own effort with 119 yards in penalties. The solid second half of the season, capped by the satisfying victory in the finale, set the tone for much more prosperous things to come in 1985.

Record: 5–11

	1	2	3	4		
Browns	7	3	7	10	=	27
Oilers	0	7	10	3	=	20

CLE-Byner 2-yd. run (Bahr kick)
CLE-Bahr 29-yd. FG
HOU-Moriarty 4-yd. run (Cooper kick)
HOU-Cooper 33-yd. FG
CLE-Byner 15-yd. run (Bahr kick)
HOU-Moriarty 4-yd. run (Cooper kick)
CLE-Davis 2-yd. run (Bahr kick)
HOU-Cooper 26-yd. FG
CLE-Bahr 29-yd. FG

Passing
CLE: McDonald 14–22–158 0 TD 1 INT
HOU: Moon 19–31–306 0 TD 0 INT

Rushing
CLE: Byner 21–188, Green 10–57, Davis 2–10, McDonald 3-(-1)
HOU: Moriarty 21–90, Moon 2–4, Edwards 4-(-2), Cooper 1-(-2)

Receiving
CLE: Holt 4–43, Feacher 2–39, Byner 3–31, Brennan 2–19, Newsome 2–18, Green 1–8
HOU: Smith 7–167, Williams 3–59, Holston 2–42, Dressel 4–32, Moriarty 3–6

1985

Sunday, September 8
St. Louis Cardinals 27, Browns 24 (OT)
Cleveland Stadium (62,107)
White jerseys/white pants

Despite a stirring rally that saw the Browns score three touchdowns in the final eight minutes, they were unable to close out the victory and lost in heartbreaking fashion in overtime in the season opener. Trailing 17–3 midway through the fourth quarter with a thunderstorm sweeping in off the lake, new starting QB Gary Danielson led the Browns on a pair of scoring drives to tie the game, then connected with TE Ozzie Newsome on a 25-yard swing pass in which Newsome dove across the goal line and into a fresh mud puddle to give the Browns a 24–17 lead with 38 seconds remaining. But the Cardinals came up with their own magic, parlaying a 43-yard screen pass to RB Ottis Anderson to set up the game-tying touchdown to force overtime. St. Louis then took the kickoff in sudden-death and drove 46 yards to kick the game-winning field goal and hand the Browns a crushing defeat.
Record: 0–1

	1	2	3	4	OT		
Cardinals	7	0	3	14	3	=	27
Browns	0	3	0	21	0	=	24

STL-Anderson 4-yd. run (O'Donoghue kick)
CLE-Bahr 33-yd. FG
STL-O'Donoghue 37-yd. FG
STL-Washington 48-yd. interception return (O'Donoghue kick)
CLE-Mack 13-yd. run (Bahr kick)
CLE-Holt 17-yd. pass from Danielson (Bahr kick)
CLE-Newsome 25-yd. pass from Danielson (Bahr kick)
STL-Tilley 5-yd. pass from Lomax (O'Donoghue kick)
STL-O'Donoghue 35-yd. FG

Passing
STL: Lomax 12–23–203 1 TD 0 INT
CLE: Danielson 17–25–202 2 TD 1 INT

Rushing
STL: Anderson 17–55, Mitchell 7–17, Ferrell 6–14, Lomax 4–14
CLE: Byner 21–68, Danielson 6–60, Mack 9–48, Baab 1–0

Receiving
STL: Anderson 2–60, Green 2–57, Ferrell 3–48, Mitchell 2–24, Marsh 2–9, Tilley 1–5
CLE: Newsome 6–79, Adams 4–65, Holt 3–33, Banks 1–9, Byner 1–9, Mack 2–7

Monday, September 15
Browns 17, Pittsburgh Steelers 7
Cleveland Stadium (79,042)
White jerseys/white pants

Clinging to a precarious three-point lead with time running out before a sellout crowd and a *Monday Night Football* television audience, the Browns' defense came up with the big play it couldn't manage the week before and the offense tacked on the game-clinching touchdown to give Cleveland its first victory of the season. Browns' LB Curtis Weathers intercepted a pass at the Pittsburgh 25 with 2:44 left, and two plays later, RB Earnest Byner exploded through the line for a 21-yard touchdown run that put the Browns in the clear. The Cleveland defense held the Steelers to just 216 total yards and Pittsburgh QB Mark Malone completed only 18 of 45 passes. Meanwhile, Byner led a consistent Cleveland offense with 82 yards rushing and another 49 receiving.
Record: 1–1

	1	2	3	4		
Steelers	0	0	0	7	=	7
Browns	0	7	3	7	=	17

CLE-Banks 17-yd. pass from Danielson (Bahr kick)
CLE-Bahr 18-yd. FG
PIT-Stallworth 6-yd. pass from Malone (Anderson kick)
CLE-Byner 21-yd. run (Bahr kick)

Passing
PIT: Malone 18–45–178 1 TD 2 INT
CLE: Danielson 18–30–206 1 TD 1 INT

Rushing
PIT: Pollard 9–38, Abercrombie 9–17, Morse 1-(-1)
CLE: Byner 18–82, Mack 12–40, Danielson 6–23

Receiving
PIT: Stallworth 8–93, Erenberg 4–35, Lipps 2–23, Pollard 2–17, Thompson 1–9, Abercrombie 1–1
CLE: Mack 4–54, Byner 5–49, Holt 2–40, Newsome 4–27, Adams 2–19, Banks 1–17

Sunday, September 22
Dallas Cowboys 20, Browns 7
Texas Stadium (61,456)
Brown jerseys/white pants

On a sunshiny afternoon in Dallas, the Browns were simply overwhelmed by the Cowboys, falling behind 20–0 before scoring a meaningless touchdown in the fourth quarter. The Browns spoiled two golden scoring opportunities when Gary Danielson threw a pair of interceptions in the end zone, the first from the Dallas 3 just before the half with the Cowboys up 10–0. Combined with four sacks allowed and nine penalties, the mistake-prone Browns couldn't keep up with the perennially powerful Cowboys and once again fell below the .500 mark.
Record: 1–2

	1	2	3	4		
Browns	0	0	0	7	=	7
Cowboys	3	7	7	3	=	20

DAL-Septien 39-yd. FG
DAL-Cosbie 10-yd. pass from White (Septien kick)
DAL-White 12-yd. pass from Jones (Septien kick)
DAL-Septien 33-yd. FG
CLE-Byner 1-yd. run (Bahr kick)

Passing
CLE: Danielson 14–26–193 0 TD 2 INT
DAL: White 20–32–182 1 TD 1 INT, Hogeboom 1–1–18 0 TD 0 INT, Jones 1–1–12 1 TD 0 INT

Rushing
CLE: Byner 15–80, Danielson 6–25, Mack 10–23
DAL: Dorsett 15–67, Newsome 10–35, White 4–18, Lavette 4–11

Receiving
CLE: Young 3–49, Adams 4–48, Newsome 4–40, Mack 2–38, Byner 1–18
DAL: Cosbie 6–71, Hill 4–35, Newsome 5–31, Dorsett 2–26, Renfro 1–21, Cornwell 2–15, White 1–12, Powe 1–1

Sunday, September 29
Browns 21, San Diego Chargers 7
Jack Murphy Stadium (52,107)
Brown jerseys/white pants

Behind a bruising running attack and a ferocious pass rush, the Browns rolled to an impressive road victory in San Diego. Setting the tone for the remainder of the season, the Browns stampeded to a whopping 275 rushing yards—and 440 total. They were paced by a brilliant performance by rookie RB Kevin Mack, who filed the first big game of his career, picking up 130 yards on just 16 carries and scoring a pair of touchdowns. Earnest Byner added another 83 on the ground and reeled in the go-ahead 11-yard touchdown reception from Gary Danielson in the third quarter as the quarterback released the football while falling backward. Meanwhile, the Cleveland defense collected six sacks—three by DE Reggie Camp—and knocked San Diego QB Dan Fouts from the game in the first quarter.
Record: 2–2

	1	2	3	4		
Browns	0	7	7	7	=	21
Chargers	7	0	0	0	=	7

SD-Bendross 54-yd. pass from Fouts (Thomas kick)
CLE-Mack 10-yd. run (Bahr kick)
CLE-Byner 11-yd. pass from Danielson (Bahr kick)
CLE-Mack 10-yd. pass from Danielson (Bahr kick)

Passing
CLE: Danielson 16–24–170 2 TD 0 INT
SD: Herrmann 16–23–178 0 TD 2 INT, Fouts 5–8–82 1 TD 0 INT

Rushing
CLE: Mack 16–130, Byner 14–83, Allen 6–28, Weathers 1–18, Danielson 3–16
SD: Spencer 7–28, James 10–27 Steels 1–1, Herrmann 2–0

Receiving
CLE: Weathers 4–88, Mack 7–49, Banks 1–15, Byner 2–12, Newsome 1–6, Holt 1–0
SD: Bendross 2–77, James 10–68, Holohan 2–27, Joiner 2–23, Chandler 1–23, Sievers 2–20, Faulkner 1–12, Spencer 1–10

Sunday, October 6
Browns 24, New England Patriots 20
Cleveland Stadium (62,139)
White jerseys/white pants

In what would prove to be a hallmark day in team history, the Browns knocked off the eventual AFC champions and witnessed the professional debut of QB Bernie Kosar. After Gary Danielson injured his shoulder late in the second quarter, the rookie entered the game and—after fumbling his first snap—played well, completing his first seven passes and leading the Browns to a go-ahead touchdown with four minutes remaining. The Patriots drove deep into Cleveland territory and had two opportunities to take back the lead in the final six minutes, but the Cleveland defense twice stopped them on fourth-and-short—the first at the goal line. Kevin Mack had another big game, rushing for 115 yards and tallying 85 more receiving, while WR Brian Brennan, playing his first game of the year after suffering an injury in the preseason finale, caught seven passes for 104 yards and threw a touchdown pass to Ozzie Newsome on a trick play in the second quarter. The Browns' offense tallied a season-high 447 total yards and overcame five turnovers to assume sole control of first place in the AFC Central.

Record: 3–2

	1	2	3	4		
Patriots	0	13	7	0	=	20
Browns	7	7	3	7	=	24

CLE-Byner 9-yd. run (Bahr kick)
NE-Rembert recovers fumble in end zone (Franklin kick)
CLE-Newsome 33-yd. pass from Brennan (Bahr kick)
NE-Franklin 29-yd. FG
NE-Franklin 33-yd. FG
CLE-Bahr 44-yd. FG
NE-Morgan 22-yd. pass from Eason (Franklin kick)
CLE-Mack 10-yd. run (Bahr kick)

Passing
NE: Eason 20–38–304 1 TD 1 INT
CLE: Danielson 11–19–164 0 TD 1 INT, Kosar 9–15–104 0 TD 1 INT, Brennan 1–1–33 1 TD 0 INT

Rushing
NE: James 12–66, Collins 6–16, Weathers 4–15, Eason 1–9, Tatupu 2–3
CLE: Mack 20–115, Byner 14–37, Danielson 1–4, Kosar 6-(-10)

Receiving
NE: Morgan 6–140, Collins 6–65, Ramsey 2–28, Williams 1–23, Fryar 1–21, Dawson 2–13, Weathers 1–13, Tatupu 1–1
CLE: Brennan 7–104, Mack 5–85, Newsome 6–73, Weathers 2–28, Byner 1–11

Sunday, October 13
Browns 21, Houston Oilers 6
Houston Astrodome (38,386)
White jerseys/white pants

Making his first pro start, Bernie Kosar overcame a difficult first half to lead the Browns to their third straight win and remain in first place in the division. Trailing 6–0 at the intermission, the Browns took the lead in the third quarter when Kosar lofted a 68-yard touchdown pass—the first of his career—to WR Clarence Weathers, who finished with 146 receiving yards on just three receptions. Kevin Mack and Earnest Byner tacked on two more touchdowns as the defense continually stymied Houston, picking up seven sacks and holding the Oilers to just 190 total yards. Meanwhile, the efficient Cleveland offense had its third straight solid performance, tallying 360. With Pittsburgh losing in Dallas, the Browns opened up a two-game lead in the AFC Central.

Record: 4–2

	1	2	3	4		
Browns	0	0	14	7	=	21
Oilers	3	3	0	0	=	6

HOU-Zendejas 50-yd. FG
HOU-Zendejas 27-yd. FG
CLE-Weathers 68-yd. pass from Kosar (Bahr kick)
CLE-Mack 4-yd. run (Bahr kick)
CLE-Byner 5-yd. run (Bahr kick)

Passing
CLE: Kosar 8–19–208 1 TD 1 INT
HOU: Moon 14–23–97 0 TD 1 INT, Moroski 1–4–11 0 TD 1 INT

Rushing
CLE: Mack 20–91, Byner 14–54, Davis 1–5, Allen 2–4, Kosar 2-(-2)
HOU: Rozier 16–49, Moriarty 6–27, Moon 3–19, Edwards 2–18, Woolfolk 6–7, Tasker 1–3

Receiving
CLE: Weathers 3–146, Brennan 2–37, Byner 2–18, Newsome 1–7
HOU: Hill 4–48, Woolfolk 8–46, Moriarty 1–8, Rozier 2–6

Sunday, October 20
Los Angeles Raiders 21, Browns 20
Cleveland Stadium (77,928)
White jerseys/white pants

The Browns had a fourth straight victory in their grasp but instead lost a heartbreaking decision to the powerful Raiders on a last-minute touchdown. In a physical, back-and-forth game, the home team forced two turnovers in the third quarter and rallied from a seven-point half-time deficit to surge ahead 20–14 on a short Kevin Mack touchdown reception from Bernie Kosar with eight minutes remaining. But the Raiders responded with a clutch drive capped by an eight-yard scoring pass to TE Todd Christensen on fourth down with 29 seconds left. While the defeat showed the Browns could hang tough with one of the NFL's best teams, it also marked the beginning of a month-long sour stretch that would nearly destroy a promising season.
Record: 4–3

	1	2	3	4		
Raiders	7	7	0	7	=	21
Browns	7	0	3	10	=	20

LA-Hawkins 21-yd. run (Bahr kick)
CLE-Byner 1-yd. run (Bahr kick)
LA-Allen 11-yd. pass from Wilson (Bahr kick)
CLE-Bahr 31-yd. FG
CLE-Bahr 31-yd. FG
CLE-Mack 7-yd. pass from Kosar (Bahr kick)
LA-Christensen 8-yd. pass from Wilson (Bahr kick)

Passing
LA: Wilson 15–36–213 2 TD 1 INT
CLE: Kosar 10–22–140 1 TD 0 INT

Rushing
LA: Allen 20–81, Hawkins 9–39, Wilson 1–0
CLE: Mack 19–56, Byner 18–41, Kosar 1–10, Davis 1–2

Receiving
LA: Christensen 6–71, Williams 2–55, Hester 4–46, Allen 3–41
CLE: Newsome 4–49, Weathers 1–32, Byner 2–28, Mack 2–22, Jefferson 1–9

Sunday, October 27
Washington Redskins 14, Browns 7
Cleveland Stadium (78,540)
White jerseys/white pants

In what became a defensive struggle, turnovers on the Browns' first two possessions led to a pair of quick Washington touchdowns and doomed the Browns to a second straight home defeat. While the Cleveland defense held the Redskins scoreless for the remainder of the game, the offense could do little, and a struggling Bernie Kosar was replaced in the second half by still-healing Gary Danielson, who led the Browns to a quick touchdown. Down by seven, the Browns had two fourth-quarter threats stall at the Washington 24, one when TE Harry Holt fumbled and the other when they failed to convert on fourth-and-14. Cleveland still clung to a one-game lead in the division ahead of the Bengals and Steelers.
Record: 4–4

	1	2	3	4		
Redskins	14	0	0	0	=	14
Browns	0	0	7	0	=	7

WAS-Riggins 1-yd. run (Moseley kick)
WAS-Clark 19-yd. pass from Theismann (Moseley kick)
CLE-Newsome 14-yd. pass from Danielson (Bahr kick)

Passing
WAS: Theismann 16–23–166 1 TD 1 INT
CLE: Danielson 9–15–99 1 TD 0 INT, Kosar 7–17–84 0 TD 2 INT

Rushing
WAS: Riggins 30–112, Rogers 8–20, Theismann 4–5, Warren 1–5
CLE: Mack 13–60, Byner 9–39, Danielson 2–0, Kosar 2-(-2)

Receiving
WAS: Clark 4–58, Griffin 3–25, Warren 2–23, Rogers 1–23, Didier 2–21, Monk 2–10, Riggins 2–6
CLE: Newsome 9–92, Byner 2–41, Mack 1–19, Jefferson 1–17, Holt 3–14

Sunday, November 3
Pittsburgh Steelers 10, Browns 9
Three Rivers Stadium (51,976)
White jerseys/white pants

Despite Browns' PR staffers sprinkling Cleveland Stadium dirt on the Three Rivers Astroturf before the game in the hopes of ending the 15-year jinx, the Steelers once again prevailed in the final seconds, handing the Browns their third straight defeat. In a cold, steady rain, the Browns struggled offensively, managing just 153 yards on the day, but still took a 6–0 halftime lead on a pair of Matt Bahr field goals. The game turned in the third quarter when Bernie Kosar turned to the officials to help quiet a roaring Pittsburgh crowd, and center Mike Baab snapped the ball right past the unsuspecting quarterback, who recovered for a 12-yard loss, but the play altered the momentum. The Steelers scored a touchdown to go ahead by a point, then Bahr kicked a third field goal with four minutes remaining in the game to put the Browns up 9–7. But Pittsburgh put together one final drive deep into Cleveland territory and kicked the game-winning field goal with nine seconds remaining. The defeat dropped the Browns into a three-way tie for first in the AFC Central with the Steelers and Bengals.

Record: 4–5

	1	2	3	4		
Browns	0	6	0	3	=	9
Steelers	0	0	7	3	=	10

CLE-Bahr 34-yd. FG
CLE-Bahr 45-yd. FG
PIT-Abercrombie 32-yd. run (Anderson kick)
CLE-Bahr 30-yd. FG
PIT-Anderson 25-yd. FG

Passing
CLE: Kosar 13–19–96 0 TD 0 INT
PIT: Woodley 9–17–91 0 TD 0 INT

Rushing
CLE: Byner 15–45, Mack 11–30, Davis 1–2, Kosar 4-(-11)
PIT: Abercrombie 19–78, Pollard 15–59, Woodley 3–15, Morse 1–3

Receiving
CLE: Brennan 2–33, Byner 6–30, Newsome 2–21, Holt 1–8, Jefferson 1–4, Mack 1–0
PIT: Lipps 3–42, Stallworth 4–37, Thompson 1–13, Erenberg 1-(-1)

Sunday, November 10
Cincinnati Bengals 27, Browns 10
Riverfront Stadium (57,293)
White jerseys/white pants

On another rainy afternoon, the Bengals scored 10 points in the fourth quarter to break open a close game and extend the Browns' losing streak to four games, tumbling them a game behind both Pittsburgh and Cincinnati. Thwarted by a trio of turnovers, the Browns tied the game at seven in the second quarter, but the Bengals took the lead for good in the final seconds of the half. In his fifth start, Bernie Kosar threw for 229 yards—hooking up with Ozzie Newsome seven times for 94—but tossed a pair of interceptions and was sacked three times. Cincinnati was paced by WR Cris Collinsworth, who snagged eight receptions for 135 yards. The Browns were now two games below .500 and were in danger of seeing their promising start to the season go for naught.

Record: 4–6

	1	2	3	4		
Browns	0	7	3	0	=	10
Bengals	7	7	3	10	=	27

CIN-Brooks 8-yd. pass from Esiason (Breech kick)
CLE-Byner 27-yd. pass from Kosar (Bahr kick)
CIN-Alexander 1-yd. run (Breech kick)
CIN-Breech 28-yd. FG
CLE-Bahr 39-yd. FG
CIN-Breech 33-yd. FG
CIN-Kinnebrew 3-yd. run (Breech kick)

Passing
CLE: Kosar 16–32–229 1 TD 2 INT
CIN: Esiason 23–33–262 1 TD 0 INT

Rushing
CLE: Mack 9–88, Byner 7–24, Kosar 1–0
CIN: Kinnebrew 17–65, Brooks 15–52, Esiason 2–1, Alexander 1–1, Jennings 1-(-1)

Receiving
CLE: Newsome 7–94, Byner 6–85, Brennan 2–38, Langhorne 1–12
CIN: Collinsworth 8–135, Brooks 6–58, Harris 2–20, Kinnebrew 1–19, Holman 3–16, Brown 2–15, Alexander 1-(-1)

Sunday, November 17
Browns 17, Buffalo Bills 7
Cleveland Stadium (50,764)
White jerseys/white pants

Despite another lackluster performance, the Browns rallied from a 7–3 halftime deficit to defeat visiting 2–8 Buffalo and snap their month-long losing streak. The power running of Earnest Byner (109 yards) and Kevin Mack (94) sparked the comeback, while the Cleveland defense held Buffalo to 217 total yards—just 55 rushing—and forced three turnovers. A Byner touchdown run in the third quarter put the Browns ahead, followed by a Bernie Kosar-to-Ozzie Newsome scoring pass in the fourth that sealed the triumph. The victory allowed the Browns to catch up to the Bengals, who fell to the Raiders, but they remained a game back of Pittsburgh, which won in Houston.
Record: 5–6

	1	2	3	4		
Bills	7	0	0	0	=	7
Browns	3	0	7	7	=	17

CLE-Bahr 40-yd. FG
BUF-Moore 1-yd. run (Norwood kick)
CLE-Byner 4-yd. run (Bahr kick)
CLE-Newsome 11-yd. pass from Kosar (Bahr kick)

Passing
BUF: Mathison 15–30–177 0 TD 2 INT
CLE: Kosar 12–25–103 1 TD 0 INT

Rushing
BUF: Cribbs 18–52, Moore 2–2, Mathison 1–1, Bell 1–0
CLE: Byner 15–109, Mack 21–94, Kosar 1-(-2)

Receiving
BUF: Burkett 4–58, Reed 2–41, Butler 3–37, Ramson 4–31, Moore 1–6, Metzelaars 1–4
CLE: Brennan 3–48, Byner 4–20, Newsome 3–17, Weathers 1–12, Mack 1–6

Sunday, November 24
Browns 24, Cincinnati Bengals 6
Cleveland Stadium (74,439)
White jerseys/white pants

Behind a ferocious defense that dominated the league's highest-scoring offense, the Browns picked up an impressive win to catapult them back into a first-place tie in the division. Setting the tone early, the Browns sprinted to a 10–0 lead, then blew the game open in the third quarter when Gary Danielson—making his first start in seven weeks—lofted a 72-yard touchdown pass to Clarence Weathers. Behind 117 rushing yards and two touchdowns by Kevin Mack, the Browns rolled to 181 yards on the ground, while the Cleveland defense limited the high-flying Bengals to 226 total yards and collected five sacks. The victory pulled the Browns back to .500 and, thanks to a Washington win over the Steelers, they stepped back atop the division and knocked the Bengals a game behind.
Record: 6–6

	1	2	3	4		
Bengals	0	3	3	0	=	6
Browns	3	7	14	0	=	24

CLE-Bahr 29-yd. FG
CLE-Mack 2-yd. run (Bahr kick)
CIN-Breech 30-yd. FG
CLE-Weathers 72-yd. pass from Danielson (Bahr kick)
CIN-Breech 29-yd. FG
CLE-Mack 35-yd. run (Bahr kick)

Passing
CIN: Schonert 10–14–109 0 TD 0 INT, Esiason 3–5–30 0 TD 1 INT
CLE: Danielson 4–7–105 1 TD 0 INT, Kosar 1–1-(-3) 0 TD 0 INT, Fontenot 0–1–0 0 TD 0 INT

Rushing
CIN: Brooks 12–90, Alexander 4–19, Esiason 1–11, Schonert 4–10, Brown 3–7, Kinnebrew 4–6, McInally 1-(-2), Jennings 1-(-5)
CLE: Mack 14–117, Byner 21–66, Danielson 1-(-2)

Receiving
CIN: Brown 3–52, Brooks 2–27, Harris 3–21, Collinsworth 1–17, Holman 2–8, Martin 1–8, Alexander 1–6
CLE: Weathers 2–84, Brennan 1–14, Newsome 2–7

Sunday, December 1
Browns 35, New York Giants 33
Giants Stadium (66,482)
White jerseys/white pants

Despite their worst defensive performance of the season, the Browns rallied from a 12-point fourth-quarter deficit to knock off the playoff-bound Giants on their own home field thanks to a missed New York field goal on the game's final play. After an interception return for a touchdown by Cleveland DB Al Gross, the Browns soared to a 21–7 lead in the second quarter but saw the Giants carve through their defense for the remainder of the game, scoring 26 straight points to go ahead 33–21 with 12 minutes remaining. But still-hurting Gary Danielson, who replaced struggling Bernie Kosar in the third quarter, led the Browns on two touchdown drives to take the lead with less than two minutes left on Earnest Byner's second touchdown of the day, giving them their highest point total in two years. But the Giants drove inside the Cleveland 20 and were poised to win the game. Kicker Eric Schubert missed a 34-yard field goal as time expired, and the Browns danced off the field with the upset and, with a Steelers' loss to Denver, sole possession of first place in the division. New York rolled to nearly 500 total yards, including 229 via a ground attack led by RB Joe Morris, who picked up 131 and three touchdowns, but the Browns persevered to pick up what would prove to be the most impressive victory of the season.

Record: 7–6

	1	2	3	4		
Browns	7	14	0	14	=	35
Giants	7	13	3	10	=	33

NYG-Morris 3-yd. run (Schubert kick)
CLE-Mack 42-yd. run (Bahr kick)
CLE-Byner 2-yd. run (Bahr kick)
CLE-Gross 37-yd. interception return (Bahr kick)
NYG-Morris 58-yd. run (kick failed)
NYG-Johnson 29-yd. pass from Simms (Schubert kick)
NYG-Schubert 35-yd. FG
NYG-Morris 5-yd. run (Schubert kick)
NYG-Schubert 40-yd. FG
CLE-Weathers 25-yd. pass from Danielson (Bahr kick)
CLE-Byner 9-yd. run (Bahr kick)

Passing
CLE: Danielson 8–17–135 1 TD 1 INT, Kosar 6–16–86 0 TD 0 INT
NYG: Simms 23–37–289 1 TD 2 INT

Rushing
CLE: Mack 14–66, Byner 14–44, Kosar 3-(-1)
NYG: Morris 22–131, Adams 3–40, Simms 3–29, Galbreath 1–13, Carpenter 2–9, Carthon 2–7

Receiving
CLE: Weathers 3–59, Byner 3–55, Newsome 3–52, Brennan 2–30, Young 1–17, Mack 2–8
NYG: Bavaro 3–60, Johnson 2–48, McConkey 3–39, Galbreath 4–37, Carpenter 3–29, Adams 5–27, Williams 2–27, Carthon 1–22

Sunday, December 8
Seattle Seahawks 31, Browns 13
Seattle Kingdome (58,477)
White jerseys/white pants

The momentum picked up during back-to-back impressive victories evaporated in Seattle as the Browns lost four fumbles—two leading to Seahawks' touchdowns and another costing the Browns points at the end of the first half—and were crushed in the Kingdome for the second straight year. Behind the hot hand of QB Dave Krieg, who threw four touchdown passes, the Seahawks took a 17–3 halftime lead and extended it to 31–6 in the fourth quarter before Bernie Kosar lofted a long touchdown pass to WR Glen Young for Cleveland's lone touchdown. The defeat once again dropped the Browns into a first-place tie in the AFC Central with Cincinnati with two games to play.

Record: 7–7

	1	2	3	4		
Browns	3	0	3	7	=	13
Seahawks	3	14	7	7	=	31

SEA-Johnson 51-yd. FG
CLE-Bahr 27-yd. FG
SEA-Ross 4-yd. pass from Krieg (Johnson kick)
SEA-Turner 8-yd. pass from Krieg (Johnson kick)
CLE-Bahr 32-yd. FG
SEA-Turner 15-yd. pass from Krieg (Johnson kick)
SEA-Largent 9-yd. pass from Krieg (Johnson kick)
CLE-Young 45-yd. pass from Kosar (Bahr kick)

Passing
CLE: Kosar 18–31–249 1 TD 0 INT
SEA: Krieg 24–34–268 4 TD 0 INT

Rushing
CLE: Mack 9–44, Byner 12–42, Dickey 2–6
SEA: Hughes 9–38, Warner 12–24, Morris 6–24, Parros 4–7, Lane 1–3, Krieg 1-(-1), Gilbert 1-(-3)

Receiving
CLE: Brennan 3–74, Byner 6–70, Young 1–45, Newsome 4–31, Banks 1–13, Tucker 1–10, Mack 1–4, Fontenot 1–2
SEA: Largent 5–89, Turner 3–40, Skansi 3–37, Warner 4–34, Lane 2–29, Hughes 2–13, Tice 2–13, Ross 2–10, Morris 1–3

Sunday, December 15
Browns 28, Houston Oilers 21
Cleveland Stadium (50,793)
White jerseys/white pants

On a dark, bitterly cold afternoon, the Browns assumed the driver's seat in the divisional race with a victory over Houston, led by new coach Jerry Glanville, who replaced Hugh Campbell earlier in the week. Controlling the football with an effective running attack, the Browns scored on the first rushing touchdown of Bernie Kosar's career and grabbed a 14–0 lead when Ozzie Newsome scored a touchdown on the five-hundredth reception of his career. Then, aided by an 81-yard return of the second-half kickoff by rookie Herman Fontenot, the Browns stretched the lead to 28–7. The Oilers scored two touchdowns in the final minutes to pull within seven, but the Browns hung on for a much-needed victory, completing their division schedule with a 4–2 record. Kosar led the way, throwing for three touchdowns in addition to his scoring scamper, and he was named AFC Offensive Player of the Week. With the Bengals losing a close game in Washington, the Browns were now a game ahead of both Pittsburgh and Cincinnati with one to play.
Record: 8–7

	1	2	3	4		
Oilers	0	7	0	14	=	21
Browns	7	7	14	0	=	28

CLE-Kosar 2-yd. run (Bahr kick)
CLE-Newsome 2-yd. pass from Kosar (Bahr kick)
HOU-Rozier 3-yd. run (Zendejas kick)
CLE-Banks 8 yd. pass from Kosar (Bahr kick)
CLE-Mack 5-yd. pass from Kosar (Bahr kick)
HOU-Woolfolk 15-yd. pass from Moon (Zendejas kick)
HOU-Smith 16-yd. pass from Moon (Zendejas kick)

Passing
HOU: Moon 22–48–339 2 TD 2 INT
CLE: Kosar 14–28–161 3 TD 0 INT

Rushing
HOU: Rozier 24–80, Moon 1–11, Woolfolk 2–9, Edwards 1-(-4)
CLE: Byner 22–87, Mack 13–72, Davis 1–0, Kosar 3-(-1)

Receiving
HOU: Smith 7–125, Woolfolk 7–96, Hill 3–62, Williams 1–20, Rozier 2–15, Edwards 1–12, Drewrey 1–9
CLE: Newsome 4–85, Brennan 4–40, Byner 3–13, Tucker 1–10, Banks 1–8, Mack 1–5

Sunday, December 22
New York Jets 37, Browns 10
Giants Stadium (59,073)
Brown jerseys/white pants

After clinching the division title the previous afternoon when Pittsburgh lost to the New York Giants, the Browns were routed on the same field by the Jets, who needed a victory to secure a wild-card spot. Aided by a punt return for a touchdown by Brian Brennan—the first by a Cleveland player in 18 years—the Browns took an early lead, and the game was tied at 10 in the second quarter before the Jets exploded for 27 unanswered points to win easily. The only Cleveland highlight of the second half came on the final play as Earnest Byner rushed for nine yards to give him 101 for the game and 1,002 for the season. He joined Kevin Mack, who'd already topped 1,000 yards, and made the Browns just the third team in NFL history to have two 1,000-yard rushers in the same season. Despite the sour finish to the season and a mediocre 8–8 record, the Browns would receive a week off before entering the playoffs against AFC East-champion Miami.
Record: 8–8

	1	2	3	4		
Browns	7	3	0	0	=	10
Jets	10	7	10	10	=	37

NYJ-Leahy 46-yd. FG
CLE-Brennan 37-yd. punt return (Bahr kick)
NYJ-Sohn 39-yd. pass from O'Brien (Leahy kick)
CLE-Bahr 32-yd. FG
NYJ-Hector 5-yd. run (Leahy kick)
NYJ-Hector 1-yd. run (Leahy kick)
NYJ-Leahy 35-yd. FG
NYJ-Leahy 32-yd. FG
NYJ-Paige 1-yd. run (Leahy kick)

Passing
CLE: Kosar 10–23–121 0 TD 1 INT, Gossett 0–1–0 0 TD 0 INT
NYJ: O'Brien 21–34–251 1 TD 1 INT

Rushing
CLE: Byner 15–101, Mack 12–30, Kosar 3–7
NYJ: McNeil 26–74, Paige 3–31, Hector 8–30, O'Brien 1–0

Receiving
CLE: Brennan 6–69, Newsome 2–31, Fontenot 1–17, Byner 1–4
NYJ: Shuler 6–83, McNeil 6–53, Sohn 2–51, Toon 4–30, Hector 1–14, Walker 1–11, Kiever 1–9

AFC Divisional Playoff
Saturday, January 4
Miami Dolphins 24, Browns 21
Orange Bowl (75,128)
Brown jerseys/white pants

	1	2	3	4		
Browns	7	7	7	0	=	21
Dolphins	3	0	14	7	=	24

MIA-Reveiz 51-yd. FG
CLE-Newsome 16-yd. pass from Kosar (Bahr kick)
CLE-Byner 21-yd. run (Bahr kick)
CLE-Byner 66-yd. run (Bahr kick)
MIA-Moore 6-yd. pass from Marino (Reveiz kick)
MIA-Davenport 31-yd. run (Reveiz kick)
MIA-Davenport 1-yd. run (Reveiz kick)

Passing
CLE: Kosar 10–19–66 1 TD 1 INT
MIA: Marino 25–45–238 1 TD 1 INT

Rushing
CLE: Byner 16–161, Mack 13–56, Dickey 6–28, Kosar 2–6
MIA: Davenport 6–48, Nathan 7–21, Bennett 4–17, Carter 2–6

Receiving
CLE: Byner 4–25, Newsome 2–22, Weathers 1–12, Fontenot 1–5, Holt 2–2
MIA: Nathan 10–101, Hardy 5–51, Moore 4–29, Johnson 2–17, Rose 1–17, Clayton 1–15, Bennett 1–6, Carter 1–2

While many observers felt the Browns had no business in the playoffs, particularly with a handful of teams with better records who didn't qualify, they assumed they'd get what was coming to them when they faced the 12–4 Dolphins, the defending AFC champions who'd finished the regular season on seven-game winning streak. But the upstart Browns had a few surprises in store.

Parlaying a nearly unstoppable running game, the Browns controlled the line of scrimmage throughout the first half and took a 7–3 lead on a Bernie Kosar-to-Ozzie Newsome touchdown pass to cap an 82-yard drive. Cleveland DB Don Rogers then halted a promising Miami drive by intercepting QB Dan Marino at the goal line and racing to midfield, setting up a 21-yard touchdown run by Earnest Byner just before the half that put the underdogs ahead by 11.

Then, five minutes into the third quarter, Byner broke free again, this time for a 66-yard touchdown jaunt that made it 21–3, and the Browns were poised for a colossal upset. But the explosive Miami offense couldn't be contained any longer, scoring on its next two possessions to cut the margin to four points going into the final quarter. The Browns drove to midfield with eight minutes left but were stopped on a key third-and-two and were forced to punt back to the Dolphins, who drove for the go-ahead touchdown on a one-yard plunge by RB Ron Davenport with 1:57 left.

The Browns' offense, not designed to score quickly, frantically plowed to midfield before time expired, and the Dolphins had escaped to advance to the AFC Championship for the second straight year on the strength of what at the time was the biggest comeback in AFC playoff history. While the Cleveland running game had been spectacular, rolling to a team playoff record 251 yards and led by Byner's 161 on 16 carries, the air attack proved to be a liability. Kosar completed just 10 of 19 passes for a mere 66 yards, and it was clear that steps would need to be taken in the offseason to elevate the offense and the team as a whole.

1986

Sunday, September 7
Chicago Bears 41, Browns 31
Soldier Field (66,030)
White jerseys/white pants

Facing the defending world champions on their own home field on opening day, the Browns hung tough with a sterling offensive performance before falling in what became a shoot-out. The Browns made history on the third play of the game when DB Al Gross recovered a fumbled snap in the end zone before going out of bounds for a touchdown, which was confirmed by the first instant-replay review in NFL history. The Browns' lead vanished as the Bears returned the following kickoff for a touchdown and scored another pair before the first quarter was over to take control of the game. Rolling to 349 yards against the vaunted Chicago defense, the Browns stayed close throughout the second half, pulling within three points on a touchdown catch by WR Brian Brennan with less than six minutes to play. But the Bears clinched victory with a long drive capped by their fifth touchdown with two minutes left. Under new offensive coordinator Lindy Infante, the Browns' passing game was suddenly vibrant, as QB Bernie Kosar threw for 289 yards, including six completions to RB Earnest Byner for 94 yards. But the Bears' offense was even better, led by RB Walter Payton, who rushed for 113 yards and scored a pair of touchdowns.

Record: 0–1

	1	2	3	4		
Browns	7	7	7	10	=	31
Bears	21	3	7	10	=	41

CLE-Gross recovered fumble in end zone (Bahr kick)
CHI-Gentry 91-yd. kickoff return (Butler kick)
CHI-Payton 2-yd. run (Butler kick)
CHI-Marshall 58-yd. interception return (Butler kick)
CLE-Mack 3-yd. run (Bahr kick)
CHI-Butler 47-yd. FG
CLE-Mack 14-yd. run (Bahr kick)
CHI-Payton 11-yd. pass from McMahon (Butler kick)
CLE-Bahr 22-yd. FG
CHI-Butler 19-yd. FG
CLE-Brennan 15-yd. pass from Kosar (Bahr kick)
CHI-Suhey 6-yd. run (Butler kick)

Passing
CLE: Kosar 23–40–289 1 TD 1 INT
CHI: McMahon 10–20–135 1 TD 0 INT, Tomczak 3–6–48 0 TD 0 INT, Payton 0–1–0 0 TD 0 INT

Rushing
CLE: Mack 10–50, Byner 13–18, Fontenot 1–1
CHI: Payton 22–113, McMahon 4–34, Suhey 7–22, Gentry 2–21, Sanders 1–2, Thomas 1–1

Receiving
CLE: Byner 6–94, Brennan 5–71, Slaughter 4–45, Fontenot 3–28, Greer 1–22, Mack 2–14, Newsome 1–14, Kosar 1–1
CHI: Suhey 6–85, Gault 3–59, Payton 2–20, Wrightman 1–14, Moorehead 1–5

Sunday, September 14
Browns 23, Houston Oilers 20
Houston Astrodome (46,049)
White jerseys/white pants

On the cusp of a second straight defeat to open the season, the Browns scored two touchdowns in the final 2:10 to pull out an important divisional victory. Down 13–9, the struggling Cleveland offense—which had tallied no first downs and minus-four total yards in the second half—drove near midfield, where Bernie Kosar lofted a 55-yard touchdown pass to WR Reggie Langhorne to put the Browns ahead. Houston fumbled the ensuing kickoff—its fifth turnover of the day—and the Browns recovered, putting the icing on the cake when Earnest Byner scored five plays later. Houston added a last-gasp touchdown, but the Browns hung on to win despite being outgained by more than 160 yards and picking up only nine first downs.

Record: 1–1

	1	2	3	4		
Browns	0	3	6	14	=	23
Oilers	7	0	0	13	=	20

HOU-Moriarty 8-yd. run (Zendejas kick)
CLE-Bahr 34-yd. FG
CLE-Bahr 29-yd. FG

CLE-Bahr 45-yd. FG
HOU-Zendejas 35-yd. FG
HOU-Zendejas 36-yd. FG
CLE-Langhorne 55-yd. pass from Kosar (Bahr kick)
CLE-Byner 1-yd. run (Bahr kick)
HOU-Woolfolk 20-yd. pass from Moon (Zendejas kick)

Passing
CLE: Kosar 11–26–180 1 TD 0 INT
HOU: Moon 22–31–264 1 TD 3 INT

Rushing
CLE: Byner 21–56, Fontenot 1–11, Dickey 4–10, Kosar 2–10
HOU: Rozier 20–69, Moriarty 16–46, Moon 3–22, Woolfolk 1–3

Receiving
CLE: Langhorne 3–115, Byner 2–19, Newsome 2–19, Slaughter 2–13, Greer 1–13, Fontenot 1–1
HOU: Woolfolk 6–60, Rozier 5–52, Givins 4–45, Pinkett 3–44, Drewrey 1–28, Williams 2–18, Moriarty 1–17

Thursday, September 18
Cincinnati Bengals 30, Browns 13
Cleveland Stadium (78,779)
White jerseys/white pants

On national television on a Thursday night, the Cleveland defense was overwhelmed for the third straight week as the Bengals blew open a tight game in the second half and coasted to a surprisingly easy victory. The Browns got off to a good start when DB Felix Wright blocked a Cincinnati punt late in the first quarter, and fellow DB Frank Minnifield recovered in the end zone to put the home team up 7–3. The game was tied at 13 midway through the third quarter when the Bengals used an almost unstoppable running attack to pull away. Rolling up 257 yards on the ground and nearly 400 total, Cincinnati scored the game's final 17 points, including two of RB Larry Kinnebrew's three touchdowns. Meanwhile, the Cleveland offense was able to move the football but, for the second straight week, struggled to put up points as the Browns dropped below .500.
Record: 1–2

	1	2	3	4		
Bengals	3	10	7	10	=	30
Browns	7	3	3	0	=	13

CIN-Breech 49-yd. FG
CLE-Minnifield recovered blocked punt in end zone (Bahr kick)
CIN-Kinnebrew 2-yd. run (Breech kick)
CIN-Breech 33-yd. FG
CLE-Bahr 19-yd. FG
CLE-Bahr 34-yd. FG
CIN-Kinnebrew 2-yd. run (Breech kick)
CIN-Kinnebrew 4-yd. run (Breech kick)
CIN-Breech 25-yd. FG

Passing
CIN: Esiason 12–21–152 0 TD 1 INT
CLE: Kosar 28–40–293 0 TD 0 INT

Rushing
CIN: Brooks 14–118, Kinnebrew 25–94, Johnson 1–34, Brown 1–13, Esiason 1-(-2)
CLE: Dickey 15–67, Byner 9–16

Receiving
CIN: Brown 3–41, Brooks 3–40, Holman 3–36, Collinsworth 2–24, Martin 1–11
CLE: Byner 10–77, Brennan 5–63, Langhorne 4–61, Fontenot 3–29, Tucker 2–29, Slaughter 2–25, Newsome 2–9

Sunday, September 28
Browns 24, Detroit Lions 21
Cleveland Stadium (72,029)
White jerseys/white pants

With the offense struggling, the Browns capitalized on a timely special-teams touchdown to pull out a narrow home victory over Detroit to even their record. The Browns caught a break on their first score when RB Kevin Mack fumbled the football into the end zone, but WR Brian Brennan pounced on it to avoid disaster and get the Browns on the board. With the game tied at seven five minutes into the second half, Cleveland WR Gerald "Ice Cube" McNeil broke free on a punt return for an 84-yard touchdown—the longest punt return for a score in team history—to give the Browns the lead and shift the game's momentum. The Lions rebounded with another touchdown to tie, but the Browns scored 10 points in the fourth quarter, then held off the Lions and closed out the victory. Outgained in total yardage for the fourth consecutive game, the Browns could manage only 254 yards of offense and were lucky to escape with the win at home against a team that wound up with a 5–11 record.
Record: 2–2

	1	2	3	4		
Lions	0	7	0	14	=	21
Browns	0	7	7	10	=	24

CLE-Brennan recovered fumble in end zone (Bahr kick)
DET-Thompson 3-yd. pass from Hipple (Murray kick)
CLE-McNeil 84-yd. punt return (Bahr kick)
DET-Jones 6-yd. pass from Hipple (Murray kick)
CLE-Bahr 24-yd. FG
CLE-Dickey 1-yd. run (Bahr kick)
DET-Bland 3-yd. pass from Hipple (Murray kick)

Passing
DET: Hipple 33–48–251 3 TD 0 INT
CLE: Kosar 17–27–139 0 TD 0 INT, Brennan 1–1–35 0 TD 0 INT

Rushing
DET: Jones 23–68, Hipple 3–27, James 4–10
CLE: Byner 12–69, Mack 4–12, Dickey 5–5, Kosar 1-(-2)

Receiving
DET: Jones 12–85, Chadwick 3–41, James 6–34, Hunter 3–31, Lewis 2–22, Mandley 2–13, Thompson 2–10, Bland 2–8, Moore 1–7
CLE: Byner 6–38, Fontenot 1–35, Mack 2–29, Langhorne 3–20, Brennan 2–20, Slaughter 2–20, Newsome 1–10, Weathers 1–2

Sunday, October 5
Browns 27, Pittsburgh Steelers 24
Three Rivers Stadium (57,327)
White jerseys/white pants

After 16 years of frustration and heartbreak, the Browns finally won for the first time at Three Rivers Stadium, knocking off the Steelers in a nail-biter. After surging to a 10–0 lead in the first quarter, the Browns fell behind before Gerald McNeil ignited a turnaround with a 100-yard kickoff return for a touchdown, Cleveland's first in 12 years. The Browns fought through a seesaw second half to take the lead with under nine minutes left on an Earnest Byner touchdown run. But when Matt Bahr missed a chip-shot field goal in the final minutes, and Pittsburgh drove into Cleveland territory with 90 seconds left, the stage seemed to be set for another Three Rivers defeat. But this time the Browns recovered a fumble, and then Bernie Kosar completed a 38-yard pass to Reggie Langhorne to give them the first down necessary to run out the clock, and the Three Rivers jinx was over. While the Cleveland offense struggled, the defense forced four turnovers and the Browns took advantage of 109 yards in penalties on the Steelers to end a frustrating chapter in team history and climb back above .500.

Record: 3–2

	1	2	3	4		
Browns	10	7	3	7	=	27
Steelers	0	14	7	3	=	24

CLE-Slaughter 15-yd. pass from Kosar (Bahr kick)
CLE-Bahr 22-yd. FG
PIT-Malone 1-yd. run (Anderson kick)
PIT-Erenberg 5-yd. pass from Malone (Anderson kick)
CLE-McNeil 100-yd. kickoff return (Bahr kick)
PIT-Lipps 6-yd. pass from Malone (Anderson kick)
CLE-Bahr 39-yd. FG
PIT-Anderson 45-yd. FG
CLE-Byner 4-yd. run

Passing
CLE: Kosar 14–23–186 1 TD 0 INT
PIT: Malone 15–23–143 2 TD 1 INT

Rushing
CLE: Byner 17–79, Dickey 5–21, Fontenot 5–11, Kosar 5-(-3)
PIT: Jackson 14–83, Erenberg 17–79, Abercrombie 4–19, Malone 3–2, Hughes 1–0, Lipps 1-(-7)

Receiving
CLE: Langhorne 4–108, Byner 5–29, Slaughter 2–20, Newsome 2–18, Brennan 1–11
PIT: Hughes 5–40, Gothard 2–31, Sweeney 2–29, Erenberg 3–23, Lipps 2–17, Jackson 1–3

Sunday, October 12
Browns 20, Kansas City Chiefs 7
Cleveland Stadium (71,278)
White jerseys/white pants

On the strength of their best defensive performance in 13 years, the Browns dominated the playoff-bound Chiefs to win their third straight game and remain tied with Cincinnati for first place in the AFC Central. Kansas City could manage just 126 total yards—only 43 rushing, though Cleveland ranked last in the NFL in ground yardage allowed—and the Browns' defense collected four sacks. Meanwhile, the offense scored the game's final 20 points to win comfortably, overcoming more than 100 yards in penalties. Bernie Kosar paced a potent air attack, throwing for 287 yards with five different receivers each topping 40 yards.

Record: 4–2

	1	2	3	4		
Chiefs	0	7	0	0	=	7
Browns	0	7	10	3	=	20

KC-Paige 26-yd. pass from Blackledge (Lowery kick)
CLE-Byner 16-yd. pass from Kosar (Bahr kick)
CLE-Newsome 6-yd. pass from Kosar (Bahr kick)
CLE-Bahr 34-yd. FG
CLE-Bahr 36-yd. FG

Passing
KC: Blackledge 11–26–109 1 TD 1 INT
CLE: Kosar 22–35–287 2 TD 1 INT

Rushing
KC: M. Pruitt 9–20, Green 4–15, Blackledge 3–6, Heard 5–2
CLE: Byner 19–35, Dickey 7–26, McNeil 1–12, Kosar 1-(-2)

Receiving
KC: Paige 2–34, Smith 3–23, Harry 1–18, Heard 2–13, M. Pruitt 2–12, Marshall 1–9
CLE: Langhorne 3–59, Brennan 3–54, Byner 5–51, Newsome 4–47, Fontenot 4–44, Slaughter 2–23, McNeil 1–9

Sunday, October 19
Green Bay Packers 17, Browns 14
Cleveland Stadium (76,438)
White jerseys/white pants

The Browns' winning streak came to a screeching halt with a stunning home loss to the 0–6 Packers, directed by former Browns' coach Forrest Gregg. The Browns took control early, surging to a 14–3 halftime lead and appeared poised for a rout, particularly after a partially blocked punt put them in position for more points just before the half. But Bernie Kosar threw a costly interception in the end zone, which turned the momentum for the rest of the sunny autumn afternoon. And when Earnest Byner left the game with an injured ankle—an injury that would sideline him for the remainder of the regular season—the Browns' offense imploded, managing just 32 rushing yards on 22 carries. Green Bay scored a pair of touchdowns in the third quarter to take the lead, while the sputtering Cleveland offense could only threaten to score on its final two possessions, both ending on failed fourth-down conversions in Green Bay territory. The defeat dropped the Browns out of first place and suggested that the season was about to become a major disappointment.
Record: 4–3

	1	2	3	4		
Packers	0	3	14	0	=	17
Browns	7	7	0	0	=	14

CLE-Byner 3-yd. pass from Kosar (Bahr kick)
GB-Del Greco 24-yd. FG
CLE-Brennan 15-yd. pass from Kosar (Bahr kick)
GB-Ellis 2-yd. run (Del Greco kick)
GB-Epps 47-yd. pass from Wright (Del Greco kick)

Passing
GB: Wright 21–27–277 1 TD 0 INT
CLE: Kosar 28–36–222 2 TD 1 INT, Gossett 1–1–30 0 TD 0 INT

Rushing
GB: Davis 10–65, Epps 1–20, Ellis 6–16, Ellerson 7–1, Carruth 4–1, Wright 1-(-7)
CLE: Mack 16–41, Byner 3–4, Kosar 1–0, Fontenot 1-(-2), Langhorne 1-(-11)

Receiving
GB: Epps 5–88, Ellis 4–65, Ivery 2–30, Lofton 2–25, Ellerson 2–18, Ross 1–16, West 1–13, Stanley 1–8, Carruth 2–7, Davis 1–7
CLE: Mack 8–68, Langhorne 6–62, Brennan 3–47, Fontenot 4–25, Newsome 3–21, Byner 3–20, Slaughter 2–9

Sunday, October 26
Browns 23, Minnesota Vikings 20
Hubert H. Humphrey Metrodome (59,133)
White jerseys/white pants

Cleveland's special teams salvaged the season as the Browns rallied from a 17–3 halftime deficit to pull out a satisfying comeback victory over a hot Vikings team that in the previous two weeks had defeated the last two Super Bowl champions. After a disastrous first half that saw the Browns manage only 55 yards of offense and allow four sacks, everything changed two minutes into the third quarter when Frank Minnifield blocked a Minnesota punt, and Felix Wright returned it 30 yards for the Browns' first touchdown. They tied the game on a Curtis Dickey touchdown run with 4:23 remaining, then Wright recovered a Minnesota fumble on the ensuing kickoff to set up the go-ahead field goal with under two minutes to play. But the Vikings quickly marched downfield and were poised to send the game to overtime with a 45-yard field-goal attempt with 12 seconds left. But Minnifield broke through to block the kick to preserve the Cleveland lead and deliver a gritty victory. The Browns were outgained by nearly 200 yards, but the offense got rolling in the second half, paced by Dickey, filling in for Byner, who turned in the only 100-yard rushing game of his Browns career. With a Cincinnati loss in Pittsburgh, the Browns surged back into a tie for first in the division. The victory also served as a turning point for the season, beginning a string of eight victories in the Browns' final nine games.

Record: 5–3

	1	2	3	4		
Browns	3	0	7	13	=	23
Vikings	3	14	3	0	=	20

MIN-Nelson 33-yd. FG
CLE-Bahr 52-yd. FG
MIN-Nelson 5-yd. run (Nelson kick)
MIN-Carter 8-yd. pass from Kramer (Nelson kick)
CLE-Wright 30-yd. blocked punt return (Bahr kick)
MIN-Nelson 32-yd. FG
CLE-Bahr 19-yd. FG
CLE-Dickey 17-yd. run (Bahr kick)
CLE-Bahr 22-yd. FG

Passing
CLE: Kosar 9–18–101 0 TD 1 INT
MIN: Kramer 18–35–261 1 TD 1 INT

Rushing
CLE: Dickey 19–106, Mack 11–44, Kosar 1-(-1)
MIN: Nelson 22–118, Anderson 3–21, Rice 4–9, Brown 3–9, Kramer 2–5, Lewis 1-(-4)

Receiving
CLE: Langhorne 2–37, Slaughter 3–29, Mack 2–25, Newsome 2–10
MIN: Rice 4–71, Lewis 3–61, Nelson 3–37, Jordan 3–26, Gustafson 1–18, Jones 1–15, Anderson 1–14, Brown 1–11, Carter 1–8

Sunday, November 2
Browns 24, Indianapolis Colts 9
Hoosier Dome (57,962)
White jerseys/white pants

Finding themselves in an identical spot as two weeks earlier against Green Bay, this time the Browns pulled away from the winless Colts after grabbing a 14–3 halftime lead and coasted to an easy victory in their first game in the Hoosier Dome. Bernie Kosar threw three touchdown passes, including a 72-yarder to RB Herman Fontenot and a nine-yard strike to TE Ozzie Newsome in the opening moments of the third quarter following an Indianapolis fumble. The Cleveland defense collected a season-high seven sacks as the Browns kept pace with the Bengals, who triumphed in Detroit.

Record: 6–3

	1	2	3	4		
Browns	14	0	10	0	=	24
Colts	0	3	0	6	=	9

CLE-Brennan 14-yd. pass from Kosar (Bahr kick)
CLE-Fontenot 72-yd. pass from Kosar (Bahr kick)
IND-Biasucci 40-yd. FG
CLE-Newsome 9-yd. pass from Kosar (Bahr kick)
CLE-Bahr 38-yd. FG
IND-Bouza 6-yd. pass from Trudeau (kick failed)

Passing
CLE: Kosar 15–25–238 3 TD 0 INT
IND: Trudeau 20–42–208 1 TD 0 INT

Rushing
CLE: Mack 17–39, Dickey 5–10, Fontenot 1-(-1), Kosar 3-(-2)
IND: Gill 13–59, McMillan 9–40, Trudeau 2–11, Wonsley 1-(-5)

Receiving
CLE: Fontenot 3–86, Newsome 3–49, Brennan 3–42, Slaughter 3–34, Langhorne 1–12, Dickey 1–11, Mack 1–4
IND: Brooks 5–63, McMillan 3–57, Bouza 5–44, LaFleur 3–21, Gill 3–20, Beach 1–3

Monday, November 10
Browns 26, Miami Dolphins 16
Cleveland Stadium (77,949)
White jerseys/white pants

Behind an amazing offensive performance, the Browns avenged their playoff loss nine months earlier with a convincing Monday-night victory over Miami. The offense rolled up 558 total yards, second-best in team history, led by 401 passing yards by Bernie Kosar in the finest game of his career to date. Kosar completed 32 passes to eight different receivers on a chilly November night but didn't throw a touchdown pass as four potential scoring throws were dropped. A touchdown run on an end-around by TE

Harry Holt gave the Browns a 10-point lead in the second quarter, then a scoring run by Curtis Dickey, who ran for 92 yards on the night, helped the Browns build a 16-point second-half lead and coast to a satisfying victory that underlined their potentially explosive passing game. A Bengals' loss in Houston the day before allowed the Browns to take over sole possession of first place with the win.

Record: 7–3

	1	2	3	4		
Dolphins	0	10	0	6	=	16
Browns	6	10	7	3	=	26

CLE-Bahr 32-yd. FG
CLE-Bahr 19-yd. FG
MIA-Reveiz 20-yd. FG
CLE-Holt 16-yd. run (Bahr kick)
MIA-Duper 24-yd. pass from Marino (Reveiz kick)
CLE-Bahr 18-yd. FG
CLE-Dickey 13-yd. run (Bahr kick)
CLE-Bahr 21-yd. FG
MIA-Clayton 22-yd. pass from Marino (kick failed)

Passing
MIA: Marino 22–39–295 2 TD 1 INT
CLE: Kosar 32–50–401 0 TD 0 INT, Gossett 0–1–0 0 TD 1 INT

Rushing
MIA: Davenport 7–33, Clayton 1–22, Marino 1–5, Nathan 1–2, Hampton 7-(-4)
CLE: Dickey 15–92, Fontenot 3–30, Mack 8–27, Holt 1–16, Everett 1–3

Receiving
MIA: Clayton 6–99, Duper 5–83, Hardy 4–45, Nathan 2–29, Davenport 2–15, Hampton 2–13, Johnson 1–11
CLE: Newsome 7–94, Mack 6–94, Fontenot 4–55, Langhorne 4–47, Dickey 5–40, Weathers 3–40, Brennan 2–18, Slaughter 1–13

Sunday, November 16
Los Angeles Raiders 27, Browns 14
Los Angeles Memorial Coliseum (65,461)
White jerseys/white pants

Following a short week of preparation and a cross-country trip, the Browns fell flat against the physical Raiders, who bullied the Browns for a convincing victory. Bernie Kosar was sacked six times, and the Browns managed only eight first downs for the game as the Raiders jumped to a 17–0 lead early in the second quarter. Cleveland cut the lead to three midway through the third quarter after a pair of short Kevin Mack touchdown runs, but QB Jim Plunkett's third touchdown pass in the opening seconds of the fourth quarter helped the Raiders put the game away. The loss, combined with a Cincinnati win over Seattle earlier that afternoon, dropped the Browns back into a tie for first place but would also represent their final defeat of the regular season.

Record: 7–4

	1	2	3	4		
Browns	0	7	7	0	=	14
Raiders	10	7	0	10	=	27

LA-Williams 46-yd. pass from Plunkett (C. Bahr kick)
LA-C. Bahr 40-yd. FG
LA-Christensen 3-yd. pass from Plunkett (C. Bahr kick)
CLE-Mack 1-yd. run (M. Bahr kick)
CLE-Mack 2-yd. run (M. Bahr kick)
LA-Williams 43-yd. pass from Plunkett (C. Bahr kick)
LA-C. Bahr 27-yd. FG

Passing
CLE: Kosar 15–34–188 0 TD 2 INT
LA: Plunkett 14–26–220 3 TD 0 INT

Rushing
CLE: Dickey 10–39, Mack 8–31, Kosar 1–2, Fontenot 1–0
LA: Allen 13–56, McCallum 16–47, Hawkins 5–13, Plunkett 3–5

Receiving
CLE: Brennan 5–74, Fontenot 5–43, Slaughter 1–35, Greer 1–16, Langhorne 1–8, Weathers 1–8, Newsome 1–4
LA: Williams 3–113, Christensen 6–52, Barksdale 1–24, Moffett 2–23, McCallum 1–5, Allen 1–3

Sunday, November 23
Browns 37, Pittsburgh Steelers 31 (OT)
Cleveland Stadium (76,452)
White jerseys/white pants

In perhaps the most exciting game of the regular season, the Browns overcame the Steelers to win an overtime thriller that saw the teams combine for nearly 900 yards of offense on a gloomy November afternoon. The teams traded touchdowns throughout the game, with the Steelers rallying for a field goal with seven seconds remaining to tie the game after the Browns had surged ahead 31–28 with under two minutes to play. The Browns collected 35 first downs and 536 yards of offense, the most ever against a Pittsburgh defense. Bernie Kosar led the charge, topping his performance against Miami two weeks earlier with a team-record 414 passing yards, connecting with nine different receivers. Webster Slaughter was his primary target, catching six for 134, including the game-winner in overtime on a 36-yard bomb six minutes into sudden-death. With the victory, the Browns completed their first season sweep of Pittsburgh in 17 years. The only bad news for the Browns coming out of the victory was a knee injury to kicker Matt Bahr that would sideline him for the remainder of the season and much of the next.

Record: 8–4

	1	2	3	4	OT		
Steelers	7	7	7	10	0	=	31
Browns	0	21	7	3	6	=	37

PIT-Abercrombie 1-yd. run (Anderson kick)
CLE-Dickey 2-yd. run (Bahr kick)
CLE-Mack 1-yd. run (Bahr kick)
PIT-Abercrombie 38-yd. run (Anderson kick)
CLE-Newsome 20-yd. pass from Kosar (Bahr kick)
PIT-Malone 1-yd. run (Anderson kick)
CLE-Dickey 4-yd. run (Bahr kick)
PIT-Malone 1-yd. run (Anderson kick)
CLE-Bahr 25-yd. FG
PIT-Anderson 40-yd. FG
CLE-Slaughter 36-yd. pass from Kosar

Passing
PIT: Malone 17–28–197 0 TD 1 INT
CLE: Kosar 28–46–414 2 TD 1 INT

Rushing
PIT: Abercrombie 15–86, Jackson 14–53, Erenberg 1–2, Malone 3–1
CLE: Mack 24–106, Dickey 9–17, Kosar 1-(-1)

Receiving
PIT: Lipps 4–85, Stallworth 4–48, Gothard 2–27, Abercrombie 4–26, Erenberg 2–13, Jackson 1-(-2)
CLE: Slaughter 6–134, Brennan 5–87, Langhorne 4–54, Fontenot 5–46, Newsome 2–32, Holt 2–26, Mack 2–15, Weathers 1–15, Dickey 1–5

Sunday, November 30
Browns 13, Houston Oilers 10 (OT)
Cleveland Stadium (62,309)
White jerseys/white pants

On a blustery, overcast afternoon, both offenses struggled to put points on the board and went through nearly five quarters of play before the Browns emerged victorious in the final minute of overtime. With the wind wreaking havoc on both teams' passing attacks—they each completed less than 50 percent of their passes and combined to throw nine interceptions—neither team scored in the first half. With Kevin Mack topping the 100-yard mark for the second straight week, the Browns crept to a 10–3 lead with less than six minutes to play. But then Houston, led by backup QB Oliver Luck, rallied for a touchdown in the final minute of regulation to send the Browns to sudden-death for the second straight week. Frank Minnifield dominated the extra session with a pair of interceptions, the second of which put the Browns in position for the game-winning field goal. New kicker Mark Moseley, signed earlier in the week to replace injured Matt Bahr, booted a 29-yard field goal with 16 seconds left in overtime to give the Browns an ugly but important victory. When Cincinnati lost in Denver later that afternoon, the Browns retook sole possession of first in the division.

Record: 9–4

	1	2	3	4	OT		
Oilers	0	0	3	7	0	=	10
Browns	0	0	0	10	3	=	13

HOU-Zendejas 47-yd. FG
CLE-Brennan 33-yd. pass from Kosar (Moseley kick)
CLE-Moseley 23-yd. FG
HOU-Wallace 11-yd. pass from Luck (Zendejas kick)
CLE-Moseley 29-yd. FG

Passing
HOU: Luck 12–15–112 1 TD 2 INT, Moon 5–23–68 0 TD 4 INT
CLE: Kosar 16–41–172 1 TD 3 INT

Rushing
HOU: Wallace 10–74, Rozier 7–26, Pinkett 11–18, Luck 1–8, Moon 3–4, Givins 1-(-2)
CLE: Mack 28–121, Fontenot 4–27, Dickey 8–15, Kosar 2–12

Receiving
HOU: Givins 3–52, Wallace 5–48, Hill 2–29, Pinkett 4–21, Rozier 1–15, Drewrey 1–11, Williams 1–4
CLE: Brennan 7–76, Fontenot 4–53, Slaughter 2–23, Langhorne 1–18, Newsome 1–3, Mack 1-(-1)

Sunday, December 7
Browns 21, Buffalo Bills 17
Rich Stadium (42,213)
White jerseys/white pants

On a cold, rainy afternoon in Buffalo, the Browns held off the Bills to win their third straight and stay a game ahead of the Bengals in the division race. A pair of Kevin Mack touchdown runs gave the Browns a 14–3 halftime lead, but Buffalo pulled back within four points with a 75-yard touchdown pass on the first play of the third quarter. A Bernie Kosar-to-WR Brian Brennan touchdown toss later that period once again gave the Browns some breathing room, and the defense kept Buffalo from scoring again until just a minute remained in the game. Despite the lousy conditions, Kosar connected with eight different receivers for 240 yards through the air, while Cleveland rolled up 141 rushing yards. The Browns now needed just one more victory to clinch their second straight playoff berth.
Record: 10–4

	1	2	3	4		
Browns	7	7	7	0	=	21
Bills	0	3	7	7	=	17

CLE-Mack 1-yd. run (Moseley kick)
BUF-Norwood 22-yd. FG
CLE-Mack 1-yd. run (Moseley kick)
BUF-Burkett 75-yd. pass from Kelly (Norwood kick)
CLE-Brennan 11-yd. pass from Kosar (Moseley kick)
BUF-Teal 4-yd. pass from Kelly (Norwood kick)

Passing
CLE: Kosar 18–33–240 1 TD 0 INT
BUF: Kelly 20–39–315 2 TD 0 INT

Rushing
CLE: Mack 16–65, Dickey 13–65, Fontenot 3–13, Everett 1–2, Kosar 4-(-4)
BUF: Riddick 14–54, Kelly 6–23, Wilkins 1–5, Harmon 1–1

Receiving
CLE: Brennan 4–66, Fontenot 4–55, Newsome 4–48, Mack 1–23, Weathers 1–16, Slaughter 1–15, Dickey 2–13, Langhorne 1–4
BUF: Burkett 3–122, Metzelaars 4–54, Reed 3–51, Teal 4–40, Riddick 3–20, Wilkins 2–17, Harmon 1–11

Sunday, December 14
Browns 34, Cincinnati Bengals 3
Riverfront Stadium (58,062)
White jerseys/white pants

In one of the most satisfying victories in team history, the Browns throttled 9–5 Cincinnati on its home field to clinch the AFC Central Division title for the second straight season by the largest margin of victory ever in a Browns–Bengals contest. The Browns set the tone on the very first play of the game, when Bernie Kosar connected with Reggie Langhorne for a 66-yard pass to the Cincinnati 1, setting up a short touchdown run by Kevin Mack. After Cincinnati's potent offense—ranked No. 1 in the NFL—responded with a quick drive that resulted in a field goal, the Browns' defense shut down the Bengals for the rest of the day, holding them to just 283 total yards after they'd topped 400 each of the previous five weeks. The Browns extended the lead to 14–3 later in the first quarter with a touchdown bomb from Kosar to Webster Slaughter, then put it away with two more scores in the third quarter, the second when Slaughter recovered a Curtis Dickey fumble in the end zone. Playing nearly a perfect game, the Browns collected 372 yards of offense while allowing no sacks and giving up no turnovers as they won in Cincinnati for the first time in five years.
Record: 11–4

	1	2	3	4		
Browns	14	3	14	3	=	34
Bengals	3	0	0	0	=	3

CLE-Mack 1-yd. run (Moseley kick)
CIN-Breech 23-yd. G
CLE-Slaughter 47-yd. pass from Kosar (Moseley kick)
CLE-Moseley 39-yd. FG
CLE-Mack 1-yd. run (Moseley kick)
CLE-Slaughter recovered fumble in end zone (Moseley kick)
CLE-Moseley 19-yd. FG

Passing
CLE: Kosar 13–29–246 1 TD 0 INT
CIN: Esiason 14–31–151 0 TD 2 INT, Anderson 1–1–17 0 TD 0 INT

Rushing
CLE: Mack 23–93, Dickey 13–37, Fontenot 1–3, Kosar 1-(-7)
CIN: Wilson 10–60, Brooks 12–43, Kinnebrew 5–35, McGee 2–2, Jennings 2-(-2), Brown 1-(-3)

Receiving
CLE: Slaughter 3–75, Langhorne 1–66, Brennan 3–33, Fontenot 2–32, Newsome 2–32, Weathers 1–5, Mack 1–3
CIN: Brooks 7–75, Brown 4–47, Holman 2–21, Kreider 1–17, Collinsworth 1–8

Sunday, December 21
Browns 47, San Diego Chargers 17
Cleveland Stadium (68,505)
White jerseys/white pants

With home-field advantage throughout the AFC playoffs clinched, the Browns opened up the playbook and closed the regular season with a blowout victory over San Diego. Cleveland opened the scoring late in the first quarter on a halfback-option touchdown pass from Herman Fontenot to Webster Slaughter, then extended the lead to 20–10 at the half with a 57-yard touchdown reception to Brian Brennan, who had a career afternoon with seven catches for 176 yards. The Browns exploded for 27 more points in the second half, collecting 462 total yards on the day, with 357 coming through the air. With their twelfth victory, the Browns finished with the most wins in a season in team history and, for the first time in 18 years, the road to the Super Bowl would go through Cleveland.
Record: 12–4

	1	2	3	4		
Chargers	0	10	7	0	=	17
Browns	7	13	17	10	=	47

CLE-Slaughter 46-yd. pass from Fontenot (Moseley kick)
CLE-Mack 2-yd. run (Moseley kick)
SD-Chandler 19-yd. pass from Fouts (Benirschke kick)
SD-Benirschke 40-yd. FG
CLE-Brennan 57-yd. pass from Kosar (kick failed)
CLE-Holt 1-yd. pass from Kosar (Moseley kick)
CLE-Fontenot 9-yd. run (Moseley kick)
CLE-Moseley 37-yd. FG
SD-Anderson 65-yd. pass from Fouts (Benirschke kick)
CLE-Dickey 2-yd. run (Moseley kick)
CLE-Moseley 32-yd. FG

Passing
SD: Fouts 15–27–236 2 TD 0 INT, Herrmann 6–8–87 0 TD 1 INT, Holohan 0–1–0 0 TD 0 INT
CLE: Kosar 21–28–258 2 TD 0 INT, Pagel 2–3–53 0 TD 0 INT, Fontenot 1–1–46 1 TD 0 INT

Rushing
SD: Spencer 5–22, Adams 11–15, Anderson 3–4, Fouts 1–0, Herrmann 1–0
CLE: Everett 10–38, Mack 9–36, Kosar 1–17, Dickey 7–13, Fontenot 4–12, Slaughter 1–1, Pagel 2–0

Receiving
SD: Chandler 6–113, Anderson 3–83, Winslow 3–52, Spencer 3–31, Joiner 3–25, Holohan 3–19
CLE: Brennan 7–176, Slaughter 4–64, Holt 2–35, Fontenot 4–27, Mack 2–18, Weathers 1–14, Dickey 1–9, Newsome 2–7, Langhorne 1–7

AFC Divisional Playoff
Saturday, January 3
Browns 23, New York Jets 20 (2 OT)
Cleveland Stadium (78,106)
White jerseys/white pants

Trailing by 10 points with four minutes to play and with their wonderful season hanging by a thread, the Browns put together a remarkable comeback, then persevered through an entire overtime session before pulling out one of the most dramatic victories in their history.

Though 10-point favorites, the Browns were evenly matched by the Jets through the first half, then New York took a 13–10 lead into the fourth quarter. A missed field goal and a costly interception in the end zone cost the Browns chances to either tie or take the lead, then Bernie Kosar's second interception set up what appeared to be the backbreaking touchdown. New York RB Freeman McNeil broke free for a 25-yard scoring run to make it 20–10 with 4:14 remaining, and it appeared the Browns' magical campaign had come to an end.

Aided by a roughing-the-passer penalty on Jets' DE Mark Gastineau, the Browns quickly drove downfield and cut the lead to three just inside the two-minute warning. The Jets recovered the ensuing onside kick, but were stuffed on three consecutive plays and forced to punt. A New York pass-interference penalty was followed by a dazzling 37-yard catch by Webster Slaughter to set up Mark Moseley's game-tying field goal with seven seconds left to send the game—all but over just minutes before—to overtime.

Though the Browns quickly drove to the New York 5 on their first possession in sudden-death, Moseley hooked a chip-shot field goal and the Jets stayed alive. The Cleveland defense maintained its dominance over the Jets, allowing the offense to put one more long drive together. This one ended when Moseley successfully booted a 27-yard field goal two minutes into the second overtime session to give the Browns their first playoff victory in 17 years.

When the dust settled on the third-longest game in NFL history, the Browns had put together their finest offensive performance ever in a postseason game, picking up 33 first downs and rolling up 558 total yards, outgaining New York by nearly 300 yards. Kosar led the way, setting an NFL playoff record with 489 passing yards as he connected with nine different receivers. The defense was nearly as dominant, collecting nine sacks to tie an NFL playoff record and holding the Jets to just 15 total yards on their final four possessions.

On the afternoon following the amazing victory, the Denver Broncos held off the New England Patriots in the other divisional playoff to earn a trip to Cleveland to face the Browns in the AFC Championship.

	1	2	3	4	OT1	OT2		
Jets	7	3	3	7	0	0	=	20
Browns	7	3	0	10	0	3	=	23

NYJ-Walker 42-yd. pass from Ryan (Leahy kick)
CLE-Fontenot 37-yd. pass from Kosar (Moseley kick)
CLE-Moseley 38-yd. FG
NYJ-Leahy 46-yd. FG
NYJ-Leahy 37-yd. FG
NYJ-McNeil 25-yd. run (Moseley kick)
CLE-Mack 1-yd. run (Moseley kick)
CLE-Moseley 22-yd. FG
CLE-Moseley 27-yd. FG

Passing
NYJ: O'Brien 11–19–134 0 TD 0 INT, Ryan 6–11–103 1 TD 0 INT
CLE: Kosar 33–64–489 1 TD 2 INT, Brennan 1–1–5 0 TD 0 INT

Rushing
NYJ: McNeil 25–71, O'Brien 3–22, Paige 3–11
CLE: Mack 20–63, Fontenot 3–8, Dickey 3–4, Kosar 1–0

Receiving
NYJ: Toon 5–93, Walker 2–49, Shuler 4–43, McNeil 4–35, Paige 1–10, Sohn 1–7
CLE: Newsome 6–114, Slaughter 6–86, Brennan 4–69, Langhorne 4–65, Fontenot 5–62, Mack 5–51, Holt 2–42, Weathers 1–3, Dickey 1–2

AFC Championship
Sunday, January 11
Denver Broncos 23, Browns 20 (OT)
Cleveland Stadium (79,915)
White jerseys/white pants

For the second straight week, the Browns found themselves immersed in a dramatic overtime thriller, but this time—after stepping to the threshold of their first Super Bowl appearance—they ran out of miracles.

The two teams were evenly matched throughout, though the Browns handed Denver three turnovers in a five-play period that allowed the Broncos to respond after a Herman Fontenot touchdown catch gave the Browns an early 7–0 lead. The game was tied at 10 at halftime, then again at 13 two minutes into the fourth quarter.

The Browns appeared to take control of the contest when Bernie Kosar hit Brian Brennan for a 48-yard touchdown pass with 5:43 to play, then Denver muffed the ensuing kickoff and began its next possession at its own 2. QB John Elway then cemented his place in football history, leading the Broncos on a 15-play, 98-yard drive to tie the game on a touchdown pass to WR Mark Jackson with 37 seconds left to send the contest to sudden-death.

With their momentum lost, the Browns went three-and-out on the first series of overtime, and Elway picked up where he left off, driving the Broncos 60 yards to the Cleveland 17. Rich Karlis then booted a 33-yard field goal to send Denver to Super Bowl XXI and deliver one of the most heartbreaking defeats in Cleveland sports history.

	1	2	3	4	OT		
Broncos	0	10	3	7	3	=	23
Browns	7	3	0	10	0	=	20

CLE-Fontenot 6-yd. pass from Kosar (Moseley kick)
DEN-Karlis 19-yd. FG
DEN-Willhite 1-yd. run (Karlis kick)
CLE-Moseley 29-yd. FG
DEN-Karlis 26-yd. FG
CLE-Moseley 24-yd. FG
CLE-Brennan 48-yd. pass from Kosar (Moseley kick)
DEN-Jackson 5-yd. pass from Elway (Karlis kick)
DEN-Karlis 33-yd. FG

Passing
DEN: Elway 22–38–244 1 TD 1 INT
CLE: Kosar 18–32–259 2 TD 2 INT

Rushing
DEN: Winder 26–83, Elway 4–56, Lang 3–9, Sewell 1–1, Willhite 3–0
CLE: Mack 26–94, Kosar 4–3, Fontenot 3–3

Receiving
DEN: Watson 3–55, Sewell 3–47, Mobley 3–36, Johnson 3–25, Jackson 2–25, Kay 2–23, Willhite 2–20, Sampson 1–10, Winder 2–2, Lang 1–1
CLE: Brennan 4–72, Fontenot 7–66, Weathers 1–42, Langhorne 2–35, Mack 2–20, Slaughter 1–20, Byner 1–4

1987

Sunday, September 13
New Orleans Saints 28, Browns 21
Louisiana Superdome (59,900)
White jerseys/white pants

A day after Pope John Paul II held mass in the Superdome, the Browns lost their fifth straight season opener to an up-and-coming Saints team. In a seesaw game, the Browns answered each New Orleans touchdown with one of their own, tying the contest at 21 early in the fourth quarter on a touchdown run by QB Bernie Kosar. Plagued by poor field position, Kosar was then hit in the end zone for safeties twice in the final 10 minutes, providing the winning points for New Orleans. While the Browns' offense collected nearly 400 yards, with Kosar throwing for 314, the Saints controlled the line of scrimmage with 191 yards on the ground.
Record: 0–1

	1	2	3	4		
Browns	0	7	7	7	=	21
Saints	7	0	14	7	=	28

NO-Brenner 5-yd. pass from Hebert (Andersen kick)
CLE-Weathers 7-yd. pass from Kosar (Jaeger kick)
NO-Brenner 7-yd. pass from Hebert (Andersen kick)
CLE-Brennan 30-yd. pass from Kosar (Jaeger kick)
NO-Hilliard 5-yd. run (Andersen kick)
CLE-Kosar 3-yd. run (Jaeger kick)
NO-Safety: Clark tackled Kosar in end zone
NO-Safety: Maxie tackled Kosar in end zone
NO-Andersen 39-yd. FG

Passing
CLE: Kosar 28–39–314 2 TD 1 INT
NO: Hebert 13–22–149 2 TD 0 INT

Rushing
CLE: Byner 10–45, Mack 11–37, Manoa 1–8, Kosar 1–3
NO: Mayes 24–147, Hebert 1–13, Jordan 5–12, Gray 1–11, Hilliard 2–5, Word 1–3

Receiving
CLE: Langhorne 5–85, Brennan 4–65, Byner 8–61, Newsome 5–43, Slaughter 2–28, Mack 2–17, Manoa 1–8, Weathers 1–7
NO: Brenner 5–68, Martin 2–29, Gray 2–18, Clark 1–11, Jones 1–11, Tice 1–10, Jordan 1–2

Sunday, September 20
Browns 34, Pittsburgh Steelers 10
Cleveland Stadium (79,543)
White jerseys/white pants

Behind a smothering defensive performance, the Browns scored 24 points in the game's final 20 minutes—all set up by turnovers—to overwhelm the Steelers and win their home opener for the first time in eight years. The Cleveland defense was magnificent, holding Pittsburgh to 58 rushing yards and just 29 total in the second half while collecting four sacks and six interceptions, including a 26-yard return for a touchdown by LB Clay Matthews six minutes into the fourth quarter. The victory evened the Browns' record—and put the AFC Central in a four-way tie for first—with a players' association strike looming.
Record: 1–1

	1	2	3	4		
Steelers	0	3	7	0	=	10
Browns	0	10	7	17	=	34

CLE-Jaeger 29-yd. FG
CLE-Mack 1-yd. run (Jaeger kick)
PIT-Anderson 27-yd. FG
PIT-Shell 19-yd. fumble return (Anderson kick)
CLE-McNeil 11-yd. pass from Kosar (Jaeger kick)
CLE-Jaeger 23-yd. FG
CLE-Matthews 26-yd. interception return (Jaeger kick)
CLE-Weathers 37-yd. pass from Kosar (Jaeger kick)

Passing
PIT: Malone 12–36–151 0 TD 5 INT, Brister 1–5–10 0 TD 1 INT
CLE: Kosar 17–29–174 2 TD 1 INT, Fontenot 1–1–14 0 TD 0 INT

Rushing
PIT: Abercrombie 6–25, Stone 1–21, Jackson 10–19, Malone 2-(-3), Pollard 4-(-4)
CLE: Mack 14–53, Byner 12–53, Manoa 5–14, Kosar 1–3, Fontenot 3–1

THE BEST OF THE "TANS"

In one of the most bizarre periods in NFL history, during the 1987 players' strike, each team fielded replacement players for three weeks of games.

While the local media referred to the Browns' replacements as the "Tans," Cleveland managed to win two of its three games thanks to the efforts of a handful of standouts (and the assistance of nine regulars who crossed the picket line to play as the strike wore on).

Several of the Tans not only excelled during their brief appearances but used the opportunity presented by the strike to break into the league.

LB Tim Crawford
Recorded 16 tackles (12 solo) and three sacks, two in the Browns' victory over New England.

LB David Grayson
Started all three replacement games, then re-signed with the team after the regulars returned and finished the season with 29 tackles (16 solo), a sack, and a fumble return for a touchdown. Went on to play three more seasons with the Browns, then another with San Diego.

LB Cliff Hanneman
Led replacement squad with 19 tackles (16 solo).

WR Perry Kemp
Caught 12 passes for 224 yards and a pair of touchdowns. Signed with Green Bay the following year (then coached by Browns' 1987 offensive coordinator Lindy Infante) and rolled up more than 2,300 yards with the Packers over the next four seasons.

RB Larry Mason
Rushed for 207 yards and scored three touchdowns, running for 133 yards and two scores in the Browns' victory over New England. Signed with Green Bay (and Infante) the following year and rushed for 194 yards in 15 games.

DB DeJuan Robinson
Defended seven passes and intercepted another.

NT Mike Rusinek
Collected 11 tackles (10 solo) along with a sack, a forced fumble, and a recovered fumble.

TE Derek Tennell
Caught five passes for 59 yards and a touchdown during the replacement games. Re-signed with the team after the regulars returned and finished the season with nine catches for 102 yards and three scores. Played two more seasons with the Browns, then three more with Detroit, Minnesota, and Dallas.

Receiving
PIT: Lipps 5–68, Abercrombie 3–24, Hoge 2–23, Stallworth 1–22, Lockett 1–17, Gothard 1–7
CLE: Mack 8–45, Slaughter 3–37, Weathers 1–37, Byner 2–35, Langhorne 1–12, McNeil 1–11, Newsome 1–6, Fontenot 1–5

Sunday, October 4
Browns 20, New England Patriots 10
Sullivan Stadium (14,830)
Brown jerseys/white pants

After their highly anticipated Monday-night rematch with Denver was canceled due to the NFL's second work stoppage, the Browns returned to action a week later with replacement players in what became one of the most bizarre chapters in team history. The "Tans," as they came to be known in the media, fell behind the Patriots 10–0 in the first half in cold, rainy Foxboro before the smallest crowd to attend a Browns game since they joined the NFL. But the new Browns turned things around and dominated the second half. RB Larry Mason, who joined the team two days earlier, tied a team record with 32 carries and rushed for 133 yards as the Cleveland ground game racked up 217 yards. Two Mason touchdowns put the Browns ahead in the fourth quarter, and the defense stymied New England from there, holding the Patriots to just 141 yards on the day, including a mere 31 rushing yards on 27 carries.

Record: 2–1

	1	2	3	4		
Browns	0	0	6	14	=	20
Patriots	0	10	0	0	=	10

NE-Schubert 23-yd. FG
NE-Linne 6-yd. pass from Bleier (Schubert kick)
CLE-Franco 28-yd. FG
CLE-Franco 21-yd. FG
CLE-Mason 1-yd. run (Kelley pass from Walters)
CLE-Mason 1-yd. run (Franco kick)

Passing
CLE: Christensen 10–30–135 0 TD 0 INT
NE: Bleier 10–26–138 1 TD 0 INT

Rushing
CLE: Mason 32–133, Everett 14–52, Christensen 7–32, Katolin 1–0
NE: Collins 15–24, McSwain 7–20, Woods 1–0, Bleier 3-(-6), LeBlanc 1-(-7)

Receiving
CLE: Kemp 2–58, Tennell 3–39, Everett 3–23, Tinsley 1–17, Mason 1-(-2)
NE: Coffey 3–66, Linne 4–45, Collins 2–16, Frain 1–11

Sunday, October 11
Houston Oilers 15, Browns 10
Cleveland Stadium (38,927)
White jerseys/white pants

The replacement Oilers dominated time of possession and limited the Browns to just 169 total yards on a mud-soaked field as Houston collected its first victory in Cleveland in six years, albeit before the smallest Browns' home crowd in nine years. Falling behind by 10 points in the second half, the Browns cut the margin to 13–10 early in the fourth quarter, but Houston struck back with a safety midway through the period. In his second start, Browns' QB Jeff Christensen connected with WR Perry Kemp five times for 96 yards, but also threw three interceptions and was sacked four times. A week after rushing for more than 130 yards, Larry Mason was held to just five on four carries. Regular DE Carl Hairston became the first Brown to cross the picket line and played in the game though wasn't much of a factor. The victory moved the Oilers into sole possession of first place in the AFC Central and dropped the Browns into a three-way tie for second.
Record: 2–2

	1	2	3	4		
Oilers	0	7	6	2	=	15
Browns	3	0	0	7	=	10

CLE-Franco 26-yd. FG
HOU-McDonald 15-yd. pass from Pease (Diettrich kick)
HOU-Diettrich 45-yd. FG
HOU-Diettrich 23-yd. FG
CLE-Mason 5-yd. pass from Christensen (Franco kick)
HOU-Safety: Baker tackled Christensen in end zone

Passing
HOU: Pease 13–25–150 1 TD 2 INT
CLE: Christensen 13–27–152 1 TD 3 INT

Rushing
HOU: Hunter 28–121, Jackson 11–40, Pease 5–10, Moore 2–3
CLE: Everett 10–27, Christensen 3–9, Mason 4–5, Verser 1–9

Receiving
HOU: Harris 6–104, Gehring 3–21, McDonald 1–15, Hunter 2–6, Jackson 1–4
CLE: Kemp 5–96, Pierce 2–21, Mason 2–16, Everett 3–10, Watson 1–9

Sunday, October 18
Browns 34, Cincinnati Bengals 0
Riverfront Stadium (40,179)
White jerseys/white pants

Though the strike came to a close on Thursday, it was past the league deadline for the regulars to play in that weekend's games, so teams played a third week of replacement football. The Browns went into Cincinnati with a huge advantage, with eight regulars crossing the picket line on Wednesday in time to play. The result was a complete slaughter on a sunshiny afternoon in Cincinnati and the Browns' first shutout in four years. With QB Gary Danielson throwing for 281 yards and four touchdowns, including 10 receptions by Brian Brennan for 139 yards, the Browns outgained the Bengals 410 yards to 95 and picked up 29 first downs to Cincinnati's six. The triumph, combined with a Houston defeat in New England to the Doug Flutie-led Patriots, allowed the Browns to pull back into a tie for first place with normalcy to return the following week.
Record: 3–2

	1	2	3	4		
Browns	7	17	3	7	=	34
Bengals	0	0	0	0	=	0

CLE-Brennan 6-yd. pass from Danielson (Jaeger kick)
CLE-Tennell 3-yd. pass from Danielson (Jaeger kick)
CLE-Jaeger 45-yd. FG
CLE-Kemp 22-yd. pass from Danielson (Jaeger kick)
CLE-Jaeger 33-yd. FG
CLE-Kemp 19-yd. pass from Danielson (Jaeger kick)

Passing
CLE: Danielson 25–31–281 4 TD 0 INT, Christensen 1–1–10 0 TD 0 INT
CIN: Bennett 2–6–25 0 TD 1 INT, Walter 2–2–15 0 TD 0 INT, Breen 0–3–0 0 TD 0 INT

Rushing
CLE: Mason 20–69, Driver 9–31, Everett 10–16, Davis 1–7, Christensen 1–0, Danielson 1–0
CIN: Walter 3–20, Bennett 2–17, Breen 2–10, Wright 4–7, Logan 7–5, McCluskey 4–5, Rice 3–1

Receiving
CLE: Brennan 10–139, Kemp 5–70, Newsome 4–29, Tennell 2–20, Watson 1–13, Mason 2–12, Everett 2–8
CIN: Logan 1–18, McCluskey 1–8, Meehan 1–7, Wright 1–7

Monday, October 26
Browns 30, Los Angeles Rams 17
Cleveland Stadium (76,933)
White jerseys/white pants

The Browns' regulars returned to deliver a rousing Monday-night victory over the Rams, highlighted by a handful of big plays. DB Felix Wright intercepted two passes in the first half, the first of which set up a field goal, and he returned the second 40 yards for a touchdown to give the Browns a 17–0 lead early in the second quarter. The margin swelled to 30–7 a minute into the third quarter on a 53-yard scoring pass from Bernie Kosar to Brian Brennan, and the Rams tacked on 10 points to round out the scoring. The Cleveland defense forced four turnovers and held All-Pro RB Eric Dickerson to just 38 yards rushing in what proved to be his final game as a member of the Rams.
Record: 4–2

	1	2	3	4		
Rams	0	7	10	0	=	17
Browns	3	20	7	0	=	30

CLE-Jaeger 23-yd. FG
CLE-Mack 16-yd. run (Jaeger kick)
CLE-Wright 40-yd. interception return (Jaeger kick)
CLE-Jaeger 48-yd. FG
LA-Dickerson 27-yd. run (Lansford kick)
CLE-Jaeger 41-yd. FG
CLE-Brennan 53-yd. pass from Kosar (Jaeger kick)
LA-White 1-yd. run (Lansford kick)
LA-Lansford 27-yd. FG

Passing
LA: Everett 21–50–227 0 TD 3 INT
CLE: Kosar 19–30–223 1 TD 1 INT

Rushing
LA: White 13–54, Dickerson 7–38, Tyrrell 2–5, McGee 2–4
CLE: Mack 14–47, Byner 7–15, Kosar 2–3

Receiving
LA: Johnson 6–69, Ellard 4–65, Young 1–26, McGee 4–18, Hill 2–14, House 1–13, Brown 2–12, Tyrrell 1–10
CLE: Brennan 4–75, Byner 5–70, Langhorne 1–20, Slaughter 3–19, Mack 3–17, McNeil 1–15, Newsome 2–7

Sunday, November 1
San Diego Chargers 27, Browns 24 (OT)
Jack Murphy Stadium (55,381)
White jerseys/white pants

After having a pair of touchdowns called back on penalties, the Browns squandered a 10-point lead in the fourth quarter and lost a frustrating game to the 5–1 Chargers in San Diego. The tone was set on the second play of the contest when Bernie Kosar was intercepted by former Cleveland LB Chip Banks, traded to the Chargers in the offseason, setting up San Diego's first touchdown. The Browns bounced back to take a 24–14 lead into the final period, but it should have been more, as a long touchdown reception by WR Webster Slaughter and punt return for a score by WR Gerald McNeil were both wiped out by Cleveland infractions. Rolling to better than 400 yards on the day, San Diego scored twice in the final six minutes to tie the game and send it to sudden-death. Kosar promptly threw his second interception of the game to set up the game-winning field goal two minutes in. The defeat dropped the Browns one game behind the first-place Oilers.
Record: 4–3

	1	2	3	4	OT		
Browns	7	7	10	0	0	=	24
Chargers	14	0	0	10	3	=	27

SD-James 15-yd. run (Abbott kick)
CLE-Slaughter 20-yd. pass from Kosar (Jaeger kick)
SD-Bernstine 10-yd. pass from Fouts (Abbott kick)
CLE-Brennan 41-yd. pass from Kosar (Jaeger kick)
CLE-Jaeger 41-yd. FG
CLE-Byner 1-yd. run (Jaeger kick)
SD-James 22-yd. pass from Fouts (Abbott kick)
SD-Abbott 20-yd. FG
SD-Abbott 33-yd. FG

Passing
CLE: Kosar 24–42–298 2 TD 2 INT
SD: Fouts 25–42–315 2 TD 1 INT

Rushing
CLE: Mack 14–61, Byner 5–9, Manoa 1–3, Kosar 1-(-1)
SD: Adams 15–66, Anderson 5–23, James 3–21, Spencer 3–19, Fouts 1-(-1)

Receiving
CLE: Brennan 4–94, Slaughter 5–74, Byner 6–62, Langhorne 2–20, Weathers 1–15, Mack 3–14, Newsome 2–10, McNeil 1–9
SD: James 4–90, Winslow 7–76, Chandler 3–49, Bernstine 4–31, Holohan 2–31, Anderson 2–19, Spencer 2–13, Adams 1–6

Sunday, November 8
Browns 38, Atlanta Falcons 3
Cleveland Stadium (71,135)
White jerseys/white pants

Behind a balanced offense and a stellar defensive effort, the Browns bounced back with a dominating victory over struggling Atlanta and pulled back into a tie for first place in the division. Aided by a long touchdown reception by Webster Slaughter, the Browns built a 14–3 halftime lead, then Earnest Byner scored three touchdowns in the third quarter to blow the game open. The Cleveland running attack controlled the contest, picking up 173 yards, while the defense added seven sacks. The Browns' special teams also got into the action, blocking a punt to set up a third-quarter touchdown.
Record: 5–3

	1	2	3	4		
Falcons	0	3	0	0	=	3
Browns	0	14	21	3	=	38

CLE-Slaughter 54-yd. pass from Kosar (Jaeger kick)
CLE-Mack 1-yd. run (Jaeger kick)
ATL-Luckhurst 42-yd. FG
CLE-Byner 3-yd. run (Jaeger kick)
CLE-Byner 5-yd. run (Jaeger kick)
CLE-Byner 4-yd. pass from Kosar (Jaeger kick)
CLE-Jaeger 38-yd. FG

Passing
ATL: Campbell 15–22–169 0 TD 1 INT
CLE: Kosar 13–23–192 2 TD 0 INT, Danielson 0–1–0 0 TD 0 INT

Rushing
ATL: Riggs 16–93, Campbell 4–22, Emery 1–5, Flowers 1–1, Matthews 1-(-4)
CLE: Manoa 7–61, Mack 18–52, Byner 10–29, Fontenot 4–24, Kosar 1–7

Receiving
ATL: Matthews 5–70, Bailey 2–36, Cox 2–18, Dixon 2–14, Riggs 2–14, Emery 1–10, Whisenhunt 1–7
CLE: Slaughter 2–70, Weathers 3–42, Byner 4–40, Newsome 3–33, Mack 1–7

Sunday, November 15
Browns 27, Buffalo Bills 21
Cleveland Stadium (78,409)
White jerseys/white pants

Behind a brilliant passing performance by Bernie Kosar, the Browns built a comfortable fourth-quarter lead and then held off the quickly improving Buffalo Bills for their sixth victory of the season. Kosar connected with nine different receivers as he threw for a season-high 346 yards and a pair of touchdowns after the teams exchanged fumble returns for touchdowns in the first half—the first by Buffalo DB Mark Kelso, the second by Browns' DB Ray Ellis. The Cleveland defense held Buffalo to only 61 rushing yards and 267 total, sacking QB Jim Kelly three times, while Gerald McNeil had a punt return for a touchdown called back on a penalty for the second time in three weeks. Meanwhile, the Browns' offense topped 400 total yards to begin a stretch in which it would do so five times in the next nine games.
Record: 6–3

	1	2	3	4		
Bills	7	0	0	14	=	21
Browns	3	14	7	3	=	27

CLE-Jaeger 22-yd. FG
BUF-Kelso 56-yd. fumble return (Norwood kick)
CLE-Ellis 27-yd. fumble return (Jaeger kick)
CLE-Langhorne 15-yd. pass from Kosar (Jaeger kick)
CLE-Slaughter 52-yd. pass from Kosar (Jaeger kick)
CLE-Jaeger 40-yd. FG
BUF-Burkett 13-yd. pass from Kelly (Norwood kick)
BUF-Reed 10-yd. pass from Kelly (Norwood kick)

Passing
BUF: Kelly 22–35–222 2 TD 0 INT
CLE: Kosar 24–34–346 2 TD 1 INT

Rushing
BUF: Kelly 4–42, Byrum 3–13, Mueller 5–4, Harmon 6–2, Porter 2–0
CLE: Mack 17–48, Byner 10–21, McNeil 1–17, Kosar 3-(-2)

Receiving
BUF: Burkett 6–91, Harmon 6–52, Reed 4–36, Johnson 2–24, Metzellars 3–15, Porter 1–4
CLE: Slaughter 4–78, Newsome 3–70, Byner 6–64, Mack 4–46, Langhorne 2–25, Tennell 1–24, Brennan 2–15, Weathers 1–14, McNeil 1–10

Sunday, November 22
Browns 40, Houston Oilers 7
Houston Astrodome (51,161)
White jerseys/white pants

In a battle for first place in the AFC Central, the Browns crushed an improved Houston team before a standing-room-only crowd in the Astrodome. After stuffing the Oilers on their first possession, the Browns marched downfield and scored the first of five touchdowns for the afternoon as they built a 26–0 halftime lead and never looked back. Cleveland rolled up a season-high 457 total yards, including 200 on the ground as Kevin Mack rushed for 114 and the Browns controlled the football for nearly 43 minutes. The defense forced six Oilers' turnovers, including three interceptions by DB Frank Minnifield, and held Houston to less than 250 total yards, a third of which came on a dazzling 83-yard touchdown reception by WR Ernest Givins in the third quarter. In the midst of a breakthrough season, Houston QB Warren Moon completed just five of 23 passes as the Oilers fell a game behind the Browns in the AFC Central.
Record: 7–3

	1	2	3	4		
Browns	9	17	14	0	=	40
Oilers	0	0	7	0	=	7

CLE-Byner 1-yd. run (pass failed)
CLE-Jaeger 21-yd. FG
CLE-Jaeger 32-yd. FG
CLE-Mack 5-yd. run (Jaeger kick)
CLE-Slaughter 27-yd. pass from Kosar (Jaeger kick)
CLE-Byner 17-yd. run (Jaeger kick)
HOU-Givins 83-yd. pass from Moon (Zendejas kick)
CLE-McNeil 39-yd. pass from Kosar (Jaeger kick)

Passing
CLE: Kosar 15–26–257 2 TD 0 INT, Danielson 0–1–0 0 TD 0 INT, Jaeger 0–1–0 0 TD 0 INT
HOU: Moon 5–23–193 1 TD 3 INT, Pease 6–11–33 0 TD 1 INT

Rushing
CLE: Mack 26–114, Byner 12–57, Manoa 6–24, Fontenot 7–5
HOU: Rozier 11–43, Moon 1–12, Highsmith 1–1, Givins 1-(-13)

Receiving
CLE: Slaughter 4–79, McNeil 3–66, Newsome 2–47, Byner 2–24, Mack 2–17, Tennell 1–15, Langhorne 1–9
HOU: Givins 3–126, Duncan 2–67, Drewrey 2–19, Hill 1–6, Jeffires 1–6, Highsmith 1–5, Rozier 1-(-3)

Sunday, November 29
San Francisco 49ers 38, Browns 24
Candlestick Park (60,248)
White jerseys/white pants

On a Sunday night, playing on ESPN for the first time, the Browns were overwhelmed by the 8–2 49ers, who scored the first 17 points of the second half to blow open a tight contest. While the Cleveland offense was effective, collecting 360 total yards, the 49ers were unstoppable, rolling up 455 as QB Joe Montana threw for 342 yards with four touchdowns—three to WR Jerry Rice. After San Francisco's lead swelled to 38–17 in the fourth quarter, the Browns closed the scoring when LB David Grayson, who'd joined the team as a replacement player two months earlier, returned a fumble 17 yards for a touchdown. With the Oilers and Steelers both losing earlier in the day, the Browns remained in sole possession of first place in the division.
Record: 7–4

	1	2	3	4		
Browns	7	10	0	7	=	24
49ers	7	14	3	14	=	38

CLE-Byner recovered own fumble in end zone (Jaeger kick)
SF-Rice 2-yd. pass from Montana (Wersching kick)
CLE-Jaeger 28-yd. FG
SF-Rice 30-yd. pass from Montana (Wersching kick)
SF-Clark 40-yd. pass from Montana (Wersching kick)
CLE-Brennan 21-yd. pass from Kosar (Jaeger kick)
SF-Wersching 38-yd. FG

SF-Rice 29-yd. pass from Montana (Wersching kick)
SF-Cribbs 9-yd. run (Wersching kick)
CLE-Grayson 17-yd. fumble return (Jaeger kick)

Passing
CLE: Kosar 26–37–275 1 TD 1 INT
SF: Montana 23–31–342 4 TD 1 INT, Young 0–1–0 0 TD 0 INT

Rushing
CLE: Byner 7–42, Mack 9–37, Kosar 3–10, Fontenot 1–3
SF: Montana 4–43, Cribbs 6–33, Craig 13–26, Rathman 7–18, Sydney 2–2, Young 2-(-3)

Receiving
CLE: Byner 8–83, Slaughter 4–66, Brennan 6–65, Langhorne 2–19, Mack 2–17, Fontenot 2–10, McNeil 1–9, Newsome 1–6
SF: Rice 7–126, Frank 6–76, Rathman 4–60, Clark 3–57, Craig 3–23

Sunday, December 6
Indianapolis Colts 9, Browns 7
Cleveland Stadium (70,661)
White jerseys/white pants

With a lifeless offensive performance, the Browns were stunned at home by the improved Colts, who managed to pull the upset without scoring a touchdown. In their worst offensive performance by the regular team in over a year, the Browns could manage only a third-quarter touchdown—set up by a blocked punt by RB Herman Fontenot—and were held to just 247 total yards. Led by Eric Dickerson, acquired from the Rams a month earlier, the Colts built a 9–0 halftime lead on a trio of field goals and were able to hang on thanks to two missed opportunities by the Browns in the second half. First came a missed chip-shot field-goal attempt by kicker Jeff Jaeger in the third quarter, followed by a critical fumble by Earnest Byner at the Indianapolis 4 three minutes into the fourth quarter. The Colts prevented the Browns from crossing midfield on their final three possessions and scored a key victory that would help them land the AFC East title. Both Houston and Pittsburgh also won, knotting the teams in a three-way tie for first atop the AFC Central.
Record: 7–5

	1	2	3	4		
Colts	0	9	0	0	=	9
Browns	0	0	7	0	=	7

IND-Biasucci 33-yd. FG
IND-Biasucci 37-yd. FG
IND-Biasucci 41-yd. FG
CLE-Brennan 19-yd. pass from Kosar (Jaeger kick)

Passing
IND: Trudeau 20–34–192 0 TD 0 INT
CLE: Kosar 16–35–178 1 TD 0 INT

Rushing
IND: Dickerson 27–98, Bentley 3–16
CLE: Mack 16–61, Byner 6–19, Manoa 3–6, Kosar 1–1

Receiving
IND: Brooks 7–85, Bentley 4–39, Boyer 5–38, Bouza 4–30
CLE: Slaughter 4–56, Brennan 4–51, Byner 4–45, Newsome 1–11, Weathers 1–8, Mack 2–7

Sunday, December 13
Browns 38, Cincinnati Bengals 24
Cleveland Stadium (77,331)
White jerseys/white pants

Rebounding from back-to-back defeats, the Browns exploded for a club-record-tying four touchdowns in the second quarter to build a comfortable lead and coast to a convincing win over the free-falling Bengals. Bernie Kosar threw a career-high four touchdown passes, including a pair to Webster Slaughter as the Browns took a 35–10 lead into the final period. A key moment came just before the half when Clay Matthews intercepted a pass by QB Boomer Esiason at the Cleveland 4 and rumbled 36 yards, then lateraled to Carl Hairston, who traveled another 40 to set up the Browns' fourth touchdown of the period. With the Cleveland offense rolling to nearly 400 yards, Kevin Mack rushed for 133 and scored a pair of touchdowns, while kicker Matt Bahr returned to action after missing the last year with a knee injury. Meanwhile, Houston lost in New Orleans, and Pittsburgh triumphed in San Diego to leave the Browns and Steelers tied atop the division.
Record: 8–5

	1	2	3	4		
Bengals	3	0	7	14	=	24
Browns	0	28	7	3	=	38

CIN-Breech 20-yd. FG
CLE-Slaughter 22-yd. pass from Kosar (Bahr kick)
CLE-Mack 22-yd. run (Bahr kick)
CLE-Mack 2-yd. pass from Kosar (Bahr kick)

CLE-Tennell 2-yd. pass from Kosar (Bahr kick)
CIN-Martin 54-yd. pass from Esiason (Breech kick)
CLE-Slaughter 18-yd. pass from Kosar (Bahr kick)
CIN-Kinnebrew 1-yd. run (Breech kick)
CIN-Kinnebrew 1-yd. run (Breech kick)
CLE-Bahr 27-yd. FG

Passing
CIN: Esiason 22–39–361 1 TD 2 INT
CLE: Kosar 17–26–241 4 TD 0 INT

Rushing
CIN: Kinnebrew 16–44, Brooks 9–11, Jennings 3–10
CLE: Mack 27–133, Byner 2–20

Receiving
CIN: McGee 4–117, Martin 3–83, Jennings 5–53, Kattus 4–34, Brown 2–34, Kinnebrew 1–19, Holman 2–17, Brooks 1–4
CLE: Slaughter 5–119, Langhorne 2–43, Byner 2–28, Mack 3–19, Newsome 3–18, Brennan 1–12, Tennell 1–2

Sunday, December 20
Browns 24, Los Angeles Raiders 17
Los Angeles Memorial Coliseum (40,275)
White jerseys/white pants

Snapping an eight-game losing streak to the Raiders and winning in Los Angeles for the first time in 29 years, the Browns clinched a playoff spot with an impressive performance. Soaring to a 17–3 halftime lead, the Browns halted the Raiders' momentum early in the third quarter when LB Mike Johnson forced a fumble at the Cleveland 7, then the Browns drove 93 yards to extend their lead to 17 points. The Raiders crept closer with a pair of scores in the fourth quarter, but a key 21-yard run on third down by Earnest Byner helped the Browns run out the final two minutes. Webster Slaughter notched his second straight 100-yard receiving game as Bernie Kosar threw for 294 yards and the Browns collected more than 400 total yards. Earlier in the afternoon, the Steelers lost in Houston to propel the Browns into sole possession of first place with one game to play.
Record: 9–5

	1	2	3	4		
Browns	7	10	7	0	=	24
Raiders	3	0	0	14	=	17

LA-C. Bahr 39-yd. FG
CLE-Byner 2-yd. pass from Kosar (M. Bahr kick)
CLE-M. Bahr 20-yd. FG
CLE-Byner 15-yd. run (M. Bahr kick)
CLE-Slaughter 18-yd. pass from Kosar (M. Bahr kick)
LA-Toran 48-yd. interception return (C. Bahr kick)
LA-Lofton 28-yd. pass from Wilson (C. Bahr)

Passing
CLE: Kosar 21–32–294 2 TD 1 INT
LA: Wilson 23–36–270 1 TD 0 INT

Rushing
CLE: Byner 12–74, Mack 17–55, Kosar 2-(-2)
LA: Allen 14–35, Wilson 4–33, Strachan 1–2, Mueller 1–1

Receiving
CLE: Slaughter 7–115, Brennan 6–79, Weathers 2–28, Langhorne 2–25, Fontenot 1–25, Byner 2–21, Newsome 1–1
LA: Allen 10–84, Lofton 4–70, Christensen 4–49, Mueller 2–27, Strachan 2–26, Woods 1–14

Saturday, December 26
Browns 19, Pittsburgh Steelers 13
Three Rivers Stadium (56,394)
White jerseys/white pants

Grinding out a tough win in Pittsburgh on the day after Christmas, the Browns clinched their third straight division title and would take a three-game winning streak into the playoffs. They built a 19–6 lead, then held on after the Steelers drew within six on an interception return for a score, but the Browns allowed Pittsburgh to run only one offensive play in the fourth quarter and ran out the final 7:27 to clinch a hard-earned victory. The Cleveland defense held the Steelers to just 221 total yards but lost NJ Bob Golic for the playoffs with a broken arm.
Record: 10–5

	1	2	3	4		
Browns	3	6	3	7	=	19
Steelers	0	3	0	10	=	13

CLE-Bahr 31-yd. FG
CLE-Tennell 2-yd. pass from Kosar (kick failed)
PIT-Anderson 39-yd. FG
CLE-Bahr 30-yd. FG
PIT-Anderson 27-yd. FG
CLE-Byner 2-yd. run (Bahr kick)
PIT-Gowdy 45-yd. interception return (Anderson kick)

Passing
CLE: Kosar 21–36–241 1 TD 1 INT
PIT: Malone 11–18–126 0 TD 2 INT

Rushing
CLE: Byner 12–48, Mack 18–37
PIT: Pollard 11–42, Jackson 6–28, Malone 4–24, Abercrombie 5–1

Receiving
CLE: Newsome 6–94, Slaughter 4–65, Langhorne 2–30, Byner 3–19, Mack 2–17, Brennan 2–12, Tennell 1–2, Weathers 1–2
PIT: Stallworth 6–53, Lipps 2–34, Thompson 1–23, Abercrombie 1–10, Young 1–6

AFC Divisional Playoff
Saturday, January 9
Browns 38, Indianapolis Colts 21
Cleveland Stadium (78,586)
White jerseys/white pants

In a rematch of the Browns' disappointing loss a month earlier, they welcomed the Colts to Cleveland once again, this time for a divisional playoff game on a frosty day in Cleveland.

While their December matchup had been a defensive struggle, the first half of the rematch forecasted an offensive shootout. The Browns drove 86 yards on their first possession to score, then added another touchdown early in the second quarter. But the Colts matched each Browns' score with one of their own as the score was knotted at 14 at the intermission.

The Colts then drove to the Cleveland 20 to open the third quarter, but Browns' LB Eddie Johnson forced a poor throw by Colts' QB Jack Trudeau that was picked off by Felix Wright to shift the momentum for the rest of the game. The Browns promptly drove 86 yards for the go-ahead touchdown, the opening salvo in a 24-point second half. With Kevin Mack sidelined with a stomach flu and rookie lineman Gregg Rakoczy filling in for injured Larry Williams, the offense didn't miss a beat. Earnest Byner led the way, scoring twice while rushing for 122 yards as the Browns rolled to more than 400 total yards, converted 11 of 14 third downs, and punted only once. The Browns' defense, meanwhile, held Eric Dickerson under 100 yards rushing for the third time on the season.

The Browns put the cap on a magnificent second half when DB Frank Minnifield returned an interception 48 yards for a touchdown in the final minute, giving the Browns their highest playoff point total in 18 years. The following afternoon, the Denver Broncos crushed Houston in the other divisional playoff to set up a rematch of the previous year's classic in the AFC Championship.

	1	2	3	4		
Colts	7	7	0	7	=	21
Browns	7	7	7	17	=	38

CLE-Byner 10-yd. pass from Kosar (Bahr kick)
IND-Beach 2-yd. pass from Trudeau (Biasucci kick)
CLE-Langhorne 39-yd. pass from Kosar (Bahr kick)
IND-Dickerson 19-yd. pass from Trudeau (Biasucci kick)
CLE-Byner 2-yd. run (Bahr kick)
CLE-Bahr 22-yd. FG
CLE-Brennan 2-yd. pass from Kosar (Bahr kick)
IND-Bentley 1-yd. run (Biasucci kick)
CLE-Minnifield 48-yd. interception return (Bahr kick)

Passing
IND: Trudeau 21–33–251 2 TD 1 INT, Salisbury 1–6–15 0 TD 1 INT
CLE: Kosar 20–31–229 3 TD 1 INT

Rushing
IND: Dickerson 15–50, Bentley 4–9, Trudeau 2–4
CLE: Byner 23–122, Mack 6–38, Manoa 4–10, Kosar 1–5

Receiving
IND: Brooks 5–78, Dickerson 7–65, Bentley 4–47, Murray 1–25, Bouza 2–24, Bellini 1–21, Beach 2–6
CLE: Newsome 4–65, Langhorne 1–39, Byner 4–36, Brennan 3–25, Fontenot 2–20, Mack 3–17, Slaughter 1–14, McNeil 1–8, Weathers 1–5

AFC Championship
Sunday, January 17
Denver Broncos 38, Browns 33
Mile High Stadium (75,993)
White jerseys/white pants

In one of the most memorable games in team history, the Browns staged an incredible rally from a monumental deficit only to fall heartbreakingly short in the final minutes in a rematch of the previous season's AFC Championship.

On a sunny, picture-perfect day for football in the Rockies, things started out disastrously for the Browns. They turned the ball over on their first two possessions, and Denver turned both into touchdowns. Things only got worse in the second quarter as the Broncos built a 21–3 halftime lead and appeared poised to coast to their second straight Super Bowl appearance.

Felix Wright intercepted John Elway to open the second half, and the Browns quickly scored their first touchdown but then surrendered an 80-yard scoring pass to WR Mark Jackson that extended Denver's lead to 28–10 five minutes into the third quarter.

But with a blowout imminent, the Browns refused to fold. They scored on their next two possessions to cut the Bronco margin to four points, then Denver tacked on a field goal to make it 31–24 going into the fourth quarter. A 53-yard, third-down reception by Earnest Byner—enjoying a career afternoon—set up the game-tying touchdown by Webster Slaughter with 11 minutes remaining.

Denver surged back into the lead with four minutes left on John Elway's third touchdown pass, but the Browns fought back and drove from their own 24 to the Denver 8 with just over a minute left. Byner broke free on a draw and appeared to score the tying touchdown but had been stripped of the football at the Denver 2 and the Broncos recovered. Denver took an intentional safety in the final seconds, and a final desperation pass by the Browns was incomplete as time expired.

It spoiled an otherwise magnificent performance by Byner, who caught seven passes for 120 yards and rushed for 67 more to lead a Cleveland offense that rolled to a season-best 464 total yards. Kosar also played one of the finest games of his career, throwing for 356 yards (246 in the second half) and three scores as the Browns scored 30 points in the final 30 minutes to turn the game into one of the most memorable—and heartbreaking—in NFL history.

	1	2	3	4		
Browns	0	3	21	9	=	33
Broncos	14	7	10	7	=	38

DEN-Nattiel 8-yd. pass from Elway (Karlis kick)
DEN-Sewell 1-yd. run (Karlis kick)
CLE-Bahr 24-yd. FG
DEN-Lang 1-yd. run (Karlis kick)
CLE-Langhorne 18-yd. pass from Kosar (Bahr kick)
DEN-Jackson 80-yd. pass from Elway (Karlis kick)
CLE-Byner 32-yd. pass from Kosar (Bahr kick)
CLE-Byner 4-yd. run (Bahr kick)
DEN-Karlis 38-yd. FG
CLE-Slaughter 4-yd. pass from Kosar (Bahr kick)
DEN-Winder 20-yd. pass from Elway (Karlis kick)
CLE-Safety: Horan ran out of end zone

Passing
CLE: Kosar 26–41–356 3 TD 1 INT
DEN: Elway 14–26–281 3 TD 1 INT

Rushing
CLE: Byner 15–67, Mack 12–61
DEN: Winder 20–72, Lang 5–51, Elway 11–36, Boddie 1–8, Sewell 1–1, Horan 1-(-12)

Receiving
CLE: Byner 7–120, Slaughter 4–53, Brennan 4–48, Langhorne 2–48, Newsome 3–35, Mack 4–28, Weathers 1–19, Tennell 1–5
DEN: Jackson 4–134, Nattiel 5–95, Winder 3–34, Sewell 1–10, Mobley 1–8

1988

Sunday, September 4
Browns 6, Kansas City Chiefs 3
Arrowhead Stadium (55,654)
White jerseys/white pants

What would become a rocky season got off to a rough start as the Browns lost five Pro Bowl players to injuries but managed to endure to pull out their first opening-day victory in six years. The most notable setback came early in the second quarter when QB Bernie Kosar was hit on a safety blitz and strained ligaments in his right elbow, knocking him out of the game and out of action for the next seven weeks. While backup Gary Danielson was able to move the Browns' offense, they struggled to put points on the board and for the first time in nearly three years were unable to score a touchdown. But the defense rose to the occasion, holding Kansas City to just 149 total yards and nine first downs. The Chiefs' only points came after they blocked a Cleveland field goal, beginning a season-long trend of Cleveland special-teams breakdowns. The Browns tied the game just before the half, and Danielson directed a clutch 72-yard drive in the final minutes that ended with Matt Bahr's second field goal of the day to put the Browns up 6–3 with 25 seconds left. It marked the first time in four years the Browns were involved in a game in which no touchdowns were scored.

Record: 1–0

	1	2	3	4		
Browns	0	3	0	3	=	6
Chiefs	0	3	0	0	=	3

KC-Lowery 33-yd. FG
CLE-Bahr 19-yd. FG
CLE-Bahr 38-yd. FG

Passing
CLE: Danielson 18–29–170 0 TD 1 INT, Kosar 3–8–39 0 TD 0 INT
KC: Kenney 11–29–106 0 TD 2 INT

Rushing
CLE: Manoa 14–70, Mack 9–41, Byner 12–33, Danielson 1-(-2)
KC: Palmer 12–28, Saxon 7–24, Moriarty 1–8

Receiving
CLE: Slaughter 5–61, Byner 3–44, Newsome 3–31, Manoa 4–25, Mack 2–20, Langhorne 2–19, Brennan 2–9
KC: Roberts 3–34, Paige 3–27, Carson 1–20, Taylor 2–16, Saxon 1–5, Palmer 1–4

Sunday, September 11
New York Jets 23, Browns 3
Cleveland Stadium (74,434)
White jerseys/white pants

With Gary Danielson at quarterback, the Browns, nine-and-a-half-point favorites, were rocked in the home opener by the mediocre Jets, who dominated time of possession and turned a tight contest into a rout with a pair of fourth-quarter touchdowns. The Cleveland offense once again failed to score a touchdown—the first time they'd failed to reach the end zone in back-to-back games in 15 years—and lost its quarterback to injury for the second straight week. Danielson broke his ankle in the third quarter, in what would mark the end of his 11-year career. Third-stringer Mike Pagel took over but had no more success as the Browns turned the ball over three times and allowed five sacks. Cleveland managed just 36 rushing yards—its lowest total in 17 years—and lost two more stars to injury in DBs Hanford Dixon and Frank Minnifield. The weary defense allowed more than 400 yards as the Browns dropped to .500.

Record: 1–1

	1	2	3	4		
Jets	3	3	3	14	=	23
Browns	3	0	0	0	=	3

NYJ-Leahy 22-yd. FG
CLE-Bahr 47-yd. FG
NYJ-Leahy 29-yd. FG
NYJ-Leahy 23-yd. FG
NYJ-Vick 1-yd. run (Leahy kick)
NYJ-Vick 3-yd. run (Leahy kick)

Passing
NYJ: O'Brien 19–30–256 0 TD 0 INT
CLE: Danielson 13–23–154 0 TD 0 INT, Pagel 7–14–73 0 TD 1 INT

Rushing
NYJ: Hector 15–56, Vick 12–45, McNeil 12–28, Walker 1–12, Leahy 1–10, O'Brien 2–3
CLE: Mack 8–26, Byner 5–5, Danielson 3–5

Receiving
NYJ: Shuler 5–73, Toon 4–55, Walker 1–49, McNeil 3–32, Vick 3–25, Hector 2–11, Griggs 1–11
CLE: Langhorne 6–75, Byner 4–46, Weathers 4–46, Newsome 2–26, Young 1–25, Brennan 1–7, Mack 2–2

Monday, September 19
Browns 23, Indianapolis Colts 17
Cleveland Stadium (75,748)
White jerseys/white pants

In a rematch of their divisional playoff eight months earlier, the Browns' offense finally got untracked against the Colts and sparked a much-needed win on *Monday Night Football.* Mike Pagel got his first Cleveland start and played well against his former team, throwing for 255 yards and a pair of touchdowns, including the Browns' first of the season, a diving 14-yard scoring catch by TE Ozzie Newsome late in the first quarter. Thanks to a close call on a touchdown reception by WR Webster Slaughter in which he and Indy DB Eugene Daniel both had possession of the football in the end zone, the Browns built a 23–10 lead early in the fourth, then held off the Colts in the final minutes after they cut the lead to six on a long punt return for a touchdown. The Cleveland defense prevented the Colts from threatening again and the Browns secured their second victory.
Record: 2–1

	1	2	3	4		
Colts	3	7	0	7	=	17
Browns	7	10	3	3	=	23

IND-Biasucci 30-yd. FG
CLE-Newsome 14-yd. pass from Pagel (Bahr kick)
CLE-Bahr 21-yd. FG
IND-Dickerson 41-yd. run (Biasucci kick)
CLE-Slaughter 17-yd. pass from Pagel (Bahr kick)
CLE-Bahr 29-yd. FG
CLE-Bahr 40-yd. FG
IND-Verdin 73-yd. punt return (Biasucci kick)

Passing
IND: Trudeau 10–19–80 0 TD 1 INT, Chandler 3–8–80 0 TD 1 INT
CLE: Pagel 23–38–255 2 TD 1 INT

Rushing
IND: Dickerson 22–117, Bentley 2–7, Chandler 1–4
CLE: Mack 23–76, Byner 10–22, Manoa 2–5, Pagel 1-(-2)

Receiving
IND: Verdin 2–55, Beach 4–30, Brooks 2–29, Bouza 2–21, Boyer 2–15, Bentley 1–10
CLE: Slaughter 6–86, Brennan 5–50, Mack 3–49, Byner 2–27, Newsome 3–20, Langhorne 3–17, McNeil 1–6

Sunday, September 25
Cincinnati Bengals 24, Browns 17
Riverfront Stadium (54,943)
White jerseys/white pants

The undefeated Bengals rolled up more than 200 rushing yards and controlled the undermanned Browns, cruising to their fourth straight victory. Cleveland dug a hole two minutes into the game when RB Kevin Mack fumbled, and Cincinnati DB Lewis Billups scooped up the loose ball and returned it 26 yards for a touchdown. The Browns would spent the rest of the day playing catch-up, and though Pagel threw for 254 yards, and the defense held Cincy scoreless in the second half, the Bengals controlled the game and took a two-game lead on Cleveland in the division race.
Record: 2–2

	1	2	3	4		
Browns	3	7	0	7	=	17
Bengals	7	17	0	0	=	24

CIN-Billups 26-yd. fumble return (Breech kick)
CLE-Bahr 27-yd. FG
CIN-Breech 34-yd. FG
CIN-Woods 1-yd. run (Breech kick)
CLE-Brennan 11-yd. pass from Pagel (Bahr kick)
CIN-Woods 1-yd. run (Breech kick)
CLE-Mack 3-yd. run (Bahr kick)

Passing
CLE: Pagel 24–48–254 1 TD 0 INT
CIN: Esiason 8–23–183 0 TD 0 INT

Rushing
CLE: Mack 14–39, Byner 4–17, Manoa 2–7, Pagel 1–5
CIN: Brooks 17–83, Wilson 11–68, Woods 13–62, Esiason 3–0

Receiving
CLE: Newsome 5–72, Byner 8–64, Slaughter 3–53, Brennan 4–31, Langhorne 3–27, Mack 1–7
CIN: Brown 4–127, McGee 1–21, Collinsworth 1–16, Riggs 1–16, Holman 1–3

Sunday, October 2
Browns 23, Pittsburgh Steelers 9
Three Rivers Stadium (56,410)
White jerseys/white pants

Thanks to a sterling defensive performance, the Browns won their third straight game at Three Rivers Stadium and moved back over the .500 mark. Trailing 9–7 at the half, the Browns controlled the final two periods, surging ahead after LB Eddie Johnson recovered a fumble and then intercepted a pass to set up Cleveland field goals. Fittingly, the defense then clinched the victory when rookie DB Brian Washington returned an interception 75 yards for a touchdown five minutes into the fourth quarter. The Cleveland defense forced five turnovers on the day and limited Pittsburgh to just 183 total yards, as the Steelers completed only 11 of 38 pass attempts. On offense, the Browns were unable to come up with the big play but controlled the line of scrimmage, rushing for 168 yards as a team as both Earnest Byner and RB Tim Manoa topped 75 yards.
Record: 3–2

	1	2	3	4		
Browns	0	7	6	10	=	23
Steelers	6	3	0	0	=	9

PIT-Anderson 49-yd. FG
PIT-Anderson 35-yd. FG
CLE-Manoa 1-yd. run (Bahr kick)
PIT-Anderson 45-yd. FG
CLE-Bahr 22-yd. FG
CLE-Bahr 21-yd. FG
CLE-Washington 75-yd. interception return (Bahr kick)
CLE-Bahr 40-yd. FG

Passing
CLE: Pagel 15–26–131 0 TD 1 INT
PIT: Bono 7–24–83 0 TD 2 INT, Brister 4–14–28 0 TD 2 INT

Rushing
CLE: Manoa 18–82, Byner 20–78, Fontenot 2–7, Mack 3–3, Pagel 2-(-2)
PIT: Williams 9–28, Jackson 8–28, Hoge 5–21, Brister 2–7, Stone 2–5

Receiving
CLE: Brennan 3–34, Tennell 2–30, Langhorne 3–29, Manoa 2–16, Newsome 2–11, Fontenot 2–9, Byner 1–2
PIT: Hoge 4–31, Stone 2–26, Lockett 1–15, Lipps 1–13, Thompson 1–12, Jackson 1–8, Williams 1–6

Sunday, October 9
Seattle Seahawks 16, Browns 10
Cleveland Stadium (78,605)
White jerseys/white pants

The Browns' tough-luck season took another bizarre turn as they lost their third quarterback in six games and dropped their second of three home games despite outplaying Seattle. After scoring a touchdown on their first possession, the Browns spent the rest of the afternoon making critical mistakes, coughing up four turnovers and allowing a blocked field goal in the second quarter that turned out to be doubly painful. Seattle DB Paul Moyer returned the blocked kick 62 yards before being tackled by Mike Pagel, who was the Browns' holder on kicking attempts. Pagel separated his shoulder on the tackle and was knocked out of the game, replaced by 37-year-old Don Strock, signed a month before in case of an emergency. With a "cheat sheet" taped to his forearm, Strock was unable to rally the Browns from a nine-point fourth-quarter deficit, and Seattle escaped despite the Browns' dominating total yardage and time of possession. The defeat dropped the Browns three games behind 6–0 Cincinnati in the division race.
Record: 3–3

	1	2	3	4		
Seahawks	7	6	0	3	=	16
Browns	7	0	0	3	=	10

CLE-Mack 1-yd. run (Bahr kick)
SEA-Warner 1-yd. run (Johnson kick)
SEA-Johnson 31-yd. FG
SEA-Johnson 38-yd. FG
SEA-Johnson 22-yd. FG
CLE-Bahr 23-yd. FG

Passing
SEA: Stouffer 9–17–112 0 TD 0 INT
CLE: Strock 12–20–151 0 TD 1 INT, Pagel 2–8–23 0 TD 1 INT

Rushing
SEA: Warner 24–96, Williams 9–29, Stouffer 3–4, Largent 1-(-3)
CLE: Mack 15–66, Byner 7–52, Manoa 4–24, Fontenot 2–13, Strock 2–5

Receiving
SEA: Blades 2–33, Warner 2–29, Skansi 1–21, Tice 2–14, Largent 1–9, Williams 1–6
CLE: Slaughter 4–59, Byner 4–42, Newsome 2–27, Langhorne 2–19, Brennan 1–16, Fontenot 1–11

Sunday, October 16
Browns 19, Philadelphia Eagles 3
Cleveland Stadium (78,787)
White jerseys/white pants

Starting their fourth different quarterback in seven games, the Browns put forth one of their finest performances of the season, dominating the playoff-bound Eagles. The Cleveland defense was magnificent, not allowing a touchdown for the third time on the season. They held Philadelphia to just 119 total yards and sacked QB Randall Cunningham nine times, while Frank Minnifield picked off two passes. Don Strock got the Browns' offense going in the second half as they blew open a 3–3 game with 16 unanswered points, including a pair of Strock scoring passes. The Cleveland offense rolled up 361 total yards, including a season-high 182 on the ground as Kevin Mack rushed for an even 100 on 16 carries. Even in victory, the Browns couldn't avoid bad luck as WR Webster Slaughter fractured his forearm in the fourth quarter and would miss the next eight games.
Record: 4–3

	1	2	3	4		
Eagles	0	3	0	0	=	3
Browns	3	0	6	10	=	19

CLE-Bahr 24-yd. FG
PHI-Zendejas 39-yd. FG
CLE-Slaughter 15-yd. pass from Strock (kick failed)
CLE-Bahr 37-yd. FG
CLE-Langhorne 18-yd. pass from Strock (Bahr kick)

Passing
PHI: Cunningham 15–27–114 0 TD 2 INT
CLE: Strock 11–18–189 2 TD 1 INT

Rushing
PHI: Toney 11–37, Cunningham 3–22, Byars 5–12
CLE: Mack 16–100, Byner 17–74, Manoa 7–9, Langhorne 1–6, Strock 3-(-7)

Receiving
PHI: Byars 7–50, Carter 2–30, Jackson 4–23, Toney 1–7, Tautalatasi 1–4
CLE: Brennan 3–79, Slaughter 4–50, Langhorne 2–39, Tennell 1–15, Newsome 1–6

Sunday, October 23
Browns 29, Phoenix Cardinals 21
Sun Devil Stadium (61,261)
Brown jerseys/white pants

On a steamy afternoon in Phoenix in which the temperature hit 110°F on the field, Bernie Kosar returned to action and led the Browns to an impressive win in their first-ever game in Arizona. Quickly returning to form, Kosar hit 10 different receivers and threw for 314 yards and a trio of touchdowns, including a tackle-eligible toss to Rickey Bolden and a brilliant diving scoring reception by Reggie Langhorne that gave the Browns a 14–0 lead midway through the second quarter. The Cardinals fought back to take a one-point lead in the fourth quarter, but the Browns surged ahead and secured victory after Langhorne's second touchdown midway through the period. They tacked on a safety recorded by DE Charles Buchanan with under two minutes to play on the Browns' sixth sack of the afternoon. The Browns' defense also forced four turnovers, balancing out four committed by the Cleveland offense.
Record: 5–3

	1	2	3	4		
Browns	7	10	3	9	=	29
Cardinals	0	14	0	7	=	21

CLE-Bolden 3-yd. pass from Kosar (Bahr kick)
CLE-Langhorne 29-yd. pass from Kosar (Bahr kick)
PHX-Ferrell 2-yd. run (Del Greco kick)
PHX-Smith 8-yd. pass from Lomax (Del Greco kick)
CLE-Bahr 46-yd. FG
CLE-Bahr 23-yd. FG
PHX-Awalt 21-yd. pass from Stoudt (Del Greco kick)
CLE-Langhorne 25-yd. pass from Kosar (Bahr kick)
CLE-Safety: Buchanan tackled Stoudt in end zone

Passing
CLE: Kosar 25–43–314 3 TD 3 INT
PHX: Lomax 11–19–120 1 TD 1 INT, Stoudt 6–13–77 1 TD 2 INT

Rushing
CLE: Manoa 15–65, Byner 4–8, Kosar 2-(-5)
PHX: Ferrell 18–110, Jordan 12–34, Lomax 2–25

Receiving
CLE: Langhorne 5–89, Byner 6–64, Brennan 3–52, Weathers 3–39, McNeil 1–23, Fontenot 2–19, Manoa 2–15, Mack 1–5, Newsome 1–5, Bolden 1–3
PHX: Green 5–69, Awalt 4–56, Smith 5–48, Ferrell 2–16, Wolfley 1–8

Sunday, October 30
Browns 23, Cincinnati Bengals 16
Cleveland Stadium (79,147)
White jerseys/white pants

In perhaps the biggest game in the history of the rivalry, the Browns outmuscled the 7–1 Bengals to move within a game of first place on a sunshiny day before Halloween. After the Browns spotted Cincinnati an early 7–3 lead on an interception return for a touchdown, the Cleveland special teams rose to the occasion. First, RB Herman Fontenot returned the ensuing kickoff 84 yards to set up the go-ahead touchdown, then midway through the third quarter, Frank Minnifield blocked a Bengals' punt, which Fontenot recovered at the Cincinnati 1 and rolled into the end zone for a score to put the Browns up 20–10. The Cleveland defense took it from there, collecting four sacks and limiting the high-powered Bengals' offense to less than 300 total yards while not allowing a touchdown. WR Clarence Weathers sparked the Cleveland offense with a marvelous day, catching seven passes for 140 yards. The victory moved the Browns into a tie for second place with the Oilers, whom they would face eight days later.
Record: 6–3

	1	2	3	4		
Bengals	0	10	3	3	=	16
Browns	3	7	10	3	=	23

CLE-Bahr 34-yd. FG
CIN-Fulcher 16-yd. interception return (Breech kick)
CLE-Manoa 2-yd. run (Bahr kick)
CIN-Breech 19-yd. FG
CLE-Bahr 39-yd. FG
CLE-Fontenot 1-yd. blocked punt return (Bahr kick)
CIN-Breech 32-yd. FG
CLE-Bahr 29-yd. FG
CIN-Breech 22-yd. FG

Passing
CIN: Esiason 12–25–173 0 TD 0 INT
CLE: Kosar 18–28–210 0 TD 2 INT

Rushing
CIN: Brooks 10–65, Woods 9–30, Esiason 5–18, Wilson 7–15
CLE: Manoa 23–89, Byner 4–14, Kosar 1-(-4)

Receiving
CIN: Brown 6–91, McGee 2–29, Collinsworth 1–18, Woods 1–16, Hillary 1–11, Riggs 1–8
CLE: Weathers 7–140, Byner 4–26, Brennan 2–22, Langhorne 1–7, Tennell 1–6, Newsome 1–5, Fontenot 1–2, Manoa 1–2

Monday, November 7
Houston Oilers 24, Browns 17
Houston Astrodome (51,467)
White jerseys/white pants

On the night before Texas native George H. W. Bush was elected the forty-first U.S. president, the Browns' three-game winning streak came to a screeching halt in the Astrodome as the Oilers physically dominated the game before a *Monday Night Football* television audience. Aided by a blocked punt—the fourth blocked kick the Browns had permitted in 1988—Houston soared to a 21–3 lead early in the third quarter and then staved off a Browns' comeback, recovering a bad shotgun snap to Bernie Kosar in Cleveland territory with 1:44 remaining after the Browns had cut the margin to 24–17. They'd clawed back on an Ozzie Newsome scoring reception and the only touchdown run of Reggie Langhorne's career, a 20-yard reverse late in the third period. The defeat once again dropped the Browns two games behind front-running Cincinnati and allowed the Oilers to take over sole possession of second place in the AFC Central.
Record: 6–4

	1	2	3	4		
Browns	3	0	7	7	=	17
Oilers	0	7	14	3	=	24

CLE-Bahr 40-yd. FG
HOU-Highsmith 1-yd. run (Zendejas kick)
HOU-Givins 8-yd. pass from Moon (Zendejas kick)
HOU-Rozier 3-yd. run (Zendejas kick)
CLE-Langhorne 20-yd. run (Bahr kick)
CLE-Newsome 4-yd. pass from Kosar (Bahr kick)
HOU-Zendejas 47-yd. FG

Passing
CLE: Kosar 16–33–219 1 TD 0 INT
HOU: Moon 11–17–182 1 TD 0 INT

Rushing
CLE: Langhorne 1–20, Byner 5–17, Mack 6–11, Manoa 2–1, Kosar 1–0, Fontenot 1-(-5)
HOU: Rozier 23–76, Highsmith 8–40, Pinkett 8–31, Moon 4–1

Receiving
CLE: Langhorne 5–93, Newsome 5–65, McNeil 2–36, Byner 3–29, Manoa 1-(-4)
HOU: Givins 6–89, Harris 4–69, Hill 1–24

Sunday, November 13
Denver Broncos 30, Browns 7
Mile High Stadium (75,806)
White jerseys/white pants

The Browns' struggles in Denver continued as they were blown away following a nightmarish first half and lost their tenth straight game to the Broncos. Aided by four Cleveland turnovers, including a fumble by Tim Manoa on the game's first play, the Broncos scored on their first six possessions to build a 30–0 halftime lead. Earnest Byner, returning to the site of his infamous fumble 10 months earlier, averted the shutout with a two-yard touchdown run late in the third quarter. Bernie Kosar was sacked six times, and the Browns racked up 86 yards in penalties as they became one of six AFC teams with a 6–5 record with five games remaining.
Record: 6–5

	1	2	3	4		
Browns	0	0	7	0	=	7
Broncos	10	20	0	0	=	30

DEN-Karlis 18-yd. FG
DEN-Mobley 11-yd. pass from Elway (Karlis kick)
DEN-Karlis 22-yd. FG
DEN-Willhite 1-yd. run (Karlis kick)
DEN-Karlis 32-yd. FG
DEN-Sewell 5-yd. pass from Elway (Karlis kick)
CLE-Byner 2-yd. run (Bahr kick)

Passing
CLE: Kosar 19–30–175 0 TD 1 INT
DEN: Elway 21–30–207 2 TD 0 INT, Kubiak 1–1–8 0 TD 0 INT, Dorsett 0–1–0 0 TD 0 INT

Rushing
CLE: Byner 11–60, Manoa 4–18, Fontenot 1–10, Kosar 1-(-1)
DEN: Dorsett 14–42, Elway 3–34, Nattiel 2–26, Winder 13–12, Sewell 5–4, Willhite 2–3, Kubiak 1-(-1)

Receiving
CLE: Brennan 6–59, Weathers 4–44, Byner 4–36, Langhorne 1–10, Young 1–9, Newsome 1–8, Tennell 1–8, Fontenot 1–1
DEN: Mobley 6–55, Johnson 3–40, Sewell 4–39, Jackson 2–31, Willhite 4–26, Kay 2–17, Nattiel 1–7

Sunday, November 20
Browns 27, Pittsburgh Steelers 7
Cleveland Stadium (77,131)
White jerseys/white pants

The struggling Browns bounced back with a convincing victory on a rainy November Sunday in Cleveland, defeating the hapless Steelers for the sixth straight time. Aided by four Pittsburgh turnovers along with a blocked punt for a touchdown and another touchdown set up by a bad punt snap, the Browns cruised to a 17–0 second-quarter lead and never looked back. They put the game away a minute into the second half when Bernie Kosar connected with Reggie Langhorne on a short sideline pass on which Langhorne broke free and turned into a 77-yard touchdown, the Browns' longest pass play in 16 years. In addition to their flurry of takeaways, the Cleveland defense collected six sacks as the Browns remained two games behind Cincinnati and a game back of Houston in the AFC Central.
Record: 7–5

	1	2	3	4		
Steelers	0	7	0	0	=	7
Browns	3	14	7	3	=	27

CLE-Bahr 32-yd. FG
CLE-Tennell 2-yd. pass from Kosar (Bahr kick)
CLE-Minnifield 11-yd. blocked punt return (Bahr kick)

PIT-Carter 1-yd. run (Anderson kick)
CLE-Langhorne 77-yd. pass from Kosar (Bahr kick)
CLE-Bahr 34-yd. FG

Passing
PIT: Brister 16–35–220 0 TD 2 INT, Carter 0–1–0 0 TD 0 INT
CLE: Kosar 12–24–204 2 TD 0 INT, Fontenot 0–1–0 0 TD 0 INT

Rushing
PIT: Hoge 17–66, Williams 8–32, Brister 4–16, Carter 2–4, Newsome 2–0
CLE: Byner 11–34, Manoa 5–13, Fontenot 7–12, Kosar 3–11, Runager 1–0

Receiving
PIT: Johnson 2–57, Lipps 2–40, Carter 2–38, Hoge 4–33, Lockett 3–33, Gothard 2–18, Williams 1–1
CLE: Langhorne 4–99, Brennan 3–66, Tennell 3–25, Newsome 1–8, Fontenot 1–6

Sunday, November 27
Browns 17, Washington Redskins 13
RFK Stadium (51,604)
Brown jerseys/white pants

The Browns kept their playoff hopes alive with a gritty, come-from-behind victory over the defending world-champion Redskins on a rainy afternoon in the nation's capital. Another blocked punt allowed by the Browns set up the Redskins' only touchdown, and Washington took a 10–3 lead into the fourth quarter. A short Kevin Mack scoring run capped a 16-play drive to tie the contest with under 10 minutes to play, but the Redskins surged ahead with a field goal on their next possession. With time running out, a crucial 21-yard completion to WR Brian Brennan on third-and-10 moved the Browns into Washington territory, then they faced another third down at the Redskins' 27 moments later. Earnest Byner exploded up the middle for a 27-yard touchdown run with 1:49 remaining to give the Browns the lead, then an interception by DB Mark Harper in the final moments clinched a satisfying victory. With the Redskins constantly pressuring Bernie Kosar—and recording six sacks—the Cleveland running game rose to the occasion, as Kevin Mack tallied the ninth (and final) 100-yard game of his career. Amazingly, it would be five years before another Cleveland running back topped 100 yards rushing in a game.
Record: 8–5

	1	2	3	4		
Browns	0	3	0	14	=	17
Redskins	0	0	10	3	=	13

CLE-Bahr 37-yd. FG
WAS-Clark 7-yd. pass from Rypien (Lohmiller kick)
WAS-Lohmiller 21-yd. FG
CLE-Mack 1-yd. run (Bahr kick)
WAS-Lohmiller 40-yd. FG
CLE-Byner 27-yd. run (Bahr kick)

Passing
CLE: Kosar 23–36–219 0 TD 1 INT
WAS: Rypien 11–24–135 1 TD 2 INT

Rushing
CLE: Mack 22–116, Byner 5–44, Manoa 1–2, Kosar 3-(-4)
WAS: Morris 19–74, Monk 1–23, Oliphant 2–5, Rypien 1–1

Receiving
CLE: Langhorne 5–57, Byner 7–48, Brennan 4–47, Weathers 3–37, Fontenot 2–22, Newsome 1–5, Mack 1–3
WAS: Sanders 3–45, Monk 2–30, Clark 3–29, Oliphant 1–16, Orr 1–8, McEwan 1–7

Sunday, December 4
Browns 24, Dallas Cowboys 21
Cleveland Stadium (77,683)
White jerseys/white pants

On a sunny December afternoon, the Browns pulled out a narrow victory over the 2–11 Cowboys in a surprisingly tight contest. The struggling Cowboys tallied 410 yards of offense and took a 14–10 lead into the fourth quarter before a pair of Bernie Kosar touchdown passes in the first two minutes of the period put the Browns ahead 24–14. The second was a dazzling one-handed reception by Clarence Weathers for a 36-yard score, bookending a 73-yard Kosar-to-Reggie Langhorne touchdown to open the scoring. The Cowboys cut the margin to three midway through the fourth and then had a chance to send the game to overtime when they connected on a 40-yard field goal with 1:43 remaining, but it was called back on a tripping penalty, and the ensuing 50-yard attempt fell short. It was a fitting end to the contest for the Cowboys, who were penalized 17 times for a whopping 142 yards. It helped counter the Browns' sudden inability to run the football, as they managed a harmless 27 yards on 20 carries and, for the first time in team history, didn't pick up a single first down rushing. Kosar threw for 308 yards and

THE TOP 10 GAMES OF BERNIE KOSAR'S CAREER

(Based on highest quarterback rating—minimum 15 attempts)

10. September 25, 1989, at Cincinnati (Browns lose, 21–14)
15 of 23 for 203 yards, 2 TD 0 INT
122.2 rating

9. September 8, 1991, at New England (Browns win, 20–0)
15 of 22 for 187 yards, 2 TD 0 INT
124.6 rating

8. December 21, 1986, vs. San Diego (Browns win, 47–17)
21 of 28 for 258 yards, 2 TD 0 INT
126.8 rating

7. October 23, 1989, vs. Chicago (Browns win, 27–7)
22 of 29 for 281 yards, 2 TD 0 INT
128.7 rating

6. January 6, 1990, vs. Buffalo* (Browns win, 34–30)
20 of 29 for 251 yards, 3 TD 0 INT
130.1 rating

5. November 2, 1986, at Indianapolis (Browns win, 24–9)
15 of 25 for 238 yards, 3 TD 0 INT
131.3 rating

4. December 13, 1987, vs. Cincinnati (Browns win, 38–24)
17 of 26 for 241 yards, 4 TD 0 INT
134.8 rating

3. November 5, 1989, at Tampa Bay (Browns win, 42–31)
18 of 22 for 164 yards, 3 TD 0 INT
137.3 rating

2. December 6, 1992, vs. Cincinnati (Browns win, 37–21)
f 23 for 239 yards, 2 TD 0 INT
138.9 rating

1. December 4, 1988, vs. Dallas (Browns win, 24–21)
19 of 27 for 308 yards, 3 TD 0 INT
145.3 rating

**AFC Divisional Playoff*

three touchdowns to help the Browns pull into a tie for second with Houston, who were upset at home by Pittsburgh that evening.

Record: 9–5

	1	2	3	4		
Cowboys	0	14	0	7	=	21
Browns	7	3	0	14	=	24

CLE-Langhorne 73-yd. pass from Kosar (Bahr kick)
DAL-Clack 7-yd. pass from Pelluer (Ruzek kick)
CLE-Bahr 25-yd. FG
DAL-Folsom 5-yd. pass from Pelluer (Ruzek kick)
CLE-Fontenot 14-yd. pass from Kosar (Bahr kick)
CLE-Weathers 36-yd. pass from Kosar (Bahr kick)
DAL-Walker 4-yd. run (Ruzek kick)

Passing
DAL: Pelluer 20–32–247 2 TD 0 INT
CLE: Kosar 19–27–308 3 TD 0 INT

Rushing
DAL: Walker 25–134, Pelluer 5–28, Clack 2–1
CLE: Byner 10–24, Mack 7–7, Fontenot 1–3, Manoa 1–1, Bahr 1-(-8)

Receiving
DAL: Gay 3–62, Burbage 1–41, Irvin 2–37, Clack 5–36, Martin 2–24, Fowler 1–12, Alexander 1–11, Walker 3–7, Folsom 1–5
CLE: Langhorne 2–79, Brennan 6–71, Weathers 3–60, Fontenot 3–41, Byner 1–29, Newsome 2–18, McNeil 1–9, Mack 1–1

Monday, December 12
Miami Dolphins 38, Browns 31
Joe Robbie Stadium (61,884)
White jerseys/white pants

In a wild Monday-night shootout in Miami, the Browns' playoff hopes were dealt a serious blow, and Bernie Kosar was lost to an injury for the second time on the season in a frustrating loss to the 5–9 Dolphins. Behind 404 passing yards by Miami QB Dan Marino—the first 400-yard passing game the Browns had allowed in eight years—the Dolphins rolled up nearly 500 total yards and built a 31–17 lead early in the fourth quarter. Then, after Kosar was knocked out of the game with a knee injury, longtime Dolphins' backup QB Don Strock entered the game and directed the Browns on a pair of touchdown drives, both ending with short scoring passes to Reggie Langhorne. The second tied the game with a minute to play. But a 46-yard Marino pass to former Browns' WR Fred Banks set up the game-winning touchdown with 34 seconds left. The Browns' quest for a playoff berth would come down to the season finale the following week.

Record: 9–6

	1	2	3	4		
Browns	0	10	7	14	=	31
Dolphins	0	17	7	14	=	38

MIA-Clayton 11-yd. pass from Marino (Reveiz kick)
CLE-Byner 39-yd. pass from Kosar (Bahr kick)
CLE-Bahr 33-yd. FG
MIA-Jensen 2-yd. pass from Marino (Reveiz kick)
MIA-Reveiz 35-yd. FG
MIA-Hampton 2-yd. pass from Marino (Reveiz kick)
CLE-Kosar 2-yd. run (Bahr kick)
MIA-Clayton 9-yd. pass from Marino (Reveiz kick)
CLE-Langhorne 3-yd. pass from Strock (Bahr kick)
CLE-Langhorne 2-yd. pass from Strock (Bahr kick)
MIA-Hampton 1-yd. run (Reveiz kick)

Passing
CLE: Kosar 21–30–202 1 TD 0 INT, Strock 7–11–70 2 TD 0 INT
MIA: Marino 30–50–404 4 TD 3 INT

Rushing
CLE: Byner 13–58, Baker 3–19, Fontenot 1–5, Manoa 1–3, Kosar 1–2
MIA: Davenport 13–42, Hampton 12–41, Jensen 1–6, Stradford 1–4

Receiving
CLE: Byner 7–88, Langhorne 7–53, Brennan 2–34, Fontenot 3–30, Newsome 4–23, Weathers 2–23, Slaughter 2–17, Tennell 1–4
MIA: Banks 6–118, Clayton 8–108, Jensen 6–76, Davenport 3–39, Edmunds 2–32, Hampton 4–27, Stradford 1–4

Sunday, December 18
Browns 28, Houston Oilers 23
Cleveland Stadium (74,610)
White jerseys/white pants

With their season hanging in the balance, the Browns rallied back through the snow to secure a playoff spot with one of the most dramatic victories in team history. Don Strock, getting his second start of the season in place of injured Bernie Kosar, was miserable in the first half, throwing three interceptions and coughing up a fumble as Houston built a 23–7 lead midway through the third quarter. But with snow beginning to fall, Strock turned things around in one of the greatest performances of his long career. A pair of Earnest Byner touchdowns pulled the Browns within two points early in the fourth quarter, then Strock connected with Webster Slaughter over the middle for a 22-yard touchdown and what proved to be the game-winning points with 6:23 remaining. The Cleveland defense held the stunned Oilers at bay in the final minutes, and the Browns wrapped up an unlikely comeback thanks to a magnificent performance by Strock, who threw for 326 yards—215 in the second half. Slaughter also had one of the finest games of his career, catching six passes for 136 yards, and rookie DT Michael Dean Perry scored the only touchdown of his career when he scooped up a fumble after a sack by LB David Grayson and rumbled 10 yards for a touchdown early in the second quarter. Ironically, the victory set up a rematch between the teams on the same field six days later in the AFC Wild Card Game.
Record: 10–6

	1	2	3	4		
Oilers	10	6	7	0	=	23
Browns	0	7	7	14	=	28

HOU-Zendejas 39-yd. FG
HOU-Bryant 36-yd. interception return (Zendejas kick)
CLE-Perry 10-yd. fumble return (Bahr kick)
HOU-Zendejas 42-yd. FG
HOU-Zendejas 35-yd. FG
HOU-Jeffires 7-yd. pass from Moon (Zendejas kick)
CLE-Byner 2-yd. pass from Strock (Bahr kick)
CLE-Byner 2-yd. run (Bahr kick)
CLE-Slaughter 22-yd. pass from Strock (Bahr kick)

Passing
HOU: Moon 20–35–287 1 TD 0 INT
CLE: Strock 25–42–326 2 TD 3 INT

Rushing
HOU: Rozier 10–17, Highsmith 4–12, Pinkett 6–10, White 1–0, Moon 2-(-2)
CLE: Fontenot 13–42, Byner 19–36, Strock 1–0

Receiving
HOU: Givins 6–119, Hill 5–59, Highsmith 2–44, Pinkett 3–34, Rozier 3–24, Jeffires 1–7
CLE: Slaughter 6–136, Langhorne 6–68, Weathers 3–47, Byner 5–31, Fontenot 3–29, Newsome 1–13, Brennan 1–2

AFC Wild Card Game
Saturday, December 24
Houston Oilers 24, Browns 23
Cleveland Stadium (74,977)
White jerseys/white pants

On a dreary Christmas Eve, the Browns lost a hard-fought rematch with the Oilers, ending both a roller-coaster season and an era in team history. Perhaps defining the entire campaign, the Browns endured one more quarterback injury—their fourth in 1988—and came from behind to take a second-half lead before faltering.

Making his third start in a Cleveland uniform, Don Strock was knocked out of the game on the first play of the second quarter with an injured wrist and was replaced by Mike Pagel, just activated from the disabled list the day before. The Oilers surged to a 14–3 lead, but the Browns battled back to go ahead 16–14 late in the third quarter on a Pagel-to-Webster Slaughter touchdown pass over the middle reminiscent of the game-winning score six days earlier.

But Houston controlled the fourth quarter, putting together a pair of long drives to score the next 10 points to go ahead 24–16 with less than two minutes remaining. The Browns frantically pulled within a point on another Slaughter touchdown with 31 seconds left, but Houston recovered the ensuing onside kick to capture its first road playoff victory since 1979.

Pagel played well in relief, throwing for 179 yards and a pair of scores, but in a recurring theme of the entire season, the Browns struggled to run the football, managing just 68 yards on 26 carries, underlined by Kevin Mack's 14 on 12 rushes. The officials became a huge part of the game as the teams combined for nearly 200 yards in penalties, and the contest hinged on a controversial ruling of what appeared to be a Houston lateral scooped up by Cleveland LB Clay Matthews and returned for a touchdown in the third quarter. It was ruled an incomplete pass and the complexion of the game changed.

Also changing was the entire Browns' organization, as three days later Marty Schottenheimer resigned as head coach under pressure from Art Modell and the front office. Houston went on to fall to Buffalo in a divisional playoff on New Year's Day.

	1	2	3	4		
Oilers	0	14	0	10	=	24
Browns	3	6	7	7	=	23

CLE-Bahr 33-yd. FG
HOU-Pinkett 14-yd. pass from Moon (Zendejas kick)
HOU-Pinkett 16-yd. run (Zendejas kick)
CLE-Bahr 26-yd. FG
CLE-Bahr 28-yd. FG
CLE-Slaughter 14-yd. pass from Pagel (Bahr kick)
HOU-White 1-yd. run (Zendejas kick)
HOU-Zendejas 49-yd. FG
CLE-Slaughter 2-yd. pass from Pagel (Bahr kick)

Passing
HOU: Moon 16–26–213 1 TD 3 INT
CLE: Pagel 17–25–179 2 TD 1 INT, Strock 2–3–13 0 TD 0 INT

Rushing
HOU: Pinkett 14–82, White 12–30, Moon 6–16, Highsmith 2–3, Givins 1-(-2)
CLE: Byner 9–57, Mack 12–14, Strock 1–0, Pagel 1-(-1), Fontenot 3-(-2)

Receiving
HOU: Hill 5–73, Jeffires 3–52, Duncan 2–33, Pinkett 2–24, Williams 1–14, Givins 1–8, Highsmith 1–8, White 1–1
CLE: Slaughter 5–58, Langhorne 6–57, Brennan 2–34, Weathers 2–27, Byner 3–10, Mack 1–6

1989

Sunday, September 10
Browns 51, Pittsburgh Steelers 0
Three Rivers Stadium (57,928)
White jerseys/white pants

In perhaps the most stunning coaching debut in NFL history, Bud Carson watched his Browns annihilate the team with which Carson rose to prominence as a defensive coordinator, handing the Steelers the worst defeat in their history. The Cleveland defense was dominant, limiting the Steelers to a record-low 53 total yards while racking up six sacks and forcing eight turnovers. The Browns turned three of the takeaways into instant touchdowns, starting with LB Clay Matthews returning a fumble three yards for a score midway through the first quarter. LB David Grayson stole the show, ripping the ball out of the arms of Steelers' WR Louis Lipps on a reverse and returning it 28 yards for a score, then intercepting a tipped pass and returning it 14 yards for another touchdown early in the fourth quarter. Grayson became the first player in Browns' history to score on a fumble return and an interception return in the same game and was named AFC Defensive Player of the Week. Meanwhile, the Cleveland offense was quietly efficient in cashing in on Pittsburgh mistakes, as RB Tim Manoa scored a pair of touchdowns and RB Mike Oliphant, acquired in a trade with Washington for Earnest Byner in the offseason, scored the only touchdown of his brief NFL career. The epic romp marked the Browns' first opening-day shutout in 18 years and propelled them into sole possession of first place hours into the new season.
Record: 1–0

	1	2	3	4		
Browns	17	13	14	7	=	51
Steelers	0	0	0	0	=	0

CLE-Matthews 3-yd. fumble return (Bahr kick)
CLE-Bahr 27-yd. FG
CLE-Grayson 28-yd. fumble return (Bahr kick)
CLE-Bahr 20-yd. FG
CLE-Manoa 3-yd. run (Bahr kick)
CLE-Bahr 27-yd. FG
CLE-Manoa 2-yd. run (Bahr kick)
CLE-Grayson 14-yd. interception return (Bahr kick)
CLE-Oliphant 21-yd. run (Bahr kick)

Passing
CLE: Kosar 16–25–207 0 TD 0 INT
PIT: Brister 10–22–84 0 TD 3 INT

Rushing
CLE: Oliphant 6–48, Jones 11–31, Redden 7–30, Metcalf 10–28, Manoa 9–20, Pagel 1-(-5)
PIT: Worley 10–36, Hoge 4–5, Lipps 1–3, Brister 2-(-8)

Receiving
CLE: Slaughter 4–75, Brennan 2–52, Langhorne 3–32, Manoa 2–31, Metcalf 4–9, Newsome 1–8
PIT: Hill 2–28, Hoge 2–25, Thompson 1–21, Carter 3–13, Lipps 1–7, Brister 1-(-10)

Sunday, September 17
Browns 38, New York Jets 24
Cleveland Stadium (73,516)
White jerseys/white pants

Facing another team for which he'd been a successful assistant, Bud Carson led the Browns to victory over the Jets in their home opener to get the team off to a 2–0 start for the first time in 10 years. While the Cleveland defense was nowhere near as dominant as the week before—allowing nearly 400 total yards—it picked off four passes, two by DB Felix Wright and scored another defensive touchdown when fellow DB Thane Gash returned an interception 36 yards for a score in the second quarter. Bernie Kosar threw three touchdown passes as the Browns pulled away after the Jets tied the game at 14 early in the third period. RB Keith Jones, signed as a free agent in the offseason, had what would prove to be his only productive day with the Browns, tallying 129 total yards and scoring the lone touchdown of his one-year career.
Record: 2–0

	1	2	3	4		
Jets	0	7	10	7	=	24
Browns	0	14	14	10	=	38

NYJ-Vick 39-yd. run (Leahy kick)
CLE-Slaughter 35-yd. pass from Kosar (Bahr kick)
CLE-Gash 36-yd. interception return (Bahr kick)

NYJ-Townsell 49-yd. pass from O'Brien (Leahy kick)
CLE-Manoa 6-yd. pass from Kosar (Bahr kick)
NYJ-Leahy 36-yd. FG
CLE-Jones 9-yd. run (Bahr kick)
NYJ-McNeil 1-yd. run (Leahy kick)
CLE-Newsome 4-yd. pass from Kosar (Bahr kick)
CLE-Bahr 21-yd. FG

Passing
NYJ: O'Brien 24–43–270 1 TD 4 INT
CLE: Kosar 15–30–196 3 TD 0 INT

Rushing
NYJ: Vick 12–80, McNeil 16–50, Hector 3–6
CLE: Jones 9–49, Manoa 8–15, Langhorne 1–14, Kosar 3–4, Metcalf 2–3

Receiving
NYJ: Shuler 6–69, Toon 5–66, Townsell 2–57, McNeil 6–40, Vick 3–24, Griggs 1–9, Hector 1–5
CLE: Slaughter 3–69, Jones 3–55, Newsome 4–31, Langhorne 3–28, Metcalf 1–7, Manoa 1–6

Monday, September 25
Cincinnati Bengals 21, Browns 14
Riverfront Stadium (55,996)
White jerseys/white pants

The Browns put up a valiant effort but were overwhelmed by the defending-AFC champion Bengals on *Monday Night Football* as Bud Carson suffered his first defeat as head coach. Despite an ineffective running game that managed just seven yards in the first half, the Browns fought to a 14–14 tie at the intermission, thanks in part to a dazzling first career touchdown catch by rookie RB Eric Metcalf, who juked and leapt past a pair of defenders and into the end zone to tie the game at seven early in the second quarter. The Bengals took the lead for good on the first series of the second half, collecting 187 yards on the ground for the night while not allowing the previously high-flying Cleveland defense to record a sack. The Browns had two chances to tie the game in the fourth quarter but twice were stopped on fourth down inside the Cincinnati 10. The second opportunity ended when a fourth-down pass for TE Ozzie Newsome was broken up in the end zone with 1:41 remaining, and the Bengals ran out the clock to move into a tie for first with the Browns.
Record: 2–1

	1	2	3	4		
Browns	0	14	0	0	=	14
Bengals	0	14	7	0	=	21

CIN-Holman 8-yd. pass from Esiason (Gallery kick)
CLE-Metcalf 5-yd. pass from Kosar (Bahr kick)
CIN-Holman 16-yd. pass from Esiason (Gallery kick)
CLE-Manoa 6-yd. pass from Kosar (Bahr kick)
CIN-Brooks 19-yd. pass from Esiason (Gallery kick)

Passing
CLE: Kosar 15–23–203 2 TD 0 INT
CIN: Esiason 14–20–184 3 TD 1 INT

Rushing
CLE: Metcalf 8–34, McNeil 2–32, Jones 6–14, Manoa 4–11, Kosar 1–1
CIN: Ball 18–78, Brooks 13–67, Esiason 9–42

Receiving
CLE: Slaughter 4–85, Newsome 2–32, McNeil 1–32, Manoa 4–28, Jones 2–11, Langhorne 1–10, Metcalf 1–5
CIN: Holman 6–50, Brooks 2–44, McGee 2–38, Martin 2–27, Brown 1–20, Kattus 1–5

Sunday, October 1
Browns 16, Denver Broncos 13
Cleveland Stadium (78,637)
Brown jerseys/white pants

In one of the wildest and most infamous games in team history, the Browns pulled out an improbable victory from the jaws of defeat and enacted some measure of revenge against the undefeated Broncos for their back-to-back AFC title-game triumphs two years before. For much of the game, the Cleveland defense was dominant, forcing nemesis QB John Elway into the worst game of his career as he completed only six passes and was sacked four times. Wearing brown jerseys at home for the first time in five years, the Browns built a 13–3 lead midway through the third quarter and appeared to be coasting to an easy victory, but—as they always seemed to—the Broncos rallied. After the officials forced the teams to switch ends of the field when the Broncos' players were pelted with eggs, rocks, and batteries thrown by fans in the bleachers, Denver tied the game with four minutes to play, then intercepted Bernie Kosar in Cleveland territory and was milking the clock in preparation for a game-winning field-goal attempt. But then Cleveland LB Mike Johnson forced a fumble that was recovered by DB Frank Minnifield at the Cleveland 16, giving the Browns new life with 1:42 remaining. Kosar quickly drove the Browns 54 yards in seven plays to the Denver 30 to set up a 48-yard field goal by Matt Bahr, which barely cleared the crossbar as time expired. The dramatic victory snapped a 10-game Cleveland losing streak to Denver and marked their first win over the Broncos in 15 years.

Record: 3–1

	1	2	3	4		
Broncos	0	3	3	7	=	13
Browns	7	3	3	3	=	16

CLE-Slaughter 9-yd. pass from Kosar (Bahr kick)
DEN-Treadwell 21-yd. FG
CLE-Bahr 36-yd. FG
CLE-Bahr 48-yd. FG
DEN-Treadwell 26-yd. FG
DEN-Johnson 7-yd. pass from Elway (Treadwell kick)
CLE-Bahr 48-yd. FG

Passing
DEN: Elway 6–19–198 1 TD 1 INT
CIN: Kosar 25–38–216 1 TD 1 INT

Rushing
DEN: Humphrey 10–44, Alexander 5–17, Winder 8–16, Elway 1–2, Jackson 1–1
CLE: Kosar 4–33, Metcalf 9–26, Jones 7–21, Manoa 4–21, Redden 1–4, Langhorne 1-(-10)

Receiving
DEN: Johnson 5–145, Sewell 1–53
CLE: Langhorne 7–67, Slaughter 5–67, Metcalf 5–24, Newsome 3–21, Brennan 2–20, Manoa 1–7, Jones 1–5, Tillman 1–5

Sunday, October 8
Miami Dolphins 13, Browns 10 (OT)
Joe Robbie Stadium (58,444)
Brown jerseys/white pants

In a game in which points were at a premium, the Browns dropped a heartbreaker in Miami in sudden-death overtime, falling a game behind Cincinnati in the AFC Central. They rallied from a 10–0 second-quarter deficit to tie the contest midway through the third on Eric Metcalf's first career rushing touchdown. The Browns had a golden opportunity to win the game in the final minute of regulation when Felix Wright returned an interception of Miami QB Dan Marino to the Dolphins' 37, but a play later Bernie Kosar returned the favor by throwing an interception. The Dolphins then missed a 45-yard field goal with three seconds left and the game went to overtime, where the Browns won the toss and quickly drove to the Miami 26. But Matt Bahr's potential game-winning 44-yard field goal drifted left. Miami then marched downfield, and rookie kicker Pete Stoyanovich booted a 35-yard field goal to win the contest. The Browns picked up a season-high 141 yards on the ground, led by Metcalf's 78 on 16 carries.

Record: 3–2

	1	2	3	4	OT		
Browns	0	3	7	0	0	=	10
Dolphins	3	7	0	0	3	=	13

MIA-Stoyanovich 43-yd. FG
MIA-Duper 35-yd. pass from Marino (Stoyanovich kick)
CLE-Bahr 50-yd. FG
CLE-Metcalf 8-yd. run (Bahr kick)
MIA-Stoyanovich 35-yd. FG

Passing
CLE: Kosar 22–35–210 0 TD 2 INT
MIA: Marino 19–33–234 1 TD 1 INT

Rushing
CLE: Metcalf 16–78, Jones 5–33, Manoa 4–28, Redden 1–3, Kosar 1-(-1)
MIA: Stradford 11–37, Smith 16–23, Logan 2–10

Receiving
CLE: Brennan 5–51, Langhorne 5–47, Newsome 3–40, Slaughter 4–39, Metcalf 3–28, Jones 1–4, Redden 1–1
MIA: Duper 5–83, Jensen 5–46, Banks 2–36, Stradford 3–21, Clayton 2–20, Edmunds 1–15, Smith 1–13

Sunday, October 15
Pittsburgh Steelers 17, Browns 7
Cleveland Stadium (78,840)
Brown jerseys/white pants

In one of the most miserable performances in team history, the Browns coughed up seven turnovers and allowed the Steelers to avenge their 51-point loss in the opener before a stunned home crowd. Sloppy from the get-go, the game saw 14 total punts and 20 combined penalties as neither team topped 300 total yards and both quarterbacks struggled. Bernie Kosar played the worst game of his career, completing just 15 of 41 passes while throwing

four interceptions, at one point tossing 11 straight incomplete passes. Pittsburgh took a 10–0 lead into the fourth quarter, but the Browns, aided by a long pass-interference penalty, cut the margin to three on an Eric Metcalf touchdown plunge with eight minutes left. But Pittsburgh RB Dwight Stone returned the ensuing kickoff 73 yards to set up a game-clinching touchdown with two minutes remaining. It marked Pittsburgh's first win in Cleveland in eight years and set up a three-way tie for second place in the division between the Steelers, Oilers, and Browns.
Record: 3–3

	1	2	3	4		
Steelers	3	0	7	7	=	17
Browns	0	0	0	7	=	7

PIT-Anderson 49-yd. FG
PIT-Carter 14-yd. pass from Blackledge (Anderson kick)
CLE-Metcalf 2-yd. run (Bahr kick)
PIT-Williams 1-yd. run (Anderson kick)

Passing
PIT: Blackledge 9–28–143 1 TD 1 INT, Carter 1–1–15 0 TD 0 INT
CLE: Kosar 15–41–162 0 TD 4 INT

Rushing
PIT: Williams 15–47, Hoge 9–35, Blackledge 6–7, Wallace 2–3, Carter 1–2, Worley 2-(-1)
CLE: Metcalf 13–57, Oliphant 5–30, Manoa 4–11, Kosar 1–9

Receiving
PIT: Thompson 2–43, Carter 3–30, Mularkey 1–30, Lipps 1–20, Hoge 1–15, Hill 1–12, Williams 1–8
CLE: Slaughter 7–106, Newsome 2–28, Metcalf 2–13, McNeil 1–9, Brennan 1–8, Jones 1–5, Kosar 1-(-7)

Monday, October 23
Browns 27, Chicago Bears 7
Cleveland Stadium (78,722)
White jerseys/white pants

The Browns surged back over the .500 mark with a convincing Monday-night victory over the Bears. After creeping to a 7–0 halftime lead, the Browns pulled away in the second half. Eric Metcalf's second touchdown of the night extended their margin to 17–0 late in the third quarter, and after a Cleveland goal-line stand midway through the fourth, the Browns regained possession at their own 3. On first down, Bernie Kosar lofted a long pass down the left sideline that Webster Slaughter reeled in near midfield and outran his defender to complete a 97-yard touchdown—the longest in both Browns' history and in the history of *Monday Night Football.* Slaughter finished the night with eight catches for a career-high 186 yards and was named NFL Player of the Week. With the Cleveland running game struggling, Kosar returned to form, throwing for 281 yards. The victory—the Browns' sixth straight Monday-night home win—pulled the Browns into a three-way tie for first atop the division with Cincinnati and Houston.
Record: 4–3

	1	2	3	4		
Bears	0	0	0	7	=	7
Browns	7	0	10	10	=	27

CLE-Metcalf 3-yd. pass from Kosar (Bahr kick)
CLE-Bahr 31-yd. FG
CLE-Metcalf 7-yd. run (Bahr kick)
CLE-Slaughter 97-yd. pass from Kosar (Bahr kick)
CHI-Davis 5-yd. pass from Harbaugh (Butler kick)
CLE-Bahr 35-yd. FG

Passing
CHI: Harbaugh 9–16–93 1 TD 0 INT, Tomczak 4–14–76 0 TD 1 INT
CLE: Kosar 22–29–281 2 TD 0 INT

Rushing
CHI: Anderson 15–69, Muster 10–48, Gentry 2–22, Harbaugh 3–7, Sanders 1–3
CLE: Metcalf 12–16, Manoa 4–10, Oliphant 2–10, Jones 2–8, Redden 2–4, Pagel 1–4, Kosar 1–1

Receiving
CHI: McKinnon 3–40, Davis 3–37, Anderson 1–31, Gentry 2–24, Thornton 1–23, Muster 2–12, Green 1–2
CLE: Slaughter 8–186, Langhorne 3–27, Newsome 2–26, Manoa 3–19, Brennan 2–15, Metcalf 4–8

Sunday, October 29
Browns 28, Houston Oilers 17
Cleveland Stadium (78,765)
White jerseys/white pants

Thanks to a bizarrely entertaining second-half performance, the Browns rallied from a 10-point halftime deficit to knock off the Oilers and remain tied for first place. After a lousy offensive showing in the first half on an unseasonably warm and sunny autumn afternoon, the Browns opened up the playbook in the third quarter. First, Bernie Kosar scored just the second rushing touchdown of his career to cut Houston's lead to three. Then three minutes later he connected with Webster Slaughter on an 80-yard flea-flicker touchdown pass down the middle of the field to give the Browns the lead. Houston scored on its next possession to surge ahead again, but a play later, Kosar fired a strike to Slaughter between two defenders that resulted in a 77-yard touchdown. A minute into the final period, the Browns added another creative score when Eric Metcalf took a handoff on a sweep from the Houston 32 but on the run fired a pass to WR Reggie Langhorne in the end zone. After forcing a Houston punt, the resurgent Browns' offense then ran out the final nine minutes of the game to secure a dazzling victory. Slaughter topped 100 receiving yards for the third straight week, but it was overshadowed somewhat by TE Ozzie Newsome's 10-year string of catching a pass in 150 consecutive games coming to an end.

Record: 5–3

	1	2	3	4		
Oilers	7	3	7	0	=	17
Browns	0	0	21	7	=	28

HOU-Jeffires 13-yd. pass from Moon (Zendejas kick)
HOU-Zendejas 23-yd. FG
CLE-Kosar 5-yd. run (Bahr kick)
CLE-Slaughter 80-yd. pass from Kosar (Bahr kick)
HOU-Rozier 1-yd. run (Zendejas kick)
CLE-Slaughter 77-yd. pass from Kosar (Bahr kick)
CLE-Langhorne 32-yd. pass from Metcalf (Bahr kick)

Passing
HOU: Moon 15–25–241 1 TD 0 INT
CLE: Kosar 14–19–262 2 TD 2 INT, Metcalf 1–1–32 1 TD 0 INT

Rushing
HOU: Highsmith 12–58, Rozier 6–13, Pinkett 5–12, Moon 2–6
CLE: Metcalf 17–48, Manoa 7–27, Langhorne 1–18, Redden 2–10, Kosar 4–0

Receiving
HOU: Hill 3–67, Duncan 2–61, Givins 3–42, Jeffires 3–30, Pinkett 2–29, Highsmith 1–6, Rozier 1–6
CLE: Slaughter 4–184, Langhorne 4–59, Metcalf 6–46, Manoa 1–5

Sunday, November 5
Browns 42, Tampa Bay Buccaneers 31
Tampa Stadium (69,162)
Brown jerseys/white pants

Exploding for four touchdowns in the second quarter, the Browns held off the Buccaneers for an exciting victory on a sunny afternoon in Tampa. After falling behind on an early Tampa Bay touchdown, the Browns lit up the scoreboard for 35 points in 15 minutes, highlighted by back-to-back interception returns for touchdowns by Felix Wright and Thane Gash. After the Bucs narrowed the Cleveland lead to 35–24 early in the third period, the Browns added another crucial touchdown a minute into the fourth when Eric Metcalf swept around left end and then maneuvered through a broken defense for a 43-yard touchdown. Metcalf finished the day with 233 total yards and scored a pair of touchdowns in the finest performance of his rookie campaign. Meanwhile, Bernie Kosar had the most accurate day of his career, completing 18 of his 22 passes, including his first eight, stretching his string begun in the Houston game the previous week to a club-record 16. And while the Cleveland defense allowed nearly 400 total yards, it also picked off four passes from Tampa QB Vinny Testaverde. With a Cincinnati loss to the Los Angeles Raiders later that afternoon, the Browns took over sole possession of first place in the AFC Central.

Record: 6–3

	1	2	3	4		
Browns	7	28	0	7	=	42
Buccaneers	7	10	7	7	=	31

TB-Tate 1-yd. run (Igwebuike kick)
CLE-Metcalf 24-yd. pass from Kosar (Bahr kick)
CLE-Tillman 7-yd. pass from Kosar (Bahr kick)
CLE-Wright 27-yd. interception return (Bahr kick)
CLE-Gash 15-yd. interception return (Bahr kick)
TB-Wilder 9-yd. pass from Testaverde (Igwebuike kick)
CLE-Tennell 4-yd. pass from Kosar (Bahr kick)
TB-Igwebuike 53-yd. FG
TB-Wilder 9-yd. pass from Testaverde (Igwebuike kick)
CLE-Metcalf 43-yd. run (Bahr kick)
TB-Tate 1-yd. run (Igwebuike kick)

Passing
CLE: Kosar 18–22–164 3 TD 0 INT
TB: Testaverde 27–50–370 2 TD 4 INT

Rushing
CLE: Metcalf 17–87, Manoa 4–15, Oliphant 1–14, Redden 2–4, Kosar 5-(-6)

TB: Wilder 6–23, Tate 6–15, Howard 1–6, Smith 1–6, Stamps 1–6, Peebles 1-(-7)

Receiving
CLE: Langhorne 3–53, Metcalf 7–52, Manoa 2–17, Slaughter 1–15, Oliphant 1–9, Jones 2–7, Tillman 1–7, Tennell 1–4
TB: Wilder 8–107, Hill 4–58, Hall 3–57, Carrier 2–33, Drewrey 3–31, Smith 2–30, Harris 1–21, Tate 1–15, Howard 1–14, Stamps 2–4

Sunday, November 12
Browns 17, Seattle Seahawks 7
Seattle Kingdome (58,978)
White jerseys/white pants

Behind a fierce defense, the Browns picked up a gritty win in Seattle to notch their fourth straight victory and stay a game ahead of Houston in the division race. After an early Seahawk touchdown, the Browns held the home team scoreless through the final three quarters and came up with three key interceptions in the second half, two of which led to the go-ahead and game-clinching scores. With the game tied at seven early in the third quarter, a Felix Wright interception set up a Bernie Kosar-to-WR Lawyer Tillman touchdown pass to give the Browns their first lead. A Clay Matthews pickoff midway through the fourth led to a Matt Bahr field goal that gave the Browns a 10-point lead with just over three minutes to play. The Cleveland defense limited Seattle to just 180 total yards for the game, its second-best performance of the season.
Record: 7–3

	1	2	3	4		
Browns	0	7	7	3	=	17
Seahawks	7	0	0	0	=	7

SEA-Blades 8-yd. pass from Krieg (Johnson kick)
CLE-Manoa 1-yd. run (Bahr kick)
CLE-Tillman 17-yd. pass from Kosar (Bahr kick)
CLE-Bahr 29-yd. FG

Passing
CLE: Kosar 16–27–173 1 TD 0 INT
SEA: Krieg 17–30–141 1 TD 3 INT

Rushing
CLE: Metcalf 19–75, Manoa 14–65, Kosar 1-(-1)
SEA: Warner 13–29, Williams 7–11, Krieg 2–6

Receiving
CLE: Langhorne 3–49, Manoa 4–35, Tillman 1–17, McNeil 1–15, Slaughter 1–15, Brennan 2–14, Jones 1–7, Metcalf 1–7, Newsome 1–7, Redden 1–7
SEA: Blades 4–57, Largent 4–33, Skansi 3–22, Williams 4–20, Clark 2–9

Sunday, November 19
Browns 10, Kansas City Chiefs 10 (OT)
Cleveland Stadium (77,922)
White jerseys/white pants

In a fierce, frustrating defensive struggle with former coach Marty Schottenheimer's Chiefs on a gloomy afternoon in Cleveland, the Browns notched their first tie in 16 years, their first since the inception of sudden-death overtime. Kansas City's lone touchdown came in the opening seconds of the second half, when DE Neil Smith recovered a fumble by Cleveland's Mike Oliphant and rolled three yards into the end zone, one of five Cleveland turnovers on the day. The Browns reclaimed the lead on an Eric Metcalf touchdown late in the third period, but a Metcalf fumble set up Kansas City's game-tying field goal with less than four minutes remaining. The Chiefs had two chances to win the game in the final seconds of regulation, but first Kansas City kicker Nick Lowery missed a 45-yard field goal wide right—wiped out when the Browns were called for a penalty—then missed the ensuing 40-yarder wide left. Lowery had another chance to win the game at the end of a long, fruitless overtime session, but his 47-yard attempt fell short. The ineptitude of the Cleveland offense washed out a marvelous performance by the defense, which held league-leading rusher Christian Okoye to just 40 yards on 21 carries. Though it wasn't a loss, the shoddy performance would be the beginning of a maddening month-long stretch of football that nearly sabotaged the Browns' season.
Record: 7–3–1

	1	2	3	4	OT		
Chiefs	0	0	7	3	0	=	10
Browns	0	3	7	0	0	=	10

CLE-Bahr 40-yd. FG
KC-Smith 3-yd. fumble return (Lowery kick)
CLE-Metcalf 1-yd. run (Bahr kick)
KC-Lowery 41-yd. FG

Passing
KC: DeBerg 17–40–209 0 TD 2 INT, Pelluer 2–4–16 0 TD 0 INT, Saxon 0–1–0 0 TD 1 INT
CLE: Kosar 21–42–198 0 TD 1 INT

Rushing
KC: Okoye 21–40, Heard 7–35, Pelluer 1–18, DeBerg 1–15, McNair 3–11
CLE: Metcalf 23–49, Manoa 13–34, Oliphant 1-(-5)

Receiving
KC: Mandley 4–56, Harry 3–47, Heard 3–40, Weathers 3–35, McNair 5–33, Paige 1–14
CLE: Slaughter 6–67, Manoa 3–41, Metcalf 4–27, Brennan 2–20, Langhorne 3–19, Oliphant 2–13, Tillman 1–11

Thursday, November 23
Detroit Lions 13, Browns 10
Pontiac Silverdome (65,624)
White jerseys/white pants

Four days after their bruising five-quarter stalemate, the Browns laid another egg on Thanksgiving Day in Detroit and dropped an ugly game to the 2–9 Lions, who had seven starters out with injuries. In a cornucopia of mistakes, the Browns missed a critical field goal in the fourth quarter and rolled up 90 yards in penalties, including two crucial ones that spoiled their final scoring opportunity. Rookie Detroit RB Barry Sanders ran wild, rushing for 145 yards to become the only running back to top triple digits against Cleveland all season. The Browns' lone touchdown came when sparingly used RB Barry Redden broke free for a 38-yard scoring run with a minute left in the half. The Browns caught a break later in the weekend when both Houston and Cincinnati lost, allowing Cleveland to keep sole possession of first place.
Record: 7–4–1

	1	2	3	4		
Browns	0	10	0	0	=	10
Lions	0	10	3	0	=	13

DET-Murray 39-yd. FG
CLE-Bahr 35-yd. FG
DET-Johnson 27-yd. pass from Gagliano (Murray kick)
CLE-Redden 38-yd. run (Bahr kick)
DET-Murray 35-yd. FG

Passing
CLE: Kosar 28–38–296 0 TD 1 INT, Metcalf 0–1–0 0 TD 0 INT
DET: Gagliano 9–19–143 1 TD 0 INT

Rushing
CLE: Redden 1–38, Metcalf 11–19, Kosar 1–5, Jones 3–4, Manoa 2–4
DET: Sanders 28–145, Gagliano 1–1

Receiving
CLE: Langhorne 5–72, Slaughter 5–60, Newsome 4–53, Jones 4–32, Metcalf 2–18, Manoa 3–17, McNeil 2–17, Redden 2–16, Tillman 1–11
DET: Johnson 3–57, Sanders 2–44, Phillips 4–42

Sunday, December 3
Cincinnati Bengals 21, Browns 0
Cleveland Stadium (76,236)
Brown jerseys/white pants

After 10 days off, the Browns hit rock bottom, getting shut out at home for the first time in 12 years and enabling the struggling Bengals to claw back into the playoff race. With a wind-chill factor of –20°F, the Cleveland offense was invisible for the third straight game, unable to penetrate the Cincinnati 20 while the Browns missed a pair of field goals and coughed up three turnovers. Bernie Kosar was replaced by Mike Pagel early in the fourth quarter, but fared no better, and RB Kevin Mack—after serving a brief jail sentence for drug possession—made his first appearance of the season. It marked the Bengals' first win in Cleveland in five years and, combined with a Houston win in Pittsburgh, dropped the Browns out of first place for the first time in two months.
Record: 7–5–1

	1	2	3	4		
Bengals	0	7	14	0	=	21
Browns	0	0	0	0	=	0

CIN-Brooks 1-yd. run (Breech kick)
CIN-McGee 38-yd. pass from Esiason (Breech kick)
CIN-Holman 9-yd. pass from Esiason (Breech kick)

Passing
CIN: Esiason 14–32–197 2 TD 2 INT
CLE: Kosar 15–30–130 0 TD 1 INT, Pagel 4–13–46 0 TD 1 INT

Rushing
CIN: Brooks 15–47, Esiason 2–19, Taylor 9–15, Ball 4–14, Jennings 3–5, Wilhelm 1–1
CLE: Metcalf 13–56, Redden 5–21, Manoa 3–14, Kosar 1–0, Mack 1-(-3)

Receiving
CIN: McGee 4–94, Brown 3–43, Hillary 2–19, Holman 2–17, Brooks 2–12, Smith 1–12
CLE: Langhorne 7–78, Slaughter 3–33, Brennan 2–22, McNeil 1–18, Newsome 2–16, Metcalf 3–5, Redden 1–4

Sunday, December 10
Indianapolis Colts 23, Browns 17 (OT)
Hoosier Dome (58,550)
White jerseys/white pants

Despite collecting nearly 500 total yards of offense, the Browns lost a maddening game in Indianapolis, squandering a 10-point second-half advantage and falling in stunning fashion in overtime. After Keith Jones blocked a Colts' punt that was recovered in the end zone by Lawyer Tillman early in the third quarter to put the Browns up 17–7, they were poised to put the game away with five minutes left in the fourth. But instead of kicking a field goal that would have put them back up by 10, Bernie Kosar was intercepted in the end zone, and a 77-yard return gave the Colts new life. They responded with the game-tying touchdown with two minutes left. The Browns quickly drove downfield and were poised to win the game with a 38-yard field goal in the final seconds, but it hooked left and the game went to overtime, where a long punt return by WR Gerald McNeil set up another short field-goal attempt. But once again, Bahr missed, this time from 35 yards as it bounced off the upright, and the game continued. The Browns were poised for the winning points once more minutes later when they regained possession at midfield, but a Kosar pass over the middle was picked off by Indy DB Mike Prior—Cleveland's fourth turnover of the day—and returned 58 yards for the game-winning touchdown. Kosar threw for a season-high 353 yards, but his two critical interceptions cost the Browns the game. Webster Slaughter quietly had another fantastic game, catching six passes for 152 yards, his fourth 100-yard game of the season. Adding insult to injury, the Oilers defeated Tampa Bay to open up a game-and-a-half lead over the Browns with two to play.
Record: 7–6–1

	1	2	3	4	OT		
Browns	0	10	7	0	0	=	17
Colts	7	0	3	7	6	=	23

IND-Rison 51-yd. pass from Trudeau (Biasucci kick)
CLE-Metcalf 12-yd. run (Bahr kick)
CLE-Bahr 48-yd. FG
CLE-Tillman recovered blocked punt in end zone (Bahr kick)
IND-Biasucci 35-yd. FG
IND-Beach 1-yd. pass from Ramsey (Biasucci kick)
IND-Prior 58-yd. interception return

Passing
CLE: Kosar 26–40–353 0 TD 2 INT
IND: Trudeau 15–32–200 1 TD 1 INT, Ramsey 8–12–71 1 TD 0 INT

Rushing
CLE: Redden 10–42, Metcalf 11–39, Mack 6–16, Manoa 5–14, Kosar 1–12
IND: Dickerson 26–137, Trudeau 2–7, Ramsey 2–1

Receiving
CLE: Slaughter 6–152, Metcalf 7–58, Newsome 3–43, Manoa 3–35, Langhorne 2–30, Brennan 2–18, McNeil 3–17
IND: Rison 5–135, Brooks 6–42, Pruitt 1–40, Dickerson 3–34, Bentley 6–13, Beach 2–7

Sunday, December 17
Browns 23, Minnesota Vikings 17 (OT)
Cleveland Stadium (70,777)
Brown jerseys/white pants

With their season hanging in the balance, the Browns pulled out a dramatic come-from-behind victory over the playoff-bound Vikings on a trick play in their fourth overtime session of the season. The wind-chill factor reached –25°F, and the offenses struggled early but picked up steam as the game went on, with Bernie Kosar snapping a string of 20 consecutive quarters without throwing a touchdown pass when he connected with TE Ron Middleton for the go-ahead score in the third quarter. After the Vikings took the lead back, Kosar hit Reggie Langhorne crossing over the middle for a 62-yard scoring strike to make it 14–10 in the final minute of the third quarter. But Minnesota endured and surged ahead on a short fourth-down touchdown pass with 3:37 remaining. Behind a patchwork offensive line, Kosar drove the Browns 51 yards in 11 plays, and Matt Bahr shook off his struggles from the week before with a 32-yard field goal with 24 seconds left to send the game to overtime. Aided by a 39-yard reception by Langhorne, who had the best game of his career, the Browns gradually drove to the Minnesota 14, where Bahr was called upon again for an apparent 31-yard field-goal attempt on third down. Instead, holder Mike Pagel took the snap, spun around, and tossed a pass to LB Van Waiters breaking off the line of scrimmage. Waiters caught it and jogged into the end zone for the game-winning score—the first time an NFL game had been won on a fake field goal in overtime in 12 years. While the Cleveland defense was once again sterling, limiting Minnesota to just one successful third-down conversion in 18 attempts, the offense showed signs of a turnaround, with Kosar throwing for 254 yards—140 to Langhorne on six receptions. Combined with Cincinnati's 61–7 massacre of Houston, the Browns managed to stay alive in the division race, and their entire up-and-down season would come down to the final week.

Record: 8–6–1

	1	2	3	4	OT		
Vikings	0	3	7	7	0	=	17
Browns	0	0	14	3	6	=	23

MIN-Karlis 44-yd. FG
CLE-Middleton 5-yd. pass from Kosar (Bahr kick)
MIN-Walker 26-yd. run (Karlis kick)
CLE-Langhorne 62-yd. pass from Kosar (Bahr kick)
MIN-Jordan 2-yd. pass from Kramer (Karlis kick)
CLE-Bahr 32-yd. FG
CLE-Waiters 14-yd. pass from Pagel

Passing
MIN: Wilson 11–32–141 0 TD 0 INT, Kramer 6–16–80 1 TD 1 INT
CLE: Kosar 17–38–254 2 TD 0 INT, Pagel 1–1–14 1 TD 0 INT

Rushing
MIN: Walker 16–57, Fenney 11–40, Carter 1–17, Anderson 1–5, Wilson 1–3
CLE: Mack 18–55, Kosar 3–6, Metcalf 2–4, Redden 3–1, Manoa 1–1, Langhorne 2-(-3)

Receiving
MIN: Jordan 6–87, Carter 4–77, Jones 2–24, Clark 1–12, Lewis 1–9, Anderson 1–7, Fenney 1–3, Novoselsky 1–2
CLE: Langhorne 6–140, Brennan 4–35, Tillman 1–19, Newsome 1–18, Slaughter 1–17, Metcalf 2–16, Waiters 1–14, Middleton 1–5, Mack 1–4

Saturday, December 23
Browns 24, Houston Oilers 20
Houston Astrodome (58,852)
White jerseys/white pants

With the AFC Central Division championship on the line, the Browns and Oilers put on a memorable show before the largest home crowd in Oilers' history. The Browns roared out of the starting gate, taking a 17–0 lead late in the second quarter on a dazzling 68-yard catch-and-run for a touchdown by Eric Metcalf and then a 40-yard scoring pass to Webster Slaughter. But the Oilers hung tough and took the lead after one of the most infamous mental lapses in Browns' history. Trailing 17–13 with six minutes to play, the Oilers drove to the Cleveland 15 before a bad center snap from the shotgun formation resulted in a fumble scooped up by the Browns' Clay Matthews at the Houston 35. Inexplicably, Matthews tried to lateral the football to teammate DE Chris Pike, but the toss went awry and Houston recovered at the Cleveland 27. On the next play, QB Warren Moon hit WR Drew Hill for a touchdown to put the Oilers ahead for the first time with 4:46 remaining. After an exchange of punts, the Browns took over at their own 41 with 2:30 remaining. Two key passes to Reggie Langhorne and a pair of big runs by Kevin Mack moved the Browns to the Houston 4 with under a minute to play. Mack then bounced off three tacklers on a draw up the middle and fell into the end zone for the game-winning touchdown with 39 seconds remaining. The Browns' big plays and Mack's late heroics helped deliver victory despite the Oilers rolling up 483 total yards—the most the Browns had allowed all season. Moon threw for 414 yards, the third-most ever against Cleveland, but Felix Wright picked off his ninth pass of the season, and with five sacks, the Browns set a new single-season record with 45. After a roller-coaster season, the thrilling finale clinched the Browns' fifth straight playoff berth and fourth division title in five years, earning them a bye week before facing Buffalo in a divisional playoff.

Record: 9–6–1

	1	2	3	4		
Browns	10	7	0	7	=	24
Oilers	0	3	7	10	=	20

CLE-Bahr 32-yd. FG
CLE-Metcalf 68-yd. pass from Kosar (Bahr kick)
CLE-Slaughter 40-yd. pass from Kosar (Bahr kick)
HOU-Zendejas 30-yd. FG
HOU-Hill 9-yd. pass from Moon (Zendejas kick)
HOU-Zendejas 37-yd. FG

HOU-Hill 27-yd. pass from Moon (Zendejas kick)
CLE-Mack 4-yd. run (Bahr kick)

Passing
CLE: Kosar 18–36–228 2 TD 0 INT
HOU: Moon 32–51–414 2 TD 1 INT

Rushing
CLE: Mack 12–62, Redden 6–23, Metcalf 4–14, Kosar 3–7, Manoa 1-(-1)
HOU: Pinkett 8–63, Moon 4–20, Highsmith 4–14, Rozier 3–5

Receiving
CLE: Metcalf 2–74, Slaughter 3–66, Langhorne 5–38, Brennan 4–34, Redden 1–6, McNeil 1–6, Mack 1–3, Newsome 1–1
HOU: Hill 10–141, Duncan 7–85, Givins 6–75, Highsmith 3–40, Verhulst 2–37, Pinkett 4–36

AFC Divisional Playoff
Saturday, January 6
Browns 34, Buffalo Bills 30
Cleveland Stadium (77,706)
Brown jerseys/white pants

Fittingly, the Browns' unpredictable regular season was followed by an equally wild playoff game against AFC East-champ Buffalo that went down to the final gun.

After Buffalo set the tone with a 72-yard QB Jim Kelly-to-WR Andre Reed scoring pass late in the first quarter, the offenses spent the rest of the afternoon rolling up and down the chewed up Stadium turf. The Browns surged to a 24–14 lead early in the third quarter after the second of two long touchdown receptions by Webster Slaughter. The Bills cut the margin to three later in the period, but then Eric Metcalf returned the ensuing kickoff 90 yards for a touchdown to stretch the lead back to 10.

The teams exchanged field goals in the first eight minutes of the fourth quarter, then Buffalo pulled within four points with four minutes remaining on Kelly's fourth touchdown pass of the day, his second to RB Thurman Thomas, who was having a career afternoon. But Buffalo kicker Scott Norwood slipped on the sandy turf and missed the extra point, which would play a huge role in the game's climax.

The Browns went three-and-out, and Buffalo picked up where it left off, quickly driving into Cleveland territory as the clock ticked down under two minutes. After converting on a pair of do-or-die fourth downs, the Bills reached the Cleveland 11 with 14 seconds left. Needing a touchdown and not a field goal, a potential scoring pass then bounced off the hands of RB Ronnie Harmon in the end zone. On the next play, Clay Matthews intercepted Kelly's fifty-fourth pass of the day at the Cleveland 1 to send the Browns back to the AFC Championship.

Behind Kelly's 405 yards passing and Thurman Thomas' 13 catches for 150 yards, the Bills rolled to 453 total yards, thwarted only by three turnovers. Meanwhile, the Cleveland offense was also effective behind three touchdown passes by Kosar and 114 receiving yards by Webster Slaughter, who'd finished the regular season with a team-record 1,236.

The following afternoon, the Denver Broncos avoided a valiant upset bid by wild-card Pittsburgh in the other AFC divisional playoff, setting up the third Browns-Broncos title-game clash in four years.

	1	2	3	4		
Bills	7	7	7	9	=	30
Browns	3	14	14	3	=	34

BUF-Reed 72-yd. pass from Kelly (Norwood kick)
CLE-Bahr 45-yd. FG
CLE-Slaughter 52-yd. pass from Kosar (Bahr kick)
BUF-Lofton 33-yd. pass from Kelly (Norwood kick)
CLE-Middleton 3-yd. pass from Kosar (Bahr kick)
CLE-Slaughter 44-yd. pass from Kosar (Bahr kick)
BUF-Thomas 6-yd. pass from Kelly (Norwood kick)
CLE-Metcalf 90-yd. kickoff return (Bahr kick)
BUF-Norwood 30-yd. FG
CLE-Bahr 47-yd. FG
BUF-Thomas 3-yd. pass from Kelly (kick failed)

Passing
BUF: Kelly 28–54–405 4 TD 2 INT
CLE: Kosar 20–29–251 3 TD 0 INT

Rushing
BUF: Thomas 10–27, Kinnebrew 7–17, Kelly 1–5
CLE: Mack 12–62, Redden 6–13, Tillman 1–8, Manoa 3–6, Metcalf 4–2, Langhorne 1–0, Kosar 3-(-1)

Receiving
BUF: Thomas 13–150, Reed 6–115, Lofton 3–66, Harmon 4–50, Beebe 1–17, Kinnebrew 1–7
CLE: Slaughter 3–114, Langhorne 6–48, Newsome 4–35, Mack 2–19, Brennan 1–15, Middleton 3–12, Metcalf 1–8

AFC Championship
Sunday, January 14
Denver Broncos 37, Browns 21
Mile High Stadium (76,046)
White jerseys/white pants

Once again, the Denver Broncos stopped the Browns one step shy of the Super Bowl, though this time no late heroics were necessary as Denver dominated Cleveland to win its fourth AFC championship.

In a completely different performance than his poor showing in Cleveland three months earlier, John Elway was unstoppable, throwing for 385 yards and three touchdowns as the Broncos picked up 497 total yards—the third straight game the Browns' defense had allowed more than 400. Denver sailed to a 24–7 lead with less than five minutes left in the third quarter, but the Browns fought back. A diving, acrobatic touchdown catch by WR Brian Brennan—his second of the day—was quickly followed by a Denver fumble recovered by Felix Wright and returned to the Broncos' 1. A play later, Tim Manoa scored to close out a 21-point third quarter and pull the Browns within three points. It appeared another climactic Browns–Broncos finish was in the works.

But Elway and Co. were just too much for the Browns' weary defense, and Denver tacked on 13 points in the fourth quarter to close out the Browns' erratic 1989 season. Playing with an injured elbow and thumb after a bruising season, Bernie Kosar struggled, completing just 19 of 44 passes while getting sacked four times. It would be the last postseason game Kosar would ever play for the Browns and marked their last appearance in a conference title game.

	1	2	3	4		
Browns	0	0	21	0	=	21
Broncos	3	7	14	13	=	37

DEN-Treadwell 29-yd. FG
DEN-Young 70-yd. pass from Elway (Treadwell kick)
CLE-Brennan 27-yd. pass from Kosar (Bahr kick)
DEN-Mobley 5-yd. pass from Elway (Treadwell kick)
DEN-Winder 7-yd. run (Treadwell kick)
CLE-Brennan 10-yd. pass from Kosar (Bahr kick)
CLE-Manoa 2-yd. run (Bahr kick)
DEN-Winder 39-yd. pass from Elway (Treadwell kick)
DEN-Treadwell 34-yd. FG
DEN-Treadwell 31-yd. FG

Passing
CLE: Kosar 19–44–210 2 TD 3 INT
DEN: Elway 20–36–385 3 TD 0 INT

Rushing
CLE: Mack 6–36, Kosar 2–22, Manoa 2–5, Metcalf 3–4, Langhorne 1-(-1)
DEN: Elway 5–39, Winder 21–37, Humphrey 8–23, Sewell 4–17, Bratton 1–4

Receiving
CLE: Langhorne 5–78, Brennan 5–58, Slaughter 3–36, Tillman 1–15, Mack 2–8, Metcalf 2–7
DEN: Young 2–123, Johnson 7–91, Sewell 3–55, Winder 2–39, Jackson 2–25, Humphrey 1–23, Mobley 2–22, Bratton 1–7

1990

Sunday, September 9
Browns 13, Pittsburgh Steelers 3
Cleveland Stadium (78,298)
White jerseys/white pants

Despite an abysmal offensive performance that saw the Browns accumulate a mere 158 yards for the game, the Cleveland defense came to the rescue to dominate Pittsburgh and propel the Browns to an ugly win in the opener. Thirteen of the game's 16 points were scored as a direct result of the defenses, including the game's only touchdown—a 30-yard fumble return by Cleveland DB Anthony Blaylock early in the third quarter. The tide of the game actually turned late in the first half after the Steelers recovered a fumble by QB Bernie Kosar—who would be sacked seven times on the day—at the Cleveland 1 but were stymied on three consecutive plays and forced to settle for a field goal. The Browns put the game out of reach with a pair of field goals, the first following a 66-yard interception return by DB Thane Gash to the Pittsburgh 9 and the second the result of a 19-play, five-minute drive resulting in new kicker Jerry Kauric's second field goal of the day with 10 minutes remaining.

Record: 1–0

	1	2	3	4		
Steelers	0	3	0	0	=	3
Browns	0	0	10	3	=	13

PIT-Anderson 19-yd. FG
CLE-Blaylock 30-yd. fumble return (Kauric kick)
CLE-Kauric 28-yd. FG
CLE-Kauric 47-yd. FG

Passing
PIT: Brister 17–32–193 0 TD 2 INT
CLE: Kosar 13–30–120 0 TD 0 INT

Rushing
PIT: Worley 11–33, Hoge 10–11, Bell 1–4, Williams 2–2, Foster 1–1, Brister 1-(-2)
CLE: Mack 6–45, Gainer 10–32, Metcalf 8–6, Redden 1-(-1), Kosar 1-(-2)

Receiving
PIT: Lipps 3–60, Mularkey 5–50, Hoge 4–40, Hill 1–17, Bell 1–13, Worley 2–11, Foster 1–2
CLE: Langhorne 5–55, Mack 4–24, Brennan 2–21, Slaughter 2–20

Sunday, September 16
New York Jets 24, Browns 21
Giants Stadium (67,354)
White jerseys/white pants

The sluggish offensive play from the week before carried over, this time compounded by an atrocious first-half effort by the Cleveland defense that saw the Jets soar to a 17-point lead at the half and then hold off the Browns in the final quarter. Things started out perfectly for the Browns as RB Eric Metcalf returned the opening kickoff 98 yards for a touchdown—the first regular-season kick return for a score in his career. The lead lasted only two minutes as the Jets quickly scored on their first possession, then added another pair of touchdowns and a field goal as they rolled up 273 yards by the intermission. Meanwhile, the Browns went three-and-out on four possessions in the first half and didn't get any rhythm until rookie RB Leroy Hoard made his NFL debut late in the third quarter and sparked the running game, stagnant without injured RB Kevin Mack. A nine-yard touchdown run by Hoard pulled the Browns to within three with just under two minutes remaining, but Jets' QB Ken O'Brien scrambled for eight yards on a critical third-and-five moments later to extinguish the Browns' comeback hopes.

Record: 1–1

	1	2	3	4		
Browns	7	0	7	7	=	21
Jets	14	10	0	0	=	24

CLE-Metcalf 98-yd. kickoff return (Kauric kick)
NYJ-McNeil 2-yd. run (Leahy kick)
NYJ-Hector 6-yd. run (Leahy kick)
NYJ-Leahy 47-yd. FG
NYJ-Baxter 1-yd. run (Leahy kick)
CLE-Langhorne 4-yd. pass from Kosar (Kauric kick)
CLE-Hoard 9-yd. run (Kauric kick)

Passing
CLE: Kosar 24–41–233 1 TD 0 INT
NYJ: O'Brien 13–21–218 0 TD 0 INT

Rushing
CLE: Hoard 6–29, Metcalf 6–9, Gainer 3–6
NYJ: McNeil 13–62, Baxter 14–47, Thomas 6–46, Hector 5–9, O'Brien 2–6

Receiving
CLE: Langhorne 5–69, Slaughter 4–63, Metcalf 9–54, Hoard 2–22, Talley 1–9, Gainer 1–7, Newsome 1–5, Joines 1–4
NYJ: McNeil 3–80, Thomas 1–55, Toon 2–21, Mathis 2–18, Wellsandt 1–13, Townsell 1–10, Baxter 1–9, Boyer 1–6, Moore 1–6

Sunday, September 23
San Diego Chargers 24, Browns 14
Cleveland Stadium (77,429)
White jerseys/white pants

The concern that had gradually arisen over the previous two weeks turned into a five-alarm fire of panic for Browns fans as they watched their team be completely outplayed on its own field by an 0–2 San Diego team coming off a 6–10 season. For the third straight week, the Cleveland offense struggled to ignite, scoring only one touchdown and giving the Chargers four turnovers, including a fumble on the second play of the game that led to a San Diego field goal. Cleveland LB Mike Johnson returned an interception 64 yards for a touchdown that gave the Browns a 7–3 lead, then Leroy Hoard capped a 90-yard drive with a one-yard touchdown plunge late in the first half to make it 14–10 Browns at the half. But their tenuous advantage dissolved in the second half. The Chargers took the lead for good with under seven minutes left in the third, then repelled a pair of Cleveland scoring threats in the fourth quarter—the first when Bernie Kosar was hit throwing a pass and was intercepted by LB Henry Rolling, who returned it 67 yards to the Cleveland 6 to set up another Chargers' touchdown to make it 24–14 with 11 minutes left. A final Browns' threat stalled at the San Diego 22 when a fourth-down pass fell incomplete. Kosar, now sacked 13 times in the first three games, was picked off three times as the Browns managed only 44 rushing yards.
Record: 1–2

	1	2	3	4		
Chargers	3	7	7	7	=	24
Browns	7	7	0	0	=	14

SD-Reveiz 42-yd. FG
CLE-Johnson 64-yd. interception return (Kauric kick)
SD-Miller 19-yd. pass from Tolliver (Reveiz kick)
CLE-Hoard 1-yd. run (Kauric kick)
SD-Miller 23-yd. pass from Tolliver (Reveiz kick)
SD-Bernstine 1-yd. run (Reveiz kick)

Passing
SD: Tolliver 12–29–139 2 TD 2 INT
CLE: Kosar 17–36–232 0 TD 3 INT

Rushing
SD: Butts 24–90, Harmon 6–30, Bernstine 5–20, Tolliver 1-(-3)
CLE: Hoard 14–34, Metcalf 5–10

Receiving
SD: McEwen 6–60, Miller 2–42, Harmon 3–36, Wilson 1–1
CLE: Metcalf 6–77, Newsome 3–47, Slaughter 1–40, Langhorne 2–35, Hoard 4–26, Brennan 1–7

Sunday, September 30
Kansas City Chiefs 34, Browns 0
Arrowhead Stadium (75,462)
White jerseys/white pants

After three lethargic performances to open the season, the Browns were massacred in week four by former coach Marty Schottenheimer and his playoff-bound Chiefs. The Cleveland special teams were abysmal, permitting two blocked punts for touchdowns and a 37-yard punt return that set up a third. The tone was set on the Browns' opening drive, when they marched to the Kansas City 3, but lost the football on a fumble by Leroy Hoard, spoiling his 42-yard run on the first play of his first NFL start. Amazingly, after that first play, Hoard would carry the ball 10 times for a total of minus-two yards. Hoard's critical cough-up was the first of three Cleveland fumbles in a disastrous first half. Trailing 24–0 at the intermission, the Browns replaced Bernie Kosar with Mike Pagel late in the third quarter, but things got no better as the Browns were shut out for just the ninth time in team history.
Record: 1–3

	1	2	3	4		
Browns	0	0	0	0	=	0
Chiefs	7	17	10	0	=	34

KC-Thomas 47-yd. pass from DeBerg (Lowery kick)
KC-Lowery 39-yd. FG
KC-Martin 31-yd. blocked punt return (Lowery kick)
KC-Harry 6-yd. pass from DeBerg (Lowery kick)
KC-Lowery 34-yd. FG
KC-Ross 4-yd. blocked punt return (Lowery kick)

Passing
CLE: Pagel 14–27–159 0 TD 1 INT, Kosar 8–17–61 0 TD 0 INT
KC: DeBerg 12–21–189 2 TD 0 INT, Pelluer 0–1–0 0 TD 0 INT

Rushing
CLE: Hoard 11–40, Mack 7–32, Metcalf 3-(-4)
KC: Okoye 17–41, Word 11–29, Jones 2–7

Receiving
CLE: Langhorne 7–82, Brennan 4–41, Metcalf 1–31, Slaughter 2–20, Talley 1–19, Gainer 2–13, Newsome 2–13, Hoard 1–6, Mack 2-(-5)
KC: Paige 4–90, Thomas 1–47, Harry 4–36, Mandley 2–16, Roberts 1–0

Monday, October 8
Browns 30, Denver Broncos 29
Mile High Stadium (74,814)
White jerseys/white pants

With the season teetering on the verge of complete disaster, the Browns pulled off a fourth-quarter rally on *Monday Night Football* to capture one of the most surprising and satisfying victories in recent memory over their nemesis, the Denver Broncos, on a frosty night at Mile High Stadium. With Bernie Kosar turning in his finest performance of the season, throwing for 318 yards and three touchdowns, the Cleveland offense finally came to life, scoring a touchdown on its first possession, then surging ahead in the second quarter on a flea-flicker touchdown pass to Webster Slaughter. Yet the problems of the previous few weeks surfaced when the Browns surrendered another blocked punt, this one for a safety, and struggled to stop the Denver running game as the Broncos took a 29–20 lead with 7:21 remaining. The Browns responded with a gutsy 80-yard drive that included a pair of fourth-down conversions and ended when Kosar hit WR Brian Brennan on a 24-yard scoring strike to cut the margin to two with just over three minutes left. The Cleveland defense forced a Denver punt, and the Browns took over at their own 39 with 2:04 showing. Kosar quickly drove his beleaguered offense 48 yards to set up Jerry Kauric's 30-yard field goal as time expired. It snapped the Browns' seven-game losing streak at Mile High, marked their first road win over the Broncos in 18 years, and appeared destined to turn the Browns' season around.
Record: 2–3

	1	2	3	4		
Browns	6	7	7	10	=	30
Broncos	7	12	0	10	=	29

DEN-Elway 13-yd. run (Treadwell kick)
CLE-Metcalf 5-yd. run (kick failed)
DEN-Treadwell 20-yd. FG
CLE-Slaughter 43-yd. pass from Kosar (Kauric kick)
DEN-Humphrey 19-yd. run (Treadwell kick)
DEN-Safety: Fletcher blocked punt out of end zone
CLE-Mack 11-yd. pass from Kosar (Kauric kick)
DEN-Jackson 16-yd. run (Treadwell kick)
DEN-Treadwell 25-yd. FG
CLE-Brennan 24-yd. pass from Kosar (Kauric kick)
CLE-Kauric 30-yd. FG

Passing
CLE: Kosar 24–38–318 3 TD 2 INT
DEN: Elway 16–33–175 0 TD 2 INT

Rushing
CLE: Mack 15–54, Slaughter 1–17, Metcalf 5–14, Hoard 7–9, Kosar 3–3
DEN: Humphrey 20–106, Elway 3–21, Jackson 1–16, Bratton 1–1, Winder 2-(-3)

Receiving
CLE: Slaughter 7–123, Brennan 5–65, Langhorne 4–60, Joines 2–39, Mack 2–17, Metcalf 3–8, Newsome 1–6
DEN: Johnson 6–90, Jackson 3–30, Bratton 2–21, Humphrey 2–15, Nattiel 1–15, Sewell 1–8, Lanier 1-(-4)

Sunday, October 14
New Orleans Saints 25, Browns 20
Louisiana Superdome (68,608)
White jerseys/white pants

The newfound momentum from the previous Monday in Denver came to a screeching halt as the Browns self-destructed time and again in the Superdome, squandering a chance to get back to the .500 mark. With the offense again reverting to its early season doldrums, the Browns fell behind 25–6 midway through the fourth quarter after allowing their fourth blocked punt in three games, this one for a safety. After a Bernie Kosar-to-WR Webster Slaughter scoring pass on the next possession, the Cleveland special teams redeemed themselves when LB Jock Jones blocked a New Orleans punt, setting up a touchdown by RB Kevin Mack that cut the margin to five with 2:56 left. But after LB Mike Johnson dropped an interception in New Orleans territory, the defense allowed a 58-yard pass from QB Steve Walsh, making his debut with the Saints, to WR Eric Martin on third-and-10, which allowed the Saints to melt away most of the final two minutes, and the Browns didn't get the ball back until just 10 seconds remained. Cleveland was now in last place in the division in mid-October for the first time in six years.

Record: 2–4

	1	2	3	4		
Browns	0	6	0	14	=	20
Saints	3	6	7	9	=	25

NO-Anderson 52-yd. FG
CLE-Kauric 37-yd. FG
NO-Hilliard 4-yd. pass from Walsh (kick failed)
CLE-Kauric 39-yd. FG
NO-Turner 49-yd. pass from Walsh (Andersen kick)
NO-Martin 13-yd. pass from Walsh (Andersen kick)
NO-Safety: Massey blocked punt out of end zone
CLE-Slaughter 13-yd. pass from Kosar (Kauric kick)
CLE-Mack 1-yd. run (Kauric kick)

Passing
CLE: Kosar 18–36–168 1 TD 0 INT
NO: Walsh 15–26–243 3 TD 1 INT, Fourcade 3–5–23 0 TD 0 INT

Rushing
CLE: Mack 13–66, Metcalf 4–6, Slaughter 1–5, Hoard 4–4
NO: Hilliard 23–84, Fourcade 1–5, Heyward 3–4, Mayes 1-(-1), Walsh 1-(-3)

Receiving
CLE: Langhorne 3–34, Gainer 2–33, Slaughter 3–32, Brennan 3–29, Mack 3–28, Joines 1–14, Hoard 1–4, Metcalf 2-(-6)
NO: Martin 8–153, Turner 3–58, Hilliard 4–36, Brenner 2–16, Tice 1–3

Monday, October 22
Cincinnati Bengals 34, Browns 13
Cleveland Stadium (78,567)
Brown jerseys/white pants

Playing their second Monday-night game in three weeks, the Browns were worn down by Cincinnati in the second half and wound up getting routed by Sam Wyche and Co. on their own home field for the second straight year. The Bengals surged to a 17–3 lead in the second quarter before the Browns clawed their way back into the game, cutting the margin to four on a Leroy Hoard touchdown plunge on the last play of the first half when they opted to run one final play from the Cincinnati 1 rather than kick a field goal. But Bernie Kosar was intercepted on the first play of the second half, leading to a Bengals' field goal, then the Browns drove to the Cincy 14, but failed to score when Mike Pagel dropped the center snap on a short field-goal attempt. The Bengals, who would roll up 233 rushing yards, responded with another long drive capped by a touchdown that put the game out of reach.

Record: 2–5

	1	2	3	4		
Bengals	7	10	3	14	=	34
Browns	3	10	0	0	=	13

CIN-Holman 19-yd. pass from Esiason (Breech kick)
CLE-Kauric 21-yd. FG
CIN-Brooks 28-yd. run (Breech kick)
CIN-Breech 20-yd. FG
CLE-Kauric 30-yd. FG
CLE-Hoard 1-yd. run (Kauric kick)
CIN-Breech 21-yd. FG
CIN-Barber 2-yd. pass from Esiason (Breech kick)
CIN-Woods 1-yd. run (Breech kick)

Passing
CIN: Esiason 7–17–85 2 TD 1 INT
CLE: Kosar 17–33–190 0 TD 2 INT, Pagel 0–1–0 0 TD 0 INT

Rushing
CIN: Green 9–75, Taylor 14–73, Brooks 6–63, Esiason 2–16, Woods 5–7, Wilhelm 1-(-1)
CLE: Mack 12–53, Hoard 9–30, Metcalf 4–10, Kosar 3–3

Receiving
CIN: Brown 3–51, Holman 1–19, Woods 1–11, Barber 1–2, Brooks 1–2
CLE: Brennan 6–83, Mack 5–67, Slaughter 4–33, Metcalf 2–7

Sunday, October 28
San Francisco 49ers 20, Browns 17
Candlestick Park (63,672)
White jerseys/white pants

With the Browns slumping, facing a short week, and traveling across the country, a blowout seemed imminent when they arrived in San Francisco to face the undefeated 49ers. As expected, the 49ers took a 14–0 halftime lead as the Browns' offense continued its slide. But late in the third quarter, trailing 17–3, Bud Carson replaced struggling Bernie Kosar with Mike Pagel. The Cleveland offense suddenly came to life as Pagel completed his first six passes and cut the margin to seven with an 11-yard strike to Webster Slaughter with just over nine minutes left. With the suddenly stalwart Cleveland defense frustrating QB Joe Montana into a sub-par performance, the Browns got the ball back with six minutes left and Pagel directed them to the end zone. Ozzie Newsome made a brilliant diving catch touchdown to tie the contest with 1:10 remaining. But on third-and-14 moments later, Montana connected with WR Mike Sherrard over the middle for 35 yards to the Browns' 41 with 38 seconds to play. It set up a 45-yard field goal by Mike Cofer with five seconds left, which gave the 49ers a narrow victory. Despite a noble effort, the Browns had lost their third straight game to an opponent that would reach the playoffs at season's end.

Record: 2–6

	1	2	3	4		
Browns	0	0	3	14	–	17
49ers	0	14	3	3	=	20

SF-Rice 14-yd. pass from Montana (Cofer kick)
SF-Rathman 1-yd. run (Cofer kick)
CLE-Kauric 45-yd. FG
SF-Cofer 40-yd. FG
CLE-Slaughter 11-yd. pass from Pagel (Kauric kick)
CLE-Newsome 4-yd. pass from Pagel (Kauric kick)
SF-Cofer 45-yd. FG

Passing
CLE: Pagel 13–21–156 2 TD 1 INT, Kosar 9–18–106 0 TD 1 INT
SF: Montana 17–37–185 1 TD 2 INT

Rushing
CLE: Mack 14–29, Metcalf 2–6, Hoard 2–3
SF: Carter 17–58, Montana 5–32, Rathman 6–27

Receiving
CLE: Metcalf 6–76, Slaughter 6–71, Brennan 4–48, Mack 2–26, Kauric 1–21, Joines 1–12, Newsome 2–8
SF: Rice 6–67, Sherrard 2–42, Jones 3–32, Rathman 3–29, Carter 3–15

Sunday, November 4
Buffalo Bills 42, Browns 0
Cleveland Stadium (78,331)
Brown jerseys/white pants

On a dreary, overcast afternoon on the lake, Browns fans witnessed Bud Carson's equivalent of Pickett's Charge. Desperately seeking any kind of spark, Carson decided to start Mike Pagel in place of Bernie Kosar—marking the first time in five years a healthy Kosar didn't start for Cleveland. The decision backfired as the 6–1 Bills rolled to a shutout victory, the worst home defeat in Browns' history. In a rematch of the previous season's AFC divisional playoff, the Bills' offense picked up where it left off 10 months earlier, using RB Thurman Thomas to carve through the Cleveland defense to sprint to a 14–0 halftime lead. After the Bills received the second-half kickoff and marched 80 yards for another score, the game was out of reach, but things would only get worse for the Browns. The home team disgusted its fans by committing 13 penalties and botching two field-goal attempts, while Pagel completed just 16 of 38 passes and didn't pick up a first down until the second quarter. The next day, Bud Carson was fired as Browns' coach and replaced by offensive coordinator Jim Shofner.

Record: 2–7

	1	2	3	4		
Bills	7	7	7	21	=	42
Browns	0	0	0	0	=	0

BUF-Thomas 3-yd. run (Norwood kick)
BUF-Thomas 11-yd. run (Norwood kick)
BUF-Mueller 1-yd. run (Norwood kick)
BUF-Thomas 11-yd. pass from Kelly (Norwood kick)
BUF-Davis 3-yd. run (Norwood kick)
BUF-Talley 60-yd. interception return (Norwood kick)

Passing
BUF: Kelly 14–19–200 1 TD 0 INT, Reich 1–1–16 0 TD 0 INT
CLE: Pagel 16–38–195 0 TD 2 INT

Rushing
BUF: Thomas 17–58, Davis 7–41, Mueller 8–21, Gardner 2–0, Reich 3-(-3), Reed 1-(-15)
CLE: Mack 11–37, Hoard 2–8, Gainer 2–5, Pagel 3-(-1), Metcalf 1-(-1), Slaughter 1-(-5)

Receiving
BUF: Reed 7–122, Thomas 5–65, Davis 1–16, McKeller 1–7, Mueller 1–6
CLE: Brennan 5–85, Newsome 3–40, Metcalf 4–34, Slaughter 2–27, Hoard 1–6, Mack 1–3

Sunday, November 18
Houston Oilers 35, Browns 23
Cleveland Stadium (76,726)
White jerseys/white pants

Following the tumultuous few days after Bud Carson's firing, the Browns received a much-needed bye week and looked like a very different team than they did two weeks earlier. For three quarters on a sunny afternoon in Cleveland, the Browns out-played the playoff-bound Oilers. Cleveland recovered a fumble on the opening kickoff that led to an Ozzie Newsome touchdown reception—what would prove to be the final score of his Hall of Fame career. Then a fumble by QB Warren Moon, who would be sacked five times, led to another Cleveland touchdown early in the second quarter. After a long Houston touchdown pass just before halftime, the Browns surged back ahead 16–14 with five minutes to play in the third on a short Jerry Kauric field goal. But Moon threw three touchdowns in a six-minute period in the fourth quarter, giving him five on the day, to wipe out the Browns' noble effort. While Bernie Kosar played well in his return to the starting lineup, throwing for 279 yards and a pair of scores, the Browns were crippled by four turnovers and a defense that permitted 10 plays of 10 yards or more.
Record: 2–8

	1	2	3	4		
Oilers	7	7	0	21	=	35
Browns	6	7	3	7	=	23

CLE-Newsome 13-yd. pass from Kosar (kick failed)
HOU-White 3-yd. pass from Moon (Garcia kick)
CLE-Gainer 1-yd. run (Kauric kick)
HOU-Jeffires 46-yd. pass from Moon (Garcia kick)
CLE-Kauric 22-yd. FG
HOU-Duncan 37-yd. pass from Moon (Garcia kick)
HOU-Jones 23-yd. pass from Moon (Garcia kick)
HOU-Givins 7-yd. pass from Moon (Garcia kick)
CLE-Langhorne 4-yd. pass from Kosar (Kauric kick)

Passing
HOU: Moon 24–32–322 5 TD 0 INT
CLE: Kosar 25–35–279 2 TD 2 INT

Rushing
HOU: Pinkett 8–45, White 8–35, Moon 2–15, Carlson 1-(-1)
CLE: Mack 14–73, Metcalf 5–21, Gainer 3–4

Receiving
HOU: Duncan 7–130, Jeffires 2–51, Pinkett 4–46, Givins 5–41, Jones 1–23, Hill 3–20, White 2–11
CLE: Slaughter 6–104, Mack 6–58, Metcalf 6–33, Langhorne 4–32, Brennan 1–28, Newsome 2–24

Sunday, November 25
Miami Dolphins 30, Browns 13
Cleveland Stadium (70,225)
Brown jerseys/white pants

There was no repeat of the inspired start of the week before as the Browns were sluggish right out of the gate and were completely dominated by a hot Miami team in the first 30 minutes. The 8–2 Dolphins converted on their first seven third downs and soared to a 27–3 halftime lead, aided by a 31-yard interception return for a touchdown by DB Kerry Glenn. Miami then nursed the advantage to an easy victory. The lone bright spot for the Browns was topping the 100-yard mark in rushing as a team for the first time all season. Additionally, this game marked the end of their gauntlet of six straight games against teams that would eventually reach the playoffs. With the defeat, Cleveland secured its first losing season in six years.
Record: 2–9

	1	2	3	4		
Dolphins	14	13	3	0	=	30
Browns	0	3	3	7	=	13

MIA-Duper 5-yd. pass from Marino (Stoyanovich kick)
MIA-Pruitt 35-yd. pass from Marino (Stoyanovich kick)
MIA-Smith 4-yd. run (kick failed)
MIA-Glenn 31-yd. interception return (Stoyanovich kick)
CLE-Kauric 36-yd. FG
CLE-Kauric 42-yd. FG
MIA-Stoyanovich 40-yd. FG
CLE-Mack 2-yd. run (Kauric kick)

Passing
MIA: Marino 16–29–245 2 TD 0 INT
CLE: Kosar 17–37–191 0 TD 2 INT

Rushing
MIA: Smith 24–96, Stradford 6–13, Limbrick 2–4, Marino 1-(-2)
CLE: Mack 13–79, Metcalf 5–29, Gainer 1–3, Slaughter 1-(-2)

Receiving
MIA: Duper 4–74, Pruitt 2–59, Jensen 4–37, Martin 2–31, Edmunds 1–20, Stradford 1–13, Schwedes 1–6, Limbrick 1–5
CLE: Brennan 4–53, Metcalf 4–39, Mack 4–29, Newsome 2–26, Slaughter 1–23, Langhorne 2–21

Sunday, December 2
Los Angeles Rams 38, Browns 23
Cleveland Stadium (61,981)
Brown jerseys/white pants

For the second straight week, the Browns were broken down early and watched a visiting opponent cruise to an easy victory. Rams' QB Jim Everett threw two of his four touchdown passes in the second quarter to push LA to a 17–3 halftime lead, then made it 24–3 on their first possession of the third quarter. The Browns scored touchdowns on their next three possessions, but also allowed the Rams to score on their next two to thwart their momentum. Bernie Kosar was again sterling in defeat, throwing for 281 yards and a pair of touchdown passes, but the Browns could muster only 37 rushing yards.
Record: 2–10

	1	2	3	4		
Rams	3	14	14	7	=	38
Browns	3	0	14	6	=	23

LA-Lansford 30-yd. FG
CLE-Kauric 37-yd. FG
LA-Holohan 1-yd. pass from Everett (Lansford kick)
LA-Green 16-yd. pass from Everett (Lansford kick)
LA-Gary 1-yd. run (Lansford kick)
CLE-Slaughter 17-yd. pass from Kosar (Kauric kick)
LA-Delpino 21-yd. pass from Everett
CLE-Mack 3-yd. pass from Kosar (Kauric kick)
LA-McGee 9-yd. pass from Everett (Lansford kick)
CLE-Mack 1-yd. run (kick failed)

Passing
LA: Everett 22–29–261 4 TD 0 INT
CLE: Kosar 23–39–281 2 TD 0 INT

Rushing
LA: Green 13–57, McGee 9–55, Gary 9–28, Dupree 2–8, Delpino 1–5, Everett 2-(-3)
CLE: Metcalf 4–17, Mack 7–15, Kosar 1–5

Receiving
LA: Ellard 6–90, Delpino 4–51, McGee 3–41, Anderson 3–31, Holohan 4–24, Green 1–16, Carter 1–8
CLE: Slaughter 7–93, Mack 7–78, Langhorne 3–60, Brennan 5–43, Metcalf 1–7

Sunday, December 9
Houston Oilers 58, Browns 14
Houston Astrodome (54,469)
White jerseys/white pants

After hanging tough with the Oilers three weeks earlier in Cleveland, the rematch in Houston was a complete massacre. The listless Browns tied a team record by allowing 45 points in the first half—extending a humiliating string of allowing opponents to score on 13 consecutive possessions—and allowed the Oilers to tally 477 total yards, 34 first downs, and eight touchdowns for the day. Outgained by nearly 300 yards, the Browns compounded matters by committing four turnovers, allowing four sacks, and being penalized 11 times while permitting Houston RB Lorenzo White to rush for four touchdowns. Eric Metcalf scored the Browns' only touchdowns, the first on a 101-yard kickoff return midway through the second quarter with the score 28–0. After scoring on seven straight possessions, the Oilers topped the 50-point plateau midway through the third quarter, at which point most of the offensive starters were pulled. It was the most points the Browns had ever allowed in a regular-season game and the most lopsided Cleveland defeat in 23 years.
Record: 2–11

	1	2	3	4		
Browns	0	7	7	0	=	14
Oilers	14	31	7	6	=	58

HOU-White 10-yd. run (Garcia kick)
HOU-White 1-yd. run (Garcia kick)
HOU-Kinard 72-yd. fumble return (Garcia kick)
HOU-Givins 6-yd. pass from Moon (Garcia kick)
CLE-Metcalf 101-yd. kickoff return (Kauric kick)

HOU-Garcia 45-yd. FG
HOU-White 7-yd. run (Garcia kick)
HOU-Harris 17-yd. pass from Moon (Garcia kick)
HOU-White 5-yd. run (Garcia kick)
CLE-Metcalf 31-yd. pass from Kosar (Kauric kick)
HOU-Jones 9-yd. pass from Carlson (kick failed)

Passing
CLE: Kosar 13–26–166 1 TD 2 INT
HOU: Moon 17–25–190 2 TD 0 INT, Carlson 11–13–92 1 TD 0 INT

Rushing
CLE: Mack 8–35, Metcalf 4–15, Gainer 2–7, Kosar 1–0
HOU: White 18–116, Jones 9–39, Carlson 4–26, Givins 1–21, Moon 2–4

Receiving
CLE: Galbraith 3–60, Metcalf 3–36, Langhorne 2–25, Slaughter 2–15, Gainer 1–13, Newsome 1–13, Mack 1–4
HOU: Hill 5–61, Jeffires 4–46, Ford 3–44, Jones 5–42, Duncan 4–32, Harris 2–24, McNeil 2–18, Givins 3–15

Sunday, December 16
Browns 13, Atlanta Falcons 10
Cleveland Stadium (46,536)
Brown jerseys/white pants

Before the smallest non-replacement-game crowd in Cleveland in six years, the Browns won for the first time in over two months, snapping an eight-game losing streak by dominating the equally miserable Falcons, who lost their eighteenth straight road game. A week after getting annihilated in Houston, the Cleveland defense was powerful, collecting eight sacks and limiting the Falcons to just 129 yards of offense over the first 55 minutes. While the Cleveland offense struggled to put points on the board, the Browns had no trouble moving the football, tallying a season-high 142 rushing yards. Trailing 3–0, the Browns turned the tide of the contest in the final moments of the second quarter, scoring 10 points in the final two minutes. A Jerry Kauric field goal midway through the third period pushed the lead to 13–3, and the defense took it from there, not allowing Atlanta to score again until the final play of the game. The victory was muted somewhat with the news that Bernie Kosar had chipped a bone in his thumb during the contest and would be forced to miss the final two games of the season. The home finale also marked the final home game for Ozzie Newsome, who caught four passes for 34 yards.
Record: 3–11

	1	2	3	4		
Falcons	0	3	0	7	=	10
Browns	0	10	3	0	=	13

ATL-Davis 30-yd. FG
CLE-Mack 5-yd. run (Kauric kick)
CLE-Kauric 23-yd. FG
CLE-Kauric 41-yd. FG
ATL-Dixon 11-yd. pass from Millen (Davis kick)

Passing
ATL: Millen 11–27–168 1 TD 0 INT, Campbell 3–9–41 0 TD 0 INT
CLE: Kosar 22–37–217 0 TD 1 INT

Rushing
ATL: Rozier 11–31, Johnson 4–23, Jones 3–10, Pringle 1–9, Campbell 1–8
CLE: Mack 13–80, Metcalf 9–51, Gainer 4–7, Kosar 1–4

Receiving
ATL: Rison 6–100, Thomas 5–62, Collins 1–25, Dixon 1–11, Haynes 1–11
CLE: Langhorne 5–70, Newsome 4–34, Slaughter 3–30, Metcalf 4–28, Gainer 1–19, Brennan 2–17, Mack 2–17, Galbraith 1–2

Sunday, December 23
Pittsburgh Steelers 35, Browns 0
Three Rivers Stadium (51,665)
White jerseys/white pants

The miserable season hit rock bottom in week 16 as the Browns tied an NFL record with eight lost fumbles, all but gift-wrapping an easy victory for the first-place Steelers two days before Christmas. Fumbling on their first three plays from scrimmage, the Browns quickly fell behind 21–0 as the Steelers began their first six possessions in Cleveland territory. Pittsburgh scored all its points in the first half and held the Browns to just 158 total yards, including a season-low 25 on the ground. It marked the Browns' first loss in Three Rivers Stadium in five years and the first time they'd been shut out three times in the same season.
Record: 3–12

	1	2	3	4		
Browns	0	0	0	0	=	0
Steelers	21	14	0	0	=	35

PIT-Mularkey 20-yd. pass from Brister (Anderson kick)
PIT-Calloway 20-yd. pass from Brister (Anderson kick)
PIT-Mularkey 2-yd. pass from Brister (Anderson kick)
PIT-Hoge 12-yd. pass from Brister (Anderson kick)
PIT-Williams 1-yd. run (Anderson kick)

Passing
CLE: Pagel 12–29–125 0 TD 1 INT, Francis 2–2–26 0 TD 0 INT
PIT: Brister 10–19–139 4 TD 0 INT, Strom 2–3–18 0 TD 1 INT

Rushing
CLE: Mack 9–19, Metcalf 3–8, Gainer 2–6, Hoard 2-(-8)
PIT: Foster 16–100, Williams 12–47, Hoge 12–39, Strom 1–10, Bell 1–1

Receiving
CLE: Langhorne 3–42, Slaughter 3–38, Brennan 2–32, Newsome 1–18, Metcalf 4–12, Hoard 1–9
PIT: Lipps 3–46, Mularkey 3–38, Calloway 2–30, Green 1–17, Hoge 1–12, Stone 1–8, Hill 1–7

Sunday, December 30
Cincinnati Bengals 21, Browns 14
Riverfront Stadium (60,041)
White jerseys/white pants

On a rainy afternoon in Cincinnati, the Browns' worst season came to a close with a surprisingly gritty performance that nearly resulted in an upset victory. The first half was disastrous, as the Browns failed to score after having first-and-goal at the Cincinnati 1, then handed the Bengals the game's first touchdown when LB James Francis returned the first of Mike Pagel's three interceptions 17 yards to the end zone. Another Pagel interception on the following series led to the Bengals' second score, and it appeared the Browns were headed for another blowout. An interception by DB Felix Wright on the first possession of the third quarter led to a short touchdown run by Kevin Mack, who turned in his finest performance of the season as the Browns notched a season-high 161 rushing yards. The Browns then tied the contest at 14 when Pagel hit Brian Brennan with a 16-yard touchdown pass on their next possession. The Bengals took the lead on a short scoring pass by QB Boomer Esiason with 8:40 left, but the Browns had two chances to tie the game in the waning minutes. First, they reached the Cincinnati 23 with just over five minutes left, but Eric Metcalf dropped a pass on fourth-and-five. The defense held, and the Browns regained possession at their own 20 with 1:36 remaining. Pagel completed two long passes to give the Browns a first down at the Bengals' 32, but then his third-down pass was intercepted by Cincinnati DB David Fulcher to clinch the victory and the AFC Central title for the Bengals.

Record: 3–13

	1	2	3	4		
Browns	0	0	14	0	=	14
Bengals	0	14	0	7	=	21

CIN-Francis 17-yd. interception return (Breech kick)
CIN-Holman 22-yd. pass from Esiason (Breech kick)
CLE-Mack 2-yd. run (Kauric kick)
CLE-Brennan 16-yd. pass from Pagel (Kauric kick)
CIN-Ball 4-yd. pass from Esiason (Breech kick)

Passing
CLE: Pagel 14–32–184 1 TD 3 INT
CIN: Esiason 10–16–154 2 TD 2 INT

Rushing
CLE: Mack 16–85, Metcalf 12–51, Slaughter 1–14, Gainer 3–11, Hoard 1–0
CIN: Brooks 17–84, Woods 14–48, Esiason 5–19

Receiving
CLE: Slaughter 6–115, Joines 1–17, Metcalf 2–16, Brennan 1–16, Mack 3–14, Newsome 1–6
CIN: Ball 1–48, McGee 3–41, Brown 2–25, Holman 1–22, Woods 2–9, Brooks 1–9

1991

Sunday, September 1
Dallas Cowboys 26, Browns 14
Cleveland Stadium (78,860)
Brown jerseys/white pants

Bill Belichick's first game as an NFL head coach ended in defeat as the Browns were overwhelmed by a vastly improved Dallas team that would reach the playoffs for the first time under coach Jimmy Johnson. With three starters in the Browns' defensive backfield injured along with LB Clay Matthews, the Cowboys had little trouble moving the football, rolling up 395 yards, and running 75 plays to the Browns' 46. Still, the Browns took an early 7–3 lead, then quickly cut a 20–7 Dallas halftime advantage to six points when QB Bernie Kosar hit WR Webster Slaughter for a 62-yard touchdown bomb on the first play of the second half. But Dallas simply had too many weapons, with RB Emmit Smith rushing for 112 yards, Michael Irvin catching nine passes for 123, and QB Troy Aikman throwing for 274. The Browns hung in until the fourth quarter, but a pair of Dallas field goals in the final period put the game away. While Kosar had a solid day with 249 yards through the air, the Cleveland ground attack was nonexistent—a trend that would continue all season—totaling just 32 yards.
Record: 0–1

	1	2	3	4		
Cowboys	3	17	0	6	=	26
Browns	7	0	7	0	=	14

DAL-Willis 38-yd. FG
CLE-Mack 1-yd. run (Stover kick)
DAL-Willis 25-yd. FG
DAL-Novacek 3-yd. pass from Aikman (Willis kick)
DAL-Irvin 4-yd. pass from Aikman (Willis kick)
CLE-Slaughter 62-yd. pass from Kosar (Stover kick)
DAL-Willis 22-yd. FG
DAL-Willis 54-yd. FG

Passing
DAL: Aikman 24–37–274 2 TD 0 INT
CLE: Kosar 22–31–249 1 TD 0 INT

Rushing
DAL: Smith 32–112, Agee 3–16, Johnston 1–2
CLE: Metcalf 3–13, Mack 7–12, Kosar 1–5, Morris 3–2

Receiving
DAL: Irvin 9–123, Novacek 4–50, Smith 6–36, Roberts 3–33, Martin 1–16, Wright 1–16
CLE: Slaughter 4–88, Metcalf 6–59, Galbraith 3–30, Jackson 2–25, Langhorne 1–21, Brennan 2–15, Mack 3–14, Morris 1-(-3)

Sunday, September 8
Browns 20, New England Patriots 0
Foxboro Stadium (35,377)
White jerseys/white pants

Ironically considering what was to come, Bill Belichick's first career coaching victory came in New England as the Browns' defense dominated a Patriots team coming off a 1–15 season and now coached by former Browns' assistant Dick MacPherson. Leading just 7–0 at the half following Leroy Hoard's first touchdown of what would be a remarkable season, the Browns pulled away in the fourth. DB Randy Hilliard intercepted New England QB Tom Hodson at the goal line with 12 minutes to play, and six plays later, Bernie Kosar lofted a 65-yard touchdown pass to rookie WR Michael Jackson to seal the victory. In addition to the interception, Hilliard added two sacks and caused a fumble as the Cleveland defense forced four turnovers and permitted the Patriots to gather only 143 total yards and eight first downs.
Record: 1–1

	1	2	3	4		
Browns	0	7	3	10	=	20
Patriots	0	0	0	0	=	0

CLE-Hoard 7-yd. pass from Kosar (Stover kick)
CLE-Stover 30-yd. FG
CLE-Stover 32-yd. FG
CLE-Jackson 65-yd. pass from Kosar (Stover kick)

Passing
CLE: Kosar 15–22–187 2 TD 0 INT
NE: Hodson 12–26–95 0 TD 2 INT

Rushing
CLE: Morris 20–70, Hoard 4–19, Metcalf 8–18, Rouson 2–9, Kosar 3-(-3)
NE: Russell 12–60, Hunter 3–7, Vaughn 1–3, Adams 1–1, Hodson 1–1

Receiving
CLE: Jackson 3–82, Metcalf 4–35, Slaughter 3–29, Galbraith 2–23, Hoard 1–7, Rouson 1–6, Morris 1–5
NE: Vaughn 2–37, Fryar 2–23, Cook 3–17, McMurtry 1–13, Carpenter 1–11, Hunter 1–2, Russell 2-(-8)

Sunday, September 15
Browns 14, Cincinnati Bengals 13
Cleveland Stadium (78,269)
Brown jerseys/white pants

After watching a lead evaporate in the fourth quarter amid record heat, the Browns rallied with a gritty drive with time running out to pick up their first win over Cincinnati in nearly three years. Behind another sterling defensive performance, the Browns surged to an 11–3 lead in the second half, highlighted by DL James Jones trapping Cincinnati RB James Brooks in the end zone for a safety in the second quarter. Rookie kicker Matt Stover then tacked on a trio of field goals to extend the Cleveland lead, which evaporated when the Bengals scored 10 points in the fourth quarter and surged ahead by two with less than seven minutes remaining. After an exchange of possessions, the Browns took over on their own 12 with 3:09 left and quickly maneuvered down the field. WR Reggie Langhorne, who hadn't caught a pass in the first two games, snagged four on the possession, and RB Kevin Mack converted on a crucial fourth-down run at midfield with less than a minute to go. With four seconds left, Stover connected from 45 yards out to give the Browns a dramatic, hard-earned victory.
Record: 2–1

	1	2	3	4		
Bengals	3	0	0	10	=	13
Browns	0	5	6	3	=	14

CIN-Breech 21-yd. FG
CLE-Safety: Jones tackled Brooks in end zone
CLE-Stover 30-yd. FG
CLE-Stover 42-yd. FG
CLE-Stover 38-yd. FG
CIN-McGee 26-yd. pass from Esiason (Breech kick)
CIN-Breech 36-yd. FG
CLE-Stover 45-yd. FG

Passing
CIN: Esiason 15–26–140 1 TD 0 INT
CLE: Kosar 20–41–197 0 TD 0 INT

Rushing
CIN: Brooks 18–111, Ball 4–10, Taylor 4–9, Esiason 3–6, Green 5-(-2)
CLE: Mack 10–37, Morris 6–25, Hoard 3–12, Metcalf 6–7, Rouson 1–5, Hansen 1–0, Kosar 1-(-2)

Receiving
CIN: McGee 3–34, Kattus 3–32, Barber 2–29, James 2–18, Ball 1–9, Taylor 2–7, Holman 1–6, Brooks 1–5
CLE: Slaughter 8–107, Langhorne 4–29, Jackson 2–26, Hoard 2–12, Metcalf 2–10, Galbraith 1–10, Morris 1–3

Sunday, September 22
New York Giants 13, Browns 10
Giants Stadium (75,891)
White jerseys/white pants

Returning to the stadium where he'd risen to stardom as the Giants' defensive coordinator, Bill Belichick watched his new team come up short in a fitting defensive struggle. The Giants, 12-point favorites, held the Browns to a meager 145 total yards of offense—just 27 in the first half—and surged to a 13–0 halftime lead. But the visitors hung around and nearly stole a victory out of the grasp of the defending world champions. Sparked by a trick play on a punt return that saw RB Eric Metcalf throw a lateral across the field to DB Frank Minnifield for a 28-yard gain, the Browns cut the margin to three on the first play of the fourth quarter, then drove to the New York 38 with five minutes to play. But Giants' LB Carl Banks sniffed out a third-down rollout to sack Bernie Kosar and end the drive, and the Browns didn't see the ball again until less than 10 seconds remained.
Record: 2–2

	1	2	3	4		
Browns	0	0	3	7	=	10
Giants	3	10	0	0	=	13

NYG-Bahr 44-yd. FG
NYG-Bahr 48-yd. FG
NYG-Hampton 28-yd. run (Bahr kick)
CLE-Stover 30-yd. FG
CLE-Mack 7-yd. pass from Kosar (Stover kick)

Passing
CLE: Kosar 13–22–107 1 TD 0 INT
NYG: Hostetler 9–15–65 0 TD 0 INT

Rushing
CLE: Mack 20–71, Metcalf 1–4, Kosar 1–2, Morris 3–1
NYG: Hampton 17–104, Tillman 14–90, Hostetler 1–12, Meggett 1–3, Carthon 1–3

Receiving
CLE: Slaughter 3–41, Brennan 3–23, Mack 4–22, Galbraith 1–21, Metcalf 2–0
NYG: Hampton 4–21, Turner 1–17, Cross 1–11, Ingram 1–9, Tillman 1–5, Meggett 1–2

Sunday, October 6
New York Jets 17, Browns 14
Cleveland Stadium (71,042)
Brown jerseys/white pants

For the second straight game, the Browns rallied from a double-digit halftime deficit and were poised to win in the final minutes only to falter. This time, it was the Jets who surged to a 14–0 lead before the Browns rallied to tie with a pair of third-quarter touchdowns. After New York took the lead back at 17–14 with 10:45 remaining, the Browns persevered. Thanks to a bold effort by the defense that held the NFL's top rushing team to just 76 yards on the ground, the Browns earned one last chance. They regained possession at their own 20 with 5:17 left and methodically marched downfield. They were near field-goal range when Bernie Kosar was stripped of the football as he scrambled across the New York 40 and the Jets recovered with 1:14 remaining.
Record: 2–3

	1	2	3	4		
Jets	0	14	0	3	=	17
Browns	0	0	14	0	=	14

NYJ-Moore 16-yd. pass from Thomas (Leahy kick)
NYJ-Baxter 1-yd. run (Leahy kick)
CLE-Mack 1-yd. run (Stover kick)
CLE-Hoard 4-yd. pass from Kosar (Stover kick)
NYJ-Leahy 28-yd. FG

Passing
NYJ: O'Brien 19–23–195 0 TD 0 INT, Thomas 1–1–16 1 TD 0 INT
CLE: Kosar 16–24–133 1 TD 0 INT, Philcox 0–1–0 0 TD 0 INT

Rushing
NYJ: Baxter 16–59, Thomas 8–13, O'Brien 3–3, McNeil 1–1
CLE: Mack 13–51, Metcalf 4–27, Morris 4–23, Kosar 2–5

Receiving
NYJ: Toon 5–88, Moore 5–57, Boyer 2–24, Thomas 4–17, Dressel 2–11, Baxter 1–10, Whisenhunt 1–4
CLE: Mack 6–41, Slaughter 3–24, Metcalf 2–21, Jackson 1–14, Brennan 1–13, Langhorne 1–13, Hoard 1–4, Rouson 1–3

Sunday, October 13
Washington Redskins 42, Browns 17
RFK Stadium (54,715)
Brown jerseys/white pants

For nearly three quarters, the Browns stood toe-to-toe with the eventual world champions, but the undefeated Redskins were too much down the stretch and pulled away for an easy victory. The Browns tied the game at seven late in the first period on a clever fake field goal in which Webster Slaughter pretended to leave the field after third down, but simply stood along the sideline, then holder Brian Hansen took the snap, stood up, and lobbed the football to Slaughter, who caught it and stepped into the end zone for a touchdown. After two more Washington touchdowns, including one by former Browns' RB Earnest Byner, Cleveland had a chance to cut the lead to seven at the half, but Eric Metcalf fumbled after a nice gain to the Washington 2, and the football hit the pylon in the corner of the end zone, giving the Redskins possession after a touchback. Still, the Browns hung around in the second half, cutting the margin to 21–17 when DB Vince Newsome scooped up a Washington fumble—his fourth recovery of the young season—and returned it 37 yards for a touchdown. But behind the effective running of RB Ricky Ervins, who picked up 133 yards on just 13 carries in relief of an injured Byner, the Redskins scored three unanswered touchdowns to turn a well-fought game into a blowout. Still, the Browns played well, rolling up 389 yards of offense, but were victimized by 103 yards in penalties and four sacks.
Record: 2–4

	1	2	3	4		
Browns	7	0	10	7	=	24
Redskins	7	14	7	14	=	42

WAS-Monk 14-yd. pass from Rypien (Lohmiller kick)
CLE-Slaughter 11-yd. pass from Hansen (Stover kick)
WAS-Riggs 1-yd. run (Lohmiller kick)

WAS-Byner 21-yd. run (Lohmiller kick)
CLE-Stover 26-yd. FG
CLE-Newsome 37-yd. fumble return (Stover kick)
WAS-Ervins 12-yd. run (Lohmiller kick)
WAS-Riggs 1-yd. run (Lohmiller kick)
WAS-Ervins 65-yd. run (Lohmiller kick)

Passing
CLE: Kosar 21–29–266 0 TD 0 INT, Philcox 4–7–49 0 TD 1 INT, Hansen 1–1–11 1 TD 0 INT
WAS: Rypien 16–22–190 1 TD 0 INT

Rushing
CLE: Mack 14–70, Morris 5–16, Kosar 2–5, Metcalf 1-(-3)
WAS: Ervins 13–133, Byner 12–65, Sanders 2–9, Riggs 7–3, Clark 1–0, Rypien 1-(-2)

Receiving
CLE: Metcalf 4–74, Mack 6–53, Jackson 4–51, Langhorne 3–47, Slaughter 2–39, Brennan 4–38, Talley 1–13, Hoard 1–8, Morris 1–3
WAS: Monk 7–106, Clark 3–44, Sanders 5–38, Byner 1–2

Sunday, October 20
Browns 30, San Diego Chargers 24 (OT)
Jack Murphy Stadium (48,440)
Brown jerseys/white pants

Trailing the 1–6 Chargers 17–3 late in the third quarter and with the season on the brink of collapse, the Browns made a stirring comeback to prevail in the most exciting game of the season. Switching to a hurry-up offense, Bernie Kosar led the Browns to two quick touchdowns to tie the game early in the fourth. Then, after San Diego took the lead back, the Browns responded and knotted it up again with 4:09 to play on Leroy Hoard's second touchdown of the day. San Diego had a chance to win on the final play of regulation, but kicker John Carney was wide on a 48-yard field goal and the game tumbled into overtime. Midway through the extra session, San Diego QB John Friesz, rushed by Browns' DL Pio Sagapolutele, hurried a throw that was picked off by Cleveland LB David Brandon and returned 30 yards for the game-winning touchdown. Brandon's play was one of three made by former Charger LBs: Richard Brown (an interception that led to Cleveland's second touchdown) and Cedric Figaro (a fourth-down tackle at the Cleveland 2), which helped bring the Browns back. Leading the comeback, Kosar threw for 297 yards and broke Milt Plum's team record for the most consecutive passes thrown without an interception (208).
Record: 3–4

	1	2	3	4	OT		
Browns	0	3	7	14	6	=	30
Chargers	3	0	14	7	0	=	24

SD-Carney 27-yd. FG
CLE-Stover 30-yd. FG
SD-Harmon 11-yd. run (Carney kick)
SD-Butts 2-yd. run (Carney kick)
CLE-Hoard 6-yd. pass from Kosar (Stover kick)
CLE-Morris 1-yd. run (Stover kick)
SD-Hendrickson 2-yd. pass from Friesz (Carney kick)
CLE-Hoard 15-yd. pass from Kosar (Stover kick)
CLE-Brandon 30-yd. interception return

Passing
CLE: Kosar 26–42–297 2 TD 0 INT
SD: Friesz 33–54–321 1 TD 2 INT

Rushing
CLE: Metcalf 6–29, Morris 9–26, Kosar 2–8, Hoard 4–7
SD: Butts 16–54, Bernstine 9–44, Harmon 4–32, Friesz 1–2

Receiving
CLE: Langhorne 6–75, Slaughter 5–75, Metcalf 6–72, Brennan 3–34, Hoard 3–29, Jackson 2–8, Morris 1–4
SD: Miller 8–82, Lewis 5–72, Harmon 6–62, McEwen 2–29, Jefferson 2–24, Walker 5–22, Butts 2–16, Taylor 2–12, Hendrickson 1–2

Sunday, October 27
Browns 17, Pittsburgh Steelers 14
Cleveland Stadium (78,285)
Brown jerseys/white pants

The Browns caught a handful of breaks to defeat the Steelers, move into sole possession of second place in the AFC Central Division, and surpass their victory total from the year before on a balmy October late afternoon that quickly turned to evening. After a 10-minute, 70-yard drive on their first possession ended in a field goal, the Browns stretched the lead to 10–0 early in the second quarter on one of the most remarkable plays in team history: a third-down Bernie Kosar pass from the Pittsburgh 2 was tipped at the line of scrimmage and fluttered into the arms of Leroy Hoard, lying flat on his back in the end zone. Pittsburgh aided the Browns' cause with three dropped interceptions, then failed on a chance to tie the game when Gary Anderson hit the upright on a 52-yard field-goal attempt with 7:47 remaining. The Browns secured the victory when Clay Matthews intercepted Pittsburgh QB Neil O'Donnell at the Cleveland 43 with 1:17 left.
Record: 4–4

	1	2	3	4		
Steelers	0	7	0	7	=	14
Browns	3	7	7	0	=	17

CLE-Stover 34-yd. FG
CLE-Hoard 2-yd. pass from Kosar (Stover kick)
PIT-O'Donnell 1-yd. run (Anderson kick)
CLE-Mack 1-yd. run (Stover kick)
PIT-Williams 1-yd. run (Anderson kick)

Passing
PIT: O'Donnell 19–35–221 0 TD 2 INT
CLE: Kosar 21–29–179 1 TD 0 INT

Rushing
PIT: Hoge 12–48, Williams 9–26, O'Donnell 2–1
CLE: Mack 19–54, Metcalf 1–12, Morris 2–9, Kosar 4–6, Hoard 1–2

Receiving
PIT: Lipps 5–69, Hoge 6–56, Stone 3–53, Green 3–25, Calloway 1–17, Cooper 1–1
CLE: Brennan 5–52, Slaughter 4–38, Jackson 1–26, Metcalf 3–23, Mack 4–21, Langhorne 2–13, Galbraith 1–4, Hoard 1–2

Sunday, November 3
Cincinnati Bengals 23, Browns 21
Riverfront Stadium (55,077)
White jerseys/white pants

In one of the most frustrating defeats in their history, the Browns squandered four golden opportunities to win in the final six minutes and lost on the final play to the 0–8 Bengals. The first two of Kevin Mack's career-high three touchdowns gave the Browns a 14–3 lead midway through the second quarter, but the Bengals rallied to take a six-point lead in the third, then a 23–21 margin two minutes into the fourth. The Browns drove to the Cincinnati 15 with 5:15 to play and were poised to take the lead right back when Mack fumbled. Their next possession ended when a gust of wind pushed Matt Stover's 47-yard field-goal attempt into the left upright with 1:47 remaining, but the resilient Browns got the ball back with just under a minute left and drove to the Bengals' 24. A perfectly thrown pass from Bernie Kosar bounced off the shoulder pads of wide-open WR Brian Brennan in the end zone with 33 seconds left, and then on the game's final play, Cincinnati DB Eric Thomas burst around the right corner to block Stover's 34-yard field-goal attempt and secure the Bengals' first win of the season. The disheartening defeat set the tone for the remainder of the season as the Browns would lose four more narrow games in the final minutes.

Record: 4–5

	1	2	3	4		
Browns	0	14	7	0	=	21
Bengals	3	10	7	3	=	23

CIN-Breech 23-yd. FG
CLE-Mack 4-yd. run (Stover kick)
CLE-Mack 2-yd. run (Stover kick)
CIN-Dingle 2-yd. pass from Esiason (Breech kick)
CIN-Breech 38-yd. FG
CIN-Brown 34-yd. pass from Esiason (Breech kick)
CLE-Mack 2-yd. run (Stover kick)
CIN-Breech 38-yd. FG

Passing
CLE: Kosar 19–31–285 0 TD 0 INT
CIN: Esiason 18–30–185 2 TD 1 INT

Rushing
CLE: Mack 26–78, Hoard 1–3, Kosar 2–2
CIN: Green 24–135, Brooks 8–23, Esiason 1–4

Receiving
CLE: Slaughter 5–107, Langhorne 4–49, Galbraith 1–42, Hoard 3–35, Brennan 4–32, Mack 1–11, Jackson 1–9
CIN: Brown 3–73, Brooks 6–47, Green 3–27, Dingle 2–11, Holman 1–11, Kattus 1–6, McGee 1–6, Barber 1–4

Sunday, November 10
Philadelphia Eagles 32, Browns 30
Cleveland Stadium (72,086)
Brown jerseys/white pants

For the second straight week, the Browns lost in a maddening fashion, this time as a result of the biggest blown lead in franchise history. On the strength of a nearly perfect offensive performance in the first half and an opportunistic defense, the Browns soared to a 23–0 lead, highlighted by a 42-yard interception return for a touchdown by rookie DB Eric Turner, making his first NFL start after missing the first half of the season to injury. Leroy Hoard added a 65-yard touchdown reception, and Webster Slaughter made a remarkable diving fingertip catch for another. But slowly, the Eagles crept back into the game, narrowing the margin to 13 points at the half, then seven going into the fourth quarter. After rolling to 234 total yards in the first half, the Browns' offense managed only 24 in the second and accumulated only 25 rushing yards for the game against a defense directed by former Browns' head coach Bud Carson, now Philadelphia's defensive coordinator. Clinging to a 30–26 lead with just under seven minutes to play, the Browns handed the Eagles the winning points when Webster Slaughter foolishly fielded a punt on his own two-yard line, then fumbled, and Philadelphia recovered at the 1. Moments later, Eagles' QB Jim McMahon, who would throw for 341 yards on the day, hit WR Calvin Williams for the winning touchdown with 5:19 showing. The lone good news for the Browns was Bernie Kosar setting a new NFL record for the most consecutive passes thrown without an interception with 308, breaking the previous record of 294 held by Green Bay's Bart Starr.

Record: 4–6

	1	2	3	4		
Eagles	0	17	6	9	=	32
Browns	16	14	0	0	=	30

CLE-Stover 50-yd. FG
CLE-Turner 42-yd. interception return (Stover kick)
CLE-Hoard 65-yd. pass from Kosar (kick failed)
CLE-Slaughter 18-yd. pass from Kosar (Stover kick)
PHI-Jackson 18-yd. pass from McMahon (Ruzek kick)
PHI-Barnett 70-yd. pass from McMahon (Ruzek kick)
PHI-Ruzek 21-yd. FG
CLE-Langhorne 24-yd. pass from Kosar (Stover kick)
PHI-Ruzek 37-yd. FG
PHI-Ruzek 24-yd. FG
PHI-Ruzek 19-yd. FG
PHI-Williams 5-yd. pass from McMahon (kick failed)

Passing
PHI: McMahon 26–43–341 3 TD 1 INT
CLE: Kosar 14–33–246 3 TD 1 INT

Rushing
PHI: Joseph 20–89, Sherman 2–6, Byars 5–3, McMahon 1-(-1)
CLE: Mack 10–23, Hoard 1–2

Receiving
PHI: Barnett 8–146, Jackson 6–76, Williams 6–76, Johnson 2–13, Green 1–9, Sherman 1–9, Byars 1–7, Joseph 1–5
CLE: Slaughter 5–74, Langhorne 4–73, Hoard 1–65, Brennan 2–22, Galbraith 1–13, Mack 1-(-1)

Sunday, November 17
Houston Oilers 28, Browns 24
Houston Astrodome (58,155)
White jerseys/white pants

Despite an admirable performance against the 8–2 Oilers, the Browns were unable to hold a 10-point second-half lead and lost in the final minute before an ESPN television audience on a Sunday night. Despite an athletic, spinning touchdown run on a reception by Leroy Hoard and a career-best 55-yard field goal by Matt Stover, the Browns' 17–7 lead evaporated, and with just over three minutes remaining, it appeared the Oilers—13-point favorites—were on their way to victory. But on fourth-and-13 from the Houston 40, Bernie Kosar connected with Reggie Langhorne for a stunning touchdown, and a minute later, Browns' DB Vince Newsome intercepted Houston QB Warren Moon to put the Browns in prime position to win. But Houston's defense held, and the Oilers got the ball back at their own 16 with 2:09 to play, then quickly marched down the field. They reached the Cleveland 1, where with nine seconds left, Moon, who threw for 399 yards, hit Drew Hill for the game-winning score. The defeat spoiled a marvelous night for Hoard, who caught 10 passes for 107 yards, but underlined continued problems with the Cleveland defense, which permitted more than 400 yards for the second straight game.

Record: 4–7

	1	2	3	4		
Browns	7	7	3	7	=	24
Oilers	0	7	7	14	=	28

CLE-Hoard 14-yd. pass from Kosar (Stover kick)
HOU-Pinkett 5-yd. run (Del Greco kick)
CLE-Morris 5-yd. run (Stover kick)
CLE-Stover 55-yd. FG
HOU-Hill 40-yd. pass from Moon (Del Greco kick)
HOU-Coleman 4-yd. pass from Moon (Del Greco kick)
CLE-Langhorne 40-yd. pass from Kosar (Stover kick)
HOU-Hill 1-yd. pass from Moon (Del Greco kick)

Passing
CLE: Kosar 21–34–279 2 TD 1 INT
HOU: Moon 31–44–399 3 TD 1 INT

Rushing
CLE: Mack 16–32, Morris 4–10, Kosar 1–9, Hoard 2–1, Hansen 1-(-3)
HOU: Pinkett 7–26, White 7–20, Moon 1-(-1)

Receiving
CLE: Hoard 10–107, Slaughter 4–78, Langhorne 1–40, Galbraith 3–39, Mack 3–15
HOU: Hill 11–144, Jeffires 6–80, Givins 5–77, Duncan 3–60, Coleman 2–13, Pinkett 1–9, Jones 1–6, White 1–6, Harris 1–4

Sunday, November 24
Browns 20, Kansas City Chiefs 15
Cleveland Stadium (63,991)
Brown jerseys/white pants

After three straight heart-wrenching defeats, the Browns finally pulled out a victory, holding on through a frigid wind in a hard-fought game with the playoff-bound Chiefs, who were led by former Browns' head coach Marty Schottenheimer. The Browns built a 17–0 lead behind the heroics of Leroy Hoard, whose amazing season continued as he scored a pair of touchdowns—the second on a makeshift 71-yard pass lobbed down the sideline by Bernie Kosar under pressure—and added a 52-yard run, what would be the Browns' longest of the season. Up 20–3 with 12 minutes to play, the Browns watched the Chiefs chip away at the lead, aiding their cause when Kosar and Kevin Mack fumbled a handoff that carried into the end zone, where Kosar covered the football for a safety. The Cleveland defense, riddled the previous two weeks, snapped back to form, forcing five turnovers and holding the ground-oriented Chiefs to just 78 yards for the game while dominating powerful RB Christian Okoye, who tallied only 33 yards on 13 carries. The unit then stopped the Chiefs at midfield on their final possession in the waning seconds and clinched victory when DB Alfred Jackson intercepted a desperation Steve DeBerg pass at the Cleveland 13.
Record: 5–7

	1	2	3	4		
Chiefs	0	0	3	12	=	15
Browns	0	10	10	0	=	20

CLE-Hoard 1-yd. run (Stover kick)
CLE-Stover 34-yd. FG
CLE-Hoard 71-yd. pass from Kosar (Stover kick)
KC-Lowery 34-yd. FG
CLE-Stover 21-yd. FG
KC-Lowery 22-yd. FG
KC-Safety: Lewis tackled Kosar in end zone
KC-Harry 5-yd. pass from DeBerg (Lowery kick)

Passing
KC: DeBerg 30–50–319 1 TD 2 INT
CLE: Kosar 13–20–170 1 TD 2 INT

Rushing
KC: Word 8–41, Okoye 13–33, McNair 1–5, DeBerg 2-(-1)
CLE: Hoard 6–61, Mack 16–46, Morris 4–9, Kosar 4–7

Receiving
KC: Harry 11–159, McNair 6–41, Stradford 5–40, Barnett 3–28, Birden 1–16, Holohan 2–14, Hayes 1–12, Jones 1–9
CLE: Hoard 2–78, Langhorne 5–50, Galbraith 3–20, Slaughter 2–17, Mack 1–5

Sunday, December 1
Browns 31, Indianapolis Colts 0
Hoosier Dome (57,539)
White jerseys/white pants

Exploding for four touchdowns in the second quarter, the Browns took a 31–0 halftime lead and coasted to an easy victory over the hapless 1–11 Colts. The Browns set the tone on the game's fourth play, forcing an Indianapolis fumble—the first of four Colts' turnovers on the afternoon, which would push the Browns' season turnover ratio to plus-20. While the offense was efficient, paced by Kevin Mack's 51-yard touchdown run in the second quarter, the defense was superb, sacking Indy QB Jeff George six times and holding the Colts to 171 total yards. The defense also added to the onslaught when James Jones returned an interception 20 yards for a touchdown. The victory pushed the Browns back into the AFC playoff race for the moment, though it would be their final win of the season. It also marked the first time the Browns had collected two shutouts in the same season since 1983.
Record: 6–7

	1	2	3	4		
Browns	3	28	0	0	=	31
Colts	0	0	0	0	=	0

CLE-Stover 41-yd. FG
CLE-Mack 3-yd. pass from Kosar (Stover kick)
CLE-Mack 51-yd. run (Stover kick)
CLE-Hoard 2-yd. run (Stover kick)
CLE-Jones 20-yd. interception return (Stover kick)

Passing
CLE: Kosar 18–23–189 1 TD 0 INT
IND: George 10–21–100 0 TD 2 INT

Rushing
CLE: Mack 9–69, Morris 19–68, Hoard 2–2
IND: Dickerson 16–117, Clark 5–23, Manoa 1–3

Receiving
CLE: Hoard 6–74, Galbraith 4–52, Mack 3–19, Slaughter 2–19, Langhorne 1–12, Brennan 1–7, Morris 1–6
IND: Hester 4–66, Brooks 2–15, Mrosko 1–13, Verdin 1–6, Dickerson 2–0

Sunday, December 8
Denver Broncos 17, Browns 7
Cleveland Stadium (73,539)
Brown jerseys/white pants

The Broncos' spell over the Browns continued as Denver broke a 7–7 tie with 10 fourth-quarter points to come out ahead in a tough defensive battle. The Browns took an early lead on a Kevin Mack touchdown run but managed little offense after that, accumulating just 181 yards for the game, including a season-low 80 passing yards. Denver quickly tied the game with the first of two touchdown passes by QB John Elway, then put it away with a field goal with just over three minutes left in the fourth quarter, set up by a 60-yard pass from Elway to RB Steve Sewell. The Cleveland defense played well, holding the Broncos to less than three yards per rush and sacking Elway four times but couldn't overcome the offense's struggles. With the defeat, the Browns' dim playoff hopes suffered a huge setback with two games to play.
Record: 6–8

	1	2	3	4		
Broncos	0	7	0	10	=	17
Browns	7	0	0	0	=	7

CLE-Mack 3-yd. run (Stover kick)
DEN-Young 30-yd. pass from Elway (Treadwell kick)
DEN-Johnson 6-yd. pass from Elway (Treadwell kick)
DEN-Treadwell 37-yd. FG

Passing
DEN: Elway 16–29–221 2 TD 1 INT
CLE: Kosar 12–24–110 0 TD 1 INT

Rushing
DEN: Green 23–51, Elway 4–25, Perryman 4–7, Sewell 2–6, Lewis 2–1
CLE: Mack 14–87, Hoard 3–11, Morris 2–3

Receiving
DEN: Sewell 1–60, Sharpe 4–59, Young 2–38, Johnson 5–35, Perryman 3–22, Russell 1–7
CLE: Langhorne 4–55, Hoard 2–19, Slaughter 2–19, Mack 3–13, Galbraith 1–4

Sunday, December 15
Houston Oilers 17, Browns 14
Cleveland Stadium (55,680)
Brown jerseys/white pants

As a heavy snow swirled through the stadium in the second half, a gritty performance by the Browns went for naught as they suffered yet another crushing defeat in the final seconds. A Cleveland lead built on two early touchdowns, including Leroy Hoard's eleventh of the season, held up through most of the second half as the defense continually thwarted Houston's powerful air attack. But the Oilers took their first lead with 2:19 to play in the game following an 82-yard drive capped by a short Warren Moon touchdown pass. Taking over at their own 18, the Browns put together a clutch drive through the snow into Houston territory. Facing third-and-19 at the Oiler 42 with 30 seconds left, Bernie Kosar connected with Brian Brennan for 30 yards to the Houston 12. After Kosar scrambled to the Houston 1, Matt Stover was called on to attempt a chip-shot 19-yard field goal that would tie the game with four seconds left. But inexplicably, Stover's kick veered wildly off to the left and the division-champion Oilers escaped, despite being outgained by the Cleveland offense and outplayed in what became an emotional contest.
Record: 6–9

	1	2	3	4		
Oilers	0	10	0	7	=	17
Browns	7	7	0	0	=	14

CLE-Hoard 8-yd. pass from Kosar (Stover kick)
HOU-Givins 7-yd. pass from Moon (Del Greco kick)
CLE-Brennan 8-yd. pass from Kosar (Stover kick)
HOU-Del Greco 27-yd. FG
HOU-Jeffires 2-yd. pass from Moon (Del Greco kick)

Passing
HOU: Moon 26–40–250 2 TD 1 INT
CLE: Kosar 28–40–258 2 TD 1 INT

Rushing
HOU: White 9–47, Pinkett 8–20, Moon 1–11, Givins 1–5
CLE: Mack 15–73, Hoard 5–17, Kosar 1–11

Receiving
HOU: Jeffires 7–91, Hill 8–60, Givins 3–43, Pinkett 5–36, Duncan 2–12, White 1–8
CLE: Brennan 5–81, Hoard 10–70, Galbraith 4–30, Langhorne 3–28, Mack 3–24, Slaughter 1–13, Morris 1–11, Kosar 1–1

Sunday, December 22
Pittsburgh Steelers 17, Browns 10
Three Rivers Stadium (47,070)
White jerseys/white pants

In Chuck Noll's final game as the Steelers' head coach, the Browns put together their finest offensive performance of the season, rolling up 401 total yards but were crippled by an endless string of mistakes that included five turnovers, five sacks allowed, and 110 yards in penalties. The Cleveland defense once again was strong, limiting the Steelers to just 225 yards of offense and 12 first downs. The most damaging Cleveland mistake came midway through the fourth quarter: a 57-yard interception return for a touchdown by Pittsburgh DB Richard Shelton, who picked off Bernie Kosar three times on the day, to give the Steelers a 17–3 lead. The Browns quickly responded with a touchdown to cut the margin back to seven, then had one last chance when they drove to the Pittsburgh 13 with six seconds to play. But Kosar was sacked by Steelers' LB Greg Lloyd to end the game and the season. Though he was intercepted three times, Kosar threw for a season-high 335 yards, including 138 to Webster Slaughter on 11 receptions. It would be the final game in a Cleveland uniform for receivers Slaughter, Reggie Langhorne, and Brian Brennan, marking the end of an era for the Browns.

Record: 6–10

	1	2	3	4		
Browns	0	3	0	7	=	10
Steelers	3	0	7	7	=	17

PIT-Anderson 34-yd. FG
CLE-Stover 19-yd. FG
PIT-Stone 65-yd. pass from Brister (Anderson kick)
PIT-Shelton 57-yd. INT return (Anderson kick)
CLE-Jackson 27-yd. pass from Kosar (Stover kick)

Passing
CLE: Kosar 28–49–335 1 TD 3 INT
PIT: Brister 7–26–113 1 TD 0 INT

Rushing
CLE: Morris 12–27, Mack 8–23, Kosar 2–19, Hoard 5–17
PIT: Worley 16–84, Hoge 11–44, Brister 3–6, Thompson 1–4, Williams 1–0

Receiving
CLE: Slaughter 11–138, Hoard 5–57, Morris 6–47, Galbraith 2–40, Jackson 1–27, Mack 2–18, Brennan 1–8
PIT: Stone 3–76, Hoge 3–25, Lipps 1–12

1992

Sunday, September 6
Indianapolis Colts 14, Browns 3
Hoosier Dome (50,766)
White jerseys/white pants

The modest expectations surrounding the Browns going into the season were obliterated on the Hoosier Dome carpet as the Colts, coming off a 1–15 campaign, completely dominated the Cleveland offense to pick up a surprising victory on opening day. Browns' QB Bernie Kosar took a horrific beating, tying a team record by getting sacked 11 times as part of a charge led by former Browns' LB Chip Banks, who collected four along with an interception to set up the Colts' first touchdown. Another former Brown, WR Reggie Langhorne, caught a 26-yard touchdown pass in the third quarter to give Indianapolis an insurmountable lead against the Browns' struggling offense, which managed only 145 total yards for the game. Cleveland's lone score came in the opening minutes of the third quarter when the Colts fumbled the second-half kickoff, but they managed to hold the Browns to a short field goal and maintain the momentum.

Record: 0–1

	1	2	3	4		
Browns	0	0	3	0	=	3
Colts	7	0	7	0	=	14

IND-Culver 1-yd. run (Biasucci kick)
CLE-Stover 20-yd. FG
IND-Langhorne 26-yd. pass from Herrmann (Biasucci kick)

Passing
CLE: Kosar 15–26–175 0 TD 2 INT
IND: Herrmann 15–24–177 1 TD 1 INT

Rushing
CLE: Vardell 9–26, Hoard 5–15, Wolfley 1–2, Metcalf 1-(-1)
IND: Culver 19–52, Johnson 6–15, Carthon 2–3, Clark 2–3, Herrmann 3-(-2), Langhorne 1-(-7)

Receiving
CLE: Jackson 3–49, Vardell 3–36, Holohan 4–30, Holland 2–27, Hoard 1–16, Metcalf 1–11, Bavaro 1–6
IND: Culver 7–78, Hester 4–55, Langhorne 2–39, Carthon 1–3, Verdin 1–2

Monday, September 14
Miami Dolphins 27, Browns 23
Cleveland Stadium (74,765)
Brown jerseys/white pants

A remarkable Browns' comeback that saw them score 20 points in the fourth quarter on *Monday Night Football* was spoiled in the final seconds as the Browns fell to 0–2 for the first time in eight years. The miserable offensive performance of the previous week continued in the first half as the Browns managed only 72 total yards and trailed 14–0 after the Dolphins scored touchdowns on their first two possessions. Down 20–3 with 12 minutes left in the game, the Browns came to life, scoring their first touchdown of the season on a fourth-down reception by WR Michael Jackson. Two plays later, Cleveland LB David Brandon scooped up a Miami fumble caused by fellow LB Mike Johnson and returned it 32 yards for another score to cut the margin to 20–17. Following a Cleveland defensive stop, the Browns quickly drove back down the field and took their first lead of the season when Bernie Kosar rolled out and hit TE Mark Bavaro, who was knocked head over heels as he crossed the goal line with 1:18 remaining. After Matt Stover's extra point hit the upright, Miami QB Dan Marino worked his magic to complete the nineteenth fourth-quarter comeback of his career. Miami quickly drove 85 yards, aided by a roughing-the-passer penalty, and scored the winning touchdown on a plunge by RB Mark Higgs with seven seconds remaining. While the loss was hard to swallow, the Browns' offense showed signs of life, notching 250 yards in the second half. The bad news was that Kosar had led the charge on a broken ankle and would be sidelined for the next eight weeks.

Record: 0–2

	1	2	3	4		
Dolphins	14	0	3	10	=	27
Browns	0	0	3	20	=	23

MIA-Duper 25-yd. pass from Marino (Stoyanovich kick)
MIA-Higgs 7-yd. run (Stoyanovich kick)
CLE-Stover 28-yd. FG
MIA-Stoyanovich 22-yd. FG
MIA-Stoyanovich 32-yd. FG

CLE-Jackson 6-yd. pass from Kosar (Stover kick)
CLE-Brandon 32-yd. fumble return (Stover kick)
CLE-Bavaro 3-yd. pass from Kosar (kick failed)
MIA-Higgs 1-yd. run (Stoyanovich kick)

Passing
MIA: Marino 25–35–322 1 TD 0 INT
CLE: Kosar 19–28–230 2 TD 0 INT

Rushing
MIA: Higgs 25–90, Humphrey 2–11, Saxon 1–0
CLE: Vardell 16–84, Metcalf 2–16, Kosar 1–8, Brooks 3–3, Hoard 2–0

Receiving
MIA: Martin 4–74, Duper 4–70, Clark 3–59, Banks 2–40, Humphrey 4–24, Edmunds 3–24, Paige 3–20, Higgs 1–6, Saxon 1–5
CLE: Jackson 5–98, Metcalf 4–59, Bavaro 4–37, Vardell 2–29, Holohan 1–6, Hoard 1–2, Brooks 2-(-1)

Sunday, September 20
Browns 28, Los Angeles Raiders 16
Los Angeles Memorial Stadium (48,102)
White jerseys/white pants

On the strength of one of the greatest individual performances in team history, the Browns avoided a 0–3 start by beating the Raiders on the road for only the second time in eight trips. Browns' RB Eric Metcalf, who had held out through most of training camp, scored four touchdowns while accumulating 177 receiving yards on just five catches, becoming the first Cleveland player to cross the goal line four times in a game since Leroy Kelly in 1968. After Metcalf's first two touchdowns—both set up by Raiders' turnovers—gave the Browns an early 14–0 lead, the Raiders crept to within a point late in the third quarter. Then Metcalf caught a pass on a slant pattern from QB Todd Philcox—in for injured Bernie Kosar—and exploded through the LA secondary for a 69-yard score. Then four minutes into the fourth, Metcalf added a 63-yard touchdown reception on a nearly identical play to put the game away. Metcalf accumulated 187 of the Browns' modest 231 yards on offense, while the Raiders—running more than twice as many plays—racked up 464 yards but were thwarted by five sacks and five turnovers, including two interceptions by Browns' DB Vince Newsome. But even in victory, the Browns could not escape bad luck—afterward Philcox was discovered to have broken his thumb during the game and would be out for six weeks.
Record: 1–2

	1	2	3	4		
Browns	14	0	7	7	=	28
Raiders	0	3	10	3	=	16

CLE-Metcalf 4-yd. pass from Philcox (Stover kick)
CLE-Metcalf 6-yd. run (Stover kick)
LA-Jaeger 27-yd. FG
LA-Gault 25-yd. pass from Marinovich (Jaeger kick)
LA-Jaeger 30-yd. FG
CLE-Metcalf 69-yd. pass from Philcox (Stover kick)
CLE-Metcalf 63-yd. pass from Philcox (Stover kick)
LA-Jaeger 43-yd. FG

Passing
CLE: Philcox 10–20–200 3 TD 0 INT
LA: Marinovich 33–59–395 1 TD 3 INT

Rushing
CLE: Brooks 6–17, Metcalf 4–10, Vardell 6–8, Hoard 6-(-4)
LA: Allen 8–52, Marinovich 2–21, Dickerson 6–22, Smith 3–20, Bell 2–5, Brown 1–2, Gossett 1-(-12)

Receiving
CLE: Metcalf 5–177, Holohan 3–13, Hoard 2–10
LA: Graddy 6–114, Allen 8–57, Gault 3–45, Horton 3–32, Brown 2–29, Smith 3–28, Jones 1–25, Bell 3–24, Dickerson 2–14, Glover 1–14, Fernandez 1–13

Sunday, September 27
Denver Broncos 12, Browns 0
Cleveland Stadium (78,064)
Brown jerseys/white pants

Fielding their third starting QB in four games, the Browns' offense reverted back to its earlier struggles, wasting an admirable effort by the Cleveland defense in a defeat to Denver that saw neither team reach the end zone. With veteran QB Mike Tomczak—signed just two weeks earlier—at the helm, the Cleveland offense managed only 216 total yards and 10 first downs and failed to put any points on the board despite three trips inside the Denver 20. Meanwhile, the Browns' defense contained longtime nemesis John Elway, sacking the Denver QB five times while limiting him to 10 completions. But a steady Denver running game that tallied 188 yards and propelled the team to four field goals was enough to drop the Browns to their third loss in four weeks. The frustration on this sunny afternoon was symbolized by the drop-off in output by Eric Metcalf: a week after tallying 187 yards of offense, he was limited to 32. One of the lone bright spots for the Browns was a 73-yard punt by Brian Hansen, the third-longest in team history.
Record: 1–3

	1	2	3	4		
Broncos	3	0	3	6	=	12
Browns	0	0	0	0	=	0

DEN-Treadwell 23-yd. FG
DEN-Treadwell 44-yd. FG
DEN-Treadwell 32-yd. FG
DEN-Treadwell 20-yd. FG

Passing
DEN: Elway 10–17–157 0 TD 1 INT
CLE: Tomczak 9–19–75 0 TD 2 INT, Stover 0–1–0 0 TD 1 INT

Rushing
DEN: Rivers 8–66, Green 18–57, Lewis 3–44, Elway 8–18, Marshall 3–5, Perryman 1-(-2)
CLE: Hoard 10–71, Metcalf 8–21, Brooks 4–18, Tomczak 2–17, Vardell 6–14

Receiving
DEN: Sharpe 2–61, Jackson 2–26, Rivers 1–17, Russell 1–15, Marshall 1–12, Tillman 1–9, Perryman 1–9, Green 1–8
CLE: Hoard 4–54, Metcalf 3–11, Holohan 2–10

Sunday, October 11
Browns 17, Pittsburgh Steelers 9
Cleveland Stadium (78,080)
Brown jerseys/white pants

With a gritty performance on a dark, damp day in Cleveland, the Browns saved their season by outmuscling the 3–1 Steelers, who were led by new head coach Bill Cowher. With the defense not allowing a touchdown for the second straight week, Mike Tomczak engineered a low-risk game plan, and the Browns' offense got rolling in the second half. They took a 10–6 lead after a 90-yard touchdown drive midway through the third quarter, then answered a Pittsburgh field goal with the play of the game. On third-and-11 from the Pittsburgh 47 with 11 minutes to play, Tomczak pump-faked and lofted a pass down the sideline for a wide-open Michael Jackson, who sprinted untouched into the end zone for the game-clinching touchdown. The Browns stuffed the Steelers on fourth-and-inches on their next possession, then forced a fumble to wrap things up with just over a minute to play. Jackson's touchdown capped a nice day for Browns' wideouts after no Cleveland wide receiver caught a pass in either of the previous two games.
Record: 2–3

	1	2	3	4		
Steelers	3	3	0	3	=	9
Browns	0	3	7	7	=	17

PIT-Anderson 25-yd. FG
PIT-Anderson 36-yd. FG
CLE-Stover 51-yd. FG
CLE-Mack 1-yd. run (Stover kick)
PIT-Anderson 40-yd. FG
CLE-Jackson 47-yd. pass from Tomczak (Stover kick)

Passing
PIT: O'Donnell 25–32–241 0 TD 0 INT
CLE: Tomczak 10–17–171 1 TD 0 INT

Rushing
PIT: Foster 24–84, Stone 1–17, Hoge 3–12, O'Donnell 3–7
CLE: Metcalf 7–49, Mack 12–32, Vardell 3–7, Tomczak 5-(-3)

Receiving
PIT: Graham 8–87, Foster 6–49, Green 3–36, Stone 3–31, Mills 2–21, Hoge 2–9, Cooper 1–8
CLE: Jackson 2–62, Metcalf 3–48, Bavaro 1–23, Smith 2–21, Mack 1–9, McCardell 1–8

Sunday, October 18
Browns 17, Green Bay Packers 6
Cleveland Stadium (69,268)
Brown jerseys/white pants

In essentially a carbon copy of the previous week's contest, the Browns' defense once again didn't allow a touchdown while the offense did just enough to notch a victory to pull the Browns to the .500 mark. Facing a Packers' offense led by new QB Brett Favre, making his third career start, and directed by first-year head coach Mike Holmgren, the Browns' defense was overpowering, limiting the Pack to just 75 rushing yards. Meanwhile, the Cleveland offense rolled up 142 yards on the ground—the team's highest total in two years—and set the tone on the game's opening drive: a 17-play march that took more than nine minutes off the clock and ended with a Matt Stover field goal. RB Kevin Mack added a pair of touchdowns in the second half, including the game-clincher to cap an 80-yard drive with six minutes left. Tomczak was efficient against the team that had released him in training camp, not throwing an interception or getting sacked.
Record: 3–3

	1	2	3	4		
Packers	0	0	3	3	=	6
Browns	3	0	7	7	=	17

CLE-Stover 26-yd. FG
GB-Jacke 44-yd. FG
CLE-Mack 1-yd. run (Stover kick)
GB-Jacke 37-yd. FG
CLE-Mack 5-yd. run (Stover kick)

Passing
GB: Favre 20–33–223 0 TD 0 INT
CLE: Tomczak 13–21–158 0 TD 0 INT

Rushing
GB: Workman 10–30, Favre 6–28, Thompson 2–8, Sydney 3–6
CLE: Mack 19–75, Vardell 9–38, Metcalf 4–21, Hoard 2–7, Tomczak 1–1

Receiving
GB: Workman 8–84, Harris 4–54, Sharpe 4–48, Beach 2–22, Brooks 1–8, Sydney 1–7
CLE: Jackson 4–43, Metcalf 3–42, Galbraith 2–29, Tillman 1–18, Collins 1–11, Bavaro 1–9, Wolfley 1–6

Sunday, October 25
Browns 19, New England Patriots 17
Foxboro Stadium (32,219)
White jerseys/white pants

With some last-minute magic, the Browns pulled out their third straight victory on a wet, chilly day in New England and surged over the .500 mark in October for the first time in three years. In the early going, it appeared the Browns would coast to an easy victory over the 0–6 Patriots, as they moved the ball at will in the first half. But despite driving inside the New England 20 on their first three possessions, the Browns were forced to settle for three field goals and a 9–0 lead. The Cleveland offense was then stymied for much of the remainder of the game, and Matt Stover missed three field-goal attempts. Meanwhile, the Patriots scored a pair of touchdowns to take the lead and snap the Browns' defense's string at 14 consecutive quarters without allowing a touchdown. Trailing 17–9 early in the fourth as darkness fell, the Browns cut the margin to five points on a field goal set up by the first of three New England fumbles on consecutive possessions. The last was recovered by the Browns' Mike Johnson, who was dominant with 20 tackles and two sacks on the day, at the New England 40 with 3:54 to play. Seven plays later, the Browns faced fourth-and-two at the Patriots' 6 with 36 seconds remaining. Under pressure, Mike Tomczak looped a pass into the corner of the end zone for TE Scott Galbraith, who made a one-handed diving catch for the game-winning touchdown. It was just Galbraith's third catch of the season and would be the only touchdown he would score in his career with the Browns, but it was a memorable one.
Record: 4–3

	1	2	3	4		
Browns	6	3	0	10	=	19
Patriots	0	7	10	0	=	17

CLE-Stover 29-yd. FG
CLE-Stover 28-yd. FG
CLE-Stover 21-yd. FG
NE-Turner 19-yd. pass from Millen (Baumann kick)
NE-Coates 22-yd. pass from Millen (Baumann kick)
NE-Baumann 30-yd. FG
CLE-Stover 32-yd. FG
CLE-Galbraith 6-yd. pass from Tomczak (Stover kick)

Passing
CLE: Tomczak 14–29–186 1 TD 0 INT
NE: Millen 17–33–194 2 TD 0 INT

Rushing
CLE: Vardell 17–80, Mack 16–38, Metcalf 1–3, Tomczak 2–2
NE: Vaughn 3–34, Stephens 5–29, Russell 8–9, Turner 2–5

Receiving
CLE: Tillman 2–71, Jackson 3–30, Metcalf 3–29, Collins 2–20, Bavaro 1–15, Hoard 1–11, Galbraith 1–6, Mack 1–4
NE: Stanley 2–48, Timpson 3–41, Cook 7–39, Coates 3–35, Turner 2–31

Sunday, November 1
Cincinnati Bengals 30, Browns 10
Riverfront Stadium (54,765)
White jerseys/white pants

Completely outplayed in all phases of the game by the slumping Bengals, the Browns dropped back to .500 with their fifth straight loss at Riverfront Stadium. After kicking a field goal on its first drive, the Browns' offense was nonexistent for the remainder of the day, while the defense was picked apart by a Cincinnati team that had lost five straight games. The turning point came in the final seconds of the first half, when the Browns, trailing 14–3, reached the Bengals' 1 but were stopped short of the goal line on third and fourth down. Cincinnati then scored on the first possession of the second half to put the game out of reach. The Browns, who were held to 58 rushing yards, scored their lone touchdown on a leaping fourth-down catch by Michael Jackson in the final period.

Record: 4–4

	1	2	3	4		
Browns	3	0	0	7	=	10
Bengals	7	7	10	6	=	30

CLE-Stover 39-yd. FG
CIN-Thompson 1-yd. pass from Esiason (Breech kick)
CIN-Holman 4-yd. pass from Esiason (Breech kick)
CIN-McGee 24-yd. pass from Esiason (Breech kick)
CIN-Breech 26-yd. FG
CIN-Breech 21-yd. FG
CLE-Jackson 30-yd. pass from Tomczak (Stover kick)
CIN-Breech 32-yd. FG

Passing
CLE: Tomczak 16–28–252 1 TD 0 INT, Goebel 2–3–32 0 TD 0 INT
CIN: Esiason 13–24–192 3 TD 0 INT, Hollas 1–2–3 0 TD 0 INT

Rushing
CLE: Mack 11–30, Hoard 3–12, Vardell 5–11, Baldwin 1–5, Tomczak 3–1, Metcalf 5-(-1)
CIN: Green 17–58, Fenner 9–31, Ball 2–16, Esiason 2–0, Hollas 2–0

Receiving
CLE: Jackson 6–96, Tillman 2–65, Baldwin 2–30, Galbraith 1–28, Metcalf 2–23, Mack 2–22, Hoard 3–20,
CIN: McGee 3–70, Green 3–37, Pickens 2–34, Brennan 1–21, Riggs 2–20, Holman 2–12, Thompson 1–1

Sunday, November 8
Browns 24, Houston Oilers 14
Houston Astrodome (57,348)
White jerseys/white pants

In their most impressive game of the season, the Browns dominated the playoff-bound Oilers in the Astrodome with a suffocating defense and a resurgent offense. With the high-flying Houston attack limited to 55 total yards in the first half and forced to go three-and-out on seven consecutive possessions, the Browns, 11-point underdogs, jumped to a 10–0 halftime lead. Their early charge was highlighted by a 46-yard touchdown strike down the middle of the field from Mike Tomczak to RB Leroy Hoard in what would be his only score of the season after collecting 11 in 1991. In the final minute of the third quarter, Houston was threatening to creep back into the game, driving to the Cleveland 25. But after WR Ernest Givins caught a pass on fourth down, he was stripped of the ball by newly acquired Browns' DB Everson Walls, and fellow DB Stevon Moore scooped up the fumble and rumbled 73 yards for the backbreaking touchdown and a 17–0 Browns' lead on the second-longest fumble return in team history. The Browns put the icing on the cake with a 12-play, 74-yard drive capped with under four minutes left when Tomczak rolled out and hit Mark Bavaro, who maneuvered through the secondary for a 17-yard touchdown. Houston QB Warren Moon, who'd riddled the Browns in their recent meetings, was forced into one of the worst games of his career, throwing for just 70 yards in 25 attempts until he was pulled late in the third quarter. The Browns' fourth victory in five weeks pulled them within a game of first place in the division.

Record: 5–4

	1	2	3	4		
Browns	3	7	7	7	=	24
Oilers	0	0	0	14	=	14

CLE-Stover 44-yd. FG
CLE-Hoard 46-yd. pass from Tomczak (Stover kick)
CLE-Moore 73-yd. fumble return (Stover kick)
HOU-Slaughter 12-yd. pass from Carlson (Del Greco kick)
CLE-Bavaro 17-yd. pass from Tomczak (Stover kick)
HOU-Givins 18-yd. pass from Carlson (Del Greco kick)

Passing
CLE: Tomczak 17–26–219 2 TD 0 INT, Metcalf 0–1–0 0 TD 0 INT
HOU: Carlson 9–11–111 2 TD 1 INT, Moon 12–25–70 0 TD 0 INT

Rushing
CLE: Mack 13–39, Vardell 5–31, Metcalf 7–23, Baldwin 2-(-1), Tomczak 3-(-6)
HOU: White 14–76, Carlson 1–8, Moon 2–6, Givins 1–2

Receiving
CLE: Hoard 2–68, Bavaro 4–57, Tillman 2–29, Metcalf 3–25, Jackson 3–19, Vardell 1–11, Mack 2–10
HOU: Givins 4–50, Duncan 5–45, Slaughter 5–31, Harris 2–28, White 3–17, Brown 1–5, Jeffires 1–5

Sunday, November 15
San Diego Chargers 14, Browns 13
Cleveland Stadium (58,396)
Brown jerseys/white pants

Despite notching a season-high in total yardage on offense on a snowy afternoon by the lake, the Browns were unable to hold off the Chargers after rallying from behind in the fourth quarter and dropped back to the .500 mark. After trailing most of the game, the Browns took a lead in the first minute of the fourth quarter on a Mike Tomczak-to-Michael Jackson touchdown pass that capped a 99-yard drive. After recovering a San Diego fumble, Cleveland extended the lead to 13–7 with five minutes remaining. But three minutes later, Chargers' QB Stan Humphries hit WR Anthony Miller for a 45-yard touchdown bomb on third-and-eight to give the Chargers back the lead. The Browns had one final chance, driving into San Diego territory in the final minute before Eric Metcalf fumbled after a reception and the Chargers recovered. Tomczak had his best game as a Brown, throwing for 322 yards as Cleveland tallied 385 total. His primary target was oft-injured WR Lawyer Tillman, who entered the contest with just seven catches for 183 yards on the season, but caught eight for 148 for the game in what would be the only 100-yard game of his career.
Record: 5–5

	1	2	3	4		
Chargers	7	0	0	7	=	14
Browns	0	3	0	10	=	13

SD-Jefferson 26-yd. pass from Humphries (Carney kick)
CLE-Stover 36-yd. FG
CLE-Jackson 24-yd. pass from Tomczak (Stover kick)
CLE-Stover 28-yd. FG
SD-Miller 45-yd. pass from Humphries (Carney kick)

Passing
SD: Humphries 19–32–234 2 TD 1 INT
CLE: Tomczak 18–32–322 1 TD 2 INT

Rushing
SD: Butts 19–61, Harmon 3–19, Bieniemy 3–9, Kidd 1–0, Humphries 1-(-1)
CLE: Mack 17–35, Metcalf 6–21, Jackson 1–21, Tomczak 3–11, Vardell 1-(-1)

Receiving
SD: Miller 7–110, Harmon 8–60, Jefferson 1–26, Walker 1–16, Butts 1–12, Lewis 1–10
CLE: Tillman 8–148, Jackson 4–84, Metcalf 3–33, Bavaro 2–32, Hoard 1–25

Sunday, November 22
Minnesota Vikings 17, Browns 13
Hubert H. Humphrey Metrodome (53,323)
White jerseys/white pants

Despite dominating the contest for three quarters, the Browns watched what would have been an inspiring victory slip through their fingers in the final 15 minutes against the eventual NFC Central champions. Controlling the game on both sides of the ball, the Browns took a 13–0 halftime lead and still were in command going into the fourth, leading 13–3. But despite leading, Bill Belichick decided to pull QB Mike Tomczak after he threw interceptions on two consecutive possessions. Though the turnovers didn't lead to points, Belichick opted to send in Todd Philcox, who hadn't played since Week Three. Fifteen seconds after the Vikings cut the lead to three points, Philcox's first pass in two months went off the hands of Mark Bavaro and right to Minnesota DB Audray McMillan for his third interception of the day. McMillan returned this one 25 yards for what would be the winning touchdown with just over nine minutes to play. The Browns failed to cross their own 35 on their final two possessions and fell to defeat despite holding Minnesota to a meager 141 total yards of offense.
Record: 5–6

	1	2	3	4		
Browns	10	3	0	0	=	13
Vikings	0	0	3	14	=	17

CLE-Stover 19-yd. FG
CLE-Mack 1-yd. run (Stover kick)
CLE-Stover 30-yd. FG
MIN-Reveiz 40-yd. FG
MIN-Johnson 3-yd. pass from Salisbury (Reveiz kick)
MIN-McMillan 25-yd. interception return (Reveiz kick)

Passing
CLE: Tomczak 15–24–169 0 TD 2 INT, Philcox 3–7–17 0 TD 1 INT
MIN: Salisbury 4–12–30 1 TD 0 INT, Gannon 5–12–26 0 TD 2 INT

Rushing
CLE: Mack 14–47, Vardell 11–29, Tomczak 4–12, Hoard 3–8, Metcalf 1-(-1)
MIN: Allen 17–45, Craig 6–36, Henderson 3–9, Gannon 2–3, Salisbury 4-(-4)

Receiving
CLE: Tillman 3–71, Metcalf 5–36, Hoard 3–31, Jackson 4–25, Bavaro 3–23

MIN: Jordan 2–26, Henderson 1–19, Carter 2–12, Johnson 2–8, Allen 1–1, Craig 1-(-10)

Sunday, November 29
Browns 27, Chicago Bears 14
Cleveland Stadium (73,578)
Brown jerseys/white pants

After missing nine games with a broken ankle, Bernie Kosar returned to the Browns' lineup, but it was the Cleveland defense and special teams that delivered a much-needed victory over the struggling Bears. The tone for the day was set on Chicago's opening possession as the Bears drove to the Browns' 10, but then QB Peter Tom Willis was intercepted by Cleveland LB David Brandon at the 8, and Brandon raced untouched into the end zone (tying a team record for the longest interception return) to turn the tide and give the Browns a 7–0 lead that swelled to 13–0 late in the first half. After the Bears cut the lead to six, Eric Metcalf sliced through the Bears' coverage on a 75-yard punt return for a touchdown—the first of his career—late in the third period. The Bears answered with a touchdown on their next offensive play, but Brandon came up big again, recovering a fumble at the Chicago 28 that led to another Browns' touchdown on a short Kevin Mack run four minutes into the final period. The Bears couldn't cross midfield on their final three possessions, and the Browns secured their sixth victory of the season despite managing only 178 yards of offense, though 131 of it came on the ground. The Cleveland defense stole the show, picking up seven sacks and four turnovers.

Record: 6–6

	1	2	3	4		
Bears	0	7	7	0	=	14
Browns	7	6	7	7	=	27

CLE-Brandon 92-yd. interception return (Stover kick)
CLE-Stover 27-yd. FG
CLE-Stover 43-yd. FG
CHI-Anderson 30-yd. pass from Willis (Butler kick)
CLE-Metcalf 75-yd. punt return (Stover kick)
CHI-Waddle 68-yd. pass from Willis (Butler kick)
CLE-Mack 1-yd. run (Stover kick)

Passing
CHI: Willis 19–26–285 2 TD 2 INT, Furrer 0–2–0 0 TD 0 INT
CLE: Kosar 8–17–59 0 TD 0 INT

Rushing
CHI: Anderson 8–34, Muster 5–25, Lewis 4–6, Green 1–6, Willis 1–2
CLE: Mack 20–53, Metcalf 5–45, Vardell 6–15, Tillman 1–15, Baldwin 1–2, Hoard 1–2, Kosar 1-(-1)

Receiving
CHI: Waddle 4–100, Muster 5–64, Anderson 4–49, Davis 2–26, Jennings 1–22, Green 2–14, Lewis 1–10
CLE: Tillman 2–29, Jackson 3–15, Holohan 1–9, Mack 1–3, Metcalf 1–3

Sunday, December 6
Browns 37, Cincinnati Bengals 21
Cleveland Stadium (68,368)
Brown jerseys/white pants

Notching their highest point total in over three years, the Browns avenged their defeat in Cincinnati with a romp over the Bengals on a frosty day in Cleveland. Leading by six midway through the third quarter, the Browns exploded for three touchdowns in 95 seconds to blow the game open. First, Eric Metcalf turned a short slant pattern into an artistic 35-yard touchdown, weaving through the Cincinnati secondary with graceful ease. It was the highlight of a magnificent day for Metcalf, who would finish with 201 total yards (53 rushing, 73 receiving, 75 on punt returns). After forcing a Cincinnati punt, the Browns struck again when Bernie Kosar lofted a 45-yard touchdown pass to Michael Jackson to extend the lead to 20. Seconds later, Mike Johnson recovered a fumble by Cincinnati rookie QB David Klingler in the end zone to give the Browns an insurmountable 34–7 lead. Kosar's sharpness returned in record-setting fashion as he set a new team mark for completion percentage in a single game, connecting on 19 of 23 attempts (82.6 percent) as the Browns rolled up 381 total yards. The victory reignited the team's playoff hopes and assured the Browns would improve their record from the season before, but it also represented their final triumph of the season.

Record: 7–6

	1	2	3	4		
Bengals	0	7	7	7	=	21
Browns	10	3	21	3	=	37

CLE-Mack 7-yd. run (Stover kick)
CLE-Stover 34-yd. FG
CIN-Holman 26-yd. pass from Klingler (Breech kick)

CLE-Stover 30-yd. FG
CLE-Metcalf 35-yd. pass from Kosar (Stover kick)
CLE-Jackson 45-yd. pass from Kosar (Stover kick)
CLE-Johnson recovers fumble in end zone (Stover kick)
CIN-Query 10-yd. pass from Klingler (Breech kick)
CLE-Stover 27-yd. FG
CIN-Query 24-yd. pass from Hollas (Breech kick)

Passing
CIN: Klingler 12–25–134 2 TD 0 INT, Hollas 5–8–64 1 TD 0 INT
CLE: Kosar 19–23–239 2 TD 0 INT

Rushing
CIN: Green 14–38, Fenner 3–23, Klingler 1–1
CLE: Metcalf 9–53, Mack 10–40, Vardell 4–27, Baldwin 6–25, Hoard 1–4, Tillman 1–0

Receiving
CIN: Query 6–85, Holman 2–34, Thompson 2–24, McGee 2–22, Pickens 2–20, Green 3–13
CLE: Metcalf 6–73, Jackson 3–64, Bavaro 2–38, Vardell 4–37, Tillman 2–17, Hoard 1–7, Mack 1–3

Sunday, December 13
Detroit Lions 24, Browns 14
Pontiac Silverdome (65,970)
White jerseys/white pants

Just as quickly as the Browns' playoff hopes were revived, they dampened as Cleveland was manhandled by the 3–10 Lions, who were playing without starting QB Rodney Peete yet still managed to take a 21–0 lead into the fourth quarter. Though the Browns' defense contained All-Pro Detroit RB Barry Sanders, limiting him to 87 yards on 30 carries, they had no answer for Andre Ware, who made his second career start at QB and completed 10 of 14 passes, two for touchdowns, while rushing for 68 yards on just five carries. The Lions rushed for 155 yards as a team and took control of the game in the third quarter. A long drive ended with a Sanders scoring run—the first rushing touchdown the Browns had allowed in 46 quarters—followed by a blocked punt that led to another score. Bernie Kosar threw a pair of touchdown passes in the fourth quarter—including a 69-yard strike in which Michael Jackson made a diving catch at the Detroit 30, then got up and ran into the end zone—but it was too little and too late to overcome three Cleveland turnovers and a season-high 11 penalties.
Record: 7–7

	1	2	3	4		
Browns	0	0	0	14	=	14
Lions	7	0	14	3	=	24

DET-Perriman 13-yd. pass from Ware (Hanson kick)
DET-Sanders 14-yd. run (Hanson kick)
DET-Barrett 19-yd. pass from Ware (Hanson kick)
CLE-Jackson 69-yd. pass from Kosar (Stover kick)
DET-Hanson 46-yd. FG
CLE-Metcalf 5-yd. pass from Kosar (Stover kick)

Passing
CLE: Kosar 20–28–276 2 TD 2 INT
DET: Ware 10–14–138 2 TD 0 INT

Rushing
CLE: Mack 6–27, Hoard 4–20, Metcalf 4–13, Kosar 1–1, Vardell 1–0
DET: Sanders 30–87, Ware 5–68

Receiving
CLE: Jackson 2–80, Holohan 6–69, Hoard 4–40, Tillman 1–30, Mack 1–23, Vardell 3–15, Bavaro 2–14, Metcalf 1–5
DET: Moore 2–52, Perriman 3–34, Barrett 1–19, Sanders 2–18, Farr 2–15

Sunday, December 20
Houston Oilers 17, Browns 14
Cleveland Stadium (59,898)
Brown jerseys/white pants

For 53 minutes, the Browns dominated the Oilers just as they had in their first meeting in Houston the month before. But in the last seven, everything fell apart, and the Browns watched an 11-point lead evaporate and suffered another heartbreaking defeat, marking the fourth time in 1992 the Browns lost a game they'd led in the fourth quarter. With the Cleveland defense once again stymieing Houston's up-tempo attack, the Browns built a 14–3 lead early in the third quarter on two Bernie Kosar touchdown passes to unlikely targets—one on a play-action toss to special-teams veteran Ron Wolfley, his first career receiving touchdown, and the other to DL James Jones, who was in the game as a blocking back, but ran a pass pattern from the Houston 1. After the Oilers were unable to score after four cracks at the end zone from the Cleveland 1 early in the fourth quarter, followed by a Houston turnover on the ensuing series, it appeared the Browns would cruise to their eighth win. But they couldn't cash in, and the Oilers cut the margin to 14–10 with three minutes left, then forced a quick Cleveland punt and regained the football at their own 26 with 1:51 to play. After a sack by Clay Matthews (giving him 70 for his career, a new team record, and the Browns' sixth of the afternoon) set up second-and-25, the Browns once again appeared in the clear. But the Oilers then pulled off the play of the day—a 65-yard screen pass to RB Lorenzo White that caught the Browns completely off guard and gave the Oilers a first down at the Cleveland 12. A play later, QB Cody Carlson hit wide-open Ernest Givins for the game-winning touchdown with 34 seconds to play, officially eliminating the Browns from playoff contention for the third consecutive year.

Record: 7–8

	1	2	3	4		
Oilers	0	3	0	14	=	17
Browns	7	0	7	0	=	14

CLE-Wolfley 2-yd. pass from Kosar (Stover kick)
HOU-Del Greco 47-yd. FG
CLE-Jones 1-yd. pass from Kosar (Stover kick)
HOU-Duncan 2-yd. pass from Carlson (Del Greco kick)
HOU-Givins 3-yd. pass from Carlson (Del Greco kick)

Passing
HOU: Carlson 19–34–248 2 TD 2 INT
CLE: Kosar 17–26–110 2 TD 3 INT

Rushing
HOU: White 16–70, Carlson 6–26, Slaughter 1–8
CLE: Mack 21–95, Hoard 10–46, Metcalf 2–4

Receiving
HOU: White 6–105, Slaughter 3–44, Duncan 4–41, Givins 4–38, Jeffires 2–20
CLE: Metcalf 3–35, Holohan 3–33, Tillman 2–20, Hoard 2–15, Smith 1–15, Mack 3–14, Jackson 1–5, Wolfley 1–2, Jones 1–1

Sunday, December 27
Pittsburgh Steelers 23, Browns 13
Three Rivers Stadium (53,776)
White jerseys/white pants

A disjointed season came to an appropriate conclusion as the Browns dug themselves into a hole that an inspired second-half performance couldn't pull them out of. Falling behind 17–3 after allowing 10 points in the final 30 seconds of the first half, the Browns also lost Bernie Kosar, who reinjured the same ankle that had sidelined him for half the season. With Mike Tomczak once again taking the controls on offense, the Browns struck on the second play of the second half with a 38-yard bomb from Tomczak to Michael Jackson to cut the deficit in half. The teams exchanged field goals before the Steelers, who'd already clinched the AFC Central title, iced the game with a 17-play, nine-minute drive that ended with a field goal to make it 23–13 with 2:35 left. A final Browns' drive ended when Tomczak was sacked and fumbled at the Pittsburgh 4 with a minute left, mirroring another thwarted scoring drive late in the third quarter when Tomczak threw an interception from the Steelers' 13. Pittsburgh RB Barry Foster notched his twelfth 100-yard rushing game of the year and the first the Cleveland defense had allowed all season. The Browns' defense also collected five sacks to set a new team record with 48 on the season. The frustrating defeat capped a third straight losing campaign for the Browns—the longest string in team history—and marked the second straight year they'd lost their last three games.

Record: 7–9

	1	2	3	4		
Browns	0	3	7	3	=	13
Steelers	7	10	3	3	=	23

PIT-Foster 7-yd. run (Anderson kick)
CLE-Stover 22-yd. FG
PIT-Jorden 2-yd. pass from Brister (Anderson kick)
PIT-Anderson 26-yd. FG
CLE-Jackson 38-yd. pass from Tomczak (Stover kick)
PIT-Anderson 29-yd. FG
CLE-Stover 22-yd. FG
PIT-Anderson 28-yd. FG

Passing
CLE: Tomczak 8–15–141 1 TD 1 INT, Kosar 5–7–41 0 TD 0 INT
PIT: Brister 18–25–223 1 TD 0 INT

Rushing
CLE: Hoard 7–55, Mack 10–32, Metcalf 7–25, Kosar 2–4, Tomczak 1–4
PIT: Foster 26–103, Stone 1–3, Hoge 1–2, Thompson 1-(-1), Brister 1-(-2)

Receiving
CLE: Jackson 4–85, Bavaro 4–61, Smith 2–28, Hoard 1–11, Metcalf 1–4, Mack 1-(-7)
PIT: Stone 5–61, Mills 3–43, Thompson 2–33, Hoge 2–31, Foster 2–29, Graham 3–24, Jorden 1–2

1993

Rushing
CIN: Fenner 13–41, Klingler 3–8, Miles 3–6, Ball 1–0
CLE: Vardell 16–60, Hoard 8–27, Metcalf 4–14, Kosar 1-(-1), Baldwin 1-(-4)

Receiving
CIN: Query 3–80, Fenner 9–64, McGee 2–39, Miles 2–13, Thompson 2–9, Pickens 1–5, Ball 1–4
CLE: Carrier 3–79, Metcalf 9–60, Dyson 3–33, Kinchen 1–8, Vardell 2–2

Sunday, September 5
Browns 27, Cincinnati Bengals 14
Cleveland Stadium (75,508)
Brown jerseys/white pants

After quickly falling behind by two touchdowns, the Browns dominated the final three quarters to capture their first opening-day win in three years. Down 14–0 after 12 minutes of play, the Browns tied the game with a pair of second-quarter touchdowns. The first came on a reception by WR Michael Jackson (who, for the only time in his career, adopted the name Michael Dyson) and the second a short run by second-year RB "Touchdown" Tommy Vardell, his first career score. Cleveland took the lead on a pair of third-quarter field goals, then put the game away a minute into the fourth quarter when DB Everson Walls sacked and stripped the football from Cincinnati QB David Klingler and Browns' DB Stevon Moore scooped it up and returned it 22 yards for a touchdown. It was one of six sacks by the Cleveland defense, which added an impressive goal-line stand at the Cleveland 1 midway through the fourth. The game was the two hundred-seventeenth of Clay Matthews's career, breaking Lou Groza's team record of 216.
Record: 1–0

	1	2	3	4		
Bengals	14	0	0	0	=	14
Browns	0	14	6	7	=	27

CIN-Miles 4-yd. run (Pelfrey kick)
CIN-Pickens 5-yd. pass from Klingler (Pelfrey kick)
CLE-Dyson 13-yd. pass from Kosar (Stover kick)
CLE-Vardell 1-yd. run (Stover kick)
CLE-Stover 28-yd. FG
CLE-Stover 34-yd. FG
CLE-Moore 22-yd. fumble return (Stover kick)

Passing
CIN: Klingler 20–28–214 1 TD 2 INT
CLE: Kosar 18–30–182 1 TD 0 INT

Monday, September 13
Browns 23, San Francisco 49ers 13
Cleveland Stadium (78,218)
Brown jerseys/white pants

In one of the most satisfying victories in recent memory, the Browns put forth an inspired performance to knock off the mighty 49ers before a packed house and a *Monday Night Football* audience. San Francisco, which had won nine straight regular-season games and entered the contest as six-and-a-half-point favorites, took an early 6–3 lead, but the Browns took control of the game in a dominating second quarter. Cleveland DL James Jones scored his third career touchdown on a surprise handoff from the San Francisco 1 to push the Browns ahead, 10–6. Then after the 49ers tied the game at 13, the Browns took the lead for good on a dazzling 30-yard touchdown strike from Bernie Kosar to Michael Jackson (back from "Dyson" the week before) with 35 seconds left in the half. Forcing four turnovers, including three interceptions of reigning NFL MVP Steve Young, the Cleveland defense thwarted the powerful 49ers' offense in the second half, and their 13 points were the fewest they'd scored in a game in nearly two years. Players drenched Bill Belichick with a bucket of water as the game ended in celebration of what appeared to be a hallmark victory for the third-year coach.
Record: 2–0

	1	2	3	4		
49ers	6	7	0	0	=	13
Browns	3	17	3	0	=	23

SF-Cofer 46-yd. FG
CLE-Stover 47-yd. FG
SF-Cofer 28-yd. FG
CLE-Jones 1-yd. run (Stover kick)
CLE-Stover 41-yd. FG
SF-Logan 4-yd. run (Cofer kick)
CLE-Jackson 30-yd. pass from Kosar (Stover kick)
CLE-Stover 33-yd. FG

Passing
SF: Young 19–33–274 0 TD 3 INT
CLE: Kosar 17–32–186 1 TD 0 INT

Rushing
SF: Watters 13–83, Logan 6–33, Young 5–11, Lee 1–3, Wilmsmeyer 1–0
CLE: Metcalf 12–71, Vardell 13–41, Kosar 3–8, Hoard 3–6, Jackson 1–1

Receiving
SF: Rice 6–82, Taylor 4–71, Watters 4–47, Jones 2–35, Logan 2–30, Williams 1–9
CLE: Jackson 5–105, Hoard 3–25, Carrier 4–24, Metcalf 4–23, Kinchen 1–9

Sunday, September 19
Browns 19, Los Angeles Raiders 16
Los Angeles Memorial Coliseum (48,617)
White jerseys/white pants

In one of the most stunning comebacks in team history, the Browns rallied from a 16–3 deficit in the final five minutes to stun the Raiders with a dramatic touchdown in the final seconds and move to 3–0 for the first time in 14 years. The Browns' offense, utterly miserable for the first 55 minutes, came alive with time running out under the direction of backup QB Vinny Testaverde, who replaced struggling Bernie Kosar early in the fourth quarter. Testaverde capped a long drive with a touchdown strike to WR Lawyer Tillman with 2:26 to play. After the Raiders were pinned deep in their own territory, they took an intentional safety to make it 16–12 with just over 90 seconds remaining. A 37-yard return on the free kick by Cleveland RB Eric Metcalf set the Browns up at midfield, and Testaverde steered them to the Raiders' 1 with six seconds left. Out of time outs and with the game riding on one play, the Browns crossed up the Raiders with a pitch to Metcalf, who sprinted untouched into the end zone to cap the comeback. Lost in the heroics was a dominating performance by the Cleveland defense, which held the Raiders to just 156 total yards and only 16 points despite four turnovers by the Browns' offense. Tommy Vardell became the first Browns' RB to top 100 yards in a game in nearly five years as he collected 104 on just 14 carries.
Record: 3–0

	1	2	3	4		
Browns	0	0	0	19	=	19
Raiders	10	3	0	3	=	16

LA-Glover 2-yd. pass from Hostetler (Jaeger kick)
LA-Jaeger 24-yd. FG
LA-Jaeger 27-yd. FG
CLE-Stover 32-yd. FG
LA-Jaeger 53-yd. FG
CLE-Tillman 12-yd. pass from Testaverde (Stover kick)
CLE-Safety: Gossett ran out of end zone
CLE-Metcalf 1-yd. run (Stover kick)

Passing
CLE: Testaverde 10–22–159 1 TD 1 INT, Kosar 8–17–71 0 TD 3 INT
LA: Hostetler 11–25–94 1 TD 0 INT, Evans 2–2–30 0 TD 0 INT

Rushing
CLE: Vardell 14–104, Testaverde 2–15, Kosar 2–0, Metcalf 7-(-2), Hoard 2-(-4)
LA: Robinson 18–59, Montgomery 4–20, Smith 2–2, Gossett 1-(-10)

Receiving
CLE: Carrier 5–73, Tillman 3–45, Hoard 3–27, Metcalf 2–26, Vardell 2–22, Kinchen 2–19, Jackson 1–18
LA: Smith 4–42, Wright 1–26, Gault 3–25, Robinson 3–15, Horton 1–14, Glover 1–2

Sunday, September 26
Indianapolis Colts 23, Browns 10
Hoosier Dome (59,654)
White jerseys/white pants

Vinny Testaverde was unable to pull off a miracle comeback for the second straight week as the Browns couldn't overcome a lethargic performance—defined by five sacks allowed and 13 penalties—and lost for the first time in 1993. Inserted to start the second half with the Browns trailing 6–0, Testaverde led them to the go-ahead touchdown, then to a fourth-quarter field goal to put the Browns up 10–9. Indianapolis took the lead back with three minutes to play, then Testaverde threw a costly interception at midfield a minute later. The Browns regained possession deep in their own territory with just over a minute remaining, but Testaverde fumbled after being sacked, and Colts' LB Jeff Herrod recovered for the game-clinching touchdown.
Record: 3–1

	1	2	3	4		
Browns	0	0	7	3	=	10
Colts	0	6	3	14	=	23

IND-Biasucci 27-yd. FG
IND-Biasucci 19-yd. FG
CLE-Kinchen 10-yd. pass from Testaverde (Stover kick)
IND-Biasucci 26-yd. FG
CLE-Stover 32-yd. FG
IND-Johnson 6-yd. run (Biasucci kick)
IND-Herrod recovered fumble in end zone (Biasucci kick)

Passing
CLE: Testaverde 9–16–127 1 TD 1 INT, Kosar 4–8–53 0 TD 0 INT
IND: Trudeau 22–38–260 0 TD 0 INT

Rushing
CLE: Vardell 11–40, Metcalf 8–23, Carrier 1–13, Testaverde 1–13, Hoard 1–6, Kosar 2–5
IND: Potts 17–64, Johnson 9–29, Verdin 1–6, Toner 1–0, Culver 2-(-1), Trudeau 2-(-1)

Receiving
CLE: Jackson 4–49, Carrier 1–46, Hoard 3–37, Tillman 1–13, Vardell 1–13, Metcalf 1–12, Kinchen 1–10
IND: Hester 7–110, Johnson 8–60, Langhorne 3–47, Cash 1–16, Cox 1–16, Potts 2–11

Sunday, October 10
Miami Dolphins 24, Browns 14
Cleveland Stadium (78,138)
Brown jerseys/white pants

For the third straight game, the Browns' offense was miserable, and Bernie Kosar was replaced by Vinny Testaverde, who was unable to rally the Browns from another disappointing defeat. The Browns started strong, marching 74 yards on their opening drive and taking a 7–0 lead on a Kosar touchdown pass to Michael Jackson, but they struggled for the remainder of the half. The Dolphins, despite losing QB Dan Marino to a season-ending Achilles tendon tear in the first half, then took control of the game. But they allowed the Browns to hang around when replacement QB Scott Mitchell was picked off by Cleveland DB Najee Mustafaa, who returned it a team-record 97 yards to put the Browns up 14–10 in the final minute of the half. Miami took the lead for good with a pair of Mitchell touchdown passes in the third quarter, and Testaverde was unable to bring the Browns back. They missed two golden scoring opportunities in the fourth quarter when Matt Stover hooked a short field goal, and a Testaverde pass into the end zone was tipped and intercepted with just under two minutes to play. Eric Metcalf was one of the lone bright spots, picking up 158 total yards, but his contributions were all but wiped out as the Browns allowed six sacks and managed just over 200 total yards for the day. Ironically, following the game, Testaverde was named the Browns' starting QB, less than five days after Kosar signed a contract extension to keep him in Cleveland through 1999.
Record: 3–2

	1	2	3	4		
Dolphins	0	10	14	0	=	24
Browns	7	7	0	0	=	14

CLE-Jackson 14-yd. pass from Kosar (Stover kick)
MIA-Stoyanovich 52-yd. FG
MIA-Ingram 13-yd. pass from Marino (Stoyanovich kick)
CLE-Mustafaa 97-yd. interception return (Stover kick)
MIA-Martin 19-yd. pass from Mitchell (Stoyanovich kick)
MIA-Jackson 3-yd. pass from Mitchell (Stoyanovich kick)

Passing
MIA: Marino 14–19–161 1 TD 0 INT, Mitchell 10–16–118 2 TD 1 INT
CLE: Kosar 15–19–82 1 TD 0 INT, Testaverde 6–13–44 0 TD 1 INT, Jackson 1–1–25 0 TD 0 INT

Rushing
MIA: Byars 8–26, Mitchell 3–14, Kirby 14–12, Higgs 5–12, Martin 1–6
CLE: Testaverde 3–37, Metcalf 7–36, Vardell 6–17

Receiving
MIA: Kirby 7–61, Byars 5–51, Fryar 2–47, Ingram 4–39, Martin 2–36, McDuffie 2–27, Jackson 2–18
CLE: Metcalf 9–66, Jackson 4–34, Vardell 5–29, Kinchen 2–13, Tillman 1–10, Carrier 1-(-1)

Sunday, October 17
Browns 28, Cincinnati Bengals 17
Riverfront Stadium (55,647)
Brown jerseys/white pants

In his first start for the Browns, Vinny Testaverde threw three first-half touchdown passes to build a commanding lead, then the Cleveland defense kept the struggling Bengals at bay for the remainder of the afternoon as the Browns picked up their first victory in Cincinnati in six years. The tone was set on the first possession as the Browns drove 80 yards for a touchdown, a 28-yard swing pass to Tommy Vardell, who would add 98 rushing yards on the day. A sack by LB Clay Matthews resulted in a fumble recovered by Browns' DT Michael Dean Perry and returned to the Cincinnati 1, where Testaverde made it 21–0 with his third scoring strike moments later. After the Bengals narrowed the lead to 11 points early in the third quarter, the Browns put the game away with another long drive, capped by a 15-yard touchdown run on a reverse by WR Mark Carrier. The Bengals, who dropped to 0–6, were held to 194 total yards and permitted four sacks, while the Cleveland offense rolled up a season-high 183 yards on the ground. The victory kept the Browns tied for first with Pittsburgh and set up a memorable showdown the following week in Cleveland.

Record: 4–2

	1	2	3	4		
Browns	7	14	0	7	=	28
Bengals	0	7	3	7	=	17

CLE-Vardell 28-yd. pass from Testaverde (Stover kick)
CLE-Baldwin 5-yd. pass from Testaverde (Stover kick)
CLE-Kinchen 1-yd. pass from Testaverde (Stover kick)
CIN-Query 11-yd. pass from Schroeder (Pelfrey kick)
CIN-Pelfrey 49-yd. FG
CLE-Carrier 15-yd. run (Stover kick)
CIN-Pickens 24-yd. pass from Schroeder (Pelfrey kick)

Passing
CLE: Testaverde 11–24–127 3 TD 1 INT
CIN: Schroeder 19–37–172 2 TD 0 INT, Klingler 3–9–25 0 TD 0 INT

Rushing
CLE: Vardell 25–98, Baldwin 6–35, Metcalf 3–33, Carrier 1–15, Testaverde 7–2
CIN: Green 8–12, Fenner 4–11, Klingler 1–9, Schroeder 1–2

Receiving
CLE: Carrier 3–55, Vardell 1–28, Hoard 2–24, Wolfley 2–7, Jackson 1–7, Baldwin 1–5, Kinchen 1–1
CIN: Pickens 6–67, Carroll 2–40, Query 4–32, Thompson 4–27, Fenner 3–17, McGee 2–14, Green 1–0

Sunday, October 24
Browns 28, Pittsburgh Steelers 23
Cleveland Stadium (78,118)
Brown jerseys/white pants

In one of their most thrilling victories of the decade, the Browns rallied from behind thanks to a remarkable performance by Eric Metcalf, who returned a pair of punts for touchdowns, including the game-winner with two minutes remaining. The Browns jumped to a 14–0 lead in the second quarter after a long touchdown reception by Michael Jackson and Metcalf's first runback—this one a team-record 91 yards. But the Steelers bounced back to take the lead in the third quarter, and the game seesawed through the second half. After Pittsburgh went up 23–21 midway through the fourth quarter in the falling darkness, Vinny Testaverde was knocked out of the game with a separated shoulder, and Bernie Kosar returned to action. It appeared Kosar would get a chance to win the game when the Browns forced a punt with just over two minutes left, but Metcalf broke free along the sideline to complete a 75-yard touchdown with 2:05 to play. Victory was secured a minute later when Stevon Moore stripped the football from Steelers' RB Dwight Stone and Cleveland LB Mike Caldwell recovered at midfield to give the Browns the victory and sole possession of first place. Metcalf finished with 237 total yards to overcome the Steelers' massive advantage in total yards (444 to 245) and time of possession. The victory marked the Browns' eleventh in their previous 12 encounters with the Steelers in Cleveland—but their last for seven years.

Record: 5–2

	1	2	3	4		
Steelers	0	14	6	3	=	23
Browns	0	14	7	7	=	28

CLE-Jackson 62-yd. pass from Testaverde (Stover kick)
CLE-Metcalf 91-yd. punt return (Stover kick)
PIT-Foster 4-yd. run (Anderson kick)
PIT-Foster 1-yd. run (Anderson kick)
PIT-Anderson 30-yd. FG
CLE-Wolfley 4-yd. pass from Testaverde (Stover kick)
PIT-Anderson 46-yd. FG
PIT-Anderson 30-yd. FG
CLE-Metcalf 75-yd. punt return (Stover kick)

Passing
PIT: O'Donnell 25–39–355 0 TD 1 INT
CLE: Testaverde 9–14–167 2 TD 0 INT, Kosar 1–2–7 0 TD 0 INT

Rushing
PIT: Foster 28–87, O'Donnell 2–11, Hoge 1–1, Mills 2-(-7)
CLE: Metcalf 7–53, Vardell 7–19, Baldwin 2–13, Testaverde 1–9, Hoard 1–3, Kosar 4–1

Receiving
PIT: Green 6–108, Graham 5–89, Stone 5–54, Hoge 4–43, Foster 3–40, Thigpen 1–13, Mills 1–8
CLE: Jackson 2–106, Hoard 2–20, Metcalf 3–18, Smith 1–17, Wolfley 2–13

Sunday, November 7
Denver Broncos 29, Browns 14
Cleveland Stadium (77,818)
Brown jerseys/white pants

In what would be the turning point of the season (and perhaps the franchise as a whole), the euphoria of the week before evaporated quickly as the Browns were utterly dominated by Denver QB John Elway and the Broncos and tumbled back into a tie for first with Pittsburgh. With their offense once again nonexistent, the Browns watched Denver score 16 second-quarter points to take command of the game, including a safety on a blocked punt out of the end zone. The Broncos controlled the line of scrimmage, rushing for 160 yards, the most allowed by the Browns all season, while Elway threw three touchdown passes. Making what turned out to be his final start with the Browns, Bernie Kosar was sacked six times but went out on a fitting note, drawing up a makeshift play in the dirt in the final seconds that became a 38-yard touchdown pass to Michael Jackson. The next day, in one of the most controversial chapters in team history, the Browns released Kosar and named third-string QB Todd Philcox the starter for the next month until Vinny Testaverde could return from his shoulder injury.
Record: 5–3

	1	2	3	4		
Broncos	0	16	7	6	=	29
Browns	0	0	7	7	=	14

DEN-Milburn 2-yd. pass from Elway (Elam kick)
DEN-Safety: Rivers blocked punt out of end zone
DEN-Russell 38-yd. pass from Elway (Elam kick)
CLE-Jackson 8-yd. pass from Kosar (Stover kick)
DEN-Sharpe 33-yd. pass from Elway (Elam kick)
DEN-Elam 22-yd. FG
DEN-Elam 38-yd. FG
CLE-Jackson 38-yd. pass from Kosar (Stover kick)

Passing
DEN: Elway 17–23–244 3 TD 0 INT
CLE: Kosar 16–30–226 2 TD 0 INT

Rushing
DEN: Bernstine 21–82, Delpino 10–39, Milburn 5–26, Rivers 3–7, Elway 2–7, Maddox 1-(-1)
CLE: Hoard 5–51, Metcalf 4–10, Vardell 3–8, Kosar 2–6

Receiving
DEN: V. Johnson 4–85, Sharpe 4–55, Russell 1–38, Delpino 1–25, Bernstine 4–22, R. Johnson 1–11, Milburn 2–8
CLE: Hoard 8–87, Jackson 4–86, Metcalf 3–41, Carrier 1–12

Sunday, November 14
Seattle Seahawks 22, Browns 5
Seattle Kingdome (54,622)
White jerseys/white pants

In an episode of symbolism impossible to ignore, new QB Todd Philcox fumbled on the very first play of the game, and it was returned for a Seattle touchdown, setting the tone for another miserable day for the Browns. The overmatched Philcox was miserable, throwing for just 85 yards with two interceptions and was pinned in the end zone for a fourth-quarter safety. Committing five of their seven turnovers in the first half, the Browns still trailed by only two going into the third quarter, thanks to a strong running game that rolled up 175 yards on the ground. But, with the beleaguered defense wearing down in the second half, the Browns allowed 15 unanswered points. It also marked the only time in team history the Browns finished a game scoring five points. Meanwhile, in Dallas, Bernie Kosar came off the bench to throw for 199 yards and a touchdown, leading the defending world-champion Cowboys—who'd signed Kosar earlier in the week—to a win over Phoenix.
Record: 5–4

	1	2	3	4		
Browns	2	3	0	0	=	5
Seahawks	7	0	7	8	=	22

SEA-Blackmon 5-yd. fumble return (Kasay kick)
CLE-Safety: Pleasant tackled Mirer in end zone
CLE-Stover 25-yd. FG
SEA-Williams 23-yd. pass from Mirer (Kasay kick)
SEA-Kasay 42-yd. FG
SEA-Kasay 47-yd. FG
SEA-Safety: Edwards tackled Philcox in end zone

Passing
CLE: Philcox 9–20–85 0 TD 2 INT
SEA: Mirer 11–27–114 1 TD 0 INT

Rushing
CLE: Metcalf 13–75, Vardell 15–61, Hoard 3–20, Baldwin 6–19, Philcox 1–0
SEA: Warren 24–112, Williams 6–5, Vaughn 1–5, Mirer 2-(-3)

Receiving
CLE: Jackson 1–56, Smith 2–25, Wolfley 1–5, Carrier 1–3, Metcalf 2-(-1), Hoard 2-(-3)
SEA: Williams 6–60, Blades 2–22, Green 1–12, Martin 1–11, Edmunds 1–9

Sunday, November 21
Houston Oilers 27, Browns 20
Cleveland Stadium (71,668)
Brown jerseys/white pants

Before a hostile home crowd demonstrating its displeasure with Bill Belichick in the aftermath of the release of Bernie Kosar, the Browns were carved up by the Oilers and suffered their third straight defeat. With the Cleveland running game struggling, Todd Philcox threw for 316 yards but completed only 22 of 47 passes and threw four costly interceptions as the Browns stretched their turnover total to 12 in two games. Behind 194 rushing yards from backup RB Gary Brown—the third-best running performance ever by a Browns' opponent—the Oilers rolled to a 27–10 lead in the fourth quarter before the Browns added 10 meaningless points in the final eight minutes. Mark Carrier was one of the few bright spots for the Browns, catching seven passes for 123 yards and a touchdown. Meanwhile, Kosar made his first start for Dallas, and though the Cowboys lost to Atlanta, he threw for 186 yards and two touchdowns without an interception.
Record: 5–5

	1	2	3	4		
Oilers	0	14	3	10	=	27
Browns	3	7	0	10	=	20

CLE-Stover 21-yd. FG
HOU-Brown 11-yd. run (Del Greco kick)
HOU-Duncan 4-yd. pass from Moon (Del Greco kick)
CLE-Metcalf 13-yd. pass from Philcox (Stover kick)
HOU-Del Greco 28-yd. FG
HOU-Moon 4-yd. run (Del Greco kick)
HOU-Del Greco 30-yd. FG
CLE-Carrier 24-yd. pass from Philcox (Stover kick)
CLE-Stover 44-yd. FG

Passing
HOU: Moon 19–40–187 1 TD 2 INT
CLE: Philcox 22–47–316 2 TD 4 INT

Rushing
HOU: Brown 34–194, Moon 4–6, Givins 1–2
CLE: Vardell 13–48, Hoard 2–9, Carrier 1-(-8)

Receiving
HOU: Duncan 7–67, Jeffires 5–52, Slaughter 5–40, Brown 2–28
CLE: Carrier 7–123, Kinchen 5–73, Jackson 4–64, Rowe 3–37, Metcalf 2–17, Hoard 1–2

Sunday, November 28
Atlanta Falcons 17, Browns 14
Georgia Dome (54,510)
White jerseys/white pants

The Browns' free fall continued as an early deficit proved too much to overcome in Atlanta, and a questionable playcall in the waning seconds secured Cleveland's fourth straight loss and sixth in eight games. Trailing 17–0 at the half, the Browns cut the margin to three points with 3:31 to play in the game and then got the ball back at their own 34 with less than a minute remaining. Facing third-and-one at their own 43 with 30 seconds left and out of time outs, the Browns called for a draw to Eric Metcalf, who was buried for a two-yard loss, bringing up fourth down and melting most of the remaining seconds away. A short fourth-down pass was completed for a first down, but time expired before the Browns could get another playoff.
Record: 5–6

	1	2	3	4		
Browns	0	0	7	7	=	14
Falcons	10	7	0	0	=	17

ATL-Johnson 51-yd. FG
ATL-Rison 14-yd. pass from Hebert (Johnson kick)
ATL-Pritchard 8-yd. pass from Hebert (Johnson kick)
CLE-Carrier 35-yd. pass from Philcox (Stover kick)
CLE-Philcox 3-yd. run (Stover kick)

Passing
CLE: Philcox 14–26–207 1 TD 0 INT
ATL: Hebert 21–29–214 2 TD 0 INT, Sanders 0–1–0 0 TD 0 INT

Rushing
CLE: Metcalf 13–61, Vardell 13–52, Philcox 1–3, Jones 1–1, Baldwin 1-(-2)
ATL: Pegram 22–58, Hebert 1–5, Pritchard 1–4

Receiving
CLE: Kinchen 4–70, Carrier 3–47, Metcalf 5–43, Jackson 1–38, Vardell 1–9
ATL: Rison 5–78, Haynes 4–47, Pritchard 4–32, Lyons 3–23, Sanders 2–13, Pegram 2–11, Hill 1–10

Sunday, December 5
Browns 17, New Orleans Saints 13
Cleveland Stadium (60,388)
Brown jerseys/white pants

Behind a dominating defensive performance, the Browns snapped their losing streak and pulled back to the .500 mark. The Browns held the Saints to just 127 total yards and collected nine sacks, but the contest remained close because Cleveland committed four turnovers and 10 penalties. Todd Philcox made his fourth consecutive start, but Vinny Testaverde returned to action in the second quarter and threw what proved to be the game-winning touchdown pass with four minutes left in the third quarter. The lead stood up thanks to the Cleveland defense, which held the Saints to minus-six yards in the fourth quarter.
Record: 6–6

	1	2	3	4		
Saints	7	0	3	3	=	13
Browns	10	0	7	0	=	17

CLE-Jackson 8-yd. pass from Philcox (Stover kick)
NO-Martin 10-yd. pass from Wilson (Andersen kick)
CLE-Stover 43-yd. FG
NO-Andersen 41-yd. FG
CLE-Jackson 4-yd. pass from Testaverde (Stover kick)
NO-Andersen 27-yd. FG

Passing
NO: Wilson 15–29–119 1 TD 0 INT
CLE: Testaverde 9–20–92 1 TD 1 INT, Philcox 7–15–91 1 TD 1 INT

Rushing
NO: Hilliard 13–47, McAfee 8–30, Muster 1–2, Wilson 2–0
CLE: Hoard 16–60, Metcalf 4–54, Vardell 8–17

Receiving
NO: Martin 4–35, Hilliard 4–22, Smith 2–21, Brenner 1–19, Early 3–16, Small 1–6
CLE: Jackson 6–65, Hoard 4–62, Kinchen 3–30, Vardell 1–18, Smith 1–13, Metcalf 1-(-5)

Sunday, December 12
Houston Oilers 19, Browns 17
Houston Astrodome (58,720)
White jerseys/white pants

Despite an admirable effort in a fiercely physical game, the Browns were haunted by a handful of key mistakes as they squandered a 10-point lead and lost a frustrating game to the red-hot Oilers, who captured their eighth straight victory. The Browns took command on the very first play, when Vinny Testaverde looped a 49-yard touchdown pass to Eric Metcalf, then made it 10–0 with a 53-yard Matt Stover field goal later in the first quarter. After the Oilers fought back with 16 straight points, the Browns scored again to take the lead into the fourth quarter but missed a scoring opportunity at the end of the first half when time expired after they reached the Houston 2. After the Oilers took the lead back at 19–17 in the fourth quarter, Stover missed a 56-yard field goal with 3:35 remaining, and the Browns blew their last chance when LB Mike Johnson jumped offside on a Houston field-goal attempt in the final minute, giving the Oilers a first down and enabling them to run out the clock. Fittingly, it gave the mistake-prone Browns an even 100 yards in penalties on the day, wiping out their decisive advantage in total yardage (410 to 257). Testaverde threw for a season-high 319 yards, while Metcalf rolled up 212 combined yards, but it was all for naught as the Browns were eliminated from the division race they'd been leading six weeks before.
Record: 6–7

	1	2	3	4		
Browns	10	0	7	0	=	17
Oilers	3	13	0	3	=	19

CLE-Metcalf 49-yd. pass from Testaverde (Stover kick)
CLE-Stover 53-yd. FG
HOU-Del Greco 27-yd. FG
HOU-Del Greco 48-yd. FG
HOU-Tillman 4-yd. pass from Moon (Del Greco kick)
HOU-Del Greco 49-yd. FG
CLE-Carrier 28-yd. pass from Testaverde (Stover kick)
HOU-Del Greco 25-yd. FG

Passing
CLE: Testaverde 19–37–319 2 TD 2 INT, Hoard 0–1–0 0 TD 0 INT
HOU: Moon 13–28–155 1 TD 1 INT

Rushing
CLE: Metcalf 18–82, Mack 4–16, Vardell 3–7, Hoard 2–0
HOU: Brown 23–109, Moon 5–19

Receiving
CLE: Metcalf 5–101, McCardell 2–55, Jackson 2–52, Kinchen 5–47, Carrier 3–45, Hoard 2–19
HOU: Givins 5–54, Slaughter 2–47, Jeffires 3–37, Wellman 1–11, Tillman 1–4, Brown 1–2

Sunday, December 19
New England Patriots 20, Browns 17
Cleveland Stadium (48,618)
Brown jerseys/white pants

The floundering Browns hit rock bottom on the Sunday before Christmas, blowing a 14–3 lead and losing to the 2–11 Patriots on their own home field. Playing before their smallest home crowd in three years, the Browns appeared on their way to an easy victory as recently acquired WR Keenan McCardell snagged the first two touchdown receptions of his career in the first half. But once again, mistakes plagued the Browns as the Patriots crept back into the game despite rookie QB Drew Bledsoe suffering nine dropped passes. The Browns appeared to have victory in their grasp with five minutes remaining when they drove to the New England 8, leading 17–13. But Vinny Testaverde was picked off in the end zone, and the Patriots drove 80 yards for the go-ahead touchdown with 2:02 remaining. Testaverde then threw another interception on his next attempt, which clinched victory for New England. Eric Metcalf was a force, tallying 212 total yards, but it wasn't enough as Bill Belichick lost to his former mentor, first-year Patriots' coach Bill Parcells.
Record: 6–8

	1	2	3	4		
Patriots	0	10	3	7	=	20
Browns	7	7	0	3	=	17

CLE-McCardell 10-yd. pass from Testaverde (Stover kick)
NE-Bahr 23-yd. FG
CLE-McCardell 10-yd. pass from Testaverde (Stover kick)
NE-Turner 6-yd. pass from Bledsoe (Bahr kick)
NE-Bahr 34-yd. FG
CLE-Stover 23-yd. FG
NE-Russell 4-yd. run (Bahr kick)

Passing
NE: Bledsoe 19–47–210 1 TD 1 INT
CLE: Testaverde 21–31–297 2 TD 2 INT

Rushing
NE: Turner 4–63, Russell 14–38, Bledsoe 4–9, Gash 3–6, Croom 2–4
CLE: Metcalf 12–48, Vardell 14–33, Testaverde 1-(-1)

Receiving
NE: Brisby 6–77, Timpson 3–42, Coates 3–36, Turner 3–17, Croom 1–14, Russell 1–11, Cook 1–7, Crittenden 1–6
CLE: Metcalf 8–81, Carrier 4–81, McCardell 4–51, Kinchen 2–46, Hoard 1–17, Williams 1–14, Vardell 1–7

Sunday, December 26
Browns 42, Los Angeles Rams 14
Anaheim Stadium (34,155)
Brown jerseys/white pants

Notching their highest single-game point total in nearly five seasons, the Browns took out two months of frustration on the lowly Rams, sparked by a record-breaking performance by Vinny Testaverde. The embattled Browns' QB set an NFL mark for completion percentage in a game by hitting on 21 of 23 passes for a clip of 91.3 percent, breaking Cincinnati QB Ken Anderson's 19-year-old record. For the second straight week, Testaverde connected with Keenan McCardell for a pair of touchdowns, and Mark Carrier, filling in for Eric Metcalf, broke the game open with a 56-yard punt return for a touchdown early in the fourth quarter. In what proved to be their last game played to date in the city of Los Angeles, the Browns closed out their scoring with a one-yard touchdown run by RB Kevin Mack, who'd suffered through an injury-plagued season—the fifty-fourth and final score of his nine-year NFL career.
Record: 7–8

	1	2	3	4		
Browns	7	7	7	21	=	42
Rams	7	0	0	7	=	14

LA-Bettis 1-yd. run (Zendejas kick)
CLE-Vardell 1-yd. run (Stover kick)
CLE-McCardell 8-yd. pass from Testaverde (Stover kick)
CLE-McCardell 28-yd. pass from Testaverde (Stover kick)
CLE-Carrier 56-yd. punt return (Stover kick)

CLE-Vardell 1-yd. run (Stover kick)
CLE-Mack 1-yd. run (Stover kick)
LA-Anderson 23-yd. pass from Rubley (Zendejas kick)

Passing
CLE: Testaverde 21–23–216 2 TD 0 INT
LA: Rubley 24–32–294 1 TD 2 INT

Rushing
CLE: Metcalf 15–56, Hoard 4–20, Mack 6–17, Vardell 6–10, Testaverde 1-(-1)
LA: Bettis 16–56, Gary 3–31, Rubley 1–5, Ellard 1–3

Receiving
CLE: McCardell 4–72, Metcalf 8–57, Carrier 3–41, Jackson 2–26, Hoard 2–12, Kinchen 1–6, Vardell 1–2
LA: Ellard 8–114, Anderson 5–58, Drayton 3–49, Lang 2–27, Carter 1–26, Bettis 2–12, Lester 1–6, Gary 2–2

Sunday, January 2
Pittsburgh Steelers 16, Browns 9
Three Rivers Stadium (49,208)
White jerseys/white pants

A wildly frustrating season ended in appropriate fashion in Pittsburgh as the Browns were unable to hold onto a fourth-quarter lead and saw a potential game-tying touchdown waved off in the final seconds. After taking the lead with three field goals in the second quarter, the Browns held the upper hand until the Steelers scored the game's lone touchdown with just over seven minutes remaining. After Pittsburgh tacked on a field goal, the Browns regained possession at their own 20 and drove to the Steelers' 17. With eight seconds left, Vinny Testaverde lobbed a pass into the corner of the end zone for Michael Jackson, who caught it for the apparent game-tying touchdown, but was ruled to have bobbled the ball and come down out of bounds. On the same pass pattern on the next play, Jackson nearly caught it again, but the ball was knocked away by Pittsburgh DB D. J. Johnson as time expired. Though it permitted 10 fourth-quarter points, the Browns' defense collected seven sacks, giving the unit 48 for the season and tying the franchise record set the year before.
Record: 7–9

	1	2	3	4		
Browns	0	9	0	0	=	9
Steelers	0	3	3	10	=	16

PIT-Anderson 36-yd. FG
CLE-Stover 36-yd. FG
CLE-Stover 47-yd. FG
CLE-Stover 44-yd. FG
PIT-Anderson 38-yd. FG
PIT-Green 14-yd. pass from O'Donnell (Anderson kick)
PIT-Anderson 26-yd. FG

Passing
CLE: Testaverde 15–30–249 0 TD 0 INT
PIT: O'Donnell 22–39–226 1 TD 0 INT

Rushing
CLE: Hoard 9–29, Vardell 4–29, Carrier 1–6, Baldwin 2–0, Testaverde 2–0, Metcalf 2-(-3)
PIT: Thompson 26–91, Hoge 4–48, O'Donnell 1-(-1), Stone 1-(-3)

Receiving
CLE: Carrier 4–118, McCardell 3–56, Hoard 2–22, Vardell 4–21, Jackson 1–17, Kinchen 1–15
PIT: Green 6–65, Stone 4–40, Thigpen 2–39, Hoge 4–36, Thompson 3–21, Graham 2–16, Cooper 1–9

1994

Sunday, September 4
Browns 28, Cincinnati Bengals 20
Riverfront Stadium (52,778)
White jerseys/white pants

The Browns parlayed a pair of touchdowns on kick returns in the second quarter into a comfortable lead, then held off the Bengals in the final minutes to pick up their second straight opening-day victory. Taking control early, the Browns surged ahead 11–0 on a touchdown reception by RB Leroy Hoard, setting the tone for an impressive season, then became the first NFL team to successfully convert a two-point conversion when punter/placekick-holder Tom Tupa took the snap on the extra-point attempt and charged up the middle and into the end zone. After the Bengals scored to cut the margin to four points, Cleveland RB Randy Baldwin returned the ensuing kickoff 85 yards for a touchdown. Then three minutes later RB Eric Metcalf scampered a team-record 92 yards for a score on a punt return—marking the first time since 1958 the Browns returned a kick and a punt for scores in the same game and the first time any NFL team had done it since 1977. Down by 18 points, the Bengals slowly chipped away at the lead, cutting the deficit to 28–20 in the fourth quarter, and drove to the Cleveland 10 with a minute to play. But Browns' rookie DB Antonio Langham, in his first pro game, intercepted Cincinnati QB David Klingler in the end zone to preserve the victory.

Record: 1–0

	1	2	3	4		
Browns	11	14	0	3	=	28
Bengals	0	10	3	7	=	20

CLE-Stover 19-yd. FG
CLE-Hoard 11-yd. pass from Testaverde (Tupa run)
CIN-Fenner 1-yd. run (Pelfrey kick)
CLE-Baldwin 85-yd. kickoff return (Stover kick)
CLE-Metcalf 92-yd. punt return (Stover kick)
CIN-Pelfrey 38-yd. FG
CIN-Pelfrey 49-yd. FG
CLE-Stover 22-yd. FG
CIN-Scott 24-yd. pass from Klingler (Pelfrey kick)

Passing
CLE: Testaverde 14–24–149 1 TD 2 INT
CIN: Klingler 27–43–224 1 TD 2 INT

Rushing
CLE: Hoard 16–92, Vardell 2–8, Baldwin 1–5, Testaverde 1–2, Metcalf 7–0
CIN: Broussard 6–48, Fenner 13–41, Klingler 4–25, Green 7–4

Receiving
CLE: Jackson 3–45, Carrier 3–33, Metcalf 2–27, Vardell 4–22, Hoard 1–11, Reeves 1–11
CIN: Fenner 7–60, Scott 3–50, Broussard 6–35, Green 5–35, Query 1–14, Tony McGee 2–12, Tim McGee 1–10, Pickens 1–6, Sadowski 1–2

Sunday, September 11
Pittsburgh Steelers 17, Browns 10
Cleveland Stadium (77,774)
Brown jerseys/white pants

Thwarted by five turnovers, the Browns squandered a 10-point lead and lost their home opener in frustrating fashion to the rival Steelers. Aided by a flurry of early Pittsburgh penalties (the Steelers would be flagged 15 times for 115 yards on the day), the Browns surged ahead 10–0 in the second quarter, but Pittsburgh scored twice—aided by a short missed field goal by the Browns—to take the lead at halftime, and the Browns' self-destructive offense was held scoreless in the second half. When it appeared they'd tied the game on a touchdown pass to WR Mark Carrier with two minutes remaining, the score was called back on a holding penalty. Three plays later, QB Vinny Testaverde threw his fourth interception of the game to clinch victory for the Steelers.

Record: 1–1

	1	2	3	4		
Steelers	0	14	0	3	=	17
Browns	7	3	0	0	=	10

CLE-Reeves 1-yd. pass from Testaverde (Stover kick)
CLE-Stover 23-yd. FG
PIT-Thigpen 31-yd. pass from O'Donnell (Anderson kick)
PIT-Foster 1-yd. run (Anderson kick)
PIT-Anderson 25-yd. FG

Passing
PIT: O'Donnell 15–25–199 1 TD 0 INT
CLE: Testaverde 19–37–211 1 TD 4 INT, Jackson 0–1–0 0 TD 0 INT

Rushing
PIT: Foster 31–84, O'Donnell 4–15 Williams 2–13, Morris 1–4
CLE: Metcalf 9–43, Hoard 5–15, Baldwin 3–13, Vardell 2–10

Receiving
PIT: Johnson 5–72, Thigpen 2–47, Williams 3–31, Foster 3–26, Green 2–23
CLE: Metcalf 3–45, Jackson 3–37, Vardell 4–36, Carrier 3–35, Alexander 2–32, Reeves 2–23, Kinchen 1–4, Hoard 1-(-1)

Sunday, September 18
Browns 32, Arizona Cardinals 0
Cleveland Stadium (62,818)
White jerseys/white pants

Despite losing both of their starting wide receivers to injuries and a shaky first half, the Browns put it together in the final two periods to crush the Cardinals and surge over .500. Up only 3–0 at halftime, Cleveland scored on its first two possessions of the third quarter, then added an 81-yard touchdown pass to rookie WR Derrick Alexander midway through the fourth quarter to make it 25–0. Cleveland DB Eric Turner preserved the shutout and put the icing on the cake when he intercepted his second pass of the quarter with two minutes left and returned it 93 yards for a touchdown. In his first pro start, Alexander stole the show with 136 yards on six receptions, while the Browns' defense held Arizona to 63 yards rushing. The game also marked the return of Browns' RB Earnest Byner, picked up as a free agent in the offseason after five years in Washington.
Record: 2–1

	1	2	3	4		
Cardinals	0	0	0	0	=	0
Browns	0	3	15	14	=	32

CLE-Stover 32-yd. FG
CLE-Testaverde 1-yd. run (Stover kick)
CLE-Vardell 16-yd. pass from Testaverde (Tupa run)
CLE-Alexander 81-yd. pass from Testaverde (Stover kick)
CLE-Turner 93-yd. interception return (Stover kick)

Passing
ARI: McMahon 19–38–169 0 TD 2 INT, Schroeder 7–20–100 0 TD 1 INT
CLE: Testaverde 17–27–248 2 TD 1 INT

Rushing
ARI: McMahon 4–31, Schroeder 1–16, Centers 6–11, Moore 6–5
CLE: Byner 8–24, Hoard 8–22, Vardell 6–22, Testaverde 3–12, Metcalf 2-(-1)

Receiving
ARI: Centers 8–62, Reeves 2–57, Proehl 4–40, Levy 4–35, Hill 2–30, Ware 3–18, Clark 2–18, Moore 1–9
CLE: Alexander 6–136, Vardell 3–28, Reeves 3–27, Carrier 1–25, Byner 1–12, Smith 1–11, Metcalf 2–9

Sunday, September 25
Browns 21, Indianapolis Colts 14
RCA Dome (55,821)
White jerseys/white pants

Aided by two long Vinny Testaverde touchdown passes to his running backs, the Browns held off the Colts and rinsed away the residue of two straight frustrating losses in Indianapolis with a solid road victory. Cleveland took control on the third play of the game when Eric Metcalf caught a short pass over the middle and turned it into a 57-yard touchdown. He added another touchdown reception to break a 7–7 tie just before the half, then Leroy Hoard provided the winning points on a 65-yard scoring catch over the middle two minutes into the fourth quarter. The Browns' defense held off the Colts for the remainder of the period, not permitting them past the Indianapolis 36. Colts' rookie RB Marshall Faulk, off to a dazzling start in his first three games, was thwarted by the Cleveland defense, held to just 61 yards on 22 carries. For the second straight year, the Browns stood at 3–1 after four games.
Record: 3–1

	1	2	3	4		
Browns	7	7	0	7	=	21
Colts	7	0	7	0	=	14

CLE-Metcalf 57-yd pass from Testaverde (Stover kick)
IND-Faulk 1-yd. run (Biasucci kick)
CLE-Metcalf 15-yd. pass from Testaverde (Stover kick)
IND-Potts 13-yd. pass from Harbaugh (Biasucci kick)
CLE-Hoard 65-yd. pass from Testaverde (Stover kick)

Passing
CLE: Testaverde 16–28–266 3 TD 1 INT
IND: Harbaugh 16–26–194 1 TD 1 INT

Rushing
CLE: Metcalf 8–42, Hoard 10–34, Byner 7–24, Alexander 1–11, Vardell 5–8
IND: Harbaugh 4–63, Faulk 22–61, Potts 3–9, Humphrey 3–8, Turner 1–5

Receiving
CLE: Hoard 2–88, Metcalf 5–74, Vardell 5–51, Alexander 2–27, McCardell 1–18, Carrier 1–8
IND: Potts 6–87, Cash 2–42, Faulk 4–27, Dawkins 1–18, Turner 2–14, Etheredge 1–6

Sunday, October 2
Browns 27, New York Jets 7
Cleveland Stadium (76,188)
Brown jerseys/white pants

On a sun-drenched autumn afternoon, the Browns blew open the game with a 17-point second quarter and coasted to their third straight victory. Aided by a pair of New York turnovers, the Browns built a 24–0 halftime lead on three rushing touchdowns by three different players—Eric Metcalf, Earnest Byner, and Leroy Hoard. Derrick Alexander notched his second 100-yard receiving game in three weeks, and the defense nearly notched its second straight home shutout before the Jets reached the end zone with seven minutes remaining. The only sour spot on the day was the loss of Cleveland RB Tommy Vardell for the season due to a knee injury.
Record: 4–1

	1	2	3	4		
Jets	0	0	0	7	=	7
Browns	7	17	3	0	=	27

CLE-Metcalf 37-yd. run (Stover kick)
CLE-Stover 23-yd. FG
CLE-Byner 1-yd. run (Stover kick)
CLE-Hoard 18-yd. run (Stover kick)
CLE-Stover 45-yd. FG
NYJ-Moore 24-yd. pass from Trudeau (Lowery kick)

Passing
NYJ: Trudeau 28–46–288 1 TD 2 INT
CLE: Testaverde 21–36–257 0 TD 0 INT

Rushing
NYJ: J. Johnson 12–34, Murrell 4–28, Baxter 2–8, Trudeau 1–2
CLE: Metcalf 5–44, Hoard 6–30, Alexander 1–25, Byner 9–15, Testaverde 5–3

Receiving
NYJ: Mitchell 5–79, Moore 5–78, Monk 6–55, A. Johnson 2–16, Yarborough 2–16, J. Johnson 3–15, Baxter 2–11, Murrell 1–11, Anderson 2–7
CLE: Alexander 7–105, Smith 1–50, Hoard 6–40, Metcalf 4–32, Kinchen 1–14, McCardell 1–13, Byner 1–3

Thursday, October 13
Browns 11, Houston Oilers 8
Houston Astrodome (50,364)
White jerseys/white pants

Behind another sterling defensive effort, the Browns held off Houston on a Thursday night to move to 5–1 for the first time since 1965. They built an 11–0 halftime lead on a 25-yard scoring reception by Mark Carrier and Tom Tupa's third two-point conversion of the season, then kept Houston off the scoreboard until 28 seconds remained in the game. The Browns then recovered the ensuing onside kick to secure their fourth straight win. Browns' DB Isaac Booth made a crucial interception at the Cleveland 8 midway through the fourth quarter to thwart a potential scoring drive. While the Browns' offense struggled, managing only 260 total yards (just 64 rushing) and 12 first downs against the 1–4 Oilers, the Cleveland defense collected five sacks and held an opponent under 10 points for the third time in four games.
Record: 5–1

	1	2	3	4		
Browns	0	11	0	0	=	11
Oilers	0	0	0	8	=	8

CLE-Carrier 25-yd. pass from Testaverde (Tupa run)
CLE-Stover 35-yd. FG
HOU-White 5-yd. pass from Tolliver (Jeffires pass from Tolliver)

Passing
CLE: Testaverde 15–25–196 1 TD 2 INT
HOU: Tolliver 9–17–115 1 TD 1 INT, Richardson 13–23–114 0 TD 0 INT

Rushing
CLE: Byner 11–25, Metcalf 8–23, Hoard 2–10, Baldwin 2–7, Testaverde 1-(-1)
HOU: White 19–58, Richardson 4–45, Tolliver 1–3

Receiving
CLE: Carrier 4–60, Metcalf 3–48, Hoard 3–40, Alexander 3–28, Byner 1–15, Kinchen 1–5
HOU: White 7–86, Jeffires 5–60, Slaughter 4–35, Givins 3–27, Coleman 2–20, Carter 1–1

Sunday, October 23
Browns 37, Cincinnati Bengals 13
Cleveland Stadium (77,588)
Brown jerseys/white pants

Two special-teams touchdowns in the third quarter pushed the Browns over the hump in an otherwise listless performance against the winless Bengals. Trailing 10–3 going into the second quarter, the Browns scored 17 points in four minutes to take control of the contest in the third period. First, they tied the score at 13 early in the second half after recovering a fumbled Cincinnati punt return. The Browns then surged ahead when LB Gerald Dixon blocked a Cincinnati punt and fellow LB Travis Hill recovered the ball in the end zone for a touchdown. Three plays later, Eric Metcalf allowed the next Cincinnati punt to roll past him, then ran back to scoop it up and returned it 73 yards for another score to make it 27–13 and put the Browns in the clear with their fourth special-teams touchdown of the season against the Bengals. Leroy Hoard added his second touchdown of the day in the waning minutes. Though the Browns lit up the scoreboard for a season-high 37 points, their offense struggled for the second straight game, managing just 240 total yards. Vinny Testaverde left the game in the second half suffering from headaches after taking a blow to the head earlier and was replaced by backup Mark Rypien, who made his Browns' debut. It was the first of five straight games in which Testaverde would miss all or portions of the contest due to the lingering effects of the injury. The 6–1 mark marked the Browns' best start since 1963.
Record: 6–1

	1	2	3	4		
Bengals	10	3	0	0	=	13
Browns	3	7	17	10	=	27

CLE-Stover 45-yd. FG
CIN-Pelfrey 36-yd. FG
CIN-Tim McGee 11-yd. pass from Klingler (Pelfrey kick)
CLE-Hoard 11-yd. pass from Testaverde (Stover kick)
CIN-Pelfrey 49-yd. FG
CLE-Stover 27-yd. FG
CLE-Hill recovered blocked punt in end zone (Stover kick)
CLE-Metcalf 73-yd. punt return (Stover kick)
CLE-Stover 35-yd. FG
CLE-Hoard 1-yd. run (Stover kick)

Passing
CIN: Klingler 18–34–200 1 TD 0 INT, Blake 0–2–0 0 TD 0 INT, Hollas 0–1–0 0 TD 0 INT
CLE: Testaverde 8–18–103 1 TD 1 INT, Rypien 3–11–31 0 TD 0 INT

Rushing
CIN: Fenner 15–50, Green 6–15, Klingler 1–8, Broussard 5–1, Cothran 3–1
CLE: Hoard 9–58, Metcalf 12–57, Byner 1–3, Baldwin 1–1, Testaverde 1–1

Receiving
CIN: Tim McGee 4–72, Scott 3–38, Green 2–37, Tony McGee 3–29, Sadowski 2–13, Broussard 2–6, Fenner 1–4, Query 1–1
CLE: Alexander 3–77, Carrier 2–28, Hoard 5–22, Metcalf 1–7

Sunday, October 30
Denver Broncos 26, Browns 14
Mile High Stadium (73,190)
White jerseys/white pants

The Browns saw their five-game winning streak come to a screeching halt as the Broncos continued their sorcery over Cleveland, picking up their fourth straight win in the series. Vinny Testaverde started the game but was forced out after receiving another blow to the head on the sixth play and did not return. Though Denver would dominate time of possession and roll up 457 total yards, the most the Browns allowed all season, Cleveland still had a chance to pull out a victory after narrowing the Broncos' lead to 20–14 with a touchdown and a two-point conversion two minutes into the fourth quarter. But Denver QB John Elway led his team on a quick scoring drive to seal the victory. Elway had another magnificent performance against the Browns, throwing for 349 yards and a pair of touchdowns, completing 18 of 20 passes in the first half. With the Steelers' loss in Arizona, the Browns maintained their one-game division lead at the season's midpoint.
Record: 6–2

John Elway vs. the Browns

Perhaps no single player victimized the Browns over the course of his career more than Denver Broncos' QB John Elway. Over the course of 12 seasons, the Browns faced Elway 12 times, including three times in the AFC Championship, and Elway's Broncos came out on top in 10 of those meetings. Along the way, Elway created a legacy, continually crushing the Browns' hopes in close games or turning otherwise even matchups into Denver romps. Here's a look at each of the Browns' 12 encounters with John Elway and how he fared:

December 4, 1983
16 of 24, 284 yards, 2 TD 0 INT
6 carries, 18 yards
134.7 QB Rating
Denver wins, 27–6

September 16, 1984
15 of 35, 170 yards, 2 TD 1 INT
6 carries, 42 yards
65.2 QB Rating
Denver wins, 24–14

***January 11, 1987**
22 of 38, 244 yards, 1 TD 1 INT
4 carries, 56 yards
74.9 QB Rating
Denver wins, 23–20 in OT

***January 17, 1988**
14 of 26, 281 yards, 3 TD 1 INT
11 carries, 36 yards
114.4 QB rating
Denver wins, 38–33

November 13, 1988
21 of 30, 207 yards, 2 TD 0 INT
3 carries, 34 yards
111.4 QB rating
Denver wins, 30–7

October 1, 1989
6 of 19, 198 yards, 1 TD 1 INT
1 carry, 2 yards
67.4 QB rating
Cleveland wins, 16–13

***January 14, 1990**
20 of 36, 385 yards, 3 TD 0 INT
5 carries, 39 yards
120.7 QB rating
Denver wins, 37–21

October 8, 1990
16 of 33, 175 yards, 0 TD 2 INT
3 carries, 21 yards, 1 TD
39.3 QB rating
Cleveland wins, 30–29

December 8, 1991
16 of 29, 221 yards, 2 TD 1 INT
4 carries, 25 yards
88.4 QB rating
Denver wins, 17–7

September 27, 1992
10 of 17, 157 yards, 0 TD 1 INT
8 carries, 18 yards
65.1 QB rating
Denver wins, 12–0

November 7, 1993
17 of 23, 244 yards, 3 TD 0 INT
2 carries, 7 yards
147.5 QB rating
Denver wins, 29–14

October 30, 1994
30 of 41, 349 yards, 2 TD 0 INT
2 carries, 14 yards
114.8 QB rating
Denver wins, 26–14

**AFC Championship Game*

COMBINED:
10–2 record
203 of 351, 2,915 yards,
21 TD 8 INT (57.8 comp %)
55 carries, 312 yards, 1 TD
(5.7 avg)
95.3 QB rating

Elway's numbers against the Browns are far better than his overall career statistics, in which he averaged 4.4 yards per rush, completed 56.9 percent of his passes, and compiled a 79.9 quarterback rating.

	1	2	3	4		
Browns	0	6	0	8	=	14
Broncos	7	7	6	6	=	26

DEN-Evans 1-yd. pass from Elway (Elam kick)
CLE-Stover 43-yd. FG
CLE-Stover 45-yd. FG
DEN-Russell 1-yd. run (Elam kick)
DEN-Elam 27-yd. FG
DEN-Elam 32-yd. FG
CLE-Carrier 6-yd. pass from Rypien (Alexander pass from Rypien)
DEN-Milburn 17-yd. pass from Elway (pass failed)

Passing
CLE: Rypien 17–30–210 1 TD 0 INT, Testaverde 6–14–74 0 TD 0 INT, Metcalf 0–1–0 0 TD 0 INT
DEN: Elway 30–41–349 2 TD 0 INT

Rushing
CLE: Metcalf 11–32, Hoard 3–6, Rypien 2–3, Alexander 1–0
DEN: Milburn 8–38, L. Russell 16–26, Rivers 6–20, Clark 5–16, Elway 2–14

Receiving
CLE: Alexander 5–76, Metcalf 8–62, Hoard 5–57, Carrier 2–48, McCardell 2–35, Kinchen 1–6
DEN: Sharpe 9–85, Miller 4–82, Milburn 8–76, D. Russell 2–47, L. Russell 3–31, Rivers 3–27, Evans 1–1

Sunday, November 6
Browns 13, New England Patriots 6
Cleveland Stadium (73,878)
Brown jerseys/white pants

On a dark, windy afternoon, the Browns' defense played magnificently while the offense parlayed a punishing ground attack into a gritty victory over the playoff-bound

Patriots. Leroy Hoard turned in the finest game of his career—and the finest by any Cleveland RB in seven years—rushing for 123 yards on 21 carries and made a bobbling running catch for the game's only touchdown to break a 3–3 tie early in the fourth quarter. Mark Rypien made his first start for the Browns for still-groggy Vinny Testaverde and paced an efficient offense, while the defense stymied the league's best passing attack, forcing QB Drew Bledsoe into four interceptions and just 20 completions in 43 attempts. The defeat dropped New England to 3–6, though the Patriots would rattle off seven straight victories from this point to set up a playoff rematch in Cleveland.

Record: 7–2

	1	2	3	4		
Patriots	0	0	3	3	=	6
Browns	0	3	0	10	=	13

CLE-Stover 33-yd. FG
NE-Bahr 20-yd. FG
CLE-Hoard 1-yd. pass from Rypien (Stover kick)
CLE-Stover 41-yd. FG
NE-Bahr 39 yd-FG

Passing
NE: Bledsoe 20–43–166 0 TD 4 INT
CLE: Rypien 14–28–164 1 TD 1 INT

Rushing
NE: Butts 25–86, Turner 7–23, Thompson 3–9, Bledsoe 1–0
CLE: Hoard 21–123, Byner 6–19, Metcalf 3–5, Rypien 1–1, Jones 1–0

Receiving
NE: Timpson 7–69, Crittenden 3–31, Coates 3–24, Hawkins 2–22, Thompson 3–10, Turner 2–10
CLE: McCardell 4–80, Metcalf 3–32, Alexander 1–20, Hoard 2–12, Kinchen 2–12, Byner 1–7, Jones 1–1

Sunday, November 13
Browns 26, Philadelphia Eagles 7
Veterans Stadium (65,233)
White jerseys/white pants

With a stunning performance, the Browns dominated the 7–2 Eagles on their own home field and cruised to one of their most impressive victories in years. The Cleveland defense controlled Philly QB Randall Cunningham, who had won 20 straight starts at Veterans Stadium, sacking him three times. After the Browns set the tone early and took a 10–0 first-quarter lead, the only Eagles' score was set up by a 46-yard pass-interference penalty. The Browns rushed for 140 yards against the league's second-ranked defense and clinched the game when Earnest Byner scooted to a four-yard touchdown four minutes into the fourth quarter, capping a drive begun when the Browns recovered a Cunningham fumble at the Cleveland 13. The Browns' eighth victory in 10 games matched the best record of any team in the NFL and kept them a game ahead of Pittsburgh in the division.

Record: 8–2

	1	2	3	4		
Browns	10	3	6	7	=	26
Eagles	0	7	0	0	=	7

CLE-Carrier 3-yd. pass from Rypien (Stover kick)
CLE-Stover 35-yd. FG
PHI-Hebron 15-yd. run (Murray kick)
CLE-Stover 41-yd. FG
CLE-Stover 22-yd. FG
CLE-Stover 36-yd. FG
CLE-Byner 4-yd. run (Stover kick)

Passing
CLE: Rypien 12–30–158 1 TD 1 INT
PHI: Cunningham 22–38–196 0 TD 1 INT

Rushing
CLE: Hoard 21–86, Baldwin 6–36, Byner 9–26, Metcalf 4-(-8)
PHI: Cunningham 7–46, Hebron 12–39, Walker 2–27

Receiving
CLE: Carrier 4–63, Hoard 2–37, Jackson 1–22, Kinchen 2–21, Hartley 1–8, Metcalf 2–7
PHI: Barnett 7–57, Hebron 6–54, Bavaro 1–22, Johnson 1–19, Walker 2–18, Williams 3–15, Bailey 1–11, Alexander 1–0

Sunday, November 20
Kansas City Chiefs 20, Browns 13
Arrowhead Stadium (69,121)
White jerseys/white pants

After taking a lead into the fourth quarter, a barrage of mistakes proved too much for the Browns to overcome on a rainy day in Kansas City as veteran QB Joe Montana led the Chiefs to a come-from-behind victory. The Browns were penalized 15 times for a whopping 142 yards and committed four turnovers, including three fumbles (the most costly at the Kansas City 5 in the first quarter) after losing only four all season going in. Alternating between Mark Rypien and Vinny Testaverde at QB, the Browns took a 13–10 lead late in the third quarter, but the Chiefs came right back to tie the game a minute into the fourth, then turned an interception into the winning touchdown with just under eight minutes remaining. The Browns drove to the Kansas City 36 with a minute left, but Rypien fumbled on a sack by LB Derrick Thomas, and the Chiefs recovered to clinch the victory. The defeat dropped the Browns into a tie for first with Pittsburgh in the AFC Central.

Record: 8–3

	1	2	3	4		
Browns	0	6	7	0	=	13
Chiefs	0	7	3	10	=	20

KC-Greene 6-yd. pass from Montana (Elliott kick)
CLE-Metcalf 15-yd. pass from Testaverde (run failed)
KC-Elliott 22-yd. FG
CLE-Jackson 15-yd. pass from Rypien (Stover kick)
KC-Elliott 28-yd. FG
KC-Anders 1-yd. run (Elliott kick)

Passing
CLE: Rypien 10–24–114 1 TD 1 INT, Testaverde 4–12–38 1 TD 0 INT, Jackson 0–1–0 0 TD 0 INT
KC: Montana 19–33–169 1 TD 0 INT

Rushing
CLE: Hoard 17–68, Byner 6–26, Rypien 2–2, Metcalf 2-(-2)
KC: Hill 12–66, Bennett 11–41, Anders 9–26, Dawson 1–2, Montana 4-(-1)

Receiving
CLE: Hoard 6–56, Jackson 3–51, Kinchen 3–24, Metcalf 1–15, Byner 1–6
KC: Martin 4–54, Hill 3–26, Dawson 2–18, Anders 2–15, Birden 2–14, Hughes 1–13, Bennett 1–12, Greene 1–6, Penn 1–6, Walker 2–5

Sunday, November 27
Browns 34, Houston Oilers 10
Cleveland Stadium (65,088)
Brown jerseys/white pants

The Browns bounced back from the tough loss in Kansas City with a big fourth quarter to put away the 1–10 Oilers and clinch their first winning season in five years. Vinny Testaverde started and played the entire game for the first time in over a month, throwing two touchdown passes and leading the Browns to 343 yards on offense. Meanwhile, the Cleveland defense limited Houston to just 182 total yards while collecting four sacks. Leading by only seven going into the fourth quarter, the Browns quickly blew it open with a pair of touchdowns by Leroy Hoard, who picked up 103 rushing yards on the day as the Browns completed their first season sweep of the Oilers since 1989.

Record: 9–3

	1	2	3	4		
Oilers	0	10	0	0	=	10
Browns	3	14	0	17	=	34

CLE-Stover 37-yd. FG
CLE-Hartley 1-yd. pass from Testaverde (Stover kick)
HOU-White 1-yd. run (Del Greco kick)
CLE-Kinchen 11-yd. pass from Testaverde (Stover kick)
HOU-Del Greco 42-yd. FG
CLE-Hoard 1-yd. run (Stover kick)
CLE-Stover 23-yd. FG
CLE-Hoard 5-yd. run (Stover kick)

Passing
HOU: Tolliver 16–33–124 0 TD 0 INT
CLE: Testaverde 15–29–199 2 TD 1 INT

Rushing
HOU: White 19–80
CLE: Hoard 23–103, Byner 7–23, Metcalf 3–14, Baldwin 2–7, Testaverde 3-(-3)

Receiving
HOU: Slaughter 5–55, Jeffires 3–34, White 4–19, Carter 2–9, Wellman 2–7
CLE: Kinchen 4–62, Jackson 3–50, Alexander 2–35, Hoard 2–20, Byner 1–15, Metcalf 1–12, Hartley 2–5

Sunday, December 4
New York Giants 16, Browns 13
Cleveland Stadium (72,068)
Brown jerseys/white pants

Once again committing a barrage of mistakes, the Browns lost a winnable game to the mediocre Giants in the final seconds and tumbled out of first place for the first time all season. Cleveland coughed up five turnovers, was flagged for 11 penalties, and, as a result, trailed 13–6 midway through the fourth quarter. With five minutes remaining, Derrick Alexander caught a 60-yard pass to set up the game-tying touchdown run by Leroy Hoard on the next snap, capping a magnificent day for the rookie wide-out with seven catches for 171 yards. But the Giants responded with a 13-play drive to set up the game-winning 33-yard field goal with 19 seconds to play. With a win in Cincinnati earlier that afternoon, the Steelers took over sole possession of first place in the division.

Record: 9–4

	1	2	3	4		
Giants	7	0	3	6	=	16
Browns	3	3	0	7	=	13

CLE-Stover 41-yd. FG
NYG-Pierce 10-yd. pass from Brown (Treadwell kick)
CLE-Stover 23-yd. FG
NYG-Daluiso 25-yd. FG
NYG-Daluiso 30-yd. FG
CLE-Hoard 5-yd. run (Stover kick)
NYG-Daluiso 33-yd. FG

Passing
NYG: Brown 17–33–226 1 TD 1 INT
CLE: Testaverde 20–38–238 0 TD 2 INT

Rushing
NYG: Hampton 23–77, Brown 5–14, Rasheed 2–8, Meggett 3-(-3)
CLE: Hoard 11–45, Metcalf 5–25, Testaverde 1–7

Receiving
NYG: Sherrard 5–101, Calloway 2–33, Rasheed 3–27, Cross 2–21, Hampton 1–17, Meggett 2–12, Pierce 1–10, Marshall 1–5
CLE: Alexander 7–171, Metcalf 3–20, Hoard 4–16, Byner 3–12, Kinchen 2–12, Carrier 1–7

Saturday, December 10
Browns 19, Dallas Cowboys 14
Texas Stadium (64,826)
Brown jerseys/white pants

Entering the game as 10-point underdogs against the 11–2 defending Super Bowl champs, the Browns played their finest game of the season and upset the Cowboys in a thrilling finish. After spoiling a golden scoring opportunity on their first drive when Leroy Hoard fumbled into the end zone from the Dallas 1, the Browns rallied from a 7–0 deficit to take a three-point advantage into the fourth quarter. They then stretched the advantage to 16–7 with two more field goals, the second after intercepting Troy Aikman for the second time. Dallas scored to cut the margin to two points on a touchdown by RB Emmitt Smith, who became the first player to top 100 rushing yards against the Browns all season. The Browns then recovered Aikman's fumble—Dallas's fourth turnover—on fourth-and-two from the Dallas 16 to set up Matt Stover's fourth field goal of the day to make it 19–14 with 1:49 remaining. The Cowboys drove to the Cleveland 6 with 10 seconds left, and Aikman hit TE Jay Novacek slanting over the middle at the 1. But as Novacek slipped on the wet turf, the Browns' Eric Turner stopped him inches short of the goal line and time expired, giving the Browns one of the most exciting victories in team history. And the following afternoon, with a Buffalo loss to Minnesota, the Browns clinched their first playoff berth in five years.

Record: 10–4

	1	2	3	4		
Browns	7	3	0	9	=	19
Cowboys	7	0	0	7	=	14

DAL-Smith 7-yd. pass from Aikman (Boniol kick)
CLE-Jackson 2-yd. pass from Testaverde (Stover kick)
CLE-Stover 34-yd. FG
CLE-Stover 32-yd. FG
CLE-Stover 43-yd. FG
DAL-Smith 4-yd. run (Boniol kick)
CLE-Stover 32-yd. FG

Passing
CLE: Testaverde 15–25–118 1 TD 1 INT
DAL: Aikman 21–36–188 1 TD 2 INT

Rushing
CLE: Hoard 25–99, Metcalf 3–19, Byner 4–8, Baldwin 4–6, Testaverde 2–2
DAL: Smith 26–112, Aikman 1–0

Receiving
CLE: Jackson 6–74, Kinchen 3–13, Metcalf 3–13, Hoard 1–9, Carrier 1–7, Baldwin 1–2
DAL: Irvin 7–88, Harper 2–27, Williams 2–26, Smith 5–22, Johnston 3–15, Novacek 2–10

Sunday, December 18
Pittsburgh Steelers 17, Browns 7
Three Rivers Stadium (60,808)
White jerseys/white pants

In a battle for first place before the largest crowd in the history of Three Rivers Stadium, three turnovers and 10 penalties doomed the Browns to their first season sweep at the hands of the Steelers in 13 years. Pittsburgh took control early, scoring touchdowns on their first two possessions and thwarted the Browns' offense for the remainder of the game. Cleveland scored its only points on a Mark Carrier touchdown reception just before the half that capped an 84-yard drive. The Browns then drove into Pittsburgh territory on the first series of the third quarter before a Leroy Hoard fumble destroyed the Browns' momentum. A Vinny Testaverde interception early in the fourth quarter set up the game-clinching field goal for Pittsburgh. With the victory, their seventh straight, the Steelers clinched their second AFC Central title in three seasons.
Record: 10–5

	1	2	3	4		
Browns	0	7	0	0	=	7
Steelers	14	0	0	3	=	17

PIT-Thigpen 40-yd. pass from O'Donnell (Anderson kick)
PIT-Foster 1-yd. run (Anderson kick)
CLE-Carrier 14-yd. pass from Testaverde (Stover kick)
PIT-Anderson 49-yd. FG

Passing
CLE: Testaverde 21–42–250 1 TD 2 INT
PIT: O'Donnell 10–18–175 1 TD 0 INT

Rushing
CLE: Metcalf 8–26, Byner 7–26, Hoard 8–25, Testaverde 1–9
PIT: Foster 32–106, Williams 5–15, Mills 1–2, O'Donnell 3–0

Receiving
CLE: Alexander 5–74, Carrier 2–40, Hoard 5–38, Byner 2–32, Jackson 2–25, Metcalf 3–21, Kinchen 2–20
PIT: Thigpen 4–74, Green 2–44, Mills 1–42, Foster 2–13, Williams 1–2

Saturday, December 24
Browns 35, Seattle Seahawks 9
Cleveland Stadium (54,180)
Brown jerseys/white pants

On Christmas Eve, before the smallest home crowd of the season, the Browns crushed Seattle to close out an impressive regular season and secure home-field advantage for their first-round playoff game the following week. Behind the hot hand of Vinny Testaverde, who completed nine of his first 11 passes and ran for a touchdown, the Browns sprinted to a 21–0 halftime lead and never looked back, stretching the margin to 35–3 early in the fourth quarter. Mark Carrier had his finest game of the season, notching 98 receiving yards and scoring a pair of touchdowns. With their first-ever home win over Seattle following three defeats, the Browns nearly became just the fifth team to permit less than 200 total points in a 16-game season. But a late Seattle touchdown gave Cleveland opponents 204 for the year, the fewest the Browns had permitted in a non-strike season since 1957.
Record: 11–5

	1	2	3	4		
Seahawks	0	0	3	6	=	9
Browns	7	14	7	7	=	35

CLE-Metcalf 6-yd. run (Stover kick)
CLE-Carrier 35-yd. pass from Testaverde (Stover kick)
CLE-Testaverde 1-yd. run (Stover kick)
SEA-Kasay 30-yd. FG
CLE-Alexander 3-yd. pass from Testaverde (Stover kick)
CLE-Carrier 14-yd. run (Stover kick)
SEA-McKnight 25-yd. pass from Gelbaugh (pass failed)

Passing
SEA: McGwire 11–26–149 0 TD 1 INT, Gelbaugh 7–11–80 1 TD 0 INT
CLE: Testaverde 16–21–228 2 TD 1 INT, Rypien 3–5–17 0 TD 0 INT

Rushing
SEA: Warren 16–61, Gelbaugh 1–10, Strong 3–7, Bryant 1–6, McGwire 2–0
CLE: Hoard 24–74, Carrier 1–14, Metcalf 3–10, Testaverde 3–5, Baldwin 4–3, Alexander 1–2, Rypien 2-(-2)

Receiving
SEA: Blades 6–80, Martin 3–49, Smith 3–33, McKnight 1–25, Thomas 1–15, Green 2–12, Bates 1–10, Johnson 1–5
CLE: Carrier 5–98, Alexander 5–47, Kinchen 2–39, McCardell 2–36, Baldwin 2–13, Metcalf 3–12

AFC Wild Card Game
Sunday, January 1
Browns 20, New England Patriots 13
Cleveland Stadium (77,452)
Brown jerseys/white pants

On New Year's Day, playing their first postseason game in five years, the Browns were paired with a red-hot New England team that stormed into the playoffs on a seven-game winning streak. Second-year Patriots' coach Bill Parcells would face his former pupil in the Browns' Bill Belichick after the pair coached together for eight years with the Giants.

The Cleveland offense set the tone for its best day of the season, driving 74 yards for a field goal on its first possession, then took back the lead at 10–7 midway through the second quarter when Vinny Testaverde rolled out from the New England 5 and hit Mark Carrier in the corner of the end zone.

After New England tied the game just before the half, the Browns took the lead for good with two minutes left in the third quarter on a 10-yard touchdown blast by Leroy Hoard. Cleveland's third interception of Drew Bledsoe set up an insurance field goal to make it 20–10 with 3:36 remaining, but the Patriots pulled back within a touchdown with 1:36 left, then recovered an onside kick. The Browns' defense forced Bledsoe into four straight incompletions to give the ball back to Cleveland, and Testaverde kneeled out the final seconds.

Just as he had in their November meeting, Bledsoe was controlled by the Browns' defense, completing just 21 of 50 passes, while Testaverde had one of his finest games as a Brown, completing 20 of 30 passes for 268 yards—at one point completing 11 straight—as the Browns rolled up a season-high 379 total yards. WR Michael Jackson, after struggling through injury for most of the season, had his finest game of the year, catching seven passes for 122 yards.

The victory, which remains the most recent postseason triumph in Browns' history, propelled them to the divisional playoffs, where Pittsburgh awaited a week later.

	1	2	3	4		
Patriots	0	10	0	3	=	13
Browns	3	7	7	3	=	20

CLE-Stover 30-yd. FG
NE-Thompson 13-yd. pass from Bledsoe (Bahr kick)
CLE-Carrier 5-yd. pass from Testaverde (Stover kick)
NE-Bahr 23-yd. FG
CLE-Hoard 10-yd. run (Stover kick)
CLE-Stover 21-yd. FG
NE-Bahr 33-yd. FG

Passing
NE: Bledsoe 21–50–235 1 TD 3 INT, O'Neill 1–1–21 0 TD 0 INT
CLE: Testaverde 20–30–268 1 TD 0 INT

Rushing
NE: Croom 9–35, Thompson 4–16, Turner 1–4, Bledsoe 2–2
CLE: Hoard 17–66, Byner 10–30, Testaverde 5–19, Metcalf 2–10

Receiving
NE: Brisby 6–83, Coates 6–79, Thompson 4–33, Brown 1–21, Timpson 2–20, Burke 1–8, Turner 1–7, Croom 1–5
CLE: Jackson 7–122, Alexander 5–69, Hoard 1–25, Hartley 2–17, Byner 2–16, Carrier 2–13, Kinchen 1–6

AFC Divisional Playoff
Saturday, January 7
Pittsburgh Steelers 29, Browns 9
Three Rivers Stadium (58,185)
White jerseys/white pants

Facing the Steelers in the playoffs for the first time in the 44-year history of the rivalry, the Browns were blown off the field and lost to a team three times in one season for the first time.

The tone was set on the Browns' first series when Derrick Alexander dropped back-to-back passes in Pittsburgh territory, forcing the Browns to punt. Pittsburgh then scored on its first three possessions to take a 17–0 lead midway through the second quarter and never looked back, stretching the advantage to 27–3 going into the fourth quarter. The Browns finally reached the end zone on a 20-yard scoring pass to WR Keenan McCardell with just under six minutes to play. Appropriately, Pittsburgh rounded out the scoring when DB Carnell Lake tackled Testaverde in the end zone for a safety, the first ever allowed by the Browns in the postseason.

The Steelers obliterated the Browns in total yardage (424 to 186) and time of possession (42:27 to 17:33) and rolled up 238 rushing yards as they picked up their first postseason win under head coach Bill Cowher. The Steelers went on to be upset by San Diego in the AFC Championship a week later.

This contest proved to be the Browns' final playoff game for eight years, when they'd return to Pittsburgh for a first-round encounter in 2002.

	1	2	3	4		
Browns	0	3	0	6	=	9
Steelers	3	21	3	2	=	29

PIT-Anderson 39-yd. FG
PIT-Green 2-yd. pass from O'Donnell (Anderson kick)
PIT-Williams 26-yd. run (Anderson kick)
CLE-Stover 22-yd. FG
PIT-Thigpen 9-yd. pass from O'Donnell (Anderson kick)
PIT-Anderson 40-yd. FG
CLE-McCardell 20-yd. pass from Testaverde (pass failed)
PIT-Safety: Lake tackled Testaverde in end zone

Passing
CLE: Testaverde 13–31–144 1 TD 2 INT
PIT: O'Donnell 16–23–186 2 TD 0 INT

Rushing
CLE: Byner 9–43, Hoard 3–8, Metcalf 5–4
PIT: Foster 24–133, Morris 22–60, Williams 2–43, Tomczak 3–2

Receiving
CLE: Jackson 3–47, McCardell 3–47, Metcalf 2–18, Byner 1–14, Carrier 2–8, Hoard 1–5, Kinchen 1–5
PIT: Mills 5–117, Green 3–21, Williams 4–20, Hastings 2–18, Thigpen 2–10

1995

Sunday, September 3
New England Patriots 17, Browns 14
Foxboro Stadium (60,126)
White jerseys/white pants

In a rematch of their playoff encounter eight months before, the Browns' defense was lit up, allowing more than 400 yards, and couldn't hold an eight-point fourth-quarter lead as New England drove 85 yards in the final minutes to score the winning touchdown. The Browns jumped to a 14–6 halftime lead on the strength of two long touchdown passes from QB Vinny Testaverde to WR Michael Jackson, who tallied 157 yards on seven receptions. But the offense struggled in the second half, putting no points on the board and accumulating only 91 total yards. Trailing 14–9, the Patriots regained possession at their own 15 with 4:29 left and drove to the Cleveland 3, where they converted on fourth-and-inches with a minute left to keep the drive alive. With 19 seconds remaining, RB Curtis Martin plowed over the goal line on a second effort to put the Patriots ahead and deliver a tough loss for the Browns, who entered the season with Super Bowl expectations.

Record: 0–1

	1	2	3	4		
Browns	7	7	0	0	=	14
Patriots	6	0	0	11	=	17

NE-Bahr 21-yd. FG
CLE-Jackson 70-yd. pass from Testaverde (Stover kick)
NE-Bahr 21-yd. FG
CLE-Jackson 30-yd. pass from Testaverde (Stover kick)
NE-Bahr 28-yd. FG
NE-Martin 1-yd. run (Meggett run)

Passing
CLE: Testaverde 20–29–254 2 TD 1 INT
NE: Bledsoe 30–47–302 0 TD 0 INT

Rushing
CLE: Hoard 9–39, Byner 3–15, White 4–6
NE: Martin 19–102, Meggett 7–23, Bledsoe 2–0

Receiving
CLE: Jackson 7–157, Hartley 1–23, Bishop 3–15, Byner 2–15, Rison 2–14, McCardell 1–14, White 2–12, Reeves 2–4
NE: Coates 9–106, Moore 6–77, Brisby 7–58, Gash 2–37, Meggett 4–16, Burke 2–8

Sunday, September 10
Browns 22, Tampa Bay Buccaneers 6
Cleveland Stadium (61,083)
White jerseys/white pants

Sparked by a defense that collected seven sacks and forced four turnovers, the Browns bounced back with a resounding victory in the home opener over Tampa Bay, coached by old Cleveland nemesis Sam Wyche. The Browns exploded for 19 points in the second quarter to take control of the game, then Cleveland DB Don Griffin came up with an interception in the end zone on the first possession of the second half to deflate any hopes of a Tampa comeback. WR Keenan McCardell scored both of Cleveland's touchdowns in the final minutes of the first half to give the Browns a commanding lead as they coasted to their fifth straight victory over the Buccaneers and their two-hundredth regular-season home victory.

Record: 1–1

	1	2	3	4		
Buccaneers	0	0	0	6	=	6
Browns	0	19	0	3	=	22

CLE-Stover 43-yd. FG
CLE-Stover 23-yd. FG
CLE-McCardell 6-yd. pass from Testaverde (pass failed)
CLE-McCardell 32-yd. pass from Testaverde (Stover kick)
TB-Rhett 2-yd. run (run failed)
CLE-Stover 20-yd. FG

Passing
TB: Dilfer 20–36–255 0 TD 2 INT
CLE: Testaverde 17–27–256 2 TD 0 INT

Rushing
TB: Rhett 23–89, Dilfer 2–12, Roby 1–0
CLE: Hoard 13–44, Hunter 7–15, Testaverde 5–9, White 6–2

Receiving
TB: Harris 8–95, Hawkins 3–67, Dawsey 2–36, Copeland 2–22, Thomas 1–16, Ellison 1–14, Rhett 2–6, Moore 1-(-1)
CLE: Alexander 3–92, McCardell 6–79, Byner 3–30, Hartley 2–25, Reeves 2–18, Rison 2–18, Hoard 1–12

Sunday, September 17
Browns 14, Houston Oilers 7
Houston Astrodome (36,077)
White jerseys/white pants

In what would prove to be their final game in the Astrodome, the Browns gutted out a tough victory over the Oilers to surge above the .500 mark. The defense forced four turnovers—including three interceptions by DB Stevon Moore in the first half, tying a team record—but the offense struggled and the game was tied at seven following a long Houston touchdown drive early in the fourth quarter. The Browns responded with a quick scoring drive of their own, capped by a Vinny Testaverde touchdown toss to Michael Jackson with nine minutes remaining to provide the winning points. The defense then came up with a crucial fourth-down stand at the Cleveland 35 with two minutes remaining to secure the victory.
Record: 2–1

	1	2	3	4		
Browns	0	7	0	7	=	14
Oilers	0	0	0	7	=	7

CLE-McCardell 15-yd. pass from Testaverde (Stover kick)
HOU-Jeffires 4-yd. pass from Furrer (Del Greco kick)
CLE-Jackson 35-yd. pass from Testaverde (Stover kick)

Passing
CLE: Testaverde 10–23–147 2 TD 0 INT
HOU: Furrer 22–41–268 1 TD 4 INT

Rushing
CLE: Hoard 20–88, Testaverde 4–18, White 4–18, Byner 2–8
HOU: Brown 12–29, Thomas 14–26, Furrer 3–16

Receiving
CLE: McCardell 3–53, Jackson 2–45, Byner 2–20, Rison 1–15, Hartley 1–12, White 1–2
HOU: Sanders 2–90, McNair 9–70, Jeffires 5–44, Thomas 2–32, Wycheck 2–22, Lewis 1–6, Russell 1–4

Sunday, September 24
Browns 35, Kansas City Chiefs 17
Cleveland Stadium (74,280)
White jerseys/white pants

Facing the undefeated Chiefs—on their way to posting the best record in the NFL for the season—the Browns controlled the game and then turned it into a rout with a pair of interception returns for touchdowns in the fourth quarter. Led by a defense that kept Kansas City out of the end zone in the first three quarters, the Browns built a 21–3 lead on a pair of scores by RB Earnest Byner and the first Browns' touchdown by heralded WR Andre Rison, a free-agent pickup in the offseason. After a Chiefs' touchdown, the Browns put the game away when LBs Gerald Dixon and Mike Caldwell both returned interceptions for touchdowns within 19 seconds. The Browns' third straight victory would prove to be the final truly happy moment of both the season and the franchise's initial regime.
Record: 3–1

	1	2	3	4		
Chiefs	0	3	0	14	=	17
Browns	7	0	7	21	=	35

CLE-Byner 7-yd. run (Stover kick)
KC-Elliott 25-yd. FG
CLE-Rison 4-yd. pass from Testaverde (Stover kick)
CLE-Byner 3-yd. pass from Testaverde (Stover kick)
KC-Cash 38-yd. pass from Bono (Elliott kick)
CLE-Dixon 18-yd. interception return (Stover kick)
CLE-Caldwell 24-yd. interception return (Stover kick)
KC-Slaughter 2-yd. pass from Bono (Elliott kick)

Passing
KC: Bono 29–49–272 2 TD 2 INT
CLE: Testaverde 21–36–204 2 TD 0 INT, Tupa 1–1–25 0 TD 0 INT

Rushing
KC: Anders 2–21, Thompson 5–18, Hill 8–17, Allen 1–3
CLE: Hoard 13–50, Byner 9–38, Hunter 5–29, White 5–7

Receiving
KC: Cash 8–111, Davis 5–53, Dawson 4–52, Anders 7–31, Slaughter 2–7, Hughes 1–9, Walker 1–7, Vanover 1–2
CLE: McCardell 6–85, Byner 7–59, Rison 4–35, Riddick 1–25, Hoard 1–11, Jackson 1–8, Hartley 1–3, Reeves 1–3

Monday, October 2
Buffalo Bills 22, Browns 19
Cleveland Stadium (76,211)
White jerseys/white pants

Twenty-four hours before the Indians would play their first postseason game in 41 years down the street, the Browns suffered a frustrating loss before a national-television audience on *Monday Night Football.* Their only touchdown on the evening came midway through the first quarter when WR Derrick Alexander returned a punt 69 yards for a score. For the rest of the night, the offense continually squandered scoring opportunities and was unable to push the ball into the end zone. Four Matt Stover field goals kept the Browns in it, his last tying the game at 16 with 3:49 left. But the Bills, who'd blown chances themselves with a missed chip-shot field goal and an extra point, drove downfield and were poised to win with a 33-yard field goal with five seconds left. Kicker Steve Christie missed the kick, but the Browns had called time out just before the play in an attempt to ice him, thus giving him another chance. He made the second and the Browns' three-game winning streak was over. One of Cleveland's lone bright spots was the first big game for Andre Rison, who caught six passes for 126 yards.

Record: 3–2

	1	2	3	4		
Bills	10	0	3	9	=	22
Browns	7	3	6	3	=	19

BUF-Armour 14-yd. pass from Kelly (Christie kick)
CLE-Alexander 69-yd. punt return (Stover kick)
BUF-Christie 38-yd. FG
CLE-Stover 32-yd. FG
BUF-Christie 31-yd. FG
CLE-Stover 47-yd. FG
CLE-Stover 23-yd. FG
BUF-Reed 41-yd. pass from Kelly (kick failed)
CLE-Stover 38-yd. FG
BUF-Christie 33-yd. FG

Passing
BUF: Kelly 27–34–256 2 TD 1 INT
CLE: Testaverde 18–34–224 0 TD 0 INT, Jackson 0–1–0 0 TD 1 INT

Rushing
BUF: Thomas 23–86, Holmes 9–62, Reed 1–8, Gardner 2–5, Kelly 1-(-1)
CLE: Alexander 1–29, Byner 7–24, White 5–24, Hoard 7–13, Testaverde 1–7

Receiving
BUF: Reed 9–97, Armour 4–46, Thomas 5–40, Copeland 2–34, Johnson 4–24, Brooks 1–8, Holmes 2–7
CLE: Rison 6–126, McCardell 5–60, Alexander 1–10, Jackson 1–9, Byner 2–8, Testaverde 1–7, Reeves 2–4

Sunday, October 8
Detroit Lions 38, Browns 20
Pontiac Silverdome (74,171)
White jerseys/white pants

Six days after a tough loss, the banged-up, demoralized Browns were crushed in Detroit as the defense permitted more than 400 yards for the second straight week and third time in five games. Lions' RB Barry Sanders ran wild, picking up 157 yards on just 18 carries along with three touchdowns, including a career-best 75-yard scoring scamper in the first quarter, as the Lions built a 31–3 lead. They then withstood a late barrage of meaningless Cleveland scores, including the first career scoring pass for rookie QB Eric Zeier. The floundering Browns' offense managed only 255 total yards as Cleveland dropped back to .500.

Record: 3–3

	1	2	3	4		
Browns	3	0	7	10	=	20
Lions	14	10	7	7	=	38

DET-Sanders 11-yd. run (Hanson kick)
CLE-Stover 22-yd. FG
DET-Sanders 75-yd. run (Hanson kick)
DET-Perriman 14-yd. pass from Mitchell (Hanson kick)
DET-Hanson 56-yd. FG
DET-Sanders 2-yd. run (Hanson kick)
CLE-Jackson 17-yd. pass from Testaverde (Stover kick)
DET-Perriman 28-yd. pass from Mitchell (Hanson kick)
CLE-Stover 38-yd. FG
CLE-Reeves 1-yd. pass from Zeier (Stover kick)

Passing
CLE: Testaverde 16–30–154 1 TD 0 INT, Zeier 6–10–46 1 TD 0 INT
DET: Mitchell 24–38–273 2 TD 1 INT

Rushing
CLE: Hunter 13–34, Hoard 7–22, White 4–3, Byner 1–0
DET: Sanders 18–157, Rivers 3–5, Majkowski 1-(-1)

Receiving
CLE: Jackson 3–54, Alexander 6–44, Hunter 4–36, Byner 3–26, McCardell 2–14, Bishop 1–12, Hoard 1–9, Kinchen 1–4, Reeves 1–1
DET: Moore 9–125, Perriman 6–78, Morton 5–43, Sanders 4–27

Sunday, October 22
Jacksonville Jaguars 23, Browns 15
Cleveland Stadium (64,405)
White jerseys/white pants

Thirteen-point favorites, the Browns watched their struggles multiply as they suffered a humiliating loss on their home field against the expansion Jaguars. The offense picked up nearly 400 total yards, but handed Jacksonville an early touchdown on an interception return—one of four Cleveland turnovers on the day—while managing only nine points on four trips inside the Jaguars' 20. Meanwhile, the Cleveland defense had trouble stopping the Jacksonville offense, ranked dead last in the NFL, giving up 20 points in the first half. The Browns cut a 14-point deficit to 20–15 going into the fourth quarter, then drove into Jacksonville territory on their final three drives, only to see them all end in turnovers. Little-used Browns' WR Rico Smith broke loose with the only big game of his career, catching six passes for 106 yards and the Browns' only touchdown. With their third straight defeat, the Browns dipped below .500, but with the Indians beginning play in their first World Series in four decades the previous evening, few Cleveland fans truly noticed.
Record: 3–4

	1	2	3	4		
Jaguars	13	7	0	3	=	23
Browns	0	12	3	0	=	15

JAX-Tillman 6-yd. pass from Brunell (Hollis kick)
JAX-Washington 48-yd. interception return (kick failed)
CLE-Stover 36-yd. FG
CLE-Stover 29-yd. FG
JAX-Dunbar 1-yd. run (Hollis kick)
CLE-Smith 29-yd. pass from Testaverde (pass failed)
CLE-Stover 21-yd. FG
JAX-Hollis 31-yd. FG

Passing
JAX: Brunell 16–28–164 1 TD 1 INT
CLE: Testaverde 20–34–299 1 TD 2 INT

Rushing
JAX: Dunbar 26–90, Brunell 11–58, Stewart 8–11
CLE: Hoard 19–74, Hunter 4–15, Byner 1–0

Receiving
JAX: Tillman 4–61, Jackson 7–53, Mitchell 2–30, Griffith 1–12, Stewart 1–10, Maston 1-(-2)
CLE: Smith 6–106, Kinchen 3–56, Byner 3–30, Hoard 2–29, Bishop 2–28, Rison 2–27, McCardell 1–12, Hartley 1–11

Sunday, October 29
Browns 29, Cincinnati Bengals 26 (OT)
Riverfront Stadium (58,639)
White jerseys/white pants

Desperately looking to find a spark, Bill Belichick benched Vinny Testaverde, though he was putting together one of the finest seasons of his career, and started rookie Eric Zeier at QB. Surprisingly, with Zeier at the controls, the Cleveland offense exploded for nearly 500 yards and appeared to have victory wrapped up when a pair of fourth-quarter touchdowns gave the Browns a 26–16 lead with less than four minutes remaining. The Bengals kicked a field goal with a minute left, then recovered an onside kick. Thanks to a pair of pass-interference penalties on the Browns, the Bengals drove to the Cleveland 1, where they scored the tying touchdown with 15 seconds showing. The game plunged into overtime, when an interception by Cleveland DB Dana Hill set up the game-winning field goal six minutes into sudden-death. Zeier threw for 310 yards, targeting sparsely used Andre Rison seven times for 173 yards. The Cleveland defense collected five sacks and forced four turnovers, but the Browns were their own worst enemy, rolling up 15 penalties for a whopping 188 yards, the second-highest total in team history.
Record: 4–4

	1	2	3	4	OT		
Browns	3	6	3	14	3	=	29
Bengals	6	3	7	10	0	=	26

CIN-Green 1-yd. pass from Blake (pass failed)
CLE-Stover 44-yd. FG
CLE-Stover 25-yd. FG
CIN-Pelfrey 37-yd. FG
CLE-Stover 36-yd. FG
CLE-Stover 38-yd. FG
CIN-Pickens 8-yd. pass from Blake (Pelfrey kick)
CLE-Rison 17-yd. pass from Zeier (Stover kick)

CLE-Byner 3-yd. run (Stover kick)
CIN-Pelfrey 41-yd. FG
CIN-Pickens 1-yd. pass from Klingler (Pelfrey kick)
CLE-Stover 28-yd. FG

Passing
CLE: Zeier 26–46–310 1 TD 1 INT
CIN: Blake 20–35–249 2 TD 2 INT, Klingler 5–11–73 1 TD 0 INT

Rushing
CLE: Byner 17–74, Hoard 8–48, Zeier 8–44, Hunter 1–7, Vardell 1–6
CIN: Green 14–66, Bieniemy 4–19, Cothran 1–4, Blake 2–3

Receiving
CLE: Rison 7–173, Byner 4–43, Smith 3–30, Bishop 4–21, Kinchen 2–21, Vardell 4–17, Hoard 2–5
CIN: Bieniemy 6–95, McGee 4–63, Scott 3–62, Dunn 3–42, Green 4–23, Pickens 3–16, Hill 1–11, Joseph 1–10

Sunday, November 5
Houston Oilers 37, Browns 10
Cleveland Stadium (57,881)
White jerseys/white pants

Just hours after news broke of the team moving to Baltimore, the Browns hosted the division-rival Oilers—for the final time ever, it would turn out—in a bizarre, toxic environment at the stadium. Art Modell, fearing for his safety, missed a home game for the first time in the 35 seasons he'd owned the team but didn't miss much as the lifeless Browns were routed. The magic Eric Zeier brought to the team the week before was gone, as he tossed three interceptions and was sacked three times. Trailing 17–7, the Browns drove to the Houston 1 on the first possession of the third quarter but were forced to settle for a field goal. The defensive stand by the Oilers changed the complexion of the game as Houston scored the final 20 points and coasted to an easy victory, beginning the most surreal period in Cleveland sports history.
Record: 4–5

	1	2	3	4		
Oilers	3	14	10	10	=	37
Browns	7	0	3	0	=	10

CLE-Rison 4-yd. pass from Zeier (Stover kick)
HOU-Del Greco 44-yd. FG
HOU-Chandler 2-yd. run (Del Greco kick)
HOU-Jeffires 23-yd. pass from Chandler (Del Greco kick)
CLE-Stover 20-yd. FG
HOU-Floyd 15-yd. pass from Chandler (Del Greco kick)
HOU-Del Greco 45-yd. FG
HOU-Del Greco 37-yd. FG
HOU-Bishop 62-yd. interception return (Del Greco kick)

Passing
HOU: Chandler 16–20–149 2 TD 0 INT, Furrer 1–2–4 0 TD 1 INT
CLE: Zeier 28–54–273 1 TD 3 INT

Rushing
HOU: Thomas 17–108, Chandler 3–10, Butts 3–9, Brown 2–5, T. McNair 1–5, S. McNair 1-(-1)
CLE: White 13–42, Zeier 4–31, Byner 4–23, Rison 1–5, Vardell 1–1

Receiving
HOU: Jeffires 4–57, Floyd 4–50, Wycheck 2–18, T. McNair 3–16, Lewis 1–6, Sanders 1–5, Thomas 2–1
CLE: Rison 3–57, White 3–45, Kinchen 6–43, McCardell 4–39, Byner 4–36, Smith 3–31, Alexander 2–18, Jackson 1–3, Vardell 2–1

Monday, November 13
Pittsburgh Steelers 20, Browns 3
Three Rivers Stadium (58,675)
White jerseys/white pants

One week after Art Modell officially announced the Browns were moving to Baltimore, despite an admirable effort by the Cleveland defense, the Browns were once again stomped, this time on *Monday Night Football* by the Super Bowl-bound Steelers. After the first NFL touchdown pass for versatile Pittsburgh QB Kordell Stewart, the Browns trailed only 7–3 at the half. But they were held to just 10 total yards and no first downs in the final two quarters as they fell in Pittsburgh for the sixth straight time. With the offense compiling only 120 yards for the game, Eric Zeier struggled once again, completing only seven passes while being sacked four times. Punter Tom Tupa was the lone bright spot, averaging better than 48 yards per kick on his nine punts.
Record: 4–6

	1	2	3	4		
Browns	0	3	0	0	=	3
Steelers	0	7	6	7	=	20

PIT-Mills 2-yd. pass from Stewart (Johnson kick)
CLE-Stover 29-yd. FG
PIT-Johnson 38-yd. FG
PIT-Johnson 34-yd. FG
PIT-Thigpen 9-yd. pass from O'Donnell (Johnson kick)

Passing
CLE: Zeier 7–19–67 0 TD 1 INT
PIT: O'Donnell 17–31–167 1 TD 0 INT, Stewart 1–1–2 1 TD 0 INT

Rushing
CLE: Hoard 7–43, Byner 5–20, White 3–11, Zeier 2–3
PIT: Pegram 26–112, Williams 6–20, Stewart 2–13, Morris 6–10, O'Donnell 1-(-2)

Receiving
CLE: Jackson 2–26, Rison 2–22, Byner 2–14, Kinchen 1–5
PIT: Johnson 4–50, Williams 2–26, Pegram 4–22, Stewart 2–21, Hayes 1–10, Hastings 2–9, Thigpen 1–9

Sunday, November 19
Green Bay Packers 31, Browns 20
Cleveland Stadium (55,388)
White jerseys/white pants

After two straight listless performances, the Browns showed signs of life when Vinny Testaverde was reinserted at quarterback at halftime but still couldn't overcome a huge deficit and lost their third straight game this time with all advertisements having been stripped from the Stadium as sponsors pulled their support of the team. Down 21–3 going into the third quarter, after Eric Zeier managed just 14 passing yards in the first half, Testaverde led the Browns to 17 second-half points and threw for nearly 250 yards in the final two quarters as Cleveland snapped a streak of 10 straight quarters without a touchdown. Trailing 24–13 midway through the fourth quarter, the Browns drove into Green Bay territory before a Testaverde interception halted the drive, and intended receiver Andre Rison didn't touch Green Bay DB LeRoy Butler after he hit the ground on the catch. Butler got up and ran 76 yards to set up a game-clinching touchdown run by Green Bay QB Brett Favre two plays later. Cleveland WR Keenan McCardell tallied 102 receiving yards while Michael Jackson caught a pair of touchdowns.

Record: 4–7

	1	2	3	4		
Packers	7	14	3	7	=	31
Browns	3	0	3	14	=	20

CLE-Stover 46-yd. FG
GB-Levens 6-yd. pass from Favre (Jacke kick)
GB-Chmura 3-yd. pass from Favre (Jacke kick)
GB-Morgan 13-yd. pass from Favre (Jacke kick)
CLE-Stover 38-yd. FG
GB-Jacke 28-yd. FG
CLE-Jackson 8-yd. pass from Testaverde (Stover kick)
GB-Favre 4-yd. run (Jacke kick)
CLE-Jackson 37-yd. pass from Testaverde (Stover kick)

Passing
GB: Favre 23–28–210 3 TD 0 INT
CLE: Testaverde 16–22–244 2 TD 1 INT, Zeier 5–10–14 0 TD 0 INT

Rushing
GB: Bennett 23–71, Levens 4–12, Favre 5-(-1)
CLE: Hoard 11–57, Byner 6–10, White 2–6, Vardell 1–2, Zeier 1–2, Testaverde 1–0

Receiving
GB: Brooks 5–48, Bennett 5–42, Levens 4–38, Morgan 2–25, Jackson 2–22, Chmura 2–16, Ingram 1–9, Freeman 1–5, Henderson 1–5
CLE: McCardell 4–102, Jackson 5–83, Hartley 2–27, Rison 3–20, Byner 4–18, Kinchen 1–4, White 1–4, Hoard 1–0

Sunday, November 26
Pittsburgh Steelers 20, Browns 17
Cleveland Stadium (67,269)
White jerseys/white pants

For the second straight week a spirited Browns' comeback went for naught as they lost their fourth consecutive game before the smallest crowd to attend a Browns–Steelers game in Cleveland in 13 years. Hampered by turnovers on their first two offensive plays, the Browns quickly fell behind 10–0 and trailed 17–3 midway through the second quarter. Vinny Testaverde, starting his first game in a month, directed the Browns to back-to-back touchdowns to tie the game, but Pittsburgh surged ahead with a field goal early in the fourth quarter, then took advantage of another Cleveland interception to hold off the Browns, controlling the football for the final nine minutes of the game. It would be the last time the teams would ever face one another in Cleveland Stadium.

Record: 4–8

	1	2	3	4		
Steelers	10	7	0	3	=	20
Browns	0	10	7	0	=	17

PIT-Johnson 33-yd. FG
PIT-Bruener 12-yd. pass from O'Donnell (Johnson kick)
CLE-Stover 44-yd. FG
PIT-Morris 1-yd. run (Johnson kick)
CLE-Jackson 11-yd. pass from Testaverde (Stover kick)
CLE-Testaverde 1-yd. run (Stover kick)
PIT-Johnson 27-yd. FG

Passing
PIT: O'Donnell 21–30–251 1 TD 0 INT, Stewart 2–2–17 0 TD 0 INT
CLE: Testaverde 20–33–178 1 TD 2 INT

Rushing
PIT: Morris 17–55, Pegram 8–6, O'Donnell 7-(-1)
CLE: Hoard 14–49, Byner 8–27, Vardell 1–0, Testaverde 2-(-1)

Receiving
PIT: Thigpen 5–106, Mills 2–41, Stewart 2–36, Bruener 5–34, Johnson 1–15, Williams 4–14, Pegram 2–11, Hayes 1–6, Morris 1–5
CLE: Byner 4–45, Jackson 6–42, Rison 5–38, McCardell 2–23, Kinchen 1–16, Hoard 2–14

Sunday, December 3
San Diego Chargers 31, Browns 13
Jack Murphy Stadium (56,358)
White jerseys/white pants

For the third straight week, the Browns dug an early hole and saw a second-half rally fall short, this time due to the beleaguered defense allowing two fourth-quarter touchdowns. After fumbling the opening kickoff, the Browns trailed 17–3 at the half before cutting the margin to a touchdown going into the fourth quarter. San Diego regained momentum with a 96-yard scoring drive to stretch the lead back to 14 points, then added another touchdown five minutes later to put the game away. The Browns tacked on the final points when Bill Belichick bizarrely called a time out and sent Matt Stover out to kick a field goal on the last play of the game with the Browns trailing 31–10. While Vinny Testaverde played well, throwing for 303 yards, the Cleveland running game was nonexistent, picking up just 26 yards on the day. The Chargers, meanwhile, rushed for 186 and topped 400 as a team.
Record: 4–9

	1	2	3	4		
Browns	0	3	7	3	=	13
Chargers	7	10	0	14	=	31

SD-Hayden 3-yd. run (Carney kick)
SD-Carney 31-yd. FG
CLE-Stover 34-yd. FG
SD-Hayden 1-yd. run (Carney kick)
CLE-Jackson 28-yd. pass from Testaverde (Stover kick)
SD-Martin 25-yd. pass from Humphries (Carney kick)
SD-Fletcher 16-yd. run (Carney kick)
CLE-Stover 40-yd. FG

Passing
CLE: Testaverde 28–41–303 1 TD 1 INT
SD: Humphries 18–25–230 1 TD 0 INT

Rushing
CLE: Hoard 8–20, Byner 5–9, Testaverde 1–1, White 1–1, Rison 1-(-5)
SD: Hayden 32–127, Fletcher 5–39, Harmon 1–10, Culver 2–9, Humphries 3–1

Receiving
CLE: McCardell 9–97, Jackson 3–51, Byner 5–32, Kinchen 2–29, Hoard 3–23, Rison 2–23, Bishop 2–21, Alexander 1–21, Hunter 1–6
SD: Martin 9–132, Seay 3–32, Jefferson 2–23, Pupunu 2–23, Harmon 2–20

Saturday, December 9
Minnesota Vikings 27, Browns 11
Hubert H. Humphrey Metrodome (47,984)
White jerseys/white pants

With bitter-cold conditions and a wind-chill factor of –50°F outside the Metrodome, inside the lifeless Browns played miserably and were dominated by the Vikings on a Saturday afternoon. The Cleveland offense was terrible, managing just 29 yards on the ground, while the Browns allowed five sacks as Eric Zeier threw four interceptions in relief of Vinny Testaverde. The Cleveland defense permitted more than 400 total yards for the fifth time on the season as the Vikings picked up 26 first downs and rolled to a 27–3 lead before the Browns scored their lone touchdown midway through the final period. It marked the Browns' sixth straight loss since the decision to move the team became public.
Record: 4–10

	1	2	3	4		
Browns	0	3	0	8	=	11
Vikings	3	10	7	7	=	27

MIN-Reveiz 23-yd. FG
MIN-Evans 1-yd. pass from Moon (Reveiz kick)
CLE-Stover 26-yd. FG
MIN-Reveiz 28-yd. FG
MIN-Reed 9-yd. pass from Moon (Reveiz kick)
MIN-Evans 2-yd. run (Reveiz kick)
CLE-Byner 29-yd. pass from Zeier (Zeier run)

Passing
CLE: Zeier 10–22–154 1 TD 4 INT, Testaverde 5–6–54 0 TD 0 INT
MIN: Moon 20–29–267 2 TD 1 INT, Johnson 9–11–72 0 TD 1 INT

Rushing
CLE: Byner 3–11, White 8–9, Tupa 1–9, Testaverde 1–0
MIN: Graham 18–77, Evans 10–22, Phillips 6–10, Palmer 2–6, Moon 3-(-4)

Receiving
CLE: Rison 1–49, Jackson 3–45, Byner 3–40, Alexander 2–31, McCardell 3–23, Kinchen 1–10, Bishop 1–9, White 1–1
MIN: Carter 8–124, Reed 4–91, Ismail 6–70, Evans 6–20, Graham 2–13, DeLong 2–12, Lee 1–9

Sunday, December 17
Browns 26, Cincinnati Bengals 10
Cleveland Stadium (55,875)
White jerseys/white pants

In the final game ever played at Cleveland Municipal Stadium, the inspired Browns gave an emotional home crowd one final victory, defeating the Bengals for the seventh straight time. A pair of Vinny Testaverde touchdown passes in a 17-point second quarter helped the Browns build a 26–3 lead in the fourth quarter, made memorable by fans sawing loose their seats and bleacher planks and tossing them onto the field, along with firecrackers and other debris. Appropriately, the star of the game for the Browns was longtime RB Earnest Byner, who rushed for 121 yards on 31 carries and added another 36 yards receiving as the offense collected 400 total yards. After the game ended, players gathered in front of the end zone bleachers, embracing and thanking fans as an era came to a heartbreaking end.
Record: 5–10

	1	2	3	4		
Bengals	0	3	0	7	=	10
Browns	0	17	6	3	=	26

CLE-Hartley 1-yd. pass from Testaverde (Stover kick)
CIN-Pelfrey 30-yd. FG
CLE-Stover 37-yd. FG
CLE-McCardell 16-yd. pass from Testaverde (Stover kick)
CLE-Stover 42-yd. FG
CLE-Stover 19-yd. FG
CLE-Stover 35-yd. FG
CIN-Bieniemy 1-yd. run (Pelfrey kick)

Passing
CIN: Blake 22–46–257 0 TD 1 INT
CLE: Testaverde 22–32–241 2 TD 0 INT

Rushing
CIN: Green 7–33, Bieniemy 5–18, Blake 4–14
CLE: Byner 31–121, Powers 9–29, Testaverde 1–9

Receiving
CIN: Pickens 5–90, McGee 2–43, Scott 4–36, Dunn 4–30, Hill 1–18, Green 2–17, Joseph 3–14, Bieniemy 1–9
CLE: Rison 6–73, Jackson 3–61, Byner 7–36, McCardell 3–33, Hartley 2 21, Bishop 1–17

Sunday, December 24
Jacksonville Jaguars 24, Browns 21
Jacksonville Municipal Stadium (66,007)
White jerseys/white pants

On Christmas Eve, the Browns closed out their first regime with a last-second loss as the expansion Jaguars completed a season sweep of the Browns, winning for the first time since their first victory over Cleveland two months earlier. The Browns' offense rolled up 450 yards—with Vinny Testaverde throwing for a season-high 325 and Michael Jackson catching seven passes for 130—but coughed up three turnovers, which allowed the Jaguars to build a 10–0 lead and then go ahead by seven in the fourth quarter. The game appeared to be headed for overtime when Testaverde scored on a one-yard run to tie the game with 1:13 left, but there was just enough time for Jacksonville to drive into Cleveland territory and attempt a 39-yard field goal. The kick hit the upright and fell away, but the Browns were called for an offside penalty, and the subsequent 34-yard kick was good, a fitting way for the season and the era to come to a close.
Record: 5–11

	1	2	3	4		
Browns	0	7	7	7	=	21
Jaguars	10	3	0	11	=	24

JAX-Hollis 42-yd. FG
JAX-Jackson 33-yd. pass from Brunell (Hollis kick)
CLE-Jackson 39-yd. pass from Testaverde (Stover kick)
JAX-Hollis 20-yd. FG
CLE-White 3-yd. run (Stover kick)
JAX-Brunell 27-yd. run (Jackson pass from Brunell)
CLE-Testaverde 1-yd. run (Stover kick)
JAX-Hollis 34-yd. FG

Passing
CLE: Testaverde 28–45–325 1 TD 3 INT
JAX: Brunell 17–29–275 1 TD 0 INT

Rushing
CLE: Byner 13–52, White 7–34, Testaverde 3–26, Powers 5–22
JAX: Brunell 5–51, Dunbar 16–36, Stewart 2–12, Maston 4–6

Receiving
CLE: Jackson 7–130, McCardell 7–75, Byner 6–42, Kinchen 2–28, Hartley 1–15, Bishop 2–12, Rison 1–11, Powers 1–6, Smith 1–6
JAX: Jackson 4–81, Marsh 3–73, Maston 5–41, Mitchell 2–29, Smith 2–27, Howard 1–24

The Lost Years

Following Art Modell's decision to move his franchise to Baltimore, starting at the conclusion of the 1995 season and for the three years that followed, there simply were no Cleveland Browns.

In 1996, 1997, and 1998, a Browns team did not take the field, and for the first time since 1936, the NFL didn't have a team in Cleveland. Quite a bit happened that affected the team and its history during that hiatus, but it all occurred off the field.

First and foremost, amid a variety of legal maneuvers by both the City of Cleveland and the NFL, in early 1996 the league ruled that while Modell could move the team, the "Browns" name, colors, and history would remain in Cleveland, to be taken up by a new version of the franchise starting in the 1999 season. Thus, Modell's original Browns adopted the "Ravens" nickname with a new logo and colors and were considered a new team by the league.

After some indecision as to whether the new Browns would be an expansion team or another NFL franchise relocated, the league announced in early 1998 that Cleveland would receive a brand-new expansion franchise.

The new team would also play in a new home. Cleveland Municipal Stadium—home to the Browns for a half-century, was demolished in 1996 and construction began on a new ballpark at the same site, eventually named Cleveland Browns Stadium, which opened with the Browns' return.

In September 1998, the NFL awarded the new Cleveland franchise to Al Lerner, the CEO of credit card company MBNA Corp., who'd submitted a winning bid of $530 million. The following winter, the primary components of the team began to come together, starting with the hiring of head coach Chris Palmer and the new players selected through the expansion and college drafts.

And finally, in September of 1999, after a 1,357-day drought, the Cleveland Browns returned to the field.

1999

Sunday, September 12
Pittsburgh Steelers 43, Browns 0
Cleveland Browns Stadium (73,138)
Brown jerseys/white pants

After a three-year absence, the Cleveland Browns were reborn before a capacity crowd at their new stadium and an ESPN national-television audience. But the party didn't last long as the Steelers annihilated the expansion Browns in what became one of the most lopsided games in NFL history. After stopping Pittsburgh on fourth-and-inches at the Cleveland 22 on the first series and a 14-yard catch by WR Leslie Shepherd on the Browns' first offensive play, it was all downhill. Cleveland was held to a team-record-low 40 total yards of offense, including a meager nine yards on the ground, and just two first downs, holding the football for just over 12 minutes of the game. Top draft pick Tim Couch relieved QB Ty Detmer early in the fourth quarter and saw his first pass intercepted, then later fumbled after being sacked. While the Cleveland offense was stymied, the defense allowed the Steelers to roll to 464 yards and 33 first downs over the course of a long night that forecasted a long season.

Record: 0–1

	1	2	3	4		
Steelers	7	13	6	17	=	43
Browns	0	0	0	0	=	0

PIT-Stewart 1-yd. run (Brown kick)
PIT-Brown 18-yd. FG
PIT-Huntley 5-yd. pass from Stewart (Brown kick)
PIT-Brown 28-yd. FG
PIT-Huntley 3-yd. run (kick failed)
PIT-Brown 19-yd. FG
PIT-Huntley 21-yd. pass from Tomczak (Brown kick)
PIT-Ward 1-yd. pass from Tomczak (Brown kick)

Passing
PIT: Stewart 15–23–173 1 TD 0 INT, Tomczak 8–8–78 2 TD 0 INT, Gonzalez 1–1–8 0 TD 0 INT
CLE: Detmer 6–13–52 0 TD 1 INT, Couch 0–3–0 0 TD 1 INT

Rushing
PIT: Bettis 18–89, Zereoue 17–44, Huntley 10–41, Stewart 7–35, Witman 3–11, Gonzalez 2-(-3)
CLE: Kirby 5–10, Edwards 1–1, Shaw 2-(-1), Detmer 1-(-1)

Receiving
PIT: Huntley 5–67, Ward 3–51, Edwards 4–45, Hawkins 3–27, Shaw 3–26, Blackwell 2–18, Zereoue 1–14, Witman 2–9, Bettis 1–2
CLE: Shepherd 2–32, Johnson 2–13, Edwards 1–5, Kirby 1–2

Sunday, September 19
Tennessee Titans 26, Browns 9
Adelphia Coliseum (65,904)
White jerseys/white pants

Following head coach Chris Palmer's decision to begin playing for the future, Tim Couch and several other young players were inserted into the starting lineup in the Browns' first-ever meeting with the Super Bowl-bound Titans. Plagued by poor field position all day, Couch was drilled in the end zone for an early safety but led the Browns to their first touchdown of the season on a 39-yard pass to fellow rookie WR Kevin Johnson late in the third quarter. After a rough first half, Couch played well in the final two quarters, completing 10 of 14 passes for 106 yards. While there was improvement, the Browns were still completely overmatched, being outgained 412 yards to 173 while allowing seven sacks.

Record: 0–2

	1	2	3	4		
Browns	0	3	6	0	=	9
Titans	2	14	3	7	=	26

TEN-Safety: Robinson tackled Couch in end zone
TEN-George 1-yd. run (Del Greco kick)
CLE-Dawson 41-yd. FG
TEN-George 1-yd. run (Del Greco kick)
TEN-Del Greco 35-yd. FG
CLE-Johnson 39-yd. pass from Couch (pass failed)
TEN-Thigpen 14-yd. pass from O'Donnell (Del Greco kick)

THE BROWNS' TRAVELING ROAD SHOW

While preseason games are generally forgettable, the Browns have a long history of traveling to unusual locations to play several exhibitions.

August 30, 1946,
at Rubber Bowl—Akron, Ohio
Browns 35, Brooklyn Dodgers 20

August 29, 1947,
at Rubber Bowl—Akron, Ohio
Browns 28, Baltimore Colts 0

August 22, 1948,
at Rubber Bowl—Akron, Ohio
Browns 35, Buffalo Bisons 21

August 27, 1948,
at Glass Bowl—Toledo, Ohio
Baltimore Colts 21, Browns 17

August 12, 1950,
at Glass Bowl—Toledo, Ohio
Browns 38, Green Bay Packers 7

August 19, 1950,
at Nippert Stadium—Cincinnati, Ohio
Browns 34, Baltimore Colts 7

August 25, 1950,
at Rubber Bowl—Akron, Ohio
Browns 35, Detroit Lions 14

September 4, 1950,
at Civic Stadium—Buffalo, New York
Browns 41, Pittsburgh Steelers 31

August 25, 1951,
at Rubber Bowl—Akron, Ohio
Browns 52, New York Yankees 0

September 6, 1952,
at Archbold Stadium—Syracuse, New York
Detroit Lions 28, Browns 21

September 13, 1952,
at Rubber Bowl—Akron, Ohio
San Francisco 49ers 35, Browns 31

September 7, 1953,
at Rubber Bowl—Akron, Ohio
Browns 23, Baltimore Colts 21

September 10, 1954,
at Cotton Bowl—Dallas, Texas
Detroit Lions 56, Browns 31

August 20, 1955,
at Rubber Bowl—Akron, Ohio
Browns 13, Green Bay Packers 7

September 15, 1956,
at Rubber Bowl—Akron, Ohio
Detroit Lions 31, Browns 14

August 24, 1957,
at Rubber Bowl—Akron, Ohio
Browns 28, Detroit Lions 13

August 16, 1958,
at Rubber Bowl—Akron, Ohio
Browns 10, Pittsburgh Steelers 0

August 22, 1959,
at Rubber Bowl—Akron, Ohio
Detroit Lions 9, Browns 3

September 3, 1960,
at Multnomah Stadium—Portland, Oregon
Browns 26, San Francisco 49ers 24

September 10, 1960,
at Rubber Bowl—Akron, Ohio
Browns 16, Chicago Bears 10

September 1, 1961,
at Rubber Bowl—Akron, Ohio
Browns 38, Pittsburgh Steelers 6

August 25, 1962,
at Multnomah Stadium—Portland, Oregon
Browns 34, San Francisco 49ers 27

September 7, 1963,
at Fawcett Stadium*—Canton, Ohio
Pittsburgh Steelers 16, Browns 7

August 22, 1964,
at Rubber Bowl—Akron, Ohio
Browns 42, Pittsburgh Steelers 7

September 11, 1965,
at Rubber Bowl—Akron, Ohio
Browns 28, Pittsburgh Steelers 16

September 3, 1966
at Legion Field—Birmingham, Alabama
Browns 13, Pittsburgh Steelers 10

August 5, 1967,
at Fawcett Stadium**—Canton, Ohio
Philadelphia Eagles 28, Browns 13

August 10, 1969,
at Husky Stadium—Seattle, Washington
Browns 21, San Francisco 49ers 16

September 10, 1969,
at Rubber Bowl—Akron, Ohio
Minnesota Vikings 23, Browns 16

August 15, 1970,
at Tampa Stadium—Tampa, Florida
Browns 17, San Francisco 49ers 10

August 22, 1970,
at Memorial Coliseum—Memphis, Tennessee
Kansas City Chiefs 16, Browns 13

August 28, 1971,
at Notre Dame Stadium—South Bend, Indiana
Chicago Bears 20, Browns 19

August 20, 1972,
at Michigan Stadium—Ann Arbor, Michigan
Detroit Lions 34, Browns 7

September 3, 1972,
at Ohio Stadium—Columbus, Ohio
Cincinnati Bengals 27, Browns 21

August 19, 1973,
at Ohio Stadium—Columbus, Ohio
Browns 24, Cincinnati Bengals 6

August 25, 1973,
at Neyland Stadium—Knoxville, Tennessee
Browns 20, Atlanta Falcons 17

September 8, 1973,
at Rubber Bowl—Akron, Ohio
New York Giants 21, Browns 10

August 17, 1974,
at Tampa Stadium—Tampa, Florida
Baltimore Colts 37, Browns 3

September 1, 1974,
at Ohio Stadium—Columbus, Ohio
Browns 21, Cincinnati Bengals 17

September 7, 1975,
at Husky Stadium—Seattle, Washington
Browns 24, New York Giants 20

July 31, 1976,
at Memorial Stadium—Lincoln, Nebraska
Baltimore Colts 21, Browns 0

August 7, 1976,
at Lewis Field—Stillwater, Oklahoma
Browns 31, Atlanta Falcons 7

August 1, 1981,
at Fawcett Stadium—Canton, Ohio**
Browns 24, Atlanta Falcons 10

August 18, 1988,
at Olympic Stadium—Montreal, Canada
New York Jets 11, Browns 7

August 6, 1989,
at Wembley Stadium—London, England
Philadelphia Eagles 17, Browns 13

August 4, 1990,
at Fawcett Stadium—Canton, Ohio**
Chicago Bears 13, Browns 0

August 14, 1993,
at SkyDome—Toronto, Canada
Browns 12, New England Patriots 9

August 9, 1999,
at Fawcett Stadium—Canton, Ohio**
Browns 20, Dallas Cowboys 17 (OT)

**Coinciding with the opening of the Pro Football Hall of Fame*

***Hall of Fame Game*

Passing
CLE: Couch 12–24–134 1 TD 0 INT
TEN: O'Donnell 31–40–310 1 TD 0 INT

Rushing
CLE: Kirby 10–40, Couch 5–40, Shaw 1–3
TEN: George 31–97, Thomas 1–6, O'Donnell 2-(-1)

Receiving
CLE: Johnson 4–62, Campbell 2–28, Kirby 2–27, Shaw 2–8, Shepherd 1–7, Smith 1–2
TEN: Thigpen 6–84, Wycheck 9–80, Dyson 5–52, George 4–27, Sanders 2–27, Harris 2–16, Thomas 2–15, Roan 1–9

Sunday, September 26
Baltimore Ravens 17, Browns 10
PSINet Stadium (68,803)
White jerseys/white pants

In their first encounter with their former selves, the Browns again showed improvement but made too many mistakes to knock off Art Modell's Baltimore Ravens. A Tim Couch fumble at the Cleveland 1 early in the second quarter led to a Ravens' touchdown as Baltimore took a 17–3 lead into the fourth quarter. The Browns pulled within seven early in the fourth quarter on Kevin Johnson's second touchdown catch in two weeks but were unable to cross their own 35 for the remainder of the game. Their final chance ended when a long Couch pass was intercepted with two minutes left, and the Ravens ran out the clock. The Browns again showed improvement, increasing their total yardage (189) while decreasing their opponent's (334) and were even in sacks (four) and turnovers (three). Cleveland also hit 100 rushing yards as a team, something that would happen just two more times over the course of the season.
Record: 0–3

	1	2	3	4		
Browns	0	0	3	7	=	10
Ravens	3	7	7	0	=	17

BAL-Stover 44-yd. FG
BAL-Case 1-yd. run (Stover kick)
CLE-Dawson 49-yd. FG
BAL-Case 1-yd. run (Stover kick)
CLE-Johnson 12-yd. pass from Couch (Dawson kick)

Passing
CLE: Couch 13–32–123 1 TD 1 INT
BAL: Case 12–25–165 0 TD 3 INT

Rushing
CLE: Kirby 18–51, Couch 6–49
BAL: Rhett 22–113, Case 11–57, Evans 3–13, Lewis 1–1

Receiving
CLE: Kirby 7–75, Johnson 2–18, Edwards 3–16, Shepherd 1–14
BAL: Ismail 2–49, Evans 2–37, Rhett 3–27, Lewis 3–23, Armour 1–16, Pierce 1–13

Sunday, October 3
New England Patriots 19, Browns 7
Cleveland Browns Stadium (72,368)
Brown jerseys/white pants

Once again the Browns showed progress, taking their first lead of the season, but made too many mistakes to keep up with the undefeated Patriots and suffered their fourth straight defeat. The Browns opened the scoring midway through the first quarter on a dazzling 64-yard touchdown catch-and-run down the sideline by Kevin Johnson and led 7–6 at the half. But the Patriots took control on the first possession of the third quarter and grabbed a 19–7 lead after a long touchdown reception by WR Terry Glenn, who had a career day with 13 receptions for 214 yards. The Browns had a chance to get back into the game when DB Marquez Pope returned an interception for a touchdown with just under 10 minutes remaining, but the play was called back on a defensive holding penalty. The Browns were then unable to cross midfield in the final minutes, and New England hung on for the victory. While the Browns topped 200 total yards for the first time on the season, they were unable to control the Patriots, who rolled to 451 yards, including 393 through the air by QB Drew Bledsoe. Johnson paced the Cleveland offense, catching six passes for 131 yards.
Record: 0–4

	1	2	3	4		
Patriots	0	6	7	6	=	19
Browns	7	0	0	0	=	7

CLE-Johnson 64-yd. pass from Couch (Dawson kick)
NE-Vinatieri 23-yd. FG
NE-Vinatieri 21-yd. FG
NE-Allen 3-yd. run (Vinatieri kick)
NE-Glenn 54-yd. pass from Bledsoe (pass failed)

Passing
NE: Bledsoe 29–43–393 1 TD 0 INT
CLE: Couch 13–28–201 1 TD 0 INT

Rushing
NE: Allen 21–68, Warren 6–10, Floyd 3–9, Carter 1–4, Bledsoe 4-(-1)
CLE: Kirby 15–71, Couch 3–11, Jones 1–2, Powell 1-(-14)

Receiving
NE: Glenn 13–214, Brown 4–59, Jefferson 1–32, Simmons 4–29, Brisby 2–27, Carter 3–13, Floyd 1–11, Warren 1–8, Allen 1–5
CLE: Johnson 6–131, Kirby 4–39, Chiaverini 2–23, Shepherd 1–8

Sunday, October 10
Cincinnati Bengals 18, Browns 17
Cleveland Browns Stadium (73,048)
Brown jerseys/white pants

The new Browns suffered their first heartbreaking loss as the 0–4 Bengals rallied with a last-minute touchdown to thwart an inspired Cleveland effort. Cleveland took control of the game early in the second quarter when kicker Phil Dawson scored the Browns' first rushing touchdown of the season on a fake field goal, then after the Browns recovered a Cincy fumble on the ensuing kickoff, they stretched the lead to 14–6 with another score. A blocked punt led to a Cleveland field goal and a 17–12 lead early in the fourth quarter. Unable to run out the clock, the Browns punted back to the Bengals with just over two minutes to play. Rookie QB Akili Smith, upset with the Browns for selecting Couch instead of him in the previous spring's draft, drove his team 80 yards and tossed the game-winning, two-yard touchdown pass to WR Carl Pickens with five seconds left. Though the Browns led most of the game, their offense struggled in the second half, managing just 50 yards and a single first down in the final two quarters. As a result, the Bengals dominated statistically, rolling to 419 total yards as RB Corey Dillon rushed for 168.
Record: 0–5

	1	2	3	4		
Bengals	6	6	0	6	=	18
Browns	0	14	0	3	=	17

CIN-Pelfrey 27-yd. FG
CIN-Pelfrey 26-yd. FG
CLE-Dawson 4-yd. run (Dawson kick)
CLE-Kirby 1-yd. run (Dawson kick)
CIN-Pickens 5-yd. pass from Smith (pass failed)
CLE-Dawson 33-yd. FG
CIN-Pickens 2-yd. pass from Smith (run failed)

Passing
CIN: Smith 25–42–221 2 TD 0 INT
CLE: Couch 15–27–164 0 TD 1 INT

Rushing
CIN: Dillon 28–168, Basnight 5–38, Smith 3–9
CLE: Kirby 15–57, Jones 6–14, Couch 1–5, Dawson 1–4

Receiving
CIN: Scott 8–110, Pickens 7–38, McGee 3–33, Groce 3–25, Griffin 2–10, Bush 1–4, Dillon 1–1
CLE: Johnson 5–73, Kirby 4–30, Edwards 2–29, Shepherd 3–22, Chiaverini 1–10

Sunday, October 17
Jacksonville Jaguars 24, Browns 7
Alltel Stadium (62,047)
White jerseys/white pants

Despite being 17-point underdogs, the Browns hung with the 4–1 Jaguars for nearly three quarters before Jacksonville took control with 18 points in the final 18 minutes to coast to victory. The Browns took the lead three minutes into the second quarter on a Tim Couch-to-RB Terry Kirby touchdown pass and held onto the advantage until the final moments of the third quarter, when a Kirby fumble set up Jacksonville's first touchdown. It proved to be the turning point as Jacksonville scored on its next two possessions while the Browns were unable to cross midfield on their last three. While Couch completed his first nine passes and hit on 18 of 23 for the afternoon against the league's top-ranked defense, Kirby paced an effective ground game that topped 100 yards for the second time on the season.
Record: 0–6

	1	2	3	4		
Browns	0	7	0	0	=	7
Jaguars	3	3	8	10	=	24

JAX-Hollis 20-yd. FG
CLE-Kirby 9-yd. pass from Couch (Dawson kick)
JAX-Hollis 36-yd. FG
JAX-Brady 7-yd. pass from Fiedler (Brady pass from Fiedler)
JAX-Stewart 2-yd. run (Hollis kick)
JAX-Hollis 24-yd. FG

Passing
CLE: Couch 18–23–161 1 TD 0 INT
JAX: Fiedler 12–14–113 1 TD 0 INT, Brunell 12–19–109 0 TD 0 INT

Rushing
CLE: Kirby 22–71, Couch 2–36, Edwards 2–5, Salaam 1–2, Jones 1-(-1)
JAX: Stewart 23–58, Fiedler 3–27, Brunell 2–8, Howard 3–7, Shelton 1–2, Banks 1–1

Receiving
CLE: Chiaverini 5–45, Johnson 3–38, Edwards 3–35, Kirby 3–21, Smith 3–18, Dunn 1–4
JAX: McCardell 7–76, Smith 6–62, Banks 5–40, Brady 2–21, Stewart 3–12, Shelton 1–11

Sunday, October 24
St. Louis Rams 34, Browns 3
TWA Dome (65,866)
White jerseys/white pants

Hoping to spark an inspired performance against the undefeated eventual Super Bowl champions, Kevin Johnson guaranteed a Browns' victory in the days before the game. Instead, the Rams, 19-point favorites, coasted to an easy victory. The Browns dug an early hole as the Rams scored on their first possession, then recovered a Cleveland fumble on the ensuing kickoff, which led to another score and a 14–0 lead. Despite gaining what to this point was a season-high in total yardage with 272, the Browns were unable to score a touchdown and permitted the Rams to roll to 436 yards, paced by RB Marshall Faulk's 200 combined yards.
Record: 0–7

	1	2	3	4		
Browns	3	0	0	0	=	3
Rams	14	7	3	10	=	34

STL-Williams 1-yd. pass from Warner (Wilkins kick)
STL-Bruce 4-yd. pass from Warner (Wilkins kick)
CLE-Dawson 47-yd. FG
STL-Williams 1-yd. pass from Warner (Wilkins kick)
STL-Wilkins 28-yd. FG
STL-Faulk 33-yd. run (Wilkins kick)
STL-Wilkins 36-yd. FG

Passing
CLE: Couch 22–40–185 0 TD 2 INT
STL: Warner 23–29–203 3 TD 0 INT, Justin 4–5–25 0 TD 0 INT

Rushing
CLE: Couch 2–50, Abdul-Jabbar 6–27, Kirby 6–12, Shepherd 1–5
STL: Faulk 16–133, Watson 9–69, Bruce 1–6, Holt 1–5, Germaine 2-(-2)

Receiving
CLE: Shepherd 6–85, Johnson 3–35, Smith 3–31, Kirby 6–18, Abdul-Jabbar 2–8, Edwards 2–8
STL: Faulk 9–67, Williams 5–50, Bruce 4–44, Proehl 5–29, Holt 2–24, Hodgins 2–14

Sunday, October 31
Browns 21, New Orleans Saints 16
Louisiana Superdome (48,817)
White jerseys/white pants

On Halloween, the Browns pulled a trick-or-treat on the Saints, scoring a last-second desperation touchdown to secure their first victory in nearly four years. Aided by five New Orleans turnovers, the Browns scored a pair of touchdowns and took a one-point lead into the fourth quarter. But the Saints endured, picking up 25 first downs to the Browns' nine and held the football for more than 40 minutes. New Orleans rookie RB Ricky Williams led the way, rushing for 179 yards on 40 carries. The Saints finally appeared poised to secure victory when they took a 16–14 lead with a field goal with 21 seconds left. The Browns regained possession at their own 25, and after a quick 18-yard pass to Leslie Shepherd to the Cleveland 44 with two seconds left, the playcall was "258 Flood Tip Right." Tim Couch lobbed a Hail Mary pass to the end zone, which was tipped and then gathered in by Kevin Johnson for the dramatic game-winning score with no time remaining. The stunning victory snapped an eight-game losing streak dating back to 1995.
Record: 1–7

	1	2	3	4		
Browns	0	7	7	7	=	21
Saints	7	3	3	3	=	16

NO-Poole 5-yd. pass from Hobert (Brien kick)
CLE-Edwards 27-yd. pass from Couch (Dawson kick)
NO-Brien 49-yd. FG
CLE-Johnson 24-yd. pass from Couch (Dawson kick)
NO-Brien 22-yd. FG
NO-Brien 46-yd. FG
CLE-Johnson 56-yd. pass from Couch (Dawson kick)

Passing
CLE: Couch 11–19–193 3 TD 0 INT
NO: Tolliver 9–20–92 0 TD 1 INT, Hobert 4–9–28 1 TD 1 INT

Rushing
CLE: Abdul-Jabbar 13–39, Kirby 6–18, Couch 2–5
NO: Williams 40–179, Tolliver 4–24, Smith 4–17, Hobert 1–9, Craver 1–2

Receiving
CLE: Johnson 4–96, Shepherd 4–52, Edwards 2–37, Kirby 1–8
NO: Craver 3–32, Kennison 2–27, Poole 3–23, Dawsey 1–11, Smith 1–11, Williams 3–8, Cleeland 1–8

Sunday, November 7
Baltimore Ravens 41, Browns 9
Cleveland Browns Stadium (72,898)
Brown jerseys/white pants

In the Baltimore Ravens' long-anticipated first visit to Cleveland, the Browns played miserably and were utterly dominated on a sunshiny November afternoon. After the Ravens scored a touchdown on their first possession, the Browns had a chance to take control of the game, recovering first a fumbled punt return that led to a field goal, then an onside kick on the ensuing kickoff. But moments later Tim Couch was intercepted in the end zone, the Ravens drove 80 yards to take a 14–3 lead, and the rout was on. In the fourth quarter, Couch was pulled from a game for the first time at any level of his career, and the Ravens' lead swelled to 34–3 before Ty Detmer finally guided the Browns into the end zone. Baltimore rolled to more than 200 rushing yards while the Browns could manage only 159 total in one of the most disappointing performances of the season.
Record: 1–8

	1	2	3	4		
Ravens	7	10	7	17	=	41
Browns	3	0	0	6	=	9

BAL-Rhett 11-yd. run (Stover kick)
CLE-Dawson 25-yd. FG
BAL-Ismail 28-yd. pass from Banks (Stover kick)
BAL-Stover 28 yd. FG
BAL-Rhett 52-yd. run (Stover kick)
BAL-Stover 44-yd. FG
BAL-Woodson 66-yd. interception return (Stover kick)
CLE-Kirby 5-yd. pass from Detmer (kick failed)
BAL-Case 20-yd. run (Stover kick)

Passing
BAL: Banks 14–25–129 1 TD 0 INT
CLE: Detmer 7–15–81 1 TD 1 INT, Couch 9–21–57 0 TD 1 INT

Rushing
BAL: Rhett 17–117, Holmes 10–40, Banks 4–23, Case 4–17, Evans 3–6
CLE: Abdul-Jabbar 9–23, Kirby 6–19, Couch 4–7, Detmer 1–7

Receiving
BAL: Ismail 2–43, Armour 5–38, Rhett 4–21, Pierce 2–17, Johnson 1–10
CLE: Kirby 5–52, Johnson 3–43, Shepherd 3–23, Edwards 2–9, Smith 2–9, Abdul-Jabbar 1–2

Sunday, November 14
Browns 16, Pittsburgh Steelers 15
Three Rivers Stadium (58,213)
White jerseys/white pants

In one of the most surprising victories in team history, the 15-point underdog Browns pulled off a last-second upset over the 5–3 Steelers to collect just their fifth all-time victory at Three Rivers Stadium. They set the tone for the afternoon by quickly driving 80 yards on the first series of the game and taking a 7–0 lead on a 35-yard touchdown pass from Tim Couch to Kevin Johnson. The Cleveland defense persevered and protected the lead until a Couch fumble inside the Cleveland 10 led to a Pittsburgh touchdown that turned the momentum. The Steelers built a 15–7 lead with 10 minutes remaining and appeared poised to complete a season sweep of the Browns. But then Cleveland LB John Thierry intercepted a pass at the Steelers' 23 to set up a short touchdown catch by FB Marc Edwards to pull the Browns within two points. After forcing a punt, the

Browns regained possession at their own 20 with 1:51 left and quickly drove downfield. Aided by a 23-yard catch by WR Darrin Chiaverini and a roughing-the-passer penalty on Pittsburgh, the Browns reached the Steelers' 22 and, with the clock ticking down under 10 seconds, rushed the kicking team onto the field. Phil Dawson booted a 39-yard kick into a swirling wind and through the uprights to give the Browns a stunning triumph over the team that had annihilated them in the opener. The Browns collected more than five times as much yardage in the second meeting with the Steelers as they did in the first and held an opponent under 300 total yards for the first time all season.

Record: 2–8

	1	2	3	4		
Browns	7	0	0	9	=	16
Steelers	3	0	9	3	=	15

CLE-Johnson 35-yd. pass from Couch (Dawson kick)
PIT-Brown 41-yd. FG
PIT-Brown 32-yd. FG
PIT-Huntley 5-yd. run (run failed)
PIT-Brown 47-yd. FG
CLE-Edwards 5-yd. pass from Couch (run failed)
CLE-Dawson 39-yd. FG

Passing
CLE: Couch 18–28–199 2 TD 1 INT
PIT: Stewart 15–32–137 0 TD 2 INT

Rushing
CLE: Abdul-Jabbar 18–56, Couch 2–15, Kirby 1–3
PIT: Bettis 26–99, Stewart 6–52, Huntley 4–12, Witman 1–5

Receiving
CLE: Johnson 5–73, Chiaverini 3–44, Shepherd 2–31, Edwards 4–22, Campbell 1–12, Kirby 2–10, Abdul-Jabbar 1–7
PIT: Ward 4–39, Hawkins 3–29, Edwards 2–29, Bruener 2–20, Bettis 1–7, Huntley 1–7, Blackwell 1–4, Witman 1–2

Sunday, November 21
Carolina Panthers 31, Browns 17
Cleveland Browns Stadium (72,818)
Brown jerseys/white pants

Despite topping 300 yards in total offense for the first time all season, the Browns were routed in their first-ever meeting with Carolina. After a false-start penalty on fourth-and-goal from the Panthers' 1 forced the Browns to settle for a game-tying field goal early in the second quarter, Carolina scored four straight touchdowns to take a commanding 31–3 lead early in the fourth. Tim Couch, who threw for a season-high 259 yards, led Cleveland to two touchdowns in the final eight minutes to make the final more respectable as the Browns dropped their fifth straight game in their new stadium.

Record: 2–9

	1	2	3	4		
Panthers	3	14	7	7	=	31
Browns	0	3	0	14	=	17

CAR-Kasay 44-yd. FG
CLE-Dawson 23-yd. FG
CAR-Floyd 1-yd. run (Kasay kick)
CAR-Walls 8-yd. pass from Beuerlein (Kasay kick)
CAR-Kinchen 1-yd. pass from Beuerlein (Kasay kick)
CAR-Floyd 1-yd. run (Kasay kick)
CLE-Kirby 2-yd. run (Dawson kick)
CLE-Chiaverini 12-yd. pass from Couch (Dawson kick)

Passing
CAR: Beuerlein 21–27–199 2 TD 0 INT, Lewis 2–3–11 0 TD 0 INT
CLE: Couch 29–46–259 1 TD 2 INT

Rushing
CAR: Biakabutuka 17–93, Lane 3–12, Floyd 6–8, Johnson 1–6, Beuerlein 1–4, Lewis 2–3, Metcalf 1–3
CLE: Kirby 6–22, Couch 6–16, Abdul-Jabbar 7–11

Receiving
CAR: Muhammad 7–72, Biakabutuka 3–42, Walls 4–39, Jeffers 3–34, Johnson 2–11, Floyd 2–10, Kinchen 2–2
CLE: Kirby 9–79, Chiaverini 8–72, Johnson 5–55, Smith 2–26, Campbell 1–21, Edwards 2–4, Abdul-Jabbar 2–2

Sunday, November 28
Tennessee Titans 33, Browns 21
Cleveland Browns Stadium (72,008)
Brown jerseys/white pants

The Browns stood up to the eventual AFC champions, again topping 300 total yards and holding a lead until the third quarter before the Titans rallied with three straight touchdowns to take control and improve to 9–2. Cleveland surged ahead 14–7 with a pair of touchdowns on three offensive plays early in the second quarter, the second a 78-yard scoring pass from Tim Couch to Terry

Kirby. The Browns still led by a point when Kevin Johnson fumbled a punt return at the Cleveland 21 three minutes into the second half, which led to the go-ahead Tennessee touchdown, and the floodgates opened. The Browns' special teams failed again minutes later when they allowed a 65-yard punt return for a touchdown by Titans' WR Derrick Mason. Tim Couch once again played well in defeat, throwing for 262 yards and a pair of touchdowns while running for his first NFL score.

Record: 2–10

	1	2	3	4		
Titans	7	6	13	7	=	33
Browns	0	14	0	7	=	21

TEN-George 14-yd. run (Del Greco kick)
CLE-Couch 4-yd. run (Dawson kick)
CLE-Kirby 78-yd. pass from Couch (Dawson kick)
TEN-Del Greco 27-yd. FG
TEN-Del Greco 31-yd. FG
TEN-McNair 1-yd. run (Del Greco kick)
TEN-Mason 65-yd. punt return (run failed)
TEN-George 5-yd. run (Del Greco kick)
CLE-Johnson 6-yd. pass from Couch (Dawson kick)

Passing
TEN: McNair 18–36–179 0 TD 0 INT
CLE: Couch 19–35–262 2 TD 0 INT

Rushing
TEN: George 26–113, McNair 7–45
CLE: Abdul-Jabbar 15–35, Couch 5–29, Kirby 4–17

Receiving
TEN: Harris 3–44, Dyson 4–42, Mason 3–28, Wycheck 3–27, George 3–21, Kent 2–17
CLE: Johnson 6–90, Kirby 4–88, Chiaverini 4–51, Campbell 2–25, Edwards 1–4, Smith 1–3, Abdul-Jabbar 1–1

Sunday, December 5
San Diego Chargers 23, Browns 10
Qualcomm Stadium (53,147)
White jerseys/white pants

Despite their finest defensive performance of the season, a handful of mistakes kept the Browns from pulling out victory in a winnable game with the Chargers, who had lost six straight. Led by John Thierry, who collected three sacks and forced a pair of fumbles, the Browns held San Diego to 277 total yards and trailed only 13–10 at the half. But the meager Cleveland offense managed just 202 yards and collapsed in the second half under the weight of six allowed sacks, while the Browns were penalized 13 times for 94 yards as a team. Still, they were within 16–10 and had reached midfield early in the fourth quarter when a Tim Couch interception led to a game-clinching Chargers' touchdown.

Record: 2–11

	1	2	3	4		
Browns	3	7	0	0	=	10
Chargers	3	10	3	7	=	23

CLE-Dawson 33-yd. FG
SD-Carney 44-yd. FG
SD-Carney 19-yd. FG
SD-Bynum 1-yd. run (Carney kick)
CLE-Johnson 19-yd. pass from Couch (Dawson kick)
SD-Carney 30-yd. FG
SD-Fazande 2-yd. run (Carney kick)

Passing
CLE: Couch 18–29–184 1 TD 2 INT, Johnson 0–1–0 0 TD 0 INT
SD: Harbaugh 16–23–161 0 TD 0 INT

Rushing
CLE: Abdul-Jabbar 10–29, Kirby 4–21, Couch 1–4, Edwards 1–1
SD: Bynum 17–60, Fazande 12–42, Fletcher 9–28, Harbaugh 6–15

Receiving
CLE: Chiaverini 4–46, Kirby 5–43, Johnson 5–41, Abdul-Jabbar 1–21, Smith 1–16, Campbell 1–12, Edwards 1–5
SD: Graham 5–82, Jones 4–42, McCrary 4–18, Ricks 2–18, Reed 1–1

Sunday, December 12
Cincinnati Bengals 44, Browns 28
Cinergy Field (59,972)
White jerseys/white pants

In their last game at Cinergy Field/Riverfront Stadium on a wet, dreary afternoon, the Browns' defense was electrified for 279 rushing yards and 459 total as the Bengals cruised to a far easier victory than their one-point triumph in the teams' first meeting in October. Corey Dillon rushed for 192 yards and three scores as Cincinnati exploded for 30 points in the first half. The Browns had pulled within

23–15 in the final minute of the second quarter, but a long kickoff return led to another Bengals' touchdown, which provided the momentum to carry them through the second half. While the Browns rolled up a season-high 323 yards and four touchdowns, they were held to just 11 yards on the ground and allowed the most points they'd permitted in a game in nine years. Kevin Johnson led the way for the Cleveland offense, catching seven passes for 135 yards.
Record: 2–12

	1	2	3	4		
Browns	7	8	6	7	=	28
Bengals	10	20	14	0	=	44

CIN-Pelfrey 28-yd. FG
CIN-Yeast 81-yd. punt return (Pelfrey kick)
CLE-Abdul-Jabbar 8-yd. pass from Couch (Dawson kick)
CIN-Groce 1-yd. run (Pelfrey kick)
CIN-Dillon 2-yd. run (kick failed)
CLE-Kirby 1-yd. run (Couch run)
CIN-Dillon 2-yd. run (Pelfrey kick)
CIN-Dillon 11-yd. run (Pelfrey kick)
CIN-Smith 16-yd. pass from Couch (pass failed)
CIN-Scott 52-yd. pass from Blake (Pelfrey kick)
CLE-Chiaverini 19-yd. pass from Detmer (Dawson kick)

Passing
CLE: Couch 16–28–239 2 TD 2 INT, Detmer 6–13–89 1 TD 0 INT
CIN: Blake 11–22–176 1 TD 0 INT, Covington 1–1–4 0 TD 0 INT

Rushing
CLE: Abdul-Jabbar 5–10, Kirby 3–5, Detmer 1–2, Edwards 1–0, Johnson 1-(-6)
CIN: Dillon 28–192, Basnight 12–44, Blake 4–28, Groce 3–14, Luchey 3–8, Yeast 1-(-3), Covington 2-(-4)

Receiving
CLE: Johnson 7–135, Chiaverini 4–48, Powell 1–45, Smith 3–33, Campbell 2–33, Kirby 2–24, Abdul-Jabbar 2–7, Edwards 1–3
CIN: Scott 2–75, Pickens 3–46, McGee 3–27, Dillon 2–20, Griffin 1–8, Basnight 1–4

Sunday, December 19
Jacksonville Jaguars 24, Browns 14
Cleveland Browns Stadium (72,038)
Brown jerseys/white pants

An admirable Browns' effort against the 12–1 Jaguars was overshadowed by one of the ugliest incidents in NFL history involving Cleveland OT Orlando Brown. After a penalty flag thrown by an official went through Brown's facemask and injured his eye, an irate Brown shoved the official to the ground and was ejected from the game. Later in the second quarter, Tim Couch's season came to an end when he was sacked for the fifty-sixth time, injuring his ankle. Ty Detmer replaced him and pulled the Browns to within 17–14 late in the third quarter, then the defense came up with a defensive stop at the Cleveland 1 early in the fourth to keep their hopes alive. But Jacksonville put the game away with 10 minutes to play on a 41-yard scoring run by RB Fred Taylor, who rushed for 136 yards. WR Darrin Chiaverini set a Browns' rookie record with 10 catches, rolling up 108 yards.
Record: 2–13

	1	2	3	4		
Jaguars	0	14	3	7	=	24
Browns	0	7	7	0	=	14

JAX-Jones 3-yd. pass from Brunell (Hollis kick)
JAX-Brunell 9-yd. run (Hollis kick)
CLE-Kirby 1-yd. run (Dawson kick)
JAX-Hollis 41-yd. FG
CLE-Chiaverini 10-yd. pass from Detmer (Dawson kick)
JAX-Taylor 41-yd. run (Hollis kick)

Passing
JAX: Brunell 21–33–267 1 TD 1 INT
CLE: Detmer 13–24–153 1 TD 0 INT, Couch 10–16–86 0 TD 0 INT, Kirby 1–1–2 0 TD 0 INT

Rushing
JAX: Taylor 26–136, Howard 4–29, Brunell 3–16
CLE: Abdul-Jabbar 13–36, Detmer 2–22, Kirby 4–14, Couch 1–0

Receiving
JAX: Smith 8–134, McCardell 8–96, Jones 2–16, Taylor 2–13, Shelton 1–8
CLE: Chiaverini 10–108, Johnson 4–54, Smith 4–36, Davis 1–25, Edwards 2–10, Kirby 2–4, Abdul-Jabbar 1–4

Sunday, December 26
Indianapolis Colts 29, Browns 28
Cleveland Browns Stadium (72,618)
Brown jerseys/white pants

A last-minute field goal enabled the 12–2 Colts to avoid a massive upset bid by the inspired Browns, who were unable to hold onto a nine-point fourth-quarter lead on a cold, snowy day after Christmas. With Ty Detmer leading an effective offense that did not permit a sack, the Browns picked up 141 yards on the ground, including a team-season-high 84 by mid-season pickup RB Karim Abdul-Jabbar. Scoring the game's first points with five minutes left in the first quarter, the Browns held the lead throughout the game, extending it to 28–19 on Terry Kirby's second touchdown of the day in the final seconds of the third quarter. The Colts cut the margin to two points with RB Edgerrin James's third touchdown of the day on their next series, then regained possession at their own 43 with four minutes left and drove to the Cleveland 3 in the final seconds. Kicker Mike Vanderjagt booted a 21-yard field goal with four seconds left to hand the Browns their fourteenth loss and secure the worst record in team history. Indy WR Marvin Harrison set a club record with 14 catches for 138 yards as the Colts rolled up nearly 400 yards of offense, topping the Browns' 314.

	1	2	3	4		
Colts	0	13	6	10	=	29
Browns	7	7	14	0	=	28

CLE-Kirby 1-yd. run (Dawson kick)
IND-James 1-yd. run (Vanderjagt kick)
CLE-Chiaverini 28-yd. pass from Detmer (Dawson kick)
IND-Vanderjagt 41-yd. FG
IND-Vanderjagt 19-yd. FG
CLE-Detmer 8-yd. run (Dawson kick)
IND-James 1-yd. run (run failed)
CLE-Kirby 1-yd. run (Dawson kick)
IND-James 2-yd. run (Vanderjagt kick)
IND-Vanderjagt 21-yd. FG

Passing
IND: Manning 27–43–276 0 TD 0 INT
CLE: Detmer 15–26–173 1 TD 0 INT

Rushing
IND: James 28–103, Manning 2–17
CLE: Abdul-Jabbar 19–84, Edwards 1–28, Kirby 5–21, Detmer 1–8

Receiving
IND: Harrison 14–138, Dilger 4–56, Wilkins 3–28, Pollard 2–24, James 3–18, Green 1–12
CLE: Smith 4–48, Chiaverini 3–40, Johnson 2–29, Edwards 1–25, Davis 1–13, Kirby 1–8, Abdul-Jabbar 2–7, Bobo 1–3

2000

Sunday, September 3
Jacksonville Jaguars 27, Browns 7
Cleveland Browns Stadium (72,418)
White jerseys/white pants

Showing notable improvement over their opening game the year before, the second-year Browns hung with the title-contending Jaguars for a half but were overwhelmed in the final 30 minutes as Jacksonville pulled away for its fifth straight win over Cleveland. The Browns tied the game at seven on a QB Tim Couch-to-WR JaJuan Dawson scoring pass late in the second quarter and were poised to take the lead on the first possession of the second half. Trailing 10–7, the Browns drove to the Jacksonville 15, but TE Aaron Shea fumbled and the Jags recovered. They then drove 85 yards to extend their lead to 17–7 and secure the momentum to win going away. Jacksonville QB Mark Brunell threw for 301 yards as the Jaguars rolled up nearly 400 total yards against the Browns' improving but still inexperienced defense, which sacked Brunell four times.
Record: 0–1

	1	2	3	4		
Jaguars	0	10	10	7	=	27
Browns	0	7	0	0	=	7

JAX-Smith 2-yd. pass from Brunell (Hollis kick)
CLE-J. Dawson 13-yd. pass from Couch (P. Dawson kick)
JAX-Hollis 50-yd. FG
JAX-Mack 3-yd. run (Hollis kick)
JAX-Hollis 25-yd. FG
JAX-Howard 9-yd. run (Hollis kick)

Passing
JAX: Brunell 24–34–301 1 TD 0 INT
CLE: Couch 19–27–160 1 TD 0 INT

Rushing
JAX: Mack 23–74, Howard 13–45, Brunell 1–5, Martin 3-(-5)
CLE: Rhett 14–64, Couch 2–32

Receiving
JAX: McCardell 9–115, Brady 5–85, Smith 6–52, Howard 1–13, Jones 1–12, Shelton 1–12, Whitted 1–12
CLE: J. Dawson 6–83, Johnson 3–32, Shea 1–24, Rhett 5–13, Patten 2–9, Northcutt 1–0, Edwards 1-(-1)

Sunday, September 10
Browns 24, Cincinnati Bengals 7
Paul Brown Stadium (64,006)
White jerseys/white pants

In the first game ever played at Paul Brown Stadium, the Browns coasted to a convincing victory over the Bengals before the largest crowd ever to attend a sporting event in the city of Cincinnati. Setting the tone from the first play—a 65-yard pass from Tim Couch to WR David Patten—the Browns surged to a 14–7 halftime lead, then pulled away in the second half as Couch hit 10 different receivers and threw for a pair of touchdown passes. The Cleveland defense was equally impressive, holding star RB Corey Dillon to just 41 yards on 12 carries after he'd ripped the Browns for 360 yards in their two meetings in 1999. Similarly, Cincinnati QB Akili Smith was held to just 15 completions in 43 attempts and was sacked seven times, three by DE Keith McKenzie. The only down moment for the Browns came after their second touchdown when LG Jim Pyne tore his ACL running into the end zone to celebrate and was lost for the year, the first of several key injuries to plague the already-thin Browns' roster.
Record: 1–1

	1	2	3	4		
Browns	7	7	3	7	=	24
Bengals	0	7	0	0	=	7

CLE-Prentice 16-yd. run (P. Dawson kick)
CIN-Dugans 4-yd. pass from Smith (Rackers kick)
CLE-Campbell 5-yd. pass from Couch (P. Dawson kick)
CLE-Dawson 30-yd. FG
CLE-Edwards 5-yd. pass from Couch (P. Dawson kick)

Passing
CLE: Couch 19–31–259 2 TD 1 INT
CIN: Smith 15–43–250 1 TD 2 INT

Rushing
CLE: Rhett 20–53, Prentice 8–46, Couch 4–7, Northcutt 1-(-1)
CIN: Dillon 12–41, Smith 2–26, Pope 1–22, Luchey 1–9, Warrick 1–8, Bennett 2–5

Receiving
CLE: Patten 3–95, Johnson 5–59, Shea 1–30, Chiaverini 1–18, J. Dawson 3–14, Northcutt 1–12, Rhett 2–11, Prentice 1–10, Campbell 1–5, Edwards 1–5
CIN: Warrick 3–80, Dillon 2–46, Yeast 2–38, McGee 1–34, Bennett 2–30, Groce 3–12, Dugans 2–10

Sunday, September 17
Browns 23, Pittsburgh Steelers 20
Cleveland Browns Stadium (73,018)
White jerseys/white pants

After nine straight defeats to open the facility, the Browns finally got their first win at Cleveland Browns Stadium in dramatic fashion, rallying from behind in the fourth quarter to take the lead and then holding off the Steelers in the final seconds. The Browns set the capacity crowd afire by scoring on their first two possessions to take a 14–0 lead, but the Steelers rebounded to take a 20–17 advantage into the fourth quarter. Pittsburgh was poised to add to the lead, but Browns' DB Corey Fuller intercepted an ill-advised option pass by Pittsburgh RB Jerome Bettis at the Cleveland 5, and the Browns drove downfield to tie the game. Then, taking over at his own 4 with less than seven minutes remaining, Tim Couch connected with WR Kevin Johnson over the middle for a 79-yard pass to set up a short field goal that gave the Browns a 23–20 lead with 2:45 left. Pittsburgh drove to the Cleveland 6 with 14 seconds remaining, but opted to run one more play rather than attempt the game-tying field goal. QB Kent Graham was sacked by rookie DE Courtney Brown—his third sack of the day—and time expired. Couch topped the 300-yard mark for the first time in his career and moved among the league leaders in passing after his third straight strong performance to start the season. With the win, the Browns moved over the .500 mark for the first time in nearly five years.
Record: 2–1

	1	2	3	4		
Steelers	0	10	10	0	=	20
Browns	14	0	3	6	=	23

CLE-Shea 2-yd. pass from Couch (P. Dawson kick)
CLE-Edwards 21-yd. pass from Couch (P. Dawson kick)
PIT-Huntley 4-yd. run (Brown kick)
PIT-Brown 41-yd. FG
PIT-Brown 31-yd. FG
CLE-P. Dawson 23-yd. FG
PIT-Bettis 10-yd. run (Brown kick)
CLE-P. Dawson 28-yd. FG
CLE-P. Dawson 19-yd. FG

Passing
PIT: Graham 13–27–172 0 TD 0 INT, Stewart 1–1–9 0 TD 0 INT, Bettis 0–1–0 0 TD 1 INT
CLE: Couch 23–31–316 2 TD 0 INT

Rushing
PIT: Bettis 24–133, Fuamatu-Ma'afala 2–22, Graham 1–7, Huntley 3–6, Witman 1–2
CLE: Rhett 18–55, Prentice 4–3, Couch 1–3

Receiving
PIT: Ward 5–75, Shaw 3–66, Witman 2–17, Bettis 1–11, Burress 1–10, Fuamatu-Ma'afala 2–8, Bruener 1–5
CLE: Johnson 4–97, Patten 3–81, Shea 4–43, Northcutt 2–27, Chiaverini 5–26, Edwards 1–21, Rhett 2–11, Prentice 2–10

Sunday, September 24
Oakland Raiders 36, Browns 10
Network Associates Coliseum (45,702)
White jerseys/white pants

Playing their first game in Oakland in 21 years, the Browns got off to a dazzling start, driving 77 yards for a touchdown on the game's opening possession. But when they tried to surprise the Raiders with an onside kick, the chicanery backfired and quickly turned the game around. Oakland recovered the onside kick and, with great field possession, quickly scored to tie the game, then added three more touchdowns before the half to take a commanding 28–7 lead. Two Tim Couch interceptions in the final two minutes of the half helped Oakland blow the game open—the first led to the Raiders' third touchdown, and the second was returned for a score. The loss dropped the Browns back to .500 and proved to be the first loss in what would become a frustrating losing streak.
Record: 2–2

	1	2	3	4		
Browns	7	0	3	0	=	10
Raiders	7	21	0	8	=	36

CLE-Chiaverini 15-yd. pass from Couch (P. Dawson kick)
OAK-Wheatley 2-yd. run (Janikowski kick)
OAK-Wheatley 2-yd. run (Janikowski kick)
OAK-Crockett 2-yd. run (Janikowski kick)
OAK-Thomas 46-yd. interception return (Janikowski kick)
CLE-P. Dawson 29-yd. FG
OAK-Janikowski 37-yd. FG
OAK-Janikowski 31-yd. FG
OAK-Safety: Couch penalized for intentional grounding in end zone

Passing
CLE: Couch 16–29–141 1 TD 2 INT, Wynn 2–5–15 0 TD 0 INT
OAK: Gannon 14–23–179 0 TD 0 INT, Hoying 0–2–0 0 TD 0 INT

Rushing
CLE: Rhett 15–85, Couch 3–3, Prentice 3–1
OAK: Wheatley 21–63, Kaufman 7–37, Gannon 1–8, Jordan 4–6, Crockett 1–2, Hoying 2-(-3)

Receiving
CLE: Prentice 5–45, Chiaverini 2–24, Rhett 2–22, Johnson 3–19, Campbell 2–16, Edwards 1–15, Northcutt 1–8, Shea 2–7
OAK: Brown 3–54, Rison 3–54, Dudley 3–44, Ritchie 3–13, Kaufman 1–13, Jordan 1–1

Sunday, October 1
Baltimore Ravens 12, Browns 0
Cleveland Browns Stadium (73,018)
Brown jerseys/white pants

Squandering a handful of scoring opportunities, the Browns were held scoreless by the improving Ravens, who posted their third shutout in five weeks. The turning point came just before the half when Browns' FB Marc Edwards lost a fumble at the goal line when Cleveland was poised to carve into Baltimore's 9–0 lead. The Browns then had two scoring opportunities in the fourth quarter, one ending when Tim Couch was intercepted by Baltimore LB Ray Lewis after reaching the Ravens' 18, the other on downs after the Browns reached the Baltimore 5. Held to just 23 rushing yards and committing four turnovers, the Browns were lucky to be in the game at all, as the Ravens rolled up 188 yards on the ground and dominated time of possession. The Browns also received another crushing blow when veteran RB Errict Rhett, signed as a free agent in the offseason, suffered a career-ending foot injury in the second quarter.
Record: 2–3

	1	2	3	4		
Ravens	3	6	3	0	=	12
Browns	0	0	0	0	=	0

BAL-Stover 45-yd. FG
BAL-Stover 30-yd. FG
BAL-Stover 44-yd. FG
BAL-Stover 22-yd. FG

Passing
BAL: Banks 18–34–169 0 TD 1 INT
CLE: Couch 20–35–203 0 TD 3 INT, Pederson 1–1–4 0 TD 0 INT

Rushing
BAL: Lewis 13–86, Holmes 20–82, Taylor 1–12, Ayanbadejo 2–8, Banks 1–0
CLE: Prentice 7–13, Edwards 2–9, Rhett 4–1

Receiving
BAL: Sharpe 6–83, Taylor 5–39, Ayanbadejo 2–14, Ismail 2–14, Holmes 2–12, Lewis 1–7
CLE: Patten 7–113, Northcutt 4–43, Rhett 3–21, Prentice 4–15, Johnson 2–11, Edwards 1–4

Sunday, October 8
Arizona Cardinals 29, Browns 21
Sun Devil Stadium (39,148)
Brown jerseys/white pants

Sprinting to a good start, the Browns squandered a two-touchdown lead and lost a winnable game in the desert to the struggling Cardinals. Rookie RB Travis Prentice scored the first two of his three touchdowns on the day to give the Browns a 14–0 lead in the second quarter, but Arizona then took command with 26 straight points. Prentice's third score cut the margin to five points two minutes into the fourth quarter, but the Browns allowed a long Cardinals' drive that ended in a field goal with three minutes to play. The Browns' last chance ended when they lost the ball on downs from their own 34 a minute later. Though Prentice rushed for 97 yards along with his three touchdowns in what proved to be the finest performance of his brief career, the Cleveland offense struggled, and it would be another two months before the Browns scored more than 20 points in a game.
Record: 2–4

	1	2	3	4		
Browns	7	7	0	7	=	21
Cardinals	0	16	10	3	=	29

CLE-Prentice 1-yd. run (P. Dawson kick)
CLE-Prentice 1-yd. run (P. Dawson kick)
ARI-Jones 10-yd. run (Blanchard kick)
ARI-Sanders 53-yd. pass from Plummer (kick failed)
ARI-Blanchard 36-yd. FG
ARI-Blanchard 47-yd. FG
ARI-Sanders 5-yd. pass from Plummer (Blanchard kick)
CLE-Prentice 6-yd. run (P. Dawson kick)
ARI-Blanchard 28-yd. FG

Passing
CLE: Couch 16–22–138 0 TD 0 INT
ARI: Plummer 17–30–171 2 TD 0 INT

Rushing
CLE: Prentice 28–97, White 2–6, Couch 1–1
ARI: Pittman 16–107, Boston 1–24, Jones 6–9, Makovicka 1–7, Plummer 7-(-1)

Receiving
CLE: Northcutt 3–67, Patten 3–27, Edwards 2–17, Shea 3–12, Prentice 3–7, Campbell 1–4, Johnson 1–4
ARI: Sanders 4–76, Boston 5–63, Pittman 2–10, Jenkins 2–8, Gedney 2–7, Hardy 1–5, Makovicka 1–2

Sunday, October 15
Denver Broncos 44, Browns 10
Mile High Stadium (75,811)
White jerseys/white pants

The Browns were no match for the Broncos, who tallied nearly 500 total yards and cashed in on several Cleveland mistakes to blow open what had been a close game after one quarter. Seventeen second-quarter points broke open a 3–3 game and gave Denver a commanding lead. Then after the Browns cut the margin to 20–10 four minutes into the second half, a long kickoff return set up a back-breaking Broncos' touchdown and opened the floodgates. While their defense was picked apart by Denver QB Brian Griese, who threw for 336 yards and three scores, the Browns hindered their own cause with 116 yards in penalties, five allowed sacks, and three turnovers.
Record: 2–5

	1	2	3	4		
Browns	3	0	7	0	=	10
Broncos	3	17	14	10	=	44

DEN-Elam 22-yd. FG
CLE-P. Dawson 45-yd. FG
DEN-Smith 22-yd. pass from Griese (Elam kick)
DEN-Smith 17-yd. pass from Griese (Elam kick)
DEN-Elam 45-yd. FG
CLE-Prentice 3-yd. pass from Couch (P. Dawson kick)
DEN-Anderson 26-yd. run (Elam kick)
DEN-Smith 32-yd. pass from Griese (Elam kick)
DEN-Jenkins 36-yd. interception return (Elam kick)
DEN-Elam 46-yd. FG

Passing
CLE: Couch 24–40–266 1 TD 3 INT, Wynn 2–5–21 0 TD 0 INT
DEN: Griese 19–34–336 3 TD 0 INT, Frerotte 3–6–17 0 TD 0 INT

Rushing
CLE: Prentice 6–27, Wynn 2–12, Couch 1-(-1)
DEN: Anderson 20–103, Harris 8–22, Griese 1–14, Smith 1–8, Frerotte 1-(-1)

Receiving
CLE: Northcutt 5–80, Shea 6–76, Johnson 8–60, Patten 4–54, Prentice 3–17
DEN: McCaffrey 5–129, Smith 5–111, Clark 4–46, Carswell 5–30, Anderson 2–28, Chamberlain 1–9

Sunday, October 22
Pittsburgh Steelers 22, Browns 0
Three Rivers Stadium (57,659)
White jerseys/white pants

In their final game at Three Rivers Stadium, the overmatched Browns were dominated by the Steelers and suffered their fifth straight defeat. With Tim Couch lost for the season with a thumb injury suffered in practice the previous week—and Ty Detmer lost for the year with a preseason injury—the Browns were forced to start journeyman Doug Pederson at QB. He threw three interceptions and, with four other offensive starters out with injuries, the Browns could manage only a meager 104 total yards and just five first downs, crossing midfield only once in the entire game. The Cleveland defense played admirably, limiting the Steelers to a single touchdown and just 248 total yards while collecting three sacks, but the efforts were lost due to the offense's impotence, which would only get worse.
Record: 2–6

	1	2	3	4		
Browns	0	0	0	0	=	0
Steelers	3	10	3	6	=	22

PIT-Brown 44-yd. FG
PIT-Bettis 1-yd. run (Brown kick)
PIT-Brown 20-yd. FG
PIT-Brown 31-yd. FG
PIT-Brown 26-yd. FG
PIT-Brown 33-yd. FG

Passing
CLE: Pederson 9–20–61 0 TD 3 INT, Wynn 1–3–2 0 TD 0 INT
PIT: Stewart 7–13–74 0 TD 0 INT, Graham 3–12–46 0 TD 0 INT

Rushing
CLE: Prentice 14–48, Pederson 2–4, White 2–0, Northcutt 1-(-3)
PIT: Bettis 33–105, Fuamatu-Ma'afala 1–20, Stewart 6–15, Huntley 4–5, Edwards 1-(-2)

Receiving
CLE: Northcutt 2–22, Shea 1–21, Prentice 3–8, Johnson 2–5, Jackson 1–5, Campbell 1–2
PIT: Shaw 3–60, Burress 2–25, Hawkins 1–16, Edwards 2–15, Ward 1–5, Huntley 1-(-1)

Sunday, October 29
Cincinnati Bengals 12, Browns 3
Cleveland Browns Stadium (73,118)
Brown jerseys/white pants

Alternating between inadequate quarterbacks Doug Pederson and Spergon Wynn, the Browns' offense was once again miserable and for the second straight week was easily beaten by a team the Browns had defeated earlier in the season, this time to the 1–6 Bengals. The struggling offense hit rock bottom late in the third quarter when it failed to score on three consecutive plays from the Cincinnati 1—all runs up the middle—and was forced to settle for a field goal that cut the Bengals' lead to 10–3. The final indignity came midway through the final period when Browns' OT Roman Oben was penalized for holding in the Cleveland end zone, an automatic safety. While the Cleveland defense played admirably, limiting the Bengals to 253 total yards and collecting four sacks, the Browns' offense managed just 182 total yards and 10 first downs. Kevin Johnson was the sole standout for Cleveland, catching six passes for 102 yards, representing more than half of the Browns' offense for the day.
Record: 2–7

	1	2	3	4		
Bengals	0	7	3	2	=	12
Browns	0	0	3	0	=	3

CIN-Dillon 1-yd. run (Rackers kick)
CIN-Rackers 39-yd. FG
CLE-P. Dawson 18-yd. FG
CIN-Safety: Oben penalized for holding in end zone

Passing
CIN: Smith 7–20–84 0 TD 1 INT
CLE: Wynn 7–16–82 0 TD 1 INT, Pederson 6–16–65 0 TD 0 INT

Rushing
CIN: Dillon 27–137, Bennett 17–39, Smith 5–12, Keaton 1–3, Warrick 1–1
CLE: Prentice 16–40, Pederson 2–10, White 2–4

Receiving
CIN: Warrick 3–25, Bennett 1–21, Yeast 1–19, McGee 1–13, Battaglia 1–6
CLE: Johnson 6–102, Northcutt 4–23, Edwards 1–12, Patten 1–7, Shea 1–3

Sunday, November 5
New York Giants 24, Browns 3
Cleveland Browns Stadium (72,718)
Brown jerseys/white pants

For the third straight game, the Browns were unable to score a touchdown and held under 200 total yards as they suffered a humiliating loss to the Super Bowl-bound Giants. Just as the week before, the Browns couldn't cross the goal line despite having a first-and-goal situation at the opponent's 1-yard line late in the first quarter and were forced to settle for a field goal, which in this case gave the Browns their first lead in nearly a month. On their next possession, they reached the New York 18, but back-to-back runs on third and fourth downs were unable to pick up the yard necessary for a first down. The Giants took the lead for good just before the half and turned away the Browns' only other scoring threat when they intercepted Doug Pederson from the Giants' 18 late in the third quarter. With their seventh straight defeat, the Browns matched their winless string to open their expansion campaign the year before.
Record: 2–8

	1	2	3	4		
Giants	0	10	7	7	=	24
Browns	3	0	0	0	=	3

CLE-P. Dawson 19-yd. FG
NYG-Daluiso 39-yd. FG
NYG-Hilliard 28-yd. pass from Collins (Daluiso kick)
NYG-Toomer 17-yd. pass from Collins (Daluiso kick)
NYG-Toomer 32-yd. pass from Collins (Daluiso kick)

Passing
NYG: Collins 19–31–257 3 TD 0 INT
CLE: Pederson 17–29–176 0 TD 1 INT

Rushing
NYG: Dayne 19–64, Barber 15–53, Toomer 1–27, Comella 3–16, Collins 5-(-5), Hilliard 1-(-6)
CLE: Prentice 11–15, Pederson 2–14, White 3–12

Receiving
NYG: Toomer 6–100, Hilliard 3–60, Comella 5–58, Barber 2–15, Davis 1–13, Jurevicius 1–10, Campbell 1–1
CLE: Johnson 5–76, Northcutt 3–34, Shea 4–27, White 2–27, Edwards 1–9, Prentice 2–3

Sunday, November 12
Browns 19, New England Patriots 11
Cleveland Browns Stadium (72,618)
Brown jerseys/white pants

Ironically, the Browns ended their disheartening losing streak by defeating former coach Bill Belichick, whose Patriots were also struggling mightily in his first season, bringing a 2–7 record into the game. The Cleveland offense showed signs of life for the first time in weeks, rushing for 139 yards as a team and snapping its 14-quarter string without a touchdown when Doug Pederson connected with Aaron Shea to give the Browns a lead they wouldn't relinquish late in the second quarter. Thanks to a defense that collected four sacks and four turnovers, the lead swelled to 19–3 early in the fourth quarter. After New England pulled within eight points with six minutes to play, the Browns came up with a key defensive stop, then came through with a surprise pitch to Travis Prentice for a 13-yard gain on third-and-one with two minutes left to enable them to run out the clock and secure their first victory in two months—and their last of the season.
Record: 3–8

	1	2	3	4		
Patriots	3	0	0	8	=	11
Browns	3	10	3	3	=	19

CLE-P. Dawson 39-yd. FG
NE-Vinatieri 38-yd. FG
CLE-Shea 9-yd. pass from Pederson (P. Dawson kick)
CLE-P. Dawson 43-yd. FG
CLE-P. Dawson 35-yd. FG
CLE-P. Dawson 35-yd. FG
NE-Rutledge 2-yd. pass from Bledsoe (Faulk run)

Passing
NE: Bledsoe 21–35–212 1 TD 1 INT
CLE: Pederson 20–37–138 1 TD 0 INT

Rushing
NE: Redmond 10–60, Faulk 5–26, Bledsoe 3–6, Carter 3–5, Shaw 1–5
CLE: Prentice 19–84, White 12–37, Pederson 4–18

Receiving
NE: Faulk 8–96, Glenn 6–65, Simmons 2–21, Rutledge 3–20, Brown 2–10
CLE: Northcutt 4–32, Edwards 4–27, Johnson 3–23, White 3–22, Prentice 4–19, Shea 1–9, Dunn 1–6

Sunday, November 19
Tennessee Titans 24, Browns 10
Adelphia Coliseum (68,498)
White jerseys/white pants

Despite collecting seven turnovers from the mistake-prone Titans, the Browns still couldn't pull out a victory as the offense's impotence proved too much to overcome. After a scoreless first half, the Browns took the lead two minutes into the third quarter when DB Percy Ellsworth intercepted Tennessee QB Steve McNair and returned it 33 yards for a touchdown, one of four interceptions thrown by McNair on the day and the Browns' first defensive touchdown since their rebirth. After the Titans tied the game on their next possession, the Browns took the lead again with a field goal after recovering a McNair fumble at the Tennessee 22. From that point on, the Titans held onto the ball, and the Browns were unable to generate any points on their own. Tennessee responded with 17 points to win the game going away, and the Browns clinched their third consecutive losing season. The miserable Cleveland offense, which crossed midfield only twice all day, managed just five first downs and only 125 yards, just under one-third of Tennessee's total yardage and less accumulated by Titans' RB Eddie George alone.
Record: 3–9

	1	2	3	4		
Browns	0	0	10	0	=	10
Titans	0	0	14	10	=	24

CLE-Ellsworth 33-yd. interception return (P. Dawson kick)
TEN-George 4-yd. run (Del Greco kick)
CLE-P. Dawson 38-yd. FG
TEN-George 1-yd. run (Del Greco kick)

TEN-Del Greco 22-yd. FG
TEN-George 1-yd. run (Del Greco kick)

Passing
CLE: Pederson 13–20–103 0 TD 1 INT
TEN: McNair 16–25–204 0 TD 4 INT

Rushing
CLE: White 8–27, Prentice 7–14, Wynn 1–3, Pederson 2–1
TEN: George 36–134, McNair 8–51, Thomas 2-(-1), Neal 1-(-2)

Receiving
CLE: Northcutt 3–30, White 3–30, Campbell 2–11, Johnson 2–9, Shea 1–9, Edwards 1–8, Prentice 1–6
TEN: Mason 6–89, Wycheck 3–55, Sanders 3–29, George 2–15, Kinney 1–10, Neal 1–6

Sunday, November 26
Baltimore Ravens 44, Browns 7
PSINet Stadium (68,361)
White jerseys/white pants

After shocking everyone in the stadium by driving 86 yards for a touchdown against Baltimore's heralded defense to open the game, the Browns were utterly annihilated for the remainder of the afternoon in the first of two consecutive humiliating blowout defeats. Baltimore quickly tied the score, then Browns' WR Dennis Northcutt fumbled a punt and the Ravens recovered, then went on to score on six of their next seven possessions. After the opening drive, sparked by a 67-yard reception by Kevin Johnson, the Browns managed only 26 yards of offense as the Ravens rolled up 461, more than four times Cleveland's total. Most of the Ravens' tally came on the ground (247 yards), led by Jamal Lewis's 170, while the Browns could manage only 28 rushing yards.
Record: 3–10

	1	2	3	4		
Browns	7	0	0	0	=	7
Ravens	7	24	6	7	=	44

CLE-Prentice 4-yd. run (P. Dawson kick)
BAL-Lewis 1-yd. run (Stover kick)
BAL-Gash 2-yd. pass from Dilfer (Stover kick)
BAL-Johnson 46-yd. pass from Dilfer (Stover kick)
BAL-Stover 39-yd. FG
BAL-Lewis 36-yd. run (Stover kick)
BAL-Stover 26-yd. FG
BAL-Stover 38-yd. FG
BAL-Holmes 3-yd. run (Stover kick)

Passing
CLE: Pederson 8–16–108 0 TD 1 INT, Wynn 5–9–30 0 TD 0 INT
BAL: Dilfer 12–23–169 2 TD 1 INT, Banks 2–3–45 0 TD 0 INT

Rushing
CLE: Prentice 11–13, White 4–12, Pederson 2–3
BAL: Lewis 30–170, Holmes 17–64, Dilfer 2–10, Johnson 1–2, Gash 1–1

Receiving
CLE: Johnson 4–85, Campbell 2–25, Patten 4–23, Edwards 1–4, Prentice 1–3, White 1-(-2)
BAL: Stokley 4–68, Johnson 2–54, Ismail 3–39, Davis 1–28, Sharpe 2–17, Gash 2–8

Sunday, December 3
Jacksonville Jaguars 48, Browns 0
Alltel Stadium (51,262)
White jerseys/white pants

In one of the most lopsided games in NFL history, the Browns were held to a team-record minus-nine yards passing and just 53 total yards as the 5–7 Jaguars cruised to an easy triumph. Rookie Spergon Wynn, making his first NFL start, completed only five of 16 passes as the Cleveland offense didn't cross midfield for the entire game and managed only two first downs. They also tied a team record with 12 punts and set a new mark with 517 punting yards. Meanwhile, Jacksonville ran 82 plays and collected nearly 400 more yards and 26 more first downs, paced by RB Fred Taylor's 181 rushing yards and three touchdowns. Adding insult to injury, the Browns also were penalized nine times and collected 30 more yards in penalties than total offense.
Record: 3–11

	1	2	3	4		
Browns	0	0	0	0	=	0
Jaguars	3	17	21	7	=	48

JAX-Hollis 40-yd. FG
JAX-Taylor 3-yd. run (Hollis kick)
JAX-Hollis 24-yd. FG
JAX-McCardell 14-yd. pass from Brunell (Hollis kick)
JAX-Taylor 2-yd. run (Hollis kick)
JAX-Brunell 8-yd. run (Hollis kick)

JAX-Taylor 1-yd. run (Hollis kick)
JAX-Stith 3-yd. run (Hollis kick)

Passing
CLE: Wynn 5–16–17 0 TD 0 INT, Pederson 1–1–8 0 TD 0 INT, Thompson 1–1–8 0 TD 0 INT
JAX: Brunell 15–31–165 1 TD 0 INT, Martin 1–2–53 0 TD 0 INT

Rushing
CLE: Prentice 10–33, White 7–29, Thompson 1–0
JAX: Taylor 30–181, Stith 11–27, Johnson 2–24, Brunell 2–14, Quinn 2-(-2)

Receiving
CLE: White 2–11, Johnson 1–8, Patten 1–8, Prentice 2–6, Northcutt 1–0
JAX: Smith 6–104, McCardell 4–46, Brady 3–41, Soward 2–21, Taylor 1–6

Sunday, December 10
Philadelphia Eagles 35, Browns 24
Cleveland Browns Stadium (72,318)
Brown jerseys/white pants

In utter desperation, the Browns installed an offensive scheme that saw WRs Kevin Johnson and Dennis Northcutt each take snaps as the QB—and it worked like a charm. Though the Browns were unable to keep up with the playoff-bound Eagles, they exploded out of their offensive doldrums by picking up 418 total yards and 25 first downs—more than they'd accumulated in their previous three games combined. After allowing opponents to score 99 consecutive points, the Browns finally got on the board early in the second quarter, then recovered a fumble on the ensuing kickoff and took the lead moments later. The surprised euphoria didn't last long as the Eagles scored 28 straight points on four touchdown passes by QB Donovan McNabb to take control of the contest. The Browns hung tough and narrowed the deficit to 35–24 midway through the fourth quarter and were driving for another score when a fumble by WR David Patten at the Philadelphia 38 halted their momentum and allowed the Eagles to hang on for the win. With Johnson and Northcutt opening up the offense, Doug Pederson had the finest game of his career, throwing for 309 yards, nearly keeping pace with McNabb's 390.
Record: 3–12

	1	2	3	4		
Eagles	7	14	14	0	=	35
Browns	0	14	0	10	=	24

PHI-Autry 3-yd. run (Akers kick)
CLE-Patten 9-yd. pass from Pederson (P. Dawson kick)
CLE-Prentice 1-yd. run (P. Dawson kick)
PHI-Small 24-yd. pass from McNabb (Akers kick)
PHI-Small 8-yd. pass from McNabb (Akers kick)
PHI-Johnson 11-yd. pass from McNabb (Akers kick)
PHI-Johnson 38-yd. pass from McNabb (Akers kick)
CLE-P. Dawson 29-yd. FG
CLE-Prentice 1-yd. run (P. Dawson kick)

Passing
PHI: McNabb 23–36–390 4 TD 0 INT
CLE: Pederson 29–40–309 1 TD 2 INT, Johnson 1–3–23 0 TD 1 INT

Rushing
PHI: Autry 10–28, McNabb 3–12, Pritchett 2–1
CLE: Prentice 17–46, Northcutt 7–37, White 3–15, Pederson 3–3

Receiving
PHI: Lewis 5–100, Johnson 5–93, Small 7–92, Pinkston 2–56, Martin 2–30, Pritchett 1–11, Thomason 1–8
CLE: Patten 7–103, Johnson 6–76, Northcutt 5–44, Shea 3–33, Prentice 4–29, Saleh 1–22, Campbell 3–17, Brown 1–8

Sunday, December 17
Tennessee Titans 24, Browns 0
Cleveland Browns Stadium (72,318)
Brown jerseys/white pants

With thick snow swirling through the stadium and blanketing the field amid a wind-chill factor of –10°F, the trickery the Browns used the week before was ineffective, and they once again saw their offense unable to put any points on the board. Shut out for a record fourth time on the season, the Browns could manage only 113 total yards and six first downs as the eventual AFC Central Division-champion Titans rolled to a 17–0 halftime lead and never looked back. Tennessee's Eddie George once again throttled the Browns, this time picking up 176 yards and all three of the game's touchdowns. Ending what had become a miserable season, the game would prove to be the final for Chris Palmer as Cleveland's head coach, as he was fired three weeks later.
Record: 3–13

	1	2	3	4		
Titans	10	7	0	7	=	24
Browns	0	0	0	0	=	0

TEN-Del Greco 33-yd. FG
TEN-George 1-yd. run (Del Greco kick)
TEN-George 2-yd. run (Del Greco kick)
TEN-George 35-yd. run (Del Greco kick)

Passing
TEN: McNair 10–18–79 0 TD 1 INT, O'Donnell 2–2–26 0 TD 0 INT
CLE: Pederson 13–30–75 0 TD 0 INT

Rushing
TEN: George 34–176, Thomas 11–27, McNair 2–9
CLE: Prentice 12–32, Pederson 1–15, White 4–3

Receiving
TEN: Mason 1–33, Thigpen 2–27, Kinney 1–15, Sanders 2–13, Wycheck 3–9, Neal 2–8, George 1–0
CLE: Patten 3–26, Prentice 2–13, White 2–12, Shea 2–8, Edwards 1–7, Brown 1–6, Johnson 2–3

2001

Sunday, September 9
Seattle Seahawks 9, Browns 6
Cleveland Browns Stadium (72,318)
White jerseys/white pants

The first game of the Butch Davis era ended in heartbreak when Seattle kicker Rian Lindell booted a 52-yard field goal with three seconds to play to give the Seahawks a narrow victory. Breakdowns by the Browns' special teams haunted them all day, particularly when they allowed a 49-yard kickoff return after tying the game at six with two minutes remaining. Neither team managed much offense as both defenses shined, neither permitting more than 260 yards of offense. The Browns collected four sacks, two by LB Jamir Miller and another by DE Gerard Warren in his first NFL game.

Record: 0–1

	1	2	3	4		
Seahawks	0	3	3	3	=	9
Browns	0	3	0	3	=	6

CLE-P. Dawson 48-yd. FG
SEA-Lindell 49-yd. FG
SEA-Lindell 23-yd. FG
CLE-P. Dawson 22-yd. FG
SEA-Lindell 52-yd. FG

Passing
SEA: Hasselbeck 20–34–178 0 TD 2 INT
CLE: Couch 17–33–176 0 TD 1 INT

Rushing
SEA: Watters 16–97, Hasselbeck 6–1, Alexander 4–3, Strong 1–0
CLE: White 10–52, Jackson 14–37, Couch 1–1

Receiving
SEA: Robinson 3–44, Watters 2–43, Mili 2–21, Strong 4–20, Engram 2–18, Jackson 5–17, Williams 2–15
CLE: Johnson 4–51, J. Dawson 5–46, Morgan 3–46, White 3–26, Dudley 1–5, Sellers 1–2

Sunday September 23
Browns 24, Detroit Lions 14
Cleveland Browns Stadium (73,168)
White jerseys/white pants

After the NFL's week two games were postponed following the September 11 terrorist attacks, the Browns returned to action with a stirring victory over Detroit highlighted by seven interceptions of former Cleveland QB Ty Detmer, tying a Cleveland record. Browns' rookie DB Anthony Henry snagged three picks as the Browns raced to a 17–0 lead, then held off the Lions in the second half. QB Tim Couch tossed three touchdown passes, including one to backup center Shaun O'Hara, with the third going to rookie WR Quincy Morgan to push the Browns' lead back to 17 points after Detroit narrowed the margin to 17–7 on an interception return for a touchdown. Cleveland RB James Jackson rolled up 124 yards on 31 carries to become the first Browns' back to top 100 yards rushing since their rebirth. Just as in the opener, the Browns accumulated less than 260 yards of total offense, but Detroit's turnovers, plus 115 yards in Lions' penalties, paved the way to a Cleveland victory.

Record: 1–1

	1	2	3	4		
Lions	0	0	7	7	=	14
Browns	7	7	10	0	=	24

CLE-Johnson 4-yd. pass from Couch (P. Dawson kick)
CLE-O'Hara 2-yd. pass from Couch (P. Dawson kick)
CLE-P. Dawson 33-yd. FG
DET-Fair 26-yd. interception return
CLE-Morgan 34-yd. pass from Couch (P. Dawson kick)
DET-Morton 14-yd. pass from Detmer (Hanson kick)

Passing
DET: Detmer 22–42–212 1 TD 7 INT
CLE: Couch 12–20–138 3 TD 2 INT

Rushing
DET: Stewart 17–71, Crowell 1–6, Detmer 2–5
CLE: Jackson 31–124, White 3–15, Couch 3–0

Receiving
DET: Morton 6–100, Schlesinger 5–37, Crowell 4–34, Foster 3–25, Stewart 4–16
CLE: Morgan 2–38, Dudley 2–37, Sellers 1–28, Johnson 4–26, White 1–4, J. Dawson 1–3, O'Hara 1–2

Sunday, September 30
Browns 23, Jacksonville Jaguars 14
Alltel Stadium (57,875)
Brown jerseys/white pants

Displaying a cocksure attitude for the first time since their return, the Browns picked up a signature victory in Jacksonville, defeating the division-rival Jaguars for the first time after six consecutive defeats. On the game's first play, Cleveland's Gerard Warren knocked Jacksonville QB Mark Brunell from the contest with a concussion (a hit for which he was later fined), while the Browns were penalized twice for taunting. Yet this fresh spirit sparked a 13–0 halftime lead, which disintegrated in the third quarter after the Jags returned a fumble for a touchdown to give them a one-point advantage. With the defense keeping an opponent under 300 total yards for the third straight game, the Browns hung tough and Phil Dawson put them back on top with a 30-yard field goal with five minutes left. Then, after Jacksonville got the ball back with just over a minute to play, Cleveland DB Daylon McCutcheon intercepted backup QB Jonathan Quinn and returned it 32 yards for the game-clinching touchdown.
Record: 2–1

	1	2	3	4		
Browns	3	10	0	10	=	23
Jaguars	0	0	14	0	=	14

CLE-P. Dawson 35-yd. FG
CLE-White 4-yd. run (P. Dawson kick)
CLE-P. Dawson 28-yd. FG
JAX-McCardell 8-yd. pass from Quinn (Hollis kick)
JAX-Beasley 40-yd. fumble return (Hollis kick)
CLE-P. Dawson 30-yd. FG
CLE-McCutcheon 32-yd. interception return (P. Dawson kick)

Passing
CLE: Couch 24–34–249 0 TD 1 INT
JAX: Quinn 15–30–136 1 TD 1 INT, Brunell 4–7–34 0 TD 1 INT

Rushing
CLE: White 23–64, Jackson 10–18, Couch 3–13
JAX: Mack 17–93, Quinn 2–5

Receiving
CLE: Johnson 6–80, German 3–34, J. Dawson 3–33, Morgan 2–32, White 5–26, Sellers 1–18, Jackson 1–16, Dudley 3–10
JAX: Smith 9–88, Mack 3–18, McCardell 2–17, Jones 1–16, Brady 1–14, Washington 1–9, Dawkins 2–8

Sunday, October 7
Browns 20, San Diego Chargers 16
Cleveland Browns Stadium (73,018)
White jerseys/white pants

In a game played beneath the shadow of that morning's launching of U.S. military action in Afghanistan in response to the September 11 terrorist attacks, the Browns rallied for a thrilling victory on a crisp, sunny afternoon before an ecstatic home crowd. After the Browns went up 10–3 at the half, the 3–0 Chargers surged to a 16–10 lead in the fourth quarter, led by rookie RB LaDainian Tomlinson, who would rush for 102 yards and a touchdown. A Phil Dawson field goal cut the margin to three, then after a key defensive stop, the Browns regained possession at midfield with just under four minutes to play. Following a key completion from Tim Couch to WR Kevin Johnson on third-and-10, the pair hooked up again, this time in the end zone on third-and-six from the Chargers' 19 to put the Browns ahead with just over a minute remaining. San Diego reached midfield, but a pair of frantic Hail Mary passes by veteran QB Doug Flutie fell incomplete, and the Browns improved to 3–1, already matching their victory total from the year before.
Record: 3–1

	1	2	3	4		
Chargers	3	0	7	6	=	16
Browns	0	10	0	10	=	20

SD-Richey 22-yd. FG
CLE-P. Dawson 31-yd. FG
CLE-Jackson 12-yd. run (P. Dawson kick)
SD-Tomlinson 2-yd. run (Richey kick)
SD-Richey 21-yd. FG
SD-Richey 38-yd. FG
CLE-P. Dawson 27-yd. FG
CLE-Johnson 19-yd. pass from Couch (P. Dawson kick)

Passing
SD: Flutie 17–37–149 0 TD 0 INT
CLE: Couch 14–27–203 1 TD 0 INT

Rushing
SD: Tomlinson 19–102, Flutie 3–9, Dwight 1–8, Fletcher 1–5, Conway 2–2
CLE: Jackson 26–68, Couch 2–24, Morgan 1–4, White 2–1

Receiving
SD: Graham 5–49, Conway 3–37, Jones 3–23, McCrary 2–13, Tomlinson 2–12, Dwight 1–8, Fletcher 1–7

CLE: Dudley 3–63, Johnson 3–38, J. Dawson 2–38, Morgan 2–26, Northcutt 1–14, Shea 1–10, German 1–8, White 1–6

Sunday, October 14
Cincinnati Bengals 24, Browns 14
Paul Brown Stadium (64,217)
White jerseys/white pants

The Browns spoiled a golden opportunity to pick up their fourth win with a sluggish second-half performance that allowed the mediocre Bengals to steamroll their way to victory. On the strength of a nifty touchdown reception by Kevin Johnson, the Browns took a 7–3 lead to the locker room at halftime only to see the Bengals score the next 21 points. RB Corey Dillon racked up 140 yards on the ground while the Browns were held to 40 as a team, relying solely on the passing game to move the ball. Johnson wound up with 153 yards on eight catches, but Cincinnati nearly doubled the Browns in total yardage with 400.
Record: 3–2

	1	2	3	4		
Browns	7	0	0	7	=	14
Bengals	3	0	10	11	=	24

CIN-Rackers 27-yd. FG
CLE-Johnson 30-yd. pass from Couch (P. Dawson kick)
CIN-Scott 5-yd. pass from Kitna (Rackers kick)
CIN-Rackers 42-yd. FG
CIN-Dillon 5-yd. run (Dugans pass from Kitna)
CIN-Rackers 21-yd. FG
CLE-Sellers 3-yd. pass from Couch (P. Dawson kick)

Passing
CLE: Couch 14–28–194 2 TD 0 INT
CIN: Kitna 20–38–201 1 TD 0 INT

Rushing
CLE: Jackson 14–22, White 3–19, Couch 2-(-1)
CIN: Dillon 31–140, Bennett 7–41, Kitna 4–18

Receiving
CLE: Johnson 8–153, White 3–27, Morgan 1–6, J. Dawson 1–5, Sellers 1–3
CIN: Warrick 4–73, Johnson 5–68, Bennett 2–18, Dillon 3–16, Neal 3–13, Dugans 1–5, Scott 1–5, Battaglia 1–3

Sunday, October 21
Browns 24, Baltimore Ravens 14
Cleveland Browns Stadium (72,818)
White jerseys/white pants

The Browns picked up one of the most satisfying victories in franchise history with a sound beating of the defending world-champion Ravens, notching the new Browns' first triumph over Art Modell's Baltimore team. The Browns set the tone on the opening drive, marching down the field over the mighty Ravens' defense and scoring on a James Jackson touchdown scamper. Behind an opportunistic Cleveland defense that collected seven sacks and three turnovers, a 10–6 Browns' lead exploded to 18 points in a matter of minutes in the third quarter when Tim Couch hit Kevin Johnson and Quincy Morgan for long touchdown passes sandwiched around a Baltimore fumble. An emotional crowd watched in joy as rain pelted the field in the fourth quarter, and the Browns hung on for a 10-point win, their third straight at home.
Record: 4–2

	1	2	3	4		
Ravens	0	6	0	8	=	14
Browns	7	3	14	0	=	24

CLE-Jackson 11-yd. run (P. Dawson kick)
BAL-Stover 21-yd. FG
CLE-P. Dawson 33-yd. FG
BAL-Stover 38-yd. FG
CLE-Johnson 28-yd. pass from Couch (P. Dawson kick)
CLE-Morgan 36-yd. pass from Couch (P. Dawson kick)
BAL-Ismail 22-yd. pass from Cunningham (Ismail pass from Cunningham)

Passing
BAL: Grbac 16–20–142 0 TD 2 INT, Cunningham 11–25–120 1 TD 0 INT
CLE: Couch 11–18–149 2 TD 0 INT

Rushing
BAL: Ayanbadejo 9–48, Brookins 13–46, Allen 3–12, Cunningham 1–5, Williams 1–2
CLE: Jackson 24–77, Couch 4–10, White 1–1

Receiving
BAL: Ismail 7–85, Stokley 5–68, Sharpe 6–61, Brookins 3–24, Ayanbadejo 5–20, Gash 1–4
CLE: Johnson 3–47, Morgan 1–36, Santiago 1–27, Jackson 2–13, Sellers 1–12, Northcutt 1–11, Shea 1–2, White 1–1

Sunday, November 4
Chicago Bears 27, Browns 21 (OT)
Soldier Field (66,944)
White jerseys/white pants

One of the greatest moments of the Browns' new era was followed by one of the most crushing as they squandered a 14-point lead in the final 30 seconds of regulation and lost to the high-flying Bears in overtime. Cleveland DE Courtney Brown started the sun-splashed afternoon by sacking Bears' QB Shane Matthews and returning the subsequent fumble 25 yards for a touchdown, the first of three sacks he would collect on the day. A pair of Tim Couch touchdown passes in the third quarter gave the Browns a 21–7 lead that they milked into the final minutes before things changed quickly. The Bears cut the margin to seven with 28 seconds left, then recovered an onside kick and Chicago RB James Allen caught a tipped ball on a Hail Mary pass in the end zone on the final play to force overtime. Then, on the Browns' first possession of sudden-death, Couch's pass was tipped and intercepted by Chicago DB Mike Brown, who returned it 16 yards for the game-winning score and the Bears' sixth straight win.

Record: 4–3

	1	2	3	4	OT		
Browns	7	0	14	0	0	=	21
Bears	0	7	0	14	6	=	27

CLE-Brown 25-yd. fumble return (P. Dawson kick)
CHI-Thomas 2-yd. run (Edinger kick)
CLE-Sellers 3-yd. pass from Couch (P. Dawson kick)
CLE-Johnson 55-yd. pass from Couch (P. Dawson kick)
CHI-Booker 9-yd. pass from Matthews (Edinger kick)
CHI-Allen 34-yd. pass from Matthews (Edinger kick)
CHI-Brown 16-yd. interception return

Passing
CLE: Couch 14–23–211 2 TD 1 INT
CHI: Matthews 30–50–357 2 TD 3 INT

Rushing
CLE: Jackson 22–71, Couch 1-(-1)
CHI: Thomas 31–96, Allen 1–3

Receiving
CLE: Johnson 5–99, Northcutt 2–34, Morgan 1–28, Santiago 2–26, White 1–10, Jackson 1–7, Shea 1–4, Sellers 1–3
CHI: White 7–92, Booker 7–85, Thomas 6–71, Allen 5–65, Terrell 3–35, Baxter 1–6, Bates 1–3

Sunday, November 11
Pittsburgh Steelers 15, Browns 12 (OT)
Cleveland Browns Stadium (73,218)
White jerseys/white pants

For the second straight week, the Browns squandered a fourth-quarter lead and lost a dispiriting game in overtime. Just as in Chicago, the Browns started fast, sprinting to a 9–0 lead in the opening minutes when former Steelers' DL Orpheus Roye pinned Pittsburgh RB Jerome Bettis in the end zone for a safety, followed by a Tim Couch touchdown pass to TE O. J. Santiago. For the remainder of the game, the Browns' offense was dominated—reflected by seven sacks of Couch in the second half—but the defense dug in to keep the team in the game. The Steelers, who would roll up 428 yards to Cleveland's meager 187, tied the game at nine on three Kris Brown field goals, then again in the fourth quarter at 12 after Phil Dawson briefly put the Browns on top again. The Browns had a chance to steal the game after Brown missed a 45-yard attempt with 1:37 left, and they drove to the Steelers' 41, but a pair of sacks ended the threat. Behind the power running of Bettis, who rolled up 163 rushing yards, the Steelers won the coin toss in overtime and easily marched into field-goal territory, setting up Brown's game-winner from 32 yards.

Record: 4–4

	1	2	3	4	OT		
Steelers	3	3	3	3	3	=	15
Browns	9	0	3	0	0	=	12

CLE-Safety: Roye tackled Bettis in end zone
CLE-Santiago 12-yd. pass from Couch (P. Dawson kick)
PIT-Brown 31-yd. FG
PIT-Brown 27-yd. FG
PIT-Brown 37-yd. FG
CLE-P. Dawson 40-yd. FG
PIT-Brown 37-yd. FG
PIT-Brown 32-yd. FG

Passing
PIT: Stewart 18–32–188 0 TD 0 INT
CLE: Couch 18–33–160 1 TD 0 INT

Rushing
PIT: Bettis 29–163, Stewart 7–65, Zereoue 4–20
CLE: Jackson 18–57, Couch 3–15, White 2–2

Receiving
PIT: Zereoue 3–77, Ward 8–55, Burress 4–44, Shaw 1–9, Bruener 1–3, Bettis 1–0
CLE: Johnson 8–62, Morgan 3–28, White 1–26, German 3–23, Santiago 2–14, Sellers 1–7

Sunday, November 18
Browns 27, Baltimore Ravens 17
PSINet Stadium (69,353)
White jerseys/white pants

The Browns completed a stunning sweep of the defending Super Bowl champions on the strength of an opportunistic defense and the heroics of previously unknown RB Ben Gay. Picking off Baltimore QB Elvis Grbac four times (including a 43-yard interception return for a touchdown by DB Devin Bush) and forcing a fumble, the Browns' defense paved the way to a 17–0 lead. After the Ravens sliced the margin to three in the third quarter, the Cleveland offense stepped up with a 12-play, 68-yard drive that melted six minutes off the clock in the fourth quarter and ended with a touchdown run by RB Jamel White to put the game away. The final march was paced by Gay, a rookie making his first NFL start, who wound up with 56 yards on 18 carries and a touchdown, along with a 42-yard kickoff return. The Ravens, who had won eight straight home games and had permitted only three rushing touchdowns all season, saw their hopes for a division title go up in smoke as the upstart Browns established themselves as a surprising contender for the AFC playoffs.
Record: 5–4

	1	2	3	4		
Browns	3	17	0	7	=	27
Ravens	0	7	10	0	=	17

CLE-P. Dawson 29-yd. FG
CLE-Gay 7-yd. run (P. Dawson kick)
CLE-Bush 43-yd. interception return (P. Dawson kick)
BAL-Stokley 21-yd. pass from Grbac (Stover kick)
CLE-P. Dawson 42-yd. FG
BAL-Heap 24-yd. pass from Grbac (Stover kick)
BAL-Stover 42-yd. FG
CLE-White 1-yd. run (P. Dawson kick)

Passing
CLE: Couch 19–30–144 0 TD 3 INT
BAL: Grbac 23–44–261 2 TD 4 INT

Rushing
CLE: Gay 18–56, White 9–29, Northcutt 1–12, Couch 2-(-2)
BAL: Brookins 21–89, Williams 5–19, Lewis 1–0

Receiving
CLE: Johnson 3–54, Northcutt 5–45, White 4–18, Morgan 2–15, Santiago 2–9, Gay 1–7, Shea 1–6, Couch 1-(-10)
BAL: Sharpe 7–78, Ismail 6–68, Taylor 5–48, Heap 1–24, Stokley 1–21, Williams 1–15, Lewis 1–5, Ayanbadejo 1–2

Sunday, November 25
Browns 18, Cincinnati Bengals 0
Cleveland Browns Stadium (72,918)
Brown jerseys/white pants

Posting their first shutout in seven years, the Browns' defense dominated Cincinnati, limiting the Bengals to 191 total yards and forcing seven turnovers while keeping All-Pro RB Corey Dillon, who had blasted the Browns for 140 yards in their first meeting a month earlier, to 63 yards on 20 carries. While the Cleveland offense, highlighted by 113 receiving yards by Kevin Johnson, struggled to put points on the board, managed only one touchdown in six trips inside the Cincinnati 20, the Browns' defense thwarted the Bengals all day. The key sequence of the game came early in the fourth quarter following a long Bengals' punt return to the Cleveland 5, when the Browns forced Cincinnati to turn the ball over on downs. The victory gave the Browns more victories in 2001 than in 1999 and 2000 combined.
Record: 6–4

	1	2	3	4		
Bengals	0	0	0	0	=	0
Browns	3	9	0	6	=	18

CLE-P. Dawson 23-yd. FG
CLE-P. Dawson 27-yd. FG
CLE-Johnson 6-yd. pass from Couch (kick failed)
CLE-P. Dawson 23-yd. FG
CLE-P. Dawson 33-yd. FG

Passing
CIN: Kitna 8–19–85 0 TD 2 INT, Mitchell 4–12–38 0 TD 3 INT, Smith 1–2–2 0 TD 0 INT
CLE: Couch 16–27–189 1 TD 2 INT

Rushing
CIN: Dillon 20–63, Bennett 2–17, Neal 1–4, Smith 1–0
CLE: Jackson 18–40, Gay 10–16, White 5–13, Northcutt 1–9, Couch 5–0

Receiving
CIN: Farmer 3–32, Scott 2–24, Warrick 1–22, Dugans 3–19, McGee 2–15, Johnson 1–7, Dillon 1–6
CLE: Johnson 6–113, Morgan 5–40, Shea 3–21, Northcutt 1–13, J. Dawson 1–2

Sunday, December 2
Tennessee Titans 31, Browns 15
Cleveland Browns Stadium (72,818)
White jerseys/white pants

Following back-to-back rousing divisional victories, the Browns returned to reality as they were thoroughly dominated by a Tennessee team already out of the playoff race. Setting the tone by fumbling the opening kickoff, the Browns quickly fell behind 17–0 and trailed 31–7 in the fourth quarter as the Cleveland defense failed to force either a sack or a turnover after notching 12 combined takeaways the previous two weeks. Titans' QB Steve McNair averaged 22 yards per completion as WRs Derrick Mason and Kevin Dyson each surpassed 100 receiving yards. QB Kelly Holcomb made his first appearance as a Brown, throwing a meaningless touchdown pass in the fourth quarter.

Record: 6–5

	1	2	3	4		
Titans	14	3	14	0	=	31
Browns	0	7	0	8	=	15

TEN-George 1-yd. run (Nedney kick)
TEN-Mason 43-yd. pass from McNair (Nedney kick)
TEN-Nedney 29-yd. FG
CLE-Johnson 10-yd. pass from Couch (P. Dawson kick)
TEN-Bennett 5-yd. pass from McNair (Nedney kick)
TEN-Mason 71-yd. pass from McNair (Nedney kick)
CLE-Johnson 20-yd. pass from Holcomb (White run)

Passing
TEN: McNair 11–17–244 3 TD 0 INT, O'Donnell 2–2–28 0 TD 0 INT
CLE: Couch 17–26–110 1 TD 1 INT, Holcomb 7–12–114 1 TD 0 INT

Rushing
TEN: George 23–51, Hicks 10–51, McNair 2–10, O'Donnell 4-(-1)
CLE: Gay 8–37, Couch 2–18, Northcutt 1–5, White 4–4, Frost 1–1, Holcomb 1–0

Receiving
TEN: Mason 3–122, Dyson 6–110, Wycheck 2–23, Bennett 2–17
CLE: Northcutt 6–65, Morgan 3–43, Johnson 4–41, Shea 6–32, J. Dawson 3–28, White 2–15

Sunday, December 9
New England Patriots 27, Browns 16
Foxboro Stadium (60,292)
White jerseys/white pants

The Browns hung tough with the eventual Super Bowl champions but couldn't take advantage of second-half opportunities to finish the job. Cleveland took a 10–3 lead in the first quarter following a 49-yard interception return for a touchdown by DB Corey Fuller but trailed by 10 at the half following an 85-yard punt return for a score by New England WR Troy Brown. The Browns whittled the lead down to four midway through the fourth quarter but couldn't take the lead on back-to-back possessions before the Patriots iced the game with a touchdown. Three Tim Couch interceptions proved costly, particularly since the Browns managed only 50 yards on the ground and didn't score an offensive touchdown.

Record: 6–6

	1	2	3	4		
Browns	10	0	3	3	=	16
Patriots	3	17	0	7	=	27

NE-Vinatieri 54-yd. FG
CLE-P. Dawson 27-yd. FG
CLE-Fuller 49-yd. interception return (P. Dawson kick)
NE-Smith 1-yd. run (Vinatieri kick)
NE-Brown 85-yd. punt return (Vinatieri kick)
NE-Vinatieri 38-yd. FG
CLE-P. Dawson 39-yd. FG
CLE-P. Dawson 22-yd. FG
NE-Smith 5-yd. run (Vinatieri kick)

Passing
CLE: Couch 20–39–244 0 TD 3 INT
NE: Brady 19–28–218 0 TD 2 INT

Rushing
CLE: Jackson 16–34, Couch 1–9, White 1–7
NE: Smith 21–76, Patten 1–7, Edwards 4–3, Faulk 2–0, Brown 1-(-2), Brady 4-(-3)

Receiving
CLE: Johnson 8–95, White 3–57, Northcutt 2–29, J. Dawson 2–26, Jackson 2–15, Santiago 2–11, Shea 1–11
NE: Brown 7–89, Glenn 4–67, Patten 3–41, Faulk 3–11, Redmond 1–8, Edwards 1–2

Sunday, December 16
Jacksonville Jaguars 15, Browns 10
Cleveland Browns Stadium (72,818)
White jerseys/white pants

The Browns' meager playoff hopes were obliterated amid controversy in the final minute of a narrow home loss to Jacksonville. Playing from behind all day, the Browns stayed in the game when Anthony Henry returned an interception 97 yards for a touchdown in the third quarter with the Jaguars on the brink of extending their lead to double digits. After the Browns cut the margin to two points midway through the fourth, Jacksonville made it 15–10 on Mike Hollis's third field goal, but the Browns had one final chance to win. Driving inside the Jaguars' 20 in the final minute, they appeared to convert on a fourth-down pass from Tim Couch to Quincy Morgan at the nine-yard line, quickly followed by an intentional spike to stop the clock with 48 seconds left. The officials then ruled that the spike did not count and retroactively reviewed the Morgan catch, ruling it was incomplete. Irate Browns fans pummeled the field and the officials with beer bottles and debris, forcing the officials to end the game early, though 25 minutes later NFL Commissioner Paul Tagliabue forced the teams back onto the field to allow Jacksonville to kneel out the final seconds. Lost in the ugliness was a strong performance by the Cleveland defense, which sacked Brunell eight times—three by Jamir Miller—and forced three turnovers.
Record: 6–7

	1	2	3	4		
Jaguars	9	0	0	6	=	15
Browns	0	0	7	3	=	10

JAX-Smith 4-yd. pass from Brunell (kick failed)
JAX-Hollis 43-yd. FG
CLE-Henry 97-yd. interception return (P. Dawson kick)
JAX-Hollis 46-yd. FG
CLE-P. Dawson 29-yd. FG
JAX-Hollis 37-yd. FG

Passing
JAX: Brunell 20–35–202 1 TD 2 INT
CLE: Couch 21–30–184 0 TD 1 INT

Rushing
JAX: Mack 28–115, Brunell 5–13
CLE: White 9–33, Couch 2–7, Jackson 2–6, Gay 2–1

Receiving
JAX: McCardell 7–61, Smith 5–52, Brady 3–44, Mack 3–24, Washington 1–12, Dawkins 1–9
CLE: J. Dawson 1–44, White 5–39, King 4–35, Johnson 3–34, Santiago 3–23, Jackson 1–5, Gay 2–2, Morgan 2–2

Sunday, December 23
Green Bay Packers 30, Browns 7
Lambeau Field (59,824)
White jerseys/white pants

With snow blanketing a slippery field, both offenses took advantage, combining for more than 700 total yards, but the Browns' five turnovers made it an easy victory for the playoff-bound Packers. Green Bay's running attack, paced by 150 yards by RB Ahman Green, was unstoppable, while Jamel White starred for the Browns, rushing for a career-high 131 yards and tallying 216 total. While Packers' QB Brett Favre tossed three touchdown passes, a trio of interceptions by Tim Couch, including one returned 69 yards for a touchdown just before the half, took the Browns out of the game as they lost their fourth straight.
Record: 6–8

	1	2	3	4		
Browns	0	7	0	0	=	7
Packers	13	10	0	7	=	30

GB-Franks 1-yd. pass from Favre (kick failed)
GB-Franks 4-yd. pass from Favre (Longwell kick)
CLE-White 3-yd. pass from Couch (P. Dawson kick)
GB-Longwell 39-yd. FG
GB-Williams 69-yd. interception return (Longwell kick)
GB-Levens 16-yd. pass from Favre (Longwell kick)

Passing
CLE: Couch 22–33–203 1 TD 3 INT
GB: Favre 18–28–139 3 TD 0 INT

Rushing
CLE: White 21–131, Couch 5–37
GB: Green 21–150, Levens 9–72, Favre 2–1, Pederson 1-(-1)

Receiving
CLE: White 9–85, Johnson 7–54, King 3–43, Morgan 2–14, Santiago 1–7
GB: Franks 4–29, Levens 2–25, Freeman 2–24, Green 3–18, Schroeder 2–15, Davis 3–14, Bradford 1–11, Henderson 1–3

Sunday, December 30
Browns 41, Tennessee Titans 38
Adelphia Coliseum (68,798)
White jerseys/white pants

Rallying from a 14-point fourth-quarter deficit, the Browns stunned the Titans with a last-minute victory four weeks after being dominated by Tennessee in Cleveland. Tim Couch played one of the finest games of his career, completing 20 of 27 passes to eight different receivers for 336 yards with three touchdowns, including the game-tying score to Kevin Johnson with 5:37 remaining, set up by a 78-yard pass to Quincy Morgan. After a key defensive stop, the Browns took over at their own 39 with 3:23 left and marched inside the Titans' 30 thanks to a Tennessee personal foul on a key third-down play, which gave the Browns a first down. Phil Dawson won it with a 44-yard field goal with 55 seconds remaining, snapping the Browns' month-long losing streak. While Cleveland's defense struggled, permitting 130 rushing yards to RB Eddie George, the Browns' offense topped 400 yards for the first time all season. Kevin Johnson surpassed the 1,000-yard mark for the year, becoming the first Browns' receiver to do so in 12 years.

Record: 7–8

	1	2	3	4		
Browns	14	10	0	17	=	41
Titans	14	10	7	7	=	38

CLE J. Dawson 33-yd. pass from Couch (P. Dawson kick)
TEN-Green 17-yd. run (Nedney kick)
CLE-Santiago 20-yd. pass from Couch (P. Dawson kick)
TEN-Dyson 40-yd. pass from McNair (Nedney kick)
CLE-P. Dawson 30-yd. FG
TEN-Mason 59-yd. pass from McNair (Nedney kick)
CLE-White 1-yd. run (P. Dawson kick)
TEN-Nedney 31-yd. FG
TEN-George 7-yd. run (Nedney kick)
TEN-George 20-yd. run (Nedney kick)
CLE-White 2-yd. run (P. Dawson kick)
CLE-Johnson 4-yd. pass from Couch (P. Dawson kick)
CLE-P. Dawson 44-yd. FG

Passing
CLE: Couch 20–27–336 3 TD 1 INT
TEN: McNair 16–25–274 2 TD 0 INT, Green 0–1–0 0 TD 1 INT

Rushing
CLE: Gay 7–46, White 21–42, Couch 1-(-1)
TEN: George 26–130, McNair 5–34, Green 4–24

Receiving
CLE: Morgan 1–78, Johnson 6–70, King 3–61, White 3–56, J. Dawson 2–37, Santiago 3–27, Moreland 1–5, Gay 1–2
TEN: Dyson 3–92, Mason 3–81, Kinney 4–43, Wycheck 3–28, George 2–20, Bennett 1–10

Sunday, January 6
Pittsburgh Steelers 28, Browns 7
Heinz Field (59,189)
White jerseys/white pants

The offensive euphoria of the week before hit a brick wall in the season finale (rescheduled from week two) as the Browns were overwhelmed in the second half by the Steelers' backups in Cleveland's first-ever game at Heinz Field. With Pittsburgh already having clinched the AFC Central title, the Steelers rested many of their starters and wound up breaking open a 7–7 game in the third quarter, starting when the Browns' Ben Gay fumbled the second-half kickoff, and Pittsburgh WR Troy Edwards returned it 32 yards for a touchdown. It was the first of three Browns' turnovers in the second half, as Cleveland was limited to 173 yards of offense. Meanwhile, Pittsburgh tallied 376, which included a whopping 221 on the ground. The loss clinched the Browns' fourth straight losing season and their eighth losing record in the previous nine seasons.

Record: 7–9

	1	2	3	4		
Browns	7	0	0	0	=	7
Steelers	0	7	14	7	=	28

CLE-White 3-yd. run (P. Dawson kick)
PIT-Fuamatu-Ma'afala 17-yd. run (Brown kick)
PIT-Edwards 32-yd. fumble return (Brown kick)
PIT-Shaw 40-yd. pass from Maddox
PIT-Bowers 21-yd. run (Brown kick)

Passing
CLE: Couch 13–26–150 0 TD 2 INT
PIT: Maddox 6–8–97 1 TD 1 INT, Stewart 8–16–72 0 TD 2 INT

Rushing
CLE: White 11–30, Morgan 1–23, Gay 6–16, Couch 1-(-1)
PIT: Fuamatu-Ma'afala 17–98, Bowers 11–67, Stewart 4–38, Maddox 1–8, Martin 1–8, Kreider 1–1, Witman 1–1

Receiving
CLE: Johnson 6–80, White 2–22, J. Dawson 1–19, Moreland 2–10, King 1–10, Santiago 1–9
PIT: Burress 3–48, Shaw 2–48, Ward 4–32, Edwards 1–21, Fuamatu-Ma'afala 2–15, Cushing 1–5, Bowers 1–0

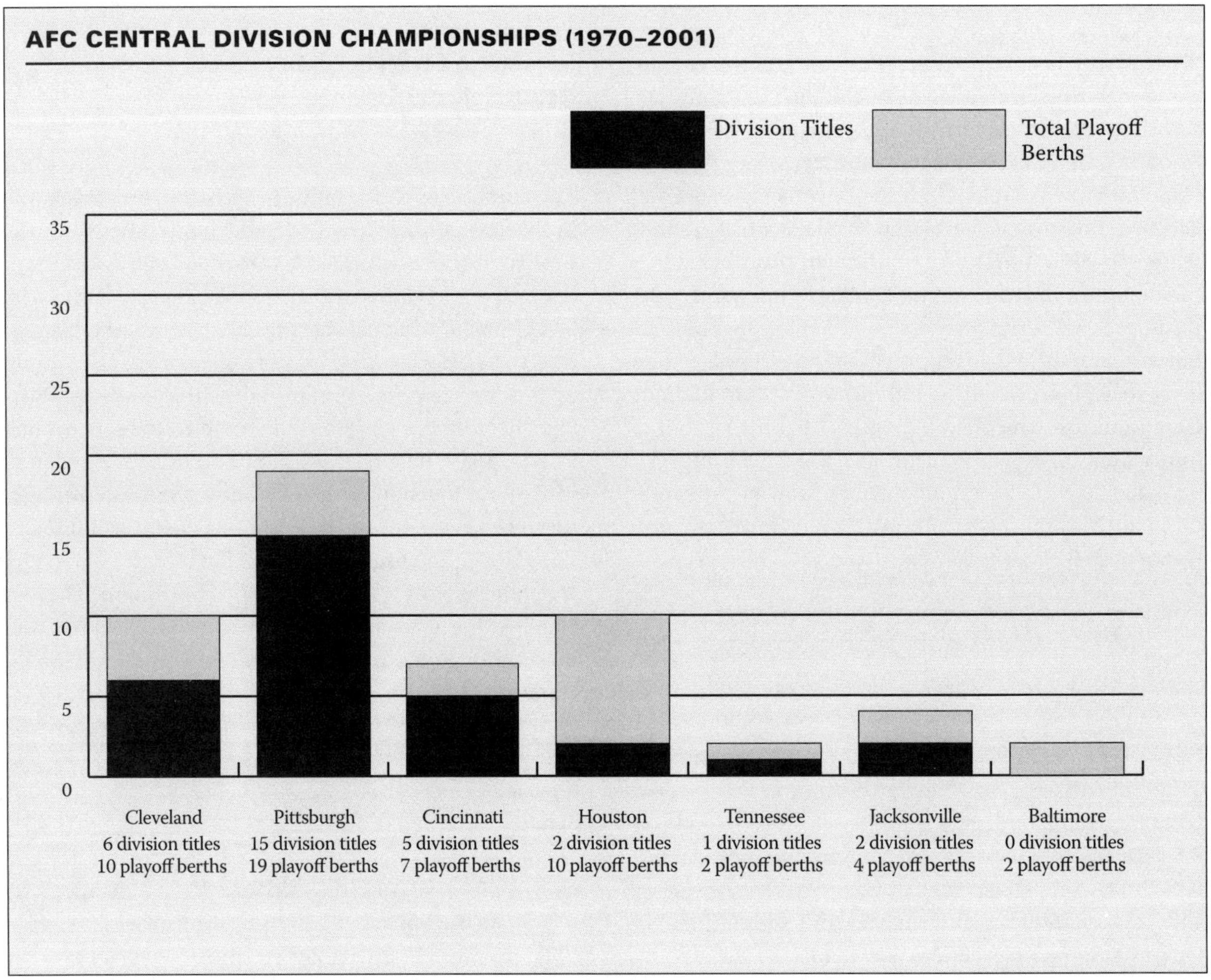

2002

Sunday, September 8
Kansas City Chiefs 40, Browns 39
Cleveland Browns Stadium (72,938)
White jerseys/white pants

In perhaps the most bizarre ending to a game in team history, the Browns lost on the final play after their celebration over an apparent victory began a few seconds too early. It had been a thrilling, seesaw game, with the teams combining for nearly 900 total yards and nine touchdowns as backup Browns' QB Kelly Holcomb, playing for an injured Tim Couch, had a magnificent performance, throwing for 326 yards and three touchdowns. Second-year WR Quincy Morgan was his primary target, reeling in nine receptions for 151 yards and a pair of scores, including a 33 yard touchdown catch on a pass from fellow WR Kevin Johnson on a trick play late in the second quarter. The Browns surged to a 30–17 lead four minutes into what became a wild fourth quarter, but Kansas City RB Priest Holmes then exploded for three of his four touchdowns on the day in the next eight minutes, and the Chiefs took a 37–36 lead with three minutes left. Holcomb directed the Browns on a gritty drive that appeared to result in the winning points when Phil Dawson kicked a 41-yard field goal with 29 seconds left to put the Browns up by two. But on the game's final play from the Chiefs' 47, after Kansas City QB Trent Green hit the turf in what looked like a game-ending sack, Browns' LB Dwayne Rudd ripped off his helmet in celebration. But Green had kept the play alive by lateraling the ball to OT John Tait, who rumbled 28 yards through the Browns' broken defense before being driven out of bounds at the Cleveland 25 with the clock at zero. But Rudd was penalized for unsportsmanlike conduct for removing his helmet before the play was over, pushing the Chiefs half the distance to the goal and giving them one more play. With their gift, they kicked a 30-yard field goal to hand the Browns an absolutely stunning defeat and set the tone for a bizarre season.

Record: 0–1

	1	2	3	4		
Chiefs	7	7	3	23	=	40
Browns	6	14	7	12	=	39

CLE-Dawson 20-yd. FG
KC-Gonzalez 17-yd. pass from Green (Andersen kick)
CLE-Dawson 32-yd. FG
CLE-Northcutt 43-yd. pass from Holcomb (Dawson kick)
KC-Holmes 5-yd. run (Andersen kick)
CLE-Morgan 33-yd. pass from Johnson (Dawson kick)
CLE-Davis 4-yd. pass from Holcomb (Dawson kick)
KC-Andersen 33-yd. FG
CLE-Dawson 34-yd. FG
KC-Holmes 26-yd. run (Andersen kick)
KC-Holmes 15-yd. run (Andersen kick)
CLE-Morgan 44-yd. pass from Holcomb (kick failed)
KC-Holmes 7-yd. run (kick failed)
CLE-Dawson 41-yd. FG
KC-Andersen 30-yd. FG

Passing
KC: Green 20–29–276 1 TD 1 INT
CLE: Holcomb 27–39–326 3 TD 0 INT, Johnson 1–1–33 1 TD 0 INT

Rushing
KC: Holmes 22–122, Tait 1–28, Green 2–17, Hall 2–14, Richardson 3–13
CLE: White 12–42, Green 8–17

Receiving
KC: Kennison 4–120, Gonzalez 5–87, Richardson 2–26, Holmes 6–19, Morton 1–15, Cloud 1–5, Hall 1–4
CLE: Morgan 9–151, Johnson 8–96, Northcutt 1–43, Campbell 2–27, White 3–20, Davis 3–14, King 2–8

Sunday, September 15
Browns 20, Cincinnati Bengals 7
Cleveland Browns Stadium (73,358)
White jerseys/white pants

The Browns bounced back from their stunning loss in the opener to control the hapless Bengals and coast to an easy triumph on a rainy afternoon. Kelly Holcomb threw two touchdowns in the second quarter to build a 17–0 lead, the second score set up when right-handed Cincinnati QB Gus Frerotte, under pressure from the Cleveland 17, tossed the ball up for grabs with his left hand. It was intercepted by Browns' DE Kenard Lang, who stampeded 71 yards to the Cincinnati 8. A play later, Holcomb connected with

Kevin Johnson in the end zone. The Cleveland defense kept the Bengals at bay from there, collecting five sacks—a trio by DE Mark Word—and three turnovers as the Browns overcame 12 penalties to break into the victory column for the first time in 2002.

Record: 1–1

	1	2	3	4		
Bengals	0	0	0	7	=	7
Browns	3	14	0	3	=	20

CLE-Dawson 52-yd. FG
CLE-Davis 15-yd. pass from Holcomb (Dawson kick)
CLE-Johnson 8-yd. pass from Holcomb (Dawson kick)
CLE-Dawson 45-yd. FG
CIN-C. Johnson 22-yd. pass from Frerotte (Rackers kick)

Passing
CIN: Frerotte 26–47–239 1 TD 3 INT
CLE: Holcomb 17–30–198 2 TD 0 INT

Rushing
CIN: Dillon 22–108, R. Johnson 5–24, Warrick 1–11, Frerotte 2–8, Neal 1–5
CLE: White 8–38, Green 17–36, Holcomb 2–1

Receiving
CIN: Dillon 8–67, Houshmandzadeh 5–58, C. Johnson 4–58, Westbrook 2–21, R. Johnson 3–16, Dugans 2–9, Neal 1–7, Warrick 1–3
CLE: Johnson 4–50, White 3–42, Morgan 2–42, Davis 4–37, Campbell 2–19, Heiden 1–8, Sanders 1–0

Sunday, September 22
Browns 31, Tennessee Titans 28 (OT)
The Coliseum (68,804)
Brown jerseys/white pants

In his first game after returning from a preseason elbow injury, QB Tim Couch rallied the Browns from 14 points down in the final five minutes to send the game to overtime, where they pulled out a hard-earned victory. Couch started hot, completing his first five passes and leading the Browns to a touchdown on their first possession, but the offense slumped after that and trailed 28–14 midway through the fourth quarter. After cutting the lead to seven with 2:35 remaining, the Browns pulled off a brilliant onside kick in which they flooded the right side, and kicker Phil Dawson pooched a looping kick to the left, where WR Dennis Northcutt gathered it in before going out of bounds at the Tennessee 42. The Browns drove to the Titans' 8, where with 12 seconds left, Northcutt—who had earlier returned a punt 74 yards for a touchdown—capped a magnificent day by catching a short pass at the 3, then spun around a defender and sprinted into the end zone to force overtime. In sudden-death, the Browns won the toss and took care of business quickly, driving 65 yards in eight plays to set up Phil Dawson's 33-yard field goal to win the game. The strong start and finish propelled Couch to a fantastic day, throwing for 326 yards to nine different receivers with three touchdowns as the Browns topped four hundred total yards while holding Tennessee to just 187. Couch also set a team record with 36 completions in a single game. But four Cleveland turnovers, including a Tennessee interception return for a touchdown, proved to be the equalizer as the Browns were forced to rally from behind for a thrilling triumph.

Record: 2–1

	1	2	3	4	OT		
Browns	7	0	7	14	3	=	31
Titans	7	14	0	7	0	=	28

CLE-Davis 14-yd. pass from Couch (Dawson kick)
TEN-George 2-yd. run (Nedney kick)
TEN-Simon 12-yd. pass from McNair (Nedney kick)
TEN-Dyson 16-yd. interception return (Nedney kick)
CLE-Northcutt 74-yd. punt return (Dawson kick)
TEN-Dyson 7-yd. pass from McNair (Nedney kick)
CLE-Davis 12-yd. pass from Couch (Dawson kick)
CLE-Northcutt 8-yd. pass from Couch
CLE-Dawson 33-yd. FG

Passing
CLE: Couch 36–50–326 3 TD 1 INT
TEN: McNair 15–23–107 2 TD 0 INT

Rushing
CLE: White 9–43, Green 8–26, Couch 3–23
TEN: George 23–59, McNair 5–17, Green 4–9, Simon 1–1, Comella 1–0

Receiving
CLE: Davis 5–99, Johnson 9–90, Morgan 5–40, White 9–38, Northcutt 3–24, Campbell 2–11, Heiden 1–11, Shea 1–8, Green 1–5
TEN: George 5–35, Mason 3–31, Simon 2–15, Comella 2–13, Dyson 1–7, Wycheck 2–6

Sunday, September 29
Pittsburgh Steelers 16, Browns 13 (OT)
Heinz Field (62,864)
White jerseys/white pants

Going to overtime for the second straight week, the Browns blew a golden opportunity to win the game and then once again lost in bizarre fashion in the one-hundredth meeting of the Cleveland–Pittsburgh rivalry. After blocking a punt, Cleveland surged to a 13–6 lead on the first play of the fourth quarter, but Pittsburgh tied the contest with a touchdown with two minutes left to force overtime. On the first play of sudden-death, Browns' LB Andra Davis intercepted Pittsburgh QB Tommy Maddox at the Steelers' 34, but three plays later, Phil Dawson's potential game-winning 45-yard field goal was grazed by a Pittsburgh defender at the line of scrimmage and fell short. With new life, the Steelers drove to the Cleveland 6, and on second down, attempted their own field goal. Browns' DL Alvin McKinley blocked it, but the football bounced backward and was scooped up by Pittsburgh kicker Todd Peterson, who then fumbled at the 13 and the Steelers recovered. Because the ball never crossed the line of scrimmage after being kicked, the Steelers maintained possession and kicked again on third down, this time connecting to end the game. It spoiled a nice effort by the Cleveland defense, which held Pittsburgh RB Jerome Bettis to just 24 yards on 14 carries while Browns' RB Jamel White rushed for 105. It marked the third time in the first four weeks of the season that a Browns game was decided on the final play.

Record: 2–2

	1	2	3	4	OT		
Browns	3	3	0	7	0	=	13
Steelers	0	6	0	7	3	=	16

CLE-Dawson 28-yd. FG
CLE-Dawson 28-yd. FG
PIT-Peterson 19-yd. FG
PIT-Peterson 27-yd. FG
CLE-White 4-yd. run (Dawson kick)
PIT-Burress 10-yd. pass from Maddox (Peterson kick)
PIT-Peterson 31-yd. FG

Passing
CLE: Couch 16–29–144 0 TD 2 INT
PIT: Stewart 15–25–143 0 TD 1 INT, Maddox 11–13–122 1 TD 1 INT, Randle El 0–1–0 0 TD 0 INT

Rushing
CLE: White 16–105, Green 7–16, Couch 1–2
PIT: Stewart 7–30, Bettis 14–24, Fuamatu-Ma'afala 5–20, Zereoue 4–10, Randle El 2–8, Maddox 2–1

Receiving
CLE: Northcutt 4–38, Davis 2–36, Johnson 3–23, Shea 2–22, White 3–14, Campbell 2–11
PIT: Ward 9–104, Burress 7–84, Randle El 5–51, Mathis 3–25, Zereoue 1–3, Bruener 1-(-2)

Sunday, October 6
Baltimore Ravens 26, Browns 21
Cleveland Browns Stadium (73,688)
Brown jerseys/white pants

Before a national-television audience on a Sunday night, a stirring Browns' rally couldn't overcome a cavalcade of mistakes and resulted in a frustrating loss to the Ravens. Coughing up five turnovers and collecting 117 yards in penalties for the night, the Browns trailed 23–0 going into the fourth quarter, then launched a furious comeback. After a touchdown and two-point conversion got the Browns on the board, Tim Couch was knocked out of the game with a concussion (and later tearfully protested the fans' booing of him as he left the game). Kelly Holcomb returned to action and promptly led the Browns on a 98-yard drive to cut the Baltimore lead to seven but then threw an interception that led to a crucial Baltimore field goal to push the lead back to 11 points. Still, the Browns weren't done, scoring again to cut the margin to 26–21 with a minute to play, then Phil Dawson recovered his own onside kick tapped directly in front of him. The Browns drove to the Baltimore 17 with 10 seconds left before Holcomb was intercepted in the end zone by Baltimore DB Ed Reed to end the game. While the Browns' defense was carved up for more than 400 yards, including 187 by Baltimore RB Jamal Lewis, the Cleveland offense rolled to 433 total yards, 396 through the air as Holcomb threw for 180 yards in the final 10 minutes, all on an injured ankle. Cleveland's primary offensive weapon was Dennis Northcutt, who accumulated a career-high 165 receiving yards. But the self-inflicted errors on both sides of the ball proved fatal as the Browns fell below .500.

Record: 2–3

	1	2	3	4		
Ravens	0	13	10	3	=	26
Browns	0	0	0	21	=	21

BAL-Stokley 30-yd. pass from Redman (Stover kick)
BAL-Stover 43-yd. FG
BAL-Stover 28-yd. FG
BAL-Stokley 35-yd. pass from Redman (Stover kick)
BAL-Stover 27-yd. FG
CLE-Campbell 2-yd. pass from Couch (Morgan run)
CLE-Northcutt 37-yd. pass from Holcomb (Dawson kick)
BAL-Stover 28-yd. FG
CLE-Northcutt 17-yd. pass from Holcomb (run failed)

Passing
BAL: Redman 19–30–208 2 TD 0 INT
CLE: Couch 16–26–216 1 TD 2 INT, Holcomb 13–23–180 2 TD 2 INT

Rushing
BAL: Lewis 26–187, Stokley 1–9, C. Taylor 3–7, Redman 2–2, T. Taylor 2-(-4)
CLE: White 7–34, Couch 2–14, Holcomb 2–9, Northcutt 1–7, Green 4–2, Morgan 1-(-4)

Receiving
BAL: Stokley 4–78, Heap 4–53, T. Taylor 4–41, Lewis 5–26, Ricard 1–5, C. Taylor 1–5
CLE: Northcutt 8–165, Davis 5–73, Morgan 5–68, Johnson 4–36, White 4–36, Campbell 2–9, Shea 1–9

Sunday, October 13
Tampa Bay Buccaneers 17, Browns 3
Raymond James Stadium (65,625)
Brown jerseys/white pants

On a sweltering afternoon in Tampa, the Browns were dominated by the eventual Super Bowl champions and lost their third straight game. Led by RB Mike Alstott's 126 rushing yards and two touchdowns, the Buccaneers nearly doubled the Browns in both first downs and total yardage as Tampa Bay held Cleveland to just 68 yards through three quarters and built a 17–0 lead. The Browns avoided a shutout when Phil Dawson booted a 50-yard field goal early in the fourth quarter. It marked the first time the Browns had ever lost to the Buccaneers after winning the first five meetings.
Record: 2–4

	1	2	3	4		
Browns	0	0	0	3	=	3
Buccaneers	7	3	0	7	=	17

TB-Alstott 1-yd. run (Gramatica kick)
TB-Gramatica 33-yd. FG
TB-Alstott 17-yd. run (Gramatica kick)
CLE-Dawson 50-yd. FG

Passing
CLE: Couch 20–40–151 0 TD 1 INT
TB: Johnson 15–32–194 0 TD 1 INT

Rushing
CLE: White 9–38, Green 8–22, Morgan 1–0
TB: Alstott 17–126, Pittman 16–53, Stecker 3–11, Johnson 1–5, Tupa 1-(-9)

Receiving
CLE: Northcutt 4–74, White 10–34, Morgan 2–16, Heiden 1–12, Johnson 2–11, Davis 1–4
TB: Pittman 5–95, Johnson 4–64, Alstott 2–13, Dilger 2–12, McCardell 1–7, Dudley 1–3

Sunday, October 20
Browns 34, Houston Texans 17
Cleveland Browns Stadium (73,248)
Orange jerseys/white pants

The Browns snapped out of nearly three quarters of lethargic play to score the game's last 17 points to streak past the expansion Texans on a crisp, sunny autumn afternoon in Cleveland. Wearing orange jerseys for the first time since 1953, the Browns were unable to muster much offense through the first half and fell behind 14–10 on a trick-play touchdown pass by Houston midway through the third quarter. Cleveland WR Andre Davis turned the game around by returning the ensuing kickoff 95 yards for a touchdown, then after the Texans tied the game with a field goal, a Tim Couch-to-Quincy Morgan scoring pass gave the Browns the lead for good with two minutes left in the third quarter. The Cleveland defense, which collected eight sacks but allowed Houston to pick up a season-high 354 yards, rose to the occasion in the fourth quarter, twice forcing the Texans into three-and-outs and recovering a fumble inside the Houston 10 to set up the game-clinching touchdown with two minutes left.
Record: 3–4

	1	2	3	4		
Texans	0	7	10	0	=	17
Browns	0	7	17	10	=	34

CLE-Green 1-yd. run (Dawson kick)
HOU-Bradford 37-yd. pass from Carr (Brown kick)
CLE-Dawson 35-yd. FG
HOU-Bradford 39-yd. pass from Gaffney (Brown kick)
CLE-Davis 95-yd. kickoff return (Dawson kick)
HOU-Brown 47-yd. FG
CLE-Morgan 25-yd. pass from Couch (Dawson kick)
CLE-Dawson 43-yd. FG
CLE-White 2-yd. run (Dawson kick)

Passing
HOU: Carr 22–36–267 1 TD 0 INT, Gaffney 1–1–39 1 TD 0 INT
CLE: Couch 21–31–148 1 TD 0 INT

Rushing
HOU: Allen 5–61, Wells 13–23, Carr 3–3, Lewis 1–2
CLE: White 12–65, Green 12–24

Receiving
HOU: Miller 6–78, Bradford 2–76, Gaffney 4–47, Allen 4–38, Black 4–31, Dawson 1–25, Wells 2–11
CLE: Morgan 7–81, White 5–34, Johnson 4–22, Northcutt 3–6, Davis 1–3, Jackson 1–2

Sunday, October 27
Browns 24, New York Jets 21
The Meadowlands (78,502)
White jerseys/white pants

Four days after the death of owner Al Lerner, the Browns rallied from a 21–3 deficit to stun the playoff-bound Jets on their home field with more last-minute heroics. Tim Couch threw a pair of touchdown passes in the third quarter, then connected with Dennis Northcutt on a desperation pass he threw into the end zone while falling backward for a critical two-point conversion that tied the game. On their next possession, the Browns drove 14 plays and took the lead on a short Phil Dawson field goal with 3:35 remaining. The Jets drove into Cleveland territory and attempted a potential game-tying 44-yard field goal with 16 seconds left, but Browns' DE Courtney Brown blocked it to secure an impressive victory. Couch had one of the finest days of his career, throwing for 294 yards, while the Cleveland defense forced three crucial turnovers to spark the comeback and give the Browns the chance to claw back to .500.
Record: 4–4

	1	2	3	4		
Browns	3	3	15	3	=	24
Jets	14	7	0	0	=	21

NYJ-Moss 63-yd. punt return (Hall kick)
CLE-Dawson 23-yd. FG
NYJ-Coles 37-yd. pass from Pennington (Hall kick)
NYJ-Chrebet 8-yd. pass from Pennington (Hall kick)
CLE-Dawson 26-yd. FG
CLE-Campbell 5-yd. pass from Couch (Dawson kick)
CLE-Davis 4-yd. pass from Couch (Northcutt pass from Couch)
CLE-Dawson 35-yd. FG

Passing
CLE: Couch 32–48–294 2 TD 0 INT
NYJ: Pennington 19–26–183 2 TD 1 INT, Chrebet 0–1–0 0 TD 0 INT

Rushing
CLE: White 14–25, Northcutt 1–13, Couch 3–9, Green 3–8
NYJ: Martin 18–65, Anderson 1–2, Pennington 1-(-1)

Receiving
CLE: Johnson 5–73, Northcutt 3–63, White 6–42, Morgan 4–40, Campbell 7–34, Davis 3–29, Shea 3–10, Jackson 1–3
NYJ: Coles 5–61, Chrebet 4–40, Martin 4–39, Moss 2–23, Anderson 3–16, Becht 1–4

Sunday, November 3
Pittsburgh Steelers 23, Browns 20
Cleveland Browns Stadium (73,718)
Brown jerseys/white pants

The Browns sprinted out to a 14–3 lead but then were overwhelmed by Pittsburgh as the Steelers completed their second straight season sweep of the Browns and assumed control of first place in the new AFC North Division. Cleveland got off to a brilliant start, stopping the Steelers on their first series, then Dennis Northcutt returned the ensuing punt 87 yards for a touchdown. Minutes later, after a 63-yard reception by Quincy Morgan, the Browns stretched the lead to 11 three minutes into the second quarter, but the Steelers scored touchdowns on their next two possessions to take control of the game. They then threatened to add another before throwing an interception at the Cleveland 1 just before the half. The Steelers squandered two more scoring opportunities in the third quarter before adding a pair of field goals in the fourth to give them enough cushion to withstand a late

Cleveland touchdown that cut the margin to 23–20 with 4:32 left. The Browns got the ball back at their own 11 with a minute to play but moved backward as time expired and dropped below .500 again. The narrow margin of victory didn't reflect Pittsburgh's dominance, as the Steelers rolled up nearly 200 more total yards and 16 more first downs while the Browns coughed up three turnovers and were penalized 11 times for 85 yards while rushing for only 36 yards as a team.

Record: 4–5

	1	2	3	4		
Steelers	3	14	0	6	=	23
Browns	7	7	0	6	=	20

CLE-Northcutt 87-yd. punt return (Dawson kick)
PIT-Peterson 43-yd. FG
CLE-Heiden 1-yd. pass from Couch (Dawson kick)
PIT-Ward 20-yd. pass from Maddox (Peterson kick)
PIT-Bruener 1-yd. pass from Maddox (Peterson kick)
PIT-Peterson 28-yd. FG
PIT-Peterson 42-yd. FG
CLE-Morgan 31-yd. pass from Couch (kick failed)

Passing
PIT: Maddox 23–42–239 2 TD 1 INT, Randle El 2–2–26 0 TD 0 INT
CLE: Couch 15–24–181 2 TD 2 INT

Rushing
PIT: Zereoue 29–111, Maddox 3–8, Ward 1–8, Haynes 4–5, Kreider 1–2, Randle El 1–2
CLE: White 6–19, Green 4–10, Northcutt 1–5, Couch 3–2

Receiving
PIT: Ward 9–79, Burress 4–69, Zereoue 5–62, Kreider 2–23, Randle El 3–18, Mathis 1–13, Bruener 1–1
CLE: Morgan 4–98, Davis 3–31, Northcutt 2–27, White 3–18, Johnson 2–7, Heiden 1–1

Sunday, November 17
Browns 27, Cincinnati Bengals 20
Paul Brown Stadium (64,060)
White jerseys/white pants

Aided by a fourth-quarter goal-line stand, the Browns held off the 1–8 Bengals to complete their first sweep of Cincinnati in seven years. The Bengals drew first blood in what became a seesaw game with a 72-yard touchdown reception by WR Chad Johnson on the third play, but the Browns bounced back with touchdowns on their first two possessions to take the lead. The Cleveland offense rolled up 382 yards on the day, fueled by a breakout game by rookie RB William Green, who rushed for 96 yards on 25 carries. After breaking a 17–17 tie with Tim Couch's third touchdown pass of the game late in the third quarter, the Browns countered a Cincinnati field goal with one of their own midway through the final stanza. The Bengals drove to the Cleveland 1 with six minutes left, but the Cleveland defense rose to the occasion, stuffing RB Corey Dillon for no gain on two straight plays to give the ball back to the offense. After fumbling a punt moments later that allowed the Browns to melt another two minutes off the clock, the Bengals frantically drove to the Cleveland 26 in the final seconds before time expired.

Record: 5–5

	1	2	3	4		
Browns	14	3	7	3	=	27
Bengals	7	7	3	3	=	20

CIN-C. Johnson 72-yd. pass from Kitna (Rackers kick)
CLE-Sanders 14-yd. pass from Couch (Dawson kick)
CLE-Davis 15-yd. pass from Couch (Dawson kick)
CIN-Kitna 3-yd. run (Rackers kick)
CLE-Dawson 27-yd. FG
CIN-Rackers 37-yd. FG
CLE-Northcutt 13-yd. pass from Couch (Dawson kick)
CIN-Rackers 31-yd. FG
CLE-Dawson 40-yd. FG

Passing
CLE: Couch 22–35–242 3 TD 1 INT, Jackson 0–1–0 0 TD 0 INT
CIN: Kitna 17–30–258 1 TD 0 INT

Rushing
CLE: Green 25–96, Jackson 7–27, Morgan 1–11, Couch 1–5, Davis 1–1
CIN: Dillon 19–92, Warrick 1–4, Bennett 1–3, Kitna 1–3

Receiving
CLE: Morgan 5–81, Northcutt 6–71, Johnson 3–32, Heiden 2–15, Davis 1–15, Sanders 1–14, Jackson 1–6, Green 2–4, Campbell 1–4
CIN: C. Johnson 4–103, Houshmandzadeh 3–59, Warrick 1–26, Dillon 2–18, Neal 2–17, Schobel 2–17, Bennett 2–9, Westbrook 1–9

Sunday, November 24
Browns 24, New Orleans Saints 15
Louisiana Superdome (68,295)
White jerseys/white pants

Forcing six turnovers and establishing a dominant running game, the Browns controlled the contest and cruised to an upset victory over the 7–3 Saints on their home field. The Saints entered the game as the league's top-scoring team, but with RB Deuce McAllister out with an injury and QB Aaron Brooks throwing three interceptions, they were held to a season-low 15 points. Meanwhile, the Browns rushed for 163 yards as William Green turned in his second straight strong performance with 114 on 28 carries. They surged to a 14–6 lead late in the second quarter on an inventive handoff to Dennis Northcutt, who slid 36 yards for a touchdown. After New Orleans cut the lead to two midway through the third quarter, the Browns responded with a 79-yard drive capped by a third-down touchdown pass from Tim Couch to Kevin Johnson, then bounced back again with a dominating seven-minute drive that resulted in the game-clinching field goal with 3:25 remaining.
Record: 6–5

	1	2	3	4		
Browns	7	7	7	3	=	24
Saints	3	3	6	3	=	15

NO-Carney 33-yd. FG
CLE-Green 1-yd. run (Dawson kick)
NO-Carney 27-yd. FG
CLE-Northcutt 36-yd. run (Dawson kick)
NO-Fenderson 17-yd. run (pass failed)
CLE-Johnson 24-yd. pass from Couch (Dawson kick)
NO-Carney 48-yd. FG
CLE-Dawson 24-yd. FG

Passing
CLE: Couch 12–21–182 1 TD 2 INT, Johnson 0–1–0 0 TD 0 INT
NO: Brooks 23–40–318 0 TD 3 INT

Rushing
CLE: Green 28–114, Northcutt 2–35, Jackson 2–11, Couch 5–3
NO: Fenderson 7–35, Keaton 10–19, McAfee 1–11, Brooks 3–9

Receiving
CLE: Northcutt 3–68, Morgan 2–57, Johnson 3–31, Sanders 1–9, Heiden 1–8, Jackson 1–5, Campbell 1–4
NO: Lewis 3–114, Horn 3–47, Williams 4–43, Pathon 4–39, Fenderson 5–33, Stallworth 2–24, Sloan 1–14, Hall 1–4

Sunday, December 1
Carolina Panthers 13, Browns 6
Cleveland Browns Stadium (72,718)
Orange jerseys/white pants

Coughing up five turnovers and managing little offense, the Browns were stunned by the 3–8 Panthers on a cold, gray afternoon in Cleveland. The first of Tim Couch's three interceptions set up the game's only touchdown late in the first quarter, and after the Browns pulled within 7–6 going into the fourth quarter, Carolina responded with a pair of field goals, the second set up by a Couch fumble. On Cleveland's final possession, with just over two minutes left, a long Couch pass was picked off by Carolina DB Emmanuel McDaniel, then appeared to be fumbled and scooped up by the Browns' Kevin Johnson and returned for a touchdown. But the officials ruled McDaniel was down before fumbling, and since the Browns were out of time outs, they couldn't challenge the call. The Panthers then ran out the clock and dealt the Browns' playoff hopes a major blow.
Record: 6–6

	1	2	3	4		
Panthers	7	0	0	6	=	13
Browns	3	0	3	0	=	6

CLE-Dawson 25-yd. FG
CAR-Walls 24-yd. pass from Peete (Graham kick)
CLE-Dawson 33-yd. FG
CAR-Graham 43-yd. FG
CAR-Graham 44-yd. FG

Passing
CAR: Peete 8–17–89 1 TD 1 INT, Fasani 0–1–0 0 TD 0 INT, Brown 0–1–0 0 TD 1 INT
CLE: Couch 12–27–130 0 TD 3 INT

Rushing
CAR: Brown 27–122, Hoover 4–20, Fasani 4–6, Peete 3-(-3)
CLE: Green 24–94, Northcutt 1–34, White 1–7, Jackson 2–5

Receiving
CAR: Muhammad 4–49, Walls 1–24, Mangum 1–9, Brown 1–4, Smith 1–3
CLE: Johnson 5–57, Green 3–44, Heiden 2–18, White 2–11

Sunday, December 8
Browns 21, Jacksonville Jaguars 20
Alltel Stadium (46,267)
White jerseys/white pants

For the second time in four years, the Browns pulled out a miracle victory with a Hail Mary touchdown pass on the game's final play to keep their playoff hopes alive. Led by another fine performance by William Green, who tallied 119 rushing yards, the Browns rolled to 417 total yards but could manage only two touchdowns over the first 59 minutes. Though the Browns outgained Jacksonville by more than 200 yards, 10 Cleveland penalties and two costly turnovers allowed the Jaguars to take a 20–14 lead when Jacksonville decided to kick a short field goal on fourth and goal from the Cleveland 4 with 50 seconds left. The ensuing squib kick on the kickoff was flubbed, and the Browns took over at their own 47. After two fruitless plays, with time running out, Tim Couch took the snap from the 50 and lofted a long pass into the right corner for Quincy Morgan, who actually ran the wrong route. Morgan, who'd already caught a 60-yard scoring pass in the third quarter, leapt up to catch the pass and pinned it against his hip as he came down, and the nose of the football appeared to touch the ground. But it was ruled a touchdown, and the replay review upheld the call, thus Phil Dawson's extra point gave the Browns a bizarre victory—the sixteenth time in Butch Davis's 29 games as head coach that a game was decided in the final minute, the seventh on the final play.
Record: 7–6

	1	2	3	4		
Browns	0	0	14	7	=	21
Jaguars	7	0	7	6	=	20

JAX-Brady 4-yd. pass from Brunell (Boyd kick)
CLE-Green 3-yd. run (Dawson kick)
JAX-Taylor 44-yd. run (Boyd kick)
CLE-Morgan 60-yd. pass from Couch (Dawson kick)
JAX-Boyd 33-yd. FG
JAX-Boyd 22-yd. FG
CLE-Morgan 50-yd. pass from Couch (Dawson kick)

Passing
CLE: Couch 21–35–264 2 TD 2 INT
JAX: Brunell 10–14–73 1 TD 0 INT

Rushing
CLE: Green 26–119, White 4–22, Couch 1–12, Jackson 1–11, Davis 1–9
JAX: Taylor 23–145, Brunell 4–6, Mack 4–6

Receiving
CLE: Morgan 3–118, Johnson 2–29, Campbell 1–26, White 4–25, Green 3–25, Heiden 5–21, Davis 3–20
JAX: Smith 2–23, Brady 3–16, Shaw 1–13, Taylor 2–12, Washington 1–5, Mack 1–4

Sunday, December 15
Indianapolis Colts 28, Browns 23
Cleveland Browns Stadium (73,098)
Brown jerseys/white pants

After surging to a 16–0 halftime lead and then leading by nine in the fourth quarter, the Browns couldn't stop a second-half surge that saw the Colts score four touchdowns to steal away victory and once again damage the Browns' playoff aspirations. The Browns lit up the scoreboard on the game's first play, when Tim Couch connected with Quincy Morgan for a 78-yard touchdown, then another Couch scoring toss and a field goal just before the half gave the Browns a seemingly comfortable lead. The Colts scored twice in the third quarter to cut the lead to two points, and then after the Browns pushed the advantage back to 23–14 early in the fourth, Indy responded with back-to-back touchdown drives to take its first lead with 6:46 to play. The Browns had one final chance as they took over at the Colts' 48 with just under three minutes to play and drove to the 5 with 37 seconds left. On fourth-and-goal, a Couch pass intended for Kevin Johnson in the end zone was inadvertently knocked away by fellow WR Andre Davis, who attempted to catch it. The stunning loss knocked the Browns back to .500, dropped them to 2–5 in Cleveland for the year, and all but extinguished their fading playoff hopes.
Record: 7–7

	1	2	3	4		
Colts	0	0	14	14	=	28
Browns	13	3	0	7	=	23

CLE-Morgan 78-yd. pass from Couch (kick failed)
CLE-Johnson 30-yd. pass from Couch (Dawson kick)
CLE-Dawson 29-yd. FG
IND-Mungro 29-yd. run (Vanderjagt kick)
IND-Harrison 25-yd. pass from Manning (Vanderjagt kick)
CLE-Green 2-yd. run (Dawson kick)
IND-Harrison 3-yd. pass from Manning (Vanderjagt kick)
IND-Mungro 3-yd. run (Vanderjagt kick)

Passing
IND: Manning 20–34–277 2 TD 1 INT
CLE: Couch 21–35–287 2 TD 0 INT

Rushing
IND: Mungro 14–75, James 10–42, Manning 6–24, Williams 3–2
CLE: Green 22–69, White 3–19, Couch 3–8

Receiving
IND: Harrison 9–172, Pollard 2–41, Davenport 1–22, James 3–20, Ismail 3–14, Mungro 2–8
CLE: Morgan 3–90, White 6–73, Johnson 5–70, Green 3–24, Campbell 2–15, King 1–13, Davis 1–2

Sunday, December 22
Browns 14, Baltimore Ravens 13
Ravens Stadium (69,348)
White jerseys/white pants

Despite a lethargic performance, the Browns hung around and pulled out another last-minute victory with an impressive desperation drive with time running out to reignite their playoff drive. Trailing 13–7 and out of time outs, the Browns took over at their own 8 with 2:18 remaining. After five quick Tim Couch completions—including a 28-yard toss to RB Jamel White—and a personal foul on the Ravens, the Browns were at the Baltimore 1, where Couch rolled out and hit TE Mark Campbell for the game-winning touchdown with 29 seconds left. Though the Browns managed only 256 total yards for the game, including just 63 rushing, they picked up their second straight victory in Baltimore and entered the final week of the season with a shot at the playoffs.
Record: 8–7

	1	2	3	4		
Browns	7	0	0	7	=	14
Ravens	3	7	3	0	=	13

CLE-White 3-yd. run (Dawson kick)
BAL-Stover 31-yd. FG
BAL-T. Taylor 17-yd. pass from Blake (Stover kick)
BAL-Stover 43-yd. FG
CLE-Campbell 1-yd. pass from Couch (Dawson kick)

Passing
CLE: Couch 22–31–209 1 TD 1 INT
BAL: Blake 16–28–143 1 TD 1 INT

Rushing
CLE: Green 20–56, White 4–11, Couch 1-(-1), Davis 1-(-3)
BAL: Lewis 21–100, Taylor 3–20, Blake 3–12, C. Taylor 1–10, Ricard 1–4

Receiving
CLE: White 4–63, Morgan 3–50, Johnson 5–44, Davis 3–21, King 2–20, Campbell 2–7, Green 2–2, Heiden 1–2
BAL: Heap 7–61, T. Taylor 3–39, Hymes 3–36, Ricard 1–4, Lewis 1–3, C. Taylor 1–0

Sunday, December 29
Browns 24, Atlanta Falcons 16
Cleveland Browns Stadium (73,528)
Brown jerseys/white pants

With a playoff berth hanging in the balance, the Browns rallied from behind for a dramatic victory and then watched the stars align to assure their first trip to the postseason since their return. After Tim Couch left the game in the second quarter with a broken leg, a rusty Kelly Holcomb struggled, but threw a third-down touchdown pass to Kevin Johnson with seven minutes left to put the Browns ahead 17–16 after they'd squandered a 10–0 lead by coughing up four turnovers. Then with four minutes to play, they pulled off the play of the day when William Green broke over right tackle for a 64-yard touchdown run to put the Browns up by eight points. It was the second score of the day for Green, who rushed for 178 yards, the highest total by a Browns' running back in 18 years. Fitting with the frantic nature of the entire Browns' season, the Falcons then drove to the Cleveland 1 in the final minute. But the Browns' defense rose to the occasion and stuffed Atlanta on three straight plays to give the ball back to the offense to run out the final seconds. Three hours later, the New York Jets completed a blowout victory over Green Bay to officially punch the Browns' playoff ticket.
Record: 9–7

	1	2	3	4		
Falcons	0	7	9	0	=	16
Browns	3	7	0	14	=	24

CLE-Dawson 40-yd. FG
CLE-Green 21-yd. run (Dawson kick)
ATL-Finneran 15-yd. pass from Vick (Feely kick)
ATL-Feely 42-yd. FG
ATL-Feely 49-yd. FG
ATL-Feely 30-yd. FG
CLE-Johnson 15-yd. pass from Holcomb (Dawson kick)
CLE-Green 64-yd. run (Dawson kick)

Passing
ATL: Vick 17–40–240 1 TD 1 INT
CLE: Holcomb 7–14–86 1 TD 2 INT, Couch 7–11–68 0 TD 1 INT

Rushing
ATL: Dunn 20–67, Vick 6–38, Duckett 1–0
CLE: Green 27–178, Northcutt 2–10, White 1–2, Holcomb 4-(-1)

Receiving
ATL: Finneran 3–77, McCord 3–65, Crumpler 2–34, Gaylor 3–30, Dunn 3–14, Layne 2–11, Kelly 1–9
CLE: Davis 2–36, Johnson 3–32, Morgan 2–32, Northcutt 1–22, Campbell 1–12, Green 2–9, Heiden 2–9, White 1–2

AFC First-Round Playoff
Sunday, January 5
Pittsburgh Steelers 36, Browns 33
Heinz Field (62,595)
White jerseys/white pants

In one of the most heartbreaking defeats in the team's postseason history, the Browns saw a 17-point second-half lead evaporate in the final minutes after they'd dominated the favored Steelers on their home field all day behind an amazing performance by Kelly Holcomb, starting in place of injured Tim Couch.

The Browns set the tone on the third play of the game when Holcomb connected with Kevin Johnson for an 83-yard gain—the longest pass in Cleveland playoff history—to set up a touchdown run by William Green on the next play. A fumbled Pittsburgh punt return led to a Holcomb scoring pass to Dennis Northcutt early in the second quarter, then a 59-yard punt return by Northcutt after the first series of the second half allowed the Browns to extend their lead to 24–7 on another Holcomb-to-Northcutt scoring pass.

With a chance to turn the game into a blowout, the Browns drove to the Pittsburgh 32 on their next series, but Holcomb was intercepted, leading to Pittsburgh's second touchdown. Still, Cleveland maintained the momentum and added what appeared would be the backbreaking score when Holcomb hit Andre Davis for a 22-yard touchdown to make it 33–21 with 10:17 remaining.

Still trailing by 12 with 5:30 to play, the Steelers regained possession at their own 23 and quickly drove for a touchdown to pull within five points. The Browns then were forced to punt on their next series when Northcutt dropped a third-down pass near midfield, which would have resulted in a first down with 2:42 left. The Steelers drove 61 yards in six plays and took their first lead on a short touchdown run by RB Chris Fuamatu-Ma'afala with 54 seconds remaining. The Browns frantically drove into Pittsburgh territory, but time expired after a pass completion to WR Andre King reached the Steelers' 29.

Northcutt's crucial drop overshadowed an otherwise marvelous performance that saw him accumulate 92 receiving yards, 70 return yards, and a pair of touchdowns, while Kevin Johnson racked up a team-playoff-record 140 receiving yards on four catches. But the Browns' star of the game was Holcomb, who threw for 429 yards and three scores. Holcomb's heroics helped atone for a miserable day by the Cleveland running game, which managed only 38 yards on the day, including a meager 30 on 25 carries by Green. Conversely, the Cleveland defense couldn't stop the Steelers when it counted, allowing 432 total yards and 30 first downs as the teams combined for nearly 900 yards and more than 50 first downs.

	1	2	3	4		
Browns	7	10	7	9	=	33
Steelers	0	7	7	22	=	36

CLE-Green 1-yd. run (Dawson kick)
CLE-Northcutt 32-yd. pass from Holcomb (Dawson kick)
PIT-Randle El 66-yd. punt return (Reed kick)
CLE-Dawson 31-yd. FG
CLE-Northcutt 15-yd. pass from Holcomb (Dawson kick)
PIT-Burress 6-yd. pass from Maddox (Reed kick)
CLE-Dawson 24-yd. FG
PIT-Tuman 3-yd. pass from Maddox (Reed kick)
CLE-Davis 22-yd. pass from Holcomb (Reed kick)
PIT-Ward 5-yd. pass from Maddox (Reed kick)
PIT-Fuamatu-Ma'afala 3-yd. run (Tuman pass from Randle El)

Passing
CLE: Holcomb 26–43–429 3 TD 1 INT
PIT: Maddox 30–48–367 3 TD 2 INT

Rushing
CLE: Green 25–30, Northcutt 1–5, Holcomb 2–3
PIT: Zereoue 13–73, Maddox 2–7, Fuamatu-Ma'afala 2–4, Ward 1–4, Randle El 1–3, Bettis 1-(-2)

Receiving
CLE: Johnson 4–140, Northcutt 6–92, Davis 2–65, White 5–45, Campbell 3–31, Morgan 2–30, King 1–16, Green 2–8, Sanders 1–2
PIT: Ward 11–104, Burress 6–100, Randle El 5–85, Mathis 3–40, Fuamatu-Ma'afala 2–20, Tuman 3–18

2003

Sunday, September 7
Indianapolis Colts 9, Browns 6
Cleveland Browns Stadium (73,358)
White jerseys/orange pants

On opening day in a season loaded with expectations, the Browns' defense rose to the occasion, containing the Colts' explosive offense, but Cleveland's own offense couldn't carry its weight, and for the third straight year, the Browns lost their opener in the final seconds. Wearing orange pants for the first time in 20 years, the Browns held the Colts under 300 yards of offense and didn't permit a touchdown, highlighted by an end-zone interception by LB Kevin Bentley of Indy QB Peyton Manning on the first possession of the game. The Browns' offense—under the direction of QB Kelly Holcomb, who won the job in training camp over Tim Couch—couldn't score despite twice having a first-and-goal situation inside the Colts' 5. After the Browns tied the game at six midway through the fourth quarter, the Colts took over for their final possession at their own 8 with under three minutes to play and drove 65 yards in 11 plays to set up a 45-yard field goal by Mike Vanderjagt with one second left to give the Browns their sixth consecutive opening-day defeat.

Record: 0–1

	1	2	3	4		
Colts	0	3	3	3	=	9
Browns	3	0	0	3	=	6

CLE-Dawson 19-yd. FG
IND-Vanderjagt 22-yd. FG
IND-Vanderjagt 46-yd. FG
CLE-Dawson 20-yd. FG
IND-Vanderjagt 45-yd. FG

Passing
IND: Manning 27–43–211 0 TD 2 INT
CLE: Holcomb 20–29–182 0 TD 2 INT

Rushing
IND: James 15–67
CLE: Green 21–86, White 2–7, J. Jackson 2–6, Northcutt 1-(-1)

Receiving
IND: Harrison 9–44, Wayne 3–39, James 5–29, Pollard 3–28, Walters 3–27, Williams 2–19, Clark 1–18, Davenport 1–7
CLE: Northcutt 5–57, Johnson 3–26, Heiden 2–22, White 4–19, Green 3–19, Davis 1–18, Morgan 1–14, Shea 1–7

Sunday, September 14
Baltimore Ravens 33, Browns 13
M&T Bank Stadium (69,473)
Brown jerseys/white pants

Baltimore RB Jamal Lewis carved up the Cleveland defense, setting an NFL single-game record with 295 rushing yards on 30 carries as the Ravens dropped the Browns to a humiliating defeat. The tone was set on the second play of the game, when Lewis took his first carry for an 82-yard touchdown. A 63-yard touchdown run would follow in the opening moments of the fourth quarter, and a 60-yard touchdown was thwarted by a holding penalty, becoming "just" a 48-yard run. For all of Lewis's heroics, the Browns trailed only 16–13 going into the fourth quarter before the Ravens pulled away in the fourth, capped by a 54-yard interception return for a touchdown by Baltimore DB Ed Reed on the game's final play. Gaining just 175 total yards, the Browns had less than half of Baltimore's total and scored their only touchdown—a Kelly Holcomb-to-WR Kevin Johnson touchdown pass—after DT Gerard Warren recovered a fumble at the Ravens' 22. The Browns were now 0–2 for the first time in four years.

Record: 0–2

	1	2	3	4		
Browns	0	3	10	0	=	13
Ravens	10	6	0	17	=	33

BAL-Lewis 82-yd. run (Stover kick)
BAL-Stover 20-yd. FG
CLE-Dawson 44-yd. FG
BAL-Stover 40-yd. FG
BAL-Richey 56-yd. FG
CLE-Dawson 35-yd. FG
CLE-Johnson 4-yd. pass from Holcomb (Dawson kick)
BAL-Lewis 63-yd. run (Stover kick)
BAL-Stover 21-yd. FG
BAL-Reed 54-yd. interception return (Stover kick)

Passing
CLE: Holcomb 17–37–147 1 TD 2 INT
BAL: Boller 7–17–78 0 TD 1 INT, Redman 0–1–0 0 TD 0 INT

Rushing
CLE: Green 17–54, Holcomb 2–6, White 1–0
BAL: Lewis 30–295, Ricard 2–36, C. Taylor 5–8, Boller 3–3, T. Taylor 1–1

Receiving
CLE: Northcutt 5–62, Johnson 6–34, Morgan 2–18, Davis 1–13, White 1–8, Green 1–7, Heiden 1–5
BAL: T. Taylor 2–27, Sanders 1–25, Robinson 1–10, Heap 1–7, Jones 1–6, C. Taylor 1–3

Sunday, September 21
Browns 13, San Francisco 49ers 12
3Com Park (67,412)
White jerseys/white pants

Thanks to a stirring rally that saw the Browns come from 12 points down in the fourth quarter, they avoided an 0–3 start with a last-minute victory by the Bay. For the second time in three weeks, the Cleveland defense didn't allow a touchdown, a performance highlighted by stopping the 49ers cold at the Browns' 1 on successive plays on San Francisco's first drive, keeping the game scoreless. After playing miserably for three quarters, the Cleveland offense came alive in the fourth, driving 75 yards to cut the lead to 12–7 with 11 minutes left. With 6:19 to play, the Browns took over at their own 9 and began a 17-play, 91-yard drive highlighted by five third-down conversions and six receptions for 51 yards by Kevin Johnson. On the fifth third-down conversion, from the San Francisco 11, WR Andre Davis made a leaping catch in the end zone for the winning touchdown with 29 seconds remaining. Making the comeback even more impressive, Kelly Holcomb had pulled it off playing on a fractured right fibula that would sideline him for the next month. Holcomb threw for 222 yards on the day, his primary target being Johnson, who finished with 11 receptions for 109 yards. It was the Browns' first win in San Francisco in 22 years.
Record: 1–2

	1	2	3	4		
Browns	0	0	0	13	=	13
49ers	0	6	3	3	=	12

SF-Pochman 38-yd. FG
SF-Pochman 44-yd. FG
SF-Pochman 46-yd. FG
SF-Pochman 36-yd. FG
CLE-Davis 2-yd. pass from Holcomb (Dawson kick)
CLE-Davis 11-yd. pass from Holcomb (pass failed)

Passing
CLE: Holcomb 25–38–222 2 TD 1 INT
SF: Garcia 21–35–198 0 TD 1 INT

Rushing
CLE: Green 15–47, Davis 1–3, Holcomb 2–1, White 1–0
SF: Garcia 5–40, Hearst 9–18, Barlow 7–14, Owens 1–3, Beasley 2–0

Receiving
CLE: Johnson 11–109, Davis 5–43, Heiden 3–25, Morgan 2–24, White 2–13, King 1–6, Shea 1–2
SF: Owens 8–90, Streets 3–44, Weaver 2–24, Wilson 2–12, Hearst 2–10, Walker 1–10, Beasley 1–5, Barlow 2–3

Sunday, September 28
Cincinnati Bengals 21, Browns 14
Cleveland Browns Stadium (73,428)
Brown jerseys/white pants

Thanks to a myriad of critical mistakes, the Browns dropped a winnable game to the 0–3 Bengals, who played the second half without injured star RB Corey Dillon and still rallied from behind to win in Cleveland. With Tim Couch starting at QB in place of injured Kelly Holcomb, the Browns drew first blood on the second play of the game when Couch hit WR Quincy Morgan on a screen pass that became a 71-yard touchdown. After Cincinnati tied the game on its first series, the Browns took the lead back and seemed in control of the game as halftime approached. But the Bengals pulled off the tide-turning play 20 seconds before the half when WR Chad Johnson slipped behind the Cleveland secondary for a 55-yard touchdown pass to tie the game and give the Bengals momentum they'd maintain through the second half. They took the lead on the first possession of the third quarter and held the Browns scoreless from there. Burdened by more than 100 yards in penalties, the Browns drove into Cincinnati territory three times in the second half but were unable to come away with points, including the final drive when Couch was intercepted from the Bengals' 45 with a minute remaining.
Record: 1–3

	1	2	3	4		
Bengals	7	7	7	0	=	21
Browns	7	7	0	0	=	14

CLE-Morgan 71-yd. pass from Couch (Dawson kick)
CIN-C. Johnson 3-yd. pass from Kitna (Graham kick)
CLE-White 4-yd. pass from Couch (Dawson kick)
CIN-C. Johnson 55-yd. pass from Kitna (Graham kick)
CIN-Kelly 1-yd. pass from Kitna (Graham kick)

Passing
CIN: Kitna 23–31–215 3 TD 0 INT
CLE: Couch 23–36–280 2 TD 1 INT

Rushing
CIN: R. Johnson 15–51, Dillon 4–20, Bennett 5–7, J. Johnson 2–3, Kitna 3-(-1)
CLE: Green 16–47, Davis 2–11, J. Jackson 2–8, Couch 2–3

Receiving
CIN: C. Johnson 3–67, Stewart 5–56, Warrick 6–41, Washington 2–28, R. Johnson 4–11, Bennett 1–8, J. Johnson 1–3, Kelly 1–1
CLE: Morgan 3–92, Johnson 5–89, Davis 3–29, Northcutt 3–23, White 4–20, Green 3–17, J. Jackson 1–7, Heiden 1–3

Sunday, October 5
Browns 33, Pittsburgh Steelers 13
Heinz Field (64,595)
White jerseys/orange pants

Before a national-television audience on a Sunday night, the Browns avenged their playoff loss in Pittsburgh exactly nine months earlier by dominating the Steelers in what would be the high point of the entire season. The Browns took command early, driving 81 yards for a touchdown on their first possession, then on Pittsburgh's first series, Cleveland DE Courtney Brown caused and recovered a fumble that led to a field goal and a 10–0 lead. Following a second Tim Couch touchdown pass and then a nine-yard touchdown run, it was 23–10 at the half, but the Steelers threatened to cut the margin five minutes into the second half. From the Cleveland 32, Pittsburgh QB Tommy Maddox was intercepted by Browns' DB Daylon McCutcheon, who returned it 75 yards for the backbreaking touchdown. While the defense limited the Steelers to just over 200 total yards while collecting three sacks and three turnovers, it was a nearly flawless performance for the entire team, which committed only two penalties on the night. Particularly impressive was the embattled Couch, who completed 16 of his first 17 passes, while RB William Green notched his first 100-yard game of the year. It was the Browns' largest margin of victory in a road game in 10 years and snapped a six-game losing streak to the Steelers.
Record: 2–3

	1	2	3	4		
Browns	10	13	7	3	=	33
Steelers	0	10	3	0	=	13

CLE-Davis 6-yd. pass from Couch (Dawson kick)
CLE-Dawson 19-yd. FG
PIT-Reed 30-yd. FG
CLE-Johnson 9-yd. pass from Couch (kick failed)
PIT-Bettis 1-yd. run (Reed kick)
CLE-Couch 9-yd. run (Dawson kick)
CLE-McCutcheon 75-yd. interception return (Dawson kick)
PIT-Reed 37-yd. FG
CLE-Dawson 22-yd. FG

Passing
CLE: Couch 20–25–208 2 TD 1 INT
PIT: Maddox 11–24–136 0 TD 2 INT, Batch 3–6–25 0 TD 0 INT

Rushing
CLE: Green 33–115, Couch 4–11, Morgan 1–1, Faine 1–0, White 1-(-3)
PIT: Zereoue 13–38, Batch 1–11, Bettis 3–8, Randle El 1–3

Receiving
CLE: Northcutt 5–58, Morgan 4–51, Davis 3–32, Heiden 2–30, Johnson 3–20, King 1–6, Sanders 1–6, Green 1–5
PIT: Zereoue 7–57, Ward 2–55, Randle El 3–25, Burress 1–19, Tuman 1–5

Sunday, October 12
Browns 13, Oakland Raiders 7
Cleveland Browns Stadium (73,318)
Brown jerseys/white pants

The Browns notched their second straight victory, prevailing in a defensive struggle that came down to a replay review in the final minute. After an early Browns' fumble led to a Raiders' touchdown, the defending AFC champions still led 7–3 late in the third quarter when William Green sparked a Browns' touchdown drive. He then helped push the team out of the shadow of its own goalpost to kick an insurance field goal with 2:29 left in the game. But the Raiders, crippled by an incredible 19 penalties for 128 yards on the day, had one final chance, and drove to the Cleveland 24, where they faced fourth-and-one with 28 seconds remaining. A pass along the sideline to WR Jerry Rice was ruled incomplete, then upheld by the replay official, and the Browns had pulled even at 3–3 on the year. While the Cleveland offense struggled for much of the day, Green was the workhorse, rushing for 145 yards on 26 carries and becoming the first Browns' back to top the century mark in back-to-back games in 17 years. The triumph also marked the Browns' first-ever win over the Raiders in Cleveland after losing their first five meetings over the previous 34 seasons.

Record: 3–3

	1	2	3	4		
Raiders	7	0	0	0	=	7
Browns	0	3	7	3	=	13

OAK-Johnson 10-yd. pass from Gannon (Janikowski kick)
CLE-Dawson 52-yd. FG
CLE-Green 5-yd. run (Dawson kick)
CLE-Dawson 32-yd. FG

Passing
OAK: Gannon 21–33–165 1 TD 0 INT
CLE: Couch 16–26–127 0 TD 0 INT

Rushing
OAK: Fargas 6–33, Garner 9–28, Wheatley 3–15, Whitted 1–10, Crockett 1–3, Gannon 1–1
CLE: Green 26–145, Dawson 1–14, Northcutt 1–8, J. Jackson 1–3, Couch 2–1, White 1–0

Receiving
OAK: Garner 9–51, Whitted 2–40, Johnson 3–21, Jolley 3–20, Rice 2–19, Brown 2–14
CLE: Northcutt 5–54, White 3–30, Johnson 2–17, Davis 1–17, Morgan 3–14, Green 1-(-2), Couch 1-(-3)

Sunday, October 19
San Diego Chargers 26, Browns 20
Cleveland Browns Stadium (73,238)
Orange jerseys/white pants

Crippled by injury on the offensive line—with two starters already out and a third going down in the first half—the Browns dug a huge hole for themselves against the 0–5 Chargers, then watched a spirited comeback attempt fall short. Aided by an interception return for a touchdown, San Diego took a 13–0 lead, then extended it to 23–6 late in the third quarter after a 70-yard touchdown run by RB LaDainian Tomlinson, who would finish the day with 200 yards on 26 carries. Struggling Tim Couch was yanked and replaced by still-hobbling Kelly Holcomb, and Holcomb quickly directed the Browns on two straight touchdown drives to cut the deficit to three points with just under 12 minutes remaining. But the Cleveland defense then allowed the Chargers to put together a 13-play, eight-minute drive that ended with a field goal and halted the Browns' momentum. Holcomb was unable to continue his magic on the Browns' final two possessions, and they fell to their fourth defeat.

Record: 3–4

	1	2	3	4		
Chargers	6	7	10	3	=	26
Browns	0	3	3	14	=	20

SD-Christie 44-yd. FG
SD-Christie 50-yd. FG
SD-Lassiter 38-yd. interception return (Christie kick)
CLE-Dawson 46-yd. FG
CLE-Dawson 42-yd. FG
SD-Tomlinson 70-yd. run (Christie kick)
SD-Christie 42-yd. FG
CLE-Northcutt 6-yd. pass from Holcomb (Dawson kick)
CLE-Sanders 1-yd. pass from Holcomb (Dawson kick)
SD-Christie 32-yd. FG

Passing
SD: Brees 9–18–74 0 TD 1 INT, Bennett 0–1–0 0 TD 0 INT
CLE: Couch 13–24–102 0 TD 2 INT, Holcomb 11–19–90 2 TD 0 INT, Johnson 0–1–0 0 TD 0 INT

Rushing
SD: Tomlinson 26–200, Neal 7–22, Dwight 1–6, Boston 1–0, Brees 1–0
CLE: Green 14–65, J. Jackson 5–27, White 3–9

Receiving
SD: Parker 2–22, Tomlinson 3–21, Dwight 1–17, Boston 2–10, Norman 1–4
CLE: Northcutt 5–54, Johnson 5–53, J. Jackson 2–22, Morgan 3–22, Heiden 3–15, White 2–11, Davis 1–8, Green 1–4, Sanders 2–3

Sunday, October 26
New England Patriots 9, Browns 3
Gillette Stadium (68,436)
White jerseys/orange pants

With four starters on the offensive line and William Green all out with injury, the Cleveland offense was once again unable to produce points, allowing the eventual Super Bowl champions to control the game on a rainy day in Foxboro. Tim Couch got the start but was pulled in the second quarter after injuring his thumb, and Kelly Holcomb couldn't provide the spark he created the week before. Thanks to a gritty performance by the Cleveland defense, the Browns hung around, tying the game at halftime and staying within one score the entire day. Despite barely accumulating 200 yards of offense, the Browns actually had a chance to win in the final two minutes, driving to the Cleveland 45 before Holcomb threw an interception with 51 seconds left.

Record: 3–5

	1	2	3	4		
Browns	0	3	0	0	=	3
Patriots	3	0	3	3	=	9

NE-Vinatieri 27-yd. FG
CLE Dawson 29-yd. FG
NE-Vinatieri 28-yd. FG
NE-Vinatieri 38-yd. FG

Passing
CLE: Holcomb 15–25–115 0 TD 1 INT, Couch 7–11–40 0 TD 0 INT
NE: Brady 20–33–259 0 TD 0 INT

Rushing
CLE: J. Jackson 15–71, Boyer 1–7, White 2–4, Morgan 1–2
NE: Faulk 23–96, Smith 3–9, Brown 1–3, Brady 2-(-2), Johnson 1-(-12)

Receiving
CLE: Davis 3–36, Heiden 6–34, Johnson 5–30, Northcutt 2–29, White 3–20, J. Jackson 2–4, Morgan 1–2
NE: Graham 7–110, Faulk 6–58, Johnson 2–51, Branch 3–30, Brown 2–10

Sunday, November 9
Kansas City Chiefs 41, Browns 20
Arrowhead Stadium (78,560)
White jerseys/white pants

Coming off a bye week, the Browns were carved up by the undefeated Chiefs, who rolled up more than 440 total yards while holding the Browns to under 200 and cruised to an easy triumph. After quickly falling behind 14–3, the Browns fought back and closed within 21–17 with five minutes left in the half but surrendered six more points before the intermission after a long kickoff return by Kansas City and then an effective two-minute drive. The Chiefs pulled away in the second half as QB Trent Green threw for 368 yards and three touchdowns. Though the Browns' defense was generally fruitless, LB Andra Davis collected three sacks.

Record: 3–6

	1	2	3	4		
Browns	3	14	3	0	=	20
Chiefs	14	13	7	7	=	41

CLE-Dawson 50-yd. FG
KC-Holmes 1-yd. run (Andersen kick)
KC-Holmes 9-yd. run (Andersen kick)
CLE-J. Jackson 1-yd. run (Dawson kick)
KC-Gonzalez 14-yd. pass from Green (Andersen kick)
CLE-Bowers 2-yd. pass from Holcomb (Dawson kick)
KC-Andersen 29-yd. FG
KC-Andersen 27-yd. FG
KC-Morton 28-yd. pass from Green (Andersen kick)
CLE-Dawson 22-yd. FG
KC-Kennison 27-yd. pass from Green (Andersen kick)

Passing
CLE: Holcomb 19–27–149 1 TD 1 INT
KC: Green 29–42–368 3 TD 0 INT

Rushing
CLE: J. Jackson 17–66, White 2–6, Northcutt 1–6, Holcomb 1–2
KC: Holmes 19–92, Richardson 2–3, Johnson 2–2, Collins 2-(-1), Hall 1-(-1)

Receiving
CLE: Davis 3–35, Morgan 2–25, Northcutt 4–24, Sanders 3–23, White 4–19, J. Jackson 1–18, Johnson 1–3, Bowers 1–2
KC: Kennison 7–115, Gonzalez 7–70, Holmes 7–66, Morton 3–49, Boerigter 2–45, Richardson 1–14, Hall 2–9

Sunday, November 16
Browns 44, Arizona Cardinals 6
Cleveland Browns Stadium (72,908)
Brown jerseys/white pants

In the midst of one of the most tumultuous weeks in team history—just after the Browns released dependable WR Kevin Johnson (citing a bad attitude) and just before starting RB William Green (already suspended for drunk driving and marijuana possession) was stabbed in the back by his fiancée in a domestic-violence dispute—the Browns rolled to one of the most dominating victories in franchise history. With red-hot Kelly Holcomb leading an unstoppable offense that tallied nearly 500 total yards, the Browns raced to a 20–0 lead over the 3–6 Cardinals and never looked back. Holcomb turned in one of the finest performances by any Browns' QB, completing 29 of 35 passes for 392 yards and three touchdowns as two Cleveland receivers—Andre Davis and Quincy Morgan—each went over the 100-yard mark. Outgained by nearly 300 yards, the Cardinals were limited to 10 first downs, turned the ball over four times, and couldn't score a touchdown. It was the Browns' largest margin of victory in 14 years, the biggest home win since 1960, and seemed to suggest the team had turned a corner.
Record: 4–6

	1	2	3	4		
Cardinals	0	3	3	0	=	6
Browns	10	10	14	10	=	44

CLE-Dawson 34-yd. FG
CLE-Davis 4-yd. pass from Holcomb (Dawson kick)
CLE-Dawson 24-yd. FG
CLE-Northcutt 1-yd. pass from Holcomb (Dawson kick)
ARI-Rackers 42-yd. FG
ARI-Rackers 26-yd. FG
CLE-J. Jackson 4-yd. run (Dawson kick)
CLE-Morgan 68-yd. pass from Holcomb (Dawson kick)
CLE-J. Jackson 4-yd. run (Dawson kick)
CLE-Dawson 29-yd. FG

Passing
ARI: Blake 9–21–121 0 TD 1 INT, McCown 4–11–31 0 TD 2 INT
CLE: Holcomb 29–35–392 3 TD 0 INT

Rushing
ARI: Shipp 9–23, McCown 2–9, Boldin 1–6, Blake 1–3
CLE: J. Jackson 19–45, White 4–27, Northcutt 2–14, Suggs 5–5, Holcomb 3-(-2)

Receiving
ARI: Boldin 4–86, Shipp 2–28, Bush 1–12, Anderson 2–10, Gilmore 1–9, Jones 3–7
CLE: Davis 7–117, Morgan 5–116, Northcutt 6–56, Heinrich 5–45, King 1–28, Mustard 2–17, J. Jackson 2–8, White 1–5

Sunday, November 23
Pittsburgh Steelers 13, Browns 6
Cleveland Browns Stadium (73,658)
Brown jerseys/white pants

The offensive fireworks of the previous week were long gone as the Browns couldn't manage a single touchdown despite driving inside the Pittsburgh 10 three times and committed five turnovers, all but handing victory to the struggling Steelers. The Browns held a 6–0 lead midway through the second quarter before two Cleveland fumbles led to 10 Pittsburgh points. The game turned on the first possession of the third quarter, as the Browns drove to the Pittsburgh 1, but couldn't cross the goal line on three successive plays, including an ill-advised double reverse on fourth-and-goal. The Browns drove to the Pittsburgh 7 on their next possession, but a third-down Kelly Holcomb pass was intercepted to thwart another scoring drive, as was their next series, killed by a fumble at the Steelers' 28 early in the fourth quarter. Fittingly, the Browns' final possession ended at midfield with their fifth turnover, another interception, with 1:41 remaining. Despite holding the Steelers to just 168 total yards and topping 300 themselves, the Browns lost for the fourth time in five games.
Record: 4–7

	1	2	3	4		
Steelers	0	10	0	3	=	13
Browns	3	3	0	0	=	6

CLE-Dawson 27-yd. FG
CLE-Dawson 31-yd FG
PIT-Bruener 1-yd. pass from Maddox (Reed kick)
PIT-Reed 23-yd. FG
PIT-Reed 46-yd. FG

Passing
PIT: Maddox 9–24–73 1 TD 0 INT
CLE: Holcomb 25–44–234 0 TD 2 INT

Rushing
PIT: Bettis 24–93, Zereoue 6–18, Haynes 1-(-2)
CLE: J. Jackson 25–94, Northcutt 2–8, White 1-(-12)

Receiving
PIT: Kreider 2–21, Burress 2–16, Ward 1–13, Bettis 1–9, Randle El 1–7, Tuman 1–6, Bruener 1–1
CLE: White 7–57, J. Jackson 5–49, Davis 3–48, Northcutt 3–24, Sanders 2–16, Morgan 1–16, King 2–12, Mustard 2–12

Sunday, November 30
Seattle Seahawks 34, Browns 7
Seahawks Stadium (64,680)
White jerseys/orange pants

In one of the ugliest games in team history, the Browns were not only thoroughly dominated but saw one of their key defensive players ejected and reignited their ongoing QB controversy. On the same play that saw the Seahawks extend their lead to 24–0 midway through the third quarter, the Browns' Gerard Warren was tossed for fighting. A play later, Tim Couch, substituting for struggling Kelly Holcomb at the start of the half, injured his elbow, and Holcomb re-entered the game, though neither was effective. The Browns avoided a shutout only through pure serendipity, when a punt by the Seahawks ricocheted off the back of their long snapper, and Browns' WR Andre King scooped up the loose ball and returned it 28 yards for a touchdown. Seattle rolled to 463 total yards, more than double the Browns' total as QB Matt Hasselbeck threw for 328 yards and three touchdowns, and RB Shaun Alexander rushed for 127. The defeat ensured the Browns a worse record than their 9–7 mark of the year before.
Record: 4–8

	1	2	3	4		
Browns	0	0	0	7	=	7
Seahawks	7	10	10	7	=	34

SEA-Mili 2-yd. pass from Hasselbeck (Brown kick)
SEA-Brown 36-yd. FG
SEA-Jackson 3-yd. pass from Hasselbeck (Brown kick)
SEA-Jackson 26-yd. pass from Hasselbeck (Brown kick)
SEA-Brown 41-yd. FG
SEA-Alexander 3-yd. run (Brown kick)
CLE-King 28-yd. blocked punt return (Dawson kick)

Passing
CLE: Holcomb 22–31–186 0 TD 1 INT, Couch 1–3–5 0 TD 0 INT
SEA: Hasselbeck 26–35–328 3 TD 1 INT

Rushing
CLE: J. Jackson 12–32, White 3–8, Davis 1–7
SEA: Alexander 27–127, Strong 4–22, Evans 1–8, Morris 4–0

Receiving
CLE: Northcutt 5–61, White 7–41, Morgan 3–30, King 3–28, Sanders 3–18, Davis 1–7, J. Jackson 1–6
SEA: Robinson 6–122, Jackson 8–102, Strong 4–56, Stevens 2–20, Alexander 2–10, Engram 2–8, Bannister 1–8, Mili 1–2

Monday, December 8
St. Louis Rams 26, Browns 20
Cleveland Browns Stadium (73,108)
Brown jerseys/orange pants

Appearing on *Monday Night Football* for the first time in eight years and wearing the brown jersey/orange pants uniform combination for the first time in two decades, the Browns once again dug a huge hole, but nearly came all the way back for a stunning victory. A two-point deficit turned into a 23–7 score within 35 seconds just before halftime when Kelly Holcomb threw two quick interceptions, the first of which was returned for a touchdown. Holcomb was yanked, and Tim Couch brought the Browns back to life with a touchdown drive on their first series of the second half, then cut the margin to 26–20 five minutes into the fourth quarter. The Browns had two more possessions with which they could have taken the lead but lost both possessions on downs, the last at the St. Louis 40 with 1:48 to play. In another fractured overall performance, Cleveland RB Jamel White was one of the few stalwarts, topping the 100-yard rushing mark for the third and final time in his career. The Browns received more bad news when it was discovered that kicker Phil Dawson had played the entire second half with a broken arm and would miss the remainder of the season.
Record: 4–9

	1	2	3	4		
Rams	3	20	3	0	=	26
Browns	7	0	6	7	=	20

STL-Wilkins 28-yd. FG
CLE-Heinrich 2-yd. pass from Holcomb (Dawson kick)
STL-Wilkins 26-yd. FG
STL-Wilkins 29-yd. FG
STL-Williams 46-yd. interception return (Wilkins kick)
STL-Bruce 16-yd. pass from Bulger (Wilkins kick)

CLE-Morgan 28-yd. pass from Couch (pass failed)
STL-Wilkins 37-yd. FG
CLE-White 2-yd. run (Dawson kick)

Passing
STL: Bulger 22–36–223 1 TD 1 INT
CLE: Couch 6–9–98 1 TD 0 INT, Holcomb 10–17–80 1 TD 2 INT

Rushing
STL: Faulk 24–102, Bulger 6–9
CLE: White 16–101, J. Jackson 4–30, Northcutt 2–16, Couch 1–8, Davis 1–7

Receiving
STL: Looker 3–50, Faulk 6–43, Holt 4–31, Bruce 3–31, Furrey 3–28, St. Clair 1–18, Manumaleuna 1–13, Cleeland 1–9
CLE: Morgan 4–64, White 4–39, Northcutt 3–33, Davis 1–17, Sanders 2–15, King 1–8, Heinrich 1–2

Sunday, December 14
Denver Broncos 23, Browns 20 (OT)
Invesco Field (75,358)
White jerseys/white pants

The Browns lost another close one, this time in a heart-wrenching fashion that brought back memories of their 1980s struggles against the Broncos. With Tim Couch reassuming the role of starting QB, the Browns stayed with the playoff-bound Broncos all afternoon, aided by a touchdown catch by TE Keith Heinrich on the last play of the half. A long return of a Denver punt by Dennis Northcutt (who also added 115 receiving yards on only three receptions) set up Couch's second touchdown pass two plays later, which tied the game at 17 midway through the fourth quarter. After a defensive stop, the Browns drove from their own 28 to the Denver 30, aided by a 33-yard pass-interference penalty, and took a 20–17 lead on a 48-yard field goal by new kicker Brett Conway with 1:11 to play. Out of time outs, the Broncos appeared on the cusp of defeat at their own 37 with 37 seconds left, but then QB Jake Plummer completed a 46-yard pass to WR Ashley Lelie to set up a game-tying field goal with six seconds left. After stopping the Browns in overtime, the Broncos began marching again, propelled by a 23-yard bootleg run by Plummer into Cleveland territory, and won the game on a 25-yard Jason Elam field goal five minutes into the extra session. It marked the Browns' sixth straight loss to the Broncos and the third time they'd fallen to Denver in overtime by a 23–20 score. Behind 139 rushing yards from RB Clinton Portis, the Broncos controlled the ball offensively, rolling up more than 400 yards and 28 first downs but allowed the Browns to stay close with 124 yards in penalties.

Record: 4–10

	1	2	3	4	OT		
Browns	0	10	0	10	0	=	20
Broncos	10	0	0	10	3	=	23

DEN-Portis 1-yd. run (Elam kick)
DEN-Elam 51-yd. FG
CLE-Conway 39-yd. FG
CLE-Heinrich 1-yd. pass from Couch (Conway kick)
DEN-Portis 13-yd. run (Elam kick)
CLE-Davis 35-yd. pass from Couch (Conway kick)
CLE-Conway 48-yd. FG
DEN-Elam 36-yd. FG
DEN-Elam 25-yd. FG

Passing
CLE: Couch 8–18–181 2 TD 1 INT, Boyer 0–1–0 0 TD 0 INT, F. Jackson 0–1–0 0 TD 0 INT, Northcutt 0–1–0 0 TD 0 INT
DEN: Plummer 22–36–269 0 TD 1 INT

Rushing
CLE: White 20–55, Suggs 5–30, Couch 1–17
DEN: Portis 38–139, Plummer 1–23, Anderson 1–3

Receiving
CLE: Northcutt 3–115, Davis 1–35, Morgan 1–12, F. Jackson 1–10, Sanders 1–8, Heinrich 1–1
DEN: Sharpe 8–97, Lelie 4–71, Smith 4–41, McCaffrey 2–26, Hape 2–21, Anderson 1–7, Portis 1–6

Sunday, December 21
Baltimore Ravens 35, Browns 0
Cleveland Browns Stadium (72,548)
Brown jerseys/white pants

Jamal Lewis became only the second RB in NFL history to rush for over 200 yards against the same opponent twice in a season as he took over the game in the second half to lead the Ravens to another easy victory over the Browns. With Baltimore leading just 7–0 in the third quarter, the Browns had done a nice job containing Lewis, holding him to 54 yards on 17 carries. Then he blew through the Cleveland line for a 72-yard touchdown run to make it 14–0, followed by a 45-yard gain on his next carry and a 24-yard touchdown run three minutes into the fourth quarter to blow the game open. Lewis finished the day with 205 yards on 22 carries, bringing his season total against Cleveland to an even 600 yards. Crippled by four turnovers and five sacks, the Browns' offense couldn't get anything going and was shut out for the first time in three years.

Record: 4–11

	1	2	3	4		
Ravens	0	7	7	21	=	35
Browns	0	0	0	0	=	0

BAL-Jones 1-yd. pass from Wright (Stover kick)
BAL-Lewis 72-yd. run (Stover kick)
BAL-Lewis 24-yd. run (Stover kick)
BAL-Williams 52-yd. interception return (Stover kick)
BAL-Smith 11-yd. run (Stover kick)

Passing
BAL: Wright 10–18–90 1 TD 1 INT, Boller 1–1–10 0 TD 0 INT
CLE: Couch 17–33–163 0 TD 1 INT

Rushing
BAL: Lewis 22–205, C. Taylor 7–22, Smith 4–21, Wright 3–16, Ricard 4–9, T. Taylor 1–3
CLE: Suggs 20–68, White 4–10

Receiving
BAL: Robinson 3–27, C. Taylor 1–23, Lewis 3–21, Heap 1–14, Jones 2–11, T. Taylor 1–4
CLE: Northcutt 7–67, Davis 1–49, White 4–21, Heinrich 1–16, Morgan 2–10, Suggs 2–0

Sunday, December 28
Browns 22, Cincinnati Bengals 14
Paul Brown Stadium (65,362)
White jerseys/white pants

A cacophony of a season ended on a sweet note as the Browns out-played the resurgent Bengals on their own home field and ended their playoff hopes with an upset victory. Emerging from obscurity into the spotlight was Browns' rookie RB Lee Suggs, who, after missing the first nine games of the season with a torn rotator cuff, exploded for 186 yards on 26 carries and a pair of tide-turning touchdowns. The first was a 78-yard jaunt to give the Browns a 13–7 lead just before the half and the second, a 25-yard run, put them ahead for good with 7:54 to play in the game. After tacking on an insurance field goal with just over a minute to play, the Browns clinched victory when DB Robert Griffith intercepted Bengals' QB Jon Kitna at the Cleveland 39. Behind Suggs, the Browns rushed for 264 yards, their highest total in 18 years.

Record: 5–11

	1	2	3	4		
Browns	3	10	0	9	=	22
Bengals	7	0	0	7	=	14

CIN-R. Johnson 5-yd. run (Graham kick)
CLE-Conway 42-yd. FG
CLE-Conway 42-yd. FG
CLE-Suggs 78-yd. run (Conway kick)
CIN-R. Johnson 2-yd. run (Graham kick)
CLE-Suggs 25-yd. run (pass failed)
CIN-Conway 18-yd. FG

Passing
CLE: Couch 9–18–115 0 TD 0 INT
CIN: Kitna 23–35–175 0 TD 1 INT

Rushing
CLE: Suggs 26–186, White 9–54, Northcutt 3–32, Couch 1-(-1), Morgan 1-(-7)
CIN: R. Johnson 14–52, Dillon 8–50, Kitna 1–9, Warrick 1–2, J. Johnson 1–2

Receiving
CLE: Davis 5–72, F. Jackson 1–19, Northcutt 1–12, Morgan 1–6, Sanders 1–6
CIN: Schobel 4–42, Bennett 5–29, C. Johnson 4–29, Warrick 4–25, R. Johnson 2–25, Dillon 1–11, Stewart 1–9, Washington 1–4, Kelly 1–1

2004

Sunday, September 12
Browns 20, Baltimore Ravens 3
Cleveland Browns Stadium (73,068)
White jerseys/white pants

With members of the 1964 world-title team on hand for a fortieth-anniversary commemoration ceremony before the game, the Browns dominated the physical Ravens in the second half to atone for two embarrassing defeats the year before and won a season opener for the first time since their return. With the game tied 3–3 late in the third quarter, QB Jeff Garcia, making his Cleveland debut, lofted a 46-yard touchdown pass to WR Quincy Morgan to give the Browns a lead they would not relinquish. The defense took it from there, holding Baltimore RB Jamal Lewis, who had torched the Browns for 600 yards rushing in two games the previous season, to just 57 yards on 20 carries. The Browns also picked off two passes in the final period to extinguish any Baltimore comeback hopes, while DE Kenard Lang collected a trio of sacks. Garcia put the game away with an athletic three-yard touchdown run with just over four minutes to play, capping a near-perfect performance on a sunshiny September afternoon.

Record: 1–0

	1	2	3	4		
Ravens	0	0	3	0	=	3
Browns	0	3	7	10	=	20

CLE-Dawson 37-yd. FG
BAL-Stover 42-yd. FG
CLE-Morgan 46-yd. pass from Garcia (Dawson kick)
CLE-Dawson 25-yd. FG
CLE-Garcia 3-yd. run (Dawson kick)

Passing
BAL: Boller 22–38–191 0 TD 2 INT
CLE: Garcia 15–24–180 1 TD 0 INT

Rushing
BAL: Lewis 20–57, Boller 2–16, C. Taylor 3–14, Ricard 1–1
CLE: Green 22–65, Garcia 3–13, J. Jackson 4–7

Receiving
BAL: Heap 9–86, Johnson 5–43, Hymes 5–39, Wilcox 2–18, T. Taylor 1–5
CLE: Davis 1–51, Morgan 1–46, Winslow 4–39, Green 4–27, Northcutt 3–12, J. Jackson 2–5

Sunday, September 19
Dallas Cowboys 19, Browns 12
Texas Stadium (63,119)
Brown jerseys/white pants

The excitement of opening day evaporated quickly as the Browns put forth a miserable performance that should have resulted in a blowout defeat, were it not for the mistake-prone Cowboys, who allowed the Browns to stay in the game. Jeff Garcia etched his name in football infamy as he tallied a passer rating of 0.0 for the game, completing only eight of 27 passes while throwing three interceptions. Dallas (and former Browns') QB Vinny Testaverde tossed for 322 yards but also fired three critical interceptions on three straight series in the second half after Dallas had stretched its lead to 17–9. The Browns could manage only a field goal from the trio of takeaways, Phil Dawson's fourth of the game. Then, after taking over at their own 1 with nine seconds left, the Browns gave the Cowboys two points when OT Joaquin Gonzalez was called for holding in the end zone—an automatic safety. Though the Browns recovered the ensuing onside free kick, the price was costly as rookie TE and No. 1 draft choice Kellen Winslow Jr. broke his leg on the play and was lost for the season. A desperation pass on the game's final play fell incomplete, and a dispiriting loss was in the books.

Record: 1–1

	1	2	3	4		
Browns	0	9	0	3	=	12
Cowboys	7	3	7	2	=	19

DAL-Robinson 1-yd. pass from Testaverde (Cundiff kick)
CLE-Dawson 45-yd. FG
CLE-Dawson 23-yd. FG
DAL-Cundiff 30-yd. FG
CLE-Dawson 49-yd. FG
DAL-George 3-yd. run (Cundiff kick)
CLE-Dawson 22-yd. FG
DAL-Safety: Gonzalez penalized for holding in end zone

Passing
CLE: Garcia 8–27–71 0 TD 3 INT, McCown 0–1–0 0 TD 0 INT
DAL: Testaverde 23–35–322 1 TD 3 INT

Rushing
CLE: Green 19–52, J. Jackson 3–50, Garcia 4–34
DAL: George 18–62, Coakley 1–33, Jones 5–16, Lee 4–15

Receiving
CLE: Davis 3–39, Morgan 1–11, Winslow 1–11, Northcutt 1–7, Green 1–2, J. Jackson 1–1
DAL: Glenn 6–90, Witten 6–82, Johnson 2–57, Bryant 3–54, George 2–17, Jones 2–14, Campbell 1–7, Robinson 1–1

Sunday, September 26
New York Giants 27, Browns 10
Giants Stadium (78,521)
White jerseys/orange pants

With seven starters out with injuries, the Browns once again were sluggish and were overwhelmed on the road. After the Giants dominated the first half, taking a 10–0 lead, the Browns had a chance to get back into the game on the first possession of the third quarter, driving to the New York 5. But Jeff Garcia fumbled the snap from center and the Giants recovered, then marched 95 yards to take a 17–0 lead and effectively end the contest. Three turnovers, four sacks allowed, and 80 yards in penalties did in the Browns, who failed to score a touchdown until just over three minutes remained in the game, snapping a string of seven consecutive quarters without reaching the end zone. RB William Green was one of the lone bright spots, rushing for 91 yards on 15 carries, and he had a 49-yard touchdown run called back on a penalty.
Record: 1–2

	1	2	3	4		
Browns	0	0	0	10	=	10
Giants	7	3	7	10	=	27

NYG-Barber 8-yd. run (Christie kick)
NYG-Christie 43-yd. FG
NYG-Warner 1-yd. run (Christie kick)
CLE-Dawson 49-yd. FG
NYG-Christie 25-yd. FG
CLE-Morgan 3-yd. pass from Garcia (Dawson kick)
NYG-Cloud 5-yd. run (Christie kick)

Passing
CLE: Garcia 21–31–180 1 TD 1 INT
NYG: Warner 19–27–286 0 TD 0 INT

Rushing
CLE: Green 15–91, J. Jackson 5–24, Garcia 3–9
NYG: Barber 23–106, Cloud 6–12, Warner 3-(-2)

Receiving
CLE: Northcutt 9–50, Morgan 3–44, Davis 3–33, King 2–28, J. Jackson 3–16, Mustard 1–9
NYG: Toomer 5–126, Barber 3–48, Carter 3–45, Shockey 5–41, Hilliard 3–26

Sunday, October 3
Browns 17, Washington Redskins 13
Cleveland Browns Stadium (73,348)
Brown jerseys/white pants

Despite a third straight lackluster performance, the Browns came from behind in the fourth quarter and evened their record at 2–2 on a bright October afternoon. With neither offense topping 280 total yards, the defenses took center stage, with the Browns holding Washington's All-Pro RB Clinton Portis to just 58 yards on 20 carries. Portis did score a touchdown in the second quarter to put the Redskins up 10–3, and after the Browns tied it early in the third on a scoring reception by TE Aaron Shea, Washington took the lead again with a field goal on the second play of the fourth quarter. Sparked by RB Lee Suggs, making his first appearance of the season after suffering a preseason neck injury, the Browns drove 80 yards and took the lead on a short Suggs touchdown run with 6:55 to play. After forcing the 'Skins to punt, the Browns were stuffed on an ill-fated fake field goal on fourth-and-four at the Washington 28 with just over two minutes to play. But a play later, Redskins' WR Laveranues Coles, who had rolled up 122 yards on the day, fumbled at the Washington 39, and the Browns recovered at the two-minute warning, then ran out the clock.
Record: 2–2

	1	2	3	4		
Redskins	3	7	0	3	=	13
Browns	3	0	7	7	=	17

WAS-Hall 31-yd. FG
CLE-Dawson 30-yd. FG
WAS-Portis 1-yd. run (Hall kick)
CLE-Shea 15-yd. pass from Garcia (Dawson kick)
WAS-Hall 26-yd. FG
CLE-Suggs 3-yd. run (Dawson kick)

Passing
WAS: Brunell 17–32–192 0 TD 0 INT
CLE: Garcia 14–21–195 1 TD 0 INT

Rushing
WAS: Portis 20–58, Brunell 3–9, Betts 2–6
CLE: Suggs 22–82, Green 4–17, Smith 1–4, Frost 1–1, Davis 1-(-3), Garcia 3-(-5)

Receiving
WAS: Coles 7–122, Rasby 3–29, Gardner 3–19, Portis 2–15, Thrash 2–7
CLE: Davis 3–93, Shea 2–28, Smith 2–20, Heiden 2–19, Morgan 2–18, Northcutt 2–11, Suggs 1–6

Sunday, October 10
Pittsburgh Steelers 34, Browns 23
Heinz Field (63,609)
White jerseys/white pants

Aided by an interception return for a touchdown, the Browns hung with the Steelers for a quarter but then were left in the dust by Pittsburgh and rookie QB Ben Roethlisberger, who threw for one touchdown and ran for another. Cleveland DB Cris Crocker got the best of Big Ben early, returning an interception 20 yards for a score to tie the score at seven three-and-a-half minutes into the game. But the Browns wouldn't reach the end zone again until the fourth quarter as the Steelers built a 27–13 halftime lead and then held off the Browns in the second half. Pittsburgh rolled up 170 yards on the ground and did not allow a sack as the Browns once again dropped below .500.
Record: 2–3

	1	2	3	4		
Browns	10	3	3	7	=	23
Steelers	14	13	7	0	=	34

PIT-Staley 25-yd. run (Reed kick)
CLE-Crocker 20-yd. interception return (Dawson kick)
PIT-Roethlisberger 6-yd. run (Reed kick)
CLE-Dawson 24-yd. FG
PIT-Reed 47-yd. FG
PIT-Burress 37-yd. pass from Roethlisberger (Reed kick)
CLE-Dawson 34-yd. FG
PIT-Reed 26-yd. FG
PIT-Bettis 3-yd. run (Reed kick)
CLE-Dawson 46-yd. FG
CLE-Davis 7-yd. pass from Garcia (Dawson kick)

Passing
CLE: Garcia 16–34–210 1 TD 0 INT
PIT: Roethlisberger 16–21–231 1 TD 1 INT

Rushing
CLE: Garcia 6–41, Suggs 11–30, Green 3–27, Northcutt 1–0
PIT: Staley 21–117, Bettis 14–34, Roethlisberger 6–13, Haynes 2–6

Receiving
CLE: Davis 5–101, Shea 1–35, Northcutt 4–33, Suggs 3–20, Morgan 1–15, Smith 1–3, Green 1–3
PIT: Burress 6–136, Ward 6–61, Randle El 2–29, Mays 1–6, Haynes 1-(-1)

Sunday, October 17
Browns 34, Cincinnati Bengals 17
Cleveland Browns Stadium (73,263)
Brown jerseys/white pants

In what would be their most impressive performance of the season, the Browns blew open a narrow game in the second half and coasted to a comfortable win over their intrastate rivals. The high point of the game was midway through the first quarter, when—pinned at his own 1—Jeff Garcia rolled to his right in the end zone and lofted a long pass for WR Andre Davis, who caught it and sprinted into the end zone for a 99-yard touchdown. It was the longest play in franchise history and just the tenth time it had ever been done in the NFL. It set the tone for a marvelous day for Garcia, who threw for 310 yards and four scores as the Browns rolled up a season-high 449 total yards. But a handful of Cleveland mistakes in the second quarter saw a 14–0 lead quickly turn into a 17–14 deficit. A risky call led to the go-ahead touchdown on a short pass to Aaron Shea on the last play of the first half. Then, with the Cleveland defense stuffing the Bengals in the second half, holding them to just 189 yards on the day, the Browns tacked on 13 more points to win going away. William Green rushed for 115 yards while fellow RB Lee Suggs added 100 receiving yards on five catches, marking the first time in 18 years the Browns had a 300-yard passer, a 100-yard rusher, and a 100-yard receiver in the same game. For as rousing as the victory was, it would be more than two months before they'd win again—and nearly a full year before winning before their home fans. It also marked Butch Davis's final victory as head coach of the Browns.
Record: 3–3

	1	2	3	4		
Bengals	0	17	0	0	=	17
Browns	7	14	3	10	=	34

CLE-Davis 99-yd. pass from Garcia (Dawson kick)
CLE-Morgan 10-yd. pass from Garcia (Dawson kick)
CIN-Kaesviharn 3-yd. fumble return (Graham kick)
CIN-Schobel 6-yd. pass from Palmer (Graham kick)
CIN-Graham 32-yd. FG
CLE-Shea 5-yd. pass from Garcia (Dawson kick)
CLE-Dawson 23-yd. FG
CLE-Suggs 59-yd. pass from Garcia (Dawson kick)
CLE-Dawson 33-yd. FG

Passing
CIN: Palmer 20–36–148 1 TD 1 INT
CLE: Garcia 16–23–310 4 TD 2 INT

Rushing
CIN: R. Johnson 16–57, Perry 2–1
CLE: Green 25–115, Suggs 13–19, Northcutt 1–2, Smith 1–2, Garcia 6–1

Receiving
CIN: C. Johnson 3–37, Watson 5–28, Russell 1–21, Washington 2–18, Schobel 3–17, Stewart 2–12, Perry 1–9, J. Johnson 2–6, R. Johnson 1–0
CLE: Suggs 5–100, Davis 1–99, Northcutt 2–59, Shea 3–25, King 2–13, Morgan 1–10, Smith 1–4, Green 1–0

Sunday, October 24
Philadelphia Eagles 34, Browns 31 (OT)
Cleveland Browns Stadium (73,394)
Brown jerseys/white pants

Trailing the undefeated Eagles by a touchdown with time running out, the Browns put together a clutch drive to tie the contest on a four-yard run by Jeff Garcia with 30 seconds remaining to force a wild game into overtime. After stopping the Eagles on the first possession of the extra session, the Browns opted to punt on fourth-and-one at their own 48 and never saw the ball again as a 28-yard run by Philly QB Donovan McNabb set up the game-winning 50-yard field goal with 5:02 remaining. The Eagles, who rolled up 488 yards on the day, had a chance to take control of the game midway through the second quarter when they drove to the Cleveland 21 leading 21–10. But Browns' LB Andra Davis intercepted McNabb, and on the ensuing possession the Browns cut the margin to four points. The contest was back-and-forth from that point on, with Cleveland taking its only lead midway through the third on a Jeff Garcia-to-TE Steve Heiden touchdown, but the Eagles took it back on the second play of the fourth quarter on the fourth touchdown pass of the day for McNabb, who threw for 376 yards.

Record: 3–4

	1	2	3	4	OT		
Eagles	14	7	0	10	3	=	34
Browns	7	10	7	7	0	=	31

PHI-Lewis 10-yd. pass from McNabb (Akers kick)
CLE-Green 11-yd. run (Dawson kick)
PHI-Owens 39-yd. pass from McNabb (Akers kick)
CLE-Dawson 38-yd. FG
PHI-Owens 40-yd. pass from McNabb (Akers kick)
CLE-Suggs 13-yd. run (Dawson kick)
CLE-Heiden 21-yd. pass from Garcia (Dawson kick)
PHI-Smith 2-yd. pass from McNabb (Akers kick)
PHI-Akers 38-yd. FG
CLE-Garcia 4-yd. run (Dawson kick)
PHI-Akers 50-yd. FG

Passing
PHI: McNabb 28–43–376 4 TD 1 INT
CLE: Garcia 21–32–236 1 TD 1 INT

Rushing
PHI: Levens 7–48, Westbrook 13–43, McNabb 2–28, Lewis 1–2
CLE: Suggs 15–78, Green 14–64, Garcia 4–21, Smith 1–2

Receiving
PHI: Owens 4–109, Pinkston 6–100, Lewis 5–37, Mitchell 2–31, Lewis 1–24, Parry 2–22, Mahe 2–18, Westbrook 3–17, Levens 1–12, Smith 2–6
CLE: Northcutt 4–70, Shea 6–45, F. Jackson 3–45, Heiden 3–42, Bryant 2–26, Suggs 2–5, Green 1–3

Sunday, November 7
Baltimore Ravens 27, Browns 13
M&T Bank Stadium (69,781)
White jerseys/white pants

Leading by one point with less than nine minutes to play, the Browns suffered two bad breaks that turned the contest in favor of the Ravens. The tone for a surprising game was set on the opening kickoff of this nationally televised Sunday-night game when WR Richard Alston, just called up from the Browns' practice squad on Thursday to help their dismal kick-return team, returned the opening kickoff 93 yards for a touchdown. The Browns' offense could add only six more points for the remainder of the night, but took a 13–12 lead on a Phil Dawson field goal on the second play of the fourth quarter. But minutes later, after being pinned back at their own 1, Browns' punter David Frost shanked a seven-yard kick from his own end zone, and the Ravens took the lead with a touchdown and two-point conversion with seven minutes to play. The Browns responded by driving to the Baltimore 5 in the final minute, but a Jeff Garcia pass glanced off the hands of Aaron Shea, who appeared to be hit by Baltimore LB Ray Lewis before the ball arrived and was picked off by Ravens' DB Ed Reed, who returned it 106 yards for a touchdown—the longest return ever by a Browns' opponent. It was a fitting conclusion for a game that saw neither team top 240 yards of offense or 15 first downs.

Record: 3–5

	1	2	3	4		
Browns	10	0	0	3	=	13
Ravens	3	9	0	15	=	27

CLE-Alston 93-yd. kickoff return (Dawson kick)
BAL-Stover 44-yd. FG
CLE-Dawson 50-yd. FG
BAL-Stover 39-yd. FG
BAL-Stover 43-yd. FG
BAL-Stover 36-yd. FG
CLE-Dawson 29-yd. FG
BAL-Lewis 2-yd. run (Moore pass from Boller)
BAL-Reed 106-yd. interception return (Stover kick)

Passing
CLE: Garcia 15–26–146 0 TD 1 INT
BAL: Boller 17–30–142 0 TD 0 INT

Rushing
CLE: Suggs 18–56, Garcia 2–25, Green 8–10
BAL: Lewis 22–81, Ricard 2–18, C. Taylor 2–6, Boller 2–1

Receiving
CLE: Bryant 4–43, Heiden 4–31, F. Jackson 2–26, Shea 2–20, Green 1–10, Northcutt 1–9, Suggs 1–7
BAL: T. Taylor 7–58, Johnson 3–24, Moore 2–24, Lewis 1–14, Wilcox 2–9, Ricard 1–7, Hymes 1–6

Sunday, November 14
Pittsburgh Steelers 24, Browns 10
Cleveland Browns Stadium (73,703)
Brown jerseys/orange pants

In one of the ugliest incidents in team history, a brawl erupted between Browns and Steelers players during opening warm-ups, resulting in the pregame ejections of William Green and Pittsburgh LB Joey Porter. With a nasty atmosphere setting the tone, Richard Alston broke free on the opening kickoff for the second straight week, sprinting 74 yards to set up a Browns' field goal. The Cleveland offense could do very little for the remainder of the game as the 7–1 Steelers gradually overwhelmed the Browns, rushing for 180 yards and building a 24–3 lead. Meanwhile, the Browns allowed four sacks and turned the ball over four times, including a fourth-quarter fumble scooped up by DB Russell Stuvaints (a Youngstown State alumnus) and returned 24 yards for Pittsburgh's final touchdown. The Browns finally reached the end zone late after Kelly Holcomb replaced Jeff Garcia at QB.

Record: 3–6

	1	2	3	4		
Steelers	7	7	0	10	=	24
Browns	3	0	0	7	=	10

CLE-Dawson 31-yd. FG
PIT-Bettis 5-yd. run (Reed kick)
PIT-Bettis 1-yd. run (Reed kick)
PIT-Reed 20-yd. FG
PIT-Stuvaints 24-yd. fumble return (Reed kick)
CLE-Shea 7-yd. pass from Holcomb (Dawson kick)

Passing
PIT: Roethlisberger 10–16–134 0 TD 1 INT
CLE: Garcia 7–16–110 0 TD 1 INT, Holcomb 5–9–64 1 TD 1 INT

Rushing
PIT: Bettis 29–103, Parker 8–44, Roethlisberger 7–38, Brown 1–2, Ward 2-(-7)
CLE: Suggs 18–38, Garcia 4–30

Receiving
PIT: Burress 5–66, Ward 3–42, Randle El 1–19, Bettis 1–7
CLE: Northcutt 2–69, F. Jackson 5–61, Bryant 2–26, Smith 1–8, Shea 1–7, Heiden 1–3

Sunday, November 21
New York Jets 10, Browns 7
Cleveland Browns Stadium (72,547)
Orange jerseys/white pants

For the third straight week, the Browns' offense was non-existent, and the defense couldn't come up with the stops it needed to hold onto a fourth-quarter lead as the Browns lost their fourth straight. A short scoring pass from Jeff Garcia to Aaron Shea gave the Browns a 7–0 lead early in the second quarter, and the Browns were still ahead early in the fourth when Phil Dawson uncharacteristically missed a 34-yard field goal that would have made Cleveland lead 10–3. Dawson, who had also missed from 42 yards in the first half, had entered the game having made his last 27 attempts. The Jets responded with a 75-yard drive and took the lead with 5:32 remaining. After the Browns were forced to punt on the ensuing possession, the Jets picked up three critical first downs to melt the last four minutes of the game and drop the Browns to another frustrating defeat. Jeff Garcia injured his shoulder late in the first half and was taken out of the game—he wouldn't start again for the remainder of his one-season tenure in Cleveland.
Record: 3–7

	1	2	3	4		
Jets	0	0	3	7	=	10
Browns	0	7	0	0	=	7

CLE-Shea 3-yd. pass from Garcia (Dawson kick)
NYJ-Brien 41-yd. FG
NYJ-McCareins 11-yd. pass from Carter (Brien kick)

Passing
NYJ: Carter 11–20–116 1 TD 1 INT
CLE: Garcia 10–17–88 1 TD 0 INT, Holcomb 4–10–32 0 TD 0 INT

Rushing
NYJ: Martin 17–88, Jordan 18–73, Carter 4-(-4)
CLE: Suggs 17–62, Green 8–32, Northcutt 2–5

Receiving
NYJ: McCareins 6–71, Moss 2–25, Jordan 1–11, Sowell 2–9
CLE: Northcutt 2–40, Bryant 3–36, Heiden 3–19, Suggs 3–15, Shea 2–7, Smith 1–3

Sunday, November 28
Cincinnati Bengals 58, Browns 48
Paul Brown Stadium (65,677)
White jerseys/white pants

In one of the most bizarre games in NFL history, the Browns' dormant offense erupted for 462 total yards and 48 points, but it wasn't enough to overcome an equally stunning performance by the Bengals, who tallied 504 yards and 58 points in what became the highest-scoring game in Browns' history and the second-highest scoring game ever played. Trailing 27–13 at the half, the Browns suddenly caught fire, scoring touchdowns on five consecutive possessions to take a 48–44 lead with 10 minutes to play. Cincinnati rebounded to take the lead back on the next possession, and after an exchange of punts, the Browns had one last chance, taking over at their own 17 with just over two minutes left. But Kelly Holcomb was picked off by Bengals' DB Deltha O'Neal, who returned it 31 yards for the game-clinching touchdown. It was one of the few mistakes of the game for Holcomb, who put together the seventh 400-yard passing game in Cleveland history and tied a team record with five touchdown passes. WR Antonio Bryant, acquired in a trade the month before, had his first big day as a Brown, catching eight passes for 131 yards and a pair of touchdowns, while Steve Heiden also came up big with 82 yards and three scores. The following evening, Browns' head coach Butch Davis resigned, and offensive coordinator Terry Robiskie was handed the reins to finish what had become a disastrous season.
Record: 3–8

	1	2	3	4		
Browns	10	3	21	14	=	48
Bengals	14	13	14	17	=	58

CLE-Heiden 7-yd. pass from Holcomb (Dawson kick)
CIN-Washington 18-yd. pass from Palmer (Graham kick)
CIN-C. Johnson 46-yd. pass from Palmer (Graham kick)
CLE-Dawson 23-yd. FG
CLE-Dawson 29-yd. FG
CIN-Houshmandzadeh 53-yd. pass from Palmer (Graham kick)
CIN-Graham 21-yd. FG
CIN-Graham 32-yd. FG
CLE-Heiden 20-yd. pass from Holcomb (Dawson kick)
CIN-Houshmandzadeh 53-yd. pass from Palmer (Graham kick)
CLE-Bryant 9-yd. pass from Holcomb (Dawson kick)
CIN-R. Johnson 7-yd. run (Graham kick)
CLE-Bryant 55-yd. pass from Holcomb (Dawson kick)

CIN-Graham 36-yd. FG
CLE-Green 1-yd. run (Dawson kick)
CLE-Heiden 1-yd. pass from Holcomb (Dawson kick)
CIN-R. Johnson 7-yd. run (Graham kick)
CIN-O'Neal 31-yd. interception return (Graham kick)

Passing
CLE: Holcomb 30–39–413 5 TD 2 INT
CIN: Palmer 22–29–251 4 TD 3 INT

Rushing
CLE: Green 15–75, Smith 1–1, Holcomb 1–0
CIN: R. Johnson 26–202, Houshmandzadeh 2–17, Watson 1–15, Palmer 2–10, C. Johnson 1–9

Receiving
CLE: Bryant 8–131, Northcutt 5–87, Heiden 7–82, Shea 5–67, F. Jackson 2–30, Green 2–15, Smith 1–1
CIN: C. Johnson 10–117, Houshmandzadeh 4–79, Washington 3–35, Walter 2–12, R. Johnson 1–5, J. Johnson 2–3

Sunday, December 5
New England Patriots 42, Browns 15
Cleveland Browns Stadium (73,028)
Brown jerseys/white pants

With an interim coach at the helm and a roster decimated by injuries, the Browns were no match for the 10–1 Patriots, who easily coasted to a blowout victory. The tone was set on the opening kickoff, when New England WR Bethel Johnson broke free for a 93-yard touchdown. After the Browns scored just before the half to cut the Patriots' advantage to 21–7, they were driving again on the first series of the second half, threatening to make a game of it. But William Green fumbled, and Pats' DB Randall Gay recovered and returned it 41 yards for the backbreaking touchdown. Rookie QB Luke McCown made his first NFL start in place of injured Kelly Holcomb and played well, throwing for 277 yards and a pair of touchdowns, but the Browns could manage only 46 rushing yards and turned the ball over four times. The defense was assaulted for the second straight week, again allowing more than 400 total yards and 200 yards on the ground. It also marked the first time in franchise history that the Browns had allowed a total of 100 points in two straight games.
Record: 3–9

	1	2	3	4		
Patriots	14	7	21	0	=	42
Browns	0	7	0	8	=	15

NE-Johnson 93-yd. kickoff return (Vinatieri kick)
NE-Dillon 4-yd. run (Vinatieri kick)
NE-Dillon 1-yd. run (Vinatieri kick)
CLE-Bryant 16-yd. pass from McCown (Dawson kick)
NE-Gay 41-yd. fumble return (Vinatieri kick)
NE-Faulk 10-yd. run (Vinatieri kick)
NE-Patten 44-yd. pass from Brady (Vinatieri kick)
CLE-Bryant 40-yd. pass from McCown (Heiden pass from McCown)

Passing
NE: Brady 11–20–157 1 TD 1 INT, Davey 3–6–44 0 TD 0 INT
CLE: McCown 20–34–277 2 TD 2 INT, F. Jackson 0–1–0 0 TD 0 INT

Rushing
NE: Dillon 18–100, Faulk 13–87, Cobbs 16–29, Brady 1–10, Pass 1–1, Davey 1-(-2)
CLE: Green 12–15, Echemandu 3–12, McCown 1–11, Northcutt 1–8

Receiving
NE: Patten 3–74, Givens 3–25, Fauria 1–25, Johnson 1–20, Pass 2–19, Graham 1–14, Branch 1–13, Weaver 1–7, Faulk 1–4
CLE: Bryant 7–115, Northcutt 5–93, Echemandu 3–25, Green 3–24, Heiden 2–20

Sunday, December 12
Buffalo Bills 37, Browns 7
Ralph Wilson Stadium (72,330)
White jerseys/white pants

It was hard to imagine things getting any worse for the Browns, but they did amid wintry conditions in Buffalo. Cleveland was held to a mere 26 yards of offense—the worst performance in team history and the fifth-worst in NFL history—and were obliterated by the Bills. Overwhelmed Luke McCown was sacked seven times, and the Browns turned the football over five times as the offense crossed midfield only once in the final three quarters. Jeff Garcia was thrust into the game at QB late in the third quarter to attempt to spark the free-falling offense. But he was knocked out of the game with a knee injury after three plays—never to take another snap with the Browns—and

McCown was thrown back into the nightmare. Reflecting the impotence, the Browns amassed more yards in penalties (40) than total offense. Amazingly, the Browns actually took a 7–3 lead into the second quarter after recovering a Buffalo fumble on a punt return at the Bills' 18 and cashed in for their only points of the game on a short McCown-to-WR Dennis Northcutt scoring toss.

Record: 3–10

	1	2	3	4		
Browns	7	0	0	0	=	7
Bills	3	14	3	17	=	37

BUF-Lindell 23-yd. FG
CLE-Northcutt 3-yd. pass from McCown (Dawson kick)
BUF-Evans 7-yd. pass from Bledsoe (Lindell kick)
BUF-McGahee 13-yd. run (Lindell kick)
BUF-Lindell 21-yd. FG
BUF-McGahee 6-yd. run (Lindell kick)
BUF-Lindell 37-yd. FG
BUF-Williams 4-yd. run (Lindell kick)

Passing
CLE: McCown 8–20–62 1 TD 2 INT, Garcia 1–1–5 0 TD 0 INT
BUF: Bledsoe 12–27–100 1 TD 1 INT, Losman 1–2–10 0 TD 0 INT, Moorman 0–1–0 0 TD 0 INT

Rushing
CLE: Echemandu 5–13, McCown 2–11, Green 11–5
BUF: McGahee 27–105, Evans 1–48, Williams 10–42, Losman 1–10, Smith 1–8, Burns 1–2, Bledsoe 1–0

Receiving
CLE: Bryant 4–37, Heiden 2–19, Northcutt 2–6, Shea 1–5
BUF: Moulds 3–38, Evans 4–33, McGahee 2–12, Trafford 1–10, Williams 1–10, Reed 1–6, Shelton 1–1

Sunday, December 19
San Diego Chargers 21, Browns 0
Cleveland Browns Stadium (72,489)
Brown jerseys/white pants

With snow swirling through the stadium and the wind-chill factor at –10°F, the Browns were stymied by the playoff-bound Chargers, led by former Browns coach Marty Schottenheimer. Attempting only six passes on the day (the fewest ever by a Browns' opponent), San Diego rushed for 174 yards and controlled the line of scrimmage. The Browns hung around for most of the first half, but the tide turned two minutes before intermission when San Diego QB Drew Brees hit TE Antonio Gates for a 72-yard touchdown pass to put the Chargers up 14–0. The lead grew to 21–0 on the first possession of the third quarter on RB LaDainian Tomlinson's second touchdown of the game. The Browns' ground game enjoyed some success as well as Lee Suggs tallied 105 yards.

Record: 3–11

	1	2	3	4		
Chargers	7	7	7	0	=	21
Browns	0	0	0	0	=	0

SD-Tomlinson 1-yd. run (Kaeding kick)
SD-Gates 72-yd. pass from Brees (Kaeding kick)
SD-Tomlinson 1-yd. run (Kaeding kick)

Passing
SD: Brees 4–6–85 1 TD 0 INT
CLE: McCown 11–27–108 0 TD 1 INT, Echemandu 0–1–0 0 TD 0 INT

Rushing
SD: Tomlinson 26–111, Chatman 14–48, Neal 4–16, Brees 6-(-1)
CLE: Suggs 21–105, Green 5–17, McCown 1–4, Northcutt 2–0

Receiving
SD: Gates 1–72, Parker 2–18, Tomlinson 1-(-5)
CLE: Northcutt 4–61, Bryant 3–30, Shea 1–8, F. Jackson 1–6, Heiden 1–5, Suggs 1-(-2)

Sunday, December 26
Miami Dolphins 10, Browns 7
Pro Player Stadium (73,169)
White jerseys/white pants

Before a national-television audience on the night after Christmas, the Browns tied a franchise record with their ninth straight loss, this one in agonizing fashion as they squandered multiple scoring opportunities and eventually lost on a 51-yard field goal by the Dolphins with seven seconds to play. Another team record fell as Lee Suggs carried the football 38 times, setting a new mark, while tallying 143 yards, but only one of his carries was truly remembered—a fumble at the Miami 2 early in the second quarter, one of four Cleveland turnovers for the contest. Midway through the third quarter, Phil Dawson missed a 43-yard field goal that would have given the Browns the lead, and two Cleveland drives inside Miami territory in the fourth quarter proved fruitless. The Browns' lone score came midway through the first quarter on a 58-yard toss from Luke McCown to Dennis Northcutt, who finished the night with 114 receiving yards.

Record: 3–12

	1	2	3	4		
Browns	7	0	0	0	=	7
Dolphins	7	0	0	3	=	10

MIA-Thompson 18-yd. pass from Feeley (Mare kick)
CLE-Northcutt 58-yd. pass from McCown (Dawson kick)
MIA-Mare 51-yd. FG

Passing
CLE: McCown 9–16–161 1 TD 2 INT
MIA: Feeley 25–43–176 1 TD 0 INT, Rosenfels 0–1–0 0 TD 0 INT

Rushing
CLE: Suggs 38–143, McCown 2-(-1)
MIA: Morris 17–69, Minor 6–30, Chambers 1–16, King 1–1

Receiving
CLE: Northcutt 4–114, Heiden 1–27, Bryant 2–15, Suggs 1–4, Heinrich 1–1
MIA: McMichael 9–59, Thompson 2–34, Booker 4–31, Chambers 3–25, Gilmore 1–13, Morris 3–5, Martin 1–5, Minor 2–4

Sunday, January 2
Browns 22, Houston Texans 14
Reliant Stadium (70,724)
White jerseys/white pants

The Browns avoided history and closed the book on a miserable campaign by overpowering Houston to snap their two-and-a-half-month losing streak. Ten-point underdogs, the Browns controlled both sides of the ball, collecting six sacks on defense while Lee Suggs notched his third straight 100-yard rushing game, though after this game would accumulate only 41 more yards in his career. Kelly Holcomb, in his final appearance with the Browns, returned to action to throw for 228 yards, while Phil Dawson kicked five field goals. After the Texans took a 7–3 lead late in the first quarter, the Browns scored the next 19 points to take command, then after Houston scored to cut the margin back to eight with 1:23 left in the fourth, the Browns recovered the ensuing onside kick and melted the final seconds. Interim coach Terry Robiskie received a Gatorade shower as the clock hit zero, and the Browns went into an offseason that promised dramatic change on a winning note.

Record: 4–12

	1	2	3	4		
Browns	3	6	7	6	=	22
Texans	7	0	0	7	=	14

CLE-Dawson 45-yd. FG
HOU-Wells 6-yd. pass from Carr (Brown kick)
CLE-Dawson 22-yd. FG
CLE-Dawson 29-yd. FG
CLE-Heiden 9-yd. pass from Holcomb (Dawson kick)
CLE-Dawson 45-yd. FG
CLE-Dawson 22-yd. FG
HOU-Davis 1-yd. run (Brown kick)

Passing
CLE: Holcomb 20–29–228 1 TD 2 INT
HOU: Carr 15–25–114 1 TD 0 INT, Banks 1–1–16 0 TD 0 INT, Gaffney 0–1–0 0 TD 1 INT

Rushing
CLE: Suggs 26–131, Northcutt 1–4, F. Jackson 1–4, Green 2–0, Holcomb 2-(-2)
HOU: Davis 17–103, Carr 5–28, Wells 2–5

Receiving
CLE: Bryant 7–87, Northcutt 5–85, Suggs 3–23, Heiden 2–20, King 1–8, Shea 2–5
HOU: Davis 5–42, Bradford 2–24, Miller 3–20, Wells 2–14, Johnson 2–13, Gaffney 1–11, Armstrong 1–6

2005

Sunday, September 11
Cincinnati Bengals 27, Browns 13
Cleveland Browns Stadium (73,013)
White jerseys/white pants

Romeo Crennel's first game as head coach saw the Browns hang tough with the eventual division-champion Bengals for most of the first half, then run out of gas in a sound defeat. A 68-yard touchdown pass from new QB Trent Dilfer to WR Frisman Jackson tied the game at 10 five minutes before the half, but the Bengals closed the second quarter and started the third with long touchdown drives to take control of the game. The Browns, meanwhile, allowed more than 400 total yards and saw touchdowns on an interception return and a punt return called back by penalties. Dilfer threw for 278 yards in his Cleveland debut but tossed a pair of interceptions and lost a fumble, while Jackson had the only 100-yard game of his career, catching eight passes for 128 yards.
Record: 0–1

	1	2	3	4		
Bengals	0	17	10	0	=	27
Browns	3	7	0	3	=	13

CLE-Dawson 29-yd. FG
CIN-R. Johnson 1-yd. run (Graham kick)
CIN-Graham 32-yd. FG
CLE-F. Jackson 68-yd. pass from Dilfer (Dawson kick)
CIN-Walter 20-yd. pass from Palmer (Graham kick)
CIN-J. Johnson 18-yd. pass from Palmer (Graham kick)
CIN-Graham 23-yd. FG
CLE-Dawson 34-yd. FG

Passing
CIN: Palmer 26–34–280 2 TD 1 INT
CLE: Dilfer 26–43–278 1 TD 2 INT

Rushing
CIN: R. Johnson 26–126, Perry 5–11, C. Johnson 1–11
CLE: Droughns 12–78, Green 4–12, Dilfer 2–5

Receiving
CIN: C. Johnson 9–91, Houshmandzadeh 5–75, Walter 4–47, Perry 5–37, J. Johnson 1–18, R. Johnson 2–12
CLE: F. Jackson 8–128, Bryant 5–65, Heiden 3–32, Droughns 3–22, Northcutt 4–16, Edwards 2–16, Faine 1-(-1)

Sunday, September 18
Browns 26, Green Bay Packers 24
Lambeau Field (70,400)
White jerseys/white pants

Two long touchdown passes in the second half helped the Browns deliver their first-ever victory at Lambeau Field and give Romeo Crennel his first win as an NFL head coach. The Browns built a 12-point lead late in the third quarter when Trent Dilfer hit rookie WR Braylon Edwards for an 80-yard touchdown pass, but Green Bay cut the margin to 19–17 with less than four minutes left in the game. With the home crowd tasting a come-from-behind victory, the Browns stunned the Packers with a short pass to TE Steve Heiden that turned into a 62-yard touchdown to put them ahead by two scores with 1:50 to play. The Packers added a desperation touchdown with four seconds left, but the Browns recovered the ensuing onside kick to clinch the victory. Dilfer played brilliantly, throwing for 336 yards and three scores, with both Heiden and Edwards topping 100 yards receiving.
Record: 1–1

	1	2	3	4		
Browns	7	6	6	7	=	26
Packers	7	0	0	17	=	24

GB-Driver 42-yd. pass from Favre (Longwell kick)
CLE-Heiden 1-yd. pass from Dilfer (Dawson kick)
CLE-Dawson 21-yd. FG
CLE-Dawson 39-yd. FG
CLE-Edwards 80-yd. pass from Dilfer (kick failed)
GB-Longwell 34-yd. FG
GB-Ferguson 19-yd. pass from Favre (Longwell kick)
CLE-Heiden 62-yd. pass from Dilfer (Dawson kick)
GB-Fisher 4-yd. pass from Favre (Longwell kick)

Passing
CLE: Dilfer 21–32–336 3 TD 0 INT
GB: Favre 32–44–342 3 TD 2 INT

Rushing
CLE: Droughns 20–50, Dilfer 3–5
GB: Green 16–54, Davenport 8–36, Favre 3–19, Chatman 1–8, Fisher 2-(-1)

Receiving
CLE: Edwards 3–107, Heiden 6–104, Northcutt 3–39, Bryant 3–32, Droughns 4–29, Green 1–14, F. Jackson 1–11
GB: Driver 6–105, Chatman 4–71, Ferguson 4–47, Green 5–45, Henderson 5–27, Murphy 3–23, Franks 3–15, Leach 1–5, Fisher 1–4

Sunday, September 25
Indianapolis Colts 13, Browns 6
RCA Dome (57,127)
White jerseys/white pants

The offensive fireworks of the week before fizzled in Indianapolis as the Browns managed just 263 total yards and were unable to score a touchdown in a mistake-riddled performance. For the second time in three weeks, a punt return for a touchdown by WR Dennis Northcutt was erased by a penalty, and a potential touchdown pass to WR Antonio Bryant that could have cut the Colt lead to three points was dropped. Indy then ran out the final 7:40 of the game to move to 3–0 in what would become a 14–2 season.
Record: 1–2

	1	2	3	4		
Browns	0	3	0	3	=	6
Colts	7	3	3	0	=	13

IND-James 2-yd. run (Vanderjagt kick)
CLE-Dawson 40-yd. FG
IND-Vanderjagt 20-yd. FG
IND-Vanderjagt 23-yd. FG
CLE-Dawson 22-yd. FG

Passing
CLE: Dilfer 22–29–208 0 TD 0 INT
IND: Manning 19–23–228 0 TD 1 INT

Rushing
CLE: Droughns 22–76, Green 1-(-1)
IND: James 27–108, Carthon 3–6, Manning 3-(-3)

Receiving
CLE: Bryant 7–75, Edwards 4–43, Droughns 3–32, F. Jackson 2–29, Heiden 2–12, Suggs 2–7, Northcutt 1–7, Green 1–3
IND: Wayne 6–97, Harrison 6–53, James 2–29, Fletcher 2–26, Clark 2–14, Stokley 1–9

Sunday, October 9
Browns 20, Chicago Bears 10
Cleveland Browns Stadium (73,079)
White jerseys/white pants

Despite playing poorly for the most of the game, the Browns put together a timely surge in the final six minutes to pull out a victory over eventual NFC North champ Chicago. Trailing 10–6, Trent Dilfer connected with Antonio Bryant for a 33-yard touchdown pass with 3:02 remaining to put the Browns ahead. Two plays later DB Cris Crocker sacked Chicago QB Kyle Orton, stripped the football, and recovered it at the Bears' 29. A play after that, Dilfer connected with Bryant again for the clinching touchdown. The Browns' defense shook off three straight sub-par performances to hold the Bears to just 266 total yards while collecting four sacks and three turnovers.
Record: 2–2

	1	2	3	4		
Bears	0	3	7	0	=	10
Browns	3	3	0	14	=	20

CLE-Dawson 19-yd. FG
CHI-Gould 44-yd. FG
CLE-Dawson 44-yd. FG
CHI-Edwards 8-yd. pass from Orton (Gould kick)
CLE-Bryant 33-yd. pass from Dilfer (Dawson kick)
CLE-Bryant 28-yd. pass from Dilfer (Dawson kick)

Passing
CHI: Orton 16–26–117 1 TD 0 INT
CLE: Dilfer 23–34–218 2 TD 2 INT

Rushing
CHI: Jones 24–137, Peterson 2–19, Orton 3–14, Benson 5–6
CLE: Droughns 17–72, Smith 1–4, Green 2–1, Dilfer 2-(-1)

Receiving
CHI: Muhammad 6–52, Bradley 4–33, Reid 1–10, Clark 2–9, Edwards 1–8, Jones 2–5
CLE: Bryant 6–83, Shea 6–65, Northcutt 3–23, Droughns 4–21, Heiden 2–11, Smith 1–8, Green 1–7

Sunday, October 16
Baltimore Ravens 16, Browns 3
M&T Bank Stadium (70,196)
White jerseys/white pants

For the second time in three games, the Browns failed to score a touchdown as the offense ran into a brick wall in

Baltimore. Trent Dilfer fumbled on the Browns' first offensive play—the first of three turnovers for him on the afternoon—leading to a Baltimore touchdown as the Ravens built a 16–0 halftime lead. The Cleveland defense held the Ravens in check in the second half, limiting nemesis RB Jamal Lewis to just 59 rushing yards for the game, but the Browns could manage only one scoring threat in the final two quarters, ending in a Phil Dawson field goal. Cleveland compiled only 186 yards of offense and 12 first downs for the game as Dilfer was sacked four times.

Record: 2–3

	1	2	3	4		
Browns	0	0	3	0	=	3
Ravens	10	6	0	0	=	16

BAL-Heap 3-yd. pass from Wright (Stover kick)
BAL-Stover 39-yd. FG
BAL-Stover 27-yd. FG
BAL-Stover 38-yd. FG
CLE-Dawson 24-yd. FG

Passing
CLE: Dilfer 16–30–147 0 TD 1 INT
BAL: Wright 23–31–213 1 TD 1 INT

Rushing
CLE: Droughns 15–55, Green 2–15, Dilfer 1–0
BAL: C. Taylor 8–92, Lewis 24–59, Wright 1-(-1)

Receiving
CLE: Northcutt 4–60, Heiden 4–38, Bryant 4–34, Shea 3–17, Droughns 1-(-2)
BAL: Mason 8–85, Heap 6–79, Hymes 1–19, Lewis 2–11, Clayton 1–9, C. Taylor 4–8, Wilcox 1–2

Sunday, October 23
Detroit Lions 13, Browns 10
Cleveland Browns Stadium (72,923)
White jerseys/white pants

The Cleveland offense was nonexistent once again, and former Browns' QB Jeff Garcia rallied the Lions to a come-from-behind victory. Managing only 174 yards of offense for the game, the Browns scored their only touchdown on a 90-yard kickoff return by rookie WR Josh Cribbs—the first of eight in his Browns career—to give them a 10–7 lead in the second quarter. With Garcia leading Detroit to a pair of second-half field goals, the Lions took a 13–10 lead early in the fourth quarter, then held off the sputtering Browns to capture the victory. While Trent Dilfer was miserable, throwing three interceptions, RB Reuben Droughns had his first big day as a Brown, picking up 100 yards on 19 carries.
Record: 2–4

	1	2	3	4		
Lions	0	7	3	3	=	13
Browns	3	7	0	0	=	10

CLE-Dawson 30-yd. FG
DET-Garcia 1-yd. run (Hanson kick)
CLE-Cribbs 90-yd. kickoff return (Dawson kick)
DET-Hanson 47-yd. FG
DET-Hanson 50-yd. FG

Passing
DET: Garcia 22–34–210 0 TD 0 INT
CLE: Dilfer 10–19–73 0 TD 3 INT

Rushing
DET: Jones 21–74, Pinner 7–24, Bryson 5–20, Garcia 4–1
CLE: Droughns 19–100, Dilfer 1–12, Bryant 1–3, Green 1–3

Receiving
DET: Williams 5–95, Vines 5–34, Bryson 4–24, Pinner 1–22, Schlesinger 2–10, Fitzsimmons 2–10, Jones 2–10, Pollard 1–5
CLE: Edwards 3–30, Bryant 1–15, Droughns 2–9, Shea 1–9, Heiden 2–8, Green 1–2

Sunday, October 30
Houston Texans 19, Browns 16
Reliant Stadium (70,064)
Brown jerseys/white pants

With spotty special-teams play and a second-half collapse, the Browns lost their third straight, this time to the 0–6 Texans. Cleveland built a 13–7 lead in the second quarter, but Houston responded with three straight field goals to take a three-point advantage early in the final period. The Browns tied the game at 16 with five minutes left, but, aided by a long kickoff return, the Texans surged back ahead with another field goal with 2:45 to play. The Browns drove to the Houston 38 with a minute left, but Trent Dilfer was sacked to take them out of field-goal range, and a fourth-down pass fell incomplete. The defeat spoiled nice performances by Antonio Bryant (four catches, 98 yards) and Reuben Droughns (99 yards on 20 carries).
Record: 2–5

	1	2	3	4		
Browns	10	3	0	3	=	16
Texans	7	3	3	6	=	19

HOU-Mathis 34-yd. pass from Carr (Brown kick)
CLE-Shea 8-yd. pass from Dilfer (Dawson kick)
CLE-Dawson 28-yd. FG
CLE-Dawson 29-yd. FG
HOU-Brown 38-yd. FG
HOU-Brown 37-yd. FG
HOU-Brown 35-yd. FG
CLE-Dawson 37-yd. FG
HOU-Brown 40-yd. FG

Passing
CLE: Dilfer 12–25–185 1 TD 0 INT
HOU: Carr 10–20–138 1 TD 1 INT

Rushing
CLE: Droughns 20–99, Green 10–48, Dilfer 3–9
HOU: Davis 28–91, Carr 8–16, Gaffney 1–10

Receiving
CLE: Bryant 4–98, Heiden 4–43, Edwards 2–32, Shea 1–8, Green 1–4
HOU: Gaffney 5–64, Mathis 1–34, Williams 2–25, Bradford 1–8, Armstrong 1–7

Sunday, November 6
Browns 20, Tennessee Titans 14
Cleveland Browns Stadium (72,594)
Brown jerseys/white pants

Battling through wind gusts of up to 50 mph, the Browns took control of the game in the third quarter and then held off the Titans in the fourth to snap their three-game losing streak. The Browns took an early lead on a long touchdown catch by Dennis Northcutt, then built a 10-point advantage after RB Jason Wright scored their first rushing touchdown in 12 games midway through the third period. A Tennessee touchdown with seven minutes remaining pulled the Titans within six, then a potential game-clinching 39-yard field goal by Phil Dawson hooked in the strong winds to give the Titans new life with 39 seconds remaining. Tennessee drove to the Cleveland 28, where on the final play QB Steve McNair was intercepted by Browns' DB Brodney Pool at the Cleveland 2 to wrap up the win. Cleveland rolled up a season-high 441 total yards as Reuben Droughns tallied 116 on the ground and 73 receiving.
Record: 3–5

	1	2	3	4		
Titans	0	7	0	7	=	14
Browns	7	0	10	3	=	20

CLE-Northcutt 58-yd. pass from Dilfer (Dawson kick)
TEN-Kinney 24-yd. pass from McNair (Bironas kick)
CLE-Dawson 37-yd. FG
CLE-Wright 6-yd. run (Dawson kick)
CLE-Dawson 19-yd. FG
TEN-Brown 15-yd. run (Bironas kick)

Passing
TEN: McNair 18–41–235 1 TD 1 INT, Hentrich 0–1–0 0 TD 0 INT
CLE: Dilfer 18–34–272 1 TD 1 INT

Rushing
TEN: Brown 22–95, McNair 1–2, Payton 1–1
CLE: Droughns 20–116, Northcutt 1–31, Wright 8–19, Dilfer 2–3, Smith 1–0

Receiving
TEN: Kinney 5–74, Williams 5–61, Scaife 5–59, Roby 1–29, Brown 1–8, Fleming 1–4
CLE: Northcutt 3–80, Bryant 3–79, Droughns 4–73, Wright 3–15, Heiden 2–15, Smith 2–8, Edwards 1–2

Sunday, November 13
Pittsburgh Steelers 34, Browns 21
Heinz Field (63,491)
White jerseys/white pants

After a quick start that saw the Browns take the lead on their opening possession, they were overwhelmed by the eventual Super Bowl champs in a nationally televised Sunday-night game. The Browns drove 66 yards on their first possession and went ahead 7–0 on a Reuben Droughns touchdown run, but the Steelers scored the next 27 points to take a comfortable lead into the fourth quarter. The Browns added a pair of touchdowns in the final period, the first when DE Orpheus Roye blocked a Pittsburgh field goal, and DB Leigh Bodden returned it 59 yards for a score. With second-year QB Ben Roethlisberger out with an injury, Pittsburgh controlled the game on the ground, rushing for 159 yards and three touchdowns.
Record: 3–6

	1	2	3	4		
Browns	7	0	0	14	=	21
Steelers	0	17	7	10	=	34

CLE-Droughns 5-yd. run (Dawson kick)
PIT-Bettis 1-yd. run (Reed kick)
PIT-Reed 42-yd. FG
PIT-Batch 1-yd. run (Reed kick)
PIT-Ward 51-yd. pass from Randle El (Reed kick)
PIT-Reed 33-yd. FG
CLE-Bodden 59-yd. return of blocked field goal (Dawson kick)
PIT-Haynes 10-yd. run (Reed kick)
CLE-Bryant 9-yd. pass from Dilfer (Dawson kick)

Passing
CLE: Dilfer 17–34–253 1 TD 1 INT
PIT: Batch 13–19–150 0 TD 0 INT, Randle El 1–1–51 1 TD 0 INT, Maddox 4–7–22 0 TD 0 INT

Rushing
CLE: Droughns 17–56, Dilfer 1–5, Smith 1–0
PIT: Staley 17–64, Haynes 9–41, Bettis 9–28, Batch 3–16, Randle El 2–10, Maddox 1–0

Receiving
CLE: Bryant 5–82, Droughns 4–67, Edwards 2–64, Northcutt 4–31, Smith 1–9, Heiden 1–0
PIT: Ward 8–124, Wilson 3–48, Randle El 2–19, Staley 2–16, Haynes 2–10, Kranchick 1–6

Sunday, November 20
Browns 22, Miami Dolphins 0
Cleveland Browns Stadium (72,773)
Brown jerseys/white pants

In their finest overall performance of the season, the Browns dominated Miami—coached by former Cleveland defensive coordinator Nick Saban—and posted their first shutout in four years. The tone was set on the Browns' first offensive play when Reuben Droughns exploded for a 75-yard touchdown run—the opening salvo in a 166-yard performance, what proved to be his finest showing as a Brown. The Cleveland defense took it from there, limiting Miami to less than 200 total yards, including just 55 through the air as the Dolphins completed just nine of 28 passes. Cleveland rookie QB Charlie Frye made his NFL debut in the second quarter and wound up completing six passes while also throwing an interception. The victory enabled the Browns to match their win total from the year before.
Record: 4–6

	1	2	3	4		
Dolphins	0	0	0	0	=	0
Browns	9	3	10	0	=	22

CLE-Droughns 75-yd. run (kick failed)
CLE-Dawson 23-yd. FG
CLE-Dawson 40-yd. FG
CLE-Smith 6-yd. pass from Dilfer (Dawson kick)
CLE-Dawson 24-yd. FG

Passing
MIA: Frerotte 4–18–53, Rosenfels 5–10–14 0 TD 2 INT
CLE: Dilfer 11–18–137 1 TD 0 INT, Frye 6–11–58 0 TD 1 INT

Rushing
MIA: Williams 13–83, Brown 12–56
CLE: Droughns 30–166, Wright 3–8, Dilfer 4–3, Northcutt 1–2, Smith 1–2

Receiving
MIA: Gilmore 1–39, Chambers 3–12, Welker 2–12, Diamond 1–7, Brown 1–2, Morris 1-(-5)
CLE: Edwards 6–90, Bryant 4–60, Heiden 4–31, Smith 1–6, Northcutt 1–5, Droughns 1–3

Sunday, November 27
Minnesota Vikings 24, Browns 12
Hubert H. Humphrey Metrodome (63,814)
White jerseys/white pants

Crippled by five turnovers and five sacks, the Browns were dominated by the Vikings in the teams' first meeting in 10 years. Minnesota WR Marcus Robinson caught three touchdown passes as the Vikings built a 24–6 lead, with all three touchdowns coming off of Cleveland turnovers. Reuben Droughns continued his stretch of effective performances, rushing for 73 yards and catching five passes for 46 more.
Record: 4–7

	1	2	3	4		
Browns	0	3	3	6	=	12
Vikings	3	7	7	7	=	24

MIN-Edinger 43-yd. FG
MIN-M. Robinson 15-yd. pass from Johnson (Edinger kick)
CLE-Dawson 32-yd. FG
MIN-M. Robinson 15-yd. pass from Johnson (Edinger kick)
CLE-Dawson 38-yd. FG
MIN-M. Robinson 2-yd. pass from Johnson (Edinger kick)
CLE-Northcutt 9-yd. pass from Dilfer (kick failed)

Passing
CLE: Dilfer 23–35–214 1 TD 2 INT, Frye 0–1–0 0 TD 1 INT
MIN: Johnson 19–28–207 3 TD 1 INT

Rushing
CLE: Droughns 19–73, Dilfer 1–5
MIN: Moore 21–67, Fason 3–14, Taylor 1–5, Johnson 3-(-2), Bennett 3-(-3)

Receiving
CLE: Heiden 5–55, Droughns 5–46, Edwards 4–42, F. Jackson 5–38, Northcutt 2–17, Bryant 2–16
MIN: Taylor 5–70, Wigins 5–67, M. Robinson 3–32, K. Robinson 4–29, Moore 2–9

Sunday, December 4
Jacksonville Jaguars 20, Browns 14
Cleveland Browns Stadium (70,941)
Brown jerseys/white pants

After surging to a 14–3 halftime lead over the playoff-bound Jaguars behind a pair of touchdown passes by Charlie Frye, making his first pro start, the Browns were dominated in the second half as Jacksonville took control of the game and coasted to victory. Frye was on fire early and hit Braylon Edwards twice in the second quarter for scores, but Edwards injured his knee in the fourth quarter and would miss the final four games of what had become a promising rookie season. Plagued by 97 yards in penalties and five sacks allowed, the Browns only threatened to score once in the second half as they compiled just 39 total yards in the final two quarters. Reuben Droughns rushed for 88 yards and became the first Cleveland RB to top the 1,000-yard mark for the season in 20 years.
Record: 4–8

	1	2	3	4		
Jaguars	3	0	17	0	=	20
Browns	0	14	0	0	=	14

JAX-Scobee 24-yd. FG
CLE-Edwards 34-yd. pass from Frye (Dawson kick)
CLE-Edwards 17-yd. pass from Frye (Dawson kick)
JAX-Scobee 29-yd. FG
JAX-Wrighster 9-yd. pass from Garrard (Scobee kick)
JAX-Smith 12-yd. pass from Garrard (Scobee kick)

Passing
JAX: Garrard 11–20–116 2 TD 1 INT
CLE: Frye 13–20–226 2 TD 0 INT

Rushing
JAX: Jones 27–103, Garrard 9–13, Jones 1–3, Pearman 1–3
CLE: Droughns 30–88, Frye 2–10

Receiving
JAX: Smith 3–49, Wilford 3–36, Brady 1–17, Wrighster 2–9, Jones 1–9, Pearman 1-(-4)
CLE: Edwards 5–86, Bryant 3–63, Northcutt 1–45, F. Jackson 2–15, Shea 1–13, Heiden 1–4

Sunday, December 11
Cincinnati Bengals 23, Browns 20
Paul Brown Stadium (65,788)
White jerseys/white pants

On a blustery day in Cincinnati, the Browns gave the 9–3 Bengals a scare before losing on a field goal on the last play of the game. Two early touchdowns helped the Browns build a one-point halftime lead, then after Cincinnati surged ahead late in the third quarter, Cleveland rebounded to tie the game at 20 on a field goal with 4:19 left. A pair of penalties on Browns' DB Leigh Bodden helped the Bengals convert on two critical third downs and set up the game-winning 37-yard field goal as time expired. The Cleveland offense could manage only 208 total yards, while the defense limited the explosive Cincinnati passing game to just 93 yards. But Bengals' RB Rudi Johnson was dominant, picking up a season-high 169 yards.
Record: 4–9

	1	2	3	4		
Browns	7	7	3	3	=	20
Bengals	7	6	7	3	=	23

CLE-Frye 3-yd. run (Dawson kick)
CIN-R. Johnson 8-yd. run (Graham kick)
CLE-Heiden 2-yd. pass from Frye (Dawson kick)
CIN-Graham 21-yd. FG
CIN-Graham 27-yd. FG
CLE-Dawson 41-yd. FG
CIN-Houshmandzadeh 4-yd. pass from Palmer (Graham kick)
CLE-Dawson 29-yd. FG
CIN-Graham 37-yd. FG

Passing
CLE: Frye 16–24–138 1 TD 1 INT
CIN: Palmer 13–27–93 1 TD 1 INT

Rushing
CLE: Droughns 21–74, Frye 4–14, Suggs 1-(-4)
CIN: R. Johnson 30–169, Perry 3–15, Palmer 1–1

Receiving
CLE: Bryant 4–48, Northcutt 3–29, Heiden 3–27, Shea 1–14, Suggs 2–13, Droughns 1–4, Smith 2–3
CIN: Houshmandzadeh 6–53, C. Johnson 2–22, R. Johnson 3–11, Kelly 2–7

Sunday, December 18
Browns 9, Oakland Raiders 7
McAfee Coliseum (41,862)
White jerseys/white pants

On a wet, windy day in Oakland, the Browns pulled out a last-second victory to snap their three-game losing streak and deliver Charlie Frye's first victory as a starting QB. The Raiders were poised to extend their 7–6 lead with just over three minutes left, but Browns' DE Alvin McKinley blocked a 46-yard field-goal attempt to keep Cleveland within a point. The Browns then drove to the Oakland 19 in the final minute and dodged a bullet when a Reuben Droughns fumble recovered by the Raiders was overturned on a replay review because it was determined his knee was down before he lost the ball. A play later, Phil Dawson booted a 37-yard field goal as time expired to give the Browns their fifth win, surpassing their victory total of the previous season.
Record: 5–9

	1	2	3	4		
Browns	0	3	3	3	=	9
Raiders	0	7	0	0	=	7

OAK-Moss 28-yd. pass from Collins (Janikowski kick)
CLE-Dawson 44-yd. FG
CLE-Dawson 24-yd. FG
CLE-Dawson 37-yd. FG

Passing
CLE: Frye 21–32–198 0 TD 1 INT
OAK: Collins 14–30–132 1 TD 1 INT

Rushing
CLE: Droughns 18–53, Frye 7–11, Suggs 1–6
OAK: Jordan 25–132, Crockett 4–10, Collins 2–1

Receiving
CLE: Bryant 5–86, Droughns 5–31, Northcutt 2–25, F. Jackson 2–21, Smith 3–16, Heiden 2–8, Cribbs 1–7, Suggs 1–4
OAK: Jordan 5–40, Porter 6–31, Moss 1–28, Williams 1–24, Gabriel 1–9

Saturday, December 24
Pittsburgh Steelers 41, Browns 0
Cleveland Browns Stadium (73,136)
Brown jerseys/white pants

On Christmas Eve, the Browns were utterly dominated by Pittsburgh on their own home field and suffered one of the most lopsided losses in team history. Pittsburgh outgained the Browns 196 yards to one in the first quarter as the Browns went three-and-out on their first five possessions, and the Steelers built a 20–0 halftime lead. The Steelers rolled up 457 total yards for the game—with more than 200 coming on the ground—and held the Browns to just 186 total as Charlie Frye was sacked eight times. Adding insult to injury, Pittsburgh's final touchdown was scored by former Browns' WR Quincy Morgan, as the Steelers picked up their fifth straight victory in Cleveland.
Record: 5–10

	1	2	3	4		
Steelers	14	6	14	7	=	41
Browns	0	0	0	0	=	0

PIT-Bettis 2-yd. run (Reed kick)
PIT-Ward 7-yd. pass from Roethlisberger (Reed kick)
PIT-Reed 26-yd. FG
PIT-Reed 31-yd. FG
PIT-Parker 80-yd. run (Reed kick)
PIT-Haynes 15-yd. run (Reed kick)
PIT-Morgan 31-yd. pass from Batch (Reed kick)

Passing
PIT: Roethlisberger 13–20–226 1 TD 0 INT, Batch 1–1–31 1 TD 0 INT
CLE: Frye 20–39–183 0 TD 0 INT

Rushing
PIT: Parker 17–130, Haynes 10–57, Bettis 7–24, Randle El 1-(-2)
CLE: Droughns 10–36, Frye 3–17, Suggs 4–7, Smith 2–3

Receiving
PIT: Ward 7–105, Wilson 2–63, Morgan 1–31, Miller 1–21, Randle El 1–20, Haynes 1–13, Kreider 1–4
CLE: Bryant 4–50, F. Jackson 3–41, Droughns 1–29, Shea 5–27, Northcutt 5–23, Heiden 2–13

Sunday, January 1
Browns 20, Baltimore Ravens 16
Cleveland Browns Stadium (69,871)
Brown jerseys/white pants

Trailing 13–0 midway through the second quarter, the Browns rallied behind their special teams to take control in the second half and hold off the Ravens for a satisfying victory in the season finale. A pair of field goals cut the Baltimore lead to seven points at the half, then the struggling Browns' offense scored its first touchdown in 12 quarters following a long kickoff return by Josh Cribbs to pull within three points. After forcing a Baltimore punt three plays later, Dennis Northcutt returned the kick 62 yards for a touchdown to provide the winning points with six minutes left in the third quarter. The Cleveland defense took it from there, and the Ravens didn't threaten to score again. An interception by Browns' DB Brian Russell clinched the victory with just over a minute to play, capping a solid performance by the Cleveland defense, which didn't allow a touchdown. Conversely, Antonio Bryant had his finest game of the season with 123 receiving yards and went over the 1,000-yard mark for the first time in his career. Meanwhile, though Reuben Droughns struggled in the finale, he finished the season with 1,232 yards, the most by any Browns' RB in 25 years.
Record: 6–10

	1	2	3	4		
Ravens	0	13	3	0	=	16
Browns	0	6	14	0	=	20

BAL-Stover 21-yd. FG
BAL-Stover 43-yd. FG
BAL-Thomas 9-yd. fumble return (Stover kick)
CLE-Dawson 21-yd. FG
CLE-Dawson 39-yd. FG
BAL-Stover 31-yd. FG
CLE-Bryant 6-yd. pass from Frye (Dawson kick)
CLE-Northcutt 62-yd. punt return (Dawson kick)

Passing
BAL: Boller 15–36–151 0 TD 2 INT
CLE: Frye 22–37–199 1 TD 1 INT

Rushing
BAL: Lewis 20–89, C. Taylor 8–36, Boller 2–4, Sanders 1–0, Zastudil 1–0
CLE: Droughns 19–40, Frye 2–8, Suggs 2–6

Receiving
BAL: Mason 3–73, Lewis 3–29, Heap 2–22, C. Taylor 4–16, Clayton 3–11
CLE: Bryant 9–123, Northcutt 6–41, Irons 2–16, Smith 2–8, Droughns 1–5, F. Jackson 1–4, Suggs 1–2

2006

Sunday, September 10
New Orleans Saints 19, Browns 14
Cleveland Browns Stadium (72,915)
White jerseys/white pants

The tone for a frustrating season was set on the Browns' first play of the opener, when a 74-yard touchdown pass from QB Charlie Frye to WR Braylon Edwards was wiped out by a holding penalty. The Browns' offense struggled from that point on and fell to an improved Saints team that wound up reaching the NFC Championship. After missing nearly two full seasons to injury, TE Kellen Winslow Jr. caught his first pro touchdown pass to pull the Browns within two points midway through the third quarter. After QB Drew Brees tossed his first scoring pass as a member of the Saints, the Browns rebounded again to make it 16–14 five minutes into the fourth quarter, then the Saints responded with a field goal. The Browns drove into New Orleans territory with less than two minutes to play, then a Frye pass bounced off the hands of Edwards and was intercepted to clinch the Saints' triumph. In a preview of things to come, Cleveland was held to a meager 186 total yards, and Frye was sacked five times. The game also marked the Browns' first helmet-design change in three decades as they reintroduced the gray facemasks the team had originally worn through 1974.

Record: 0–1

	1	2	3	4		
Saints	3	6	7	3	=	19
Browns	0	0	7	7	=	14

NO-Carney 43-yd. FG
NO-Carney 25-yd. FG
NO-Carney 21-yd. FG
CLE-Winslow 18-yd. pass from Frye (Dawson kick)
NO-Colston 12-yd. pass from Brees (Carney kick)
CLE-Frye 1-yd. run (Dawson kick)
NO-Carney 20-yd. FG

Passing
NO: Brees 16–30–170 1 TD 1 INT
CLE: Frye 16–27–132 1 TD 2 INT

Rushing
NO: McAllister 22–90, Bush 15–67, Karney 1–1, Brees 3-(-2)
CLE: Frye 6–44, Droughns 11–27, Harrison 2–14, Vickers 2–0, Smith 1–0

Receiving
NO: Bush 7–52, Colston 4–49, Henderson 3–44, Horn 2–25
CLE: Winslow 8–63, Northcutt 4–37, Edwards 2–23, Heiden 1–7, Smith 1–2

Sunday, September 17
Cincinnati Bengals 34, Browns 17
Paul Brown Stadium (66,072)
Brown jerseys/white pants

While the offense showed signs of improvement, the Cleveland defense was bombed for nearly 500 total yards as the Bengals rolled to an easy victory. Cincinnati QB Carson Palmer threw for 352 yards while RB Rudi Johnson ran for 145 and a pair of scores in the fourth quarter as the Bengals picked up 27 first downs and ran 76 plays to Cleveland's 53. The Browns topped 300 yards, paced by Braylon Edwards's 110 receiving, but Charlie Frye was sacked four times as the Browns lost to the Bengals for the fourth straight time.

Record: 0–2

	1	2	3	4		
Browns	3	0	0	14	=	17
Bengals	14	3	0	17	=	34

CIN-Washington 22-yd. pass from Palmer (Graham kick)
CLE-Dawson 30-yd. FG
CIN-C. Johnson 8-yd. pass from Palmer (Graham kick)
CIN-Graham 37-yd. FG
CIN-Graham 37-yd. FG
CLE-Droughns 1-yd. run (Dawson kick)
CIN-R. Johnson 1-yd. run (Graham kick)
CIN-R. Johnson 9-yd. (Graham kick)
CLE-Frye 2-yd. run (Dawson kick)

Passing
CLE: Frye 20–33–244 0 TD 2 INT
CIN: Palmer 24–40–352 2 TD 2 INT

Rushing
CLE: Droughns 14–32, Northcutt 1–16, Frye 4–10, Wright 1-(-1)
CIN: R. Johnson 26–145, Watson 1–10, Perry 2–4, Palmer 3–1

Receiving
CLE: Edwards 4–110, Winslow 4–42, Droughns 3–30, Northcutt 3–18, Harrison 2–17, Heiden 2–13, Cribbs 1–11, Smith 1–3
CIN: Henry 5–113, C. Johnson 6–78, Washington 5–77, Perry 3–37, Kelly 2–35, Stewart 1–9, R. Johnson 2–3

Sunday, September 24
Baltimore Ravens 15, Browns 14
Cleveland Browns Stadium (72,474)
Brown jerseys/white pants

Thanks to a series of critical mistakes, the Browns squandered an 11-point second-half lead and lost on a last-minute field goal to drop to 0–3 for the first time in seven years. The Browns soared to a 14–3 halftime lead, and after Baltimore pulled within 14–12 in the fourth quarter, the Browns were poised to land the knockout punch when they drove to the Baltimore 4 with just over three minutes to play. But Charlie Frye was hit as he attempted a second-down pass and was intercepted in the end zone, giving the Ravens new life. They drove to the Cleveland 33, then former Brown Matt Stover kicked a 52-yard field goal with 20 seconds left to hand the Browns a heart-wrenching defeat. While Frye played well, throwing for 298 yards—including 116 to Braylon Edwards and 92 to Kellen Winslow Jr.—he was sacked seven times as the Browns failed to score in the second half.
Record: 0–3

	1	2	3	4		
Ravens	3	0	0	12	=	15
Browns	0	14	0	0	=	14

BAL-Stover 32-yd. FG
CLE-Edwards 58-yd. pass from Frye (Dawson kick)
CLE-Frye 1-yd. run (Dawson kick)
BAL-Heap 3-yd. pass from McNair (pass failed)
BAL-Stover 43-yd. FG
BAL-Stover 52-yd. FG

Passing
BAL: McNair 23–41–264 1 TD 0 INT
CLE: Frye 21–33–298 1 TD 1 INT

Rushing
BAL: Lewis 21–86, Smith 3–8, McNair 2-(-2), Clayton 1-(-6)
CLE: Wright 15–31, Frye 2–6, Harrison 2–1

Receiving
BAL: Mason 7–132, Clayton 8–74, Heap 5–36, Smith 2–12, Wilcox 1–10
CLE: Edwards 5–116, Winslow 7–92, Northcutt 3–32, Vickers 1–29, Heiden 2–18, Cribbs 1–6, Wright 1–3, Harrison 1–2

Sunday, October 1
Browns 24, Oakland Raiders 21
McAfee Coliseum (61,426)
White jerseys/white pants

Apparently on their way to a fourth straight loss to open the season, the Browns rallied from a 21–3 second-quarter deficit to stun the Raiders on their home field for the second time in 10 months. Down by 18 points with four minutes left in the first half, a 53-yard kickoff return by WR Josh Cribbs helped spark a quick scoring drive to halt Oakland's momentum, then a 22-yard fourth-down pass to Kellen Winslow in the third quarter set up a Winslow touchdown catch a play later to cut the margin to 21–17. Five minutes later, Dennis Northcutt returned a punt 58 yards to propel the Browns to the go-ahead touchdown reception by WR Joe Jurevicius. The Browns' defense took it from there, halting Oakland on a fourth-and-one play at the Cleveland 30 early in the fourth quarter. After Frye was picked off the end zone with less than four minutes showing for the second straight week, the Browns forced the Raiders into a three-and-out. Frye and Co. then ran out the final three minutes to secure their first win of the season and cap the second-largest comeback in team history.
Record: 1–3

	1	2	3	4		
Browns	0	10	14	0	=	24
Raiders	7	14	0	0	=	21

OAK-Williams 30-yd. fumble return (Janikowski kick)
OAK-Moss 5-yd. pass from Walter (Janikowski kick)
CLE-Dawson 28-yd. FG
OAK-Jordan 59-yd. run (Janikowski kick)
CLE-Dinkins 3-yd. pass from Frye (Dawson kick)
CLE-Winslow 2-yd. pass from Frye (Dawson kick)
CLE-Jurevicius 5-yd. pass from Frye (Dawson kick)

Passing
CLE: Frye 22–32–192 3 TD 2 INT
OAK: Walter 9–23–68 1 TD 1 INT, Curry 0–1–0 0 TD 0 INT

Rushing
CLE: Droughns 25–100, Wright 2–9, Harrison 3-(-3), Frye 5-(-2)
OAK: Jordan 20–128, Fargas 3–54, Walter 1–12

Receiving
CLE: Edwards 6–75, Winslow 3–31, Droughns 2–24, Jurevicius 3–22, Harrison 1–12, Northcutt 2–10, Smith 3–9, Heiden 1–6, Dinkins 1–3
OAK: Curry 3–27, Jordan 2–13, Anderson 1–8, Williams 1–8, Whitted 1–7, Moss 1–5

Sunday, October 8
Carolina Panthers 20, Browns 12
Bank of America Stadium (73,520)
Brown jerseys/white pants

A good start quickly evaporated as the Browns wasted a sterling defensive effort and were unable to score a touchdown in an ugly loss in Charlotte. After kicking a field goal on their first possession and stuffing Carolina on its first two, a pass went off Dennis Northcutt's hands and into the arms of Carolina DB Richard Marshall, who returned it 30 yards for a touchdown to give the Panthers a lead they would not relinquish. Stuffing the Cleveland offense for the remainder of the game, Carolina built a 17–3 lead and then held off the self-destructive Browns in the second half. The Browns' offense managed just 248 total yards, while coughing up three turnovers and being flagged five times for offensive holding. It spoiled an admirable performance by the defense, which limited Carolina to less than 300 total yards and prevented the Panthers from converting a first down on 11 third-down opportunities.
Record: 1–4

	1	2	3	4		
Browns	3	0	3	6	=	12
Panthers	7	7	3	3	=	20

CLE-Dawson 41-yd. FG
CAR-Marshall 30-yd. interception return (Kasay kick)
CAR-Johnson 17-yd. pass from Delhomme (Kasay kick)
CAR-Kasay 24-yd. FG
CLE-Dawson 47-yd. FG
CLE-Dawson 22-yd. FG
CAR-Kasay 19-yd. FG
CLE-Dawson 32-yd. FG

Passing
CLE: Frye 26–43–173 0 TD 2 INT
CAR: Delhomme 20–29–170 1 TD 0 INT

Rushing
CLE: Droughns 18–65, Harrison 3–14, Frye 2–12
CAR: Foster 24–106, Smith 1–7, Williams 1–4, Goings 1–3, Delhomme 1-(-1)

Receiving
CLE: Winslow 8–55, Jurevicius 3–28, Edwards 3–27, Heiden 2–21, Cribbs 2–18, Northcutt 1–11, Harrison 4–10, Droughns 3–3
CAR: Johnson 5–67, Smith 6–62, Mangum 5–21, Foster 3–12, Gaines 1–8

Sunday, October 22
Denver Broncos 17, Browns 7
Cleveland Browns Stadium (73,024)
Brown jerseys/white pants

On an overcast afternoon, the struggling Cleveland offense put forth another miserable performance as the 4–1 Broncos built a 17–0 lead and never looked back, defeating the Browns for the seventh straight time. Cleveland was held to a season-low 165 total yards—less than half Denver's total—and managed only 10 first downs as Charlie Frye was sacked five times. The Browns were held scoreless until a fourth-quarter interception by LB Andra Davis set up a Joe Jurevicius touchdown catch four minutes into the fourth quarter. The Browns drove into Denver territory on their next possession but were unable to convert on a fourth-down pass with eight minutes to play, ending their final chance to claw back into the game.
Record: 1–5

	1	2	3	4		
Broncos	0	10	7	0	=	17
Browns	0	0	0	7	=	7

DEN-Elam 32-yd. FG
DEN-Bell 9-yd. run (Elam kick)
DEN-Marshall 9-yd. pass from Plummer (Elam kick)
CLE-Jurevicius 6-yd. pass from Frye (Dawson kick)

Passing
DEN: Plummer 20–41–209 1 TD 2 INT
CLE: Frye 19–33–149 1 TD 1 INT

Rushing
DEN: T. Bell 24–115, M. Bell 10–25, Plummer 3–10
CLE: Droughns 12–33, Frye 1–1

Receiving
DEN: Walker 9–107, Smith 6–69, Marshall 2–22, T. Bell 3–11
CLE: Jurevicius 4–40, Winslow 3–34, Cribbs 4–32, Droughns 4–27, Heiden 2–10, Edwards 2–6

Sunday, October 29
Browns 20, New York Jets 13
Cleveland Browns Stadium (72,507)
Brown jerseys/white pants

Following a tumultuous week that saw the resignation of embattled offensive coordinator Maurice Carthon, the Browns picked up an impressive victory, building a 20–3 lead in the falling October darkness and then holding off the playoff-bound Jets. With RB Reuben Droughns rushing for a season-high 125 yards, the Browns took control in the third quarter, then survived a kickoff return for a touchdown by New York to secure the victory following a questionable decision by the officials with a minute to play. Jets' TE Chris Barker caught a fourth-down pass from the Cleveland 24 in the end zone but was knocked out of bounds before he could get his feet down. The officials opted not to give Barker credit for the catch, which by the rule at the time they could have if they decided he would have gotten his feet down in bounds before getting knocked out of bounds. Thus, the Browns were able to run out the clock and pick up their second victory, thanks to a defense that permitted just 193 total yards and limited the Jets to only 11 pass completions in 28 attempts. Cleveland DB Sean Jones picked off a pair of passes, earning him AFC Defensive Player of the Week honors.
Record: 2–5

	1	2	3	4		
Jets	3	0	7	3	=	13
Browns	3	7	10	0	=	20

NYJ-Nugent 27-yd. FG
CLE-Dawson 47-yd. FG
CLE-Droughns 2-yd. run (Dawson kick)
CLE-Winslow 30-yd. pass from Frye (Dawson kick)
CLE-Dawson 21-yd. FG
NYJ-Miller 99-yd. kickoff return (Nugent kick)
NYJ-Nugent 47-yd. FG

Passing
NYJ: Pennington 11–28–108 0 TD 2 INT
CLE: Frye 15–22–141 1 TD 1 INT

Rushing
NYJ: Washington 15–51, Barlow 5–16, Pennington 3–9, Cotchery 1–8, Smith 3–4
CLE: Droughns 33–125, Frye 5–19, Smith 1–3

Receiving
NYJ: Cotchery 5–43, Coles 4–40, Baker 1–17, Barlow 1–8
CLE: Winslow 7–76, Heiden 3–23, Edwards 2–21, Cribbs 1–14, Droughns 2–7

Sunday, November 5
San Diego Chargers 32, Browns 25
Qualcomm Stadium (65,558)
White jerseys/white pants

Despite not scoring a touchdown until the final moments, the Browns went toe-to-toe with a San Diego team led by former Browns' coach Marty Schottenheimer that would post a 14–2 record. But a marvelous fourth-quarter performance by one of the league's best players propelled the Chargers to victory. The Browns held a 12–10 lead late in the third quarter when San Diego RB LaDainian Tomlinson exploded for a 41-yard touchdown to give the Chargers a lead they would not relinquish. The Browns stayed close with field goals on their next two possessions but Tomlinson was unstoppable, rushing for 84 yards and two more touchdowns in the fourth quarter and 172 yards for the day. After Phil Dawson kicked a team-record six field goals, the Browns finally reached the end zone with a minute left, but it was too little, too late. While the offense struggled inside the Chargers' 20, it was effective overall, aided by a career-high 11 catches by Kellen Winslow Jr. and an 81-yard punt return by Dennis Northcutt at the end of the first quarter, which set up the Browns' first points. Aided by 113 yards in San Diego penalties, the Browns handed the Chargers what amounted to the winning points when Charlie Frye was sacked and fumbled into the end zone, where it was recovered for a touchdown six minutes before the half.
Record: 2–6

	1	2	3	4		
Browns	3	9	0	13	=	25
Chargers	3	7	7	15	=	32

SD-Kaeding 29-yd. FG
CLE-Dawson 37-yd. FG
CLE-Dawson 20-yd. FG
SD-Harris recovered fumble in end zone (Kaeding kick)
CLE-Dawson 42-yd. FG
CLE-Dawson 30-yd. FG
SD-Tomlinson 41-yd. run (Kaeding kick)
CLE-Dawson 36-yd. FG
SD-Tomlinson 7-yd. run (Kaeding kick)
CLE-Dawson 35-yd. FG
SD-Tomlinson 8-yd. run (Jackson pass from Rivers)
CLE-Edwards 4-yd. pass from Frye (Dawson kick)

Passing
CLE: Frye 26–44–241 1 TD 1 INT
SD: Rivers 19–28–211 0 TD 0 INT

Rushing
CLE: Droughns 19–36, Frye 5–27, Harrison 2–13, Edwards 1–8
SD: Tomlinson 18–172, Turner 2–21, Rivers 3-(-3)

Receiving
CLE: Winslow 11–78, Jurevicius 3–76, Edwards 7–66, Heiden 2–14, Northcutt 1–7, Droughns 1–0, Smith 1–0
SD: Parker 5–65, McCardell 5–64, Gates 2–22, Neal 1–21, Tomlinson 3–20, Jackson 1–11, Floyd 2–8

Sunday, November 12
Browns 17, Atlanta Falcons 13
Georgia Dome (70,793)
White jerseys/white pants

The Browns built an early two-touchdown lead and then held off the 5–3 Falcons to deliver Romeo Crennel's first road victory over a team with a winning record. After surging to a 14–0 advantage early in the second quarter, the Browns watched the Falcons creep within a single point midway through the final period. Then a dazzling 36-yard reception by Kellen Winslow Jr. set up an insurance field goal with 5:35 remaining to make it 17–13, but the Browns still weren't out of the woods. Atlanta drove to the Cleveland 17 with less than three minutes to play, then after an offensive holding penalty, QB Michael Vick fumbled, and Browns' DB Jereme Perry recovered. Cleveland ran out all but the final 17 seconds and then stopped a desperation play as time expired to clinch their third victory. The Cleveland offense struggled, picking up a mere nine first downs and just 236 total yards as Charlie Frye was sacked five times. But the defense rose to the occasion, forcing three turnovers and limiting Atlanta to just 16 pass completions in 41 attempts.

Record: 3–6

	1	2	3	4		
Browns	7	7	0	3	=	17
Falcons	0	3	7	3	=	13

CLE-Droughns 1-yd. run (Dawson kick)
CLE-Edwards 19-yd. pass from Frye (Dawson kick)
ATL-Andersen 44-yd. FG
ATL-Jenkins 12-yd. pass from Vick (Andersen kick)
ATL-Andersen 41-yd. FG
CLE-Dawson 43-yd. FG

Passing
CLE: Frye 16–22–165 1 TD 0 INT
ATL: Vick 16–40–197 1 TD 2 INT, Schaub 0–1–0 0 TD 0 INT

Rushing
CLE: Droughns 21–54, Frye 4–28, Northcutt 1–7, Smith 1–2
ATL: Vick 7–74, Dunn 21–73, Jackson 1–2

Receiving
CLE: Winslow 5–90, Edwards 3–31, Heiden 4–24, Cribbs 1–10, Northcutt 1–6, Jurevicius 2–4
ATL: White 5–99, Crumpler 4–37, Dunn 4–35, Jenkins 2–17, Lelie 1–9

Sunday, November 19
Pittsburgh Steelers 24, Browns 20
Cleveland Browns Stadium (73,296)
Brown jerseys/white pants

After dominating the struggling Steelers for three quarters on a gloomy afternoon, the Browns blew a 10-point lead in the final nine minutes and lost to Pittsburgh at home for the sixth straight time. Though the Cleveland offense struggled, the defense and special teams helped build a comfortable lead when DB Daven Holly returned the first of two interceptions 57 yards for a touchdown in the second quarter, then Josh Cribbs ran back a kickoff for a score to make it 20–10 with 9:21 to play. Pittsburgh QB Ben Roethlisberger then took over. Held to 48 passing yards with three interceptions through the first three quarters, he threw for 224 in the fourth quarter and led the Steelers on scoring drives of 79 and 77 yards to take the lead on a short touchdown pass to RB Willie Parker with 32 seconds remaining. The

Browns scampered to the Pittsburgh 22 in the final moments, but a pass to Braylon Edwards on the final play fell incomplete. The suddenly potent Pittsburgh offense had controlled the football for 12 of the final 15 minutes as the Steelers picked up their first road win of the season. The defeat spoiled a great day for Edwards, who caught seven passes for 137 yards and a score.

Record: 3–7

	1	2	3	4		
Steelers	0	0	3	21	=	24
Browns	0	10	0	10	=	20

CLE-Holly 57-yd. interception return (Dawson kick)
CLE-Dawson 23-yd. FG
PIT-Reed 43-yd. FG
CLE-Dawson 35-yd. FG
PIT-Holmes 20-yd. pass from Roethlisberger (Reed kick)
CLE-Cribbs 92-yd. kickoff return (Dawson kick)
PIT-Parker 1-yd. run (Reed kick)
PIT-Parker 4-yd. pass from Roethlisberger (Reed kick)

Passing
PIT: Roethlisberger 25–44–272 2 TD 3 INT
CLE: Frye 17–27–224 0 TD 0 INT

Rushing
PIT: Parker 16–46, Roethlisberger 2–20, Davenport 2–11
CLE: Wright 18–74, Frye 5–27, Harrison 4–5, Smith 1–1, Edwards 1-(-8)

Receiving
PIT: Ward 7–81, Holmes 5–75, Miller 2–32, Wilson 3–27, Washington 2–24, Parker 4–17, Davenport 2–16
CLE: Edwards 7–137, Winslow 4–36, Jurevicius 1–16, Heiden 2–14, Vickers 1–12, Wright 1–6, Northcutt 1–3

Sunday, November 26
Cincinnati Bengals 30, Browns 0
Cleveland Browns Stadium (72,926)
Brown jerseys/white pants

Despite facing the worst defense in the league—one that had allowed 65 points in its previous two games—the Browns were dominated at home by the Bengals, who posted their first shutout in 17 years. Charlie Frye played miserably, throwing four interceptions while getting sacked five times and getting in a heated argument with Braylon Edwards on the sideline. Picking up only nine first downs for the game, the Browns racked up more yards in penalties (93) than they did rushing (51), falling behind 17–0 at the half and crossed midfield only twice in the most humiliating defeat of the season. Commemorating their sixtieth anniversary season, the Browns wore special throwback helmets with a single white stripe down the middle and, for the first time since 1960, numbers on the sides.

Record: 3–8

	1	2	3	4		
Bengals	7	10	6	7	=	30
Browns	0	0	0	0	=	0

CIN-R. Johnson 1-yd. run (Graham kick)
CIN-Henry 7-yd. pass from Palmer (Graham kick)
CIN-Graham 24-yd. FG
CIN-Houshmandzadeh 6-yd. pass from Palmer (kick failed)
CIN-Henry 10-yd. pass from Palmer (Graham kick)

Passing
CIN: Palmer 25–32–275 3 TD 1 INT, Wright 2–2–25 0 TD 0 INT
CLE: Frye 18–29–186 0 TD 4 INT

Rushing
CIN: R. Johnson 25–64, Watson 5–12, Perry 1–10, C. Johnson 1–6, J. Johnson 2–5, Palmer 2–0, Wright 1-(-9)
CLE: Harrison 3–18, Wright 5–12, Northcutt 1–9, Frye 2–5, Droughns 2–4, Smith 1–3

Receiving
CIN: C. Johnson 7–123, Houshmandzadeh 7–79, Henry 5–41, Kelly 3–25, Stewart 2–15, Watson 1–14, R. Johnson 1–0
CLE: Northcutt 3–61, Winslow 6–52, Edwards 2–29, Jurevicius 2–19, Heiden 2–14, Harrison 1–6, Droughns 1–5, Wright 1–0

Sunday, December 3
Browns 31, Kansas City Chiefs 28 (OT)
Cleveland Browns Stadium (71,927)
Brown jerseys/white pants

On the cusp of a third straight disheartening defeat, backup QB Derek Anderson rallied the Browns from a 14-point fourth-quarter deficit to send the game to overtime, where the Browns prevailed for their first sudden-death victory in four years. Charlie Frye injured his wrist on Cleveland's first series but returned to action to pull the Browns into a 14–14 tie at the intermission. In the second half, Anderson replaced the dinged-up Frye, but the playoff-bound

Chiefs built a 28–14 advantage with 12 minutes left. Anderson then led the Browns on scoring drives of 81 and 70 yards, connecting with TE Steve Heiden for short touchdown passes each time to tie the contest with 35 seconds remaining. After the Browns forced a Kansas City punt in overtime, Anderson connected with Kellen Winslow Jr. for 26 yards, then rumbled for a 33-yard gain to the Chiefs' 12 to set up the game-winning 33-yard field goal by Phil Dawson. Anderson threw for 171 yards in relief as the Browns rolled up a season-high 438 yards.

Record: 4–8

	1	2	3	4	OT		
Chiefs	0	14	7	7	0	=	28
Browns	7	7	0	14	3	=	31

CLE-Edwards 23-yd. pass from Frye (Dawson kick)
KC-Kennison 22-yd. pass from Green (Tynes kick)
KC-Gonzalez 9-yd. pass from Green (Tynes kick)
CLE-Droughns 1-yd. run (Dawson kick)
KC-Wilson 6-yd. pass from Green (Tynes kick)
KC-Gonzalez 23-yd. pass from Green (Tynes kick)
CLE-Heiden 6-yd. pass from Anderson (Dawson kick)
CLE-Heiden 3-yd. pass from Anderson (Dawson kick)
CLE-Dawson 33-yd. FG

Passing
KC: Green 24–32–297 4 TD 1 INT
CLE: Anderson 12–21–171 2 TD 1 INT, Frye 11–13–122 1 TD 0 INT

Rushing
KC: Johnson 28–110, Bennett 3–14, Green 1–0
CLE: Droughns 14–70, Anderson 2–44, Wright 11–25, Cribbs 1–9, Frye 1–2

Receiving
KC: Kennison 7–117, Gonzalez 9–105, Bennett 4–33, Johnson 2–26, Parker 1–10, Wilson 1–6
CLE: Jurevicius 6–75, Wright 2–70, Droughns 5–48, Edwards 3–36, Heiden 5–27, Winslow 1–26, Dinkins 1–11

Thursday, December 7
Pittsburgh Steelers 27, Browns 7
Heinz Field (55,246)
White jerseys/white pants

On a frigid Thursday night in Pittsburgh, in their first-ever telecast on the NFL Network, the overmatched Browns were routed by the Steelers. Pittsburgh picked up a whopping 528 total yards—303 rushing—as RB Willie Parker set a team record with 223 on the ground. Derek Anderson made his first NFL start and played well, throwing for 276 yards despite seven dropped passes. WR Joe Jurevicius was the primary target, catching seven for 111 yards. But the Cleveland running game was nonexistent, picking up a mere 18 yards as the Steelers ran 25 more offensive plays than the Browns in collecting their seventh straight victory in the series.

Record: 4–9

	1	2	3	4		
Browns	0	0	0	7	=	7
Steelers	7	3	14	3	=	27

PIT-Washington 49-yd. pass from Roethlisberger (Reed kick)
PIT-Reed 23-yd. FG
PIT-Roethlisberger 2-yd. run (Reed kick)
PIT-Parker 3-yd. run (Reed kick)
PIT-Reed 28-yd. FG
CLE-Edwards 45-yd. pass from Anderson (Dawson kick)

Passing
CLE: Anderson 21–37–276 1 TD 1 INT
PIT: Roethlisberger 11–21–225 1 TD 0 INT

Rushing
CLE: Droughns 5–6, Smith 2–4, Anderson 1–4, Wright 2–2, Vickers 1–2
PIT: Parker 32–223, Davenport 14–62, Kuhn 1–16, Roethlisberger 3–4, Batch 2-(-2)

Receiving
CLE: Jurevicius 7–111, Edwards 4–86, Droughns 2–23, Heiden 2–21, Winslow 4–19, Northcutt 1–12, Vickers 1–4
PIT: Holmes 4–81, Washington 2–67, Davenport 1–21, Tuman 1–18, Young 1–17, Morey 1–15, Kreider 1–6

Sunday, December 17
Baltimore Ravens 27, Browns 17
M&T Bank Stadium (70,857)
White jerseys/white pants

For the first time in team history, the Browns completed a season without winning a single game within their division as the Ravens rolled to a triumph that dropped the Browns to 0–6 against their AFC North opponents. Things actually started well for the Browns, as Phil Dawson kicked a 51-yard field goal on their first possession to take an early lead, then Baltimore QB Steve McNair left the game with an injury on the next series. But backup Kyle Boller led the Ravens to 17 straight points to take a commanding lead. The Browns rebounded with a pair of Derek Anderson touchdown passes to tie the contest midway through the third quarter, but the Ravens answered with a 77-yard touchdown pass to WR Demetrius Williams to take the lead right back moments later. The Baltimore defense then took over, not allowing the Browns to cross the Ravens' 47 for the remainder of the game, and the Ravens tacked on a late field goal to put the game away. Despite throwing a pair of interceptions and being sacked six times, Anderson was effective, at one point completing 13 straight passes, but it wasn't enough to prevent the Browns from making dubious team history.

Record: 4–10

	1	2	3	4		
Browns	3	7	7	0	=	17
Ravens	7	10	7	3	=	27

CLE-Dawson 51-yd. FG
BAL-Lewis 7-yd. run (Stover kick)
BAL-Mughelli 9-yd. pass from Boller (Stover kick)
BAL-Stover 38-yd. FG
CLE-Jurevicius 3-yd. pass from Anderson (Dawson kick)
CLE-Edwards 14-yd. pass from Anderson (Dawson kick)
BAL-Williams 77-yd. pass from Boller (Stover kick)
BAL-Stover 22-yd. FG

Passing
CLE: Anderson 23–32–223 2 TD 2 INT, Cribbs 0–1–0 0 TD 0 INT
BAL: Boller 13–21–238 2 TD 1 INT, McNair 0–4–0 0 TD 0 INT

Rushing
CLE: Wright 8–37, Droughns 8–31
BAL: Lewis 22–109, Anderson 3–22, Boller 9–12, Clayton 1-(-1)

Receiving
CLE: Edwards 5–68, Winslow 5–61, Jurevicius 5–46, Heiden 3–20, Wilson 1–16, Vickers 2–9, Wright 1–3, Droughns 1–0
BAL: Williams 2–100, Heap 5–58, Clayton 1–42, Mason 2–20, Mughelli 2–13, Lewis 1–5

Sunday, December 24
Tampa Bay Buccaneers 22, Browns 7
Cleveland Browns Stadium (69,603)
Brown jerseys/white pants

For the second straight year, the Browns were humiliated on Christmas Eve, this time getting overwhelmed by a woeful Tampa Bay team that entered the game with a 3–11 record and a winless mark on the road for the season. The Buccaneers dominated the Browns, holding the home team to less than 200 yards of offense while picking off four passes thrown by Derek Anderson, who was then knocked out the game with a separated shoulder. After Anderson's third interception was returned for a Tampa touchdown, the Browns' lone score came early in the fourth quarter when DB Daven Holly scooped up a fumble and returned it 40 yards for a touchdown. Adding insult to injury, the loss ensured the Browns would finish with a worse record than the year before.

Record: 4–11

	1	2	3	4		
Buccaneers	3	3	6	10	=	22
Browns	0	0	0	7	=	7

TB-Bryant 23-yd. FG
TB-Bryant 24-yd. FG
TB-Pittman 11-yd. run (kick failed)
TB-Brooks 21-yd. interception return (Bryant kick)
CLE-Holly 40-yd. fumble return (Dawson kick)
TB-Bryant 37-yd. FG

Passing
TB: Rattay 16–26–212 0 TD 1 INT
CLE: Anderson 10–27–123 0 TD 4 INT, Dorsey 0–1–0 0 TD 0 INT

Rushing
TB: Pittman 16–86, Alstott 22–56, Graham 5–12, Rattay 1-(-1)
CLE: Droughns 19–92, Anderson 1-(-1)

Receiving
TB: Hilliard 4–67, Smith 4–45, Stovall 2–45, Galloway 2–34, Pittman 4–21
CLE: Jurevicius 4–58, Northcutt 2–31, Winslow 2–27, Edwards 2–7

Sunday, December 31
Houston Texans 14, Browns 6
Reliant Stadium (70,097)
White jerseys/white pants

The Browns closed out a miserable season with a fittingly frustrating loss in Houston on New Year's Eve. Despite holding the Texans to just 177 yards—the Browns' best defensive performance of the year—the Cleveland offense was unable to score a touchdown for the second straight week, while again handing their opponents a defensive score. After the Texans surged ahead 7–3 on the first series of the second half, Charlie Frye—playing with an injured wrist in place of sidelined Derek Anderson—was sacked and fumbled, and Houston DT Anthony Maddox scooped up the loose ball and rumbled 47 yards for a score and a 14–3 lead. The Browns, who crossed midfield seven times, cut the margin to eight with a field goal midway through the fourth quarter. But they went nowhere on their final possession in the last two minutes, securing their twelfth loss of the season and their first defeat in a regular-season finale in five years. Kellen Winslow Jr. caught a career-best 11 passes and finished the season with 89 receptions, tying a team record set by Ozzie Newsome in 1983 and 1984.
Record: 4–12

	1	2	3	4		
Browns	0	3	0	3	=	6
Texans	0	0	14	0	=	14

CLE-Dawson 43-yd. FG
HOU-Taylor 5-yd. run (Brown kick)
HOU-Maddox 47-yd. fumble return (Brown kick)
CLE-Dawson 36-yd. FG

Passing
CLE: Frye 25–35–187 0 TD 1 INT
HOU: Carr 9–15–86 0 TD 1 INT

Rushing
CLE: Droughns 19–83, Frye 5–36, Edwards 1–7, Cribbs 1–2, Smith 1–1, Harrison 1-(-2)
HOU: Taylor 20–99, Lundy 1–3, Carr 5-(-6)

Receiving
CLE: Winslow 11–93, Edwards 4–46, Heiden 3–17, Wilson 1–16, Smith 2–7, Vickers 1–6, Droughns 3–2
HOU: Leach 2–33, Johnson 2–12, Taylor 1–12, Moulds 2–11, Bruener 1–10, Lundy 1–8

2007

Sunday, September 9
Pittsburgh Steelers 34, Browns 7
Cleveland Browns Stadium (73,089)
Brown jerseys/white pants

In one of the most disastrous season openers in team history, the Browns were throttled on their home field by the Steelers, who notched their seventh straight victory in Cleveland and pulled ahead in the all-time series for the first time. The tone was set early when the Browns committed four penalties on one play on their first possession, as the Steelers scored on their first three possessions to sprint to a 17–0 lead. Browns' QB Charlie Frye was pulled in the third quarter after getting sacked five times, and backup Derek Anderson led the team to its only touchdown. The Browns turned the ball over five times, and the defense was chewed up by Pittsburgh, as QB Ben Roethlisberger threw a career-best four touchdown passes, and the Steelers rolled to better than 200 rushing yards in the debut of new head coach Mike Tomlin. Two days later, the embarrassed Browns traded Frye to Seattle and handed the starting QB job to Anderson.

Record: 0–1

	1	2	3	4		
Steelers	17	0	14	3	=	34
Browns	0	0	7	0	=	7

PIT-Ward 5-yd. pass from Roethlisberger (Reed kick)
PIT-Reed 26-yd. FG
PIT-Holmes 40-yd. pass from Roethlisberger (Reed kick)
PIT-Spaeth 5-yd. pass from Roethlisberger (Reed kick)
CLE-Vickers 1-yd. pass from Anderson (Dawson kick)
PIT-Miller 22-yd. pass from Roethlisberger (Reed kick)
PIT-Reed 31-yd. FG

Passing
PIT: Roethlisberger 12–23–161 4 TD 0 INT
CLE: Anderson 13–28–184 1 TD 1 INT, Frye 4–10–34 0 TD 1 INT

Rushing
PIT: Parker 27–109, Davenport 8–43, Wilson 1–37, Holmes 1–11, Davis 3–5, Roethlisberger 1–2, Batch 1-(-1)
CLE: Lewis 11–35, Vickers 2–8, Wright 1–3, Frye 1–1, Anderson 1-(-1)

Receiving
PIT: Holmes 2–55, Ward 3–51, Miller 4–35, Davenport 1–17, Spaeth 1–5, Parker 1-(-2)
CLE: Winslow 4–83, Edwards 3–49, Jurevicius 2–28, Carter 1–22, Lewis 2–11, Dinkins 1–8, Vickers 2–7, Cribbs 1–7, Heiden 1–3

Sunday, September 16
Browns 51, Cincinnati Bengals 45
Cleveland Browns Stadium (72,801)
Brown jerseys/white pants

The Browns bounced back by winning one of the most incredible games in franchise history, outlasting Cincinnati in a surprising offensive shootout. Making his first start as the Browns' full-time QB, Derek Anderson missed on his first five pass attempts but then caught fire to turn in one of the finest performances in team history. He threw five touchdown passes, bringing the Browns back from an early deficit and sparking an unstoppable offense that rolled up 554 total yards, the most they'd tallied in 21 years. Two scoring tosses to Cleveland native WR Joe Jurevicius gave the Browns their first lead midway through the second quarter, then two more to WR Braylon Edwards (who totaled 146 receiving yards for the day) helped propel the Browns to a 51–38 lead with less than six minutes to play. The Bengals pulled back within a touchdown on QB Carson Palmer's sixth scoring pass of the day, then regained possession at their own 9 with 1:03 remaining. They quickly drove to midfield, then Cleveland DB Leigh Bodden intercepted a pass along the sideline at the Browns' 27 with 20 seconds remaining to clinch a thrilling victory. RB Jamal Lewis, acquired by the Browns as a free agent in the offseason, turned in one of the finest games of his career, exploding for 216 rushing yards, including a 66-yard touchdown in the third quarter. The wild victory cemented Anderson's role as QB and set the tone for an unexpectedly exciting season.

Record: 1–1

	1	2	3	4		
Bengals	7	14	17	7	=	45
Browns	6	21	14	10	=	51

CIN-R. Johnson 13-yd. pass from Palmer (Graham kick)
CLE-Dawson 39-yd. FG
CLE-Dawson 39-yd. FG
CLE-Jurevicius 17-yd. pass from Anderson (Dawson kick)
CIN-Houshmandzadeh 23-yd. pass from Palmer (Graham kick)
CLE-Jurevicius 9-yd. pass from Anderson (Dawson kick)
CIN-C. Johnson 22-yd. pass from Palmer (Graham kick)
CLE-Winslow 25-yd. pass from Anderson (Dawson kick)
CIN-Graham 20-yd. FG
CLE-Edwards 34-yd. pass from Anderson (Dawson kick)
CIN-C. Johnson 14-yd. pass from Palmer (Graham kick)
CLE-Lewis 66-yd. run (Dawson kick)
CIN-Houshmandzadeh 5-yd. pass from Palmer (Graham kick)
CLE-Edwards 37-yd. pass from Anderson (Dawson kick)
CLE-Dawson 18-yd. FG
CIN-Holt 7-yd. pass from Palmer (Graham kick)

Passing
CIN: Palmer 33–50–401 6 TD 2 INT
CLE: Anderson 20–33–328 5 TD 1 INT

Rushing
CIN: R. Johnson 23–118, Palmer 2–10, Perry 1–9
CLE: Lewis 28–216, Cribbs 1–11, Vickers 1–0

Receiving
CIN: C. Johnson 11–209, Houshmandzadeh 8–69, Holt 5–52, R. Johnson 4–33, Green 1–18, Kelly 1–8, Perry 1 7, Coats 1–4, Watson 1–1
CLE: Edwards 8–146, Winslow 6–100, Jurevicius 4–44, Heiden 1–27, Vickers 1–11

Sunday, September 23
Oakland Raiders 26, Browns 24
McAfee Coliseum (51,075)
White jerseys/white pants

Despite a sloppy performance, the Browns had a chance to win on the final play of the game, only to see Phil Dawson's 40-yard field-goal attempt blocked as time expired and they dropped to 1–2. Behind a strong running game, the Raiders soared to a 16–0 lead late in the second quarter, but the Browns fought back with two scores in the final two minutes of the half after WR Josh Cribbs returned the ensuing kickoff 99 yards for a touchdown and an Oakland fumble led to a field goal. After Cleveland surged ahead briefly in the third quarter, the Raiders took a 26–17 lead midway through the fourth. The Browns cut the margin to two with 3:33 remaining, then regained possession at their own 9 with just over a minute left and quickly drove to the Raiders' 22 with three seconds showing. The Raiders called time out just before Dawson attempted his final kick, which sailed through the uprights in vain, then his actual attempt was blocked to secure the Raiders' victory.
Record: 1–2

	1	2	3	4		
Browns	0	10	7	7	=	24
Raiders	3	13	7	3	=	26

OAK-Janikowski 32-yd. FG
OAK-Janikowski 22-yd. FG
OAK-Curry 41-yd. pass from McCown (Janikowski kick)
OAK-Janikowski 23-yd. FG
CLE-Cribbs 99-yd. kickoff return (Dawson kick)
CLE-Dawson 23-yd. FG
CLE-Edwards 21-yd. pass from Anderson (Dawson kick)
OAK-Jordan 1-yd. run (Janikowski kick)
OAK-Janikowski 48-yd. FG
CLE-Anderson 1-yd. run (Dawson kick)

Passing
CLE: Anderson 18–37–248 1 TD 2 INT
OAK: Culpepper 8–14–118 0 TD 0 INT, McCown 6–12–108 1 TD 0 INT

Rushing
CLE: Lewis 15–56, Wright 1–13, Anderson 2–12, Cribbs 1–7
OAK: Jordan 29–121, Fargas 8–50, McCown 4–15

Receiving
CLE: Winslow 6–88, Edwards 4–83, Jurevicius 3–33, Lewis 2–22, Carter 1–14, Wright 2–8
OAK: Curry 3–62, Madsen 3–61, Jordan 2–32, Williams 1–24, Porter 1–20, Miller 1–13, Griffith 2–7, Fargas 1–7

Sunday, September 30
Browns 27, Baltimore Ravens 13
Cleveland Browns Stadium (73,024)
Brown jerseys/white pants

Taking control with two touchdowns in the first 10 minutes, the Browns cruised to an easy victory over Baltimore despite permitting more than 400 total yards. After a Derek Anderson-to-Joe Jurevicius touchdown pass on the game's first possession, an interception by Leigh Bodden was followed by a 78-yard strike from Anderson to Braylon

Edwards to put the Browns up 14–0. Thanks to a fumble on a Baltimore kickoff return, the lead swelled to 27–6 going into the fourth quarter, though the Cleveland offense managed only a field goal in the second half. Anderson averaged better than 20 yards per completion as Edwards collected 97 receiving yards, and TE Kellen Winslow Jr. notched 96. Baltimore tallied more than 100 more yards than the Browns but also ran 25 additional plays against a Cleveland defense that allowed only one touchdown.
Record: 2–2

	1	2	3	4		
Ravens	0	6	0	7	=	13
Browns	14	10	3	0	=	27

CLE-Jurevicius 2-yd. pass from Anderson (Dawson kick)
CLE-Edwards 78-yd. pass from Anderson (Dawson kick)
BAL-Stover 21-yd. FG
CLE-Dawson 41-yd. FG
CLE-Lewis 1-yd. run (Dawson kick)
BAL-Stover 29-yd. FG
CLE-Dawson 20-yd. FG
BAL-Sypniewski 4-yd. pass from McNair (Stover kick)

Passing
BAL: McNair 34–53–307 1 TD 1 INT
CLE: Anderson 10–18–204 2 TD 1 INT

Rushing
BAL: McGahee 14–104, Smith 5–5, McNair 1–2
CLE: Lewis 23–64, Wright 2–27, Vickers 1–6, Cribbs 1–2, Anderson 3–0

Receiving
BAL: Mason 10–78, Williams 5–63, Clayton 3–43, Heap 4–36, Sypniewski 6–34, McGahee 2–32, Smith 3–19, Wilcox 1–2
CLE: Edwards 3–97, Winslow 4–96, Jurevicius 2–10, Heiden 1–1

Sunday, October 7
New England Patriots 34, Browns 17
Gillette Stadium (68,756)
White jerseys/white pants

Crippled by four turnovers, including three first-half interceptions by Derek Anderson, the Browns were no match for the 16-point-favorite Patriots, who won their fifth game in what would be a perfect regular season. The Browns squandered a chance to take an early lead when Anderson was picked off in the end zone on a play from the New England 1. Anderson's next pass was also intercepted, setting up the Patriots' first touchdown, and his third pickoff set up another score as New England took a 20–0 halftime lead. The Browns made a game of it in the second half as they tallied 353 total yards against the league's best defense and twice pulled within 10 points. New England added another score on a fumble return for a touchdown in the final minute. The Cleveland defense was lit up once again, permitting more than 400 yards for the third time in four games.
Record: 2–3

	1	2	3	4		
Browns	0	0	3	14	=	17
Patriots	10	10	0	14	=	34

NE-Gostkowski 20-yd. FG
NE-Stallworth 34-yd. pass from Brady (Gostkowski kick)
NE-Gostkowski 25-yd. FG
NE-Watson 7-yd. pass from Brady (Gostkowski kick)
CLE-Dawson 42-yd. FG
CLE-Carter 21-yd. pass from Anderson (Dawson kick)
NE-Watson 25-yd. pass from Brady (Gostkowski kick)
CLE-Winslow 14-yd. pass from Anderson (Dawson kick)
NE-Gay 15-yd. fumble return (Gostkowski kick)

Passing
CLE: Anderson 22–43–287 2 TD 3 INT
NE: Brady 22–38–265 3 TD 0 INT

Rushing
CLE: Wright 15–59, Cribbs 1–11, Lewis 1–11, Anderson 3–7, Vickers 1–4
NE: Morris 21–102, Eckel 6–16, Stallworth 1–12, Watson 1–11, Faulk 3–6

Receiving
CLE: Edwards 6–110, Carter 3–50, Winslow 4–49, Wright 4–43, Jurevicius 1–17, Heiden 2–10, Vickers 2–8
NE: Watson 6–107, Stallworth 4–65, Moss 3–46, Welker 4–19, Morris 2–9, Brady 1–7, Faulk 1–7, Gaffney 1–5

Sunday, October 14
Browns 41, Miami Dolphins 31
Cleveland Browns Stadium (73,198)
Brown jerseys/white pants

Behind an unstoppable offense, the Browns held off the 0–5 Dolphins and surged back to the .500 mark on a crisp, sunny autumn afternoon in Cleveland. Scoring on five of six possessions in the first half even without injured RB Jamal Lewis, the Browns built a 24–3 lead. Miami pulled within

three points in the second half, but Braylon Edwards caught two of his three touchdown passes on consecutive possessions in the fourth quarter to put the game away. The red-hot Cleveland offense picked up 384 total yards and 24 first downs as the Browns won their third straight home game.
Record: 3–3

	1	2	3	4		
Dolphins	3	7	14	7	=	31
Browns	14	13	0	14	=	41

CLE-Wright 1-yd. run (Dawson kick)
MIA-Feely 43-yd. FG
CLE-Anderson 1-yd. run (Dawson kick)
CLE-Dawson 40-yd. FG
CLE-Edwards 24-yd. pass from Anderson (Dawson kick)
MIA-Martin 14-yd. pass from Lemon (Feely kick)
CLE-Dawson 20-yd. FG
MIA-Lemon 5-yd. run (Feely kick)
MIA-Lemon 1-yd. run (Feely kick)
CLE-Edwards 5-yd. pass from Anderson (Dawson kick)
CLE-Edwards 16-yd. pass from Anderson (Dawson kick)
MIA-Martin 4-yd. pass from Lemon (Feely kick)

Passing
MIA: Lemon 24–43–256 2 TD 2 INT
CLE: Anderson 18–25–245 3 TD 0 INT

Rushing
MIA: Brown 19–101, Lemon 4–9
CLE: Wright 20–59, Harrison 8–57, Anderson 5–13, Vickers 1–7, Cribbs 1–4

Receiving
MIA: Chambers 6–73, Brown 9–69, Booker 2–34, Ginn 1–32, Hagan 3–30, Martin 3–18
CLE: Winslow 5–90, Edwards 5–67, Wright 3–39, Jurevicius 3–28, Harrison 1–15, Vickers 1–6

Sunday, October 28
Browns 27, St. Louis Rams 20
Edward Jones Dome (62,777)
White jerseys/white pants

After quickly falling behind 14–0, the Browns rallied to pull out a tough victory over the 0–7 Rams to vault over the .500 mark for the first time in three years and win back-to-back games in the same season for the first time in 64 games. Three Derek Anderson touchdown passes propelled the Browns to a seven-point lead in the fourth quarter, then a critical defensive stop on fourth-and-inches at the Cleveland 16 with two minutes left and an interception at the Cleveland 28 in the final minute helped the Browns emerge victorious. Though the offense was once again effective, the Browns allowed the struggling Rams to roll up nearly 400 total yards and maligned their own cause with 14 penalties for 102 yards. Braylon Edwards notched his third 100-yard game of the season, and Anderson pushed his touchdown-pass total to 17 in seven games.
Record: 4–3

	1	2	3	4		
Browns	3	14	7	3	=	27
Rams	14	3	3	0	=	20

STL-Jackson 2-yd. run (Wilkins kick)
STL-Holt 1-yd. pass from Bulger (Wilkins kick)
CLE-Dawson 35-yd. FG
CLE-Edwards 12-yd. pass from Anderson (Dawson kick)
CLE-Winslow 21-yd. pass from Anderson (Dawson kick)
STL-Wilkins 40-yd. FG
CLE-Edwards 5-yd. pass from Anderson (Dawson kick)
STL-Wilkins 46-yd. FG
CLE-Dawson 45-yd. FG

Passing
CLE: Anderson 18–25–248 3 TD 0 INT
STL: Bulger 24–36–310 1 TD 1 INT, Frerotte 1–3–12 0 TD 0 INT

Rushing
CLE: Lewis 17–61, Harrison 5–32, Wright 4–19, Cribbs 1–18, Vickers 1–3, Anderson 1-(-1)
STL: Jackson 8–41, Leonard 15–33, Minor 1–5

Receiving
CLE: Edwards 8–117, Jurevicius 5–76, Winslow 2–26, Carter 1–14, Heiden 1–8, Wright 1–7
STL: Holt 6–110, Bruce 6–70, Bennett 6–63, McMichael 2–39, Leonard 3–31, Jackson 2–9

Sunday, November 4
Browns 33, Seattle Seahawks 30 (OT)
Cleveland Browns Stadium (72,927)
Brown jerseys/white pants

In another thrilling offensive shootout, the Browns rallied from a 21–6 deficit to catch the playoff-bound Seahawks and send the game to overtime, where a defensive stop led to a dramatic victory in the falling darkness. After a disastrous start that included allowing the longest punt return for a touchdown in team history, the Browns gradually clawed back behind a career-high four touchdowns by Jamal Lewis, the last with 2:21 remaining to give the Browns their first lead. Seattle responded with a last-second field goal to send the game to sudden-death, where the Cleveland defense stuffed Seattle on fourth-and-inches from the Browns' 44 on the first series. Lewis then capped his career day a play later when he rumbled 34 yards with a screen pass to set up Phil Dawson's winning 25-yard field goal. Both teams topped 400 total yards, with Derek Anderson throwing for a career-best 364, including 11 connections with Kellen Winslow Jr. for 125 yards. The victory extended the Browns' winning streak to three games, their longest in six years.

Record: 5–3

	1	2	3	4	OT		
Seahawks	7	14	3	6	0	=	30
Browns	0	9	7	14	3	=	33

SEA-Engram 5-yd. pass from Hasselbeck (Brown kick)
CLE-Lewis 2-yd. run (kick failed)
SEA-Hackett 6-yd. pass from Hasselbeck (Brown kick)
SEA-Burleson 94-yd. punt return (Brown kick)
CLE-Dawson 19-yd. FG
CLE-Lewis 1-yd. run (Dawson kick)
SEA-Brown 39-yd. FG
CLE-Lewis 2-yd. run (pass failed)
SEA-Brown 26-yd. FG
CLE-Lewis 1-yd. run (Jurevicius pass from Anderson)
SEA-Brown 22-yd. FG
CLE-Dawson 25-yd. FG

Passing
SEA: Hasselbeck 30–47–318 2 TD 1 INT
CLE: Anderson 29–48–364 0 TD 1 INT

Rushing
SEA: Morris 9–55, Alexander 14–32, Hasselbeck 4–17, Weaver 1–1
CLE: Lewis 20–37, Anderson 2–21, Wright 3–6

Receiving
SEA: Engram 14–139, Burleson 4–59, Hackett 6–58, Morris 2–43, Weaver 2–11, Obomanu 1–7, Alexander 1–1
CLE: Winslow 11–125, Jurevicius 4–69, Edwards 5–67, Lewis 4–67, Vickers 3–17, Wright 1–13, Heiden 1–6

Sunday, November 11
Pittsburgh Steelers 31, Browns 28
Heinz Field (64,781)
White jerseys/white pants

Despite being dominated statistically, the Browns sprinted to a 21–6 lead before a fourth-quarter surge by Pittsburgh dropped the Browns two games behind the Steelers in the AFC North. After a long scoring drive on their first possession, the Browns scored again moments later when Josh Cribbs started a magnificent day with a 90-yard kickoff return to set up a second touchdown. A brilliant catch along the sideline in the end zone by Braylon Edwards gave the Browns a 15-point lead five minutes before the half, but the Cleveland offense was controlled in the final two periods as the Steelers surged ahead 24–21 early in the fourth quarter. After allowing the ensuing kickoff to skip past him, Cribbs scooped it up and motored along the sideline for a 100-yard touchdown to put the Browns ahead again. The Steelers answered with a 14-play touchdown drive to take a 31–28 lead with 3:13 left. After an exchange of punts, the Browns regained possession at their own 33 with a minute left and drove to the Pittsburgh 35, where Phil Dawson attempted a 52-yard field goal that fell short with six seconds left. While the Cleveland defense collected four sacks, it allowed more than 400 yards, compared with the offense's meager 163. But Cribbs rode to the rescue, tallying 204 yards on returns, the second-best day in the Browns' history.

Record: 5–4

	1	2	3	4		
Browns	7	14	0	7	=	28
Steelers	3	6	7	15	=	31

CLE-Winslow 4-yd. pass from Anderson (Dawson kick)
PIT-Reed 28-yd. FG
CLE-Vickers 2-yd. pass from Anderson (Dawson kick)
PIT-Reed 35-yd. FG
CLE-Edwards 16-yd. pass from Anderson (Dawson kick)
PIT-Reed 30-yd. FG
PIT-Roethlisberger 30-yd. run (Ward pass from Roethlisberger)
CLE-Cribbs 100-yard kickoff return (Dawson kick)
PIT-Miller 2-yd. pass from Roethlisberger (Reed kick)

Passing
CLE: Anderson 16–35–123 3 TD 0 INT
PIT: Roethlisberger 23–34–278 2 TD 1 INT, Parker 0–1–0 0 TD 0 INT

Rushing
CLE: Lewis 16–35, Anderson 2–5
PIT: Parker 25–105, Roethlisberger 5–49, Davenport 4–7, Holmes 1-(-2)

Receiving
CLE: Winslow 5–46, Jurevicius 5–44, Edwards 1–16, Lewis 3–8, Wright 1–7, Vickers 1–2
PIT: Ward 7–80, Miller 5–71, Washington 4–56, Holmes 4–53, Davenport 1–10, Parker 2–8

Sunday, November 18
Browns 33, Baltimore Ravens 30 (OT)
M&T Bank Stadium (71,055)
White jerseys/white pants

In one of the most bizarre finishes to a game in NFL history, the Browns sent the contest to overtime with a ping-pong field goal by Phil Dawson originally ruled no good on the final play of regulation, then secured victory over the stunned Ravens minutes later. The Browns appeared to be in control, taking a 27–14 lead into the fourth quarter following a franchise-record 100-yard interception return for a touchdown by DB Brodney Pool. But the Ravens endured and scored 16 straight points to take a 30–27 lead with 26 seconds remaining to apparently clinch a comeback victory. But Josh Cribbs returned the ensuing kickoff 39 yards and a long pass to Braylon Edwards with three seconds left set up a 51-yard field-goal attempt by Dawson. The kick hit the left upright, then bounced through and off the crossbar support before landing in the end zone. The officials originally ruled the kick was no good, and the Ravens left the field apparently victorious. But after conferring, the officials reversed the call since the ball had passed through the goalposts. The Browns won the coin toss, and Cribbs returned the kickoff 41 yards—setting a new team record with 245 return yards for the day—to set up the game-winning field goal six minutes into sudden-death. The teams combined for more than 700 total yards, though the Browns' defense racked up six sacks and forced four turnovers as they completed their first season sweep of Baltimore in six years.
Record: 6–4

	1	2	3	4	OT		
Browns	3	10	14	3	3	=	33
Ravens	0	7	7	16	0	=	30

CLE-Dawson 28-yd. FG
CLE-Lewis 1-yd. run (Dawson kick)
BAL-Lewis 35-yd. interception return (Stover kick)
CLE-Dawson 39-yd. FG
BAL-McGahee 2-yd. run (Stover kick)
CLE-Anderson 1-yd. run (Dawson kick)
CLE-Pool 100-yd. interception return (Dawson kick)
BAL-Stover 34-yd. FG
BAL-Stover 41-yd. FG
BAL-Darling 27-yd. pass from Boller (Stover kick)
BAL-Stover 47-yd. FG
CLE-Dawson 51-yd. FG
CLE-Dawson 33-yd. FG

Passing
CLE: Anderson 24–38–274 0 TD 1 INT
BAL: Boller 22–41–279 1 TD 2 INT

Rushing
CLE: Lewis 22–92, Wright 4–19, Vickers 3–4, Cribbs 1–3, Zastudil 1-(-3), Anderson 4-(-4)
BAL: McGahee 21–102, Boller 2–19, Smith 1–7, McClain 1–0

Receiving
CLE: Edwards 8–85, Jurevicius 4–82, Winslow 5–64, Lewis 4–30, Carter 1–10, Heiden 1–2, Wright 1–1
BAL: Darling 4–107, Mason 6–83, Sypniewski 6–53, McGahee 2–24, Clayton 2–9, Smith 2–3

Sunday, November 25
Browns 27, Houston Texans 17
Cleveland Browns Stadium (72,926)
Brown jerseys/white pants

Once again wearing the throwback white-striped helmets with the numerals on the side, the Browns rolled up nearly 400 yards of offense with a balanced attack and cruised to their fifth straight home victory to stay within a game of the first-place Steelers. Jamal Lewis rushed for 134 yards and the game-clinching touchdown, set up by a Brodney Pool interception, with less than six minutes remaining to put the Browns up by 17 points. Houston had crept to a 10–7 lead midway through the second quarter before the Browns exploded for 20 straight points to take control. Kellen Winslow Jr. caught 10 passes for 107 yards and a touchdown as the Cleveland offense piled up 397 total yards.
Record: 7–4

	1	2	3	4		
Texans	7	3	0	7	=	17
Browns	0	14	3	10	=	27

HOU-Walter 17-yd. pass from Schaub (Brown kick)
CLE-Edwards 19-yd. pass from Anderson (Dawson kick)
HOU-Brown 41-yd. FG
CLE-Winslow 7-yd. pass from Anderson (Dawson kick)
CLE-Dawson 25-yd. FG
CLE-Dawson 27-yd. FG
CLE-Lewis 1-yd. run (Dawson kick)
HOU-Daniels 6-yd. pass from Schaub (Brown kick)

Passing
HOU: Schaub 22–36–256 2 TD 2 INT
CLE: Anderson 24–35–253 2 TD 1 INT

Rushing
HOU: Dayne 16–78, Schaub 1–7, Jones 1-(-8)
CLE: Lewis 29–134, Wright 3–14, Vickers 1–0

Receiving
HOU: Daniels 7–82, Walter 6–65, Davis 3–51, Johnson 3–37, Jones 1–14, Dayne 2–7
CLE: Winslow 10–107, Edwards 4–57, Jurevicius 5–55, Wright 3–21, Lewis 2–13

Sunday, December 2
Arizona Cardinals 27, Browns 21
University of Phoenix Stadium (64,791)
White jerseys/white pants

Despite a sloppy performance defined by four turnovers and 10 penalties, the Browns still had a chance to win but were denied on the game's final play. After falling behind 14–3 in the first quarter and then 21–10 early in the third, the Browns fought back on the strength of a 67-yard touchdown reception by Braylon Edwards, who finished with 149 yards on the day. After Arizona extended the lead to six points with under two minutes left, the Browns drove to the Cardinals' 37 with six seconds remaining. Kellen Winslow Jr. leapt over two defenders to catch Derek Anderson's final pass in the end zone as time expired but was unable to come down in bounds, and the officials did not rule he was forced out. Anderson topped 300 yards passing for the third time on the season, but had an interception returned for a touchdown on Cleveland's first series and lost a fumble on the second that led to Arizona's second score.
Record: 7–5

	1	2	3	4		
Browns	3	7	8	3	=	21
Cardinals	14	0	7	6	=	27

ARI-Hood 71-yd. interception return (Rackers kick)
ARI-Pope 5-yd. pass from Warner (Rackers kick)
CLE-Dawson 37-yd. FG
CLE-Lewis 6-yd. pass from Anderson (Dawson kick)
ARI-Johnson 1-yd. pass from Warner (Rackers kick)
CLE-Edwards 67-yd. pass from Anderson (Winslow pass from Cribbs)
ARI-Rackers 33-yd. FG
CLE-Dawson 22-yd. FG
ARI-Rackers 19-yd. FG

Passing
CLE: Anderson 21–41–304 2 TD 2 INT
ARI: Warner 18–30–169 2 TD 1 INT

Rushing
CLE: Lewis 16–62, Anderson 2–10, Wright 1–9, Vickers 1–2, Cribbs 1–1
ARI: James 24–114, Arrington 2–19, Warner 1–0

Receiving
CLE: Edwards 7–149, Jurevicius 4–44, Winslow 3–35, Vickers 2–30, Lewis 3–24, Heiden 1–12, Wright 1–10
ARI: Johnson 6–56, Morey 2–29, Boldin 2–25, Breaston 2–24, Arrington 2–15, Pope 2–14, Patrick 1–5, Shipp 1–1

Sunday, December 9
Browns 24, New York Jets 18
The Meadowlands (76,822)
White jerseys/white pants

In a cold, driving rain, the Browns held off the struggling Jets, coached by Eric Mangini, who would take over as Cleveland's head coach 13 months later. After building a 17–6 fourth-quarter lead, the Browns allowed the Jets to recover an onside kick and claw back within two points with 1:43 remaining. After the Browns recovered the Jets' second onside kick of the period, Jamal Lewis broke four tackles and carried three defenders into the end zone on an exclamatory third-down, 31-yard touchdown run two plays later. The Jets cut the margin back to six with a quick drive and a field goal, then the Browns recovered New York's third onside kick to clinch the victory. Lewis finished with 118 rushing yards as the Browns pulled back within a game of first place in the division.
Record: 8–5

	1	2	3	4		
Browns	0	7	7	10	=	24
Jets	0	3	3	12	=	18

CLE-Lewis 7-yd. pass from Anderson (Dawson kick)
NYJ-Nugent 35-yd. FG
CLE-Edwards 4-yd. pass from Anderson (Dawson kick)
NYJ-Nugent 41-yd. FG
CLE-Dawson 49-yd. FG
NYJ-Clemens 1-yd. run (pass failed)
NYJ-Nugent 38-yd. FG
CLE-Lewis 31-yd. run (Dawson kick)
NYJ-Nugent 35-yd. FG

Passing
CLE: Anderson 16–29–185 2 TD 1 INT
NYJ: Clemens 24–41–286 0 TD 2 INT

Rushing
CLE: Lewis 21–118, Harrison 2–21, Vickers 2–6, Cribbs 1–4, Anderson 3–3
NYJ: Jones 24–106, Clemens 3–8, Washington 3–5

Receiving
CLE: Edwards 3–63, Winslow 4–34, Heiden 2–20, Lewis 3–19, Cribbs 1–18, Wright 1–14, Vickers 1–10, Jurevicius 1 7
NYJ: Cotchery 6–119, Coles 7–48, Baker 3–48, Washington 4–31, Smith 3–27, Jones 1–13

Sunday, December 16
Browns 8, Buffalo Bills 0
Cleveland Browns Stadium (73,196)
Brown jerseys/white pants

Through blinding snow and 40 mph wind gusts, the Browns posted their first shutout in two years and strengthened their playoff hopes with a memorable victory. Phil Dawson kicked a pair of difficult field goals through the brutal wind, the second of which ticked off the crossbar support he'd made famous a month earlier. The Browns added two more points when a bad Buffalo punt snap went out of the end zone for a Cleveland safety early in the second quarter. Jamal Lewis paced a simplified Cleveland offense with 163 yards on 33 carries, including 69 yards in the fourth quarter. After the Browns' defense contained Buffalo the entire game, a late drive gave the Bills once last chance, but the Browns stopped a fourth-down pass short of a first down with three seconds left. It marked the first NFL game decided by an 8–0 score since 1929 as the Browns clinched their first winning record in five years.

Record: 9–5

	1	2	3	4		
Bills	0	0	0	0	=	0
Browns	3	5	0	0	=	8

CLE-Dawson 35-yd. FG
CLE-Safety: Neill fumbled ball out of end zone
CLE-Dawson 49-yd. FG

Passing
BUF: Edwards 13–33–124 0 TD 0 INT
CLE: Anderson 9–24–137 0 TD 0 INT

Rushing
BUF: Lynch 21–82, Jackson 7–16, Edwards 1–12, Moorman 2–4, Reed 1-(-6)
CLE: Lewis 33–163, Wright 3–11, Anderson 1–0

Receiving
BUF: Evans 4–36, Jackson 3–36, Reed 3–29, Gaines 2–14, Royal 1–9
CLE: Edwards 4–64, Jurevicius 2–34, Winslow 2–28, Lewis 1–11

Sunday, December 23
Cincinnati Bengals 19, Browns 14
Paul Brown Stadium (66,023)
White jerseys/white pants

With a chance to clinch their first playoff spot in five years, the Browns played miserably on a windy afternoon in Cincinnati and lost to the 5–9 Bengals. Crippled by four Derek Anderson interceptions—one after being tipped in the end zone—and a botched field-goal attempt, the Browns fell behind 19–0 at the half before clawing back to within five points following a pair of Braylon Edwards touchdown receptions. After Cleveland LB D'Qwell Jackson recovered a Cincinnati fumble at the Cleveland 17 with 1:48 remaining, the Browns drove to the Cincinnati 29 with a second to play. A desperation pass to Kellen Winslow Jr. in the end zone fell incomplete, and the Browns' playoff hopes dimmed.

Record: 9–6

	1	2	3	4		
Browns	0	0	7	7	=	14
Bengals	0	19	0	0	=	19

CIN-Graham 29-yd. FG
CIN-Graham 38-yd. FG
CIN-Houshmandzadeh 5-yd. pass from Palmer (Graham kick)
CIN-Watson 1-yd. run (pass failed)
CLE-Edwards 2-yd. pass from Anderson (Dawson kick)
CLE-Edwards 5-yd. pass from Anderson (Dawson kick)

Passing
CLE: Anderson 29–48–251 2 TD 4 INT
CIN: Palmer 11–21–115 1 TD 2 INT

Rushing
CLE: Lewis 21–92, Wright 3–38, Anderson 1–6, Zastudil 1–0
CIN: Watson 30–130, Johnson 1–16, Dorsey 1–8, Holt 1–1

Receiving
CLE: Winslow 7–73, Edwards 8–52, Lewis 5–42, Wright 3–34, Jurevicius 4–31, Cribbs 1–12, Carter 1–7
CIN: Johnson 4–44, Houshmandzadeh 2–25, Kelly 1–24, Watson 3–20, Chatman 1–2

Sunday, December 30
Browns 20, San Francisco 49ers 7
Cleveland Browns Stadium (73,041)
Brown jerseys/white pants

The Browns made one final push for a playoff berth with a solid win over the 49ers in the finale but were denied the postseason when Tennessee defeated Indianapolis that evening, giving the Titans the tie-breaker over the Browns with a better record against common opponents (4–1 to 3–2). The Browns took control early on a 76-yard punt return for a touchdown by Josh Cribbs, his third kick return for a score on the season. Minutes later, a 45-yard touchdown strike from Derek Anderson to Braylon Edwards put the Browns up 14–0 and marked Edwards's sixteenth touchdown of the season, setting a team record. Edwards also set a team single-season mark for receiving yardage, finishing with 1,289. Rookie QB Brady Quinn made his NFL debut late in the first half after Anderson was knocked out of the game briefly with an injured finger and completed three passes. Jamal Lewis topped the 100-yard mark for the fifth time in 2007 and finished the year with 1,304 yards, the most ever by any Cleveland RB other than Jim Brown. The Cleveland defense quietly had its finest game of the year, holding San Francisco to 185 total yards and nine first downs while collecting five sacks. The victory marked the Browns' seventh straight in Cleveland, the most home victories in a single season by any Browns team, and gave Cleveland its first double-digit win total in a season in 13 years.
Record: 10–6

	1	2	3	4		
49ers	0	7	0	0	=	7
Browns	7	10	0	3	=	20

CLE-Cribbs 76-yd. punt return (Dawson kick)
CLE-Edwards 45-yd. pass from Anderson (Dawson kick)
SF-Jackson 7-yd. pass from Weinke (Nedney kick)
CLE-Dawson 23-yd. FG
CLE-Dawson 49-yd. FG

Passing
SF: Weinke 13–22–104 1 TD 0 INT
CLE: Anderson 11–20–152 1 TD 1 INT, Quinn 3–8–45 0 TD 0 INT

Rushing
SF: Gore 23–94, Hicks 1–18
CLE: Lewis 26–128, Harrison 8–32, Vickers 1–3, Anderson 1–0

Receiving
SF: Jackson 3–28, Gore 2–21, Davis 2–20, Battle 3–19, Walker 2–14, Hicks 1–2
CLE: Edwards 3–67, Winslow 4–62, Wright 3–36, Heiden 1–15, Jurevicius 1–12, Harrison 1–4, Lewis 1–1

2008

Sunday, September 7
Dallas Cowboys 28, Browns 10
Cleveland Browns Stadium (73,012)
White jerseys/white pants

In one of the most highly anticipated openers in club history, the Browns put forth a miserable performance and were dominated by a seasoned Dallas squad. The Cowboys rolled up 487 total yards and collected 30 first downs as they blew open a tie game with three touchdowns in a 16-minute period. The Browns' offense, which entered the season with great expectations, was limited to 205 yards and ran only 16 plays in the second half. Dallas QB Tony Romo threw for 320 yards as the Cowboys controlled time of possession and ran 20 more offensive plays than Cleveland. After Dallas marched 80 yards for a touchdown on its first possession, the Browns knotted the score with their only touchdown early in the second quarter. The Cowboys surged back ahead two plays later and never looked back as Cleveland lost its fourth straight season opener and tenth in 11 seasons.

Record: 0–1

	1	2	3	4		
Cowboys	7	14	7	0	=	28
Browns	0	7	0	3	=	10

DAL-Barber 1-yd. run (Folk kick)
CLE-Winslow 2-yd. pass from Anderson (Dawson kick)
DAL-Owens 35-yd. pass from Romo (Folk kick)
DAL-Barber 1-yd. run (Folk kick)
DAL-Jones 11-yd. run (Folk kick)
CLE-Dawson 34-yd. FG

Passing
DAL: Romo 24–32–320 1 TD 1 INT
CLE: Anderson 11–24–114 1 TD 0 INT

Rushing
DAL: Barber 16–80, Jones 9–62, Choice 5–26, Romo 1-(-1)
CLE: Lewis 13–62, Anderson 4–24, Wright 1–5

Receiving
DAL: Witten 6–96, Owens 5–87, Crayton 6–82, Stanback 2–24, Barber 3–21, Curtis 1–8, Choice 1–2
CLE: Winslow 5–47, Sanders 1–18, Edwards 2–14, Lewis 1–14, Steptoe 1–12, Heiden 1–9

Sunday, September 14
Pittsburgh Steelers 10, Browns 6
Cleveland Browns Stadium (73,048)
Brown jerseys/white pants

Playing through a steady rain and 60 mph wind gusts in the aftermath of Hurricane Ike, the Browns were once again completely out-played on their home field and lost in the first of five prime-time appearances in the season. In what proved to be the turning point of the game, Cleveland QB Derek Anderson was intercepted at the Pittsburgh 2 in the final seconds of the first half, spoiling a golden scoring opportunity that would haunt the team later. Trailing by seven with just over three minutes remaining, Browns' head coach Romeo Crennel opted to kick a field goal on fourth-and-seven from the Pittsburgh 20 rather than go for the first down. Still up by four, the Steelers controlled the ball for the next three minutes, giving the Browns just enough time for three desperate plays. For the second straight week, Cleveland's heralded offense was unable to find any rhythm, being limited to just 208 total yards despite running more plays and controlling the ball longer than Pittsburgh. The Browns' defense kept them in the game, limiting the Steelers to less than 300 yards and collecting three sacks of QB Ben Roethlisberger, who played the game with a separated shoulder.

Record: 0–2

	1	2	3	4		
Steelers	0	7	3	0	=	10
Browns	0	0	3	3	=	6

PIT-Ward 11-yd. pass from Roethlisberger (Reed kick)
PIT-Reed 48-yd. FG
CLE-Dawson 31-yd. FG
CLE-Dawson 38-yd. FG

Passing
PIT: Roethlisberger 12–19–186 1 TD 0 INT
CLE: Anderson 18–32–166 0 TD 0 INT

Rushing
PIT: Parker 28–105, Holmes 1–10, Davis 1–2, Roethlisberger 1–0
CLE: Lewis 19–38, Anderson 3–6, Cribbs 1–5, Harrison 1–2, Vickers 1–2

Receiving
PIT: Holmes 5–94, Ward 5–59, Miller 2–33
CLE: Winslow 7–55, Edwards 3–32, Lewis 3–28, Harrison 1–23, Steptoe 2–16, Wright 1–9, Vickers 1–3

Sunday, September 21
Baltimore Ravens 28, Browns 10
M&T Bank Stadium (71,104)
White jerseys/white pants

A halftime lead quickly vanished in the third quarter when a pair of Derek Anderson interceptions in a three-minute period swung the momentum to the Ravens, who then cruised to an easy victory. With the Browns ahead 10–7 to start the second half on the strength of a third-down touchdown pass to RB Jerome Harrison, Anderson's third pass of the third quarter was picked off and returned to the Cleveland 12, setting up the go-ahead touchdown. Two plays later, another Anderson interception by DB Ed Reed was returned 32 yards for score, and the Browns never again crossed midfield. For the third straight week, the Cleveland offense struggled, this time managing only 169 yards of offense as Anderson finished with a miserable passer rating of 22.9. With the defeat, the Browns dropped to 0–3 for the second time in three years.
Record: 0–3

	1	2	3	4		
Browns	0	10	0	0	=	10
Ravens	0	7	21	0	=	28

CLE-Harrison 19-yd. pass from Anderson (Dawson kick)
BAL-McGahee 5-yd. run (Stover kick)
CLE-Dawson 38-yd. FG
BAL-McClain 1-yd. run (Stover kick)
BAL-Reed 32-yd. interception return (Stover kick)
BAL-McClain 1-yd. run (Stover kick)

Passing
CLE: Anderson 14–37–125 1 TD 3 INT
BAL: Flacco 13–19–129 0 TD 2 INT

Rushing
CLE: Lewis 12–56, Wright 1–11, Vickers 1–4, Anderson 1–2
BAL: McClain 17–66, McGahee 15–64, Rice 5–21, Neal 1–2, Flacco 6-(-2)

Receiving
CLE: Edwards 3–27, Lewis 3–21, Vickers 2–21, Harrison 1–19, Cribbs 1–17, Winslow 2–14, Steptoe 2–6
BAL: Mason 4–42, Heap 2–32, Williams 3–26, Clayton 2–14, McGahee 1–11, McClain 1–4

Sunday, September 28
Browns 20, Cincinnati Bengals 12
Paul Brown Stadium (65,541)
White jerseys/white pants

In a sloppy game between two struggling teams, the Browns exploded for 17 fourth-quarter points to pull out their initial victory of the season and first win in Cincinnati in five years. With Cincinnati QB Carson Palmer sidelined with an elbow injury, the Browns' defense dominated the Bengals. But, with the Cleveland offense still playing poorly, Cincy still took a 6–3 lead into the fourth quarter. The momentum swung in the first four minutes of the final period as a one-handed touchdown catch by WR Braylon Edwards gave the Browns the lead, then on the Bengals' next play, Cleveland DB Mike Adams recovered a fumble to set up a short touchdown run by Jamal Lewis. After the Bengals cut the margin to 17–12 midway through the fourth quarter, the Browns recovered a fumble at the Cincinnati 19 with two minutes remaining and tacked on an insurance field goal with 32 seconds left. While the Browns were held under 275 yards of offense for the fourth straight week, the defense limited the Bengals to just 211 while forcing five turnovers.
Record: 1–3

	1	2	3	4		
Browns	3	0	0	17	=	20
Bengals	0	6	0	6	=	12

CLE-Dawson 25-yd. FG
CIN-Graham 42-yd. FG
CIN-Graham 45-yd. FG
CLE-Edwards 4-yd. pass from Anderson (Dawson kick)
CLE-Lewis 1-yd. run (Dawson kick)
CIN-Johnson 4-yd. pass from Fitzpatrick (pass failed)
CLE-Dawson 29-yd. FG

Passing
CLE: Anderson 15–24–138 1 TD 1 INT
CIN: Fitzpatrick 21–35–156 1 TD 3 INT

Rushing
CLE: Lewis 25–79, Harrison 4–20, Wright 5–18, Anderson 4–11, Vickers 1–6, Cribbs 1–0
CIN: Fitzpatrick 4–41, Perry 12–28

Receiving
CLE: Winslow 5–54, Steptoe 2–24, Edwards 3–22, Lewis 2–15, Wright 1–10, Vickers 1–8, Harrison 1–5
CIN: Houshmandzadeh 6–50, Chatman 2–32, Johnson 3–28, Kelly 3–21, Perry 5–15, Utecht 2–10

Monday, October 13
Browns 35, New York Giants 14
Cleveland Browns Stadium (73,102)
Brown jerseys/white pants

In what proved to be the highlight of the season, the Browns rolled over the defending Super Bowl champions before a raucous home crowd and under a full harvest moon on *Monday Night Football.* Wearing their throwback numeral helmets, after taking a 17–14 halftime lead, the Browns pulled away in the second half, holding the 4–0 Giants scoreless and controlling the game. Derek Anderson played his finest game of the year, throwing for 310 yards, while Braylon Edwards tallied a career-best 154 receiving yards—129 in the first half. Altogether, the offense rolled up a season-best 454 total yards and allowed no sacks or interceptions. The defense also rose to the occasion, intercepting Giants' QB Eli Manning three times, the last resulting in a game-clinching 94-yard return for a touchdown by DB Eric Wright midway through the fourth quarter. It marked the Browns' first Monday-night victory in 15 years and what would prove to be their only home win in 2008.
Record: 2–3

	1	2	3	4		
Giants	0	14	0	0	=	14
Browns	3	14	3	15	=	35

CLE-Dawson 28-yd. FG
NYG-Jacobs 7-yd. run (Carney kick)
CLE-Lewis 4-yd. run (Dawson kick)
CLE-Dinkins 22-yd. pass from Anderson (Dawson kick)
NYG-Burress 3-yd. pass from Manning (Carney kick)
CLE-Dawson 26-yd. FG
CLE-Edwards 11-yd. pass from Anderson (Dawson kick)
CLE-Wright 94-yd. interception return (Edwards pass from Anderson)

Passing
NYG: Manning 18–28–196 1 TD 3 INT
CLE: Anderson 18–29–310 2 TD 0 INT

Rushing
NYG: Ward 10–101, Jacobs 14–67, Manning 1–13
CLE: Lewis 21–88, Harrison 2–41, Cribbs 1–12, Wright 1–3, Vickers 1–2, Anderson 4-(-2)

Receiving
NYG: Smith 9–94, Burress 4–58, Boss 1–24, Matthews 1–13, Hixon 1–6, Ward 2–1
CLE: Edwards 5–154, Heiden 5–59, Harrison 2–26, Dinkins 1–22, Steptoe 1–20, Stallworth 2–19, Wright 1–6, Lewis 1–4

Sunday, October 19
Washington Redskins 14, Browns 11
FedEx Field (90,487)
Brown jerseys/white pants

Before the largest crowd ever to attend a Browns' regular-season game (and trailing only the 1951 College All-Star Game throng of 92,180 in overall team history), the momentum gained with the Monday-night victory evaporated with a poor performance in the nation's capital, as a late rally wasn't enough to rescue the Browns from losing to the Redskins for the first time in 17 years. After neither team scored in the first half, Washington rolled to a 14–3 advantage early in the fourth quarter. The Cleveland offense, sluggish all afternoon, clawed back into the game after Cleveland DB Brodney Pool recovered a Washington fumble at the Redskins' 29 with 5:36 left. After a touchdown catch by WR Josh Cribbs and a two-point conversion with less than three minutes remaining, the Cleveland defense quickly forced a punt. The Browns regained possession at their own 29 with 1:51 left and drove to the Washington 36. A 54-yard field-goal attempt by Phil Dawson with 25 seconds remaining sliced wide right, handing the Browns their fourth loss. While the offense barely managed half the total yardage of the week before, the defense was lit up by Washington RB Clinton Portis, who rushed for 175 yards.
Record: 2–4

	1	2	3	4		
Browns	0	0	3	8	=	11
Redskins	0	0	7	7	=	14

WAS-Portis 3-yd. run (Suisham kick)
CLE-Dawson 37-yd. FG
WAS-Moss 18-yd. pass from Campbell (Suisham kick)
CLE-Cribbs 1-yd. pass from Anderson (Edwards pass from Anderson)

Passing
CLE: Anderson 14–37–136 1 TD 0 INT
WAS: Campbell 14–23–164 1 TD 0 INT

Rushing
CLE: Lewis 19–80, Harrison 3–12, Anderson 3–4, Cribbs 1–2, Vickers 1–2, Wright 1–2
WAS: Portis 27–175, Cartwright 3–12, Alexander 3–8, Campbell 2–1, Davis 1-(-3)

Receiving
CLE: Edwards 4–58, Stallworth 2–24, Lewis 1–18, Winslow 2–17, Heiden 1–10, Vickers 1–6, Dinkins 1–4, Cribbs 1–1, Ali 1-(-2)
WAS: Moss 4–75, Randle El 4–56, Cooley 4–32, Portis 1–8, Cartwright 1-(-7)

Sunday, October 26
Browns 23, Jacksonville Jaguars 17
Jacksonville Municipal Stadium (64,775)
White jerseys/white pants

After squandering a 10-point halftime lead, the Browns scratched out a narrow victory thanks to a pair of fourth-quarter field goals by Phil Dawson and a defensive stand in the final seconds. After the Jaguars tied the game at 17 midway through the fourth quarter, the Browns responded with a 77-yard drive that resulted in a field goal with 4:27 remaining, then recovered a fumble on the ensuing kickoff and cashed in for another Dawson field goal less than a minute later to put them up 23–17. The Jaguars drove to the Cleveland 26 in the final seconds, then Browns' DB Nick Sorenson broke up a potential touchdown pass with a second left, and a final desperation toss sailed out of the end zone after time expired. The key play of the game was a blocked 38-yard field goal by Browns' DL Shaun Rogers early in the fourth quarter that would have tied the game and changed the complexion of the final period. With their third victory in four games, the Browns appeared on the brink of atoning for their miserable start to the season.
Record: 3–4

	1	2	3	4		
Browns	7	10	0	6	=	23
Jaguars	0	7	7	3	=	17

CLE-Stallworth 3-yd. pass from Anderson (Dawson kick)
JAX-Williams 5-yd. pass from Garrard (Scobee kick)
CLE-Lewis 2-yd. run (Dawson kick)
CLE-Dawson 32-yd. FG
JAX-M. Jones 8-yd. pass from Garrard (Scobee kick)
JAX-Scobee 53-yd. FG
CLE-Dawson 20-yd. FG
CLE-Dawson 42-yd. FG

Passing
CLE: Anderson 14–27–246 1 TD 0 INT
JAX: Garrard 25–42–283 2 TD 0 INT

Rushing
CLE: Lewis 20–81, Vickers 2–10, Wright 1–1, Harrison 1-(-1)
JAX: Garrard 7–59, Jones-Drew 12–29, Taylor 8–24, Williamson 1–1, G. Jones 1–0

Receiving
CLE: Heiden 3–73, Edwards 2–64, Steptoe 1–53, Wright 2–18, Stallworth 3–13, Vickers 1–13, Lewis 1–7, Dinkins 1–5
JAX: M. Jones 8–117, Northcutt 5–49, Williams 3–42, Lewis 3–34, Jones-Drew 3–19, G. Jones 1–11, Williamson 1–6, Angulo 1–5

Sunday, November 2
Baltimore Ravens 37, Browns 27
Cleveland Browns Stadium (73,078)
Brown jerseys/white pants

In what proved to be a microcosm of the entire season, the Browns rallied from a 10-point deficit, then blew a 14-point second-half lead and lost by 10 on their home field following one of the most incredible collapses in team history. Cleveland appeared to have the game in control by scoring touchdowns on the first two possessions of the third quarter to take a 27–13 lead, but the Ravens rallied back with touchdowns on their next two series to tie the game again. On the next possession, a wide-open Braylon Edwards dropped what would have been a 77-yard touchdown pass, and the stunned Browns were forced to punt. The Ravens then took the lead on a field goal with less than six minutes to play, but the Browns had one last chance, taking over at midfield with three minutes left. A third-down screen pass by Derek

Anderson was picked off by Baltimore LB Terrell Suggs and returned 42 yards for the game-clinching touchdown. The Cleveland defense played one of its worst games of the season, allowing 429 total yards, including 154 rushing on just 21 carries by RB Ray Rice. Aside from a 54-yard field goal by Phil Dawson, the lone bright spot for the Browns was Josh Cribbs, who tallied 278 return yards, including a 92-yard kickoff return for a touchdown in the first quarter.
Record: 3–5

	1	2	3	4		
Ravens	10	3	7	17	=	37
Browns	7	6	14	0	=	27

BAL-Stover 41-yd. FG
BAL-Clayton 47-yd. pass from Flacco (Stover kick)
CLE-Cribbs 92-yd. kickoff return (Dawson kick)
CLE-Dawson 23-yd. FG
BAL-Stover 32-yd. FG
CLE-Dawson 54-yd. FG
CLE-Edwards 28-yd. pass from Anderson (Dawson kick)
CLE-Wright 7-yd. pass from Anderson (Dawson kick)
BAL-McClain 1-yd. run (Stover kick)
BAL-Mason 28-yd. pass from Flacco (Stover kick)
BAL-Stover 22-yd. FG
BAL-Suggs 42-yd. interception return (Stover kick)

Passing
BAL: Flacco 17–29–248 2 TD 0 INT
CLE: Anderson 17–33–219 2 TD 1 INT

Rushing
BAL: Rice 21–154, McClain 14–34, Flacco 4–2, Neal 1–2, Smith 1–1
CLE: Lewis 19–49, Anderson 2–8, Harrison 1–5, Wright 1–2

Receiving
BAL: Mason 9–136, Clayton 4–87, Rice 3–22, McClain 1–3
CLE: Edwards 4–86, Winslow 5–64, Heiden 2–25, Wright 3–22, Lewis 1–13, Steptoe 2–9

Thursday, November 6
Denver Broncos 34, Browns 30
Cleveland Browns Stadium (73,141)
Brown jerseys/white pants

Two days after Barack Obama was elected president of the United States, the Browns squandered a double-digit lead in the second half for the second straight game as they lost a nationally televised Thursday-night game with Denver. With erratic Derek Anderson benched, Browns' QB Brady Quinn made his first NFL start and played well, throwing for 239 yards and a pair of touchdowns, but it was for naught. The Cleveland defense was ripped apart, allowing 564 total yards—the third-most ever against the Browns—as Denver QB Jay Cutler threw for 447 and three scores. The Browns built a 23–10 lead early in the third quarter and took a 10-point advantage into the fourth before falling apart. They allowed three touchdowns in the final period, including a 93-yard touchdown pass to WR Eddie Royal. The Broncos surged to a 27–23 lead, but the Browns responded with a 78-yard drive capped by a short Jamal Lewis touchdown run to put them back ahead with five minutes left. Denver then drove 80 yards in 13 plays to score the game-winning touchdown with 1:14 left and clinched victory when Browns' TE Kellen Winslow Jr. dropped a fourth-down pass near midfield. It spoiled an otherwise nice game for Winslow, who caught 10 passes for 111 yards and two scores, sparking a Cleveland offense that tallied nearly 400 total yards, but was ultimately overshadowed.
Record: 3–6

	1	2	3	4		
Broncos	7	3	3	21	=	34
Browns	7	13	3	7	=	30

DEN-Torain 1-yd. run (Prater kick)
CLE-Winslow 5-yd. pass from Quinn (Dawson kick)
CLE-Dawson 24-yd. FG
CLE-Winslow 16-yd. pass from Quinn (Dawson kick)
DEN-Prater 35-yd. FG
CLE-Dawson 52-yd. FG
CLE-Dawson 33-yd. FG
DEN-Prater 30-yd. FG
DEN-Royal 93-yd. pass from Cutler (Prater kick)
DEN-Graham 28-yd. pass from Cutler (Prater kick)
CLE-Lewis 1-yd. run (Dawson kick)
DEN-Marshall 11-yd. pass from Cutler (Prater kick)

Passing
DEN: Cutler 24–42–447 3 TD 1 INT
CLE: Quinn 23–35–239 2 TD 0 INT

Rushing
DEN: Torain 12–68, Cutler 7–29, Hillis 8–24, Young 1–2
CLE: Lewis 19–60, Harrison 5–48, Cribbs 3–48, Quinn 1–3, Wright 1–1

Receiving
DEN: Royal 6–164, Scheffler 4–92, Marshall 6–89, Graham 3–50, Jackson 3–36, Stokley 2–16
CLE: Winslow 10–111, Stallworth 4–48, Heiden 3–24, Lewis 2–24, Edwards 1–15, Harrison 1–9, Steptoe 1–7, Ali 1–1

Monday, November 17
Browns 29, Buffalo Bills 27
Ralph Wilson Stadium (71,645)
White jerseys/white pants

Coming close to becoming the first NFL team to blow double-digit leads to lose three consecutive games, the Browns managed to pull out a narrow Monday-night victory thanks to some late heroics. After Buffalo threw three first-quarter interceptions to allow the Browns to sprint to a 13–0 advantage, Buffalo narrowed it to three points in the third quarter. Browns' RB Jerome Harrison then broke through for a 72-yard touchdown on the first play of what promised to be a wild fourth quarter, but the Bills returned the ensuing kickoff for a touchdown to narrow the margin again. The Bills took their first lead with a touchdown with just over two minutes left, then the Browns drove to the Buffalo 39, where Phil Dawson kicked a career-best 56-yard field goal to give the Browns a 29–27 lead with 1:39 left. Yet after another nice kickoff return, the Bills marched to the Cleveland 29 and were poised to steal the victory. But Rian Lindell missed a 47-yard field goal wide right with 38 seconds left to secure what proved to be the Browns' final victory of the season. While the Browns' offense was effective once again, the defense struggled, particularly in stopping RB Marshawn Lynch, who rushed for 119 yards and caught 10 passes for 58 more.
Record: 4–6

	1	2	3	4		
Browns	6	7	3	13	=	29
Bills	0	10	3	14	=	27

CLE-Dawson 40-yd. FG
CLE-Dawson 33-yd. FG
CLE-Cribbs 2-yd. run (Dawson kick)
BUF-Lynch 18-yd. pass from Edwards (Lindell kick)
BUF-Lindell 26-yd. FG
CLE-Dawson 43-yd. FG
BUF-Lindell 31-yd. FG
CLE-Harrison 72-yd. run (Dawson kick)
BUF-McKelvin 98-yd. kickoff return (Lindell kick)
CLE-Dawson 22-yd. FG
BUF-Edwards 1-yd. run (Lindell kick)
CLE-Dawson 56-yd. FG

Passing
CLE: Quinn 14–36–185 0 TD 0 INT
BUF: Edwards 16–26–148 1 TD 3 INT

Rushing
CLE: Harrison 3–80, Lewis 18–65, Quinn 4–18, Cribbs 1–2, Stallworth 1-(-4)
BUF: Lynch 23–119, Jackson 12–60, Edwards 3–7

Receiving
CLE: Edwards 8–104, Winslow 3–40, Harrison 1–21, Ali 1–12, Steptoe 1–8
BUF: Lynch 10–58, Johnson 3–41, Royal 1–22, Parrish 1–21, Fine 1–6

Sunday, November 23
Houston Texans 16, Browns 6
Cleveland Browns Stadium (72,077)
Brown jerseys/white pants

With a horrible performance, the Browns were dominated by the struggling Texans and dropped to 1–5 at home on the season. The Browns coughed up five turnovers, including three interceptions by Brady Quinn, who was benched late in the third quarter. Houston scored on its first two possessions to take a 10–0 lead, but the Browns sandwiched a pair of field goals around a blocked field goal by Shaun Rogers to narrow the margin to 10–6. After Houston upped the margin to 10 points, a Browns' drive to the Houston 12 ended with Quinn's third interception, then Phil Dawson missed a 39-yard field goal midway through the fourth quarter to spoil their final scoring opportunity. It marked the first of what would become six consecutive games in which the Cleveland offense failed to score a touchdown.
Record: 4–7

	1	2	3	4		
Texans	7	6	3	0	=	16
Browns	0	6	0	0	=	6

HOU-Walter 17-yd. pass from Rosenfels (Brown kick)
HOU-Brown 31-yd. FG
CLE-Dawson 32-yd. FG
CLE-Dawson 32-yd. FG
HOU-Brown 31-yd. FG
HOU-Brown 36-yd. FG

Passing
HOU: Rosenfels 24–32–275 1 TD 2 INT
CLE: Quinn 8–18–94 0 TD 2 INT, Anderson 5–14–51 0 TD 1 INT

Rushing
HOU: Slaton 21–73, Green 13–39, Rosenfels 2–0
CLE: Lewis 10–58, Harrison 7–31, Cribbs 2–6, Anderson 1–0

Receiving
HOU: Johnson 10–116, Walter 7–93, Daniels 3–28, Anderson 1–11, Davis 1–10, Leach 1–9, Green 1–8
CLE: Edwards 5–85, Stallworth 1–18, Winslow 1–11, Lewis 2–10, Harrison 1–8, Heiden 1–5, Steptoe 1–4, Vickers 1–4

Sunday, November 30
Indianapolis Colts 10, Browns 6
Cleveland Browns Stadium (72,411)
Brown jerseys/white pants

Despite another lousy offensive performance, the Browns were on the brink of victory midway through the fourth quarter before a fumble return for a touchdown handed them their fourth loss in five games. With the Cleveland defense containing Indianapolis QB Peyton Manning and the playoff-bound Colts, a pair of Phil Dawson field goals gave the Browns a 6–3 halftime lead that lasted into the final period. The defense came up with the highlight of the day when it stopped the Colts on consecutive plays from the Cleveland 1 late in the second quarter, including a fourth-down stuff of Manning at the goal line. Then, with 10 minutes to play in the game, Derek Anderson—starting in place of Brady Quinn, who was lost for the season with a fractured finger—was sacked and fumbled. Indy DE Robert Mathis scooped up the loose ball and returned it 37 yards for what proved to be the game-winning score. Cleveland's final two possessions stalled, and Anderson was lost for the season when he injured his knee on a sack with a minute left. The Cleveland offense managed only 193 total yards, beginning a string of five consecutive games in which the Browns failed to accumulate 200 yards. Making matters worse, third-stringer Ken Dorsey was thrust into the role of starting QB.
Record: 4–8

	1	2	3	4		
Colts	3	0	0	7	=	10
Browns	3	3	0	0	=	6

CLE-Dawson 34-yd. FG
IND-Vinatieri 30-yd. FG
CLE-Dawson 25-yd. FG
IND-Mathis 37-yd. fumble return (Vinatieri kick)

Passing
IND: Manning 15–21–125 0 TD 2 INT
CLE: Anderson 16–26–110 0 TD 0 INT, Dorsey 0–3–0 0 TD 1 INT

Rushing
IND: Addai 15–57, Rhodes 11–35, Manning 3-(-2)
CLE: Lewis 24–77, Wright 2–11, Harrison 2–6, Anderson 2–5, Vickers 1–2, Cribbs 1–0

Receiving
IND: Wayne 4–46, Harrison 3–27, Clark 2–24, Gonzalez 2–13, Rhodes 2–6, Addai 1–6, Robinson 1–3
CLE: Edwards 2–36, Wright 3–18, Heiden 3–15, Winslow 3–15, Rucker 1–9, Lewis 1–7, Stallworth 1–4, Steptoe 1–3, Vickers 1–3

Sunday, December 7
Tennessee Titans 28, Browns 9
LP Field (69,143)
White jerseys/white pants

The floundering Browns were no match for the 11–1 Titans, who picked up more than twice as much total yardage and won easily despite committing three turnovers and 131 yards in penalties. With Ken Dorsey making his first start in three years, the offense once again failed to score a touchdown, managing just 178 total yards and three field goals, though the Browns took a 6–0 lead into the second quarter. The Titans controlled the line of scrimmage, rolling up more than 200 rushing yards as RB Chris Johnson ran for 136, and RB LenDale White added 99 more. Conversely, Browns' RB Jamal Lewis was corralled for just seven yards on seven carries. The defeat guaranteed a losing record for the Browns in 2008 after entering the season with playoff expectations.
Record: 4–9

	1	2	3	4		
Browns	6	0	0	3	=	9
Titans	0	14	7	7	=	28

CLE-Dawson 47-yd. FG
CLE-Dawson 41-yd. FG
TEN-Hall 28-yd. pass from Collins (Bironas kick)

TEN-White 3-yd. run (Bironas kick)
TEN-Gage 9-yd. pass from Collins (Bironas kick)
CLE-Dawson 39-yd. FG
TEN-Johnson 25-yd. run (Bironas kick)

Passing
CLE: Dorsey 22–43–150 0 TD 1 INT, Cribbs 0–1–0 0 TD 0 INT
TEN: Collins 14–23–155 2 TD 2 INT

Rushing
CLE: Cribbs 6–24, Lewis 7–7, Harrison 2–2, Wright 2–1, Vickers 1–1, Dorsey 1–0
TEN: Johnson 19–136, White 24–99

Receiving
CLE: Wright 5–40, Edwards 3–38, Heiden 4–29, Steptoe 4–20, Stallworth 1–15, Harrison 2–6, Lewis 2–3, Vickers 1-(-1)
TEN: Johnson 4–30, Hall 1–28, Crumpler 1–20, McCareins 1–20, Scaife 2–19, Gage 2–18, Jones 2–18, White 1–2

Monday, December 15
Philadelphia Eagles 30, Browns 10
Lincoln Financial Field (69,144)
White jerseys/white pants

An interception return for a touchdown midway through the fourth quarter was all that prevented the Browns from extending their string to four consecutive games without scoring a touchdown as the Eagles rolled to an easy triumph on *Monday Night Football.* Once again held under 200 total yards, the Cleveland offense was miserable, managing just a single field goal (on which Phil Dawson set a franchise record for most field goals in a season with 30) and handing the Eagles seven points on a 50-yard interception return for a score. Things would have been much worse were it not for a big night from Browns' DB Brandon McDonald, who returned an interception 24 yards for Cleveland's only touchdown and also picked off a pass with one hand in the end zone just before the half and returned it 98 yards to the Philadelphia 7 as time expired—the second-longest interception return in team history. McDonald's score snapped a string of 16 consecutive quarters without a touchdown for the Browns, their first in over 245 minutes of play. The only other highlight was Braylon Edwards cracking the 100-yard barrier for the third time on the season, all on *Monday Night Football.*
Record: 4–10

	1	2	3	4		
Browns	3	0	0	7	=	10
Eagles	10	7	3	10	=	30

PHI-Curtis 14-yd. pass from McNabb (Akers kick)
CLE-Dawson 27-yd. FG
PHI-Akers 24-yd. FG
PHI-Samuel 50-yd. interception return (Akers kick)
PHI-Akers 34-yd. FG
PHI-Akers 34-yd. FG
PHI-Lewis 10-yd. pass from McNabb (Akers kick)
CLE-McDonald 24-yd. interception return (Dawson kick)

Passing
CLE: Dorsey 11–28–156 0 TD 2 INT, Cribbs 0–1–0 0 TD 0 INT
PHI: McNabb 26–35–290 2 TD 1 INT, Kolb 0–2–0 0 TD 1 INT, Jackson 0–1–0 0 TD 1 INT

Rushing
CLE: Lewis 14–32, Cribbs 5–25, Dorsey 1–0
PHI: Buckhalter 6–55, Westbrook 16–53, Eckel 9–28, Kolb 2-(-2)

Receiving
CLE: Edwards 5–102, Vickers 1–21, Lewis 3–14, Stallworth 1–13, Dinkins 1–6
PHI: Avant 5–101, Jackson 5–77, Curtis 4–45, Baskett 3–15, Westbrook 3–14, Smith 2–13, Lewis 1–10, Celek 2–9, Klecko 1–6

Sunday, December 21
Cincinnati Bengals 14, Browns 0
Cleveland Browns Stadium (72,361)
Brown jerseys/white pants

On a bitterly cold afternoon—with wind gusts over 25 mph and the chill factor at 0°F—the Browns closed out an abysmal home season with a lifeless shutout defeat to the 2–11–1 Bengals, who avenged their September loss to the Browns. The punchless Cleveland offense managed only 182 yards and coughed up four turnovers, including one for a touchdown for the third straight week. This one was a 50-yard interception return by DB Leon Hall, who picked off three passes on the day. The Bengals, who were without starting QB Carson Palmer and WR Chad Johnson, attempted only nine passes for the game and were paced by RB Cedric Benson, who carried the football 38 times for 171 yards. Adding insult to injury, the Browns

ONE-START WONDERS

Generally thrust into the spotlight in either indifference or utter desperation, seven quarterbacks have started one game and one game only for the Browns since they joined the NFL in 1950:

Len Dawson
October 22, 1961
6 of 12 for 68 yards, 0 TD 2 INT
Browns beat Steelers, 30–28
With starter Milt Plum nursing a sore thumb, future Hall of Famer Dawson's only start with the Browns ended in victory, but only after Dawson was pulled and replaced by Plum in the second half after the Steelers rebounded from a 10-point deficit to take the lead.

Gary Lane
December 17, 1967
19 of 39 for 211 yards, 2 TD 1 INT
Browns lose to Eagles, 28–24
Blanton Collier opted to rest many of his starters in a meaningless regular-season finale in preparation for the playoffs, and Lane started in place of Frank Ryan. After the Browns fell behind by 18 points, Lane tossed a pair of scoring passes in the fourth quarter to lead a late charge, but it was for naught.

Don Gault
October 3, 1970
1 of 16 for 44 yards, 0 TD 2 INT
Browns beat Steelers, 15–7
After Bill Nelsen went down with a knee injury the week before, Gault got the start in a Saturday-night game with the Steelers and put forth one of the worst performances in NFL history. But rookie Mike Phipps, making his NFL debut, replaced him in the second half and helped rally the Browns to victory after trailing 7–2 at the half.

Will Cureton
November 9, 1975
10 of 32 for 95 yards, 1 TD 1 INT
Browns lose to Lions, 21–10
With both Mike Phipps and Brian Sipe dinged up and ineffective, Cureton was called upon in desperation to try to deliver the 0–7 Browns' first victory of the season. It proved to be not only his lone start but the only appearance of Cureton's brief NFL career.

Terry Luck
December 18, 1977
6 of 15 for 105 yards, 0 TD 4 INT
Browns lose to Seahawks, 20–19
In the season finale, with both Brian Sipe and Dave Mays lost for the season to injury, Terry Luck made the only start of his career for interim head coach Dick Modzelewski, who filled in after Forrest Gregg resigned earlier in the week. Luck caught a touchdown on a halfback-option pass from Greg Pruitt, but his four interceptions proved to be the difference in a narrow defeat.

Spergon Wynn
December 3, 2000
5 of 16 for 17 yards, 0 TD 0 INT
Browns lose to Jaguars, 48–0
In what proved to be the final appearance of his brief Cleveland career, Wynn was tossed to the wolves in a humiliating defeat as the injury-riddled Browns were held to 53 total yards, punted 12 times, collected only two first downs, and didn't cross midfield.

Bruce Gradkowski
December 28, 2008
5 of 16 for 18 yards, 0 TD 2 INT
Browns lose to Steelers, 31–0
With their top three QBs all unavailable due to injury, in desperation the Browns turned to Gradkowski to close out a disastrous season. The results weren't surprising as the Browns were crushed by the eventual Super Bowl champions, crossing midfield just once.

lost another QB as Ken Dorsey left the game dazed in the fourth quarter (after throwing three interceptions) and was replaced by Bruce Gradkowski. The sole offensive highlight for Cleveland was Jamal Lewis surpassing the 10,000-rushing-yard mark for his career.

Record: 4–11

	1	2	3	4		
Bengals	7	7	0	0	=	14
Browns	0	0	0	0	=	0

CIN-Hall 50-yd. interception return (Graham kick)
CIN-Henry 20-yd. pass from Fitzpatrick (Graham kick)

Passing
CIN: Fitzpatrick 5–9–55 1 TD 0 INT
CLE: Dorsey 10–17–64 0 TD 3 INT, Gradkowski 2–5–8 0 TD 1 INT

Rushing
CIN: Benson 38–171, Fitzpatrick 5–10, J. Johnson 3–10
CLE: Lewis 16–76, Cribbs 5–36, Wright 7–30, Harrison 1-(-1)

Receiving
CIN: J. Johnson 3–27, Henry 1–20, Caldwell 1–8
CLE: Wright 6–33, Edwards 4–31, Dinkins 1–4, Stallworth 1–4

Sunday, December 28
Pittsburgh Steelers 31, Browns 0
Heinz Field (63,553)
White jerseys/white pants

A terrible season finally came to a close with a pathetic defeat in Pittsburgh as the Browns were shut out for the second straight week and completed their sixth straight game without an offensive touchdown, setting an NFL record. Managing just 126 total yards and eight first downs, the Browns crossed midfield only on their first possession as starting QB Bruce Gradkowski completed only five of 16 passes and was picked off twice, the second of which resulted in a defensive touchdown allowed by the Browns for the fourth straight game. Though he didn't compile 100 yards in a single game all season, Jamal Lewis surpassed the 1,000-yard mark for the second straight year, tallying a season-high 94 yards in the finale. He became the first Browns' RB to top four digits in two straight years since Mike Pruitt 27 years earlier. Before the game was over, Browns' GM Phil Savage was fired and returned to Cleveland, and Romeo Crennel was fired as head coach the next day. With his final defeat, Crennel finished his Cleveland career with a 0–8 record against Pittsburgh, becoming the only Browns' coach never to defeat the Steelers.
Record: 4–12

	1	2	3	4		
Browns	0	0	0	0	=	0
Steelers	0	14	3	14	=	31

PIT-Parker 34-yd. run (Reed kick)
PIT-Leftwich 8-yd. run (Reed kick)
PIT-Reed 22-yd. FG
PIT-Russell 3-yd. run (Reed kick)
PIT-Carter 32-yd. interception return (Reed kick)

Passing
CLE: Gradkowski 5–16–18 0 TD 2 INT, Cribbs 1–2–8 0 TD 0 INT
PIT: Roethlisberger 9–14–110 0 TD 1 INT, Leftwich 7–12–80 0 TD 0 INT, Dixon 1–1–3 0 TD 0 INT

Rushing
CLE: Lewis 23–94, Cribbs 2–7, Gradkowski 1–2, Vickers 1–2, Harrison 2–1
PIT: Parker 23–116, Moore 4–23, Russell 4–21, Davis 1–11, Leftwich 1–8, Dixon 2-(-3)

Receiving
CLE: Stallworth 1–12, Rucker 1–8, Edwards 1–5, Ali 1–2, Harrison 2-(-1)
PIT: Ward 6–70, Miller 5–55, Holmes 3–31, Davis 1–14, Washington 1–13, Moore 1–10

2009

Sunday, September 13
Minnesota Vikings 34, Browns 20
Cleveland Browns Stadium (70,560)
Brown jerseys/white pants

In Eric Mangini's first game as Cleveland head coach, the Browns clawed to a three-point halftime lead but were overwhelmed in the second half by the eventual NFC North champs. Just before the intermission, WR Josh Cribbs returned a Minnesota punt 67 yards for a touchdown to give the Browns a 13–10 advantage and tie him with Eric Metcalf for the franchise record of seven kick returns for touchdowns, but the Vikings dominated the game from there. Led by QB Brett Favre, making his Minnesota debut (after playing for Mangini with the Jets the year before), the Vikes scored 24 straight points to take a commanding lead. Minnesota RB Adrian Peterson was dominant, rushing for a whopping 180 yards—155 in the second half alone—and three touchdowns.

Record: 0–1

	1	2	3	4		
Vikings	3	7	14	10	=	34
Browns	3	10	0	7	=	20

CLE-Dawson 37-yd. FG
MIN-Longwell 21-yd. FG
MIN-Peterson 1-yd. run (Longwell kick)
CLE-Dawson 20-yd. FG
CLE-Cribbs 67-yd. punt return (Dawson kick)
MIN-Peterson 1-yd. run (Longwell kick)
MIN-Harvin 6-yd. pass from Favre (Longwell kick)
MIN-Longwell 37-yd. FG
MIN-Peterson 64-yd. run (Longwell kick)
CLE-Royal 26-yd. pass from Quinn (Dawson kick)

Passing
MIN: Favre 14–21–110 1 TD 0 INT, Jackson 0–1–0 0 TD 0 INT
CLE: Quinn 21–35–205 1 TD 1 INT

Rushing
MIN: Peterson 25–180, Harvin 2–22, Taylor 7–17, Dugan 1–5, Tahi 1–2, Jackson 1-(-1)
CLE: Lewis 11–57, Quinn 2–21, Cribbs 3–6, Davis 4–5

Receiving
MIN: Harvin 3–36, Shiancoe 3–26, Peterson 1–18, Rice 2–17, Taylor 5–13
CLE: Royal 4–60, Lewis 3–47, Furrey 4–28, Massaquoi 1–18, Heiden 2–14, Edwards 1–12, Vickers 1–12, Cribbs 2–10, Davis 3–4

Sunday, September 20
Denver Broncos 27, Browns 6
Invesco Field (73,931)
White jerseys/brown pants

After recovering a fumble on the opening kickoff (by future Browns' RB Peyton Hillis) that led to an early field goal, the Browns were blown away by the Broncos, who cruised to an easy victory. Denver rolled up 449 total yards while holding the Browns to just 200, while Cleveland (wearing brown pants in a regular-season game for the first time) coughed up three turnovers and allowed four sacks in a miserable performance that forecasted the next two months. All four sacks were recorded by Denver DE Elvis Dumervil in a performance that sparked a dominating, 17-sack season. Despite a poor offensive showing—and a Brady Quinn fumble that led to Denver's first touchdown—the Browns hung close, staying within four points at the half. But a fumble on the first possession of the third quarter led to a Denver field goal, and then a pair of Broncos' touchdowns in the first seven minutes of the fourth quarter put the game away. It marked the Browns' ninth consecutive loss to Denver in a losing streak that now stretched 19 years.

Record: 0–2

	1	2	3	4		
Browns	6	0	0	0	=	6
Broncos	7	3	3	14	=	27

CLE-Dawson 22-yd. FG
DEN-Scheffler 2-yd. pass from Orton (Prater kick)
CLE-Dawson 47-yd. FG
DEN-Prater 23-yd. FG
DEN-Prater 38-yd. FG
DEN-Hillis 2-yd. run (Prater kick)
DEN-Buckhalter 45-yd. run (Prater kick)

Passing
CLE: Quinn 18–31–161 0 TD 1 INT
DEN: Orton 19–37–263 1 TD 0 INT

Rushing
CLE: Lewis 14–38, Harrison 3–8, Quinn 3–4, Cribbs 1–4
DEN: Buckhalter 9–76, Moreno 17–75, Jordan 7–19, Marshall 1–14, Hillis 1–2, Orton 2–0

Receiving
CLE: Edwards 6–92, Harrison 4–24, Cribbs 5–22, Royal 1–13, Lewis 1–8, Furrey 1–2
DEN: Gaffney 3–82, Stokley 5–70, Marshall 3–34, Buckhalter 1–30, Royal 3–20, Moreno 2–22, Graham 1–3, Scheffler 1–2

Sunday, September 27
Baltimore Ravens 34, Browns 3
M&T Bank Stadium (70,950)
White jerseys/brown pants

The Browns were completely dominated from start to finish as the Ravens improved to 3–0 and dropped the Browns to 0–3 for the third time in four years. Holding the Browns to just 78 total yards in the first half and just 186 for the game, Baltimore cruised to a 20–0 halftime lead and never looked back. Brady Quinn was replaced by Derek Anderson in the second half, but the offense fared no better as Anderson was intercepted three times. The Cleveland defense was ravaged for 479 total yards as QB Joe Flacco threw for 342 yards. It marked the second straight week the Browns failed to score a touchdown, with four more touchdown-less games to follow in 2009. The Browns' lone score came on a field goal by newly acquired kicker Billy Cundiff, signed to replace Phil Dawson, who would miss the next six weeks with a calf injury.
Record: 0–3

	1	2	3	4		
Browns	0	0	0	3	=	3
Ravens	10	10	7	7	=	34

BAL-McGahee 7-yd. run (Hauschka kick)
BAL-Hauschka 36-yd. FG
BAL-Hauschka 33-yd. FG
BAL-McGahee 15-yd. run (Hauschka kick)
BAL-Rice 9-yd. run (Hauschka kick)
CLE-Cundiff 29-yd. FG
BAL-Mason 72-yd. pass from Flacco (Hauschka kick)

Passing
CLE: Anderson 11–19–92 0 TD 3 INT, Quinn 6–8–34 0 TD 1 INT
BAL: Flacco 25–35–342 1 TD 0 INT, Smith 1–2–4 0 TD 0 INT

Rushing
CLE: Harrison 16–52, Davis 5–10, Quinn 2–9
BAL: McGahee 7–67, Rice 11–48, Clayton 2–15, McClain 2–7, Flacco 2–5, Lawrence 4–0

Receiving
CLE: Furrey 4–40, Edwards 3–35, Harrison 5–33, Massaquoi 1–13, Royal 1–7, Cribbs 1–2, Davis 1–1, Vickers 1-(-5)
BAL: Mason 5–118, Washington 5–66, Heap 4–41, Clayton 3–35, McClain 3–29, Rice 4–27, Smith 1–26, Lawrence 1–4

Sunday, October 4
Cincinnati Bengals 23, Browns 20 (OT)
Cleveland Browns Stadium (69,844)
Brown jerseys/white pants

Despite an inspired effort and gritty comeback against the eventual division champions, the Browns dropped to 0–4 with a heartbreaking loss on an overcast afternoon. The Bengals roared to a 14–0 lead following a 75-yard fumble return for a touchdown, but the Browns fought back to surge ahead 20–14 with 6:34 remaining in the game. Cincinnati then drove 70 yards, converting on a key third-and-14 and tied the game on a short touchdown catch by WR Chad Ochocinco (formerly "Johnson") with 1:55 to play. But the Browns stayed alive when NT Shaun Rogers blocked the ensuing extra point to keep the game knotted. After a Cleveland drive stalled at the Cincinnati 40 in the final seconds, the contest tumbled into overtime. The teams exchanged punts three times in sudden-death before the Bengals got rolling with under three minutes remaining, driving to the Cleveland 13. Seven seconds away from a tie, Cincy kicker Shayne Graham connected on a 31-yard field goal—which he nearly missed trying to avoid the oncoming Rogers, who'd already blocked two kicks on the day—to give the Bengals a narrow victory. The Browns' offense finally came to life, rolling up nearly 400 yards as RB Jerome Harrison rushed for 121 yards, and WR Mohamed Massaquoi caught eight passes for 148 yards. Josh Cribbs added 223 yards in returns.
Record: 0–4

	1	2	3	4	OT		
Bengals	7	7	0	6	3	=	23
Browns	0	7	7	6	0	=	20

CIN-Ochocinco 5-yd. pass from Palmer (Graham kick)
CIN-Geathers 75-yd. fumble return (Graham kick)
CLE-Heiden 1-yd. pass from Anderson (Cundiff kick)
CLE-Anderson 1-yd. run (Cundiff kick)
CLE-Cundiff 26-yd. FG
CLE-Cundiff 31-yd. FG
CIN-Ochocinco 2-yd. pass from Palmer (kick failed)
CIN-Graham 31-yd. FG

Passing
CIN: Palmer 23–44–230 2 TD 1 INT
CLE: Anderson 26–48–269 1 TD 1 INT

Rushing
CIN: Benson 18–74, Scott 6–41, Palmer 3–20, Caldwell 1–11, Johnson 1–4, Leonard 1–4
CLE: Harrison 29–121, Cribbs 1–15, Jennings 1–8, Anderson 2–2

Receiving
CIN: Foschi 3–44, Coats 4–36, Henry 2–36, Leonard 6–28, Caldwell 2–26, Ochocinco 3–24, Coles 2–24, Benson 1 12
CLE: Massaquoi 8–148, Furrey 4–37, Heiden 5–33, Harrison 5–31, Royal 2–13, Cribbs 1–5, Jennings 1–2

Sunday, October 11
Browns 6, Buffalo Bills 3
Ralph Wilson Stadium (70,526)
White jerseys/brown pants

In one of the ugliest games in team history, the Browns pulled out their first victory of the season without scoring a touchdown on a blustery day in Buffalo. With both offenses ineffective, it appeared the 3–3 game would head into overtime before Browns' LB Blake Costanzo recovered a fumbled punt return by the Bills at the Buffalo 16 with three minutes remaining. Six straight runs by RB Jamal Lewis pushed the ball to the Buffalo 1, and Billy Cundiff kicked the game-winning field goal with 23 seconds left. Though they managed 171 yards on the ground, including 117 from Lewis, the Browns became the first NFL team in 10 years to win a game while completing two or fewer passes. Derek Anderson went two for 17 for just 23 yards on the day as his receivers dropped nine passes, which was particularly ironic since the team traded erratic WR Braylon Edwards to the New York Jets the previous week. Punter Dave Zastudil also set a franchise record by placing seven punts inside the Buffalo 20. The victory snapped a 10-game Cleveland losing streak and marked the Browns' first triumph since their last visit to Buffalo the previous November.
Record: 1–4

	1	2	3	4		
Browns	0	3	0	3	=	6
Bills	0	0	3	0	=	3

CLE-Cundiff 24-yd. FG
BUF-Lindell 36-yd. FG
CLE-Cundiff 18-yd. FG

Passing
CLE: Anderson 2–17–23 0 TD 1 INT
BUF: Edwards 16–31–152 0 TD 1 INT

Rushing
CLE: Lewis 31–117, Cribbs 1–31, Harrison 8–21, Anderson 1–2
BUF: Lynch 17–69, Edwards 4–40, Jackson 13–30, Owens 1–6

Receiving
CLE: Massaquoi 1–16, Heiden 1–7
BUF: Lynch 6–56, Owens 4–44, Jackson 2–17, Evans 2–11, Fine 1–8, Nelson 1–0

Sunday, October 18
Pittsburgh Steelers 27, Browns 14
Heinz Field (64,398)
White jerseys/brown pants

In a contest that was far more one-sided than the final score indicated, the Steelers dominated the Browns and picked up their twelfth straight victory over their turnpike rivals. Pittsburgh rolled to 543 yards, its highest total in 14 years, as QB Ben Roethlisberger threw for 417 yards and improved to 10–0 all-time against Cleveland. Meanwhile, Derek Anderson fumbled twice, suffered seven dropped passes, and threw a costly interception at the Pittsburgh 1 to wipe out the Browns' final scoring opportunity with four minutes remaining. Despite managing nearly 350 fewer yards of offense, the Browns clawed within 17–14 early in the third quarter and stayed within striking distance until the final minutes. Josh Cribbs sparked the rally with a 98-yard kickoff return for a touchdown, the eighth scoring return of his career.
Record: 1–5

	1	2	3	4		
Browns	0	7	7	0	=	14
Steelers	0	17	7	3	=	27

PIT-Miller 8-yd. pass from Roethlisberger (Reed kick)
PIT-Ward 52-yd. pass from Roethlisberger (Reed kick)
CLE-Cribbs 98-yd. kickoff return (Cundiff kick)
PIT-Reed 32-yd. FG
CLE-Vickers 1-yd. pass from Anderson (Cundiff kick)
PIT-Mendenhall 2-yd. run (Reed kick)
PIT-Reed 39-yd. FG

Passing
CLE: Anderson 9–24–122 1 TD 1 INT, Cribbs 0–2–0 0 TD 1 INT
PIT: Roethlisberger 23–35–417 2 TD 1 INT

Rushing
CLE: Cribbs 6–45, Harrison 5–26, Lewis 11–21, Anderson 1-(-1)
PIT: Mendenhall 17–62, Parker 7–26, Wallace 1–21, Moore 5–20, Roethlisberger 6–11

Receiving
CLE: Massaquoi 5–83, Robiskie 1–23, Lewis 2–15, Vickers 1–1
PIT: Ward 8–159, Holmes 5–104, Miller 5–80, Wallace 2–50, Mendenhall 2–15, Parker 1–9

Sunday, October 25
Green Bay Packers 31, Browns 3
Cleveland Browns Stadium (69,797)
Brown jerseys/white pants

For the second straight week, the Browns were statistically dominated, but this time were unable to hang close and were crushed by the playoff-bound Packers. Green Bay rolled to 460 total yards and soared to a 21–3 halftime lead, while the Browns managed just 139 yards for the game. The Browns actually took a 3–0 lead on the first play of the second quarter but only threatened to score on one other possession, coming up empty when a fourth-down pass from the Green Bay 1 fell incomplete early in the final period. Fittingly, the Packers responded with a 99-yard touchdown drive.
Record: 1–5

	1	2	3	4		
Packers	0	21	3	7	=	31
Browns	0	3	0	0	=	3

CLE-Cundiff 22-yd. FG
GB-Havner 45-yd. pass from Rodgers (Crosby kick)
GB-Driver 71-yd. pass from Rodgers (Crosby kick)
GB-Grant 1-yd. run (Crosby kick)
GB-Crosby 18-yd. FG
GB-Jones 5-yd. pass from Rodgers (Crosby kick)

Passing
GB: Rodgers 15–20–246 3 TD 0 INT, Flynn 1–2–12 0 TD 0 INT
CLE: Anderson 12–29–99 0 TD 1 INT

Rushing
GB: Grant 27–148, Jackson 9–31, Rodgers 4–23, Kuhn 1–0
CLE: Lewis 15–47, Harrison 3–7, Anderson 2–3, Cribbs 1–1

Receiving
GB: Driver 2–84, Havner 2–59, Jennings 5–52, Lee 3–39, Finley 1–16, Jones 1–5, Grant 1–3, Johnson 1–0
CLE: Gaines 2–30, Harrison 4–23, Massaquoi 1–22, Estandia 2–10, Vickers 1–10, Furrey 1–5, Cribbs 1-(-1)

Sunday, November 1
Chicago Bears 30, Browns 6
Soldier Field (62,262)
White jerseys/brown pants

For the fourth straight week the Browns failed to top 200 total yards as they suffered another blowout defeat in Chicago. After completing just six of 17 passes and throwing an interception that was returned for Chicago's final touchdown, Derek Anderson was replaced once again by Brady Quinn. The return for a score was Anderson's second interception of the game and the Browns' fifth turnover, which set up 20 of the Bears' 30 points. The lone bright spot for the Browns was the return of kicker Phil Dawson, though his lone kick of the day—an extra-point attempt after the Browns' lone touchdown—was blocked.
Record: 1–7

	1	2	3	4		
Browns	0	0	6	0	=	6
Bears	6	10	7	7	=	30

CHI-Gould 37-yd. FG
CHI-Gould 29-yd. FG
CHI-Gould 32-yd. FG
CHI-Forte 1-yd. run (Gould kick)
CLE-Anderson 1-yd. run (kick failed)
CHI-Forte 10-yd. run (Gould kick)
CHI-Tillman 21-yd. interception return (Gould kick)

Passing
CLE: Anderson 6–17–76 0 TD 2 INT, Quinn 1–3–9 0 TD 0 INT
CHI: Cutler 17–30–225 0 TD 1 INT

Rushing
CLE: Lewis 16–69, Cribbs 6–28, Harrison 5–19, Anderson 2–1
CHI: Forte 26–90, Wolfe 5–53, Cutler 5–32, Hester 1-(-5)

Receiving
CLE: Massaquoi 2–28, Cribbs 1–23, Stuckey 1–11, Heiden 1–10, Furrey 1–9, Vickers 1–4
CHI: Hester 7–81, Knox 3–44, Olsen 3–40, Forte 2–31, Bennett 2–29

Monday, November 16
Baltimore Ravens 16, Browns 0
Cleveland Browns Stadium (69,023)
Brown jerseys/white pants

Before a disenchanted home crowd and *Monday Night Football* audience, the Browns were shut out for the first time in 2009 and lost for the fourteenth time in 15 games. The Cleveland offense was miserable, picking up just 160 total yards and not crossing the Baltimore 45 all night. The Browns' defense kept the team in the game through a scoreless first half, but the Ravens took control in the first three minutes of the third quarter with a pair of touchdowns, the second on an interception return. The Browns' Shaun Rogers blocked the ensuing extra point to provide the Browns' sole highlight of the evening, his third blocked kick of the season. Brady Quinn got his first start in six weeks but was sacked four times, completed only 13 of 31 passes, and was picked off twice.
Record: 1–8

	1	2	3	4		
Ravens	0	0	16	0	=	16
Browns	0	0	0	0	=	0

BAL-Rice 13-yd. run (Hauschka kick)
BAL-Landry 48-yd. interception return (kick failed)
BAL-Hauschka 44-yd. FG

Passing
BAL: Flacco 13–18–155 0 TD 0 INT, Rice 0–1–0 0 TD 0 INT
CLE: Quinn 13–31–99 0 TD 2 INT

Rushing
BAL: Rice 20–89, McGahee 13–35, McClain 3–10, Flacco 1-(-6)
CLE: Lewis 10–36, Cribbs 6–34, Jennings 7–18, Quinn 2–1, Massaquoi 1-(-3)

Receiving
BAL: Mason 3–78, Heap 4–43, McClain 3–19, Rice 3–15
CLE: Furrey 6–30, Massaquoi 1–30, Cribbs 1–10, Jennings 1–10, Heiden 1–9, Royal 1–7, Lewis 1–5, Vickers 1-(-2)

Sunday, November 22
Detroit Lions 38, Browns 37
Ford Field (43,170)
White jerseys/brown pants

In one of the wildest games in team history, the Browns squandered a 21-point lead and then allowed the winning points after a series of three plays after time had expired to lose once again. In a battle between two 1–8 teams, the Browns roared to a 24–3 lead in the first 12 minutes behind three touchdown passes by Brady Quinn. Detroit rallied to tie the game at 24 midway through the second quarter, then the game seesawed through the second half. Detroit took a 31–27 lead late in the third period, but the Browns clawed back with a safety on an intentional-grounding penalty on the Lions in the end zone to pull within two points. Cleveland then surged back ahead on a Quinn touchdown toss to TE Michael Gaines with 5:44 remaining. Trailing 37–31, the Lions regained possession at their own 12 with 1:46 left and reached the Cleveland 32 with eight seconds remaining. The Browns appeared to seal the victory when DB Brodney Pool intercepted a desperation pass as the clock hit zero, but Cleveland DB Hank Poteat was penalized for pass interference in the end zone, giving the Lions a first down at the Cleveland 1. After an ill-advised time out by the Browns that gave Lions' QB Matthew Stafford a chance to recover after suffering an injury on the previous play, Stafford connected with TE Brandon Pettigrew in the end zone for the tying touchdown, and Jason Hanson kicked the extra point to give Detroit a one-point win. The teams combined for more than 900 total yards, with the Browns compiling a season-high 439, including 304 passing and four touchdowns by Quinn. Mohamed Massaquoi also had a big day, catching five passes for 115 yards, but the Cleveland defense was ravaged for 473 yards—422 through the air by Stafford along with five touchdown passes.
Record: 1–9

	1	2	3	4		
Browns	24	3	2	8	=	37
Lions	10	14	7	7	=	38

CLE-Dawson 44-yd. FG
DET-Hanson 31-yd. FG
CLE-Massaquoi 59-yd. pass from Quinn (Dawson kick)
CLE-Stuckey 40-yd. pass from Quinn (Dawson kick)
CLE-Cribbs 4-yd. pass from Quinn (Dawson kick)
DET-Brown 26-yd. pass from Stafford (Hanson kick)
DET-Smith 25-yd. pass from Stafford (Hanson kick)
DET-C. Johnson 75-yd. pass from Stafford (Hanson kick)
CLE-Dawson 29-yd. FG
DET-Heller 1-yd. pass from Stafford (Hanson kick)
CLE-Safety: Stafford penalized for intentional grounding in end zone
CLE-Gaines 2-yd. pass from Quinn (Lewis run)
DET-Pettigrew 1-yd. pass from Stafford (Hanson kick)

Passing
CLE: Quinn 21–33–304 4 TD 0 INT, Dawson 1–1–10 0 TD 0 INT
DET: Stafford 26–43–422 5 TD 2 INT

Rushing
CLE: Lewis 24–75, Jennings 10–36, Cribbs 4–16, Quinn 2–4
DET: Smith 12–45, Stafford 2–7, Morris 2–5

Receiving
CLE: Massaquoi 5–115, Stuckey 5–76, Cribbs 2–39, Jennings 5–38, Estandia 1–18, Lewis 1–13, Furrey 1–10, Gaines 2–5
DET: C. Johnson 7–161, Smith 4–104, Pettigrew 6–72, Brown 1–26, B. Johnson 2–23, Northcutt 3–17, Heller 2–12, Felton 1–7

Sunday, November 29
Cincinnati Bengals 16, Browns 7
Paul Brown Stadium (64,553)
White jerseys/brown pants

The offensive fireworks of the previous Sunday vanished as the Browns lost their sixth straight game and dropped to 1–10 for the first time in team history. Cincinnati rushed for more than 200 yards and held Cleveland to just 169 total in the Bengals' best defensive showing in 26 years. Though Brady Quinn completed only 15 of 34 passes for just 100 yards, he rushed for the Browns' only touchdown and caught a pass in a game for the first time since high school—an 18-yard completion from Josh Cribbs on a trick play that led to the score. Adding insult to injury, the Browns lost four starters to injury during the game.

Record: 1–10

	1	2	3	4		
Browns	0	0	7	0	=	7
Bengals	3	10	3	0	=	16

CIN-Graham 37-yd. FG
CIN-Foschi 4-yd. pass from Palmer (Graham kick)
CIN-Graham 53-yd. FG
CLE-Quinn 9-yd. run (Dawson kick)
CIN-Graham 28-yd. FG

Passing
CLE: Quinn 15–34–100 0 TD 0 INT, Cribbs 1–1–18 0 TD 0 INT
CIN: Palmer 13–24–110 1 TD 0 INT

Rushing
CLE: Lewis 11–40, Quinn 2–10, Jennings 2–5, Harrison 2–3, Cribbs 1–0
CIN: Johnson 22–107, Scott 18–87, Palmer 4–15, Leonard 1–1

Receiving
CLE: Stuckey 4–44, Quinn 1–18, Estandia 1–17, Massaquoi 1–12, Furrey 1–9, Cribbs 3–7, Harrison 3–5, Jennings 1–4, Vickers 1–2
CIN: Ochocinco 3–38, Caldwell 3–33, Coles 2–24, Foschi 2–11, Leonard 1–6, Johnson 2-(-2)

Sunday, December 6
San Diego Chargers 30, Browns 23
Cleveland Browns Stadium (67,978)
Brown jerseys/white pants

A frantic Browns' rally in the fourth quarter couldn't overcome a terrible defensive performance as the Chargers built a 20-point lead and improved to 9–3 on the year. After the Browns scored a touchdown on their first possession for the first time in two years, San Diego scored 27 straight points to take control. Cleveland rallied for 16 points in the final nine minutes on a pair of Brady Quinn touchdown passes and a long Phil Dawson field goal. The Chargers finished the game with 477 total yards, including 373 passing yards by QB Philip Rivers and 167 on eight catches by TE Antonio Gates. With 64 yards on the ground, San Diego RB LaDainian Tomlinson passed Jim Brown for eighth place on the NFL's all-time rushing list.

Conversely, the Cleveland offense showed signs of life, with 271 yards passing and three touchdowns by Brady Quinn but couldn't avoid their seventeenth loss in their last 18 games—but their final defeat of the season.

Record: 1–11

	1	2	3	4		
Chargers	10	3	14	3	=	30
Browns	7	0	0	16	=	23

CLE-Massaquoi 11-yd. pass from Quinn (Dawson kick)
SD-Kaeding 32-yd. FG
SD-Tolbert 66-yd. pass from Rivers (Kaeding kick)
SD-Kaeding 42-yd. FG
SD-Sproles 31-yd. pass from Rivers (Kaeding kick)
SD-Tomlinson 4-yd. run (Kaeding kick)
CLE-Harrison 8-yd. pass from Quinn (Dawson kick)
SD-Kaeding 22-yd. FG
CLE-Harrison 8-yd. pass from Quinn (run failed)
CLE-Dawson 49-yd. FG

Passing
SD: Rivers 18–25–373 2 TD 0 INT, Naanee 1–1–21 0 TD 0 INT
CLE: Quinn 25–45–271 3 TD 0 INT

Rushing
SD: Tomlinson 20–64, Sproles 7–27, Rivers 4–0, Hester 1–0
CLE: Cribbs 4–38, Harrison 10–35, Jennings 5–28, Quinn 2–8, Stuckey 1–6

Receiving
SD: Gates 8–167, Tolbert 1–66, Sproles 4–56, Jackson 2–54, Floyd 3–30, Tomlinson 1–21
CLE: Moore 6–80, Robiskie 4–69, Harrison 7–62, Massaquoi 2–24, Stuckey 3–23, Cribbs 1–6, Vickers 1–5, Jennings 1–2

Thursday, December 10
Browns 13, Pittsburgh Steelers 6
Cleveland Browns Stadium (69,009)
Brown jerseys/white pants

A myriad of streaks came to an end with a stunning Browns' victory over the defending Super Bowl champions on a frigid Thursday night in Cleveland. Behind a fierce defensive performance that racked up eight sacks and held Pittsburgh to just 218 total yards, the Browns controlled the game from the outset, building a 13–0 lead in the second quarter and then holding off the Steelers in the second half. A long punt return by Josh Cribbs set up a field goal, and then a long Cribbs run out of the wildcat formation set up the game's only touchdown, a 10-yard burst by RB Chris Jennings (the first rushing touchdown by a Cleveland RB all season) just before the half. Cribbs finished the night with a season-high 87 rushing yards on just eight carries. After the Steelers pulled within seven points in the final minute of the third quarter, two trips into Cleveland territory in the final period were thwarted, including a key fourth-down play from the Cleveland 39 with 1:43 remaining. The victory snapped the Browns' seven-game losing streak in 2009, their 10-game losing streak at home, and was their first triumph over Pittsburgh in their last 12 meetings. It also marked Pittsburgh QB Ben Roethlisberger's first career loss to the Browns.

Record: 2–11

	1	2	3	4		
Steelers	0	3	3	0	=	6
Browns	3	10	0	0	=	13

CLE-Dawson 29-yd. FG
CLE-Dawson 29-yd. FG
CLE-Jennings 10-yd. run (Dawson kick)
PIT-Reed 27-yd. FG
PIT-Reed 42-yd. FG

Passing
PIT: Roethlisberger 18–32–201 0 TD 0 INT
CLE: Quinn 6–19–90 0 TD 0 INT

Rushing
PIT: Mendenhall 16–53, Parker 3–12, Roethlisberger 3–12
CLE: Cribbs 8–87, Jennings 20–73, Harrison 7–9, Quinn 1–2, Stuckey 1–0

Receiving
PIT: Holmes 6–93, Miller 5–59, Ward 4–21, Mendenhall 1–17, Wallace 2–11
CLE: Massaquoi 1–37, Moore 2–34, Harrison 2–10, Cribbs 1–9

Sunday, December 20
Browns 41, Kansas City Chiefs 34
Arrowhead Stadium (53,315)
White jerseys/brown pants

The Browns picked up their third victory in another wild game that saw a handful of records broken. Mirroring the bizarre contest in Detroit a month earlier, the struggling Browns and Chiefs put on an offensive show that saw the teams combine for more than 900 total yards and 75 points. Despite entering the game with the NFL's worst offense, the Browns exploded for 417 yards—351 on the ground behind a historic performance by sparingly used RB Jerome Harrison. Picking up 286 yards on 34 carries with three touchdowns, Harrison broke Jim Brown's franchise record for rushing yards in a game and posted the third-best day of any back in NFL history. Somewhat overshadowed by Harrison's heroics, Josh Cribbs became the first player in NFL history to return two kickoffs at least 100 yards for a touchdown in the same game and set a team record for kickoff-return and total yardage in a single contest with 269 and 316, respectively. But for all the offensive fireworks, the game was still in doubt as the 3–10 Chiefs, who tallied nearly 500 yards of offense themselves, surged ahead by 11 late in the second quarter. Then after the Browns rebounded with three straight touchdowns, Kansas City tied the contest at 34 with just over two minutes left. A key third-down scramble for 24 yards by Brady Quinn pushed the Browns into Kansas City territory, then Harrison scored from 20 yards out with 52 seconds left to put Cleveland ahead. A last-gasp drive by Kansas City reached the Cleveland 26, where a desperation pass to the end zone fell incomplete as time expired.

Record: 3–11

	1	2	3	4		
Browns	10	10	7	14	=	41
Chiefs	3	21	0	10	=	34

CLE-Dawson 47-yd. FG
KC-Succop 30-yd. FG
CLE-Cribbs 100-yd. kickoff return (Dawson kick)
CLE-Dawson 30-yd. FG
KC-Chambers 9-yd. pass from Cassel (Succop kick)
KC-Charles 47-yd. run (Succop kick)
KC-Studebaker 21-yd. fumble return (Succop kick)
CLE-Cribbs 103-yd. kickoff return (Dawson kick)
CLE-Harrison 71-yd. run (Dawson kick)
CLE-Harrison 8-yd. run (Dawson kick)
KC-Succop 27-yd. FG
KC-Bradley 12-yd. pass from Cassel (Succop kick)
CLE-Harrison 28-yd. run (Dawson kick)

Passing
CLE: Quinn 10–17–66 0 TD 2 INT, Cribbs 0–1–0 0 TD 0 INT
KC: Cassel 22–40–331 2 TD 0 INT

Rushing
CLE: Harrison 34–286, Quinn 4–39, Jennings 7–18, Cribbs 3–8, Hodges 1–0
KC: Charles 25–154, Cassel 2–10, Castille 2–3, Williams 1–1

Receiving
CLE: Stuckey 5–41, Harrison 2–12, Moore 1–7, Cribbs 1–3, Massaquoi 1–3
KC: Chambers 5–114, Cottam 4–62, Bowe 4–56, Bradley 3–52, Pope 3–23, Charles 2–16, Cox 1–8

Sunday, December 27
Browns 23, Oakland Raiders 9
Cleveland Stadium (67,964)
Brown jerseys/white pants

After Mike Holmgren had been hired as team president the previous week, the Browns extended a winning streak to three games for the first time in two years as they coasted to victory over the mistake-prone Raiders. With Derek Anderson starting at QB, the Browns once again rode Jerome Harrison, who set a team record with 39 carries and wound up with 148 rushing yards to go along with a touchdown 90 seconds into the game. Aided by a 61-yard field goal by Sebastian Janikowski, the Raiders stayed close, but a pair of Phil Dawson field goals in the second half put the game away. Though Oakland tallied nearly 400 yards of offense, including 333 passing by former Browns' QB Charlie Frye, the Raiders committed 13 penalties for 126 yards and had two players ejected for fighting. It marked the second time in three games the Browns' defense didn't allow a touchdown.

Record: 4–11

	1	2	3	4		
Raiders	3	6	0	0	=	9
Browns	10	7	3	3	=	23

CLE-Harrison 17-yd. run (Dawson kick)
CLE-Dawson 42-yd. FG
OAK-Janikowski 44-yd. FG
OAK-Janikowski 34-yd. FG
CLE-Massaquoi 19-yd. pass from Anderson (Dawson kick)
OAK-Janikowski 61-yd. FG
CLE-Dawson 33-yd. FG
CLE-Dawson 34-yd. FG

Passing
OAK: Frye 26–45–333 0 TD 3 INT
CLE: Anderson 8–17–121 1 TD 0 INT

Rushing
OAK: Bush 10–52, McFadden 7–23, Frye 2–13
CLE: Harrison 39–148, Cribbs 4–21, Anderson 1-(-1), Jennings 2-(-4)

Receiving
OAK: Miller 9–110, Schilens 4–64, McFadden 4–55, Higgins 1–33, Murphy 2–22, Watkins 2–19, Russell 2–14, Reece 1–9, Bush 1–7
CLE: Massaquoi 3–61, Gaines 1–24, Moore 1–19, Robiskie 2–14, Stuckey 1–3

Sunday, January 3
Browns 23, Jacksonville Jaguars 17
Cleveland Browns Stadium (66,935)
Brown jerseys/white pants

Closing out an incredibly unbalanced season, the Browns won their fourth straight game on a frigid, snowy afternoon in Cleveland. Behind another strong performance by Jerome Harrison (33 carries, 127 yards), the Browns took a 20–3 lead into the fourth quarter before allowing a touchdown at home for the first time in 12 quarters, which pulled the Jaguars within 10 points with 10 minutes left. Cleveland responded with a 14-play, eight-minute drive that ended with a Phil Dawson field goal, then Jacksonville added a meaningless touchdown on the game's final play. At the game's conclusion, Browns' players dumped a bucket of Gatorade over embattled head coach Eric Mangini, who would return for 2010 after his job was rumored to be in jeopardy throughout his tumultuous first season.
Record: 5–11

	1	2	3	4		
Jaguars	3	0	0	14	=	17
Browns	3	10	7	3	=	23

CLE-Dawson 27-yd. FG
JAX-Scobee 47-yd. FG
CLE-Cribbs 14-yd. run (Dawson kick)
CLE-Dawson 21-yd. FG
CLE-Harrison 6-yd. run (Dawson kick)
JAX-Miller 6-yd. pass from Garrard (Scobee kick)
CLE-Dawson 33-yd. FG
JAX-Miller 15-yd. pass from Garrard (Scobee kick)

Passing
JAX: Garrard 22–39–202 2 TD 1 INT
CLE: Anderson 7–11–86 0 TD 1 INT

Rushing
JAX: Jones-Drew 16–82, Garrard 5–40, Jennings 3–9
CLE: Harrison 33–127, Cribbs 6–47, Jennings 9–38, Anderson 1–2

Receiving
JAX: Miller 8–69, Thomas 7–65, Jennings 3–31, Sims-Walker 2–28, Jones-Drew 1–6, Potter 1–3
CLE: Royal 2–34, Harrison 2–20, Moore 2–18, Massaquoi 1–14

2010

Sunday, September 12
Tampa Bay Buccaneers 17, Browns 14
Raymond James Stadium (47,211)
Brown jerseys/white pants

For the eleventh time in 12 seasons since their rebirth, the Browns lost their opening game, this time squandering an 11-point lead and losing on a steamy afternoon in Tampa. Cleveland dominated play in the first half, rolling up more than 200 total yards and soaring to a 14–3 lead, but the game turned when new Browns' QB Jake Delhomme was intercepted in Tampa Bay territory in the final minute of the first half, and it was returned to the Cleveland 3, setting up a Buccaneers' touchdown. The Browns then drove to the Tampa 15 on the first series of the third quarter, but RB Peyton Hillis fumbled, giving the Bucs new life. Tampa Bay surged ahead on a touchdown pass with 6:45 remaining, and the Browns were unable to move the ball past their own 33 on their final three possessions. The loss spoiled a nice effort by the Cleveland offense, which rolled up 340 total yards, with nine different players catching passes.
Record: 0–1

	1	2	3	4		
Browns	7	7	0	0	=	14
Buccaneers	3	7	0	7	=	17

CLE-Massaquoi 41-yd. pass from Delhomme (Dawson kick)
TB-Barth 49-yd. FG
CLE-Hillis 10-yd. run (Dawson kick)
TB-Williams 3-yd. pass from Freeman (Barth kick)
TB-Spurlock 33-yd. pass from Freeman (Barth kick)

Passing
CLE: Delhomme 20–37–227 1 TD 2 INT, Cribbs 1–1–9 0 TD 0 INT
TB: Freeman 17–28–182 2 TD 1 INT

Rushing
CLE: Harrison 9–52, Hillis 9–41, Cribbs 3–11, Delhomme 1–1, Watson 1-(-1)
TB: C. Williams 22–75, Freeman 2–34, Graham 6–10

Receiving
CLE: Moore 3–87, Massaquoi 2–46, Stuckey 4–30, Hillis 4–24, Watson 3–16, Cribbs 2–11, Wallace 1–9, Harrison 1–7, Robiskie 1–6
TB: Spurlock 2–49, Winslow 4–32, Stroughter 2–32, M. Williams 5–30, C. Williams 2–23, Graham 1–8, Stevens 1–8

Sunday, September 19
Kansas City Chiefs 16, Browns 14
Cleveland Browns Stadium (65,377)
Brown jerseys/white pants

Following a script nearly identical to the week before, the Browns built a 14–10 halftime lead, then watched it disappear in the second half as the Cleveland offense failed to put any points on the board after the intermission. Peyton Hillis opened the Browns' scoring with a short touchdown run early in the second quarter. After Kansas City took the lead back on an interception return for a touchdown, Cleveland QB Seneca Wallace—starting in place of injured Jake Delhomme—hit Josh Cribbs for a 65-yard score for the game's third touchdown in less than four minutes. The Browns' offense stalled for the remainder of the game, and the Chiefs kicked the game-winning field goal with 7:41 remaining, then prevented the Browns from crossing midfield on their final two possessions. The Cleveland running game managed just 73 yards, typified by RB Jerome Harrison, who was held to 33 yards on 16 carries after exploding for 286 in the teams' previous meeting nine months earlier.
Record: 0–2

	1	2	3	4		
Chiefs	3	7	3	3	=	16
Browns	0	14	0	0	=	14

KC-Succop 35-yd. FG
CLE-Hillis 1-yd. run (Dawson kick)
KC-Flowers 33-yd. interception return (Succop kick)
CLE-Cribbs 65-yd. pass from Wallace (Dawson kick)
KC-Succop 26-yd. FG
KC-Succop 23-yd. FG

Passing
KC: Cassel 16–28–176 0 TD 2 INT
CLE: Wallace 16–31–229 1 TD 1 INT

Rushing
KC: Jones 22–83, Charles 11–49, Cassel 4–5, McCluster 1–3, Castille 1–0
CLE: Hillis 8–35, Harrison 16–33, Wallace 1–4, Cribbs 1–1

Receiving
KC: Moeaki 5–58, Bowe 4–45, Chambers 3–33, Charles 1–27, Castille 2–8, Jones 1–5
CLE: Cribbs 3–74, Watson 4–62, Harrison 3–35, Hillis 3–26, Robiskie 1–12, Stuckey 1–11, Massaquoi 1–9

Sunday, September 26
Baltimore Ravens 24, Browns 17
M&T Bank Stadium (71,119)
White jerseys/white pants

For the third straight week, the Browns were unable to hold onto a fourth-quarter lead and squandered a golden opportunity to pick up a huge upset on the road against a division rival. A gritty overall team performance was personified by Peyton Hillis, who rushed for 144 yards against Baltimore's vaunted defense—the first Cleveland RB ever to do so against the Ravens. After a short touchdown catch by TE Ben Watson on the first play of the fourth quarter capped an 86-yard drive, the Browns took a 17–14 lead. The Ravens surged back ahead with nine minutes remaining on the third touchdown of the day by WR Anquan Boldin, who finished with 142 receiving yards. The Browns then punted after three plays, and Baltimore successfully ran out the final four minutes. Cleveland dropped to 0–3 for the third straight year.
Record: 0–3

	1	2	3	4		
Browns	3	7	0	7	=	17
Ravens	7	7	0	10	=	24

CLE-Dawson 38-yd. FG
BAL-Boldin 8-yd. pass from Flacco (Cundiff kick)
BAL-Boldin 12-yd. pass from Flacco (Cundiff kick)
CLE-Hillis 1-yd. run (Dawson kick)
CLE-Watson 1-yd. pass from Wallace (Dawson kick)
BAL-Boldin 27-yd. pass from Flacco (Cundiff kick)
BAL-Cundiff 49-yd. FG

Passing
CLE: Wallace 18–24–141 1 TD 0 INT
BAL: Flacco 22–31–262 3 TD 0 INT, Boldin 1-1-(-6)

Rushing
CLE: Hillis 22–144, Cribbs 2–20, Davis 4–9, Wallace 1–0
BAL: Rice 15–80, McGahee 7–29, McClain 1–4, Flacco 4-(-4)

Receiving
CLE: Cribbs 5–58, Watson 5–47, Hillis 7–36, Vickers 1–0
BAL: Boldin 8–142, Heap 4–46, Mason 4–30, McClain 2–18, Rice 4–16, Houshmandzadeh 1–4

Sunday, October 3
Browns 23, Cincinnati Bengals 20
Cleveland Browns Stadium (66,731)
Brown jerseys/white pants

The Browns broke into the win column with an inspired performance against the defending division champions, building a 13-point second-half lead and then holding off the Bengals in the final minutes. After Cincinnati rallied from an early 10-point deficit to tie the game on a 78-yard touchdown catch by WR Terrell Owens, the Browns scored 13 straight points to take a 23–10 lead midway through the third period. Cincinnati chipped away and pulled within 23–20 early in the fourth quarter, then drove into Cleveland territory on its next possession. But a key third-down sack by Cleveland LB Matt Roth forced a punt, then a key 24-yard run by Peyton Hillis enabled the Browns to run out the final 4:41 and clinch their first victory of the season. Though the defense was lit up for 413 total yards—including 371 passing by Cincy QB Carson Palmer and 222 receiving by Owens—the Browns ran more plays and held a slight advantage in time of possession, sparked by Hillis's 102 rushing yards. DE Kenyon Coleman added a sack to a pair of fumble recoveries, and the Browns' special teams got into the act when LB Scott Fujita blocked a Cincinnati field goal late in the first half.
Record: 1–3

	1	2	3	4		
Bengals	0	10	3	7	=	20
Browns	3	10	10	0	=	23

CLE-Dawson 30-yd. FG
CLE-Moore 24-yd. pass from Wallace (Dawson kick)
CIN-Nugent 24-yd. FG
CIN-Owens 78-yd. pass from Palmer (Nugent kick)
CLE-Dawson 31-yd. FG
CLE-Hillis 1-yd. run (Dawson kick)
CLE-Dawson 22-yd. FG
CIN-Nugent 25-yd. FG
CIN-Leonard 3-yd. pass from Palmer (Nugent kick)

Passing
CIN: Palmer 25–36–371 2 TD 0 INT
CLE: Wallace 18–30–184 1 TD 1 INT

Rushing
CIN: Benson 15–60, Scott 2–7, Palmer 1–0
CLE: Hillis 27–102, Cribbs 3–9, Wallace 5–5

Receiving
CIN: Owens 10–222, Ochocinco 3–59, Gresham 5–35, Shipley 2–29, Caldwell 3–15, Leonard 2–11
CLE: Watson 6–60, Stuckey 5–56, Cribbs 2–24, Moore 1–24, Hillis 2–8, Aiken 1–7, Massaquoi 1–5

Sunday, October 10
Atlanta Falcons 20, Browns 10
Cleveland Browns Stadium (65,290)
Brown jerseys/white pants

The Browns hung close with the eventual NFC South champions for much of the afternoon, but costly mistakes in the second half proved too much to overcome. Cleveland took a 7–6 lead early in the second quarter on a terrific one-handed touchdown reception by Peyton Hillis, then stretched the advantage to 10–6 midway through the third before the Falcons responded with a long touchdown pass moments later. When Seneca Wallace left the game with an ankle injury, still-injured Jake Delhomme hobbled in and threw two interceptions in the fourth quarter, the first of which was returned for the game-clinching touchdown with four minutes to play. The Browns were held to 48 yards rushing on the afternoon, while Atlanta RB Michael Turner sprinted to 140 yards on 19 carries.
Record: 1–4

	1	2	3	4		
Falcons	0	6	7	7	=	20
Browns	0	7	3	0	=	10

ATL-Bryant 24-yd. FG
CLE-Hillis 19-yd. pass from Wallace (Dawson kick)
ATL-Bryant 30-yd. FG
CLE-Dawson 19-yd. FG
ATL-White 45-yd. pass from Ryan (Bryant kick)
ATL-Biermann 31-yd. interception return (Bryant kick)

Passing
ATL: Ryan 16–28–187 1 TD 0 INT
CLE: Wallace 11–15–139 1 TD 0 INT, Delhomme 13–23–97 0 TD 2 INT, Cribbs 1–1–10 0 TD 0 INT

Rushing
ATL: Turner 19–140, Snelling 6–18, Ryan 5–5, Mughelli 1–2
CLE: Hillis 10–28, Cribbs 2–11, Harrison 6–6, Vickers 1–3, Delhomme 1–0

Receiving
ATL: White 5–101, Gonzalez 5–41, Douglas 2–17, Peelle 1–15, Palmer 1–11, Snelling 2–2
CLE: Massaquoi 5–55, Stuckey 5–54, Hillis 4–49, Watson 5–45, Royal 2–13, Vickers 1–10, Cribbs 1–8, Moore 1–7, Robiskie 1–5

Sunday, October 17
Pittsburgh Steelers 28, Browns 10
Heinz Field (65,168)
White jerseys/white pants

Though the overmatched Browns were handled by the Super Bowl-bound Steelers, the day proved positive thanks to the surprisingly effective performance by rookie QB Colt McCoy in his NFL debut. With both Jake Delhomme and Seneca Wallace injured, third-stringer McCoy started and played well, completing 23 of 33 passes for 281 yards despite being sacked six times. Only two other times all season would Pittsburgh's defense allow more passing yards in a game. McCoy also lost a pair of his primary targets when Josh Cribbs and Mohamed Massaquoi both left the game with head injuries after helmet-to-helmet hits by Pittsburgh LB James Harrison. After the Browns took a 3–0 lead into the second quarter, the Steelers—led by QB Ben Roethlisberger, making his season debut after serving a four-game suspension following a rape conviction—scored three straight touchdowns before McCoy tossed his first career scoring pass, a 12-yarder, to TE Ben Watson in the fourth quarter.
Record: 1–5

	1	2	3	4		
Browns	3	0	0	7	=	10
Steelers	0	7	7	14	=	28

CLE-Dawson 39-yd. FG
PIT-Wallace 29-yd. pass from Roethlisberger (Reed kick)
PIT-Ward 8-yd. pass from Roethlisberger (Reed kick)
PIT-Mendenhall 2-yd. run (Reed kick)
CLE-Watson 12-yd. pass from McCoy (Dawson kick)
PIT-Miller 14-yd. pass from Roethlisberger (Reed kick)

Passing
CLE: McCoy 23–33–281 1 TD 2 INT
PIT: Roethlisberger 16–27–257 3 TD 1 INT

Rushing
CLE: Hillis 12–41, McCoy 4–22, Bell 2–3, Stuckey 1–2, Cribbs 2–1
PIT: Mendenhall 27–84, Redman 6–31, Roethlisberger 1–5, Moore 1–1

Receiving
CLE: Watson 6–88, Moore 4–84, Hillis 6–49, Stuckey 4–46, Robiskie 2–13, Vickers 1–1
PIT: Wallace 3–90, Ward 5–54, Miller 2–50, Sanders 2–37, Mendenhall 3–15, Randle El 1–11

Sunday, October 24
Browns 30, New Orleans Saints 17
Louisiana Superdome (70,077)
Brown jerseys/white pants

In perhaps the biggest upset of the entire NFL season, the Browns took down the defending Super Bowl champions on their home field by pulling off a handful of surprises. The trickery began in the opening minutes when Josh Cribbs threw a cross-field lateral to DB Eric Wright on a punt return and Wright scampered 62 yards to set up a field goal. The Browns extended their lead to 10–0, then 13–3 late in the second quarter following a 68-yard run by punter Reggie Hodges on a fake punt. Then just before the half, Cleveland LB David Bowens picked off a pass from New Orleans QB Drew Brees and returned it 30 yards for a touchdown to make it 20–3. It was one of four interceptions by Brees on the afternoon, the final a tipped screen also gathered in by Bowens, who rumbled 64 yards for the game-clinching touchdown with three minutes remaining. The Saints rolled up nearly 400 yards of offense, with Brees throwing for 356, but the four turnovers and three allowed sacks allowed the Browns to control the game despite collecting just over 200 yards on offense themselves.
Record: 2–5

	1	2	3	4		
Browns	10	10	0	10	=	30
Saints	0	3	0	14	=	17

CLE-Dawson 23-yd. FG
CLE-Hillis 4-yd. run (Dawson kick)
NO-Hartley 32-yd. FG
CLE-Dawson 21-yd. FG
CLE-Bowens 30-yd. interception return (Dawson kick)
NO-Thomas 11-yd. pass from Brees (Hartley kick)
CLE-Dawson 48-yd. FG
CLE-Bowens 64-yd. interception return (Dawson kick)
NO-Colston 8-yd. pass from Brees (Hartley kick)

Passing
CLE: McCoy 9–16–74 0 TD 0 INT, Hillis 1–1–13 0 TD 0 INT
NO: Brees 37–56–356 2 TD 4 INT

Rushing
CLE: Hillis 16–69, Hodges 1–68, Bell 5-(-3), Figurs 1-(-4), McCoy 5-(-5)
NO: Ivory 15–48, Jones 1–6, Evans 1–2, Meachem 1–2

Receiving
CLE: Robiskie 3–25, Watson 1–18, Stuckey 2–16, McCoy 1–13, Cribbs 1–10, Vickers 1–4, Hillis 1–1
NO: Colston 10–112, Betts 8–48, Moore 5–43, Graham 4–38, Thomas 3–33, Meachem 2–31, Shockey 2–30, Henderson 2–20, Jones 1–1

Sunday, November 7
Browns 34, New England Patriots 14
Cleveland Browns Stadium (66,292)
Brown jerseys/white pants

Playing nearly a perfect game, the Browns dominated the 6–1 Patriots and rolled to a blowout victory before a euphoric home crowd on a sunny November afternoon. The Browns grabbed a 10–0 lead before New England even ran a play as the Browns kicked a field goal on their first possession, then recovered a fumble on the ensuing kickoff and cashed in for a touchdown by Peyton Hillis, who would have a career day. After a Patriots' score cut the lead to three, the Browns pushed it back to 10 late in the first half on a trick play from the New England 11 in which Josh Cribbs lined up at QB and handed off to WR Chansi Stuckey on an end around, and Stuckey scampered into the end zone for a touchdown. The Browns put the icing on the cake in the second half with a broken-field touchdown scramble by Colt McCoy, then Hillis broke free for a 35-yard scoring jaunt to cap his brilliant afternoon with 2:38 remaining. Hillis finished with a career-best 184 rushing yards as the Browns topped 400 yards of offense for the only time all season. At the game's conclusion, Browns' players drenched head coach Eric Mangini with Gatorade to cap the most impressive victory of his coaching career, coming at the expense of his former tutor, Bill Belichick. The Patriots would go on to win their final eight games and post the NFL's best record at 14–2.
Record: 3–5

	1	2	3	4		
Patriots	0	7	0	7	=	14
Browns	10	7	7	10	=	34

CLE-Dawson 38-yd. FG
CLE-Hillis 2-yd. run (Dawson kick)
NE-Hernandez 2-yd. pass from Brady (Gostkowski kick)
CLE-Stuckey 11-yd. run (Dawson kick)
CLE-McCoy 16-yd. run (Dawson kick)
CLE-Dawson 37-yd. FG
NE-Hernandez 1-yd. pass from Brady (Welker kick)
CLE-Hillis 35-yd. run (Dawson kick)

Passing
NE: Brady 19–36–224 2 TD 0 INT, Hoyer 0–2–0 0 TD 1 INT
CLE: McCoy 14–19–174 0 TD 0 INT

Rushing
NE: Woodhead 9–54, Green-Ellis 9–14, Brady 1–1, Hoyer 1-(-1)
CLE: Hillis 29–184, McCoy 3–20, Stuckey 1–11, Bell 6–7, Vickers 3–6, Cribbs 2–2

Receiving
NE: Hernandez 5–48, Gronkowski 4–47, Woodhead 2–38, Welker 4–36, Morris 1–22, Branch 2–21, Tate 1–12
CLE: Massaquoi 4–58, Hillis 3–36, Watson 1–24, Robiskie 1–20, Moore 1–17, Cribbs 2–13, Stuckey 2–6

WHEN THE BROWNS BEAT THE BEST

Browns' wins over that year's eventual world champion
1951: Beat Los Angeles Rams 38–23
1956: Beat New York Giants 24–7
1959: Beat Baltimore Colts 38–31
1960: Beat Philadelphia Eagles 41–24
1981: Beat San Francisco 49ers 15–12

Browns' wins over the defending world champion
1950: Beat Philadelphia Eagles 35–10 and 13–7
1952: Beat Los Angeles Rams 37–7
1954: Beat Detroit Lions 56–10*
1957: Beat New York Giants 6–3 and 34–28
1959: Beat Baltimore Colts 38–31
1961: Beat Philadelphia Eagles 45–24
1971: Beat Baltimore Colts 14–13
1976: Beat Pittsburgh Steelers 18–16
1980: Beat Pittsburgh Steelers 27–26
1988: Beat Washington Redskins 17–13
1994: Beat Dallas Cowboys 19–14
2001: Beat Baltimore Ravens 24–14 and 27–17
2008: Beat New York Giants 35–14
2009: Beat Pittsburgh Steelers 13–6
2010: Beat New Orleans Saints 30–17

**NFL Championship Game*

Sunday, November 14
New York Jets 26, Browns 20 (OT)
Cleveland Browns Stadium (67,449)
Brown jerseys/white pants

Another inspired performance by the Browns fell short as they dropped a marathon contest with the playoff-bound Jets. After the Browns took a 10–3 lead into the second quarter, the Jets seized control of the game, surging to a seven-point lead after controlling the football for 23 minutes of the second half. But three missed field goals haunted New York and allowed the Browns to hang close. Colt McCoy directed a clutch drive to tie the game with 44 seconds remaining on a short touchdown pass to Mohamed Massaquoi. Cleveland was then poised to win the game on its first possession of overtime, but Chansi Stuckey fumbled after catching a pass at the New York 32 and the Jets recovered. New York then squandered a chance to win when kicker Nick Folk was wide right on a 47-yard field-goal attempt on the ensuing possession. The teams continued to battle, and an interception by Browns' DB Joe Haden gave them the ball at the Cleveland 3 with less than two minutes remaining. Opting not to play for the tie, the Browns ran three fruitless plays and then punted back to the Jets, who regained possession at the Cleveland 37 with 24 seconds left. On the next play, WR Santonio Holmes caught a short pass and blasted through an exhausted Cleveland defense for the game-winning touchdown. Running 32 more offensive plays than the Browns, the Jets gathered 456 total yards and 28 first downs and controlled the football for more than 47 minutes. But in playing their fifth consecutive game against a playoff-bound team, the Browns endured and nearly pulled off a third straight upset.
Record: 3–6

	1	2	3	4	OT		
Jets	3	14	0	3	6	=	26
Browns	10	3	0	7	0	=	20

CLE-Dawson 34-yd. FG
NYJ-Folk 27-yd. FG
CLE-Hillis 12-yd. run (Dawson kick)
NYJ-Cotchery 25-yd. pass from Sanchez (Folk kick)
CLE-Dawson 23-yd. FG

NYJ-Sanchez 1-yd. run (Folk kick)
NYJ-Folk 25-yd. FG
CLE-Massaquoi 3-yd. pass from McCoy (Dawson kick)
NYJ-Holmes 37-yd. pass from Sanchez

Passing
NYJ: Sanchez 27–44–299 2 TD 1 INT
CLE: McCoy 18–31–205 1 TD 0 INT

Rushing
NYJ: Greene 20–72, Tomlinson 18–57, Smith 5–39, Sanchez 2–4
CLE: Hillis 19–82, Cribbs 1–14, McCoy 4–11, Clayton 1–0

Receiving
NYJ: Holmes 5–76, Edwards 4–59, Tomlinson 6–53, Cotchery 3–43, Keller 3–25, Greene 3–22, Richardson 2–15, Smith 1–6
CLE: Watson 5–74, Cribbs 1–37, Hillis 4–27, Stuckey 4–27, Moore 1–18, Royal 1–14, Massaquoi 2–8

Sunday, November 21
Jacksonville Jaguars 24, Browns 20
EverBank Field (62,254)
White jerseys/white pants

Despite forcing six turnovers and holding a lead with less than three minutes remaining, the Browns were unable to pull out a victory in Jacksonville. With the offense struggling, and Peyton Hillis limited to just over two yards per carry, four interceptions, and two fumble recoveries by the Cleveland defense—including a string of five straight possessions in the second half—resulted in just 10 points, including a fumble return for a touchdown by DB Abram Elam early in the third quarter. After the Jaguars tied the game at 17 with under four minutes to play, a 38-yard catch by TE Evan Moore and an 18-yard, third-down scramble by Colt McCoy, hobbling on an injured ankle, set up the go-ahead field goal with 2:46 remaining. Moments later, a screen pass to Jacksonville RB Maurice Jones-Drew (who compiled more than 200 total yards for the game) turned into a 75-yard gain to the Cleveland 1, leading to the winning touchdown a play later with 1:20 left. Out of time outs, the Browns hurriedly drove to the Jacksonville 29 in the final seconds, but a long McCoy pass was tipped and intercepted at the 5 to seal the Jags' victory.
Record: 3–7

	1	2	3	4		
Browns	0	7	10	3	=	20
Jaguars	3	7	0	14	=	24

JAX-Scobee 47-yd. FG
CLE-Hillis 11-yd. pass from McCoy (Dawson kick)
JAX-Thomas 5-yd. pass from Garrard (Scobee kick)
CLE-Elam 18-yd. fumble return (Dawson kick)
CLE-Dawson 38-yd. FG
JAX-Lewis 14-yd. pass from Garrard (Scobee kick)
CLE-Dawson 41-yd. FG
JAX-Jones-Drew 1-yd. run (Scobee kick)

Passing
CLE: McCoy 17–28–241 1 TD 1 INT
JAX: Garrard 20–34–254 2 TD 3 INT, Jones-Drew 0–1–0 0 TD 1 INT

Rushing
CLE: Hillis 21–48, McCoy 4–39, Bell 1–1
JAX: Jones-Drew 23–133, Garrard 3–9, Jennings 2–3

Receiving
CLE: Hillis 6–95, Moore 3–69, Massaquoi 4–51, Stuckey 4–26
JAX: Jones-Drew 3–87, Lewis 5–66, Thomas 5–36, Miller 3–27, Osgood 2–22, Jennings 1–9, Underwood 1–7

Sunday, November 28
Browns 24, Carolina Panthers 23
Cleveland Browns Stadium (64,463)
Brown jerseys/white pants

Once again going down to the wire, the Browns escaped with a narrow victory over the 1–9 Panthers despite a shaky second-half performance. Behind three rushing touchdowns by Peyton Hillis, the Browns roared to a 21–7 lead midway through the second quarter, but Carolina slowly chipped away, aided by two key interceptions early in the third quarter thrown by Jake Delhomme, starting in place of injured Colt McCoy. The second was returned for a touchdown and pulled Carolina within one point, then the Panthers took the lead midway through the fourth after the Browns failed to convert on a fourth-and-one play at the Carolina 25 early in the period. Delhomme redeemed himself with a clutch drive to set up the go-ahead field goal with 2:47 remaining, and it appeared the Browns had the game wrapped up when Joe Haden pulled down an interception at midfield with just over a minute left. But the Browns were unable to pick up a first down and punted back to the Panthers, who took over at their own 5 with 59 seconds left and quickly reached midfield. A circus catch along the sideline at the Cleveland 24 by WR Brandon LaFell (which should have been the last play of the game, but the officials incorrectly ruled LaFell made it out of bounds before being downed) set up a 42-yard field-goal attempt as time expired. But John Kasay's kick sliced at the last second, grazing the left upright and giving the Browns their first victory in three weeks. It rewarded another spectacular effort by Hillis, who rushed for 131 yards and collected another 63 receiving.

Record: 4–7

	1	2	3	4		
Panthers	7	6	7	3	=	23
Browns	14	7	0	3	=	24

CAR-Goodson 26-yd. run (Kasay kick)
CLE-Hillis 9-yd. run (Dawson kick)
CLE-Hillis 5-yd. run (Dawson kick)
CLE-Hillis 6-yd. run (Dawson kick)
CAR-Kasay 43-yd. FG
CAR-Kasay 42-yd. FG
CAR-Munnerlyn 37-yd. interception return (Kasay kick)
CAR-Kasay 43-yd. FG
CLE-Dawson 41-yd. FG

Passing
CAR: Clausen 16–28–195 0 TD 1 INT
CLE: Delhomme 24–35–245 0 TD 2 INT, Hillis 0–1–0 0 TD 0 INT

Rushing
CAR: Stewart 12–98, Goodson 14–55, Rosario 1-(-2)
CLE: Hillis 26–131, Bell 2–14, Mitchell 1–9, Delhomme 2–2, Stuckey 1-(-4)

Receiving
CAR: Goodson 8–81, LaFell 2–37, Rosario 3–33, Smith 2–33, Fiammetta 1–11
CLE: Hillis 6–63, Massaquoi 4–52, Robiskie 7–50, Watson 4–40, Stuckey 1–24, Moore 2–16

Sunday, December 5
Browns 13, Miami Dolphins 10
Sun Life Stadium (65,942)
Brown jerseys/white pants

Thanks to a timely Miami mistake in the final moments, the Browns were able to pull out a victory in an ugly, low-scoring contest in south Florida. With neither offense able to get untracked, the Browns broke a 3–3 tie late in the third quarter with a 94-yard drive capped by a three-yard touchdown pass from Jake Delhomme to Ben Watson, who tallied 100 yards on 10 catches. The Dolphins responded with a scoring drive to tie the game, and the teams exchanged punts through the fourth quarter (combining for 16 in the game) until a third-down pass by Miami QB Chad Henne was tipped by David Bowens and intercepted at the Miami 27 by Browns' DB Mike Adams, who returned it to the Dolphins' 2 with 54 seconds remaining. The Browns ran three plays to milk the clock, and then Phil Dawson booted a 23-yard field goal as time expired to give them their fourth victory in six games. The Cleveland defense stood tall once again with three interceptions, while Shaun Rogers blocked the fourteenth field-goal attempt of his career to keep Miami from scoring on the first possession of the contest. Though it pulled the Browns within two games of .500, it would prove to be their final victory of the season and Eric Mangini's last as Cleveland head coach.

Record: 5–7

	1	2	3	4		
Browns	0	3	7	3	=	13
Dolphins	0	3	0	7	=	10

CLE-Dawson 32-yd. FG
MIA-Carpenter 60-yd. FG
CLE-Watson 3-yd. pass from Delhomme (Dawson kick)
MIA-Fasano 11-yd. pass from Henne (Carpenter kick)
CLE-Dawson 23-yd. FG

Passing
CLE: Delhomme 24–34–217 1 TD 0 INT
MIA: Henne 16–32–174 1 TD 3 INT

Rushing
CLE: Hillis 18–57, Delhomme 4-(-5)
MIA: Brown 16–50, Williams 10–48, Henne 5–17, Polite 1-(-1)

Receiving
CLE: Watson 10–100, Massaquoi 4–81, Hillis 7–22, Robiskie 2–10, Stuckey 1–4
MIA: Bess 6–67, Fasano 4–41, Brown 2–27, Williams 2–19, Cobbs 1–11, Wallace 1–9

Sunday, December 12
Buffalo Bills 13, Browns 6
Ralph Wilson Stadium (50,861)
White jerseys/white pants

With a sloppy offensive performance on a rainy day in Buffalo, the Browns failed to score a touchdown and lost to the 2–10 Bills. Things started well as Peyton Hillis rushed for 49 yards on the opening drive, going over the 1,000-yard mark for the season, to set up a field goal.

Moments later the Browns recovered a Buffalo fumble and were poised to take control of the game, but on the next play, Hillis fumbled back to the Bills. After a Buffalo touchdown, the Browns pulled within a point with another field goal, but that marked the end of their offensive production as they failed to cross midfield in the second half. Cleveland finished with just 187 total yards—108 rushing by Hillis—and managed only nine first downs for the game.

Record: 5–8

	1	2	3	4		
Browns	3	3	0	0	=	6
Bills	0	10	0	3	=	13

CLE-Dawson 19-yd. FG
BUF-Nelson 11-yd. pass from Fitzpatrick (Lindell kick)
CLE-Dawson 25-yd. FG
BUF-Lindell 30-yd. FG
BUF-Lindell 19-yd. FG

Passing
CLE: Delhomme 12–20–86 0 TD 1 INT
BUF: Fitzpatrick 14–23–142 1 TD 0 INT

Rushing
CLE: Hillis 21–108, Bell 3–8, Cribbs 1-(-11)
BUF: Jackson 29–112, Fitzpatrick 4–49, Spiller 8–33, Jones 1-(-2)

Receiving
CLE: Massaquoi 3–43, Robiskie 2–17, Hillis 4–10, Watson 1–8, Cribbs 1–7, Stuckey 1–1
BUF: Stupar 3–45, Johnson 5–42, Jones 2–14, McIntyre 1–14, Martin 1–13, Nelson 1–11, Jackson 1–3

Sunday, December 19
Cincinnati Bengals 19, Browns 17
Paul Brown Stadium (56,342)
White jerseys/white pants

Entering the game in the midst of a 10-game losing streak, the Bengals dominated time of possession and held off the Browns for their first victory in nearly three months. With Colt McCoy back in the lineup, the Browns scored touchdowns on their first and last possessions of the game, but the offense was ineffective in between, managing just over 100 total yards and seven first downs on their middle six possessions. Cincinnati rolled to 188 rushing yards—150 by RB Cedric Benson—and held the football for over 38 minutes as the Bengals built a 19–10 lead midway through the fourth quarter. A long McCoy touchdown pass to WR Brian Robiskie pulled the Browns within two points with just over two minutes left, but Cincinnati recovered the ensuing onside kick to secure the victory.

Record: 3–11

	1	2	3	4		
Browns	7	0	0	10	=	17
Bengals	0	10	6	3	=	19

CLE-Royal 20-yd. pass from McCoy (Dawson kick)
CIN-Benson 18-yd. run (Stitser kick)
CIN-Stitser 25-yd. FG
CIN-Stitser 39-yd. FG
CIN-Stitser 34-yd. FG
CLE-Dawson 23-yd. FG
CIN-Stitser 20-yd. FG
CLE-Robiskie 46-yd. pass from McCoy (Dawson kick)

Passing
CLE: McCoy 19–25–243 2 TD 0 INT
CIN: Palmer 14–23–209 0 TD 0 INT

Rushing
CLE: Hillis 14–59
CIN: Benson 31–150, Scott 8–40, Palmer 5-(-1), Leonard 1-(-1)

Receiving
CLE: Watson 7–92, Robiskie 5–82, Royal 2–29, Hillis 2–23, Massaquoi 1–11, Cribbs 1–4, Stuckey 1–2
CIN: Caldwell 4–89, Ochocinco 2–36, Simpson 2–30, Leonard 1–20, Shipley 2–14, Cosby 1–11, Gresham 1–6, Kelly 1–3

Sunday, December 26
Baltimore Ravens 20, Browns 10
Cleveland Browns Stadium (65,028)
Brown jerseys/white pants

After a spirited first-half performance, the Browns ran out of gas in the second half against the playoff-bound Ravens. Cleveland drew first blood midway through the first quarter on a razzle-dazzle touchdown that saw Mohamed Massaquoi throw a 29-yard touchdown pass to fellow WR Brian Robiskie. The Ravens bounced back with 13 points to take the lead, but the Browns narrowed the margin to three with a field goal in the final seconds of the half. They then attempted a surprise onside kick on the opening kickoff of the second half, but the kick went out of bounds and Baltimore took over at the Cleveland 38. The Ravens scored a touchdown two plays later to swing the momentum back in their favor. While the Cleveland defense hung tough, keeping the Ravens off the board for the remainder of the game, the Browns only threatened to score one other time, reaching the Baltimore 27 before Colt McCoy threw his third interception of the game. The Browns actually put forth their finest defensive performance of the season, limiting Baltimore to 258 total yards, but the Cleveland offense—hindered by four turnovers and Peyton Hillis's rib injury early in the game—couldn't take advantage.

Record: 5–10

	1	2	3	4		
Ravens	0	13	7	0	=	20
Browns	7	3	0	0	=	10

CLE-Robiskie 29-yd. pass from Massaquoi (Dawson kick)
BAL-Cundiff 27-yd. FG
BAL-Houshmandzadeh 15-yd. pass from Flacco (Cundiff kick)
BAL-Cundiff 40-yd. FG
CLE-Dawson 30-yd. FG
BAL-Mason 22-yd. pass from Flacco (Cundiff kick)

Passing
BAL: Flacco 12–19–102 2 TD 1 INT
CLE: McCoy 15–29–149 0 TD 3 INT, Massaquoi 1–1–29 1 TD 0 INT

Rushing
BAL: Rice 25–92, McGahee 8–34, McClain 2–19, Flacco 3–16
CLE: Hillis 12–35, McCoy 4–30, Bell 7–27, Cribbs 2–8, Vickers 1–2

Receiving
BAL: Mason 4–50, Houshmandzadeh 4–32, Boldin 2–15, McClain 1–5, Rice 1–0
CLE: Bell 2–48, Stuckey 4–39, Robiskie 2–35, Watson 3–22, Massaquoi 2–14, Cribbs 1–9, Smith 1–6, Hillis 1–5

Sunday, January 2
Pittsburgh Steelers 41, Browns 9
Cleveland Browns Stadium (68,303)
Brown jerseys/white pants

Suffering their worst defeat of the season, the Browns dropped their fourth straight game as Pittsburgh dominated from the outset and clinched the No. 2 seed in the AFC playoffs. The tone was set in the opening seconds when Colt McCoy's second pass was intercepted, and on the next play, Ben Roethlisberger threw a 56-yard touchdown pass. The Steelers added touchdowns on their next three possessions as they built a 31–3 halftime lead and cruised through a meaningless second half. It was another tough day for McCoy, who wrapped up an otherwise promising rookie campaign with three interceptions and four sacks as the Browns were held to 225 total yards. Brian Robiskie finished the season with a flourish, catching a touchdown pass for the third straight game. It proved to be the final game for Browns' head coach Eric Mangini, who was fired the next day after posting a 10–22 record in two seasons.

Record: 5–11

	1	2	3	4		
Steelers	14	17	7	3	=	41
Browns	0	3	0	6	=	9

PIT-Wallace 56-yd. pass from Roethlisberger (Suisham kick)
PIT-Mendenhall 1-yd. run (Suisham kick)
CLE-Dawson 19-yd. FG
PIT-Mendenhall 1-yd. run (Suisham kick)
PIT-Miller 4-yd. pass from Roethlisberger (Suisham kick)
PIT-Suisham 41-yd. FG
PIT-Ward 3-yd. pass from Randle El (Suisham kick)
PIT-Suisham 24-yd. FG
CLE-Robiskie 20-yd. pass from McCoy (pass failed)

Passing
PIT: Roethlisberger 15–22–280 2 TD 0 INT, Leftwich 5–7–42 0 TD 0 INT, Randle El 1–1–3 1 TD 0 INT
CLE: McCoy 20–41–209 1 TD 3 INT, Wallace 1–1–1 0 TD 0 INT, Cribbs 0–1–0 0 TD 0 INT

Rushing
PIT: Mendenhall 14–36, Dwyer 9–28, Roethlisberger 4–24, Redman 3–12
CLE: McCoy 4–19, Bell 5–14, Hillis 6–13, Cribbs 1–0, Massaquoi 1-(-3)

Receiving
PIT: Wallace 3–105, Miller 4–55, Brown 4–52, Ward 5–45, Mendenhall 1–24, Randle El 2–21, Sanders 1–16, Redman 1–7
CLE: Watson 7–67, Massaquoi 3–50, Cribbs 3–37, Robiskie 2–35, Bell 4–14, Stuckey 1–4, Hillis 1–3

2011

Sunday, September 11
Cincinnati Bengals 27, Browns 17
Cleveland Browns Stadium (67,321)
White jerseys/white pants

After rallying from a 13-point deficit to take a four-point lead into the fourth quarter, the Browns and new head coach Pat Shurmur lost their opener in maddening fashion. The Bengals scored on their first three possessions to go up 13–0 early in the second quarter, but the Browns stormed back with a pair of touchdown passes by QB Colt McCoy on back-to-back series to take a 14–13 lead at the half. They stretched the lead to 17–13 going into the fourth and were poised to clinch victory when the sputtering Bengals' offense faced third-and-11 at the Cleveland 41. Backup Cincy QB (and former Brown) Bruce Gradkowski—in for injured starter Andy Dalton—orchestrated a quick snap before the Browns' defense could break the huddle and floated a long pass to wide-open WR A. J. Green for a 41-yard touchdown to give the Bengals the lead with 4:28 remaining. The Browns managed only one first down on their next two possessions, and the Bengals put the game away when RB Cedric Benson broke free for a 39-yard touchdown run with less than two minutes to play. The loss marked the Browns' seventh straight defeat on opening day and thirteenth in 14 seasons as Shurmur became the sixth straight Browns head coach to lose his first game.

Record: 0–1

	1	2	3	4		
Bengals	10	3	0	14	=	27
Browns	0	14	3	0	=	17

CIN-Nugent 24-yd. FG
CIN-Gresham 2-yd. pass from Dalton (Nugent kick)
CIN-Nugent 47-yd. FG
CLE-Watson 34-yd. pass from McCoy (Dawson kick)
CLE-Moore 2-yd. pass from McCoy (Dawson kick)
CLE-Dawson 20-yd. FG
CIN-Green 41-yd. pass from Gradkowski (Nugent kick)
CIN-Benson 39-yd. run (Nugent kick)

Passing
CIN: Gradkowski 5–12–92 1 TD 0 INT, Dalton 10–15–81 1 TD 0 INT
CLE: McCoy 19–40–213 2 TD 1 INT

Rushing
CIN: Benson 25–121, Leonard 2–15, Scott 4–3, Gradkowski 2–0
CLE: Hillis 17–57, Hardesty 5–18, McCoy 3–11, Cribbs 1-(-3)

Receiving
CIN: Gresham 6–58, Simpson 4–44, Green 1–41, Leonard 2–29, Benson 1–2, Shipley 1-(-1)
CLE: Massaquoi 3–77, Watson 3–45, Moore 3–35, Hillis 6–30, Cribbs 1–13, Little 1–12, Norwood 1–6, McCoy 1-(-5)

Sunday, September 18
Browns 27, Indianapolis Colts 19
Lucas Oil Stadium (65,035)
White jerseys/white pants

Against the hapless Colts, who would fall to 2–14 after losing star QB Peyton Manning for the season due to injury, the Browns took control in the second half behind the power running of RB Peyton Hillis, who exploded for the game-clinching, third-down touchdown run from 24 yards out with under four minutes to play. Hillis finished the day with 94 yards on the ground—60 in the second half—and a pair of scores, the first of which came just before the half and gave the Browns the lead for good. His second score was set up by a 43-yard punt return by WR Josh Cribbs, who also set up Cleveland's first touchdown with a 52-yard kickoff return. The Cleveland defense held its opponent under 300 total yards for the second straight week.

Record: 1–1

	1	2	3	4		
Browns	0	14	0	13	=	27
Colts	3	6	3	7	=	19

IND-Vinatieri 39-yd. FG
IND-Vinatieri 27-yd. FG
CLE-Moore 16-yd. pass from McCoy (Dawson kick)

IND-Vinatieri 52-yd. FG
CLE-Hillis 1-yd. run (Dawson kick)
IND-Vinatieri 36-yd. FG
CLE-Dawson 20-yd. FG
CLE-Hillis 24-yd. run (Dawson kick)
CLE-Dawson 23-yd. FG
IND-Clark 6-yd. pass from Collins (Vinatieri kick)

Passing
CLE: McCoy 22–32–211 1 TD 0 INT
IND: Collins 19–38–191 1 TD 1 INT

Rushing
CLE: Hillis 27–94, McCoy 3–10, Hardesty 3–1, Marecic 1–1
IND: Addai 14–64, Carter 11–46, Collins 1-(-1)

Receiving
CLE: Massaquoi 3–45, Cribbs 3–41, Little 4–38, Hillis 4–23, Smith 3–19, Watson 2–16, Moore 1–16, Marecic 2–13
IND: Wayne 4–66, Addai 4–37, Clark 4–32, Garcon 3–28, Collie 3–24, Eldridge 1–4

Sunday, September 25
Browns 17, Miami Dolphins 16
Cleveland Browns Stadium (66,651)
White jerseys/white pants

Overcoming a lethargic offensive performance, the Browns pulled out a dramatic last-minute victory to surge over the .500 mark for the first time in four years. With Peyton Hillis missing the game with strep throat, the Browns managed little offense throughout the afternoon and trailed 16–10 when they regained possession at their own 20 with 3:23 remaining. Colt McCoy directed the Browns on a 13-play drive that ended when WR Mohamed Massaquoi made an acrobatic leaping catch along the sideline in the end zone for the go-ahead touchdown with 43 seconds to play. But the Browns were penalized for excessive celebration after the touchdown, then were flagged for a personal foul on the ensuing kickoff return. Miami took over at the Cleveland 47, but the Browns' defense forced three straight incompletions, then DB Mike Adams intercepted a fourth-down pass with 13 seconds left to clinch the narrow victory. Though the Browns' defense allowed 369 total yards, it collected five sacks and didn't allow a touchdown in the final three quarters.
Record: 2–1

	1	2	3	4		
Dolphins	7	3	3	3	=	16
Browns	0	7	3	7	=	17

MIA-Thomas 10-yd. pass from Henne (Carpenter kick)
CLE-Cribbs 33-yd. pass from McCoy (Dawson kick)
MIA-Carpenter 23-yd. FG
CLE-Dawson 30-yd. FG
MIA-Carpenter 41-yd. FG
MIA-Carpenter 38-yd. FG
CLE-Massaquoi 14-yd. pass from McCoy (Dawson kick)

Passing
MIA: Henne 19–29–255 1 TD 1 INT
CLE: McCoy 19–39–210 2 TD 1 INT

Rushing
MIA: Thomas 23–95, Henne 4–26, Bush 10–13, Hilliard 1–4
CLE: Hardesty 14–67, Marecic 1–3, Smith 2–2, McCoy 2-(-2)

Receiving
MIA: Hartline 4–87, Bess 5–52, Marshall 4–43, Thomas 3–27, Fasano 1–26, Bush 1–12, Hilliard 1–8
CLE: Watson 5–64, Cribbs 3–49, Massaquoi 2–26, Little 3–24, Hardesty 3–19, Moore 2–19, Smith 1–9

Sunday, October 2
Tennessee Titans 31, Browns 13
Cleveland Browns Stadium (66,240)
White jerseys/white pants

Amid a myriad of big mistakes, the Browns were dominated by the visiting Titans on a wet and windy afternoon in Cleveland. Thanks to a pair of long Phil Dawson field goals, the Browns hung close through the first quarter before Tennessee pulled off an 80-yard touchdown pass, then completed a 57-yard pass just before the half, which led to another score. The Titans then capped their scoring with a 97-yard interception return for a touchdown to extend their lead to 31–6 late in the third quarter. While the Cleveland offense racked up more than 400 yards, it struggled to put points on the board. Colt McCoy completed 40 of 61 passes—both team records—for 350 yards, hitting 11 different receivers.
Record: 2–2

	1	2	3	4		
Titans	7	14	10	0	=	31
Browns	3	3	0	7	=	13

CLE-Dawson 48-yd. FG
TEN-Stevens 12-yd. pass from Hasselbeck (Bironas kick)
CLE-Dawson 51-yd. FG
TEN-Cook 80-yd. pass from Hasselbeck (Bironas kick)
TEN-Williams 4-yd. pass from Hasselbeck (Bironas kick)
TEN-Bironas 39-yd. FG
TEN-Babineaux 97-yd. interception return (Bironas kick)
CLE-Watson 10-yd. pass from McCoy (Dawson kick)

Passing
TEN: Hasselbeck 10–20–220 3 TD 1 INT, Locker 0–1–0 0 TD 0 INT
CLE: McCoy 40–61–350 1 TD 1 INT

Rushing
TEN: Johnson 23–101, Hasselbeck 1–5, Ringer 4–4, Harper 1–2
CLE: Hillis 10–46, Hardesty 7–22, McCoy 4–16

Receiving
TEN: Cook 2–93, Washington 2–62, Hawkins 2–38, Stevens 1–12, Johnson 2–11, Williams 1–4
CLE: Little 6–57, Cribbs 5–50, Hardesty 5–49, Watson 6–48, Massaquoi 6–46, Robiskie 3–25, Hillis 5–23, Norwood 1–19, Moore 1–15, Smith 1–13, Marecic 1–5

Sunday, October 16
Oakland Raiders 24, Browns 17
O.Co Coliseum (57,300)
White jerseys/white pants

A handful of earlier mistakes outweighed a frenzied comeback attempt in the final minutes as the Browns dropped back under the .500 mark. The Raiders—playing in tribute to longtime owner Al Davis, who died the previous week—took a 24–7 lead into the fourth quarter aided by a pair of big plays on special teams. A 101-yard kickoff return for a score thwarted a tying Cleveland touchdown early in the second quarter, then Oakland made the lead 17 points on a touchdown pass on a fake field goal late in the third. The Browns cut the margin to three points with just over a minute left, then recovered an onside kick, but were unable to pick up a first down and the Raiders escaped. With Peyton Hillis leaving the game early with an injured hamstring, the Cleveland offense struggled, and Colt McCoy completed only 21 of 45 passes. Meanwhile, the Raiders lost starting QB Jason Campbell for the rest of the season with a broken collarbone in the first half, but backup Kyle Boller played well in relief to deliver the win.
Record: 2–3

	1	2	3	4		
Browns	0	7	0	10	=	17
Raiders	7	7	10	0	=	24

OAK-McFadden 4-yd. run (Janikowski kick)
CLE-Smith 1-yd. pass from McCoy (Dawson kick)
OAK-Ford 101-yd. kickoff return (Janikowski kick)
OAK-Janikowski 48-yd. FG
OAK-Boss 35-yd. pass from Lechler (Janikowski kick)
CLE-Dawson 47-yd. FG
CLE-Massaquoi 12-yd. pass from McCoy (Dawson kick)

Passing
CLE: McCoy 21–45–216 2 TD 0 INT
OAK: Boller 8–14–100 0 TD 0 INT, Campbell 6–9–52 0 TD 0 INT, Lechler 1–1–35 1 TD 0 INT

Rushing
CLE: Hardesty 11–35, McCoy 4–16, Hillis 6–14
OAK: McFadden 20–91, Bush 10–28, Campbell 2–16, Tonga 1–12, Boller 5–9, Ausberry 1-(-2), Moore 1-(-3)

Receiving
CLE: Little 6–72, Watson 3–35, Massaquoi 3–30, Cribbs 2–30, Hardesty 2–18, Moore 3–16, Smith 2–14
OAK: Heyward-Bey 6–82, Ford 3–43, Boss 1–35, Bush 1–9, Moore 1–9, Ausberry 1–4, Myers 1–3, McFadden 1–2

Sunday, October 23
Browns 6, Seattle Seahawks 3
Cleveland Browns Stadium (66,350)
White jerseys/white pants

Behind a magnificent defensive performance, the Browns pulled back to the .500 mark in the fourth 6–3 game in team history. The Seahawks managed just 137 total yards—the least allowed by the Browns in 18 years—while the Cleveland offense held the football for nearly 43 minutes despite once again playing without Peyton Hillis. In his place, Montario Hardesty carried the football 33 times for 95 yards and propelled the Browns to two long field goals by Phil Dawson. Two other Cleveland field-goal attempts were blocked, including a 24-yard shot with three minutes remaining in the game. But after the Seattle offense picked up a first down on a Cleveland penalty, the Seahawks were unable to pick up another, and the Browns ran out the clock for their third victory.
Record: 3–3

	1	2	3	4		
Seahawks	0	0	3	0	=	3
Browns	0	3	0	3	=	6

CLE-Dawson 52-yd. FG
SEA-Hauschka 20-yd. FG
CLE-Dawson 53-yd. FG

Passing
SEA: Whitehurst 12–30–97 0 TD 1 INT
CLE: McCoy 20–35–178 0 TD 1 INT

Rushing
SEA: Washington 7–39, Forsett 8–23, Whitehurst 1–6
CLE: Hardesty 33–95, McCoy 9–29, Ogbonnaya 3–15

Receiving
SEA: Rice 2–38, Morrah 2–18, Tate 1–11, Washington 4–10, McCoy 2–10, Williams 1–10
CLE: Ogbonnaya 5–43, Moore 4–35, Little 5–31, Hardesty 2–27, Massaquoi 1–13, Cribbs 1–9, Watson 1–5

Sunday, October 30
San Francisco 49ers 20, Browns 10
Candlestick Park (69,732)
White jerseys/white pants

Just like two weeks before, the Browns dug an early hole and then saw a comeback attempt fall short in northern California as the 49ers improved to 6–1 on the season. A Colt McCoy fumble on the game's second play led to San Francisco's first touchdown, and after Montario Hardesty left the game with an injured calf, the 49ers extended the margin to 17–0 late in the first half. A long Phil Dawson field goal got the Browns on the board before the half, then a 45-yard touchdown catch by Josh Cribbs pulled the Browns within seven points with six minutes left in the game. The Cleveland defense, which had played well throughout the second half, appeared to force a three-and-out moments later, but LB D'Qwell Jackson was called for a third-down facemask penalty, which gave the 49ers a first down and kept the drive alive. It ended with a game-clinching field goal with two minutes left. With their top two RBs hurt, the Browns' ground game managed only 66 yards, but McCoy threw for 241 yards to keep them in the game.
Record: 3–4

	1	2	3	4		
Browns	0	3	0	7	=	10
49ers	10	7	0	3	=	20

SF-Gore 4-yd. run (Akers kick)
SF-Akers 29-yd. FG
SF-Crabtree 2-yd. pass from Smith (Akers kick)
CLE-Dawson 52-yd. FG
CLE-Cribbs 45-yd. pass from McCoy (Dawson kick)
SF-Akers 26-yd. FG

Passing
CLE: McCoy 22–34–241 1 TD 1 INT
SF: Smith 15–24–177 1 TD 0 INT

Rushing
CLE: Ogbonnaya 11–37, McCoy 8–30, Hardesty 2–6, Marecic 1–1, Little 1-(-8)
SF: Gore 31–134, Smith 4–22, Hunter 3–26, Ginn 1-(-8)

Receiving
CLE: Watson 3–64, Cribbs 2–56, Norwood 5–32, Little 4–28, Ogbonnaya 5–24, Smith 1–20, Moore 2–17
SF: Crabtree 5–54, Edwards 4–42, Davis 3–27, Peelle 1–19, Sopoaga 1–18, Staley 1–17

Sunday, November 6
Houston Texans 30, Browns 12
Reliant Stadium (71,511)
White jerseys/white pants

With a horrific performance, the Browns were dominated by the playoff-bound Texans, who more than doubled Cleveland in first downs and total yardage. The Browns were held to a season-low 172 yards and once again fell behind early, giving up a touchdown on Houston's first possession. The Browns then compounded the problem when third-string RB Chris Ogbonnaya fumbled on Cleveland's first offensive play, leading to another Houston touchdown. The Texans had their way with the Browns up front, rolling up 261 yards on the ground as RBs Arian Foster and Ben Tate both topped 100 yards, the first time a Cleveland opponent had accomplished that in the same game in 55 years. Phil Dawson kicked two more field goals of 50 yards or more, giving him six on the season, but the Browns didn't reach the end zone until the final five minutes of the contest, when they trailed by 24 points.
Record: 3–5

	1	2	3	4		
Browns	3	0	3	6	=	12
Texans	14	10	3	3	=	30

HOU-Tate 27-yd. run (Rackers kick)
HOU-Schaub 2-yd. run (Rackers kick)

CLE-Dawson 50-yd. FG
HOU-Foster 19-yd. run (Rackers kick)
HOU-Rackers 28-yd. FG
HOU-Rackers 21-yd. FG
CLE-Dawson 51-yd. FG
HOU-Rackers 50-yd. FG
CLE-Cribbs 2-yd. pass from McCoy (pass failed)

Passing
CLE: McCoy 14–22–146 1 TD 1 INT
HOU: Schaub 14–23–119 0 TD 1 INT

Rushing
CLE: Ogbonnaya 13–28, Clayton 5–10, McCoy 3–6
HOU: Foster 19–124, Tate 12–115, Ward 6–22, Schaub 3–0

Receiving
CLE: Cribbs 5–50, Little 2–33, Watson 2–26, Ogbonnaya 1–13, Moore 2–11, Cameron 1–7, Norwood 1–6
HOU: Daniels 3–32, Jones 2–28, Dreessen 2–27, Foster 5–26, Walter 1–5, Casey 1–1

Sunday, November 13
St. Louis Rams 13, Browns 12
Cleveland Browns Stadium (64,900)
White jerseys/white pants

The Browns suffered another frustrating home defeat, this time to the 1–7 Rams as the offense couldn't score a touchdown, and the special teams suffered an untimely breakdown in the waning moments. Though the Browns made four trips inside the St. Louis 20, they failed to reach the end zone, settling for four Phil Dawson field goals to take a 12–10 lead into the fourth quarter. A fumbled punt return by Josh Cribbs set up the go-ahead St. Louis field goal midway through the fourth quarter, but the Browns responded with a drive to the St. Louis 4. With just over two minutes remaining, they lined up for the go-ahead field goal, but a bad snap by Ryan Pontbriand threw off Phil Dawson's timing and the kick sailed wide left. The Rams then ran out the clock and escaped with just their second victory of the season. The defeat spoiled solid performances by Colt McCoy, who completed 20 of 27 passes, and Chris Ogbonnaya, who rushed for 90 yards.
Record: 3–6

	1	2	3	4		
Rams	0	10	0	3	=	13
Browns	3	6	3	0	=	12

CLE-Dawson 44-yd. FG
STL-Lloyd 7-yd. pass from Bradford (Brown kick)
CLE-Dawson 32-yd. FG
STL-Brown 29-yd. FG
CLE-Dawson 43-yd. FG
CLE-Dawson 27-yd. FG
STL-Brown 34-yd. FG

Passing
STL: Bradford 15–25–155 1 TD 1 INT
CLE: McCoy 20–27–218 0 TD 0 INT

Rushing
STL: Jackson 27–128, Bradford 4–3, Miller 1–2
CLE: Ogbonnaya 19–90, Cribbs 3–21, Little 1–10, McCoy 4–4, Marecic 1–3, Clayton 2-(-2)

Receiving
STL: Lloyd 4–48, Pettis 3–31, Jackson 3–23, Hoomanawanui 2–21, Miller 1–20, Bajema 2–12
CLE: Little 6–84, Cribbs 3–32, Watson 3–30, Wallace 1–21, Ogbonnaya 2–19, Smith 2–15, Norwood 2–14, Clayton 1–3

Sunday, November 20
Browns 14, Jacksonville Jaguars 10
Cleveland Browns Stadium (63,498)
White jerseys/white pants

Thanks to a last-second goal-line stand, the Browns snapped their three-game losing streak and captured what would prove to be their final victory of the season. In a low-scoring affair, the Browns tied the game at seven late in the second quarter on a short touchdown run by Chris Ogbonnaya, who had the best day of his brief career, tallying 115 yards on 21 carries. The Browns then took the lead on a short Josh Cribbs touchdown reception early in the fourth quarter. After the Rams cut the margin to 14–10, the Browns had an opportunity to push the lead back to seven points, but Phil Dawson missed a 38-yard field goal with just over two minutes to play. The Jaguars quickly drove downfield, aided by two key penalties on Cleveland that resulted in first downs, and reached the Browns' 2 with 13 seconds left. After stuffing RB Maurice Jones-Drew at the 1, the Cleveland defense rose up to force two straight incompletions, including a final pass into the end zone as time expired.
Record: 4–6

	1	2	3	4		
Jaguars	0	7	0	3	=	10
Browns	0	7	0	7	=	14

JAX-Jones-Drew 6-yd. run (Scobee kick)
CLE-Ogbonnaya 1-yd. run (Dawson kick)
CLE-Cribbs 3-yd. pass from McCoy (Dawson kick)
JAX-Scobee 42-yd. FG

Passing
JAX: Gabbert 22–41–210 0 TD 0 INT
CLE: McCoy 17–24–199 1 TD 1 INT

Rushing
JAX: Jones-Drew 21–87, Gabbert 2–10, Owens 2–10, Karim 4–1
CLE: Ogbonnaya 21–115, McCoy 5–27, Clayton 1–4, Cribbs 1–2

Receiving
JAX: Lewis 7–64, Hill 3–49, Jones-Drew 4–31, Dillard 3–29, Thomas 3–23, West 2–14
CLE: Little 5–59, Norwood 1–51, Cribbs 3–20, Massaquoi 2–19, Ogbonnaya 2–19, Watson 2–18, Marecic 2–13

Sunday, November 27
Cincinnati Bengals 23, Browns 20
Paul Brown Stadium (48,260)
White jerseys/white pants

Squandering a 10-point third-quarter lead, the Browns were unable to make or prevent the big play down the stretch and lost another close one to Cincinnati. Colt McCoy threw a pair of touchdown passes in the first half, then Phil Dawson booted a 54-yard field goal to give the Browns a 20–10 advantage late in the third quarter. But the Bengals, aided by a McCoy interception, roared back with scores on their next two possessions to tie the contest early in the fourth. The Browns were poised to take the lead when they drove into Cincinnati territory with less than two minutes left, but WR Greg Little dropped a pass on third down, and Dawson's subsequent 55-yard field-goal attempt fell short. Bengals' WR A. J. Green then made a terrific third-down catch for a 51-yard gain to the Cleveland 2 with a minute remaining to set up the game-winning field goal with 38 seconds to play.
Record: 4–7

	1	2	3	4		
Browns	7	10	3	0	=	20
Bengals	7	0	10	6	=	23

CLE-Norwood 24-yd. pass from McCoy (Dawson kick)
CIN-Benson 16-yd. run (Nugent kick)
CLE-Dawson 32-yd. FG
CLE-Little 3-yd. pass from McCoy (Dawson kick)
CIN-Nugent 23-yd. FG
CLE-Dawson 54-yd. FG
CIN-Gresham 22-yd. pass from Dalton (Nugent kick)
CIN-Nugent 40-yd. FG
CIN-Nugent 26-yd. FG

Passing
CLE: McCoy 16–34–151 2 TD 1 INT
CIN: Dalton 21–31–270 1 TD 0 INT

Rushing
CLE: Hillis 19–65, McCoy 6–38, Ogbonnaya 3–16, Little 1–13, Cribbs 1–2
CIN: Benson 21–106, Dalton 6–23, Leonard 1–2, Scott 4–1

Receiving
CLE: Norwood 4–69, Little 5–57, Watson 2–14, Cribbs 1–8, Ogbonnaya 1–4, Moore 1–3, Hillis 2-(-4)
CIN: Green 3–110, Gresham 5–68, Hawkins 2–27, Benson 4–24, Caldwell 3–24, Simpson 2–15, Scott 2–2

Sunday, December 4
Baltimore Ravens 24, Browns 10
Cleveland Browns Stadium (63,648)
White jerseys/white pants

Through a steady rain, the Cleveland defense was shredded by a powerful Baltimore running game that tallied nearly 300 yards and propelled the Ravens to an easy victory. Led by Ray Rice's 204 rushing yards, Baltimore set a franchise record with 55 running attempts and took a 17–3 lead into the fourth quarter before putting the contest away on a punt return for a touchdown with seven minutes remaining. The Ravens' defense was also effective, holding the Browns to just over half of Baltimore's total yardage and keeping the Browns out of the end zone until the final five minutes, when Colt McCoy threw a meaningless touchdown pass to TE Evan Moore.
Record: 4–8

	1	2	3	4		
Ravens	0	10	7	7	=	24
Browns	0	0	3	7	=	10

BAL-Rice 6-yd. run (Cundiff kick)
BAL-Cundiff 21-yd. FG
CLE-Dawson 21-yd. FG
BAL-Williams 1-yd. run (Cundiff kick)

BAL-Webb 68-yd. punt return (Cundiff kick)
CLE-Moore 22-yd. pass from McCoy (Dawson kick)

Passing
BAL: Flacco 10–23–158 0 TD 0 INT
CLE: McCoy 17–35–192 1 TD 1 INT, Wallace 1–1–4 0 TD 0 INT

Rushing
BAL: Rice 29–204, Williams 16–76, Leach 4–12, Taylor 1–2, Flacco 4-(-1), Smith 1-(-3)
CLE: Hillis 12–45, McCoy 4–12, Ogbonnaya 1–2

Receiving
BAL: Dickson 3–47, Boldin 2–32, Smith 1–32, Pitta 1–26, Leach 1–11, Rice 2–10
CLE: Hillis 1–52, Watson 3–34, Norwood 3–29, Ogbonnaya 5–28, Moore 2–28, Little 3–18, Massaquoi 1–7

Thursday, December 8
Pittsburgh Steelers 14, Browns 3
Heinz Field (60,754)
White jerseys/white pants

On a Thursday night in Pittsburgh, both teams lost their starting QBs to injury, but the Browns hung close with the 9–3 Steelers until the final minutes before falling. On the first series of the game, the Browns drove to the Pittsburgh 2, then after a Colt McCoy touchdown run was overturned on replay review, they settled for a short field goal that proved to be the only points they'd score all night. Pittsburgh answered with a touchdown on its first possession, then the game became a defensive struggle with neither team threatening to score until the fourth quarter. The Browns made a defensive stand at the Cleveland 1 in the opening minutes of the final period, then following an interception on the Steelers' next series, the Browns drove to the Pittsburgh 5 with four minutes left. Along the way, McCoy was drilled in the head by Pittsburgh LB James Harrison and left the game for a play, then returned, though he had suffered a concussion. On his next play, the jarred McCoy was intercepted in the end zone, ending the scoring threat. A play after that, Pittsburgh QB Ben Roethlisberger, who left the game in the first half with an injured knee but returned, threw a 79-yard touchdown pass to WR Antonio Brown that secured the Steelers' eighth straight home victory over the Browns. The Cleveland defense allowed more than 400 yards for the second straight game, but the Steelers helped even things out with three turnovers and 97 yards in penalties.
Record: 4–9

	1	2	3	4		
Browns	3	0	0	0	=	3
Steelers	7	0	0	7	=	14

CLE-Dawson 20-yd. FG
PIT-Cotchery 11-yd. pass from Roethlisberger (Suisham kick)
PIT-Brown 79-yd. pass from Roethlisberger (Suisham kick)

Passing
CLE: McCoy 18–35–209 0 TD 2 INT, Wallace 1–1–13 0 TD 0 INT
PIT: Roethlisberger 16–21–280 2 TD 1 INT, Batch 0–2–0 0 TD 0 INT

Rushing
CLE: Ogbonnaya 2–31, Hillis 10–25, Hardesty 11–24, McCoy 6–15, Cribbs 1–3
PIT: Mendenhall 18–76, Redman 6–35, Wallace 1–21, Moore 3–15

Receiving
CLE: Moore 4–55, Massaquoi 3–44, Cribbs 2–38, Little 2–25, Norwood 2–21, Smith 2–19, Watson 2–11, Hardesty 2–9
PIT: Brown 5–151, Wallace 4–57, Cotchery 2–33, Johnson 2–22, Miller 2–11, Ward 1–6

Sunday, December 18
Arizona Cardinals 20, Browns 17 (OT)
University of Phoenix Stadium (60,443)
White jerseys/white pants

For the fourth time in 2011, the Browns were unable to hold a fourth-quarter lead and fell to defeat, this time in overtime to the Cardinals, who captured their fourth straight victory. The Browns controlled the game through three quarters, surging to a 17–7 lead after a dynamic 76-yard touchdown pass from a running Seneca Wallace, starting for injured Colt McCoy, to Greg Little. After the Cardinals scored a touchdown to pull within three points midway through the fourth, Wallace was sacked and fumbled, and Arizona recovered at the Cleveland 5, setting up the game-tying field goal. Neither team was able to score on its final two possessions of regulation, and after the Browns were forced to punt on the first series of overtime, a 32-yard return by Arizona DB Patrick Peterson gave the Cardinals a first down in Cleveland territory. Two plays later, a 32-yard catch by WR Larry Fitzgerald set up the game-winning field goal. It spoiled a breakthrough performance by Little, who tallied 131 receiving yards on five catches, while Peyton Hillis rushed for 99 yards and the Browns' first touchdown.

Record: 4–10

	1	2	3	4	OT		
Browns	7	3	7	0	0	=	17
Cardinals	0	7	0	10	3	=	20

CLE-Hillis 1-yd. run (Dawson kick)
CLE-Dawson 44-yd. FG
ARI-Roberts 9-yd. pass from Skelton (Feely kick)
CLE-Little 76-yd. pass from Wallace (Dawson kick)
ARI-Wells 1-yd. run (Feely kick)
ARI-Feely 33-yd. FG
ARI-Feely 22-yd. FG

Passing
CLE: Wallace 18–31–226 1 TD 0 INT
ARI: Skelton 28–46–313 1 TD 1 INT

Rushing
CLE: Hillis 26–99, Wallace 3–21
ARI: Wells 15–51, Skelton 2–7, Roberts 1–7, Stephens-Howling 3–6, Taylor 2–3, Smith 1–0

Receiving
CLE: Little 5–131, Massaquoi 3–42, Norwood 3–21, Hillis 1–9, Smith 1–9, Cameron 3–8, Cribbs 1–3, Ogbonnaya 1–3
ARI: Heap 7–69, Fitzgerald 3–65, Roberts 6–60, Doucet 3–37, King 1–24, Stephens-Howling 2–18, Taylor 3–17, Wells 1–10, Stuckey 1–7, Sherman 1–6

Saturday, December 24
Baltimore Ravens 20, Browns 14
M&T Stadium (71,083)
White jerseys/white pants

Mistakes doomed the Browns' bid for a fourth-quarter comeback on Christmas Eve, and instead they lost to Baltimore for the eighth straight time. After the Ravens sprinted to a 17–0 lead, the Browns showed signs of life just before the half, driving to the Baltimore 3. But with the clock ticking down and the Browns out of time outs, Peyton Hillis was stopped for no gain on an ill-advised handoff, and time expired before the Browns could get another playoff. After another Baltimore field goal, the Browns got on the board when Josh Cribbs returned a punt for a touchdown for the first time in nearly three seasons, then cut the margin to 20–14 with just over eight minutes remaining on a touchdown catch by Evan Moore. After a defensive stop, the Browns drove to their own 45 before a fourth-down pass fell incomplete to halt the march. They had one final chance with two minutes left as the Ravens lined up for a fourth-down play at the Cleveland 37, but Cleveland DT Phil Taylor jumped offside, giving the Ravens a first down and the opportunity to kneel out the clock. The miscues spoiled an otherwise admirable performance by the Browns' defense, which held the Ravens under 300 total yards, while Hillis rushed for 112.

Record: 4–11

	1	2	3	4		
Browns	0	0	7	7	=	14
Ravens	10	7	3	0	=	20

BAL-Dickson 5-yd. pass from Flacco (Graham kick)
BAL-Graham 48-yd. FG
BAL-Rice 42-yd. pass from Flacco (Graham kick)
BAL-Graham 43-yd. FG
CLE-Cribbs 84-yd. punt return (Dawson kick)
CLE-Moore 6-yd. pass from Wallace (Dawson kick)

Passing
CLE: Wallace 19–33–147 1 TD 1 INT
BAL: Flacco 11–24–132 2 TD 1 INT

Rushing
CLE: Hillis 24–112, Wallace 1–5
BAL: Rice 23–87, Williams 10–45, Flacco 4–30

Receiving
CLE: Little 4–40, Moore 5–35, Cribbs 2–28, Massaquoi 2–17, Mitchell 2–12, Ogbonnaya 1–12, Cameron 1–3, Hillis 2–0
BAL: Rice 3–48, Smith 2–38, Williams 2–21, Dickson 2–14, Leach 2–11

Sunday, January 1
Pittsburgh Steelers 13, Browns 9
Cleveland Browns Stadium (68,266)
White jerseys/white pants

On a gloomy, blustery New Year's Day, the Browns put forth a noble effort, but fell short to the 11–4 Steelers to complete a winless division schedule for just the second time in team history. After sneaking to a 6–3 halftime lead, the Browns lost control of the game in the third quarter as the Steelers scored 10 points to surge ahead. A Phil Dawson field goal cut the margin to 13–9 in the final minute of the third quarter, then the Browns' defense recovered fumbles on back-to-back possessions to keep them in the game. With less than two minutes to play and the afternoon's steady rain turning to snow, the Browns drove from their own 24 to the Pittsburgh 24, where Seneca Wallace's final pass as time expired fell incomplete off the hands of Greg Little in the flat. It marked the first time in 21 years the Browns failed to score an offensive touchdown against Pittsburgh in a season and closed out the team's lowest-scoring season in 11 years on a six-game losing streak.

Record: 4–12

	1	2	3	4		
Steelers	0	3	10	0	=	13
Browns	0	6	3	0	=	9

CLE-Dawson 26-yd. FG
CLE-Dawson 45-yd. FG
PIT-Suisham 19-yd. FG
PIT-Suisham 29-yd. FG
PIT-Redman 7-yd. run (Suisham kick)
CLE-Dawson 49-yd. FG

Passing
PIT: Roethlisberger 23–40–221 0 TD 0 INT
CLE: Wallace 16–41–177 0 TD 1 INT

Rushing
PIT: Redman 19–92, Mendenhall 8–38, Clay 9–31
CLE: Wallace 3–44, Hillis 10–30, Hardesty 2-(-2)

Receiving
PIT: Brown 6–90, Cotchery 3–28, Ward 5–24, Miller 2–23, Redman 3–18, Sanders 1–14, Wallace 1–11, Mendenhall 1–7, Johnson 1–6
CLE: Cribbs 7–91, Moore 4–39, Mitchell 1–19, Massaquoi 2–16, Cameron 1–15, Hillis 1-(-3)

2012

Sunday, September 9
Philadelphia Eagles 17, Browns 16
Cleveland Browns Stadium (68,693)
White jerseys/white pants

Pulled down by a disastrous professional debut by rookie QB Brandon Weeden, the Browns blew a fourth-quarter lead and lost a heartbreaker in the final minutes for their seventh consecutive opening-day defeat. Completing only 12 of 35 passes and throwing four interceptions, Weeden notched a passer rating of just 5.1 as the Cleveland offense managed just over 200 total yards for the game. Meanwhile, the Cleveland defense allowed a whopping 456 yards, but also forced five turnovers, including a 27-yard interception return for a touchdown by LB D'Qwell Jackson a minute into the fourth quarter that gave the Browns a 16–10 lead. But the Eagles, also hindered by 110 yards in penalties, rallied with time running out to put together a 16-play, 91-yard drive. After Cleveland LB L. J. Fort dropped what could have been a game-clinching interception in the end zone the play before, Philadelphia surged ahead with 1:18 remaining on a touchdown pass by QB Michael Vick, who had thrown four interceptions in the game. The Browns had one final chance to win, but on their next offensive play, Weeden tossed his fourth interception to seal the Philadelphia victory. Fellow Browns' rookie RB Trent Richardson also began his career unimpressively, managing just 39 yards on 19 carries.

Record: 0–1

	1	2	3	4		
Eagles	0	10	0	7	=	17
Browns	3	0	3	10	=	16

CLE-Dawson 43-yd. FG
PHI-Henery 42-yd. FG
PHI-Maclin 18-yd. pass from Vick (Henery kick)
CLE-Dawson 42-yd. FG
CLE-Dawson 22-yd. FG
CLE-Jackson 27-yd. interception return (Dawson kick)
PHI-Harbor 4-yd. pass from Vick (Henery kick)

Passing
PHI: Vick 29–56–317 2 TD 4 INT
CLE: Weeden 12–35–118 0 TD 4 INT

Rushing
PHI: McCoy 20–110, Vick 7–32, Jackson 1–5, Brown 2–3
CLE: Richardson 19–39, Benjamin 1–35, Weeden 2–25

Receiving
PHI: Maclin 7–96, Jackson 4–77, Celek 4–65, Avant 4–27, McCoy 6–26, Harbor 3–16, Johnson 1–10
CLE: Massaquoi 3–41, Gordon 2–32, Jackson 2–20, Benjamin 1–12, Watson 2–9, Richardson 1–5, Smith 1-(-1)

Sunday, September 16
Cincinnati Bengals 34, Browns 27
Paul Brown Stadium (63,036)
Brown jerseys/white pants

Tallying more than twice as much total yardage as it did the week before, the Browns' offense made dramatic improvements after its miserable showing in the opener, but it still wasn't enough as the defense permitted big plays all afternoon and allowed the Bengals to control the game. After Cincinnati surged to a lead on a punt return for a touchdown in the opening minutes, the Cleveland offense got rolling behind impressive performances from Brandon Weeden (322 passing yards) and Trent Richardson (109 rushing yards, two touchdowns). But the Bengals, aided by second-half touchdown passes of 44 and 50 yards by QB Andy Dalton, stayed one step ahead of the Browns all afternoon. After a short Phil Dawson field goal pulled the Browns within seven points with 20 seconds remaining, the Bengals secured the victory when they recovered the ensuing onside-kick attempt. The victory gave them a six-game lead in the all-time series between the teams, the largest advantage either team had ever held.

Record: 0–2

	1	2	3	4		
Browns	3	7	7	10	=	27
Bengals	7	10	7	10	=	34

CIN-Jones 81-yd. punt return (Nugent kick)
CLE-Dawson 50-yd. FG
CIN-Green 10-yd. pass from Dalton (Nugent kick)
CLE-Richardson 32-yd. run (Dawson kick)
CIN-Nugent 39-yd. FG
CIN-Tate 44-yd. pass from Dalton (Nugent kick)
CLE-Richardson 23-yd. pass from Weeden (Dawson kick)

CIN-Hawkins 50-yd. pass from Dalton (Nugent kick)
CLE-Little 24-yd. pass from Weeden (Dawson kick)
CIN-Nugent 37-yd. FG
CLE-Dawson 25-yd. FG

Passing
CLE: Weeden 26–37–322 2 TD 0 INT
CIN: Dalton 24–31–318 3 TD 1 INT

Rushing
CLE: Richardson 19–109, Benjamin 2–15, Weeden 2–6
CIN: Green-Ellis 21–75, Dalton 3–4, Peerman 1–1

Receiving
CLE: Massaquoi 5–90, Ogbonnaya 6–73, Little 5–57, Richardson 4–36, Smith 3–30, Watson 1–27, Gordon 1–5, Cribbs 1–4
CIN: Tate 3–71, Binns 5–66, Green 7–58, Hawkins 2–56, Gresham 4–37, Green-Ellis 3–30

Sunday, September 23
Buffalo Bills 24, Browns 14
Cleveland Browns Stadium (69,353)
White jerseys/white pants

With the offense reverting back to its opening-day struggles and the defense permitting touchdowns on Buffalo's first two possessions, the Browns quickly dug a deep hole they were unable to climb out of and dropped to 0–3 for the fourth time in five years. Though the Cleveland offense managed just 240 total yards for the game, it put together two scoring drives to pull the Browns within three points late in the third quarter after a touchdown reception by WR Travis Benjamin. But Buffalo—playing without league-leading RB C. J. Spiller, who left the game in the first quarter with a shoulder injury—pushed the lead back to double digits with a touchdown midway through the final period, then intercepted two Brandon Weeden passes in the final five minutes to secure the victory. After a breakthrough performance the week before, Trent Richardson was held to just 27 yards on 12 carries as the Browns managed a harmless 33 yards rushing for the game as a team.
Record: 0–3

	1	2	3	4		
Bills	14	0	3	7	=	24
Browns	0	7	7	0	=	14

BUF-Graham 9-yd. pass from Fitzpatrick (Lindell kick)
BUF-Spiller 32-yd. pass from Fitzpatrick (Lindell kick)
CLE-Richardson 6-yd. run (Dawson kick)
BUF-Lindell 37-yd. FG
CLE-Benjamin 22-yd. pass from Weeden (Dawson kick)
BUF-Johnson 9-yd. pass from Fitzpatrick (Lindell kick)

Passing
BUF: Fitzpatrick 22–35–208 3 TD 0 INT
CLE: Weeden 27–43–237 1 TD 2 INT

Rushing
BUF: Choice 20–91, Spiller 4–16, White 2–15, Fitzpatrick 6–10, Smith 2–6
CLE: Richardson 12–27, Ogbonnaya 1–6

Receiving
BUF: Johnson 7–61, Jones 5–42, Spiller 2–42, Graham 3–24, Chandler 2–22, McIntyre 1–9, Choice 2–8
CLE: Cameron 5–45, Benjamin 2–44, Gordon 3–40, Richardson 6–24, Cribbs 1–24, Little 2–17, Watson 4–15, Ogbonnaya 3–14, Massaquoi 1–14

Thursday, September 27
Baltimore Ravens 23, Browns 16
M&T Bank Stadium (70,944)
White jerseys/white pants

Following the same script to defeat as four days earlier, the Browns fell behind by two scores early and were unable to overcome in a Thursday-night battle in Baltimore. The key play came in the final seconds of the third quarter when Ravens' DB Cary Williams intercepted a Brandon Weeden pass and returned it 63 yards for a touchdown to put Baltimore up 23–10. The Browns pulled back within seven points with 4:33 remaining, then drove from their own 10 to the Baltimore 18 in the final minute before Weeden's final pass sailed out of the end zone as time expired, securing the Ravens' ninth straight win over the Browns. Despite completing less than half of his passes, Weeden threw for 320 yards, while Baltimore QB Joe Flacco tossed for 356, and the Ravens rolled up 438 total yards. Phil Dawson became just the seventh kicker in NFL history to kick three field goals of 50 or more yards in the same game and the first to do it in the same half. The contest also marked the return of the regular NFL officials, who went back to work after the resolution of a three-week labor dispute with the league.
Record: 0–4

	1	2	3	4		
Browns	0	7	3	6	=	16
Ravens	0	9	14	0	=	23

BAL-Smith 18-yd. pass from Flacco (kick failed)
BAL-Tucker 45-yd. FG
CLE-Richardson 1-yd. run (Dawson kick)
BAL-Flacco 1-yd. run (Tucker kick)
CLE-Dawson 51-yd. FG
BAL-Williams 63-yd. interception return (Tucker kick)
CLE-Dawson 50-yd. FG
CLE-Dawson 52-yd. FG

Passing
CLE: Weeden 25–52–320 0 TD 1 INT
BAL: Flacco 28–46–356 1 TD 1 INT

Rushing
CLE: Richardson 14–47, Benjamin 1–0, Little 1-(-2), Ogbonnaya 1-(-2)
BAL: Rice 18–49, Pierce 6–48, Flacco 2–4, Smith 1–0

Receiving
CLE: Little 4–77, Richardson 4–57, Norwood 4–56, Watson 5–52, Benjamin 2–26, Gordon 1–16, Cameron 1–15, Cribbs 2–11, Ogbonnaya 2–10
BAL: Boldin 9–131, Smith 6–97, Rice 8–47, Doss 1–39, Leach 2–25, Jones 2–17

Sunday, October 7
New York Giants 41, Browns 27
MetLife Stadium (79,911)
White jerseys/white pants

After getting off to a dazzling start and soaring to a 14–0 lead in the game's first five minutes, the Browns were dominated for the remainder of the afternoon and lost a lopsided game to the defending world champions. After recovering a fumble by New York RB Ahmad Bradshaw on the game's first play from scrimmage, the Browns cashed in one play later with a scoring run by Trent Richardson, then added another score on a 62-yard touchdown bomb from Brandon Weeden to rookie WR Josh Gordon four minutes later. But the Giants outscored the Browns 27–3 for the rest of the half and built a 21-point lead in the fourth quarter before the Browns pulled back within 14 on Gordon's second scoring catch in the final minutes of the game. The turning point came late in the first half with the Browns still leading 17–10, when Weeden threw an ill-advised pass on third-and-one at the New York 25 that was intercepted to set up the tying touchdown. Josh Cribbs then fumbled the ensuing kickoff to spark the Giants' go-ahead touchdown, and they never looked back. New York simply overwhelmed the Cleveland defense, rolling up more than 500 yards of offense and 30 first downs, led by 200 rushing yards by Bradshaw and three touchdown catches by WR Victor Cruz. Weeden threw for 291 yards, and the Browns rolled up nearly 400 yards of offense themselves but still couldn't keep up with the red-hot Giants. The defeat was the Browns' eleventh straight, matching a franchise record set in 1974–75.

Record: 0–5

	1	2	3	4		
Browns	14	3	3	7	=	27
Giants	7	20	7	7	=	41

CLE-Richardson 15-yd. run (Dawson kick)
CLE-Gordon 62-yd. pass from Weeden (Dawson kick)
NYG-Cruz 3-yd. pass from Manning (Tynes kick)
CLE-Dawson 32-yd. FG
NYG-Tynes 29-yd. FG
NYG-Bradshaw 4-yd. run (Tynes kick)
NYG-Cruz 7-yd. pass from Manning (Tynes kick)
NYG-Tynes 40-yd. FG
NYG-Cruz 28-yd. pass from Manning (Tynes kick)
CLE-Dawson 41-yd. FG
NYG-Wilson 40-yd. run (Tynes kick)
CLE-Gordon 20-yd. pass from Weeden (Dawson kick)

Passing
CLE: Weeden 22–35–291 2 TD 2 INT
NYG: Manning 25–37–259 3 TD 1 INT

Rushing
CLE: Richardson 17–81, Weeden 1–2, Norwood 1–1
NYG: Bradshaw 30–200, Wilson 2–44, Manning 2-(-1)

Receiving
CLE: Gordon 2–82, Norwood 9–81, Ogbonnaya 3–54, Richardson 5–47, Cameron 2–26, Watson 1–1
NYG: Randle 6–82, Hixon 5–55, Cruz 5–50, Bennett 3–30, Bradshaw 4–29, Pascoe 1–7, Jernigan 1–6

Sunday, October 14
Browns 34, Cincinnati Bengals 24
Cleveland Browns Stadium (67,060)
White jerseys/white pants

Thanks to a 21-point explosion in the fourth quarter, the Browns' long losing streak came to an end as they picked up their first win of the season. Trailing 14–13 going into the fourth quarter, the Browns scored three touchdowns in just over seven minutes, taking their first lead of the game on the first play of the final period on a short scoring run by RB Montario Hardesty, filling in for a banged-up Trent Richardson. After a Cincinnati field goal, the Browns drove 63 yards for another score on a three-yard Brandon Weeden pass to TE Ben Watson, then on the next play from scrimmage, DB Sheldon Brown intercepted Bengals' QB Andy Dalton and returned it 19 yards for a touchdown to make it 34–17. The Bengals quickly cut the margin back to 10 points with a long scoring pass, then drove to the Cleveland 9 with just under three minutes remaining before Cleveland DL Emmanuel Stephens sacked Dalton and stripped the football, which was recovered by fellow lineman Billy Winn and returned to the Cincinnati 42 to seal the victory. Though the Cleveland defense permitted 438 yards—381 passing by Dalton and seven catches for 135 by WR A. J. Green—it also forced four key turnovers. Meanwhile, Hardesty came off the bench to rush for 56 yards and spark the offense in the second half, while Josh Gordon reeled in a long pass for a touchdown for the second straight week to give the Browns their only points of the first half.

Record: 1–5

	1	2	3	4		
Bengals	7	7	0	10	=	24
Browns	0	7	6	21	=	34

CIN-Gresham 55-yd. pass from Dalton (Nugent kick)
CLE-Gordon 71-yd. pass from Weeden (Dawson kick)
CIN-Green 4-yd. pass from Dalton (Nugent kick)
CLE-Dawson 41-yd. FG
CLE-Dawson 38-yd. FG
CLE-Hardesty 1 yd. run (Dawson kick)
CIN-Nugent 44-yd. FG
CLE-Watson 3-yd. pass from Weeden (Dawson kick)
CLE-Brown 19-yd. interception return (Dawson kick)
CIN-Green 57-yd. pass from Dalton (Nugent kick)

Passing
CIN: Dalton 31–46–381 3 TD 3 INT
CLE: Weeden 17–29–231 2 TD 1 INT

Rushing
CIN: Green-Ellis 16–62, Peerman 1–7, Dalton 2–5, Hawkins 1–2
CLE: Hardesty 15–56, Richardson 14–37, Cribbs 1–8, Ogbonnaya 1–6, Weeden 3–3

Receiving
CIN: Green 7–135, Peerman 8–76, Gresham 3–68, Hawkins 5–35, Jones 2–21, Binns 2–12, Charles 1–12, Tate 1–11, Green-Ellis 1–8, Leonard 1–3
CLE: Gordon 3–99, Cooper 2–39, Cameron 2–38, Little 3–18, Richardson 2–17, Hardesty 1–9, Watson 2–6, Ogbonnaya 2–5

Sunday, October 21
Indianapolis Colts 17, Browns 13
Lucas Oil Stadium (64,560)
White jerseys/white pants

A series of missed opportunities cost the Browns a chance to win their first game under new owner Jimmy Haslam, who officially purchased the team the previous week. Each team scored a touchdown on its first possession, including a juggling touchdown reception by Browns' WR Greg Little, but the Browns blew their extra-point attempt when holder Reggie Hodges bobbled the center snap, and the Colts would keep the lead for the remainder of the game. Indianapolis added another touchdown run by rookie QB Andrew Luck on its next possession and held an eight-point lead until a long touchdown pass from Brandon Weeden to Josh Gordon on the first series of the second half. After a field goal pushed the Colts' lead to 17–13, the Browns squandered two chances to take the lead in the fourth quarter. First, Gordon dropped a sure touchdown pass on third down from the Indy 41, and Pat Shurmur opted to punt on fourth and one with 6:38 remaining. The Browns drove into Colts' territory again on their next possession, but a fourth-down pass from the 39 fell incomplete with less than two minutes to play, and the Colts held the football for all but the final second, securing the victory. Trent Richardson, nursing sore ribs, was held to just eight yards on eight carries before being pulled from the game at the half, and the Browns managed only 55 yards on the ground. The Browns were also playing without LG Jason Pinkston, who had been hospitalized due to life-threatening blood clots in his lung two days earlier.

Record: 1–6

	1	2	3	4		
Browns	0	6	7	0	=	13
Colts	7	7	3	0	=	17

IND-Luck 3-yd. run (Vinatieri kick)
CLE-Little 14-yd. pass from Weeden (kick failed)
IND-Luck 5-yd. run (Vinatieri kick)
CLE-Gordon 33-yd. pass from Weeden (Dawson kick)
IND-Vinatieri 38-yd. FG

Passing
CLE: Weeden 25–41–264 2 TD 0 INT
IND: Luck 16–29–186 0 TD 0 INT

Rushing
CLE: Hardesty 7–28, Weeden 1–13, Richardson 8–8, Ogbonnaya 1–6
IND: Ballard 20–84, Carter 11–41, Luck 3–12, Moore 3–11

Receiving
CLE: Gordon 2–59, Cooper 4–53, Little 6–52, Watson 3–36, Benjamin 3–33, Ogbonnaya 3–17, Richardson 2–11, Cribbs 1–8, Cameron 1–4
IND: Wayne 6–73, Avery 4–46, Hilton 2–22, Ballard 1–19, Fleener 2–17, Allen 1–9

Sunday, October 28
Browns 7, San Diego Chargers 6
Cleveland Browns Stadium (65,337)
Brown jerseys/white pants

On a rainy, blustery afternoon, the Browns scored a touchdown on their opening possession and then held off the Chargers for the rest of the contest to pick up their second victory in three weeks. Behind the power running of Trent Richardson, the Browns drove 70 yards the first time they had the ball and took a 7–0 lead when Richardson broke two tackles and sloshed for a 26-yard touchdown. Meanwhile, the Cleveland defense kept the Chargers out of the end zone, starting with key fourth-down stops in Cleveland territory on San Diego's first and last possessions, the latter at the Cleveland 44 with just over a minute to play. The Browns held San Diego to just 265 total yards—a season low for Cleveland's defense—while Richardson paced the Browns' offense with a season-high 122 rushing yards on 24 carries. The victory marked the team's first under Jimmy Haslam's ownership.
Record: 2–6

	1	2	3	4		
Chargers	0	3	3	0	=	6
Browns	7	0	0	0	=	7

CLE-Richardson 26-yd. run (Dawson kick)
SD-Novak 43-yd. FG
SD-Novak 31-yd. FG

Passing
SD: Rivers 18–34–154 0 TD 0 INT
CLE: Weeden 11–27–129 0 TD 0 INT

Rushing
SD: Mathews 24–95, Brown 4–17, Battle 3–6, McClain 2–5, Meachem 1-(-6)
CLE: Richardson 24–122, Weeden 4–4, Ogbonnaya 1–4, Hardesty 3–3, Cribbs 1–0

Receiving
SD: Brown 7–85, Floyd 4–43, Gates 2–14, Rosario 2–11, Mathews 2–9
CLE: Gordon 3–46, Little 2–28, Watson 1–14, Cameron 1–12, Richardson 1–12, Ogbonnaya 1–9, Cribbs 1–7, Smith 1–1

Sunday, November 4
Baltimore Ravens 25, Browns 15
Cleveland Browns Stadium (65,449)
Brown jerseys/white pants

After digging a quick hole, the Browns gradually fought back to take a fourth-quarter lead, only to see it evaporate in the final minutes as they lost to the Ravens for the tenth straight time. Baltimore scored touchdowns on its first two possessions to build a 14–0 lead, but the Cleveland defense stymied the Ravens over the next two quarters, allowing the Browns to slowly claw back into the game on the strength of five Phil Dawson field goals. Dawson remained perfect for the season, extending his streak to 23 straight successful field-goal attempts. His fifth on the day gave the Browns a 15–14 lead with just under nine minutes remaining but came after a touchdown reception by Josh Gordon was wiped out by an illegal-formation penalty. The Ravens responded with a touchdown of their own and two-point conversion to surge back to a seven-point advantage. The Browns then spoiled their last chance when they failed to convert on fourth-and-two from their own 28 with 3:50 remaining. Baltimore tacked on an insurance field goal in the final minutes, and a Brandon Weeden interception wrapped up the Ravens' victory. Though Trent Richardson rushed for more than 100 yards for the second straight week, the Cleveland offense struggled, picking up less than 300 total yards and failing to punch the ball into the end zone despite five trips inside the Baltimore 20.
Record: 2–7

	1	2	3	4		
Ravens	14	0	0	11	=	25
Browns	0	9	3	3	=	15

BAL-Rice 8-yd. run (Tucker kick)
BAL-Pierce 12-yd. run (Tucker kick)
CLE-Dawson 32-yd. FG
CLE-Dawson 28-yd. FG
CLE-Dawson 29-yd. FG
CLE-Dawson 33-yd. FG
CLE-Dawson 41-yd. FG
BAL-Smith 19-yd. pass from Flacco (Boldin pass from Flacco)
BAL-Tucker 43-yd. FG

Passing
BAL: Flacco 15–24–153 1 TD 0 INT
CLE: Weeden 20–37–176 0 TD 2 INT

Rushing
BAL: Rice 25–98, Pierce 7–26, Leach 2–8, Taylor 1–4, Flacco 2–1
CLE: Richardson 25–105, Weeden 2–11

Receiving
BAL: Boldin 5–57, Smith 4–46, Pitta 2–33, Dickson 2–11, Rice 2–6
CLE: Little 5–52, Gordon 2–38, Richardson 6–31, Watson 2–22, Benjamin 1–19, Smith 3–8, Massaquoi 1–6

Sunday, November 18
Dallas Cowboys 23, Browns 20 (OT)
Cowboys Stadium (81,936)
Brown jerseys/white pants

The Browns got off to a great start and controlled the game through the first half but then squandered two fourth-quarter leads and lost a wild game in overtime. Holding Dallas scoreless in the first two quarters, the Browns built a 13-point lead on the strength of a ferocious pass rush that recorded seven sacks on the day. They took a 13–3 advantage into the final period before Dallas surged ahead with a pair of touchdowns. The Browns endured and were poised to take the lead back but were stopped on downs at the Dallas 1 with 1:42 left. Again, Cleveland fought back, forcing a punt, and after a 21-yard return by Josh Cribbs, Brandon Weeden hit TE Ben Watson for a 17-yard touchdown pass to put the Browns ahead with 1:10 remaining. The Cowboys responded with a quick drive downfield, aided by a 35-yard pass-interference penalty on the Browns, and tied the game with a field goal with two seconds left. After an exchange of possessions in overtime, the Cowboys marched deep into Cleveland territory, catching a break when an apparent Dallas fumble was instead ruled an incomplete pass and won the game with a short field goal. Nearly identical in total yardage, the teams combined for more than 200 yards in penalties, including 129 by the Browns, 92 committed by a struggling defensive secondary.
Record: 2–8

	1	2	3	4	OT		
Browns	7	6	0	7	0	=	20
Cowboys	0	0	3	17	3	=	23

CLE-Watson 10-yd. pass from Weeden (Dawson kick)
CLE-Dawson 51-yd. FG
CLE-Dawson 37-yd. FG
DAL-Bailey 44-yd. FG
DAL-Jones 2-yd. run (Bailey kick)
DAL-Bryant 28-yd. pass from Romo (Bailey kick)
CLE-Watson 17-yd. pass from Weeden (Dawson kick)
DAL-Bailey 32-yd. FG
DAL-Bailey 38-yd. FG

Passing
CLE: Weeden 20–35–210 2 TD 0 INT
DAL: Romo 35–50–313 1 TD 0 INT

Rushing
CLE: Richardson 28–95, Hardesty 4–23, Ogbonnaya 1–1
DAL: Jones 14–43, Dunbar 5–10, Romo 2–10

Receiving
CLE: Gordon 5–53, Little 3–53, Richardson 6–49, Watson 4–47, Cooper 1–6, Smith 1–2
DAL: Bryant 12–145, Austin 6–58, Witten 7–51, Harris 3–20, Jones 2–12, Ogletree 1–10, Beasley 1–8, Dunbar 2–6, Vickers 1–3

Sunday, November 25
Browns 20, Pittsburgh Steelers 14
Cleveland Browns Stadium (69,661)
Brown jerseys/white pants

Thanks to an opportunistic defense, the Browns put a dent in Pittsburgh's postseason drive and picked up their first victory over the Steelers in nearly three years. Pittsburgh committed eight turnovers, including five fumbles, to help the Browns overcome a critical mistake of their own in the opening minutes. After an interception return for a touchdown by the Steelers on the fourth play of the game, the Browns fought back to take the lead in the second quarter but then lost it again when Pittsburgh drove 84 yards in the final two minutes of the half to make it 14–13. One of three interceptions of Pittsburgh third-string QB Charlie Batch—starting because of injuries to Ben Roethlisberger and backup Byron Leftwich—gave the Browns possession in Pittsburgh territory midway through the third quarter. Two plays later, Trent Richardson burst over left tackle for a 15-yard touchdown run to give the Browns a lead they would not relinquish. The defenses slugged it out from there, with the Browns halting the most promising Pittsburgh drive at the Cleveland 30 three minutes into the fourth quarter when lineman Billy Winn picked off a pass. Fellow lineman Phil Taylor also recovered a fumble at the Pittsburgh 40 with 2:25 left, and the Steelers didn't get the ball back until a perfect Browns' punt pinned them at their own 3 in the final seconds. The game ended, fittingly, with one last Pittsburgh fumble recovered by the Browns as time expired. Neither offense tallied 250 yards of offense as the Browns held the Steelers to just 49 rushing yards. Trent Richardson picked up 85 yards on the ground in a physical game that saw Brandon Weeden sidelined in the final minutes after receiving a blow to the head. The victory represented just the Browns' second victory over Pittsburgh in their last 18 meetings.

Record: 3–8

	1	2	3	4		
Steelers	7	7	0	0	=	14
Browns	3	10	7	0	=	20

PIT-Timmons 53-yd. interception return (Suisham kick)
CLE-Dawson 28-yd. FG
CLE-Cameron 5-yd. pass from Weeden (Dawson kick)
CLE-Dawson 32-yd. FG
PIT-Rainey 1-yd. run (Suisham kick)
CLE-Richardson 15-yd. run (Dawson kick)

Passing
PIT: Batch 20–34–199 0 TD 3 INT
CLE: Weeden 17–26–158 1 TD 1 INT

Rushing
PIT: Dwyer 9–19, Rainey 5–17, Redman 2–7, Mendenhall 4–6
CLE: Richardson 29–85, Hardesty 2–14, Weeden 2–8, Benjamin 1–1

Receiving
PIT: Sanders 5–75, Miller 6–63, Rainey 4–15, Redman 1–15, Johnson 1–13, Dwyer 2–9, Wallace 1–9
CLE: Gordon 4–60, Richardson 4–27, Massaquoi 3–27, Watson 3–26, Cameron 2–12, Little 1–6

Sunday, December 2
Browns 20, Oakland Raiders 17
O.Co Coliseum (43,641)
White jerseys/white pants

Behind an efficient offense, the Browns took control of the game early and held off the Raiders to snap their franchise-record 12-game road losing streak. The Browns rolled up 475 total yards, their highest total in five years, and built a 10-point lead following a 44-yard touchdown pass from Brandon Weeden to Josh Gordon. A pair of Weeden interceptions squandered scoring opportunities in the first half, then the Browns saw momentum shift when Oakland blocked a field goal, breaking Phil Dawson's string of 29 consecutive made field goals. Moments later, the Raiders scored a touchdown to cut the margin to three points. Oakland threatened to take the lead on its next possession, but Browns' DB Sheldon Brown intercepted a pass at the Cleveland 6 with just under 10 minutes to play. The Browns then embarked on an impressive 14-play, 94-yard drive that ate up six minutes and delivered the game-clinching points when Trent Richardson scored from three yards out with 3:31 left. The Raiders added another touchdown in the final seconds, but the Browns recovered the ensuing onside kick to secure their second straight win. Weeden tossed for a season-high 364 yards, while Gordon became the first Browns' receiver to top 100 yards in 2012. The victory marked the Browns' fourth in seven games and matched their win total from the year before.

Record: 4–8

	1	2	3	4		
Browns	0	10	3	7	=	20
Raiders	0	3	7	7	=	17

CLE-Dawson 41-yd. FG
CLE-Gordon 44-yd. pass from Weeden (Dawson kick)
OAK-Janikowski 51-yd. FG
CLE-Dawson 35-yd. FG
OAK-Streater 64-yd. pass from Palmer (Janikowski kick)
CLE-Richardson 3-yd. run (Dawson kick)
OAK-Myers 17-yd. pass from Palmer (Janikowski kick)

Passing
CLE: Weeden 25–36–364 1 TD 2 INT
OAK: Palmer 34–54–351 2 TD 1 INT

Rushing
CLE: Richardson 20–72, Hardesty 5–39, Weeden 5–11
OAK: Stewart 9–46, Reece 7–36, Palmer 1–3

Receiving
CLE: Gordon 6–116, Watson 6–80, Massaquoi 2–60, Little 4–48, Cameron 2–30, Richardson 3–23, Benjamin 1–6, Smith 1–1
OAK: Myers 14–130, Streater 3–96, Heyward-Bey 4–40, Moore 2–31, Criner 4–26, Reece 5–20, Hagan 1–6, Stewart 1–2

Sunday, December 9
Browns 30, Kansas City Chiefs 7
Cleveland Browns Stadium (62,422)
Brown jerseys/white pants

Before their smallest home crowd in 17 years, the Browns bounced back from a disastrous start to roll to a blowout win, posting their largest margin of victory in nine years while surpassing their victory total from the year before. After scoring a touchdown on the game's first play, the Chiefs were poised to make it 10–0 after driving deep into Cleveland territory on their second possession, only to miss a chip-shot field goal. From then on, the Chiefs were shut out, and the Browns opened the floodgates on the first play of the second quarter with a franchise-record 93-yard punt return for a touchdown by rookie WR Travis Benjamin. They then pulled away in the second half behind a pair of short touchdown runs by Trent Richardson, who tied Jim Brown's team record for touchdowns by a rookie. Phil Dawson added three field goals, becoming just the twenty-fifth player in NFL history to kick 300 in his career. The contest also marked a homecoming for former Browns' head coach Romeo Crennel, former starting QB Brady Quinn, and former 1,000-yard RB Peyton Hillis, all now with the Chiefs.
Record: 5–8

	1	2	3	4		
Chiefs	7	0	0	0	=	7
Browns	3	7	10	10	=	30

KC Charles 80-yd. run (Succop kick)
CLE-Dawson 23-yd. FG
CLE-Benjamin 93-yd. punt return (Dawson kick)
CLE-Richardson 1-yd. run (Dawson kick)
CLE-Dawson 24-yd. FG
CLE-Richardson 1-yd. run (Dawson kick)
CLE-Dawson 34-yd. FG

Passing
KC: Quinn 10–21–159 0 TD 1 INT
CLE: Weeden 17–30–217 0 TD 0 INT

Rushing
KC: Charles 18–165, Hillis 5–11, Quinn 1–4, Draughn 1–0, McCluster 1–0
CLE: Hardesty 10–52, Richardson 18–42, Little 1–17, Cribbs 2–15, Benjamin 1–15, Weeden 1–15, McCoy 2-(-2)

Receiving
KC: Bowe 2–70, Copper 3–32, Newsome 1–25, Moeaki 1–10, Draughn 1–8, McCluster 1–8, Hillis 1–6
CLE: Gordon 8–86, Little 4–69, Watson 3–43, Cameron 1–10, Richardson 1–9

Sunday, December 16
Washington Redskins 38, Browns 21
Cleveland Browns Stadium (65,083)
Brown jerseys/white pants

After sprinting to an early lead, the Browns faded as the game wore on and were overwhelmed in their home finale by a Washington team fighting for a playoff spot. An interception by Browns' safety T. J. Ward on the Redskins' second possession set up a short touchdown run by Trent Richardson on the next play to give the Browns a 7–0 lead, as Richardson set a new franchise rookie record for rushing touchdowns in a season. After Washington scored the next 10 points, the Browns put together a long drive capped by another Richardson score to make it 14–10 just before the half. But a Brandon Weeden interception on the Browns' first possession of the third quarter set up the go-ahead touchdown for the Redskins, who went on to dominate the second half. Washington backup QB Kirk Cousins, playing for injured rookie Robert Griffin III, was superb, throwing for 329 yards and a pair of touchdowns as Washington rolled up 430 yards of offense. Meanwhile, the Cleveland offense struggled, particularly on the ground as Richardson was held to just 28 yards on 11 carries. One of the only high points for the Browns was a 69-yard touchdown bomb from Weeden to Travis Benjamin, which pulled them within 10 points with 10 minutes remaining. But it was followed by a five-minute, 76-yard touchdown drive by the 'Skins that put the game away.
Record: 5–9

	1	2	3	4		
Redskins	7	3	14	14	=	38
Browns	7	7	0	7	=	21

CLE-Richardson 6-yd. run (Dawson kick)
WAS-Hankerson 54-yd. pass from Cousins (Forbath kick)
WAS-Forbath 44-yd. FG
CLE-Richardson 1-yd. run (Dawson kick)
WAS-Morris 3-yd. run (Forbath kick)
WAS-Hankerson 2-yd. pass from Cousins (Forbath kick)
WAS-Royster 4-yd. run (Forbath kick)
CLE-Benjamin 69-yd. pass from Weeden (Dawson kick)
WAS-Morris 8-yd. run (Forbath kick)

Passing
WAS: Cousins 26–37–329 2 TD 1 INT
CLE: Weeden 21–35–244 1 TD 2 INT

Rushing
WAS: Morris 27–87, Cousins 3–22, Young 3–10, Royster 2–3
CLE: Richardson 11–28, Cribbs 1–16, Weeden 1–9, Hardesty 2–5

Receiving
WAS: Garcon 6–65, Morgan 4–60, Moss 5–57, Hankerson 2–56, Paulsen 4–47, Royster 2–30, Young 1–8, Morris 2–6
CLE: Little 5–74, Benjamin 1–69, Cameron 3–34, Gordon 3–27, Massaquoi 2–16, Watson 2–12, Smith 2–8, Richardson 3–4

Sunday, December 23
Denver Broncos 34, Browns 12
Sports Authority Field at Mile High (76,351)
White jerseys/white pants

Unable to stop veteran QB Peyton Manning, the Browns were no match for the red-hot Denver Broncos, who moved to 12–3 on the year with their tenth straight victory over the Browns. Manning, who moved to 6–0 in his career against Cleveland, threw for 339 yards and three scores, leading the Broncos to touchdowns on their first two possessions. The Browns tried to keep up with a field goal on their first possession of each half, the second a 53-yard kick by Phil Dawson that cut the Denver lead to 14–6. But the Broncos rebounded to score on their next three series to put the game away. While Denver rolled up 457 total yards of offense, the Browns could manage just 233, and Brandon Weeden left the game with a shoulder injury in the third quarter. In his first extensive action of the year, backup Colt McCoy directed the Browns to their only touchdown—a short pass to WR Greg Little—but it was too little, too late. Weeden and McCoy were sacked a combined six times, the most allowed by the Browns in a game all season.
Record: 5–10

	1	2	3	4		
Browns	3	0	3	6	=	12
Broncos	7	7	7	13	=	34

DEN-Thomas 22-yd. pass from Manning (Prater kick)
CLE-Dawson 27-yd. FG
DEN-Decker 10-yd. pass from Manning (Prater kick)
CLE-Dawson 53-yd. FG
DEN-Decker 8-yd. pass from Manning (Prater kick)
DEN-Prater 27-yd. FG
DEN-Hester 1-yd. run (Prater kick)
CLE-Little 6-yd. pass from McCoy (run failed)
DEN-Prater 41-yd. FG

Passing
CLE: Weeden 12–19–104 0 TD 0 INT, McCoy 9–17–79 1 TD 0 INT
DEN: Manning 30–43–339 3 TD 1 INT

Rushing
CLE: Richardson 9–53, McCoy 2–17, Hardesty 3–14, Weeden 3–4, Cribbs 1–3
DEN: Moreno 22–78, Hillman 6–35, Hester 3–6, Osweiler 1-(-1)

Receiving
CLE: Little 6–58, Watson 3–47, Benjamin 3–46, Richardson 3–15, Hardesty 1–7, Gordon 1–7, Smelley 1–3, Ogbonnaya 2–2, Smith 1–(–2)
DEN: Thomas 9–102, Tamme 2–69, Decker 6–65, Moreno 5–49, Stokley 5–32, Dreessen 3–22

Sunday, December 30
Pittsburgh Steelers 24, Browns 10
Heinz Field (51,831)
White jerseys/white pants

The Browns closed out another disappointing season and another head coach's tenure with their tenth straight loss in Pittsburgh. Despite outgaining the Steelers by more than 100 total yards, the Browns coughed up four costly turnovers, two of which led to Pittsburgh touchdowns. With starting QB Brandon Weeden and backup QB Colt McCoy both sidelined with injuries, third-stringer Thaddeus Lewis played well in his NFL debut, throwing for 204 yards and tossing a touchdown pass to Greg Little that tied the game at 10 early in the third quarter. The score was set up by a gutsy fake punt call from the Cleveland 25 that resulted in a 35-yard gain. The Steelers responded with an 80-yard touchdown drive to take the lead back, and the Browns drove into Pittsburgh territory three times in the fourth quarter but were unable to score any points. Before the smallest crowd in Heinz Field history, the Steelers put the game away with a touchdown with just over three minutes remaining after recovering a Travis Benjamin fumble in Cleveland territory. With Trent Richardson also injured, RB Brandon Jackson made his Cleveland debut and picked up 54 yards on the ground. The following morning, head coach Pat Shurmur and general manager Tom Heckert were fired by new owner Jimmy Haslam.
Record: 5–11

FACING THEIR OLD BOSS

Since Paul Brown's departure as the team's original coach—and his subsequent founding of the Cincinnati Bengals—the Browns have established a long history of going head to head with former head coaches who have gone on to take the same role with other teams.

Browns vs. Paul Brown (7–3)

October 11, 1970	vs. Cincinnati	W 30–27
November 15, 1970	at Cincinnati	L 10–14
October 17, 1971	at Cincinnati	W 27–24
December 5, 1971	vs. Cincinnati	W 31–27
October 1, 1972	vs. Cincinnati	W 27–6
December 9, 1972	at Cincinnati	W 27–24
October 7, 1973	vs. Cincinnati	W 17–10
December 9, 1973	at Cincinnati	L 17–34
September 15, 1974	at Cincinnati	L 7–33
October 13, 1974	vs. Cincinnati	L 24–34
September 21, 1975	at Cincinnati	L 17–24
November 23, 1975	vs. Cincinnati	W 35–23

Browns vs. Forrest Gregg (4–4)

November 23, 1980	vs. Cincinnati	W 31–7
December 21, 1980	at Cincinnati	W 27–24
September 20, 1981	at Cincinnati	W 20–17
November 29, 1981	vs. Cincinnati	L 21–41
December 12, 1982	at Cincinnati	L 10–23
September 15, 1983	vs. Cincinnati	W 17–7
October 23, 1983	at Cincinnati	L 21–28
October 19, 1986	vs. Green Bay	L 14–17

Browns vs. Marty Schottenheimer (2–5–1)

November 19, 1989	vs. Kansas City	T 10–10
September 30, 1990	at Kansas City	L 0–34
November 24, 1991	vs. Kansas City	W 20–15
November 20, 1994	at Kansas City	L 13–20
September 24, 1995	vs. Kansas City	W 35–17
October 26, 2003	vs. San Diego	L 20–26
December 19, 2004	vs. San Diego	L 0–21
November 5, 2006	at San Diego	L 25–32

Browns vs. Bill Belichick (2–4)

November 12, 2000	vs. New England	W 19–11
December 9, 2001	at New England	L 16–27
October 26, 2003	at New England	L 3–9
December 5, 2004	vs. New England	L 15–42
October 7, 2007	at New England	L 17–34
November 7, 2010	vs. New England	W 35–14

Browns vs. Romeo Crennel (1–0)

December 9, 2012	vs. Kansas City	W 30–7

Browns' all-time record against former head coaches: 16–16–1

The Browns have also been involved in the converse, facing a head coach who would eventually become their own head coach:

Browns vs. Nick Skorich (3–2–1)

September 17, 1961	at Philadelphia	L 20–27
November 19, 1961	vs. Philadelphia	W 45–24
September 30, 1962	at Philadelphia	L 7–35
November 4, 1962	vs. Philadelphia	T 14 14
October 20, 1963	vs. Philadelphia	W 37–7
November 3, 1963	at Philadelphia	W 23–17

Browns vs. Eric Mangini (2–0)

October 29, 2006	vs. NY Jets	W 20–13
December 9, 2007	at NY Jets	W 24–18

	1	2	3	4		
Browns	0	3	7	0	=	10
Steelers	0	10	7	7	=	24

PIT-Suisham 41-yd. FG
CLE-Dawson 51-yd. FG
PIT-Pope 1-yd. pass from Roethlisberger (Suisham kick)
CLE-Little 7-yd. pass from Lewis (Dawson kick)
PIT-Brown 9-yd. pass from Roethlisberger (Suisham kick)
PIT-Burress 12-yd. pass from Roethlisberger (Suisham kick)

Passing
CLE: Lewis 22–32–204 1 TD 1 INT
PIT: Roethlisberger 15–23–134 3 TD 0 INT

Rushing
CLE: Jackson 8–54, Hardesty 14–37, Ventrone 1–35, Ogbonnaya 2–9, Lewis 1–3
PIT: Dwyer 11–52, Redman 6–26, Mendenhall 6–19, Rainey 1–2, Roethlisberger 2-(-2), Brown 2-(-6)

Receiving
CLE: Watson 7–64, Benjamin 4–43, Gordon 4–39, Little 3–38, Cribbs 1–9, Cooper 1–8, Ogbonnaya 2–3
PIT: Sanders 2–28, Burress 2–24, Brown 2–22, Cotchery 2–21, Johnson 2–17, Redman 1–11, Dwyer 1–9, Mendenhall 2–1, Pope 1–1

Appendix

Browns' 100-Yard Rushing Games

(Since joining NFL, including postseason)

Player	Games
Jim Brown	58
Leroy Kelly	27
Greg Pruitt	17
Mike Pruitt	16
Kevin Mack	9
Bobby Mitchell	8
Earnest Byner	7
William Green	6
Peyton Hillis	6
Jamal Lewis	6
Reuben Droughn	5
Jerome Harrison	4
Fred Morrison	4
Marion Motley	4
Lee Suggs	4
Ken Carpenter	3
Boyce Green	3
Harry Jagade	3
Trent Richardson	3
Jamel White	3
Lew Carpenter	2
Preston Carpenter	2
Ernie Green	2
Leroy Hoard	2
Dub Jones	2
Emerson Cole	1
Curtis Dickey	1
James Jackson	1
Ron Johnson	1
Larry Mason	1
Cleo Miller	1
Ed Modzelewski	1
Reece Morrison	1
Chris Ogbonnaya	1
Ray Renfro	1
Bo Scott	1
Tommy Vardell	1

Browns' 300-Yard Passing Games

(Since joining NFL, including postseason)

Player	Games
Brian Sipe	18
Bernie Kosar	11
Otto Graham	7
Derek Anderson	4
Kelly Holcomb	4
Tim Couch	3
Paul McDonald	3
Milt Plum	3
Frank Ryan	3
Vinny Testaverde	3
Brandon Weeden	3
Bill Nelsen	2
Trent Dilfer	1
Jeff Garcia	1
Colt McCoy	1
Jim Ninowski	1
Tommy O'Connell	1
Doug Pederson	1
Todd Philcox	1
Brady Quinn	1
Don Strock	1
Mike Tomczak	1
Eric Zeier	1

Browns' 100-Yard Receiving Games

(Since joining NFL, including postseason)

Player	Games
Webster Slaughter	15
Ray Renfro	14
Gary Collins	12
Paul Warfield	12
Braylon Edwards	11
Darrel Brewster	10
Dante Lavelli	10
Ozzie Newsome	10
Reggie Rucker	8
Kevin Johnson	7
Milt Morin	6
Mac Speedie	6
Michael Jackson	5
Dave Logan	5
Dub Jones	4
Derrick Alexander	3
Brian Brennan	3
Antonio Bryant	3
Preston Carpenter	3
Reggie Langhorne	3
Quincy Morgan	3
Dennis Northcutt	3
Frank Pitts	3
Greg Pruitt	3
Kellen Winslow Jr.	3
Mark Carrier	2
Andre Davis	2
Ricky Feacher	2
Duriel Harris	2
Rich Kreitling	2
Eric Metcalf	2
Bobby Mitchell	2
Mohamed Massaquoi	2
Andre Rison	2
Clarence Weathers	2
Jim Brown	1
Earnest Byner	1
Darrin Chiaverini	1
Chip Glass	1
Josh Gordon	1
Ernie Green	1
Steve Heiden	1
Calvin Hill	1
Leroy Hoard	1
Fair Hooker	1
Frisman Jackson	1
Harry Jagade	1
Joe Jurevicius	1
Greg Little	1
Keenan McCardell	1
Hugh McKinnis	1
Gern Nagler	1
David Patten	1
Rico Smith	1
Lee Suggs	1
Lawyer Tillman	1
Benjamin Watson	1
Charles White	1

Browns' 1,000-Yard Rushing Seasons

PLAYER	YEAR	YARDS	AVERAGE PER CARRY	AVERAGE PER GAME	TEAM'S RECORD
Jim Brown	1963	1,863	6.4	133.1	10–4
Jim Brown	1965	1,544	5.3	110.3	11–3
Jim Brown	1958	1,527	5.9	127.3	9–3*
Jim Brown	1964	1,446	5.2	103.3	10–3–1**
Jim Brown	1961	1,408	4.6	100.6	8–5–1
Jim Brown	1959	1,329	4.6	110.8	7–5
Jamal Lewis	2007	1,304	4.4	86.9	10–6
Mike Pruitt	1979	1,294	4.9	80.9	9–7
Jim Brown	1960	1,257	5.8	89.8	8–3–1
Leroy Kelly	1968	1,239	5.0	88.5	10–4*
Reuben Droughns	2005	1,232	4.0	77.0	6–10
Leroy Kelly	1967	1,205	5.1	86.1	9–5*
Mike Pruitt	1983	1,184	4.0	78.9	9–7
Peyton Hillis	2010	1,177	4.4	73.6	5–11
Leroy Kelly	1966	1,141	5.5	81.5	9–5
Kevin Mack	1985	1,104	5.0	69.0	8–8*
Mike Pruitt	1981	1,103	4.5	68.9	5–11
Greg Pruitt	1977	1,086	4.6	77.6	6–8
Greg Pruitt	1975	1,067	4.9	76.2	3–11
Mike Pruitt	1980	1,034	4.2	64.6	11–5*
Earnest Byner	1985	1,002	4.1	62.6	8–8*
Jamal Lewis	2008	1,002	3.6	62.6	4–12
Greg Pruitt	1976	1,000	4.8	71.4	9–5

** Reached postseason*

*** Won NFL Championship*

Browns' 1,000-Yard Receiving Seasons

PLAYER	YEAR	YARDS	AVERAGE PER CATCH	AVERAGE PER GAME	TEAM'S RECORD
Braylon Edwards	2007	1,289	16.1	80.6	10–6
Webster Slaughter	1989	1,236	19.0	77.3	9–6–1*
Kellen Winslow Jr.	2007	1,106	13.5	69.1	10–6
Kevin Johnson	2001	1,097	13.1	68.6	7–9
Paul Warfield	1968	1,067	21.3	76.2	10–4
Antonio Bryant	2005	1,009	14.6	63.1	6–10
Ozzie Newsome	1981	1,002	14.5	62.6	5–11
Ozzie Newsome	1984	1,001	11.2	62.6	5–11

** Reached postseason*

Browns' 3,000-Yard Passing Seasons

PLAYER	YEAR	YARDS	AVERAGE PER GAME	RATING	TEAM'S RECORD
Brian Sipe	1980	4,132	258.3	91.4	11–5*
Brian Sipe	1981	3,876	242.3	68.2	5–11
Bernie Kosar	1986	3,854	240.1	83.8	12–4*
Brian Sipe	1979	3,793	237.1	73.4	9–7
Derek Anderson	2007	3,787	236.7	82.5	10–6
Brian Sipe	1983	3,566	237.7	79.1	9–7
Bernie Kosar	1989	3,533	220.8	80.3	9–6–1*
Bernie Kosar	1991	3,487	217.9	87.8	6–10
Paul McDonald	1984	3,472	217.0	67.3	5–11
Brandon Weeden	2012	3,385	225.7	72.6	5–11
Tim Couch	2001	3,040	190.0	73.1	7–9
Bernie Kosar	1987	3,033	252.8	95.4	10–5*

**Reached postseason*

The Top 25 Quarterback Performances in the Browns' NFL History

(Based on highest passer rating—minimum 15 attempts)

25. Brady Quinn
November 22, 2009, at Detroit (Browns lost, 38–37)
21 of 33 for 304 yards, 4 TD 0 INT
133.1 rating

24. Frank Ryan
September 29, 1963, vs. LA Rams (Browns win, 20–6)
9 of 15 for 152 yards, 2 TD 0 INT
133.9 rating

23. Bernie Kosar
December 13, 1987, vs. Cincinnati (Browns win, 38–24)
17 of 26 for 241 yards, 4 TD 0 INT
134.8 rating

22. Vinny Testaverde
December 26, 1993, at LA Rams (Browns win, 42–14)
21 of 23 for 216 yards, 2 TD 0 INT
134.8 rating

21. Otto Graham
November 9, 1952, vs. Chicago Cardinals (Browns win, 28–13)
18 of 24 for 249 yards, 2 TD 0 INT
135.6 rating

20. Charlie Frye
December 4, 2005, vs. Jacksonville (Browns lose, 20–14)
13 of 20 for 226 yards, 2 TD 0 INT
136.7 rating

19. Bernie Kosar
November 5, 1989, at Tampa Bay (Browns win, 42–31)
18 of 22 for 164 yards, 3 TD 0 INT
137.3 rating

18. Tim Couch
December 30, 2001, at Tennessee (Browns win, 41–38)
20 of 27 for 336 yards, 3 TD 1 INT
137.3 rating

17. Bernie Kosar
December 6, 1992, vs. Cincinnati (Browns win, 37–21)
19 of 23 for 239 yards, 2 TD 0 INT
138.9 rating

16. Jim Ninowski
October 21, 1962, at St. Louis (Browns win, 34–7)
19 of 29 for 339 yards, 3 TD 0 INT
139.9 rating

15. Frank Ryan
December 17, 1966, at St. Louis (Browns win, 38–10)
17 of 30 for 367 yards, 4 TD 0 INT
139.9 rating

14. Otto Graham
October 9, 1955, vs. Philadelphia (Browns win, 21–17)
16 of 21 for 223 yards, 2 TD 0 INT
141.6 rating

13. Kelly Holcomb
November 16, 2003, vs. Arizona (Browns win, 44–6)
29 of 35 for 392 yards, 3 TD 0 INT
141.9 rating

12. Derek Anderson
October 14, 2007, vs. Miami (Browns win, 41–31)
18 of 25 for 245 yards, 2 TD 0 INT
142.5 rating

11. Derek Anderson
October 28, 2007, at St. Louis (Browns win, 27–20)
18 of 25 for 248 yards, 3 TD 0 INT
143 rating

10. Gary Danielson
October 18, 1987, at Cincinnati (Browns win, 34–0)
25 of 31 for 281 yards, 4 TD 0 INT
144 rating

9. Milt Plum
October 23, 1960, vs. Philadelphia (Browns lost, 31–29)
16 of 22 for 289 yards, 2 TD 0 INT
145.1 rating

8. Bernie Kosar
December 4, 1988, vs. Dallas (Browns win, 24–21)
19 of 27 for 308 yards, 3 TD 0 INT
145.3 rating

7. Frank Ryan
October 24, 1965, at NY Giants (Browns win, 38–14)
10 of 15 for 177 yards, 3 TD 0 INT
146.4 rating

t5. Otto Graham
October 4, 1953, at Chicago Cardinals (Browns win, 27–7)
15 of 22 for 310 yards 3 TD 0 INT
150.6 rating

t5. Brian Sipe
November 19, 1978, at Baltimore (Browns win, 45–24)
15 of 22 for 309 yards, 4 TD 0 INT
150.6 rating

4. Milt Plum
October 25, 1959, vs. Washington (Browns win, 34–7)
13 of 18 for 253 yards, 4 TD 0 INT
153.9 rating

3. Milt Plum
November 13, 1960, vs. St. Louis (Browns win, 28–27)
11 of 15 for 194 yards, 2 TD 0 INT
154.9 rating

t1. Otto Graham
October 10, 1954, vs. Chicago
14 of 18 for 266 yards, 3 TD 0 INT
158.3* rating

t1. Brian Sipe
October 29, 1978, vs. Buffalo (Browns win, 41–20)
12 of 15 for 217 yards, 3 TD 0 INT
158.3* rating

**Perfect rating*

Browns' Assistant Coaches Who Became NFL Head Coaches

A handful of Browns' assistant coaches have gone on to become full-time head coaches in the NFL:

Raymond Berry (Browns' wide receivers coach, 1976–77)
Head coach of New England Patriots, 1984–89 (48–39)

Blanton Collier (Browns' backfield coach, 1946–53/Browns' offensive backs coach, 1962/Browns' quarterbacks coach, 1975–76)
Head coach of Cleveland Browns, 1963–70 (76–34)

Bill Cowher (Browns' special teams coach, 1985–86/Browns' secondary coach 1987–88)
Head coach of Pittsburgh Steelers, 1992–2006 (149–90–1)

Romeo Crennel (Browns' defensive coordinator, 2000)
Head coach of Cleveland Browns, 2005–08 (24–40)
Head coach of Kansas City Chiefs, 2011–12 (4–15)

Weeb Ewbank (Browns' line coach, 1949–53)
Head coach of Baltimore Colts, 1954–62 (59–52–1)
Head coach of New York Jets, 1963–73 (71–77–6)

Forrest Gregg (Browns' offensive line coach, 1974)
Head coach of Cleveland Browns, 1975–77 (18–23)
Head coach of Cincinnati Bengals, 1980–83 (32–25)
Head coach of Green Bay Packers, 1984–87 (25–37–1)

Rich Kotite (Browns' receivers coach, 1978–82)
Head coach of Philadelphia Eagles, 1991–94 (36–28)
Head coach of New York Jets, 1995–96 (4–28)

Dick MacPherson (Browns' linebackers coach, 1978–80)
Head coach of New England Patriots, 1991–92 (8–24)

Eric Mangini (Browns' coaches assistant, 1995)
Head coach of New York Jets, 2006–08 (23–25)
Head coach of Cleveland Browns, 2009–10 (10–22)

Nick Saban (Browns' defensive coordinator, 1991–94)
Head coach of Miami Dolphins, 2005–06 (15–17)

Marty Schottenheimer (Browns' defensive coordinator, 1980–84)
Head coach of Cleveland Browns, 1984–88 (44–27)
Head coach of Kansas City Chiefs, 1989–98 (101–58–1)
Head coach of Washington Redskins, 2001 (8–8)
Head coach of San Diego Chargers, 2002–06 (47–33)

Tony Sparano (Browns' offensive quality control/offensive line coach, 1999–2000)
Head coach of Miami Dolphins, 2008–11 (29–32)

Ken Whisenhunt (Browns' special teams coach, 1999)
Head coach of Arizona Cardinals, 2007–12 (45–51)

Several others have become Browns' assistants after serving as NFL head coaches:

Dave Campo (Browns' defensive coordinator, 2003–04)
Head coach of Dallas Cowboys, 2000–02 (15–33)

Brad Childress (Browns' offensive coordinator, 2012)
Head coach of Minnesota Vikings, 2006–10 (39–35)

Rod Dowhower (Browns' quarterbacks coach, 1994)
Head coach of Indianapolis Colts, 1985–86 (5–24)

Bill Edwards (Browns' tackles coach, 1947–48)
Head coach of Detroit Lions, 1941–42 (4–9–1)

Dick Jauron (Browns' defensive coordinator, 2011–12)
Head coach of Chicago Bears, 1999–2003 (35–45)
Head coach of Buffalo Bills, 2006–09 (24–33)

Ray Perkins (Browns' tight ends coach, 1999–2000)
Head coach of New York Giants, 1979–82 (23–34)
Head coach of Tampa Bay Buccaneers, 1987–90 (19–41)

Ray Rhodes (Browns' senior assistant-defense, 2011–12)
Head coach of Philadelphia Eagles, 1995–98 (29–34–1)
Head coach of Green Bay Packers, 1999 (8–8)

Nick Skorich (Browns' offensive coach, 1964–70)
Head coach of Philadelphia Eagles, 1961–63 (15–24–3)
Head coach of Cleveland Browns, 1971–74 (30–24–2)

Jerry Williams (Browns' passing offense coach, 1971)
Head coach of Philadelphia Eagles, 1969–71 (7–22–2)

Browns vs. Former Assistants

Raymond Berry (2–1)
October 7, 1984: New England Patriots 17, Browns 16
October 6, 1985: Browns 24, New England Patriots 20
October 4, 1987: Browns 20, New England Patriots 10

Bill Cowher (5–21)
October 11, 1992: Browns 17, Pittsburgh Steelers 9
December 27, 1992: Pittsburgh Steelers 23, Browns 13
October 24, 1993: Browns 28, Pittsburgh Steelers 23
January 2, 1994: Pittsburgh Steelers 16, Browns 9
September 11, 1994: Pittsburgh Steelers 17, Browns 10
December 18, 1994: Pittsburgh Steelers 17, Browns 7
January 7, 1995: Pittsburgh Steelers 29, Browns 9*
November 13, 1995: Pittsburgh Steelers 20, Browns 3
November 26, 1995: Pittsburgh Steelers 20, Browns 17
September 12, 1999: Pittsburgh Steelers 43, Browns 0
November 14, 1999: Browns 16, Pittsburgh Steelers 15
September 17, 2000: Browns 23, Pittsburgh Steelers 20
October 29, 2000: Pittsburgh Steelers 22, Browns 0
November 11, 2001: Pittsburgh Steelers 15, Browns 12 (OT)
January 6, 2002: Pittsburgh Steelers 28, Browns 7
September 29, 2002: Pittsburgh Steelers 16, Browns 13 (OT)
November 3, 2002: Pittsburgh Steelers 23, Browns 20
January 5, 2003: Pittsburgh Steelers 36, Browns 33*
October 5, 2003: Browns 33, Pittsburgh Steelers 13
November 23, 2003: Pittsburgh Steelers 13, Browns 6
October 10, 2004: Pittsburgh Steelers 34, Browns 23
November 14, 2004: Pittsburgh Steelers 24, Browns 10
November 13, 2005: Pittsburgh Steelers 34, Browns 21
December 24, 2005: Pittsburgh Steelers 41, Browns 0
November 19, 2006: Pittsburgh Steelers 24, Browns 20
December 7, 2006: Pittsburgh Steelers 27, Browns 7

Weeb Ewbank (3–2)
November 11, 1956: Baltimore Colts 21, Browns 7
November 1, 1959: Browns 38, Baltimore Colts 31
October 14, 1962: Baltimore Colts 36, Browns 14
September 21, 1970: Browns 31, New York Jets 21
December 17, 1972: Browns 26, New York Jets 10

Rich Kotite (0–1)
November 10, 1991: Philadelphia Eagles 32, Browns 30

Dick MacPherson (2–0)
September 8, 1991: Browns 20, New England Patriots 0
October 25, 1992: Browns 19, New England Patriots 17

Nick Saban (1–0)
November 20, 2005: Browns 22, Miami Dolphins 0

Tony Sparano (2–0)
December 5, 2010: Browns 13, Miami Dolphins 10
September 25, 2011: Browns 17, Miami Dolphins 16

Romeo Crennel (1–0)
December 9, 2012: Browns 30, Kansas City Chiefs 7

Browns' Head Coaches' Records Ranked by Winning Percentage

COACH	RECORD*	WIN %	POSTSEASON APPEARANCES
Paul Brown (1946–62)	167–53–8	.750	12
Blanton Collier (1963–70)	79–38–2	.672	5
Marty Schottenheimer (1984–88)	46–31	.597	4
Nick Skorich (1971–74)	30–26–2	.534	2
Sam Rutigliano (1978–84)	47–52	.475	2
Bud Carson (1989–90)	12–14–1	.463	1
Bill Belichick (1991–95)	37–45	.451	1
Forrest Gregg (1975–77)	18–23	.439	0
Butch Davis (2001–04)	24–36	.400	1
Romeo Crennel (2005–08)	24–40	.375	0
Eric Mangini (2009–10)	10–22	.313	0
Pat Shurmur (2011–12)	9–23	.281	0
Terry Robiskie (2004)**	1–4	.200	0
Chris Palmer (1999–2000)	5–27	.156	0
Jim Shofner (1990)**	1–6	.143	0
Dick Modzelewski (1977)**	0–1	.000	0

**Including postseason games*

***Interim coach*

The Browns' 10 Largest Home Crowds

10.	84,213	vs. NY Giants	October 27, 1963
9.	84,236	vs. Green Bay*	September 2, 1967
8.	84,285	vs. Oakland	October 4, 1971
7.	84,349	vs. Pittsburgh	October 3, 1970
6.	84,684	vs. Pittsburgh	October 5, 1963
5.	84,721	vs. Dallas	October 23, 1966
4.	84,850	vs. Dallas	November 2, 1969
3.	84,918	vs. Green Bay*	September 7, 1968
2.	85,532	vs. Green Bay*	August 30, 1969
1.	85,703	vs. NY Jets**	September 21, 1970

**Preseason doubleheader*

***First* Monday Night Football *game*

There have been 64 home crowds over 80,000; the last was in 1980.

The Browns' 10 Largest Road Crowds

10.	78,196	at Miami*	December 24, 1972
9.	78,266	at Buffalo	November 1, 1981
8.	78,502	at NY Jets	October 27, 2002
7.	78,521	at NY Giants	September 26, 2004
6.	78,560	at Kansas City	November 9, 2003
5.	79,911	at NY Giants	October 7, 2012
4.	84,816	vs. Cincinnati‡	September 3, 1972
3.	87,695	at L.A. Rams**	December 26, 1955
2.	90,487	at Washington	October 19, 2008
1.	92,180	vs. College All-Stars†	August 17, 1951

**Divisional playoff game*

***NFL Championship Game*

†At Soldier Field, Chicago

‡Preseason game at Ohio Stadium in Columbus, Ohio

The Browns' 10 Smallest Home Crowds

10.	22,878	vs. Washington	November 25, 1956
9.	22,550	vs. San Francisco*	December 11, 1949
8.	22,511	vs. Buffalo	November 13, 1949
7.	21,908	vs. Washington	November 19, 1950
6.	21,621	vs. Baltimore	September 11, 1949
5.	20,645	vs. Philadelphia	December 2, 1956
4.	17,631	vs. Chicago**	September 18, 1954
3.	17,270	vs. Buffalo†	December 4, 1949
2.	16,506	vs. Chicago	November 6, 1949
1.	15,456	vs. Green Bay**	September 1, 1956

**AAFC Championship*

***Preseason game*

[†]AAFC playoff game

The Browns' 10 Smallest Road Crowds

Regular Season

10.	19,742	at Chicago	November 4, 1951
9.	18,876	at Brooklyn	September 12, 1947
8.	18,450	at Chicago	September 26, 1947
7.	16,263	at Philadelphia	December 16, 1951
6.	15,201	at Baltimore	September 24, 1950
5.	14,830	at New England*	October 4, 1987
4.	14,600	at Miami	December 8, 1946
3.	9,821	at Brooklyn	December 5, 1947
2.	9,083	at Brooklyn	December 3, 1946
1.	5,031	at Chicago	November 24, 1949

**Strike replacement game*

Preseason

10.	19,441	vs. NY Yankees (at Akron)	August 26, 1949
9.	18,462	vs. Pittsburgh (at Canton)	September 7, 1963
8.	17,500	vs. Philadelphia (at Canton)	August 5, 1967
7.	16,360	at Pittsburgh	August 18, 1960
6.	15,747	at Green Bay	August 21, 1954
5.	15,513	at Washington	August 22, 1975
4.	15,259	vs. Pittsburgh (at Buffalo)	September 4, 1950
3.	13,500	vs. Chicago (at Toledo)	August 14, 1949
2.	13,433	vs. Baltimore (at Toledo)	August 27, 1948
1.	10,000	vs. Green Bay (at Toledo)	August 12, 1950

Browns' Average Attendance Per Home Game (By season)

1946: 47,554
1947: 56,109
1948: 42,700
1949: 30,301
1950: 32,891
1951: 38,569
1952: 41,591
1953: 45,779
1954: 32,472
1955: 41,907
1956: 36,941
1957: 54,028
1958: 61,797
1959: 56,397
1960: 56,329
1961: 60,983
1962: 60,292
1963: 69,633
1964: 78,610
1965: 79,612
1966: 77,750
1967: 77,830
1968: 76,581
1969: 82,623
1970: 81,054
1971: 76,948
1972: 75,513
1973: 70,058
1974: 60,630
1975: 55,777
1976: 67,515
1977: 68,686
1978: 63,756
1979: 74,228
1980: 77,572
1981: 75,216
1982: 62,829
1983: 70,580
1984: 57,304
1985: 66,969
1986: 74,176
1987: 71,441
1988: 76,725
1989: 76,791
1990: 71,012
1991: 71,469
1992: 70,052
1993: 71,059
1994: 70,782
1995: 64,049
1999: 72,617
2000: 72,693
2001: 72,887
2002: 73,287
2003: 73,196
2004: 73,105
2005: 72,291
2006: 72,334
2007: 73,001
2008: 72,779
2009: 68,889
2010: 66,117
2011: 65,859
2012: 66,632

The Evolution of the Brown and Orange

The Browns' uniform is often considered not only one of the simplest in all of sports but also one that hasn't changed much over the years.

While that's true in a broad sense, the Browns' uniform has evolved quite a bit in the team's long history.

1946

The Browns debut with plain white leather helmets, white jerseys with brown numerals trimmed in orange, and brown jerseys with white numerals. (Orange numerals trimmed in white were used on the brown jerseys, but only in 1946.) The sleeves on the white jerseys have three brown stripes interspersed with two orange stripes on the forearms; the sleeves on the brown jerseys have three white stripes interspersed with two orange stripes on the forearms. The pants are white with one brown stripe between two orange stripes going down the legs. The socks worn with white jerseys are white from knee to calf with three brown stripes interspersed with two orange stripes; the socks worn with brown jerseys are brown from knee to calf with three white stripes interspersed with two white stripes.

1947

The socks worn with brown jerseys are still brown from knee to calf but now have three orange stripes interspersed with two white stripes.

1950

Orange leather helmets are introduced, but the white leather helmets are still used. The socks worn with brown jerseys are still brown from knee to calf but are switched back to three white stripes interspersed with two orange stripes.

1952

After using white leather helmets for the entire 1951 season, they are eliminated for a full-time switch to orange plastic helmets with a white stripe down the middle.

1953

Orange jerseys with white numerals trimmed in brown are worn once, for a night game with Philadelphia on October 10. (They were also worn in the preseason, then again for exhibition games in 1954 and 1955, though with brown numerals.) The sleeves of the orange jerseys have three brown stripes interspersed with two white stripes on the forearms. The socks worn with orange jerseys are orange from knee to calf with three brown stripes interspersed with two white stripes.

1954

All helmets are equipped with gray facemasks.

1957

Jersey numbers are added to the helmets.

1960

Two brown stripes flank the existing white stripe down the middle of helmet.

1961

Jersey numbers are removed from the helmets.

1968

Four thin brown lines are added as borders to the two orange stripes on the sleeves of the brown jerseys.

1969

The NFL fiftieth anniversary patch is added to the left shoulder. Four thin white lines are added as borders to the two orange stripes on the white jerseys.

1970

Last names are added to the back of the jerseys. Four thin white lines are added as borders to the two orange stripes on the socks worn with white jerseys. Four thin brown lines are added as borders to the two orange stripes on the socks worn with brown jerseys.

1974

Socks worn with white jerseys are now the same as those worn with brown jerseys: brown from knee to calf with three white stripes interspersed with two orange stripes, with the two orange stripes flanked by four thin brown stripes.

1975

The pants are changed from white to orange with the three-toned stripe down the side now mirroring the stripe pattern down the middle of the helmet: two brown stripes around a white stripe. The socks worn with white jerseys revert back to white from knee to calf with three brown stripes interspersed with two orange stripes, with the two orange stripes flanked by four thin white stripes. The facemasks on the helmets are changed from gray to white.

1984

The pants are changed from orange back to white, but now have two brown stripes around an orange stripe down the side. The socks worn with brown jerseys are now solid brown; the socks worn with white jerseys are now solid orange. The numbers on both the brown and white jerseys are trimmed in orange. The sleeves on the white jerseys now have one thick brown stripe on the forearm flanked by two thin orange stripes; the sleeves on the brown jerseys now have one thick orange stripe flanked by two thin white stripes. (Orange numerals with white trim were worn on the brown jerseys in the preseason.)

1985

The entire uniform reverts back almost completely to that worn through most of the 1960s: white jerseys with brown numerals with no trim and three brown stripes interspersed with two orange stripes on the sleeves. The socks worn with the white jerseys are white from knee to calf with three brown stripes interspersed with two orange stripes. The brown jerseys have white numerals with no trim and three white stripes interspersed with two orange stripes (and the two orange stripes are flanked by four thin brown stripes). The socks worn with the brown jerseys are brown from knee to calf with three white stripes interspersed with two orange stripes (and the orange stripes are flanked by four thin brown stripes). The stripe pattern down the side of the pants goes back to one brown stripe flanked by two orange stripes.

1991

A small NFL shield is added to the middle of the front collar and on the left hip of the pants.

1992

Stripes on the sleeves of the white jerseys are changed to two brown stripes around one orange stripe; the stripes on the sleeves of the brown jerseys are changed to two white stripes around one orange stripe (which is flanked by two thin brown stripes).

1994

The NFL seventy-fifth anniversary patch is worn on the left shoulder.

1999

The 1999 expansion patch is worn on the left shoulder. Stripes on sleeves revert back to pre-1992: white jerseys now have three brown stripes interspersed with two orange stripes; brown jerseys now have three white stripes interspersed with two orange stripes (which are flanked by four thin brown stripes).

2002

Orange jerseys are reintroduced and worn twice, then twice more over the next two years: they have white numerals with brown trim, and the sleeves have three brown stripes interspersed with two white stripes. Solid brown socks are worn with the orange jerseys. Following owner Al Lerner's death on October 23, an "AL" commemorative patch is worn on the left shoulder for the remainder of the season.

2003

The "AL" patch is made smaller and included as a permanent part of the uniform, placed in the middle of the forearm stripes. The orange pants are reintroduced and worn five times, then twice the following season. The stripe pattern on the white pants, when worn with brown jerseys, is changed to include two thin white stripes between the one orange stripe and two brown stripes. Solid brown socks are also now used as an option on various jersey/pants combinations. A small "Browns" is added on the upper chest just beneath the NFL logo on the front collar.

2005

The stripe pattern variable on the white pants is removed, back to one orange stripe flanked by two brown stripes.

2006

The team's sixtieth anniversary patch is placed on the left shoulder. The thin brown stripes flanking the two orange stripes on the sleeves on the brown jerseys are removed. The facemasks on the helmets revert from white to gray. A throwback uniform is introduced and worn once, then twice over the next two seasons: numerals on the helmets, a single white stripe down the middle of the helmet, and socks brown from knee to calf and three white stripes interspersed with two orange stripes.

2008

Solid brown socks are used for all combinations other than the throwback uniform. Solid brown pants with no stripe down the side are introduced and worn in the preseason.

2009

The solid brown pants are worn with the white jerseys through the entire season. With the brown pants, the white-to-calf, three-brown-stripe, two-orange-stripe socks are worn. These socks will be used as an option with the all-white combination each of the next two years.

2010

The brown pants are replaced by the white pants when the white jerseys are worn.

2012

The Pro Football Hall of Fame fiftieth anniversary patch is worn on the left shoulder in Weeks 14 and 15.

What They've Worn at Home

Throughout their history, the Browns have alternated back and forth as to what jerseys and uniform combinations they wear for home games, often times mixing it up within the course of a single season.

Here's a breakdown of what uniforms the Browns have worn for home games by season:

Same Uniform for the Entire Home Season

White jerseys/white pants

1948
1949
1950
1951
1952
1954
1955
1956
1964
1965
1966
1967
1969
1970
1971
1972
1973
1974
1985
1986
1987
1988
1995
2011

Brown jerseys/white pants

1957
1958
1959
1960
1961
1962
1963
1984
1991
1992
1993
1999
2007
2009
2010

Brown jerseys/orange pants

1975

White jerseys/orange pants

1976
1977

Different Uniforms Throughout the Home Season

White jerseys/white pants and orange jerseys/white pants

1953 (5 games white, 1 game orange)

White jerseys/white pants and brown jerseys/white pants

1946 (4 games white, 4 games brown)
1947 (6 games white, 1 game brown)
1968 (8 games white, 1 game brown)
1989 (4 games white, 5 games brown)
1990 (3 games white, 5 games brown)
1994 (1 game white, 8 games brown)
2000 (2 games white, 6 games brown)
2001 (7 games white, 1 game brown)
2005 (3 games white, 5 games brown)
2006 (1 game white, 7 games brown)
2008 (1 game white, 7 games brown)
2012 (3 games white, 5 games brown)

White jerseys/white pants, brown jerseys/white pants, and orange jerseys/white pants

2002 (2 games white, 4 games brown, 2 games orange)

White jerseys/orange pants and brown jerseys/orange pants

1978 (4 games white, 4 games brown)
1979 (4 games white, 4 games brown)
1980 (4 games white, 5 games brown)
1981 (3 games white, 5 games brown)
1982 (1 game white, 3 games brown)
1983 (3 games white, 5 games brown)

White jerseys/orange pants, brown jerseys/white pants, orange jerseys/white pants, and brown jerseys/orange pants

2003 (1 game white/orange, 5 games brown/white, 1 game orange/white, 1 game brown/orange)

White jerseys/white pants, brown jerseys/white pants, brown jerseys/orange pants, and orange jerseys/white pants

2004 (1 game white/white, 5 games brown/white, 1 game brown/orange, 1 game orange/white)

Records of Every Starting Quarterback in the Browns' NFL History by Winning Percentage

(Record includes regular season and postseason games)

Rank. Quarterback	Record	Pct.
t1. Len Dawson (1960–61)	1–0	1.000
t1. Don Gault (1970)	1–0	1.000
3. Otto Graham (1950–55)	61–16–1	.789 (4–3 postseason)
4. Tommy O'Connell (1956–57)	10–4–1	.700 (0–1 postseason)
5. Frank Ryan (1962–68)	53–24–2	.684 (1–2 postseason)
t6. Mark Rypien (1994)	2–1	.667
t6. Don Strock (1988)	2–1	.667 (0–1 postseason)
8. Milt Plum (1957–61)	33–17–2	.654 (0–1 postseason)
9. Bill Nelsen (1968–72)	36–19–1	.652 (2–3 postseason)
10. Gary Danielson (1985–88)	5–3	.625
11. Vinny Testaverde (1993–95)	17–16	.515 (1–1 postseason)
12. Bernie Kosar (1985–93)	56–55–1	.505 (3–4 postseason)
13. Brian Sipe (1974–83)	57–56	.504 (0–1 postseason)
t14. Mike Tomczak (1992)	4–4	.500
t14. Jake Delhomme (2010)	2–2	.500
t14. Jeff Christensen (1987)	1–1	.500
17. Mike Phipps (1970–76)	24–26–2	.481 (0–1 postseason)
18. Derek Anderson (2006–09)	16–18	.471
19. Jim Ninowski (1958–59, 1962–66)	5–6	.455
t20. Todd Philcox (1992–93)	2–3	.400
t20. George Ratterman (1952–56)	2–3	.400
22. Tim Couch (1999–2003)	22–37	.373
t23. Paul McDonald (1980–84)	8–14	.364 (0–1 postseason)
t23. Trent Dilfer (2005)	4–7	.364
t25. Brandon Weeden (2012)	5–10	.333
t25. Babe Parilli (1956)	1–2	.333
27. Charlie Frye (2005–07)	6–13	.316
28. Kelly Holcomb (2001–04)	4–9	.308 (0–1 postseason)
29. Jeff Garcia (2004)	3–7	.300
t30. Colt McCoy (2010–11)	6–15	.286
t30. Mike Pagel (1986–90)	2–5	.286
t32. Brady Quinn (2007–09)	3–9	.250
t32. Dave Mays (197677)	1–3	.250
t32. Eric Zeier (1995)	1–3	.250
35. Seneca Wallace (2010–11)	1–6	.143
36. Doug Pederson (2000)	1–7	.125
t37. Luke McCown (2004)	0–4	.000
t37. Ken Dorsey (2008)	0–3	.000
t37. Ty Detmer (1999–2000)	0–2	.000
t40. Will Cureton (1975)	0–1	.000
t40. Bruce Gradkowski (2008)	0–1	.000
t40. Gary Lane (1966–67)	0–1	.000
t40. Thaddeus Lewis (2012)	0–1	.000
t40. Terry Luck (1977)	0–1	.000
t40. Spergon Wynn (2000)	0–1	.000

Browns' Record by Decade*

1940s:	52–4–3 (.907)
1950s:	92–35–2 (.721)
1960s:	95–45–5 (.672)
1970s:	72–72–2 (.500)
1980s:	86–75–1 (.534)
1990s:	42–72 (.368)
2000s:	57–104 (.354)
2010s:	14–34 (.292)

TOTAL: 510–441–13 (.536)

**Including postseason games*

Browns' All-Time Record by Month*

SEPTEMBER:	96–89–2 (.519)
OCTOBER:	156–104–2 (.599)
NOVEMBER:	146–113–7 (.562)
DECEMBER:	105–120–2 (.467)
JANUARY:	7–15 (.318)

**Including postseason games*

Browns' All-Time Record by Day of the Week*

SUNDAY:	454–405–12
MONDAY.	16–15–1
TUESDAY:	2–0
THURSDAY:	5–9
FRIDAY:	8–0
SATURDAY:	25–12

*Including postseason games

Browns' All-Time Record at Home: 281–195–6 (.589)

Cleveland Stadium: 240–124–6 (.657)
Cleveland Browns Stadium: 41–71 (.366)

Browns' All-Time Record on the Road: 229–246–7 (.482)

Browns' All-Time Record by Uniform

White Jersey:	**353–297–11 (.542)**
Home:	171–88–5 (.657)
Road:	182–209–6 (.466)
Brown Jersey:	**155–141–2 (.524)**
Home:	108–104–1 (.509)
Road:	47–37–1 (.559)
Orange Jersey:	**2–3 (.400)**
Home:	2–3
White Pants:	**443–360–13 (.551)**
Home:	243–164–6 (.596)
Road:	200–196–7 (.505)
Orange Pants:	**65–75 (.464)**
Home:	38–31
Road:	27–44
Brown Pants:	**2–6 (.250)**
Road:	2–6

Browns' All-Time Record by Uniform Combination

White Jersey/White Pants: 314–236–11 (.570)

Home:	155–70–5 (.685)
Road:	159–166–6 (.489)

Brown Jersey/White Pants: 127–121–2 (.512)

Home:	86–91–1 (.486)
Road:	41–30–1 (.576)

White Jersey/Orange Pants: 37–55 (.402)

Home:	16–18 (.471)
Road:	21–37 (.362)

Brown Jersey/Orange Pants: 28–20 (.583)

Home:	22–13 (.629)
Road:	6–7 (.462)

Orange Jersey/White Pants: 2–3 (.400)

Home:	2–3 (.400)

White Jersey/Brown Pants: 2–6 (.250)

Road:	2–6 (.250)

Browns' Record Day by Day

SEPTEMBER

September 1: 0–1
1991–L
September 2: 1–0
1979–W
September 3: 2–3
1948–W, 1978–W, 1984–L, 1995–L, 2000–L
September 4: 2–1
1983–L, 1988–W, 1994–W
September 5: 2–0–1
1947–W, 1949–T, 1993–W
September 6: 1–1
1946–W, 1992–L
September 7: 0–5
1980–L, 1981–L, 1986–L, 2003–L, 2008–L
September 8: 1–2
1985–L, 1991–W, 2002–L
September 9: 2–4
1979–W, 1984–L, 1990–W, 2001–L, 2007–L, 2012–L
September 10: 4–1
1978–W, 1989–W, 1995–W, 2000–W, 2006–L
September 11: 3–4
1949–W, 1966–W, 1983–W, 1988–L, 1994–L, 2005–L, 2011–L
September 12: 5–2
1947–W, 1948–W, 1976–W, 1982–W, 1999–L, 2004–W, 2010–L
September 13: 3–3
1946–W, 1964–W, 1981–L, 1987–L, 1993–W, 2009–L
September 14: 1–3
1986–W, 1992–L, 2003–L, 2008–L
September 15: 5–2
1963–W, 1968–W, 1974–L, 1980–L, 1983–W, 1991–W, 2002–W
September 16: 6–3
1950–W, 1962–W, 1973–W, 1979–W, 1984–L, 1985–W, 1990–L, 2007–W, 2012–L
September 17: 5–4
1948–W, 1961–L, 1967–L, 1972–L, 1978–W, 1989–W, 1995–W, 2000–W, 2006–L
September 18: 5–2
1949–W, 1966–L, 1977–W, 1986–L, 1994–W, 2005–W, 2011–W
September 19: 4–5
1965–W, 1971–W, 1976–L, 1982–L, 1988–W, 1993–W, 1999–L, 2004–L, 2010–L
September 20: 3–1–1
1964–T, 1981–W, 1987–W, 1992–W, 2009–L
September 21: 5–2
1947–W, 1969–W, 1970–W, 1975–L, 1980–W, 2003–W, 2008–L
September 22: 4–3
1946–W, 1963–W, 1968–L, 1974–W, 1985–L, 1991–L, 2002–W
September 23: 2–5
1962–L, 1973–L, 1984–W, 1990–L, 2001–W, 2007–L, 2012–L
September 24: 5–4
1950–W, 1961–W, 1967–L, 1972–W, 1978–L, 1979–W, 1995–W, 2000–L, 2006–L
September 25: 5–5
1949–W, 1955–L, 1960–W, 1966–L, 1983–W, 1988–L, 1989–L, 1994–W, 2005–L, 2011–W
September 26: 4–8
1947–W, 1948–W, 1954–L, 1959–L, 1965–L, 1971–W, 1976–L, 1977–W, 1993–L, 1999–L, 2004–L, 2010–L
September 27: 3–4
1953–W, 1964–W, 1970–L, 1981–W, 1992–L, 2009–L, 2012–L
September 28: 6–2
1952–W, 1958–W, 1969–W, 1975–L, 1980–W, 1986–W, 2003–L, 2008–W
September 29: 4–3
1946–W, 1957–W, 1963–W, 1968–L, 1974–L, 1985–W, 2002–L
September 30: 3–6
1951–L, 1956–L, 1962–L, 1973–W, 1979–L, 1984–L, 1990–L, 2001–W, 2007–W

OCTOBER

October 1: 5–3
1950–L, 1961–W, 1967–W, 1972–W, 1978–L, 1989–W, 2000–L, 2006–W
October 2: 6–4
1949–W, 1955–W, 1960–W, 1966–W, 1977–L, 1983–L, 1988–W, 1994–W, 1995–L, 2011–L
October 3: 4–2
1965–W, 1970–W, 1976–L, 1999–L, 2004–W, 2010–W
October 4: 5–3
1952–W, 1953–W, 1959–W, 1964–W, 1971–L, 1981–L, 1987–W, 2009–L
October 5: 8–3
1947–W, 1948–W, 1957–W, 1958–W, 1963–W, 1968–W, 1969–L, 1975–L, 1980–L, 1986–W, 2003–W
October 6: 3–3
1946–W, 1956–W, 1974–L, 1985–W, 1991–L, 2002–L
October 7: 6–4
1950–W, 1951–W, 1962–W, 1967–W, 1973–W, 1979–L, 1984–L, 2001–W, 2007–L, 2012–L
October 8: 4–5
1961–W, 1966–W, 1972–L, 1978–W, 1989–L, 1990–W, 1995–L, 2000–L, 2006–L
October 9: 4–3
1949–L, 1955–W, 1965–W, 1977–L, 1983–W, 1988–L, 2005–W

October 10: 5–5
1948–W, 1953–W, 1954–W, 1964–L, 1971–W, 1976–W, 1993–L, 1999–L, 2004–L, 2010–L

October 11: 3–3
1959–L, 1970–W, 1981–L, 1987–L, 1992–W, 2009–W

October 12: 6–3
1946–W, 1947–L, 1952–L, 1958–W, 1969–W, 1975–L, 1980–W, 1986–W, 2003–W

October 13: 5–4
1957–W, 1963–W, 1968–L, 1974–L, 1985–W, 1991–L, 1994–W, 2002–L, 2008–W

October 14: 4–6
1949–W, 1951–W, 1956–L, 1962–L, 1979–L, 1984–L, 1990–L, 2001–L, 2007–W, 2012–W

October 15: 2–6
1950–W, 1961–L, 1967–W, 1972–L, 1973–L, 1978–L, 1989–L, 2000–L

October 16: 4–3
1955–W, 1960–W, 1977–W, 1983–L, 1988–W, 2005–L, 2011–L

October 17: 6–3
1948–W, 1954–L, 1965–W, 1971–W, 1976–W, 1993–W, 1999–L, 2004–W, 2010–L

October 18: 7–2
1951–W, 1959–W, 1964–W, 1969–W, 1970–L, 1981–W, 1987–W, 1992–W, 2009–L

October 19: 4–4
1947–W, 1952–W, 1958–W, 1975–L, 1980–W, 1986–L, 2003–L, 2008–L

October 20: 5–3
1946–W, 1957–L, 1963–W, 1968–W, 1974–L, 1985–L, 1991–W, 2002–W

October 21: 5–3
1951–W, 1956–L, 1962–W, 1973–W, 1979–W, 1984–L, 2001–W, 2012–L

October 22: 3–6
1950–L, 1961–W, 1967–W, 1972–W, 1978–L, 1990–L, 1995–L, 2000–L, 2006–L

October 23: 7–3
1955–W, 1960–L, 1966–W, 1977–W, 1983–L, 1988–W, 1989–W, 1994–W, 2005–L, 2011–W

October 24: 6–3
1948–W, 1954–W, 1965–W, 1971–L, 1976–W, 1993–W, 1999–L, 2004–L, 2010–W

October 25: 6–1
1953–W, 1959–W, 1964–W, 1970–W, 1981–W, 1992–W, 2009–L

October 26: 7–2–1
1947–W, 1952–W, 1958–W, 1969–T, 1975–L, 1980–W, 1986–W, 1987–W, 2003–L, 2008–W

October 27: 6–3
1946–L, 1951–W, 1957–W, 1963–L, 1968–W, 1974–W, 1985–L, 1991–W, 2002–W

October 28: 4–3–1
1956–L, 1962–W, 1973–T, 1979–W, 1984–L, 1990–L, 2007–W, 2012–W

October 29: 7–2
1950–W, 1961–W, 1967–L, 1972–W, 1978–W, 1989–W, 1995–W, 2000–L, 2006–W

October 30: 7–3
1949–W, 1955–W, 1960–W, 1966–W, 1977–W, 1983–W, 1988–W, 1994–L, 2005–L, 2011–L

October 31: 2–3
1954–W, 1965–L, 1971–L, 1976–L, 1999–W

NOVEMBER

November 1: 3–5
1953–W, 1959–W, 1964–W, 1970–L, 1981–L, 1987–L, 1992–L, 2009–L

November 2: 3–4
1947–W, 1952–L, 1958–L, 1969–W, 1975–L, 1986–W, 2008–L

November 3: 4–5
1946–L, 1957–W, 1963–W, 1968–W, 1974–L, 1980–W, 1985–L, 1991–L, 2002–L

November 4: 5–4–1
1951–W, 1956–W, 1962–T, 1973–L, 1979–W, 1984–W, 1990–L, 2001–L, 2007–W, 2012–L

November 5: 4–5
1950–W, 1961–L, 1967–W, 1972–W, 1978–L, 1989–W, 1995–L, 2000–L, 2006–L

November 6: 4–6
1949–W, 1955–W, 1960–L, 1966–L, 1977–L, 1983–L, 1994–W, 2005–W, 2008–L, 2011–L

November 7: 5–5
1948–W, 1954–W, 1965–W, 1971–L, 1976–W, 1988–L, 1993–L, 1999–L, 2004–L, 2010–W

November 8: 5–2
1953–W, 1959–W, 1964–W, 1970–L, 1981–L, 1987–W, 1992–W

November 9: 3–4
1947–W, 1952–W, 1958–L, 1969–L, 1975–L, 1980–W, 2003–L

November 10: 5–3
1946–W, 1957–W, 1963–L, 1968–W, 1974–W, 1985–L, 1986–W, 1991–L

November 11: 2–6
1951–W, 1956–L, 1962–L, 1973–W, 1979–L, 1984–L, 2001–L, 2007–L

November 12: 5–2
1950–W, 1961–W, 1967–L, 1978–L, 1989–W, 2000–W, 2006–W

November 13: 5–6–1
1949–T, 1955–L, 1960–W, 1966–W, 1972–W, 1977–L, 1983–W, 1988–L, 1994–W, 1995–L, 2005–L, 2011–L

November 14: 5–4
1948–W, 1954–W, 1965–W, 1971–L, 1976–W, 1993–L, 1999–W, 2004–L, 2010–L
November 15: 5–2
1953–W, 1959–W, 1964–W, 1970–L, 1981–W, 1987–W, 1992–L
November 16: 5–4
1947–W, 1952–W, 1958–W, 1969–W, 1975–L, 1980–L, 1986–L, 2003–W, 2009–L
November 17: 5–3–1
1946–W, 1957–T, 1963–L, 1968–W, 1974–L, 1985–W, 1991–L, 2002–W, 2008–W
November 18: 8–2
1951–W, 1956–W, 1962–W, 1973–W, 1979–W, 1984–W, 1990–L, 2001–W, 2007–W, 2012–L
November 19: 5–3–1
1950–W, 1961–W, 1967–W, 1972–W, 1978–W, 1989–T, 1995–L, 2000–L, 2006–L
November 20: 8–2
1949–W, 1955–W, 1960–L, 1966–W, 1977–W, 1983–W, 1988–W, 1994–L, 2005–W, 2011–W
November 21: 6–4
1948–W, 1954–W, 1965–W, 1971–W, 1976–W, 1982–W, 1993–L, 1999–L, 2004–L, 2010–L
November 22: 3–5
1953–W, 1959–L, 1964–L, 1970–W, 1981–L, 1987–W, 1992–L, 2009–L
November 23: 5–4–1
1947–T, 1952–L, 1958–W, 1969–W, 1975–W, 1980–W, 1986–W, 1989–L, 2003–L, 2008–L
November 24: 8–2
1946–W, 1949–W, 1957–W, 1963–W, 1966–L, 1968–W, 1974–L, 1985–W, 1991–W, 2002–W
November 25: 8–4
1948–W, 1951–W, 1956–L, 1962–W, 1973–W, 1979–L, 1982–L, 1984–W, 1990–L, 2001–W, 2007–W, 2012–W
November 26: 3–4
1961–L, 1967–W, 1972–W, 1978–W, 1995–L, 2000–L, 2006–L
November 27: 4–3–2
1947–W, 1955–T, 1960–T, 1977–L, 1983–W, 1988–W, 1994–W, 2005–L, 2011–L
November 28: 6–3
1948–W, 1954–W, 1965–W, 1971–W, 1976–W, 1993–L, 1999–L, 2004–L, 2010–W
November 29: 3–5
1953–W, 1959–L, 1964–W, 1970–L, 1981–L, 1987–L, 1992–W, 2009–L
November 30: 6–2
1952–W, 1958–W, 1969–W, 1975–W, 1980–W, 1986–W, 2003–L, 2008–L

DECEMBER

December 1: 6–1
1957–W, 1963–W, 1968–W, 1974–W, 1985–W, 1991–W, 2002–L
December 2: 4–5–1
1951–W, 1956–W, 1962–L, 1973–T, 1979–W, 1984–L, 1990–L, 2001–L, 2007–L, 2012–W
December 3: 5–6
1946–W, 1950–W, 1961–W, 1967–W, 1972–L, 1978–L, 1981–L, 1989–L, 1995–L, 2000–L, 2006–W
December 4: 5–5
1949–W,* 1955–W, 1960–W, 1966–W, 1977–L, 1983–L, 1988–W, 1994–L, 2005–L, 2011–L
December 5: 7–3
1948–W, 1954–W, 1965–W, 1971–W, 1976–W, 1982–L, 1993–W, 1999–L, 2004–L, 2010–W
December 6: 2–4
1953–W, 1959–L, 1964–L, 1987–L, 1992–W, 2009–L
December 7: 7–4
1947–W, 1952–W, 1958–W, 1969–W, 1971–W, 1974–L, 1975–L, 1980–W, 1986–W, 2006–L, 2008–L
December 8: 3–6
1946–W, 1957–L, 1963–L, 1968–W, 1985–L, 1991–L, 2002–W, 2003–L, 2011–L
December 9: 5–7
1951–W, 1956–W, 1962–L, 1972–W, 1973–L, 1979–L, 1984–L, 1990–L, 1995–L, 2001–L, 2007–W, 2012–W
December 10: 5–3
1950–W, 1961–L, 1967–W, 1978–W, 1989–L, 1994–W, 2000–L, 2009–W
December 11: 3–4
1949–W,* 1955–W, 1960–W, 1966–L, 1977–L, 1983–L, 2005–L
December 12: 3–10
1954–W, 1964–W, 1965–L, 1970–L, 1971–W, 1976–L, 1981–L, 1982–L, 1988–L, 1993–L, 1999–L, 2004–L, 2010–L
December 13: 2–2
1953–L, 1959–W, 1987–W, 1992–L
December 14: 4–5
1947–W,* 1952–L, 1958–L, 1968–L, 1969–W, 1975–W, 1980–L, 1986–W, 2003–L
December 15: 5–4
1957–W, 1960–W, 1962–W, 1963–W, 1974–L, 1985–W, 1991–L, 2002–L, 2008–L
December 16: 4–5
1951–W, 1956–L, 1973–L, 1979–L, 1984–W, 1990–W, 2001–L, 2007–W, 2012–L
December 17: 5–4–1
1949–L,† 1950–W,* 1961–T, 1966–W, 1967–L, 1972–W, 1978–L, 1989–W, 1995–W, 2000–L, 2006–L
December 18: 3–3
1977–L, 1983–W, 1988–W, 1994–L, 2005–W, 2011–L

December 19: 4–5
1948–W,* 1954–L, 1965–W, 1971–W, 1982–W, 1993–L, 1999–L, 2004–L, 2010–L

December 20: 3–2
1970–W, 1981–L, 1987–W, 1992–L, 2009–W

December 21: 3–5
1958–L,* 1968–W,* 1969–L, 1975–L, 1980–W, 1986–W, 2003–L, 2008–L

December 22: 2–2
1946–W,* 1985–L, 1991–L, 2002–W

December 23: 1–5
1951–L,* 1989–W, 1990–L, 2001–L, 2007–L, 2012–L

December 24: 2–7
1950–W,* 1967–L,* 1972–L,* 1988–L,* 1994–W, 1995–L, 2005–L, 2006–L, 2011–L

December 26: 5–4
1954–W,* 1955–W,* 1971–L,* 1982–W, 1987–W, 1993–W, 1999–L, 2004–L, 2010–L

December 27: 2–2
1953–L,* 1964–W,* 1992–L, 2009–W

December 28: 2–2
1952–L,* 1969–W,* 2003–W, 2008–L

December 29: 1–2
1957–L,* 1968–L,* 2002–W

December 30: 2–2
1990–L, 2001–W, 2007–W, 2012–L

December 31: 0–1
2006–L

JANUARY

January 1: 1–1
1995–W,* 2012–L

January 2: 1–4
1966–L,* 1983–L, 1994–L, 2005–W, 2011–L

January 3: 2–0
1987–W,* 2010–W

January 4: 0–3
1970–L,* 1981–L,* 1986–L*

January 5: 0–2
1964–L,** 2003–L*

January 6: 2–1
1990–W,* 2002–L, 2006–W

January 7: 0–3
1961–L,** 1968–L,** 1995–L*

January 8: 0–1
1983–L*

January 9: 1–0
1988–W*

January 11: 0–1
1987–L*

January 14: 0–1
1990–L*

January 17: 0–1
1988–L*

**Postseason game*

***Playoff Bowl*

†Shamrock Bowl

Index